READINGS IN MEDIEVAL PHILOSOPHY

READINGS
IN
MEDIEVAL PHILOSOPHY

Andrew B. Schoedinger

New York   Oxford
OXFORD UNIVERSITY PRESS
1996

FOR BELLE AND CHELSEY

OXFORD UNIVERSITY PRESS

Oxford New York
Athens Auckland Bangkok Bombay
Calcutta Cape Town Dar es Salaam Delhi
Florence Hong Kong Istanbul Karachi
Kuala Lumpur Madras Madrid Melbourne
Mexico City Nairobi Paris Singapore
Taipei Tokyo Toronto

and associated companies in
Berlin Ibadan

Copyright © 1996 by Oxford University Press, Inc.

Published by Oxford University Press, Inc.
198 Madison Avenue, New York, New York 10016

Oxford is a registered trademark of Oxford University Press

Library of Congress Cataloging-in-Publication Data
Readings in medieval philosophy / [edited by] Andrew B. Schoedinger.
p.   cm.
ISBN 0-19-509292-9
ISBN 0-19-509293-7 (pbk.)
1. Philosophy, Medieval.   I. Schoedinger, Andrew B.
B720.R43 1996   95-14118
189—dc20

1 3 5 7 9 8 6 4 2
Printed in the United States of America
on acid free paper

Preface

Contained within the covers of this volume is the most extensive and complete collection of readings in medieval philosophy published to date. The readings are arranged chronologically within nine thematic sections. Until now many of the readings have not been widely available. This change is due, in part, to a renaissance of interest in medieval studies in general and medieval philosophy in particular. Previous anthologies of readings in medieval philosophy have presented the material chronologically by author, are highly edited, and therefore the offerings tend to be brief. This procedure carries liabilities on both counts. Such a chronological presentation precludes a thematic approach to the subject matter, thus creating pedagogical difficulties. Highly edited material prevents the reader from observing the medieval mind at work and is therefore self-defeating. After all, the goal of such a book is to make possible not only an understanding of what the medievals had to say concerning philosophical problems but to foster an appreciation of their work, at the very least, and hopefully sheer delight in their acuity and nimbleness of mind. I have taken a laissez-faire approach to the readings. Only by doing so can the "flavor" of the selections be fully savored, for the medieval mind was indeed different from ours. I have also been quite liberal in the number of readings included within each section. This was done to ensure a modicum of thoroughness for the topic being studied. The outcome has been a rather imposing volume of fifty-four readings of selected works of thirty-seven philosophers. Nevertheless, it does offer a professor considerable flexibility relative to both breadth and depth of subject matter. In this sense, it is a one-size-fits-all book. In addition, each selection is prefaced by a biographical sketch of its author and a summary of the chosen reading.

I wish to express my profound appreciation to the following individuals for so graciously contributing translations to this volume: Paul Vincent Spade for William of Ockham and Walter Burley on universals, Fridugisus of Tours, *On the Being of Nothing and Shadows,* and St. Peter Damian, *On Divine Omnipotence*; Richard Ingardia for selections from St. Thomas Aquinas' *De Malo*; Theodore Kermit Scott for Jean Buridan's Chapter VIII of *Sophismata*; Norman Kretzmann and Eleonore Stump for the selections of Boethius and Kilwardby in the section on "Logic and the Philosophy of Language"; Daniel D. McGarry for selections from *The Metalogicon of John of Salisbury*; Jean M. Manninger, trustee of the Ernest A. Moody Estate for the two letters of Nicolaus of Autrecourt; Peter G. Sobol for Jean Buridan's *Commentary on Aristotle's De Anima* and for the summary accompanying that reading; and my colleague and friend Warren G. Harbison for the selection of Matthew of Aquasparta and its attendant compendium.

In addition, I want to thank the administration of Boise State University and the department of philosophy for their monetary support of this project, including a faculty research grant.

A very special "thank you" goes to Faith Brigham, for whose assistance in the development of this manuscript I am eternally grateful. Finally, my wife Belle more than deserves recognition for her omnipresent sense of perspective and sense of humor demonstrated throughout this project.

Boise, Idaho   A.B.S.
May 1995

Contents

PART IV
THEOLOGY

PART V
POLITICAL PHILOSOPHY

PART VI
KNOWLEDGE AND SENSATION

PART VII
UNIVERSALS

PART VIII
LOGIC AND THE PHILOSOPHY OF LANGUAGE

PART IX
PHYSICS

PART I

THE EXISTENCE OF GOD

CHAPTER 1

St. Augustine

Aurelius Augustinus was born on November 13, 354, at Tagaste, in North Africa (modern Souk-Ahras, Algeria). The child was raised in the Christian tradition of his mother even though his father was a pagan. As a child he learned the fundamentals of Latin and arithmetic from a schoolmaster of his hometown. He also studied Greek but never learned to read it with ease. In 370 Augustine moved to Carthage to study rhetoric. He subsequently opened a school to teach that discipline and lived there for thirteen years (save for a year-long return to Tagaste in 374). This great port city and center of government provided for this passionate and robust young man fertile soil in which to sow wild oats. It was there that he took a mistress with whom he lived for better than ten years and by whom he fathered a son named Adeodatus. Nevertheless, the quest to satiate his strong carnal needs did not detract from his intellectual life. "At the age of nineteen," he wrote, "on reading in the school of rhetoric Cicero's *Hortensius*, I was inflamed by such a love of philosophy that I considered devoting myself to it at once." Soon thereafter he rejected Christianity (a) because of its simplistic and anthropomorphic conception of God, and (b) because it provided no acceptable solution to the problem of evil.

It was at this point in his life that Augustine found the doctrine of Manichaeism to provide satisfactory answers to his philo-theological concerns. The followers of Mani maintained a dualistic theory believing that the world is governed by two basic principles, (a) good (literally that of light) and understood to be God or Ormuzd, and (b) evil (literally that of darkness). These two principles are locked in eternal strife. This strife is reflected in this world via mankind. Man's soul is composed of light and is representative of the good principle, whereas man's body is a product of the evil principle. Furthermore, this doctrine was appealing to Augustine because it was by nature materialistic. He had not yet evolved intellectually to appreciate the possibility of an immaterial reality. This is most important in ultimately understanding Augustine's intellectual development.

In time Augustine became rather disenchanted with Manichaeism, most notably concerning the reason why the two aforementioned principles were in eternal conflict. Being intellectually unfulfilled and disenchanted with his Carthage students, he moved to Rome in 383, where he opened a school in rhetoric. However, he faced a predominance of students transferring to other schools just before tuition was due. Thus, to protect his livelihood, the following year he sought and acquired a position at Milan as a municipal professor of rhetoric. During his year in Rome he lost most of his belief in Manichaeism and turned briefly to the skepticism of Cicero.

At Milan Augustine was exposed to the sermons of Ambrose, the bishop of Milan. These sermons presented Christianity in a manner more acceptable to Augustine. Also during this time he had most probably read the *Enneads* of Plotinus, a Neoplatonic work. This set the stage for Augustine's ultimate and final return to Christianity. Neoplatonism provided answers to the problem of evil as well as freeing him from the shackles of materialism. Plotinus understood evil as privation of good rather than a substantive positive. Reality in the Platonic tradition is immaterial. That which is physical is only apparent (i.e., appearances) to our (five) senses. Reality is within the world of Forms, namely, Ideas in the mind of God, and as such the ultimate truth is immaterial.

The upshot of this rather torturous intellectual journey was his dramatic conversion to Christianity, which he recounted in his *Confessions*. Following a year of prayer at Cassiciacum (A.D. 388), he returned to Tagaste, sold his property, and set up a small monastic community. (He had left his mistress and mother of his son while at Milan in an attempt to follow the wishes of his mother and marry someone acceptable. This, however, did not come to pass. While at Cassiciacum he resolved not to marry.) During a visit to the seaport town of Hippo in 391, he was ordained by the bishop of that diocese, apparently against his wishes. The ailing bishop desired Augustine's help, and in compliance he moved to Hippo and established a monastery there. He was consecrated coadjutor in 395 and the following year became bishop of Hippo upon the death of Valerius. He remained in that position until his death on August 28, 430. During his tenure as bishop he became a most prolific writer. Not only was Augustine a spiritual leader, but he also stands out as a pillar of intellectualism during a period of strong anti-intellectualism within the church (viz., the influence of Tertullian). No one dominated the thought of Latin Christendom more so than Augustine until the thirteenth century, which witnessed the rise of Aristotelianism through the works of Thomas Aquinas.

St. Augustine on the Existence of God

In scrutinizing St. Augustine's argument for the existence of God one cannot help but notice the influence of Plato. Not only is the argument presented as a dialogue, but, more importantly, it possesses as its core the unchanging nature of numbers, a fact upon which Plato extrapolated to justify his claim that the essential nature of all Forms is immutability.

In the first stage of the argument St. Augustine extracts from Evodius the concession that life presupposes existence and understanding presupposes life. A being which possesses all three is superior to one which does not.

The second stage establishes understanding (viz., reasoning) as superior to the bodily senses since the latter cannot perceive themselves even though they, being what they are, perceive bodily things. However, we know that judgment can be passed on the bodily senses. Consequently, there must be some other sense, an inner sense that performs this function. This we call reason. Reason itself dictates its superiority over the bodily senses.

It is at this point that St. Augustine extracts a concession from his longtime friend Evodius, namely, that which, if anything, can be determined superior to reason would properly be called God. The remainder of the argument is devoted to making such a determination.

The Argument

1. Is anything incorruptible (i.e., unchanging)?

2. *Yes.* (a) The meanings of numbers and (b) truth. The true meanings of numbers are unchangeable.

3. No bodily sense makes contact with all of the numbers. Therefore, numbers are not the types of things that are perceived, but are the subjects of reason.

4. Augustine quotes from Ecclesiastes to the effect that a knowledge of numbers and wisdom are on a par. But what is wisdom?

5. Evodius suggests that wisdom is in the mind of the beholder (i.e., there is no one agreed upon definition of wisdom).

6. Augustine counters that even though judgments about wisdom differ among individuals, the very notion of it has been impressed upon their minds verified by the fact that they universally claim to desire it. Therefore the concept of wisdom is common to all people even though their characterizations of it vary widely.

7. Surely wisdom is the highest good of mankind. How so? Such a claim is true by universal agreement in the same way that there is universal agreement regarding the proposition that "we ought to live justly".

8. In like manner we can agree that that which is incorrupt (i.e., unchangeable) is better than that which is corrupt. (This is presumably a norm of wisdom.)

9. The norms of wisdom are as true and unchangeable as the rules regarding numbers.

10. Therefore the norms of wisdom are eternal truths which are unchangeable and eternal and therefore are not a matter of opinion.

11. The truth transcends reason and is to be understood by reason. It was agreed that that which transcends reason is God. If there be something superior to truth, then whatever that may be would be God, otherwise God must be (eternal) truth. In either case, God exists, QED.

THE FREE CHOICE OF THE WILL

Book II

Chapter 3

Let us pursue our inquiry, if you will, according to this order: first, what evidence is there that God exists;[1] next, do all things, insofar as they are good, come from God; lastly, should free will be numbered among

From St. Augustine, *The Free Choice of the Will*, from *The Fathers of the Church: St. Augustine; The Teacher, The Free Choice of the Will, Grace and Free Will*, translated by Robert P. Russell, O.S.A. (Washington, D.C.: The Catholic University of America Press, 1968), pp. 113–150. Reprinted by permission of The Catholic University of America Press.

things good. Once these questions have been answered, I think it will become clear enough whether it was right to give free will to man.

Hence, to begin with what is most evident, I will ask you whether you yourself exist. Possibly, you are afraid of being mistaken by this kind of a question when, actually, you could not be mistaken at all if you did not exist?[2]

Evodius. Go on instead to the other questions.

Augustine. Then, since it is evident that you exist, and that this could not be so unless you were living, then the fact that you are living is also evident. Do you understand that these two points are absolutely true?

Ev. I understand that perfectly well.

Aug. Then this third point is also evident, namely, that you understand.

Ev. It is evident.

Aug. Which of these three, in your opinion, is the most excellent?

Ev. Understanding.

Aug. Why do you think so?

Ev. Because, while these are three in number, existence, life, and understanding, and though the stone exists and the animal lives, yet I do not think that the stone lives or that the animal understands, whereas it is absolutely certain that whoever understands also exists and is living. That is why I have no hesitation in concluding that the one which contains all three is more excellent than that which is lacking in one or both of these. Now whatever is living is certainly also existing, but it does not follow that it also understands. This kind of life, I think, is proper to animals. But it certainly does not follow that what exists must also live and understand, for I can admit that a corpse exists, but no one would say it lives. And still less can something understand if it is not living.

Aug. We maintain, then, that two of these three are lacking in a corpse, one in the animal, and none in man.

Ev. That is true.

Aug. We likewise maintain that the most excellent among the three is what man possesses together with the other two, namely, understanding, and that having this, he must also exist and live.

Ev. We do, indeed.

Aug. Now tell me whether you know you have these well known senses of the body, sight, hearing, smell, taste, and touch.

Ev. I do.

Aug. What do you think is the function of sight, that is, what do we perceive when we see?

Ev. Anything corporeal.

Aug. When we see, we do not likewise perceive what is hard and soft, do we?

Ev. No.

Aug. What then is the proper function of the eyes, that is, what do we perceive with them?

Ev. Color.

Aug. Of the ears?

Ev. Sound.

Aug. Of smell?

Ev. Odors.

Aug. Of taste?

Ev. Flavor.

Aug. Of touch?

Ev. Soft or hard, smooth or rough, and many such qualities.

Aug. And what of the shapes of bodies? Do we not perceive that they are large, small, square, round, and so on, both by touch and sight? Consequently, these qualities are not proper either to sight or vision alone, but belong to both.

Ev. I understand.

Aug. Then you further understand that each sense has its own proper object to report while some senses have certain objects in common.

Ev. I understand that also.

Aug. Can we, therefore, determine by any of these senses what is the proper object of each sense or what those objects are which some or all of them have in common?

Ev. Not at all. This is discerned by some power within.

Aug. Might not this be the reason itself, which is wanting in beasts? For, in my opinion, reason enables us to grasp these and to know just what they are.

Ev. I think it is rather reason that enables us to know that there is a kind of internal sense to which everything is referred by those well-known five senses. Now the power enabling the animal to see is one thing, that by which it shuns or seeks what it perceives by seeing is something else.

The former is located in the eye, the latter within, in the soul itself. The inner sense enables the animal to seek and acquire things that delight and to repel and avoid things that are obnoxious, not only those that are perceived by sight and hearing, but all those which are grasped by the other bodily senses. But this power cannot be called either sight or hearing or smell or taste or touch, but is some other kind of power that presides over all of them together. Although, as I mentioned, we do grasp this power by our reason, yet we may not call it reason, since it is obviously present in beasts.

Aug. I acknowledge that this power, whatever it is, does exist, and I do not hesitate to call it the inner sense. But unless the impressions brought to us by the bodily senses pass beyond even this inner sense, they cannot result in knowledge. For it is by reason that we grasp whatever we know. To mention but a few instances, we know that color cannot be perceived by hearing nor sound by sight. And this is something that we do not know by sight or hearing or by that inner sense which is not lacking in beasts. We are not to suppose that beasts know that light is not perceived by the ear or sound by the eye, since we discern this only by rational reflection and thought.

Ev. I could not say that I have grasped this point. Suppose that beasts do discern that color cannot be perceived by hearing or sound by sight by means of that inner sense which you admit they do possess.

Aug. You do not suppose, do you, that animals can distinguish one from another the color they perceive, the power of sense in the eye, the inner sense within the soul, and reason by which all these are enumerated and defined, one by one?

Ev. Not at all.

Aug. But could reason distinguish these four things one from another and assign their limits by definition unless color was referred to it by the sense of sight, and this sense, in turn, by that inner sense which presides over it, and this inner sense, in turn, by its direct action upon reason, provided, however, that there is no other power interposed?

Ev. I fail to see how it could be otherwise.

Aug. Are you aware of this, that color is perceived by the sense of sight, whereas this sense of sight is not perceived by sight itself? For you do not see the act of seeing itself by the same sense by which you see color.

Ev. Absolutely not.

Aug. Try now to make these further distinctions. You will not deny, I think, that color and seeing color are different, and also that the power is different by which color can be perceived in its absence as if it were present.

Ev. I draw a distinction between these two, and admit that they are distinct from one another.

Aug. Except for color, you do not see any of these three with the eyes, do you?

Ev. Nothing else but color.

Aug. Tell me then what it is that enables you to see the other two, for you could not distinguish them if they were not seen.

Ev. I do not know the nature of that other power. I know it exists but nothing more.

Aug. Then you do not know whether it is reason itself or that vital power, called the inner sense, which presides over the bodily senses, or something else?

Ev. I do not know.

Aug. But this much you do know, that reason alone can define these powers and that it can only do so with what is presented for its scrutiny.

Ev. That is certain.

Aug. It follows that this other power, whatever it is, which enables us to perceive all that we know, is the servant of reason. It presents and reports to reason whatever has come within its reach so that the objects of sense perception can be assigned their proper limits and be grasped not only by sensation but also by knowledge.

Ev.   That is right.

Aug.   Reason itself distinguishes between its servants and the impressions they convey to it, and likewise recognizes what a difference there is between these and itself and asserts its primacy over them. Now does reason know reason in another way than by reason itself? Or how would you otherwise know that you had reason unless you perceived it by reason?

Ev.   That is very true.

Aug.   Consequently, in perceiving color, we do not perceive by the same sense our act of seeing; in hearing we do not hear our act of hearing; in smelling a rose, the act itself of smelling imparts no fragrance to us; in tasting a flavor, the act itself has no taste in our mouth, and in touching something, we cannot touch the act itself of touching. It is evident that those five senses cannot be perceived by any one of them, though all corporeal qualities can be perceived by them.

Ev.   It is evident.

Chapter 4

Aug.   I think it is likewise clear that the inner sense perceives not only what it receives from the five bodily senses but also the senses themselves. For if the beast were not aware of its act of perception, it could not otherwise direct its movements toward something, or away from it. This awareness is not ordered towards knowledge, which is the function of reason, but towards movement which it does not perceive by any of the five senses.

If this is still obscure, it may become clear if you note the single example of what occurs in any one of the senses, such as sight. The beast could not open its eyes at all or turn its gaze towards the thing it wants to see were it not for the fact that while its eyes were closed or not fixed upon the object, it perceived that it was not seeing. But if it is conscious of its not seeing when in fact it does not see, it must also be aware of its seeing when it does see. The fact that, while seeing, the beast does not alter its gaze by that desire which moves it to turn its gaze when it does not see something, shows that it is aware of both states.

But whether this vital power, which is aware of its perceiving corporeal things, also perceives itself, is not so clear, except for the fact that when a person raises the question in his own mind, he comes to see that all living things shun death. Since death is the contrary of life, we must infer that the vital power is aware of itself since it shuns what is contrary to it. But if this point is still not clear, then disregard it, so that our effort to reach the desired conclusion will be based solely on clear and evident proofs.

These points are clear: corporeal qualities are perceived by the bodily senses; one and the same sense cannot perceive itself; the inner sense perceives that corporeal qualities are perceived by the bodily sense and also the bodily sense itself; all these things of sense, as well as reason itself, are known by reason and come under the heading of knowledge. Do you not think so?

Ev.   I do indeed.

Aug.   Come, tell me how this question arose, for we have been pursuing this avenue of inquiry a long time in our desire to reach a solution.

Chapter 5

Ev.   So far as I recall, we are now dealing with the first of those three questions which we proposed a while ago when we arranged a plan for this discussion, namely, how the existence of God can be made evident, though we must believe it with a strong and persevering faith.

Aug.   You have recalled this very well. But I want you also to keep carefully in mind that when I asked whether you were existing, it was made clear that you knew not only this but also two other things.

Ev. I remember that too.

Aug. Now see which one of these three you think is that one to which pertains everything perceived by the bodily senses, that is, in what class of things you think we should locate whatever is perceived by our senses, by the eyes or by any other organ of the body. Should it be with things that merely exist, with those that also live, or with those that also understand?

Ev. With those that merely exist.

Aug. In which of the three classes do you think the sense power itself should be placed?

Ev. In the class of things living.

Aug. Which of these two do you think is better, the sense itself or its object?

Ev. The sense, of course.

Aug. Why is that?

Ev. Because whatever also has life is better than something which merely exists.

Aug. And what of that inner sense which we found was inferior to reason and which we still share in common with beasts? Would you hesitate to rank this sense above that by which we perceive a body, which you said should be ranked above the body itself?

Ev. I would have no hesitation whatever.

Aug. I should like you to tell me why you have no hesitation on this point. For you cannot say that this inner sense should be placed in that one of the three classes which also includes understanding, but rather in the class of things which exist and live, although they lack understanding. This inner sense is found also in beasts which are without understanding. If this is so, I would like to know why you rank the inner sense above that which perceives corporeal qualities, since both are found in the class of things that live. You ranked the sense which perceives bodies above bodies because the latter are in the class of things

which only exist, while the former are in the class of things that also live. Since the inner sense is also found in this class, tell me why you think it is better.

If you say it is because the inner sense perceives the bodily sense, I do not believe you will find any rule that we could rely upon for holding that the subject perceiving is better than what it perceives. Otherwise, we might also be forced to conclude that the person understanding is better than what he understands. This, of course, is untrue because man understands wisdom but he is not better than wisdom itself. Consider, then, why you thought that the inner sense should be ranked above the sense by which we perceive things corporeal.

Ev. It is because I look upon the inner sense as a ruler and kind of judge of the latter. For if there is any shortcoming in the discharge of their function, the inner sense demands this service from the bodily senses as a kind of debt owed by its servant, as was pointed out a short time ago. The sense of sight does not see that it is seeing or not seeing and, failing to do so, it cannot judge what is missing or what is sufficient. This is done by the inner sense which directs the soul of the beast to open its eyes when they are closed and to supply what it perceives is missing. There can be no doubt in anyone's mind that what judges is better than what is judged.

Aug. Do you understand then that even the bodily senses pass a kind of judgment on bodies? Pleasure and pain are theirs to experience whenever they come in contact gently or roughly with a body. Just as the inner sense judges as to what is missing or what is sufficient in visual perception, so the eyes themselves judge as to what is deficient or sufficient in the matter of color. So too in the case of hearing, just as the inner sense judges whether or not it is attentive enough, so the auditory sense judges concerning sounds, discerning those which either flow gently into the ear or which produce a harsh dissonance.

There is no need to continue with the rest of the bodily senses. I think you know already what I am trying to say, namely, that just as the inner sense judges the bodily senses, approving what is complete in them and requiring what is deficient, so too the bodily senses themselves judge bodies, admitting pleasurable sensations of touch found in them, while rejecting the opposite.

Ev. I see these points clearly and agree that they are perfectly true.

Chapter 6

Aug. See now whether reason also judges the inner sense. I am not asking whether you have any doubt that reason is better than the inner sense because I am sure that this is your judgment. Yet I feel that now we should not even have to ask whether reason passes judgment on the inner sense. For in the case of things inferior to it, namely, bodies, the bodily senses, and the inner sense, is it not, after all, reason itself that tells us how one is better than the other and how far superior reason itself is to all of them? This would not be possible at all unless reason were to judge them.

Ev. Obviously.

Aug. Consequently, that nature which not only exists but also lives, though it does not understand, such as the soul of beasts, is superior to one that merely exists and neither lives nor understands, such as the inanimate body. Again, that nature which at once exists and lives and understands, such as the rational mind in man, is superior to the animal nature. Do you think that anything can be found in us, namely, something among those elements which complete our nature and make us men, that is more excellent than that very thing which we made the third in those three classes of things? It is clear that we have a body and a kind of living principle which quickens the body itself and makes it grow, and we recognize that these two are also found in beasts. And it is also clear that there is a third something, the apex, so to speak, or eye of the soul, or whatever more

appropriate term may be employed to designate reason and understanding, which the animal nature does not possess. So I ask you to consider whether there is anything in man's nature more excellent than reason.

Ev. I see nothing at all that is better.

Aug. But suppose we could find something which you are certain not only exists but is also superior to our reason, would you hesitate to call this reality, whatever it is, God?

Ev. If I were able to find something which is better than what is best in my nature, I would not immediately call it God. I do not like to call something God because my reason is inferior to it, but rather to call that reality God which has nothing superior to it.

Aug. That is perfectly true. For God Himself has given this reason of yours the power to think of Him with such reverence and truth. But I will ask you this: if you should find that there is nothing above our reason but an eternal and changeless reality, would you hesitate to say that this is God? You notice how bodies are subject to change, and it is clear that the living principle animating the body is not free from change but passes through various states. And reason itself is clearly shown to be changeable, seeing that at one time it endeavors to reach the truth, and at another time it does not, sometimes it arrives at the truth, sometimes it does not. If reason sees something eternal and changeless not by any bodily organ, neither by touch nor taste nor smell nor hearing nor sight, nor by any sense inferior to it, but sees this of itself, and sees at the same time its own inferiority, it will have to acknowledge that this being is its God.

Ev. I will openly acknowledge that to be God, if, as all agree, there is nothing higher existing.

Aug. Good! It will be enough for me to show that something of this kind exists. Either you will admit that *this* is God or, if there is something higher, you will admit that *it* is God. Accordingly, whether there exists something higher or not, it will become clear that God exists, when, with His assistance, I shall prove, as I promised, that there exists something above reason.

Ev. Prove then what you are promising.

Chapter 7

Aug. I shall do so. But first I shall ask you whether my bodily senses are the same as yours, or whether mine are mine alone and yours are yours alone. If this latter were not so, I would be unable to see anything with my eyes which you would not see.

Ev. I fully agree that though the senses are of the same nature, yet each one of us has his own sense of sight or hearing, and so forth. One man cannot only see but also hear something that another man does not hear, and one man can perceive by any one of the senses something different from what another perceives. So it is obvious that your senses are yours alone and mine are mine alone.

Aug. Would you give the same or a different answer concerning the inner sense?

Ev. Not a different answer, certainly. My inner sense perceives my bodily sensations and your inner sense perceives yours. I am often asked by a man who sees something whether I also see it, simply because I am conscious of seeing or not seeing it, while he is not.

Aug. What of reason itself? Does not each one of us have his own since, actually, it can happen that I understand something while you do not, and you may be unable to know whether I do understand, although I do know.

Ev. It is also clear that each one of us has his own rational mind.

Aug. You could not possibly say, could you, that we possess individually our own sun or moon, or morning star, or other such things that we see, though each one of us sees these things with his own sense?

Ev. I could never say such a thing.

Aug. So it is possible for many of us to see some one thing at one and the same time, though each of us has his own individual senses with which he perceives the same thing which we all see at the same time. Consequently, though my senses are distinct from yours, it may happen that what we see is not something different for both, but the one thing which is present to each of us and which is seen by both of us at the same time.

Ev. That is perfectly clear.

Aug. We can also hear the same voice at the same time so that, while my hearing is distinct from yours, yet it is not a different voice that we are hearing at the same time. Neither is one part of the voice heard by me and another part by you, but whatever sound is made is within the hearing of both of us, perceived as one sound in its entirety.

Ev. That too is clear.

Aug. With regard to the other senses, you must now take note that what we have to say in this connection holds for them in a way neither entirely the same nor entirely different from what was said about the two senses of sight and hearing. You and I can inhale the same air and perceive the quality of the air by its odor. Again, we can both taste the same honey, or any other kind of food and drink, and perceive its quality from the taste. Although the taste is the same, yet our senses are individual to us, yours belong to you, and mine to me. So when both perceive the one odor or taste, you do not perceive it with my sense nor do I perceive it with yours. Neither do I perceive it by a single sense which we can share in common, but my sense is mine entirely and so is yours, though it is the one odor or taste that is perceived by both of us.

Accordingly, these two senses of smell and taste are found to have something similar to the two senses of sight and hearing. But they differ in a way which has a bearing on the subject we are presently considering. For, though we both inhale the same air with our nostrils or taste the same food that we take, I do not breathe in that part of the air which you do, or eat the same portion of food that you eat, but I take one part, and you, another. Therefore, when I breathe, I inhale as much of all the air as I need, and you do the same. And though the same food is all eaten by both of us, yet it cannot be taken wholly by both of us in the way that we both hear a whole word at the same time and both see the same sight equally well. But in the case of food and drink, different portions have to pass into each of us. Do you have some faint understanding of all this?

Ev. On the contrary, I agree that it is perfectly clear and certain.

Aug. You would not say, would you, that we should compare the sense of touch with those of sight and hearing with reference to the point now under discussion? We can both perceive by the sense of touch not only the same body, but also the same part of the body. It is different with food, for each one of us cannot take all the food placed before us when we are both eating it. But you and I can touch the same body in its entirety, not just different parts of it, but the whole body.

Ev. I admit that in this respect the sense of touch is very much like the two previous senses. But I see it differs in this, that both of us can see and hear all of the same thing together, that is, at the same time. Now both of us can touch a whole body at one time, but only in different parts, and only the same part at different times. I cannot apply my sense of touch to the part you are touching unless you remove yours.

Aug. A very astute answer! But you should note this point too, that though some objects perceived by us are perceived together and others separately, yet each of us has an individual awareness of his own sense perceptions of the objects he perceives through the bodily sense. I am neither aware of your sensations nor are you aware of mine. In other words, with regard to things corporeal, what we can perceive

individually but not together is that alone which so becomes part of us that we can change and transform it into ourselves. So it is with food and drink where both of us cannot taste the same portion. Although nurses actually serve food already masticated to infants, yet the portion which is taken to be tasted and is assimilated into the body of the nurse chewing it cannot be returned and given back as food for the infant. When the palate tastes something pleasant, no matter how small a portion it is, it claims this for itself once and for all, and makes it become part of the body's nature. If this were not the case, no taste could remain in the mouth after masticated food was rejected from the mouth. We may say the same of the parts of the air we breathe. Though you can inhale some of the air which I exhale, you cannot do so with that part which has become nourishment for me because it cannot be returned. Physicians point out that we take in nourishment even with our nostrils. When I breathe, I am the only one who can perceive this nourishment and I cannot return it by exhaling it for you to inhale it again and perceive it with your nostrils.

Although we perceive other sense objects, our perception of them does not destroy their nature and change them into our bodily substance. We can both perceive them either together or at different times, so that what I perceive, either in whole or in part, can also be perceived by you. Light, sound, and bodily objects are examples of things with which we can come in contact, but without altering their nature.

Ev. I understand.

Aug. It is clear, therefore, that those things which are not changed by us, though we perceive them with our bodily senses, are not the property of our senses and hence are all the more common to us, seeing that they are not changed or converted into our own individual or, so to speak, private property.

Ev. I am in full agreement.

Aug. We are to understand by individual and, so to speak, private property, that which is identified with each one of us and which each one alone can perceive within himself as belonging properly to his own nature. By common and, so to speak, public, we understand that which is experienced by all who perceive something, without any deterioration or change in the thing itself.

Ev. That is correct.

Chapter 8

Aug. Come now, and let me have your attention. Tell me whether anything can be found which all thinking men perceive in common, each one making use of his own mind and reason. Something which is seen is present to everybody and is not changed into something else useful for those to whom it is present, like food and drink, but remains whole and entire, whether it is seen or not. Or do you think that perhaps no such thing exists?

Ev. On the contrary, I see there are many, but it is sufficient to single out one of them, the nature and truth of number which are present to all who make use of reason. Everyone engaged in computing them strives to grasp their nature with his own reason and intelligence. Some do this rather easily, others with more difficulty, while others cannot do it at all, though the truth makes itself equally available to all who can grasp it. And whenever someone experiences this, it is not altered or changed into a kind of nourishment for the one who perceives it. When anyone errs in judgment about it, the reality itself, which remains true and intact, is not at fault; rather, his own error is measured by his failure to behold the reality itself.

Aug. That is certainly true. I see you were quick to find an answer as becomes a man not unfamiliar with such matters. But suppose I were to tell you that these numbers have not been impressed upon our mind by any nature of their own but come from things which we grasp with the bodily senses and are a kind of sense-image of

things visible, how would you reply? Or would you also be of the same opinion?

Ev. I could never think of such a thing. Even if I could perceive numbers by the bodily senses, I could not on this account also perceive the nature of numerical division and addition by the bodily sense. It is by the light of the mind that I show a man to be wrong whose computation indicates an incorrect total either in addition or subtraction. Besides, I cannot tell how long anything will endure which comes in contact with my bodily senses, such as the heavens and the earth, and all the other bodies which I see are contained in them. But seven and three are ten, not only now, but forever. And there has never been, nor will there ever be a time when seven and three were not ten. This is why I have said that the indestructible truth of number is common to me and to anyone at all who uses his reason.

Aug. I cannot gainsay the absolute truth and certainty of your answer. But you will readily see that even the numbers themselves have not been brought in through the bodily senses if you realize that all numbers are designated as multiples of the number one. For example, twice one is two, one tripled is three, and ten times one is ten. No matter what the number, it is so designated according to the number of times it contains the number one. But anyone with a true notion of "one" will doubtless discover that it cannot be perceived by the bodily senses. Whatever comes in contact with the bodily senses can be shown to be many, and not one, since, being a body, it also has numberless parts. To say nothing of the minute and barely discernible particles, no matter how small the tiny body, it has one part on the right, another on the left, one above and another below, one to the far side and another on the near side, parts at the extremes and parts in between. We have to admit that such parts are found in any body, no matter how small it is. Accordingly, we acknowledge that no bodily reality is one, truly and simply, and yet it would be impossible to enumerate so many parts within the body unless these were differentiated by the concept of one.

Whenever I look for this "one" in a body, though I am sure I will not find it, I certainly know what I am looking for and what it is that I do not find there. I know it cannot be found, or better, that it is not present there at all. Consequently, when I recognize that a bodily reality is not one, I know the meaning of one; otherwise, I could not number the many parts in the body. Wherever it is that I come to know one, I certainly do not know it by the bodily senses, for by these I know only bodies, which, as we have shown, are not one, truly and simply. Furthermore, if we have not perceived one by the bodily sense, then neither have we perceived any number by them, none at least of those numbers which we can discern with the understanding. For there is not one of them that does not get its name from its being a given multiple of one, which is not perceived by the bodily senses. The half of any small body has itself its own half, although the whole body is made up of two halves. Hence those two parts of the body are such that even they are not simply two. But the number we call two, because it is twice that which is simply one, has one for its half, namely, that which is simply one, and this in turn cannot have a half or a third, or any other fraction, because it lacks parts and is truly one.

Since we are following numerical order, we see next that two follows one and that it is related to one as its double. The double of two does not follow at once, but three, and then four, which is the double of two. And this ordered sequence extends to all the remaining numbers according to a fixed and changeless law. Thus, after one, the first of all numbers, the first number, apart from one, which follows next is two, the double of one. After this second number, namely, two, the second number, apart from the number two, is the double of two, since the first number after two is three, while the second after two is four, the double of two. After the third number, apart from three, is the double of three, since af-ter three, the first number is four, the second is five, and the third is six, which is the double of three. So too, after number four, the fourth number, apart from four, is the double of four, since following the fourth number, namely, after four, the first number is five, the second is six, the third is seven, and the fourth is eight, which is the double of four. You will also find that the same thing holds for all the other numbers, which we discovered when we combined the first two, that is, numbers one and two, namely, that the double of any number is as many times removed from that number as the number doubled is removed from the beginning of number.

How, then, do we discern that this numerical relationship, which we observe to prevail throughout the whole range of numbers, is changeless, fixed, and indestructible? No one perceives all numbers by any bodily sense, for they are innumerable. I say, then, how do we know that this holds true for all numbers? What idea or image enables us to see with such assurance that this fixed law governing number holds throughout innumerable instances, unless it be that inner light of which the senses have no knowledge?

Men endowed with the God-given ability to reason and not blinded by stubbornness, are constrained by these and many other such proofs to acknowledge that the law and truth of numbers do not pertain to the bodily sense, that they remain changeless and incorruptible, and belong to all who use their reason to perceive them. Many other things possibly come to mind which, as the common and, as it were, public possession of all who use reason, are there to be seen by the mind and reason of each one who perceives them, though the realities themselves remain intact and unchanging. However, I was delighted to hear that the law and truth of numbers came especially to your mind when you wanted to give an answer to my question. It is not without some intent that number and wisdom are brought together in the Sacred Scriptures, where it is said: "I have gone round—I and my heart—to know and to consider, and to search out wisdom and number."[3]

Chapter 9

But let me ask you this: What, in your opinion, should be our view of wisdom itself? Do you think that each man has his own individual wisdom, or that there is one wisdom present to all alike, and that a man becomes wiser the more he shares in it?

Ev. I do not yet know to what wisdom you refer, for I notice that wise actions and words are looked at differently by men. Those who wage war think they are acting wisely, while those who spurn war to devote care and effort to tilling the soil, prefer to extol this activity and to regard it as wisdom. Those shrewd enough to devise schemes for acquiring money are wise in their own eyes. Those uninterested in such things and who renounce them and all such temporal goods, to direct all their effort to the search for truth so as to know themselves and God, judge that this is the one great task of wisdom. Those who are unwilling to allow themselves such leisure for the quest and contemplation of truth, preferring to work for the welfare of men amidst burdensome cares and duties and are occupied with the task of providing just rule and government for human affairs, think that they are wise. And those who combine both of these, living part of their life in the contemplation of truth and part in the discharge of official duties, which they feel are owing to human society, think they have won the prize for wisdom. I make no mention of the countless sects where each one sets its own followers above the rest and would have it that they alone are wise.

Consequently, since the answer to our present problem must not be what we believe but what we grasp with a clear understanding, I cannot possibly reply to your question about the nature of wisdom unless I know by reflection and rational discernment what I already hold on faith.

Aug. Do you think there can be any wisdom but the truth wherein the highest good is seen and possessed? Now those men whom you mentioned as pursuing different goals, all seek good and shun evil, but they pursue different goals because they have different ideas about the good. Any man, then, who seeks what should not be sought is still in error, even though he would not be seeking it unless he thought it was good. A man who seeks nothing, or who seeks what ought to be sought, is not in error.

Insofar, therefore, as all men seek the happy life, they are not in error. But to the extent that a man fails to hold to that way of life which leads to happiness, by so much is he in error, though he avows and professes that he is seeking only happiness. For there is error whenever we follow something which does not lead us where we want to go. And the more one errs in his way of life, the less wise he is, for he is all the farther from the truth wherein the highest good is seen and possessed. It is by attaining to the possession of the highest good that a man becomes happy, which is unquestionably what all of us desire.

Just as we agree that we want to be happy, so do we agree that we want to be wise since, without wisdom, no one is happy. For no one is happy except by the highest good which is found in the contemplation and possession of that truth which we call wisdom. So, just as the notion of happiness is impressed on our minds even before we are happy—this enables us to have the assurance and to state unhesitatingly that we want to be happy—so too, even before we are wise, we have the notion of wisdom impressed on our minds. And if any one of us is asked whether he wants to be happy, it is this notion that enables him to reply that he does, beyond any shadow of doubt.

We agree then about the nature of wisdom, though you were not able to put it in words. For if you did not perceive it at all in your mind, you simply could not know that you want to be wise or that this was your duty, which I do not think you will deny. If, then, we are in agreement about wisdom, I want you to tell me whether, as in the case of the law and truth of numbers, you think that wisdom too is present to all alike who use their reason, or whether you feel there are as many wisdoms as there are men capable of becoming wise. For there are as many minds as there are men, so that we do not perceive anything with one another's mind.

Ev. If the highest good is one for all men, then that truth wherein we can contemplate and possess it, namely, wisdom, must also be common to all.

Aug. Do you doubt that the highest good, whatever it is, is the same for all men?

Ev. I really do, because I notice that different men take delight in different things as their highest good.

Aug. I only wish that no one had any doubt about the highest good, just as no one doubts that it is only by the possession of this good, whatever it is, that man can become happy. But as this is an important question and may require a lengthy discussion, let us go all the way and suppose that there are just as many highest goods as there are different classes of things which different men seek as their highest good. It does not follow, does it, that wisdom itself is not something one and common to all alike, simply because those goods which they see and choose in the light of this wisdom are many and varied? If you think it does, you could also doubt that the sunlight is something one, since the objects we see in it are many and varied. From among these objects each one freely chooses something to enjoy through his sense of sight. One man likes to look at a mountain height and finds delight in such a view; another, at the level expanse of a meadow; another, at the slope of a valley; another, at the green forest; another, at the undulating surface of the sea; another gathers in all or several of these at once for the sheer delight of looking at them.

The things which men see in the light of the sun and which they choose for their enjoyment are many and varied, yet there is the one sunlight in which each viewer sees and takes hold of an object for his enjoyment. Similarly, the goods are many and varied from which each one chooses what he wants, and it is by contemplating and taking hold of this object of his choice that each one really and truly makes this the highest good wherein to find his enjoyment. It is still possible that the light of wisdom itself, in which these things are seen and grasped, may be one and shared by all alike who are wise.

Ev. I acknowledge that this is possible and that there is nothing to prevent the one wisdom from being common to all, even though the highest goods are many and varied. But I would like to know whether this is the case, since, by granting that it is possible, it does not necessarily follow that it is so.

Aug. We know for now that wisdom does exist. But whether there is one wisdom common to all, or whether each wise man has his own wisdom in the way that he has his own soul or mind, is something that we do not yet comprehend.

Ev. That is true.

Chapter 10

Aug. Well then, where do we see the truth of what we now know, namely, that wisdom or wise men exist, and that all men want to be happy? I certainly have no doubt whatever that you do see this and that it is true. Do you see then that this is true just as you see your own thoughts which are completely unknown to me unless you disclose them to me? Or do you see it in such a way as to understand that it can also be seen as true by me, though you did not tell it to me?

Ev. I have no doubt indeed that you could also see it, even against my will.

Aug. Is not this one truth, then, which we both see with our individual minds, common to both of us.

Ev. Quite evidently.

Aug. I also believe you will not deny that we should have a zeal for wisdom and will agree that this in fact is true.

Ev. I do not deny this at all.

Aug. Can we possibly deny that this truth is likewise one and that it is something to be seen by all alike who know it? Yet each one sees it with his own mind, not with mine or yours, or with anyone else's mind, since what is seen is present to all alike who behold it.

Ev. We could never deny that.

Aug. Will you not also admit that these statements have an absolute truth which is present and common to you as well as to me, and to all who see it, namely: we ought to live justly, the less perfect should be subordinated to the more perfect, like things should be equally esteemed, each one should be given his due?

Ev. I agree.

Aug. Can you deny that something incorrupt is better than the corrupt, the eternal better than the temporal, the inviolable better than what is subject to injury?

Ev. Who could possibly deny it?

Aug. Can anyone say, therefore, that this truth belongs to him alone when its changeless character is there to be seen by all who have the power to behold it?

Ev. No one could truly say that this truth belongs to him alone, since it is just as much one and common to all as it is true.

Aug. Who, again, is there to deny that the soul should turn from what is corrupt to the incorrupt, and should love, not the corrupt, but the incorrupt? Or how can anyone, once he acknowledges that something is true, fail to understand its changeless character or to see that it is present to all alike who are able to behold it?

Ev. That is perfectly true.

Aug. Well then, will anyone doubt that a life which does not turn away from its firm and moral convictions by any adversity is better than one which is easily broken and overcome by temporal misfortune?

Ev. Who could doubt it?

Aug. I will look for no further examples of this kind. It is enough that together we see and admit as an absolute certainty that those truths are so many rules and beacons of virtue, that they are true and changeless, and, whether taken singly or collectively, that they are present in common for all to see who can do so, each one viewing them with his own mind and reason. But what I am really asking is whether you think that these truths pertain to wisdom. I believe that in your opinion a man is wise who has acquired wisdom.

Ev. I certainly think so.

Aug. Could a man who lives justly live this way unless he knew which are the lower things that he subordinates to the higher, which the things of equal rank that he brings together, and what things he assigns as appropriate to each class?

Ev. He could not.

Aug. Then you will not deny, will you, that a man who sees these things does so wisely?

Ev. I do not deny it.

Aug. Does not the man who lives prudently choose the incorrupt and judge that it should be preferred to the corrupt?

Ev. Quite clearly.

Aug. Then when a man chooses to turn his soul to what everybody admits should be chosen, can we deny that he is making a wise choice?

Ev. I could never deny that.

Aug. Therefore, when he turns his soul to what was a wise choice, he does so wisely.

Ev. Most certainly.

Aug. And the man who is undeterred by fear or punishment from what he has wisely chosen, and to which it was wise of him to turn, is undoubtedly acting wisely.

Ev. Beyond any doubt.

Aug. It is perfectly clear then that all those truths which we call rules and beacons pertain to wisdom. The more a man uses them in the conduct of his life and lives in conformity with them, the more wisely does he live and act. And we cannot really say that what is done wisely is found apart from wisdom.

Ev. That is absolutely true.

Aug. Accordingly, just as there are true and changeless rules governing numbers whose law and truth are, as you said, unalterably present and common to all who see them, so, too, are the rules of wisdom likewise true and changeless. When you were asked just now about a few of them, one by one, you replied that they were true and evident and admitted that they are common for all to see who are capable of beholding them.

Chapter 11

Ev. I cannot doubt it. But I would very much like to know whether these two, namely, wisdom and number, fall under some one class since you mentioned that they are placed together even in the Sacred Scriptures. Is one derived from the other, or is it contained in the other; does number, for example, derive from wisdom, or is it contained in wisdom? For I would not dare assert that wisdom derives from number or is contained in it. I do not see how I could do so because I am acquainted with many mathematicians or accountants, or whatever else they may be called, who work out perfectly accurate and remarkable calculations. But of wise men, I either know very few, or possibly none at all. Wisdom, it strikes me, is far nobler than number.

Aug. You mention a subject at which I am also wont to marvel. For whenever I go over in my mind the unchanging truth of number, and consider, so to speak, its abode or sanctuary or sphere, or however else we may suitably indicate somehow the seat and dwelling-place of number, I am far removed from the body.[4] And when I chance to find something that I can think of, but not something that I can adequately express in words, I return wearily to the familiar things about us in order to be able to speak, and I speak in the usual way of things that confront our gaze. This happens to me even when I do all I can to think carefully and intently about wisdom. That is why I marvel exceedingly at the fact that, while wisdom and number occupy a hidden and certain abode in Truth, and while there is also the additional scriptural testimony which I cited, linking them together—I marvel exceedingly, as I said, why number is of little value for most men, while wisdom is dear to them.

But it doubtless comes down to this, that they are one and the same thing. Yet, since the Sacred Scripture has this to say of wisdom that "it reaches from end to end strongly and orders all things gently,"[5] then, possibly, the power whereby "it reaches from end to end strongly," is called number, while that whereby "it orders all things gently" is here called wisdom, though both belong to one and the same wisdom.

Wisdom has endowed all things with number, even the least and those at the lowest confines of the universe. Though they hold the lowest place in existence, bodies all possess these numbers. But the capacity for wisdom has not been given to bodily things or to every kind of soul, but only to rational souls. It is there that wisdom has, so to speak, taken up its abode and from where it orders all things it has endowed with number, even the lowest. Since it is easy for us to judge about bodily things, occupying, as they do, a place beneath us, and to see that they have numbers impressed on them which we also judge to be below us, we therefore set a lower value upon numbers.

But once we begin to change our course, as it were, to an upward direction, we discover that number transcends even our minds and abides unchangingly in truth itself. But since few men are capable of wisdom, whereas the ability to count has been given even to fools, men admire wisdom and have little regard for number. There are, on the other hand, men learned and devoted to study, and the more these withdraw from the taint of earthly things, the more clearly they behold in the truth itself both number and wisdom and hold both in high esteem. And when they compare truth with gold and silver and the other things for which men struggle, then not only these, but even they themselves, appear vile in their sight.

It should not surprise you that men have belittled number and set a high value on wisdom simply because it is easier for them to count than to acquire wisdom, when you stop to consider how much more they value gold than the light of a lamp, compared to which gold is something trivial. But greater honor is given something far inferior simply because even a beggar can light himself a candle, whereas only a few can possess gold. This is far from implying that, in comparison with number, wisdom is found inferior, since it is the same; but it must find an eye capable of discerning this identity.

Light and heat are perceived coexistent, so to speak, in the one fire and cannot be separated from each other. Yet, the heat reaches objects placed near it, while the light is spread even over a larger area. In like manner, the power of understanding, present in wisdom, warms what is near it, such as rational souls, whereas, for things farther removed, such as bodies, it does not reach them with the warmth of its wisdom, but permeates them with the light of number. Perhaps you find this obscure, for no analogy drawn from visible things to illustrate an invisible reality can be made to fit perfectly.

Only take note of this point which is enough for our problem at hand and is clear even to more lowly minds, such as ours. Though we are unable to see clearly whether number is contained in wisdom, or is derived from it, or whether wisdom itself derives from number, and is contained in it, or whether it can be shown that both are names of the same thing, this much at least is clear, that both are true and are unchangeably true.

Chapter 12

You would in no way deny, then, that there exists unchangeable truth that

embraces all things that are immutably true. You cannot call this truth mine or yours, or anyone else's. Rather, it is there to manifest itself as something common to all who behold immutable truths, as a light that in wondrous ways is both hidden and public. But how could anyone say that anything which is present in common to all endowed with reason and understanding is something that belongs to the nature of any one of these in particular? You recall, I believe, the result of our discussion a short time ago concerning the bodily senses,[6] namely, that the objects perceived by us in common by sight and hearing, such as color and sound, which you and I see and hear together, are not identified with the nature of our eyes or ears, but are common objects of our perception. So too, you would never say that the things each one of us perceives in common with his own mind, belong to the nature of either of our minds. You cannot say that what two people perceive at the same time with their eyes is identified with the eyes of either one; it is a third something toward which the view of both is directed.

Ev. That is perfectly clear and true.

Aug. This truth, therefore, which we have discussed at length and in which, though it is one, we perceive so many things—do you think that compared to our minds it is more excellent, equally excellent, or inferior? Now if it were inferior, we would not be making judgments according to it, but about it. We do make judgments, for example, about bodies because they are lower, and we often state not only that they exist or do not exist this way, but also that they ought or ought not so to exist. So too with our souls; we not only know that our soul is in a certain state, but often know besides that this is the way it ought to be. We also make similar judgments about bodies, as when we say that a body is not so bright or so square as it ought to be, and so on, and also of souls, when we say the soul is not so well disposed as it ought to be, or that it is not so gentle or not so forceful, according to the dictates of our moral norms.

We make these judgments according to those rules of truth within us which we see in common, but no one ever passes judgment on the rules themselves. For whenever anyone affirms that the eternal ought to be valued above the things of time, or that seven and three are ten, no one judges that it ought to be so, but merely recognizes that it is so. He is not an examiner making corrections, but merely a discoverer, rejoicing over his discovery.

But if this truth were of equal standing with our minds, it would itself also be changeable. At times our minds see more of it, at other times less, thereby acknowledging that they are subject to change. But the truth which abides in itself, does not increase or decrease by our seeing more or less of it, but, remaining whole or inviolable, its light brings delight to those who have turned to it, and punishes with blindness those who have turned from it.

And what of the fact that we judge about our own minds in the light of this truth, though we are unable to judge at all about the truth itself? We say that our mind does not understand as well as it ought, or that it understands as much as it ought. But the mind's understanding should be in proportion to its ability to be drawn more closely and to cling to the unchangeable truth. Consequently, if truth is neither inferior nor equal to our minds, it has to be higher and more excellent.

Chapter 13

I had promised to show you, if you recall, that there is something higher than our mind and reason. There you have it—truth itself! Embrace it, if you can, and enjoy it; "find delight in the Lord and He will grant you the petitions of your heart."[7] For what more do you desire than to be happy? And who is happier than the man who finds joy in the firm, changeless, and most excellent truth?

Men proclaim they are happy when they embrace the beautiful bodies of their wives and even of harlots, which they desire so passionately, and shall we doubt that we are happy in the embrace of truth? Men proclaim they are happy when, suffering from parched throats, they come to a copious spring of healthful waters, or, when hungry, they come upon a big dinner or supper sumptuously prepared. Shall we deny we are happy when we are refreshed and nourished by truth? We often hear men proclaim they are happy if they recline amid roses and other flowers, or delight in the fragrance of ointments. But what is more fragrant, what more delightful, than the breath of truth? And shall we hesitate to say we are happy when we are filled with the breath of truth? Many decide that for them the happy life is found in vocal music and in the sounds of string instruments and flutes. Whenever these are absent, they account themselves unhappy, whereas when they are at hand, they are thrilled with joy. When truth steals into our minds with a kind of eloquent silence without, as it were, the noisy intrusion of words, shall we look for another happy life and not enjoy that which is so sure and intimately present to us? Men delight in the glitter of gold and silver, in the lustre of gems, and are delighted by the charm and splendor of light, whether it be the light in our own eyes, or that of fires on earth, or the light in the stars, the moon, or the sun. And they think themselves happy when they are not withdrawn from these enjoyments by some kind of trouble or penury, and they would like to go on living forever for the sake of those delights. And shall we be afraid to find our happiness in the light of truth?

Quite the contrary. Since it is in truth that we know and possess the highest good, and since that truth is wisdom, let us see in wisdom our highest good. Let us make it our aim to enjoy fully, for happy indeed is the man whose delight is in the highest good.

It is this truth which throws light on all things that are truly good and which men choose according to their mental capacity, either singly or severally, for their enjoyment. By the light of the sun men choose what they like to look at and find delight in it. If some of them are perchance endowed with a sound, healthy, and powerful vision, they will like nothing better than to gaze at the sun itself which also sheds its light on other things in which weaker eyes find delight. Similarly, when the sharp and strong vision of the mind beholds a number of immutable truths known with certainty, it directs its gaze to truth itself, which illumines all that is true.[8] As if unmindful of all else, it clings to this truth and, in enjoying it, enjoys everything else at the same time. For whatever is delightful in other truths is made delightful by the truth itself.

Our freedom is found in submission to this truth. And it is our God Himself who frees us from death, namely, from our sinful condition. It is the Truth Himself, speaking also as a man with men, who says to those believing in him: "If you remain in my word, you are indeed my disciples, and you shall know the truth and the truth shall make you free."[9] But the soul is not free in the enjoyment of anything unless it is secure in that enjoyment.

Chapter 14

Now no one is secure in the possession of goods which can be lost against his will. But no one loses truth or wisdom against his will, for he cannot be separated from them by spatial distances. What we call separation from truth and wisdom is a perverse will which makes inferior things the object of its love. But no one wills anything unwillingly.

In possessing truth, therefore, we have something which all of us can equally enjoy in common, for there is nothing wanting or defective in it. It welcomes all its lovers without any envy on their part; it is available to all, yet chaste with each. No one of them says to another: step back so I too may come close; take your hands away so

I may also embrace it. All cling to it; all touch the selfsame thing. It is a food never divided into portions; you drink nothing from it that I cannot drink. By sharing in it, you make no part of it your personal possession. I do not have to wait for you to exhale its fragrance so that I too may draw it in. No part of it ever becomes the exclusive possession of any one man, or of a few, but is common to all at the same time in its entirety.[10]

Consequently, the objects we touch or taste or smell bear less resemblance to such truth than those which we perceive by hearing and sight. Every word is fully heard by all who hear it and by each one at the same time; every visible object before our eyes is seen at the same time as much by one as by another.

But these analogies are quite remote. No spoken word, for instance, emits all its sound at the same time, since its sound is prolonged over intervals of time, one part coming before another. And every visible object protrudes, so to speak, through space and is not wholly present everywhere. In any case, these things can all be taken from us against our will, and there are obstacles which stand in the way of our being able to enjoy them.

And even if the beautiful singing of a vocalist were to last forever, his admirers would vie with one another to come to hear him; they would press about each other, and, as the crowd became larger, would fight over seats so that each might be closer to the singer. And as they listened, they could not take any of the sound to keep for themselves but could only be caressed by all the fleeting sounds. And if I should wish to gaze at the sun, and were able to do so uninterruptedly, it would leave me at sunset and could be covered over by a cloud, and I could be forced to give up the pleasure of seeing it because of many other hindrances. Finally, even if the delights attached to seeing light and hearing sound were to be ever present, what great advantage would be mine since I share this in common with brute animals?

But the beauty of truth and wisdom

does not turn away any who come because the audience is already overcrowded, provided only that there is a steadfast will to enjoy them. This beauty does not pass with time or move from place to place; it is not interrupted by nightfall or concealed by shadows, and is not at the mercy of the bodily senses. It is near to all throughout the world who have made it the object of their love, and belongs to them forever. It occupies no one place and is nowhere absent; outwardly, it admonishes us, inwardly, it teaches us.[11] All who behold it are changed for the better, and no one can change it for the worse. No one passes judgment on it, and without it no one can judge aright. Hence it is clear, beyond doubt, that truth is superior to our minds, each one of which is made wise by it alone, and is made a judge, not of truth itself, but of all other things in the light of truth.

Chapter 15

You granted that if I could prove that there was something above our minds, you would admit it was God, provided that there was still nothing higher. I agreed and stated that it would be enough for me to prove this point. For if there is anything more excellent, then this is God; if not, then truth itself is God. In either case, you cannot deny that God exists, which was the question we proposed to examine in our discussion. If you are uneasy because of what we have received on faith through the hallowed teaching of Christ, namely, that there is a Father of Wisdom, then remember that we have accepted this also on faith, namely, that the Wisdom begotten of the eternal Father is equal to Him. We are not to inquire further about this just now, but only to accept it with an unshaken faith.

God exists indeed, and He exists truly and most perfectly. As I see it, we not only hold this as certain by our faith, but we also arrive at it by a sure, though, as yet, very inadequate form of knowledge. But this is sufficient for the matter at hand and will enable us to explain the other points

that have a bearing on the subject, unless, of course, you have some objections to raise.

Ev. I accept all this, overwhelmed as I am with an incredible joy which I am unable to express to you in words. I declare that it is absolutely certain. I do so, prompted by that inner voice which makes me want to hear the truth itself and to cling to it. I not only grant that this is good, but also that it is the highest good and the source of happiness.

Aug. You are certainly right. I too rejoice exceedingly. But I will ask you whether we are already wise and happy, or whether we are still striving to make this our goal.

Ev. I think rather we are striving toward it.

Aug. How then do you grasp those things which you rejoice in as being true and certain? You do grant that an understanding of them pertains to wisdom. Can a foolish man know wisdom?

Ev. Not while he remains foolish.

Aug. Then you must now be wise, or else you do not yet know wisdom.

Ev. I am, to be sure, not yet wise, but, insofar as I do know wisdom, I would say that I am not foolish. For I cannot deny that the things I know are certain, and that this is wisdom.

Aug. Please answer me this question: will you not grant that a man who is not just is unjust, and the man who is not prudent is imprudent, and the man who is not temperate is intemperate? Can there be any doubt about it?

Ev. I grant that when a man is not just, he is unjust, and I would give the same answer regarding the prudent and temperate man.

Aug. Why, then, is a man not foolish when he is not wise?

Ev. This I will also admit, that when a man is not wise, he is foolish.

Aug. Now which one of the two are you?

Ev. Whichever one you want to call

me, for I dare not say that I am wise. Yet, I see how it follows from what I have admitted that I should not hesitate to say I am foolish.

Aug. Then the foolish man knows wisdom. For, as we have stated, he would not be sure he wanted to be wise, and that

he ought to be so, unless the notion of wisdom were fixed in his mind; fixed in his mind, as are those things pertaining to wisdom itself about which, when questioned one by one, you replied, and in the knowledge of which you found delight.

Ev. It is just as you say.

NOTES

1. The beginning of Augustine's rational dialectic to prove God's existence from the existence and nature of truth. Nowhere else in his writings is the problem dealt with *ex professo* or in such detail. The connection between the problem of certitude and God's existence, as here evidenced, strongly supports Gilson's observation ". . . that in Saint Augustine the problem of God's existence cannot be distinguished from the problem of knowledge; knowing how we apprehend truth and knowing the existence of Truth are one and the same thing" *(The Christian Philosophy of Saint Augustine 18).*
2. Although suggested as early as the Cassiciacum period in *De beata vita* (2.7) and the *Soliloquia* (2.1.1), this is the first formal statement of Augustine's own argument against the Skeptics based on the immediate evidence of personal existence. Similar formulations appear later in *De vera religione* (39.73), *De Trinitate* (15.12.21), and *De civitate Dei* (11.26). For a comparison with the "cogito" of Descartes, cf. G. Lewis, "Augustinisme et Cartésianisme," *Augustinus Magister* (Paris 1954) 2.1087–1104.
3. 1 Eccles. 7.26.
4. The Pythagorean influence on Augustine's treatment of number is apparent in the early dialogue *De ordine*, where the "science of number" is assigned a kind of primacy in the order of knowledge (2.18.47). His sermons and scriptural commentaries often reflect the attitude of an age fascinated by the sacramental aspect of number and occasion ingenious pieces of exegesis which at times appear fanciful and extravagant to men of a later day. On the scriptural influence on Augustine's notion of number, cf. W. Most, "The Scriptural Basis of Saint Augustine's Arithmology," *The Catholic Biblical Quarterly* 13 (1951) 284–295.
5. Wis. 8.1.
6. Cf. 2.7.
7. Ps. 36.4.
8. Augustine's earlier effort to prove the existence of God by rational argument would seem to exclude an Ontologistic interpretation of this passage. For if man's intellect enjoys in this life a natural and intuitive vision of God, then His existence can be neither an object of faith nor of rational demonstration. In the *De Genesi ad litteram* (12.27–28, 55–56), he had allowed the vision of God to Moses and St. Paul, but later rejected this view entirely. Cf. *De Trinitate* 2.16.27.
9. John 8.31–32.
10. The theoretic principles for Augustine's view of Christian humanism, expounded in *De doctrina christiana* (2.40), stem in part from this conception of truth, which belongs to all because it belongs to none. *Rationem autem veritatis quae nec mea nec tua est sed utrique nostrum ad contemplandum proposita . . . (C. Secundinum Manichaeum 2).*
11. The same theme is developed in *De magistro*, a dialogue between Augustine and his son, Adeodatus, composed about the year 389.

CHAPTER 2

Avicenna

Avicenna, or Ibn Sīnā, is considered by many to be the greatest and most influential medieval Islamic philosopher. He was most likely of Persian ancestry and was born in Bukhara in 980. He demonstrated a great appetite for learning. He first received the basics of Islamic religious education, then proceeded to master logic, geometry, astronomy, medicine, and philosophy. However, he himself admitted that Aristotle's *Metaphysics* was beyond his comprehension until he chanced upon a commentary on it by al-Fārābī.

As a young man he was appointed court physician to the sultan of Bukhara, a position which allowed him access to an excellent royal library. However, his political fortunes diminished when in 999 the Sāmānid rule in Bukhara collapsed with the onslaught of a Turkish Ghaznawid invasion. Thus he entered a rather nomadic period traveling from city to city in Transoxiana and Iran, serving local warring princes. The latter part of his life was spent in relative calm in Isfaham as the physician to 'Alā al-Dawlah. He died in 1037 from ill health while accompanying his patron on a campaign against the city of Hamadan.

Avicenna was a prolific writer, and although some of his works were pillaged and lost when the Ghaznawids sacked Isfahan in 1030, over one hundred of his works have survived.

Avicenna on the Necessary Existent

At the outset much credit is to be given Avicenna for understanding the fundamental link between essence and causation. Typically, these are treated as if they function independently of one another. Such is not the case, and his argument for the existence of God reflects his awareness of the intimate relationship between the two. Avicenna's deduction that God exists rests on an analysis of (a) essence versus existence and (b) the relationship between causation and existence.

An examination of any given species or type of thing reveals that nothing concerning its essence entails its existence. From *what* a species as type of thing is one cannot infer *that* it exists, even though it, in fact, exists.

Something must function as the cause of its existence. Furthermore, this cause must be the species' necessitating cause, for if it were not, an infinite regress is generated. That is, if the cause of a species or type of thing was not necessitating, it would be

24

such that it may or may not produce its effect, namely, the species or type of thing in question. If such were the case, another cause would need be supposed and if this cause were not necessitating yet another, and so on ad infinitum. The upshot is that whether taken singly or as an infinite chain, nonnecessitating causes are such that they cannot "specify" the possible with existence, that is, to give it form via existence. Only a necessitating cause can "specify" something with its existence. That is, it is necessarily the case that of all possible causes only one is such that it has the power of creating a given effect as the type of thing (i.e., species) that it is. It is in this sense that a necessitating cause "specifies" something with existence. Consequently, each and every existent must be necessitated by another. Now it is impossible to proceed to infinity in the chain of necessitating or essential causes where such causes derive their existence externally; that is, from some cause other than itself. There must be some Necessary Existent which is such that its essence is identical to its existence and is the necessitating cause of all existents. This Necessary Existent Avicenna understands to be God. Furthermore, this Being must be eternal, unitary, and atomic, namely, devoid of all multiplicity.

THE METAPHYSICA OF AVICENNA (IBN SĪNĀ)
THE NECESSARY EXISTENT

18. Analysis of the condition of being as being necessary and being contingent

The being of that entity which has being, is either necessary in itself due to its own nature, or it is not necessary.[1] The being of that which is not necessary in itself is either an impossibility or a contingency. Whatever is impossible in itself can never be realized as we indicated previously.[2]

Consequently, it must be contingent due to itself and necessary due to the condition that its cause exists, whereas it is an impossibility due to the condition that its cause does not exist. One factor is its being, and another distinct factor is the condition of the existence or the non-existence of a cause. When one considers its being-qua-being without any other conditions, it is neither a necessity nor an impossibility. When one considers that determined cause which is the condition for realizing its cause, it becomes a necessity, whereas it becomes an impossibility if one considers as

From *The Metaphysica of Avicenna (ibn Sīnā)*, translated by Parviz Morewedge, Persian Heritage Series No. 13 (New York: Columbia University Press, 1973), pp. 47–60. Reprinted by permission of Bibliotheca Persica, New York.

its cause the condition of the non-realization of its cause. Hence, if one considers number without regard to any conditions which are usually associated with it, its nature cannot be an impossibility, for as such it would never exist. But, if one regards the state of the number four which results from two times two, the result must be a necessity, for its non-realization as four is an impossibility. Hence, any existing entity, for which existence is not intrinsically necessary is contingent in itself.[3] Therefore, this entity is a contingent being in itself and a non-contingent being with regard to something else. Its existence is not yet realized in such a manner that it must exist due to that reason. Since becoming an existent is a contingency, and since a contingency in itself is never realized because it has not come from a cause, it is necessary, therefore, that the contingency be realized by means of a cause so that it may become necessary to that cause as an existent. And that entity, or that existent, is of such a nature that its union with its cause is completed and that all its conditions are fulfilled when it becomes an existent. Furthermore, a cause becomes a cause due to its acting. Hence, a cause becomes a cause due to action when it must be active so that an effect may necessarily result from it.[4]

19. Finding that the Necessary Existent is not essentially united with anything[5]

In Itself, the Necessary Existent cannot be united with any cause. Since its being is necessary in Itself without being caused, Its being cannot be due to a cause. Thus, It is not united with any cause. If Its being were not necessary without a cause, It would not be the Necessary Existent in Itself.

The necessary Existent cannot be united with something in a reciprocal union. If It were in a reciprocal relation with another entity, and if one were the cause of the other, each would then be prior to the other, and the being of each would henceforth be prior to that of the other. As its cause, therefore, the being of one would be posterior to that of the other. Consequently, its being would then be conditioned by another being which could be realized only posterior to its own realization. Therefore, its being could never be.

If two entities are not causes of each other, though one is necessarily related to the other, they are then simultaneous, being neither posterior nor prior to one another, as in the case of two (twin) brothers. The essence of each is either necessary in itself, or it is not necessary in itself. If one entity were necessary in itself, the non-being of the other would not then constitute a harm to it. Thus, such a union between two necessary entities could not be possible. If the non-being of one entity would harm the existence of the other, it would not be necessary in itself, and, hence, it would be contingent in itself. Considered only by itself, the being of any contingent entity is not superior to its non-being. Consequently, its existence is caused by the existence of its cause, and its non-existence is similarly due to the non-existence of its cause. If it existed due to itself, then nothing but its intrinsic nature would be necessary for it to exist.

Therefore, there is a cause for the existence of any contingent being, and this cause is prior to it in essence. Accordingly, within the being of each one of the two entities (in the reciprocal relation) there must be a cause other than its companion to which it corresponds. One of the two cannot be prior to the other, for, like its companion, it is necessary on account of its cause, and unnecessary in itself without the cause. If one were a cause and the other an effect, essentially both would not be necessary.

From this reasoning we learn that Necessary Existent does not have an element nor a part, because elements and parts are due to material causes as we have indicated.[6]

For this reason, the Necessary Existent is not united with anything essentially.

20. Finding the nature of contingent being

The existence of that which is contingent in itself is necessitated and can be realized by something other than itself. The meaning of 'the existence of something is realized due to the existence of another thing' can have two senses. Either something can bring something else into existence, as someone who builds a house, or the existence of something can be realized through another thing, as when the being of the patient (i.e., the thing made) subsists because of the being of the agent as the illumination from the sun subsists in the earth.

There is a general belief on the part of the people that a maker of something is he who actualizes the being of a thing which, once it is realized, will no longer depend on him. But they are misled by an invalid argument and an improper example. The argument they offer is the following: the being of that which already has been actualized is no longer in need of a cause for its being, because that which has already been made does not need to be remade.[7] The example they use is this: once a house has been made by someone, it is no longer dependent on its maker. But the mistake in this reasoning is due to this fact: no one claims that a thing made is thereafter still in need of a maker. We do assert, however, that what is made continues to be in need of a supporter.[8] As regards the analogy of the house, the mistake in the reasoning is apparent, for the builder of the house is not actually the cause of the house, though he is responsible for the movement of wood to the place of the house. This condition; namely, the transport of clay and wood) terminates after the builder, or the maker, of the house has left. The actual cause realizing the form of a house is the superimposition of the elements which constitute the house and their intrinsic nature which necessitates the persistence of the house having that form. Though by itself each element has a downward movement, when the elements are retained, they stand as upholders of the house. Thus, the cause actualizing the form of the house is a synthesis of these two causes. As long as a house exists, these two causes exist also. It is to be noted that in this reasoning no causality is attributed to the builder. He is to be regarded as a cause only inasmuch as he gathers the elements constituting the house and constructs them so that they support one another. And when the cause (i.e., the builder) has disappeared the cause of a house cannot continue to exist as a cause. Consequently, the builder constructing the clay is in reality not the builder of the house, but only its apparent maker, as we stated previously. Likewise, a father is in reality not the maker of the son, but rather, his apparent maker, for nothing has come from him but a movement which led to the issue of the sperm. For this reason, the act by which the sperm partakes of the form of man is due to other factors related to the sperm. The actualization of the form of humanity is due to an existent, as will be known from forthcoming discussions.

Though we have discussed two mistakes in popular arguments, our discussion is still incomplete, for we should also know why the causal relationship cannot be otherwise. Any patient has two properties and any agent also has two properties. The first one is that the being of the patient is due to the maker, and the second is that the patient cannot be prior to the agent. Henceforth, the union between the patient and the agent is either due to the existence of the maker, to his nonexistence, or to both. But, obviously, the union cannot be realized due both to existence and to non-existence. It can result only from one or the other. If we were to suppose that the agent did not exist, then its effect could obviously not be united with anything. And were it not united with something due to the fact that it exists, then it would not be united for any other reason. For the very reason that it exists, the patient has no choice but to be united with something else and to depend on this entity in order to persist.

That existent which is due to non-existence is an entity which cannot have a cause. Its suggested cause cannot exist, for if it existed, it would not be non-existence. It is certainly possible for the patient not to exist, but the existence of that which is not posterior to non-existence cannot exist. Thus, from that aspect that it is a being, the patient depends on the maker because its existence is due to this maker. However, from another aspect, that its existence is posterior to its non-existence, it is not in need of a maker, for from this point of view it is necessary in itself. An entity that is dependent in respect to being cannot be independent since it is united with a cause. Other correct arguments can be upheld for this subject, but this discussion is sufficient.

As regards the maker (the agent), however, functioning as a cause is not due to its own making if we consider as an agent that entity from which something originates that did not exist previously. Being a cause is due to the fact that something is realized from it. The patient did not exist before because the agent was previously not a cause.

We have, then, asserted the existence of two conditions. The first is that the agent is not the cause of the existence of a thing, and the second is that it functions as a cause at a given time. The first condition is its non-causality rather than its causality, whereas the second condition is its causality. For example, someone can will the existence of an entity in order that it may be realized from the other entities whose existence depend on his will. Since there is a will as well as a capability on the part of the agent, that entity is actualized. When it is actualized, it is true that that entity is an existent whose causality is due to the realization of that which was willed. When the will is realized and that which is willed is realized posterior to its 'non-existence', then the former has no influence on the latter because the object willed must be as it is. Consequently, the realization of something into an existent is due to the fact that its agent becomes a cause, and that its being is due to its causation. But one should note that being a cause is one thing, whereas becoming a cause is another thing. Likewise, that being is one state, whereas becoming an existent is a different state. Being a cause corresponds, therefore, to being, but not to becoming an existent.

If one means by an agent that by means of which something becomes an existent (due to itself), rather than that by means of which something that already is continues to exist, then being an agent is not being a cause but becoming a cause. Let us suppose, however, and this we regard as a correct interpretation, that being an agent meant one thing, and that becoming an agent meant something else. Hence, there will be no relation between the state of being an agent and the condition of becoming an existent, posterior to the non-existence of the agent. Agentness would then have to correspond to being an existent because something existed due to another cause from which it was separated either permanently or only temporarily after becoming an existent. Although the patient would actually be different from the agent, 'being a cause' is commonly regarded as becoming an agent. Although people generally fail to distinguish between being an agent and becoming one, they believe, nonetheless, that being an agent cannot be separated from becoming an agent. From the context of this discussion it becomes evident, therefore, that the essence of an effect is not an actuality (i.e., its essence alone does not imply its existence) unless the cause exists. If the effect should persist, though that which is regarded as a cause would not exist, then that cause would have to be the cause for something other than the existence of that effect. It has also become evident that the agent is in reality that from which the being of the patient is realized separately from the essence of the agent, for if the patient were a part of the agent's essence, then the latter would be a receptacle rather than a maker.

21. Finding that there cannot be a multiplicity in the Necessary Existent

The Necessary Existent cannot contain a multiplicity as though it were composed of many elements, as a man's body consists of many parts. The Necessary Existent cannot have different kinds of parts, each standing by itself and forming a unit, such as wood and clay in a house.[9] Nor can such parts be separate in idea but not in essence in the manner matter and form are 'separate' in natural bodies. Hence, the possibilities mentioned here are ruled out, for if any of them were accurate, then the Necessary Existent would have to be united with the causes as we explained before. Different properties cannot be contained in the Necessary Existent, for if Its essence were realized with such properties, they would be together as parts. If Its essence were realized and the properties were accidental, then they would subsist in the Necessary Existent for their essence due to another cause. Consequently, the Necessary Existent would be a receptacle. But from what we have asserted it has become evident that the Necessary Existent is not the receptacle in essence. It cannot, moreover, be the case that these attributes are due to the Necessary Existent Itself, for It would then be a receptacle. From one idea no more than one thing can be realized, for we have proved that whatever comes from a cause is not realized until it becomes necessary. Consequently, when one entity becomes a necessity from a single idea and another entity also becomes a necessity from the same idea, then something must become a necessity due to something else because of the nature of the former due to which something becomes a necessity. It becomes a necessity due to two reasons. One of these originates, for example, from this nature and this will, whereas the other comes from that nature and that will. Another duality is then placed into this context. Discourse would then be directed at this duality and the argument would start anew. Hence, there is no multiplicity in the Necessary Existent.

22. Finding that the characteristic 'Necessary Existent' cannot be applied to more than one entity[10]

We have found that if two entities were called 'Necessary Existent,' then without a doubt there would be a differentia or a distinguishing mark for each. We have also found that both the differentia and the distinguishing mark do not occur in the essence (reality) of that which is universal. Hence, the Necessary Existent is a Necessary Existent without that differentia and that distinguishing mark. If we imagine only the nonexistence of that differentia and that distinguishing mark, one of these two cases would follow. Either each would be like the Necessary Existent or each would not be like It. If they were like the Necessary Existent, they would be two different things without, however, the distinctions of differentia and distinguishing mark, which is impossible. If they were not like It, then having a differentia and a distinguishing mark would be an essential condition for the necessary existence of the Necessary Existent, and this condition would have to be the essence of the Necessary Existent. Thus, differentia and distinguishing mark would come under the common idea of essence, which is absurd.

Indeed, if existence were other than essence, then this could be a legitimate alternative. But, for the Necessary Existent, existence is either due to essence or it is essence. Consequently, the Necessary Existent cannot be a duality in essence, in differentia, or in the distinguishing mark.[11] For this reason, the 'Necessary Existent' cannot be a characteristic that is applied to two things. Yet we have found that a cause is contained in the elements of any universal idea. For this reason, the Necessary Existent is not universal. If It were a universal, It would be an effect, and would not, therefore, be different from being a contingent being, which is impossible according to our demonstration.

23. Finding that the Necessary Existent is not receptive to change and that it necessarily persists in every mode

Whatever is receptive to change is also receptive to a cause. It is in a given condition due to one cause, and in another condition due to another cause. Its being is not devoid of the property of 'being in union with these causes'. Thus, its being depends on 'being in union with' the object with which it is united. We have established, however, that the Necessary Existent is not in union (with any other entity). Consequently, the Necessary Existent is not receptive to change.[12]

24. Finding that the essence of the Necessary Existent can be no other than existence

That whose essence is other than existence is not the Necessary Existent. It has become evident that existence has an accidental meaning for that whose essence is other than existence.[13] And it has also become evident that there is a cause for that which has an accidental idea (i.e., for that which has a contingent being). The cause of such a being is either the essence of that entity in which it subsists or something else.[14]

The Necessary Existent cannot have an essence as the cause of Its existence for the following reasons. If such an essence should have being so that the existence of the Necessary Existent could be derived from it, or that this being were the cause of Its existence, then the being of the essence would have to be realized prior to itself. Since the second hypothesis could not be the reason for Its being, an inquiry into the first explanation would be legitimate. On the other hand, if the essence had no being, it could not be the cause of anything. For whatever does not exist is not the cause of the existence of anything. Thus, the essence of the Necessary Existent is not the cause of its existence. Its cause is, therefore, something else. Henceforth, there must be a cause for the existence of the Necessary Existent. The Necessary Existent must exist, therefore, due to something else. This, however, is impossible.

25. Finding that the Necessary Existent is neither a substance nor an accident

A substance is that whose essence does not exist in a subject when the substance exists. Furthermore, it is that which can be realized only in a subject matter. From this point of view, there is no doubt that a body is a substance, though one can doubt the actual existence of that body which is a substance until one knows whether or not it is in a subject. Hence, substance is that which has an essence, such as materiality, spirituality, humanity, and horseness.[15] The condition of such an essence specifies that one does not know whether or not it has existence until its existence is realized in a subject. Whatever is of such a nature possesses an essence other than existence. Consequently, whatever has no essence other than existence is not a substance. And with regard to accidentality it is obvious that the Necessary Existent does not subsist in anything. Since the existence of the Necessary Existent is not related by way of correspondence or generically to the existence of other things, this essence is neither in the subject (due to the subject), as it is for hu-

manity and what is other than humanity, nor is the idea of genus applied to it, since existence is applied to what is posterior and prior, having neither opposite nor genus. And whatever is not in a subject has neither posteriority nor priority. Accordingly, an existent which does not subsist in a subject cannot be a genus of things other than in the sense described previously, whereas substance is the genus of those things which are substances. The Necessary Existent is, therefore, not a substance.[16] In brief, It is not in any category because existence is external to essence for each category, and hence it would only be an accidental addition to the essence of the Necessary Existent if the Necessary Existent belonged to a category. Existence, however, is the essence of the Necessary Existent. From our discussion it becomes evident that there is no genus for the Necessary Existent. Consequently, It does not have a differentia and, thus, It does not have a definition. Since it has neither a place nor a subject, it has no opposite and no species. It has neither companion nor resemblance. Finally, it has become evident that It does not have a cause. Hence, It is not receptive to change or to divisibility.

26. Analysis of the possibility that the Necessary Existent may have multiple characteristics without having multiplicity in its essence

There are four kinds of characteristics for things. One is that which is attributed to a body. It is an accidental characteristic which subsists in a substance although it is not united with another thing external to it. Another is that which is said of the color white. It is an accidental characteristic subsisting in a substance, although it is not united with another thing external to it. The third is that characteristic by which we describe the 'knower.' It is characteristic for a substance such as man, such that the aspect it contains is something external to the accidentality which brings about a union between that thing and other things. For example, there is a union between the knower and the known in which the form of knowledge is applied to the former. There is also the union between knowledge and things that are known. The fourth characteristic may be asserted of a 'father' and of 'being complete.' For the father has no characteristic as 'father-qua-father' other than being united with a child. Due to the existence of the child he is considered a father and is therefore made complete.

In addition to these four cases, there are characteristics for things which actually lack a characteristic.[17] Such is true of inertness when it is applied to a rock. The assertion that inertness subsists in a rock is meaningless, except for its implication that living is impossible for that to which 'inertness' applies. Thus, there cannot be multiple characteristics for the Necessary Existent, whether they are essential or accidental. The case for the accidental characteristic which subsists in an essence is self-evident. Let us consider, for instance, the characteristic of union of these characteristics; the Necessary Existent has no alternative but to exist with many things just as all things must exist due to it. While these characteristics refer to positive features of the Necessary Existent, there are many other characteristics describing the Necessary Existent in terms of what it lacks. For example, the characteristic of unity is attributed to the Necessary Existent, whereas this characteristic actually means that It has no companion. In another case it is said that It contains neither constituent nor part. There is also mention of 'being eternal' which in reality means that Its being has no beginning. Both of these characteristics are such that they do not imply multiplicity to the essence of the Necessary Existent. These characteristics refer essentially to nothing but (1) union, where 'union' is an idea in the intelligence rather than in the essence, or (2) negation and denial. In so doing they do not imply the existence of many characteristics, but rather an omission of many characteristics. Yet the term 'characteristic' induces the imagination to believe that there is a characteristic which subsists in essence. For example, the characteristic 'a rich man' can be

attributed to someone. This descriptive name is due to the existence of something else with which the person is united, but it is not a characteristic which refers to the essence of the person. The label 'a poor man' is applied to someone on account of the non-existence of a thing, rather than on account of a characteristic which refers to his essence. Enough has been said on this topic.

27. Finding that the Necessary Existent is a unity in reality and that the existence of all things is due to It[18]

As we have stated, the Necessary Existent is in fact a unity, and all other things are non-necessary beings. Thus, they are contingent beings. All have a cause, and causes are infinite series. Accordingly, they either attempt to return to a primary cause, the Necessary Existent, or they return to themselves (i.e., the chain of causation is circular). For example, if A is the cause of B, B the cause of J, and J the cause of D, then D will be the cause of A. Taken together, therefore, this group will be a group of effects. Hence, it has become evident that there must be an external cause for them. The absurdity of the argument for the circularity of causes is also apparent in another proof. If D were the cause of A, then the effect of the effect of A, and the effect of the effect of the effect of A would be the effect of A. For the one thing, another thing would have to act both as cause and effect, which is impossible. Therefore, each effect must return to the Necessary Existent which is unique. Consequently, all effects and contingencies return to the one Necessary Existent.

28. Finding that the Necessary Existent is eternal and that all other things are transitory

In brief, the being of bodies (i.e., substances), accidents, and the categories is evident in this sensible world.[19] And for all entities in this realm which belong to the ten categories, essence is different from existence.[20] We have asserted that they are all contingent beings. And accident subsists in substances which are receptive to change. Matter and form, the components of bodies, are also constituents of the body. By its own nature, matter is incapable of action. The same holds true for form. We have also made the assertion that any entity having this nature is a contingent being which exists due to a cause, rather than due to its own nature. Being dependent means that the contingent being exists due to something other than itself. We have likewise asserted that the causes culminate in a Necessary Existent and that the Necessary Existent is one. It has become evident, therefore, that there is a primary entity in the world which is not in the world though the being of the world comes from It. Its existence, which is necessary, is due to Itself. In reality It is absolute being and absolute existence. All things exist due to It in the same manner as the light of the sun is due to itself, whereas the illumination all other things receive from the sun is accidental. This analogy would have been correct if the sun were the basis of its own illumination.[21] This is not the case, however, because the illumination of the sun has a subject whereas the being of the Necessary Existent has no subject but stands by Itself.

NOTES

1. The first sentence is highly ambiguous. If one were to translate it literally, it would read as follows: 'The being of that which possesses being is either a necessity due to itself or is not such a necessity.' But in ibn Sīnā's philosophy there is nothing that is not 'a being.' In view of his philosophical system it would be more correct to render this proposition as: 'Self-necessity applies to some beings but not to other beings.' In this context ibn Sīnā introduces the concept of 'the Necessary Existent' by syntactical a priori means, rather than by an a posteriori proof. In a similar vein he asserts in the Shifā' (pp. 37–8) that it is impossible for the Necessary Existent not to be. In the Ishārāt III, 19 he repeats the thesis that that which exists must be either a necessity or a contingency, and only the former kind persists. This view finds its expression also in the Ishārāt, though wujūd appears here, rather than hastī, as the latter Persian term could not be employed in his Arabic texts. Ibn Sīnā's type of 'a priori' argumentation differs from Aristotle's presentation of his argument for the first mover (in Metaphysica 1072 b 10 and Physica 242 b 34). The convergent views of these two philosophers on 'contingent beings' are displayed in Aristotle's mention of 'entities' which are capable of both being and not being (De Caelo 281 a 27) and ibn Sīnā's reference to entities as actual contingent beings.
2. This proposition displays definitely that ibn Sīnā discriminates between wujūd and hastī by using the former in the sense of 'existence' and the latter in the sense of 'being.' The former, which is included in the latter, consists of nothing but actualized, persisting entities.
3. See Shifā', p. 37, where it is asserted that the Necessary Existent is uncaused.
4. Here ibn Sīnā means that a cause is a feature of an entity but is not identical with it. For instance, an entity may exist for a duration without being the cause of anything; it becomes a cause, however, when something is produced by it.
5. The same doctrine is expressed in the Shifā', p. 38, as well as in the Ishārāt III, 49.
6. There is a logical shade of difference between a bahra, meaning 'part,' and a juz', meaning 'constituent.' The former belongs to the same category as the whole of which it is a part, as a piece of paper is the same kind of paper as the sheet from which it was torn. The latter is merely an aspect of the entity apart from which it cannot exist, as for instance, the surface of a ball which cannot exist by itself, or the substratum-matter of a body which cannot exist in separation from its form.
7. Ibn Sīnā differentiates between two senses of 'cause': (1) where the cause is distinct from its effect, as is a moving cause which precedes its effect, and (2) where it is not necessary for the cause to be distinct from its effect, as in the case of a definition where the cause is the essence of the effect. A similar discussion of causation appears in Aristotle's Metaphysica (1070 a 21) and in his Analytica Posteriora (91 a 1). In the first work cited, Aristotle points out that a cause may be simultaneous with its effect, as in the case of a definition. He affirms in the second work that the definition of a concept discloses the essential nature of this concept. It is debatable whether these two formulations of his doctrine can be said to be consistent; for some apparent differences between them, see W.D. Ross, Aristotle's Prior and Posterior Analytics, Oxford, 1965, p. 79. Similar to the treatment ibn Sīnā gives to causality in this chapter of the Dānish Nāma are several analyses of this notion in the Shifā' (pp. 327, 343, 364) and the Hudūd (defs. 67–8).

8. Ibn Sīnā makes use of the term supporter [in Persian, *dāranda*] with reference to the Necessary Existent in the following sense. The Necessary Existent is not distinct from the world but is an aspect of it, namely that aspect by which it is 'upheld.' As such, It is the principle of sufficient reason for the world.

9. The same argument is advanced in the *Shifā'*, p. 37, and in the *Ishārāt* III, 44–5. Aristotle, too, argues that God (his prime mover, a non-sensible, eternal substance) is without part and indivisible for the reason that He has no magnitude (*Metaphysica* 1073 a 5). While Aristotle attempts to prove his argument on the basis of the non-infinity of magnitude, ibn Sīnā derives his conclusion from the analytic nature of the Necessary Existent.

10. That the Necessary Existent is unique is mentioned also in the *Shifā'*, p. 343, p. 43, p. 37, and in the *Ishārāt* III, 36-41, 116.

11. To replace Mo'in's incorrect reading, '. . . consequently, the Necessary Existent cannot be a duality in essence, in actuality *(fi'l)*, or in the possession of distinguishing marks,' we suggest the emendation 'differentia' *(faṣl)* for his 'actuality' *(fi'l)*, for the context in which this sentence appears makes it obvious that Mo'in's reading is mistaken—very likely—on account of a printing error.

12. Similar features of the Necessary Existent are described in the *Shifā'*, p. 37, and the *Ishārāt* III, 53. Aristotle ascribes the same features to his God in *Metaphysica* 1073 a 13.

13. As regards the controversy over ibn Sīnā's essence-existence distinction, see A.M. Goichon, *La distinction de l'essence et de l'existence d'après Ibn Sīnā (Avicenne)*, Paris, 1937; Hernandez M. Cruz, "La distinctión avicenniana de la escencia y la existencia y su interpretacion en la filosofia occidental," *Homenaje a Millas-Vallicrosa*, i (1954), pp. 351–74; F. Rahman, "Essence and Existence in Avicenna," *Med. Ren. Stud.*, iv (1958), pp. 1–16. For the relationship between ibn Sīnā, Aristotle and al-Fārābī on this distinction, see N. Rescher, *Studies in the History of Arabic Logic*, Pittsburgh, 1963, pp. 39–42; Aristotle's *Analytica Posteriora* 92 b 3–18, 93 a 18–20; and J. Owens, *The Doctrine of Being in the Aristotelian 'Metaphysics,'* Toronto, 1963, p. 309. The same doctrine is mentioned in ibn Sīnā's *Ishārāt* (III, 15) in illustrating the concept of a triangle and the existence *(wujūd)* of a particular triangle. The distinction between the idea *(ma'nā)*, the reality-essence *(māhiyya)* and existence *(wujūd)* is upheld in the *Ishārāt*, loc. cit.

14. In the *Ishārāt* III, 46, ibn Sīnā uses an epistemic approach in his analysis of this issue when he states that an understanding of the essence of the Necessary Existent entails an understanding of Its existence. Though this point is not mentioned explicitly in the *Dānish Nāma*, it is implicit in many arguments presented in this text. In the *Shifā'* (p. 344) he affirms also that the essence of the Necessary Existent is no other than Its existence *(anniyya)*.

15. Ibn Sīnā distinguishes here clearly between two senses of 'substance'; the first is an 'essence' which corresponds to Aristotle's secondary sense of substance (*Categoriae* 5; *Metaphysica* 1017 b 21; bk. VII, ch. 17), while the second refers to an actual individual particular (*Categoriae* 5). There is no causal connection between the realms of substances. In the *Shifā'*, p. 228, ibn Sīnā even asserts that 'a species is realized concomitantly in nature and intelligence.'

16. His view, that the Necessary Existent is not a substance, differentiates ibn Sīnā's Necessary Existent from Aristotle's God. From Aristotle's classification of substances into non-sensible eternals, sensible eternals, and sensible perishables, it is evident that he regards his God as a substance, in the sense that a body can be said to be a substance (*Metaphysica* 1073 a 3; 1072 b 20; 1069 a 30). Except for the passages noted, ibn Sīnā asserts in no other work that the Necessary Existent is not a substance. The specifications to which he subjects It preclude Its inclusion in the category of substance. For instance, in the *Ishārāt* (III, 53) ibn Sina avows that the Necessary Existent has neither a genus nor a differentia. Various similar points about the Necessary Existent find their expression in the *Shifā'*. There he affirms that numerous qualities, such as genus, essence, quality, quantity, place, time, definition, and explanation among others, are excluded from It by means of privation (p. 354). On the grounds that It has neither a genus nor a differentia, It cannot have a definition and cannot be demonstrated (p. 348). Its essence is existence *('inn wa maujūd)* itself (p. 367), and Its existence, in turn, is described as the essence of Its existence (p. 342). Other existents emanate from It (ibid.). In a peculiar passage (p. 367) ibn Sīnā does refer to the Necessary Existent as a substance, but he construes this reference as a privation in the sense that the Necessary Existent cannot be contained in a subject. The last point is also made in the *Dānish Nāma*, ch. 28.

17. Ibn Sīnā's notion of 'privation' *('adam)*, which is also expressed in the *Dānish Nāma* (ch. 13), is similar to that of Aristotle's *(stérēsis)* which appears repeatedly in Aristotle's *opera*, e.g. *Metaphysica* 1022 b 22, *Categoriae* 11 b 18. Ibn Sīnā employs this concept in order to clarify the features of the Necessary Existent by enumerating the qualities It lacks. He asserts accordingly in the *Shifā'* that the statement 'the Necessary Existent is an intelligence' implies that It is not a material entity (or that It is fixed with respect to place).

18. Observe the similar doctrines held by ibn Sīnā and Proclus who proclaims (*Elements*, p. 13), 'All that exists proceeds from a single first cause (prop. 11). For otherwise all things are uncaused; or else the sum of existence is limited, and there is a circuit of causation within the sum; or else there will be regress to infinity, cause lying behind cause, so that the positing of prior causes will never cease.' Aristotle

proffers similar arguments on several occasions in his *opera*, e.g. *Metaphysica* 994 a 1–19, 1072 b 12, and *Physica* 242 b 34. In the works listed below and elsewhere, ibn Sīnā either reiterates the very same arguments, or singles out the Necessary Existent as the first cause. *Shifā'*, pp. 342–43, 367; *Ishārāt* III, 18, 27; *'Ishq*, p. 20.

19. In a manner that brings to mind ibn Sīnā's exposition of the Necessary Existent, Aristotle attributes 'eternity' *(aidios)* to his God (*Metaphysica* 1072 b 27) in the context of his discussion of the first cause, and asserts, moreover, that any absolute existence is necessarily imperishable and ungenerated (*De Caelo* 281 b 27). In the Aristotelian system form and substratum-matter are alien to God with regard to their origin; they are linked to Him only in terms of movement. Ibn Sīnā's doctrine of emanation links bodies and the heavens more intimately to the Necessary Existent (from which they emanate) than they are so linked to God in the Aristotelian system.

20. Ibn Sīnā excludes the Necessary Existent from the categories by classifying It as a 'being' rather than as a 'substance' or as an 'accident.' Aristotle places his God in the category of substance. Unlike the theories of both ibn Sīnā and Aristotle is the theory held by Plotinus and Proclus who regard the One as being beyond 'being,' or beyond that which exists, though It is the generator of everything that has being (*Enneads* V [1]; *Elements*, p. 9).

21. This passage is of particular significance for the reason that it does not identify the Necessary Existent with the source of light, such as the sun, as which It is generally depicted by the mystics, but relates the metaphor to the receptivity of the mystic who allegedly becomes receptive to the eternal light when his soul is united with the active intelligence. In this context, then, the Necessary Existent is experienced by the mystic. Among other references to the 'light of lights' is that which is found in the *Ishārāt* II, 391 where this *terminus technicus* of the sūfic language refers to the goal to which the soul hopes to attain at the highest stage of its ascent. Ibn Sīnā repeatedly employs the light metaphor in connection with the Necessary Existent, e.g. *Ishārāt* IV, 60.

CHAPTER 3

St. Anselm

St. Anselm was born in 1033 of a noble family at Aosta, northern Italy. He completed his preliminary studies in France, at Avranches. He then decided to become a Benedictine monk against the objections of his father and in 1059 went to Bec in Normandy to study under Lanfranc, a noteworthy teacher. The following year he entered the Benedictine Order. He succeeded Lanfranc as prior of Bec in 1063 and was made abbot in 1078. He composed his main works during this fifteen-year period.

In 1093 he once again succeeded Lanfranc, this time as archbishop of Canterbury and Primate of England. He held that important position until his death in 1109. His tenure as Archbishop was distinguished by a vigorous defense of the rights of the church against the king.

To St. Anselm's credit, he was a bastion of intellectualism, standing firm against the anti-intellectualism of his day. He promoted a rational analysis of the faith, arguing that rather than leading to skepticism reason does none other than strengthen one's faith. His argument for the existence of God is a rational demonstration designed to bolster one's faith in divinity.

St. Anselm on the Existence of God

One best approaches St. Anselm's argument not so much as a proof but rather as a demonstration of God's existence. After all, if God is a necessary being, one is, strictly speaking, not in any position whatsoever of proving (i.e., establishing) the existence of such a being. Steps 1–4 demonstrate God's exemplified existence, and the subsequent three steps establish His necessary existence.

1. The first premise states that God is something nothing greater than which can be conceived. This is a claim as to the nature (i.e., understanding) of the Judeo-Christian (and Islamic) concept of God. In other words, God is the most perfect of possible conceptions. There are two important points concerning this premise: (a) The word 'can' does not mean 'does.' Just as no human has the ability to totally grasp the concept of infinity, that fact does not render the concept meaningless. So, too, with the concept of perfection. (b) This premise pertains solely to the nature of the *concept* of God.

But who is to say what God is? St. Anselm's concern was to demonstrate the existence of the God of his Christian belief. There is no doubt as to the nature of the Judeo-

Christian God verified by reference to the scriptures of those religions. It is a factual matter that in concept the God of those religious persuasions is infinite and one of all perfections.

2. The second premise states that that which exists in an exemplified way is greater (i.e., more perfect) than that which exists merely in an unexemplified way. The truth of this premise is based on the medieval analysis of the concept of dependency. That which is dependent is in some sense or other lacking, that is, it relies on something other than itself to be complete or whole. Unexemplified existence is that type of existence the object of which is dependent upon an act of thought whereas an object of exemplified existence is independent of an act of thought. Therefore, the former, by virtue of its dependency status, is inferior to the latter type of existence.

3. The third premise is a conditional statement the antecedent being a conjunction of the first two premises and the consequent being that God exists. This results in a modus ponens argument form the conclusion of which is 4.

4. God exists (in an exemplified manner). A contemporary, Gaunilon, objected by observing that the mere conception of a perfect island does not entail its (exemplified) existence. The import of this objection is that Anselm's argument must be fallacious, namely that the mere concept of perfection does not entail exemplification of the object of that conception. Anslem's response to Gaunilon's criticism is seen in steps 5–7 of his argument.

5. That which cannot be conceived not to exist is greater (i.e., more perfect) than that which can be conceived not to exist. This means that that which exists necessarily is more perfect than that which exists in a contingent manner. The truth of premise 5 is determined once one understands the difference between necessary and contingent existence; that is, indestructibility is a more perfect state of existence than destructibility. It is not the case that one must be able to imagine something that exists necessarily. One need only to understand the characteristics of necessary versus contingent existence to understand that the former is a more perfect form of existence than the latter. Islands, no matter how perfect, are contingent.

6. The sixth premise is a conditional statement the antecedent being a conjunction of premise 1 and premise 5 and the consequent being that God necessarily exists. Once again, this results in a modus ponens form of argument the conclusion of which is 7.

7. God exists (and necessarily so!).

ANSELM'S PROSLOGIUM OR DISCOURSE ON THE EXISTENCE OF GOD

Preface

After I had published, at the solicitous entreaties of certain brethren, a brief work (the *Monologium*) as an example of meditation on the grounds of faith, in the person

From St. Anselm, *Proslogium; Monologium; An Appendix in Behalf of the Fool by Gaunilon; and Cur Deus Homo*, translated by Sidney Norton Deane, B.A. (Chicago: Open Court Publishing Co., 1903), pp. 1–10, 145–170.

of one who investigates, in a course of silent reasoning with himself, matters of which he is ignorant; considering that this book was knit together by the linking of many arguments, I began to ask myself whether there might be found a single argument which would require no other for its proof than itself alone; and alone would suffice to demonstrate that God truly exists, and that there is a supreme good requiring nothing else, which all other things require for their existence and well-being; and whatever we believe regarding the divine Being.

Although I often and earnestly directed my thought to this end, and at some times that which I sought seemed to be just within my reach, while again it wholly evaded my mental vision, at last in despair I was about to cease, as if from the search for a thing which could not be found. But when I wished to exclude this thought altogether, lest, by busying my mind to no purpose, it should keep me from other thoughts, in which I might be successful; then more and more, though I was unwilling and shunned it, it began to force itself upon me, with a kind of importunity. So, one day, when I was exceedingly wearied with resisting its importunity, in the very conflict of my thoughts, the proof of which I had despaired offered itself, so that I eagerly embraced the thoughts which I was strenuously repelling.

Thinking, therefore, that what I rejoiced to have found, would, if put in writing, be welcome to some readers, of this very matter, and of some others, I have written the following treatise, in the person of one who strives to lift his mind to the contemplation of God, and seeks to understand what he believes. In my judgment, neither this work nor the other, which I mentioned above, deserved to be called a book, or to bear the name of an author; and yet I thought they ought not to be sent forth without some title by which they might, in some sort, invite one into whose hands they fell to their perusal. I accordingly gave each a title, that the first might be known as, An Example of Meditation on the Grounds of Faith, and its sequel as, Faith Seeking Understanding. But, after both had been copied by many under these titles, many urged me, and especially Hugo, the reverend Archbishop of Lyons, who discharges the apostolic office in Gaul, who instructed me to this effect on his apostolic authority—to prefix my name to these writings. And that this might be done more fitly, I named the first, *Monologium*, that is, A Soliloquy; but the second, *Proslogium*, that is, A Discourse.

Chapter I

Up now, slight man! flee, for a little while, thy occupations; hide thyself, for a time, from thy disturbing thoughts. Cast aside, now, thy burdensome cares, and put away thy toilsome business. Yield room for some little time to God; and rest for a little time in him. Enter the inner chamber of thy mind; shut out all thoughts save that of God, and such as can aid thee in seeking him; close thy door and seek him. Speak now, my whole heart! speak now to God, saying, I seek thy face; thy face, Lord, will I seek (Psalms xxvii. 8). And come thou now, O Lord my God, teach my heart where and how it may seek thee, where and how it may find thee.

Lord, if thou art not here, where shall I seek thee, being absent? But if thou art everywhere, why do I not see thee present? Truly thou dwellest in unapproachable light. But where is unapproachable light, or how shall I come to it? Or who shall lead me to that light and into it, that I may see thee in it? Again, by what marks, under what form, shall I seek thee? I have never seen thee, O Lord, my God; I do not know thy form. What, O most high Lord, shall this man do, an exile far from thee? What shall thy servant do, anxious in his love of thee, and cast out afar from thy face? He pants to see thee, and thy face is too far from him. He longs to come to thee, and thy dwelling-place is inaccessible. He is eager to find thee, and knows not thy place. He desires to seek thee, and does not know thy face. Lord, thou art my God, and thou art my Lord, and never have I seen thee. It is thou that hast made me, and hast made me anew, and hast bestowed upon me all the blessings I enjoy; and not yet do I know thee. Finally, I was created to see thee, and not yet have I done that for which I was made.

O wretched lot of man, when he hath lost that for which he was made! O hard and terrible fate! Alas, what has he lost, and what has he found? What has departed, and what remains? He has lost the blessedness for which he was made, and has found the misery for which he was not made. That has departed without which nothing is happy, and that remains which, in itself, is only miserable. Man once did eat the bread of angels, for which he hungers now; he eateth now the bread of sorrows, of which he knew not then. Alas! for the mourning of all mankind, for the universal lamentation of the sons of Hades! He choked with satiety, we sigh with hunger. He abounded, we beg. He possessed in happiness, and miserably forsook his possession; we suffer want in unhappiness, and feel a miserable longing, and alas! we remain empty.

Why did he not keep for us, when he could so easily, that whose lack we should feel so heavily? Why did he shut us away from the light, and cover us over with darkness? With what purpose did he rob us of life, and inflict death upon us? Wretches that we are, whence have we been driven out; whither are we driven on? Whence hurled? Whither consigned to ruin? From a native country into exile, from the vision of God into our present blindness, from the joy of immortality into the bitterness and horror of death. Miserable exchange of how great a good, for how great an evil! Heavy loss, heavy grief heavy all our fate!

But alas! wretched that I am, one of the sons of Eve, far removed from God! What have I undertaken? What have I accomplished? Whither was I striving? How far have I come? To what did I aspire? Amid what thoughts am I sighing? I sought blessings, and lo! confusion. I strove toward God, and I stumbled on myself. I sought calm in privacy, and I found tribulation and grief, in my inmost thoughts. I wished to smile in the joy of my mind, and I am compelled to frown by the sorrow of my heart. Gladness was hoped for, and lo! a source of frequent sighs!

And thou too, O Lord, how long? How long, O Lord, dost thou forget us; how long dost thou turn thy face from us? When wilt thou look upon us, and hear us? When wilt thou enlighten our eyes, and show us thy face? When wilt thou restore thyself to us? Look upon us, Lord; hear us, enlighten us,

reveal thyself to us. Restore thyself to us, that it may be well with us,—thyself, without whom it is so ill with us. Pity our toilings and strivings toward thee, since we can do nothing without thee. Thou dost invite us; do thou help us. I beseech thee, O Lord, that I may not lose hope in sighs, but may breathe anew in hope. Lord, my heart is made bitter by its desolation; sweeten thou it, I beseech thee, with thy consolation. Lord, in hunger I began to seek thee; I beseech thee that I may not cease to hunger for thee. In hunger I have come to thee; let me not go unfed. I have come in poverty to the Rich, in misery to the Compassionate; let me not return empty and despised. And if, before I eat, I sigh, grant, even after sighs, that which I may eat. Lord, I am bowed down and can only look downward; raise me up that I may look upward. My iniquities have gone over my head; they overwhelm me; and, like a heavy load, they weigh me down. Free me from them; unburden me, that the pit of iniquities may not close over me.

Be it mine to look up to thy light, even from afar, even from the depths. Teach me to seek thee, and reveal thyself to me, when I seek thee, for I cannot seek thee, except thou teach me, nor find thee, except thou reveal thyself. Let me seek thee in longing, let me long for thee in seeking; let me find thee in love, and love thee in finding. Lord, I acknowledge and I thank thee that thou hast created me in this thine image, in order that I may be mindful of thee, may conceive of thee, and love thee; but that image has been so consumed and wasted away by vices, and obscured by the smoke of wrong-doing, that it cannot achieve that for which it was made, except thou renew it, and create it anew. I do not endeavor, O Lord, to penetrate thy sublimity, for in no wise do I compare my understanding with that; but I long to understand in some degree thy truth, which my heart believes and loves. For I do not seek to understand that I may believe, but I believe in order to understand. For this also I believe,—that unless I believed, I should not understand.

Chapter II

And so, Lord, do thou, who dost give understanding to faith, give me, so far as thou knowest it to be profitable, to understand that thou art as we believe; and that thou art that which we believe. And, indeed, we believe that thou art a being than which nothing greater can be conceived. Or is there no such nature, since the fool hath said in his heart, there is no God? (Psalms xiv. I). But, at any rate, this very fool, when he hears of this being of which I speak—a being than which nothing greater can be conceived—understands what he hears, and what he understands is in his understanding; although he does not understand it to exist.

For, it is one thing for an object to be in the understanding, and another to understand that the object exists. When a painter first conceives of what he will afterwards perform, he has it in his understanding, but he does not yet understand it to be, because he has not yet performed it. But after he has made the painting, he both has it in his understanding, and he understands that it exists, because he has made it.

Hence, even the fool is convinced that something exists in the understanding, at least, than which nothing greater can be conceived. For, when he hears of this, he understands it. And whatever is understood, exists in the understanding. And assuredly that, than which nothing greater can be conceived, cannot exist in the understanding alone. For, suppose it exists in the understanding alone: then it can be conceived to exist in reality; which is greater.

Therefore, if that, than which nothing greater can be conceived, exists in the understanding alone, the very being, than which nothing greater can be conceived, is one, than which a greater can be conceived. But obviously this is impossible. Hence, there is no doubt that there exists a being, than which nothing greater can be conceived, and it exists both in the understanding and in reality.

Chapter III

And it assuredly exists so truly, that it cannot be conceived not to exist. For, it is possible to conceive of a being which cannot be conceived not to exist; and this is greater than one which can be conceived not to exist. Hence, if that, than which nothing greater can be conceived, can be conceived not to exist, it is not that, than which nothing greater can be conceived. But this is an irreconcilable contradiction. There is, then, so truly a being than which nothing greater can be conceived to exist, that it cannot even be conceived not to exist; and this being thou art, O Lord, our God.

So truly, therefore, dost thou exist, O Lord, my God, that thou canst not be conceived not to exist; and rightly. For, if a mind could conceive of a being better than thee, the creature would rise above the Creator; and this is most absurd. And, indeed, whatever else there is, except thee alone, can be conceived not to exist. To thee alone, therefore, it belongs to exist more truly than all other beings, and hence in a higher degree than all others. For, whatever else exists does not exist so truly, and hence in a less degree it belongs to it to exist. Why, then, has the fool said in his heart, there is no God (Psalms xiv. 1), since it is so evident, to a rational mind, that thou dost exist in the highest degree of all? Why, except that he is dull and a fool?

Chapter IV

But how has the fool said in his heart what he could not conceive; or how is it that he could not conceive what he said in his heart? since it is the same to say in the heart, and to conceive.

But, if really, nay, since really, he both conceived, because he said in his heart; and did not say in his heart, because he could not conceive; there is more than one way in which a thing is said in the heart or conceived. For, in one sense, an object is conceived, when the word signifying it is conceived; and in another, when the very entity, which the object is, is understood.

In the former sense, then, God can be conceived not to exist; but in the latter, not at all. For no one who understands what fire and water are can conceive fire to be water, in accordance with the nature of the facts themselves, although this is possible according to the words. So, then, no one who understands what God is can conceive that God does not exist; although he says these words in his heart, either without any, or with some foreign, signification.

For, God is that than which a greater cannot be conceived. And he who thoroughly understands this, assuredly understands that this being so truly exists, that not even in concept can it be non-existent. Therefore, he who understands that God so exists, cannot conceive that he does not exist.

I thank thee, gracious Lord, I thank thee; because what I formerly believed by thy bounty, I now so understand by thine illumination, that if I were unwilling to believe that thou dost exist, I should not be able not to understand this to be true.

APPENDIX
IN BEHALF OF THE FOOL
AN ANSWER TO THE ARGUMENT OF ANSELM
IN THE *PROSLOGIUM*
BY GAUNILON, A MONK OF MARMOUTIER

1. If one doubts or denies the existence of a being of such a nature that nothing greater than it can be conceived, he receives this answer:

The existence of this being is proved, in the first place, by the fact that he himself, in his doubt or denial regarding this being, already has it in his understanding; for in hearing it spoken of he understands what is spoken of. It is proved, therefore, by the fact that what he understands must exist not only in his understanding, but in reality also.

And the proof of this is as follows.—It is a greater thing to exist both in the understanding and in reality than to be in the understanding alone. And if this being is in the understanding alone, whatever has even in the past existed in reality will be greater than this being. And so that which was greater than all beings will be less than some being, and will not be greater than all: which is a manifest contradiction.

And hence, that which is greater than all, already proved to be in the understanding, must exist not only in the understanding, but also in reality: for otherwise it will not be greater than all other beings.

2. The fool might make this reply:

This being is said to be in my understanding already, only because I understand what is said. Now could it not with equal justice be said that I have in my understanding all manner of unreal objects, having absolutely no existence in themselves, because I understand these things if one speaks of them, whatever they may be?

Unless indeed it is shown that this being is of such a character that it cannot be held in concept like all unreal objects, or objects whose existence is uncertain: and hence I am not able to conceive of it when I hear of it, or to hold it in concept; but I must understand it and have it in my understanding; because, it seems, I cannot conceive of it in any other way than by understanding it, that is, by comprehending in my knowledge its existence in reality.

But if this is the case, in the first place there will be no distinction between what has precedence in time—namely, the having of an object in the understanding—and what is subsequent in time—namely, the understanding that an object exists; as in the example of the picture, which exists first in the mind of the painter, and afterwards in his work.

Moreover, the following assertion can

hardly be accepted: that this being, when it is spoken of and heard of, cannot be conceived not to exist in the way in which even God can be conceived not to exist. For if this is impossible, what was the object of this argument against one who doubts or denies the existence of such a being?

Finally, that this being so exists that it cannot be perceived by an understanding convinced of its own indubitable existence, unless this being is afterwards conceived of—this should be proved to me by an indisputable argument, but not by that which you have advanced: namely, that what I understand, when I hear it, already is in my understanding. For thus in my understanding, as I still think, could be all sorts of things whose existence is uncertain, or which do not exist at all, if some one whose words I should understand mentioned them. And so much the more if I should be deceived, as often happens, and believe in them: though I do not yet believe in the being whose existence you would prove.

3. Hence, your example of the painter who already has in his understanding what he is to paint cannot agree with this argument. For the picture, before it is made, is contained in the artificer's art itself; and any such thing, existing in the art of an artificer, is nothing but a part of his understanding itself. A joiner, St. Augustine says, when he is about to make a box in fact, first has it in his art. The box which is made in fact is not life; but the box which exists in his art is life. For the artificer's soul lives, in which all these things are, before they are produced. Why, then, are these things life in the living soul of the artificer, unless because they are nothing else than the knowledge or understanding of the soul itself?

With the exception, however, of those facts which are known to pertain to the mental nature, whatever, on being heard and thought out by the understanding, is perceived to be real, undoubtedly that real object is one thing, and the understanding itself, by which the object is grasped, is another. Hence, even if it were true that there is a being than which a greater is inconceivable: yet to this being, when heard of and understood, the not yet created picture in the mind of the painter is not analogous.

4. Let us notice also the point touched on above, with regard to this being which is greater than all which can be conceived, and which, it is said, can be none other than God himself. I, so far as actual knowledge of the object, either from its specific or general character, is concerned, am as little able to conceive of this being when I hear of it, or to have it in my understanding, as I am to conceive of or understand God himself: whom, indeed, for this very reason I can conceive not to exist. For I do not know that reality itself which God is, nor can I form a conjecture of that reality from some other like reality. For you yourself assert that that reality is such that there can be nothing else like it.

For, suppose that I should hear something said of a man absolutely unknown to me, of whose very existence I was unaware. Through that special or general knowledge by which I know what man is, or what men are, I could conceive of him also, according to the reality itself, which man is. And yet it would be possible, if the person who told me of him deceived me, that the man himself, of whom I conceived, did not exist; since that reality according to which I conceived of him, though a no less indisputable fact, was not that man, but any man.

Hence, I am not able, in the way in which I should have this unreal being in concept or in understanding, to have that being of which you speak in concept or in understanding, when I hear the word *God* or the words, a *being greater than all other beings*. For I can conceive of the man according to a fact that is real and familiar to me: but of God, or a being greater than all others, I could not conceive at all, except merely according to the word. And an object can hardly or never be conceived according to the word alone.

For when it is so conceived, it is not so much the word itself (which is, indeed, a real thing—that is, the sound of the letters and syllables) as the signification of the word, when heard, that is conceived. But it is not conceived as by one who knows what is generally signified by the word; by whom, that is, it is conceived according to a reality and in true conception alone. It is conceived as by a man who does not know the object, and conceives of it only in accordance with the movement of his mind produced by hearing the word, the mind attempting to image for itself the signification of the word that is heard. And it would be surprising if in the reality of fact it could ever attain to this.

Thus, it appears, and in no other way, this being is also in my understanding, when I hear and understand a person who says that there is a being greater than all conceivable beings. So much for the assertion that this supreme nature already is in my understanding.

5. But that this being must exist, not only in the understanding but also in reality, is thus proved to me:

If it did not so exist, whatever exists in reality would be greater than it. And so the being which has been already proved to exist in my understanding, will not be greater than all other beings.

I still answer: if it should be said that a being which cannot be even conceived in terms of any fact, is in the understanding, I do not deny that this being is, accordingly, in my understanding. But since through this fact it can in no wise attain to real existence also, I do not yet concede to it that existence at all, until some certain proof of it shall be given.

For he who says that this being exists, because otherwise the being which is greater than all will not be greater than all, does not attend strictly enough to what he is saying. For I do not yet say, no, I even deny or doubt that this being is greater than any real object. Nor do I concede to it any other existence than this (if it should be called existence) which it has when the mind, according to a word merely heard, tries to form the image of an object absolutely unknown to it.

How, then, is the veritable existence of that being proved to me from the assumption, by hypothesis, that it is greater than all other beings? For I should still deny this, or doubt your demonstration of it, to this extent, that I should not admit that this being is in my understanding and concept even in the way in which many objects whose real existence is uncertain and doubtful, are in my understanding and concept. For it should be proved first that this being itself really exists somewhere; and then, from the fact that it is greater than all, we shall not hesitate to infer that it also subsists in itself.

6. For example: it is said that somewhere in the ocean is an island, which, because of the difficulty, or rather the impossibility, of discovering what does not exist, is called the lost island. And they say that this island has an inestimable wealth of all manner of riches and delicacies in greater abundance than is told of the Islands of the Blest; and that having no owner or inhabitant, it is more excellent than all other countries, which are inhabited by mankind, in the abundance with which it is stored.

Now if some one should tell me that there is such an island, I should easily understand his words, in which there is no difficulty. But suppose that he went on to say, as if by a logical inference: "You can no longer doubt that this island which is more excellent than all lands exists somewhere, since you have no doubt that it is in your understanding. And since it is more excellent not to be in the understanding alone, but to exist both in the understanding and in reality, for this reason it must exist. For if it does not exist, any land which really exists will be more excellent than it; and so the island already understood by you to be more excellent will not be more excellent."

If a man should try to prove to me by such reasoning that this island truly exists, and that its existence should no longer be doubted, either I should believe that he was jesting, or I know not which I ought to regard as the greater fool: myself, supposing that I should allow this proof; or him, if he should suppose that he had established with any certainty the existence of this island. For he ought to show first that the hypothetical excellence of this island exists as a real and indubitable fact, and in no wise as any unreal object, or one whose existence is uncertain, in my understanding.

7. This, in the meantime, is the answer the fool could make to the arguments urged against him. When he is assured in the first place that this being is so great that its non-existence is not even conceivable, and that this in turn is proved on no other ground than the fact that otherwise it will not be greater than all things, the fool may make the same answer, and say:

When did I say that any such being exists in reality, that is, a being greater than all others?–that on this ground it should be proved to me that it also exists in reality to such a degree that it cannot even be conceived not to exist? Whereas in the first place it should be in some way proved that a nature which is higher, that is, greater and better, than all other natures, exists; in order that from this we may then be able to prove all attributes which necessarily the being that is greater and better than all possesses.

Moreover, it is said that the non-existence of this being is inconceivable. It might better be said, perhaps, that its non-existence, or the possibility of its non-existence, is unintelligible. For according to the true meaning of the word, unreal objects are unintelligible. Yet their existence is conceivable in the way in which the fool conceived of the non-existence of God. I am most certainly aware of my own existence; but I know, nevertheless, that my non-existence is possible. As to that supreme being, moreover, which God is, I understand without any doubt both his existence, and the impossibility of his non-existence. Whether, however, so long as I am most positively aware of my existence, I can conceive of my non-existence, I am not sure. But if I can, why can I not conceive of the non-existence of whatever else I know with the same certainty? If, however, I cannot, God will not be the only being of which it can be said, it is impossible to conceive of his non-existence.

8. The other parts of this book are argued with such truth, such brilliancy, such grandeur; and are so replete with usefulness, so fragrant with a certain perfume of devout and holy feeling, that though there are matters in the beginning which, however rightly sensed, are weakly presented, the rest of the work should not be rejected on this account. The rather ought these earlier matters to be reasoned more cogently, and the whole to be received with great respect and honor.

ANSELM'S APOLOGETIC
IN REPLY TO GAUNILON'S ANSWER IN BEHALF OF THE FOOL

It was a fool against whom the argument of my Proslogium was directed. Seeing, however, that the author of these objections is by no means a fool, and is a Catholic, speaking in behalf of the fool, I think it sufficient that I answer the Catholic.

Chapter 1

You say—whosoever you may be, who say that a fool is capable of making these statements that a being than which a greater cannot be conceived is not in the understanding in any other sense than that in which a being that is altogether inconceivable in terms of reality, is in the understanding. You say that the inference that this being exists in reality, from the fact that it is in the understanding, is no more just than the inference that a lost island most certainly exists, from the fact that when it is described the hearer does not doubt that it is in his understanding.

But I say: if a being than which a greater is inconceivable is not understood or conceived, and is not in the understanding or in concept, certainly either God is not a being than which a greater is inconceivable, or else he is not understood or conceived, and is not in the understanding or in concept. But I call on your faith and conscience to attest that this is most false. Hence, that than which a greater cannot be conceived is truly understood and conceived, and is in the understanding and in concept. Therefore either the grounds on which you try to controvert me are not true, or else the inference which you think to base logically on those grounds is not justified.

But you hold, moreover, that supposing that a being than which a greater cannot be conceived is understood, it does not follow that this being is in the understanding; nor, if it is in the understanding, does it therefore exist in reality.

In answer to this, I maintain positively: if that being can be even conceived to be, it must exist in reality. For that than which a greater is inconceivable cannot be conceived except as without beginning. But whatever can be conceived to exist, and does not exist, can be conceived to exist through a beginning. Hence what can be conceived to exist, but does not exist, is not the being than which a greater cannot be conceived. Therefore, if such a being can be conceived to exist, necessarily it does exist.

Furthermore: if it can be conceived at all, it must exist. For no one who denies or doubts the existence of a being than which a greater is inconceivable, denies or doubts that if it did exist, its non-existence, either in reality or in the understanding, would be impossible. For otherwise it would not be a being than which a greater cannot be conceived. But as to whatever can be conceived, but does not exist—if there were such a being, its non-existence, either in reality or in the understanding, would be possible. Therefore if a being than which a greater is inconceivable can be even conceived, it cannot be nonexistent.

But let us suppose that it does not exist, even if it can be conceived. Whatever can be conceived, but does not exist, if it existed, would not be a being than which a greater is inconceivable. If, then, there were a being a greater than which is inconceivable, it would not be a being than which a greater is inconceivable: which is most absurd. Hence, it is false to deny that a being

than which a greater cannot be conceived exists, if it can be even conceived; much the more, therefore, if it can be understood or can be in the understanding.

Moreover, I will venture to make this assertion: without doubt, whatever at any place or at any time does not exist—even if it does exist at some place or at some time—can be conceived to exist nowhere and never, as at some place and at some time it does not exist. For what did not exist yesterday, and exists today, as it is understood not to have existed yesterday, so it can be apprehended by the intelligence that it never exists. And what is not here, and is elsewhere, can be conceived to be nowhere, just as it is not here. So with regard to an object of which the individual parts do not exist at the same places or times: all its parts and therefore its very whole can be conceived to exist nowhere or never.

For, although time is said to exist always, and the world everywhere, yet time does not as a whole exist always, nor the world as a whole everywhere. And as individual parts of time do not exist when others exist, so they can be conceived never to exist. And so it can be apprehended by the intelligence that individual parts of the world exist nowhere, as they do not exist where other parts exist. Moreover, what is composed of parts can be dissolved in concept, and be non-existent. Therefore, whatever at any place or at any time does not exist as a whole, even if it is existent, can be conceived not to exist.

But that than which a greater cannot be conceived, if it exists, cannot be conceived not to exist. Otherwise, it is not a being than which a greater cannot be conceived: which is inconsistent. By no means, then, does it at any place or at any time fail to exist as a whole: but it exists as a whole everywhere and always.

Do you believe that this being can in some way be conceived or understood, or that the being with regard to which these things are understood can be in concept or in the understanding? For if it cannot, these things cannot be understood with reference to it. But if you say that it is not understood and that it is not in the understanding, because it is not thoroughly understood; you should say that a man who cannot face the direct rays of the sun does not see the light of day, which is none other than the sunlight. Assuredly a being than which a greater cannot be conceived exists, and is in the understanding, at least to this extent—that these statements regarding it are understood.

Chapter II

I have said, then, in the argument which you dispute, that when the fool hears mentioned a being than which a greater is inconceivable, he understands what he hears. Certainly a man who does not understand when a familiar language is spoken, has no understanding at all, or a very dull one. Moreover, I have said that if this being is understood, it is in the understanding. Is that in no understanding which has been proved necessarily to exist in the reality of fact?

But you will say that although it is in the understanding, it does not follow that it is understood. But observe that the fact of its being understood does necessitate its being in the understanding. For as what is conceived, is conceived by conception, and what is conceived by conception, as it is conceived, so is in conception; so what is understood, is understood by understanding, and what is understood by understanding, as it is understood, so is in the understanding. What can be more clear than this?

After this, I have said that if it is even in the understanding alone, it can be conceived also to exist in reality, which is greater. If, then, it is in the understanding alone, obviously the very being than which a greater cannot be conceived is one than which a greater can be conceived. What is more logical? For if it exists even in the understanding alone, can it not be conceived also to exist in reality? And if it can be so conceived, does not he who conceives of this conceive of a thing greater than that

being, if it exists in the understanding alone? What more consistent inference, then, can be made than this: that if a being than which a greater cannot be conceived is in the understanding alone, it is not that than which a greater cannot be conceived?

But, assuredly, in no understanding is a being than which a greater is conceivable a being than which a greater is inconceivable. Does it not follow, then, that if a being than which a greater cannot be conceived is in any understanding, it does not exist in the understanding alone? For if it is in the understanding alone, it is a being than which a greater can be conceived, which is inconsistent with the hypothesis.

Chapter III

But, you say, it is as if one should suppose an island in the ocean, which surpasses all lands in its fertility, and which, because of the difficulty, or rather the impossibility, of discovering what does not exist, is called a lost island; and should say that there can be no doubt that this island truly exists in reality, for this reason, that one who hears it described easily understands what he hears.

Now I promise confidently that if any man shall devise anything existing either in reality or in concept alone (except that than which a greater cannot be conceived) to which he can adapt the sequence of my reasoning, I will discover that thing, and will give him his lost island, not to be lost again.

But it now appears that this being than which a greater is inconceivable cannot be conceived not to be, because it exists on so assured a ground of truth; for otherwise it would not exist at all.

Hence, if any one says that he conceives this being not to exist, I say that at the time when he conceives of this either he conceives of a being than which a greater is inconceivable, or he does not conceive at all. If he does not conceive, he does not conceive of the non-existence of that of which he does not conceive. But if he does conceive, he certainly conceives of a being which cannot be even conceived not to exist. For if it could be conceived not to exist, it could be conceived to have a beginning and an end. But this is impossible.

He, then, who conceives of this being conceives of a being which cannot be even conceived not to exist; but he who conceives of this being does not conceive that it does not exist; else he conceives what is inconceivable. The non-existence, then, of that than which a greater cannot be conceived is inconceivable.

Chapter IV

You say, moreover, that whereas I assert that this supreme being cannot be *conceived* not to exist, it might better be said that its non-existence, or even the possibility of its non-existence, cannot be *understood.*

But it was more proper to say, it cannot be conceived. For if I had said that the object itself cannot be understood not to exist, possibly you yourself, who say that in accordance with the true meaning of the term what is unreal cannot be understood, would offer the objection that nothing which is can be understood not to be, for the non-existence of what exists is unreal: hence God would not be the only being of which it could be said, it is impossible to understand its non-existence. For thus one of those beings which most certainly exist can be understood not to exist in the same way in which certain other real objects can be understood not to exist.

But this objection, assuredly, cannot be urged against the term *conception,* if one considers the matter well. For although no objects which exist can be understood not to exist, yet all objects, except that which exists in the highest degree, can be conceived not to exist. For all those objects, and those alone, can be conceived not to exist, which have a beginning or end or composition of parts: also, as I have already said, whatever at any place or at any time does not exist as a whole.

That being alone, on the other hand, cannot be conceived not to exist, in which any

conception discovers neither beginning nor end nor composition of parts, and which any conception finds always and everywhere as a whole.

Be assured, then, that you can conceive of your own non-existence, although you are most certain that you exist. I am surprised that you should have admitted that you are ignorant of this. For we conceive of the non-existence of many objects which we know to exist, and of the existence of many which we know not to exist; not by forming the opinion that they so exist, but by imagining that they exist as we conceive of them.

And indeed, we can conceive of the non-existence of an object, although we know it to exist, because at the same time we can conceive of the former and know the latter. And we cannot conceive of the non-existence of an object, so long as we know it to exist, because we cannot conceive at the same time of existence and non-existence.

If, then, one will thus distinguish these two senses of this statement, he will understand that nothing, so long as it is known to exist, can be conceived not to exist; and that whatever exists, except that being than which a greater cannot be conceived, can be conceived not to exist, even when it is known to exist.

So, then, of God alone it can be said that it is impossible to conceive of his non-existence; and yet many objects, so long as they exist, in one sense cannot be conceived not to exist. But in what sense God is to be conceived not to exist, I think has been shown clearly enough in my book.

Chapter V

The nature of the other objections which you, in behalf of the fool, urge against me it is easy, even for a man of small wisdom, to detect; and I had therefore thought it unnecessary to show this. But since I hear that some readers of these objections think they have some weight against me, I will discuss them briefly.

In the first place, you often repeat that I

assert that what is greater than all other beings is in the understanding; and if it is in the understanding, it exists also in reality, for otherwise the being which is greater than all would not be greater than all.

Nowhere in all my writings is such a demonstration found. For the real existence of a being which is said to be *greater than all other beings* cannot be demonstrated in the same way with the real existence of one that is said to be *a being than which a greater cannot be conceived.*

If it should be said that a being than which a greater cannot be conceived has no real existence, or that it is possible that it does not exist, or even that it can be conceived not to exist, such an assertion can be easily refuted. For the non-existence of what does not exist is possible, and that whose non-existence is possible can be conceived not to exist. But whatever can be conceived not to exist, if it exists, is not a being than which a greater cannot be conceived; but if it does not exist, it would not, even if it existed, be a being than which a greater cannot be conceived. But it cannot be said that a being than which a greater is inconceivable, if it exists, is not a being than which a greater is inconceivable; or that if it existed, it would not be a being than which a greater is inconceivable.

It is evident, then, that neither is it non-existent, nor is it possible that it does not exist, nor can it be conceived not to exist. For otherwise, if it exists, it is not that which it is said to be in the hypothesis; and if it existed, it would not be what it is said to be in the hypothesis.

But this, it appears, cannot be so easily proved of a being which is said to be *greater than all other beings.* For it is not so evident that what can be conceived not to exist is not greater than all existing beings, as it is evident that it is not a being than which a greater cannot be conceived. Nor is it so indubitable that if a being greater than all other beings exists, it is no other than the being than which a greater cannot be conceived; or that if it were such a being, some other might not be this being in like manner; as it is certain with regard to a being which is hypothetically posited as one than which a greater cannot be conceived.

For consider: if one should say that there is a being greater than all other beings, and that this being can nevertheless be conceived not to exist; and that a being greater than this, although it does not exist, can be conceived to exist: can it be so clearly inferred in this case that this being is therefore not a being greater than all other existing beings, as it would be most positively affirmed in the other case, that the being under discussion is not, therefore, a being than which a greater cannot be conceived?

For the former conclusion requires another premise than the predication, *greater than all other beings.* In my argument, on the other hand, there is no need of any other than this very predication, *a being than which a greater cannot be conceived.*

If the same proof cannot be applied when the being in question is predicated to be greater than all others, which can be applied when it is predicated to be a being than which a greater cannot be conceived, you have unjustly censured me for saying what I did not say; since such a predication differs so greatly from that which I actually made. If, on the other hand, the other argument is valid, you ought not to blame me so for having said what can be proved.

Whether this can be proved, however, he will easily decide who recognizes that this being than which a greater cannot be conceived is demonstrable. For by no means can this being than which a greater cannot be conceived be understood as any other than that which alone is greater than all. Hence, just as that than which a greater cannot be conceived is understood, and is in the understanding, and for that reason is asserted to exist in the reality of fact: so what is said to be greater than all other beings is understood and is in the understanding, and therefore it is necessarily inferred that it exists in reality.

You see, then, with how much justice you have compared me with your fool, who, on the sole ground that he understands what is described to him, would affirm that a lost island exists.

Chapter VI

Another of your objections is that any unreal beings, or beings whose existence is uncertain, can be understood and be in the understanding in the same way with that being which I discussed. I am surprised that you should have conceived this objection, for I was attempting to prove what was still uncertain, and contented myself at first with showing that this being is understood in any way, and is in the understanding. It was my intention to consider, on these grounds, whether this being is in the understanding alone, like an unreal object, or whether it also exists in fact, as a real being. For if unreal objects, or objects whose existence is uncertain, in this way are understood and are in the understanding, because, when they are spoken of, the hearer understands what the speaker means, there is no reason why that being of which I spoke should not be understood and be in the understanding.

How, moreover, can these two statements of yours be reconciled: (1) the assertion that if a man should speak of any unreal objects, whatever they might be, you would understand, and (2) the assertion that on hearing of that being which does exist, and not in that way in which even unreal objects are held in concept, you would not say that you conceive of it or have it in concept; since, as you say, you cannot conceive of it in any other way than by understanding it, that is, by comprehending in your knowledge its real existence?

How, I ask, can these two things be reconciled: that unreal objects are understood, and that understanding an object is comprehending in knowledge its real existence? The contradiction does not concern me: do you see to it. But if unreal objects are also in some sort understood, and your definition is applicable, not to every understanding, but to a certain sort of understanding, I ought not to be blamed for saying that a being than which a greater cannot be conceived is understood and is

in the understanding, even before I reached the certain conclusion that this being exists in reality.

Chapter VII

Again, you say that it can probably never be believed that this being, when it is spoken of and heard of, cannot be conceived not to exist in the same way in which even God may be conceived not to exist.

Such an objection could be answered by those who have attained but little skill in disputation and argument. For is it compatible with reason for a man to deny the existence of what he understands, because it is said to be that being whose existence he denies because he does not understand it? Or, if at some times its existence is denied, because only to a certain extent is it understood, and that which is not at all understood is the same to him: is not what is still undetermined more easily proved of a being which exists in some understanding than of one which exists in no understanding?

Hence it cannot be credible that any man denies the existence of a being than which a greater cannot be conceived, which, when he hears of it, he understands in a certain degree: it is incredible, I say, that any man denies the existence of this being because he denies the existence of God, the sensory perception of whom he in no wise conceives of.

Or if the existence of another object, because it is not at all understood, is denied, yet is not the existence of what is understood in some degree more easily proved than the existence of an object which is in no wise understood?

Not irrationally, then, has the hypothesis of a being a greater than which cannot be conceived been employed in controverting the fool, for the proof of the existence of God: since in some degree he would understand such a being, but in no wise could he understand God.

Chapter VIII

Moreover, your so careful demonstration that the being than which a greater cannot be conceived is not analogous to the not yet executed picture in the understanding of the painter, is quite unnecessary. It was not for this purpose that I suggested the preconceived picture. I had no thought of asserting that the being which I was discussing is of such a nature; but I wished to show that what is not understood to exist can be in the understanding.

Again, you say that when you hear of a being than which a greater is inconceivable, you cannot conceive of it in terms of any real object known to you either specifically or generally, nor have it in your understanding. For, you say, you neither know such a being in itself, nor can you form an idea of it from anything like it.

But obviously this is not true. For everything that is less good, in so far as it is good, is like the greater good. It is therefore evident to any rational mind, that by ascending from the lesser good to the greater, we can form a considerable notion of a being than which a greater is inconceivable.

For instance, who (even if he does not believe that what he conceives of exists in reality) supposing that there is some good which has a beginning and an end, does not conceive that a good is much better, which, if it begins, does not cease to be? And that as the second good is better than the first, so that good which has neither beginning nor end, though it is ever passing from the past through the present to the future, is better than the second? And that far better than this is a being—whether any being of such a nature exists or not—which in no wise requires change or motion, nor is compelled to undergo change or motion?

Is this inconceivable, or is some being greater than this conceivable? Or is not this to form a notion from objects than which a greater is conceivable, of the being than which a greater cannot be conceived? There is, then, a means of forming a notion of a being than which a greater is inconceivable.

So easily, then, can the fool who does not accept sacred authority be refuted, if he denies that a notion may be formed from other objects of a being than which a greater is inconceivable. But if any Catholic would deny this, let him remember that the invisible things of God, from the creation of the world, are clearly seen, being understood by the things that are made, even his eternal power and Godhead. (Romans i. 20.)

Chapter IX

But even if it were true that a being than which a greater is inconceivable cannot be conceived or understood; yet it would not be untrue that a being than which a greater cannot be conceived is conceivable and intelligible. There is nothing to prevent one's saying *ineffable*, although what is said to be ineffable cannot be spoken of. *Inconceivable* is conceivable, although that to which the word *inconceivable* can be applied is not conceivable. So, when one says, *that than which nothing greater is conceivable,* undoubtedly what is heard is conceivable and intelligible, although that being itself, than which a greater is inconceivable, cannot be conceived or understood.

Or, though there is a man so foolish as to say that there is no being than which a greater is inconceivable, he will not be so shameless as to say that he cannot understand or conceive of what he says. Or, if such a man is found, not only ought his words to be rejected, but he himself should be condemned.

Whoever, then, denies the existence of a being than which a greater cannot be conceived, at least understands and conceives of the denial which he makes. But this denial he cannot understand or conceive of without its component terms; and a term of this statement is *a being than which a greater cannot be conceived.* Whoever, then, makes this denial, understands and conceives of that than which a greater is inconceivable.

Moreover, it is evident that in the same

way it is possible to conceive of and understand a being whose non-existence is impossible; but he who conceives of this conceives of a greater being than one whose non-existence is possible. Hence, when a being than which a greater is inconceivable is conceived, if it is a being whose non-existence is possible that is conceived, it is not a being than which a greater cannot be conceived. But an object cannot be at once conceived and not conceived. Hence he who conceives of a being than which a greater is inconceivable, does not conceive of that whose non-existence is possible, but of that whose non-existence is impossible. Therefore, what he conceives of must exist; for anything whose non-existence is possible, is not that of which he conceives.

Chapter X

I believe that I have shown by an argument which is not weak, but sufficiently cogent, that in my former book I proved the real existence of a being than which a greater cannot be conceived; and I believe that this argument cannot be invalidated by the validity of any objection. For so great force does the signification of this reasoning contain in itself, that this being which is the subject of discussion, is of necessity, from the very fact that it is understood or conceived, proved also to exist in reality, and to be whatever we should believe of the divine substance.

For we attribute to the divine substance anything of which it can be conceived that it is better to be than not to be that thing. For example: it is better to be eternal than not eternal; good, than not good; nay, goodness itself, than not goodness itself. But it cannot be that anything of this nature is not a property of the being than which a greater is inconceivable. Hence, the being than which a greater is inconceivable must be whatever should be attributed to the divine essence.

I thank you for your kindness both in your blame and in your praise for my book. For since you have commended so generously those parts of it which seem to you worthy of acceptance, it is quite evident that you have criticized in no unkind spirit those parts of it which seemed to you weak.

CHAPTER 4

William of Auvergne

William of Auvergne (or Paris) was born at Aurillac around 1180. He taught theology at Paris and was consecrated bishop of that city in 1228 by Pope Gregory IX. Under this pope there was initiated a considerable adjustment concerning Catholic theology and Aristotelianism, whereby it became understood that the latter must be rejected when it was inconsistent with the former but accepted when in conformity with the teachings of the church.

William was a scholar not only of the works of Plato and Aristotle but also of the writings of Arabian and Jewish philosophers. As a result, he was very much aware of the points in which the Arabians and the writings of Aristotle were at odds with Christian doctrine. He was careful to draw a clear distinction between philosophy and theology, noting that they are separate disciplines governed by two separate and distinct sets of rules. In this regard he was somewhat ahead of his time; namely, in advance of Albert the Great and Thomas Aquinas, each of whom understood the value of treating philosophy and theology as separate disciplines. He expired in 1249.

William of Auvergne on the Existence of God

William of Auvergne provides an ontological argument. He observes that being (*esse*) has two intentions: (1) one is the essence or quiddity of a thing signified by a defining expression or by the name of a species; (2) the second intention pertains to the word 'is' (*est*). That these two are different is established by observing that the defining expression of a thing does not include existence. In other words, the being and the essence of a thing are distinct.

Now a thing typically derives its being from something else. "But if for each thing the being (*esse*) is other than the thing itself, it is necessary that this proceed in a circle or in a straight line, and it will go on to infinity." William argues that this is untenable. We must conclude that there is a being whose existence and essence are one and the same. This we call God. It should be noted that such a Being is atomic, absolutely simple. In other words, no distinction can be made between its existence and essence.

THE TRINITY, OR THE FIRST PRINCIPLE

Chapter I

Know that a being *(ens)* and being *(esse)* have many intentions and that they do not have an account or definition, as you will learn in what follows.[1] They seem to have intentions similar to what men assign to good. For they speak of good either by substance or by participation. In this way a color is said to be white substantially or essentially because its essence is whiteness, but the surface is said to be white by participation, that is, in having or participating in whiteness, not in being whiteness itself.[2] In like manner something is said to be good essentially, because its essence is goodness itself in virtue of which it is said to be good. Something else is said to be good by participation insofar as it has or participates in goodness, which is not the essence of that which participates in it.

In this way there is also the being whose essence is for it being *(esse)* and whose essence we predicate, when we say, "It is,"[3] so that it itself and its being *(esse)*, which we assert when we say, "It is" are one thing in every way. Something else is said [to be] by participation, insofar as it has something which is in no way one with the essence of the being and does not pertain to its essence. In fact, it is utterly beyond the account of the substance of the being.

Concerning this matter you read in the book, *The Hebdomads* of Boethius[4] that "every simple has its being *(esse)* and what it is as one." Otherwise, the simple would itself be divisible into that which it is and its being *(esse)*. This being would be resolvable into what participates and what is participated, since this being would be other than its being *(esse)*. Thus they would be participant and participated as though joined together from the two, that is, the

From William of Auvergne, *The Trinity, or the First Principle,* translated by Roland J. Teske, S.J., and Francis C. Wade, S.J. (Milwaukee, Wis.: Marquette University Press, 1989), pp. 65–73. Reprinted by permission of Marquette University Press.

being would not itself be simple in the ultimate degree.

You also find in the same book this division of the good.[5] Now the reason demanding that this be so is that everything that is said of a thing is either essential to it or accidental to it. That is, either it is its essence or part of the essence, or it is entirely beyond the essence. This latter is what we call accidental, and we say that it is had or is said by participation. Being, then, is said of everything either by substance or by participation. Or rather it will be said of one thing substantially, of another accidentally.[6] Since it cannot be said of everything by participation, it is necessary that it be said of something according to essence. For if it were said of everything by participation, no intellect could grasp it, because there would never be an end. For example, if good were never said except by participation, there would be no intention for this name "good." For on this showing something is said to be good by its having a good which is good. If it itself is something that has good, A will be good in having a good, which is B. But again B is good in having a good: either the good which is A or another good which is C. If B is good in having A, then A will be good in having a good which has A. Thus it will be good by participating in that which participates in A. The goodness of A will then be the cause of its own cause, for it will be, according to this, the cause of the goodness of B, but the goodness of B will be the cause of the goodness of A, since A was good in having a good, namely, B. Thus the same thing is the cause of its cause, and it will give to that which gives to it naturally prior to its having what it gives. For it will give it to this one before it will receive it from the same one, because it is necessary that B receive the goodness before it gives it. Thus it will receive it before it gives it to A. Thus A will have the goodness before B, and the converse as well. This is manifestly impossible and frivolous.

Consequently, B is good in having the good, which is C, and this goes on to infinity. Thus there is a complicated and involved infinity of participateds and participants in the intention of this word "good." For it says that "good" means "having good." Explain this second good, and its intention will be "having good," and this goes on to infinity. Hence, nothing is left in the intention of the name "good" except "having" infinitely repeated. This infinity neither determines nor settles the intellect. If someone contends that there is something left in the intention of the name "good," because it is called "having" an infinite number of times, this is clearly false. The reason is that nothing falls within its intention except the participating and the participated, and the latter is "having" and "good." But it still includes in its intention the "having," since it is said only according to participation. And so "good" is not what is left apart from "having," but is the whole intention of "having" and "good." Given, therefore, that every good is good by participation, [the participation] is infinite, and there is nothing that is called good. It is clear then that something is said to be good according to essence. In the same way it will be shown that being cannot be said of everything by participation. Thus, it is necessary that it be said of something according to essence, so that its intention and understanding have a limit.

Know that the modes of speaking which we have given, that is, the modes of speaking according to essence and according to participation, necessarily follow from each other. For the modes of speaking according to essence and according to participation, as we showed, cannot be one without the other, just as that which participates, insofar as it is participating, cannot be without the participated. To this mode of speaking are tied the modes of speaking essentially (per se) and accidentally (per accidens), so that the mode of speaking accidentally can in no way stand alone. It is not possible that something be said of something accidentally and said essentially of nothing; a subject that is a subject accidentally is extraneous to everything and not a proper subject. If it were a proper subject, a predicate would be due to it essentially because

it would be essentially and not accidentally the subject of that predication. But if it is extraneous and not a proper and primary subject, then something else is prior and proper. This is the subject that is said to be the subject essentially, and of it the predicate is said essentially. For example, a white thing is not the proper subject of healing; [healing] is said of it accidentally and not primarily. Hence, there will necessarily be something else of which it is said essentially and primarily, and this will be the primary and proper subject of being healed. Therefore, the mode of speaking that is accidental cannot stand by itself, just as an affection cannot be without its proper and primary subject.

In like manner, the qualified (secundum quid) mode of speaking cannot be without the unqualified (simpliciter) mode of speaking. If nothing is said unqualifiedly, it is impossible to speak qualifiedly of something. For unless something were said unqualifiedly of the First, it would be said qualifiedly of the whole. The reason is that, if it were said qualifiedly of the First, it would not be more worthy of such predication than the whole. Thus it should be said to have been predicated of the whole according to it rather than according to the whole. For it is no more said of the First than of the whole, since it is said only qualifiedly of both. Thus it will not be true that something is said qualifiedly of the whole unless it is said unqualifiedly of that according to which it is said of the whole.

When you find one of the three modes of speaking, it is necessary that you also discover the primary manner of speaking in that mode. Otherwise the secondary manner of speaking cannot stand, as we have shown, because the primary is like the roots and foundations of the others, which I have already called secondary.

Chapter II

You should know that being (esse) has two intentions. One of them is what is left from the variety of accidents that clothe it.[7] This is what is properly called the essence or substance, and in this intention there is grasped along with this sort of determination the intention that is all being (esse). In another determination it signifies only that which is signified by a defining expression or by the name of a species. This, then, is what is called the substance of a thing, its being (esse) and its quiddity, and this is the being (esse) the definition signifies and expresses. This is called the essence of a thing.

The second intention of that which is being (esse) is that which is said of each thing by this word "is" (est), and it is beyond the definition of each thing. Being (esse) is not included in any definition; for whatever we imagine, whether a man or an ass or anything else, we do not understand being (esse) in its definition. To this there is one sole exception, where being (esse) is said essentially, because its essence cannot be understood except through being itself (ipsum esse) since the essence and its being (esse) are in every way one thing.[8]

There is another way of showing these two modes of speaking of being (esse) in the second of the intentions that we have just pointed out. For everything that is either is its own being (esse) or something else is being (esse) for it. This means that what is said of anything by the word "is" is either the thing itself or something else; it is, however, in each thing in one respect the thing itself, in another respect something else. But if for each thing the being (esse) is other than the thing itself, it is necessary that this proceed in a circle or in a straight line, and it will go on to infinity.

If it proceeds in a circle, then A will be being (esse) for B, and B for A. A then will be being (esse) for its own being (esse). Hence, it will be before its own being (esse) and precede in being (in essendo) its own being (esse), and it will have being (esse) before its being (esse), and it will have being (esse) before it is. Also it turns out that from the fact that it is the cause of being (essendi) to its own being (esse), and the converse as well, being (esse) will be prior to the cause of being (causa essendi). Hence, it is prior to what is prior to itself. Much worse, it will be before itself and after itself in one and

the same respect, since it will be this whole [of A and B] to the extent it is. For, to the extent it is, it is only if there is first part A, and this is only to the extent that B is, for B is not the cause of being (essendi) for A except to the extent B is. But B is only through A and to the extent A is. Therefore, A will only be if it itself is and to the extent it is, and thus the same thing will be the cause of itself, and both prior and posterior to itself. And this is only one respect.

If this went in a straight line and to infinity, so that B is being (esse) for A and C for B, and this has no end, the result of this is that every being (esse) is both infinite and never closed off or terminated by any thought or expression. For the being (esse) of A is B, but not B absolutely and precisely, nor in just any respect and intention, but to the extent it is a being (ens), for A cannot be by it except to the extent it is already a being (ens). B is, therefore, being (esse) for A, insofar as B already has being (esse), which is to say, already having C. Thus in order to explain its being (esse), we would say that it, as already having C and insofar as it has C, is being (esse) for A. Then C will be being (esse) for B in the same manner, namely, insofar as it already has the being (esse) which is D. Thus the being of A is having B, which has C, C, I mean, having D, and of D the same explanation will hold. Hence, the whole being (esse) of A is not explained and explicated. An explanation of this sort has no end, and on this account neither does the very being (esse) of A. And so the being (esse) of A is infinite. Hence, no thought or expression can attain it. But this is a whole, because in the being (ens) A there is understood the being (ens) B, and in the being (ens) B there is understood the being (ens) C, and this has no end. Nor is the being (ens) of B understood unless this infinite complication and convolution is understood.

Either infinity, then, will be grasped and encompassed in our intellect—a thing every intellect knows is impossible—or it will be impossible that anything be understood to be (esse), since every being (esse) on this showing is infinite.[9] But in no sense will we enter into argument with those who destroy the intellect and the limitation or determination of the intellect.[10] For in this way they block the path to philosophizing and destroy the principle and root of knowledge, which the intellect truly is, while they posit infinities and unintelligibilities and ineffabilities. Rather we will dismiss them to follow their own devices, that is, the huge expanse of error and the darkness of infinity and incertitude, and we will hold what the necessity of knowing requires us to affirm, namely, that "is" (est) is said of something according to essence and of something not according to essence. The same holds for being (ens). We will bring you to see that everything of which it is said according to essence is not caused.[11] (This is taken in the sense of external causation, which is the only one philosophers consider. For they do not consider the internal effective causation of which we shall say something later and which we shall describe later.)[12] On the other hand, it is necessary that it be said of every created thing not according to essence.

First, one should recall that those names which are said according to essence are properly names, since they alone name. Accidental predicates do not name, but are properly said to denominate. For example, the name "man" is proper to the species and is common to all men; consequently, it ought not to be said to belong to one and it does not properly name one of them. "White" is the name of nothing and does not name a white thing; rather it denominates a white thing. For this reason, then, it should be said that the name "man" names and is properly a name, but "white" cannot rightly be a name, but rather a denomination.

Then let us go back and say that, when being (ens) is said of something essentially, it is the proper name of that of which it is said essentially, and it properly names its essence. Hence, it is the essential name of one or of many in common. It is said of that according to the truth, because it is said according to the essence or substance, which

in each thing is said to be the truth of that very thing. Likewise, it is inseparable from the same thing, since it is said essentially of it; neither in actuality nor in thought is it separable from it. For whether being (esse) is the essence of that of which it is said or a part of the essence, it is inseparable both in actuality or in thought from it. But the essential is either the whole essence or a part of the essence of that to which it is said to be essential. Hence, it is clear that there is some being (esse) which not only cannot not be, but also cannot be understood not to be.

Likewise, affirmation is not only not receptive of negation, but also, when the negation of something has been known by the intellect, it is unintelligible for an affirmation to be made concerning it. Hence, it is clear that a being (ens) of this sort cannot possibly admit the negation of its own essence. For this reason it is impossible to know a being (ens) of this sort as not a being (non ens) or not being (non esse). Moreover, every caused thing, where "caused" and "cause" are taken as we have explained them, has being (esse) that is acquired and drawn by its cause from not being (non esse) into being (esse) to the extent that it can. (For it does not exclude from itself its not being [non esse], and it does not give to itself its own being (esse), but it has and receives it.) Therefore, it is in itself possible and receptive of both [being and not being].

For this reason being (esse) of this sort, of which being (esse) is said according to essence, is not created, since from its side it cannot admit affirmation and negation of being (essendi), as we said, but it is its own being (esse) and is essentially opposed to its not being (non esse), just as an affirmation is opposed to its negation and, therefore, cannot admit negation, for no opposite can admit its opposite insofar as it is opposed to it. Moreover, affirmation has no being (esse) or becoming regarding negation or in negation. Since they in no way admit each other in the same thing, much less can one admit the other in itself.

Being (esse) about which or in which affirmation and negation have being (esse) and becoming is other than its affirmation and negation. Thus everything caused is other than its own being (*esse*) or not being (*non esse*), for it is necessary that receptive being (*esse*) is other than what is received, and that which acquires is other than that which is acquired. For this reason it is necessary that everything caused is other than its own being (*esse*). Thus what is the same as its being (*being*) necessarily is not caused.

Chapter III

It already begins to be clear to us that an essential being is necessary, eternal and incorruptible. It is not caused. I mean that it is not caused by an external cause, that is, a cause external in the sense of not sharing an essence with it and thus not causing out of itself or through itself alone. This latter sort of causality is called perfect.[13] It is, then, ungenerated and simple in the highest degree of simplicity, that is, in every way. For were it composed or resolvable in any way, it would necessarily be caused as well, for every composite is the effect of the component parts and of what brings them together, conjoining and ordering the parts in the composite.

In what follows we shall in many ways bring you to the knowledge of such being (*esse*), when we speak of possible and acquired being (*esse*). In the meantime, then, let us hold that this is the first being (*ens*) and first being (*esse*) to which there is nothing prior or superior. The reason is that, if there were anything prior or superior, it would necessarily be more simple and its cause. For the prior things are the causes of those that follow, if they are prior in the same order. But we have already shown that it is not caused. If there is something superior and prior to it in another order, it is frivolous and vain, since priority and su-

periority are said according to the same order, and this would be, so to speak, from another domain. We shall bring you to see in what follows that neither being (*esse*) nor being (*ens*) belong to another domain and that there is no order or ordering apart from that which begins from it and ends in it.

Also it is already clear to you from what went before, that this being (*esse*) and this being (*ens*) is most bare, since it has no essential clothing whatsoever. For such clothing is a composition, and we have excluded from it all composition and essential causation. I mean clothing such as there is in a species which contains the essence of its genus cloaked with the differences. If someone should say that nothing prevents such being (*esse*) from being clothed by the variety and adornment of accidents, he ought to know that between accidents and a being (*esse*) of this sort there must be substances in the order of being (*essendi*). Thus no accident is naturally suited to be joined to this sort of essence or this sort of being (*esse*), since substances necessarily stand in between in the order of being (*essendi*). For example, accidents, which are naturally suited to come to be in Socrates and follow upon Socrates, cannot possibly be joined to the species or genus under which Socrates stands.[14] This is so because Socrates comes in between and receives this union and excludes it from more remote subjects. The reason for this is that an accident demands a subject as close as possible for its own congruence and order. Thus no accident can be joined to the first and second being (*esse*) because of the excessive distance and disagreement with them in being (*in essendo*); for example, knowledge is not naturally suited to come to be in a body nor white in the soul. This will become clearer when we speak of the being (*esse*) of accidents in what follows.

NOTES

1. From the first page William's debt to Avicenna, Boethius and the Bible are apparent. Cf. Avicenna, *Metaphysics* I, 5, p. 35, 59–61 and p. 40, 46–49, as well as I, 6, pp. 43–47. For William's use of "intention," cf. *The Cambridge History of Later Medieval Philosophy from the Discovery of Aristotle to the Disintegration of Scholasticism*, ed. by Norman Kretzmann, Anthony Kenny and Jan Pinborg (Cambridge: Cambridge University Press, 1982), pp. 479–480. The Latin *"intentio"* translated two Arabic words in the writings of Al-farabi and Avicenna *"ma'qul" and "ma'na."* Avicenna used the latter "to signify the reality of the known considered as known" (p. 479). Given William's indebtedness to Avicenna, it would seem likely that he is using the term in much the same way.

2. Boethius, *De Hebdomadibus*, or *The Hebdomads*, lines 60–64. This is a common title, stemming from Boethius himself (PL 64, 1311A), for the theological treatise, "How Substances Can Be Good in Virtue of Their Existence Without Being Absolute Goods." References to the Boethian theological treatises will be to the lines of the Loeb Classical Library edition by H. F. Stewart and E. K. Rand. William may also have used the commentaries of Gilbert of Poitiers on Boethius' theological works. Cf. N. M. Häring, *The Commentaries on Boethius by Gilbert of Poitiers* (Toronto: Pontifical Institute of Mediaeval Studies, 1966) in *Texts and Studies* 13, *Expositio in Boecii Librum de Bonorum Hebdomade*, nos. 95–119, pp. 208–213.

3. William may here be alluding to Exodus 3:14, where God tells Moses that his name is, "He who is." Augustine used "Is" (*Est*) as a name for God. Thus in *Confessions* 13, 31, 46 (CCL 27, 269–270), he says, "We see that whatever is in any way is good, for it is from him who is not in some way, but is Is." So too in commenting on Psalm 134, he says, "He is Is, as the good of goods is good" (PL 37, 1341) and in commenting on Psalm 101, he says, "Behold a great Is, a great Is" (PL 37, 1311). Cf. *Dieu et l'etre: exégèse d'Exode 3, 14 et de Coran 20, 11–24* (Paris: Etudes Augustiniennes, 1978) for a series of articles on God as being in both the Christian and Moslem traditions.

4. Boethius, *De heb.*, lines 45f.

5. Ibid., lines 56–174.

6. Cf. Joseph Owens, "The Accidental and Essential Character of Being in the Doctrine of St. Thomas Aquinas," MS 20 (1958), 1–40, for an excellent discussion of the senses in which being can be accidental and yet essential to each created thing.

7. William thinks of accidental and substantial forms as a kind of clothing. He carries this metaphor throughout *De trinitate* and other works. A passage from his *De universo* both provides an excellent example of this metaphor and reveals much about how William viewed the structure of created being and its relation to God. "The Creator is most close and most present to you, indeed he is interior to, each created thing. This can become apparent to you by abstracting and stripping off all conditions and accidental and substantial forms. For when you have abstracted all these from each created thing last of all there will be found being (*esse*) or entity (*entitas*) and, hence, its giver. For example, when you have stripped Socrates of his singular form by which he is Socrates, and of his specific [form] by which he is man, and of his generic [forms] by which he is animal, body and substance, there will still remain being (*ens*). Hence, there will remain for him his being (*esse*) and entity (*entitas*), like his inner garment or undershirt with which the Creator first clothed him. When you withdraw from him being itself (*ipsum esse*) and entity (*entitas*), there will be withdrawn from him all causes of being (*essendi*) and helps, except the Creator. Hence, it is clear that of all the helps and aids toward being (*essendi*) the first and interior one is the Creator. I have written you all these things in order that they might raise you up in some way to ponder the sublimity of the Creator. Complete knowledge of him is beatitude and the glory of our intellective power" (*De universo* 1–1, 30, *Opera Omnia*, vol. 2, p. 625). The imagery of forms as clothing is also found in Avicebron, *Fons vitae* 3, 10, p. 101, 9–10; 5, 8, p. 271, 7; 5, 26, p. 305, 15; 5, 42, p. 334, 21, and Avicenna, *Metaphysics* 4, 2, p. 210, 98.

8. Cf. Augustine, *De doctrina christiana* 1, 5, 5 (CCL 32, 9), where he speaks of "one supreme reality; *una quaedam summa res.*" This phrase was used by the Fourth Lateran Council's condemnation of the Abbot Joachim of Flora (d. 1202) who had accused Peter Lombard of heresy for saying in his *Sentences* that "a supreme reality is the Father, the Son and the Holy Spirit, and it is not generating, nor born, nor proceeding." Joachim claimed that Peter Lombard had thereby introduced a quaternity into the trinity. With the Council's approval, Innocent III said, "we believe and confess, with Peter Lombard, that there is one supreme reality . . . which truly is the Father, the Son and the Holy Spirit, . . . " (DS 803–804). This extraordinary endorsement of a theological doctrine seems to have—at least in part—been aimed at the school of Gilbert of Poitier (d. 1154). Peter Lombard was, after all, one of those who along with St. Bernard attacked Gilbert at the Council of Rheims (1148), and Eugenius III had approved only one decree of that council, thus permitting the followers of Gilbert to continue; cf. DS 745. As we shall see in dealing with the trinitarian notions, William is very much aware of the Porretan doctrine and is fairly sympathetic to it in some respects, though his insistence upon "one reality: *una res*" shows his concern to abide by Lateran IV's decree. Cf. Antoine Dondaine, *Ecrits de la 'petite ecole' porretaine* (Montreal: Institut d'études medievales; Paris: J. Vrin, 1962), pp. 9–11.

9. The language reflects that of *Liber de causis* 5 (6), pp. 59–61, but William's point is quite different. References to this work are to *Le Liber de causis*. Edition établie à l'aide de 90 manuscrits avec introduction et notes par Adriaan Pattin (Leuven: Tijdschrift voor Filosofie, n.d.).

10. Bruno Switalski, in *William of Auvergne: De trinitate: An Edition of the Latin Text with an Introduction*

(Toronto: Pontifical Institute of Medieval Studies, 1976), suggests that William is referring to Aristotle and the Moslem philosophers who accepted matter as eternal and independent of the first being. However, William is rather arguing that the intellect cannot accept an infinite regress in causal dependence—a point on which he is in agreement with Avicenna.

11. Cf. Avicenna, *Metaphysics* 1, 6, p. 43, 14–15 and p. 44, 24–37.
12. These philosophers are not Christians. Hence, they are not familiar with the internal or perfect causality by which the Son and the Holy Spirit arise from the Father.
13. The Son and the Holy Spirit are produced by such perfect causality.
14. That is, forms must come to a being in the proper order.

CHAPTER 5

St. Thomas Aquinas

St. Thomas, known as the Angelic Doctor, was born at the castle of Roccasicca near Naples in 1225, the son of the count of Aquino. His early studies came at the local Benedictine Abbey of Monte Cassino. At age fourteen he went to the University of Naples, where he was immersed in the liberal arts program until 1244. He then decided to enter the teaching order of the Dominicans, much to the dissatisfaction of his family. While on his way to Paris to study theology, he was abducted by two of his brothers, who held him captive for a year at the castle of St. Giovanni and tried in vain to convince him to change his mind. At Paris he came under the influence of Albert the Great and accompanied his master to Cologne in 1248. There he entered the priesthood. In 1252 he returned to Paris to study for the degree of master of theology. During this period he became embroiled in a controversy between the secular masters at Paris and the mendicants (Franciscans and Dominicans). Only after intervention on behalf of Pope Alexander IV in 1256 was Thomas permitted to give his inaugural lecture as master of theology. It was during this period that he had published several works, most notably his commentary on the Sentences of Peter Lombard, De principius natural and De ente et essentia.

In 1259 he returned to Italy, where he spent the next nine years teaching and writing at various Dominican priories. In 1268 he was appointed to lecture on theology at the University of Paris. During the next three years he was once again involved in scholastic controversy, this time between the conservative theologians in the Augustinian tradition and followers of a speculative theology known as Latin Averroism, an Averroistic interpretation of Aristotle, the principle advocate of which was Siger of Brabant. In the spring of 1272 Thomas was once more recalled to Italy, where he was charged with overseeing the theological curriculum for the Dominican order in that country. He resided in Naples during this period. In 1274 Pope Gregory X invited Thomas to take part in the Council of Lyons, the purpose of which was to discuss the unity of the Church. During the journey he became ill, and on March 7, 1274, he died at the Cistercian Abbey of Fossanuova.

St. Thomas Aquinas on the Five Ways

St. Thomas Aquinas provided five arguments for the existence of God, the first three of which are cosmological in nature. The first two ways are identical in form and differ only with respect to the type of causation involved. It should be noted that St. Thomas adopted these two arguments from those formulated by Aristotle.

The first way establishes the existence of an unmoved mover, the second an uncaused cause. The former pertains to animate causation, whereas the latter concerns inanimate causation. Together the two are inclusive of causation throughout the universe. The conclusions of these two arguments can be viewed as the lesser of two evils. The only alternative to a first cause of the universe is an infinite regress, namely proceeding backward in the order of causes and things caused and never reaching a beginning. Without a *beginning*, it is inconceivable how the universe could be (i.e., exist). Since it does exist (verified by sense experience), it follows that the universe must have had a beginning. Therefore there must be a first cause—inconceivable as that may be.

Regarding the first argument, it rests on the thesis that any given thing cannot be at once in actuality and potentiality in the same respect. Specifically, a thing is either actually in motion or potentially in motion. The things of which we possess knowledge are such that their potentiality to motion is actualized by something other than themselves. That is, nothing merely potential has the power to actualize itself. To proceed to infinity in the order of movers and things moved results in the untenable position that what we know to be moved could not be so moved for there would not be a first mover. But things are moved. Therefore there must be a first mover.

Regarding the second argument, it rests on the thesis that nothing with which we are familiar is the efficient cause of itself but rather is caused by something other than itself. By parity of reasoning with the first argument, St. Thomas concludes that there must be a (first) uncaused cause.

The third way establishes the first cause as a necessary being. It is a reductio ad absurdum argument that demonstrates that if all things in the universe were contingent, the universe and all that therein is would have already ceased to exist since all possibilities are realized over infinite time. One of the possibilities of a totally contingent universe is that everything in it ceases to exist at the same instant. Since time is infinite regarding the past, this possibility would already have been actualized and there would presently be absolutely nothing. Since such is not the case, it follows that not everything in the universe is contingent. In other words, something must be necessary. This we call God.

The fourth way proceeds from the degrees of perfection we perceive in things to a paradigm of that perfection which we call God. Two things are noteworthy about this argument: (a) it is Platonic in origin and is based on the view that (sensible) particulars by virtue of their accidental characteristics can only possess degrees of perfection. Only that which is pure Form (essence) can be absolutely perfect. (b) Furthermore, particulars possess whatever degree of perfection they have by participation in the relevant Form (i.e., truth, goodness, being). In other words, the Forms provide the causal basis regarding the degrees of perfection in (sensible) things. "Now the maximum in any order is the cause of all the other realities of that order. Therefore there is a real cause of being and goodness and all perfections whatsoever in everything; and this we term God."

The fifth way is a teleological argument. We observe organic objects functioning for some end or other. This is not haphazard. Rather, such objects cooperate in a manner that suggests a unification of purpose via the functioning of the universe. Now, objects that lack consciousness cannot be the origin of their cooperation and purposefulness. This presupposes "directed unification, as the order of battle of a whole army hangs on the plan of the commander-in-chief". Only one being could warrant such a title, namely God.

SUMMA THEOLOGICA

Part I
Question I
The Nature and Extent of Sacred Doctrine
(In Ten Articles)

To place our purpose within proper limits, we first endeavour to investigate the nature and extent of this Sacred Doctrine. Concerning this there are ten points of inquiry:—
(1) Whether it is necessary? (2) Whether it is a Science? (3) Whether it is one or many? (4) Whether it is speculative or practical? (5) How it is compared with other sciences? (6) Whether it is the same as Wisdom? (7) Whether God is its subject-matter? (8) Whether it is a matter of argument? (9) Whether it rightly employs metaphors and similes? (10) Whether the Sacred Scripture of this Doctrine may be expounded in different senses?

First Article

Whether, Besides Philosophy, Any Further Doctrine Is Required?

We proceed thus to the First Article:—
Objection 1. It seems that, besides philosophical science, we have no need of any further knowledge. Man should not seek to know what is above reason: *Seek not the things that are too high for thee* (Ecclus. iii. 22). But whatever is not above reason is fully treated of in philosophical science. Therefore any other knowledge besides philosophical science is superfluous.
Obj. 2. Further, knowledge can only be concerned with being, for nothing can be known, save what is true; and all that is, is true. But everything that is, is treated of in philosphical science—even God Himself; so that there is a part of philosophy called

From *The "Summa Theologica" of St. Thomas Aquinas*, translated by Fathers of the English Dominican Province (London: R. & T. Washbourne, Ltd., 1911), pp. 1–3, 19–27.

Theology, or the Divine Science, as Aristotle has proved. Therefore, besides philosophical science, there is no need of any further knowledge.

On the contrary, It is said, *All Scripture inspired of God is profitable to teach, to reprove, to correct, to instruct in justice* (2 Tim. iii. 16). Scripture, inspired of God, is no part of philosophical science, which has been built up by human reason. Therefore it is useful that besides philosophical science there should be other knowledge—i.e., inspired of God.

I answer that, It was necessary for man's salvation that there should be a knowledge revealed by God, besides philosophical science built up by human reason. Firstly, indeed, because man is ordained to God, as to an end that surpasses the grasp of his reason; *The eye hath not seen, besides Thee, O God, what things Thou hast prepared for them that wait for Thee* (Isa. lxiv. 4). But the end must first be known by men who are to direct their thoughts and actions to the end. Hence it was necessary for the salvation of man that certain truths which exceed human reason should be made known to him by Divine Revelation. Even as regards those truths about God which human reason could have discovered, it was necessary that man should be taught by a Divine Revelation; because the Truth about God such as reason could discover, would only be known by a few, and that after a long time, and with the admixture of many errors. Whereas man's whole salvation, which is in God, depends upon the knowledge of this Truth. Therefore, in order that the salvation of men might be brought about more fitly and more surely, it was necessary that they should be taught Divine Truths by Divine Revelation. It was therefore necessary that, besides philosophical science built up by reason, there should be a sacred science learnt through Revelation.

Reply Obj. 1. Although those things which are beyond man's knowledge may not be sought for by man through his reason, nevertheless, once they are revealed by God, they must be accepted by faith. Hence the sacred text continues, *For many things are shown to thee above the understanding of man* (Ecclus. iii. 25). And in this the Sacred Science consists.

Reply Obj. 2. Sciences are differentiated according to the various means through which knowledge is obtained. The astronomer and the physicist both may prove the same conclusion—that the earth, for instance, is round: the astronomer by means of mathematics (i.e., abstracting from matter), but the physicist by means of matter itself. Hence there is no reason why those things which may be learnt from philosophical science, so far as they can be known by natural reason, may not also be taught us by another science so far as they fall within revelation. Hence theology included in Sacred Doctrine differs in kind from that theology which is part of philosophy.

Second Article

Whether Sacred Doctrine Is a Science?

We proceed thus to the Second Article—

Objection 1. It seems that Sacred Doctrine is not Science. For every science proceeds from self-evident principles. But Sacred Doctrine proceeds from articles of Faith which are not self-evident, since their truth is not admitted by all. *For all men have not faith* (2 Thess. iii. 2). Therefore Sacred Doctrine is not a science.

Obj. 2. Further, no science deals with individual facts. But this Sacred Science treats of individual facts, such as the deeds of Abraham, Isaac, and Jacob. Therefore Sacred Doctrine is not a science.

On the contrary, Augustine says, *to this science alone belongs that whereby saving faith is begotten, nourished, protected, and strengthened.* But this can be said of no science except Sacred Doctrine. Therefore Sacred Doctrine is a science.

Question II
The Existence of God
(in Three Articles)

Because the chief aim of Sacred Doctrine is to teach the knowledge of God, not only as He is in Himself, but also as He is the beginning of things and their last end, and especially of rational creatures, as is clear from what has been already said; therefore, in our endeavour to expound this science:—

(1) We shall treat of God. (2) Of the rational creature's advance towards God. (3) Of Christ, Who as man, is our way to God.

In treating of God there will be a threefold division:—

(1) For we shall consider whatever concerns the Divine Essence. (2) Whatever concerns the distinctions of Persons. (3) Whatever concerns the issue of creatures from Him.

Concerning the Divine Essence, we must consider:—

(1) Whether God exists? (2) The manner of His existence, or, rather, what is *not* the manner of His existence. (3) Whatever concerns His operations—namely, His Knowledge, Will, Power.

Concerning the first, three points are to be discussed:—

(1) Whether the proposition 'God exists' is self-evident? (2) Whether it is demonstrable? (3) Whether God exists?

First Article
Whether the Existence of God
Is Self-Evident?

We proceed thus to the First Article:—

Objection 1. It seems that the Existence of God is self-evident. Those things are said to be self-evident to us the knowledge of which is naturally implanted in us, as we can see in regard to first principles. But the Damascene says that, *the knowledge of God is naturally implanted in all*. Therefore the Existence of God is self-evident.

Obj. 2. Further, those things are said to be self-evident which are known as soon as the terms are known, which the Philosopher says is true of the first principles of demonstration. Thus, when the nature of a whole and of a part is known, it is at once recognized that every whole is greater than its part. But as soon as the signification of the word 'God' is understood, it is at once seen that God exists. For by this word is signified that thing than which nothing greater can exist. But that which exists actually and mentally is greater than that which exists only mentally. Therefore, because as soon as the word 'God' is understood it exists mentally, it also follows that it exists actually. Therefore the proposition that God exists is self-evident.

Obj. 3. Further, the existence of Truth is self-evident; for whoever denies the existence of Truth concedes that Truth does not exist. Now, if Truth does not exist, then the propostion 'Truth does not exist' is true. But if there is anything true, there must be Truth. God is Truth itself: *I am the way, the truth, and the life* (John xiv. 6). Therefore the proposition that God exists is self-evident.

On the contrary, No one can mentally admit the opposite of what is self-evident; as is clear from the Philosopher, concerning the first principles of demonstration. The opposite of the proposition 'God is' can be mentally admitted: *The fool hath said in his heart, There is no God* (Ps. lii. 1). Therefore, that God exists is not self-evident.

I answer that, A thing can be self-evident in either of two ways; on the one hand, self-evident in itself, though not to us; on the other, self-evident in itself, and to us. A proposition is self-evident because the predicate is included in the notion of the subject, as 'Man is an animal,' for animal is contained in the formal idea of man. If, therefore, the essence of the predicate and subject be known to all, the proposition will be self-evident to all; as is clear with regard to the first principles of demonstra-

tion, the terms of which are common things that no one is ignorant of, such as being and non-being, whole and part, and such like. If there are some to whom the essence of the predicate and subject are unknown, the proposition will be self-evident in itself, but not to those who do not know the meaning of the predicate and subject of the proposition. Therefore, it happens, as Boethius says, that there are some mental concepts self-evident only to the learned, as that incorporeal substances are not in space. Therefore I say that this proposition, 'God exists,' of itself is self-evident, for the predicate is the same as the subject; because God is His Own Existence. Forasmuch as we do not know the Essence of God, the proposition is not self-evident to us; but needs to be proved by such things as are more evident to us, though less evident in their nature—namely, by effects.

Reply Obj. 1. To know that God exists in a general and indefinite way is implanted in us by nature, inasmuch as God is man's beatitude. For man naturally desires happiness, and what is naturally desired by a man must be naturally known to him. This, however, is not to know absolutely that God exists; as to know that someone is approaching is not the same as to know that Peter is approaching, even though it is Peter who is approaching; for many there are who imagine that man's perfect good (which is happiness) consists in riches, and others in pleasures, and others in something else.

Reply Obj. 2. Perhaps not everyone who hears of this word 'God' may understand it to signify something than which nothing better can be imagined, seeing that some have believed God to be a body. Yet, granted that everyone understands that by this word 'God' is signified something than which nothing greater can be imagined, nevertheless, it does not therefore follow that he understands that what the word signifies exists actually, but only that it exists mentally. Nor can it be argued logically that it actually exists, unless it be admitted that there exists something than which nothing greater can be imagined; and this precisely is not admitted by those who hold that God does not exist.

Reply Obj. 3. The existence of truth in a general way is self-evident, but the existence of a Primal Truth is not self-evident to us.

Second Article

Whether It Can Be Demonstrated That God Exists?

We proceed thus to the Second Article:—

Objection 1. It seems that the existence of God cannot be demonstrated; for it is an article of Faith that God exists. But what is of Faith cannot be demonstrated, because a demonstration produces knowledge; whereas Faith is of the unseen (Heb. xi. 1). Therefore it cannot be demonstrated that God exists.

Obj. 2. Further, the essence is the middle term of demonstration. But we cannot know in what God's essence consists, but solely in what it does not consist; as the Damascene says. Therefore we cannot demonstrate that God exists.

Obj. 3. Further, if the existence of God were demonstrated, this could only be from His effects. But the effects are not proportionate to Him, since He is infinite and His effects are finite; and between the finite and infinite there is no proportion. Therefore, since a cause cannot be demonstrated by an effect not proportionate to it, it seems that the existence of God cannot be demonstrated.

On the contrary, The Apostle says: *The invisible things of God are clearly seen, being understood by the things that are made* (Rom. i. 20). But this would not be unless the existence of God could be demonstrated through the things that are made; for the first thing we must know of anything is, whether it exists.

I answer that, Demonstrations can be made in two ways: One is through the cause, and is called a priori, and this is to argue from what is prior absolutely. The other is through the effect, and is called a demonstration a posteriori; this is to argue from what is prior relatively only to us. When an effect is better known to us than its cause, from the effect we proceed to the knowledge of the cause. From every effect the existence of a proportionate cause can be demonstrated, so long as its effects are better known to us. Since every effect depends upon its cause, if the effect exists, the cause must have pre-existed. Hence the existence of God, in so far as it is not self-evident to us, can be demonstrated from those of His effects which are known to us.

Reply Obj. 1. The existence of God and other like truths about God, which can be known by natural reason, are not articles of Faith, but are preambles to the articles; for Faith presupposes natural knowledge, even as grace presupposes nature, and perfection supposes something that can be perfected. Nevertheless, there is nothing to prevent a man, who cannot grasp its proof, accepting, as a matter of Faith, something in itself capable of being known and demonstrated.

Reply Obj. 2. When the existence of a cause is demonstrated from an effect, this effect takes the place of the definition of the cause in proof of the cause's existence. This is especially the case in regard to God, because, in order to prove the existence of anything, it is necessary to accept as a middle term the meaning of the word, and not its essence, for the question of its essence follows on the question of its existence. The names given to God are derived from His effects; consequently, in demonstrating the existence of God from His effects, we may take for the middle term the meaning of the word 'God.'

Reply Obj. 3. From effects not proportionate to the cause no perfect knowledge of that cause can be obtained. Yet from every effect the existence of the cause can be demonstrated, and so we can demonstrate the existence of God from His effects; though from them we cannot perfectly know God as He is in His own Essence.

Third Article

Whether God Exists?

We proceed thus to the Third Article:—

Objection 1. It seems that God does not exist; because if one of two contraries be infinite, the other would be altogether destroyed. But the word 'God' means that He is infinite goodness. If, therefore, God existed, there would be no evil discoverable; but there is evil in the world. Therefore God does not exist.

Obj. 2. Further, it is superfluous to suppose that, what can be accounted for by a few principles has been produced by many. But it seems that everything that appears in the world can be accounted for by other principles, supposing God did not exist. For all natural things can be reduced to one principle, which is nature; and all things that happen intentionally can be reduced to one principle, which is human reason, or will. Therefore there is no need to suppose God's existence.

On the contrary, It is said in the person of God: *I am Who am* (Exod. iii. 14).

I answer that, The existence of God can be proved in five ways.

The first and more manifest way is the argument from motion. It is certain and evident to our senses that some things are in motion. Whatever is in motion is moved by another, for nothing can be in motion except it have a potentiality for that towards which it is being moved; whereas a thing moves inasmuch as it is in act. By 'motion' we mean nothing else than the reduction of something from a state of potentiality into a state of actuality. Nothing, however, can be reduced from a state of potentiality into a state of actuality, unless by something already in a state of actuality. Thus that which is actually hot as fire, makes wood, which is potentially hot, to be actually hot, and thereby moves and changes it. It is not possible that the same thing should be at once in a state of actuality and potentiality from the same point of view, but only from different points of view. What is actually hot cannot simultaneously be only potentially hot; still, it is simultaneously potentially cold. It is therefore impossible that from the same point of view and in the same way anything should be both moved and mover, or that it should move itself. Therefore, whatever is in motion must be put in motion by another. If that by which it is put in motion be itself put in motion, then this also must needs be put in motion by another, and that by another again. This cannot go on to infinity, because then there would be no first mover, and, consequently, no other mover—seeing that subsequent movers only move inasmuch as they are put in motion by the first mover; as the staff only moves because it is put in motion by the hand. Therefore it is necessary to arrive at a First Mover, put in motion by no other; and this everyone understands to be God.

The second way is from the formality of efficient causation. In the world of sense we find there is an order of efficient causation. There is no case known (neither is it, indeed, possible) in which a thing is found to be the efficient cause of itself; for so it would be prior to itself, which is impossible. In efficient causes it is not possible to go on to infinity, because in all efficient causes following in order, the first is the cause of the intermediate cause, and the intermediate is the cause of the ultimate cause, whether the intermediate cause be several, or one only. To take away the cause is to take away the effect. Therefore, if there be no first cause among efficient causes, there will be no ultimate cause, nor any intermediate. If in efficient causes it is possible to go on to infinity, there will be no first efficient cause, neither will there be an ultimate effect, nor any intermediate efficient causes; all of which is plainly false. Therefore it is necessary to put forward a First Efficient Cause, to which everyone gives the name of God.

The third way is taken from possibility and necessity, and runs thus. We find in nature things that could either exist or not exist, since they are found to be generated, and then to corrupt; and, consequently, they can exist, and then not exist. It is impossible for these always to exist, for that which can one day cease to exist must at some time have not existed. Therefore, if everything could cease to exist, then at one time there could have been nothing in existence. If this were true, even now there would be nothing in existence, because that which does not exist only begins to exist by something already existing. Therefore, if at one time nothing was in existence, it would have been impossible for anything to have begun to exist; and thus even now nothing would be in existence—which is absurd. Therefore, not all beings are merely possible, but there must exist something the existence of which is necessary. Every necessary thing either has its necessity caused by another, or not. It is impossible to go on to infinity in necessary things which have their necessity caused by another, as has been already proved in regard to efficient causes. Therefore we cannot but postulate the existence of some being having of itself its own necessity, and not receiving it from another, but rather causing in others their necessity. This all men speak of as God.

The fourth way is taken from the gradation to be found in things. Among beings there are some more and some less good, true, noble, and the like. But 'more' and 'less' are predicated of different things, according as they resemble in their different ways something which is in the degree of 'most,' as a thing is said to be hotter according as it more nearly resembles that which is hottest; so that there is something which is truest, something best, something noblest, and, consequently, something which is uttermost being; for the truer things are, the more truly they exist. What is most complete in any genus is the cause of all in that genus; as fire, which is the most complete form of heat, is the cause whereby all things are made hot. Therefore there must also be something which is to all beings the cause of their being, goodness, and every other perfection; and this we call God.

The fifth way is taken from the governance of the world; for we see that things which lack intelligence, such as natural bodies, act for some purpose, which fact is evident from their acting always, or nearly always, in the same way, so as to obtain the best result. Hence it is plain that not fortuitously, but designedly, do they achieve their purpose. Whatever lacks intelligence cannot fulfil some purpose, unless it be directed by some being endowed with intelligence and knowledge; as the arrow is shot to its mark by the archer. Therefore some intelligent being exists by whom all natural things are ordained towards a definite purpose; and this being we call God.

Reply Obj. 1. As Augustine says: *Since God is wholly good, He would not allow any evil to exist in His works, unless His omnipotence and goodness were such as to bring good even out of evil.* This is part of the infinite goodness of God, that He should allow evil to exist, and out of it produce good.

Reply Obj. 2. Since nature works out its determinate end under the direction of a higher agent, whatever is done by nature must needs be traced back to God, as to its first cause. So also whatever is done designedly must also be traced back to some higher cause other than human reason or will, for these can suffer change and are defective; whereas things capable of motion and of defect must be traced back to an immovable and self-necessary first principle.

CHAPTER 6

John Duns Scotus

John Duns Scotus, known as the Subtle Doctor, was born in Scotland probably in 1265 either at Duns in Berwickshire or at Maxton in the county of Roxburgh. There is some evidence that he was taken to the Franciscan friary at Dumfries at an early age (in 1278), where in 1281 he took his vows. He then studied at Oxford. On March 17, 1291, he was ordained a priest at Northhampton by Oliver Sutton, bishop of Lincoln. He then studied at the University of Paris from roughly 1293 to 1296, after which he returned to Oxford, where he taught and in 1301 completed the rigorous thirteen-year master of theology program, yet was not incepted as a master there because the Franciscan chair of theology was occupied. In 1302 Scotus assumed the Franciscan chair of theology at Paris. The following year he became embroiled in a dispute between King Philip the Fair and Pope Boniface over taxation of church property to support the French armies. Having sided with the pope, Scotus was exiled, albeit briefly, from France (where he went is unknown); he was back teaching at Oxford during the year 1303–4. In late 1304 he was back at Paris to teach and continue his interrupted studies, and in 1305 he received the degree of doctor of theology. Two years later he was sent to Cologne to teach. There his brilliant career was cut short when he died on November 8, 1308.

John Duns Scotus on the Existence of God

One can approach the issue of God's existence from an a priori or an a posteriori point of view. If one utilizes the former, no proof, strictly speaking, can be had. If the proposition "God exists" is true by definition then it is not self-evident since the definition "borrows its evidence" from something other than the definiendum. This point can be understood by analyzing definitions by genus and difference (e.g., ice is frozen water). Secondly, definitions are not self-evident by virtue of their complexity. Only that which is truly simple can be self-evident. (No definition so qualifies except ostensive ones and God clearly is not defined in such a manner.) So if God's existence is self-evident, the claim "God exists" must be synthetic and absolutely simple. The claim can only be simple if God's nature (*essentia*) and His existence (*existentia*) are identical. Since it is simple, its truth cannot be derived by logical demonstration. Rather, it is a matter of intuition. An enlightened person merely intuits that the proposition "God exists" is self-evident. Hence, a rational demonstration of God's existence can only proceed from an a posteriori point of view.

The a posteriori approach Scotus takes is principally by way of efficient causation. He is quick to observe that the infinite regress generated by the order of causes and things caused is not in and of itself a sufficient basis from which to conclude the existence of an uncaused cause, much less a necessary one. To so conclude begs the question. That is, there is nothing about a causal claim that dictates that within the chain itself there must be an uncaused cause. One can proceed to infinity within the chain. Now the issue arises as to the origin of the chain (i.e., universe) itself. If the chain is contingent (as indeed our senses concerning causation tell us it is), then it, the chain, can cease to exist. If this potentiality is actualized there would then be nothing. But something cannot come from nothing. Therefore, there must be a necessary cause external to the chain that provides the basis for its existence. This necessary cause is itself uncaused because necessity entails self-sufficiency. This necessary first cause we call God.

"ON THE EXISTENCE OF GOD" FROM *A TREATISE ON GOD AS FIRST PRINCIPLE*

Question One: Does an Infinite Being Exist?

1. The first question raised in connection with the second distinction is this: "In the realm of beings is there some being which is actually infinite?"

Pro et Contra

It would seem not, for:

[Arg. I] If one of two contraries were actually infinite, it would be incompatible with anything other than itself. But good and evil are contraries. Hence, if some good were actually infinite, nothing would be actually evil, which is false.

2. In answer to this some say that the evil in the universe is not a true contrary to God or the infinite good, because he has no true contrary. But this is no solution, for whether the contrariety be formal or only virtual between two things, if one of the two be infinite, it will tolerate nothing contrary either to itself or to its effect. If the sun, for instance, possessed infinite heat either formally or virtually, nothing would be cold. Consequently, if some good were

From *John Duns Scotus: A Treatise on God as First Principle*, edited and translated by Allan B. Wolter (Quincy, Ill.: Franciscan Press at Quincy University, 1965), pp. 392–410. Reprinted by permission of the Franciscan Press.

actually infinite either virtually or formally, then throughout the universe evil, as the contrary of some good, would be simply non-existent.

3. [Arg. II] An infinite body would not allow another body to coexist; therefore an infinite spirit will not allow another spirit to coexist. The antecedent is evident from Bk. IV of the *Physics*.[1]

The consequence is thus proved: just as two bodies cannot coexist in one place because of their opposed dimensions, so neither does it seem possible for two spirits because their actualizations are opposed.

4. Another proof of the same consequence is this: If another body could coexist with an infinite body, then there would be something larger than an infinite body. It would seem then that if another spirit existed in addition to the infinite, there would be something virtually greater than the infinite.

5. [Arg. III] Furthermore, whatever is here and nowhere else is limited in its whereabouts; what exists now but not then is of limited time; and what acts by this action and no other is limited in action, and so on. But whatever exists is a "this" in such a way that it is no other; therefore it is finite, whatever it be.

6. [Arg. IV] Furthermore, if some power were infinite, it would cause movement in-

stantaneously, as Bk. VIII of the *Physics* proves.[2] Motion, therefore, would occur instantaneously, which is impossible.

7. *To the contrary*:

In Bk. VIII of the *Physics*,[3] the Philosopher [Aristotle] says that the first mover is infinite. And therefore his power does not reside in any magnitude—not in an infinite magnitude, because there is no such thing, nor in a finite magnitude, because something of greater magnitude would have a greater power. But this argument is not valid unless it be understood of something that is infinite in power, because a body, like the sun, would be infinite in duration.

Question Two: Is It Self-Evident That an Infinite Being Exists?

8. This poses the further question: Is the existence of something infinite, such as God's existence, a fact that is self-evident?

Pro et Contra

The arguments that it is are these:

[Arg. I] Damascene says in the first chapter:[4] "The knowledge that God exists is implanted in everyone." Such knowledge, however, is self-evident, as is clear from Bk. II of the *Metaphysics*,[5] where first principles, which are like the [proverbial] door, are presented as something self-evident.

9. [Arg. II] Furthermore, the existence of a thing is self-evident if it is impossible to think of anything greater than it. For if one were to grant the opposite of the predicate, it would destroy the subject; because if the thing in question did not exist one could think of something greater, viz. its existence, which is greater than its nonexistence. And this seems to be Anselm's argument in chapter two of the *Proslogion*.[6]

10. [Arg. III] That truth exists is self-evident; therefore etc. Proof of the antecedent: Whatever follows from its own denial is self-evident. But truth is such, because if you affirm that truth exists, then it is true that you affirm this and hence truth exists; if you may deny that truth exists, then it

would be true that truth does not exist. And therefore some truth still exists.

11. [Arg. IV] Furthermore, those propositions are self-evident which derive their necessity from that fact that their terms have at least that qualified existence that comes from being in the mind. All the more then is that proposition self-evident which owes its necessity to the being of the thing and terms in an unqualified sense. But "God exists" is such a proposition. Proof of the antecedent: Suppose that neither a whole nor its part existed. The very fact that these terms in the mind are related the way they are, guarantees "Every whole is greater than its part" to be a necessary truth. In such a case, however, the terms would have only a qualified existence in the mind.

12. *To the contrary*:

No mind can deny what is self-evident; but God's existence can be denied for "The fool says in his heart, 'There is no God'" [Psalms 13,1].

I. Reply to the Second Question

13. We must answer this second question first. To solve it, we must understand first of all what is meant by a self-evident proposition. Then it will be clear if "God exists" (or some other proposition in which "existence" is predicated of something belonging to God, such as "An infinite being exists") is self-evident.

14. To understand the meaning of "self-evident proposition," know that when a proposition is said to be such, the word "self" does not rule out every cause whatsoever, because it does not exclude knowledge of the terms. For no proposition is self-evident unless there is knowledge of its terms. What is excluded is any cause or reason which is not essentially included in the concepts of the terms of the self-evident proposition. Hence, that proposition is self-evident which does not need to borrow knowledge elsewhere, but draws the evidence of its own truth from the knowledge of its terms and has the sole source of its certitude within itself.

15. But the name, now, is one term and

the concept associated with it is another, the difference between them being that of a name and its definition. Proof: In a demonstration, the definition of one of the extremes serves as a middle term, the remaining term in the premises being the same as in the conclusion. The extreme differs from the middle term as the defined differs from the definition. If the term and concept of the thing defined were the same as that of the definition, then the most cogent form of demonstration would involve a begging of the question. What is more, it would have but two terms. Consequently, the concept of the definition is different from that of the thing defined in so far as the latter is expressed by the name which is defined.

16. Furthermore, Bk. I of the *Physics*[7] says that much the same thing happens in the relation of names to their definitions as does in the relation of the whole to its parts. The thing defined is known even before its definition is discovered by an analysis of the parts it has. Wherefore, in so far as the concept of the definition is expressed by the name of the thing defined, it is something confused and is known before [the definition]. But it is expressed more distinctly by the name of the definition, which distinguishes the several parts of the defined. Hence the concept associated with the name of the thing defined is other than that of the definition.

17. From this it follows that a proposition is not self-evident if our only knowledge of it stems from a definition of its terms. For, inasmuch as only that proposition is self-evident which is evident from a knowledge of its terms, and the definition and the name are different terms, it follows that a proposition whose evidence stems exclusively from the definition of its terms, is not self-evident, since it borrows its evidence from something beyond itself and it can be a conclusion with reference to some other proposition.

18. Likewise, if a proposition whose evidence stemmed from the definition of its terms were self-evident, then every proposition would be self-evident that is in the first mode of per se predication, such as "Man is an animal, and a body" and so on, up to "substance." Consequently, knowledge of the definition is not enough to make a proposition self-evident.

19. Therefore that proposition only is self-evident which draws its evidence solely from the knowledge of its terms and does not borrow it from the evidence for other concepts.

20. From this we see there is no point or purpose in distinguishing propositions which are self-evident by their nature from those which are self-evident to us; or among the latter, those which are self-evident to the wise from those which are self-evident to the foolish; or those which are self-evident of the first order from those which are self-evident of the second order. For a proposition is not called self-evident because it happens to be in a particular mind, but because its terms are by their nature apt to cause self-evident knowledge in any intellect which conceives them as self-evident in themselves. And therefore nothing is self-evident which can be demonstrated to any intellect. Nevertheless, grades do exist among self-evident propositions according to their value or lack of it. Thus, "It is impossible for the same thing to both be and not be" is of more value than this: "Every whole is greater than its part," etc.

21. Secondly, turning now to the question at issue, I say this: Suppose one means by the name "God" something which we do not conceive perfectly—such as "this divine essence" where the latter term is grasped as self-evident, as would be the case, for instance, if God, seeing himself, were to impose this name "God" upon his essence. Then one might ask whether "God exists" or "This essence exists" would be self-evident. I say that they would be, because the terms in this case are such that they are able to make such a proposition evident to anyone who grasped the terms of the proposition perfectly, and "self-evident" could not be more aptly applied than to this essence.

22. But suppose you ask whether exis-

tence is predicated of any concept which we have of God's essence, so that such a proposition would be self-evident wherein existence is predicated of such a concept, as when we say for example that "The infinite exists." To this I say: No! For nothing which can be the conclusion of a demonstration is self-evident from the knowledge of its terms. But every proposition predicating existence of any concept we have of God is just such, viz. the conclusion of a demonstration. Proof: Anything which pertains to a more comprehensive but less extensive concept according to the first mode of per se predication, can also be shown to pertain per se to a broader concept by using the more comprehensive concept as a middle term. For instance, if some attribute pertains primarily to "triangle," it can be demonstrated to be an attribute of "figure" by means of "triangle." Every concept that we use to conceive of God, however, is less comprehensive than "this essence." Therefore, by using as middle term "this essence" to which existence primarily pertains, one could demonstrate existence of every concept that we use to conceive of God. Consequently, no proposition such as "An infinite being exists" is self-evident from a knowledge of its terms but it borrows its evidence from something else, and hence is not self-evident.—The major of this argument, however, can be asserted in an even more universal form, viz. whatever pertains to something primarily, does not pertain to another except in virtue of that nature to which it belongs primarily. But "existence" belongs primarily to "this divine nature." Therefore it is not ascribed [primarily] to some property [of this essence], neither does it pertain to any other [divine attribute] except in virtue of the nature of [the divine] essence. Therefore, no proposition in which existence is predicated of some property of this [divine] essence which we conceive is primarily true, but it is true only by reason of some other truth, and consequently it is not a primary or self-evident proposition.

23. Furthermore, if a proposition is self-evident, then any intellect which conceives its terms, will by that very fact know that the proposition is true. But this is not the case with such a proposition as "God exists"—where by God is meant not this essence which we conceive, but some concept which we have about this essence—or "God is infinite" or "An infinite being exists." Therefore, it is not self-evident. The major is evident. The minor is established as follows. Everyone who assents to any proposition either because of faith or belief or because it is demonstrated, grasps the meaning of the terms. But we assent to this: "God exists" either because of faith or because of a demonstration. Therefore, the meaning of the terms are known prior to faith or demonstration. But this apprehending of the terms does not make us assent to the proposition, otherwise we should not know it only by faith or demonstration.

24. What is more, there is a third argument. To understand it, you must keep in mind first of all that some concepts are *simply simple* and others are not. That concept is simply simple which is not reduced to some prior or simpler concept, nor is it fully resolved into more than one concept. Such are the concepts of being, and of the ultimate differences. But a concept that is not simply simple is one which, though it be simply grasped, i.e. nothing is affirmed or denied about it, is nevertheless resolved into more than one concept of which the one can be conceived without the other. Such is the concept of the species which can be resolved into a genus and a difference. Consequently, even though a concept be simple in the sense that nothing is affirmed or denied, one must distinguish further whether it is simply simple or not in the aforesaid sense. From this it is clear how one should understand or explain the statement of the Philosopher in Bk. IX of the *Metaphysics*[8] where we read that so far as simple concepts are concerned the deception characteristic of what is composite is absent. It is not a question here of an affirmation or negation of anything, for one can err by asserting something of a simple concept just as one can say something true or

false of a composite concept. What he has in mind is that "the definition of the composite is a long rigmarole,"[9] in which many concepts are lumped together and error can arise concerning their conjunction. Sometimes the combination may even include contradictory elements as is the case with "dead man" [i.e. a man without a soul] or "irrational man" [where man is defined as a rational animal]. But such is not the case where simple notions are concerned, for here either one grasps the whole or he grasps nothing.

25. Keeping this explanation in mind, I argue as follows: No proposition about a concept which is not simply simple will be self-evident, unless it also be self-evident that the components of such a concept go together, as I shall prove. Every proper concept that we have of God, however, is not simply simple and consequently, nothing is self-evident of such a concept unless we know that the parts of such a concept essentially go together. But, as I shall prove shortly, it is not self-evident that this is the case. As a consequence, no proposition in which anything is asserted of any concept we have of God will be self-evident, e.g. "God exists" or "An infinite God exists."

26. Proof of the major: no notion is true *of* anything unless it first be true in itself. For if it is false in itself, it will not be true of anything. This is clear from Bk. V of the *Metaphysics* in the chapter "About the False,"[10] where the Philosopher intends to say that the false in itself includes a contradiction, whereas what is false of something is that which is not false of everything whatsoever, as is the case with the false in itself. Consequently, it is necessary that one must first know that a thing is true in itself before one can know that it is true of something. But if one does not grasp that the parts of a concept that is not simply simple go together, he does not conceive something that is true in itself and hence does not conceive it as being in something or as true of something. Nothing therefore is self-evidently known about a concept which is not simply simple unless one first recognizes that the parts of this concept go together.

27. The other proposition assumed in the argument is also true, viz. that every concept which we have of God is not simply simple, because every such concept I have of God has to do with what is common to me and to him, as will become clear later.[11]

28. The other assumption is true too, viz. that it is not self-evident that the parts of the concept we use to think of God go together, because it can be demonstrated that one part goes with the other, as is the case, for example, when we demonstrate "God is infinite" or "God exists" (where by "God" we mean what we conceive God to be).

29. From this it is clear that they are incorrect who claim such propositions as "God exists," "A necessary being exists," or "What is operating is in act" are self-evidently known on the grounds that the opposite of the predicate is inconsistent with the subject, and therefore the proposition is self-evident.

I say that they are not self-evident, because whenever you use a concept that is not simply simple as the subject you must have self-evident knowledge that the parts go together, which is not the case with "A necessary being exists" and "What is operating is in act," for it is not self-evident that something necessary exists, but this can be demonstrated. That is why the Heracliteans were wont to deny "necessary being" and assert that all is in continuous motion. It is the same with "What is operating is in act," because it is not self-evident that there is actually anything which is operating. Hence it does not follow from the fact that the opposite of the predicate is inconsistent with the subject that the proposition in question is necessary. Indeed, it may even be that such a proposition is false, as is the case with "An irrational man is an animal": for this is inconsistent: "No animal exists, yet an irrational man exists." It is the same with the proposition: "Something greater than God exists," which is false, even though the opposite of the predicate is inconsistent with the subject.

30. If you insist that the predicate is already posited in the subject in the proposition like "A necessary being exists" or

"What is operating is in act" and consequently they are self-evident, I reply that this does not follow, because it is not self-evidently known that the notions which are presumed to be present in the subject can actually go together.

31. To this it is objected on logical grounds that if the opposite of the predicate of some proposition is inconsistent with the subject, then from the existence of the subject follows the existence of the predicate. For example, in the proposition "Man is an animal," the opposite of animal is inconsistent with man; therefore this follows: "If a man exists, an animal exists." Hence, if in the proposition "An irrational man is an animal," the opposite of the predicate is inconsistent with the subject, then this would follow: "An irrational man exists, therefore an animal exists." Hence the medium used to infer this, viz. "An irrational man is an animal," is true. Therefore, if the opposite of the predicate is inconsistent with the subject, the proposition will be true and necessary.

To this I say: the inference does not follow, because those extremes must be united for which the inference holds. But in this: "An irrational man exists, therefore an animal exists," the consequence holds solely because of "man" and not because of "irrational," and therefore it is by virtue of "Man is an animal" that it holds. Consequently, the following is not an inference: "An irrational man exists, therefore a man exists," because "irrational" adds nothing to the inference, and to go from one thing to the same thing is not an inference; neither then is this: "A necessary being exists, therefore it exists."

32. And so it is clear, then, first of all what a self-evident proposition is, seeing that it is one which draws its evidence from the concepts of its terms and from nothing else, whatever be the intellect which conceives those terms. For this follows what was said above [cf. 14–20].

33. It is also clear in what way "God exists" is self-evident and in what way it is not. For if we mean by God "this divine essence" which we do not conceive, it is a self-evident truth; but if we mean by God, that which we first conceive God to be in such universal terms as "first principle" and "infinite" and many such like, then the truth is not self-evidently known, as has already been shown.

II. To the Arguments at the Beginning of the Second Question (par. 8–11)

34. [To Arg. I] As for the first reason, based on Damascene's statement that the knowledge of God is implanted in all, I say that in the same place he says that "no one knows God except by revelation" so that it is necessary to gloss his statement. Therefore it can be said that the cognition of God is implanted in everybody, not in particular but in universal terms and according to common notions which are most appropriately applied to God, and therefore by way of appropriation it is said that the knowledge of him is implanted in all. Hence "being" and "act," etc. are most appropriately applied to God. Or one could say that the knowledge of God is implanted in everyone by reason of their knowledge of creatures, from which they come to know God. But even for him the knowledge of God is not self-evident.

35. [To Arg. II] As for the other, where it is argued that according to Anselm the existence of a thing is self-evident, if it is impossible to think of anything greater, I reply that such is not the case. Hence Anselm's intention there is not to show that the existence of God is self-evident, but that it is true. And he makes two syllogisms, of which the first is: "Something is greater than anything which does not exist; but nothing is greater than the highest; therefore the highest is not nonbeing." There is another syllogism: "What is not a nonbeing, exists; but the highest is not a nonbeing, therefore the highest exists."

36. [To Arg. III] As for the other reason, where it is claimed: "That truth exists is self-evident," I say for one thing the argument fallaciously affirms the consequent, since it proceeds from truth in general to this "Truth" which is God. For another, I say that it is not self-evident that "truth exists." And when it is argued that "If truth does not exist, it is true that truth does not

exist," I say that the consequence does not follow, because there is no truth except fundamentally in things and formally in the intellect. But if nothing is true, then nothing exists and consequently in nothing is there truth. Hence, it doesn't follow that if truth does not exist, therefore this dictum "Truth does not exist" is true.

37. [To Arg. IV] As for the next argument, when it is claimed that the proposition "God exists" has terms which are purely necessary, whereas this is not the case with "Every whole is greater than a part thereof" I say that the necessity of the proposition is not a necessity characteristic of real things, but it consists of the evidence for the proposition which is in the mind because the terms are there. "God exists," however, has a necessity and an evidence that stems from reality, but the other proposition has the greater evidence in the mind, once its terms are known, and consequently it is self-evident, whereas the other is not.

III. Reply to the First Question

38. In answer to the first question one must say this. Some properties of the infinite being have reference to creatures and from the existence of their referents, the existence of these properties can be inferred. From this it follows that the proper way to know the existence of God and his infinity is by way of such divine properties as have reference to creatures.

A. God's Existence Demonstrated from Properties Which Refer to Creatures

39. Now there are two properties of God which have reference to creatures, one is eminence in goodness, the other is causality. Eminence is not subdivided further, but causality is. According to some,[12] its divisions are: exemplar, efficient and final cause. Such say that the exemplar cause gives a thing its essential being. But I say here (and later on in more detail)[13] that the exemplar cause is not to be numbered alongside of the efficient cause, for it is only

as a concomitant factor of an efficient cause that the exemplar in the mind of the artisan gives any being to a thing. And if [the exemplar in view of its effect] can be considered as a formal cause, then it would pertain to eminence rather than to causality, for the more excellent being contains virtually the forms of other things and contains them unitively. Hence in God there are these three: eminence, efficiency and finality.

1. The Argument from Efficiency

40. Now efficiency can be considered either as a metaphysical or as a physical property. The metaphysical property is more extensive than the physical for "to give existence to another" is of broader scope than "to give existence by way of movement or change." And even if all existence were given in the latter fashion, the notion of the one is still not that of the other.

It is not efficiency as a physical attribute, however, but efficiency as the metaphysician considers it that provides a more effective way of proving God's existence, for there are more attributes in metaphysics than in physics whereby the existence of God can be established. It can be shown, for example, from "composition and simplicity," from "act and potency," from "one and many," from those features which are properties of being. Wherefore, if you find one extreme of the disjunction imperfectly realized in a creature, you conclude that the alternate, the perfect extreme exists in God.

Averroës, therefore, in attacking Avicenna at the end of Bk. I of the *Physics*,[14] is incorrect when he claims that to prove that God exists is the job of the physicist alone, because this can be established only by way of motion, and in no other way—as if metaphysics began with a conclusion which was not evident in itself, but needed to be proved in physics (for Averroës asserts this falsehood at the end of the first book of the *Physics*). In point of fact, however, [God's existence] can be shown more truly and in a greater variety of ways by means of those metaphysical attributes which characterize being. The proof lies in this that the first efficient cause imparts not merely this fluid existence [called motion] but existence in an unqualified sense, which is still more perfect and widespread. Now the existence of a primacy in the higher class does not follow logically from the existence of a primary in a lower [or more specific] class, unless that member is the most noble. For example, this does not follow: "The most noble donkey exists, therefore the most noble animal exists." Consequently, from the property of being the most noble being, one can argue better to a primacy among beings than from the primacy characteristic of a prime mover.

41. Hence, we omit the physical argument by which a prime mover is shown to exist and, using the efficiency characteristic of beings, we argue that among beings there is one which is a first efficient cause. And this is Richard's argument in Bk. I, chapter eight *On the Trinity*.[15]

Some being is not eternal, and therefore it does not exist of itself, neither is it caused by nothing, because nothing produces itself. Hence, it is from some other being. The latter either gives existence in virtue of something other than itself or not. And its existence, too, it either gets from another or not. If neither be true—i.e., if it neither imparts existence in virtue of another nor receives its own existence from another—then this is the first efficient cause, for such is the meaning of the term. But if either of the above alternatives holds [viz. if it receives existence, or imparts it to others only in virtue of another], then I inquire about the latter as I did before. One cannot go on his way ad infinitum. Hence, we end up with some first efficient cause, which neither imparts existence in virtue of another nor receives its own existence from another.

42. Objections, however, are raised against this argument. To begin with, it seems to beg the question, for it assumes that there is an order and a first among causes. But if no efficient cause is first, then both the order and the terminus in such causes would have to be denied.

43. Furthermore, inasmuch as the argument begins with a contingent premise, it does not seem to be a demonstration. For a demonstration proceeds from necessary premises, and everything exists contingently which owes its existence to God. Consequently, with reference to God this statement is contingent: "Some being is non-eternal," because from it this statement follows: "Some non-eternal being exists," and this latter is contingent.

44. Furthermore, since there is no demonstration of the reasoned fact, neither does there seem to be any demonstration of the simple fact.[16] For, whenever some conclusion is established by a demonstration of the latter type, one can always set up a converse demonstration of the reasoned fact (from cause to effect). But from the existence of the first cause, the existence of other things cannot be inferred by a demonstration of the reasoned fact; therefore, neither is the converse relation demonstrable as a simple fact.

45. To solve these objections, then, know this to begin with. Incidental [*per accidens*] causes are not the same as causes that are ordered to one another incidentally, just as essential [per se] causes are not the same as causes essentially ordered to one another. For when I speak of essential [i.e., per se] and incidental [i.e., *per accidens*] causes, I express a one to one relationship, viz. between a cause and its effect. But when causes are said to be incidentally or essentially ordered, two causes are being considered with reference to a single effect, so that we have a two to one relationship. Now causes are essentially ordered if one is ordered to the other so that [together] they cause a third thing, the effect. But causes are incidentally ordered if one is not ordered to the other in the very act of causing the effect. This would be the case with father and grandfather with regard to the son.

46. Secondly, it follows from this that essentially ordered causes differ from incidentally ordered causes in a threefold way:

The first difference is this: one cause depends essentially upon the other in order to produce an effect, which is not the case with causes that are ordered to a single effect only incidentally. Wherefore, the single causality of one of the incidentally ordered causes suffices to produce the single effect, whereas the causality of only one of the essentially ordered causes does not suffice.

47. From this, the second difference follows, viz. where essentially ordered causes are concerned, their causality differs in kind and they are not related to their effect in the same way. But the causality of all the incidentally ordered causes is of the same kind, since they can be referred immediately to the same effect.

48. From this, too, the third difference arises, viz. that the causalities of all of the essentially ordered causes concur simultaneously to produce the effect. For what is needed to cause an effect is that all its necessary causes concur. But all the essentially ordered causes are necessary causes. Therefore, all such must actually concur to bring about the effect. But this is not required where incidentally ordered causes are concerned, because each of itself possesses perfect causality as regards its effect, and they are of one kind so far as their immediate effect is concerned.

49. With these things presupposed, then, what remains to be shown is that the proof for a first cause does not involve a begging of the question. Therefore, I first prove that there is such a first where essentially ordered causes are concerned. I do this:

First, by the argument of the Philosopher, Bk. II of the *Metaphysics*[17] (and that of Avicenna, too, Bk. VIII, chapter one)[18] which seems to be this: All causes intermediate between the first and the last, cause by virtue of the first, so that their causality is derived from the first. As the Philosopher points out there, it is not derived from the last but from the first, for if "to cause" pertains to any of them, a fortiori it will pertain to the first. Now the minor of his argument seems to be this: "If the series of causes is infinite then all are intermediate causes." Consequently they all cause in virtue of some first cause, so that it is necessary to assume a first among efficient causes.

50. But you may object: When you say in the minor, "Every cause in an infinite series is an intermediate cause," either you mean by intermediate such causes as lie between a first and a last in the series, and so assume that there is a first, or else you mean it in a purely negative sense [i.e., as being neither the first nor last], in which case there are four terms, and again the conclusion does not follow.

51. I say, therefore, that the statement first assumed by the Philosopher is not the major in the argument, but is antecedent thereto. The argument, consequently, goes in this way. Every intermediary cause having a first and a last, derives its causality from the first. Hence the causality of the intermediary causes comes from the first. But if there were an infinity of such causes, they would all be intermediary. Hence, their causality is derived from some first. But if they are infinite, then there is no first. Hence, there is and there is not a first cause!

Proof of the aforesaid consequence:

All causes in any way intermediate, be they positively or negatively so, are caused. Therefore, the whole concatenation of intermediary causes is caused. Hence, it is caused by something which is outside the concatenated series. Hence, there is a first.

52. What is more, the causalities of all the essential causes must concur simultaneously to produce their effect, as was pointed out above. But an infinity of things cannot so concur to produce one thing, hence there is not an infinity of such causes and therefore a first cause does exist.

53. Furthermore, a cause which is prior as regards the causation has a more perfect causality, and the more it is prior, the more perfect its causality. Hence, a cause with infinite priority would have an infinite causality. But if there were an infinite regress in essentially ordered causes, then there is a cause with infinite priority. To assume an infinite regress, then, is to grant a cause whose causality is infinite. But surely a cause which exercises infinite causality when it causes, does not depend upon anything else, and as such it would be the first. Therefore, etc.

54. Furthermore, to be able to produce something is not a property which of itself entails imperfection. But whatever is of such like is able to exist in something without imperfection. And thus there must be an efficient cause in which it can exist in this way, which is impossible if the cause does not produce its effect independently, and this means it is the first efficient cause. Therefore, etc.

55. Likewise, if one assumes an infinity of incidentally ordered causes, it still follows that there is a first in essentially ordered causes, for those causes which are incidentally ordered are in individuals of the same species. Then [one argues] as follows: No deformity is perpetual, unless it is brought about by a perpetual cause—outside this coordination—which perpetuates this deformity. Proof: Nothing that is part of this concatenation can be the cause of the whole of this perpetuated deformity, because in such incidentally ordered [causes], one is the cause of one only. Therefore, it is necessary to postulate—beyond this deformed concatenation—some first essential cause which perpetuates it. The deformation, then, is due to the deformed cause, but the continual uniformity of this deformity will be due to a cause outside this concatenation. And thus, if there is a process in incidentally ordered causes, there will still be a terminal point in some first essential cause upon which all the incidentally ordered causes depend.

In this way we avoid begging the question as regards a terminus and order of essential causes.

56. Now for the second objection raised against the aforesaid argument, viz. that it proceeds from something contingent, scil. "Something other than God exists." The philosophers would say that this is something necessary because of the essential order that holds between the cause and what it produces.

But I say, first, that even though it be contingent with reference to God, it is nevertheless most evident, so that anyone who would deny the existence of some being which is not eternal needs senses and pun-

ishment.[19] And therefore, from what is contingent in this way we can establish something necessary, for from the contingent something necessary follows, but not vice versa.

57. Also, I say that although things other than God are actually contingent as regards their actual existence, this is not true with regard to potential existence. Wherefore, those things which are said to be contingent with reference to actual existence are necessary with respect to potential existence. Thus, though "Man exists" is contingent, "It is possible for man to exist" is necessary, because it does not include a contradiction as regards existence. For, for something other than God to be possible, then, is necessary. Being is divided into what must exist and what can but need not be. And just as necessity is of the very essence or constitution of what must be, so possibility is of the very essence of what can but need not be. Therefore, let the former argument be couched in terms of possible being and the proposition will become necessary. Thus: It is possible that something other than God exist which neither exists of itself (for then it would not be possible being) nor exists by reason of nothing. Therefore, it can exist by reason of another. Either this other can both exist and act in virtue of itself and not in virtue of another, or it cannot do so. If it can, then it can be the first cause, and if it can exist, it does exist—as was proved above. If it cannot [both be and act independently of every other thing] and there is no infinite regress, then at some point we end up [with a first cause].

58. To the other objection (viz. that whenever an argument proceeds by way of a demonstration of simple fact, a converse demonstration of the reasoned fact can be constructed), one must say that such is not always true, because when we argue from the effect to the existence of a cause our argument may merely prove that the latter is a necessary condition rather than a sufficient reason for the effect. But it is only when the argument from effect to cause establishes [in addition] that the latter is a sufficient reason that the

above principle [of converse demonstration] holds good.

59. And so we show from efficiency, to begin with, that something which is first exists, for—as we have made clear—something exists which makes all possible things possible. But that which makes all possibles possible cannot fail to exist of itself, for otherwise it would be from nothing. Therefore, it must needs be actually self-existent. And so our thesis is proved.

2. The Argument from Finality

60. That something first exists is established secondly from finality. Something is suited by its very nature to be an end. Hence it so functions either in virtue of itself or in virtue of another. If the first be the case, we have something which is first; if it functions as an end only in virtue of another then this other is suited by its very nature to be an end, and since there is no infinite regress, we arrive at some end which is first. This is the argument of the Philosopher in *Metaphysics*, Bk. II[20] and Bk XII[21] about the most perfect good, and it is also the argument of Augustine in *On the Trinity*, Bk. VIII, chapter three:[22] "Consider this good and that good, abstract from the 'this' and the 'that,' and consider, if you can, simply the good itself, and thus you will see God, who is not good by reason of some other good but is the goodness of all that is good."

3. The Argument from Eminent Perfection

61. The third way is that of eminence. Some good is exceeded in perfection, or is able to be exceeded if you prefer to argue from possibility. Therefore, there is something which exceeds or is able to exceed something else in perfection. The latter either is or is not able to be exceeded or is actually exceeded in perfection by something else. If it is not, then it is first in the order of eminence, if it is not first and there is no regress ad infinitum, then we argue the same as before.

62. And so we show that something is first in three ways, first in the order of efficiency, first in the order of eminence and first in the order of ends.

And this triple "first" is one and the same because the first efficient cause is fully actualized, while the most eminent is the best of things. But what is fully actualized is also the best, with no mixture of evil or potentiality. Then too, the first efficient cause does not act for the sake of anything other than itself, for if it did, this other would be better than it. Consequently, it is the ultimate end, and hence first in the order of ends. The same thing, then, enjoys [a triple primacy].

63. Before establishing that some being is infinite, we prove God is his own knowledge, for if his knowledge were not his nature but something accidental to it, then as the first efficient cause of everything, he would produce his knowledge. But God acts with knowledge; hence he would have to know about this knowledge beforehand. About this prior knowledge we inquire as before. Either there will be an infinite regress before something is known—and then nothing will be known—[or we admit finally that God is his own knowledge].

NOTES

1. Aristotle, *Physic.* III, c. 5 (204b 19–22).
2. Ibid., VIII, c. 10 (266a 24–266b 6).
3. Ibid., (266a 10–24).
4. *De fide orthodoxa,* c. 1 (ed. Buytaert, Franciscan Institute Publ. Text series No. 8, p. 12; PG 94. col. 790).
5. Aristotle, *Metaphysica* II, c. 1 (993b 4–5).
6. Anselm, *Proslogion,* c. 2 (PL 158 227–28).
7. Aristotle, *Physic.* I, c. 1 (184a 26–184b 3).
8. Aristotle, *Metaphy.* IX, c. 10 (1051b 25–28, 13–15).
9. Ibid., VIII, c. 3 (1043b 23–32).
10. Ibid., V, c. 29 (1024b 31–32).

11. The reference is to the first question of distinction 3 where he shows that every simple concept that applies to God is univocally predicable of God and some creature and every concept which applies exclusively to God is composite and is constructed by affirming, denying and interrelating conceptual elements that are simple and univocally predicable of creatures. Confer A. Wolter, *Duns Scotus: Philosophical Writings* (Edinburgh: Nelson and Sons, 1962), 19–28.

12. Henry of Ghent, *Summa quaestionum ordinariarum*, art. 22, q. 4 vol. I (Parisiis, 1520), fol. 132M.

13. *Lectura oxoniensis I*, dist. 26, n. 19.

14. Averroës, *Physica I*, com. 83 (*Commentaria in Aristotelis opera*, Venetiis, 1483).

15. Richard of St. Victor, *De Trinitate 1*, c. 8 (PL 196, col. 894).

16. See Aristotle, *Prior Analytics I*, c. 13 (78a 22–78b 34) for the distinction between a demonstration of the reasoned fact and of the simple fact. The former roughly corresponds to an a priori demonstration, e.g. from cause to effect, the latter gives no cause or prior reason why such a fact occurs but only why we know the fact to be the case.

17. Aristotle, *Metaphys.* II, c. 2 (994a 11–13).

18. Avicenna, *Opera* (Venetiis, 1508), fol. 97rb–va.

19. See Aristotle, *Topica I*, c. 9 (105a 4–5).

20. Aristotle, *Metaphys.* II, c. 2 (994b 9–13).

21. Ibid., XII, c. 10 (1075a 11–23).

22. Augustine, *De Trinitate*, VIII, c. 3 (PL 42, col. 949).

PART II

ETHICS AND THE PROBLEM OF EVIL

CHAPTER 7

Pseudo-Dionysius

Pseudo-Dionysius is so named because he was wrongly identified as Dionysius the Areopagite, who St. Paul converted to Christianity in Athens (Acts 17:34). He was also misidentified as St. Denis, the patron saint of France. But it was not until the sixteenth century that these beliefs concerning Pseudo-Dionysius were discovered to be false. Although his origins are unknown, the Pseudo-Dionysius had a tremendous influence on later thinkers of the Middle Ages, including such notables as John of Damascus, Thomas Aquinas, Peter Lombard, Robert Grosseteste, and Albert the Great.

His writings began to appear toward the close of the fifth century. Four of his treatises, *The Celestial Hierarchy, The Ecclesiastical Hierarchy, The Divine Names*, and *The Mystical Theology*, as well as ten of his letters are extant. We see in these works a clear and distinct Neoplatonic influence which had already had a tremendous effect on St. Augustine. The dualism of Plato's metaphysics as expressed in Neoplatonism was most compatible with Christianity. Both, for example, placed emphasis on the contrast between the visible and invisible worlds. In *The Divine Names* Pseudo-Dionysius proposes a Neoplatonic solution to the problem of evil.

Pseudo-Dionysius on the Nature of Evil

In Book VI of *The Republic* Plato draws an analogy between the highest of the forms, the Good, and the sun. Just as sunlight is a prerequisite for seeing, the Good is a prerequisite for understanding all other Forms. Pseudo-Dionysius employs the same reasoning with the addition of identifying the Good with God. God is Good and the ground of all being. All that is emanates from God. God is the ultimate cause of all being. Therefore, all that exists is good.

Another Platonic notion is utilized. Things as we know them participate in the Good to varying degrees. Evil is not a thing, for Good cannot create evil. " . . . evil (qua evil) causes no existence or birth, but only debases and corrupts, so far as its power extends, the substance of things that have being." All created things are good by virtue of their being *(ens)*. That there are degrees of Goodness in things is necessitated by the fact that otherwise "the divinest and most honorable things would be no higher than the lowest." But such lower things are not evil. Rather, they are simply imperfectly good.

Pseudo-Dionysius observes that there is a difference between moral evil (viz., man's

83

inhumanity to man) and natural evil (viz., natural disasters such as earthquakes). Regarding the former he argues that the evil we observe does not exist in mankind *as* evil, "but only as a deficiency and lack of the perfection of our proper virtues". As for natural evil there is understood to be none when Nature is considered as a whole, taking into account the integration of the laws of nature. It is only when isolated incidents are considered out of context with the universal system of Nature that they appear evil. But such are not really evil, only appearances as such.

"THE NATURE OF EVIL"
FROM *THE DIVINE NAMES*

Chapter Four
Concerning Good, Light, Beauty, Love, Ecstasy, Jealousy, and that the Evil is neither existent, nor from existent, nor in things being.

Section I

Be it so then. Let us come to the appellation "Good," already mentioned in our discourse, which the Theologians ascribe pre-eminently and exclusively to the super-Divine Deity, as I conjecture, by calling the supremely Divine Subsistence, Goodness; and because the Good, as essential Good, by Its being, extends Its Goodness to all things that be.

For, even as our sun—not as calculating or choosing, but by its very being, enlightens all things able to partake of its light in their own degree—so too the Good—as superior to a sun, as the archetype par excellence, is above an obscure image—by Its very existence sends to all things that be, the rays of Its whole goodness, according to their capacity. By reason of these (rays) subsisted all the intelligible and intelligent essences and powers and energies. By reason of these they are, and have their life, continuous and undiminished, purified from all corruption and death and matter, and generation; and separated from the unstable and fluctuating and vacillating mutability, and are conceived of as incorporeal and immaterial, and as minds they think in

From *The Works of Dionysius The Areopagite, Part I. Divine Names, Mystic Theology, Letters, & c.*, translated by the Rev. John Parker, M. A. (Merrick, N. Y.: Richwood Publishing Co., reprinted 1976), pp. 32–72.

a manner supermundane, and are illuminated as to the reasons of things, in a manner peculiar to themselves; and they again convey to their kindred spirits things appropriate to them; and they have their abiding from Goodness; and thence comes to them stability and consistence and protection, and sanctuary of good things; and whilst aspiring to It, they have both being and good being; and being conformed to It, as is attainable, they are both patterns of good, and impart to those after them, as the Divine Law directs, the gifts which have passed through to themselves from the Good.

Section II

Thence come to them the supermundane orders, the unions amongst themselves, the mutual penetrations, the unconfused distinctions, the powers elevating the inferior to the superior, the providences of the more exalted for those below them; the guardings of things pertaining to each power; and unbroken convolutions around themselves; the identities and sublimities around the aspiration after the Good; and whatever is said in our Treatise concerning the angelic properties and orders. Further also, whatever things belong to the heavenly Hierarchy, the purifications befitting angels, the supermundane illuminations, and the things perfecting the whole angelic perfection, are from the all-creative and fontal Goodness; from which was given to them the form of Goodness, and the revealing in themselves the hidden Goodness, and that angels are, as it were, heralds of the Divine silence, and project, as it were, luminous lights revealing Him Who is in secret. Further, after these—the sacred and holy minds—the souls, and whatever is good in souls is by reason of the super-good Goodness—the fact that they are intellectual—that they have essential life—indestructible—the very being itself—and that they are able, whilst elevated themselves to the angelic lives, to be conducted by them as good guides to the good Origin of all good things, and to become partakers of the illuminations, thence bubbling forth, according to the capacity of each, and to participate in the goodlike gift, as they are able, and whatever else we have enumerated in our Treatise concerning the soul. But also, if one may be permitted to speak of the irrational souls, or living creatures, such as cleave the air, and such as walk on earth, and such as creep along earth, and those whose life is in waters, or amphibious, and such as live concealed under earth, and burrow within it, and in one word, such as have the sensible soul or life, even all these have their soul and life, by reason of the Good. Moreover, all plants have their growing and moving life from the Good; and even soulless and lifeless substance is by reason of the Good, and by reason of It, has inherited its substantial condition.

Section III

But, if the Good is above all things being, as indeed it is, and formulates the formless, even in Itself alone, both the non-essential is a pre-eminence of essence, and the non-living is a superior life, and the mindless a superior wisdom, and whatever is in the Good is of a superlative formation of the formless, and if one may venture to say so, even the nonexistent itself aspires to the Good above all things existing, and struggles somehow to be even itself in the Good,—the really Superessential—to the exclusion of all things.

Section IV

But what slipped from our view in the midst of our discourse, the Good is Cause of the celestial movements in their commencements and terminations, of their not increasing, not diminishing, and completely changeless, course, and of the noiseless movements, if one may so speak, of the vast celestial transit, and of the astral orders, and the beauties and lights, and stabilities, and the progressive swift motion of certain stars, and of the periodical return of the two luminaries, which the Oracles call "great," from the same to the same quarter, after which our days and nights being marked, and months and years being measured, mark and number and arrange and comprehend the circular movements of time and things temporal. But, what would any one say of the very ray of the sun? For the light is from the Good, and an image of the Goodness, wherefore also the Good is celebrated under the name of Light; as in a portrait the original is manifested. For, as the goodness of the Deity, beyond all, permeates from the highest and most honoured substances even to the lowest, and yet is above all, neither the foremost outstripping its superiority, nor the things below eluding its grasp, but it both enlightens all that are capable, and forms and enlivens, and grasps, and perfects, and is measure of things existing, and age, and number, and order, and grasp, and cause, and end; so, too, the brilliant likeness of the Divine Goodness, this our great sun, wholly bright and ever luminous, as a most distant echo of the Good, both enlightens whatever is capable of participating in it, and possesses the light in the highest degree of purity, unfolding to the visible universe, above and beneath, the splendours of its own rays, and if anything does not participate in them, this is not owing to the inertness of deficiency of its distribution of light, but is owing to the inaptitude for light-reception of the things which do not unfold themselves for the participation of light. No doubt the ray passing over many things in such condition, enlightens the things after them, and there is no visible thing which it does not reach, with the surpassing greatness of its own splendour. Further also, it contributes to the generation of sensible bodies, and moves them to life, and nourishes, and increases, and perfects, and purifies and renews; and the light is both measure and number of hours, days, and all our time. For it is the light itself, even though it was then without form, which the divine Moses declared to have fixed that first Triad of our days. And, just as Goodness turns all things to Itself, and is chief collector of things scattered, as One-springing and One-making Deity, and all things aspire to It, as Source and Bond and End, and it is the Good, as the Oracles say, from Which all things subsisted, and are being brought into being by an all-perfect Cause; and in Which all things consisted, as guarded and governed in an all-controlling-route; and to Which things are turned, as to their own proper end; and to Which all aspire—the intellectual and rational indeed, through knowledge, and the sensible through the senses, and those bereft of sensible perception by the innate movement of the aspiration after life, and those without life, and merely being, by their aptitude for mere substantial participation; after the same method of its illustrious original, the light also collects and turns to itself all things existing—things with sight—things with motion—things enlightened—things heated—things wholly held together by its brilliant splendours—whence also, Helios, because it makes all things altogether (ἀολλῆ), and collects things scattered. And all creatures, endowed with sensible perceptions, aspire to it, as aspiring either to see, or to be moved and enlightened, and heated, and to be wholly held together by the light. By no means do I affirm, after the statement of antiquity, that as being God and Creator of the universe, the sun, by itself, governs the luminous world, but that the invisible things of God are clearly seen from the foundation of the world, being understood by the things that are made, even His eternal power and Deity.

Section V

But we have spoken of these things in our *Symbolical Theology*. Let us now then celebrate the spirital Name of Light, under Which we contemplate the Good, and declare that He, the Good, is called spiritual[1]

Light, on the ground that He fills every supercelestial mind with spiritual light, and expels all ignorance and error from all souls in which they may be, and imparts to them all sacred light, and cleanses their mental vision from the mist which envelops them, from ignorance, and stirs up and unfolds those enclosed by the great weight of darkness, and imparts, at first, a measured radiance; then, whilst they taste, as it were, the light, and desire it more, more fully gives Itself, and more abundantly enlightens them, because "they have loved much," and ever elevates them to things in advance, as befits the analogy of each for aspiration.

Section VI

The Good then above every light is called spiritual Light, as fontal ray, and stream of light welling over, shining upon every mind, above, around, and in the world, from its fulness, and renewing their whole mental powers, and embracing them all by its over-shadowing; and being above all by its exaltation; and in one word, by embracing and having previously and pre-eminently the whole sovereignty of the light-dispensing faculty, as being source of light and above all light, and by comprehending in itself all things intellectual, and all things rational, and making them one altogether. For as ignorance puts asunder those who have gone astray, so the presence of the spiritual light is collective and unifying of those being enlightened, both perfecting and further turning them towards the true Being, by turning them from the many notions and collecting the various views, or, to speak more correctly, fancies, into one true, pure and uniform knowledge, and by filling them with light, one and unifying.

Section VII

This Good is celebrated by the sacred theologians, both as beautiful and as Beauty, and as Love, and as Beloved; and all the other Divine Names which beseem the beautifying and highly-favoured comeliness. But the beautiful and Beauty are not to be divided, as regards the Cause which has embraced the whole in one. For, with regard to all created things, by dividing them into participations and participants, we call beautiful that which participates in Beauty; but beauty, the participation of the beautifying Cause of all the beautiful things. But, the superessential Beautiful is called Beauty, on account of the beauty communicated from Itself to all beautiful things, in a manner appropriate to each, and as Cause of the good harmony and brightness of all things which flashes like light to all the beautifying distributions of its fontal ray, and as calling (καλοῦν) all things to Itself (whence also it is called Beauty) (κάλλος), and as collecting all in all to Itself. (And it is called) Beautiful, as (being) at once beautiful and super-beautiful, and always being under the same conditions and in the same manner beautiful, and neither coming into being nor perishing, neither waxing nor waning; neither in this beautiful, nor in that ugly, nor at one time beautiful, and at another not; nor in relation to one thing beautiful, and in relation to another ugly, nor here, and not here, as being beautiful to some, and not beautiful to others; but as Itself, in Itself, with Itself, uniform, always being beautiful, and as having beforehand in Itself preeminently the fontal beauty of everything beautiful. For, by the simplex and supernatural nature of all beautiful things, all beauty, and everything beautiful, pre-existed uniquely as to Cause. From this Beautiful (comes) being to all existing things,— that each is beautiful in its own proper order; and by reason of the Beautiful are the adaptations of all things, and friendships, and inter-communions, and by the Beautiful all things are made one, and the Beautiful is origin of all things, as a creating Cause, both by moving the whole and holding it together by the love of its own peculiar Beauty; and end of all things, and beloved, as final Cause (for all things exist for the sake of the Beautiful) and exemplary (Cause), because all things are determined according to It. Wherefore, also, the Beautiful is identical with the Good, because all things aspire to the Beautiful and Good, on every account, and there is no ex-

isting thing which does not participate in the Beautiful and the Good. Yea, reason will dare to say even this, that even the non-existing participates in the Beautiful and Good. For then even it is beautiful and good, when in God it is celebrated super-essentially to the exclusion of all. This, the one Good and Beautiful, is uniquely Cause of all the many things beautiful and good. From this are all the substantial beginnings of things existing, the unions, the distinctions, the identities, the diversities, the similarities, the dissimilarities, the communions of the contraries, the commingling of things unified, the providences of the superior, the mutual cohesions of those of the same rank; the attentions of the more needy, the protecting and immoveable abidings and stabilities of their whole selves and, on the other hand, the communions of all things among all, in a manner peculiar to each, and adaptations and unmingled friendships and harmonies of the whole, the blendings in the whole, and the undissolved connections of existing things, the never-failing successions of the generations, all rests and movements, of the minds, of the souls, of the bodies. For, that which is established above every rest, and every movement, and moves each thing in the law of its own being to its proper movement, is a rest and movement to all.

Section VIII

Now, the divine minds[2] are said to be moved circularly indeed, by being united to the illuminations of the Beautiful and Good, without beginning and without end; but in a direct line, whenever they advance to the succour of a subordinate, by accomplishing all things directly; but spirally, because even in providing for the more indigent, they remain fixedly, in identity, around the good and beautiful Cause of their identity, ceaselessly dancing around.

Section IX

Further, there is a movement of soul, circular indeed,—the entrance into itself from things without, and the unified convolution of its intellectual powers, bequeathing to it inerrancy, as it were, in a sort of circle, and turning and collecting itself, from the many things without, first to itself, then, as having become single, uniting with the uniquely unified powers, and thus conducting to the Beautiful and Good, which is above all things being, and One and the Same, and without beginning and without end. But a soul is moved spirally, in so far as it is illuminated, as to the divine kinds of knowledge, in a manner proper to itself, not intuitively and at once, but logically and discursively; and, as it were, by mingled and relative operations; but in a straight line, when, not entering into itself, and being moved by unique intuition (for this, as I said, is the circular), but advancing to things around itself, and from things without, it is, as it were, conducted from certain symbols, varied and multiplied, to the simple and unified contemplations.

Section X

Of these three motions then in everything perceptible here below, and much more of the abidings and repose and fixity of each, the Beautiful and Good, which is above all repose and movement, is Cause and Bond and End; by reason of which, and from which, and in which, and towards which, and for sake of which, is every repose and movement. For, both from It and through It is both Essence and every life, and both of mind and soul and every nature, the minutiae, the equalities, the magnitudes, all the standards and the analogies of beings, and harmonies and compositions; the entireties, the parts, every one thing, and multitude, the connections of parts, the unions of every multitude, the perfections of the entireties, the quality, the weight, the size, the infinitude, the compounds, the distinctions, every infinitude, every term, all the bounds, the orders, the pre-eminences, the elements, the forms, every essence, every power, every energy, every condition, every sensible perception, every reason, every conception, every contact, every science, every union, and in one word, all things existing are from the Beautiful and Good, and in the Beautiful and Good, and turn themselves to the Beautiful and Good.

Moreover, all things whatever, which are and come to being, are and come to being by reason of the Beautiful and Good; and to It all things look, and by It are moved and held together, and for the sake of It, and by reason of It, and in It, is every source exemplary, final, creative, formative, elemental, and in one word, every beginning, every bond, every term, or to speak summarily, all things existing are from the Beautiful and Good; and all things non-existing are superessentially in the Beautiful and Good; and it is of all, beginning and term, above beginning and above term, because from It, and through It, and in It, and to It, are all things, as says the Sacred Word.

By all things, then, the Beautiful and Good is desired and beloved and cherished; and, by reason of It, and for the sake of It, the less love the greater suppliantly; and those of the same rank, their fellows brotherly; and the greater, the less considerately; and these severally love the things of themselves continuously; and all things by aspiring to the Beautiful and Good, do and wish all things whatever they do and wish. Further, it may be boldly said with truth, that even the very Author of all things, by reason of overflowing Goodness, loves all, makes all, perfects all, sustains all, attracts all; and even the Divine Love is Good of Good, by reason of the Good. For Love itself, the benefactor of things that be, pre-existing overflowingly in the Good, did not permit itself to remain unproductive in itself, but moved itself to creation,[3] as befits the overflow which is generative of all.

Section XI

And let no one fancy that we honour the Name of Love beyond the Oracles, for it is, in my opinion, irrational and stupid not to cling to the force of the meaning, but to the mere words; and this is not the characteristic of those who have wished to comprehend things Divine, but of those who receive empty sounds and keep the same just at the ears from passing through from outside, and are not willing to know what such a word signifies, and in what way one ought to distinctly represent it, through other words of the same force and more explanatory, but who specially affect sounds and signs without meaning, and syllables, and words unknown, which do not pass through to the mental part of their soul, but buzz without, around their lips and ears, as though it were not permitted to signify the number four, by twice two, or straight lines by direct lines, or motherland by fatherland, or any other, which signify the self-same thing, by many parts of speech.

We ought to know, according to the correct account, that we use sounds, and syllables, and phrases, and descriptions, and words, on account of the sensible perceptions; since when our soul is moved by the intellectual energies to the things contemplated, the sensible perceptions by aid of sensible objects are superfluous; just as also the intellectual powers, when the soul, having become godlike, throws itself, through a union beyond knowledge, against the rays of the unapproachable light, by sightless efforts. But, when the mind strives to be moved upwards, through objects of sense, to contemplative conceptions, the clearer interpretations are altogether preferable to the sensible perceptions, and the more definite descriptions are things more distinct than things seen; since when objects near are not made clear to the sensible perceptions, neither will these perceptions be well able to present the things perceived to the mind. But that we may not seem, in speaking thus, to be pushing aside the Divine Oracles, let those who libel the Name of Love (Ἔρωτος) hear them. "Be in love with It," they say, "and It will keep thee—Rejoice over It, and It will exalt thee—Honour It, in order that It may encompass thee,"—and whatever else is sung respecting Love, in the Word of God.

Section XII

And yet it seemed to some of our sacred expounders that the Name of Love is more Divine than that of loving-kindness (ἀγάπης). But even the Divine Ignatius writes, "my own Love (ἔρως) is crucified"; and in the introductions to the Oracles you will find a certain One saying of the Divine Wisdom, "I became enamoured of her Beauty." So that we, certainly, need not be afraid of this Name of Love, nor let any alarming statement about it terrify us. For the theologians seem to me to treat as equivalent the name of Loving-kindness, and that of Love; and on this ground, to attribute, by preference, the veritable Love, to things Divine, because of the misplaced prejudice of such men as these. For, since the veritable Love is sung of in a sense befitting God, not by us only, but also by the Oracles themselves, the multitude, not having comprehended the Oneness of the Divine Name of Love, fell away, as might be expected of them, to the divided and corporeal and sundered, seeing it is not a real love, but a shadow, or rather a falling from the veritable Love. For the Oneness of the Divine and one Love is incomprehensible to the multitude, wherefore also, as seeming a very hard name to the multitude, it is assigned to the Divine Wisdom, for the purpose of leading back and restoring them to the knowledge of the veritable Love; and for their liberation from the difficulty respecting it. And again, as regards ourselves, where it happened often that men of an earthly character imagined something out of place, (there is used) what appears more euphonius. A certain one says, "Thy affection fell upon me, as the affection of the women." For those who have rightly listened to things Divine, the name of Loving-kindness and of Love is placed by the holy theologians in the same category throughout the Divine revelations, and this is a power unifying, and binding together, and mingling pre-eminently in the Beautiful and Good; pre-existing by reason of the beautiful and good, and imparted from the beautiful and good, by reason of the Beautiful and Good; and sustaining things of the same rank, within their mutual coherence, but moving the first to forethought for the inferior, and attaching the inferior to the superior by respect.

Section XIII

But Divine Love is extatic, not permitting (any) to be lovers of themselves, but of those beloved. They shew this too, the superior by becoming mindful of the inferior; and the equals by their mutual coherence; and the inferior, by a more divine respect towards things superior. Wherefore also, Paul the Great, when possessed by the Divine Love, and participating in its extatic power, says with inspired lips, "I live no longer, but Christ lives in me." As a true lover, and beside himself, as he says, to Almighty God, and not living the life of himself, but the life of the Beloved, as a life excessively esteemed. One might make bold to say even this, on behalf of truth, that the very Author of all things, by the beautiful and good love of everything, through an overflow of His loving goodness, becomes out of Himself, by His providences for all existing things, and is, as it were, cozened by goodness and affection and love, and is led down from the Eminence above all, and surpassing all, to being in all, as befits an extatic superessential power centred in Himself. Wherefore, those skilled in Divine things call Him even Jealous, as (being) that vast good Love towards all beings, and as rousing His loving inclination to jealousy,—and as proclaiming Himself Jealous—to Whom the things desired are objects of jealousy, and as though the objects of His providential care were objects of jealousy for Him. And, in short, the lovable is of the Beautiful and Good, and Love preexisted both in the Beautiful and Good, and on account of the Beautiful and Good, is and takes Being.

Section XIV

But what do the theologians mean when at one time they call Him Love, and Loving-kindness, and at another, Loved and Esteemed? For, of the one, He is Author and, as it were, Producer and Father; but the other, He Himself is; and by one He

is moved, but by the other He moves; or (when they say), that He Himself is Procurer and Mover of Himself and by Himself. In this sense, they call Him esteemed and loved, as Beautiful and Good: but again Love and Loving-kindness, as being at once moving and conducting Power to Himself;—the alone—self Beautiful and Good, by reason of Itself, and, being, as it were, a manifestation of Itself through Itself, and a good Progression of the surpassing union, and a loving Movement, simplex, self-moved, self-operating, preexisting in the Good, and from the Good bubbling forth to things existing, and again returning to the Good, in which also the Divine Love indicates distinctly Its own unending and unbeginning, as it were a sort of everlasting circle whirling round in unerring combination, by reason of the Good, from the Good, and in the Good, and to the Good, and ever advancing and remaining and returning in the same and throughout the same. And these things our illustrious initiator divinely set forth throughout His Hymns of Love, of which we may appropriately make mention, and, as it were, place as a certain sacred chapter to our treatise concerning Love.

Section XV

Extract from the "Hymns of Love," by the most holy Hierotheus:— Love, whether we speak of Divine, or Angelic or intelligent, or psychical, or physical, let us regard as a certain unifying and combining power, moving the superior to forethought for the inferior, and the equals to a mutual fellowship, and lastly, the inferior to respect towards the higher and superior.

Section XVI

Of the same, from the same Erotic Hymns. Since we have arranged the many loves from the one, by telling, in due order, what are the kinds of knowledge and powers of the mundane and super-mundane loves; over which, according to the defined purpose of the discourse, the orders and ranks of the mental and intelligible loves preside; next after[4] which are placed the self-existent intelligible and divine, over the really beautiful loves there which have been appropriately celebrated by us; now, on the other hand, by restoring all back to the One and enfolded Love, and Father of them all, let us collect and gather them together from the many, by contracting It into two Powers entirely lovable, over which rules and precedes altogether the Cause, resistless from Its universal Love beyond all, and to which is elevated, according to the nature of each severally, the whole love from all existing things.

Section XVII

Of the same, from the same Hymns of Love. Come then, whilst collecting these again into one, let us say, that it is a certain simplex power, which of itself moves to a sort of unifying combination from the Good, to the lowest of things existing, and from that again in due order, circling round again, through all to the Good from Itself, and through Itself and by Itself, and rolling back to Itself always in the same way.

Section XVIII

And yet, any one might say, "if the Beautiful and Good is beloved and desired, and esteemed by all (for even that which is non-existing desires It, as we have said, and struggles how to be in It; and Itself is the form-giving, even of things without form, and by It alone, even the non-existing is said to be, and is superessentially)—How is it that the host of demons do not desire the Beautiful and Good, but, through their earthly proclivities, having fallen away from the angelic identity, as regards the desire of the Good, have become cause of all evils both to themselves and to all the others who are said to be corrupted? and why, in short, when the tribes of demons have been brought into being from the Good, are they not like the Good? or how, after being a good production from the Good, were they changed? and what is that which depraved them, and in short, what is evil?

and from what source did it spring? and in which of things existing is it? and how did He, Who is Good, will to bring it into being? and how, when He willed it, was He able? And if evil is from another cause, what other cause is there for things existing, beside the Good? Further, how, when there is a Providence, is there evil, either coming into existence at all, or not destroyed? And how does any existing thing desire it, in comparison with the Good?"

Section XIX

Such a statement as this might be alleged by way of objection. We, however, on our part, will pray the objector to look to the truth of the facts, and will make bold to say this first. The Evil is not from the Good, and if it is from the Good, it is not the Evil. For, it is not the nature of fire to make cold, nor of good to bring into being things not good; and if all things that be are from the Good (for to produce and to preserve is natural to the Good, but to destroy and to dissolve, to the Evil), there is no existing thing from the Evil, nor will the Evil itself be, if it should be evil even to itself. And, if it be not so, the Evil is not altogether evil, but has some portion of the Good, in consequence of which it wholly is. Now, if the things existing desire the Beautiful and Good, and whatever they do, they do for the sake of that which seems good, and every purpose of things existing has the Good for its beginning and end (for nothing looking to the Evil qua evil, does what it does), how shall the Evil be in things existing; or, wholly being, how has it been seduced from such a good yearning? Also if all the things existing are from the Good, and the Good is above all things existing, then there is existing in the Good even the non-existing; but the Evil is not existing; and, if this be not the case, it is not altogether evil, nor non-existing, for the absolutely non-existing will be nothing, unless it should be spoken of as in the Good superessentially. The Good, then, will be fixed far above both the absolutely existing and the non-existing; but the Evil is neither in things existing, nor in things non-existing, but, being further distant from the Good than the non-existing itself, it is alien and more unsubstantial. Where then is the Evil? some one may perchance say. For if the Evil is not,—virtue and vice are the same, both universally and particularly. Or, not even that which opposes itself to virtue will be evil, and yet sobriety and license, and righteousness and unrighteousness, are contraries. And I, by no means, speak in reference to the just and unjust man, and the temperate and intemperate man; but also, long before the difference between the just man and his opposite is made manifest externally, in the very soul itself the vices stand altogether apart from the virtues, and the passions rebel against the reason; and from this we must grant some evil contrary to the Good. For the Good is not contrary to Itself, but as the product from one Source and one Cause, It rejoices in fellowship and unity and friendship. Nor yet is the lesser good opposed to the greater, for neither is the less heat or cold opposed to the greater. The Evil[5] then is in things existing, and is existing, and is opposed, and is in opposition to, the Good; and if it is the destruction of things existing, this does not expel the Evil from existence; but it will be, both itself existing, and generator of things existing. Does not frequently the destruction of one become birth of another? and the Evil will be contributing to the completion of the whole, and supplying through itself non-imperfection to the whole.

Section XX

Now to all this true reason will answer, that the Evil qua evil makes no single essence or birth, but only, as far as it can, pollutes and destroys the subsistence of things existing. But, if any one says, that it is productive of being, and that by destruction of one it gives birth to another, we must truly answer, that not qua destruction it gives birth, but qua destruction and evil, it destroys and pollutes only, but it becomes birth and essence, by reason of the Good; and the Evil will be destruction indeed, by reason of itself; but producer of birth by

reason of the Good; and qua evil, it is neither existing, nor productive of things existing; but, by reason of the Good, it is both existing and good-existing, and productive of things good. Yea, rather (for neither will the same by itself be both good and evil, nor the self-same power be of itself destruction and birth—neither as self-acting power, nor as self-acting destruction), the absolutely Evil is neither existing nor good, nor generative, nor productive of things being and good; but the Good in whatever things it may be perfectly engendered, makes them perfect and pure, and thoroughly good,—but the things which partake of it in a less degree are both imperfectly good, and impure, by reason of the lack of the Good. And (thus) the Evil altogether, is not, nor is good, nor good producing; but that which approaches more or less near the Good will be proportionately good; since the All-perfect Goodness, in passing through all, not only passes to the All-good beings around Itself, but extends Itself to the most remote, by being present to some thoroughly, to others subordinately, but to the rest, in the most remote degree, as each existing thing is able to participate in It. And some things, indeed, participate in the Good entirely, whilst others are deprived of It, in a more or less degree, but others possess a more obscure participation in the Good; and to the rest, the Good is present as a most distant echo. For if the good were not present according to the capacity of each, the most Divine and honoured would occupy the rank of the lowest. And how were it possible that all should participate in the Good uniformly, when not all are in the same way adapted to its whole participation?

Now, this is the exceeding greatness of the power of the Good, and It empowers, both things deprived, and the deprivation of Itself, with a view to the entire participation of itself. And, if one must make bold to speak the truth, even the things fighting against It, both are, and are able to fight, by Its power. Yea rather, in order that I may speak summarily, all things which are, in so far as they are, both are good, and from the Good; but, in so far as they are deprived of the Good, are neither good, nor do they exist. For, even with regard to the other conditions, such as heat or cold, there are things which have been heated, and when the heat has departed from them, many of them are deprived both of life and intelligence (now Almighty God is outside essence, and is, superessentially), and, in one word, with regard to the rest, even when the condition has departed, or has not become completely developed, things exist, and are able to subsist; but that which is every way deprived of the Good, in no way or manner ever was, or is, or will be, nor is able to be. For example, the licentious man, even if he have been deprived of the Good, as regards his irrational lust, in this respect he neither is, nor desires realities, but nevertheless he participates in the Good, in his very obscure echo of union and friendship. And, even Anger participates in the Good, by the very movement and desire to direct and turn the seeming evils to the seeming good. And the very man, who desires the very worst life, as wholly desirous of life and that which seems best to him, by the very fact of desiring, and desiring life, and looking to a best life, participates in the Good. And, if you should entirely take away the Good, there will be neither essence, nor life, nor yearning, nor movement, nor anything else. So that the fact, that birth is born from destruction, is not a power of evil, but a presence of a lesser good, even as disease is a defect of order, not total—for, if this should be, not even the disease itself will continue to exist, but the disease remains and is, by having the lowest possible order of essence, and in this continues to exist as a parasite. For that which is altogether deprived of the Good, is neither existing, nor in things existing; but the compound, by reason of the Good in things existing, and in consequence of this in things existing, is also existing in so far as it participates in the Good. Yea rather, all things existing will so far be, more or less, as they participate in the Good; for, even as respects the self-existing Being, that which in no ways is at all, will

not be at all; but that which partially is, but partially is not, in so far as it has fallen from the ever Being, is not; but so far as it has participated in the Being, so far it is, and its whole being, and its non-being, is sustained and preserved. And the Evil,—that which has altogether fallen from the Good—will be good, neither in the more nor in the less; but the partially good, and partially not good, fight no doubt against a certain good, but not against the whole Good, and, even it is sustained by the participation of the Good, and the Good gives essence even to the privation of Itself, wholly by the participation of Itself; for, when the Good has entirely departed, there will be neither anything altogether good, nor compound, nor absolute evil. For, if the Evil is an imperfect good, (then) by the entire absence of the Good, both the imperfect and the perfect Good will be absent; and then only will be, and be seen, the Evil, when on the one hand, it is an evil to those things to which it was opposed, and, on the other, is expelled from other things on account of their goodness. For, it is impossible that the same things, under the same conditions in every respect, should fight against each other. The Evil then is not an actual thing.

Section XXI

But neither is the Evil in things existing. For, if all things existing are from the Good, and the Good is in all things existing, and embraces all, either the Evil will not be in things existing, or it will be in the Good; and certainly it will not be in the Good, for neither is cold in fire, nor to do evil in Him, Who turns even the evil to good. But, if it shall be, how will the Evil be in the Good? If forsooth, from Itself, it is absurd and impossible. For it is not possible, as the infallibility of the Oracles affirms, that a "good tree should bring forth evil fruits," nor certainly, vice versa. But, if not from Itself, it is evident that it will be from another source and cause. For, either the Evil will be from the Good, or the Good from the Evil; or, if this be not possible, both the Good and the Evil will be from another source and cause, for no dual is source, but a Unit will be source of every dual. Further, it is absurd that two entirely contraries should proceed and be from one and the same, and that the self-same source should be, not simplex and unique, but divided and double, and contrary to itself, and be changed; and certainly it is not possible that there should be two contrary sources of things existing, and that these should be contending in each other, and in the whole. For, if this were granted, even Almighty God will not be in repose, nor free from disquietude, if there were indeed something bringing disturbance even to Him. Then, everything will be in disorder, and always fighting; and yet the Good distributes friendship to all existing things, and is celebrated by the holy theologians, both as very Peace, and Giver of Peace. Wherefore, things good are both friendly and harmonious, every one, and products of one life, and marshalled to one good; and kind, and similar, and affable to each other. So that the Evil is not in God, and the Evil is not inspired by God. But neither is the Evil from God, for, either He is not good, or He does good, and produces good things; and, not once in a way, and some; and at another time not, and not all; for this would argue transition and change, even as regards the very Divinest thing of all, the Cause. But, if in God, the Good is sustaining essence, God, when changing from the Good, will be sometimes Being, and sometimes not Being. But, if He has the Good by participation, He will then have it from another; and sometimes He will have it, and sometimes not. The Evil, then, is not from God, nor in God, neither absolutely nor occasionally.

Section XXII

But neither is the Evil in Angels; for if the goodlike angel proclaims the goodness of God, being by participation in a secondary degree that which the Announced is in the first degree as Cause, the Angel is a likeness of Almighty God—a manifestation of the unmanifested light—a mirror untarnished—most transparent—without

flaw—pure—without spot—receiving, if I may so speak, the full beauty of the Good-stamped likeness of God—and without stain, shedding forth undefiledly in itself, so far as is possible, the goodness of the Silence, which dwells in innermost shrines. The Evil, then, is not even in Angels. But by punishing sinners are they evil? By this rule, then, the punishers of transgressors are evil, and those of the priests who shut out the profane from the Divine Mysteries. And yet, the being punished is not an evil, but the becoming worthy of punishment; nor the being deservedly expelled from Holy things, but the becoming accursed of God, and unholy and unfit for things undefiled.

Section XXIII

But, neither are the demons evil by nature; for, if they are evil by nature, neither are they from the Good, nor amongst things existing; nor, in fact, did they change from good, being by nature, and always, evil. Then, are they evil to themselves or to others? If to themselves, they also destroy themselves; but if to others, how destroying, or what destroying?—Essence, or power, or energy? If indeed Essence, in the first place, it is not contrary to nature; for they do not destroy things indestructible by nature, but things receptive of destruction. Then, neither is this an evil for every one, and in every case; but, not even any existing thing is destroyed, in so far as it is essence and nature, but by the defect of nature's order, the principle of harmony and proportion lacks the power to remain as it was. But the lack of strength is not complete, for the complete lack of power takes away even the disease and the subject; and such a disease will be even a destruction of itself; so that, such a thing is not an evil, but a defective good, for that which has no part of the Good will not be amongst things which exist. And with regard to the destruction of power and energy the principle is the same. Then, how are the demons, seeing they come into being from God, evil? For the Good brings forth and sustains good things. Yet they are called evil, some one may say. But not as they are (for they are from the Good, and obtained a good being), but, as they are not, by not having had strength, as the Oracles affirm, "to keep their first estate." For in what, tell me, do we affirm that the demons become evil, except in the ceasing in the habit and energy for good things Divine? Otherwise, if the demons are evil by nature, they are always evil; yet evil is unstable. Therefore, if they are always in the same condition, they are not evil; for to be ever the same is a characteristic of the Good. But, if they are not always evil, they are not evil by nature, but by wavering from the angelic good qualities. And they are not altogether without part in the good, in so far as they both are, and live and think, and in one word— as there is a sort of movement of aspiration in them. But they are said to be evil, by reason of their weakness as regards their action according to nature. The evil then, in them, is a turning aside and a stepping out of things befitting themselves, and a missing of aim, and imperfection and impotence, and a weakness and departure, and falling away from the power which preserves their integrity in them. Otherwise, what is evil in demons? An irrational anger—a senseless desire—a headlong fancy.—But these, even if they are in demons, are not altogether, nor in every respect, nor in themselves alone, evils. For even with regard to other living creatures, not the possession of these, but the loss, is both destruction to the creature, and an evil. But the possession saves, and makes to be, the nature of the living creature which possesses them. The tribe of demons then is not evil, so far as it is according to nature, but so far as it is not; and the whole good which was given to them was not changed, but themselves fell from the whole good given. And the angelic gifts which were given to them, we by no means affirm that they were changed, but they exist, and are complete, and all luminous, although the demons themselves do not see, through having blunted their powers of seeing good. So far as they are, they are both from the Good, and are good, and as-

pire to the Beautiful and the Good, by aspiring to the realities, Being, and Life, and Thought; and by the privation and departure and declension from the good things befitting them, they are called evil, and are evil as regards what they are not: and by aspiring to the non-existent, they aspire to the Evil.

Section XXIV

But does some one say that souls are evil? If it be that they meet with evil things providentially, and with a view to their preservation, this is not an evil, but a good, and from the Good, Who makes even the evil good. But, if we say that souls become evil, in what respect do they become evil, except in the failure of their good habits and energies; and, by reason of their own lack of strength, missing their aim and tripping? For we also say, that the air around us becomes dark by failure and absence of light, and yet the light itself is always light, that which enlightens even the darkness. The Evil, then, is neither in demons nor in us, as an *existent* evil, but as a failure and dearth of the perfection of our own proper goods.

Section XXV

But neither is the Evil in irrational creatures, for if you should take away anger and lust, and the other things which we speak of, and which are not absolutely evil in their own nature, the lion having lost his boldness and fierceness will not be a lion; and the dog, when he has become gentle to every body, will not be a dog, since to keep guard is a dog's duty, and to admit those of the household, but to drive away the stranger. So the fact that nature is not destroyed is not an evil, but a destruction of nature, weakness, and failure of the natural habitudes and energies and powers. And, if all things through generation in time have their perfection, the imperfect is not altogether contrary to universal nature.

Section XXVI

But neither is the Evil in nature throughout, for if all the methods of nature are from universal nature, there is nothing contrary to it. But in each individual (nature) one thing will be according to nature, and another not according to nature. For one thing is contrary to nature in one, and another in another, and that which is according to nature to one, is to the other, contrary to nature. But malady of nature, that which is the contrary to nature, is the deprivation of things of nature. So that there is not an evil nature; but this is evil to nature, the inability to accomplish the things of one's proper nature.

Section XXVII

But, neither is the Evil in bodies. For deformity and disease are a defect of form, and a deprivation of order. And this is not altogether an evil, but a less good; for if a dissolution of beauty and form and order become complete, the body itself will be gone. But that the body is not cause of baseness to the soul is evident, from the fact that baseness continues to coexist even without a body, as in demons. For this is evil to minds and souls and bodies, (viz.) the weakness and declension from the habitude of their own proper goods.

Section XXVIII

But neither (a thing which they say over and over again) is the evil in matter, so far as it is matter. For even it participates in ornament and beauty and form. But if matter, being without these, by itself is without quality and without form, how does matter produce anything—matter, which, by itself, is impassive? Besides how is matter an evil? for, if it does not exist in any way whatever, it is neither good nor evil; but if it is any how existing, and all things existing are from the Good, even it would be from the Good; and either the Good is productive of the Evil, or the Evil, as being from the Good, is good; or the Evil is capable of producing the Good; or even the Good, as from the Evil, is evil; or further, there are two first principles, and these suspended from another one head. And, if they say that matter is necessary, for a completion of the whole Cosmos, how is matter an evil? For the Evil is one thing, and the necessary is another. But, how does He, Who is Good, bring anything to birth from the Evil? or, how is that, which needs the Good, evil? For the Evil shuns the nature of the Good. And how does matter, being evil, generate and nourish nature? For the Evil, qua evil, neither generates, nor nourishes, nor solely produces, nor preserves anything.

But, if they should say, that it does not make baseness in souls, but that they are dragged to it, how will this be true? for many of them look towards the good; and yet how did this take place, when matter was dragging them entirely to the Evil? So that the Evil in souls is not from matter, but from a disordered and discordant movement. But, if they say this further, that they invariably follow matter, and unstable matter is necessary for those who are unable to stand firmly by themselves, how is the Evil necessary, or the necessary an evil?

Section XXIX

But neither is it this which we affirm— the "privation fights against the Good by its own power"; for the complete privation is altogether powerless, and the partial has the power, not in respect of privation, but in so far as it is not a complete privation. For, whilst privation of good is partial, it is not, as yet, an evil, and when it has become an accomplished fact, the nature of the evil has departed also.

Section XXX

But, to speak briefly, the Good is from the one and the whole Cause, but the Evil is from many and partial defects. Almighty God knows the Evil qua good; and, with Him, the causes of the evils are powers producing good.[6] But, if the Evil is eternal, and creates, and has power, and is, and does, whence do these come to it? Is it either from the Good, or by the Good from the Evil, or by both from another cause? Everything that is according to nature comes into being from a defined cause. And if the Evil is

without cause, and undefined, it is not according to nature. For there is not in nature
what is contrary to nature; nor is there any
raison d'être for want of art in art. Is then
the soul cause of things evil, as fire of burning, and does it fill everything that it happens to touch with baseness? Or, is the nature of the soul then good, but, by its
energies, exists sometimes in one condition, and sometimes in another? If indeed
by nature, even its existence is an evil, and
whence then does it derive its existence?
Or, is it from the good Cause creative of the
whole universe? But, if from this, how is it
essentially evil? For good are all things
born of this. But if by energies, neither is
this invariable, and if not, whence are the
virtues? Since it (the soul) comes into being
without even seeming good. It remains
then that the Evil is a weakness and a falling short of the Good.

Section XXXI

The Cause of things good is One. If the
Evil is contrary to the Good, the many
causes of the Evil, certainly those productive of things evil, are not principles and
powers, but want of power, and want of
strength, and a mixing of things dissimilar
without proportion. Neither are things evil
unmoved, and always in the same condition, but endless and undefined, and borne
along in the different things, and those
endless. The Good will be beginning and
end of all, even things evil, for, for the sake
of the Good, are all things, both those that
are good, and those that are contrary. For
we do even these as desiring the Good (for
no one does what he does with a view to
the Evil), wherefore the Evil has not a subsistence, but a parasitical subsistence, coming into being for the sake of the Good, and
not of itself.

Section XXXII

It is to be laid down that being belongs
to the Evil as an accident and by reason of
something else, and not from its own origin, and thus that that which comes into
being appears to be right, because it comes
into being for the sake of the Good, but that
in reality it is not right for the reason that
we think that which is not good to be good.
The desired is shewn to be one thing, and
that which comes to pass is another. The
Evil, then, is beside the path, and beside the
mark, and beside nature, and beside cause,
and beside beginning, and beside end, and
beside limit, and beside intention, and beside purpose. The Evil then is privation and
failure, and want of strength, and want of
proportion, and want of attainment, and
want of purpose; and without beauty, and
without life, and without mind, and without reason, and without completeness, and
without stability, and without cause, and
without limit, and without production; and
inactive, and without result, and disordered, and dissimilar, and limitless, and
dark, and unessential, and being itself
nothing in any manner of way whatever.
How, in short, can evil do anything by its
mixture with the Good? For that which is
altogether without participation in the
Good, neither is anything, nor is capable of
anything. For, if the Good is both an actual
thing and an object of desire, and powerful
and effective, how will the contrary to the
Good,—that which has been deprived of
essence, and intention, and power, and energy,—be capable of anything? Not all
things are evil to all, nor the same things
evil in every respect. To a demon, evil is to
be contrary to the good-like mind—to a
soul, to be contrary to reason—to a body,
to be contrary to nature.

Section XXXIII

How, in short, are there evils when there
is a Providence? The Evil, qua evil, is not,
neither as an actual thing nor as in things
existing. And no single thing is without a
Providence. For neither is the Evil an actual
thing existing unmixed with the Good.
And, if no single thing is without participation in the Good, but the lack of the Good
is an evil, and no existing thing is deprived
absolutely of the Good, the Divine Providence is in all existing things, and no single
thing is without Providence. But Providence, as befits Its goodness, uses even

evils which happen for the benefit, either individual or general, of themselves or others, and suitably provides for each being. Wherefore we will not admit the vain statement of the multitude, who say that Providence ought to lead us to virtue, even against our will. For to destroy nature is not a function of Providence. Hence, as Providence is conservative of the nature of each, it provides for the free, as free; and for the whole, and individuals, according to the wants of all and each, as far as the nature of those provided for admits the providential benefits of its universal and manifold Providence, distributed proportionably to each.

Section XXXIV

The Evil, then, is not an actual thing, nor is the Evil in things existing. For the Evil, qua evil, is nowhere, and the fact that evil comes into being is not in consequence of power, but by reason of weakness. And, as for the demons, what they are is both from the Good, and good. But their evil is from the declension from their own proper goods, and a change—the weakness, as regards their indentity and condition, of the angelic perfection befitting them. And they aspire to the Good, in so far as they aspire to be and to live and to think. And in so far as they do not aspire to the Good, they aspire to the non-existent; and this is not aspiration, but a missing of the true aspiration.

Section XXXV

Now the Oracles call conscious transgressors those who are thoroughly weak as regards the ever memorable knowledge or the practise of the Good, and who, know-

ing the will, do not perform it,—those who are hearers indeed, but are weak concerning the faith, or the energy of the Good. And for some, it is against their will to understand to do good, by reason of the deviation or weakness of the will. And in short, the Evil (as we have often said) is want of strength and want of power, and defect, either of the knowledge, or the never to be forgotten knowledge, or of the faith, or of the aspiration, or of the energy of the Good. Yet, some one may say, the weakness is not punishable, but on the contrary is pardonable. Now, if the power were not granted, the statement might hold good; but, if power comes from the Good, Who giveth, according to the Oracles, the things suitable to all absolutely, the failure and deviation, and departure and declension of the possession from the Good of our own proper goods is not praiseworthy. But let these things suffice to have been sufficiently said according to our ability in our writings *"Concerning just and Divine chastisement,"* throughout which sacred treatise the infallibility of the Oracles has cast aside those sophistical statements as senseless words, speaking injustice and falsehood against Almighty God. But now, according to our ability, the Good has been sufficiently praised, as really lovable,—as beginning and end of all—as embracing things existing—as giving form to things not existing—as Cause of all good things—as guiltless of things evil—as Providence and Goodness complete—and soaring above things that are and things that are not—and turning to good things evil, and the privation of Itself—as by all desired, and loved, and esteemed, and whatever else, the true statement, as I deem, has demonstrated in the preceding.

NOTES

1. The Greek work is νοητὸν, which is in connection with Φῶς is rendered here "spiritual light."
2. Angels.
3. Creation through Goodness not necessity.
4. I.e. in ascending order.
5. Plato, Theaet., 176a.
6. Out of evil forth producing good.

CHAPTER 8

Solomon Ibn Gabirol

Data are sparse on the life of Solomon Ibn Gabirol. It is assumed that he was born in Málaga, Spain, circa 1021. Reared in Saragossa, he was orphaned at an early age. He was both a philosopher and a poet, to which some four hundred extant secular and religious poems attest. One such poem, powerful in both style and content, *The Kingly Crown*, has become a part of the Sephardic Jewish liturgy for the Day of Atonement. Gabirol's commitment to pure philosophy is demonstrated in both his ontological work *The Fountain of Life* and his ethical treatise *The Improvement of the Moral Qualities*. The former is a dialogue detailing in five parts his account of matter and form. The goal of the latter work was the development of a purely physiopsychological ethics, an autonomous system independent of theological dogma. This pure but unorthodox approach to philosophy resulted in his ostracism by many of his colleagues. Nevertheless, he managed to acquire two patrons during his lifetime: Yequtiel ben Ishaq ibn Hasan at the court in Saragossa and later with Samuel ibn Nagrella at the court of Zirid in Granada.

The date of his demise is not certain. It is generally accepted that he died circa 1058, although the Jewish philosopher Abraham ibn Daud (c. 1110–1180) claimed he died in 1070.

It is interesting to note that Gabirol had a far greater influence on Christian philosophers of the Middle Ages than on his Jewish counterparts. References to Gabirol are found in the works of Thomas Aquinas, William of Auverogne, Bonaventure, Alexander Hales, Albertus Magnus, and Duns Scotus.

Solomon Ibn Gabirol on the Improvement of the Moral Qualities

The Improvement of the Moral Qualities is a dissertation on what Gabirol takes to be the virtues and vices of human behavior. Notwithstanding repeated references to the Bible, Gabirol attempts to establish a purely physiopsychological system of ethics. In this regard he demonstrated independence from the typical Hebrew view of ethics, namely, as an extension of divine law. Man possesses purely animal qualities which manifest themselves via the five senses. These qualities are virtues and vices in groupings of four, with each group attributed specifically to one of the five physical senses. In addition, man has higher qualities. These are intellectual in nature. Gabirol likens them to inner or concealed senses, namely, reason and understanding. These inner senses are a function of man's soul highly reminiscent of Plato's conception of it as constituting the psychological dimension of man. Construed in this manner, the soul does not connote the divine within man.

Nevertheless, the inner senses are divine endowments. On the surface, this appears contradictory, but it is not. God endows mankind with the powers of reason and understanding, yet it is up to individuals to exercise these powers. Reason and understanding constitute the psychological dimension of man. There is an important dichotomy in Gabirol's view concerning the relationship between these two sets of virtues. On the one hand, the qualities of the soul are derived from the physical (or animal) qualities of man. The qualities of the soul can only be developed relative to the part played by the physical senses. In this way Gabirol is able to demonstrate that ethics is autonomous; that is, it is not a function of religion. On the other hand, he draws a sharp distinction between these two sets of qualities by which is made possible the control of the soul over the animal nature of man.

It is reason or intelligence that functions as the principal agent of this control. He who makes his intelligence master over his natural (viz., base) inclinations will be the benefactor of a blissful life. "Let not man suppose the passage, 'The steps of a good man are ordered by the Lord' implies any compulsion to obedience (to God) or disobedience; (it does point) however, to the bliss and misery (which are their respective reward and punishment). In saying, 'The steps of a good man are ordered by the Lord,' he means that God created his soul perfect, not wanting anything; and when it inclines to virtue, to wholesome practice and good conduct, the expression 'are ordered' implies that he merits the approval of God; and this is meant by the expression, 'And He delighteth in his way.' "

THE IMPROVEMENT OF THE MORAL QUALITIES

Part I

Chapter I

Treating of Pride (Haughtiness).

How good it is that this chapter happens to be the first of all the chapters, as required by the connection. For I have seen many of the elect exercise this quality unnecessarily and give it preference over their other qualities; so much so, that the masses take it unto themselves and make use of it in cases where it is needless to do so, until it gains the upper hand over their nature. I also observe this quality frequently present in young men, i.e., in the child and the youth, especially if the temperament happens to be "yellow-hot." For it is characteristic of

From Solomon ibn Gabirol, *The Improvement of the Moral Qualities*, translated by Stephen S. Wise (New York: Columbia University Press, 1901), pp. 55–101.

the yellow gall to rise. In its excitement it accustoms the nature of man to exercise this quality until he almost comes to exercise it amid circumstances unsuited to its appearance. Among the special branches of this quality are vanity (presumptuousness), boastfulness, and haughtiness. These are not (included) among the qualities of the ancient saints, of whom their noble virtues testified that they were opposed to them. Now, as we see, some men, who were known to exercise these qualities out of place, have thereby become despicable. Others aim to exercise the praiseworthy aspects of the quality of Pride, and are praised therefor. I shall not go to the length of recounting their names, for they are well known. This being so, we must carefully consider how to acquire the means of exercising this quality in the right place, and subduing it out of season; and we must make mention of the loathing, which ensues as a result of its blameworthiness.

When we perceive this quality beginning to affect the nature of a man, it becomes necessary for us to call attention to serious matters, such as lead to reflection on the origin of existent things and their end, i.e., the coming into being of things, their beginnings, their transitoriness, and their destruction. When he learns that all existent things are changeable, and finally that his own being will change (waste away) and his body become extinct, then the quality of his soul, which was haughty throughout the course of his life, will become meek and penitent at (the thought of) death. Since we are forced to accept this logical conclusion and traditional reasoning, it behooves the wise man to avoid preferring this quality of his own free will, since it is detestable and there results no benefit whatever from pursuing it. On the contrary, it is the cause of many dangers, especially if man's arrogance urge him not to incline to the advice of any man; and although in (seeking) advice is the essence of good counsel, he turn away from it and abide by his own opinion. Of such a man Solomon the Wise, peace be upon him, said (Prov. xii. 15), "The way of a fool is right in his own eyes." Thou knowest also what befell Korach and Rehoboam and others like them, who cared only for their own opinion. Man must remember that if he realize not his own sins but consider his course correct, there will surely befall him what befell them. Concerning this the sage saith (Prov.xvi. 2), "All the ways of a man are clean in his own eyes, but the Lord weigheth the spirits"; and he saith of pride (id. xvi. 18), "Pride goeth before destruction," i.e., the result of pride and pomp is overthrow and degradation. Thus it happened to Pharaoh, who said (Ex. v. 2), "Who is the Lord?" and Goliath when he spake (I Sam. xvii. 10), "I defy the armies of Israel"; and Sennacherib for his boastfulness in saying (II Kings xviii. 35), "Who are they among all the gods of the countries"; and Nebuchadnezzar in that he said (Dan. iii. 15), "Who is that God that shall

deliver you out of my hands?" and others who follow them in the manner of their speech and whose end was complete abasement and utter obscurity. Whosoever is in this state is not secure from error and sin. Thus saith the sage (Prov. xxi. 24), "Proud and haughty scorner is his name." He mentions craftiness, because it is the source of boastfulness. Whoever acts in this wise ought to be ashamed, and remember that according to the measure of his superciliousness will he experience contempt, and in proportion to his power will humiliation suddenly befall him. Thus the sage saith (id., xxix. 23), "A man's pride shall bring him low," i.e., boastfulness and arrogance are the main causes of man's humiliation, and these, by my life, are characteristic of the wicked, as he saith (id., xxi. 4), "A high look and a proud heart." Some of the proud vaunt themselves in the exercise of this blameworthy quality, because they delight therein (and try to excuse themselves by) arguing, that the soul inclines to distinction, and finds lowliness irksome. Again, they hold that domineering (supremacy) strengthens it, while submission weakens it, and were there no domination, the world would not be well adjusted.[1] They further say that the prayers of the excellent had the attainment thereof in view when they said (Gen. xxvii. 29), "Let people serve thee and nations bow down to thee." Yea, in this way God distinguished His prophet when He spake to him (Gen. xxxv. 11), "And kings shall come out of thy loins." On the other hand, he punished those who deserved punishment by humbling their power; thus it is said (Isa. ix. 14), "Therefore the Lord will cut off from Israel head and foot, branch and rush in one day," and so forth. Simpletons, discussing this superciliousness, do not consider that, when they resort thereto, their souls become unduly great, that they overstep their bounds, become overbearing toward their relatives, turn away from their companions, deride the advice of every man, for as much as they rely upon their own opinions and go their own way. But when it is so exercised as to keep one away from baseness, to enable one to rise unto the exellences, and to be firm in devotion to God, exalted be He,—which is His highest gift, exalted and magnified may He be, to His servants,—then this becomes the means whereby men gain the grace of God and reach the everlasting kingdom. Of these it is said (Job xxxvi. 7), "He withdraweth not his eyes from the righteous, but with kings are they on the throne; yea, he doth establish them forever, and they are exalted." But he, who resorts to superciliousness unnecessarily and takes only his own counsel, is like him of whom it was said (Prov. xviii. 1), "He intermeddleth with all wisdom." Men disregard such a man and desire not his presence: of such as these the sage saith (Prov. xxvi. 16), "The sluggard is wiser in his own conceit than seven men that can render a reason." And often, moreover, his vanity impels him to undertake something outside of his usual course of action, because he relies upon his opinion saving him and upon his counsel protecting him. It is this that causes him to stumble; thus it is said (Job v. 12), "He disappointeth the devices of the crafty, so that their hands cannot perform their enterprise." Having progressed thus far in our description of the quality of superciliousness, the way in which to make use thereof moderately, and the mode of suppressing its use in the wrong place, we must now proceed to quote very sparingly a few prose utterances of the wise concerning this quality, and whatever verses concerning it we can.

The divine[2] Socrates said: "From whom doth disappointment never part? He who seeks a rank for which his ability is too feeble." Again he said, "He who sets himself up as wise will be set down by others for a fool." I hold that bad manners are attributable to superciliousness. Socrates said, "Aversion is always felt for him who has an evil nature, so that men flee away from him." Aristotle says, "As the beauty of form is a light for the body, so is beauty of character a light for the soul." Again he said in his testament to Alexander his pupil, "It does not show much nobility of pur-

pose on the part of a king to lord it over men; (the less so) for one man over a fellow-man." A certain haughty man is said to have been journeying-along with his effects; some of them fell down, whereupon he threw the others out of the wagon. The ancients say, "With him who is pleased with himself, many become displeased." A poet composed these lines concerning the blameworthiness of haughtiness and arrogance:

"Let him who shows great vanity concerning his beauty consider this! If men would but consider what is within them, neither young nor old would feel proud. Are there not in the head of every son of man five orifices from which come forth effluvia? The nose exudes, the ear gives forth an unpleasant odor, the eye sheds tears, and the mouth salivates. O son of earth, to be consumed of earth on the morrow, desist from thy pride, for thou wilt be food and drink (to the earth)!"

It is told of Ardeshir,[3] the king, that he gave a book to a man accustomed to stand at his side, and said unto him, "When thou seest me become violently angry give it to me," and in the book (was written), "Restrain thyself, for thou art not God; thou art but a body, one part of which is on the point of consuming the other, and in a short while it will turn into the worm and dust and nothingness."

Chapter II

Treating of Meekness.

This quality is more nearly a virtue than that which was mentioned just before, because the possessor of this attribute, i.e., modesty and humility, withholds his desire from seeking gratification. When one attains this precious rank, the praiseworthy character in man is made perfect. This, in my opinion, is a disposition which merits praise for him who acquires it. Verily, he is accorded the loftiest praise. Dost thou not see that humility is the highest degree of the nobles and of the prophets, distinguished by their divine rank? One of them said (Gen. xviii. 27), "I am but dust and ashes"; another said (Ps. xxii. 7), "I am a worm and no man"; and so forth. They were praised for their actions and were honored. A man of intelligence should know that lowliness and meekness cause him to realize his desire in regard to present things, as thou knowest from the account of what happened to the captains of Achaziah, because of their folly; and what happened to the third captain who gently spake to Elijah (II Kings i. 13), "I pray thee let my life and the life of these thy fifty servants be precious in thy sight." Him there befell the reverse of what had befallen the former. Verily, fame and glory will be the reward of whosoever is lowly. The recompense of meekness is honor and prosperity, and also the deserving of honor. Thus it is said (Prov. xxii. 4), "The reward of humility and the fear of God are riches, and honor, and life."

The most excellent of the ancient nobles (may God guide thee aright) were accustomed to exercise the quality of meekness, and preferred it to their natural impulses. It is related of an illustrious king, that one night while a number of people were assembled about him, he arose to trim the lamp. Whereupon it was said to him, "Why didst thou not utter a command, which would have sufficed?" And he answered them, "As king I rose, and as king I resume my seat." He was wont to say that "Every grace (of man) is envied, except meekness." The philosopher Buzurjmihr said, "The fruits of lowliness are love and tranquillity." Know thou that in honoring his brother or his neighbor, man honors himself. Some one has remarked that "lowliness consists in being beforehand with greetings to whomsoever one may meet, and in descending to the lowest rank." Contentment is of a kind with this quality. When one is gifted with its presence, he has already gained superiority. It is said, "Whomsoever the Lord loveth he inspireth with contentment." Scripture says of the contented servant of God (Prov. xiii. 25), "The righteous eateth to the satisfying of the soul." And it says of the reverse, "But

the belly of the wicked shall want." He who possesses strength, health, and a sense of security ought never to feel sad. The fruit of contentment is tranquillity. The greatest riches are contentment and patience. One of the sages has said, "He who desires of this world only that which is sufficient for him, will be content with the very least thereof." Another sage was wont to admonish his son, "He who cannot bear with one word, will be compelled to listen to many. He who esteems his rank but slightly, enhances men's estimation of his dignity." In holding the view that it may be right (at times) to repudiate this quality, I mean thereby that a man should not abase himself before the wicked. With reference to such a case it is said (Prov. xxv. 26), "A righteous man, falling down before the wicked, is as a troubled fountain and a corrupt stream." It was said concerning this, "He who deserves (the greatest) compassion is the wise man lost among fools." In the ethical sayings of Lokman (we find), "When the noble man forsakes the world, he becomes humble: the ignoble in forsaking the world becomes haughty." In the book of al-Ḳuṭi (it is said), "Be humble without cringing, and manly without being arrogant. Know thou that arrogance is a wilderness and haughtiness a taking refuge therein, and, altogether, a going astray."

Chapter III

On the Qualities of Pudency and Modesty.

A wise man was asked, "What is intelligence?" and he answered, "Modesty." Again he was asked, "What is modesty?" and he replied, "Intelligence." This quality, although like unto meekness and agreeing therewith, is of a nobler rank than the latter, for it is kindred to intelligence. To every man of understanding the nobility of the intellect is patent, for it is the dividing line between man and beast, in that it masters man's natural impulses and subdues passion. With the help of intelligence man realizes the benefit of knowledge and gets to understand the true nature of things; he comes to acknowledge the Unity of God, to worship his Master, and to bear a striking resemblance to the character of the angels. Since this precious quality is of so noble a kind, it follows that modesty which resembles it is almost equally so. The proof of its being thus related is, that thou wilt never see a modest man lacking intelligence, or an intelligent man devoid of modesty. This being so, man must direct all his efforts to the attainment of this wonderful and highly considered quality.

He must prefer it to all his natural impulses, and regard it as superior to all his other qualities, for by means of it he acquires many virtues, and all vice becomes hidden from him. Thus it is said, "The faults of him, whom modesty clothes with dignity, will not be remarked by men." Dignity and honor follow upon him. Thus it is said (Prov. xv. 33), "Before honor is humility." The meek find acceptance before God because of their modesty; He brings them unto everlasting bliss. Concerning him who understands its ways, it is said (Ps. xxv. 9), "The meek will He guide in judgment: and the meek will He teach His way." Even as it is necessary that the intelligent man be pudent in the presence of others, so must he be pudent when alone. It was said that, "Pudency and faith are interdependent, and either cannot be complete without the other." A poet said, "Keep guard over thy modesty: truly pudency marks the countenance of a nobleman." It is said that "Impudence and a lack of pudency are offshoots of unbelief." He who wishes to acquire pudency should associate with those who are modest with respect to him. An Arab was wont to say, "Pay no regard to any man unless he show thee that he cannot do without thee, even when thou needest him most, so that, if thou sin, he will forgive and act as though he were the sinner; and if thou wrong him, he will demean himself as though he had been the offender." Another said, "Finally, one learns from the words of prophecy. 'If

thou art not pudent, do whatsoe'er thou wilt.' " In the course of a characterization of modesty, the poet said,

"Upon him reposes the mantel of piety: and, in truth, a light streams from between his eyes."

Al-faḍil says: "By reason of belief and piety, men dwell together for a time. Afterward they are kept together by reason of modesty, pudency, and blamelessness." Aristotle said in his discourse, "As a result of modesty (one's) helpers are multiplied." He was accustomed to say, "In chaste children modesty clearly rules over their countenance." It was termed pudency[4] only because it is the way to eternal life. A philospher said, "Modesty asserts itself in the midst of wrath." Again it was said, "The enmity of the modest man is less harmful to thee than the friendship of the fool." He who desires to guard this quality should not trifle away his dignity when asked to serve men, for when thou hast once worn out thy dignity, thou wilt find no one to renew it for thee. To make use of pudency (that is, to be overpudent), in speaking the truth or enjoining good acts, in spreading religion and devotion, is blameworthy. In such cases one must not make use of it; thus the saint said (Ps. cxix. 46), "I will speak of thy testimonies also before kings, and will not be ashamed." But it is necessary for man to cover his face with the mantle of modesty before all men, as thou knowest from the case of Saul when he hid himself, (as) it is written (I Sam. x. 23), "Behold he is hidden among the vessels." God selected him for kingship, as it is written (I Sam. x. 24), "Behold whom the Lord hath chosen." To sum up, according to the opinion of the philosophers and the sages, this quality is one of the virtues of the noble soul, and its relation to these is as that of the spirit to the body. A philosopher said, "Modesty consists in conducting affairs in the best way wherein it is possible for them to be conducted, and in leaving them in their best aspects." He who is modest will attain to power.

Chapter IV

Treating of the Quality of Impudence.

We had much to say on the praiseworthiness of the quality of pudency, but the quantity of blame which we shall mete out to the quality of impudence is small. He who is possessed of the quality of shamelessness is culpable in the eyes of God, as are those of whom it is said (Jer. v. 3), "They have made their faces harder than a rock; they have refused to return." The Saint says with reference to the impudent (Prov. xi. 2), "When pride cometh, then cometh shame," which means that when impudence prevails over the qualities of man, he is scorned by men and not respected. He is not taken seriously, nor is he regarded with that consideration for his wisdom, even though he be learned, which is paid to the pudent. Thus it is written (ib.), "But with the lowly is wisdom." If one is wise and desires to pursue the goodly course which is acceptable unto God, let him abandon this quality, refrain from exercising it, and keep it afar from the character of his soul. Of him who is impudent the prince saith (id. xxi. 24), "Proud and haughty scorner is his name," by which he means that God will requite according to his doing, whosoever is impudent, as it is written (ib.), "Who dealeth in proud wrath." It is possible also that "Who dealeth in proud wrath" refers to such an impudent one as, by reason of the quality of impudence, provokes the displeasure and annoyance of others, and so forth. When this disposition becomes part of man's nature, whosoever is familiar with him must turn him away from it by rebuking him as much as he is able, and by annoying him, until he be rid of all that was in him. Thus it is said (id. xxi. 29), "A wicked man hardeneth his face." Yet impudence (boldness) may be commendable when supporting religion, when performing "service" and speaking the truth. But to oppose thereby the righteous and the Prophets and God is reprehensible. Thus it is said (Ez. ii. 4), "Impudent children and stiff-hearted." If the man who practises this quality be of a yellow (bilious) constitution, and if in the course of his youth he give strong evidence of its possession, he must oppose to it its very reverse. Let him trust in God, and he will accustom himself to avoid this blameworthy quality and subdue it.

PART II

Chapter I

On the Quality of Love.

It is almost impossible for any man to be secure from this "accident," O God, save he whose intellect is master over his nature. None such exists; and if any (be found to) exist, he is undoubtedly one of the most excellent (men). Lust is a constituent element in the nature of man, and if he desire to be master and ruler, let him cast away lust (passion), make no use of it whatever, ignore it and do without it, for it is one of the baser qualities. It is well known that the qualities of the wise are not perfected until their souls gain the mastery over their desires. The deeds of him whose intellect prevails over his lustfulness are commendable. Upon the realization of desires, there ensues the penalty of misfortune. One of the signs of him, who is overcome by his lust, is that he is very changeable, restless, and fickle of speech. Especially if, added to this, the bloody temper prevail in his constitution and he be in the period of youth and the season of spring, then it proves too strong for him. Therefore the wise man must shrink from this quality lest he make use of it and turn away from it, for there is connected with it no inconsiderable harm. Thou knowest how contempt, obscurity, and abasement come upon its devotee, and that finally its outcome is evil. This thou knowest from the story of Amnon and what happened to him when he hastened after his desire. Man ought to employ this quality only in the service of God and His divine Law, as it is written (Ps. i. 2), "And his delight is in the law of the Lord," and again (id., cxix. 97), "How I love thy law," etc. Necessarily, one who occupies himself with the quest of knowledge and moral science (theoretical science and the practical arts), will be (so busy as to be) kept from his lusts. The wise one said, "If aught befall thee and no one occur to thee whom thou mightest consult with reference thereto, avoid it and bring it not near to thy passion, for passion is an enemy of the heart." And he said, "He who is submissive to his lust is routed, and he who rebels against it gains the victory." This quality is preferred by foolish men only because of the imminence (immediateness) of its delight and for the sake of the amusement and merriment and the hearing of mirthful songs which they get through it. They heed not the suffering and the wretchedness that follow in its train, and therefore incline in accord with their natural impulses to the attainment of present pleasure, as it is said (Prov. xiii. 19), "The desire accomplished is sweet to the soul"—turning aside from wisdom and the service of the Lord, because of what appears to be the remoteness of the delight and pleasureableness of these things. Verily, in their opinion, these are remote. Yet these are not remote, but near at hand. They are remote only in their mind. Therefore man must devote this quality of love to God, exalted may He be, as it is written (Deut. xi. I), "Thou shalt love the Lord thy God"; and to his soul, as it is written (I Sam. xx. 17), "For he loved him as he loved his own soul"; to his relatives, as it is written (Gen. xxix. 18), "And Jacob loved Rachel"; to his offspring, as it is written (id., xxxvii. 3), "Israel loved Joseph"; to his country, as it is written (Num. x. 30), "But I will depart to my own land and to my kindred"; to his companion, as spake David to Jonathan (II Sam. i. 26), "Very pleasant hast thou been unto me"; to his wife (Prov. v. 19), "Let her be

as the loving hind and the pleasant roe"; to wisdom, as it is written (Prov. xxix. 3), "The man that loveth wisdom rejoiceth his father." The moral application of this quality is, man must evince it (in his dealings) with all men. It has been said, "He who desires to be endeared to men should conduct himself with regard to them in the best possible manner. Benefit occasions love even as injury begets hatred." Moreover, included under this quality are wishes and unattainable desires. It is right for the man of understanding that he train himself (to keep aloof) therefrom. The following is part of what the poets have said concerning such wishes as cannot be realized, and wherefrom the soul realizes naught except possibly weariness of spirit, continual disquietude, and protracted restlessness:

"My day is a day which is common to men until the darkness of the night is fallen, and then my couch wearies me. I spent my day in entertainment and in desire but the night brought me altogether to grief."

Among other things which have been said with reference to devoting one's self wholly to pleasure and passion, the blameworthy outcome of this, and the trouble which is associated therewith, the poet says:

"We have drunk of the dregs of the wine as if we were kings of the two Iraks and the sea; but when the sun shone brightly, thou mightest have found me with my riches flown, and poverty once more my own."

When this quality obtains the mastery of the soul, the senses become blunted and man is not conscious because of his being given over to pleasure. He is as those of whom it is said (Isa. v. 20), "Woe unto them that call evil good and good evil." The maxim of the sage is, "Thy love of anything renders thee blind and deaf." One sage, writing to another on the subject of subduing the lusts, said, "Thou shalt not attain what thou lovest until thou suffer much from what thou loathest. And thou shalt not be delivered from that which thou loathest, until thou suffer much through that which thou lovest."

Chapter II

(Treating of) Hate.

Thou shouldst know that he who hates men is hated by them, and when this quality takes firm hold of the soul, it destroys it, because it leads to the hatred of the very food and drink with which man sustains life. Besides, he suffers injury through the hostility of men. When excessive love is expended on other than divine things, it is changed into the most violent hatred. As thou knowest from the expression (II Sam. xiii. 15), "Then Amnon hated her exceedingly." He who loves thee for some reason will turn his back, simultaneously with its disappearance and ending. Thou must not trust in the counsel of the enemy, the "Hater." Thus it is written (Prov. xxvii. 6), "The kisses of an enemy are deceitful." From this quality there branches out fretfulness. Thou knowest how the prevalence of fretfulness has been censured, the blameworthiness which attaches to its use and the repugnance the soul feels therefor. It has been said that the fretful cannot abide by one state; he has not a friend; his circumstances are always disturbed, and misery never parts company with him. He is like one of whom it is said (Prov. xii. 27), "The slothful (listless) man roasteth not that which he took in hunting." Thou knowest that many men make a show of friendship in their speech and yet frequently are enemies at heart. Do not trust them, as it is written (id., xxvi. 24), "He that hateth, dissembleth with his lips," Even though he be gentle in discourse with thee, do not associate with him, as it is written (id., 25), "When he speaketh fair, believe him not." Thus Jacob also made a show of kind-heartedness and affection for Abner and Amasa before killing them. So also did Ismael favor Guedaliah ben Achikam ere he killed him. It is said, "He who sows hatred will reap regret." He who is of this character is ill-disposed to his fellow-man in matters concerning himself and another. So much the more will he be so in those affecting him and his Lord. He acts as though he were praying, but his secret thoughts are quite different. Thus it is written of them (Ps. lxxviii. 36), "Nevertheless they did flatter him with their mouth and they did lie unto him with their tongues," and so forth. The divine Socrates spake unto his disciples, bidding them "Beware of whomsoever your heart hate, for the hearts of men are like a mirror." Thus the sage said (Prov. xxvii. 19), "As in water, face answereth to face, so the heart of man to man." Souls are alike, and the most harmful and persistent form of hatred is that caused by envy. The poet saith, "Thou canst cure all manner of enmity except he enmity which comes to thee through envy."

In the book of al-Kuṭi (it is said), "The very best that thou canst look forward to in regard to thy enemies is that thou bring them back to the love of thee, if that be possible."

Chapter III

Treating of the Quality of Mercy and Compassion (Pity), The Praise of Its Possessors, and an Exhortation to Give Preference Thereto.

Since this quality is of a kind with the nature of the Creator, may He be greatly praised and mightily exalted, it is complementary to the twelve attributes especially characteristic of Him, i.e., the thirteen qualities which are ascribed to the Lord of Worlds, viz., "The Lord eternal is a merciful and gracious God," and so forth. That which it is possible for the wise man to aim at in action is,—being slow to anger, "long-suffering," and largely generous, as it is said, "abundant in loving-kindnesses," tolerant of sin, as it is said, "Forgiving iniquity," and so forth. The upright and wise man must emulate these as far as he is able to do. Even as man desires that he be dealt with mercifully, when compelled to seek help, so must he be merciful to whosoever seeks his help. This quality is extremely praiseworthy, and God, exalted may He be, has distinguished His righteous servants through their love therefor. As thou knowest of Joseph, where it is said (Gen. xliii. 30), "His bowels did yearn upon his brother." The intelligent man has the qualities of pity and compassion implanted in his soul and ever present therein. The sage said, "Mercy is the result of kindliness and honesty." In regard to it, Solomon the Wise spake when he exhorted to mercy and compassion (Prov. xxiv. 11), "If thou forbear to deliver them that are born unto death." A beautiful feature of this quality in connection with the Creator, exalted and hallowed may He be, is that He is merciful in dealing with all His creatures. Thus it is said (Ps. cxlv. 9), "The Lord is good to all, and His tender mercies are over all His works." In the book of Al-Ḳuṭi, it is said, "Spare no effort to deliver those who are confronted with death." Again he said, "Do not wrong the weak, for their Protector is God, the mighty One." He said, "Prosperous are they whose heart is ever merciful and meek," and again we find therein, "He who is not merciful will die by the hand of one who is merciless."

Chapter IV

Treating of Hard-Heartedness.

I do not find this quality among righteous or superior men. But it is (to be found) in him whose nature resembles that of a lion, for he is one who is never sated. These are the ones of whom it is said (Deut. xxviii. 50), "A nation of fierce countenance." Upon my soul, this is a wholly detestable quality, whether (its measure be) great or small. It comes into being when the spirit of wrath prevails over a man. This quality is exercised for the purpose of wreaking vengeance upon enemies. There is no harm in making use of it in this manner, although the intelligent man ought not endeavor to be avenged upon his enemies. For this is not befitting. Thus saith the sage (Prov. xxiv. 17), "Rejoice not when thy enemy falleth." To make use of it in order that one may do evil to his fellow-man, to kill him, or to lay hold of the possessions of one who has given no offence, is reprehensible. From such as these may God preserve me, for of their ilk, the Saint said (Ps. cxxiv., 1 and 3), "If it had not been the Lord who was on our side, now may Israel say": "Then they had swallowed us up quick, when their wrath was kindled against us." A proof that this quality is only found in the wicked is the expression (Prov. xii. 10), "But the tender mercies of the wicked are cruel." Plato, the author of the laws in regard to vengeance, said, "He who desires to be revenged upon his enemies should add (a degree of) excellence to himself."

PART III

Chapter I

Treating of Joy (Cheerfulness).

This quality is found to differ in various men. Sometimes, it is natural; this is the case in him whose temper is humid-hot as is that of blood; especially when his hopes are well ordered and never confounded, and who, in addition, is far from experiencing suffering and free from affliction. It is but meet that in the nature of him who is of this character there appear the sign of this quality—that his exterior be sound, his health robust, and old age without haste in overtaking him. Thus it is said of such an one (Prov. xvii. 22), "A merry heart doeth good like a medicine, but a broken spirit dries the bones." Sometimes it is coincident with the attainment of the desire and the realization of a wish. Peculiar to it is continual smiling without (apparent) cause. Very often lightmindedness accompanies it, whereof it is written (Eccl. vii. 6), "For as the crackling of thorns under a pot, so is the laughter of the fool." It has been said that one of the distinguishing marks of the fool is his laughing when there is no occasion for laughter. I hold that this quality is to be found in the souls of those, above all, who are free from defilement, the righteous, the pious, the pure, destined for the Heavenly Kingdom, rising to spirituality, i.e., the souls of the upright for they are in perfect enjoyment of their condition of service and greatly rejoiced because of their worship, as it is written (Ps. xxxii. 11), "Be glad in the Lord and rejoice, ye righteous; and shout for joy, all ye that are upright in heart." The well-bred man ought not to indulge in laughter when seated in an assembly, for it was said that for him who laughs much, but little respect is felt. Facetiousness takes away the veil of dignity. Even as anxiety (apprehensiveness) when it is aroused gives rise to weeping, so gladness, when it is stirred, incites to laughter. Therefore the intelligent man ought to understand that this quality and some other qualities are not of the rational soul, as Galen holds, but of the animal soul. The proof of this is that thou seest laughter break out in spite of dreadful events. Often, too, man is unable to refrain therefrom. The same is held with regard to wrath and other qualities. Considering this, man should urgently seek to render his animal soul submissive to his rational soul: namely, that his intellect guide his nature. When he does this, he becomes included among the most excellent men. Wherefore Socrates says in regard to joy, "Whatever causes joy causes sorrow." In the ethics of Diogenes, treating of joy, he states: "Joy is life and exaltation to the heart, whereas grief is distress and destruction."

Chapter II

Treating of Grief (Apprehensiveness).

This quality usually succeeds in establishing itself in the soul when wishes fail of realization, and then the soul is brought to such a point as almost to be killed when it loses the objects of its love. Oh, what a quality is this! How serious a matter when it comes into evidence, and how waste is its place when it prevails! Thus it was said, "Apprehensiveness is a living death." I

have determined to linger here a little in the discussion of this chapter. Perhaps God will grant us His grace and inspire us with excellent words, which may relieve the sadness of man, so that he may find healing in our discourse, because it is impossible to find healing for psychical ills other than in spiritual remedies. As this takes firmer hold of the soul, so also it becomes more diffcult to find the remedy. Of God we pray that He protect us therefrom in His graciousness.

The constitution of apprehensiveness is cold and dry, like the black gull (humor). No man can absolutely escape it. In some it attains immense proportions, so that they thereby become afflicted with psychical ailments. Thus it is said (Prov. xii. 25), "Gloom in the heart of man maketh it stoop, but a good word maketh it glad." Know thou that this quality is generally visible in the countenance, as thou hast seen in the case of Joseph, who discerned what was in the heart of "the servants of Pharaoh," when he beheld their austere countenances; it being said (Gen. xl. 6), "And he looked upon them, and behold they were sad," and as Artaxerxes said to Nehemiah (Neh. ii. 2), "Why is thy countenance sad, seeing thou art not sick." Thus it is obvious that this quality is generally distinctly visible in the countenance. Thou shouldst know that if a man be madly in love with this world, which is a world *de generatione et corruptione*, he never omits to seek the gratification of the senses, constantly moving on from one thing to another. If he attain them and then lose them, gloom overcomes him. On the other hand, if he be made to forget this world, and apply himself to the world of intellect, then it becomes possible for him to escape the psychical ills, which are (occasioned by) worldly acquisitions,—that is, if he turn away from vain works and incline in the fulness of the soul to ethical science and religious laws. Therefore the intellectual man ought to cast away the lowly quality of the masses and the grandiose manner of kings. If it be impossible for a man to have what he desires, he must desire what he has. Let him not prefer continual gloom. We ought to strive to cure our souls of this evil (disease), in the same way as we must suffer hardships in trying to cure our bodies and to rid them of diseases by means of burning and cutting (fire and iron), and so forth. Rather must we gradually accustom ourselves to improve our souls through strength of purpose, and to endure a little difficulty in order that, as a result of this, we may pursue a praiseworthy course. We know, moreover, that if we represent to ourselves that no misfortune will befall us, it is as though we desired not to exist at all. Because misfortunes are a necessary condition of the passing of wordly things. If this were not, there could be no becoming. *Ergo*, to wish that no accident should come to pass is like wishing not to exist. But existence is (a part) of nature, and annihilation likewise is (a part) of nature. Then if we desire that this be not (a part) of nature, we desire the impossible; he who desires the impossible will have his wish denied, and he whose wish is denied is miserable. We ought to be ashamed to give the preference to this quality, grief, and we should yearn to rise unto a state of beatitude. Let him who would not mourn represent to his soul the things that lead to mourning, as though they already were; thus, for example, let man say, "A certain possession of mine will be destroyed and I will mourn for it," accounting it as already destroyed, or (considering) as already lost that which he loves. Concerning this, the poet-philosopher said:

"The man of prudence grows up, representing to himself his mishaps before they befall him; if they befall him suddenly, they will not terrify him because of the things already pictured in his soul. He sees that one thing will lead to another, and therefore he knows the end from the beginning."

But not the least trace of apprehensiveness is to be found in those who are of lofty souls and noble aspirations. Socrates was asked, "Why do we never perceive in thee any sign of apprehensiveness?" And he an-

swered, "Because I have never possessed anything over the loss of which I would grieve." Wherefore let the intelligent man consider that there is nothing in this world of all that grows, save it be insignificant at the outset, and afterward develops, except grief, which is greatest on the day it comes into being, and the longer it continues the less it becomes, until it entirely disappears. The firm and resolute man is he who braces himself up with all his might in the hour of his affliction. Alexander, in order to console his mother about himself (in the event of his death), wrote to her as follows: "My mother, order a great and fortified city to be built when the news of Alexander's death reaches you. Prepare therein for eating and drinking, and gather together in it, on an appointed day, men from all the lands to eat and drink. When that has been done and all the men are ready to eat and drink what the queen has prepared, let it be proclaimed at that moment that no man should enter her abode whom misfortune has befallen." And thus she did upon the death of Alexander. But when she ordered that no one whom misfortune had befallen should enter her house, she noticed (that) no one (came). Then she felt sure that he had only wished to comfort her about himself.

Alexander had heard from Aristotle, his master, that "Grief injures the heart and destroys it." He wished to ascertain the truth of this. He therefore decided upon an animal, the nature of which was nearest to that of man, confined it in a dark place, and allotted to it nourishment only sufficient to sustain its body. Afterward he led it forth and slaughtered it: whereupon he found its heart dissolved and melted away. Then he knew that Aristotle had spoken nothing but the truth. Among the words spoken by Galen on grief (we find), "Apprehensiveness is a consuming of the heart, and sadness is a sickness of the heart." Afterward he explained this, saying, "Sadness is felt for what is past, and apprehensiveness for what may occur." In another place again (he said), "Sadness (is occasioned) by what has occurred, and apprehensiveness is (felt) for what may come to pass. Therefore beware of sadness, for sadness is the end of life." Dost thou not see that when the face of man is overclouded (with sadness), he will perish of grief. One of the sages said, "Drinking poison is easier (to endure) than apprehensiveness." Now, if one should ask what benefit is derived from choosing this quality at the occurrence of misfortune and its appearance, I would answer that in shedding the tears which have become spoiled and stagnant, and which nature is incapable of returning to their place, we pour out the putrid humors, which have become rotten, the chyme, and we remedy it through purifying drugs, and thus we cleanse the humor in such a manner as to cause it to return to its orignal state. Thus it is known that in some small children there is a spoiled excess, which cannot be passed off save through weeping. This, then, is the natural use of weeping. Wherefore Socrates said, "Sorrows are a species of ills of the heart, as diseases are ills of the body." Among the words of Ptolemy on this (subject are), "Let him who wishes to live long, prepare to meet misfortunes with a patient heart."

Chapter III

Treating of Tranquillity.

This quality is commendable when a man directs it in faith in the Lord, and places his reliance and his confidence in Him. Thus it is said (Prov. xxii. 19), "That thy trust may be in the Lord." This is a praiseworthy disposition: its possessor is worthy of very good fortune and abundant mercy from God, as it is written (Ps. xxxii. 10), "He that trusteth in the Lord, mercy shall compass him about." He who is in this state deserves to be blest, as it is said (Jer. xvii. 7), "Blessed is the man that trusteth in the Lord and whose hope the Lord is." This quality is usually found in the upright, those who fear God and who are referred to in the command, which declares (Ps. cxv. 11), "Ye that fear the Lord, trust in the Lord." The excellence of this quality and its merit before God, exalted be He, (is seen in the fact that) He promised it to Jacob during his sleep, as it is said (Isa. xliv. 2), "Fear not, O Jacob, my servant," and as it is said of the righteous man who trusts in the Lord and who confides in Him (Ps. cxii. 7), "He shall not be afraid of evil tidings: his heart is fixed, trusting in the Lord."

Chapter IV

Treating of Penitence (Remorse) and Guarding Against (The Need of) It.

This quality comes into being, when a man quits a sinful state and repents. When he gives evidence of the quality of penitence, then his repentance is complete. It must be preceded by three conditions, namely, penitence, seeking pardon, and guaranteeing to abandon one's wonted course. Thus our master Saadya Alfayumi, may God be gracious unto him, explained that one of the righteous was wont to say, "He who repents of his past sins is as though he had not sinned." This trait is commendable from this point of view. But the reprehensible side of it comes to light in the case of him who says "Yes" to-day in some matter and after a time regrets what he has said and retracts, or who vows to fast or to give alms and repents of his vow. All this is blameworthy. The reasonable way, in my opinion, is for man to beware of placing himself in a position which he may be compelled to regret. Although men have not the power so to control themselves, that they can choose (all) their qualities, nevertheless they can desire to rise gradually from a base to a lofty course, and from faulty qualities to sound ones. The acme of bliss for man is to be able to bridle his soul, to rule it, to lead it along the right way. He whose nature yields to his intellect becomes lordly; his merit becomes high and profitable, and his deeds are praised.

PART IV

Chapter I

Treating of Wrath.

This quality, although among the forces of the animal soul, we have set down as one of the qualities of man, because of its analogy to his other qualities. Let us begin by describing its useful side, although the latter is inseparable from its baneful aspect. There is no quality so reprehensible, but that it at time serves a use, even as no quality is so praiseworthy, but that it frequently becomes detrimental. Thus thou knowest that silence is a commendable trait, but it becomes detestable when resorted to while listening to absurdities. Wrath is a reprehensible quality, but when employed to correct or to reprove, or because of indignation at the performance of transgressions, it becomes laudable. Therefore the thoroughly wise and ethically trained man must abandon both extremes and set about the right mean. Galen said in his book on the qualities of the soul, "Wrath and anger are two words with one meaning." "Sometimes it appears, (to judge) from the countenance of the wrathful, that he is distressed, his body feverishly inflamed, his heart throbbing violently, his pulse beating strongly and swiftly." He said again, "Dignity becomes apparent in him who indulges in wrath only after reflection. But he who indulges therein unadvisedly gives evidence of stupidity." Wherefore the saying, "He who is mighty in wrath and violent in anger is not far removed from the mad." In the book of Al-Ḳuṭi (it is said) that the man of wrath is never seen to be joyful. We would classify the wrathful soul as of four kinds.[5] He who is quickly angered and (as) quickly appeased is of an even-balanced disposition. This is mainly characteristic of a man possessed of a yellow (bilious) temperament. He who is slow to anger and difficult to appease is likewise of an evenbalanced disposition. But he who is difficult to appease and quickly angered is in a reprehensible condition because he has

overstepped the boundaries of moderation. But he who is slow to anger and quickly appeased is most praiseworthy. This is one of the virtues of the noble and excellent men, among whose qualities wrath rarely ever appears. Those who subdue their souls' anger and prevail upon their nature to restrain it, have been described as noble and characterized as exalted. Thus the sage said (Prov. xvi. 32), "He that is slow to anger is better than the mighty." This is one of the thirteen attributes ascribed to God, exalted is He, in the passage (Ex. xxxiv. 6), "And the Lord passed by before him," etc. It is said that as scab is a disease of the body, so is wrath a disease of the soul. The moral man must not become wrathful often, because, by reason of his wrath, he is compelled to bear burdens. Thus saith the sage (Prov. xix. 19), "A man of great wrath shall bear punishment." The sage has forbidden it, saying (Eccl. vii. 9), "Be not hasty in thy spirit to be angry." Furthermore the verse makes clear the reason for his forbidding it in the expression (ib.), "For anger resteth in the bosom of fools." The wrathful deserves to be called "fool." It is impossible in most cases for the man of violent wrath to be secure from grave sin and serious transgression. Thus the sage spake (Prov. xxix. 22): "A wrathful man aboundeth in transgression." Thou wilt notice that most men, when they become wroth and violently angry, take no heed of the disaster which they may incur through the violence of their anger, like him of whom it is said (id., 11), "A fool uttereth all his mind," and on the other hand (ib.), "But a wise man keepeth it till afterward." Therefore our masters, peace be upon them, sought to interdict the immoderate exercise of this quality, saying, "He who rends his garments in wrath is like unto an idolator." According to this, a superior man must not be violent in wrath, for he accustoms himself to the qualities of the wild and wicked beast. Nor must he be so gentle as never to become wrathful, for this were characteristic of little boys. The discreet stand with reference to this is to take the intermediate course. Thou must know that man's reason is perfected when it subdues his wrath. Thus Scripture says (Prov. xix. 11), "The discretion of a man deferreth his anger." Ptolemy, the sage, said of wrath, "When thou becomest wrathful, pardon, for if thou dost not yield, the taking of vengeance is a sign of weakness."

Chapter II

Treating of the Quality of Good-Will (Suavity).

This is one of the praiseworthy qualities, since it is rarely to be met with, except in the case of a noble-minded person, who accepts things just as they come to him and looks not for better ones. The quality of contentment is also derived therefrom. This is, as thou knowest, reader, an excellent quality, which we have portrayed and extolled above in the second chapter of Part I., whilst treating of the quality of meekness. If the righteous man be well disposed toward his fellow men and the latter similarly disposed toward him, it is certain that he will be acceptable unto God. Yea, more, even his enemies will make peace with him. Thus the sage saith (Prov. xvi. 7), "When a man's ways please the Lord, he maketh even his enemies to be at peace with him," as thou knowest from the good-will Abimelech bore Abraham, peace be upon him, and the latter's making peace with him; thus also in the speech of our sainted Rabbi to R. Ḥiyya, and so forth. Wherefore the excellence of good-will is related to life, being a source of superiority and a fount of good fortune according to the saying (id., xvi. 15), "In the light of the king's countenance is life; and his favor is as a cloud of the latter rain." So also in that of man; thus Pharaoh bore good-will to Joseph, even bringing him unto kingly power. Thus Ahasuerus, too, bore good-will to Mordecai. Thou seest how such a man is treated and exalted; how much more he to whom God bears good-will,—

therefore the saying (Isa. xlviii. 17), "I am the Lord thy God which teacheth thee to profit, which leadeth thee by the way that thou shouldst go." The sage said, "Whosoever is contented is rich: whosoever is obedient is joyous: whosoever is rebellious is sad." He was wont to say, "He who is not content of his own accord with his condition will be (compelled to be) satisfied despite himself." From this quality there branch out forbearance and forgiveness, which are of the attributes of the Creator, exalted is He and blest, and of the wise and noble man. The poet spake, "If I were not to pardon a brother's fault, and if I were to say that I would exact vengeance from him, where then would be the superiority? And if I were to cut myself from my brethren because of their sins, I would be alone, and have none with whom to associate."

It is related: "A king once became angry at a company of men and commanded that they be slain. Then spake one of them, 'Verily we have sinned grievously. Will not thy goodliness manifest itself in forgiveness?' Whereupon he forgave them and slew them not."

Chapter III

Treating of Jealousy.

This quality is an offshoot of wrath. Most rational beings are not exempt from it: but it is in them all, for we see men seeking to imitate the actions of their companions. For instance, when one (man) sees that his friend has acquired some worldly gain, mineral, animal, or vegetable, or other possessions, he likewise endeavors to acquire similar things, although he be able to dispense with them or compensate himself with other things in their stead. Let him not protract his endeavor, nor set his heart upon attaining such possessions. This is the expression to which the sage, peace be upon him, gave utterance (Eccl. iv. 4), "Again I considered all travail and every right work, that for this a man is envied of his neighbor." He whose nature is overcome by this disposition is blameworthy, for it leads him to envy, and a noble man is never found to be envious. Books (i.e., of poetry) have been filled with the censure of envy, and every man of intelligence knows how much has been said as to its baseness. It is necessary to turn from it, for frequently the affairs of the envious lead him to use violence. Thus it is said of such as these (Micah ii. 2), "And they covet fields and take them by violence." Enviousness is a loathsome trait. The wise man must keep himself as far from it as he can, for he gains no advantage through it: on the contrary, continued depression and fatigue of the spirit through desires and the constant hatred of men, scantiness of repose, preoccupation of the mind, apprehensiveness and the punishment of God, for transgressing that which He forbade in His revealed Scripture. Man must not be jealous of unrighteous men, because he sees them devote themselves to pleasure and (the gratifying of) passions. But let him employ his zeal in the service of God. Thus the sage said (Prov. xxiii. 17), "Let not thy heart be envious of the sinners." Again he spake (Ps. xxxvii. 1), "Be thou not envious against the workers of iniquity." Zeal is goodly only in the service of God, as thou knowest from (the case of) Phinehas, of whom it is said (Num. xxv. 11), "While he was zealous for may sake," and the good reward which he merited thereby, as it is said (id., 12), "Wherefore, say, behold I give unto him my covenant of peace." Among the things which have been said with reference to the jealous and envious (we find), "Thou wilt observe the envious man effusive in his affection (for thee) when he meets thee, but hating thee in thy absence. His name is friend, his intention unfriendly." Again it has been said, "It appears as though the envious were created in order to be angered." Furthermore it has been said, "Let it suffice for thee that the envious man is grieved at the time of thy joy." It is incumbent upon man to mount to such an exalted rank with the aid of his powers and gifts, that he be envied therefor." Let him ponder over this, as saith the poet:

"Lo, I was envied, but God increased men's enviousness touching me. Let man rather not live at all than live for a single day unenvied. Man is not envied save for his excellences, which are forbearance, scholarship, nobility, and generosity."

Chapter IV

Treating of Wide-Awakedness.

I must preface, in treating of this quality, of what nature it is derived. I would hold that it is of the yellow-gall species. This quality appears usually when the soul is free from other blamable qualities and when it is not mingled with aught of grief, and most frequently it is (found) in pure and noble souls. It is a commendable quality, and man ought to make use of it in whatsoever work of art or science he be engrossed. Was it not said of him (Prov. xii. 27), "The substance of a wide-awake man is precious," which means that the most precious virtue of the lofty is wide-awakedness, both in the present and future life. In the world *de generatione et corruptione*, he is wide-awake in his quest of knowledge as well as goodness of service and faith, and in the attempt to attain to the world of intellect. With reference to the reverse of this quality, i.e., weakness of purpose in worldly affairs and in the attempt to save souls, it has been said (Prov. xxiv. 10), "If thou faint in the day of adversity thy strength is small"; and again (id., xii. 27), "The slothful man roasteth not that which he took in hunting." However, we have mentioned the languid while treating of the quality of hatred. He who is one of the estimable, and administers his affairs with alacrity, will succeed in them. Thus it is said (Prov. xii. 24), "The hand of the diligent shall bear rule; but the slothful shall be under tribute." Concerning this the poet spake:

"If the souls become too greatly ambitious, the bodies will be wearied thereby."

This is a beautiful maxim. The sage, peace be upon him, exhorted to wide-awakedness in matters religious and worldly in saying (Prov. xix. 15), "Sloth-fulness casteth into a deep sleep." This say-ing is very evident, for slothfulness neces-sarily induces lethargy. For when the vapors, which are designed to exude from the pores of the body through forcible movements, are motionless and do not dis-solve, they mount to the brain, and bring about constant drowsiness. In the book of Al-Kuṭi it is said of wide-awakedness, "He who satisfies his land in respect of culti-vation, will be statisfied by it with bread." The ethical aspect of this quality is, "Man must not display it in his lust." He shall not be rash through this in his wrath, for rash-ness is blameworthy since it is not one of the qualities of the wise. The excellent do not make use of it. But one ought to employ wide-awakedness in matters relating to re-ligion and law. The surest reason for the success of a man is (to be found in) the wide-awakedness with which he conducts his affairs, and the greatest sign of misfor-tune is his slothfulness with regard to them. The poet has said:

"The pure and noble souls are wakeful, watchful, and sound of judgment, while the stupid and heavy souls are drowsy, mean and low."

But that intense wide-awakedness which leads to hastiness is culpable. Let the intel-ligent man beware of using it, for it is the very worst of evils.[6] He who is hasty, rushes to destruction, and the man of hast-iness is not secure from disappointment. A verse reads:

"A cautious man will realize his desires. But he who hastens unduly is bound to stumble."

Man must not make undue haste in his affairs, because no good result can be ob-tained by haste, but through deliberation ends are (more) easily attained. The beauty of the state of wide-awakedness lies in its being potential in the soul and not appear-ing quickly in action.

PART V

Chapter I

Treating of the Quality of Liberality (Generosity).

This quality, when it is employed with moderation and does not lapse into prodi-gality, is commendable. Man must prefer this quality to its antithesis, i.e., the quality of niggardliness, since the great men who are renowned by reason of their excellences are not convinced that niggardliness is a praiseworthy quality. Dost thou not see, may God guide thee aright, in how many places the sage extols the man who is gen-erous? In one place he says that liberality brings a man to many degrees of eminence in this world and in the world to come. Thus it is said (Prov. xviii. 16), "A man's gift maketh room for him and bringeth him before great men"—in this world, because it brings him near to kings whose good-will he gains through gifts; as thou knowest from the respect of Ben Hadad for Asa, and Tiglath for Ahaz, because presents were made to them—and in the world to come he will attain the merited (share of its) bliss, which man realizes because of his serving the Lord with his substance in almsgiving. Thus it is said (Isa. liii. 12), "Therefore will I divide him a portion with the great." Since liberality was a virtue of our father Abraham, peace be upon him, he became known thereby and it was ascribed to him. This quality is attributed to him in the Holy Scripture in several places, and thus is to be understood the explanation of (Ps. xlvii. 9), "The generous of the people are gath-ered together, even the people of the God of Abraham." This is a commendable qual-ity because it secures honor for him who exercises it. Thus it is said (Prov. xix. 6), "Many will entreat the favor of the gener-ous, and every man is a friend to him that giveth gifts." Through this a man merits his fellow-men's praise when he gives gener-ously, and he is lauded therefor. Thus spake a poet:

"When thou goest to him, thou wilt find

him of pleasant demeanor as it thou wert about to give him what he will give thee. Had he naught but his life to give, he would give this. Wherefore, let the fear of God be upon whomsoever would ask this of him."

But the unseemly side of this quality appears when man wastes his substance needlessly and mismanages it; as, for instance, he who spends it in devotion to pleasures and in gratifying his lust. This is squandering and is not characteristic of the wise. A gift in the right place is a treasure put aside. It perisheth not in the course of time, but abideth with the ages. This is the opinion of Solomon, peace be upon him, who said (Eccl. xi. 1), "Cast thy bread upon the waters; for thou shalt find it after many days." This verse evidently exhorts to generosity, for if man be generous and bountiful, he will reap the fruit thereof. Thus spake the poet:

"Sow thou generosity in the field of gifts, and noble deeds shall be harvested by thee early."

Wherefore man ought to know that if he be in a prosperous condition, then his generosity will not impair his prosperity, and if he be in a straitened condition, his adversity will not continue on that account. It is peculiar to this noble quality, that he who employs it never feels the want of anything; on the contrary, his abundance is much increased. Thus it is said (Prov. xxviii. 27): "He that giveth unto the poor shall not lack." Furthermore, David the Saint, peace be upon him, says of generous and liberal men (Ps. cxii. 9), "He hath dispersed, he hath given to the poor: his righteousness endureth forever." What is your opinion with reference to the use of this gracious virtue? It is like lending unto God, exalted and magnified is He. Thus the saying (Prov. xix. 17), "He that hath pity upon the poor lendeth unto the Lord." Thus it was said in the book on Ethics: "Bestow kindness on those who are worthy and upon those who are unworthy. In the case of the worthy, thy kindness will be in the right place; and in the case

of the unworthy, prove thou thy worth." Again it was said with reference to liberality, "It is a part of the noble qualities to give liberally to him who asks." In the book of Al-Ḳuṭi (it is said): "Know thou that resolution consists in doing things with firmness. Consider well when to yield and when to deny, when to grant and when to promise. For a gift after denying is better than denying after (promising) a gift and favor. Setting out to do after consideration is better than to abandon after setting out. Know that thou shouldst be more prompt to do what thou hast not promised, than to promise what thou wilt not do. Therefore beware of hastily promising what thou fearest thou mayest be unable to perform. Adorn thy promise with truth and thy deed with justice."

Chapter II

Treating of Niggardliness.

Know thou that this is a reprehensible quality. Among the host of reprehensible qualities there is none more abominable than this. For thou seest that he who is lavishly bountiful of his substance, although blameworthy, is statisfied with the pleasure he derives and men's goodly praise which is his. But niggardliness is accompanied by evil repute without even the attainment of pleasure; and to be of evil repute is not one of the qualities desired by the excellent. The noble-minded man ought to shrink from this quality and not employ it on any occasion. The sages are at one in thinking that manliness does not go well with prodigality, nor religion with an inordinate desire (for gain). He who is of this character may well despair of a good repute and a fair record. Thus it was said (Isa. xxxii. 5), "The vile person shall be no more called liberal, nor the churl said to be bountiful." This "vile person" is like him, in the wilderness of Maon, who said (I Sam. xxv. 11), "Shall I then take my bread and my water, ... and give it unto men whom I know not whence they be?" Thou knowest the severe punishment with which he met. But the good feature of this state is that man does not squander his substance, be it great or small, but guards it by means of this quality. He must not overdo this, however, lest he pass over to the quality of greed, which is not of the qualities of the noble. Thus the sage spake in condemning niggardliness (Prov. xi. 26), "He that withholdeth corn, the people shall curse him"; and, on the contrary, "Blessing shall be on the head of him that selleth it." This verse outwardly refers to "charity," but its hidden implication is knowledge. The wise man ought not be niggardly in dealing out his knowledge, for knowledge is not lessened by imparting it (to others), as little as the brightness of the fire dies away when a light is kindled therefrom. The best rule with regard to the employment of this quality is to accustom one's self to beneficence toward kinsmen, until one gradually habituate one's self to benevolence toward strangers, and thus train one's self to choose generosity.

Chapter III

Treating of Valor.

The man who prevails over the temperament of the blood-nature, who is large-hearted, full-veined, and long-armed, thou wilt generally find to be a man of valor, especially if, combined with that, he be master of the art of war. This quality is praiseworthy (in man), when it is manifested in his strength, and in accordance with his determination to be saved from what might befall him. But when he departs from a moderate course and unites valor with the quality of folly and it becomes the cause of a man's throwing himself into dangerous places then it is reprehensible. Of these two dispositions the sage saith (Prov. xxviii. 14), "Happy is the man that feareth always; but he that hardeneth his heart shall fall into mischief." But as regards the great men who are mentioned as possessors of this quality, heavenly signs

gave evidence of their possessing this power,—thus Joshua, Gideon, Samson, Saul, David, Jonathan, Joab, and Abner, and others like them, whose power gave evidence of the quality of valor, were praised therefor; and those whose weakness, in contradistinction to the former, gave evidence of the quality of cowardice, were not commended for it, as I will show in regard to them in the following chapter. It is necessary to devote this quality to the service of God, as thou knowest from (the story of) Moses, peace be upon him, when he retaliated upon the people by saying to the children of Levi (Ex. xxxii. 27), "Put every man his sword by his side"; and as thou knowest from Phinehas in the matter of his zeal. Thus it is said (Num. xxv. 7), "And when Phinehas, the son of Aaron the priest, saw it, he rose up from among the congregation and took a javelin in his hand." This quality of valor never fails to be conspicuous in the souls of mighty men and courageous heroes. With reference to valor and patience in facing danger, the poet spake:

"There came a day in the heat of which some people warmed themselves, but though there was no fire, they acted as if in the fire's midst. But we had patience until the day was done. Likewise, a case of misfortune can be brought to a close only through patience."

Among the things which have been said in order to encourage the use of valor is: "Crave death, and life will be granted thee." The Arabs were accustomed to call the man of valor "safe." Among the things which have been said on the emboldening of the spirit in combat is the word of the poet:

"I went to the rear to preserve my life (in battle), but I found that I could not preserve my life unless I went forward."

Thus the noble man must make use of this quality in such a way as not to overstep the middle path lest he be called demented (foolhardy). But he must pursue an excellent course in regard to this quality. The philosopher spake, "The extreme limit of valor is strength and endurance with respect to what thou abhorrest." Valor cannot go hand-in-hand with vanity (untruth), nor firmness with absurdity, nor patience with weariness, for these are of the qualities of asses and swine. Valor consists in persevering in the right and overcoming thy desires, until thou feel that to die in the best way thou hast found is more desirable than to live in the opposite (i.e., evil) way, which the power of understanding may have revealed to thee. According to Al-Ḳuṭi, "Valor is the nature of a noble soul, corresponding to the strength of the body."

Chapter IV

Treating of Cowardice.

This quality is generally found in spirits that are abject and downcast, poor and wretched. It is a reprehensible quality. Let the wise man be on his guard against it, let him make no use of it, exert himself to keep away and abstain from it, since he derives no benefit from it; on the contrary, he reaps ill-repute, a vile record, and a diminution of praise. Men of lofty purpose must dread it when they have learned to employ their power of distinguishing in the use of things, so that it may be the means of escaping serious danger. Among the offshoots of the quality is slothfulness, of which we have already treated. Thou knowest what was said with regard to its ignominy and baseness. Thus the sage, peace to upon him, said (Prov. xxvi. 15), "A slothful man hideth his hand in his bosom, and will not so much as bring it to his mouth again." This is the uttermost that can be said of the shame thereof. The slothful coward is known to say: "I will not travel, for fear of highwaymen and wild beasts. I will no engage in business, lest I meet with losses. I will not fast, lest I become ill. I will give no alms, lest I become poor," and similar words that put an end to all activity, until there remains nothing for him to do, but living on without moving

from his place, as it is said (id., xxvi. 14), "As the door turneth upon its hinges, so doth the slothful upon his bed." A wise man should not choose this quality of cowardice or make use thereof in preference to his other qualities, lest he become known thereby and be as one who fancies that he will be killed before the expiration of the appointed time, as was said exaggeratedly of the slothful coward by the poet, who spake thus:

"If a little bird merely raises its voice, the heart of the coward is consumed (leaps with terror). But his teeth are sharp as iron,—at meal times."

But in a case where escape is impossible, it is permissible for the quality of cowardice to come into play—as in the case of him, concerning whom it is said: "The king dispatched him to a dangerous place. He refused to go. The king reviled him, whereupon he said, 'It is better that thou revile me when living than bless me when dead.' " It has been said that this quality has been made use of by those who prefer repose in this world to all other qualities, not knowing that repose can be enjoyed to the full, only after zealous care in the regulating of affairs and the attainment of whatsoever be needed. Thus it is said (Prov. xxiv. 27), "Prepare thy work without, and make it fit for thyself in the field." Repose in and of itself signifies slothfulness and cowardice. Thou knowest what happens to a man by reason of his slothfulness: namely, he is deprived of all his honor through utter poverty. Thus it is said (id., xxiv. 33–34): "Yet a little sleep, a little slumber, a little folding of the hands to sleep: so shall thy poverty come as one that travelleth, and thy want as an armed man." Again this quality engenders in the body not a few ills and diseases, thus flabbiness, dulness, swelling, gout, sciatica, and elephantiasis, and similarly whatsoever results from indigestion: in fact, this quality becomes habitual to a man and he considers everything else as faulty and worthless; especially if this feeble coward be of a phlegmatic disposition and on the way to old age, then it weighs him down even more.[7]

NOTES

1. Guttmann ("Saadya," pp. 276, 277, note 2, Emunoth we-Deoth, x. 9) points out that Gabirol closely follows the teaching of Saadya with respect to the love of dominion; it is worthy of notice that Gabirol quotes the same scriptural passages.
2. The appellation "divine," as applied to Socrates and other Greek philosophers, was not uncommon.
3. Called an "Indian King" in the "Choice of Pearls."
4. Play upon the similarity of the words "pudency" and "life" in the Arabic.
5. Aristotelian; cf. "Moral Philosophy of Aristotle," by W. M. Hatch (London, 1879, p. 223 et seq.).
6. Attributed to Plato.
7. We have here a reminiscence of Saadya's distinction between the results of tranquillity and slothfulness, between the reposeful and the indolent, as found in the "Emunoth weDeoth," x.

CHAPTER 9

Peter Abelard

Peter Abelard was born in 1079 at Pallet, Brittany. He learned the art of dialectic as a youth while studying under the nominalist Rocelin, after which he made his way to Paris, where he received instruction from William of Champeaux, a realist. He soon became unwelcome as a result of a public disagreement with William concerning the nature of universals. Such controversy was to follow him throughout his life. His ruthlessness in public debate earned him many enemies, as well as the nickname of *rhinocerus indomitus.*

Nevertheless, his reputation as a brilliant teacher and philosopher brought him a great following of students. He opened his first school at Melun, then one at Corbeil, and finally one at Paris. At the age of thirty-four he lost interest in dialectics and turned to the study of theology, entering the school of Anselm of Laon. But in no time he was once again at odds with his masters. His solution was once again his own school, which he opened at Mont Sainte-Geneviève and then at Paris in 1113.

It was also during this period that he met Héloïse, with whom he had the most celebrated love affair of the Middle Ages. The physical dimension of the affair ended after several thugs hired by Héloïse's uncle battered Abelard and in the process castrated him. Subsequently, he entered the monastery of Saint-Denis, where he continued to teach until 1121, and she entered a nunnery. Nevertheless, they continued their romance on a cerebral level through a prolific correspondence.

In 1121 Abelard's book *On the Trinity* was condemned at a special session called at Soissons. This, plus his constant bickering with the monks at Saint-Denis, made his residence there intolerable, and he obtained permission to retire. He sought solitude at Maisoncelle near Nogent-sur-Seine. It was only a short time, however, until students gathered around him to form yet another school. His popularity once again caught the attention of his enemies. After a brief tenure as abbot of St. Gildas in his native Brittany (1128), he returned to Paris. Here his controversial teachings brought him into direct conflict with Bernard of Clairvaux, whose influence caused Peter to be summoned before the Council of Sens (1141), where a number of his views were condemned. He set out for Rome to plead his case, not knowing his fate was sealed due to Bernard's influence with the pope. On his way he stayed at the Abbey of Cluny, where his friend and abbot Peter the Venerable persuaded him to give up the struggle and remain there. Having been condemned to silence, Abelard devoted the last two years of his life to prayer and other monastic exercises.

Abelard on Ethics

Abelard understands evil as a necessary fact of human existence. It was created by God for the purpose of testing mankind. For example, it is a fact that men lust after women. Abelard sees no sin attached to the will for intercourse; that lust is presumably there to test men's resolve. The ethical issue is whether or not a man consents to his will to engage in an evil act. It is the giving in to one's will to do evil that is evil, not (so much) the overt act itself. Coveting lends itself particularly well to this analysis. The tenth commandment states, "Thou shalt not covet." Coveting is a stronger (mental) state than a genuine appreciation of another man's oxen or wife. Coveting is the desire of owning that person's oxen or having his wife to the extent that one is in the planning stages of stealing the one or seducing the other. Consequently, "Whosoever looketh on a woman to lust after her hath committed adultery with her already in his heart" (Matthew 5:28). The mechanics of coveting consist of four steps:

1. Consent to will an evil deed leads to
2. intent to do the evil deed, which entails
3. knowledge that what one is intending to do is evil, which implies that
4. that which one is intending to do is, in fact, evil.

It is important to note that Abelard understands that there are, in fact, evil deeds. He, however, is primarily concerned with the ascriptive aspect of evil as opposed to the descriptive elements of it. It is for him not so much a matter of whether one commits adultery. Clearly, that one does not know that the person with whom he has intercourse is married does not negate the act as adulterous. And adultery is evil. Such ignorance, however, relieves one of responsibility for engaging in the evil deed. One must know that he is engaged in adultery for him to be guilty of so sinning. One can consent to engage in an adulterous act only if one knows that the willing party is married. Obviously, then, knowledge as well as consent plays a major role in Abelard's ethics. This is why he maintains that children and idiots cannot sin. "God considers only the mind in rewarding good or evil, not the results of deeds."

ETHICS OR *KNOW THYSELF*

Prologue

In the study of morals we deal with the defects or qualities of the mind which dispose us to bad or good actions. Defects and qualities are not only mental, but also physical. There is bodily weakness; there is also the endurance which we call strength. There is sluggishness or speed; blindness or sight. When we now speak of defects, therefore, we pre-suppose defects of the

From *Abelard's Ethics*, translated by J. Ramsay McCallum, M.A. (Merrick, N.Y.: Richwood Publishing Co., 1976), pp. 15, 17–61.

mind, so as to distinguish them from the physical ones. The defects of the mind are opposed to the qualities; injustice to justice; cowardice to constancy; intemperance to temperance.

Chapter I

The Defect of Mind Bearing Upon Conduct

Certain defects or merits of mind have no connection with morals. They do not make human life a matter of praise or blame.

Such are dull wits or quick insight; a good or a bad memory; ignorance or knowledge. Each of these features is found in good and bad alike. They have nothing to do with the system of morals, nor with making life base or honourable. To exclude these we safeguarded above the phrase 'defects of mind' by adding 'which dispose to bad actions,' that is, those defects which incline the will to what least of all either should be done or should be left undone.

Chapter II

How Does Sin Differ from a Disposition to Evil?

Defect of this mental kind is not the same thing as sin. Sin, too, is not the same as a bad action. For example, to be irascible, that is, prone or easily roused to the agitation of anger is a defect and moves the mind to unpleasantly impetuous and irrational action. This defect, however, is in the mind so that the mind is liable to wrath, even when it is not actually roused to it. Similarly, lameness, by reason of which a man is said to be lame, is in the man himself even when he does not walk and reveal his lameness. For the defect is there though action be lacking. So, also, nature or constitution renders many liable to luxury. Yet they do not sin because they are like this, but from this very fact they have the material of a struggle whereby they may, in the virtue of temperance, triumph over themselves and win the crown.

As Solomon says: 'Better a patient than a strong man; and the Lord of his soul than he that taketh a city.' (Prov. xvi, 32.) For religion does not think it degrading to be beaten by man; but it is degrading to be beaten by one's lower self. The former defeat has been the fate of good men. But, in the latter, we fall below ourselves. The Apostle commends victory of this sort; 'No one shall be crowned who has not truly striven.' (2 Tim. ii, 5.) This striving, I repeat, means standing less against men than against myself, so that defects may not lure me into base consent. Though men cease to

oppose us, our defects do not cease. The fight with them is the more dangerous because of its repetition. And as it is the more difficult, so victory is the more glorious. Men, however much they prevail over us, do not force baseness upon us, unless by their practice of vice they turn us also to it and overcome us through our own wretched consent. They may dominate our body; but while our mind is free, there is no danger to true freedom. We run no risk of base servitude. Subservience to vice, not to man, is degradation. It is the overlordship of defects and not physical serfdom which debases of soul.

Chapter III

Definition of 'Defect' and of Sin

Defect, then, is that whereby we are disposed to sin. We are, that is, inclined to consent to what we ought not to do, or to leave undone what we ought to do. Consent of this kind we rightly call sin. Here is the reproach of the soul meriting damnation or being declared guilty by God. What is that consent but to despise God and to violate his laws? God cannot be set at enmity by injury, but by contempt. He is the highest power, and is not diminished by any injury, but He avenges contempt of Himself. Our sin, therefore, is contempt of the Creator. To sin is to despise the Creator; that is, not to do for Him what we believe we should do for Him, or, not to renounce what we think should be renounced on His behalf. We have defined sin negatively by saying that it means not doing or not renouncing what we ought to do or renounce. Clearly, then, we have shown that sin has no reality. It exists rather in *not being* than in *being*. Similarly we could define shadows by saying: The absence of light where light usually is.

Perhaps you object that sin is the desire or will to do an evil deed, and that this will or desire condemns us before God in the same way as the will to do a good deed justifies us. There is as much quality, you suggest, in the good will as there is sin in the evil will; and it is no less 'in being' in the latter than in the former. By willing to do what we believe to be pleasing to God we please Him. Equally, by willing to do what we believe to be displeasing to God, we displease Him and seem either to violate or despise His nature.

But diligent attention will show that we must think far otherwise of this point. We frequently err; and from no evil will at all. Indeed, the evil will itself, when restrained, though it may not be quenched, procures the palm-wreath for those who resist it. It provides, no merely the materials for combat, but also the crwon of glory. It should be spoken of rather as a certain inevitable weakness than as sin. Take, for example, the case of an innocent servant whose harsh master is moved with fury against him. He pursues the servant, drawing his sword with intent to kill him. For a while the servant flies and avoids death as best he can. At last, forced all unwillingly to it, he kills his master so as not to be killed by him. Let anyone say what sort of evil will there was in this deed. His will was only to flee from death and preserve his own life. Was this an evil will? You reply: 'I do not think this was an evil will. But the will that he had to kill the master who was pursuing him was evil.' Your answer would be admirable and acute if you could show that the servant really willed what you say that he did. But, as I insisted, he was unwillingly forced to his deed. He protracted his master's life as long as he could, knowing that danger also threatened his own life from such a crime. How, then was a deed done voluntarily by which he incurred danger to his own life?

Your reply may be that the action was voluntary because the man's will was to escape death even though it may not have been to kill his master. This charge might easily be preferred against him. I do not rebut it. Nevertheless, as has been said, that will by which he sought to evade death, as you urge, and not to kill his master, cannot at all be condemned as bad. He did, however, fail by consenting, though driven to it through fear of death, to an unjust murder which he ought rather to have endured than committed. Of his own will, I mean, he took the sword. It was not handed to him by authority. The Truth saith: 'Everyone that taketh the sword shall perish by the sword.' (Matt. xxvi. 52.) By his rashness he risked the death and damnation of his soul. The servant's wish, then, was not to kill his master, but to avoid death. Because he *consented*, however, as he should not have done, to murder, this wrongful consent preceding the crime was sin.

Someone may interpose: 'But you cannot conclude that he wished to kill his master because, in order to escape death, he was willing to kill his master. I might say to a man; I am willing for you to have my cape so that you may give me five shillings. Or, I am glad for you to have it at this price. But I do not hand it over because I desire you to have possession of it.' No, and if a man in prison desired under duresse, to put his son there in his place that he might secure his own ransom, should we therefore admit that he wished to send his son to prison?

It was only with many a tear and groan that he consented to such a course.

The fact is that this kind of will, existing with much internal regret, is not, if I may so say, *will*, but a passive submission of mind. It is so because the man wills one thing on account of another. He puts up with *this* because he really desires *that*. A patient is said to submit to cautery or lancet that he may obtain health. Martyrs endured that they might come to Christ; and Christ, too, that we may be saved by his passion.

Yet we are not bound to admit simply that these people therefore wish for this mental unease. Such unease can only be where something occurs contrary to wish. No man suffers so long as he fulfils his wish and does what he likes to experience. The Apostle says: 'I desire to depart and to be with Christ' (Phil. i, 23), that is, to die so that I may attain to him. Elsewhere this apostle says: 'We desire not to be despoiled of our garments, but to be clothed from above, that our mortal part may be swallowed up in life.' This notion, Blessed Augustine reminds us, was contained in the Lord's address to Peter: 'Thou shalt extend thy hands and another shall gird thee, and lead thee wither thou willest not.' (John xxi, 18.) The Lord also spoke to the Father out of the weakness of the human nature which he had taken upon himself: 'If it be possible, let this cup pass from me; nevertheless not as I will, but as thou willest.' (Matt. xxvi, 39.) His spirit naturally trembled before the great terror of death: and he could not speak of what he knew to be punishment as a matter of his own will. When elsewhere it is written of Him: 'He was offered because He himself willed it' (Isaiah liii, 7), it must be understood either of His divine nature, in whose will it was that he should suffer as a man, or 'He himself willed it' must be taken according to the Psalmist's phrase: 'Whatsoever he willed, that he did.' (Ps. cxiii, 3.)

Sin, therefore, is sometimes committed without an evil will. Thus sin cannot be defined as 'will.' True, you will say, when we sin under constraint, but not when we sin willingly, for instance, when we will to do something which we know ought not to be done by us. There the evil will and sin seem to be the same thing. For example a man sees a woman; his concupiscence is aroused; his mind is enticed by fleshly lust and stirred to base desire. This wish, this lascivious longing, what else can it be, you say, than sin?

I reply: What if that wish may be bridled by the power of temperance? What if its nature is never to be entirely extinguished but to persist in struggle and not fully fail even in defeat? For where is the battle if the antagonist is away? Whence the great reward without grave endurance? When the fight is over nothing remains but to reap the reward. Here we strive in contest in order elsewhere to obtain as victors a crown. Now, for a contest, an opponent is needed who will resist, not one who simply submits. This opponent is our evil will over which we triumph when we subjugate it to the divine will. But we do not entirely destroy it. For we needs must ever expect to

encounter our enemy. What achievement before God is it if we undergo nothing contrary to our own will, but merely practice what we please? Who will be grateful to us if in what we say we do for him we merely satisfy our own fancy?

You will say, what merit have we with God in acting willingly or unwillingly? Certainly none: I reply. He weighs the intention rather than the deed in his recompense. Nor does the deed, whether it proceed from a good or an evil will, add anything to the merit, as we shall show shortly. But when we set His will before our own so as to follow His and not ours, our merit with God is magnified, in accordance with that perfect word of Truth: 'I came not to do mine own will, but the will of Him that sent me.' (John vi, 38.) To this end He exhorts us: 'If anyone comes to me, and does not hate father, and mother . . . yea his own soul also, he is not worthy of me.' (Luke xiv, 26.) That is to say, 'unless a man renounces his parents' influence and his own will and submits himself to my teaching, he is not worthy of me.' Thus we are bidden to hate our father, not to destroy him. Similarly with our own will. We must not be led by it; at the same time, we are not asked to root it out altogether.

When the Scripture says: 'Go not after your own desires' (Eccles. xviii, 30), and: 'Turn from your own will' (ibid.), it instructs us not to fulfil our desires. Yet it does not say that we are to be wholly without them. It is vicious to give in to our desires; but not to have any desires at all is impossible for our weak nature.

The sin, then, consists not in desiring a woman, but in consent to the desire, and not the wish for whoredom, but the consent to the wish is damnation.

Let us see how our conclusions about sexual intemperance apply to theft. A man crosses another's garden. At the sight of the delectable fruit his desire is aroused. He does not, however, give way to desire so as to take anything by theft or rapine, although his mind was moved to strong inclination by the thought of the delight of eating. Where there is desire, there, without doubt, will exists. The man desires the eating of that fruit wherein he doubts not that there will be delight. The weakness of nature in this man is compelled to desire the fruit which, without the master's permission, he has no right to take. He conquers the desire, but does no extinguish it. Since, however, he is not enticed into consent, he does not descend to sin.

What, then, of your objection? It should be clear from such instances, that the wish or desire itself of doing what is not seemly is never to be called sin, but rather, as we said, the consent is sin. We consent to what is not seemly when we do not draw ourselves back from such a deed, and are prepared, should opportunity offer, to perform it completely. Whoever is discovered in this intention, though his guilt has yet to be completed in deed, is already guilty before God in so far as he strives with all his might to sin, and accomplishes within himself, as the blessed Augustine reminds us, as much as if he were actually taken in the act.

But while wish is not sin, and, as we have said, we sometimes commit sin unwillingly, there are nevertheless those who assert that every sin is voluntary. In this respect they discover a certain difference between sin and will. Will is one thing, they say, but a voluntary act is another. They mean that there is a distinction between will and what is done willingly. If, however, we call sin what we have already decided that it essentially is, namely, contempt of God or consent to that which we believe should not, for God's sake, be done how can we say that sin is voluntary? I mean, how can we say that we wish to despise God?[1] What is sin but sinking below a standard, or becoming liable to damnation? For although we desire to do what we know deserves punishment, yet we do not desire to be punished. Thus plainly we are reprobate. We are willing to do wrong; but we are unwilling to bear the just punishment of wrong-doing. The punishment which is just displeases: the deed which is unjust pleases. Often we woo a married woman because of her charm. Our wish is

not so much to commit adultery as a longing that she were unmarried. On the other hand, many covet the wives of influential men for the sake of their own fame, and not for the natural attractiveness of these ladies. Their wish is for adultery rather than sexual relationship, the major in preference to the minor excess. Some, too, are ashamed altogether of being betrayed into any consent to concupiscence or evil will; and thus from the weakness of the flesh are compelled to wish what they least of all wish to wish.

How, then, a wish which we do not wish to have can be called voluntary, as it is according to those thinkers I have mentioned, so that all sin becomes a matter of voluntary action, I assuredly do not understand unless by voluntary is meant that no action is determined, since a sin is never a predestined event. Or perhaps we are to take 'voluntary' to be that which proceeds from some kind of will. For although the man who slew his master had no will to perform the actual murder, nevertheless he did it from some sort of will, because he certainly wished to escape or defer death.

Some are intensely indignant when they hear us assert that the act of sinning adds nothing to guilt or damnation before God. Their contention is that in this act of sinning a certain delight supervenes, which increases the sin, as in sexual intercourse or indulgence in food which we referred to above. Their statement is absurd unless they can prove that physical delight of this kind is itself sin, and that such pleasure cannot be taken without a sin being thereby committed. If it be as they suppose, then no one is permitted to enjoy physical pleasure. The married do not escape sin when they employ their physical privilege; nor yet the man who eats with relish his own fruits.

Invalids, too, who are treated to more delicate dishes to aid their recovery of strength would likewise be guilty, since they are not able to eat without a sense of delight and should this be lacking, the food does them no good. Finally, God, the Creator of nourishment and of the bodies which receive it, would not be without guilt for having instilled savours which necessarily involve in sin those who ignorantly use them. Yet how should He supply such things for our consumption, or permit them to be consumed, if it were impossible for us to eat them without sin? How, again, can it be said that there is sin in doing what is allowed? In regard to those matters which once were unlawful and forbidden, if they are later allowed and made lawful, they can be done entirely without sin. For instance, the eating of pork and many other things once out of bounds to the Jew are now free to us Christians. When, therefore, we see Jews turned Christian gladly eating food of this sort which the law had prohibited, how can we defend their rectitude except by affirming that this latitude has now been conceded to them by God?

Well, in what was formerly a food restriction and is now food freedom, the concession of freedom excludes sin and eliminates contempt of God. Who then shall say that a man sins in respect of a matter which the divine permission has made lawful for him? If the marriage-bed or the eating of even delicate food was permitted from the first day of our creation, when we lived in Paradise without sin, who can prove that we transgress in these enjoyments, so long as we do not pass the limits of the permission? Another objection is that matrimonial intercourse and the eating of tasty food are only allowed on condition of being taken without pleasure. But, if this is so, then they are allowed to be done in a way in which they never can be done. That concession is not reasonable which concedes that a thing shall be so done as it is certain that it cannot be done. By what reasoning did the law aforetime enforce matrimony so that each might leave his seed to Israel? Or, how did the Apostle oblige wives to fulfil the mutual debt if these acts could not be done without sinning? How can he refer to this debt when already it is of necessity sin? Or how should a man be compelled to do what he will grieve God by doing? Hence, I think that it is plain that no natural physical delight can be set down as sin, nor can it be called guilt for men to delight in what,

when it is done, must involve the feeling of delight.

For example, if anyone obliged a monk, bound in chains, to lie among women, and the monk by the softness of the couch and by contact with his fair flatterers is allured into delight, though not into consent, who shall presume to designate guilt the delight which is naturally awakened?

You may urge, with some thinkers, that the carnal pleasure, even in lawful intercourse, involves sin. Thus David says: 'Behold in sin was I conceived.' (Ps. l, 7.) And the Apostle, when he had said: 'Ye return to it again' (I Cor. vii, 5), adds, nevertheless, 'This I say by way of concession, not of command.' (ibid., v, 6.) Yet authority rather than reason, seems to dictate the view that we should allow simple physical delight to be sin. For, assuredly, David was conceived not in fornication, but in matrimony: and concession, that is forgiveness, does not, as this standpoint avers, condone when there is no guilt to forgive. As for what David meant when he says that he had been conceived 'in iniquity' or 'in sin' and does not say 'whose' sin, he referred to the general curse of original sin, wherein from the guilt of our first parents each is subject to damnation, as it is elsewhere stated: 'None are pure of stain, not the infant a day old, if he has life on this earth.' As the blessed Jerome reminds us and as manifest reason teaches, the soul of a young child is without sin. If, then, it is pure of sin, how is it also impure by sinful corruption? We must understand the infant's purity from sin in reference to its personal guilt. But its contact with sinful corruption, its 'stain,' is in reference to penalty owed by mankind because of Adam's sin. He who has not yet perceived by reason what he ought to do cannot be guilty of contempt of God. Yet he is not free from the contamination of the sin of his first parents, from which he contracts the penalty, though not the guilt, and bears in penalty what they committed in guilt. When, therefore, David says that he was conceived in iniquity or sin, he sees himself subject to the general sentence of damnation from the guilt of his racial parents, and he assigns these sins, not to his fatther and mother but to his first parents.

When the Apostle speaks of indulgence, he must not be understood as some would wish to understand him, to mean permission to be equivalent to pardon for sin. His statement is: 'By way of indulgence not of command.' He might equally have said: 'By permission, not by force.' If husband and wife wish and decide upon mutual agreement they can abstain altogether from intercourse, and may not be compelled to it by command. But should they not so decide they have indulgence, that is, permission to substitute a less perfect for a more perfect rule of life. The Apostle, in this passage, did not therefore refer to pardon for sin, but to the permission of a less strict life for the avoidance of fornication. He meant that this lower level might elude the peaks of sin, and by its inferior standing escape the greater guilt.

We come, then, to this conclusion, that no one who sets out to assert that all fleshly desire is sin may say that the sin itself is increased by the doing of it. For this would mean extending the consent of the soul into the exercise of the action. In short, one would be stained not only by consent to baseness, but also by the mire of the deed, as if what happens externally in the body could possibly soil the soul. Sin is not, therefore, increased by the doing of an action: and nothing mars the soul except what is of its own nature, namely consent. This we affirmed was alone sin, preceding action in will, or subsequent to the performance of action. Although we wish for, or do, what is unseemly, we do not therefore sin. For such deeds not uncommonly occur without there being any sin. On the other hand, there may be consent without the external effects, as we have indicated. There was wish without consent in the case of the man who was attracted by a woman whom he caught sight of, or who was tempted by his neighbour's fruit, but who was not enticed into consent. There was evil consent without evil desire in the servant who unwillingly killed his master.

Certain acts which ought not to be done

often are done, and without any sin, when, for instance, they are committed under force or ignorance. No one, I think, ignores this fact. A woman under constraint of violence, lies with another's husband. A man, taken by some trick, sleeps with one whom he supposed to be his wife, or kills a man, in the belief that he himself has the right to be both judge and executioner. Thus to desire the wife of another or actually to lie with her is not sin. But to consent to that desire or to that action is sin. This consent to covetousness the law calls covetousness in saying: 'Thou shalt not covet.' (Deut. v, 21.) Yet that which we cannot avoid ought not to be forbidden, nor that wherein, as we said, we do not sin. But we should be cautioned about the consent to covetousness. So, too, the saying of the Lord must be understood: 'Whosoever shall look upon a woman to desire her.' (Matt. v, 28.) That is, whosoever shall so look upon her as to slip into consent to covetousness, 'has already committed adultery with her in his heart' (Matt. v, 28), even though he may not have committed adultery in deed. He is guilty of sin, though there be no sequel to his intention.

Careful account will reveal that wherever actions are restricted by some precept or prohibition, these refer rather to will and consent than to the deeds themselves. Otherwise nothing relative to a person's moral merit could be included under a precept. Indeed, actions are so much the less worth prescribing as they are less in our power to do. At the same time, many things we are forbidden to do for which there exists in our will both the inclination and the consent.

The Lord God says: 'Thou shalt not kill. Thou shalt not bear false witness.' (Deut. v, 17, 20.) If we accept these cautions as being only about actions, as the words suggest, then guilt is not forbidden, but simply the activity of guilt. For we have seen that actions may be carried out without sin, as that it is not sin to kill a man or to lie with another's wife. And even the man who desires to bear false testimony, and is willing to utter it, so long as he is silent for some reason and does not speak, is innocent before the law, that is, if the prohibition in this matter be accepted literally of the action. It is not said that we should not *wish* to give false witness, or that we should not *consent* in bearing it, but simply that we should not bear false witness.[2]

Similarly, when the law forbids us to marry or have intercourse with our sisters, if this prohibition relates to deed rather than to intention, no one can keep the commandment, for a sister unless we recognize her, is just a woman. If a man, then, marries his sister in error, is he a transgressor for doing what the law forbade? He is not, you will reply, because, in acting ignorantly in what he did, he did not consent to a transgression. Thus a transgressor is not one who *does* what is prohibited. He is one who *consents* to what is prohibited. The prohibition is, therefore, not about action, but about consent. It is as though in saying: 'Do not do this or that,' we meant: 'Do not consent to do this or that,' or, 'Do not wittingly do this.'

Blessed Augustine,[3] in his careful view of this question, reduces every sin or command to terms of charity and covetousness, and not to works. 'The law,' he says, 'inculcates nothing but charity, and forbids nothing but covetousness.' The Apostle, also, asserts: 'All the law is contained in one word: thou shalt love thy neighbour as thyself,' (Rom. xiii, 8, 10), and again, 'Love is the fulfilling of the law.' (ibid.)

Whether you actually give alms to a needy person, or charity makes you ready to give, makes no difference to the merit of the deed. The will may be there when the opportunity is not. Nor does it rest entirely with you to deal with every case of need which you encounter. Actions which are right and actions which are far from right are done by good and bad men alike. The intention alone separates the two classes of men.

Augustine reminds us that in the selfsame action we find God the Father, the Lord Jesus Christ, and also Judas the betrayer. The betrayal of the Son was accomplished by God the Father, and by the Son, and by the betrayer. For 'the Father delivered up the Son, and the Son Himself' (Rom. viii, 32; Gal. ii, 22), as the Apostle says, and Judas delivered up his Master. The traitor, therefore, did the same thing as God Himself. But did Judas do anything well? No. Good certainly came of his act; but his act was not well done, nor was it destined to benefit him.

God considers not the action, but the spirit of the action. It is the intention, not the deed wherein the merit or praise of the doer consists. Often, indeed, the same action is done from different motives: for justice sake by one man, for an evil reason by another. Two men, for instance, hang a guilty person. The one does it out of zeal for justice; the other in resentment for an earlier enmity. The action of hanging is the same. Both men do what is good and what justice demands. Yet the diversity of their intentions causes the same deed to be done from different motives, in the one case good, in the other bad.

Everyone knows that the devil himself does nothing without God's permission, when he either punishes a wicked man according to his deserts, or is allowed to afflict a just man for moral cleansing or for an example of endurance. Since, however, in doing what God permits the devil moves at the spur of his own malice, the power which he has may be called good, or even just, while his will is for ever unjust. He receives, that is, the power from God, but his will is of himself.

Who, among the elect, can ever emulate the deeds of hypocrites? Who, for the love of God, ever endures or undertakes so much as they do from thirst for human praise? Who does not agree that sometimes what God forbids may rightly be done, while, contrarily, He may counsel certain things which of all things are least convenient? We note how He forbade certain miracles, whereby He had healed infirmities, to be made public. He set an example of humility lest any man should claim glory for the grace bestowed on him. Nevertheless, the recipients of those benefits did not cease to broadcast them, to the praise of

Him who had done such things, and yet had forbidden them to be revealed. Thus we read: 'As much as He bade them not to speak, so much the more did they publish abroad, etc.' Will you judge these men guilty of a fault who acted contrary to the command which they had received, and did so wittingly? Who can acquit them of wrong-doing, unless by finding that they did not act out of contempt for the One who commanded, but decided to do what was to His honour? How, then, did the matter stand? Did Christ command what ought not to have been commanded? Or, did the newly-healed men disobey when they should have obeyed? The command was a good thing; yet it was not good for it to be obeyed.

In the case of Abraham, also, you will accuse God for first enjoining the sacrifice of Abraham's son, and then revoking the command. Has, then, God never *wisely commanded* anything which, if *it had come about*, would not have been good? If good, you will object, why was it afterwards forbidden? But conceive that it was good for the same thing to be prescribed and also to be prohibited. God, we know, permits nothing, and does not himself consent to achieve anything apart from rational cause. Thus it is the pure intention of the command, not the execution of the action which justifies God in wisely commanding what would not in actual fact be good. God did no intend Abraham to sacrifice his son, or command this sacrifice to be put into effect. His aim was to test Abraham's obedience, constancy of faith, and love towards Him, so that these qualities should be left to us as an example. This intention the Lord God plainly asserts afterwards in saying: 'Now know I that thou fearest the Lord.' (Gen. xxii, 12.) It is as if he frankly said: 'I commanded you: you showed yourself ready to obey Me. Both these things were done so that others might know what I had Myself known of you from the beginning.' There was a right intention on God's part; but it was not right for it to be put in practice. The prohibition, too, in the case of the miracles of healing was right. The object of this prohibition was not for it to be obeyed, but for an example to be given to our weak spirit in avoiding empty applause. God, in the one case enjoined an action which, if obeyed, would not have been good. In the other case, He forbade what was worth putting into fact, namely, a knowledge of Christ's miracles. The intention excuses Him in the first matter, just as the intention excuses the men who, in the second instance, were healed and did not carry out his injunction. They knew that the precept was not given to be practised, but in order that the aforenamed example of moderation in a successful miracle might be set. In keeping, then, the spirit of the command they showed, by actually disobeying no contempt for Him with whose intention they knew that they were acting.

A scrutiny of the deed rather than of the intention will reveal, then, cases where men frequently not only wish to go against God's bidding, but carry their wish knowingly into effect, and do so without any guilt of sin. An action or a wish must not be called bad because it does not in actual fact fall in with God's command. It may well be that the doer's intention does not at all differ from the will of his divine superior. The intention exonerates Him who gave a practically unseemly command: the intention excuses the man who, out of kindness, disobeyed the command to conceal the miracle.

Briefly to summarize the above argument: Four things ere postulated which must be carefully distinguished from one another.

1.   Imperfection of soul, making us liable to sin.
2.   Sin itself, which we decided is consent to evil or contempt of God.
3.   The will or desire of evil.
4.   The evil deed.

To wish is not the same thing as to fulfil a wish. Equally, to sin is not the same as to carry out a sin. In the first case, we sin by consent of the soul: the second is a matter of the external effect of an action, namely, when we fulfil in deed that whereunto we have previously consented. When, therefore, temptation is said to proceed through three stages, suggestion, delight, consent, it must be understood that, like our first parents, we are frequently led along these three paths to the commission of sin. The devil's persuasion comes *first* promising from the taste of the forbidden fruit immortality. Delight follows. When the woman sees the beautiful tree, and perceives that the fruit is good, her appetite is whetted by the anticipated pleasure of tasting. This desire she ought to have repressed, so as to obey God's command. But in consenting to it, she was drawn *secondly* into sin. By penitence she should have put right this fault, and obtained pardon. Instead, she *thirdly* consummated the sin by the deed. Eve thus passed through the three stages to the commission of sin.

By the same avenues we also arrive not at sin, but at the action of sin, namely, the doing of an unseemly deed through the suggestion or prompting of something within us. If we already know that such a deed will be pleasant, our imagination is held by anticipatory delight and we are tempted thereby in thought. So long as we give consent to such delight, we sin. Lastly, we pass to the third stage, and actually commit the sin.

It is agreed by some thinkers that carnal suggestion, even though the person causing the suggestion be not present, should be included under sinful suggestion. For example, a man having seen a woman falls into a sensual desire of her. But it seems that this kind of suggestion should simply be called delight. This delight, and other delights of the like kind, arise naturally and, as we said above, they are not sinful. The Apostle calls them 'human temptations.' 'No temptation has taken you yet which was not common to men. God is faithful, and will not suffer you to be tempted above what you are able; but will, with the temptation make a way of escape, that you may be able to bear it.' By temptation is meant, in general, any movement of the soul to do something unseemly, whether in wish or consent. We speak of human temptation without which it is hardly or never possible for human weakness to exist. Such are sexual desire, or the pleasures of the table. From these the Psalmist asks to be delivered when he says: 'Deliver me from my wants, O Lord' (Ps. xxiv, 17); that is, from the temptations of natural and necessary appetites that they may not influence him into sinful consent. Or, he may mean: 'When this life is over, grant me to be without those temptations of which life has been full.'

When the Apostle says: 'No temptation has taken you but what is human,' his statement amounts to this: Even if the soul be stirred by that delight which is, as we said, human temptation, yet God would not lead the soul into that consent wherein sin consists. Someone may object: But by what power of our own are we able to resist those desires? We may reply: 'God is faithful, who will not allow you to be tempted,' as the Scripture says. In other words: We should rather trust him than rely upon ourselves. He promises help, and is true to his promises. He is faithful, so that we should have complete faith in him. Out of pity God diminishes the degree of human temptation, 'does not suffer us to be tempted above what we are able,' in order that it may not drive us to sin at a pace we cannot endure, when, that is, we strive to resist it. Then, too, God turns the temptation to our advantage: for He trains us thereby so that the recurrence of temptation causes us less care, and we fear less the onset of a foe over whom we have already triumphed, and whom we know how to meet.

Every encounter, not as yet undertaken, is for that reason, to us, a matter of more anxiety and dismay. But when such an encounter comes to those accustomed to victory, its force and terror alike vanish.

Chapter IV

Diabolical Suggestion

There are suggestions of demons, as well as of men. Demons stimulate to sin not so much by words as by opportunities. Skilled in natural matters, both by subtlety of spirit and long experience, whence they are called 'daemones,' i.e., *skilful*,[4] they know the inherent nature or force of things whereby human frailty can easily be led into lust and other impulses.

With God's permission they also often send men into a stupor and provide remedies for it when men ask their aid. When they cease to injure 'tis said, they begin to cure. In Egypt they were allowed, through magicians, to work wonderfully against Moses. Indeed, by their insight into the nature of things they must be named 'promoters' rather than creators of what they accomplish; just as the man who, in Virgil (*Georg.*, Bk. IV, v, 310), made bees come out of the tanned hide of a bull, would be called not a creator of bees, so much as a fitter of nature's parts.

Demons, by this skill in the nature of things, bewitch us into lust or other passions, arousing them by some art we wot not of, bestirring them as we eat or lie a-bed; or somehow insinuating them from within or without. In herbs or seeds, or in the nature of trees and stones, are many powers apt to stimulate or mollify the mind. Diligent study of them brings facility in their use.

Chapter V

Crime and Inward Guilt: Their Respective Punishments

'The sinful action is not strictly sin; it adds nothing to the sum of sin.' Our axiom, so enunciated, falls on dissentient ears. 'Why, then,' it is asked 'give a more severe penance for sins of commission than for guilty thoughts?' But let them reflect whether sometimes a grave penance be not imposed where no guilt called for pardon. Are there not times when we must punish those whom we know to be innocent?

A poor woman has a child at the breast. She lacks the clothing needful for herself and for the babe in the cradle. Prompted by pity, she lays the infant in her own bed so as to cherish him with her clothes. Nature, however, overcomes her, and, in sleep, she stifles the child whom she yet embraces with the greatest love. 'Have love,' says Augustine, 'and do as thou wilt.' Yet when she goes to the bishop for penance, a heavy penalty is pronounced upon her, not for the fault, but that she herself a second time, and other women, may be more careful in such a situation.

Again, a man may be accused by his enemies before the judge, and a charge made against him whereof the judge knows that the man is innocent. His enemies, however, persist and are importunate for a hearing. On the appointed day they begin the case and adduce false witnesses to get their man convicted. By no clear reasons can the judge take exception to these witnesses; and he is compelled by law to admit them. Their proof prevails. The judge has to punish an innocent man who ought not to be punished. The accused merited no penalty; but the judge, justly in the legal aspect, had to impose one. Plainly, therefore, a man may frequently be the subject of a justifiable sentence without the anterior fault. Is it any wonder, then, if there be preceding guilt, that the subsequent act of crime should increase the penalty required by men in this life, although the guilt and not the act of crime is what begets the penalty required by God in a future life? Men judge of visible, and not of invisible fact. They do not estimate the error, so much as the effect of an action. God alone considers the spirit in which a thing is done, rather than merely what is done. He weighs accurately the guilt in our intention, and assesses our fault by a true test. Hence he 'proves the heart and reins' (Jer. xx, 12), and 'sees in secret.' (Matt. vi, 4.) Where no man sees, there God sees. In punishing sin he regards not the work, but the will. We, contrarily, regard not the will, which we do not see, but the work which we do see. Frequently, therefore, by mistake, or, as we have said, under stress of law, we punish the innocent or acquit the guilty. 'He tries the heart and reins.' God discerns, that is to say, the *intentions*, of whatever sort, which spring from the disposition or weakness of the soul, or from physical delight.

Chapter VI

Spiritual and Carnal Sins

All sins are of the mind only, for there alone can be the crime and the contempt of God, where is the seat of the knowledge of Him, and where reason resides. Certain sins, nevertheless, are called spiritual, others carnal. The spiritual sins proceed from the imperfection of the mind, the carnal from the weakness of the flesh. Now it is impossible to lust after or desire anything except by an act of will. Although, therefore, desire belongs to the mind alone, will concerns both the flesh and also the spirit. 'The flesh,' says the Apostle, 'lusteth against the spirit, and the spirit against the flesh.' (Gal. v, 7.) Out of fleshly delight the soul desires certain things which, on the verdict of reason, it either recoils from or rebukes.

Chapter VII

Why Is God Called 'Inspector Cordis et Renum,' i.e., Said to Try the Heart and Reins?

These two desires of the flesh, and of the spirit are, then, distinguished. Now God has been called the 'one who tries the heart and reins.' He scrutinizes, that is to say, intentions and the consents which proceed from them. We on our part cannnot discuss and decide these issues of intention, but address our censure to deeds. We punish facts rather than faults. Injury to the soul we do not regard as so much a matter for punishment as injury to others. Our object is to avoid public mischief, rather than to correct personal mistakes. The Lord said to Peter: 'If thy brother sin against thee, correct him between thyself and him.' (Matt. xviii, 15.) 'Sin against thee.' Is the meaning here that we ought to correct and punish injuries done to us and not those done to others, as though 'against thee' meant 'not against another?' By no means. The phrase 'if he sin against thee' means that he acts publicly so as to corrupt you by his example. For if

he sins against himself only, his sin, being hidden, involves in guilt merely the man himself. The sin does not, by the sinner's bad example, induce others to indiscretion. Although the evil action has no imitators, or even none who recognize it as wrong, nevertheless, in so far as it is a public act it must, in human society, be chastised more than private guilt, because it can occasion greater mischief, and can be more destructive, by the example it sets, than the hidden failing. Everything which is likely to lead to common loss or to public harm must be punished by a greater requital. Where a sin involves more serious injury the penalty must therefore be heavier. The greater the social stumbling-block, the more stringent must be the social correction, even though the original guilt be relatively light.

Suppose, for example, that someone has, by evil intercourse, corrupted a woman in a church. The people hear of the incident. But they are not roused so much by the violation of a woman, the true temple of God, as by the desecration of the material temple, the church. This is the case even though, admittedly, a wall is of less consequence than a woman, and it is more grievous to harm a human being than a place. Again, the setting fire to houses we punish more severely than fornication. But with God the latter incurs a far greater sentence.

The punishment of public guilt is not so much a debt paid to justice as the exercise of economy. We consult the common interest, as has been said by checking social mischief. Frequently we punish minor misdeeds with major penalties. In doing so, we do not, in a spirit of pure justice ponder what guilt preceded; but, by shrewd foresight, we estimate the damage which may ensue if the deed be lightly dealt with. We reserve, therefore, sins of the soul for the divine judgment. But the effect of these sins, about which we have to determine, we follow up, by our own judgment, employing a certain economy, that is, the rule of prudence referred to above, rather than the precept of equity.

God assigns the penalty of each crime according to the measure of guilt. The degree of contempt displayed by men to God is afterwards proportionately punished, whatever be their condition or calling. Suppose that a monk and a lay-brother both fall into consent to an act of fornication. If the mind of the lay-brother be so inflamed that he would not abstain from shame out of reverence for God, even if he had been a monk, then the lay-brother deserves the same penalty as the monk.

The same notion applies where one man, sinning openly, offends many, and corrupts them by his example; while another man sins in secret, and injures only himself. For the secret sinner, if his intention and his contempt of God are identical with those of the open sinner, rather by accident does not corrupt others. The man who does not restrain himself out of respect for God would hardly refrain, for the same reason from public crime. In God's sight, assuredly, he is committed on a similar charge to that of the open sinner. For, in the recompense of good or evil, God notes the soul alone, not its external effects, and counts what comes from our guilt or good will. It is the soul in its scheme of intention, not in the outward result of its action, that God assesses. There are actions, as we said, common to sinners and saints, all of them in themselves indifferent and only to be called bad or good according to the intention of the agent. Such actions are so described not because it is good or bad for them to be done, but because they are done *well*, or *ill*; that is, they are performed with a seemly, or unseemly intention.

For, as Blessed Augustine reminds us, it is good for a man to be bad since God may use him for a good end, and may not allow him to be otherwise even though his condition be altogether evil.

When, therefore, we call the intention of a man good, and his deed good also, we distinguish two things, intention and deed. Nevertheless, there is only one goodness of intention. It is like speaking of a good man, and the son of a good man. We imagine two men, but not two goodnesses. A man is called good because of his own goodness. But when the son of a good man is spoken of, it is clear that he cannot have good in him just because he is a good man's son. Similarly, everyone's intention is called good in itself. But the deed is not called good in itself, for it only proceeds from a good intention. Thus, there is one goodness, whence both intention and deed are designated good, just as there is one goodness from which a good man and the son of a good man are named; or one goodness by which a good man, and the will of a good man can each be explained.

The objection of some who say that the deed merits equal recompense with the intention, or even an additional recompense, may be proved nonsensical. 'There are two goods,' they exclaim, 'the good intention, and the carrying out of the good intention. Good added to good ought to be worth more than a single good.'

Our reply is: 'Granted that the whole is worth more than the separate parts, must we admit that it merits greater reward?' Not at all. There are many animate and inanimate things which, in large numbers, are useful for more purposes than any one of the number would be alone. Nevertheless, no additional reward is thought to be due to them on that account. For instance, an ox joined to another ox or a horse to a horse; or, again, wood added to wood or iron to iron; these things are good, and a number of them is worth more than each singly. Yet they are not more highly praised when it is seen that two of them put together can do more than one by itself.

True, you say, it is so; but only because these things could never deserve anything, being without reason. Well; but has our deed any reason, so as to be able to deserve praise or blame? None, you say; by our action is said to have merit because it imparts merit to us, making us worthy of reward, or, at any rate, or greater reward. Now it is this very statement which we have denied above. Consider why it is false, apart from what we have already said. Two men set about the same scheme of building poorhouses. One man completes the object to which he devotes himself. The other has the money which he put by stolen forcibly from him, and through no fault of his own—prevented simply by burglary—is not able to conclude what he intended to do. Can the external fact, that the almshouses are unbuilt, lessen his merit with God, or shall the malice of another make the man who did what he could for God less acceptable to God?

Otherwise, the size of his purse could make a man better and worthier, if property had any bearing upon moral merit or the increase of merit. The richer men were, the better they could be, since from their stock of wealth they would be able to augment their piety by their philanthropy.[5] But it is the height of insanity to assume that wealth can confer true bliss or dignity of the soul, or detract from the merit of poor men. If property cannot make a soul better, then it cannot make the soul dearer to God, nor get any bliss of moral merit.

Chapter VIII

Recompense of Actions

We do not, however, deny that in this life some recompense should be made for good and bad deeds, so that by means of reward and punishment in the present we may be stirred to good actions or restrained from bad ones. People may also profit by the examples of others in this way. They can copy what is fit and agreeable, and avoid what is not.

Chapter IX

God and Man United in Christ Is Not Something Better than God Alone

Let us resume the argument (Ch. VII). When it is asserted that good added to good achieves something better than one of these goods by itself, beware of being led to say that Christ, that is, God and man united mutually in a person, is something better than the divinity of Christ or than the humanity of Christ, that is to say that this union is more than God united with man, or man's nature taken by God. It is agreed that, in Christ, man's nature was assumed, and that

God, who assumed it, was good. Both substances, human and divine, can only be understood as good. Similarly in individual men, the body and the soul, the corporeal and the incorporeal, are alike good. The goodness of the body does not effect the honour or merit of the soul. But who will dare to prefer the whole which is called Christ, namely, God and man, or any group of things to God Himself, as though there could be anything better than Him, Who is the highest good, and from Whom all things receive whatever good they possess? For although some things seem to be so necessary to achieving action that God cannot, as it were, do without them, as being auxiliary or originative casues, yet let there be the largest assembly of things imaginable, nothing can possibly surpass God. Suppose that the number of good things be known, so that we have goodness in many particular cases, still it does not come about, for that reason, that the goodness itself is greater. The same is true of knowledge, which may exist in many minds; or the number of known things may increase, but on that account, knowledge itself does not necessarily grow and become greater than it was before. So, since God is good in Himself, and creates innumerable things, which would neither exist or be good apart from Him, goodness exists in many things through Him, and the number of good things may get greater, yet no goodness can be preferred to or equal His goodness. Goodness exists in man, and goodness exists in God. The substances or natures wherein goodness exists are different: and the goodness of a thing can never be preferred to or equal the divine goodness. For this reason, we cannot speak of anything as better, that is to say, a greater good than God, or of anything equally good.

Chapter X

A Number of Good Things Is Not Better than One of These Good Things

The number of actions is of no importance for their intention. For to speak of good intention and good action, that is action proceeding from good intention, is to refer merely to the goodness of the intention. We cannot retain the term good in this same sense and talk of many 'goods.'

When we say that a man is simple, and speech simple, we do not therefore allow that there exist many 'simples' just because this word 'simple' is employed in the first instance of a man, and in the second instance of speech. No one can then compel us to concede that when the good act is added to the good intention, good is added to good, as though there could be many goods in proportion to whose number recompense ought to be increased. As we have said, we cannot call those actions 'additional goods,' for the word 'good' does not properly apply to them.

Chapter XI

The Good Action Springs from the Good Intention

We call the intention good which is right in itself, but the action is good, not because it contains within it some good, but because it issues from a good intention. The same act may be done by the same man at different times. According to the diversity of his intention, however, this act may be at one time good, at another bad. So goodness and badness vary. Compare the proposition: 'Socrates sits.' One conceives this statement either truly or falsely according as Socrates actually does sit, or stands. This alteration in truth and falsity, Aristotle affirms, comes about not from any change in the circumstances which compose the true or false situation, but because the subject-matter of the statement (that is, Socrates) moves in itself, I mean changes from sitting to standing or vice versa.[6]

Chapter XII

What Are the Grounds of Good Intention?

Good or right intention is held by some to be when anyone believes that he acts

well, and that what he does pleases God. An example is supplied by those who persecuted the martyrs. About them the Gospel Truth says: 'The hour comes when everyone who kills you will think that he is obedient to God.' (John xvi, 2.) In sympathy with the ignorance of such the Apostle exclaims: 'I bear this testimony on their behalf, that they are zealous for God but not according to knowledge.' That is to say, they are fervently eager to do what they believe pleases God. Since, however, in this desire or keenness of mind they are deceived, their intention is a mistake. The eye of the heart is not so simple as to be capable of seeing clearly and to guard itself from error. For this reason the Lord, when he distinguished works according to right and wrong intention, spoke of the eye of the mind, that is the intention, as either *single*, pure, as it were, from spot, so that it could see clearly, or, on the contrary, as *clouded*. 'If thine eye be single, thy whole body shall be full of light.' This means that, provided the intention was right, all the acts proceeding from the intention which can possibly be foreseen in the manner of mortal affairs, will be worthy of the light; that is to say, good. And, contrarily, from wrong intention arise dark deeds.

The intention, therefore, must not be called good, merely because it seems good, but over and above this, because it is such as it is estimated to be. I mean that, if it thinks to please God in what it aims at its aim therein should not be mistaken. Otherwise the heathen, just like us, could count their good works, since they no less than we believe themselves either to be saved or to please God by their deeds.[7]

Chapter XIII

No Sin Save That Against Conscience

The question may be asked whether the persecutors of the martyrs or of Christ erred because they believed that they were pleasing God, or whether they could do without sin what they at heart thought should never be done, especially in view of the above analysis of sin as 'contempt of God,' or 'consent to that whereto consent ought not to be given.' We cannot say that they did sin in this respect: nor can we call anyone's ignorance or even the infidelity (having which no man may be saved) a sin. They who know not Christ, and reject the Christian faith because they believe that it is contrary to God, what contempt of God do they show in this act which is really done on behalf of God? On this latter account, indeed, they think to do well, particularly when the Apostle says: 'If our heart does not condemn us, we have confidence with God.' (I John iii, 2), as though he said: 'when we do not violate our conscience, we have little fear of God holding us guilty of a fault.' If ignorance must least of all be reckoned as sin, how, it may be urged, does the Lord Himself pray for those who crucify Him saying: 'Father, forgive them: for they know not what they do.'—(Luke xxiii, 34) or, taught by this example, how can Stephen supplicate for the men who stone him: 'Father, lay not this sin to their charge.' (Acts vii, 59)? We must proceed to deal with this question. For, it will be insisted, where guilt does not go first there is no need, later, of pardon. And to be pardoned is simply to have the penalty remitted which the crime warranted. Moreover, Stephen clearly calls sin that which came about from ignorance.

Chapter XIV

Various Uses of the Word 'Sin'

To reply more fully to these objections it must be understood that the term 'sin' can be taken in different ways, although, properly speaking, sin is the actual *contempt of God*, or *consent to evil* as we recalled just now. The young are immune from sin; so, too, are idiots. These two classes, lacking reason, cannot claim merit and nothing can be imputed to them for sin. They are saved only by the sacraments. Sin is spoken of with the meaning 'a sacrifice for sin.' The Apostle, for instance, says that our Lord Je-

sus Christ was made 'sin.'[8] The 'penalty of sin' is called simply sin or 'curse' when we say sin is destroyed, that is the penalty remitted; and, again, when it is said that Jesus Christ bore our sins, that is, He endured the punishment of our sins or their possible punishment.

The statement that infants have original sin or that all, as the Apostle says, have sinned in Adam is the same as saying that from Adam's sin arose the sense of our punishment or damnation for sin. Sinful deeds, provided we either do not rightly know them as such, or do not really wish to do them, are not at all to be termed sins. For what is sinning against anyone but the putting into effect of the evil intention? It is not unusual when, contrariwise, we refer, with Athanasius, to sins as if they were deeds. 'And they shall give an account,' he says, 'of their own deeds. They who have done good deeds shall go into enternal life; they who have done evil, into everlasting fire.' What, then, is 'their own deeds'? Is judgment merely to be about what has been fulfilled in action, that a man may receive more in recompense in proportion as he offers more in effects? Is he who came short in effecting what he intended immune from damnation, like the devil who designed cunningly, but failed in fact? Certainly not. In speaking of 'their own deeds' the scripture means what they consented to, what they determined to carry out, that is, about sins of intention, the things which, in God's sight, they are considered to have actually done, since He punishes intentions as we punish deeds.

Stephen, however, speaks of the sin which the Jews, out of ignorance, committed against him. By this he means the punishment itself which he was enduring and which resulted from the sin of our first parent, just like other punishment issuing from the same source, or, in a word, the injustice of their action in stoning him. And when Stephen prayed that it might not be laid to their charge, he meant that they should not be physically punished for it. For not seldom God punishes some people physically when no fault of theirs warrants it. God does so not without a reason, as when He sends affliction upon the just to purge or prove them; or gain, when he permits some to be in distress that they may afterwards be freed and glorify God for the benefit obtained. We have, for instance, the case of the blind man about whom the Saviour says: 'Neither did this man sin, nor his parents that he was born blind, but that the works of God might become manifest in him.' (John ix, 2.)

You may notice, too, that innocent sons may be endangered or afflicted along with their evil parents and because of their parents' guilt, as was the case at Sodom, and as often occurs. The object is to inspire the wicked to greater terror as they see the punishment more widely extended. It was therefore this kind of sin, namely the punishment which he endured from the Jews and which they unjustly put into effect, which Blessed Stephen contemplated with patience. He prayed that it might not be laid to their charge. That is, that they should not suffer the physical punishment which God gives for peoples' well-being even though they have not sinned in intention.

Our Master also was of this mind in saying: 'Father, forgive them.' (Luke xxiii, 34.) He meant: 'Do not avenge their action against Me with a physical penalty.' This could reasonably have come about even had no guilt of theirs gone before. By such punishment other people, and those Jews themselves, would have realized that in their deed they had not done rightly. Well did the Lord by this example of His prayer exhort us to the power of patience and to an expression of the highest love. Thereby through His own example he showed to us in deed what He had taught in word, that we also should pray for our enemies. The saying, 'forgive,' did not refer to preceding guilt or contempt of God, but to God's reasonable right of inflicting punishment. A divine penalty might, as we said, ensue for which there could be good reason even though actual guilt had not preceded it. An instance occurs in the case of the prophet sent to speak against Samaria, who passed

the time in eating, God having forbidden him to do this. He was tricked by another prophet, and could not be charged with contempt of God. He incurred death innocently, and more because he had done a deed than from real guilt. For Blessed Gregory reminds us: 'God sometimes alters his sentence, but never His plan.' God often withdraws from effect a lesson or threat which he had been disposed to employ. His plan, however, remains firm. What He wills, in prescience, to accomplish never comes short of attainment. He did not abide, for instance, by His injuction to Abraham to immolate his son, nor by his threat against the Ninevites. He changed, as we said, his sentence. Similarly the aforementioned prophet, whom God had forbidden to eat on his journey, believed that God had altered his resolution. The prophet thought that he would be in the wrong if he gave no heed to the other prophet, who asserted that he had been sent by God for the very purpose of refreshing that prophet's faintness with food. He acted without fault, therefore, in as much as he determined to avoid a fault. The sudden death did not harm him. It set him free from the cares of this life and was a salutary caution to many. For they might behold the punishment of a man, just and faultless, and the fulfilment of the saying: 'Thou, O God, art just and disposest all things justly: him also who deserves no penalty thou dost condemn.'[9] 'Thou condemnest,' the scripture implies, 'not to eternal, but to physical death.' We may compare the fact that some are saved without merit of their own, as for instance, infants, and attain eternal life by grace alone. Equally, it is not fantastic that some should endure physical penalties which they have not merited. This is the case with infants deceased without the grace of baptism. They are damned, physically and eternally. Many innocent people are also afflicted. What wonder, therefore, if those who crucified the Lord should reasonably incur punishment, though not eternal, albeit their ignorance excuses them from real guilt! Thus was said: 'forgive them,' or 'do not put into effect the punishment which they may, with good reason, incur from this insult.'

The actions which those men committed out of ignorance, or, if you will, ignorance itself is not properly called sin, that is contempt of God. Nor, also, is infidelity, under these circumstances, to be called sin, although of necessity it involves exclusion from eternal life for those who are rationally full-grown. Disbelief in the Gospel, not to recognize Christ, refusal of the Church sacraments, each of these, though they come less from malice than as a result of ignorance are reasons for damnation. The Truth speaks of such: 'He who believes not is already judged.' (John iii, 18.) The Apostle also: 'He who does not know shall not be known,' (I Cor. xiv, 38.) But when we say that we sin ignorantly, that is, do what is not seemly, we take sin of this sort to be not in real contempt, but in action only. Philosophers call it a fault to express an idea in unfitting fashion, even though this mistake may not seem to do offence to God. Aristotle, for instance, speaks somewhere about the wrong description of relations. Unless the terms of a statement are properly placed a wrong notion will be the result. Thus a wing may be predicated as 'of a bird,' but it would be a fault to make a phrase 'the bird of a wing.'

Now, if in this sort of fashion we can speak of sin, then everything which we do unsuitably or which we cling to contrary to our well-being—infidelity and ignorance of beliefs which are necessary to salvation—all this we can speak of as 'sins,' although no contempt of God appears in them. But I feel that, properly speaking, sin is that which can never come about without personal guilt. Not to know God, to have no belief in Him, to do wrongly under a misapprehension—such things can be found in many a life without there being real fault. A man, for example, may not believe in the Gospel or in Christ because he has heard no preacher. 'How shall they believe who have not heard? How shall they hear without a preacher.' (Romans x, 14.) What blame is to be attributed to such a

man for not believing? Cornelius did not believe in Christ until Peter came and gave him instruction. He had known and loved God before by natural law, and, by reason of this, deserved to be heard in his prayer and to find favour in his almsgiving. But if, prior to faith in Christ, he had perchance been untrue to the light of conscience, we should not dare to promise him life, however good his deeds, and we should have to count him not among the faithful, but rather, despite his zeal of salvation, among the unfaithful. Many of God's decisions are a mystery. He draws to Himself those who hold back or are least concerned with their own salvation, but, in the profound wisdom of his plan he rejects the forward convert and the overwilling believer. Thus the zealous volunteer—'Master, I will follow thee withersoever thou goest'—met with reproof. When another excused himself on the ground of solicitude for his father, the Saviour did not even for a moment admit this plea of filial regard. Again, in his onslaught on the obstinacy of certain cities the Lord says: 'Woe to thee, Chorazin! woe to thee, Bethsaida! For if the mighty works had been done in Tyre and Sidon which have been done among you, they would have repented long ago in sackcloth and ashes.' (Matt. xi. 21.) He confronted these cities, Bethsaida and Chorazin, not only with his preaching, but also with his miracles, though he had anticipated that they would not receive them with respect. The other Gentile cities, Tyre and Sidon, as he knew, would easily have received the evangel. While he thought that a visit to them was unwarranted, he knew that certain people in these cities had been ready to accept the word of preaching. And yet these people perished with their cities. Who, then, can impute to their guilt the destruction which undoubtedly came about through no disregard of theirs?[10] Nevertheless, we affirm that their infidelity, wherein they died, suffices for damnation, although the reason for this blindness in which the Lord left them remains less clear. One may, perhaps, set it down to their sin, which was a mistake but not a guilty mistake. For, is it not absurd for such persons to be damned if they have not done some kind of sinful deed?

The contention, however, which for some time we have kept in mind is that sin is simply guilty neglect. It cannot exist in anyone, young or old, without their deserving damnation thereby. I do not see how it can be ascribed to guilt if infants or those to whom the Gospel has not been announced do not believe in Christ. It is infidelity; but not guilt, any more than anything which occurs through invincible ignorance, and which we cannot foresee is guilt, e.g., when a man accidentally kills another in a forest with an arrow, not seeing the man and thinking to slay only birds or wild beasts. In such a case we say that he 'sins' from ignorance just as we may say that we 'sin' not only in consent, but in imagination. But we do not here mean sin to be the same as guilt. We use the term 'sin' widely for what little beseems us to do, whether it come about from a mistake, from neglect, or from some other remissness. This, then, is our definition of the sin of ignorance: to do without guilt what we should not do: to do or, if you like, sin in imagination, i.e., to wish for what is not fitting for us; or in speech, or in act, speaking or doing what we ought not; and to do such things out of ignorance and unwittingly. The persecutors of Christ and of their own kinsfolk whom they thought ought to be persecuted, may be said to have sinned in action only (*per operationem*). But they would have sinned really and more grievously, had they contrary to their conscience, permitted their victims to go free.

Chapter XV

Is Every Sin Prohibited?

It may be asked whether God forbids us altogether to sin. If so, then He appears to act unreasonably. This life of ours cannot be lived without at least venial sins.[11] If God meant us to avoid all sins, which is impossible, He would then have promised us no easy yoke and placed on us no light burden, but one which exceeds our strength and which we should support feebly like that yoke of the law of which the apostle Peter spoke. For who can provide against the idle word so as ever without contumely to preserve that perfection whereof James says: 'If any stumbleth not in word, the same is a perfect man.' (James iii, 2.) The same writer, however, observes: 'In many things we have all offended.' And another apostle of great excellence says: 'If we say that we have no sin we deceive ourselves and the truth is not in us.' (I John i, 18.) All, I think, are aware how difficult and, indeed, impossible, it seems to our weak nature for us to remain entirely immune from sin. Thus, if we take the term 'sin' generally we shall affirm sin to be everything which we do unfittingly. On the other hand, if strictly speaking we understand by sin simply contempt of God, then it is truly possible for our life to be passed without sin, though this will involve the greatest difficulty. Sin, as we said, is not prohibited by God, but only consent to evil whereby we despise God: and this is forbidden even though it seems, in the practice of it, to give moral instruction. This has been explained above, where we have also shown that in no other way can we keep God's commandments.

Some sins are spoken of as venial or light, and others are called damnable or grave. Again of damnable sins some are called criminous, which can make a person infamous or criminous if they become known; while others are hardly of this sort at all. Venial sins are such as we consent to, knowing that we should not give consent. But the memory of what we know does not at the moment recur to our mind. For we can know many things even when asleep or when we are unconscious of knowing them. We do not lose our knowledge in sleep. If we did, we should become fools, or else develop wisdom by keeping awake. When, therefore, we give way to flippancy or excessive eating or drinking, we know that this ought not to be done. But at the time we are least aware of the restriction. Such consent, arising from absent-mindedness, is called venial or slight; and not needing correction by a grave penalty. For such sin we are not excluded from the Church, or put under the strain of severe self-denial. These peccadillos are remitted for the penitent by the words of daily confession wherein is no mention of the more grievous but only of small faults; and in daily prayer we are not to avow: 'I have sinned by perjury, homicide, adultery, and the like,' which are mortal and more serious sins. These latter, unlike the former, are not entered upon from short-sightedness. We commit that kind of crime with close attention and set purpose: and become anathema to God, as the Psalmist says: 'They have become abominable in their ways.' (Ps. xiii, 2.) He refers to men who were unholy and hateful inasmuch as they offended wittingly. Of this sort of sin some is called criminous which, being of known effect, demoralizes a man by the stain of great guilt. Such are conscious perjury, homicide or adultery, which chief of all are a scandal to the Church. If, however, we exceed sufficiency by over-eating at table, or adorn our person, out of vain glory, in extravagant attire, and are conscious of going to an excess in this way, our fault is not commonly reckoned criminous.[12] Many, indeed, give these foibles more praise than blame.

Chapter XVI

Slight and Serious Sins. Of Which Is It Best to Beware?[13]

The avoidance of venial in contrast to criminal sins is by some thinkers insisted on, because, as they hold, such is the more complete and the better method of conduct, and in its greater difficulty calls for a stricter effort. Our immediate reply to this argument is in a line of Cicero. *The laborious is not therefore the glorious.* But if they are right, then those who bore the heavy weight of the law had more worth before God than those who serve Him with the Gospel freedom. Fear has punishment which perfect love casteth out, and to be

driven by fear makes men drudge more than they would if they acted spontaneously out of love. For this reason the heavy-laden are urged by the Lord to His easy yoke, and to take up a light burden. They are to leave the slavery of the law whereby they are weighted down, for the liberty of the Gospel: so that though beginning in fear they may end in love which, without difficulty, 'beareth all things, endureth all things.' Nothing is hard to one who loves. The love of God is spiritual, not carnal, and all the stronger because it is truer.

Who doubts that it is harder for us to guard against a flea than an enemy, or the injury of a little flint than of a large stone?

But as to that which gives us greater difficulty in guarding against it, do we consider it to be therefore the better and more sound achievement? We do not. And why not? Because what is more difficult to beware of is less likely to injure. Although, then, our view is that it is harder to be rid of venial than of criminal faults, yet it is the latter that should be avoided as compared with the former. We ought to steer clear of those sins by which we believe that God is most likely to be offended. These merit the greater condemnation and displease Him the more. As love brings us nearer to God we should be more carefully averse from giving Him an affront and from doing what He more plainly disapproves. The lover is anxious less on account of his own loss than for any injury or contempt of his friend. Thus the Apostle: 'Love seeketh not her own.' (I Cor. xiii, 5); and again: 'Let no one look to the things of himself, but to those of others.' If it is our duty, then, to avoid faults not so much in view of our own loss, but of their offence to God, it is evident that those sins should be guarded against whereby God will be the more grieved. We may listen to the line of the poet on moral honour:

From love of virtue good men hate to sin.[14]

It is evident that certain things must give rise to particular disgust as being objectionable in themselves and causing hurt to other people.

Finally, in order to distinguish faults by

a closer inspection, let us compare the venial and the criminous. Take, for instance, over-indulgence at the table and compare it with perjury and adultery. Let us ask, by which of these trespasses is the greater sin committed, or by which of them is God the more despised and affronted. 'I know not,' you may perhaps reply, 'for some philosophers have thought all faults to be equal.' But if you desire to follow this philosophy or rather avowed foolishness, then it is equally good to abstain either from criminous or venial faults, for to commit either the one or the other is alike bad. Why, too, should anyone aver that it is preferable to abstain from venial rather than from criminal faults? Should anyone ask how we can tell that the transgression of adultery displeases God more than excess of eating, it is, as I think, the divine law which instructs us. For the punishment of over-eating there has been laid down no penalty, whereas adultery is to be avenged not by this or that punishment but by death. In proportion as love—which the Apostle calls 'fulfilling of the law'—is injured, by so much is the action contrary to love, and therefore the sin is the more grievous.

Even when we set particular sins of a venial and criminous kind side by side and compare them so as to satisfy every possibility I still hold to my point. Assume that a man uses every care to abstain from the venial and yet makes no attempt to avoid criminal faults. Now because he keeps clear of all light contamination there arises this question: who shall decide that he sins more lightly or is better for avoiding venial sin, but being liable to criminal? There is no 'worse' or 'better' in his case because he has left the light sins and given an opening for the grave ones. In fact, should we compare sins singly, as I said, or in general, the conclusion is that to avoid the venial rather than the criminal is not a superior way or the sign of greater perfection. Anyone, however, who by avoiding first the venial fault is strengthened to combat later the criminal has, in this respect, come towards perfection. But we must beware of regarding these later victories, which elicit the height of courage, as overtopping the earlier points of valour or meriting a great recompense. Often in the building of an edifice those do less who bring the job to a finish than the men who have toiled from the first. For they lay the coping and carry the work to its conclusion, so that the house is builded. But while the house was in building there was no need of their finishing touches.

To endeavour to know our faults so far as memory directs us is enough. Where we recognize a thing more closely we can be the more cautious over it. Knowledge of evil cannot be lacking to a just man: and there is no sense in avoiding sins which are not known.[15]

NOTES

1. Compare Socrates' recorded saying: οὐδεὶς ἑκὼν κακός, No man is voluntarily base.
2. Cf. Augustine, *Enchiridion*, ch. xvii: Non consideratis itaque rebus ipsis, de quibus aliquid dicitur, sed sola intentione dicentis, melior est, qui nesciens falsum dicit, quoniam id verum putat, quam qui mentiendi animum sciens gerit, nesciens verum esse quod dicit. The intention of the speaker rather than his action must be considered, and the man who tells a lie thinking it to be the truth is better than one who, wishing to tell a lie tells the truth by mistake. Augustine here introduces a moral test which is not developed in his general doctrine.
3. Abelard cites the Fathers to buttress particular points without implying their full agreement with his main argument. In the *Sic et Non* he showed that the Fathers frequently contradicted themselves!
4. Cf. the Greek legendary figure, Daedalus, whose name with the same root, signifies 'cunning workman.' Abelard is mediaeval rather than modern in this chapter; but there is a scientific view in his notion of incitement through material objects.
5. Two almshouses built by a very rich man would be of greater merit to him than one built by a well-off man, even though the piety of both, in their motive of serving God and man, was the same.
6. We may do the same action twice, just as we may say 'Socrates sits' twice. But just as the same statement

will be true when Socrates sits and false when he stands, so the same action will be good when the intention is good, and bad when the intention is bad.

7. This Chapter bears closely upon the 'Group Movement' doctrine of the twentieth century. A sense of divine guidance must be grounded in a recognition of divine reason.

8. I.e., 'a sacrifice for sin.'

9. Text, badly quoted by Abelard, of Is., ch. xii, 15. 'Since, then, thou art just, thou disposest everything justly. The condemnation of him who deserves no punishment thou reckonest contrary to thy power.'

10. The people of Tyre and Sidon sinned in not knowing Christ, but they did so in ignorance, and their sin has, therefore, not the guilt of the cities of Bethsaida and Chorazin, who sinned knowingly, since Christ had preached to them.

11. Cf. Augustine: peccatis venalibus sine quis non potest vivere, *Ench.*, 2.

12. Abelard suggests a new view of mortal sin. It is not merely the tabulated offences of patristic moralists, such as perjury, adultery, etc., but *any deliberate contempt* of God. Venial sins are those which, knowing them to be wrong, we commit in a moment of forgetfulness. Mortal sins are sins which we know to be wrong and yet commit with deliberate intent. See for a full discussion of this point, K. E. Kirk, *Vision of God* (Bampton Lectures), 1931, Appendix Note, p. 540 ff.

13. This chapter discusses an orthodox contemporary point of moral theology.

14. Hor., *Epist.*, xvi, 57.

15. This somewhat hesitant argument should be compared with the Fragment of a second Book at the end of this treatise. There Abelard defines more clearly his idea of personal intention, and shows how the psychological 'content' of an individual can indicate his development and duties. It is this aspect of conduct to which the notion of intention points, rather than to meticulous regard to stated crimes and faults.

CHAPTER 10

Moses Maimonides

Maimonides, the most celebrated Jewish philosopher of the Middle Ages, was born at Córdoba on March 30, 1135. His father was a distinguished scholar, and from him and other teachers Maimonides received a thorough education in philosophy and science as well as theology. In 1148 Córdoba was conquered by the Almohads, religious zealots who forced non-Muslims to convert to Islam. Consequently, Maimonides fled the city with his family. After wandering in Spain for an unknown period of time, they settled at Fez in present-day Morocco. This move was temporary, however, as this area of North Africa was also under the domination of the Almohads. After a brief stay in Palestine, the family finally settled in Egypt in 1165. His brother David, a merchant, supported the family at this time.

Upon David's untimely death during a voyage on the Indian Ocean, Maimonides turned to the practice of medicine to support the entire family. He gained renown as a physician and eventually became physician to the vizier of Saladin at the sultan's palace in Cairo. The contacts Maimonides made at the court were invaluable. Generally, Jews were vulnerable in any Muslim-dominated society. Specifically, these contacts protected him from challenges to the unorthodox character of his thought, which was believed by some Muslims to be pernicious. Within the Jewish community, however, Maimonides achieved tremendous respect for his biblical and rabbinic scholarship.

He was and remains one of the premier authorities on Jewish religious law. He began his first major work, the *Book of Illumination*, at the age of twenty-three. He completed this commentary on the *Mishneh* ten years later in 1168. Within this work are two "Introductions." The first, known as the "Eight Chapters," addresses the health of the soul. It is an overview of Maimonides' psychological views. Within the second one are found his thirteen principles of Jewish belief as well as his eschatological views.

The *Mishneh Torah* was Maimonides' second major work. It is his great Code, consisting of fourteen books in which he classifies the vastness of Jewish Oral Law, according to subject. Maimonides maintained that the Oral Law was handed down from Moses and recorded primarily in the *Babylonian* and *Jerusalem Talmuds*. It is to be distinguished from the Written Law of the Pentateuch. The Oral Law is intended to be an explanation of the Written Law. The first book of the *Mishneh Torah* is "The Book of Knowledge," within which are found the *Laws Concerning Character Traits*. These laws or commandments concern the well-being of both individuals and society.

Maimonides' third major work was his *Guide of the Perplexed*. The "Introductory Epistle" is addressed to the semi-intellectuals of his day who were of the opinion that the

Greek sciences contradict religious faith. It is they who are perplexed. It is the mission of the *Guide* to demonstrate to these individuals that no such contradiction exists.

Maimonides was also the author of the short *Treatise on the Art of Logic*, as well as a number of medical treatises. On December 13, 1204, he died and was buried at Tiberias. It was oft said of him, "From Moses (the prophet) to Moses (ben Maimon) there had arisen no one like him."

Maimonides on Laws Concerning Character Traits

One of several works of Maimonides is the *Mishneh Torah*, which is a compilation of traditional Jewish Oral Law, as distinct from the Written Law of the Pentateuch. According to Maimonides, the Oral Law originated with Moses and over the generations was recorded in the *Babylonian* and *Jerusalem Talmuds*. These two bodies of law are complementary. Indeed, Maimonides intended his codification of the Oral Law to be an explanation of the Written Law. The *Mishneh Torah* consists of fourteen books, the first of which is "The Book of Knowledge," within which are found the *Laws Concerning Character Traits (Hilkhot De'ot)*. In this regard he was unique, for he was the first Jewish thinker to construe the shaping of character as a function of the Law. Furthermore, he classifies ethics as a part of political science. Man is by nature a social and therefore necessarily a political creature. His needs of food, shelter, and other necessities of life require that he live in society. The existence of society is dependent upon laws. The concept of law entails political authority through which specific laws are defined and promulgated. Without a body of laws, a society would disintegrate into chaos. Nevertheless, it is individuals who constitute society. Maimonides understands that the health of a community therefore depends upon its members possessing good moral habits. However, the well-being of society is not the only purpose of morality. Moral virtue curbs carnal desire so that one can enjoy the fruits of a contemplative life. Living a virtuous life provides one the freedom to successfully pursue intellectual concerns. Consequently, man's political and rational natures both presuppose ethics.

Eleven commandments constitute the *Laws Concerning Character Traits*. The first is to imitate God's ways, which Maimonides interprets to mean living according to the mean. This is detailed in Chapters One through Five, wherein both temperament and physical health are discussed. It is interesting that ethics is understood to be dependent, in part, upon the art of medicine. Living according to the mean satisfies the two primary goals of the Code *(Mishneh Torah)*, namely, personal tranquillity and the well-being of society. The remaining ten commandments pertain primarily to the latter. The second commandment instructs one to cleave to those who know Him; that is, to emulate the behavior of those whom we respect. Here Maimonides brings into focus the traditional esteem of those men who are wise and just. Third, "And you shall love your neighbor as yourself." This entails a respect not only for other people but for their possessions as well. Fourth, "He [God] commanded the love of the convert, just as He commanded the love of His name." The fifth commandment is a corollary of the third and fourth. One must not hate others, specifically those who have sinned against one. The sixth commandment instructs one to rebuke his neighbor; that is, to reprimand the sinner. The purpose of a rebuke is twofold; it contributes to the well-being of the sinner by helping to set him straight, and it helps to prevent the use of hatred in him who has been sinned against and who is presumably engaged in the rebuke. Not to put anyone to shame is the seventh commandment, and the eighth is not to afflict the distressed. Ninth, one must not be a talebearer. The tenth and eleventh commandments are not to take revenge and not be bear a grudge. Although Maimonides presents these as separate commandments, it is perfectly reasonable to subsume those regulating man's relations with his fellow man under the commandment to love one's neighbor.

A reading of the *Laws* demonstrates an intellectual kinship between Maimonides and Aristotle. Both view ethics as part of practical philosophy or political science. Both understand and appreciate the importance of engaging in one's daily activities according to the mean.

LAWS CONCERNING CHARACTER TRAITS

They include altogether eleven commandments, five positive commandments and six negative commandments. These are: (1) to imitate His ways, (2) to cleave to those who know Him, (3) to love neighbors, (4) to love the converts, (5) not to hate brothers, (6) to rebuke, (7) not to put [anyone] to shame, (8) not to afflict the distressed, (9) not to go about as a talebearer, (10) not to take revenge, (11) not to bear a grudge.[1] The explanation of all these commandments is in the following chapters.

Chapter One

Every single human being has many character traits. [As for character traits in general,] one differs from another and they are exceedingly far apart from each other. One man is irascible, perpetually angry, and another man has a tranquil mind and does not become angry at all; if he does become angry, his anger is mild and only rarely aroused during a period of several years. One man has an exceedingly haughty heart, and another has an extremely lowly spirit. One is so full of desire that his soul is never satisfied by pursuing its desire; another has a body so exceedingly pure that he does not

From the *Ethical Writings of Maimonides*, translated by Raymond L. Weiss with Charles E. Butterworth (New York: New York University Press, 1975), pp. 27–52. Reprinted by permission of New York University Press.

even desire the few things the body needs. One has a desire[2] so great that his soul would not be satisfied with all the wealth in the world. As it is said: "He that loves silver shall not be satisfied with silver."[3] Another is so constrained that he would be satisfied with some small thing not adequate for him, and he does not press to acquire whatever he needs.

One torments himself with hunger and is so tightfisted that he does not eat the worth of a small coin except when in great pain; another intentionally squanders all his wealth. All the rest of the character traits follow these patterns, which are [also] exemplified by the gay and the mournful, the miserly and the prodigal, the cruel and the merciful, the soft-hearted and the hard-hearted, and so on.

Between two character traits at opposite extremes, there is a character trait in the middle, equidistant from the extremes. Some character traits a man has from the beginning of his creation,[4] depending upon the nature of his body; some character traits a certain man's nature is disposed to receive in the future more quickly than other character traits; and some a man does not have from the beginning of his creation but learns from others, or he himself turns to them due to a thought that arose in his heart, or he hears that a certain character trait is good for him and that it is proper to acquire it and he trains himself in it until it is firmly established within him.

For any character trait, the two opposite extremes are not the good way, and it is not proper for a man to follow them nor to teach them to himself. If he finds his nature inclined toward one extreme or if he is disposed to receive one of them or if he has already learned one of them and has become accustomed to it, he shall make himself return to the good way and follow the way of good men, which is the right way.[5]

The right way is the mean[6] in every single one of a man's character traits. It is the character trait that is equally distant from the two extremes, not close to one or the other. Therefore the wise men of old[7] commanded that a man continuously appraise his character traits and evaluate them and direct them in the middle way so that he becomes perfect.[8]

How so? A man shall not be irascible and easily angered, nor like a corpse which feels nothing, but in between; he shall only become angry about a large matter that deserves anger so that something like it not be done again.

So too, he shall only desire the things which the body needs and without which it is impossible to live. As it is said: "A just man eats to satisfy his desire."[9] Likewise, he shall only labor at his work to acquire what he needs for the present. As it is said: "Good is a little for the just man."[10] He shall not be exceedingly tightfisted, nor squander all his wealth, but he shall give charity according to his means and lend a fitting amount to the needy. He shall not be gay and buffoonish nor sad and mournful, but rejoice all his days, calmly, with a cheerful demeanor. And thus shall he order the rest of his character traits. This way is the way of the wise men.

Every man whose character traits all lie in the mean is called a wise man. Whoever is exceedingly scrupulous with himself and moves a little toward one side or the other, away from the character trait in the mean, is called a pious man.

How so? Whoever moves away from a haughty heart to the opposite extreme so that he is exceedingly lowly in spirit is called a pious man; this is the measure of piety. If he moves only to the mean and is humble, he is called a wise man; this is the measure of wisdom. The same applies to all the rest of the character traits. The pious men of old[11] used to direct their character traits from the middle way toward [one of] the two extremes; some character traits toward the last extreme, and some toward the first extreme. This is the meaning of "inside the line of the law."[12]

We are commanded to walk in these middle ways, which are the good and right[13] ways. As it is said: "And you shall walk in His ways."[14] Thus they taught in explaining this commandment: Just as He is called gracious, you too be gracious; just as He is called merciful, you too be merciful; just as He is called holy, you too be holy.[15]

In like manner, the prophets applied all these terms to God: slow to anger and abundant in loving-kindness, just and righteous, perfect, powerful, strong, and the like. They did so to proclaim that these ways are good and right,[16] and a man is obliged to train himself to follow them and to imitate according to his strength.

How so? A man shall habituate himself in these character traits until they are firmly established in him. Time after time, he shall perform actions in accordance with the character traits that are in the mean. He shall repeat them continually until performing them is easy for him and they are not burdensome and these character traits are firmly established in his soul.

Since these terms applied to the Creator refer to the middle way that we are obliged to follow, this way is called the way of the Lord. That is what Abraham taught to his sons. As it is said: "For I have known him so that he will command his sons and his household after him to keep the way of the Lord, to do justice and righteousness."[17] Whoever walks in this way brings good and blessing upon himself. As it is said: "In order that the Lord render unto Abraham that which He said concerning him."[18]

Chapter Two

Those whose bodies are sick taste the bitter as sweet and the sweet as bitter. Some of the sick desire and long for foods that are not fit to eat, such as soil and charcoal, and they hate good foods, such as bread and meat. It all depends upon the extent of the illness. Likewise, people with sick souls crave and love the bad character traits and hate the good way. They are careless about following it, and it is very difficult for them, depending upon the extent of their illness. Thus says Isaiah about these men: "Woe unto them who call evil good, and good evil; who turn darkness into light, and light into darkness; who turn the bitter into the sweet, and the sweet into the bitter."[19] Of them it is said: "They forsake the paths of righteousness to walk in the ways of darkness."[20]

What is the remedy for those whose souls are sick? Let them go to the wise men—who are physicians of the soul—and they will cure their disease by means of the character traits that they shall teach them, until they make them return to the middle way. Solomon said about those who recognize their bad character traits and do not go to the wise men to be cured: "Fools despise admonition."[21]

How are they to be cured? Whoever is irascible is told to train himself so that if he is beaten and cursed, he will not feel anything. He shall follow this way for a long time until the rage is uprooted from his heart. If his heart is haughty, he shall train himself to endure much degradation. He shall sit lower than anyone else and wear worn-out, shabby garments, which make the wearer despised, and do similar things, until his haughty heart is uprooted. Then he shall return to the middle way, which is the good way, and when he returns to the middle way he shall follow it all his days.

He shall do the same with all the other character traits. If he is at one extreme, he shall move to the other extreme and accustom himself to it for a long time until he returns to the good way, which is the mean[22] in every single character trait.

In the case of some character traits, a man is forbidden to accustom himself to the mean. Rather, he shall move to the other [i.e., far] extreme. One such [character trait] is a haughty heart, for the good way is not that a man be merely humble, but that he have a lowly spirit, that his spirit be very submissive.[23] Therefore it was said of Moses our master that he was "very humble," and not merely humble.[24] And therefore the wise men commanded: "Have a very, very lowly spirit."[25] Moreover they said that everyone who makes his heart haughty denies the existence of God.[26] As it is said: "And your heart shall swell, and you shall forget the Lord your God."[27] In addition they said: "Whoever has an arrogant spirit—even a little—deserves excommunication."[28] Likewise, anger is an extremely bad character trait, and it is proper for a man to move away from it to the other extreme and to teach himself not to become angry, even over something it is proper to be angry about. Now, he might wish to arouse fear in his children and the members of his household or in the community (if he is a leader) and to become angry at them in order that they return to what is good. Then he shall pretend to be angry in their presence in order to admonish them, but his mind shall be tranquil within himself, like a man who feigns anger but is not angry. The wise men of old[29] said: "Anyone who is angry—it is as if he worships idols."[30] They said about anyone who is angry: If he is a wise man, his wisdom departs from him, and if he is a prophet, his prophecy departs from him.[31] And [they said] the life of irascible men is no life.[32] Therefore they commanded a man to refrain from becoming angry, until he trains himself not to feel anything even in response to things that provoke anger; this is the good way. The way of the just men is to be insulted but not to insult; they hear themselves reviled and do not reply; they act out of love and rejoice in afflictions. Scripture says about them: "And those who love Him are like the sun rising in its power."[33]

There shall always be much silence in a man's conduct. He shall speak only about a matter concerned with wisdom or matters that are necessary to keep his body alive. They said about Rav, a student of our holy master, that during his entire life he did not engage in idle conversation.[34] The latter is characteristic of most men. A man shall not use many words, even in connection with the needs of the body. Concerning this, the wise men commanded, saying: "Anyone who multiplies words brings about sin."[35] They also said: "I have found nothing better for the body than silence."[36] Likewise, concerning words of Torah and words of wisdom, the words of the wise man shall be few, but full of content. This is what the wise men commanded, saying: "A man shall always teach his students by the shortest path."[37] But if the words are many and the content slight, that is indeed foolishness. Concerning this it is said: "For a dream comes with much content, but a fool's voice with many words."[38]

Silence is a fence around wisdom.[39] Therefore he shall not hasten to reply, nor speak much; he shall teach his students quietly and calmly, without shouting or prolixity. That is in keeping with the saying of Solomon: "Words of wise men, spoken calmly, are listened to."[40]

A man is forbidden to make a habit of using smooth and deceptive language. There shall not be one thing in his mouth and another in his heart, but what is within shall be like what is without. The matter in his heart shall be the same as what is in his mouth. It is forbidden to delude[41] one's fellow creatures, even a Gentile.

How so? He shall not sell to a Gentile meat not ritually slaughtered as though it were ritually slaughtered, nor a shoe made from an animal that died by itself in place of one ritually slaughtered. He shall not urge his friend to eat with him when he knows he will not eat, nor press refreshment upon him when he knows it will not be accepted, nor open casks of wine (which

he needs to open to sell anyway) to deceive him into thinking they were opened to honor him. Likewise with everything like that—even one word of deception and fraud is forbidden. Rather, he shall have lips of truth, a steadfast spirit, and a heart pure of all mischief and intrigue.

A man shall not be full of laughter and mockery, nor sad and mournful, but joyful. Thus the wise men said: "Laughter and levity bring about illicit sexual conduct."[42] They commanded that a man not be unrestrained in laughter, nor sad and mournful, but that he receive every man with a cheerful demeanor.[43] Likewise his desire[44] shall not be so great that he rushes for wealth, nor shall he be lazy and refrain from working. But he shall live in contentment,[45] have a modest occupation, and be occupied [mainly] with the Torah.[46] No matter how small his portion, let him rejoice in it.[47] He shall not be full of contention, envy, or desire, nor shall he seek honor. Thus the wise men said: "Envy, desire, and honor remove a man from the world."[48] The general rule is that he follow the mean[49] for every single character trait, until all his character traits are ordered according to the mean. That is in keeping with what Solomon says: "And all your ways will be upright."[50]

Chapter Three

Perhaps a man will say: "Since desire, honor, and the like constitute a bad way and remove a man from the world, I shall completely separate myself from them and go to the other extreme." So he does not eat meat, nor drink wine, nor take a wife, nor live in a decent[51] dwelling, nor wear decent clothing, but sackcloth, coarse wool, and so on, like the priests of Edom.[52] This, too, is a bad way and it is forbidden to follow it.

Whoever follows this way is called a sinner. Indeed, He [God] says about the Nazirite: "He [the priest] shall make atonement for him because he sinned against the soul."[53] The wise men said: "If the Nazirite who only abstained from wine needs atonement, how much more does one who abstains from every thing [need atonement]."[54]

Therefore the wise men commanded that a man only abstain from things forbidden by the Torah alone. He shall not prohibit for himself, by vows and oaths, things that are permitted. Thus the wise men said: "Is what the Torah has prohibited not enough for you, that you prohibit other things for yourself?"[55]

Those who fast continually are in this class; they do not follow the good way. The wise men prohibited a man from tormenting himself by fasting. Concerning all these things and others like them, Solomon commanded, saying: "Do not be overly righteous and do not be excessively wise; why should you destroy yourself?"[56]

Man needs to direct every single one of his deeds solely toward attaining knowledge of the Name, blessed be He. His sitting down, his standing up, and his speech, everything shall be directed toward this goal. How so? When he conducts business or works to receive a wage, his heart shall not only be set upon taking in money, but he shall do these things in order to acquire what the body needs, such as food, drink, shelter, and a wife.

Likewise when he eats, drinks, and has sexual intercourse, his purpose[57] shall not be to do these things only for pleasure, eating and drinking only what is sweet to the palate and having sexual intercourse only for pleasure. Rather, his only purpose in eating and drinking shall be to keep his body and limbs healthy. Therefore he shall not eat everything that the palate desires, like a dog or an ass, but he shall eat things that are useful for him, whether bitter or sweet, and he shall not eat things bad for the body, even if they are sweet to the palate.

How so? Whoever has warm flesh shall not eat meat or honey, nor drink wine. As Solomon, for example, said: "It is not good to eat much honey, etc."[58] He shall drink chicory water, even though it is bitter. Since it is impossible for a man to live except by eating and drinking, he shall eat and drink only in accordance with the directive of medicine, in order that he become healthy and remain perfect. Likewise when he has sexual intercourse, he shall do so only to keep his body healthy and to have offspring. Therefore he shall not have sexual intercourse every time he has the desire, but whenever he knows that he needs to discharge sperm in accordance with the directive of medicine, or to have offspring.

If one conducts himself in accordance with the [art of] medicine and sets his heart only upon making his body and limbs perfect and strong, and upon having sons who will do his work and labor for his needs, this is not a good way. Rather, he shall set his heart upon making his body perfect and strong so that his soul will be upright to know the Lord. For it is impossible for him to understand and reflect upon wisdom[59] when he is sick or when one of his limbs is in pain. He shall set his heart upon having a son who perhaps will be a wise and great man in Israel. Whoever follows this way all his days serves the Lord continuously, even when he engages in business and even when he has sexual intercourse, because his thought in everything is to fulfill his needs so that his body will be perfect to serve the Lord.

Even when he sleeps, if he sleeps with the intention of resting his mind and his body so that he does not become sick—for he is unable to serve the Lord when he is sick—his sleep shall become a service of the Lord,[60] blessed be He. Concerning this subject, the wise men commanded, saying:"Let all your deeds be for the sake of Heaven."[61] That is what Solomon said in his wisdom: "In all your ways know Him, and He will make your paths straight."[62]

Chapter Four

Since preserving the body's health and strength is among the ways of the Lord—for to attain understanding and knowledge is impossible when one is sick—a man

needs to keep away from things that destroy the body and to accustom himself to
things that make him healthy and vigorous. They are as follows. A man should eat
only when he is hungry and drink only
when he is thirsty. Whenever he needs to
urinate or defecate, he should do so at once;
he should not delay for even a single moment.

A man should not eat until his stomach
is full, but about one-fourth less than
would make him sated. He should not
drink water with the food, except a little
mixed with wine. When the food begins to
be digested in his intestines, he should
drink what he needs to drink. He should
not drink an excessive amount of water
even when the food is being digested. He
should not eat until he has examined himself very well, lest he needs to ease himself.

A man should not eat unless he first
takes a walk so that his body becomes
heated, or he should work or exert himself
in some other way. The general rule is that
he should afflict his body and exert himself
every day in the morning until his body
starts to become hot. Then he should rest a
little until his soul is tranquil, and then eat.
If he washes with warm water after his exertion, that is good. Afterward, he should
wait a little and then eat.

While he is eating, a man should always
sit at his place or incline to the left, and
should neither walk nor ride. He should
not exert himself nor shake his body nor
take a long walk until all the food in his
intestines is digested. Anyone who takes
long walks or exerts himself immediately
after eating brings bad and severe illnesses
upon himself.

Day and night have altogether twenty-
four hours. It suffices for a man to sleep
one-third of them, i.e., eight hours, at the
end of the night, so that there be eight
hours from the beginning of his sleep until
the sun rises. He should stand up from his
bed before the sun rises.

A man should not sleep upon his face,
nor upon his back, but upon his side; at the
beginning of the night, on the left side, and
at the end of the night, on the right side.

He should not go to sleep shortly after eating. He should not sleep during the day.

Things which loosen the bowels, such as
grapes, figs, mulberries, pears, melons, and
the pulp of cucumbers and gherkins, are
eaten before the meal. One should not mix
them with the meal, but wait a little until
they leave the upper stomach, and then eat
the meal. Things which harden the bowels,
such as pomegranates, quinces, apples, and
small pears, are eaten immediately after the
meal, and not in excess.

When a man wants to eat poultry and the
meat of cattle together, he should first eat
the poultry. In the case of eggs and poultry,
he should first eat the eggs. In the case of
the meat of lean cattle and of heavy cattle,
he should first eat the meat of the lean cattle. He should always have light food before heavy food.

In hot weather he should eat cold foods,
without much condiment, and sour food.
In the rainy season[63] he should eat warm
foods, with a lot of condiment, and a little
mustard and asafetida. He should do so in
cold as well as hot places, in accordance
with what is appropriate for each place.

There are foods that are exceedingly bad
and it is never proper for a man to eat them,
such as large, salted, stale fish; salted, stale
cheese; truffles and mushrooms; salted,
stale meat; wine from the press; cooked
food kept until its odor disappears; and
likewise every food whose odor is bad or
exceedingly bitter—these are like poison
for the body.

There are foods that are bad, but not as
bad as the above. Consequently, it is proper
for a man to eat only a little of them, at long
intervals, and not to accustom himself to
make a meal of them or continually to eat
them with his food. For example: large fish,
cheese, milk kept twenty-four hours after
milking, meat of large oxen and large
goats, beans, lentils, chickpeas, barley
bread, unleavened bread, cabbage, leeks,
onions, garlic, mustard, and radishes. All
these are bad foods.

It is proper for a man to eat only very
little of them and then only in the rainy season; he should not eat them at all outside

of the rainy season. It is not proper to eat beans and lentils in either hot weather or the rainy season. Gourds may be eaten a little in hot weather.

There are foods that are bad, but not as bad as the above. They are: water fowl, young pigeons, dates, meat juice, fish brine, and bread baked in oil or kneaded in oil and fine flour sifted to such an extent that no trace of coarse bran remains. It is not proper to eat much of these foods. A man who is wise and conquers his impulse does not succumb to his desire to eat from any of the above-mentioned at all, except if he has need of them for medicine. He is indeed a powerful man.[64]

A man should always restrain himself from eating the fruit of trees. He should not eat much of them even when they are dried and, needless to say, when they are fresh.[65] For before they are cooked sufficiently, they are like daggers to the body. Likewise carob-pods are always bad. All sour fruit is bad and should not be eaten, except for a little in hot weather or in hot places. Figs, grapes, and almonds are always good, whether fresh or dried, and a man may eat of them whatever he needs. But he should not eat them continually, even though they are the best of all the fruit from trees. Honey and wine are bad for children, but fine for old people, especially in the rainy season. In hot weather, a man needs to eat two-thirds of what he eats in the rainy season.

All his days a man should try always to keep his bowels loose and be a bit close to diarrhea. This is an important general rule in medicine, for whenever the stool is blocked or expelled with difficulty, many illnesses result.

What should he loosen his bowels with if they are a little firm? If he is a youth, he should eat salted, boiled food, seasoned with oil, fish brine, and salt, and not eat bread; or he should drink the juice of boiled spinach or cabbage, with oil, salt, and fish brine. If he is old, he should drink honey mixed with warm water in the morning, and wait about four hours, after which he should eat his meal. He should do so day after day, for three or four days if necessary, until his bowels are loosened.

Still another general rule: they said about the health of the body that if a man does much exercise and hard work and is not sated and his bowels are loose, he will not become sick and his strength will increase, even if he eats bad food. Whoever leads a sedentary life and does not exercise, or delays excretion or has hard bowels, even if he eats good food and guards himself in accordance with medical practice, all his days will be painful and his strength will diminish. Gross eating is like deadly poison for the body of any man; it is a root of all illness.

Most of the illnesses that come to a man are due either to bad foods or to stuffing the stomach. Solomon, in his wisdom, says about the one who eats in a gross manner (even though the food is good): "He who guards his mouth and his tongue guards his soul from troubles."[66] That is to say, he guards his mouth from eating bad food or from being sated, and his tongue from speaking, except in connection with his needs.

The way to bathe is to enter the bath every seven days, and not enter shortly before eating or when hungry, but when the food begins to be digested. A man should wash his whole body with water that is not so hot that the body would be burned by it, but wash only his head with water so hot it would burn the body. Afterward he should wash his body with lukewarm water, and after that with water even less warm, until he washes with cold water. He should not let any lukewarm or cold water pass over his head. He should not wash with cold water in the rainy season, nor wash until his whole body perspires and becomes pliant, nor remain long in the bath, but when he perspires and his body becomes pliant he should rinse and leave.

He should test himself before he enters the bath and after he leaves, lest he needs to ease himself; likewise a man should inspect himself before and after eating, before and after sexual intercourse, before and after he exerts himself with exercise, before he goes to sleep and after he awakens—ten times in all.

When a man leaves the bath, he should put on his clothes and cover his head in the anteroom, so that a cold breeze does not overcome him. Even in hot weather, he needs to be careful and pause after he leaves the bath until his soul is tranquil, his body is at rest, and he is no longer warm. Afterward he should eat, and if he sleeps a little when he leaves the bath before eating, that is indeed very fine. A man should not drink cold water when he leaves the bath and, needless to say, he should not drink in the bath. If he is thirsty when he leaves the bath and is unable to restrain himself, he should mix water with wine or honey and drink it. During the rainy season if he has a massage with oil at the bath after he rinses, that is good.

A man should not accustom himself to have blood let continually; he should not have blood let unless there is an extraordinary need. He should not have blood let in either hot weather or the rainy season, except during the month of Nissan and a little during the month of Tishri. After age fifty, he should not have blood let at all. A man should not have blood let and enter the bath on the same day. He should not have blood let when he sets out on a trip, nor when he returns from a trip. On the day of bloodletting, he should eat and drink less than what he is accustomed to; he should rest and neither exercise nor take a long walk.

Semen is the strength of the body and its life, and is the light of the eyes. Whenever too much is ejaculated, the body decays, its strength is spent, and its life destroyed. As Solomon said in his wisdom: "Do not give your strength to women, and your years to that which destroys kings."[67]

As for anyone who overindulges in sexual intercourse: old age pounces upon him; his strength fails; his eyes become dim; a bad odor spreads from his mouth and armpits; the hair on his head, his eyebrows, and his eyelashes fall out; the hair of his beard, armpits, and legs grows excessively; his teeth fall out; and many pains in addition to these come to him.

The wise men among the physicians said: one in a thousand dies from other illnesses, and the rest from excessive copulation. Therefore a man needs to be careful in this matter if he wishes to live well. He should only have sexual intercourse when his body is healthy and exceedingly strong and he has a continuous, involuntary erection and he distracts himself with something else, but the erection remains as it was, and he finds a heaviness in his loins and below, as if the cords of the testicles were drawn out, and his flesh is hot. Such a man needs to have sexual intercourse and his medicine is to have sexual intercourse.

A man should not have sexual intercourse when he is sated or hungry, but after the food is digested in his intestines. Before and after sexual intercourse, he should test to see whether he needs to ease himself. He should not have sexual intercourse in either a standing or sitting position, nor in the bathhouse, nor on the day he enters the bath, nor on the day of bloodletting, nor on the day of departure or return from a trip—neither before nor afterward.

Whoever conducts himself along the paths we have taught, I guarantee will not become ill all his days, until he is very old and dies. He will not need a physician and his body will be perfect and remain healthy all his days, unless it is defective from the beginning of its creation, or he has become accustomed to a bad habit from the time of birth, or a pestilence or drought comes to the world.

It is only proper for a healthy man to adhere to these good habits about which we have spoken. But as for a sick man, or one with a sick organ, or one who is accustomed to a bad habit for many years—for each of them there are other paths and practices, depending upon his illness, as is explained in the medical books. "A change of custom is the beginning of illness."[68]

Whether a man is healthy or sick, if he lives in a place where there is no physician, it is not proper for him to depart from any of the paths we have discussed in this chapter, for every one of them results in some good.

A disciple of wise men[69] is not permitted to live in any city that does not have these ten things: a physician, a surgeon, a bathhouse, a bathroom, a fixed source of water such as a river or spring, a synagogue, a teacher of children, a scribe, a collector of charity, and a court that can punish with lashes and imprisonment.[70]

Chapter Five

The wise man is identified by his wisdom and his character traits, which distinguish him from the rest of the people. Similarly, he needs to be identified by his actions: by his eating, his drinking, his sexual intercourse, his relieving himself, his speech, his walking, his dress, the management of his affairs, and his business conduct. All of these actions are to be exceptionally decent and fitting.

How so? A disciple of wise men shall not be a glutton, but eat food that is suitable for making the body healthy. He shall not eat in a gross manner, nor run to fill his stomach, like those who stuff themselves with food and drink until their belly swells. The tradition applies the following verse to such people: "And I will spread dung on your faces, even the dung of your holiday sacrifices (haggeikhem)."[71] The wise men said: "These are the people who eat and drink and make all their days like holidays (haggim)."[72]

They are the same people who say: "Eat and drink for tomorrow we die."[73] This is how the wicked eat, whose tables Scripture censured by saying: "For all tables are full of filthy vomit, and no place is clean."[74]

However, the wise man only eats one or two courses, eating from them what suffices for life, which is enough for him. That is what Solomon said: "A just man eats to satisfy his desire."[75]

When the wise man eats the little that is suitable for him, he shall eat it only in his house, at his table. He shall not eat in a store nor in the marketplace, except in case of great need, so that he is not degraded before his fellow creatures. He shall not eat with ignoramuses nor at those tables full of "filthy vomit." He shall not frequent feasts at a variety of places, even with the wise men. He shall not eat at feasts where there is a large gathering. It is not proper for him to eat at a feast unless it involves fulfilling a commandment, such as a feast of betrothal or marriage, and then only if a disciple of wise men marries the daughter of a disciple of wise men. The just men and[76] the pious men of old[77] never ate at a feast not their own.

When the wise man drinks wine, he drinks only in order to loosen the food in his intestines. Anyone who becomes drunk commits a sin, is contemptible, and loses his wisdom. If he becomes drunk before ignoramuses, he profanes the Name. It is forbidden to drink at noon, even a little, unless it is part of the meal, for drinking which is part of the meal does not make one drunk. They [the wise men] warn only about wine that comes after the meal.

Even though a man's wife is always permitted to him, it is proper for a disciple of wise men to conduct himself in holiness and not be with his wife like a rooster, but [be with her] only on the night of the Sabbath, if he has the strength. When he cohabits with her, he shall not cohabit at the beginning of the night when he is sated, nor at the end of the night when he is hungry, but in the middle of the night when the food in his intestines is digested.

He shall not be frivolous, nor dirty his mouth with obscenity,[78] even between himself and her. Indeed, it says in the tradition: "He [God] tells a man what his conversation was."[79] The wise men said: "Judgment is made in the future even upon a frivolous conversation between a man and his wife."[80]

Both of them (or one of them) shall not be drunk, lethargic, or sad. She should not be asleep and he should not force her if she is unwilling, but [intercourse shall take place] when both wish it and in state of mutual joy. He shall converse and play with her a little so that their souls become tranquil, and he shall have sexual intercourse modestly, not shamelessly, and separate [from her] at once.

Anyone accustomed to this conduct not only makes his soul holy, purifies himself, and improves his character traits, but also, if he has sons, they will be decent and modest,[81] fit for wisdom and piety. Anyone accustomed to the conduct of the rest of the people, who walk in darkness, will have sons like those people.

Disciples of wise men are accustomed to behave with great modesty.[82] They do not degrade themselves; they uncover neither their heads nor their bodies. Even after entering the toilet, one must be modest and not uncover his garments until he sits down. He shall not wipe with the right hand. He shall move away from everyone and [for example] enter the innermost room of a cave and relieve himself there. If he relieves himself behind a fence, he shall go far away so that his fellow man will not hear a sound if he breaks wind. If he relieves himself in a plain, he shall go far away so that his fellow man will not see him uncovered. He shall not speak when he relieves himself, even in case of great need. He conducts himself with the same modesty in the toilet at night as by day. A man shall forever train himself to relieve himself only in the morning and the evening, so that he does not have to go off at a distance.

A disciple of wise men shall not shout and scream when he speaks, like cattle and wild beasts. He shall not raise his voice much, but speak calmly with all his fellow creatures. When he speaks calmly, he shall be careful not to be aloof, lest his words appear to be like the words of the arrogant. He greets every man first,[83] so that they will be pleasantly disposed toward him. He judges every man in a favorable light.[84] He speaks in praise of his fellow man, never disparagingly. He loves peace and seeks peace.[85]

If he sees a place where his words would be useful and listened to, he speaks and, if not, he remains silent. How so? He does not appease his friend in the hour of his anger; he does not ask about his vow at the time he makes the vow, but waits until his mind becomes cool and is calm; he does not comfort [his friend] while his dead lie before him because he is in a state of shock until the burial;[86] and so too, in all similar circumstances. He does not appear before his friend in the hour of his disgrace, but hides his eyes from him.[87]

He shall not alter what he says; he shall neither add nor detract, except in matters concerning peace and the like. The general rule is that he speaks only in performing deeds of loving-kindness or about matters of wisdom and the like. He shall not converse with a woman in the marketplace, even if she is his wife, sister, or daughter.[88]

A disciple of wise men shall not walk with an erect carriage[89] and outstretched neck. As it is said: "And they walk with outstretched necks and wanton eyes."[90] He shall not walk mincingly and smugly, like the women and the arrogant about whom it is said: "Walking and tripping along, making a tinkling sound with their feet."[91]

He shall not run in a public place and behave in a crazy manner, nor bend over like hunchbacks. Rather he looks down, like someone praying, and walks straight ahead, like a man preoccupied with his affairs.

In his manner of walking, too, a man is recognized as wise and sensible,[92] or else a simpleton and a fool. Thus, Solomon said in his wisdom: "Also in the way the fool walks he lacks thought, and he says to everyone that he is a fool."[93] He announces about himself to all that he is a fool.

The dress of a disciple of wise men is becoming[94] and clean. It is forbidden for a stain, a fatty spot, and the like to be found on his garment. He shall not wear the dress of the poor, which degrades those who wear it, but garments that are becoming and in the middle [way]. His flesh must not show from beneath his clothing, as happens with the exceedingly light, linen garments that they make in Egypt, nor shall his garments drag on the earth, as do the garments of the arrogant, but they shall extend down to his heel and his sleeve extend down to his fingertips. He shall not let his garment hang down because he would appear like the arrogant, except on the Sabbath, if he has no change of clothing. In hot weather he shall not wear patched shoes and a garment with patch over patch, but in the rainy season this is permitted if he is poor.

He shall not go perfumed to the marketplace, with perfumed garments or with perfume on his hair, but if his skin is massaged with perfume to remove a foul smell, it is permitted. So too, he shall not go out alone at night, unless he has a set time to go out in order to study. All these [laws] are to avoid suspicion.[95]

A disciple of wise men conducts his affairs judiciously. His eating and drinking and his support of the members of his household depend upon his income and his success. He shall not burden himself excessively. The wise men commanded concerning the proper regimen that a man eat meat only when he has the desire.[96] As it is said: "Because your soul desires to eat meat."[97] It is enough for a healthy man to eat meat on the eve of the Sabbath. If he is rich enough to eat meat every day, he may do so.

The wise men commanded, saying: "A man shall always eat less than is suitable for him according to his income, dress as is suitable for him, and honor his wife and children more than is suitable for him."[98]

A sensible man[99] first establishes himself in an occupation which supports him, afterward he buys a home, and after that he marries a woman. As it is said: "What man is there who has planted a vineyard and has not used the fruit thereof; who has built a new house and has not dedicated it; who is betrothed to a woman and has not taken her?"[100] But the fool begins by marrying a woman after which, if he can, he buys a house and, after that, at the end

of his days, he finally seeks a trade or he is supported by charity. Thus it says in the [enumeration of] curses: "A woman shall you betroth . . . a house shall you build . . . a vineyard shall you plant."[101] That is to say, your deeds shall be the reverse [of what is proper], so that you shall not make your paths prosper. In the blessing, what does it say? "And David had success in all his paths, and the Lord was with him."[102]

A man is forbidden to renounce ownership of all his possessions and to dedicate them to the Temple, and then to become a burden upon his fellow creatures. He shall not sell a field and buy a house, nor sell a house and then either buy movable goods or do business with the funds from his house, but he may sell movable goods and buy a field. The general rule is that he set his goal to improve his possessions, not to have a little pleasure for the moment, or to have a little pleasure and then suffer a great loss.

The business conduct of the disciples of wise men is truthful and faithful. His "no" is no and his "yes" yes. He is scrupulous with himself in his reckoning. He gives in and yields to others when he buys from them and is not exacting of them. He gives the sale-price on the spot. He does not allow himself to be made a surety or a guarantor and does not accept the power of attorney. He obligates himself in matters of buying and selling in circumstances where the Torah does not obligate him, so that he stands by his word and does not change it.[103] If others are obligated to him by law, he gives them time and is forgiving. He lends money and is gracious. He shall not take away business from his fellow man[104] nor bring grief to any man in the world during his lifetime.

The general rule is that he be among the oppressed and not the oppressors, among the insulted and not those who insult.[105] Scripture says about a man who performs all these actions and their like: "And He said to me, 'You are My servant Israel, in whom I will be glorified.' "[106]

Chapter Six

Man is created in such a way that his character traits and actions are influenced by his neighbors and friends, and he follows the custom of the people in his city. Therefore a man needs to associate with the just and be with the wise continually in order to learn [from] their actions, and to keep away from the wicked, who walk in darkness, so that he avoids learning from their actions. That is what Solomon said: "He who walks with wise men will become wise, but he who associates with fools will become evil."[107] And it says: "Blessed is the man who does not walk in the council of the wicked, etc."[108] Likewise, if he is in a city with evil customs where men do not follow the right way, he shall go to a place where men are just and they follow the way of good men. If all the cities he knows or hears about follow a way that is not good, as in our time, or if because of military conscription or illness, he is unable to go to a city with good customs, he shall dwell alone in solitude. As it is said: "Let him dwell alone and be silent."[109] If there are evil men and sinners who do not let him live in the city unless he mingles with them and follows their evil customs, he shall go off to the caves, the briers, or the desert, and not accustom himself to the way of sinners. As it is said: "O that I were in the desert, in a lodging place of wayfaring men."[110]

It is a positive commandment to cleave to the wise men in order to learn from their actions. As it is said: "And to Him shall you cleave."[111] Is it possible for a man to cleave to the *Shekhinah* [Presence]? But thus said the wise men in explaining this commandment: cleave to the wise men and their disciples.[112] Therefore a man needs to try to marry the daughter of a disciple of wise men; to give his daughter in marriage to a disciple of wise men; to eat and drink with the disciples of wise men; to do business on behalf of the disciples of wise men; and to associate with them in all kinds of associations. As it is said: "And cleave to Him."[113] Thus the wise men commanded,

saying: "Sit in the dust of their feet and drink in thirst their words."[114]

It is a commandment for every man to love every single individual of Israel like his own body. As it is said: "And you shall love your neighbor as yourself."[115] Therefore he needs to speak in praise of him and to have concern for his possessions, just as he has concern for his own possessions and wants to be honored himself. Whoever glorifies himself through the humiliation of his fellow man has no portion in the world-to-come.[116]

There are two positive commandments to love the convert[117] who comes under the wings of the *Shekhinah;* one, because he is in the class of neighbors, and the other, because he is a convert and the Torah said: "And you shall love the stranger."[118] He [God] commanded the love of the convert, just as He commanded the love of His Name. As it is said: "And you shall love the Lord your God."[119] The Holy One Himself, blessed be He, loves the converts. As it is said: "And He loves the stranger."[120]

Anyone who hates one Israelite in his heart transgresses a prohibition. As it is said: "You shall not hate your brother in your heart."[121] They do not give lashes in connection with this prohibition, since it does not refer to an action. The Torah warned [here] only about hatred in the heart, but whoever strikes his fellow man and reviles him, even though it is not permitted, does not transgress what is prohibited by the verse, "You shall not hate. . . ."

When a man sins against another man, he [the latter] shall not hate him and remain silent. As it is said about the wicked: "And Absalom spoke to Amnon neither good nor evil, although Absalom hated Amnon."[122] Rather, he is commanded to speak to him, and to say to him: "Why did you do such-and-such to me? Why did you sin against me in such-and-such a matter?" As it is said: "You shall surely rebuke your neighbor."[123] If he repents and requests forgiveness from him, he needs to forgive and shall not be cruel. As it is said: "And Abraham prayed to God, etc."[124]

If someone sees his fellow man who has sinned or who follows a way that is not good, it is a commandment to make him return to the good and to make known to him that he sins against himself by his evil actions. As it is said: "You shall surely rebuke your neighbor."[125]

Whoever rebukes his fellow man, whether concerning matters between the two of them or between him [the fellow man] and God,[126] needs to rebuke him in private. He shall speak to him calmly and gently, and make known to him that he talks to him only for his own good, to bring him to the life of the world-to-come. If he accepts it from him, good; if not, he shall rebuke him a second and a third time. Thus he is always obliged to rebuke him until the sinner strikes him and says to him, "I will not listen."[127] If he does not prevent everything he can possibly prevent, he is ensnared in the sin of all those he could have prevented from sinning.

Whoever rebukes his fellow man shall not at first speak harshly so as to put him to shame. As it is said: "You shall not bear sin on his account."[128] Thus said the wise men: "Are we to assume he should rebuke him until his face changes [its expression or color]? The text therefore says: 'You shall not bear sin on his account.' "[129] From this we learn it is forbidden to humiliate an Israelite; all the more [is it forbidden] in public.

Even though the one who humiliates his fellow man is not given lashes, it is a great sin. Thus said the wise men: "Whoever puts his fellow man to shame in public has no portion in the world-to-come."[130]

Therefore a man needs to be careful that he not shame his fellow man—be he young or old—in public, nor call him by a name he is ashamed of, nor speak about something in front of him that would make him ashamed.

To what matters does the above refer? To matters between a man and his fellow man, but in matters of Heaven if he does not repent in private, he is to be humiliated in public, his sin is proclaimed, and he is reviled to his face and degraded and cursed

until he returns to the good. That is what all the prophets did with Israel.

If someone is sinned against by his fellow man and does not wish to rebuke him or to say anything to him—because the sinner is exceedingly simple or his mind is distraught—and if he forgives him in his heart and bears no animosity toward him and does not rebuke him, this is indeed the measure of piety. The Torah was particularly concerned only about animosity.

A man is obliged to be careful about widows and orphans because their souls are very lowly and their spirits submissive, even if they are wealthy. We are even warned about the widow and the orphans of a king. As it is said: "You shall not afflict any widow or orphan."[131]

How should we conduct ourselves toward them? A man shall speak only softly to them, treat them only with honor, and not afflict their bodies with labor nor their hearts with words. He shall have more concern for their possessions than for his own. If anyone belittles them, vexes them, afflicts their hearts, subjugates them, or loses their money, he transgresses a prohibition, and all the more if he strikes or curses them. Although lashes are not given in such cases, the punishment is expressly stated in the Torah: "My wrath shall wax hot, and I will slay you with the sword."[132]

A covenant was made for them by Him who spoke and the world came to be. Whenever they cry out because of violence, they are answered. As it is said: "For if they cry out at all to Me, I will surely hear their cry."[133] To what do these words refer? To a man's afflicting them for his own needs, but if a teacher afflicts them in order to teach them Torah or a craft or to guide them on the right way,[134] this is indeed permitted. Nevertheless, he shall not treat them the way he is accustomed to treat every man, but shall make a distinction and guide them calmly, with great mercy and honor—"For the Lord will plead their cause"[135]—whether the orphan has lost his father or mother. For how long are they called orphans with respect to this matter? Until they have no need of an adult to depend upon for their nurture and their care, but the orphan can fulfill all his own needs like any other adult.

Chapter Seven

Whoever speaks ill of his fellow man transgresses a prohibition. As it is said: "You shall not go about as a talebearer among My people."[136] Even though they do not give lashes in connection with this prohibition, it is a great sin and causes many people of Israel to be killed. Therefore it is followed by the verse: "And you shall not stand idly by the blood of your neighbor."[137] Go and learn what happened in the case of Doeg the Edomite.[138]

Who is a talebearer? He who carries words and goes from one person to another, saying: "A certain individual said such-and-such"; "I heard such-and-such about a certain individual." Even though he speaks the truth, this man destroys the world.

There is a far greater sin that falls under this prohibition. It is "the evil tongue," which refers to whoever speaks disparagingly of his fellow man, even though he speaks the truth. But whoever tells a lie is called, "one who gives his fellow man a bad name." However, the one who possesses an "evil tongue" sits and says: "A certain individual did such-and-such"; "his ancestors were so-and-so"; "I heard such-and-such about him." Scripture says concerning whoever speaks disparagingly about someone: "May the Lord cut off all smooth lips, the tongue that speaks proud things."[139]

The wise men said: "For three transgressions punishment is exacted from a man in this world and he has no portion in the world-to-come: idol worship, illicit sexual unions, and the shedding of blood. And the evil tongue is equal to all of them put together."[140] Moreover, the wise men said: "Whoever speaks with an evil tongue [behaves] as if he denied God.[141] As it is said: 'They said, "With our tongues we will prevail, our lips are with us. Who is lord over

us?" '[142] Furthermore, the wise men said: "The evil tongue slays three: the one who speaks, the one who accepts it, and the one who is spoken about; the one who accepts it more so than the one who speaks."[143]

There are also words that are "dust of the evil tongue." For example: "Who would have thought that so-and-so would become like he is now?" Or someone says: "Be still about so-and-so; I do not wish to tell about what happened and what took place." And words like these. So too, the one who speaks well of someone before his enemies; this too is "dust of the evil tongue," for that would cause them to speak disparagingly of him. Concerning this matter, Solomon said: "He who blesses his neighbor with a loud voice, rising early in the morning, will be regarded as cursing."[144] For out of the good [said] of him comes evil.

It is also [dust of the evil tongue] if one speaks with an evil tongue in jest and levity, that is, speaks without hatred. This is what Solomon says: "Like a madman who throws firebrands, arrows, and death is the man who deceives his neighbor and says, 'I am jesting.' "[145] And, so too, if one speaks with an evil tongue deceitfully, feigning innocence, as though he does not know that it is evil speech.[146] When they protest about it, he says: "I did not know that these are the deeds of so-and-so or that this is evil speech."

It is all the same whether he speaks with an evil tongue in the presence of his fellow man or not in his presence. Whoever relates things which, if repeated, would harm the body or possessions of his fellow man, or would only distress or frighten him—this is the evil tongue! If these words are spoken in the presence of three people, the matter is regarded as public knowledge. If one of the three relates it once again, it is not classified as the evil tongue, assuming that he does not intend to make a proclamation and to be excessive in the disclosure.

It is forbidden to dwell in the vicinity of any of those with an evil tongue, and all the more to sit with them and to listen to their words. The judgment against our fathers in the desert was decreed solely because of the evil tongue.[147]

One who takes vengeance against his fellow man transgresses a prohibition. As it is said: "You shall not take vengeance."[148] Even though he is not given lashes, this is an extremely bad character trait.[149] It is proper for a man to overlook all the things of the world, for according to those who understand, everything is vain and empty and not worth taking vengeance for.

What is vengeance? His friend says: "Lend me your axe." He says: "I will not lend it to you." The next day, [the other] needs to borrow from him and says: "Lend me your axe." He says: "I will not lend it to you, for you did not lend your axe to me when I asked you for it." This is taking vengeance.[150] Rather, when someone comes to him to borrow, he shall give with a perfect heart and not repay in kind. So too, with all things like these. So too, David said, referring to his good character traits: "If I have repaid my friend with evil or plundered my enemy without cause, etc."[151]

Likewise, whoever bears a grudge against any Israelite transgresses a prohibition. As it is said: "You shall not bear a grudge against the sons of your people."[152] How so? Reuben said to Simon: "Rent this house to me" or "Lend this ox to me." Simon did not wish to. After several days, Simon needed to borrow from Reuben or to rent from him. Reuben said to him: "Here you are, I will lend it to you. I am not like you. I will not pay you back in kind." The one who acts like this transgresses the verse: "You shall not bear a grudge."[153]

Rather, he shall blot out the matter from his heart and not bear a grudge. If he bears a grudge over something[154] and remembers it, he might come to take vengeance. Therefore the Torah was particularly concerned with grudge-bearing so that the wrong done be completely blotted out from a man's heart and he not remember it. This is the appropriate character trait; it makes possible the settlement of the earth and social relations[155] among human beings.[156]

●

*Blessed be the Merciful One
who has helped us.*

NOTES

1. These commandments are all based upon verses from Scripture cited in the text.
2. The primary meaning of the word is "soul."
3. Eccles. 5:9.
4. I.e., conception. Cf. Hilkhot De'ot, IV 20, where the beginning of a man's creation is contrasted with the time of his birth.
5. Or: straight path.
6. Literally: a middle measure.
7. Literally: the first wise men.
8. Cf. *Babylonian Talmud* (cited henceforth as B.T.), Mo'ed Qatan, 5a; Sotath, 5b.
9. Prov. 13:25. The last word in the verse could also be translated as "soul."
10. Ps. 37:16.
11. Literally: the first pious men.
12. A rabbinic expression for going beyond what is required by the Law.
13. Or: straight.
14. Deut. 28:9.
15. According to B.T., Shabbat, 133b, just as God is gracious and merciful, man must be gracious and merciful. Cf. *Sifre* to Deut. 10:12, which teaches that just as God is merciful, gracious, just and pious (*hasid*), so too, man must acquire these qualities. The command to imitate the holiness of God is based on Lev. 19:2.
16. Or: straight (yashar).
17. Gen. 18:19.
18. Ibid.
19. Isa. 5:20.
20. Prov. 2:13.

21. Prov. 1:7.
22. Literally: middle measure.
23. Literally: low.
24. Num. 12:3.
25. *Mishnah*, Avot, IV 4.
26. Literally: the root.
27. *B.T.*, Sotah, 4b; Deut. 8:14.
28. *B.T.*, Sotah, 5a.
29. Literally: the first wise men.
30. Cf. *B.T.*, Shabbat, 115b.
31. *B.T.*, Pesahim, 66b.
32. Ibid., 113b.
33. *B.T.*, Yoma, 23a; Gittin 36b.
34. Cf. *B.T.*, Sukkah, 28a, where this is reported about R. Yohanan ben Zakkai. "Our holy master" refers to R. Judah the Prince.
35. *Mishnah*, Avot, I 16.
36. Ibid. Maimonides interprets the word *guf* in the rabbinic passage quite literally as "body." It might also mean something like "principle," in which case the passage would read: "I have found no better principle than silence."
37. *B.T.*, Pesahim, 3b.
38. Eccles. 5:2.
39. *Mishnah*, Avot, III 16.
40. Eccles. 9:17.
41. Literally: steal the opinion of.
42. *Mishnah*, avot, III 16.
43. Cf. ibid.
44. The primary meaning of this word is "soul."
45. Literally: possess a good eye. This refers to the virtue of contentment, according to Maimonides' Commentary on *Avot*, II 12.
46. *Mishnah*, Avot, IV 12.
47. Cf. ibid., IV 1.
48. Ibid., IV 27.
49. Literally: the middle measure.
50. Prov. 4:26. The full verse reads: "Balance the course of your steps, and all your ways will be upright."
51. Na'eh, which can have the connotation of being suitable, attractive, or becoming.
52. I.e., Christian monks.
53. Num. 6:11.
54. *B.T.*, Ta'anit 11a; Nedarim, 10a; Nazir, 19a, 22a; Baba Qamma, 91b.
55. *Jerusalem Talmund*, Nedarim, IX 1.
56. Eccles. 7:16.
57. Literally: he shall place upon his heart. According to the Jewish tradition, the heart is the location of both thought and will.
58. Prov. 25:27.
59. The next has the plural and (presumably) the definite article: the wisdoms.
60. Literally: the Place (a talmudic term for God).
61. *Mishnah*, Avot, II 15.
62. Prov. 3:6.
63. The rainy season refers to the winter months.
64. Cf. *Mishnah*, Avot, IV 1: "Who is a powerful man *(gibbor)*? He who conquers his impulse."
65. Literally: wet.
66. Prov. 21:23.
67. Prov. 31:3. The biblical verse reads, "your ways"; the edition of Hyamson reads, "your years."
68. *B.T.*, Baba Barta, 146a; Ketuvot, 110b.
69. *Talmind ha-hakhamim*, which refers to an advanced student of the law, who might even be elderly.
70. *B.T.*, Sanhedrin, 17b. The passage there reads: "A disciple of a wise man [or a wise disciple] is not permitted to live in a city that does not have these ten things: a court that can give lashes and exact penalties, charity collected by two [men] and distributed by three, a synagogue, a bathhouse, a bathroom, a physician, a surgeon, a scribe, a butcher, and a teacher of children."
71. Malachi 2:3.
72. *B.T.*, Shabbat, 151b. The passage there reads: "These are the people who foresake the words of Torah and make all their days like holidays."

73. Isa. 22:13.
74. Isa. 28:8.
75. Prov. 13:25. The last word in this verse could also be translated as "soul."
76. Readings with the traditional version, the Rome edition, the Constantinople edition, and many manuscripts cited in Lieberman; Hyamson has "the pious, just men of old."
77. Literally: the first pious men.
78. Literally: the words of vanity (or exaggeration).
79. Amos 4:13.
80. B.T., Hagigah, 5b.
81. Or: have a sense of shame (bayyshanin).
82. *Seniy'ut*, as distinct from *bushah*, which is found at the end of V 4. *Bushah* can have the connotation of a "sense of shame."
83. *Mishnah*, Avot, IV 20.
84. Ibid., I 6. More literally: he inclines toward judging every man as being on the scale of merit.
85. Ibid., I 12.
86. Ibid., IV 23.
87. Ibid.
88. B.T., Berakhot, 43b.
89. B.T., Kiddushin, 31a. Cf. *Guide*, III 52.
90. Isa. 3:16.
91. Ibid.
92. *Ba'al de'ah*. Literally: a master of intellect, or of character trait.
93. Eccles. 10:3.
94. See supra, chapter three, note fifty-one.
95. B.T., Berakhot, 43b. If he is perfumed, he might be suspected of being a homosexual. If he is not accustomed to go out alone at night, he might be suspected of some other improper conduct.
96. B.T., Hullin, 84a.
97. Deut. 12:20.
98. B.T., Hullin, 84b.
99. The text has the plural (ba'alei de'ah). Cf. note ninety-two.
100. Cf. Deut. 20:6,5,7. Maimonides changes the order found in the Bible.
101. Deut. 28:30. The complete verse reads: "A woman shall you betroth and another man shall lie with her; a house shall you build and you shall not dwell in it; a vineyard shall you plant and not use the fruit thereof."
102. I Sam. 18:14.
103. According to Jewish law, "a purchase is made with words." The sale must be consummated by the payment of money, signing a contract, or some other legally binding method (M.T., Laws of Selling, I). The disciples of the wise go beyond what the Law requires.
104. Or: his friend. The word *haver*, usually translated as "fellow man," does not have universalistic overtones. It means "friend," "associate," "fellow."
105. Cf. supra, Chapter Two, paragraph five.
106. Isa. 49:3. This verse is also quoted at the end of the fifth chapter in M.T., Laws of the Foundation of Torah. That chapter deals with the sanctification of God's name and ends with an exhortation to wise men to be scrupulous in all their conduct.
107. Prov. 13:20.
108. Ps. 1:1.
109. Lam. 3:28.
110. Jer. 9:1.
111. Deut. 10:20.
112. *Sifre* to Deut. 10:12.
113. Deut. 11:22; B.T., Ketuvot, 111b.
114. *Mishnah*, Avot. I 4.
115. Lev. 19:18.
116. *Jerusalem Talmund*, Hagigah, II 1.
117. *Ger*, which also means "stranger." Maimonides interprets the commandment, "To love the stranger," as requiring a love of the convert. Cf. Sifra to Lev. 19:33–34.
118. Deut. 10:19. This is the conventional translation of the verse. According to the interpretation of Maimonides, it means: "And you shall love the convert."
119. Deut. 6:5.
120. Deut. 10:18. This is the conventional translation of the verse. According to the interpretation of Maimonides, it means: "And He loves the convert."
121. Lev. 19:17.

122. II Sam. 13:22. After Amnon had forced their sister, Tamar, to lie with him, Absolom hated Amnon and did not rebuke him.
123. Lev. 19:17.
124. Gen. 20:17. After Abimelech showed regret for having taken Sarah, whom he had supposed to be Abraham's sister, Abraham asked God not to punish Abimelech.
125. Lev. 19:17.
126. Literally: the Place (a talmudic term for God).
127. *B.T.*, 'Arakhin, 16b.
128. Lev. 19:17.
129. *B.T.*, 'Arkhin, 16b.
130. *Mishnah*, Avot, III 14.
131. Exod. 22:21.
132. Exod. 22:23.
133. Exod. 22:22.
134. Or: straight path.
135. Prov. 22:23.
136. Lev. 19:16.
137. Ibid.
138. When Saul was in pursuit of David, Doeg the Edomite reported to Saul that David had been aided by the priest, Ahimelech of Nob. As a result, Saul had eighty-five priests of Nob put to death by the hand of Doeg. All the inhabitants of Nob were also exterminated by Doeg. I Sam. 22:6–19.
139. Ps. 12:4.
140. Cf. *B.T.*, 'Arakhin, 15b.
141. Literally: the root.
142. *B.T.*, 'Arakhin, 15b; Ps. 12:5.
143. Cf. *Jerusalem Talmund*, Pe'ah, I 1; *B.T.*, 'Arakhin, 15b.
144. Prov. 27:14.
145. Prov. 26:18–19.
146. Literally: the evil tongue.
147. *B.T.*, 'Arakhin, 15a. According to the Talmund, the Hebrews were not permitted to enter the promised land because they accepted the evil report of the spies concerning the land of Canaan. Cf. Num. 13:31–14:23.
148. Lev. 19:18.
149. Reading *de'ah* with the traditional version, the Rome edition, and other editions listed in Liberman; Hyamson has *da'at*.
150. *B.T.*, Yoma, 23a; *Sifra* to Lev. 19:18.
151. Ps. 7:5. The next verse continues: "Let the enemy pursue my soul and overtake it, and tread my life down to the earth; let him lay my glory in the dust."
152. Lev. 19:18.
153. *B.T.*, Yoma, 23a; *Sifra* to Lev. 19:18.
154. More literally: If he guards *(noter)* the thing. The primary meaning of the Hebrew word that refers to bearing a grudge is to "guard" or "keep."
155. *Masa' umatan*, a Hebrew idiom meaning literally, "carrying and giving."
156. Maimonides closes the work as he had begun, with a reference to "human beings" *(benei 'adam)* and an allusion to man's political nature.

CHAPTER 11

St. Thomas Aquinas

(See Chapter Five for biography.)

St. Thomas Aquinas on Concerning Evil

At the outset, it should be noted that Aquinas continues in the tradition of St. Augustine and the Pseudo-Dionysius concerning the nature of evil. Evil is the privation of good. Construing evil as such makes it possible to accommodate God as essentially good and the creator of the universe and all that therein is. Were Aquinas to argue that evil is some thing, it would follow that God is ultimately responsible for its creation which is unacceptable. Article 1 begins with the question "Is evil something?" Evil can be understood in one of two ways: (a) as that which is the subject of evil, namely, as something or (b) as evil itself. In the first case Aquinas argues that evil is not a thing and in the second case that evil is to be understood as the privation of some particular good. The second article asks, "Does evil exist in the good?" There are two ways of understanding the good; (a) as the absolute good and (b) as a particular good. (a) The absolute good is essentially goodness and therefore evil does not exist in it. (b) Any given particular good is good by virtue of having the potential to be good. Evil exists in this way of understanding good as obstructing such potential to become fully actualized. Therefore, such evil is privation of actualized good.

"Is the good the cause of evil?" Good is the cause of evil only accidentally. The good by virtue of its essential nature cannot "intend" to cause evil. Consequently, any evil caused by good occurs only accidentally and manifests itself as a privation of the good that was intended by its good cause.

Evil is reasonably construed as (a) sin and (b) punishment. Is God the cause of sin? He is not because sin is caused by free choice. From the proposition that God is the cause of free choice, it does not follow that He is the cause of sin which is the consequence of (misguided) free choice.

"DISPUTED QUESTIONS CONCERNING EVIL" FROM *DE MALO*

Question One: Concerning Evil

The following problems are to be treated: (1) Is evil something?; (2) Does evil exist in the good?; (3) Is the good the cause of evil?; (4) Is the division of evil into sin and punishment adequately done?; (5) Which contains the greater character of evil—sin or punishment?

Article 1: Is evil something?

Arguments in Favor

It seems that evil is something because:

Evil is contrary to good. Now because contraries are defined in relationship to each other, since they are in the same category, they are something in nature. Thus evil is something.

Furthermore, contrary forms and privations are not found together in nature. However, physical evil is not said to be contrary to good, but only evil in moral matters, because evil and good, insofar as they are opposed, are contained within virtue and vice. Thus the contrariety of evil and good is not to be understood absolutely.

Again, all things that cause corruption, act. But evil as such causes corruption, as Dionysius says in the fourth chapter of *The Divine Names*. Thus evil as evil acts. Now nothing acts except insofar as it is something. Thus evil as such is something.

Moreover, what is not something cannot be the constitutive difference of anything, because every difference is both one and being, as stated in the Third Book of the *Metaphysics*. But good and evil are the constitutive differences of virtue and vice. Thus evil is something.

Besides, that which is not something cannot be increased and diminished. Now evil is increased and diminished, since homi-

From St. Thomas Aquinas, *De Malo* (Parma edition), translated by Richard Ingardia. Reprinted by kind permission of Richard Ingardia.

cide is a greater evil than adultery. Further, it cannot be said that an evil is called greater or more intense as it is more destructive of good, because corruption of the good is a consequent of evil, and a cause is not amplified or lessened owing to the effect, but conversely. Thus evil is something.

Furthermore, because the good is that which all desire, as is said in the First Book of the *Nicomachean Ethics*, the good has the nature of that which is desirable. For the same reason evil is that which is to be avoided. As the lamb by nature flees the wolf and desires its absence, it happens that something negatively signified is naturally sought and that something affirmatively signified is naturally fled. Thus evil is as much something as good.

Arguments Against

1. In the Eleventh Book of *The City of God* (Chapter IX), Augustine says that evil is a natural thing, but the word "evil" indicates a lack of good.

2. Again, John (1:3) says, "All things are made through Him." As Augustine says (Commentary on John, 1) evil is not made through the Word. Thus evil is not something.

3. Besides, in the same place Augustine states: "Without Him nothing is made— that is, sin; for sin is nothing, and men become nothing when they sin." For this reason, then, any evil at all is nothing. Thus evil is not something.

Resolution

I answer that 'evil' like 'white' can be said in two ways. For in one way when something is called 'white', we can understand the subject in which whiteness is located; in another way when the word 'white' is used, we can understand white as such, that is, the accident itself. Similarly 'evil' can be, in one way, understood as that which is the subject of evil, and this is

something. In another way, we can understand evil itself; and this is not any thing,
but is the very privation of some particular
good. In order to clarify this we must realize that, properly speaking, the good is
something insofar as it is desirable, because, according to the Philosopher in the
First Book of the *Nicomachean Ethics*, they
best give a definition of good who say that
the good is that which all desire. However,
evil is said to be opposite of good. Thus evil
is opposed to the desirable as such.

Now that which is opposed to the desirable as such cannot be anything, for three
reasons. First, the desirable has the nature
of an end. However, the order of ends corresponds to agents, because to the extent to
which an agent is higher and more universal, to the same extent the end for which it
acts is more of a universal good. This is so
because every agent acts for the sake of an
end and this is something good. This is especially clear in human actions. Thus the
ruler of a city aims for some particular
good, namely the good of the city, while
the king, who is superior, aims at a universal good, namely, the peace of the entire
kingdom. Thus, because among agent
causes (efficient causes) we cannot proceed
to infinity but must stop at one that is first,
which is the universal cause of being, so
also there must be some universal good to
which all other goods are ordered. And this
cannot be anything other than the first and
universal agent, because the desirable
moves the appetite and since the first
mover must be unmoved by any other, the
first and universal must be the first and
universal good, which does all things owing to a desire for itself. Thus just as everything in the real order must be caused by
the first and universal cause of being, so too
whatever is real must be caused from the
first and universal good. But what is from
the first and universal good can be only a
particular good, just as what comes from
the first and universal being can be only
some definite being. Thus whatever is in
reality must be some particular good, and
inasmuch as it exists is not able to be opposed to good. Hence the result of this is

that evil, insofar as it is evil, is not something in the real order but is the privation
of some particular good, inhering in some
particular good.

The second reason supporting the same
conclusion is that whatever exists in reality
has some inclination toward and tendency
for something agreeable to itself. However,
whatever has the nature of desirableness
has the nature of a good. Thus every real
thing is directed to a suitable good. However, evil as such is incompatible with the
good, but is opposed to it. Thus evil is not
any real thing. But if evil were some thing,
it would seek nothing, nor would it be
sought by anything. Consequently, because
nothing acts or is moved unless an end is
sought, an evil thing would have neither
action nor motion.

The third reason supports the same conclusion because existence itself especially
has the nature to be most desirable. Thus
we see that anything naturally tends to preserve its own existence, and flees things destructive of its existence and resists those
things as much as it is able. And so existence itself, inasmuch as it is desirable, is
good. Thus it necessarily follows that evil,
which is universally opposed to good, is
opposed to that which is existence. However, what is opposed to existence cannot
be something. Thus I conclude that that
which is evil happens is something, inasmuch as evil takes from its subject some
particular good, just as blindness itself is
not something, but the subject to which
blindness happens is something.

Replies to Arguments in Favor

Good and evil are properly contrasted as
privation, because, as Simplicius says
(*Commentary on the Categories*) contraries
properly exist as something in the real order, as hot and cold, white and black, but
other contrasts are such that one is in the
real order and the other withdrawn from
reality, and this is a relative opposition,
namely privations. But privations are of
two kinds: one is the privation of the perfection of existence, death and blindness.
The other privation is reductive of such

perfection, illness or ophthalmia, which put a being on the way to death or blindness; and this kind of privation prohibits being called a contrary inasmuch as it retains something from what has been stripped.

In moral matters more than in material things is evil said to be contrary to good, because moral matters depend on free choice, and the object of choice is good and evil. However, each act receives its designation and species from an object. Thus if an act of the will tends to what is evil, it receives its character as evil and is called evil. This evil is most properly the contrary of good.

Evil considered generally, that is evil itself, is said to corrupt, not actively corrupt but formally, insofar as the corruption of the good is evidently just what it is. Similarly, blindness is said to corrupt vision inasmuch as it consists in the very corruption or privation of sight. But that which is evil, if it is evil absolutely, that is, evil itself, does corrupt in that it introduces evil into an act and an effect. This is done not efficiently but deficiently, according to a defect in the active power. Similarly, the seed that is improperly received in the progenitor produces a defective offspring, which is a corruption of nature. But if that something is not evil absolutely and purely, then, according to its own active power, it can produce complete corruption, not unqualifiedly but only in another.

Only in moral matters are good and evil differences, in that evil is said to be something positive, as the very act of choice is characterized as evil from what is chosen; though evil itself cannot be chosen except under the aspect of good.

One thing is more evil than another, yet not because of a proximity to some highest evil or because of diverse participation in some form as something is said to be more or less white through diverse participation in whiteness. Rather, something is said to be more or less evil according as it is more or less defective of the good, not, certainly, efficiently but formally. For homicide is said to be a greater sin than adultery, not

because it destroys more the natural good of the soul, but because it more removes goodness from activity of the soul. Murder, more than adultery, is opposed to the good of charity with which the virtuous act ought to be informed.

Non-existence is never sought after except insofar as through some particular non-existence one's proper being is conserved. For example, the lamb seeks the absence of the wolf so as to maintain its own life; and the presence of the wolf is not fled except as it is a threat to the lamb's life. Thus it is clear that being is desired for its own sake and fled from only accidentally, while non-being of itself is avoided and sought after only accidentally. Thus the good as good is something and that evil as evil is privation.

Article 2: Does evil exist in the good?

Arguments in Favor

Evil and good are opposites. But each opposite is not in the other: the cold is not in the hot. Thus evil is not in the good.

Furthermore, that which is not a being cannot be in anything. But evil is not a being. Thus evil is not in the good.

Arguments Against

1. Augustine says (*Enchiridion*, ch. 14) that evil cannot exist except in the good.
2. Again, evil is a privation of the good, as Augustine says in *Enchiridion* (ch. 11). But a privation determines its subject, because it is a negation in a subject, as stated in the Fourth Book of the *Metaphysics*. Thus evil determines for itself a subject. Because it is existing, every subject is good, since the good and being are convertible. Thus evil exists in the good.

Resolution

Evil exists only in the good. In order to make this clear we should distinguish two ways of talking about the good: one way is an absolute good, the other way as this or that particular good, for example, a good man or a good eye.

Speaking about an absolute good, as the Platonists were pleased to say, the good has the broadest extension, even broader than being. Because the good is that which is desirable, that which of itself is desirable is of itself good. Such is the end. And from the fact that we seek an end, it follows that we seek what is ordered to the end. As a consequence of this those things ordered to the end as means acquire the character of goods because they are ordered to the end or the good. Thus useful things are included in the understanding of the good. Now everything that is in potency to the good has, from this fact itself, an order to the good, since to be in potency is nothing other than to be ordered to act. Clearly, therefore, the potential has, from the fact that it is potential, the character of a good. Now every subject, insofar as it is in potency to some perfection, even primary matter, has from the very fact that it is in potency, the character of a good. And because the Platonists did not distinguish matter and privation and placed matter in the category of non-being, they maintained that the good has greater extension than being. And this position Dionysius took in the *Divine Names* (ch. 5) in which he made the good prior to being. And although matter is to be distinguished from privation and is not non-being except accidentally, nevertheless, this position contains some truth. For primary matter is called being only to the extent that it is potential, and has absolute existence through form, while it has the potential through itself. Now because potency pertains to the character of the good, as has been said, it follows that matter is of itself good.

Now although any being at all, whether in act or in potency, can be called an absolute good, nevertheless, it does not follow that anything whatsoever is this good. For example, if some man is an absolute good it does not follow that he has achieved excellence as a zither player, since to achieve this he must perfect himself in the art. Thus, although man, from the very fact that he is man, is something good, still from this fact he is not a good man; rather, that which makes anything good is its proper virtue. For virtue is what makes its possessor good, according to the Philosopher in the Second Book of the *Nicomachean Ethics*. Now, as is said in the First Book of *The Heavens*, virtue is the ultimate potency of a thing. Thus it becomes clear that something is called good having the perfection proper to it, as man is called good when he has the perfection of a man and an eye is called good when it has the perfection of an eye.

Thus from the above the good can be spoken about in three ways. In the first way the very perfection of a thing is called its good, as sharpness of vision is said to be the good of the eye and as virtue is said to be the good of man. In the second way the very thing possessing its proper perfection is called good, for example, the virtuous man, the eye that sees clearly. In the third way good is said of the subject itself, insofar as it is in potency to perfection, for example, the soul is directed to virtue and the substance of the eye to keenness of sight.

Now, as has been said, evil is nothing other than the privation of a due perfection. However, privation exists only in that which is potential, since we speak of something being deficient when it lacks that which it is natural to have. It follows that evil exists in the good, insofar as being in potency is called good. Yet that good which is the very perfection of a thing is destroyed by evil; thus it is not in such good that evil exists. Yet there is a good that is a combination of the subject and its perfection. Such a good is diminished by evil insofar as the perfection is taken away while the subject remains. For example, blindness destroys sight, impairs the seeing eye, and exists in the substance of the eye, or in the animal itself, as in a subject.

Thus if there is a good that is pure act, having no admixture of potency, and this is so of God, in such a good evil can in no way exist.

Replies to Arguments in Favor

Evil is not opposed to the good in which it exists, because it exists in the good which is potential. But evil is a privation, and the potency is the opposite of neither privation nor perfection; it underlies both. Nevertheless, Dionysius does use this reason to show that evil is not in the good as an existing something. (*The Divine Names*, ch. 4)

Evil is not said to be in the good as something positive but as a privation.

Article 3: Is the good the cause of evil?

Arguments in Favor

It seems that the good is not the cause of evil because:

As stated in the Gospel of Matthew: "The good tree does not bear evil fruit." For the fruit is called an efficient cause. Thus good is not the cause of evil.

Yet it can be stated that the good, insofar as it is deficient, is the cause of evil. But, on the other hand, everything deficient has the character of evil. Thus if good is the cause of evil, insofar as it is deficient, then the good is the cause of evil, inasmuch as it possesses in itself evil; hence the original problem returns regarding that evil. Thus one proceeds either to infinity, or one is led back to a first evil that causes evil, or it is argued that the good, insofar as it is deficient, is the cause of evil.

Moreover, every good, insofar as it is created, is defective. Thus if good, insofar as it is limited, is the cause of evil, it follows that good, insofar as it is created, is the cause of evil. However, a created good remains always created. Thus for all time the good causes evil, which is absurd.

Besides, if good, insofar as it is either actually or potentially deficient, is the cause of evil, it follows that God, who in no way is either actually or potentially deficient, can be the cause of evil. Yet this is what is opposed to what is said in Scripture. Thus good is not the cause of evil, insofar as it is deficient.

Again, if the will, insofar as it is deficient, is the cause of evil, then the will is punishable for its acts of itself, as this constitutes

punishment, so punishment precedes blame, or the will is not responsible for its own acts, and so from such defect, no evil would ensue; for it does not follow that, for example, a stone is evil because it lacks sight. Thus no good is the cause of evil, insofar as it is deficient.

Arguments Against

1. In *Enchiridion* (chapters 14 and 15), Augustine says that evil cannot arise except from the good.
2. Besides, in *The Divine Names* (ch. 4), Dionysius says that the source and end of all evils is a good.

Resolution

In the manner in which evil can have a cause, that cause is the good. But evil cannot have an essential cause. This is seen in three ways.

Now the first reason is that a thing having an essential cause is intended by its cause, because that which arises apart from the agent's intention is not a direct effect but an accidental one. For example, the digging of a grave is accidentally the cause of the uncovering of a treasure, since it happens without the intention of the gravedigger. Yet evil, insofar as it is evil, cannot be intended nor in any way willed or desired. The reason is that every object of appetite has the character of a good, to which evil as evil is opposed. Thus we see that no one produces some evil unless intending what seems to him as a good. For example, to the adulterer experiencing sense pleasures seems good, and it is for this reason he commits adultery. Thus we are left with the conclusion that evil does not have an essential cause.

The second reason is that every direct or essential effect has a likeness to its cause in some manner, either according to the same nature, as with univocal agents, or according to a deficient nature, as with equivocal agents. For every agent cause (efficient cause) acts according as it is in act. Actuality, however, pertains to the nature of the good. Thus evil as such is not assimilated to the agent cause insofar as the agent is acting. It remains, therefore, that evil does not have an essential cause.

The third reason is that every essential cause has a certain, specified order to its effect. But that which occurs according to an order is not evil; rather evil occurs when there is a neglecting of order. Hence evil does not have a direct cause.

While it is clear that evil does not have a direct cause, still it must in some way have a cause. The reason is clear because evil is not something existing by itself but something inhering as a privation (which is the lack of that which ought naturally be present), that which is evil does not naturally enter into that in which it inheres. For if any defect belongs to a thing naturally, it cannot be said that this is an evil for it, for it is not bad for a man to be deprived of wings or for a stone to lack vision, since such lacks follow from nature. Now everything that exists in another without being natural to it must have some cause; for water would not be hot without some cause. Thus it turns out that every evil has some cause, not essentially but accidentally. Now every thing that exists accidentally is reduced to that which is an essential cause. Now if evil does not have an essential cause, as has been shown, it follows that only good has an essential cause. But there cannot be any essential cause of the good except the good, because every essential cause causes its likeness. From all of this it follows that for any evil good is the cause accidentally.

However, it happens that evil, which is a defective good, is the cause of evil. Nevertheless, it still comes down to holding that the first cause of evil is not evil but good. Thus there are two ways in which good causes evil. One way is to the extent that the good is deficient; the other way, is to the extent that the good is accidental.

It is easy to see these points established among natural things. For of that evil that is destructive of water the cause is the ac-

tive power of fire. Now, the fire is not principally and essentially inclined to the destruction of water; rather fire is principally tending to produce its own form in matter, which tending necessarily brings about the elimination of water; and so it is accidentally that fire makes water cease to exist. Now of the evil that produces the birth of a defective child, the cause is the deficient power in the seed. Yet if we seek a cause of this deformity, the evil of the seed, it will be discovered that some good is the cause of the evil accidentally, and not insofar as it is deficient. For the deficiency in the seed the cause is some variable principle that brings about a quality contrary to what is proper for the good disposition of the seed. The stronger the alternative power of this principle, so much the more does it bring out the contrary quality and consequently the defect in the seed. Thus the evil of the seed is not caused by the good insofar as it is deficient; rather, it is caused by the good insofar as the good is perfect but operating accidentally.

A similar situation exists in the voluntary order, though not with respect to all matters. For it is clear that the sensible pleasure moves the will of the adulterer in such a way to revel in pleasure that excludes the order of reason and the divine law. This is moral evil. If, therefore, the situation were such that the will was necessarily subject to the influence of such enticing pleasure, as a natural body is necessarily subject to an exterior power, the situation of voluntary acts and natural acts would be like each other. However, the two acts are not identical. For it is in the power of the will to accept or not to accept the attraction of the exterior sensible lure, no matter how much it may attract. Thus of the evil that occurs when the will accepts, the cause of the evil is not the exterior detectible but the will itself. The will, then, is the cause of evil both ways: by accident and according as it is a deficient good. The will causes evil accidentally insofar as it seeks in something what is good relatively but has conjoined to it that which is simply evil. But as a deficient good the will causes evil to the extent that in the will there is presupposed some defect preceding the deficient choice through which is chosen that relative good which is simply evil.

Now in all things wherever one ought to be the rule and measure of the other, the good in that which is ruled and measured in conformity to the rule and measure, while evil consists in not being ruled or measured. Thus, if any artisan must cut a piece of wood in a straight line according to some rule and fails to cut in a straight line—which is to make a bad cut—this bad cutting will result from the fact that the artisan was without his rule and measure. Similarly, pleasure and every other thing in human affairs ought to be measured and ruled according to the rule of reason and divine law. Accordingly, that the will does not use reason and divine law is presupposed in the will prior to an inordinate choice.

However, in this matter, in the failure to use the rule of reason it is not necessary to seek a cause, since the very freedom of the will, by which it is can act or not act, is sufficient. Now this very lack of actual attention to the rule, considered in itself, is not an evil; neither is it a fault (sin) or a punishment, because the soul is not required, nor is it able, constantly to attend to a rule of this sort, in act. Now the first element of fault appears in the fact that, without the actual consideration of the rule, the will, nonetheless, proceeds to a choice of this kind. Similarly, the artisan does not err by the fact that he does not hold onto his measure always; rather, he errs in that not holding the measure he proceeds along in the cutting. Similarly, the fault of the will is not in this that it does not actually attend to the rule of reason or divine law. Rather it consists in this that, not having this rule or measure, it proceeds to choose. And so it is that Augustine says (Twelfth Book of *The City of God*, chapters 6–7) that the will is the cause of sin insofar as it is deficient, but that defect he compares to silence and darkness because that defect is solely a negation.

Replies to Arguments in Favor

Augustine resolved this problem in *Enchiridion* (ch. 15) by distinguishing that the tree symbolizes the will and the fruit symbolizes the exterior work. It is understood that the good tree cannot bear evil fruit, since an evil work does not come from a good will any more than a good work comes from an evil will. Nevertheless, the will itself comes from some good, just as the bad tree is produced from the good soil. For, as was said above, if any evil effect arises from an evil cause, which is a deficient good, nevertheless it is imperative to conclude that evil is caused accidentally by a good that is not deficient.

Some good is the cause of evil insofar as it is deficient; yet this is not the sole way in which good causes evil. Somehow good also causes evil accidentally and not just insofar as it is deficient. In voluntary acts the cause of evil, which is sin, is a deficient will. However, this deficiency does not have the character of a fault or punishment, since it is presupposed by sin, as has been shown. And for such a deficiency no further cause need be sought, so it is not necessary to proceed to infinity. Thus it is said that good is the cause of evil insofar as it is deficient. If by "insofar as" is designated something pre-existing, then the statement is not universally true. If, however, it designates something concomitant, then it is universally true, because everything that causes evil is deficient, that is, a deficiency causing. In the same way it might be said that every hot thing heats to the extent that it is hot.

Good, from the fact that it is created, can fail by the sort of deficiency from which voluntary evil proceeds. For from the fact that a thing is created it follows that it is subject to another as to a rule and measure. However, if it were its own rule and measure, it could not begin to operate without a rule and measure. Precisely for this reason God, who is His own rule, cannot sin, just as an artisan could not err in cutting a piece of wood if his hand were its own rule for cutting.

As previously argued, it is not necessary that good, which is the cause of evil accidentally, be a deficient good. For God is the cause of the evil of punishment, because He does not intend evil to that which He punishes but rather the imposition of His justice on things, which results in evil for that which is punished. For example, the form of fire entails the privation of water.

The defect that sin presupposes in the will is not itself a fault or a punishment but is a pure negation; it acquires the nature of a fault from the fact that with this negation the will begins to operate. For out of the very application of the will to a task arises the need of that good which it lacks—namely, actual attention to the rule of reason and of divine law.

Article 4: Is the division of evil into sin and punishment adequately done?

Arguments in Favor

It seems that the division of evil into sin and punishment is not adequately done because:

Some evil is neither sin nor punishment, for example, natural evil. Thus the division of evil into punishment and sin is not adequately done.

Furthermore, as the Philosopher says in the *Topics* (Bk. I, ch. 13), as often as one division is stated, so many times it is corrected. For the good is spoken about in three ways: virtue, utility, and pleasure. And so evil must be divided in three, not two, ways.

Again, according to the Philosopher (*Nicomachean Ethics*, Bk. II, ch. 6), evil is as multiple as good. But the good is threefold: nature, grace, glory. Thus it seems that evil must be multiple, and so evil cannot be properly divided into just two categories.

Resolution

In comparison with other creatures the rational or intellectual nature possesses good and evil in a special manner. For every other creature is naturally directed to some particular good, whereas the intellectual nature alone apprehends the nature of common good itself through the intellect and moves towards the common good through the desire of the will. Thus the evil of the rational creature is divided specially into sin and punishment. For this division of evil is not made except according to what is in rational nature, as is clear from what Augustine stated. Also, from this source, the rationale is accepted that whereas it is of the nature of sin that it follows from the will, it is of the nature of punishment that it is opposed to the will. For the will is located in the intellectual nature alone. This twofold distinction can be accepted here for the moment.

For, as evil is opposed to good, it is necessary that evil be divided according to the division of good. For the good designates a certain perfection. Now perfection is twofold: the first is a form or ability, and the second is an operation. With respect to the first perfection, the exercise of which is operation, is able to be led back to each thing we use in acting. Conversely, evil also is found in a twofold way. In the first way, evil is found in the agent itself, which lacks form, or ability, or whatever is required for its operation; blindness or crookedness of limb is some evil.

Now just as it occurs that these two types of evil are found in other things, so too it is discovered that it is in the intellectual nature that acts through the will. It is clear here that an inordinate action of the will has the character of sin, because from this anyone is blamed and is made culpable, in that such a person voluntarily performs an inordinate action. It is, however, in this way that evil is found in intellectual creatures according to a deficiency of form or ability, or of any other thing required for acting well, whether it pertains to the soul, the body, or to external things. According to the Catholic faith, such evil must be called punishment. For, concerning the nature of punishment, three items are present. The first one is that punishment has a relation to sin, since someone is said to be punished when he suffers evil for something he has committed. Moreover, the tradition of the Catholic faith holds that the rational creature cannot incur anything harmful, neither with respect to the soul, the body, or any external things, unless sin existed either in the person or at least in his nature. Thus it follows that each deficiency of a good that anyone can use for acting properly is called punishment in men, and for the same reason, in Angels. Thus every evil of the rational creature falls under either sin or punishment.

Now the second item that pertains to the character of punishment is that it opposes the will. The desire of every single thing has an inclination to its proper good; hence, to be deprived of its proper good is repulsive to the will. . . . The third point pertaining to the nature of punishment is that it consists of a certain suffering. For in those things which are opposed to the will occur not as the consequent of an intrinsic principle, namely, the will itself, but from an extrinsic principle from which suffering is said to be an effect.

Thus sin and punishment differ in three ways. First, whereas sin is an evil of the action itself, punishment, however, is an evil of the acting. For these two evils are differently ordered in nature and voluntary being. For in natural things from the evil of the agent follows the evil of the action, for example, from a crooked leg limping follows. However, in voluntary being, on the

contrary, from the evil of action, which is sin, follows the evil of the agent, which is punishment, Divine Providence rectified sin through punishment. In the second way, punishment differs from sin because of this, that one is according to the will, and the other is contrary to the will, as Augustine said above. And in the third way, as Augustine saw (*On Free Choice*, bk. 1), sin is called evil in the acting, punishment in the suffering.

Replies to Arguments in Favor

As is stated, such a division of evil is not commonly accepted, but evil is not found in rational creatures, for there cannot be any evil that is not sin or punishment. Nevertheless, it is understood that not every deficiency has the character of evil, as natural things possess deficiencies of good; for it is not a defect of man that he cannot fly, and so consequently, this is neither sin nor punishment.

Besides, the useful good is directed to pleasure and the virtuous as to an end. And so there are two chief goods, namely, the virtuous and pleasure. To these two goods are opposed two evils: sin compared with the virtuous, punishment with pleasure.

As the good is threefold, namely, nature, grace, and glory, according to form and act, so too, sin and punishment are distinguished in the same way, as is stated.

QUESTION THREE: CONCERNING THE CAUSE OF SIN

Article 1: Is God the cause of evil?

Arguments in Favor

It seems that God is the cause of evil because:

As the Apostle says (Rom. 1: 28): "God delivered them to their reprobate sense, that they might do unsuitable things." The gloss of Augustine taken from the book, *On Grace and Free Choice*, says: "It is clear that God works in the hearts of men by inclining their wills to whatever He wills,

whether to good or evil." But the inclination of the will to evil is sin. Thus God causes sin.

Besides, that which is the cause of the cause is cause of the caused. But free choice, the cause of which is God, is the cause of sin. Thus God causes sin.

Furthermore, that to which a power disposes—which power comes from God—is itself caused by God. Yet some powers that are caused by God are inclined towards sin, as the irascible appetite inclines us to murder, and the concupiscible power to adultery. Thus God is the cause of sin.

Again, it belongs to the same thing to act and to be able to act. For, as the Philosopher says (*On Dreams*, ch. 1), to whom the power exists, so too does the act. But God is the cause of the power to sin.

Arguments Against

1. Augustine says in *The Eighty-Three Questions* that it is not God's origination that man deteriorates. But man is deformed because of sin. Thus God is not the author of sin.

2. Besides, Fulgentius (*Ad Monimum*, bk. 1) says that God is not the cause of that which He is the punisher. For God punishes sin. Thus God is not the cause of sin.

3. Again, as stated in *Wisdom* xi, 25, "God loves all the things that exist, and He hates none of the things He has made." It is for this reason that God causes only what He loves. Yet, according to *Wisdom*, xiv, 9, "In like manner, God hates the wicked and that which springs from the wicked." Thus God is not the cause of sin.

Resolution

There are two ways that one is the cause of sin. One way is that one commits the sin himself; the other way is that one makes another person commit sin. Neither of these two ways pertains to God.

It is clear that God cannot cause sin both from the common meaning of sin and from the proper meaning of sin, as a culpability. Sin spoken about in a common way, according as it is found in natural and artificial things, arises from the fact that in acting one does not achieve the end for the sake of which it acts. This defect arises in the active principle, as is the case in the grammarian's failure to write correctly, when he intends to do so, results from a failure of his art; and that nature sins in the formation of an animal, as occurs in the birth of a deformed animal, results from a defect in the power of the seed.

Sin, as it is properly said in moral matters, has the character of culpability and arises in that the will falls short of its end, tending to an unsuitable end. In God, however, neither can the active principle be deficient, because the power of God is infinite, nor can God's will fail to achieve its proper end, because the divine will, which is the divine nature, is the highest end and the first rule of all wills. Thus naturally the divine will is contained in the supreme good; and this cannot be deficient. In like manner, the appetite of any thing cannot be deficient, when it seeks its natural good. Thus God cannot cause sin in the sense that He Himself should sin.

Similarly, God cannot cause sin making others sin. For sin, as we now speak of it, consists in the aversion of the created will from the ultimate end. It is impossible, however, that God prevent the will of another from the ultimate end, because that which is commonly discovered in all created agents is possessed by imitating the first agent, which produces its likeness on all things insofar as they are able to receive it, as Dionysius points in the ninth chapter of *The Divine Names*. Now any created agent is found by its action to attract somehow other things to itself, making them like itself. This assimilating occurs through a likeness in form, as when hot heats or ordering other things to its own end, as when man by his commands orders others to the end he intends. Thus it is fitting for God to direct all things to Himself and consequently to prevent nothing from coming to Himself. For God is the highest good. Thus God cannot be the cause of the aversion of will from the highest good, which constitutes the nature of sin, as we are now speaking of it. Therefore, it is impossible that God is the cause of evil.

Replies to Arguments in Favor

God is said to hand over some to their reprobate sense, or to incline their wills to evil, not by acting or moving them, but by not impeding them and allowing them to be alone. Thus, if someone did not lend a helping hand to one who was falling, he could be said to be the cause of that fall. But God out of His judgment, establishes that for some men, His aid will not prevent them from falling.

The effect of a cause, insofar as it is a cause, is reduced to the latter's cause. If, however, something arises from a cause other than as the caused, it does not have to be reduced to the cause of the cause. Thus the motion of the knee is caused by the motive power of the animal, which moves the knee; but a limited walk does not come from the knee, as it is subject to that motive power, but rather it fails to receive the influence of that motive power because of some defect of its own. Thus the limping is not caused by the motive power. So it is, there-fore, that sin is caused by free choice as it falls short of God. Thus, despite the fact that God is the cause of free choice, nevertheless, God need not be the cause of sin.

Sins do not arise from the irascible or concupiscible tendencies according to these have been instituted by God, but rather as they fail to comply with God's established order. Thus they are grounded in man that they be subject to reason. When they pre-cede human reason, therefore, and tend to sin, this inclination is not from God.

As the Philosopher says, it is understood that it is the same thing that can act and that acts but not that whatever is the cause of a power is the cause also of the act.

CHAPTER 12

John Duns Scotus

(See Chapter Six for biography.)

John Duns Scotus on Ethical Theory

Man's reason, guided by its "affection for justice" in conjunction with free will, is an essential feature of the ethical theory of Duns Scotus. Together they constitute a necessary, though not sufficient, condition for any action to have moral value. Without reason the will of man would be totally unfettered, resulting in capricious and therefore irrational behavior. Were he possessed of a "natural will," the sort that guides lower animals, man would be in the peculiar position of making errors of judgment, yet at the same time incapable of sinning. Such would be an untenable view for the likes of Duns Scotus, a member of the Franciscan Order of Friars. It is the "affection for justice" that aids man in his free choice to override his natural inclination for self-indulgence and opt for the more noble dictates of justice. It is because of his powers of reflective choice that man is responsible for the outcome of his decisions, be they good or evil.

The moral goodness of an action entails more than its being chosen freely. An action possesses moral worth both essentially and accidentally. The former pertains to the genetic character of an action, the latter to the circumstances surrounding its performance. For example, conceptually, one ought to tell the truth. However, there may well be specific circumstances which mitigate the moral goodness of such behavior.

Four factors contribute to "goodness from circumstance". "The first goodness comes, it seems, from the circumstances of the end, for given the nature of the agent, of the action, of the object, one immediately concludes that such an action ought to be performed by this agent for such an end, and that it ought to be chosen and wanted for the sake of such an end." To fully appreciate this requirement one must employ the distinction Duns Scotus draws between the internal and the external act. Consider, for example, the act of telling the truth. One can freely choose to tell the truth. Such is an internal act. It is an act of will. One's moving his *orbicularis oris* in such a way to form speech by which he tells the truth is an external act. In such a case, the will commands the mouth to move. Concerning the ends of actions, the "circumstance is not precisely characteristic of the act as actually performed or not, but rather of the act as willed and related to this end by an act of the will. Indeed, the decision to do something for a worthy purpose is no less good when the external act that ensues fails to achieve that end than when it succeeds."

The second circumstance contributing to the moral goodness of an action is the manner in which the action is performed. One must be concerned with how he performs an intended action. There is a difference between gently telling the truth and doing it in a cruel manner.

Third and fourth, there is an appropriate time and place to tell the truth. ". . . To be perfectly good, an act must be faultless on all counts." Moral goodness boils down to what Duns Scotus calls *integral suitability*. It is right reason that determines this suitability.

Since the role of right reason is different for internal and external acts, it follows that the goodness or badness relative to each also differs. This being the case, and because both are ultimately controlled by free will, that is, both internal and external acts are voluntary, it follows that both types of act are praiseworthy or blameworthy as the case may be. Were not acts voluntary, there would be no basis to ascribe either laudability or culpability to them.

GOD AND CREATURES; THE QUODLIBETAL QUESTIONS

Question 18
Does the Exterior Act Add Some Goodness or Badness to the Interior Act?

18.1   The next question concerns the interrelation of the extrinsic and intrinsic acts and asks whether the extrinsic adds some goodness or badness to the intrinsic.[1]

Arguments Pro and Con

Argument for the negative:[2]
That which is not voluntary is neither good nor bad. Now the external act insofar as it is distinct from the internal is not voluntary. It derives what "voluntary" character it has from the internal act. Therefore, the external act has no goodness or badness of its own and, having none, it cannot add any to the internal act.

18.2   Against this it is argued that what is forbidden by a distinct negative precept includes its own distinct illicitness. But the external act is forbidden by one precept and the internal act by another. This is clearly the case with the precepts "You shall not commit adultery" and "You shall not covet your neighbor's wife"[3] as well as

From John Duns Scotus, *God and Creatures, the Quodlibetal Questions*, translated by Felix Alluntis, O.F.M., and Allan B. Wolter, O.F.M. (Princeton, N.J.: Princeton University Press, 1975), pp. 399–417. Reprinted by permission of Princeton University Press.

with the precepts "You shall not steal" and "You shall not covet your neighbor's goods."[4]

Body of the Question

18.3   It is moral, not natural, goodness that poses the major difficulty, for the answer is clear enough as regards natural goodness, no matter how you understand this term, since internal and external acts are by nature different. Indeed, they are elicited immediately by different powers, the internal by the will and the external by some external power subject to the will's command.

18.4   Neither does the question pose a problem where the external and internal are distinct acts either because they are elicited by different persons (where one has the internal act, for instance, and the other the external) or because they are performed by the same person at different times (for instance, the same subject has only an internal act at one time and an external act at another). Only when the two acts are conjoined does the question become difficult (when, for example, in the same person the internal act is followed by an external act).

18.5   Third, the question must be understood extensionally and not as the addition of intensive goodness or badness. For as regards both good and bad actions, it frequently happens that desire for the absent is a weaker act than an act concerned with something present, which Augustine calls "love." "Wanting what is present," he says, "is love in the one who enjoys it."[5] But whether they be one or distinct, love is more perfect intensively than desire, since it satisfies the will in a way desire cannot do. When there is an exterior act, then, it can happen that the interior act is intensified. But this is not what the question is about. The issue is whether the external act of itself adds additional goodness to that which is proper to the internal act.

18.6   The sense in which the question creates the most difficulty, then, is this: Does the external act, when united with the internal act in one and the same person, have a moral goodness of its own distinct from that of the internal act?

18.7   To solve this question, three points require investigation: (1) Whence comes the moral goodness or badness of an act? (2) Does its laudability or its culpability spring from the same source? (3) Is the goodness or laudability of the external action distinct from that of the interior act?

Article I
The Source of Moral Goodness or Badness

18.8   [Description of moral goodness] The moral goodness of an act consists in its having all that the agent's right reason declares must pertain to the act or the agent in acting.

18.9   [Clarification] This description is explained as follows: Just as the primary goodness of a being, called "essential" and consisting in the integrity or perfection of the being itself, implies positively that there is no imperfection so that all lack or diminution of perfection is excluded, so the being's secondary goodness, which is something over and above, or "accidental," consists in its being perfectly suited to or in complete harmony with something else—

something which ought to have it or which it ought to have. And this two-way suitability is commonly connected. As an example of the first, health is said to be good for man because it suits him. [As an example of the second,] food is called good because it has an appropriate taste. Augustine gives examples of both.[6] "Health without pain or fatigue is good," he says. This refers to the first type of suitability, since health is good for man because it suits him. Then Augustine adds: "Good is the face of a man with regular features, a cheerful expression, and glowing color." This is an instance of the second, because here the face is called good for having what is appropriate to it.

There is this difference between the two. What suits someone is said to be good for him, that is, for him it is a good or a perfection, but we do not speak of it as being accidentally or denominatively good in itself. That to which something is appropriate, on the other hand, is called good denominatively because it has what is suited to it. In the first case, the form takes its name from the subject in which it is. As the soul is called "human," so something is called "good for man" because it is a human good. In the second case, the subject gets its designation from the form. Thus we say a man is good because of some good he has.

Now an act is by nature apt to be in agreement with its agent as well as to have something suited to itself. On both counts then it can be called "good" with a goodness that is accidental. This is true in general of a natural act as well, so that this goodness, which consists in having what is appropriate to it, is not only an accidental, but also a natural, goodness.[7]

18.10   Furthermore, some agents [are] without intellect and will neither judge nor can judge what is appropriate to their acts. In such a case, what is suitable is determined by natural causes alone and they incline the agent to act. Or if in addition there be the judgment of some mind and the movement of some will, it would be that of God alone as universal director and mover of the whole of nature. Now the goodness in the act of an agent without intellect and will is merely natural.

18.11 Over and above this general judgment [of God] about the suitability of the action (which concerns agents alike that act with or without knowledge), a general judgment is involved in the case of agents endowed with an intrinsic knowledge of their actions. Those with sense knowledge alone somehow apprehend the suitability of the object of their action. But whether or not they judge the action appropriate, the goodness of the action does not transcend the natural. Others act by virtue of intellectual knowledge, which alone is able to pass judgment, properly speaking, upon the appropriateness of the action. Such agents are suited by nature to have an intrinsic rule of rectitude for their actions. Only they can have an act whose goodness is moral.

18.12 But for this it is not enough that the agent have the ability to adjudicate the appropriateness of his acts. He must actually pass judgment upon the act and carry it out in accord with that judgment. If one is in error and still acts in accord with the correct judgment of another, he is not acting rightly, for by his own knowledge he was meant to regulate his actions and in this case he is not acting in accord with it but against it, and hence he does not act rightly. Similarly, such an agent elicits the sort of act as lies in his power. Now he has in his power the sort of act he deliberately elicits, for the power of free choice consists either formally or concomitantly in knowledge and election. And so it appears clear how the moral goodness of the act lies in its suitability judged according to the agent's right reason.

18.13 [Explanation of all that right reason demands of the act] We explain the added qualification [in 18.8], "all that must pertain to the act," in this way: Every judgment begins with something certain. Now the first judgment about the appropriateness cannot presuppose some knowledge determined by another intellect; otherwise it would not be first. Hence it presupposes

something certain but judged by this intellect, namely: the nature of the agent and the power by which he acts together with the essential notion of the act. If these three notions are given, no other knowledge is needed to judge whether or not this particular act is suited to this agent and this faculty. For instance, if one knows what man is, what his intellectual powers are, and what an act of understanding is, then it is clear to him that it befits man to understand with his intellect. Knowing what it means to attain knowledge, it would also be clear to him what it is not appropriate for his mind to reach. Similarly, it is evident from the notions of the nature, the potency, and the act why understanding does not befit the brute, or rather why it is not compatible with his nature. For this first judgment, based precisely on the nature of the agent, the operative power and the act, reveals not something just ill-matched, i.e., some unbecoming or disorderly connection, but a simple inconsistency, i.e., the absolute impossibility of any such union.

18.14 What is more, from these three notions one can conclude what object is appropriate to a given act of a certain agent. Take the act of eating, for example. Food capable of restoring what man has lost would be its appropriate object, whereas a stone or something nourishing for animals but not for man would not be.

This delimitation introduced by the object first brings the act under the generic heading of moral. Not that the nature of its object determines its moral species; rather it opens it to further moral determination, for when an act has an appropriate object, it is capable of further moral specification in view of the circumstances in which it is performed. That is why an act is said to receive its generic goodness from its object, for just as genus is potential with respect to differences, so the goodness derived from its object first puts it into the generic class of moral acts. Only goodness of nature is presupposed. And once it has generic goodness, the way is open to all the additional moral specifications.

18.15 The procedure for determining specific goodness, called "goodness from circumstances," is as follows: The first goodness comes, it seems, from the circumstances of the end, for given the nature of the agent, of the action, of the object, one immediately concludes that such an action ought to be performed by this agent for such an end, and that it ought to be chosen and wanted for the sake of such an end. This circumstance is not precisely characteristic of the act as actually performed or not, but rather of the act as willed and related to this end by an act of the will. Indeed, the decision to do something for a worthy purpose is no less good when the external act that ensues fails to achieve that end than when it succeeds.

The next circumstance seems to be the manner in which the action is performed. How it ought to be performed we infer from all or from some of the aforementioned considerations.

Next come our conclusions regarding the appropriate time. For a given action done for such a purpose and in such a manner is not always befitting such an agent; it is appropriate only when the act can be directed to or can attain such an end.

Last of all is the circumstance of place. Indeed there are many acts with complete moral goodness in which place plays no part.[8]

18.16 It is clear then how many conditions right reason sets down, for according to the description given above [in 18.8], to be perfectly good, an act must be faultless on all counts. Hence Dionysius[9] declares: "Good requires that everything about the act be right, whereas evil stems from any single defect." "Everything," he explains, includes all the circumstances.

18.17 Objection: Circumstances are relations whereas good is a quality, according to the *Ethics*;[10] virtue is also a quality, according to the *Categories*.[11]

I answer: According to the *Physics*:[12] "All virtue and malice are relative." That acts be good or virtuous, therefore, implies one or several relations. But like "healthy" or "beautiful," "good" or "virtuous" are spoken of, and predicated, as qualities, and this commonly happens with the fourth type of quality.

18.18 [The source of moral badness] In view of the second part of the citation [in 18.16] from Dionysius we ought to look into the source of moral badness in an act.

Badness can be opposed to goodness in an act either privatively or as its contrary. Man is said to be bad in this second sense if he has some vice, for though this implies a privation of a perfection that should be there, a vice is certainly a positive habit. In the other sense, man is said to be bad privatively if he lacks the goodness he ought to have, even if he does not have the contrary vice or vicious habit.[13]

18.19 We find this distinction in Boethius[14] where he explains the first characteristic of quality: "They say justice is not contrary to injustice, for they think injustice is a privation and not a contrary state." And he adds in refutation: "Many habits are expressed in privative terms such as 'illiberality' and 'imprudence.' These would never be contrasted with virtues, which are habits, if they themselves were not habits."

18.20 Reason also justifies this distinction. For it can happen that an act is performed under circumstances that are not all they should be [to make the act morally good], yet neither are they so improper that they ought not to be there, for instance, when an action is neither directed to an appropriate end nor to an inappropriate one. In such a case the act is bad only privatively, not contrarily as it would be if it were performed for some unlawful purpose. And from many similar acts, a corresponding habit would arise, namely, one whose "badness" is privative rather than a positive contrary. For example, to give alms, not for a good end such as the love of God or to help one's neighbor, but not for a bad end either such as out of vainglory or to hurt someone, is an act of this sort that is privatively, not contrarily, bad.

It is to such privative "badness" that Dionysius refers when he states that the absence of any one of the required circumstances suffices to render the act bad. But for it to be bad contrarily there must be some positive circumstance present that involves some deformity.

18.21   Briefly, then, just as moral goodness is integral suitability, so moral badness is unsuitability. Privative badness is a lack of suitability, i.e., the absence of what ought to be there, whereas badness as the contrary of goodness is unsuitability as a contrary state, i.e., as some condition that is incompatible with suitability.

18.22   [Corollary] From what has been said this corollary follows: The same fundamental act can have a manifold moral goodness. It is not just that it is correct in all its circumstances (something which invests the act not with many goodnesses but with one integral goodness), but it can also have at the same time all that is needed for two distinct virtues, and thus be directed to several ends according to different dictates of perfect prudence. For example, I go to church to fulfill an obligation in justice, because of obedience or some vow. And I also go out of charity or love of God, to pray or to worship him. And I also go out of fraternal charity to edify my neighbor. In short the more morally good motives there are, the better the act is. This is true whether the goodness in question be moral goodness alone or that additional goodness we call meritorious.

18.23   In like fashion, badness multiplies if one and the same act violates several dictates of reason.

Article II
The Source of Laudability and Culpability

18.24   [Meaning of the terms, especially "imputable"] In regard to the second main problem [in 18.7] let me say that "praiseworthy" and "blameworthy," and more generally "remunerable" or "punishable," come under the general designation "imputable." What all these have in common is that the acts to which they refer are in the

free power of the agent. Now although this power involves both intellect and will, it is only the will, I say, that can completely account for the indifference or indeterminacy as regards the alternative—the indifference, namely, that consists in the fact that the action which occurred might not have occurred, or vice versa ("indifference to the alternative" must be understood here disjunctively, not conjunctively, that is to say, *in sensu diviso*, not *in sensu composito*).

Every other active potency acts naturally, and of itself is thus determined to one effect, i.e., to one of two contradictories. Even if its activity ranges over disparate effects as is the case of the manifold terrestrial effects produced by the sun, if we consider one particular effect or its contradictory, we see the cause is determined to produce this. Thus the sun is determined to cause this herb to grow or this worm to be produced, and the same with other effects.

The will alone is indeterminate as regards contradictory effects, and it determines itself to one of the two, as is clear from the *Metaphysics*;[15] otherwise it would cause contrary effects at the same time.

It is because the will has its act in its power indeterminately, presupposing only knowledge, that the act is essentially imputable to the agent. Hence St. Augustine says:[16] "It is clear that if this movement is called culpable, it is not natural but voluntary." And then the disciple's comment follows: "If the movement by which the will turns in different directions were not voluntary and under our control, man would not deserve praise or blame," as we said in the question [in 16.47 ff.] on the natural necessity in the will.

18.25   "Imputable," then, implies a dual relationship, one to the dominion or power of the agent, the other to something which in justice corresponds to the act or to the agent because of the act. The first relation remains unchanged whether the act be good or bad; whereas the second varies. Not, indeed, that it changes formally from good to bad, but given the difference between good and bad judged in terms of suitability or lack thereof, as explained in the first article [in 16.8 ff.], the second relation varies accordingly. For good is imputable for praise or reward, whereas evil is imputable for blame or punishment. A neutral or indifferent act is imputed to the agent in whose power it lies as somehow blameworthy because he could have acted according to the dictates of right reason, or at least it is credited to him as unpraiseworthy and this because of a defect on his part, for he could have acted in a praiseworthy fashion.

18.26 From all this it is clear that an act is not imputable and formally good in a moral sense for the same reason. It has moral goodness because it conforms to a rule or norm as it should. It is imputable because it lies in the free power of the agent. Praiseworthy and blameworthy presuppose both. For while they formally assert the act is imputable (specifying that for which it is imputable), they connote materially the reason why the act is imputable in one way or the other, namely, the goodness or badness, which are the grounds for its being imputed for praise or punishment.

18.27 [Two types of imputable acts] We can distinguish two senses of "imputable." What is most properly imputable lies immediately in the power of the will, and in this sense only volition itself is imputable since it alone is immediately in the will's power.

In another sense, anything is imputable that falls simply, though not immediately, under the control of the will. If the will by its command can make another power elicit an action or can prevent it from doing so, then that action is also imputable to the will, for the whole causal chain leading up to and including that act lies in the power of the will.

18.28 There is a difference between what is imputable in the first and second ways. For the first, only the potency of the will and the intellection which the act of the will presupposes are needed, because volition is an immediate effect of the will. In this sense Augustine's statement should be understood:[17] "Nothing is so in the power

of the will as the will itself." By "will" we should understand not its entity but its proper act. For the execution of an act imputable in the second way, however, another potency besides the will is required.

18.29 From this it follows that the contingency or indeterminacy of the act imputable in the first sense is somehow greater, since only the will plus sufficient intellectual light is needed for it. Consequently nothing posterior can impede its execution. An act imputable in the second way requires another faculty whose impotence can impede the will's power over the act. Its contingency does not depend only on the indifference of the will as does the contingency of the first act. And since the contingency of any other cause or power is more removed from the single contingency characteristic of the will's causation, it follows that the contingency of an act imputable in the first way is simply greater than that of an act imputable in the second way. Nevertheless, since an act imputable in the second sense depends on different factors and any one of them or their absence can impede the effect, we could say that such an effect is more contingent or, better, is contingent on more than one count.

Article III
Is the Goodness or Laudability of the External Action Distinct from That of the Interior Act?

18.30 [Two points must be studied] As for the third main problem [in 18.7] we can say first of all that the external or commanded act has some moral goodness of its own distinct from that of the interior elicited act. Second, we shall see whether it has its own imputability or not.

1. The Exterior Act Has Its Own Moral Goodness

18.31 [Two proofs] The first conclusion is established in two ways.

First by a text from Augustine:[18] "For though everyone is made wretched by the bad will alone, he becomes more wretched by the power whereby the desire of the bad will is satisfied. And though he would be wretched by the bad will alone, yet he would be less wretched if he could have had nothing of those things which he has wrongfully willed." "Wretchedness" obviously does not refer to pain or suffering, for he who wants something and cannot get what he desires has more pain than he who satisfies his desires. Hence it must be understood of the wretchedness of guilt. Therefore, the evil of the external act adds to the misery of guilt present in the internal act.

18.32   Reason proves the same point. From the first article [18.8 ff.], we know that moral goodness consists in an act having all that the agent's right reason declares must pertain to the act. But the demands of right reason are different for the internal and external acts. Therefore, their moral goodness or badness is also different. This holds true whether the badness be privative (because something is missing that should be there) or contrary (because something is present that is incompatible with what should be there).

18.33   Proof of the minor: Right reason does not demand the impossible. Now what suits or can suit the internal act cannot possibly also suit the external act if we consider both acts in their real being and what is appropriate to this. For while the external act as an object willed, but not as an elicited act, does in some sense pertain denominatively (by a kind of extrinsic denomination) to what is appropriate in reality to the internal act, still the same thing does not suit each in the same way. Since the potencies responsible for the internal and external acts are incapable of having the same act, indeed their natures differ, it follows that what suits their respective acts must also differ in nature, or at least—and this suffices for our purpose—what is appropriate to each is different.

With this in mind, the answers to certain objections to our position become clear.

18.34   [Objections] Against the foregoing it is argued:

First, the truth of the act of understand-ing and of the object understood is one and the same. For like reasons the goodness of the act of willing and of the object willed should be the same.

The antecedent seems clear from these examples: As the truth of a principle is immediate, so the knowledge of it can be called immediate in contrast to the mediate knowledge of the conclusion. Similarly, the knowledge of a principle is derived from its terms, and the knowledge of a conclusion is derived from principles. In this same way truth pertains to principles and truth pertains to conclusions.

18.35   Confirmation of the same point: Where one thing exists because of another, we have but one thing. Now the external act has goodness only because of the goodness present in the internal act. Therefore, the goodness of one is not distinct from that of the other.

18.36   Besides, according to Anselm,[19] sin is lack of due justice. But there is but one such lack in the internal and external acts, for justice and injustice—according to him—are by their nature able to exist only in the will.

18.37   Besides, where there is but one act of aversion and inordinate desire, there seems to be but one formal reason for sin. In the internal and external act, however, there is but a single act of aversion, for the will is the only faculty capable both of turning towards or turning away from the end. The same should be said of inordinate desire which Augustine[20] sometimes calls cupidity and defines it properly as "the venom of charity." Hence it is properly in that faculty in which charity is apt to be, which is the will alone.

18.38   [Answer to the objections] Reply to the first [in 18.34]: The same truth which pertains formally to the act of understanding does belong in some other way (viz., objectively) to the object known insofar as this exists in the intellect. Similarly, that goodness which pertains formally to volition does belong in some derivative fashion to the willed object qua willed. Yet for all that, the [external] act, insofar as it has real being apart from the will, can have a goodness of its own just as it can have a real suitability or inappropriateness of its own.

18.39   And the argument [of 18.35] cited in confirmation can lead to the opposite conclusion. If the interior act is really the means whereby the exterior act acquires an appropriateness by being in agreement with a rule of its own, then this appropriateness must be other than that characteristic of the interior act, for nothing functions as a cause or means with respect to itself.

We have an example of this in the acts of the intellect. Even though a conclusion derives its truth from the principle used to prove it, it still has a truth of its own, for the agreement between what exists and what it affirms to be the case in virtue of its own terms is something proper to itself. It is not the truth of the principle that formally constitutes its own truth, for the conclusion is a mediate and demonstrated truth, and the truth it possesses is formally demonstrable truth.

Similarly, where many different conclusions follow in a certain sequence from the same principle, each has its own distinct truth. It may even be that the prior conclusion is truer and more necessary since it does not depend for its necessity upon the subsequent conclusions but vice versa.

In like manner, every false conclusion which conflicts with the same truth has its own distinct falsity, for what each asserts disagrees in a different way with what is actually the case.

It is the same with the acts of the will. Volition is not the only act that is able by nature to be in conformity or in disagreement with what right reason dictates. This is also true of the commanded act by reason of its being willed. And though the norm to which each act must conform is the same, the acts themselves are different and so too are their respective agreements, even though these be to the same norm.

18.40   You may object: Truth pertains to nothing outside the mind. It belongs solely to the act of the intellect or to the object insofar as it is in the mind. Analogously, then, goodness pertains to the external act only as the object of volition and not as elicited externally.

I reply: The analogy could be denied according to those words of the *Metaphysics*:[21] "Falsity and truth are not in things—it is not as if the good were true and the bad were in itself false—but in thought."

Another way of answering would be to deny the antecedent. For if some intellect were to function as the norm for what is understood in the way the divine intellect is the rule and exemplar for the creature, then one could maintain that the object is true not only as actually known but also in itself, since in its very being it is modeled on and conformed to its exemplar.

18.41   [To the second objection] As for the other [in 18.36], I say: Justice may mean habitual rectitude or refer to a habit of the will, in virtue of which the will would be said to be habitually righteous even when it is not actually willing something. Thus we would call a sleeper "just" if he had the habit, and we would call him "unjust" if he lacked it or had a contrary habit of injustice. In another sense, however, rectitude could be understood to mean that which is actualized or in act and it would consist in the conformity of the elicited act with a norm. The first type of justice is quite generally admitted. For the second we give some proof. An action is not said to be formally right or just simply because the will is in the habitual state of justice, for this state is compatible with an act that is indifferent or even venially sinful, neither of which is just or right. What is needed is that the rectitude, by reason of which the act is formally called just, be present in the act while the action is going on. Perhaps it is not immediately in the will but in the act itself and by means of the act it is mediately in the will. For what the nature of the will is able to receive immediately is the habit and the act of volition. But actual justice is neither of these. It is rather a certain condition of the act itself, such as its conformity to a rule.

18.42   This would be more obvious if the action were not over in an instant but remained for a while. For just as one and the same movement numerically and specifically can be rapid at first and slow later (from which it follows that neither its rapidity nor its slowness is absolutely identical with the movement), so an action that continued for some time might at first be elicited in conformity to right reason and afterwards not, and so would be righteous at first and afterwards not. But the action is over in a moment or, if it continues awhile, its rectitude commonly remains, so that there is no switch from right to wrong. Consequently, the distinction between the act and its rectitude is not so evident.

Nevertheless, we can infer its existence in the ways mentioned above. It can be proved also in this way. If a relation is not a necessary consequence of the nature of its foundation, then it is not completely identical with the foundation. But rectitude is not a necessary consequence of the nature of the act. Also, actual justice of a secondary kind can be present in the commanded act (even though its primary form exists only in the act of volition), for the commanded act has a rightness of its own even though this is dependent upon the volition being right.

The statement, then, that justice is only in the will refers to habitual justice, which, as Anselm puts it, is rightness preserved for its own sake. For what is preserved pertains to the habit, or if we extend the meaning of "preserved," then the definition would be true of primary actual justice for this also is "preserved for its own sake," i.e., the will keeps it in its act, which it elicits rightly by means of [habitual] justice. If we are speaking about actual justice in the secondary sense, however, it must be admitted that this is only causally, not subjectively, in the will. So that even here the definition that justice is rectitude of will can somehow be saved, not indeed in the sense that rightness formally inheres in the will, but that it pertains to the will as causing or commanding, and this rightness is wanted or "preserved for its own sake," namely, as an effect caused voluntarily.

18.43 [Corollaries] From this some corollaries follow that clarify our thesis.

First corollary: Given the same habitual justice, there are as many actual justices as there are elicited acts. And if one is elicited with greater effort than another, one can be more intense than the other, even though the habit remains equal. The first act can be elicited with more effort (in which case its actual justice will be correspondingly more intense), whereas the second act can be done with less effort, even though it is certain the habitual justice is not less.

18.44 Second corollary: Each evil act has an actual badness of its own. For just as each act is able to have its own goodness because it conforms to the same or different dictates of reason, so too each may be lacking such conformity.

18.45 Third corollary: Instances of badness differ in the same way as do the corresponding instances of goodness that ought to have been there. If the difference is specific or numerical in the one case, it is the same in the other. For privations are distinguished in terms of the corresponding habits that might have been there. For instance, deafness and blindness are specifically different privations even as hearing and vision are specifically different positively. This and that case of blindness are numerically distinct privations, even as this and that case of seeing are numerically distinct in a positive way.[22]

18.46 [Additional corollaries] From this it is clear how not only vices, speaking physically, but also sins, speaking theologically, can be distinguished numerically, specifically, and even generically. It is not just in terms of the distinction of things to which one turns in sinning, for this neither constitutes the sin nor distinguishes one sin from another; rather it is the proper nature of the privation which provides the formal grounds for distinguishing privatively, just as it is the proper nature of the corresponding virtue that is the basis for positive distinctions.

18.47 It is also clear why one sin is more grievous than another, whether their differences in gravity be specific or within the same species. For the greater, specifically or intensively, the goodness that should be there, the worse the act that lacks it. If it is a simple lack, the act is privatively worse; if something positively incompatible be present, the act is contrarily worse.[23]

18.48 Third, we see why the damned can continue to sin ad infinitum and still their nature is not consumed, nor is any natural aptitude or anything else in their nature. For nothing created can cause an intellectual nature or anything in it to perish, and if it could diminish such a nature, it could eventually destroy it completely.[24]

18.49 Similarly, the contingent effect does not accompany its cause necessarily. Hence the opposite of that effect or of something in the effect does not destroy or diminish the cause. Now the badness of the act is a privation in a contingent effect of the will. Therefore, it does not diminish anything pertaining to the will itself.

18.50 What then does sin added to sin take away? For according to Augustine:[25] "Evil is there to the extent that it takes away a measure of goodness."

I answer: Obviously the actual badness of an elicited act does not take away some good that is there at the same time; neither does it destroy some good that was there, for as we said above [in 18.42], the act takes place too quickly to change from good to evil.

But if a "good that was there" refers to the gratuitous habit [of grace or charity] that sin destroys, Augustine's dictum cannot mean every sin removes this; the second sin does not, for the first already destroyed it. Yet there is nothing essential to the first sin that makes it more destructive than the second. If there were, then the first would be simply more heinous than the second, since it takes away a greater good. But the second sin is sometimes more serious than the first and is by nature apt to take away even more. What it does take away essentially [per se] is actual goodness, and it would also remove the habitual or gratuitous goodness if it were present. What sin in general destroys, then, is something which should have been there, just as blindness in one born blind does not take away sight that was there but which should

have been there. Thus Augustine[26] says of the angel who sinned that "he fell not from a state he had received, but from what he would have received had he chosen to submit to God." And if sin were heaped upon sin ad infinitum, each would take away some goodness of its own which should have been there. Neither is it incongruous that a finite good which contains virtually, so to say, an infinity of effects to be elicited successively, also have an unlimited amount of righteousness corresponding to them.

18.51 [To the third objection] As for the objection [in 18.37] that there is but one act of aversion, we can take aversion to the end in several senses. For one thing, it can mean an actual nolition of the end. In this sense, it is clear that not every sinner has aversion for the end. Perhaps the sinner often does not actually think of it, or if he does, he does not view it with any malice.

Another way would be to understand this turning from the end, not as formal, but as a kind of virtual aversion, which would consist in the will's accepting something incompatible with any effective volition or attainment of the end. Such would be the case if the will wanted something absolutely inordinate that would prevent any attainment of the end, for instance, something in violation of a divine command which must be observed if the end is to be reached. In this sense also, aversion pertains solely to the will.

In a third and larger sense, however, aversion can refer to any sort of malice which keeps one effectively from willing or attaining the end. Now an act commanded by the will can be bad in this sense, for if it is evil to command such an act, the will no longer efficaciously wills the ultimate end nor its attainment.[27]

18.52 Now just as the ability to be related or directed to the end can be called "conversion," so the ability to be directed away from it can be called "aversion." When it is claimed there is but one aversion in the external and internal act, this would be true of aversion taken in the first two senses, since this is present only in the internal act. But the further claim that aversion, so understood, is the formal ground for sin must be denied. The way a commanded act can be "turned away"—which can be called aversion in the third sense—suffices.

18.53   As for what is said [in 18.37] about "inordinate desire," if this means "bad will," i.e., immoderate volition, then inordinate desire is not formally present in all sin; it is only present with sin either formally or causally. To make inordinate desire or cupidity coextensive with sin, therefore, one must extend its meaning to cover not only the interior acts but also the commanded acts of the will that are immoderate.

2. The External Act Is Imputable

18.54   As for the second point of this article [in 18.30], viz., concerning imputability, it is clear from the distinction made [in 18.27] of article two, that only what is immediately in the will's power is strictly speaking imputable, and that is volition and nolition.

But if "imputable" be taken in general as anything that is simply in the will's power, then a commanded act is properly imputable. For even though it is not immediately in the power of the will, it is put into execution by volition which falls under the will's control not only qua volition but also qua principle of the external act, for the will can place the external act by means of the internal. For example, if a servant kills on the command of his master, the death is imputed mediately to the master, for the servant's action was in his power.

18.55   If one objects, as before, that the external act is imputable only by means of the internal, I reply: From this our thesis follows, viz., that the imputability of one is not that of the other, for nothing functions as cause or means with respect to itself. We

can also explain this the way we explained the proper goodness of the external act [in 18.31 f.]. Though the term be the same, different foundations bear different relationships to it. Now the external and internal acts represent different foundations. And even though imputability pertains to each with reference to the same will, it will be different in each even as the way they are caused and the way in which they fall under the control of the same will is different.[28]

Reply to the Initial Argument

18.56   Answer to the argument at the beginning [in 18.1]: "Voluntary" can mean: (a) what is the will as in a subject, (b) what is willed by the will, or (c) what is commanded by the will. The first is not enough to make something completely voluntary, for a habit can exist in the will and be there involuntarily, as when the will is sad. The second is called "voluntary" in a participated sense because its acceptation as an object is voluntary. It should be called "willed," however, rather than "voluntary." Properly speaking, then, voluntary is what lies in the power of the will, which is the third sense. And thus the external act would be as simply voluntary as the internal act, even though it is not equally first since it presupposes the internal act.[29]

Proof of the minor: I say that while the external act apart from the internal (i.e., when it is performed without the latter) is not voluntary, for a more remote effect is not called "voluntary" if it is not actualized by the more proximate effect (i.e., the internal act), nevertheless when the external act is joined to the internal and proceeds from the latter, it not only becomes a voluntary act, but has a distinctive ground for being so, for it is "mediately voluntary," whereas the interior act is "immediately voluntary."

NOTES

1. Cf. Duns Scotus, *Ord.* II, d.42, q.5 (ed. Vivès XIII, 448–77).
2. Aristotle, *Ethica ad Nic.* III, c.7 (1113b5–19).
3. Exodus 20:17.
4. Ibid.
5. Augustine, *De Trin.* IX, c.12, n.18: PL 42, 971–72; CCSL 50, 309–10.
6. Ibid., VIII, c.3, n.4: PL 42, 949; CCSL 50, 272.
7. There is an addition found in M_1 at the end of 18.9. In M_2 and W it follows 18.10:

   And this suitability stems either from the nature of the terms or if it must generally be traced back to the judgment of some intellect (since the intellect is the measure of suitability), this judgment will be that of the intellect which is the rule of the whole of nature, viz., the divine intellect. Indeed this intellect, just as it knows perfectly every being, so it knows perfectly the harmony or disagreement of one thing with another.

8. Cf. Duns Scotus, *Ord.,* II, d.40, q.un. (ed. Vivès XIII, 424–27).
9. Ps. Dionysius, *De div. nomin.,* c.4, 30: PG 3, 806; *Dionysiaca* I, 298–99.
10. Aristotle, *Ethica ad Nic.* X, c.2 (1173a13–22).
11. Aristotle, *Praedicam,* c.8 (8b30).
12. Aristotle, *Physic.* VII, c.3 (246b2–8).
13. Cf. Duns Scotus, *Ord.* II, d.7, q.un., n.12 (ed. Vivès XII, 387).
14. Boethius, *In categorias Aristot.* III: PL 64, 255.
15. Aristotle, *Metaph.* IX, c.5 (1048a5–15).
16. Augustine, *De libero arbitr.* III, c.1, nn.2–3: PL 32, 1271–72; CCSL 29, 275–76.
17. Augustine, *Retract.* I, c.9 (8), n.3, and c.22 (21), n.4: PL 32, 596, 620; CSEL 36, 39.
18. Augustine, *De Trin.* XIII, c.5, n.8; PL 42, 1020; CCSL 50a, 392.
19. Anselm, *De conceptu virg.* c.5: PL 158, 438–39.
20. Augustine, *De diversis quaest.* 83, q.36, n.1: PL 40, 25.
21. Aristotle, *Metaph.* V, c.4 (1027b25–30).
22. Cf. Duns Scotus, *Ord.* II, d.37, q.1, n.9 (ed. Vivès XIII, 359).
23. Cf. ibid., IV, d.50, q.6, nn. 12–13 (ed. Vivès XXI, 569–70); II, d.21, q.2, n.3 (ed. Vivès XIII, 141); d.37, q.1, nn.8–10 (ibid., 358–60).
24. Cf. ibid., II, d.37, q.1, n.4 (ed. Vivès XIII, 354).
25. Augustine, *Enchirid.,* c.4, n.12: PL 40, 237; CCSL 96, 54.
26. Augustine, *Super Gen.* XI, c.23, n.30: PL 34, 441.
27. Cf. Duns Scotus, *Ord.* II, d.41, q.un., nn.2–3 (ed. Vivès XIII, 434–35); d.43, q.1, n.2 (ibid., 483); d.37, q.1, n.8 (ibid., 358–59).
28. There is an addition found in M_1 and M_2 only: On the contrary: Those who do not differ in the power of their will do not differ in sinning, but he who sins and he would equally want to sin but is powerless to do so are equal as regards that which is in the power of their will and differ only in that which is not in their power. Therefore, etc.
29. M_2 and W have the following addition: Therefore, *voluntary* must mean that which is caused by the will and this either directly or by command, although that which is elicited by the will is called voluntary in the primary sense rather than that which is commanded. Therefore, let the major be conceded, but understand *voluntary* generally, and in this sense the minor is false.

PART III

GOD'S FOREKNOWLEDGE AND FREE WILL

CHAPTER 13

Boethius

Boethius was born in Rome about 480 into the distinguished senatorial family of the Anicii. His father had been consul in 487 and twice prefect of the city but died when Boethius was a young boy. He was adopted by the even more distinguished Symmachus, whose daughter Rusticiana he later married. Boethius was educated in Athens, where he was exposed to the various schools of Greek philosophy. One of his life's goals was to translate the complete works of Plato and Aristotle into Latin with the intention of exposing their essential agreement via commentary. The demands of public life plus his early demise undermined this goal. Nevertheless, he was very prolific, translating the whole of Aristotle's *Orgonon* plus Porphyry's *Introduction to the Categories of Aristotle* with commentary. He commented at length on Aristotle's *Categories* and *De Interpretatione*. In addition, he wrote five essays of his own on logic. He also wrote works on arithmetic, geometry, and music, as well as several theological treatises.

He was in agreement with Plato that only the educated elite, and more specifically philosophers, should run government. With this and his aristocratic background, Boethius entered the Roman administrative system when he was still a young man. At this time Theodoric, king of the Ostrogoths, ruled the western Roman Empire as the deputy of the Eastern emperors in Constantinople. Boethius became consul to Theodoric in 510 and also held the position of Master of the King's Officers, a most prestigious position. He was a staunch supporter of the Roman senate and diligently sought to eliminate corruption in government.

Not surprisingly, given his principles and zeal, he made many enemies, and the very senate he defended condemned both him and Symmachus of treason (by way of perjured testimony). Theodoric also turned against Boethius and his adopted father. Boethius was stripped of his honor and possessions and thrown into a remote prison at Pavia in 523. He remained there for a year, during which time he was tortured and finally executed. It was during his stint in prison that he wrote his most celebrated work, *The Consolation of Philosophy*, a dialogue on Christian stoicism.

Boethius on Foreknowledge

At the outset Boethius establishes that human beings possess free will. Lady Philosophy observes that creatures which are naturally capable of reasoning are endowed with the power to judge and make decisions. This entails that they can ascertain what ought to be avoided as well as what ought to be desired. Due to the capacity to reason, human beings choose to pursue that which they find desirable and likewise choose to avoid what is believed ought to be shunned. Such constitutes free will. In other words, human action is voluntary.

The argument employed by Boethius that God's foreknowledge is compatible with free will is based on an analogy. Disregarding the past and the future, a person in the present can see simultaneously the sun rising in the sky and a man walking on the ground. Furthermore, that person can determine and therefore be said to know that the former is a necessary occurrence whereas the latter is voluntary. His knowledge in no way determines and is therefore independent of the necessity and voluntariness of these happenings. By virtue of the fact that God is infinite, the concept of time does not apply to Him as it does to human beings. There is no past or future relative to God. His infinity entails that He functions in an eternal now. He can (and does) know that certain occurrences in the here and now are necessary (such as the sun rising) and some are voluntary (such as a man walking on the ground). Analogous to the human counterpart, we can understand that therefore His knowledge in no way interferes with the voluntariness of human action.

THE CONSOLATION OF PHILOSOPHY

Book V

Here she made an end and was for turning the course of her speaking to the handling and explaining of other subjects. Then said I: "Your encouragement is right and most worthy in truth of your name and weight. But I am learning by experience what you just now said of Providence; that the question is bound up in others. I would ask you whether you think that chance exists at all, and what you think it is?"

Then she answered: "I am eager to fulfil my promised debt, and to show you the path by which you may seek your home. But these things, though all-expedient for knowledge, are none the less rather apart from our path, and we must be careful lest you become wearied by our turnings aside, and so be not strong enough to complete the straight journey."

"Have no fear at all thereof," said I. "It will be restful to know these things in which I have so great a pleasure; and when

From Boethius, *The Consolation of Philosophy*, translated by W. V. Cooper from *The Consolation of Philosophy*, with an introduction by Irwin Edman (New York: Random House, 1943), pp. 101–120.

every view of your reasoning has stood firm with unshaken credit, so let there be no doubt of what shall follow."

"I will do your pleasure," she made answer, and thus she began to speak:

(Philosophy discusses "chance")

"If chance is defined as an outcome of random influence, produced by no sequence of causes, I am sure that there is no such thing as chance, and I consider that it is but an empty word, beyond showing the meaning of the matter which we have in hand. For what place can be left for anything happening at random, so long as God controls everything in order? It is a true saying that nothing can come out of nothing. None of the old philosophers has denied that, though they did not apply it to the effective principle, but to the matter operated upon—that is to say, to nature; and this was the foundation upon which they built all their reasoning. If anything arises from no causes, it will appear to have risen out of nothing. But if this is impossible, then chance also cannot be anything of that sort, which is stated in the definition which we mentioned."

"Then is there nothing which can be justly called chance, nor anything 'by chance'?" I asked. "Or is there anything which common people know not, but which those words do suit?"

"My philosopher, Aristotle, defined it in his *Physics*[1] shortly and well-nigh truly."

"How?" I asked.

"Whenever anything is done with one intention, but something else, other than was intended, results from certain causes, that is called chance: as, for instance, if a man digs the ground for the sake of cultivating it, and finds a heap of buried gold. Such a thing is believed to have happened by chance, but it does not come from nothing, for it has its own causes, whose unforeseen and unexpected coincidence seem to have brought about a chance. For if the cultivator did not dig the ground, if the owner had not buried his money, the gold would not have been found. These are the causes of the chance piece of good fortune, which comes about from the causes which meet it, and move along with it, not from the intention of the actor. For neither the burier nor the tiller intended that the gold should be found; but, as I said, it was a coincidence, and it happened that the one dug up what the other buried. We may therefore define chance as an unexpected result from the coincidence of certain causes in matters where there was another purpose. The order of the universe, advancing with its inevitable sequences, brings about this coincidence of causes. This order itself emanates from its source, which is Providence, and disposes all things in their proper time and place.

In the land where the Parthian, as he turns in flight, shoots his arrows into the pursuer's breast, from the rocks of the crag of Achaemenia, the Tigris and Euphrates flow from out one source, but quickly with divided streams are separate. If they should come together and again be joined in a single course, all, that the two streams bear along, would flow in one together. Boats would meet boats, and trees meet trees torn up by the currents, and the mingled waters would together entwine their streams by chance; but their sloping beds restrain these chances vague, and the downward order of the falling torrent guides their courses. Thus does chance, which seems to rush onward without rein, bear the bit, and take its way by rule."

(Philosophy asserts the existence of free will.)

"I have listened to you," I said, "and agree that it is as you say. But in this close sequence of causes, is there any freedom for our judgment, or does this chain of fate bind the very feelings of our minds too?"

"There is free will," she answered. "Nor could there be any reasoning nature without freedom of judgment. For any being that can use its reason by nature, has a power of judgment by which it can without further aid decide each point, and so distinguish between objects to be desired and objects to be shunned. Each therefore seeks what it deems desirable, and flies from what it considers should be shunned. Wherefore all who have reason have also freedom of desiring and refusing in themselves. But I do not lay down that this is equal in all beings. Heavenly and divine beings have with them a judgment of great insight, an imperturbable will, and a power which can effect their desires. But human spirits must be more free when they keep themselves safe in the contemplation of the mind of God; but less free when they sink into bodies, and less still when they are bound by their earthly members. The last stage is mere slavery, when the spirit is given over to vices and has fallen away from the possession of its reason. For when the mind turns its eyes from the light of truth on high to lower darkness, soon they are dimmed by the clouds of ignorance, and become turbid through ruinous passions; by yielding to these passions and consenting to them, men increase the slavery which they have brought upon themselves, and their true liberty is lost in captivity. But God, looking upon all out of the infinite, perceives the views of providence, and disposes each as its destiny has already fated for it according to its merits: 'He looketh over all and heareth all'.[2]

Homer with his honeyed lips sang of the bright sun's clear light; yet the sun cannot burst with his feeble rays the bowels of the earth or the depths of the sea. Not so with the Creator of this great sphere. No masses of earth can block His vision as He looks over all. Night's cloudy darkness cannot resist Him. With one glance of His intelligence He sees all that has been, that is, and that is to come. He alone can see all things, so truly He may be called the Sun.'[3]

Then said I, "Again am I plunged in yet more doubt and difficulty."

(Boethius cannot reconcile God's foreknowledge with man's free will.)

"What are they," she asked, "though I have already my idea of what your trouble consists?"

"There seems to me," I said, "to be such incompatibility between the existence of God's universal foreknowledge and that of any freedom of judgment. For if God foresees all things and cannot in anything be mistaken, that, which His Providence sees will happen, must result. Wherefore if it knows beforehand not only men's deeds but even their designs and wishes, there will be no freedom of judgment. For there can neither be any deed done, nor wish formed, except such as the infallible Providence of God has foreseen. For if matters could ever so be turned that they resulted otherwise than was foreseen of Providence, this foreknowledge would cease to be sure. But, rather than knowledge, it is opinion which is uncertain; and that, I deem, is not applicable to God. And, further, I cannot approve of an argument by which some men think that they can cut this knot; for they say that a result does not come to pass for the reason that Providence has foreseen it, but the opposite rather, namely, that because it is about to come to pass, therefore it cannot be hidden from God's Providence. In that way it seems to me that the argument must resolve itself into an argument on the other side. For in that case it is not

necessary that that should happen which is foreseen, but that that which is about to happen should be foreseen; as though, indeed, our doubt was whether God's foreknowledge is the certain cause of future events, or the certainty of future events is the cause of Providence. But let our aim be to prove that, whatever be the shape which this series of causes takes, the fulfillment of God's foreknowledge is necessary, even if this knowledge may not seem to induce the necessity for the occurrence of future events. For instance, if a man sits down, it must be that the opinion, which conjectures that he is sitting, is true; but conversely, if the opinion concerning the man is true because he is sitting, he must be sitting down. There is therefore necessity in both cases: the man must be sitting, and the opinion must be true. But he does not sit because the opinion is true, but rather the opinion is true because his sitting down has preceded it. Thus, though the cause of the truth of the opinion proceeds from the other fact, yet there is a common necessity on both parts. In like manner we must reason of Providence and future events. For even though they are foreseen because they are about to happen, yet they do not happen because they are foreseen. None the less it is necessary that either what is about to happen should be foreseen of God, or that what has been foreseen should happen; and this alone is enough to destroy all free will.

Yet how absurd it is that we should say that the result of temporal affairs is the cause of eternal foreknowledge! And to think that God foresees future events because they are about to happen, is nothing else than to hold events of past time to be the cause of that highest Providence. Besides, just as, when I know a present fact, that fact must be so; so also when I know of something that will happen, that must come to pass. Thus it follows that the fulfillment of a foreknown event must be inevitable.

Lastly, if any one believes that any matter is otherwise than the fact is, he not only has not knowledge, but his opinion is false also, and that is very far from the truth of knowledge. Wherefore, if any future event is such that its fulfillment is not sure or necessary, how can it possibly be known beforehand that it will occur? For just as absolute knowledge has no taint of falsity, so also that which is conceived by knowledge cannot be otherwise than as it is conceived. That is the reason why knowledge cannot lie, because each matter must be just as knowledge knows that it is. What then? How can God know beforehand these uncertain future events? For if He thinks inevitable the fulfillment of such things as may possibly not result, He is wrong; and that we may not believe, nor even utter, rightly. But if He perceives that they will result as they are in such a manner that He only knows that they may or may not occur, equally, how is this foreknowledge, this which knows nothing for sure, nothing absolutely? How is such a foreknowledge different from the absurd prophecy which Horace puts in the mouth of Tiresias: 'Whatever I shall say, will either come to pass, or it will not'?[4] How, too, would God's Providence be better than man's opinion, if, as men do, He only sees to be uncertain such things as have an uncertain result? But if there can be no uncertainty with God, the most sure source of all things, then the fulfillment of all that He has surely foreknown, is certain. Thus we are led to see that there is no freedom for the intentions or actions of men; for the mind of God, foreseeing all things without error or deception, binds all together and controls their results. And when we have once allowed this, it is plain how complete is the fall of all human actions in consequence. In vain are rewards or punishments set before good or bad, for there is no free or voluntary action of the mind to deserve them; and what we just now determined was most fair, will prove to be most unfair of all, namely to punish the dishonest or reward the honest, since their own will does not put them in the way of honesty or dishonesty, but the unfailing necessity of development constrains them. Wherefore neither virtues nor vices are

anything, but there is rather an indiscriminate confusion of all deserts. And nothing could be more vicious than this; since the whole order of all comes from Providence, and nothing is left to human intention, it follows that our crimes, as well as our good deeds, must all be held due to the author of all good. Hence it is unreasonable to hope for or pray against aught. For what could any man hope for or pray against, if an undeviating chain links together all that we can desire? Thus will the only understanding between God and man, the right of prayer, be taken away. We suppose that at the price of our deservedly humbling ourselves before Him we may win a right to the inestimable reward of His divine grace: this is the only manner in which men can seem to deal with God, so to speak, and by virtue of prayer to join ourselves to that inaccessible light, before it is granted to us; but if we allow the inevitability of the future, and believe that we have no power, what means shall we have to join ourselves to the Lord of all, or how can we cling to Him? Therefore, as you sang but a little while ago,[5] the human race must be cut off from its source and ever fall away.

What cause of discord is it breaks the bonds of agreement here? What heavenly power has set such strife between two truths? Thus, though apart each brings no doubt, yet can they not be linked together? Comes there no discord between these truths? Stand they for ever sure by one another? Yes, 'tis the mind, o'erwhelmed by the body's blindness, which cannot see by the light of that dimmed brightness the finest threads that bind the truth. But wherefore burns the spirit with so strong desire to learn the hidden signs of truth? Knows it the very object of its careful search? Then why seeks it to learn anew what it already knows? If it knows it not, why searches it in blindness? For who would desire aught unwitting? Or who could seek after that which is unknown? How should he find it, or recognize its form when found, if he knows it not? And when the mind of man perceived the mind of God did it then know the whole and parts alike? Now is the mind buried in the cloudy darkness of the body, yet has not altogether forgotten his own self, and keeps the whole though it has lost the parts. Whosoever, therefore, seeks the truth, is not wholly in ignorance, nor yet has knowledge wholly; for he knows not all, yet is not ignorant of all. He takes thought for the whole which he keeps in memory, handling again what he saw on high, so that he may add to that which he has kept, that which he has forgotten."

(Philosophy tries to show how they may be reconciled.)

Then said she, "This is the old plaint concerning Providence which was so strongly urged by Cicero when treating of Divination,[6] and you yourself have often and at length questioned the same subject. But so far, none of you have explained it with enough diligence or certainty. The cause of this obscurity is that the working of human reason cannot approach the directness of divine foreknowledge. If this could be understood at all, there would be no doubt left. And this especially will I try to make plain, if I can first explain your difficulties.

Tell me why you think abortive the reasoning of those who solve the question thus; they argue that foreknowledge cannot be held to be a cause for the necessity of future results, and therefore free will is not in any way shackled by foreknowledge.[7] Whence do you draw your proof of the necessity of future results if not from the fact that such things as are known beforehand cannot but come to pass? If, then (as you yourself admitted just now), foreknowledge brings no necessity to bear upon future events, how is it that the voluntary results of such events are bound to find a fixed end? Now for the sake of the argument, that you may turn your attention to what follows, let us state that there is no foreknowledge at all. Then are the events which are decided by free will, bound by any necessity, so far as this goes? Of course not. Secondly, let us state that foreknowledge exists, but brings no necessity to bear upon events; then, I think, the same free will will be left, intact and ab-

solute. 'But,' you will say, 'though foreknowledge is no necessity for a result in the future, yet it is a sign that it will necessarily come to pass.' Thus, therefore, even if there had been no foreknowledge, it would be plain that future results were under necessity; for every sign can only show what it is that it points out; it does not bring it to pass. Wherefore we must first prove that nothing happens but of necessity, in order that it may be plain that foreknowledge is a sign of this necessity. Otherwise, if there is no necessity, then foreknowledge will not be a sign of that which does not exist. Now it is allowed that proof rests upon firm reasoning, not upon signs or external arguments; it must be deduced from suitable and binding causes. How can it possibly be that things, which are foreseen as about to happen, should not occur? That would be as though we were to believe that events would not occur which Providence foreknows as about to occur, and as though we did not rather think this, that though they occur, yet they have had no necessity in their own natures which brought them about. We can see many actions developing before our eyes; just as chariot drivers see the development of their actions as they control and guide their chariots, and many other things likewise. Does any necessity compel any of those things to occur as they do? Of course not. All art, craft, and intention would be in vain, if everything took place by compulsion. Therefore, if things have no necessity for coming to pass when they do, they cannot have any necessity to be about to come to pass before they do. Wherefore there are things whose results are entirely free from necessity. For I think not that there is any man who will say this, that things, which are done in the present, were not about to be done in the past, before they are done. Thus these foreknown events have their free results. Just as foreknowledge of present things brings no necessity to bear upon them as they come to pass, so also foreknowledge of future things brings no necessity to bear upon things which are to come.

But you will say that there is no doubt of

this too, whether there can be any fore-knowledge of things which have not results bounden by necessity. For they do seem to lack harmony: and you think that if they are foreseen, the necessity follows; if there is no necessity, then they cannot be fore-seen; nothing can be perceived certainly by knowledge, unless it be certain. But if things have uncertainty of result, but are foreseen as though certain, this is plainly the obscurity of opinion, and not the truth of knowledge. For you believe that to think aught other than it is, is the opposite of true knowledge. The cause of this error is that every man believes that all the subjects, that he knows, are known by their own force or nature alone, which are known; but it is quite the opposite. For every subject, that is known, is comprehended not ac-cording to its own force, but rather accord-ing to the nature of those who know it. Let me make this plain to you by a brief ex-ample: the roundness of a body may be known in one way by sight, in another way by touch. Sight can take in the whole body at once from a distance by judging its radii, while touch clings, as it were, to the outside of the sphere, and from close at hand per-ceives through the material parts the roundness of the body as it passes over the actual circumference. A man himself is dif-ferently comprehended by the senses, by imagination, by reason, and by intelligence. For the senses distinguish the form as set in the matter operated upon by the form; imagination distinguishes the appearance alone without the matter. Reason goes even further than imagination; by a general and universal contemplation it investigates the actual kind which is represented in indi-vidual specimens. Higher still is the view of the intelligence, which reaches above the sphere of the universal, and with the un-sullied eye of the mind gazes upon that very form of the kind in its absolute sim-plicity. Herein the chief point for our con-sideration is this: the higher power of un-derstanding includes the lower, but the lower never rises to the higher. For the senses are capable of understanding naught but the matter; imagination cannot

look upon universal or natural kinds; rea-son cannot comprehend the absolute form; whereas the intelligence seems to look down from above and comprehend the form, and distinguishes all that lie below, but in such a way that it grasps the very form which could not be known to any other than itself. For it perceives and knows the general kind, as does reason; the ap-pearance, as does the imagination; and the matter, as do the senses, but with one grasp of the mind it looks upon all with a clear conception of the whole. And reason too, as it views general kinds, does not make use of the imagination nor the senses, but yet does perceive the objects both of the imagination and of the senses. It is reason which thus defines a general kind accord-ing to its conception: Man, for instance, is an animal, biped and reasoning. This is a general notion of a natural kind, but no man denies that the subject can be ap-proached by the imagination and by the senses, just because reason investigates it by a reasonable conception and not by the imagination or senses. Likewise, though imagination takes its beginning of seeing and forming appearances from the senses, yet without their aid it surveys each subject by an imaginative faculty of distinguish-ing, not by the distinguishing faculty of the senses.

Do you see then, how in knowledge of all things, the subject uses its own standard of capability, and not those of the objects known? And this is but reasonable, for every judgment formed is an act of the per-son who judges, and therefore each man must of necessity perform his own action from his own capability and not the capa-bility of any other.

In days of old the Porch at Athens[8] gave us men, seeing dimly as in old age, who could believe that the feelings of the senses and the imagination were but impressions on the mind from bodies without them, just as the old custom was to impress with swift-running pens letters upon the surface of a waxen tablet which bore no marks be-fore. But if the mind with its own force can bring forth naught by its own exertions; if it does but lie passive and subject to the marks of other bodies; if it reflects, as does, forsooth, a mirror, the vain reflections of other things; whence thrives there in the soul an all-seeing power of knowledge? What is the force that sees the single parts, or which distinguishes the facts it knows? What is the force that gathers up the parts it has distinguished, that takes its course in order due, now rises to mingle with the things on high, and now sinks down among the things below, and then to itself brings back itself, and, so examining, refuses the false with truth? This is a cause of greater power, of more effective force by far than that which only receives the impressions of material bodies. Yet does the passive reception come first, rousing and stirring all the strength of the mind in the living body. When the eyes are smitten with a light, or the ears are struck with a voice's sound, then is the spirit's energy aroused, and, thus moved, calls upon like forms, such as it holds within itself, fits them to signs without and mingles the forms of its imagination with those which it has stored within."

(Human reasoning, being lower than divine intelligence, can at best only strive to approach thereto.)

"With regard to feeling the effects of bodies, natures which are brought into contact from without may affect the organs of the senses, and the body's passive affection may precede the active energy of the spirit, and call forth to itself the activity of the mind; if then, when the effects of bodies are felt, the mind is not marked in any way by its passive reception thereof, but declares that reception subject to the body of its own force, how much less do those subjects, which are free from all affections of bodies, follow external objects in their perceptions, and how much more do they make clear the way for the action of their mind? By this argument many different manners of understanding have fallen to widely different natures of things. For the senses are incapable of any knowledge but their own, and they alone fall to those living beings which

are incapable of motion, as are sea shell-fish, and other low forms of life which live by clinging to rocks; while imagination is granted to animals with the power of motion, who seem to be affected by some desire to seek or avoid certain things. But reason belongs to the human race alone, just as the true intelligence is God's alone. Wherefore that manner of knowledge is better than others, for it can comprehend of its own nature not only the subject peculiar to itself, but also the subjects of the other kinds of knowledge. Suppose that the senses and imagination thus oppose reasoning, saying, 'The universal natural kinds, which reason believes that it can perceive, are nothing; for what is comprehensible to the senses and the imagination cannot be universal: therefore either the judgment of reason is true, and that which can be perceived by the senses is nothing; or, since reason knows well that there are many subjects comprehensible to the senses and imagination, the conception of reason is vain, for it holds to be universal what is an individual matter comprehensible to the senses.' To this reason might answer, that 'it sees from a general point of view what is comprehensible to the senses and the imagination, but they cannot aspire to a knowledge of universals, since their manner of knowledge cannot go further than material or bodily appearances; and in the matter of knowledge it is better to trust to the stronger and more nearly perfect judgment.' If such a trail of argument occurred, should not we, who have within us the force of reasoning as well as the powers of the senses and imagination, approve of the cause of reason rather than that of the others? It is in like manner that human reason thinks that the divine intelligence cannot perceive the things of the future except as it conceives them itself. For you argue thus: 'If there are events which do not appear to have sure or necessary results, their results cannot be known for certain beforehand: therefore there can be no foreknowledge of these events; for if we believe that there is any foreknowledge thereof, there can exist nothing but such as is brought forth of necessity.' If therefore we, who have our share in possession of reason, could go further and possess the judgment of the mind of God, we should then think it most just that human reason should yield itself to the mind of God, just as we have determined that the senses and imagination ought to yield to reason.

Let us therefore raise ourselves, if so be that we can, to that height of the loftiest intelligence. For there reason will see what it cannot of itself perceive, and that is to know how even such things as have uncertain results are perceived definitely and for certain by foreknowledge; and such foreknowledge will not be mere opinion, but rather the single and direct form of the highest knowledge unlimited by any finite bounds.

In what different shapes do living beings move upon the earth! Some make flat their bodies, sweeping through the dust and using their strength to make therein a furrow without break; some flit here and there upon light wings which beat the breeze, and they float through vast tracks of air in their easy flight. Tis others' wont to plant their footsteps on the ground, and pass with their paces over green fields or under trees. Though all these thou seest move in different shapes, yet all have their faces downward along the ground, and this doth draw downward and dull their senses. Alone of all, the human race lifts up its head on high, and stands in easy balance with the body upright, and so looks down to spurn the earth. If thou art not too earthly by an evil folly, this pose is as a lesson. Thy glance is upward, and thou dost carry high thy head, and thus thy search is heavenward: then lead thy soul too upward, lest while the body is higher raised, the mind sink lower to the earth."

(Philosophy explains that God's divine intelligence can view all things from its eternal mind, while human reason can only see them from a temporal point of view.)

"Since then all that is known is apprehended, as we just now showed, not according to its own nature but according to the nature of the knower, let us examine, so far as we lawfully may, the character of the divine nature, so that we may be able to learn what its knowledge is.

The common opinion, according to all men living, is that God is eternal. Let us therefore consider what is eternity. For eternity will, I think, make clear to us at the same time the divine nature and knowledge.

Eternity is the simultaneous and complete possession of infinite life. This will appear more clearly if we compare it with temporal things. All that lives under the conditions of time moves through the present from the past to the future; there is nothing set in time which can at one moment grasp the whole space of its lifetime. It cannot yet comprehend tomorrow; yesterday it has already lost. And in this life of today your life is no more than a changing, passing moment. And as Aristotle[9] said of the universe, so it is of all that is subject to time; though it never began to be, nor will ever cease, and its life is coextensive with the infinity of time, yet it is not such as can be held to be eternal. For though it apprehends and grasps a space of infinite lifetime, it does not embrace the whole simultaneously; it has not yet experienced the future. What we should rightly call eternal is that which grasps and possesses wholly and simultaneously the fullness of unending life, which lacks naught of the future, and has lost naught of the fleeting past; and such an existence must be ever present in itself to control and aid itself, and also must keep present with itself the infinity of changing time. Therefore, people who hear that Plato thought that this universe had no beginning of time and will have no end, are not right in thinking that in this way the created world is coeternal with its creator.[10] For to pass through unending life, the attribute which Plato ascribes to the universe is one thing; but it is another thing to grasp simultaneously the whole of unending life in the present; this is plainly a peculiar property of the mind of God.

And further, God should not be regarded as older than His creations by any
period of time, but rather by the peculiar
property of His own single nature. For the
infinite changing of temporal things tries to
imitate the ever simultaneously present immutability of His life: it cannot succeed in
imitating or equalling this, but sinks from
immutability into change, and falls from
the single directness of the present into an
infinite space of future and past. And since
this temporal state cannot possess its life
completely and simultaneously, but it does
in the same manner exist for ever without
ceasing, it therefore seems to try in some
degree to rival that which it cannot fulfil or
represent, for it binds itself to some sort of
present time out of this small and fleeting
moment; but inasmuch as this temporal
present bears a certain appearance of that
abiding present, it somehow makes those,
to whom it comes, seem to be in truth what
they imitate. But since this imitation could
not be abiding, the unending march of time
has swept it away, and thus we find that it
has bound together, as it passes, a chain of
life, which it could not by abiding embrace
in its fullness. And thus if we would apply
proper epithets to those subjects, we can
say, following Plato, that God is eternal,
but the universe is continual.

Since then all judgment apprehends the
subjects of its thought according to its own
nature, and God has a condition of ever-
present eternity, His knowledge, which
passes over every change of time, embracing infinite lengths of past and future, views
in its own direct comprehension everything
as though it were taking place in the present.
If you would weigh the foreknowledge by
which God distinguishes all things, you will
more rightly hold it to be a knowledge of a
never-failing constancy in the present, than
a foreknowledge of the future. Whence
Providence is more rightly to be understood
as a looking forth than a looking forward,
because it is set far from low matters and
looks forth upon all things as from a lofty
mountain-top above all. Why then do you
demand that all things occur by necessity,

if divine light rests upon them, while men
do not render necessary such things as they
can see? Because you can see things of the
present, does your sight therefore put upon
them any necessity? Surely not. If one may
not unworthily compare this present time
with the divine, just as you can see things
in this your temporal present, so God sees
all things in His eternal present. Wherefore
this divine foreknowledge does not change
the nature or individual qualities of things:
it sees things present in its understanding
just as they will result some time in the future. It makes no confusion in its distinctions, and with one view of its mind it discerns all that shall come to pass whether of
necessity or not. For instance, when you see
at the same time a man walking on the earth
and the sun rising in the heavens, you see
each sight simultaneously, yet you distinguish between them, and decide that one is
moving voluntarily, the other of necessity.
In like manner the perception of God looks
down upon all things without disturbing at
all their nature, though they are present to
Him but future under the conditions of
time. Wherefore this foreknowledge is not
opinion but knowledge resting upon truth,
since He knows that a future event is,
though He knows too that it will not occur
of necessity. If you answer here that what
God sees about to happen, cannot but happen, and that what cannot but happen is
bound by necessity, you fasten me down to
the word necessity, I will grant that we have
a matter of most firm truth, but it is one to
which scarce any man can approach unless
he be a contemplator of the divine. For I
shall answer that such a thing will occur of
necessity, when it is viewed from the point
of divine knowledge; but when it is examined in its own nature, it seems perfectly
free and unrestrained. For there are two
kinds of necessities; one is simple: for instance, a necessary fact, 'all men are mortal';
the other is conditional; for instance, if you
know that a man is walking, he must be
walking: for what each man knows cannot
be otherwise than it is known to be; but the
conditional one is by no means followed by

this simple and direct necessity; for there is no necessity to compel a voluntary walker to proceed, though it is necessary that, if he walks, he should be proceeding. In the same way, if Providence sees an event in its present, that thing must be, though it has no necessity of its own nature. And God looks in His present upon those future things which come to pass through free will. Therefore if these things be looked at from the point of view of God's insight, they come to pass of necessity under the condition of divine knowledge; if, on the other hand, they are viewed by themselves, they do not lose the perfect freedom of their nature. Without doubt, then, all things that God foreknows do come to pass, but some of them proceed from free will; and though they result by coming into existence, yet they do not lose their own nature, because before they came to pass they could also not have come to pass.

'What then,' you may ask, 'is the difference in their not being bound by necessity, since they result under all circumstances as by necessity, on account of the condition of divine knowledge?' This is the difference, as I just now put forward: take the sun rising and a man walking; while these operations are occurring, they cannot but occur: but the one was bound to occur before it did; the other was not so bound. What God has in His present, does exist without doubt; but of such things some follow by necessity, others by their authors' wills. Wherefore I was justified in saying that if these things be regarded from the view of divine knowledge, they are necessary, but if they are viewed by themselves, they are perfectly free from all ties of necessity: just as when you refer all, that is clear to the senses, to the reason, it becomes general truth, but it remains particular if regarded by itself. 'But,' you will say, 'if it is in my power to change a purpose of mine, I will disregard Providence, since I may change what Providence foresees.' To which I answer, 'You can change your purpose, but since the truth of Providence knows in its present that you can

do so, and whether you do so, and in what direction you may change it, therefore you cannot escape that divine foreknowledge: just as you cannot avoid the glance of a present eye, though you may by your free will turn yourself to all kinds of different actions.' 'What?' you will say, 'can I by my own action change divine knowledge, so that if I choose now one thing, now another, Providence too will seem to change its knowledge?' No; divine insight precedes all future things, turning them back and recalling them to the present time of its own peculiar knowledge. It does not change, as you may think, between this and that alternation of foreknowledge. It is constant in preceding and embracing by one glance all your changes. And God does not receive this ever-present grasp of all things and vision of the present at the occurrence of future events, but from His own peculiar directness. Whence also is that difficulty solved which you laid down a little while ago, that it was not worthy to say that our future events were the cause of God's knowledge. For this power of knowledge, ever in the present and embracing all things in its perception, does itself constrain all things, and owes naught to following events from which it has received naught. Thus, therefore, mortal men have their freedom of judgement intact. And since their wills are freed from all binding necessity, laws do not set rewards or punishments unjustly. God is ever the constant foreknowing overseer, and the ever-present eternity of His sight moves in harmony with the future nature of our actions, as it dispenses rewards to the good, and punishments to the bad. Hopes are not vainly put in God, nor prayers in vain offered: if these are right, they cannot but be answered. Turn therefore from vice: ensue virtue: raise your soul to upright hopes: send up on high your prayers from this earth. If you would be honest, great is the necessity enjoined upon your goodness, since all you do is done before the eyes of an all-seeing Judge."

NOTES

1. Aristotle, *Physics*, ii.3.
2. A phrase from Homer (*Iliad*, iii, 277, and *Odyssey*, xi. 109), where it is said of the sun.
3. This sentence, besides referring to the application of Homer's words used above, contains also a play on words in the Latin, which can only be clumsily reproduced in English by some such words as "The sole power which can see all is justly to be called the solar."
4. Horace, *Satires*, II, v. 59.
5. Supra, Book IV, Met. vi. p. 135.
6. Cicero, *De Divinatione*, II.
7. Referring to Boethius's words on p. 194.
8. Zeno, of Citium (342–270 B.C.), the founder of the Stoic school, taught in the Stoa Poekile, whence the name of the school. The following lines refer to their doctrine of presentations and impressions.
9. Aristotle, *De Caelo*, I.
10. Boethius speaks of people who "hear that Plato thought, etc.," because this was the teaching of some of Plato's successors at the Academy. Plato himself thought otherwise, as may be seen in the *Timaeus*, e.g. ch. xi, 38 B., "Time then has come into being along with the universe, that being generated together, together they may be dissolved, should a dissolution of them ever come to pass; and it was made after the pattern of the eternal nature that it might be as like to it as possible. For the pattern is existent for all eternity, but the copy has been, and is, and shall be, throughout all time continually." (Mr. Archer Hind's translation.)

CHAPTER 14

St. Anselm

(See Chapter Three for biography.)

St. Anselm on Foreknowledge and Free Choice

St. Anselm utilizes the notion of necessity to solve the problem of divine foreknowledge. He first of all observes that if God possesses foreknowledge, it is necessary that what is foreknown will occur. Free Will entails that that which is a result of free will does not occur necessarily. There is no incompatibility, for God can foreknow that something is going to occur without any necessity. In other words, God knows that some actions are going to be a result of free choice, which is to say that He knows that some actions will occur in the future without necessity, that is, without His compulsion. To clarify this view, Anselm introduces a distinction between preceding necessity and subsequent necessity. The former is causal necessity, the latter logical necessity. The apparent incompatibility between God's foreknowledge and free will is resolved via subsequent necessity; for example, it is necessarily the case that what is going to happen is going to happen in the same way that it is necessarily the case that every man is a man. The necessity is of a logical character, for "if it were not necessary that everything which is going to happen were going to happen, then something which is going to happen would not be going to happen—a contradiction." This sense of necessity has nothing to do with compulsion. God's foreknowledge pertains to subsequent necessity, not preceding necessity. So long as God's foreknowledge does not require preceding or causal necessity, there is no incompatibility between His foreknowledge and free will. When we say that God foreknows the future "we are not asserting that every event is going to occur by necessity; rather we are asserting that the event which is going to occur is, necessarily, going to occur. For although God foreknows all future events, He does not foreknow that all of them are going to occur by necessity. Rather, He foreknows that some of them will occur as the result of the free will of a rational creature".

FOREKNOWLEDGE AND FREE CHOICE

1

Admittedly, free choice and the foreknowledge of God seem incompatible; for it is necessary that the things foreknown by God be going to occur, whereas the things done by free choice occur without any necessity. Now, if these two are incompatible, then it is impossible that God's all-foreseeing foreknowledge should coexist with something's being done by freedom of choice. In turn, if this impossibility is regarded as not obtaining, then the incompatibility which seems to be present is completely eliminated.

Therefore, let us posit as existing together both God's foreknowledge (from which the necessity of future things seems to follow) and freedom of choice (by which many actions are performed, we believe, without any necessity); and let us see whether it is impossible for these two to coexist. If this coexistence is impossible, then some other impossibility arises from it. For, indeed, an impossible thing is one from which, when posited, some other impossible thing follows. Now, on the assumption that some action is going to occur without necessity, God foreknows this, since he foreknows all future events. And that which is foreknown by God is, necessarily, going to occur, as is foreknown. Therefore, it is necessary that something be going to occur without necessity. Hence, the foreknowledge from which necessity follows and the freedom of choice from which necessity is absent are here seen (for one who rightly understands it) to be not at all incompatible. For, on the one hand, it is necessary that what is foreknown by God be going to occur; and, on the other hand, God foreknows that something is going to occur without any necessity.

From St. Anselm, *The Harmony of the Foreknowledge, The Predestination, and the Grace of God with Free Choice* from *Anselm of Canterbury*, Vol. 2, edited and translated by Jasper Hopkins and Herbert Richardson (Toronto and New York: The Edwin Mellen Press, 1976), pp. 181–188. Reprinted by permission of The Edwin Mellen Press.

But you will say to me: "You still do not remove from me the necessity of sinning or the necessity of not sinning. For God foreknows that I am going to sin or foreknows that I am not going to sin. And so, if I sin, it is necessary that I sin; or if I do not sin, it is necessary that I do not sin." To this claim I reply: You ought to say not merely "God foreknows that I am going to sin" or "God foreknows that I am not going to sin" but "God foreknows that it is without necessity that I am going to sin" or "God foreknows that it is without necessity that I am not going to sin." And thus it follows that whether you sin or do not sin, in either case it will be without necessity; for God foreknows that what will occur will occur without necessity. Do you see, then, that it is not impossible for God's foreknowledge (according to which future things, which God foreknows, are said to occur of necessity) to coexist with freedom of choice (by which many actions are performed without necessity)? For if this coexistence were impossible, then something impossible would follow. But no impossibility arises from this coexistence.

Perhaps you will claim: "You still do not remove the constraint of necessity from my heart when you say that, because of God's foreknowledge, it is necessary for me to be going to sin without necessity or it is necessary for me to be not going to sin without necessity. For necessity seems to imply coercion or restraint. Therefore, if it is necessary that I sin willingly, I interpret this as indicating that I am compelled by some hidden power to will to sin; and if I do not sin, [I interpret this as indicating that] I am restrained from willing to sin. Therefore, it seems to me that if I sin I sin by necessity, and if I do not sin it is by necessity that I do not sin."

2

And I [reply]: We must realize that we often say "necessary to be" of what is not compelled-to-be by any force, and "necessary not to be" of what is not excluded by any preventing factor. For example, we say "It is necessary for God to be immortal" and "It is necessary for God not to be unjust." [We say this] not because some force compels Him to be immortal or prohibits Him from being unjust, but because nothing can cause Him not to be immortal or can cause Him to be unjust.[1] Similarly, then, I might say: "It is necessary that you are going to sin voluntarily" or "It is necessary that, voluntarily, you are not going to sin"—just as God foreknows. But these statements must not be construed to mean that something prevents the act of will which shall not occur, or compels that act of will which shall occur. For God, who foresees that some action is going to occur voluntarily, foreknows the very fact that the will is neither compelled nor prevented by anything. Hence, what is done voluntarily is done freely. Therefore, if these matters are carefully pondered, I think that no inconsistency prevents freedom of choice and God's foreknowledge from coexisting.

Indeed, (if someone properly considers the meaning of the word), by the very fact that something is said to be *foreknown*, it is declared to be going to occur.[2] For only what is going to occur is foreknown, since knowledge is only of the truth. Therefore, when I say "If God foreknows something, it is necessary that this thing be going to occur," it is as if I were to say: "If this thing will occur, of necessity it will occur." But this necessity neither compels nor prevents a thing's existence or nonexistence. For because the thing is presumed to exist, it is said to exist of necessity; or because it is presumed not to exist, it is said to not-exist of necessity. [But our reason for saying these things is] not that necessity compels or prevents the thing's existence or nonexistence. For when I say "If it will occur, of necessity it will occur," here the necessity follows, rather than precedes, the presumed existence of the thing.[3] The sense is the same if we say "What will be, of necessity will be." For this necessity signifies nothing other than that what will occur will not be able not to occur at the same time.

Likewise, the following statements are equally true: (1) that some thing did exist and does exist and will exist, but not out of necessity, and (2) that all that was, necessarily was, all that is, necessarily is, and all that will be, necessarily will be. Indeed, for a thing to be past is not the same as for a past thing to be past; and for a thing to be present is not the same as for a present thing to be present; and for a thing to be future is not the same as for a future thing to be future. By comparison, for a thing to be white is not the same as for a white thing to be white. For example, a staff is not always necessarily white, because at some time before it became white it was able not to become white; and after it has become white, it is able to become not-white. But it is necessary that a white staff always be white. For neither before a white thing was white nor after it has become white can it happen that a white thing is not-white at the same time. Similarly, it is not by necessity that a thing is temporally present. For before the thing was present, it was able to happen that it would not be present: and after it has become present, it can happen that it not remain present. But it is necessary that a present thing always be present, because neither before it is present nor after it has become present is a present thing able to be not-present at the same time. In the same way, some event—e.g., an action—is going to occur without necessity, because before the action occurs, it can happen that it not be going to occur.[4] On the other hand, it is necessary that a future event be future, because what is future is not able at the same time to be not-future. Of the past it is similarly true (1) that some event is not necessarily past, because before it occurred, there was the possibility of its not occurring, and (2) that, necessarily, what is past is always past, since it is not able at the same time not to be past. Now, a past event has a characteristic which a present event or a future event does not have. For it is never possible for a past event to become not-past, as a present event is able to become not-present, and as an event which is not necessarily going to happen has the possibility of not happening in the future. Thus, when we say of what is going to happen that it is going to happen, this statement must be true, because it is never the case that what is going to happen is not going to happen. (Similarly, whenever we predicate something of itself, [the statement is true]. For when we say "Every man is a man," or "If he is a man, he is a man," or "Every white thing is white," or "If it is a white thing, it is white": these statements must be true because something cannot both be and not be the case at the same time.) Indeed, if it were not necessary that everything which is going to happen were going to happen, then something which is going to happen would not be going to happen—a contradiction. Therefore, *necessarily*, everything which is going to happen is going to happen; and if it is going to happen, it is going to happen. (For we are saying of what is going to happen that it is going to happen.) But ["necessarily" here signifies] subsequent necessity, which does not compel anything to be.

3

However, when an event is said to be going to occur, it is not always the case that the event occurs by necessity, even though it is going to occur. For example, if I say "Tomorrow there will be an insurrection among the people," it is not the case that the insurrection will occur by necessity. For before it occurs, it is possible that it not occur even if it is going to occur. On the other hand, it is sometimes the case that the thing which is said to be going to occur does occur by necessity—for example, if I say that tomorrow there will be a sunrise. Therefore, if of an event which is going to occur I state that it must be going to occur, [I do so] either in the way that the insurrection which is going to occur tomorrow is, necessarily, going to occur, or else in the way that the sunrise which is going to occur tomorrow is going to occur by necessity. Indeed, the insurrection (which will occur but not by necessity) is said necessarily to be going to occur—but only in the sense of subsequent necessity. For we are saying of what is going to happen that it is going

to happen. For if the insurrection is going to occur tomorrow, then—necessarily—it is going to occur. On the other hand, the sunrise is understood to be going to occur with two necessities: (1) with a preceding necessity, which causes the event to occur (for the event will occur because it is necessary that it occur), and (2) with a subsequent necessity which does not compel anything to occur (for because the sunrise is going to occur, it is—necessarily—going to occur).

Therefore, when of what God foreknows to be going to occur we say that it is necessary that it be going to occur, we are not in every case asserting that the event is going to occur by necessity; rather, we are asserting that an event which is going to occur is, necessarily, going to occur. For something which is going to occur cannot at the same time be not going to occur. The meaning is the same when we say "If God foreknows such-and-such an event"—without adding "which is going to occur." For in the verb "to foreknow" the notion of future occurrence is included, since to foreknow is nothing other than to know the future; and so if God foreknows some event, it is necessary that this event be going to occur. Therefore, from the fact of God's foreknowledge it does not in every case follow that an event is going to occur by necessity. For although God foreknows all future events, He does not foreknow that all of them are going to occur by necessity. Rather, He foreknows that some of them will occur as the result of the free will of a rational creature.

Indeed, we must note that just as it is not necessary for God to will what He does will, so in many cases it is not necessary for a man to will what he does will. And just as whatever God wills must occur, so what a man wills must occur—in the case, that is, of the things which God so subordinates to the human will that if it wills them they occur and if it does not will them they do not occur. For since what God wills is not able not to occur: when He wills for no necessity either to compel the human will to will or to prevent it from willing, and when He wills that the effect follow from the act of human willing, it is necessary that the human will be free and that there occur what it wills. In this respect, then, it is true that the sinful deed which a man wills to do occurs by necessity, even though the man does not will it by necessity. Now, with respect to the human will's sin when it wills to sin: if someone asks whether this sin occurs by necessity, then he must be told that just as the will does not will by necessity, so the will's sin does not occur by necessity. Nor does the human will act by necessity; for if it did not will freely, it would not act—even though what it wills must come to pass, as I have just said. For since, in the present case, to sin is nothing other than to will what ought not [to be willed]: just as willing is not necessary, so sinful willing is not necessary. Nevertheless, it is true that if a man wills to sin, it is necessary that he sin—in terms, that is, of that necessity which (as I have said)[5] neither compels nor prevents anything.

Thus, on the one hand, free will is able to keep from willing what it wills; and, on the other hand, it is not able to keep from willing what it wills—rather, it is necessary for free will to will what it wills. For, indeed, before it wills, it is able to keep from willing, because it is free. And while it wills, it is not able not to will; rather, it is necessary that it will, since it is impossible for it to will and not to will the same thing at the same time. Now, it is the will's prerogative that what it wills occurs and that what it does not will does not occur. And the will's deeds are voluntary and free because they are done by a free will. But these deeds are necessary in two respects: (1) because the will compels them to be done, and (2) because what is being done cannot at the same time not be done. But these two necessities are produced by freedom-of-will; and the free will is able to avoid them before they occur. Now, God (who knows all truth and only truth) sees all these things as they are—whether they be free or necessary; and as He sees them, so they are. In this way, then, and without any inconsistency, it is evident both that God foreknows all things and that many things are done by free will. And before these things

occur it is possible that they never occur. Nevertheless, in a certain sense they occur necessarily; and this necessity (as I said)[6] derives from free will.

4

Moreover, that not everything foreknown by God occurs of necessity but that some events occur as the result of freedom-of-will can be recognized from the following consideration. When God wills or causes something, He cannot be denied to know what He wills and causes, and to foreknow what He shall will and shall cause. ([It makes no difference here] whether we speak in accordance with eternity's immutable present, in which there is nothing past or future, but in which all things exist at once without any change (e.g., if we say only that He wills and causes something and deny that He has willed or has caused and shall will or shall cause something), or whether we speak in accordance with temporality as when we state that He shall will or shall cause that which we know has not yet occurred). Therefore, if God's knowledge or foreknowledge imposes necessity on everything He knows or foreknows, then He does not freely will or cause anything (either in accordance with eternity or in accordance with a temporal mode); rather, He wills and causes everything by necessity. Now, if this conclusion is absurd even to suppose, then it is not the case that everything known or foreknown to be or not to be occurs or fails to occur by necessity. Therefore, nothing prevents God's knowing or foreknowing that in our wills and actions something occurs or will occur by free choice. Thus, although it is necessary that what He knows or foreknows, occur, nevertheless many events occur not by necessity but by free will—as I have shown above.[7]

Indeed, why is it strange if in this way something occurs both freely and necessarily? For there are many things which admit of opposite characteristics in different respects.[8] Indeed, what is more opposed than coming and going? Nevertheless, when someone moves from one place to another, we see that his movement is both a coming and a going. For he goes away from one place and comes toward another. Likewise, if we consider the sun at some point in the heavens, as it is hastening toward this same point while always illuminating the heavens: we see that the point to which it is coming is the same point from which it is going away; and it is constantly and simultaneously approaching the point from which it is departing. Moreover, to those who know the sun's course, it is evident that in relation to the heavens, the sun always moves from the western sector to the

eastern sector; but in relation to the earth, it always moves only from east to west. Thus, the sun always moves both counter to the firmament and—although more slowly [than the firmament]—with the firmament.[9] This same phenomenon is witnessed in the case of all the planets. So then, no inconsistency arises if (in accordance with the considerations just presented) we assert of one and the same event (1) that, necessarily, it is going to occur (simply because it *is* going to occur) and (2) that it is not compelled to be going to occur by any necessity—except for the necessity which (as I said above)[10] derives from free will.

NOTES

1. Note *Cur Deus Homo* II, 17 (S II, 123:31–124:2) and *Ein neues unvollendetes Werk des hl. Anselm von Canterbury* (Philosophical Fragments) 24:16–25.
2. Note *De Casu Diaboli* 21 (S 1, 266:16–22).
3. On the distinction between antecedent and subsequent necessity, see *Cur Deus Homo* II, 17.
4. Anselm continues to use the word *"res"* (i.e., "thing"), which we now translate as *event*.
5. *De Concordia Praescientiae et Praedestinationis et Gratiae Dei cum Libero Arbitrio* I, 2 (S II, 249:2–3).
6. A few lines earlier.
7. Note the last portion of *De Concordia Praescientiae et Praedestinationis et Gratiae Dei cum Libero Arbitrio* I, 3.
8. Note *De Veritate* 8 (S I, 187:2–17).
9. Anselm is referring to the fact that the sun appears to revolve around the earth from *east to west* (i.e., "with the firmament") once every day. At the same time, the sun actually moves among the stars from *west to east* (i.e., "counter to the firmament"), making one complete circuit of the heavens in a year. Because the sun changes its position in the heavens constantly at a uniform rate, it requires a few more minutes than do the stars to complete its daily apparent revolution about the earth. A similar effect is generally true for the planets as well.
10. *De Concordia Praescientiae et Praedestinationis et Gratiae Dei cum Libero Arbitrio* I, 3 (S II, 251:27).

CHAPTER 15

Averroës

Averroës, or Ibn Rushd, is most certainly among the outstanding figures of medieval Islamic philosophy. His preeminence is due not only to his own extraordinary abilities but to his enormous influence on certain Christian philosophers from 1200 to 1650.

He was born at Córdoba, Spain, circa 1126 to a family of prominent judges and lawyers. Both his grandfather and father held the position of chief *qādī* (judge) of Córdoba. That Islam is a theocracy, training in the law was (and is) both civil and religious. Not surprisingly, Averroës was also trained in this tradition as well as in medicine. Little, however, is known regarding his early philosophical training.

Sometime between 1153 and 1169, Averroës' mentor, philosopher and court physician Ibn-Tufail, introduced the young scholar to the sultan of Marrakesh, Caliph Abū Ya qūb, a great patron of scholarship, research, and learning. The caliph was most impressed by Averroës' philosophical acuity, and with the caliph's encouragement Averroës commenced the long series of commentaries on Aristotle. These works had such an enormous effect on subsequent Latin thought that he became known as the Commentator.

The undertaking of these commentaries began in 1169, coincidental to his appointment as *qādī* of Seville. In 1171 he returned to Córdoba, where he eventually became chief *qādī*. During this time he made frequent visits to Marrakesh and in 1182 became court physician to the caliph. He continued to enjoy high favor until about 1195, when he was suddenly banished to a small village outside Seville.

Details surrounding Averroës' ouster are scant, but it is speculated that at this time conservative (Islamic) theologians began to flex their muscles in a general reaction against philosophy. That his exile was for his own protection is substantiated by the fact that it was short-lived and he was recalled to Marrakesh and restored to a position of honor. He died there in 1198.

Averroës on God's Knowledge

The problem of foreknowledge is a function of "originated" or human knowledge. This is knowledge of the sensible world and presupposes change, specifically the coming of things into being and of their going out of being. In short, originated knowledge pertains to contingency. Contingency presupposes the distinction between exemplified and unexemplified existence. If one, by analogy, concludes that God's knowledge is similarly affected by this ontological distinction, then His (eternal) knowledge is subject to change which would undermine His foreknowledge. That is, at time t_1 God knows that a thing exists in an unexemplified way and at time t_2 He knows that it exists in an exemplified way. The change in existential status of the thing in question would necessarily entail a change in God's knowledge. Averroës understands foreknowledge as incompatible with change in existential status when such a status is tantamount to contingency.

Averroës suggests that this dilemma is based on an analogy between eternal knowledge and originated knowledge; that is, between the suprasensible and the sensible. The dilemma is resolved by realizing that such is a false analogy. As for originated knowledge, namely, human knowledge, the existence of beings is a cause of and basis for that knowledge. That is, were it not for the fact that things are (by virtue of becoming) exemplified, there would be no human knowledge, namely, knowledge of the sensible world. Eternal knowledge, on the other hand, is not dependent upon the existence of things. Rather, it is a cause of and the basis for beings. As the ground of being of all things, eternal knowledge is unaffected (i.e., unchanged) by the change in status of a being existing unexemplified at time t_1 and exemplified at time t_2. In essence, change in the ontological status of a thing affects (i.e., influences, changes) originated knowledge, whereas it has no effect on eternal knowledge, for any such change in ontological status is dependent (for its existence) on eternal knowledge in the first place. In other words, existence is a predicate with respect to originated knowledge. Existence is not a predicate with respect to God's knowledge. Consequently, what God knows is eternal and not subject to change because His knowledge is the ground of all being. The different "modes" of existence do not affect the suprasensible. They only affect the sensible world.

"ON GOD'S KNOWLEDGE,"
FROM *ON THE HARMONY OF RELIGION AND PHILOSOPHY*

Selection I

[We shall try to solve your problem about God's Knowledge.]

May God prolong your power, continue to bless you, and keep you out of sight of misfortunes!

By your superior intelligence and abundant talents you have surpassed many of those who devote their lives to these sciences, and your sure insight has led you to become aware of the difficulty that arises

From Averroës, *On the Harmony of Religion and Philosophy*, translated and edited by George F. Hourani. (Printed for the Trustees of the "E.J.W. Gibb Memorial" and published by Messrs. Luzac and Co., London, 1961), pp. 72–75.

about the eternal, Glorious Knowledge, on account of Its being connected with the things originated by It. It is therefore our obligation, in the interests of truth and of ending your perplexity, to resolve this difficulty, after formulating it; for he who does not know how to tie a knot cannot untie it.

[The problem: How can God be aware of a change in reality without a corresponding change occurring in His eternal Knowledge?]

The difficulty is compelling, as follows. If all these things were in the Knowledge of God the Glorious before they existed, are they in their state of existence [the same] in His Knowledge as they were before their existence, or are they in their state of existence other in His Knowledge than they were before they existed? If we say that in their state of existence they are other in God's knowledge than they were before they existed, it follows that the eternal Knowledge is subject to change, and that when they pass from nonexistence to existence, there comes into existence additional Knowledge: but that is impossible for the eternal Knowledge. If on the other hand we say that the Knowledge of them in both states is one and the same, it will be asked, 'Are they in themselves', i.e. the beings which come into existence, 'the same before they exist as when they exist?' The answer will have to be 'No, in themselves they are not the same before they exist as when they exist'; otherwise the existent and the non-existent would be one and the same. If the adversary admits this, he can be asked, 'Is not true Knowledge acquaintance with existence as it really is?' If he says 'Yes', it will be said, 'Consequently if the object varies in itself, the knowledge of it must vary; otherwise it will not be known as it really is'. Thus one of two alternatives is necessary: either the eternal Knowledge varies in Itself, or the things that come into existence are not known to It. But both alternatives are impossible for God the Glorious.

This difficulty is confirmed by what appears in the case of man: His knowledge of non-existent things depends on the supposition of existence, while his knowledge of them when they exist depends [on existence itself]. For it is self-evident that the two states of knowledge are different; otherwise he would be ignorant of things' existence at the time when they exist.

[God's foreknowledge of all change does not solve the problem, as the theologians think, for the actual occurrence of the change presumably adds something new to His knowledge.]

It is impossible to escape from this [difficulty] by the usual answer of the theologians about it, that God the Exalted knows things before their existence as they will be at the time of their existence, in respect of time, place and other attributes proper to each being. For it can be said to them: 'Then when they come to exist, does there occur any change or not?'—with reference to the passage of the thing from non-existence to existence. If they say 'No change occurs', they are merely being supercilious. But if they say 'There does occur a change', it can be said to them: 'Then is the occurrence of this change known to the eternal Knowledge or not?' Thus the difficulty is compelling. In sum, it can hardly be conceived that the knowledge of a thing before it exists can be identical with the knowledge of it after it exists. Such, then, is the formulation of this problem in its strongest possible form, as we have explained it to you in conversation.

[Nor is Ghazālī's solution satisfactory. He regards God's Knowledge as a term in a relation, which does not change in itself when that to which it is related, the known object, changes its relation to it. But knowledge is a relation, not a related term.]

The [full] solution of this difficulty would call for a lengthy discourse; but here we shall only go into the decisive point of the solution. Abū Ḥāmid in his book entitled *The disintegration* wanted to resolve this difficulty in a way which carries no conviction. He stated an argument the gist of which is as follows. He asserted that knowledge and the object known are related; and as one of two related things may change without the other changing in itself, this is just what seems to happen to things in the Knowledge of God the Glorious: they change in themselves, but the Knowledge of God the Glorious about them does not change. A parallel case of related things would be if a single column were first on the right of Zayd and then came to be on his left: meanwhile Zayd would not have changed in himself. But this [argument] is not correct. For the relation has changed in itself: the relation which was a right-handed one has become a left-handed one, and the only thing which has not changed is the subject of the relation, i.e. its bearer, Zayd. If this is so, and knowledge is the relation itself, it must necessarily change when the object known changes, just as, when the column changes [its position], the relation of the column to Zayd changes, coming to be a left-handed relation after having been a right-handed one.

[The correct solution is that the eternal Knowledge is the cause of beings, not their effect as originated knowledge is. Therefore It does not change when they change.]

The way to resolve this difficulty, in our opinion, is to recognize that the position of the eternal Knowledge with respect to beings is different from the position of originated knowledge with respect to beings, in that the existence of beings is a cause and reason for our knowledge, while the eternal Knowledge is a cause and reason for beings. If, when beings come to exist after not having existed, there occurred an addition in the eternal Knowledge such as occurs in originated knowledge, it would follow that the eternal Knowledge would be an effect of beings, not their cause. Therefore there must not occur any change such as occurs in originated knowledge. The mistake in this matter has arisen simply from making an analogy between the eternal Knowledge and originated knowledge, i.e. between the suprasensible and the sensible; and the falsity of this analogy is well known. Just as no change occurs in an agent when his act comes into being, i.e. no change which has not already occurred, so no change occurs in the eternal Glorious Knowledge when the object of Its Knowledge results from It.

Thus the difficulty is resolved, and we do not have to admit that if there occurs no change, i.e. in the eternal Knowledge, He does not know beings at the time of their coming into existence just as they are; we only have to admit that He does not know them with originated knowledge but with eternal Knowledge. For the occurrence of change in knowledge when beings change is a condition only of knowledge which is caused by beings, i.e. originated knowledge.

[The philosophers hold that God knows particulars with eternal Knowledge, not that He does not know them at all. Indeed, they consider that His knowledge is the cause of their coming into existence, also that It sends premonitions of particulars in dreams.]

Therefore eternal Knowledge is only connected with beings in a manner other than that in which originated knowledge is connected with them. This does not mean that It is not connected at all, as the philosophers have been accused of saying, in the context of this difficulty, that the Glorious One does not know particulars. Their position is not what has been imputed to them; rather they hold that He does not know particulars with originated knowledge, the occurrence of which is conditioned by their occurrence, since He is a cause of them, not caused by them as originated knowledge is. This is the furthest extent to which purification [of concepts] ought to be admitted.

For demonstration compels the conclusion that He knows things, because their issuing from Him is solely due to His knowing; it is not due to His being merely Existent or Existent with a certain attribute, but to His knowing, as the Exalted has said: "Does He not know, He who created? He is the Penetrating, the Omniscient!" But demonstration also compels the conclusion that He does not know things with a knowledge of the same character as originated knowledge. Therefore there must be another knowledge of beings which is unqualified, the eternal Glorious Knowledge. And how is it conceivable that the Peripatetic philosophers could have held that the eternal Knowledge does not comprehend particulars, when they held that It is the cause of warning in dreams, of revelation, and of other kinds of inspiration?

[Conclusion]

This is the way to resolve this difficulty, as it appears to us; and what has been said is incontestable and indubitable. It is God who helps us to follow the right course and directs us to the truth. Peace on you, with the mercy and blessings of God.

CHAPTER 16

William of Ockham

William of Ockham, known as the Venerable Inceptor, was born around 1280, presumably at Ockham, a village in the county of Surrey, near present-day London. (There is only evidence of his name in support of his birthplace.) He entered the Franciscan order and was ordained a subdeacon in 1306. He pursued a normal course of study at Oxford, where he lectured on the *Sentences* (of Peter Lombard) from 1317 to 1319. He was prevented from becoming a regent master in theology by John Lutterell, the chancellor of the university and an overzealous Thomist who challenged the empirical leanings of William. Consequently, William remained an inceptor, namely, a student who had completed most of the requirements for teaching as a master in theology. This caused a controversy within the university, and the bishop of Lincoln, upon request of the university itself, deposed Lutterell in 1322.

Apparently aware of the controversy, the king refused to allow Ockham to leave the country. Nevertheless, Lutterell's accusation of heresy against William made a permission to visit the papal court in Avignon possible. In 1324, Pope John XXII summoned Ockham to Avignon to respond to the accusations, and a commission was appointed to examine his teachings. The commission's investigations dragged on for the better part of two years. Two lists of suspect theses were compiled, often blatantly misrepresenting Ockham's views. This incurred the pope's ire, and the commission was unable to achieve agreement concerning the orthodoxy of Ockham's teachings.

In 1327 Michael of Cesena, the general of the Franciscan order, arrived at Avignon to defend his position supporting evangelical poverty. He directed Ockham to study the issue. Central to the debate was whether Jesus and his disciples owned property. William's investigation revealed inconsistences between statements of Pope John and earlier papal documents. Consequently, he sided with his superior against the pope. Pope John then attempted to replace Michael with a new general. On May 26, 1328, evidently fearing the worst, Ockham, Cesena, and two other friars fled Avignon to Pira, Italy, to seek the protection of Louis of Bavaria, another papal enemy. Louis was returning to Munich from Rome, where he had installed an antipope. In a reciprocal gesture the antipope had crowned Louis emperor. Not surprisingly, Pope John XXII promptly excommunicated the refugees. Nevertheless, they continued to live in Munich under Louis' protection.

Ockham's retaliation was in the form of a series of polemical works directed not only toward Pope John but also to his successors, Clement XII and Benedict VI. The battle of the pen lasted more than two decades. However, the power of Louis waned, which made

Ockham's position somewhat tenuous. Thus, upon the death of Louis in 1347, William attempted a reconciliation with the papacy. A formulae of submission was drawn up. It is noteworthy that the theological issues for which he was originally summoned to Avignon were absent from it. It is not known whether he subscribed to his formulae. It is believed that he died in 1349, most likely a victim of the Black Death.

It should be noted that none of Ockham's philosophical or theological writings were ever officially condemned by the church. Furthermore, his nonpolitical writings set the stage for the empirical trend that ultimately dominated the thought of the late Middle Ages.

William of Ockham on Foreknowledge

Ockham approaches the problem of free will and foreknowledge by first arguing that God is the efficient cause of the universe and all that therein is. By efficient cause he means that God is either the immediate (i.e., proximate) or mediate (i.e., distal) cause of effects. (The former may be either a total or a partial cause.) Although God's causality cannot be (physically) demonstrated, it follows from both authority and reason. As evidence in support of the former he cites the Gospel of St. John and the Creed. Reason dictates that God must be the first cause and therefore the efficient cause of all else, otherwise "something different from God would be uncreated, or one could go on *ad infinitum* in the series of causes".

Notwithstanding that impossibilities (e.g., chimeras), logical entities (e.g., mental words), thought-objects, propositional truths, and privations are from God, Ockham must explain how God as efficient cause is compatible with free will. In Quodlibeta, I, question xvi he observes that free will is known by experience because "a man experiences the fact that however much his reason dictates some action, his will can will, or not will, this act". An act can be performed with either evil or good intent. The nature of the intent by which an act is performed is a product of individual free will. However, the act in either case regardless of the intent by which it is performed is the same. Thus Ockham argues that God can be the immediate partial cause of such acts "since numerically the same act may be caused by one cause with guilt and by another cause without guilt". In other words, God is the causal basis for acts whereas (human) free will provides the intent which properly characterizes the (objective) act as either good or evil.

Having dealt with the issue of free will relative to God's efficiency, Ockham turns to the problem of foreknowledge. Reason dictates that a future contingent is such that "That which is not true in itself cannot be known at that time when it is not true". In other words, future contingency means that there is no factual component to "back up" a statement about the future. No such statement can be true (or false) until the fact referred to by the statement becomes exemplified (or not). The exemplification of facts is necessary for knowledge. Therefore, since there is no factual "backup" relative to foreknowledge no such knowledge exists. However, Ockham continues, it must be the case that God knows all future contingent facts. How can this be? With characteristic honesty and forthrightness he says, "it is impossible for any [created] intellect, in this life, to explain or evidently know how God knows all future contingent events" (*Commentary on the Sentences*, d. 38, q. 1).

"GOD'S CAUSALITY AND FOREKNOWLEDGE"

From Quodlibeta, III, Question III

Whether God is the Efficient Cause of All Things Outside of Him?

No: For God is not the efficient cause of logical entities; otherwise such entities would actually exist in the universe.

On the contrary: Everything that is not from God as its efficient cause, is uncaused; and everything of this nature is God; therefore everything different from God is from God as its efficient cause.

Concerning this question, I first shall distinguish senses of the term 'cause', and secondly I shall answer the question.

Concerning the first point I say that one sort of cause is immediate, whether it be a total or a partial cause; whereas another is mediate. The latter is called 'cause' in that it is cause of a cause, just as Abraham is said to be father and cause of Jacob, since he is the father of his father. However, I take the question as regarding not the immediate cause only, but both mediate and immediate causes.

Concerning the second point I first state that God is the mediate or immediate cause of all things. Though this cannot be demonstrated, yet I argue persuasively for it on the basis of authority and reason.

By authority: In the first chapter of the St. John's Gospel it is said: 'All things were made through Him', etc. This term 'all things' cannot be understood of God, since the distribution of this term is not here extended to God. Hence the meaning is that all things *besides* God are made through Him. Again in the Creed: 'I believe in God the Father almighty'; and then follows 'creator of heaven and earth, of all things visible and invisible', etc. Again, in the Decretal *Extra de summa Trinitate et fide catholica,*

From Ockham, *Philosophical Writings,* edited and translated by Philotheus Boehner, O.F.M. (Edinburgh: Thomas Nelson and Sons, Ltd., 1957), pp. 128–135. Reprinted by permission of Hackett Publishing Co., Inc.

firmiter: 'He is the creator of all things visible and invisible, corporeal and incorporeal'.

Furthermore, I prove this by reason in the following manner: All things essentially depend on God. This would not be true if God were not the cause of them. Again, if God were not the efficient cause of all things, then something different from God would be uncreated, or one could go on ad infinitum in the series of causes. For let me select something which you do not admit to be caused by God and let me ask: Is it caused or uncaused? If the first is conceded, I ask again about its cause, and about the cause of that in the same manner, and so ad infinitum. If the second alternative is conceded, then I have the intended thesis.

Secondly, I state that God is the immediate cause of all things. I prove this as follows. Everything different from God depends more on God than one creature on any other creature; but one creature is so dependent on another that this other is its immediate cause; therefore, etc.

Furthermore, if God were not the immediate cause of all things, this should be true above all for a wrongful action. But this case raises no difficulty, since numerically the same act may be caused by one cause with guilt and by another cause without guilt. For instance, the same act of will comes from a natural cause, viz. cognition, and from a free cause, viz. the will. Therefore the same act may have God as its immediate part-cause without His incurring guilt, and also be caused by a will that does incur guilt.

Nevertheless, some doubts arise against this solution. First: Impossibilities are not from God and nevertheless they are not God.

Second: Fictions and logical entities as opposed to real entities are not God and are not from God.

Third: The existence of things as thought-objects, and likewise sins, are not from God.

Fourth: Propositional truths, and also privations, are not God, nor are they from God as their efficient cause.

To the first of these doubts I answer that all impossibilities are from God, because all impossibilities are either complex or non-complex terms, and all such terms are from God.

You may object that the chimera is an impossibility, and nevertheless is not from God, because if it were from God, it would be something. I answer: The proposition 'A chimera is possible or impossible' has to have its senses distinguished. For 'possible' in one sense can mean all that which can be, whether it be complex or non-complex. In this sense the proposition 'Man is a donkey' is possible since the proposition can exist. In this way 'chimera' (taken in simple *suppositio*)[1] can be and is possible, because such a concept or word can exist. In another sense, 'possible' is predicated of a proposition that is not impossible, and in this sense it is not predicated of 'chimera'. Likewise 'impossible', in one sense, is predicated of a term which in its signification is equivalent to a phrase about which no true affirmative predication is affirmed. In this sense a 'chimera' (in personal *suppositio*) can be made. In this manner it is not improper [to say] that the same term is possible and impossible according to a different *suppositio*. Similarly the propositions 'A chimera is something', 'A chimera is a being', are false in their literal meaning, since 'chimera' has personal *suppositio*. However, if it has simple *suppositio*, both these propositions are true.

To the second I reply that fictions are from God, because some of them are mental entities, some vocal, some written signs, and all of these are real beings and thus are from God, just as lies are from God, since they are real entities. Likewise logical entities are from God, since they are mental words, either non-complex or complex.

You object, however, that logical being *(ens rationis)* is contrasted with real being *(ens reale)*, hence they are not the same. I answer first with the Commentator[2] on the sixth book of the *Metaphysics, ad fin.*: 'The Philosopher[3] speaks of beings which are propositions. They are contrasted with beings which of themselves fall under the categories; and also with non-complex terms. Later the Philosopher divides non-complex terms into the ten categories'. We could answer in another way by saying that this is the division of a name in relation to the things it signifies, and not by opposites. And there is nothing improper in the fact that here subdivisions coincide. For in like manner the Philosopher, in the first book of the *Prior Analytics*, divides 'contingent' in general into 'contingent as regards being and non-being', 'necessary' and 'possible'. Nevertheless what is contingent as regards being and non-being is possible and what is necessary is possible also. Now it is the same in our case.

To the third I reply that there are no such thought-objects *(esse objectiva)*; they neither are nor can be real beings. Nor is there another little world made up of thought-objects. But whatever is not a thing is absolutely nothing, as St. Augustine says in the first book of his *De doctrine Christiana*.

If you object that according to St. Augustine in the *De Trinitate* I can mentally picture such a man as I have seen, I reply: Such a mental picturing is an act of thinking which refers to all men; and if nothing in reality corresponds to it, it is a faulty act of thinking.

In a similar manner, the objections concerning sins can be answered. Everything that is a sin is from God. But God does not sin, since He is not obliged to do the opposite of that which is a sin, because He is debtor to no one.

To the fourth I reply: privations, being intelligible, are something, because they are either concepts of the mind or words or things outside the mind; for it seems that 'blind' and 'blindness' signify absolutely the same and can stand for the same. Therefore, just as we concede that a blind man is something outside the soul, so also is blindness, provided it has personal *suppositio*; not, however, if it has simple *suppositio*.

To the other part of this objection, that concerning truth, I reply: the truth of the proposition 'God causes nothing' can be caused by God, since the truth of this proposition is only the proposition itself, and that can be caused by God.

If you reply, 'Let us assume that this possibility is a fact', I answer, it is not possible to do so, since assuming it as a fact involves a contradiction, viz. that God causes nothing, and that God causes something. For if it is assumed as a fact, then this proposition is true, 'God causes the truth "God causes nothing";' consequently, God causes something. But if God causes the truth 'God causes nothing', then the proposition 'God causes nothing' is true. An example may explain this. The proposition 'Something white can be black' is true; nevertheless, the possibility cannot be assumed as a fact, since then the proposition 'Something white is black' would be true. Another answer would be the following: If our proposition is assumed as a fact, it must not be done like this, 'God causes this truth', but like this, 'God causes this proposition (for which the term "truth" stands): "God causes nothing". But in that case the proposition will not be truth but falsity; just as the proposition, 'Something white can be black', has to be assumed to be a fact thus, 'This proposition is possible: "Socrates (for whom 'white' stands in fact) is black" '.

The answer to the main argument is clear from the aforesaid.

"God's Foreknowledge of Future Contingent Facts" From Ordinatio, D. xxxviii, Question unica

Therefore I reply to the question that it has to be held without any doubt that God knows all future contingent facts evidently and with certainty. But to explain this evidently, and to express the manner in which He knows all future contingent facts, is impossible for any intellect in this life.

And I say that the Philosopher would maintain that God does not know all future contingent facts evidently and with certitude, and he would maintain this for the following reason: That which is not true in itself cannot be known at that time when it is not true. But a future contingent fact simply depends on a free power and hence is not true in itself, because, according to the Philosopher, no reason can be assigned why one side of the contradiction is true rather than the other, and therefore either each part is true, or neither one is true. But it is not possible that each part be true; therefore neither part is true, consequently neither part is known as true.

This proof is conclusive, according to the way of the Philosopher, only as regards facts which are in the power of the will. As regards those facts which are not in the power of the will but which simply depend on natural causes, as for instance that the sun will rise, and the like, the argument is not conclusive. The reason for this is that a natural cause is determined to one side [of a contradiction], nor can any natural causes be impeded except by a free cause, by which, however, they can be impeded only in regard to one determinate effect, not in regard to every effect.

Notwithstanding this argument, it has to be held that God evidently knows all future contingent facts. The manner in which he knows them, I, however, do not know. Yet it can be said that God Himself or the divine essence is an intuitive cognition both of Himself and of all things which can or cannot be made, and that this intuitive cognition is so perfect and so clear that it is also an evident knowledge of past, future and present facts. Just as our intellect is able to know contingent propositions from our intuitive intellectual cognition of their terms, so the divine essence itself is an intuitive cognition by which are known not only necessary truth and contingent truth about a present fact, but also which side of a contradiction will be true and which will be false. The reason for this, perhaps, is not determination by God's will. But even if we made the impossible assumption that God's will is not the total or partial effective cause of contingent effects, and nevertheless the divine cognition remained just as perfect as it is now, that cognition would still be the means by which God would evidently know which side of a contradiction was going to be false and which true. And this is probably not because the future contingent facts are present to Him, nor because of ideas that are the means of this knowledge, but because of the divine essence or the divine knowledge, which is a cognition by which He knows what is true and what is false, what was true and what was false, what will be true and what will be false.

Although this conclusion cannot be proved by any a priori natural reason possible to us, yet it can be proved from authentic texts of the Bible and from the saints, which are well known. But I omit them for the present.

But for certain members of the Faculty of Arts it must be pointed out that no matter how much God knows about all future contingent facts, and as to which side of a contradiction will be true and which false, nevertheless the proposition 'God knows that this side will be true' is not a necessary but a contingent proposition. This means that no matter how true the proposition 'God knows that this side of the contradiction will be true' may be, nevertheless it is possible that this never was true. And in this case there is a possibility of the other side without any succession, because it is possible this proposition should never have been true. But it is different as regards a created will. For after a created will has had an act it is not possible that it should later on be true to say that it never had this act.

NOTES

1. See p. 603.
2. Reference to Averroës.
3. Reference to Aristotle.

CHAPTER 17

Levi ben Gerson

Levi ben Gerson (Gershom), or Gersonides, was a French Jewish philosopher born at Bagnols in Languedoc, probably in 1288. As is the case of other medieval Jewish philosophers, not much is known about his life other than his writings. His supercommentaries on Averroëan works cover the latter's commentaries on Aristotle's logical, physical, psychological, and metaphysical writings. His major work, *The Wars of the Lord*, he wrote to "wage the Lord's war against the false opinions found among his predecessors" and promulgate those opinions he considered correct.

In addition to his interest in philosophy, he was a biblical exegete of note; of particular importance are his commentaries on the Pentateuch and on the Book of Job. It is therefore surprising that he never held a rabbinic post. It is speculated that the freedom of his opinions was a stumbling block in this regard.

Ben Gerson also made many scientific contributions, mainly in mathematics, most particularly in astronomy. He invented two astronomical instruments, an improved camera obscura and the Jacob's staff.

It is known that he was active in the Provençal towns of Avignon and Orange. He died at Perpignan in 1344.

Levi ben Gerson on the Nature of Divine Knowledge

Ben Gerson, or Gersonides, begins by examining the views of the Aristotelians concerning the issue of God's foreknowledge of future contingents. Aristotelian analysis holds that particulars are composed of both essential and accidental characteristics. Contingent particulars are potential or yet to be realized particulars. Within this tradition are two groups: (1) There are those that deny that God knows contingent particulars altogether, that is, that God does not know either the essence or accidents of contingent particulars. In other words, God has no knowledge of future contingents. (2) There are those who maintain that God knows contingent particulars according to their essence while denying that He knows them according to their particularity (viz., accidental characteristics). He knows them not only according to their eternal and immutable essences but according to the necessary laws of nature and unchanging order of the universe.

Next, ben Gerson reviews Maimonides' analysis of future contingents. Maimonides argued that God knows contingent particulars according to both their particularity and their essence. By casting the problem of future contingents within the framework of essential and accidental characteristics, the issue turns not on immutable essences but on accidental characteristics which change, thus establishing contingency. God's knowledge is eternal and immutable. Therefore, He knows particulars from eternity. This rules out any sort of genuine contingency, since God knows future contingents before they exist. How is it possible for this analysis to accommodate freedom of human choice? Maimonides concludes that God's knowledge is different than human knowledge. It is this difference that makes possible His knowledge of future contingents and human free will. God's knowledge is the opposite of human knowledge, allowing His foreknowledge to be consistent with human free will. Thus the term 'knowledge' is equivocal. Gersonides argues that there is only theological justification for this claim. The distinction is philosophically unjustified.

Nevertheless, ben Gerson does believe there exists a pertinent distinction concerning knowledge regarding this problem. The term 'knowledge' can predicate in two ways. Prior knowledge is properly predicated of God, for within God knowledge is identical with His essence. Posterior knowledge is properly predicated of humans, since human knowledge is the effect of God's knowledge.

The difference between prior and posterior knowledge is one of degree. God's knowledge is perfect. The most perfect knowledge is with respect to specificity and determinateness. God knows particulars by which they are ordered and determinate. "On the other hand, the sense in which God does not know particulars is the sense in which they are not ordered, i.e. the sense in which they are contingent. Nevertheless, the fact that God does not have the knowledge of which possible outcome will be realized does not imply any defect in God, for perfect knowledge of some thing is the knowledge of what that thing is in reality. . . . Hence, God knows all these things in the best manner possible; for He knows them in so far as they are ordered in a determinate and certain way, and He knows in addition that these events are contingent, in so far as they fall within the domain of human choice." In the final analysis, Gersonides' analysis is remarkably similar to that of the second group of Aristotelians discussed previously.

THE WARS OF THE LORD

Book III, Divine Knowledge

Chapter I

The Views of Our Predecessors
Concerning This Question

It is appropriate to examine whether or not God knows particular, contingent things[1] in the sublunar world, and if He

From Levi ben Gerson, *The Wars of the Lord*, Vol. 2, translated by Seymour Feldman (Philadelphia, New York, and Jerusalem: The Jewish Publication Society, 1987), pp. 89–137. Reprinted by permission of The Jewish Publication Society.

does know them [there is still the question], how He knows them. Since the philosophers and the sages of our Torah have differed with respect to this problem, it is proper that we first examine their views. Whatever truth we find in them we shall accept, and in whatever falsity we find we shall indicate the truth that is to be found in refuting it.

There are two main views on this topic among the ancients that are worthy of discussion: (1) the views of Aristotle and his followers, and (2) the views of the great sages of the Torah. Aristotle maintained that God (may He be blessed) does not know particular things in the sublunar world.[2] Those who followed him are divided into two camps on this question, the first group maintaining that Aristotle believed that God (may He be blessed) has no knowledge of these things in the sublunar world, either universals or particulars, for if He were to know either universals or particulars, there would be multiplicity in His knowledge and hence in His essence. In short, His essence would be divided into a more perfect part and a less perfect part. This is similar to the case of things with definitions; some part of the definition is the perfection of the other part of the definition.[3] The second camp holds that Aristotle's view is that God (may He be blessed) knows the things in the sublunar world with respect to their general natures, i.e., their essences, but not insofar as they are particulars, i.e., contingents. Nor is there any multiplicity in His essence on this view, since He knows only Himself and in this knowledge He knows all things with respect to their general natures. For He is the principle of law, order, and regularity in the universe.[4] But God [according to this view] does not know particulars; hence there is no order to them by virtue of [His not knowing them as particulars], although they do exhibit some order and regularity insofar as God knows them [i.e., their general natures]. It shall be demonstrated (with God's help) in Book Five of this treatise that this is the authentic view of Aristotle.[5]

However, the great sages of our Torah, such as the outstanding philosopher Maimonides (may he be blessed) and others of our Torah who have followed him, maintain that God (may He be blessed) does know all particular and contingent things insofar as they are particular. Indeed, they believe that in one piece of knowledge He knows all these things, which in fact are infinite. This is indeed the view of Maimonides (may his memory be blessed), who in Chapter 20 of Part III of his great

book *The Guide of the Perplexed* says the following: "Similarly we say that the various things that occur are known to Him before they take place and that He doesn't cease knowing them. Hence, no new knowledge accrues to Him at all. For example, He knows that a particular person is now nonexistent but will exist at some later date, and will continue to exist for some time and then will be nonexistent. Now when this person actually does exist according to [God's prior] knowledge of him, there is no addition to His knowledge and no new piece of information has arisen which was not already known to Him. But something has in fact taken place that previously was known would take place and exactly in the same way [as He knew it would]. This belief implies that [God's] knowledge refers to the nonexistent and encompasses the infinite. We accept this belief. And we say that the nonexistent things, the bringing forth of which pre-exists in His knowledge and falls within His power to bring about, can be objects of God's knowledge."[6] It is clear from this that Maimonides maintains that God (may He be blessed) knows particular, contingent things insofar as they are particular.

Chapter II

The Arguments in Favor of These Views, as We Have Found Them Explicitly or Implicitly in the Statements of Their Proponents

After having mentioned these opinions on this question, let us now examine them to see which is the true one. It will be necessary to examine the arguments in behalf of these views as well as those that purport to refute them.

Artistotle's thesis that God (may He be blessed) does not know particulars has been thought to be quite plausible. First, a particular is not apprehended except by means of a corporeal faculty, for example, the senses or the imagination. But it is obvious that God (may He be blessed) has no corporeal powers. Hence, God does not know these particulars. The following syllogism can be constructed: God has no corporeal powers; anything that apprehends a particular possesses a corporeal power; hence, God cannot apprehend particulars.[7]

Second, a particular is a temporal phenomenon, i.e., its existence is in some portion of time. But someone who cannot be described as in motion or at rest cannot apprehend temporal phenomena. Now God cannot be described as in motion or at rest; hence He cannot apprehend particulars. The following syllogism can be constructed: God cannot be described as in motion or at rest; anyone who cannot be described as in motion or at rest cannot apprehend temporal phenomena; hence God cannot apprehend temporal phenomena. To this conclusion we add a self-evident premise, namely, that particulars are temporal phenomena. From this it follows that God cannot apprehend particulars.

Third, if it were claimed that God knows these things, it might be thought that it would follow that the superior is perfected by the inferior, for knowledge is a perfection of the knower. But this is utterly absurd [with respect to God], and whatever leads to an absurdity is itself absurd. Hence, God clearly does not know these things. This argument, it would seem, also implies that God knows only Himself, i.e., that He knows neither universals nor particulars.[8]

Fourth, if God (may He be blessed) did know particulars, since the intellect is constituted by its knowledge, it would seem that God would not be one but many because of the many cognitions [of particulars] by virtue of which He is constituted. This, however, is completely false, and hence the hypothesis that led to it is also false. From this it is obvious that God does not know particulars; indeed, it would also seem that God knows only Himself.[9]

Fifth, particulars are infinite [in number]. Knowledge, however, is something comprehensive and inclusive. But what is infinite cannot be comprehended or incorporated in some cognition.[10] This argument implies that there is no knowledge of particulars in their entirety insofar as they are particulars, neither by God (may He be blessed) nor by anyone else.

Sixth, if it were alleged that God (may He be blessed) knows things that are generated, the following dilemma ensues: either He knows them *before* they occur, or He knows them only *simultaneously* with their occurrence, not beforehand. Now, if we assume that He knows them before their occurrence, His knowledge would refer to nonbeing. But this is absurd, for knowledge is necessarily [the cognition] of an existent, apprehended thing.[11] Moreover, this divine foreknowledge of generated things implies the following dilemma. If He knows generated things as genuine contingents, then His knowledge that one of these contingencies is to occur is compatible with the occurrence of the alternative. If, on the other hand, He knows precisely[12] *which* of the two alternative states of affairs will occur, its alternative will not be genuinely possible. Now, if we assume that God has knowledge of these events as genuine contingencies [the first horn of this dilemma], His foreknowledge of them would change when they actually occurred, for prior to their occurrence they could or could not have happened, but after their occurrence this possibility is removed.[13] And since the intellect is constituted by what it knows, God would be continually changing—but this is utterly absurd. If, on the other hand, God knows *precisely* which of these contingencies will occur [the second horn of this dilemma], it follows that there is no genuine contingency at all; hence everything would be necessary. But this, too, is absurd and repugnant. It is clear, then, that it is false to say that God has knowledge of these generated events before they occur.[14] But if we say that He has knowledge of them simultaneously with their occurrence [the second horn of the original dilemma], new knowledge would continually arise in Him. And since the intellect is constituted by what it knows, the divine essence would be continually changing, which is utterly impossible.[15]

Seventh, if God has knowledge of these

particulars, the following three alternatives ensue: (1) God guides and orders them in a good and perfect manner; (2) or He is incapable of ordering them and has no power over them; or (3) He has the power to order them properly but He neglects and forgets them either because they are despicable, lowly, and trivial in His eyes or because He is jealous. Now the latter two of these three alternatives are obviously false. It is evident that God can do whatever He pleases and that He does not refrain from giving perfection to each existing thing as much as possible. This is clearly and marvelously exhibited by the widsom evident in the creation of animals and in the great power of God has in bringing about greatest possible perfection in them, so that it is impossible for them to be any more perfect than they are. Hence, only the first of these alternatives remains, i.e., God orders these particulars in a perfect and complete way if He knows them at all. But this is contrary to what we in fact observe of these particulars. They frequently exhibit evil and disorder, so that many evils befall the righteous and many favorable things befall the sinners. Indeed, this is the strongest argument in the eyes of those who deny divine knowledge of particulars. It seems that it was this argument that led Artistotle to say that God (may He be blessed) does not know particulars. This is evident from what he says in the *Metaphysics*.[16] [In sum,] these are the arguments that we have been able to extract from the words of the philosophers, explicitly, in support of the thesis that God does not know particulars.

There is, in addition, an eighth argument on behalf of the claim that God does not know particulars which we have encountered among some of the modern thinkers, from which claim they deduce that a continuous magnitude can be divided into an indivisible [quantum]. We think it appropriate to discuss it here, since it might be thought that such argument establishes the claim that God has no knowledge of particulars. It is argued that if God did know particulars, it would seem to follow that the impossible becomes possible. It has been shown that a continuous magnitude is divisible into divisible parts. But if it is alleged that God has complete knowledge of that into which this magnitude, insofar as it is a magnitude, can be divided, there will be in this magnitude parts that are known by God and that are indivisible. For if they were divisible, God would not know completely that into which this magnitude can be divided. But it is absurd to say about a continuous magnitude as such that it contains indivisible quanta. Some of the recent philosophers have considered this argument and deduced from it the consequence that a continuous magnitude is divisible into indivisible quanta. What brought them to this conclusion was their belief, previously received from tradition, that God knows *everything*; hence, given this argument, they concluded that a continuous magnitude is divisible into indivisible quanta. These are then the arguments in behalf of the thesis that God (may He be blessed) does not know any of these particulars; they are sufficient, [it is alleged], to refute the claim of those who assert that God (may He be blessed) does know particulars.[17]

Nevertheless, the view of our sages of the Torah (of blessed memory) that God (may He be blessed) does know particulars also has arguments in its favor. First, since it is admitted by all who philosophize that God is the most perfect being, it is improper to attribute to Him the defect of ignorance, i.e., that He does not know *some* thing; for ignorance is one of the greatest defects. Someone who chooses to attribute to Him ignorance of particulars rather than to ascribe to Him the inability to arrange these particulars in an orderly manner escapes from one evil and falls into something worse. For it could be the case that the recipient[18] cannot receive more perfection than it actually does, and this is not a defect with respect to God (may He be blessed).[19]

Second, it is not proper to ascribe to the agent who produces something ignorance of his product. Rather, his knowledge of the product is more perfect than that possessed by someone else. For the knows through one cognition everything that will derive from the produced thing by virtue of the disposition [i.e., structure] according to which he made it. Someone else, however, acquires his knowledge of it from the product, and when he observes that the object exhibits some new property resulting from the nature with which it has been endowed, he acquires new knowledge of that new property. And so new properties of a thing give rise to successive cognitions in the observer, and it is possible that the observer will never obtain complete knowledge of the properties that accrue to this object, [especially] if the properties are quite numerous. Thus, since God (may He be blessed) is the creator of the whole world, He has a complete knowledge of what shall happen to that which He has made, a knowledge that cannot be compared to our knowledge. For He knows in one cognition everything that will happen with respect to the world according to the nature with which He has endowed it; whereas we know these things only as they occur. Hence, it is not proper to compare our knowledge and His knowledge, saying that if God (may He be blessed) were to have this knowledge, He would have many cognitions, and hence His essence would be subject to plurality. What we know by many cognitions is known to God (may He be blessed) in one cognition, as we have seen. Indeed, God knows through one cognition [many things of] these particulars, of which we can have knowledge [only] by means of a plurality of cognitions. For our knowledge does not encompass the many things that are generated in the world according to the nature with which God (may He be blessed) has endowed the world.

These two arguments are given by Maimonides (of blessed memory) in Part III of his celebrated book *The Guide of the Perplexed* in behalf of the claim that God (may He be blessed) knows all these particulars.[20] It is clear that the second argument, in addition to proving that God knows all the things that happen, refutes some of the arguments of the philosophers against the

view that God knows particulars. On the other hand, some of the philosophers have countered the first argument in behalf of divine knowledge of all particulars by saying that the denial of this claim does not entail any defect in God. For not every privation is a defect; it is a defect only when the thing is able to have the characteristic in question, not when it cannot. For example, motion is a perfection of animate creatures; when we deny motion of God, however, it is not a defect in Him but a perfection. Similarly, they say that in claiming that God does not know particulars, no imperfection in Him results, only perfection; for His knowledge concerns superior things, not these trivial matters. And so Artistotle says in Book XII of the *Metaphysics* that it is better not to see some things than to see them.[21]

Maimonides (of blessed memory) countered all those difficulties that have been believed to entail the rejection of divine knowledge of particulars by means of his dictum that it is not appropriate to compare divine cognition with human cognition. For to the extent that His being is greater than ours, so, too, is His knowledge greater than ours. And this is a necessary truth, since His knowledge is identical with Himself, as the philosophers have explained.[22] Accordingly, Maimonides frequently rebukes the philosophers for comparing divine knowledge with human knowledge and inferring therefrom that God does not know particulars. They themselves have shown us in some sense that when applied to both God and men, the term "knowledge" is equivocal. And it is obvious that with respect to things having equivocal predicates, inferences from one to the other cannot be made. By means of this argument, Maimonides claimed that it is not impossible, despite the arguments of the philosophers, for God to know all particulars. And when it has been shown that there is no impossibility in this supposition, it is clearly proper then to ascribe this power to Him in order to remove the defect of ignorance from Him.[23]

According to Maimonides, there are five

factors by virtue of which God's knowledge differs from our knowledge, i.e., each one of these factors that is present in divine cognition cannot obtain in human cognition. I shall explain this in discussing these five factors.

First, a cognition that is numerically one [i.e., God's knowledge] agrees with and corresponds to many things different in species. But it is important to realize that this kind of knowledge cannot be attributed to man as long as the many things known are not unified i.e., in a unified system in which one particular is the perfection of the other. Only in this way can a plurality of things become a unity. For example, when "man" is defined as "a body having nutritive, perceptual and rational powers," a thing that is numerically one is indicated, even if the parts of the definition are many, since one part of the definition is the perfection of the other part.[24] However, in a plurality of individuals where it is impossible for one to be the perfection of another, as in the case of particulars that are infinite insofar as they are particular, it is evident that they cannot be unified in our knowledge, if it is assumed that we have knowledge of them. For there is no aspect by virtue of which they can be unified. It is all the more impossible for them to become one in the sense of absolute simplicity, as is the case with divine knowledge, since God (may He be blessed) is one in the sense of absolute simplicity.[25] That these particulars are such that one is not the perfection and form of the other is obvious from the fact that they are infinite, whereas things of which one is the form of the other must be finite, as is explained in the *Metaphysics*.[26] Moreover, they occur cyclically in species, although not individually, and it is clearly impossible among things that are cyclical for one of them to be the form and perfection of all the rest of them.[27] If it were possible, one and the same thing would be the form of itself, which is absurd. For example, let the generated events be A, B, and C, and let them occur cyclically ad infinitum such that B would be the perfection [i.e., terminus ad quem] of A and C the per-

fection of B, and [then] A is again reached, which is then the perfection of C. In such a situation A is the perfection of A, and B the perfection of B, and C the perfection of C.[28] Since with respect to human knowledge it is inconceivable that an ununified plurality can become unified in a completely simple manner, Maimonides (may he be blessed) concluded that in this respect divine cognition differs from human cognition. This was consistent with his view that the term "knowledge" is equivocal when applied to God (may He be blessed) and man.

The second of these factors that differentiate divine cognition from human cognition is, according to Maimonides, that divine knowledge refers to things that are nonexistent. It should be realized that Maimonides had to introduce this difference between divine and human cognition because he had already assumed that God (may He be blessed) knows *all* particulars and hence knows those that are now nonexistent and will exist at some other time and those that will not exist at another time. Accordingly, His knowledge of this event that is nonexistent now is actually present, whereas the object of knowledge to which this knowledge refers is nonexistent. This kind of cognition cannot be at all attributed to our cognition, for, since the object of knowledge and the act of knowledge are numerically one, when the object is not present the knowledge of it is necessarily lacking. Hence, in our cognition, if there is an actual cognitive act, the object of cognition to which it refers must also be present.

It will not do to object that in human cognition there are cases in which the act of cognition is present but the object of cognition is not, such as in many examples of mathematical figures about which we have knowledge but which do not exist outside the mind at all. We have already demonstrated in Book One of this treatise that our knowledge of these figures is grounded in the intelligible order pertaining to these things in the Agent Intellect, in which this order is always present.[29] Moreover, it would not be possible for Maimonides to say that the divine knowledge of particulars is grounded in the intelligible order pertaining to them in God's mind, in which this order is eternally [present]. For if this were so, God would not have knowledge of particulars as particulars but only as they are [components] in the intelligible order pertaining to them in His mind; however, in the latter sense they are not particulars. Therefore, Maimonides concluded that in this respect, too, God's knowledge differs from our knowledge. And this was consistent with his idea that the term "knowledge" is utterly equivocal with respect to God (may He be blessed) and man.

Now it seems that Maimonides' second argument, which we cited above, in behalf of the claim that God does know particulars as particulars implies that this divine knowledge is grounded in the intelligible order of the world that is eternally in His mind [and which] corresponds to the nature with which He has endowed [the world]. Accordingly, he says that the agent's knowledge of the product is more perfect than the knowledge of it possessed by someone else. For the various properties that will accrue to the product are grounded in this prior knowledge of it, since he made the product in such a way that these properties will happen to it. In the case of human beings, however, who observe the product, their knowledge [of the product] results from the [various] properties that accrue to it.[30] Thus, it might be thought that Maimonides' views are inconsistent. For the second argument suggests that God (may He be blessed) does not know particulars as particulars but only insofar as they are part of the intelligible order pertaining to them inherent in His mind. In attempting to solve this problem we should point out that Maimonides did not intend in this argument to explain to us *how* God (may He be blessed) actually knows particulars, for this is impossible for man to know, as Maimonides has frequently mentioned. Rather, he did want to show in this argument that God (may He be blessed) does know these things and that there is a great difference between His

knowledge and our knowledge. Hence, it is not proper for us to make any analogies between His knowledge and our knowledge, as the philosophers have done. This is quite evident to those who carefully consider Maimonides' discussion on this topic.

The third differentiating feature is that divine knowledge encompasses an infinite number of things insofar as they are infinite. Maimonides had to accept this principle because he assumed that God (may He be blessed) knows particulars as particulars, and in this respect they are infinite. But this feature cannot be attributed to human cognition. For knowledge as such requires that the object of knowledge be limited and definite, while that which is infinite cannot be comprehended and encompassed by knowledge.[31] And so, Maimonides concluded, in this respect, too, God's knowledge differs from human knowledge. [Again,] this is consistent with his view that the term "knowledge" is utterly equivocal with respect to God and man.

It will not do to object that human knowledge also encompasses the infinite, i.e., definitions and universal propositions range over an infinite number of individuals. A close analysis of this claim reveals its falsity. For individuals are not known as individuals (and this is the sense in which they are infinite) through definitions and universal propositions. Rather [in these ways], they are known as a unit, i.e., as [instances of] a common nature; this is obvious.[32] Nor would it do to object that human knowledge encompasses the infinite because of our knowledge that a continuous magnitude is infinitely divisible and a number is infinitely augmentable. [On the contrary,] we know these parts as a unit, not as a plurality, for we do not know these parts in the sense that, for example, one part is a hand-breadth, another half of a hand-breadth, and a third a quarter of a hand-breadth, that is, the sense in which these parts constitute a multiplicity. Rather, [we know them] insofar as we know that each part is a continuous quantity, and that all continuous quantities are divisible. Similarly, with numbers: we do not know [all these numbers] in the sense that, for example, one number is 20, another 21, and a third 22, i.e., the sense in which they are many. Rather [we know them] in the sense that each is *a* number, and that any number can be augmented.

The fourth differentiating factor is that the divine knowledge of future events does not entail that the predicted event will occur; rather, its opposite is still possible.[33] Maimonides was led to this belief because he could not deny the existence of contingency, for both philosophy and the Torah assert the existence of contingent events. Hence, it would follow that when it is claimed that God has foreknowledge of future events, the opposite of the event predicted by God could occur and the predicted event could [then] not occur. For if [it were maintained] that the predicted event will undoubtedly occur, its opposite could not occur at all, and contingency would thereby be eliminated. And this is what Maimonides wanted to avoid. Now this feature cannot be attributed to human cognition. For if Maimonides meant that God (may He be blessed) knows with respect to two opposite possibilities which one will occur but also that it may not occur (i.e., its possible)—and this seems to be how his position should be construed—this [kind of cognition] would obviously not be considered by us to be *knowledge* but opinion.[34] For when we say that we *know* that one particular possibility of two contradictory possibilities will occur, we thereby imply that it is impossible that it not occur, whereas if we *think* that it cannot occur, we call this "opinion," not "knowledge." That is, we would then say "we *think* that this possibility will happen" and not "we *know* that it will occur." And if what we thought would occur turns out not to occur, our opinion would be considered by us to have been erroneous; this is obviously not knowledge.

[On the other hand,] if Maimonides meant that God knows determinately which possibility will occur but does not know that it may not occur, and it is the case that the latter is really possible (i.e., the

opposite of this event is possible), we would not consider this to be knowledge but error. That is, if the opposite of what we judged would occur happens instead, [we would] obviously [consider our judgment to be mistaken]. Hence, it is evident that according to this principle, what is knowledge with respect to God (may He be blessed) with respect to us is the opposite of knowledge; for error is the contrary of knowledge, and opinion, too, is in some sense the opposite of knowledge. For this reason, then, Maimonides claimed that divine knowledge differs from human knowledge. This difference in these two cognitions is consistent with Maimonides' thesis that the term "knowledge" is absolutely equivocal when applied to God (may He be blessed) and to us.

It will not do to object that Maimonides did not mean that God (may He be blessed) determines by His knowledge which possibility will occur. For he did believe that God knows distinctly and precisely which event will occur. This is clearly indicated by the language he uses in stating this difference.[35] Indeed, even if we were to concede this objection, this feature would also be inconceivable in human cognition. For we consider such a state to be perplexity and confusion. We would say that we are perplexed and would not [be able] to opine which possibility among several will occur. And if the alternatives are many, the perplexity is greater. Perplexity and confusion are opposites of knowledge. This is especially the case when the [perplexity][36] is construed in this manner. For with respect to a contingent event that is preceded by a thousand years, for example, there are almost an infinite number of possibilities preceding it. When it is supposed that each one of the intermediary events is such that it could or could not occur, and that if it could occur[37] it could be this or that, then (if this is the way the matter stands) it is the case that [prior to] the last event, which occurs as the result of the intermediary events (if they have occurred), there is an infinite set of contrary possibilities. We would consider such a situation to be absolutely perplexing and confusing, that is, we would be uncertain whether this or that possibility [ad infinitum] would occur. Perplexity and uncertainty are less frequent when the possibilities are fewer. Hence the answer that specifies precisely something [as distinct] from something else is the most perfect answer, although it may not specify the thing completely. For example, in the statement "A boat is a material object, made from wood by a craft, hollow inside, and uncovered," each one of these [additional] specifications affords new knowledge, since it removes the vagueness that is implicit in each of the preceding specifications [but] that is not included in it, even though no one of these specifications completely particularizes [and distinguishes] the boat from any other boat.[38]

The fifth of these differentiating factors is that God's knowledge does not change with the occurrence of any of these events about which He has foreknowledge, although the event, to which this knowledge refers, does change insofar as before its occurrence it was [merely] possible, whereas afterward it actually occurred.[39] Maimonides was led to this view because God's knowledge is identical with His essence, as has been indubitably demonstrated in the proper place, and since God's essence does not change, His knowledge also does not change. When we consider this factor, it will be seen that it is impossible to ascribe such a feature to human cognition and knowledge. Maimonides assumed that God (may He be blessed) knows that the event in question is nonexistent now but will occur at some particular time and then be nonexistent at another time.[40] And this is true also of any contingent thing that occurs in the world. When the event actually occurs [Maimonides claims], no new knowledge is acquired by God that He did not possess previously. Rather, what does in fact occur is exactly what was known previously would occur. Thus, it is evident that according to this hypothesis God (may He be blessed) knows everything that will happen and everything that has happened. This belief is also incumbent upon anyone who wants to avoid attributing to God ignorance of these matters, for ignorance of

what has happened is a more serious defect than ignorance of what will happen, as is obvious.

Now, if this is the case, the following dilemma ensues: either God knows that the possibility, whose occurrence He had foreknown, has already occurred; or, He knows that one of the [contradictory] possibilities has occurred, although it is not the possibility whose eventuality had been foreknown to Him before the occurrence of what has in fact happened. It we say He knows that the possiblity whose occurrence He had foreknown has taken place, it would follow that His knowledge of many of these things would be considered by us to be error, not knowledge. For, since the possibility whose occurrence He foreknew *could not have occurred*, it could happen in many of these things that what takes place is *not* the event that God foreknew would happen. Someone who thinks that something has occurred that actually has not occurred is undoubtedly in error. On the other hand, if we say that God knows the possibility that has in fact occurred although it is not the possibility that He had known would occur prior to its actualization, this is certainly a novelty and change in God's knowledge. This is precisely what Maimonides (of blessed memory) wanted to avoid by means of this principle that he introduced concerning divine knowledge. Nor would it do to say that the event originally known by God is without a doubt the event that actually occurred. For if this were so, everything would be necessary and no contingencies would exist at all. Maimonides wanted to avoid this falsehood; hence, he declared that the opposite of what God predicts is still possible.

Now it is quite clear that this cannot be a feature of human cognition. For such "knowledge" is considered by us to be error or to be subject to novelty and change; it is not, as Maimonides maintained, immune from change and novelty. In no way can this be attributed to human knowledge, for that which with respect to God [in this case] is called "immutable knowledge" is called with respect to us "error" or "novel and changeable knowledge." Each of its features is the opposite of immutable knowledge, for error is considered by us to be the opposite of knowledge, and changeable knowledge is considered by us to be the opposite of immutable knowledge. Since human cognition cannot be characterized in this way, Maimonides concluded that herein lies another difference between divine and human knowledge. Again, this is consistent with his view that the term "knowledge" is absolutely equivocal with respect to God and men. Moreover, according to Maimonides, we cannot comprehend the nature of divine knowledge because of its extreme perfection, for in trying to understand the nature of His knowledge, it is as if we were trying to become identical with Him and to identify our knowledge with His knowledge. For this reason, many serious difficulties will arise in our investigation of the nature of the divine knowledge of particulars. The nature of this cognition implies that we cannot understand or comprehend it.[41]

Chapter III

A Critical Examination of the Adequacy of the Arguments Advanced by the "Master of the *Guide*" [i.e., Maimonides on This Topic]

It is proper that we determine whether Maimonides' efforts to counter all the possible arguments of the philosophers who differ from him are successful before we examine whether or not these arguments are correct and, it they are correct, whether [or not] they entail what the philosophers concluded from them. For if Maimonides' replies to these arguments are adequate, there will be no need for us to examine them by means of another method.

We claim that the first thing to do is to examine whether the term "knowledge" is equivocal with respect to divine and human knowledge, such that the difference between them is as Maimonides thought— i.e., that divine knowledge is the opposite of our knowledge, so that what we consider to be opinion, error, or confusion is

knowledge with respect to God—or whether the equivocation involved here is such that this difference cannot be such [as Maimonides claimed]. It seems to us that Maimonides' position on this question of divine cognition is not implied by any philosophical principles; indeed, reason denies this view, as I will show. It seems rather that theological considerations have forced him to this view. The question of whether the Torah requires this doctrine will be considered after our philosophical analysis of this problem.

That philosophical argument rules out Maimonides' position on this topic will be demonstrated as follows. It would seem that God's knowledge is equivocal with respect to our knowledge in the sense of prior and posterior predication, that is, the term "knowledge" is predicated of God (may He be blessed) *primarily* and of others *secondarily*.[42] For in God knowledge is identical with His essence, whereas in anyone else knowledge is the effect of God's knowledge. In such a case the term is applied to God in a prior sense and to other things in a posterior sense. The same is true with respect to such terms as "exists," "one," "essence," and the like, i.e., they are predicated of God primarily and of other things secondarily. For His existence, unity, and essence belong to Him essentially, whereas the existence, unity, and essence of every [other] existent thing emanate from Him. Now when something is of this kind, the predicate applies to it in a prior sense, whereas the predicate applies in a posterior sense to the other things that are called by it insofar as they are given this property directly[43] by the substance that has the property in the prior sense. All of this is obvious to the reader of this treatise, and it will be discussed in detail in Book Five.[44] Hence, it seems that the difference between divine and human cognition is a difference in terms of greater perfection, for this is what is implied by prior and posterior predication. Now if what we have said is true, and since it is obvious that the most perfect knowledge is more true with respect to specificity and determinateness, it would follow that God's knowledge is more true with respect to specificity and determinateness. Hence, it cannot be that what is considered knowledge with respect to God can be called "belief," "error," or "confusion" with respect to man.

We can show in another way that the difference between divine and human cognition is not as Maimonides thought. It is evident that we proceed to affirm attributes of God from that with which we are familiar. That is, we say that God knows because of the knowledge found in us. For example, since we apprehend that the knowledge belonging to our intellect is a perfection of our intellect—without which it could not be an intellect in act [i.e., perfect]—we predicate of God that he knows by virtue of the fact, which we have demonstrated concerning Him, that God (may He be blessed) is indubitably an intellect in act.[45] It is self-evident that when a predicate is affirmed of some object because it is true of some other thing, it is not predicated of both things in an absolutely equivocal sense, for between things that are absolutely equivocal there is no analogy.[46] For example, just as it would be impossible to infer that man is intelligent from the fact that body is a continuous imagnitude, so, too, would it be impossible [even] if we were to posit [arbitrarily] a term that is predicable of both [attributes] *intelligent* and *continuous* in an absolutely equivocal sense.[47] Hence, it is clear that the term "knowledge" is not completely equivocal when applied to God (may He be blessed) and man. Since this term cannot be applied univocally with respect to God and man, it must be predicated in the sense of priority and posteriority. The same holds for other attributes that are predicated of both God (may He be blessed) and man. Thus, the difference between divine and human knowledge is one of greater perfection, albeit exceedingly so, and this type of knowledge is more precise and clear. In general, the kind of equivocation with respect to divine and human knowledge is analogous to the equivocation involved in the attribute of essence in God and in the acquired intellect among men, since the knowledge and the knower are numerically identical (as has been previously explained). And just as God's essence is more perfect than the essence of the acquired intellect in us, so, too, is His knowledge [more perfect] that our knowledge.

The inadequacy of Maimonides' contention about the [absolute] difference between our knowledge and God's knowledge can be shown in another way. With respect to those attributes concerning which we want to know whether or not they can be predicated of God, it is evident that such predicates have one meaning regardless whether we affirm or deny them. For example, if we want to know whether God is corporeal or incorporeal, the term "corporeal" has the same meaning in some sense in either case. For if the term "body" has a completely different connotation in the negation from the meaning it has in the affirmation, these statements would not be considered genuine contradictions, as is obvious.[48] For example, just as one could not say "I will investigate whether the wall is a body or whether it is not a color," so, too, one could not say this [i.e., "I will examine whether the wall is a body or whether it is not a color"] even if he introduces [arbitrarily] a term that [connotes both] bodies and colors, for there would be no [genuine] contradictories.[49] Hence, since it is clear when we deny attributes of God that are found in us that such attributes are not completely equivocal with respect to God (may He be blessed) and us, the same is true when we affirm of God predicates that are true of us. For example, we say that God is immovable, since if He were movable He would be a body, for all movable objects [are bodies]. Now it is evident that in this proposition the term "movable" is not completely equivocal with respect to the term "movable" when it is applied to nondivine things. For if it were, there would be no proof that God is not movable, since the movable object that must be a body is that which is movable in the domain of human phenomena, whereas the term "movable" (in the completely equivocal sense) would not imply that it is a body. Hence, since it is evident that the predicates we deny of God are not absolutely equivocal, neither are the terms that we affirm of Him. For at first we were uncertain whether to affirm or deny such predicates of God (may He be blessed). Then when the inquiry was completed, we were able to affirm or deny such predicates of Him. In general, if the terms used in affirming predicates of Him were absolutely equivocal, there would be no term applicable to things in our world that would be more appropriate to deny than to affirm of God or [more appropriate] to affirm than to deny of Him. For example, someone could say "God is a body" but not mean by the term "body," "a magnitude"; rather he would mean something that is completely equivocal with the term "body" as we usually use it. Similarly, someone could say "God does not have knowledge," since the term "knowledge" would not [on this view] have the same meaning for him in this statement as it does for us. It will not do to object that we indeed deny corporeality of God because it is an imperfection for us, whereas we affirm knowledge of Him because it is a perfection for us.[50] For the *term* "corporeality" is not [itself] an imperfection, and it is the term that we deny of Him, but the content of the term is the imperfection. Similarly, the *term* "knowledge" is not [itelf] a perfection; its content is. The proof of this is as follows. If by the term "corporeality" we were to connote what the term "knowledge" connotes, and conversely, corporeality would be a perfection of us and knowledge an imperfection. Moreover, we do not affirm or deny anything of God except by determining at the outset whether it is proper or improper for *Him*; we do not ask whether or not it is a perfection for *us*. Thus, it is clear that reason shows that the term "knowledge" is not completely equivocal with respect to God (may He be blessed) and man.

Maimonides' conception of divine knowledge can be shown to be inadequate from a different perspective. If we were to concede that divine knowledge is completely equivocal with respect to human knowledge, it would be impossible for contrary predicates to be simultaneously applied to it, e.g., that divine knowledge is both ungenerated and not changeable and generated and changeable. But Maimonides (of blessed memory) did admit that this knowledge is capable of these contrary features, as we have explained in our discussion of his theory of divine knowledge.[51] Furthermore, Maimonides wanted to avoid ascribing the term "ignorance" to God, and hence he said that God knows everything. [Nevertheless,] the content, i.e., ignorance itself, is still applicable to Him, as can be seen from his theory of divine knowledge, i.e., such a knowledge as this would be called by us "ignorance" and not "knowledge." However, the Torah compelled Maimonides (of blessed memory) to accept this particular belief with respect to divine knowledge, as we have mentioned. In recognizing that there was a considerable philosophical controversy concerning this doctrine, he tried to meet the philosophical objections and to establish the doctrine dictated (in his view) by the Torah [by means of] this theory. We shall investigate (with God's help) the doctrine of the Torah after we have completed our philosophical analysis of this problem.

There is, however, a sense in which Maimonides' claim that the term "knowledge" is absolutely equivocal when applied to God (may He be blessed) and to us is plausible. For it has been shown that there is no relationship [i.e., similarity] between God and any existing thing; hence, it is not possible to predicate of Him anything that is predicable of His creatures, except by way of absolute equivocation. Nor is it proper to ascribe to Him *any* attribute, since every attribute would imply a plurality [in His essence], i.e., the attribute itself and the subject of the attribute. It is also evident that when any attribute is ascribed to God, that attribute is completely equivocal with reference to Him and us. For with respect to God, this [attribute] denotes something that is identical with the essence of that of which it is predicated. Maimonides has given a lengthy analysis of this point in his famous book, *The Guide of the Perplexed*.[52] Now it would seem that from this argument all attributes are absolutely equivocal with respect to God and man. Nevertheless, the arguments we have previously adduced indicate just the opposite! Would that I knew the truth of this matter!

Upon further reflection it appears, however, that there are attributes that can be predicated of God and man in the sense of prior and posterior predication without implying any plurality in Him. For not every proposition about the essence of something implies a plurality in that thing. It does imply a plurality in the thing if one part of [the proposition] serves as a real subject [i.e., genus] for the other part [of the proposition]. But if [the former part] is not a real subject, although it is a linguistic subject, the proposition does not imply a plurality. For example, when we say "this redness is a red color," it does not follow from this assertion that the redness is composed of color and red, for the color is not a thing existing [by itself and serving as] a [real] subject for red. It is only a linguistic subject.[53] The same is true for any other properties that particularize this thing. For example, when it is said "this [redness] is a color between black and white but more like black than white," these properties denote only one simple thing; the multiplicity of conditons and particular properties serves to point out which simple color is the color [referred to in this proposition]. The very same thing is also true in things that have no subject [i.e., common genus or matter]: the proposition asserted of them does not imply any plurality in them. For example, if we say "the intellect that moves the sphere of the sun is the intellect that apprehends the particular order according to which the movements of that sphere are ordered," no plurality is implied by this proposition, since the term "intellect" is only a linguistic subject,[54] not a real subject. Although this term can be applied to other

separate intelligences, this does not mean that they [i.e., these intelligences] agree in subject [i.e., genus] and differ [only] in their specific differences. Rather, in this statement [the term "intellect"] denotes which of the simple [intellects] that are encompassed by the term "intellect" [is the referent in this proposition]. For these intellects differ from each other *essentially* without having anything [i.e., genus] in common. If they had something in common, they would be composite, not simple entities. They differ in exactly the same way in which their cognitions differ.[55] Accordingly, it is evident that when God (may He be blessed) is described by any attribute or by many attributes, these attributes do not imply in Him any plurality, for He has no subject [i.e., genus]. Hence, all of these attributes denote only one simple thing.

Indeed, it can be verified that the attributes of God (may He be blessed) are predicated of Him primarily but of other things secondarily, even though it be conceded that there is no similarity[56] between God (may He be blessed) and His creatures. There are several predicates that are predicated of some things primarily and others secondarily in this way [i.e., even though these things are not similar]. For example, the term "existent" is predicated of a substance primarily but secondarily of accidents, as has been shown in the *Metaphysics*; yet it is evident that there is no similarity between substance and its accidents.[57] It is important to realize that there are attributes that *must* be attributed to God, for example, that He is a substance. The term "substance," however, is not predicated of God and other beings univocally but [of God] primarily and [of everything else] secondarily. For, that which makes all things describable by some attribute in such a way that they are [truly] describable by that attribute—[namely], by virtue of what these things have acquired essentially and primarily [i.e., directly] from it—is itself more appropriately called by that term.[58] Now God (may He be blessed) makes all other things in such a way that they are substances, for He endows them with their substantiality; accordingly, He is more appropriately describable as "substance." Moreover, the divine substance is self-subsistent, whereas all other substances derive their existence from something else, and whatever is self-subsistent is more appropriately described as "substance" than something whose existence derives from another thing.

In this way it can be shown that God (may He be blessed) is more properly described as a "being" and as "one" than any other thing. We have already indicated in our commentary on the *Metaphysics* the defect in Avicenna's rejection of these predicates with respect to God (may He be blessed).[59] Indeed, the Torah agrees that these two predicates are more properly attributable to the divine essence than to anything else. Thus, the Torah uniquely ascribes to God the Tetragrammaton ["YHVH"], which connotes being and existence, as well as the predicate "one." This is evident in the passage "Hear Oh Israel, the Lord our God the Lord is one."[60] This is also indicated when Moses, our teacher (may he rest in peace) said: "They will ask me, 'what is His name'; what shall I say to them?"[61] He received the reply: "I shall be whatever I shall be," the predicate of which connotes being and existence. In this way it can be shown that God must be described as "intellect," "alive," "knowing," "provident," "beneficent," "powerful," and "willing," for He is more properly described by these attributes than any other being. This is obvious with a little reflection to the reader of this treatise, especially as the result of the preceding remarks. This will be demonstrated in detail in Book Five of this treatise, with God's help.[62] In all these predicates, however, only one absolutely simple substance is referred to, as we have explained. The disparity between the meaning of these predicates and the like when applied to God (may He be blessed) and their meaning when applied to creatures is comparable to the disparity between the perfect and noble essence of God and their essence, i.e., these predicates are

predicated of God (may He be blessed) implying greater perfection than when predicated of creatures.

On the basis of this entire discussion, it is now evident that reason shows that the term "knowledge" is predicated of God (may He be blessed) primarily and of creatures secondarily, not absolutely equivocally, and that the principles [of religious language] adopted by Maimonides in order to remove the objections of the philosophers concerning the problem of divine knowledge are not acceptable.

Chapter IV

The Completion of Our Theory of Divine Knowledge, Philosophically Demonstrated; Refutation of the Opposing Arguments

Now that we have philosophically proved that Maimonides' counterargument against the objections of the philosophers is not satisfactory—it is evident that the dispute with them should be philosophical and not from the Torah only—it is proper that we ourselves examine the objections of the philosophers against the thesis of divine knowledge of contingent particulars to see whether they are true or not and if true whether the conclusions they drew from them are valid or invalid. But before we analyze these objections, we want to complete our inquiry, as far as we can, into the nature of divine knowledge, for in this way our discussion of the arguments of the philosophers will be more complete and better understood by the reader. Now there are several arguments in favor of the thesis that God (may He be blessed) knows particulars.

First, it will be proved that God (may He be blessed) is the agent of everything that occurs in the sublunar world with respect to substances and accidents and that the Agent Intellect and the heavenly bodies serve as instruments for Him; for, from the emanation that the heavenly bodies receive from God (may He be blessed), all the sublunar things are derived.[63] Now from the very nature of an instrument qua instrument it is clear that it does not move itself to perform its function without the knowledge of the artisan. From this it is apparent that God (may He be blessed) knows all particular things.

Second, since God necessarily knows His essence according to His level of being, and since from His essence all other existent things hierarchically emanate, it follows that God (may He be blessed) knows all the things that emanate from Him. For if He did not know them, His knowledge of His essence would be defective in the sense that He would not know what can emanate from His essence according to His [level of] being. Hence, since it is evident that all substances and accidents emanate from Him, it is clear that He knows all substances and accidents. Therefore, it is clear that God (may He be blessed) necessarily knows *all* particulars.

Third, it has already been shown that the Agent Intellect has some knowledge of the events that occur in the sublunar world. Now, since God (may He be blessed) is the agent, the form and the final end of all the other separate intelligences, as has been explained in the *Metaphysics*,[64] it follows that God has all knowledge possessed by the other intelligences, for the knowledge possessed by them is related to the divine knowledge as matter is related to form. Similarly, one who knows the form of the house necessarily knows the forms of the bricks and of the beams, which are understood by the craftsmen who are subordinate to the craft of building the house itself [i.e., the master craft, architecture]; but the master craftsman knows all these [forms] in a more perfect manner, i.e., insofar as they are parts of the [complete] house. This has been explained previously.[65] Hence, it is evident that the knowledge of sublunar events possessed by the Agent Intellect— which it indubitably has—is possessed by God in a more perfect manner. From this it would seem that God (may He be blessed) knows particulars.

Now, when we consider these arguments that have been brought forth in favor of divine knowledge of particulars and the arguments adduced by the philosophers against this thesis, there is no alternative but to say that God knows particulars in one respect but does not know them in another respect. But what these respects are, would that I knew!

It has been previously shown that these particulars are ordered and determined in one sense, yet contingent in another sense.[66] Accordingly, it is evident that the sense in which God knows these particulars is the sense in which they are ordered and determined, as the case with the Agent Intellect, according to the results previously established. For from this aspect it is possible to have knowledge of them. On the other hand, the sense in which God does not know particulars is the sense in which they are not ordered, i.e., the sense in which they are contingent. For in the latter sense knowledge of them is not possible. However, God does know from this aspect that these events may not occur because of the choice, which He has given man to compensate for the deficiencies in the supervision coming from the heavenly bodies, as has been explained in Book Two.[67] But He does not know which of the contradictory outcomes will be realized insofar as they are [genuinely] contingent affairs; for if He did, there would not be any contingency at all. [Nevertheless,] the fact that God does not have the knowledge of which possible outcome will be realized does not imply any defect in God (may He be blessed). For perfect knowledge of something is the knowledge of what that thing is in reality; when the thing is not apprehended as it is, this is error, not knowledge. Hence, God knows these things in the best manner possible, for He knows them insofar as they are ordered in a determinate and certain way, and He knows in addition that these events are contingent, insofar as they fall within the domain of human choice, [and as such knows them] truly as contingent. Thus, God (may He be blessed), by means of the Prophets, commands men who are about to suffer evil fortune that they mend their ways so that they will avert this punishment, as in the case of King Zedekiah who was commanded to make peace with the King of Babylonia.[68] Now this indicates that what God knows of future events is known by Him as not necessarily occurring; however, He knows these events in the sense that they are part of the general order and also as possibly not occurring insofar as they are contingent.[69]

We shall now show that the previously mentioned arguments in favor of divine knowlege of [all] particulars do not establish that God knows more than what we have just indicated and that the philosophical arguments against divine knowledge of particulars do not at all refute the position we have just advanced with respect to divine knowledge of particulars. That the arguments previously cited do not establish that God knows more than what [we have claimed He knows] can be seen as follows.

The first argument claims that God has knowledge of all particulars because the Agent Intellect and the heavenly bodies are His instruments for His activities in the sublunar world. This argument proves, however, only that God knows the general patterns from which these activities derive. A separate substance insofar as it is a separate substance performs its activity upon anything that is prepared to receive it without having individual knowledge of the recipient as a particular. It is in this way that the Agent Intellect performs its operations on all sublunar phenomena, as has been previously explained.[70] It is true, however, that a corporeal agent, insofar as it is corporeal, does not perform his craft without having a knowledge of the recipient as a particular. Thus, the practical arts make use of the intellect *and* the imagination, as has been explained in *On the Soul*.[71] This is the case because the [corporeal] agent must approach the recipient, for the latter will not be subject to his will unless the agent comes near it; then the agent will shape it as he wishes. Matter receives the will of an incorporeal agent, however, much more easily, and hence it is not required that the in-

corporeal agent know the object on whom its action is directed as a particular individual. We can appreciate the ease with which matter receives the will of a form when we consider the way in which the movements of a man are regulated by his acts of conception. For example, when a man wants to sing a song that he has conceived in his mind, the vocal cords are immediately set in motion by this conception, producing such marvelous movements that instrumental music cannot reproduce them. Similarly, the fingers of an instrumentalist rapidly move over the instrument according to the conception [of the music] in his mind without having to consider each particular movement that is required. This is also true for speech: a man easily pronounces and says the letters he wants without considering which letter requires which movement of his vocal cords for its proper pronunciation.[72] Hence, it is evident that it is possible for God (may He be blessed) to be the agent of all particulars without knowing them as particulars. Nevertheless, He does know them in a more perfect way.[73]

The second argument claims to prove that God (may He be blessed) has knowledge of particulars from the fact that He knows His essence. Nevertheless, it is evident that this argument establishes merely that God knows the intelligible order inherent in these particulars from which they emanate.

The third argument argues that God (may He be blessed) knows particulars because the Agent Intellect has such knowledge. But this argument proves only that God knows the order inherent in them, for this is all that the Agent Intellect knows, as has been explained.[74] God's knowledge of this order differs from the knowledge possessed by the Agent Intellect in that it is more perfect, as has been explained and will be discussed in greater depth in Book Five of this treatise with God's help.[75]

Nor do Maimonides' arguments establish the claim that God knows more than what we have maintained and that He knows *all* particulars. His first argument maintains that God knows sublunar phenomena, for otherwise He would be ignorant. It is clear [however] that if God knows these things in the way we have claimed, there is not ignorance in Him; indeed, He knows them just as they are [i.e., as contingent]. Concerning his second argument [i.e., the analogy with the artisan], we pointed out, while we were discussing this argument, that God's knowledge of particulars is the knowledge of their intelligible order from which they emanate, and no more; and this is what we have maintained here concerning this topic.

Having established this point, we shall now show that none of the aforementioned arguments of the philosophers against divine knowledge of particulars is valid against our own theory.

The first of these arguments of the philosophers—since God has no corporeal powers, He has no knowledge of particulars—does not prove that God has no knowledge of the intelligible order inherent in them and in terms of which they are ordered and determinate. This argument implies only that He does not know them as particulars in their very individuality. This is evident. Similarly, the second argument—God has no knowledge of particulars because they are temporal phenomena—does not refute our theory. For we have not claimed that His knowledge encompasses their temporal aspects; rather we have claimed that it is concerned with the intelligible order in terms of which these particulars are ordered, and from this aspect they are not temporally specified.

The third argument claims that it is impossible for God to have knowledge of particulars either in a general or in a particular way, for if He did, that which is superior would be perfected by that which is inferior, and this is absurd. On close examination, however, this argument is invalid. It does not follow from our hypothesis that God knows the intelligible order obtaining in substances and accidents within the sublunar world that He is perfected by these phenomena. For He does not acquire His

knowledge from these phenomena; rather, His knowledge of them is based upon the intelligible order pertaining to them in His mind. Therefore, it is evident that by this knowledge God is not perfected through something else. Indeed, the intelligible order in the divine mind is that which gives existence to all these phenomena. Thus, this argument is clearly not valid.

The fourth argument claims that if God knew these particulars His essence would admit multiplicity. From this it is concluded that God does not know particulars, neither in the sense in which they have something in common, i.e., their essences, nor in the sense in which they are particulars, i.e., as contingents. Examination reveals, however, that this argument is invalid. From our theory that God knows particulars it does not follow that His essence admits multiplicity. For the various patterns exhibited by these particulars are unified, i.e., they exhibit an aspect in terms of which they are one, as we have pointed out many times.[76] It is with respect to this aspect that God knows particulars; He does not know them insofar as they are not unified, i.e., as particulars and individuals. For as particulars they would have to be known by means of a corporeal capacity [e.g., sensation]. And such a cognition would be defective, for this kind of cognition is not knowledge of the essence but only of the accidental features. Accordingly, it cannot be attributed to God. Nor is it true that if God knows particulars [in some sense] that His essence would be divided into the perfect and the imperfect.[77] For both the Agent Intellect and the acquired intellect are simple and one, even though this kind of plurality is a feature of their concepts. This point will be discussed in detail in Book Five of this treatise, if God wills.[78]

The fifth argument claims that since particulars are infinite, there cannot be any knowledge comprehending them. It is evident, however, that this does not refute our thesis that God knows particulars. For the intelligible patterns exhibited by these particulars are not infinite but limited, and in this sense it is possible to have knowledge of them. This argument entails only the impossiblity of knowing them as particulars, and it is in this sense that they are infinite.

The sixth argument maintains that God cannot know generated events [i.e., particular events], for if He did, He would know them either *before* their occurrence or only simultaneously with their occurrence. If He knows them before their occurrence, His knowledge would refer to nonexistents. Moreover, if this is indeed the case, either He knows them as they really are, i.e., as contingents, and then it is still possible that the opposite of what He predicted will occur; or He knows definitely which alternative of two contradictory states of affairs will occur, such that the other alternative is not possible. If we say that He knows them as genuine contingents, His foreknowledge of these events would be subject to change when the event in question has occurred; for prior to its occurrence the event in question has occurred; for prior to its occurrence the event could or could not have occurred, whereas after its occurence this possibility has disappeared. And since the intellect is constituted by its knowledge, God's essence would be continually subject to change, which is absurd. On the other hand, if we say that He knows definitely which of two contradictory events will occur, no contingency would exist. Finally, if we say that God knows particulars only as they occur, His knowledge would always be generated and His essence subject to change. Since all of these suppositions are absurd, it follows that God does not know particulars at all.

Nevertheless, this argument does not invalidate our version of the thesis that God knows particulars. In saying that God knows particulars insofar as they are ordered and that He knows them as contingent insofar as human choice is involved, we are not subject to any of the abovementioned absurdities. [In the first place], His knowledge does not refer to nonexistents, since we maintain that His knowledge of particulars is grounded in the intelligible order pertaining to them as it is present in His mind, but not in these particulars themselves. [In the second place], it does not follow that His knowledge is subject to change when any of these events has occurred, for we have not claimed that His knowledge is based upon any of these events; rather, it is grounded in their intelligible order in His mind. And this order is eternally in His mind and never changes. [In the third place], it does not follow from our hypothesis that there is no contingency [merely because] we maintain that God has foreknowledge of which of two contradictory events will occur. According to our theory God knows that a particular event *should* occur given the ordering of phenomena [in the intelligible order of things], but not that it *must absolutely* occur; for God recognizes that by virtue of human choice this event might not occur, and this is the sense in which these things are contingent.

The seventh argument claims that if God had knowledge of particulars, He would have arranged them equitably and perfectly. However, this is contrary to what we observe of these things, since they exhibit much injustice and disorder. This argument will be refuted when we show that the order obtaining among contingent affairs and the contingency exhibited in them manifest the best order and perfection possible. We have already demonstrated this in our commentary on Job and we shall, with God's help, prove it in Book Four of this treatise.[79]

The eighth objection was that if God knows all these particulars, that which is impossible would become possible. It has been demonstrated that a continuous magnitude as such is divisible indefinitely. But if God is assumed to have knowledge of *all* particulars, He would have knowledge of all the divisions that can possibly be made of that continuous magnitude. If this were so, a continuous magnitude would have parts that are not capable of further division, i.e., the parts at which God's knowledge of these parts terminates, otherwise, God's knowledge of this [process of] division would be deficient.[80] We claim that this argument is not valid. If we were to admit, for example, that with respect to any given body God has knowledge of the nature [i.e., the capacity] for division in the body, it does not follow that the division will end. He knows the nature of this division, i.e., He knows that whatever is divisible can be divided further insofar as it is a quantity. God has no knowledge of an end of division, which by its very nature has no end, for such knowledge would be considered error, not knowledge. Moreover, on our hypothesis concerning God's knowledge, as we have explained, God has knowledge of the general nature of quantity insofar as it is always divisible, but He has no knowledge of divisibility with respect to any particular magnitudes. If He had, His knowledge in this regard would be defective, since it would not be a knowledge of the essence, i.e., the divisibility of any particulars follows from their nature as quantities, not from the fact that [the body] is, for example, wood or copper.

Some modern thinkers[81] have inferred from this argument that a magnitude is composed of indivisible parts [i.e., atoms], because of their admission that God knows completely the division that a magnitude is capable of. For if, [as they argue,] the parts are capable of division [ad infinitum], God's knowledge will not encompass all the parts into which the magnitude could be divided. This argument is clearly absurd. It does not follow from the admission that God knows *all* particulars that He knows all the divisions that a particular magnitude is capable of. For the phrase "all the divisions" is obviously absurd; in this phrase we have generalized something into one class that cannot be so generalized, because the infinite cannot be comprehended in one class. Yet it does follow from this that God does know that every magnitude is indefinitely divisible insofar as it is a quantity; in this manner the natural capacity of a body for limitless division is known by God. But He does not know the limit of what naturally has no limit, for this would be error, not knowledge!

This problem is similar to the problem discussed by Aristotle in his *On Generation and Corruption*, in which it is alleged [in the name of the Atomists] that a body is divisible into entities that are not capable of further division. For if it were assumed that a body is divisible exhaustively at each of the parts into which it is capable of being divided, this might be false yet possible, [but] not false and impossible. Yet, if it is alleged [that a body is divisible exhaustively], it would follow that a body is divisible into indivisible entities; for if these entities were divisible, the body would not be divisible [exhaustively] at each part into which it is capable of being divided, as was originally assumed. Thus, it has been inferred from this that a body is divisible into indivisible entities.[82]

There is no value in adopting Averroës' solution to this problem, which he believed was Aristotle's own solution in this discussion. For Averroës' solution is incorrect; moreover, it leaves the problem standing, as we shall show. Averroës' solution to this difficulty is as follows: "Exhaustive infinite divisibility of a body is not completely impossible, but is possible in one sense although impossible in another. The sense in which it is, in our opinion, possible is the potential division, not the actual division, at all its points simultaneously. For if [the actual division] were possible, a body would then be decomposable into indivisible entities. But it does not follow if the body is divisible exhaustively [but only] potentially at every one of its points ad infinitum that it is [so] divisible actually. For it does not follow if each point in a body can equally be divided that all of them are divided simultaneously and that the body itself is divided at all of these points simultaneously, even if it is divisible equally at each of these points. Just as it does not follow from the statement "A man can learn all sciences" that he learns all of them at the same time. For whatever may be true of something in its divided sense may not be true in its composite sense, as has been explained in Aristotle's *On Sophistical Refutations*.[83] Indeed, this is the fallacy in this argument."

"On the other hand, the body would be capable of simultaneous division at all of its points *if* one point were immediately next to another point. But it has been demonstrated in Book VI of the *Physics* that one point is not consecutive to another point.[84] Hence, it would appear that when we divide a magnitude at a point, the division cannot occur at the point consecutive to it, [for there is no such point]. It would have been possible at the outset to have divided the magnitude at another point, just as it was possible for the division to have fallen at the point [where it did in fact occur]. But once the division has occurred at [the first] point, the possibility of the division's occurring at another point consecutive to it was thereby precluded. Thus, when we have chosen a point at any desired place where the magnitude can be divided, once we have divided the magnitude at that point, it is impossible to divide it at any second point at a place we might choose, for it is impossible to divide it at a point consecutive to the first point."[85]

That Averröes' solution is inadequate is evident. From the nature of quantity [as such] it is not impossible to divide a quantity at any one of its points, i.e., it is not impossible to divide it at a given point just because it has already been divided at a point consecutive to it. However, if this is impossible in a body, this is because it is a natural [i.e., an actual] body, for from this aspect the division terminates at a definite magnitude. Any smaller part will not receive the form of that body, as has been explained in the *Physics*.[86] That the [original] difficulty has not been removed by Averröes is [also] clear. For that which is in between any two points (among the infinite points that ex hypothesi the body potentially possesses) would not itself be divisible; hence, the body would be composed of indivisible entities, and these entities would exist potentially in the body.[87] Nor would it do to say, in order to escape from this difficulty, that it is not possible in actuality for it [i.e., the magnitude] to be divided into these indivisibles, as Averröes' solution suggests.[88]

Our own solution to this difficulty is as follows. To suppose that a possible state of affairs exists without entailing an impossibility is to assume that such an existent is *genuinely* possible. However, if an existent is assumed that is genuinely impossible, an impossibility results therefrom. Now we shall show in this passage [from Aristotle] an existent has been postulated that is really an impossiblity. For it is evident that when it is assumed that a continuous magnitude is divisible into that which is itself divisible, as has been demonstrated in the proper place,[89] it follows that it cannot be divided into that which is indivisible. When we posit a body *actually* divided at *every* place where it can be divided, we have postulated as existent something that is impossible, for it cannot be divided except into that which is [capable] of [further] division. The cause of the error in this argument is that they [i.e., the Atomists] assumed that the possibility [for division] simultaneously exists and is exhausted, [a possibility] that cannot by its very essence be encompassed or exhausted.[90]

This solution can also remove the previously cited difficulty raised by those recent thinkers with respect to God's knowledge of the division of a continuous magnitude. Our hypothesis that God has complete knowledge of the divisiblity of a continuous magnitude does not entail that by virtue of this knowledge this division terminates in indivisibles. What it entails, however, is that God knows this division in its true nature, i.e., that anything into which the continuous magnitude has been divided can be divided further *indefinitely*; but God does not know the end of a division that by nature has no end. Indeed, in the same manner a similar difficulty with respect to number could be raised: it could be said that it is possible for there to be a number incapable of further increase and that this number is known by God. For a number is augmentable ad infinitum, and if we assume that God knows completely all these increments or that the potential [increments] in them have [all] been actualized, there would then be a number that is no longer augmentable. But this is false. The fallacy in this objection is the assumption of an existent that is logically impossible [i.e., the greatest number]. It is not proper for something to be called "knowledge" unless it agrees with the nature of the thing that is known; what does not agree with the nature of this thing is more properly called "ignorance" and "error."

We should also realize that Averroës' interpretation of Aristotle is erroneous from another point of view. The assumption that in a body there are potentially and simultaneously an infinite number of points such that the body can be divided at each one of them is clearly false. For if in a finite body there were potentially an infinite number of points,[91] then, since these points are not consecutive to each other (as has been explained in Book VI of the *Physics*), there would be some quantity between any two points. And since ex hypothesi these points are infinite, the quantities between any two points among them would be infinite in number. And since it is evident that when any quantity whatever is infinitely multiplied, an infinite magnitude thereby results, from this hypothesis it would follow that a finite body is infinite, which is utterly absurd. Thus, it is evident that a continuous magnitude does not have an infinite number of points, neither potentially nor actually. The absence of a limit, however, that is present in the division of a continuous magnitude pertains to the *act of division*, not the number of parts. For the number of parts into which the magnitude can be divided is always finite, although this number is indefinitely augmentable. For example, when we conceive of a division of some magnitude into two parts, each of these parts can be divided [again] into two parts, resulting in four parts, each of which in turn can be divided by half, resulting in eight parts, and the process can be carried on *indefinitely*, although the number of parts is always finite. This kind of lack of limit in division is also true of the lack of limit in numbers; for just as a number is not augmentable, either potentially or actually, into that which is infinite in number [i.e.,

an infinite aggregate or infinite number], so, too, is this the case in the division of a continuous magnitude. That a number is not augmentable potentially into that which is infinite in number can be demonstrated from two principles. First, every number is finite, since every number is either even or odd, and each of these numbers is finite.[92] Second, in augmentation a number has no potentiality for becoming a non-number but the potentiality for becoming a greater number that it is.[93] Hence, it is clear that a number has no potentiality in this power of inexhaustible augmentation of becoming an infinte number. From this it can be shown that a continuous magnitude does not potentially have an infinite number of parts; hence it is evident that it does not potentially have an infinite number of points. We have provided a detailed proof of this in our commentary on the *Physics*.[94] It was incumbent upon us here, however, to refute the assumption employed by Averroës in the solution offered by him to this difficulty, i.e., the principle that in a body there are potentially and simultaneously an infinite number of points at each one of which a body can be divided. For if this assumption were true, the difficulties that have been raised with respect to [God's] knowledge and to the postulation of a possibility as real[95] would still remain.[96]

It has therefore been demonstrated that the arguments of the philosophers do not invalidate the thesis that God does know particulars as we have construed this thesis about divine cognition of particulars.[97]

Chapter V

The Advantages of Our Theory

One of the evident advantages of our theory of divine knowledge of particulars is that none of the absurdities that ensue from Maimonides' account of divine knowledge is applicable to it, i.e., the difficulties deriving from the five features that allegedly differentiate divine knowledge from human knowledge.

The first of these features—in divine knowledge one piece of knowledge is proper to and encompasses many things different in species—is a feature characteristic of our knowledge as well, [i.e.,] when we know these many things from the aspect by which they are unified. This is the case when we know their intelligible patterns [i.e., their orderliness] and when we recognize that they are hierarchically ordered with respect to form and perfection [i.e., some things are the perfections of others.]. Since we have claimed that God's knowledge of the plurality of particulars is of this sort (that is, He knows the intelligible order of things insofar as they are so ordered and knows them as unified in terms of this order), it is evidently not necessary for us to accept the difference between divine and human knowledge postulated by Maimonides. The difference between these two cognitions lies, according to our theory, in the difference in the way in which these things are unified in God; for the difference between the unity of which our intellect is capable and the unity in the divine intellect is very great, so that there is no similarity between them.[98] This is evident from what we have said in Book One of this treatise.[99]

The second feature—i.e., divine knowledge refers to the nonexistent—does not follow from our account of this kind of knowledge. For we have claimed that God's knowledge of particulars as ordered is based upon the intelligible order pertaining to them which is eternally inherent in His intellect and is not based upon these contingent things. For God does not acquire His knowledge from them; rather they acquire their existence from His knowledge of them, since their existence is an effect of the intelligible order pertaining to them inherent in the divine intellect. Hence, it does not follow from this that divine knowledge is grounded in nonexistence; rather it is grounded in something that eternally and immutably exists.[100]

The third feature—divine knowledge encompasses the infinite insofar as it is infinite—is also not part of our theory of divine cognition. For God knows particulars

insofar as they are one, not insofar as they are infinite and not unified. The latter is the sense in which they are particular.

The fourth feature—God's knowledge of future events does not imply that the event foreknown will necessarily occur; rather its opposite is still possible—is also a characteristic of our knowledge insofar as we have knowledge of these events through dreams, divination, or prophecy. For we do possess such knowledge insofar as such events are ordered. Yet they remain contingent by virtue of the factor of choice. This is the reason why this knowledge has been given to us, that we can recognize the evil that has been prepared for us and take measures to avoid it, as has been fully explained in the preceding Book.[101] This can be understood if we examine the practice of the Prophets (may they rest in peace), who warn us of some [imminent] evil. For it is the case that they give advice on how to prevent this evil from coming. Similarly, Joseph warns Pharoah, by interpreting his dream, about the famine and suggests a relief measure so that the famine will not be as calamitous as it was originally predicted in the dream.[102] Daniel, for example, tells Nebuchadnezzar, by interpreting his dream, that he will lose his reason and be like an animal for seven years, but he also suggests a way in which this evil can be averted.[103] Since we have claimed that God has knowledge of these events insofar as they are ordered, it is not strange that they are still contigent with respect to human choice. In this way, the difficulty that has continually plagued men—i.e., how can God know future events without these events being necessary—disappears; for these events exhibit two aspects [i.e., an ordered, or regular, pattern and a free, or voluntary, dimension], and not just one aspect.

[Finally, with respect to] the fifth feature—God's knowledge of generated events does not change with the actual generation of these events—even if the event in question has changed from a possible state of affairs to a state of affairs that actually has occurred, this, too, is a feature of our own knowledge when we obtain such knowledge insofar as it is ordered. For even though the opposite of what was predicted actually happens, our original knowlede remains unchanged with respect to the general ordering of these events, i.e., from this aspect the event should have occurred as predicted were it not for human choice, which is the factor that prevents what should have occurred from occurring.[104] Since God's knowledge of these events is based upon the intelligible order in His intellect, and since this order is immutable, His knowledge does not change when one of these events is realized, for His knowledge is not based upon them; rather they are based upon the order pertaining to them in His intellect. Nor is it the case that God's knowledge that these events are possible [i.e., from the aspect of human choice] changes when they have actually occurred. For we do not claim that His knowledge is derived from these events or that He knows them as definite particulars; rather He knows them in a common, general way. And in this way [their] contingency, of which God has knowledge, is preserved. This is quite obvious to the reader of this book.

Chapter VI

The Identity of Our View with the Doctrine of the Torah

It is now incumbent upon us to show that the theory we have established by philosophical argument is identical with the view of our Torah. It is a fundamental and pivotal belief of the Torah that there are contingent events in the world. Accordingly, the Torah commands us to perform certain things and prohibits other things. It is [also] a fundamental principle implicit in all the Prophets (may they rest in peace) that God informs them of these contingent events before they actually occur, as it is said, "God does nothing without having revealed His purpose to His servants the prophets."[105] Yet it is not necessary that any evil predicted by them must occur, as it is said, "God is gracious . . . [abounding in kindness] and renouncing punish-

ment."[106] These principles are reconcilable only on the hypothesis that [first] these contingent events are in some sense ordered, and it is in this respect that knowledge of them is possible, but in another sense not ordered, and it is in the latter sense that they are contingent; and [second] that God (may He be blessed) knows all future contingent events insofar as they are ordered and [in addition] knows that they are contingent. It is, therefore, clear that the view of our Torah is identical with the theory that philosophical argument has proved with respect to divine knowledge. Moreover, it can be shown that the view of the Torah is that God knows these things in a general manner, not as particulars, for it is said "He who fashions the hearts of them *all*, who discerns *all* their doings."[107] That is, God created the hearts and thoughts of men *at the same time* insofar as He endowed the heavenly bodies with those patterns from which [these thoughts] are in their entirety derived. In this way God considers *all* their deeds, i.e., simultaneously, not in the sense that His knowledge refers to the particular as particular. This shows that [according to the Torah] God understands all human affairs in a general way.

Moreover, the Torah maintains that the will of God does not change, as it said, "I am the Lord—I have not changed."[108] And Balaam, when he was a prophet, said: "God is not man to be capricious, or mortal to change His mind."[109] [Yet] in some of the Prophets [it is related that] God does repent of His acts, as it is said, "The Lord renounced the punishment He had planned to bring upon His people";[110] "For God is gracious . . . renouncing punishment."[111] Since this difficulty cannot be removed when it is assumed that God (may He be blessed) knows particulars as particulars but can be easily removed when it is assumed that He knows them as we have argued [i.e., generally], it is proper, according to the Torah, that we should interpret the doctrine of divine knowledge according to our philosophical theory.

That our theory of divine cognition can easily solve this problem can be shown as follows. God's knowledge does not imply that a particular event will occur to a particular man, but that it may occur to *any* man who falls under this [general] ordering of events, insofar as these events are ordered; in addition, God knows that this event may *not* occur because of human choice. But if we were to claim that God knows this affair with respect to this particular man as a definite individual, it would follow that His will would be subject to change.

In short, there is nothing in the words of the Prophets (may they rest in peace) that implies anything incompatible with the theory we have developed by means of philosophy. Hence, it is incumbent upon us to follow philosophy in this matter. For, when the Torah, interpreted literally, seems to conflict with doctrines that have been proved by reason, it is proper to interpret these passages according to philosophical understanding, so long as none of the fundamental principles of the Torah are destroyed. Maimonides, too, followed this practice in many cases, as his famous book *The Guide of the Perplexed* shows. It is even

more proper that we not disagree with philosophy when the Torah itself does not disagree with it. Maimonides relates further in Chapter 20 of Part 3 of the celebrated *Guide of the Perplexed*: "Some thinkers have been inclined to say that God's knowledge refers to the species and uniformly encompasses all members of the species. This is the view of any believer in a revealed religion who is guided by the necessity of reason." This [passage] shows that Maimonides believed that this view [i.e., God knows particulars only generally] agrees with the view of the Torah. It seems, too, that the sage Abraham ibn Ezra was of this opinion, for in his *Commentary on the Torah*, he says; "The truth is that He knows every particular generally, not as a particular."[112] The agreement between our philosophically established theory of divine knowledge and the Torah will be more fully appreciated after we have examined the question of divine providence in the Torah, which will be treated in the next book. This book has now been completed.

NOTES

1. "*Ēlu ha-devarim ha-peratiyim ha-'efshariyim.*" This phrase expresses the main theme of Book Three: God's knowledge of particular items and events in our world. The two key terms in this phrase are "*peratiyim*" and "'*efshariyim,*" which I translate as "particulars" and "contingents," respectively. (Touati renders these terms as "*les choses singulières et contingentes.*" C. Touati, *Les Guerres Du Seigneur: Livres III et IV* [Paris 1968], p. 41.)

   The term "*peratiyim*" corresponds to two Arabic terms that are interchangeably used in this context in the medieval Arabic philosophical literature: "*ashkhās*" and "*ju'zīyāt*"—literally, "individuals" and "parts." (*Al-Farabi's Commentary on Aristotle's De Interpretatione*, edited by W. Kutsch and S. Marrow [Beirut, 1971], ad 18a, 33–34; *Al-Farabi's Commentary and Short Treatise on Aristotle's De Interpretatione*, translated by F. W. Zimmerman [Oxford, 1981], p. 76. A-M. Goichon, *Lexique Philosophique D'Ibn Sina* [Paris, 1938], entries 94, 309–311. Al-Ghazali, *Tahāfut al-Falāsifa*, edited by M. Bouyges [Beirut, 1927], Discussion XIII, pp. 223–227. Sometimes the Hebrew " '*ishiyim*" ("individuals") is used for "*ashkhās*"; sometimes the Hebrew "*helaqīm*" ("parts") is used for "*ju'zīyāt.*" In the ibn Tibbon translation of Maimonides' *Guide* we find all three Hebrew words used interchangeably to express the same idea: particular things or events occurring in our world. Indeed, for the term "occurrence" another technical term is used—"*mithadesh*" (Arabic *hadath*)—literally, "generated thing." (In his translation of the *Guide*, Pines translates *ashkhās* as "individual circumstances," *ju'zīyāt* as "particulars," and *hawādith* as "things produced in time.") All these Arabic and Hebrew words go back to the Greek terms τὰ μέρη (parts) and τὰ ἕκαστα (individuals), which were used in Greek philosophical literature to connote particular items as opposed to universals, such as genera or species or Platonic Forms. (Plotinus, *Enneads* III:1,5 and III:2,14. Aristotle, *On Interpretation*, 17a, 38 ff., 17b, 26–30).

   The term *'efsharī* literally means "possible." However, as Gersonides' subsequent discussion will show, the term is used in this context to express a contrast with the necessary (*hekhrahī*; Arabic, *darūrī*; 'αναΥκαˆῦος i.e., that which may or may not be the case as opposed to that which cannot not happen (Aristotle, *Metaphysics*, V:5). It is thus better to render *'efsharī* in this context as "contingent" (ἐνδεχομένος), or that which can be otherwise as opposed to that which cannot be otherwise (J. Hintikka, "Aristotle's Different Possibilities," *Inquiry* 3 [1960], pp. 18–28).

2. Aristotle, *Metaphysics*, XII:9.
3. In the definition of "man" as "rational animal," rationality completes, or perfects, the generic property animality.
4. Since God is the principle of order in the universe, He knows the various patterns of order in the universe.
5. Gersonides, *The Wars*, vol. 3, Bk. 5, pt. 3, chap. 3. These two divergent interpretations of Aristotle were found among the Muslim Falāsifa, Averröes and Avicenna. Averröes maintained that God does not know things either generally or particularly, that is, the divine knowledge is sui generis, unique and indescribable (Averröes, *Commentary on Aristotle's Metaphysics, Book XII*, recently translated into English as *Ibn Rushd's Metaphysics* by Charles Genequand [Leiden, 1984], pp. 197–198). Avicenna, however, claimed that God knows particulars but only in a universal, or general, way, i.e., as representatives of species and genera (M. Marmura, "Some Aspects of Avicenna's Theory of God's Knowledge of Particulars," *Journal of the American Oriental Society* 82 [1962]; id., "Divine Omniscience and Future Contingents in Al-Farabi and Avicenna," in *Divine Omniscience and Omnipotence in Medieval Philosophy*, edited by T. Rudavsky [Dordrecht, 1985], pp. 81–94).
6. Maimonides, *The Guide of the Perplexed*, III:20; chaps. 16–21 are all relevant to this topic.
7. These various arguments of "the Philosophers" are reported and discussed in Maimonides' *Guide*, III:16 and 20, Aquinas' *Summa Contra Gentiles*, 1:63, and Averröes' *Tahāfut al-Tahāfut*, Discussion XIII.
8. S. van den Bergh, *Die Epitome der Metaphysik des Averröes* (Leiden, 1924), p. 124.
9. Ibid., pp. 125–128.
10. Aristotle, *Posterior Analytics*, I:18.
11. Idem.
12. *Bishlēmūt*; This Hebrew term corresponds to the Arabic *bitaḥṣīl*, which has recently been rendered into English as "definitely" by Fritz Zimmerman in his translation of *Al-Farabi's Commentary on Aristotle's On Interpretation*, pp. 91, 96, 244 (cf. A-M. Goichon, *Lexicon Philosophique D'Ibn Sina*, entry 162). The Hebrew and Arabic terms connote precise and definite knowledge of something. In this context they connote the exact knowledge of the outcome of a pair of alternative contradictory future contingent events; for example, there will be a sea battle tomorrow in the Mediterranean or there will not be a sea battle tomorrow in the Mediterranean. To have precise knowledge of either alternative is to imply that the truth value of that alternative is *determinate* (cf. Gersonides, *The Wars*, Bk. 2, chap. I, especially n. 6; and Gersonides, *Supercommentary on Averröes' Commentary on Aristotle's On Interpretation*, chap. 9, Bodleian Hebrew Manuscript Neubauer 1361, Michael 347). In the Latin literature on this topic, the terms "definitive" and "determinate" were used. (Boethius, *In Librum De Interpretatione, Editio Prima*, Migne, *Patrologia Latina*, vol. 64, cols. 329–342. Peter Abelard, *Dialectica*, edited by L. M. de Rijk [Assen, 1956], pp. 193–222. For a good recent survey of this issue in Latin Scholasticism, see Calvin Normore's essay in the *Cambridge History of Late Medieval Philosophy*, edited by N. Kretzmann, A. Kenny, and J. Pinborg [Cambridge, 1982], pp. 358–381.) All these Hebrew, Arabic, and Latin terms are probably derived from Aristotle's word ὁιελότα in *On Interpretation*, 9, 19a, 28, which has been translated as "determinately" by Harold Cooke in the Loeb Classical Library edition of this treatise (Cambridge, Mass., 1938). Alexander of Aphrodisias used the term πάντως ("completely," "perfectly"), which comes quite close to Gersonides' *bishlēmūt* (Richard Sharples, *Alexander of Aphrodisias: de Fato*, text, translation and commentary [Duckworth, England, 1983], especially p. 165).
13. When the event has already occurred, it is no longer a contingent event, since it has then acquired a determinate status; the sentence referring to it now has a definite truth value. Once true, this statement is in a sense necessarily true, since its truth status can no longer change. As Aristotle put it, "It is necessary whenever something exists that it exist, and whenever something is not that it not exist" (Aristotle, *On Interpretation*, 9, 19a, 24–25). This formula became an established logical principle for some of the Latin Scholastics such as William of Ockham (William of Ockham, *Predestination, God's Foreknowledge, and Future Contingents*, translated by M. M. Adams and N. Kretzmann [New York, 1969], Question II).
14. The first horn of the original dilemma has therefore been shown to be false, no matter how it is construed. If God knows these events as genuine contingents, He has no foreknowledge of them. If He has foreknowledge of them, they are not genuinely contingent.
15. Averröes, *On The Harmony of Religion and Philosophy*: Appendix (*Ḍamīma*), translated by G. Hourani (London, 1961), pp. 72–75.
16. Aristotle, *Metaphysics*, XII:9–10.
17. This argument connecting the question of divine knowledge and the problem of continuous magnitudes has a venerable history. In late antiquity Alexander of Aphrodisias had suggested that if the gods do know the infinite, the infinite would then terminate in indivisibles, since that which is known must be definite. Since the consequent is absurd, so is the antecedent (R. Sharples, *Alexander of Aphro-*

disias: de Fato, Chap. 30). This theme is even more prominent in some of the Mutakallimun; Ibn Hazm, for example, records an argument that God's omniscience implies that He knows all the parts of a body. Hence, since knowledge is definite, these parts must terminate in indivisibles, or atoms. This argument was rejected by Nazzam, who maintained that God's knowledge does not encompass the infinite. (Cf. S. Pines, *Beiträge Zur Islamischen Atomenlehre* [Berlin, 1936], pp. 11–14. M. Horten, *Die Philosophischen Systeme Der Speculativen Theologen im Islam* [Bonn, 1912], p. 204. J. Guttmann, "The Problem of Free-Will in Hasdai Crescas and the Muslim Aristotelians," in his *Dat U-mad'a* [Jerusalem, 1955], pp. 166–168. Averröes, *Theologie und Philosophie*, p. 32. C. Touati, *Les Guerres Du Seigneur*, p. 50, n. 1. H. Wolfson, *The Philosophy of the Kalam* [Cambridge, Mass., 1976], pp. 470–471.)

18. *Ha-meqabel.* In this context this term refers to matter, out of which particulars are generated.
19. Maimonides, *Guide*, III:16 and 19.
20. Maimonides, *Guide*, III:20–21.
21. Aristotle, *Metaphysics*, 1074b, 25–34. Abraham ibn Daud, *Ha-'Emunab ha-Ramab*, edited by S. Weil (Frankfurt, 1852), p. 96.
22. Aristotle, op. cit., 1072b, 19–23.
23. If the term "know" is equivocal with respect to its application to God and to man, such that whatever is true in its use in the human situation need not be true in its use in the divine context, then, Maimonides claims, the alleged dilemma between God's omniscience and human freedom is spurious (Maimonides, *Guide*, III:20. This is also the solution suggested by Averröes in his *Tahāfut al-Tahāfut*, Thirteenth Discussion, and in his *Damīma*.
24. Aristotle, *Metaphysics*, VII:12; *Posterior Analytics*, II:13.
25. Maimonides, *Guide*, II:1.
26. Aristotle, *Metaphysics*, II:2.
27. Averröes, *Middle Commentary and Epitome on Aristotle's De Generatione et Corruptione*, Hebrew and English editions, edited by S. Kurland (Cambridge, Mass., 1958), pp. 136–138, in English translation; pp. 125–126 in Hebrew. Aristotle, *On Generation and Corruption*, 338b, 7ff.
28. Events and particulars in the sublunar world are determined by the cyclical motions of the heavenly bodies, whose revolutions bring about the elemental mixtures and transformations among terrestrial phenomena. The four sublunar elements, for example, are *mutually transformable*, or reversible, such that no one of them can be said to be the form of the other. Accordingly, individual terrestrial substances qua mixtures of these basic elements are not hierarchically ordered such that one is the form or perfection of the other. In his symbolization of this argument, Gersonides construes the relation "x is the perfection of y" as transitive (cf. M. Steinschneider, *Hebraische Übersetzungen* [Berlin, 1893], pp. 287–288. Touati, *Les Guerres Du Seigneur*, p. 57, n. 2).
29. Gersonides, *The Wars*, Bk. 1, chaps. 10–11, especially n. 50 in chap. 10.
30. Maimonides, *Guide*, III:21.
31. Aristotle, *Metaphysics*, II:2, 994b, 20ff.
32. Gersonides, *The Wars*, vol. 1, Bk. 1, chap. 10.
33. Actually, this is the fifth of these factors, as enumerated in both the ibn Tibbon Hebrew translation and the Arabic text of the *Guide*.
34. That is, in human predictions, if an event *e* is forecasted with the understanding that *not-e* is also possible, this would be considered opinion, not knowledge. Gersonides is operating with the Platonic-Aristotelian conception of knowledge, according to which knowledge implies certainty (Plato, *Republic*, V; Aristotle, *Posterior Analytics*, 1:33).
35. Maimonides, *Guide*, III:20.
36. Cf. Touati, *Les Guerres Du Seigneur*, p. 62, n. 2.
37. I adopt Touati's emendation of *ve-'im lo yiyeh* to *ve'im yiyeh*, which is in fact a reading in a Parma manuscript cited by Kellermann, *Die Kämpfe Gottes* (Berlin, 1936), found Part 2, *ad locum*.
38. If a boat is defined merely as a material object, we would be in doubt as to whether it is made of wood or stone. When we are told that it is wooden, the initial vagueness has been removed, and the same for any of the other properties.
39. Maimonides, *Treatise on Logic*, c. 4.
40. Maimonides, *Guide*, III:20, beginning.
41. Maimonides, *Guide*, III:21.
42. *Bequōdem ve-'īhūr* (Arabic, *betaqdīm wa-ta'khīr*), "prior and posterior." We are now entering into one of the more controversial and difficult medieval metaphysical issues, the problem of divine attributes. As Gersonides' subsequent treatment shows, he subscribes to the view of Averröes that most, if not all, of the divine attributes are equivocal, but not absolutely equivocal, as Maimonides had claimed. That is, there is some common core meaning when we predicate "good" of God and of Abraham, but the term signifies differently when it is applied to the former. In God's case the predicate signifies good primarily *(bequōdem)*, whereas in Abraham's case it signifies good secondarily *(be'īhur)*. This distinction goes back to Aristotle's *Physics*, VII:4. (See Harry Wolfson's essays, "Maimonides and Ger-

sonides on Divine Attributes," *Mordecai M. Kaplan Jubilee Volume*, English Section [New York, 1953], pp. 515–530; and "The Amphibolous Terms in Aristotle, Arabic Philosophy and Maimonides," *Harvard Theological Review 30* [1936], pp. 151–173.) A version of this theory is also found in Thomas Aquinas, *Summa Theologiae*, I:I, q. 13 a.4.

43. *Be-'azmut*. Cf. Touati, *Les Guerres Du Seigneur*, p. 76, n. 3.

44. Gersonides, *The Wars*, vol. 3, Bk. 5, pt. 3, chap. 12.

45. Wolfson, "Maimonides and Gersonides on Divine Attributes," p. 521.

46. Maimonides, *Treatise on Logic*, c. 13.

47. If inferences from effects to causes are admissible—as they are for Maimonides, e.g., proofs for God's existence—then it cannot be maintained that the terms in the inference are absolutely equivocal. For if they were, any inference would be permissible simply by using a term in the premise that is absolutely equivocal. For example, it is obvious that from the statement "All bodies are continuous" one cannot infer "All men are intelligent," even if it is true that all men have bodies. Suppose, however, that one were to replace the predicate "continuous" in "All bodies are continuous" with the predicate "intelligent," which now connotes both intelligence and continuousness; then the above inference would seem to be valid. But this is a mistake, Gersonides insists, because the term "intelligent" in the premise is absolutely equivocal, and no inferences involving absolutely equivocal premises are licit.

48. Aristotle, *On Interpretation*, c. 6.

49. Here Gersonides employs the logic of his earlier argument about the impossibility of making inferences when the terms of the propositions are absolutely equivocal. In the present context we are concerned with affirmative and negative statements: "S is P" and "S is not-P." Gersonides insists that in both the affirmation and the negation the predicate "P" cannot be completely equivocal, for if it were, no genuine contradiction between the affirmation and the negation would obtain. In Gersonides' own example, it is obvious that the predicates "is a body" and "is a color" are totally different, such that the affirmation "the wall is a body" and the negation "the wall is not a color" are not genuine contradictories. Suppose, however, we replace the predicate "is a color" with a new predicate that is equally true of bodies and colors: "ϕ." We would then get "the wall is ϕ" and "the wall is not ϕ," which *appear* to be contradictory statements. But they are not, Gersonides insists, since the term "ϕ" is absolutely equivocal.

50. Maimonides, *Guide*, I:26.

51. Gersonides, *The Wars*, Bk. 3, chap. 2, end.

52. Maimonides, *Guide*, I:51–66.

53. The key technical terms in this difficult discussion are *"noseh be-mezi'ut"* and *"noseh ba-ma'amar,"* which have been variously translated. In his earlier essay on Crescas' theory of divine attributes, Wolfson translated these phrases as "the subject with respect to existence" or "existent subject" and "subject in the proposition" or "subject of discourse," respectively (Wolfson, "Crescas on Divine Attributes," *JQR* VII [1916], p. 39). In a later essay he used "subject of existence" or "something existent as a subject" and "subject of discourse," respectively (Wolfson, "Maimonides and Gersonides on Divine Attributes," *Mordecai M. Kaplan Jubilee Volume*, English Section [New York, 1953], pp. 526–527). Touati uses the terms *"substrat réel"* and *"substrat logique"* in *Les Guerres Du Seigneur*, pp. 74–75.

According to Wolfson, this passage is based upon the theory, current among the Muslim philosophers, that in predication *per prius et posterius* there is no essential, or definitional, predication, such that one part of the predication would be the genus ["subject"], while the other part would be the specific difference. Predication *per prius et posterius* does not constitute a genuine definition (*gader; hadd*) but is only a description (*roshem; rasm'*) of the thing (Wolfson, "Maimonides and Gersonides on Divine Attributes," p. 528; Goichon, *Lexique De La Langue Philosophique D'Ibn Sina* [Paris, 1938], par. 276, p. 143). This distinction is in turn based upon Aristotle's distinction between real and nominal definitions: the former gives the essence of the thing defined, while the latter merely provides recognitional marks of the thing. (Wolfson, ibid., p. 529; Aristotle, *Posterior Analytics*, II:7–10.)

Now in the case before us, Gersonides argues that since our predications about God are *per prius et posterius*, such characterizations are not definitional and hence do not connote distinct properties, i.e., the genus and the specific difference, in that which is being described. With respect to God there is no genus in which He belongs and hence no specific difference that would differentiate Him from any other members of that genus. On this point he agrees with Maimonides. But since our language about God is based upon *descriptions*, or *nominal definitions*, which do not have the ontological weight carried by real definitions, no internal plurality or compositeness is implied by such language.

54. Here Gersonides refers to the term "intellect" as it appears in the phrase "the intellect that apprehends . . . ."

55. Gersonides, *The Wars*, vol. 3, Bk. 5, pt. 3, chaps. 8 and 13.

56. I have here translated *yahas*, which strictly speaking means "relation," as "similarity" in order to make sense of the subsequent analogy with substance and accident. If *yahas* were translated as "relation" the analogy would not make sense, since there is a relation between substance and accident—inherence.

57. Aristotle, *Metaphysics*, IV:2, 1003b, 6–9; VII:I, 1028a, 10–30. Wolfson, "Maimonides and Gersonides on Divine Attributes," pp. 527–528; Wolfson, "Crescas on Divine Attributes," p. 40.

58. Aristotle, *Metaphysics*, II:I, 993b 23–25; *Posterior Analytics*, I:2, 72a 28–29. Aristotle gives the example of fire: Since fire makes all other hot things hot, it is more appropriately described as 'hot.' For Gersonides, this principle implies that since God is the source of the existence and the substance of all other things, He is more appropriately described by the terms 'existent' and 'substance.'

59. Avicenna, *Die Metaphysik*, edited by M. Horten, p. 512. Gersonides' Commentary on *Aristotle's Metaphysics* is lost, but he gives a full discussion of this problem in Bk. 5, pt. 3, chap. 12.

60. Deut. 6:4.

61. Ex. 3:13.

62. Gersonides, *The Wars*, Bk. 5, pt. 3, chap. 12.

63. Gersonides, *The Wars*, Bk. 5, pt. 3, chaps. I, 5, 7–10.

64. Aristotle, *Metaphysics*, XII:7.

65. Gersonides, *The Wars*, vol. 1, Bk. 1, chaps. 6–7. For the metaphor of the master builder, see Aristotle, *Metaphysics*, I:1.

66. Ibid., Bk. 2, chap. 2.

67. Ibid., Bk. 2, chap. 2. Gersonides, *Commentary on Genesis*, p. 16a, column 2.

68. Jer. 38:17–18.

69. Gersonides' position, then, is the thesis that God knows future contingents only insofar as they are different *possibilities* within the general scheme of things, which He does know. Moreover, God knows that these events are contingent. Hence, His knowledge is a true reflection of reality. (Abraham ibn Daud, *Ha-Emunah ha-Ramah* [Frankfurt, 1852[, p. 96.)

70. Gersonides, *The Wars*, Bk. 2, chap. 6.

71. Aristotle, *On the Soul*, III:3 and 7. Whereas the intellect apprehends universals, the imagination, like perception, is concerned with particulars.

72. Jehuda Halevi, *Kuzari*, III:11 (cf. Kol Jehudah's quotation).

73. That is, as part of the general order of things. In the Aristotelian tradition there is a definite bias in favor of the general, at least in epistemology. (Aristotle, *Posterior Analytics*, I:4 and 31; *Metaphysics*, I:1.)

74. Gersonides, *The Wars*, Bk. 2, chap. 2.

75. Ibid., Bk. 5, pt. 3, chap. 13.

76. Ibid., Bk. 1, chap. 12.

77. Ibid., Bk. 3, chap. 1. This argument of the philosophers claimed that if God knew particulars, His knowledge would reflect the ordered arrangement of these particulars, some of which are more perfect than others. Hence, God's knowledge would mirror these gradations in perfection. But since His knowledge is identical with His essence, different and multiple levels of perfection and imperfection would enter into the divine essence. But this is unacceptable. So the philosophers denied that God can know particulars.

78. Ibid., Bk. 5, pt. 3, chap. 3.

79. Ibid., Bk. 4, chap. 2.

80. That is, perfect knowledge is determinate and finite. If God knew *all* the divisions a magnitude can sustain, He would know a determinate number of such divisions. Hence, the magnitude is *not* indefinitely divisible, which is *contra hypothesem*.

81. This is the eighth argument discussed by Gersonides in chap. 2 of this book.

82. Aristotle, *On Generation and Corruption*, 316a, 15–317a, 2. This text is both important and difficult. (For a discussion of the textual problems, see H. Joachim, *Aristotle on Coming-to-Be and Passing-Away* [Oxford, 1922], ad locum; W. J. Verdenius and J. H. Waszink, *Aristotle on Coming-to-Be and Passing-Away; Some Comments* [Leiden, 1966], pp. 9–16.) The crucial phrase "πάντη διαρετόν [*bikhlalūtō*] is variously translated as "divisible throughout" (Forster, Loeb edition), "divisible through and through" (Joachim), "divisible everywhere" (Furley, *Two Studies in the Greek Atomists* [Princeton, 1967], pp. 84–94), "divisible in all directions" (Verdenius and Waszink), and "exhaustively" (Vlastos, "Zeno of Elea," *Encyclopedia of Philosophy* [New York, 1967], vol. 8, p. 371b.) To understand this phrase, the context of the argument must be set out.

Aristotle is presenting an argument *in behalf of* the Atomist theory of indivisible magnitudes. This theory argues by a *redutio ad absurdum* that the thesis of πάντη διαρετόν leads to the theory of indivisible magnitudes. For if a magnitude is πάντη διαρετόν, either nothing at all remains when the division has been completed, and thus the magnitude dissolves; or if something remains, the remainder will be an entity that is not a magnitude, for example, a point. In either case, no magnitude would ensue if the end-products of the division were compounded; for from nothings or points no magnitude results. Thus, the Atomists conclude, the thesis that a magnitude is πάντη διαρετόν is false. A magnitude, then, is ultimately analyzable into indivisible quanta, or atoms. Aristotle then criticizes this argument in 317a, 2–13. For some contemporary discussions of this issue, see the essays in *Infinity and Continuity in Ancient and Medieval Thought*, edited by N. Kretzmann (Ithaca, 1982) and R. Sorabji, *Time, Creation and the Continuum* (Ithaca, 1983), Part V.

83. Aristotle, *On Sophistical Refutations*, 166a, 23–33, 177a, 33, 177b, 34. This fallacy is often referred to as the fallacy of composition—asserting of the whole what is true only of the part. In this particular argument, Averroës claims that even if each point is indifferently divisible, the whole collection of points need not be divisible at the same time.

84. The terms "immediately next to" and "consecutive to" are technical terms in Aristotle's physics (*Aristotle*, Physics, V:3). The latter term is the more general, and it needs to be defined first. In a series with a generating relation and a first member, "β *is consecutive* (*tilvah*; ἐφεξῆς; *tulāqi*) to α" if and only if nothing of the same genus is between α and β. Thus, if α and β are the natural numbers 1 and 2, they are consecutive to each other, since there is no other natural number between them. Now, if in a consecutive series any member is in contact with (*meshūsh*; ἅπτεσθαι; *māss*) the member to which it is consecutive, then it is immediately next (*pogeshet*; ἐχόμενον; *talqā*) to it. For *x* to be in contact with *y* means that their extremes, i.e., boundaries, are contiguous, or together. (H. H. Joachim, *Aristotle on Coming-to-Be and Passing-Away*, pp. 80–81; Wolfson, *Crescas' Critique of Aristotle*, pp. 375–376.) Now a point is not *consecutive* to another point, since between any two points something of the same genus intervenes, i.e., a line (*Physics*, VI:1, 231b, 8–9). Hence, points cannot be immediately next to each other.

85. Averroës, *Commentaries on De Generatione et Corruptione*, translated and edited by S. Kurland (Cambridge, Mass., 1958), p. 10 Hebrew, p. 13 English. Gersonides' citation from the Averroës Hebrew text is not complete. I have translated Gersonides' quotation. Cf. Philoponus, *In Aristotelis Libros de Generatione et Corruptione Commentaria*, edited by H. Vitelli [Berlin, 1896], in the *Commentaria in Aristotelem Graeca* [Berlin, 1901], vol. XIV, pt. 2, pp. 34–41, translated in part in W. Böhm, *Johannes Philoponus* (München, 1967), pp. 74–75.

86. Touati cites a passage from Averroës' *Middle Commentary on the Physics*, fol. 18, that is instructive:

> One could reply that a line is divisible ad infinitum insofar as it is simply a line; nevertheless, insofar as it is a line of fire or water, it is not divisible ad infinitum, but only up to an indivisible magnitude, which is the minimum magnitude that could receive the form of fire [or water]; for this magnitude is delimited by nature (Touati, *Les Guerres Du Seigneur*, p. 91; n. 3; my translation).

That is, when we are dealing with actual pieces of wood or gold, there is a definite limit to the division, or a minimum part. To divide further is to obtain something that is no longer wood or gold.

Gersonides' distinction between the infinite division of a quantity as such at every one of its points and the division of an actual body terminating at a *minimum part* parallels analogous distinctions made by many Latin scholastics in the late 13th and 14th centuries. Gilles of Rome (Aegidio Colonna), for example, distinguished between pure extension, which is divisible ad infinitum, and extension as embodied in a particular substance such as water, where the division terminates at a minimum part (P. Duhem, *Études Sur Léonard De Vinci*, 2nd edition (Paris, 1955), II, pp. 11 ff.).

87. This argument is not transparent. I understand it as follows. Averroës' solution assumes that an exhaustive division of a body can actually and simultaneously be effected at each one of its points *if and only if* each point is immediately next to another point. But according to the Aristotelian theory of extension, points are not immediately next to each other; rather, between any two points there is a line (Aristotle, *Physics*, VI:1). Hence, when a body is divided at point α, it can only be divided simultaneously at another point β that is *not* immediately next to it. Thus, for Averroës, actual and simultaneous exhaustive division of a body is not possible.

Gersonides claims that this solution achieves nothing. For, if between two points α and β there exists a line *AB*, then although the body can in moment *t* be simultaneously divided at *both* α and β, *AB* is still undivided. And this is the case for each and every division of the magnitude: there will always be an undivided line between the points of division. Hence, at *t* there are undivided magnitudes, which would be infinite in number, since *ex hypothesi* the number of points is potentially infinite. Thus, Averroës' solution does not eliminate the Atomist residue of indivisible magnitudes.

88. Three paragraphs later Gersonides supplies the reason why this latter route is really a dead end.

89. Aristotle, Physics, III:6; *On Generation and Corruption*, I:2.

90. That is, the argument in behalf of the Atomists assumes as possible that a magnitude can be completely divided such that no further division is possible. This assumption, Gersonides argues, is illegitimate.

The Latin Scholastics also distinguished between the potentiality that will some time or another actually be realized—*in facto esse*—and the potentiality that can never be realized completely—*in fieri esse*. Infinite divisibility was for many of them of the second type. The Scholastic logicians designated the propositions dealing with the former type of infinites "categorematic," whereas propositions dealing with the latter type were called "syncategorematic" (Duhem, *Études Sur Léonard De Vinci*, pp. 18–21). For some modern discussions of this Atomist argument, see G. Vlastos' article on Zeno in the

Encyclopedia of Philosophy, vol. 8, p. 372, and A. Grünbaum, *Philosophical Problems of Space and Time* (New York, 1963), pp. 167–168.

91. *Gevulim*, corresponding to the Greek ἔσχατα, which in this context connote *points* (Aristotle, *Physics*, IV:11, 220a, 9, ff.).

92. Wolfson, *Crescas' Critique of Aristotle*, p. 477.

93. If a number could become infinite, it would not be a number, since a number is by the first principle a *definite* magnitude.

94. Gersonides, Commentary on Averröes' *Middle Commentary of the Physics*, Book VI:1, folio 37.

95. That is, the hypothesis of atomism, which was raised by Aristotle in his *On Generation and Corruption*.

96. The upshot of this most difficult discussion is that the argument in favor of atomism from divine omniscience of all particular events is invalid for several reasons, not the least of which is the falsity of atomism on independent grounds. If atomism is false, then divine omniscience in the strong sense of encompassing all particular facts is also false by contraposition.

It might be useful to understand this digress on atomism in its appropriate historical context. At some stage in pre-Socratic philosophical thought, it was advanced (perhaps by Anaxagoras) that a magnitude could be divided to infinity such that all of its infinite parts simultaneously coexist as the result of a completed process of division. In reply to this thesis, the notorious Zeno argued that this notion of a completed infinite division, indeed division in general, is absurd; this was the point of his famous paradox "the dichotomy." Two solutions to this paradox were offered in Greek philosophy: the Atomists' denial of infinite divisibility altogether and their affirmation of indivisible atoms, and the alternative account by Aristotle of infinite divisibility as potential divisibility (D. Furley, *Two Studies in the Greek Atomists*, pp. 44–130).

Gersonides' own account of this matter is superficially a criticism of Averröes' interpretation of Aristotle's alternative answer to the Atomists. But in essence it constitutes a significant modification of Aristotle's answer. The substance of Gersonides' objection to Averröes, and by implication to Aristotle as well, is that the notion of potential infinite divisibility is seriously misleading. For, according to Aristotle, all potentialities are sooner or later realized (Aristotle, *On the Heavens*, I:12); if this is so, then at one time all the possible divisions of a magnitude, which are *ex hypothesi* infinite, will have been completed, and an actually infinite magnitude will have resulted, which is contrary to Aristotle's physics. The term "potentially infinite" is then, according to Gersonides, ambiguous, for it suggests that at some time or another the potentially infinite can become actually infinite. To avoid this ambiguity, we should realize that what is infinite in the divisibility of matter, for example, is the absence of any a priori limitation upon the *act of division*; given any amount of divisions, there is always another that can be performed, and so in *indefinitely*.

Actually, Aristotle himself understood this point, although his terminology betrayed him. In his *Metaphysics*, IX, he observed that genuine infinities do not exist potentially in the way in which, say, a cure for cancer is potentially realizable or the occurrence of a snowstorm in May in New York City is possible. In these latter cases the putative state of affairs is (1) logically possible, and (2) is realizable as a distinct and individual fact or event. (Aristotle, *Metaphysics*, IX:6, 1048b, 9–17.) Now in the case of an infinite, its being is different; it exists in the way in which a day exists. For just as a day comes into being progressively, or successively, such that each part of the day constitutes the actual being of the day, so, too, the infinite is progressively generated such that it exists in each of its parts. No one part of the infinite is *the infinite*, any more than one hour of the day is *the day*. Or, more generally, the infinite is not a definite, particular entity all of whose parts or identity can be found to exist all at once. Rather, it is an entity that is progressively and continuously being generated. (Aristotle, *Physics*, III:6, 206a 18 ff.; Philoponus, op. cit., p. 36, line 13; Böhm, *Johannes Philoponus*, p. 77; J. Hintikka, "Aristotelian Infinity," *Philosophical Review* LXXV (1966), pp. 197–218.) Unfortunately, Aristotle used the term "potential," whose richness occasions all kinds of ambiguities and, in this context, mistakes. What is needed is a different word that connotes the core of Aristotle's notion of the infinite as a kind of entity whose being is always coming to be and yet exists at each stage of this progressive process. Perhaps Descartes' suggestion that matter is *indefinitely divisible* is better; it does capture the meaning of Gersonides' theory of infinite divisibility (Descartes, *Principles of Philosophy*, I:26–27.)

97. Gersonides' theory of divine knowledge reaches the same conclusion suggested by Alexander of Aphrodisias, who also denied that God knows future contingents (Alexander of Aphrodisias, *On Destiny*, c. 30, pp. 124–125, 127–129). Among Jewish thinkers this view was advanced by Abraham ben David, in his *Ha-'Emunah ha-Ramah*, pp. 96–98 (S. Pines, *Scholasticism After Thomas Aquinas and the Teaching of Hasdai Crescas and His Predecessors*, Appendix II).

98. This cannot be taken literally, as Touati rightly observes (Touati, *Les Guerres Du Seigneur*, p. 97, n. 3). For according to Gersonides' theory of religious language, predicates can be applied in a not absolutely equivocal way to both God and man. Gersonides' point here is that there is a great disparity between divine and human cognition, a difference in degree but not in kind.

99. Gersonides, *The Wars*, vol. 1, Bk. 1, chap. 12.

100. Wolfson, *Philosophy of Spinoza* (New York, 1958), vol. II, pp. 27–31.

101. Gersonides, *The Wars*, Bk. 2, chap. 5.

102. Gen. 41:25–26.

103. Dan. 4:16–24.

104. That is, the prediction was warranted in terms of this general pattern.

105. Amos 3:7.

106. Joel 2:13.

107. Ps. 33:15 [my italics].

108. Mal. 3:6.

109. Num. 23:19.

110. Ex. 32:14.

111. Joel 2:13.

112. The passage in question is Gen. 18:21, in which God is about to punish Sodom and Gomorrah. The key word is *'ēda'ah*, "I shall know." Ibn Ezra's own language is cryptic, as usual. Gersonides' interpretation of this passage in his own *Commentary on the Torah* should be consulted (28d).

CHAPTER 18

Peter de Rivo

Peter de Rivo was born at Assche, near Alost (present-day Aalst in the Belgian province of East Flanders), circa 1420. Records indicate that he matriculated at the University of Louvain in 1437. He became a bachelor of arts in 1441, then master of arts the following year. In 1443 he was named professor of philosophy at the College du Faucon, during which time he commenced his studies in theology. In 1460 he succeeded Hugues de Harlem as professor of rhetoric. Peter was naturally eloquent and nimble of mind, and had acquired the skill of controlling his temper in the heat of debate, always being courteous albeit charming. This generally earned him the esteem of his colleagues. His sphere of influence was greatly enhanced by the fact that the course in rhetoric was open to all students of the faculty of arts, and they flocked to it.

Historically, Peter gained notoriety because of a protracted dispute over the issue of future contingents. It began in 1446 when the Promoter of the faculty of arts, John Block, denounced masters guilty of "teaching for some time now propositions offensive to the ears, contrary to the common opinion of doctors and philosophers, and prejudicial to the honor of the faculty and even of the University". One of these propositions had to do with the truth of future contingents and had apparently been defended by Henry de Zomeren. Peter was drawn into the conflict opposing Henry's views. The issue became dormant in 1448 when Henry left for Rome on official university business, after which he went to Paris. He returned to Louvain in 1460. The agitation over the issue of future contingents resumed in 1465 and blossomed into a full-scale medieval quarrel which lasted until 1477, almost five years after the death of Henry de Zomeren. Although Peter's views were endorsed by the faculty of theology at the University of Cologne and had the support of twenty-four professors at the University of Paris, Henry had an "in" with Rome and specifically with the pope (Sixtus IV). On March 19, 1473, Peter signed a retraction of five propositions drawn from his works, thus allowing him to continue to teach. Undaunted, he continued to pursue the topic and concluded, "I did not dare and I still do not dare say that propositions stating a future contingent are true with the truth Aristotle spoke of, because this truth requires that their object happen necessarily". Not surprisingly, news of this got back to Rome, resulting in a papal bull, sent January 14, 1474, charging the deans of the chapters of Saint-Gery at Cambrai and of Soignies to ascertain whether Peter had publicly taught his formerly retracted errors. If the results of the investigation demonstrated that he had, Peter was to promptly recant and he would be deprived for ten years of the right to teach theology, to take new degrees, and to preach. This investigation was not completed until 1476, at which point Peter signed a new retraction.

In March 1477 the Holy See lifted its prohibition against Peter. He died in either 1499 or 1500, bequeathing his house to the College du Chateau.

Peter De Rivo on Future Contingents

There are two aspects to Peter de Rivo's solution to the problem of future contingents: (a) He analyzes the nature of statements, and (b) he argues that God's knowledge is compatible with (a).

(a) De Rivo asserts that ". . . before the occurrence of the actual thing in being there is no truth or falsity in a proposition about a future contingent; but, once the thing has occurred in being there is truth in the proposition". In other words, statements are not such that they confer truth or falsity to facts. Rather, facts determine whether statements about them are either true or false. Consequently, statements about future contingents are neither true nor false because the facts purportedly referred to by such statements have yet to be exemplified. That is, there is no factual referent to a statement about future contingents. Two important points follow from this: (1) If (part of) the definition of a statement is that it, the statement, is true or false, then claims about future contingents are not, strictly speaking, statements but rather some other sort of linguistic expression. (2) Concerning any (conceivable) future contingent, it is the case that whatever is said about it will be either true or false. This in no way denies contingency, for such a claim is not about the future. It is a tautology and therefore has no determining effect whatsoever concerning facts, future or otherwise.

(b) Foreknowledge as it is normally understood only applies to mortals because the very notion of foreknowledge presupposes the future. In one sense, God does not possess foreknowledge since He is "aware of all things, even those that in the course of time are future . . . for in respect of God no things are future, nor are any expected as coming". Consequently, the subject of God's knowledge is that of which is present to Him by way of Him existing in an eternal "now". In a different sense, however, God does possess foreknowledge, since "all things present, past, and future are immediately present to divine perception". He knows the future in a passive way as the future is presented to Him in the eternal present. He can be aware of what is in this eternal state of being without having any determining effect upon it in the same way that a mortal can be aware (i.e., possess knowledge) of the (present) facts without being instrumental in their determination. Any statement concerning God's knowledge is therefore true or false due to the instance of a corresponding state of affairs made possible by God's existing only in what for Him is an eternal present.

A QUODLIBETAL QUESTION ON FUTURE CONTINGENTS

Disputed at Louvain in the year 1465

Was It in Peter's Power to Deny Christ After Christ Had said to Him, "Thou Wilt Deny Me Thrice"?

First I proved that the contingency of things is of the number of things that are manifest per se, partly on the basis of theological, partly on philosophical considerations. And stating my method I said that, just as it is manifest per se that nature is, as is said in *Physics* II, so is it also that there is contingency in things; for each is immediately deduced by means of a kind of imperceptible syllogism on the basis of things that are manifest to sense, etc.

Three things appear to stand in the way of contingency. The first is logical; for if there is determinate truth as regards future contingents, nothing will come about contingently, but all things of necessity. The second is physical; for if fated dispositions or natural inclinations impose necessity on things, those things will not come about contingently. The third is metaphysical; for if God foreknows all future things, as is totally to be believed, no future thing will be contingent, because there is no knowledge of contingents.

In this whole determination, my argument was based on the fact that nothing precedes the coming about of a future contingent in an intervening line of succession that could entail such a coming about in a necessary consequence. For if anything could have preceded the coming about of a future contingent in this way, then that thing would be unimpedible, because there is no power over the past; but in a necessary consequence only what is unimpedible follows from the unimpedible, otherwise the false could follow from the true;

Reprinted from *The Quarrel over Future Contingents* (Louvain 1465–1475). Unpublished texts collected by Leon Baudry, translated by Rita Guerlac (Dordrecht, Boston, London: Kluwer Academic Publishers, 1989), pp. 36–45. Reprinted by permission of Kluwer Academic Publishers.

for this reason the future coming about of the actual thing would be unimpedible; therefore all things would come about unimpedibly and of necessity, and there would be no contingency in things. I do not see how I could resolve this argument.

Following up on the three above arguments that seem to stand in the way of contingency, I first stated that the first opinion about the truth of propositions about the future contingent was that of poets, who posited three fatal goddesses, who from eternity fated or foretold of any future thing what would finally happen with regard to its rise, its fall, and its duration. And, because the poets thought unimpedible truth was inherent in those things foretold from eternity, they said that all things come about by fate. Therefore, according to them, there is no contingency in things, but all things come about of necessity.

Then, touching upon the opinion of the philosophers, I showed from Tully's book *De fato* that there was a question among them over the way in which truth and falsity are opposed with respect to a proposition. And it was the opinion of Chrysippus that they are directly opposed, and so he said that every proposition is either true or false. But Epicurus' opinion was that they are indirectly opposed so that there would be some propositions that are true, some false, and some neutral, neither true nor false, and he said that all propositions about a future contingent are of this kind. Tully adhered to Chrysippus' opinion, but Aristotle in the first book of *De interpretatione* seems rather to have followed Epicurus.

Now there seem to be two arguments that can be drawn from Tully's book which confirm Chrysippus' opinion. One is that if a proposition about a future contingent were not true, then something could have happened about which it was not true to say that it was going to be—which seems absurd. For of anything that has already happened it seems it was formerly true that would happen. The other is that a proposition about the past is true because for an earlier time its corresponding proposition about the present was true; therefore by analogy it seems that a proposition about the future is true because for a later time its corresponding proposition about the present will be true.

I resolved these arguments by saying in reply to the first that, with regard to what has already happened it was formerly neither true nor false to say that it would happen. I explained this by analogy with a puppy which, although on the day determined by nature it has sight, yet on the previous days it was neither blind nor sighted. And I thought, following Aristotle's opinion, that there is an analogy to be drawn from this because, just as before the time determined by nature there is in the susceptible subject neither possession nor privation, so before the occurrence of a thing in being there is no truth or falsity in a proposition about a future contingent; but once the thing has occurred in being there is truth in the proposition—not, indeed, in the one about the future, but in the one about the present whose truth succeeds the one about the future as the completion of it. In successive things, moreover, when something is completed it is no more, as motion, when it is completed, is no more, and similarly with a game.

To the other argument I said that past things and future things are not alike because, before the occurrence of a thing in being it is in the power of the cause to bring it or not bring it into being; but after its occurrence the cause has no power over it. Therefore after a thing has occurred in being its occurrence is unimpedible; for this reason a truth so caused is unimpedible; accordingly, unimpedible truth is suited to a proposition about the past. But before a contingent thing occurs in being its future occurrence is impedible; accordingly the truth that would be caused thereby would be impedible. But what is impedibly now does not exist, because a present effect is

unimpedible. Therefore in a proposition about the future there is no presential truth.

I added two other arguments for Chrysippus' opinion. The first was that a statement is defined as a sentence in which there is truth or falsity; if therefore a statement about the future were neither true nor false, the definition of a statement would not apply to it. The other was that about any subject there is a true affirmation or negation, as the first principle says; therefore, since a proposition about a future contingent is an affirmation or a negation, it follows that it will be true or false.

In reply to the first I said that the definition of statement is not to be understood as if truth and falsity are formally in a statement, but as if something is true or false in the signifying. For in every affirmative there is truth in this way, because it signifies that the composition of predicate with subject is true; and in every negative there is falsity, because it signifies that the composition of predicate with subject is false. Thus as we find in *Metaphysics* V, 'is' signifies that something is true, and 'is not' that it is false. But Aristotle and Epicurus on this problem meant that a statement about a future contingent is formally neither true or false.

In reply to the other I said that affirmation or negation about any subject is true in the compounded sense, so that plainly it is truly said about any subject that the predicate is affirmative, or its negation. Thus an affirmation or negation is truly said about future contingents conjointly, not separately, as it is truly said about the sea battle that it will or will not be, but it is said neither truly that it will take place nor truly that it will not.

On these matters I said that whoever wants to uphold Aristotle's opinion on future contingents must necessarily erase from his mind the opinion by which it is commonly granted and believed that every proposition is true or false, since whoever thinks that seems unable to support it. Moreover whoever thinks with Aristotle that there is not determinate truth in future contingents is not obliged because of this kind of truth to deny contingency, because there is not such truth in propositions about a future contingent. And I believe that in confirming Aristotle's opinion I have satisfactorily adduced his own opinions.

Having stated that the truth of propositions about a future contingent is no barrier to contingency, I moved on to the second apparent barrier, where I showed that neither the fated dispositions that inhere in heavenly bodies, nor the natural inclinations which are constitutionally in us impose necessity on things. This is clear first because heavenly bodies, with respect to their movements by which, according to Aristotle, causality combines with them in regard to things below, are under divine power, as I stated about the retardation of the sun in the time of Hezekiah, and of the moon in the time of Joshua, and the miraculous eclipse at the time of Christ's passion. If then the heavenly bodies can be impeded in their movements, they can also be impeded in the causation of their effects. And second it is clear that natural inclinations are under our power. Thus no men who were naturally inclined to wickedness were found [to] be good men, as I stated about Socrates, etc.

Against the first point the objection was made that astronomy deals with the movements of the celestial bodies. Since, therefore, knowledge is of necessary things, it seems that movements of the heavenly bodies are necessary and unimpedible. Solution: According to Aristotle, the movements of the heavenly bodies were absolutely necessary. According to the faith, however, they are frequently contingent. But as we see in *Posterior Analytics* I, knowledge is not only of things that always are, but frequently are, etc.

Finally I tried to show that divine foreknowledge does not abolish the contingency of things. To begin with, I advanced the idea that all things, present, past, and future, are immediately present in the divine sight. Because this is extremely difficult to understand, for a little help in imagining it I brought up Plato's opinion about

Ideas. For he thought ideas are apart from any local condition, whence in *Physics* III it is said of them that they are indefinable. Nonetheless he said they are indistant from all their singulars however much they are locally distant. Thus we imagine God as separate from any situation or temporal difference and yet having all things immediately present to him, however much they are temporally distant from each other. Because, then, all things that in the course of time are past, present, or future are, with respect to their real existence, immediately present to God, therefore the divine essence is, as it were, an image of them. For just as images of things in a mirror are immediate to themselves, so it is in God. Therefore the divine view, which is turned toward its own essence as towards its primary object, looking upon it as an example of all existing things, is said to be aware of all things, even those that in the course of time are future, not indeed with expectative cognition, for in respect of God no things are future nor are any expected to come about. Indeed such cognition is, rather, intuitive, not in such a way that it is fixed directly upon the thing, but upon his own essence exemplifying the thing. Whence God is to be understood as a sort of mirror in which all things succeeding one another in the whole course of time have images shining back, a mirror indeed directly beholding itself and all the images existing in it. And thus he is said to know the things whose images he beholds. And we are speaking in accordance with the opinion of ordinary people who think that an image is something in the mirror; but according to those who know optics, it is nothing, etc.

And because future things, as to their actuality or existence, are immediately present to the divine sight, and his cognition in respect of such things is not expectative, therefore God's cognition of this kind is not properly said to be foreknowledge in the way our cognition in respect of a future eclipse is customarily called foreknowledge. For between our cognition and such an eclipse there is an intervening line of succession which makes the eclipse distant from our cognition. But all future things are, in respect of divine cognition, immediately present. Yet the divine cognition of future things can in one way be called foreknowledge because, presiding over the whole course of time, it knows all things in it as immediate in its sight. Therefore because divine foreknowledge is not to be understood as anteceding the occurrence of future events through an intervening line of succession, even though it infers an occurrence of this kind in a necessary consequence as immediately present, it does not infer it as future. And so, although the foreknowledge itself is unimpedible, it does not infer that the thing unimpedibly and of necessity will be. And, consequently it does not abolish contingency. For even if something infers that a thing already is of necessity, it still does not infer that the thing for a preceding time would be of necessity, as the vision by which at the present moment I see your being seated infers that you are for that moment unimpedibly seated, but does not infer that yesterday it was unimpedible that you would be seated, etc.

From the foregoing the solution is clear by which it is customarily argued thus: Everything foreknown will come about of necessity, but all things that are future are foreknown at least by God; therefore they will come about of necessity. To the major the answer is, if the foreknowledge is understood to antecede the thing foreknown, the major is true because it thus looks to the thing as going to happen; but if the thing foreknown is quite immediate to it, then the major is denied. For then the foreknowledge by which the thing is said to be foreknown infers the actuality of the thing to be immediately present to him, but it does not infer it will necessarily happen because he does not look to it as going to happen.

Some people solve this argument in another way, separating the major into the compounded and divided sense, and saying that in the divided sense it is false and in the compounded sense true. Others distinguish a double necessity: absolute and conditional. Now they say the major is true, speaking of conditional, not absolute, necessity. Neither of the solutions seems to work. Not the first, because propositions to which a concrete accident is inseparably added, though they can be divided into the compounded and divided sense, are yet never in one sense true and in the other false. For example, suppose that nothing is white but a swan. Then 'It is possible that white is black' is false in both senses, and 'It is impossible that white is black' is true in both senses. Because then 'foreknown' is an accident inseparable from the thing assumed to be foreknown, it appears that the major will not be true in the compounded and false in the divided sense unless something else is added.

The second solution does not work either because, if the major is true speaking of the necessity of the consequence, then this consequence is necessary: This is foreknown; therefore it will happen. The antecedent is inevitable. For what is foreknown is inevitably foreknown because by no power is it avoidable that the past be past. Therefore the consequent will be inevitable, for in a necessary consequence the avoidable does not follow from the unavoidable any more than the contingent does from the necessary. Because if the foreknown will inevitably happen, it follows that it will happen necessarily with the necessity of the consequence, not indeed with logical but with physical necessity, that of course by which something is so necessary that by no power can it be impeded.

And so I have been astonished at some people who have explored the greatest causes with the utmost subtlety, so that they scarcely left a particle undiscussed, and yet are satisfied with these solutions. From the foregoing I have drawn a conclusion under this or an equivalent form of words. Contingency is among the things manifest per se, which is impeded neither by the truth of propositions about future contingents because there is no truth in them; nor by fated dispositions or natural instincts because they are all impedible; nor by divine foreknowledge because it is immediately present and not expectative of future things.

A corollary reply to the Question. It was still in Peter's power not to deny Christ after Christ said to him: Thou wilt deny me thrice. It is evident, because the proposition spoken by Christ seems no more to have taken away his power of not denying Christ than the proposition: Tomorrow you will die, spoken by Isaiah to Hezekiah, took away the power of not dying, or than the proposition spoken by Jonah, "Yet forty days and Nineveh will be destroyed," took away from Nineveh the power of not being destroyed. For they say that in propositions about a future contingent there is no truth that takes away the contingency of things. Not even the cunning of Satan, who wanted Peter, or Peter's weakness, took away his power of not denying Christ, since he could, through his free will, with God's help, have impeded both causes. Nor, third, did the foreknowledge with which Christ, by his divine cognition, foreknew Peter's denial, because he did not regard it as in the future, but as immediately present, as was said above.

So far I have spoken philosophically, as is appropriate in the School of Arts. But because I feared some of my hearers might perhaps be disturbed in their faith by the foregoing, because they had earlier heard me state that there is not determinate truth in future contingents, and it might perhaps seem to them that the propositions about the future contingent contained in the prophetic Scriptures and in the Creed, such as 'Antichrist will be born', 'The dead will rise again', 'Christ will judge the world', and the like, are not determinately true and consequently not firmly to be believed (since nothing, it seems, is firmly believed unless it is held to be determinately true), lest it happen that the weak in faith be scandalized by this conclusion of mine, I stated two things.

The first was that the cognition God has of future contingents is not properly expressed by any proposition. And though it appears it can be better expressed by a future-tense proposition, yet that it is not

properly expressed by it is evident thus, because such a proposition, by its own nature and by logical rigor, expresses expectative cognition. For example, the proposition: The sun will be eclipsed, expresses cognition of the eclipse as we expect it as future to us. Since then there is no expectative cognition in God, as was evident, it seems to follow that his cognition is not properly expressible by a future-tense proposition. And so it happens that the prophets, desiring to express the cognition by which God knows future contingents, expressed it not only by future-tense propositions but sometimes by the past tense, as in Isaiah 9: 'Unto us a child is born', etc. It is believed the reason for this was that they found no proposition by which they could properly express God's cognition of future things.

The second was that propositions of this kind which, merely by the intention of the authors of sacred Scripture and not by their own nature or mode of stating, signify the divine cognition of future contingents, are not true in virtue of their own truth and by logical rigor; nevertheless they are true with the truth of the divine cognition which the prophets and authors intended to express through them, that is by uncreated Truth. And, as it appears, it is enough for them to be true in this way to be believed in the faith, because uncreated Truth, according to catholic doctors, is the formal object of faith. Accordingly for propositions to be believed in the faith as its material objects, it is enough that they be true with uncreated Truth or revealed by the same Truth. But speaking of created truth, it does not appear that they should, if they are about a future contingent, in Aristotle's sense and his way of stating, be actually and formally true. Nevertheless, every catholic must unhesitatingly believe they are to be made true, and that the things signified by them will eventually happen. In this way it seems possible to reconcile Aristotle's teaching about future contingents with our catholic faith.

Just as I have not admitted any expectative foreknowledge in God, so I said in another conclusion that there is no prevolition in God, speaking of expectative prevolition; for example, in God there is no act of desire by which one wishes anything with respect to the future, expecting it as distant from himself through an intervening line of succession, as in a contest one has with an enemy, by desiring he forewishes a victory still distant from him by an intervening time. For God expects nothing as future, indeed all things are immediately present to him, as we have shown. Therefore, etc.

Again, when someone argued against Aristotle's opinion of future contingents on the basis of authoritative passages of Holy Scripture, I jokingly suggested that not all sentences contained in Holy Scripture are true sentences, adding that, though little old women and the common people are wont to say, 'It is as true as the Our Father' in fact in the Lord's Prayer there seem not to be any true sentences; for there are eight complete sentences in it: one vocative, i.e., 'Our Father, who art in heaven,' and seven precative. But according to all the logicians, neither vocative nor precative sentences are true or false. If someone says that there are indicative sentences in it, such as 'who art in heaven,' and 'as we forgive our debtors', and that those are true or false, here is the answer: Those two sentences are in-

complete, because the first is only a qualifying clause added to the vocative 'father' as its completion, and the second is added to the verb 'forgive' as its completion. But everyone knows that incomplete sentences are not true. For it happens that indicative propositions become incomplete sentences by the addition of terms or syncategoremata. For example, the sentence, 'Socrates runs', is complete and indicative, but through an addition it sometimes becomes incomplete, as when one says, 'if Socrates runs', or 'as Socrates runs', neither of which is true or false. Having said this, I added the solution that when the Scriptural authorities say that some propositions about a future contingent are true, they mean that they are true with the uncreated Truth which they express, or with the truth of the one uttering or revealing them, or with the truth that is faithfully expected, etc.

The foregoing things, as far as I can remember, I said in the School of Arts at the time of quodlibetals and under the prescribed order, having always relied upon the customary protestation of submitting myself to the edict of the Holy Apostolic See and of my mother the Faculty of Theology.

PART IV
THEOLOGY

CHAPTER 19

St. Augustine

(See Chapter One for biography.)

St. Augustine on the Immortality of the Soul

A scrutiny of Augustine's thesis on the immortality of the soul reveals (1) that he was greatly influenced by Plato's writings on the subject and (2) that he identifies the soul with the mind. Consistent with his theory of knowledge (see chapter 31), there is a dichotomy between body and mind. The activity of the body is sensation. The activity of the mind is reason. "Surely, reason either is the mind or is in the mind. Our reason, moreover, is better than our body, and body is a substance, and it is better to be a substance than to be nothing. Therefore, reason is not nothing." From this Augustine argues that the mind qua soul is a substance in its own right. It is an immaterial substance versus the body, which is material and mutable in nature. The mind is stimulated by the data of sensation for the purpose of (ultimately) understanding eternal and immutable ideas. The dichotomy here is between a posteriori and a priori knowledge qua reasoning. The subject matter of the latter (e.g., mathematics) is immutable. "This sort of reasoning, then, is immutable. Therefore, reason is immutable. . . . death [cannot] befall unchangeable things. Consequently, the mind always lives, and either the mind is reason itself or has reason in it inseparably." Furthermore, argues Augustine, "The soul is prior to the body in connection with those supreme and eternal principles which survive unchangeably and are not contained in space. . . ." One such principle is Life. No principle admits of its contrary. Life is the antithesis of death. Consequently, the principle of Life entails life everlasting. The soul participates in Life. It is that which gives life to the body. And it survives the demise of the body which is mutable. In other words, the soul is immortal.

ON THE IMMORTALITY OF THE SOUL

Chapter I

The First Reason Why the Soul Is
Immortal: It Is the Subject of Science
Which Is Eternal

If science [*disciplina*] exists anywhere, and cannot exist except in that which lives; and if it is eternal, and nothing in which an eternal thing exists can be non-eternal; then that in which science exists lives eternally. If we exist who reason, that is, if our mind does, and if our mind cannot reason rightly without science, and if without science no mind can exist except as a mind without science, then science is in the mind of man. Science, moreover, is somewhere, for it exists, and whatever exists cannot be nowhere. Further, science cannot exist except in that which lives. For nothing which is not alive learns anything, and science cannot be in a thing which does not learn.

Again, science is eternal. For what exists and is unchangeable must be eternal. But no one denies that science exists. And whoever admits that it is impossible that a line drawn through the midpoint of a circle is not greater than all lines which are not drawn through the midpoint, and admits that this is a part of science, does not deny that science is unchangeable. Further, nothing in which an eternal thing exists can be non-eternal. For nothing which is eternal ever allows to be taken from it that in which it exists eternally.

Now, truly, when we reason it is the mind which reasons. For only he who thinks reasons. Neither does the body think, nor does the mind receive the help of the body in thinking, since when the mind wishes to think it turns away from the body. For what is thought is thus eternal, and nothing pertaining to the body is thus eternal, therefore the body cannot help the mind as it strives to understand;

Reprinted from *St. Aurelius Augustine: Concerning the Teacher and On the Immortality of the Soul*, translated by George G. Leckie (New York: Appleton-Century–Crofts, Inc., 1938), pp. 59–84.

for it is sufficient if the body does not hamper the mind. Again, without science [*disciplina*] nobody reasons rightly. For thought is right reasoning moving from things certain to the investigation of things uncertain, and there is nothing certain in an ignorant mind. All that the mind knows, moreover, it contains within itself, nor does knowledge consist in anything which does not pertain to some science. For science is the knowledge of any things whatsoever. Therefore the human mind always lives.

Chapter II

Another Reason: It Is the Subject of
Reason Which Is Not Changed

Surely, reason either is the mind or is in the mind. Our reason, moreover, is better than our body, and body is a substance, and it is better to be a substance than to be nothing. Therefore, reason is not nothing.

Again, whatever the harmony of the body is, it must be in the body inseparably as in a subject; and nothing may be held to be in the harmony unless it is also necessarily in that body inseparably as in a subject. But the human body is mutable and reason is immutable. For all which does not exist always in the same mode is mutable, but that two and two are four exists always in the same mode, and also that four contains two and two exists always in the same mode, but two does not contain four, therefore two is not four. This sort of reasoning, then, is immutable. Therefore, reason is immutable.

Moreover, if the subject is changed, there is no way in which that which is in the subject remains unchanged. Hence, it follows that the mind is not a harmony of the body. Nor can death befall unchangeable things. Consequently, the mind always lives, and either the mind is reason itself or has reason in it inseparably.

Chapter III

Mind Is Living Substance and Immutable;
and If It Is in Some Mode Mutable, It
Does Not on That Account Become
Mortal

Some power [*virtus*] is constant, and all
constancy is unchangeable, and all power
can act, nor does it cease to be power when
it acts. Further, all action is moved or
moves. Therefore, not all which is moved,
or surely not all which moves, is changeable. But all which is moved by another
and does not move itself is a mortal thing.
Nor is anything immutable which is mortal. Hence, certainly and without any disjunction, it is concluded that not all which
moves is changed.

There is, moreover, no motion without
substance, and any substance either is alive
or is not alive, and all which does not live
is inanimate. But no action is inanimate.
Therefore, that which moves so as not to be
changed can be only living substance. Any
action, moreover, moves the body through
a number of steps; therefore, not all which
moves the body is changeable. The body,
moreover, is not moved except in time; and
to the body pertains being moved faster
and slower; therefore, there is shown to be
a certain thing which moves in time and is
not changed. Moreover, every body which
moves in time, although it tends towards
one end, yet can neither accomplish simultaneously all the steps which lead to this
end, nor can avoid the several steps. For by
whatever impulse it is moved, a body cannot be perfectly one, because it can be divided into parts; and there is no body without parts, as there is no time without an
interval of delay, even if it is expressed by
a very short syllable of which you hear neither the beginning nor the end. Further,
what occurs thus needs expectation that it
may be accomplished and memory that it
may be understood as much as possible.
And expectation is of future things, while
memory is of things past. But intention to
act belongs to present time, through which
the future moves into the past. And without memory we cannot expect the end of a

motion which has begun. For how can that
be expected to cease which forgets either
that it has begun or that it is in motion?
Again, the intention of accomplishing
which is present cannot be without expectation of the end which is future: nor does
anything exist which does not yet exist or
which has already ceased to exist. Therefore, there can be something in acting
which pertains to those things which do
not yet exist. There can be several things
simultaneously in the agent, although these
several acts when executed cannot exist
simultaneously. Likewise, they can exist simultaneously in the mover, although they
cannot in the thing moved. But whatever
things cannot exist simultaneously in time,
and yet are transmitted from future into
past, must of necessity be mutable.

From the above we have already gathered
that there can be a certain thing which is not
changed when it moves changeable things.
For when the intention of the mover to bring
the body which it moves to the end it desires
is not changed, while the body which is
acted upon is changed by this motion from
moment to moment, and when that intention of accomplishment, which obviously
remains unchanged, moves both the members of the artificer and the wood or stone
which are subject to the artificer, who may
doubt that what we have said follows as a
logical consequence? Therefore, if any
change in bodies be effected by the mind as
mover, however intent upon the change the
mind may be, we should not think that the
mind is changed necessarily by this, or that
the mind dies. For along with this intention
it can have memory of past things and expectation of future things, none of which
can exist without life. And even if there be
no destruction without change, and no
change without motion, yet not all change is
engaged in destruction, nor is all motion engaged in change. For we can say that this
body of ours has been for the most part
moved by an action, and that it has undoubtedly been changed especially by age;
still it has not yet perished, that is, is not
without life. Therefore, from this it follows
immediately that the mind is not deprived

of life, even though some change does perchance occur to it through motion.

Chapter IV

Art and the Unchangeable Principle of Numbers, Which Do Not Inhere in the Mind Without Life

For if there persists anything in the mind unchangeable, which cannot exist without life, then life must also remain in the mind eternally. For indeed the mind is so constituted that if the antecedent is true, the consequent is true. Moreover, the antecedent is true. For who dares say, not to mention other things, either that the principle [*ratio*] of number is changeable or that there is any art which does not depend upon this principle [*ratio*]; or that an art is not in the artist even if he be not applying it; or that it is in him other than as being in the mind; or that it can be where there is no life; or that what is unchangeable cannot be anywhere; or that art is other than a principle [*ratio*]? For although an art is said to be a sort of assemblage of many principles [*rationes*], yet an art can in truth be called one principle [*ratio*] and can be so thought. But whether it be the former or the latter, it follows none the less that art is unchangeable. Moreover, it is clear not only that an art is in the mind of the artist, but also that it is nowhere else except in the mind, and in it inseparably. For if art is separated from the mind it will be other than in the mind, or will be nowhere, or will pass immediately from the mind. But just as there is no seat of art without life, so there is no life according to a principle [*ratio*] anywhere except in the soul. Further, that which is cannot be nowhere nor can that which is immutable be non-existent at any time. But if art passes from mind to mind, it would leave one mind and abide in another; in this case nobody would teach an art except by losing it, or further, nobody would become skilled except through the forgetting of his teacher, or by the teacher's death. If these things are utterly absurd and false, as they are, then the human mind is immortal.

And if indeed art exists at some time, it does not so exist in a mind which is conspicuous for its forgetfulness and ignorance. The conclusion of this argument adds nothing to the mind's immortality unless the preceding be denied in the following way. Either there is something in the mind which is not in present thought or else the art of music is not in the educated mind when it thinks of geometry alone. And this latter is false. Hence the former is true. Moreover, the mind does not perceive that it contains anything except what comes into thought. Therefore, there can be something in the mind, which the mind itself does not perceive to be in it. But as long as it is there, this makes no difference. For if the mind has been occupied with other things too long to be able to turn its attention back to things thought of before, this is called forgetting or ignorance. But since, when we reason with ourselves or when we are skilfully questioned by another concerning certain liberal arts, we then discover the things which we discover nowhere else but in the mind; and since to discover is not to make or to cause, as otherwise the mind would cause eternal things through temporal discovery (for it often discovers eternal things, as the principle [*ratio*] of the circle, or anything else of this sort in the arts, which is not understood either to have been non-existent at some time or ever to be about to be); hence it is also evident that the human mind is immortal, and all true principles [*rationes*] are in its hidden places, although, either because of ignorance or forgetting, it seems not to contain them or to have lost them.

Chapter V

Mind Is Not Changed So That It Ceases to Be Mind

But now let us see to what extent we should accept the statement that the mind changes. For if the mind is the subject, with art existing in the subject, and if a subject cannot be changed unless that which is in it as in a subject be changed also, who can hold that art and principle [*ratio*] are unchangeable in the mind if the mind in which they exist is shown to be changeable? Moreover, where is there greater change than that in contraries? And who denies that the mind is, to say the least, at times stupid and at other times wise? Therefore, let us see in how many ways that which is called change of the soul may be taken. Of these I think there are found two genera quite evident or at least quite clear to us, though there are found several species. For the soul is said to be changed either according to passions of the body or according to its own passions. According to the passions of the body, as through age, disease, sorrow, work, hatred, or carnal desires; according to its own passions, however, as by desiring, enjoying, fearing, worrying, striving, or learning.

All these changes, if they are not necessarily proof that the soul dies, ought not to be feared at all taken separately each by each; but it should be seen whether they oppose our reasoning in which we said that when a subject is changed all which is in the subject is necessarily changed. But they do not oppose it. For this is said of a subject according to such a change as makes the name change entirely. For if wax changes to a black color from white, it is none the less wax; and also if it assumes a round shape after being square, becomes hard when it has been soft, cools after being hot. These are all in the subject, and wax is the subject. But wax remains not more or less wax when these things are changed. Therefore, some change of the things in the subject can occur, when the subject itself is not changed with regard to what it is and is called. But if so much change occurs in those things which are in the subject that that which was said to be the subject cannot any longer be so called, as, for example, when from the heat of fire wax disappears into the air, and suffers such change that it may rightly be understood that the subject is changed, since it was wax, and is no longer wax; then by no reasoning of any kind whatever would we think that any of those things would remain, which were in that subject because it was what it was.

Consequently, if, as we said above, the soul is a subject in which reason is insepa-

rably (by that necessity also by which it is shown to be in the subject) neither can there be any soul except a living soul, nor can reason be in a soul without life, and reason is immortal; hence, the soul is immortal. For in absolutely no way could the soul remain immutable if its subject did not exist. This would happen if so great a change should befall the soul as would make it not a soul, that is, would compel it to die. Moreover, not one of those changes which occur to the soul, either through the body or through itself (although there is not a little question whether any occur through itself, that is, of which it is itself the cause) causes the soul not to be a soul. Therefore, they need not be feared per se; nor because they may oppose our reasoning.

Chapter VI

Unchangeable Reason, Whether It Be in the Mind or With the Mind, or Whether the Mind Be in It, Cannot Be Separated from the Very Same Mind

Hence I see that all men of reason ought to take pains to know what reason is and in how many ways it can be defined, so that it may remain firm according to all modes and with regard to the immortality of the soul. Reason is the aspect of the mind which perceives the true per se and not through the body; or it is the contemplation of the true, not through the body; or it is the true itself which is contemplated. Nobody doubts that the first of these is in the mind. There can be a question about the second and third; but even the second cannot exist without the mind. Concerning the third the great question is whether the true which is perceived by the mind without the instrument of the body exists per se, and is not in the mind, or whether it can exist without the mind. Moreover, in whatever mode the true may be, the mind cannot contemplate it per se except through some connection with it. For all that we contemplate we either perceive through cogitation [*cogitatio*], or through a sense or through the intellect. But those things which are perceived through sense we also sense to be outside us, and to be contained in places apart from which it is established that they cannot be perceived. But those things which are thought are not thought as being in another place other than the very mind which thinks them: for at the same time they also are thought as not being contained in any place.

Consequently, the connection between the mind which perceives and the true which it perceives is either such that the mind is the subject with the true in it as in a subject; or on the other hand the true is the subject with the mind in it as in a subject; or else each is a substance. Moreover, if the connection is of the first sort, the mind is as immortal as reason, according to the preceding argument, since reason can be in nothing but a living thing. The same necessity lies in the second sort of connection. For if the true, which is called reason, contains nothing which is changeable, as it appears, then nothing can be changed which is in it as in a subject. Therefore, all the struggle is left to the third. For if mind is one substance and reason another substance to which it is joined, he is not absurd who would think it possible for the former to remain while the latter perishes. But it is evident that as long as the mind is not separated from reason and remains connected with it, the mind necessarily survives and lives. But by what force can it be separated? By bodily force, whose power is weaker, whose origin is inferior, whose order is more disparate? Not at all. Then by animate strength? But how so? Cannot a more powerful mind contemplate reason without separating another mind from it? Reason is not lacking in any mind which contemplates, if all minds contemplate; and since nothing is more powerful than reason itself, than which nothing is more immutable, by no means will there be a mind not joined to reason and yet more powerful than one which is so joined. It remains that either reason separates itself from mind, or else the mind itself is separated by will. But there is no envy in that nature, and, therefore, it offers itself for mind's enjoyment; and, what is more, whatever it joins to itself it causes to be, which is contrary to destruction. Moreover, it is too absurd for someone to say that the mind is separated from reason by the mind's own will, provided there can be any mutual separation of things which space does not contain. Indeed this can be said in contradiction to all we have argued above in meeting other opposition. What then? Should it be concluded that the mind is immortal? Or, even though it cannot be separated, can it perhaps be extinguished? But if the very strength of reason affects the mind by its connection (and it cannot fail to affect it), then it at once causes being to be ascribed to mind. For it is in great measure reason itself in which the supreme immutability is thought. Therefore, that which reason affects by virtue of itself it causes to exist in a certain respect. Hence the mind cannot be extinguished unless it be separated from reason, and it cannot be separated, as we have proved above. Therefore it cannot perish.

Chapter VII

And If the Mind Tends Through Substance Towards Defection, Still It Does Not on This Account Perish

But that very turning away from reason by which stupidity enters the mind cannot occur without a defect in the mind. For if the mind has more being when turned towards reason and inhering in it, thus adhering to the unchangeable thing which is truth, both greatest and first; so when turned away from reason it has less being, with constitutes a defection. Moreover, every defect tends towards nothing [non-being], nor do we ever speak more properly of destruction than when that which was something becomes nothing. Therefore, to tend towards nothing [non-being] is to tend towards destruction. It is hard to say why this does not occur to the soul in which defect occurs. We grant all the above, but we deny that it follows that what tends towards nothing [non-being] perishes, that is, that it reaches nothing. This can be observed in the body also. For any body is part of the sensible world, and for this reason the larger it is and the more space it occupies the nearer it is to the universe; and the more it does this, the greater it is. For the whole is greater than the part. Hence, necessarily, it is less when it is diminished; that is, it suffers a defect when it is lessened. Moreover, it is lessened when something is taken from it by cutting away, and it follows from this that because of such subtraction it tends to nothing. But no cutting away leads to nothing as such. For every part which remains is a body, and whatever is a body occupies a place in some space. Nor would this be possible unless it were to have parts into which it might be cut again and again. Therefore, it can be infinitely diminished through infinite division, and hence can suffer defection and tend towards nothing, although it can never reach nothing. Further, this can be said and understood of space itself and of any interval whatever. For by taking, let us say, a half part from the limits, and always a half part from what is left, the interval is diminished and approaches a limit which yet it can in no mode attain. Accordingly, even less should it be feared that the mind may become nothing, for the mind is indeed better and more lively than the body.

Chapter VIII

Just as That Cannot Be Taken from Body by Which It Is Body, So Neither Can That Be Taken from Mind by Which It Is Mind

But if that which causes the body to be is not in the matter of the body but in the form (which point is established by quite irrefutable reasoning, for a body is greater according as it has better form and is more excellent, and it is less according as it is uglier and is more deformed, which defect occurs not from a taking away of matter, about which enough has been said, but from a privation of form), then this should be questioned and discussed, lest someone assert that mind perishes through defect of form; for seeing that when it is stupid mind is deprived of some of its form, it may be believed that this privation can be increased so much as to deprive the mind of form in every mode, by this misfortune re-

ducing it to nothing and causing it to perish. Hence, if we can succeed in showing that not even the body can be deprived of that by virtue of which it is body, perhaps we shall rightly maintain that the mind can much less have that taken from it by virtue of which it is mind. For whoever considers carefully will admit that any kind of mind whatever must be preferred to every body.

Let this, then, be the beginning of our argument, namely, that no thing makes or begets itself, unless it was before it existed: if the latter is false, the former is true. Again, that which has not been made or begotten, and yet is, must be everlasting. Whoever attributes this nature and this excellence to any body, errs indeed greatly. But why do we dispute? For even were we to attribute it to body we should be forced to attribute it much more to the mind. Thus if any body is everlasting, there is no mind which is not everlasting; seeing that any mind is to be preferred to any body and eternal things to non-eternal things. But if it is truly said that the body is made, it was made by some maker, nor was the maker inferior to body. For an inferior maker would not have power to give to that which he was making whatever it is that makes it what it is. But the maker and the body are not equals, since it is necessary for a maker to have something better for making than that which he makes. For we do not make the absurd statement that the begetter is that thing which is begotten by him. Therefore, a whole body has been made by some force which is more powerful and better, or at least not corporeal. For if a body be made by a body, it cannot be made whole; for it is very true, as we stated in the beginning of this argument, that no thing can be made by itself. Moreover, this force or incorporeal nature being the producer of the whole body preserves the whole by its abiding power. For it did not make a thing and then vanish and desert the thing made. Indeed that substance which is not body is not, if I may speak thus, moved in space so that it can be separated from that substance which is localized; and this effecting strength cannot be idle, but preserves that which it has made, and does not allow it to lack the form by virtue of which it is to whatever extent it is. For since the thing made does not exist per se, if it is abandoned by that through which it exists, it will immediately cease to exist, and we cannot say that when the body was made it received the power to be sufficient by virtue of itself when it is deserted by its maker.

And if this is so, the mind which clearly excels the body has power to a greater degree. And thus the mind is proved immortal, if it can exist per se. For whatever exists thus must be incorruptible, and therefore unable to perish, since nothing abandons itself. But the changeability of the body is manifest, which the whole motion of the entire body indicates adequately. Hence, it is found by those who investigate carefully, in so far as such a nature can be investigated, that ordered changeableness imitates that which is unchangeable. Moreover, that which exists per se has no need of anything, not even of motion, since it has all it needs existing in itself; for all motion is towards another thing which is that which is lacked by that which is moved. Therefore, form is present in the whole body while a better nature which made it provides for and sustains it, hence, that changeability does not take away from a body its being a body, but causes it to pass from one form to another by a well-ordered motion. For not one of its parts is allowed to be reduced to nothing, since that effective power with its force, neither striving nor inactive, aims at a whole, permitting the body to be all which through the power it is, in so far as it is. Consequently, there should be no one so devoid of reason as not to be certain that the mind is better than the body, or when this has been granted, to think that it does not happen to the body that the body is not body, yet happens to the mind that it is not mind. If this does not happen, and a mind cannot exist unless it lives, surely a mind can never die.

Chapter IX

Mind Is Life, and Thus It Cannot Lack Life

If anyone asserts that the mind ought not to fear that destruction in which that which was something becomes nothing, but ought to fear that in which we call those things dead which lack life, let him notice that there is no thing which lacks itself. Moreover, mind is a certain life, so that all which is animated lives. But every inanimate thing which can be animated is understood to be dead, that is, deprived of life. Hence the mind cannot die. For if anything can lack life, this thing is not mind which animates, but a thing which has been animated. If this is absurd, this kind of destruction should be feared much less by the mind, since destruction of life is surely not to be feared. For if the mind dies wholly when life abandons it, that very life which deserts it is understood much better as mind, as now mind is not something deserted by life, but the very life itself which deserted. For whatever dead thing is said to be abandoned by life, is understood to be deserted by the soul. Moreover, this life which deserts the things which die is itself the mind, and it does not abandon itself; hence the mind does not die.

Chapter X

Mind Is Not the Organization of Body

Unless perhaps we ought to believe that life is some organization [temperatio] of the body, as some have held. It would never have seemed so to them if they had been able to see those things which exist truly and which remain unchangeable when the same mind has been freed from the habit of bodies and cleansed. For who has looked well within himself without having experienced that the more earnestly he had thought something, the more he was able to move and draw the attention of the mind away from the senses of the body? If the mind were an organization of the body, this would absolutely not happen. For a thing which did not have a nature of its own and was not a substance, but which like color and shape was in the body inseparably as in a subject, would not try in any way to turn itself away from that same body in order to perceive intelligible things; and only inasmuch as it could do this would it be able to look upon intelligible things and be made by this vision better and more excellent. Indeed, in no way can shape or color, or the very organization of the body, which is a certain mixture of four natures in which the same body consists, turn from the thing in which they are inseparably as in a subject. In comparison with these things, those things which the mind thinks when it turns away from the body are not wholly corporeal, and yet they exist, and that in great degree, for they maintain themselves always in the same mode. For nothing more absurd can be said than that those things which we see with the eyes exist, while those things which we perceive by the intellect do not; for it is mad to doubt that the intellect is incomparably superior to the eyes. Moreover, while these things which are thought maintain themselves in the same mode, when the mind sees them it shows well enough that it is joined to them in a certain miraculous and likewise incorporeal way, that is, not locally. For either they are in it, or it is in them. And whichever one of these is true, either the one is in the other as in a subject, or each one is a substance. But if the first is true, the mind is not in the body as in a subject, as color and shape are, since either it is substance itself or it is in another substance which is not body. Moreover, if the second is true, mind is not in body as in a subject, as color is in body, because the mind is a substance. Further, the organization of a body is in the body as in a subject, just as color is; therefore, mind is not the organization of the body, but the mind is life. No thing deserts itself, and that dies which is deserted by life. Therefore, the mind cannot die.

Chapter XI

Even Though Truth Is the Cause of the Mind, Mind Does Not Perish Through Falsehood, the Contrary of Truth

And so again, if anything should be feared, it is that the mind may perish by defection, that is, may be deprived of the very form of existence. Although I think enough has been said about this, and it has been shown by clear reasoning that this

cannot be done, yet it should also be observed that there is no other reason for this fear except that we have admitted that the stupid mind exists defectively, while the wise mind exists in more certain and fuller essence. But if, as nobody doubts, the mind is most wise when it looks upon truth which is always in the same mode, and clings immovable to it, joined by divine love; and if all things which exist in any mode whatever exist by that essence which exists in the highest and greatest degree; then either the mind exists by virtue of that essence, inasmuch as it does exist, or it exists per se. But if it exists per se, since it is itself the cause of its existing and never deserts itself, it never perishes, as we also argued above. But if we exist from that essence there is need to inquire carefully what thing can be contrary to it, which may rob the mind of being the mind which the essence causes. So, then, what is it? Falsity, perhaps, because the essence is truth? But it is manifest and clearly established to what extent falsity can harm the mind. For can it do more than deceive? And except he live is any deceived? Therefore, falsity cannot destroy the mind. But if what is contrary to truth cannot rob the mind of that being mind which truth gave it (for truth is thus unconquerable) what else may be found which may take from the mind that which is mind? Nothing, surely; for nothing is more able than a contrary to take away that which is made by its contrary.

Chapter XII

There Is No Contrary to the Truth by Which Mind Exists in So Far as It Exists

But suppose we seek the contrary of truth, not inasmuch as it is truth as the contrary of falsity, but inasmuch as it exists in the greatest and highest degree (although truth exists thus to the extent that it is truth, if we call that truth by which all things are true, in whatever degree they may exist, they exist inasmuch as they are true); yet by no means shall I seek to avoid that which this suggests to me so clearly. For if there is no contrary to any essence inasmuch as it is an essence, then much less is there a contrary to that first essence inasmuch as it is essence. Moreover, the antecedent is true. For no essence exists for any other reason than that it exists. Being, moreover, has no contrary except non-being; hence nothing is the contrary of essence. Therefore, in no way can anything exist as a contrary to that substance which exists first and in highest degree. If the mind has its very essence from that essence (for since it does not have it from itself [ex se] it cannot have it otherwise than from that thing which is superior to the mind itself); then there is no thing by which it may lose its existence (being), because there is nothing contrary to that thing from which it has it. Hence the mind cannot cease to exist. But since the mind has wisdom because of turning to that by virtue of which it exists, so also when it turns away it can lose this wisdom. For turning away is the contrary of turning toward. But what it has from that to which there is no contrary is not a thing which it can lose. Therefore, it cannot perish.

Chapter XIII

Nor Is Mind Changed into Body

Here perhaps some question may appear as to whether the mind which does not perish is not changed into a lower essence. For it can appear to some, and not unjustly, that this reasoning proves that the mind cannot reach nothing, yet can be perhaps changed into body. For if what was formerly mind becomes body it will not yet be wholly non-existent. But this is impossible unless the mind desires it or else is compelled by another. Yet mind will not necessarily be able to be body, even if it desires it, or if it is compelled. For if it is body it follows that it desires this or is compelled. But it does not follow that if it desires or is compelled, it is body. Moreover, it will never desire to be body: for all the mind desires in regard to body is that it may possess it, or make it live, or fashion it in a certain manner, or look out for it in some way or other. Moreover, none of these things is possible if

mind is not better than body. But if mind is body, it follows that it will not be better than body. Therefore, it will not wish to be body. Nor is there any surer proof of this than when the mind questions itself about this point. For thus the mind easily discovers that it has no desire except for some action, either knowing or sensing, or only living to the fullest extent of its power.

But if it is compelled to be body, by what, pray, is it compelled? Whatever it is it must surely be more powerful than mind, hence it cannot be compelled by body itself; for no body can in any way be more powerful than mind. Moreover, a more powerful mind compels only that which is set under its power, and no mind can in any way be set under the power of another mind except by the former's own desire. Hence, one mind does not compel another mind more than the desires of the other allow. Moreover, it has been said that mind cannot have desire to be body. Also it is clear that the mind attains no satisfaction of its desire while it loses all desire, which happens when it is made body. Therefore, a mind cannot be compelled to become body by one whose only right to compel lies in the desires of the one compelled. Then whatever mind has another mind in its power must prefer having it to having a body in its power, and must wish to promote its goodness or to have power over evil. Therefore, it will not wish it to be body.

Finally, the mind which compels either is animal or it lacks body. But if it lacks body it is not in this world. And if it is thus, it is supremely good and cannot wish another to suffer such a wicked change. But if it is animal, either the mind it compels is animal or it is not. But if it is not, it cannot be compelled to anything by another. For none is more powerful than that which exists in the greatest degree. On the other hand, if it is body, again it is forced through body to whatever extent it is forced. But who believes that in any way such a change can be made in mind through body? For it would be made if the body were greater than it; although no matter what it is to which it is compelled by body it is not compelled wholly through body, but is compelled through its own desires, about which enough has been said. Moreover, that which is better than a rational soul is God, as all agree. He surely looks after the soul, and, therefore, the soul cannot be forced by Him to be changed into body.

Chapter XIV

Nor Is the Strength of the Mind Diminished by Sleep or Any Other Similar Affection of the Body

Hence, if the mind does not suffer this change by its own will, or because it is compelled by another, by what means can it suffer it? Or, because sleep for the most part overtakes us against our will, should it be feared that by some such defect the mind may be changed to body? As if when our limbs are overwhelmed by sleep to say that the mind is made weaker in some sense. Sensible things only it does not sense, because whatever causes sleep pertains to the body and works in the body. Sleep lulls and shuts off the corporeal senses so soundly that the soul submits with pleasure to such a change of the body. Such a change is according to nature and refreshes the body after its labors, yet it does not take from the mind the power of sensing and thinking. For it still has images of sensible things at hand of such evident similarity that at the time they cannot be distinguished from the things of which they are the images. If the mind thinks anything, it is as true in sleeping as in waking. For, to give an example, if it should argue to itself in a dream, and following true principles in argument should learn something, when it is awakened the same principles remain immutable, although other things may be found false, such as the place where the argument seemed to have occurred, the person with whom it seemed to have been held, even, as far as sound is concerned, the words themselves by which it seemed the argument was made, and other things of this sort. Likewise when

these things are perceived and discussed by those who are awake, they pass away and in no sense attain the eternal presence of true principles. From this it is inferred that when a body changes as in sleep the soul's use of that body can be diminished, but not its own life.

Chapter XV

Again, Mind Cannot Be Changed into Body

Finally, however much the soul is joined to a body occupying space, still it is not joined locally. The soul is prior to the body in connection with those supreme and eternal principles which survive unchangeably and are not contained in space; and the soul's connection is not only prior but also greater; as much prior as it is nearer, and for the same reason as much greater as it is better than body. And this nearness is not in place but in the order of nature. According to this order it is understood that the supreme essence bestows form upon the body through the soul by which it exists in whatever degree it does exist. Therefore, the body subsists through the soul, and it exists to the extent that it is animated, whether universally, as the world, or particularly, as some animal or other within the world. Therefore, the conclusion was that a soul would become body through a soul, or else not at all. Since it does not become body, and the soul remains soul in that in which it is the soul, the body subsists through the soul which gives it form and does not take this form away; hence the soul cannot be changed into body. For if it does not give up the form which it takes from the Supreme Good, it does not become body through that form; and if it does not become body through that, either it does not become body at all, or else takes a form as near the Supreme Good as soul. But if, when it became body, it assumed a form as near the Supreme Good as soul, that form would be a soul; for this is important, that the soul is better to the extent to which it takes a form nearer the Supreme

Good. Moreover, body would take a form of the corporeal order even if it did not take its form through soul. For if nothing intervened it would still take a form in this order. Nor is there found anything which exists between the Supreme Life which is wisdom and truth unchangeable and that remote thing which is made alive (that is, body) except the soul which makes the body live. If the soul gives form to body, so that body may exist to the extent that it does exist, it does not take the form away by giving. Moreover, it takes the soul into the body by transmutation. Therefore, the soul does not become body, either per se, because body is not made by soul unless the soul remains, or through another, because not except by giving form is body made through soul, and by taking away form soul would be changed into body, if it were changed.

Chapter XVI

Nor Even Is the Rational Soul Changed into the Irrational. The Whole Soul Is in the Body as a Whole and in Each Part

Likewise it can be said that the rational soul is not changed into the irrational soul or life. For the irrational soul, even were it not held in a lower order by the rational soul, would nevertheless assume the same form it does assume and be moved as it is. Therefore, more powerful things receive form from the Supreme Excellence and give it to things in the natural order. And when they give, surely, they do not take away. And to whatever extent the things which are inferior exist, they exist because the form in which they exist is given to them by those more powerful than they. And, indeed, the more powerful are also better. For to these natures it has been granted, not that through greater mass they have more power over things of lesser mass, but that without any increase of local magnitude they are more powerful than and better than the lower forms. In this way the soul is better than and greater than the body. Therefore, since the body, as has

been said, subsists through the soul, the soul can in no way be changed into body; for no body is made except by receiving its form from the soul. The soul, if it became body, would become body through losing form, not through receiving it; therefore, it is not possible, unless perhaps the soul be contained in a place and joined locally to the body. For if this were true, although the soul is more perfect in form, perhaps a greater mass could change the soul into its lower form, just as the greater air changes the lesser fire. But it is not true. Indeed, every mass which occupies a place is not a separate whole in each of its parts, but the whole consists of all the parts. Consequently, one part of such a whole is in one place, and another in another. But the soul is present as a whole not only in the entire mass of a body, but also in every least part of the body at the same time. For the soul senses the suffering of a part of a body as a whole, and yet not in the whole body. For when there is a pain in the foot the eye turns, the tongue speaks, the hand moves forward. This would not happen unless the soul which senses in these parts, also senses in the foot, nor could it while absent sense what was happening there. For it is not to be believed that it happens through any agent of communication which does not sense what it communicates; for the suffering which occurs does not run through the whole extent of the mass in such a way as to involve all the other parts of the soul which are elsewhere. Rather, the whole soul senses what happens to the foot in particular, and only senses it at the place at which it happens. The whole soul, therefore, is present simultaneously in each part, and simultaneously senses in each. Yet the soul is not wholly present in the way in which whiteness or any other quality of this sort is wholly present in each part of a body. For what a body suffers in one part by change of whiteness cannot pertain to the whiteness which is in another part. Hence, it is shown that a mass itself is differentiated according as its parts are differentiated. But we have proved above that this is not the case with the soul as it senses.

CHAPTER 20

Fridugisus of Tours

Very little is known of Fridugisus (also Fridigis, Fredegis, Fredegisus) the deacon, including his date of birth. He was of Anglo-Saxon origin and studied under Alcuin at York (England). In circa 796 he ventured to Charlemagne's palace school in the capacity as a teacher, where he joined his mentor. Upon Alcuin's death in 804, Fridugisus succeeded him as abbot of St. Martin of Tours. He was appointed chancellor in 819 under Charlemagne's son, Louis the Pious, and continued in this capacity until 832. He died in 834. His only extant writing is his *Epistola de nihil et tenebris* to Charlemagne, composed during his tenure at the palace school.

Fridugisus of Tours on the Being of Nothing and Shadows

Fridugisus establishes the origins of the universe from an analysis of language. It is via such an analysis that he demonstrates that something, the universe, can come from nothing. The word 'nothing' is a definite noun, and therefore there must be some thing which is its referent. That is to say, there is some definite thing which is the referent of the word 'nothing'. So 'nothing' refers to something. What is that something? It is nothing. Where did that something we call the universe come from? It must have come from that thing we call nothing. The creation of the universe is thus explained.

In a similar vein, Fridugisus argues that 'shadows' (or 'darkness') is a definite noun. Furthermore, when a definite noun appears as the subject in a positive declarative statement, it must be the case that the referent of the definite noun exists. He cites examples of such statements from the Bible: "...there was darkness over the deep" (Genesis 1:2). Darkness is as much something as is light. An analysis of language, therefore, dispels any and all mysteries surrounding such notions as darkness and nothing.

It should be noted, however, that the word 'nothing' is an indefinite noun and as such undermines Fridugisus' analysis. 'Nothing' means no thing; that is, the absence of thingness. It is because 'nothing' is an indefinite noun that the claim "something can come from nothing" is logically impossible and therefore absurd.

LETTER TO CHARLEMAGNE
ON THE BEING *(SUBSTANTIA)* OF NOTHING AND SHADOWS

On the Being of Nothing

Fridugisus the deacon, to all the faithful of God and of our most fair lord Charles, gathered together at his sacred palace.

I diligently turned it over [in my mind] and considered the matter, and at last it seemed right to me to undertake the question about nothing, which has been bandied about by a great many people for a long time, but which they have abandoned without [seriously] discussing or examining it, as if it were impossible to explain. Breaking the powerful bonds in which it seemed to be tangled up, I have resolved [the question] and untied [the knot]. Dispersing the cloud, I have brought [the matter] back into the light, and have taken care that it be entrusted to the memory of posterity for all ages to come.

Now the question is as follows: Is nothing something or not?

If one answers "It seems to me to be nothing", his very denial, as he supposes it, compels him to say that something is nothing, since he says "It seems to me to be nothing", which is as if he were to say, "It seems to me that nothing is something". But if it seems to be something, it cannot appear not to be in any way at all. Hence, the only remaining alternative is that it seems to be something.

But if this is the answer given, "It seems to me to be nothing and not something",[1] this answer is to be countered first by reasoning, to the extent that human reason allows, and then by authority—not just any [authority], but only by divine [authority], which alone is [truly] an authority and [which] alone reaches unshakable certitude.

Let us proceed therefore by reason. Every finite name signifies something. For

instance, 'man', 'stone', 'wood'. As soon as these [words] are said, at the same time we understand the things they signify. Thus, the name 'man', uttered without any differentiating [word], designates the universality of men. 'Stone' and 'wood' include their generality in the same way. So, if 'nothing' is a name at all, as the grammarians claim [it is], it is a finite name. But every finite name signifies something. Now it is impossible that this finite something is not anything. It is impossible, therefore, that nothing, which is finite, is not anything. And in this way it can be proved that it exists.

Again, 'nothing' is a significative word. But every signifying is related to what it signifies. [Hence,] on these grounds too it is proved that nothing is unable not to be anything [at all].

Again, another [argument]. Every signifying is a signifying of that which is. But 'nothing' signifies something. Therefore, 'nothing'-'s signifying is of that which is— that is, of an existing thing.

Now because we have provided only a few points from reason to demonstrate that nothing is not only something but even something great, although nevertheless countless such examples could be brought into the discussion, we wish to turn [now] to divine authority, which is the safeguard and fixed foundation of reason.

For indeed the whole divinely instructed Church, which arose from the side of Christ, was raised on the food of his most sacred flesh and the drink of his precious blood, [and] was educated from the cradle in the mysteries of secret things, confesses that it holds with unshakable faith that the divine power produced earth, water, air and fire, along with light and the angels and man's soul, out of "nothing".

The edge of the mind, therefore, must be lifted up to the authority of so great a summit, which no reason [can] shake, no arguments [can] refute, no powers can oppose.

For this is [the authority] that declares that the things first and foremost among creatures are produced out of nothing. Therefore, nothing is a great and distinguished something. It cannot be assessed how great is that from which so many and so distinguished things come, since not one of the things generated from it can be assessed for what it is worth or be defined.

For who has measured the nature of the elements in detail? Who has grasped the being and nature of light, of angelic nature, or of the soul?

Therefore, if we are unable to comprehend by human reason these things I [just] mentioned, how shall we [ever] reach [the knowledge of] how great and what kind of thing it is from which they draw their origin and their genus?

I could have added a great many other things. But we think that, from the points [above], enough has [already] penetrated into the breasts of whoever can be taught.

On the Being of Shadows

Since I have appropriately put an end [to the previous discussion] after saying the [few] brief things [above], I have next turned [my] attention to [other] matters that must be explained, [matters] that have not undeservedly seemed to inquisitive readers [to be] worth asking about.

There is the opinion, then, among some people that shadows do not exist, and that it is impossible that they exist. How easily this [opinion] can be refuted, the prudent reader will recognize from the authority of Sacred Scripture, once it has been brought into the discussion.

So let us see what the story in the book of Genesis thinks about this.

It says, "And the shadows were over the face of the deep" (Gen. 1:2).

If they did not exist, by what inference is it said that they "were" [over the face of the deep]? He who says that shadows "are", by affirming a thing, posits [it]; but he who [says they] "are not", by denying the thing, takes [it] away. For example, when we say "Man is" we affirm a thing— namely, man. When we say "Man is not", by denying the thing—namely, man—we take [it] away. For a substantial verb[2] has it in its nature that, whatever subject it is joined to without a negation, it makes known the being of that subject. Therefore, in saying 'were' in the quotation "the shadows were over the face of the deep", a thing is affirmed that no negation separates or divides from being.

Again, 'shadows' is the subject, [and] 'were' makes [it] known. For it makes [it] known by declaring that shadows in some way are.

Observe how invincible authority, accompanied by reason, together with reason acknowledging authority, declare the same thing, namely, that shadows exist.

But, although the above points, given for the sake of example, are enough to demonstrate what we claimed, nevertheless in order that there remain no opportunity for enemies to contradict [us], let us bring out into the open a few [other] passages from Scripture, gathering [them] from among the many [possible], [so that,] shaken by the fear of them, [such people] will not dare to hurl their ridiculous words against them any more.

When the Lord punished Egypt with terrible plagues because of [its] oppressing the people of Israel, he enveloped it with shadows so thick they could be felt. Not only did they deprive men's sight of [its] objects, but because of their density, they could even be touched by the hands. Now whatever can be touched and felt must be. Whatever must be, it is impossible for it not to be. And so it is impossible for shadows not to be because it is necessary for [them] to be, as is proved from the fact that it[3] can be felt.

Moreover, the fact is not to be ignored that when the Lord made the division into light and shadows, he called the light "day" and the shadows "night" (Gen. 1:5). For if the name 'day' signifies something, the name 'night' cannot help but signify something. Now 'day' signifies the light, and light is a great something. For the day both is and is something great. What then? Do shadows signify nothing when the name 'night' is imposed on them by the same maker who imposed the title 'day' on the light?[4] Is divine authority to be shaken [in this way]? No indeed! It is easier for heaven and earth to pass away than for divine authority to be moved from its station.

The creator stamped names on the things he made, so that each thing would be known when it is called by its name. Neither did he form any thing without its [corresponding] word, nor did he establish any word unless that for which it was established existed. If it were the case [that God had established a word with no corresponding thing, the word] would seem entirely superfluous. And it is wicked to say God has done that. But if it is wicked to say God has established something superfluous, [then] the name God imposed on the shadows cannot appear in any way to be superfluous. But if it is not superfluous, [then] it is in accordance with [some] method. And if it [is] in accordance with a method, it [is] also necessary, since it is needed in order to distinguish the thing signified by it. And so it is certain that God has established things and names, which are necessary for one another, in accordance with a method.

And the holy prophet David, filled with the Holy Spirit and knowing that "shadows" does not mean something empty and like a wind, plainly expresses [the fact that] they are something. Thus he says, "He sent shadows" (Psalms 104:28). If they do not exist, how are they sent? What is can be sent, and can be sent to where it is not. But what is not cannot be sent anywhere, since it is nowhere. Therefore, the shadows are said to have been sent because they were.

Again, the passage: "He put the shadows as his hiding place" (Psalms 17:12). Of course he put what existed, and he put [it] a certain way, so that he put the shadows, which were his hiding place.[5]

Again, another [passage]: "Like his shadows" (Psalms 138:12). Here it is indicated that they are in [his] possession, and therefore it is made plain that they exist. For everything that is possessed exists. But the shadows are in [his] possession. Therefore, they exist.

Although these passages are enough, as many and as great as they are, and offer a secure fortress against all attacks, so that with an easy rebuff they can turn missiles back on those who threw them, nevertheless certain passages from the steadfastness of the Gospel should be required [too].

Therefore, let us set down the words of the Savior himself. "The children of the kingdom," he says, "will be cast forth into the shadows outside" (Matt. 8:12). Now observe that he calls the shadows "outside". For 'out' (extra), from which 'outside' (exterius) is derived, signifies a place. Therefore, when he says "outside", he is indicating that shadows have locations. There would not be shadows "outside" unless there were also [others] "inside". Now whatever is outside must be in a place; what does not exist is nowhere. Therefore, the shadows outside not only exist but also have locations.

Also, in the Lord's passion the evangelist declares that shadows were made from the sixth hour of the day until the ninth hour. Since they were made, how can they be said not to exist? What has been made cannot be caused not to have been made; rather what does not always exist, and is never made, never exists. But shadows are made. Hence it cannot be brought about that they do not exist.[6]

Again, another [passage]: "If the light that is in you is shadows, how great those shadows will be!" (Matt. 6:23). I believe no one doubts that quantity is attributed to bodies, which are divided [from one another] by quantity. And quantity is accidental to bodies. But accidents are either in a subject or predicated of a subject. Therefore, in the quotation 'how great those shadows will be', quantity is shown to be in a subject.[7] Hence it is inferred, by a persuasive argument, that shadows not only exist, they are also corporeal.

And so I have taken the trouble to write to Your Dignity and Prudence these few points collected from reason and authority together, so that, adhering fast and immovably to them, no false opinion will be able to seduce you to stray from the path of truth.

But if perhaps something in disagreement with this reasoning of ours should be said by anyone, you will, by having recourse to this [letter] as if to a rule, be able to overthrow foolish contrivances on the basis of its statements.

The end

NOTES

1. The second clause in this formulation is intended to prevent the kind of objection raised to the first answer, in the preceding paragraph. In other words, I take both of these answers to be on the negative side of the question.
2. A "substantial verb" is a form of the verb 'to be' when not used as a copula—that is, when it means "to exist". Other verbs, which can be resolved into a copula plus a participle (e.g., runs = is + running), are called "adjectival verbs". The exact metaphysical importance of this distinction is of course subject to discussion. But the terminology itself was standard.
3. The text has the singular here, presumably referring to 'whatever can be touched and felt' two sentences earlier. One would have expected a plural, agreeing with 'shadows'.
4. There seems to be some confusion here about what is signifying what. The point would be clearer, and the parallel with the fact that 'day' signifies the light would be stronger, if the text read: "Are shadows nothing when the name 'night' is imposed on them by the same creator . . ."
5. The general point of the paragraph is clear enough, but I find the exact sense a little shaky.
6. Presumably this is not supposed to mean that things that are made cannot be destroyed, but only that what is made exists, and nothing can change that fact.
7. As it stands, this is of course a blatant non sequitur. But the words 'or at least predicated of a subject' could be added to the sentence without spoiling the point of the paragraph.

CHAPTER 21

John Scotus Eriugena

John Scotus Eriugena was born in Ireland about 810. "Eriugena" means belonging to the people of Erin. He was not a Scot, as "Scotus" would lead one to believe, since in the ninth century Ireland was known as *Scotia Maior* and the Irish as *Scoti*. He was educated in an Irish monastery, where he became proficient in Greek. During this period the study of Greek was peculiar to Irish monasteries. By 850 he had made his way to the court of the Frankish emperor Charles the Bald, where he occupied a prominent position teaching at the Palatine School. His first work of note, *De Praedestinatione*, was written at the request of Hincmar, bishop of Rheims, to settle a theological dispute concerning predestination. Rather than quelling the controversy, the work brought its author under suspicion of heresy. In 858, at the request of his patron, John Scotus began to translate from Greek to Latin the writings of the Christian Neoplatonist known as the Pseudo-Dionysius. In the process Eriugena prepared a series of commentaries on them as well. He also published translations of the *De Hominis Opificio* of St. Gregory of Nyssa and the *Ambigua* of Maximus the Confessor. In addition, he wrote commentaries on the Gospel according to John and on the *De Consolatione Philosophiae* of Boethius. His own monumental systematic treatise, the *Periphyseon*, or *De Divisione Naturae*, was most likely composed between 862 and 866. The place and date of his death are unknown. However, data suggest that he did not outlive Charles the Bold, who died in 877.

John Scotus Eriugena on the Division of Nature

In the *Periphyseon*, or *On the Division of Nature*, John Scotus divides nature into four species, namely (1) Nature which creates and is not created, (2) Nature which is created and creates, (3) Nature which is created and does not create, and (4) Nature which neither creates nor is created. From this it is apparent he means by Nature the sum total of Reality. This Reality includes God and the metaphysical (or supernatural) world as well as the natural world. There is but one Reality by whom and with whom all participate as emanations of God. From this it would be tempting to conclude that Eriugena was promoting a doctrine of pantheistic monism, but such is not the case, as is indicated in Book II, where he denies that creatures are actually a part of God or that God is a genus of which creatures are a species. The *Periphyseon* is a difficult work to interpret because of its complexity. Not content with grappling with isolated problems, John Scotus produced a system, the first great speculative system of the Middle

Ages, and throughout it he attempts to enunciate Christian teaching and the philosophical doctrine of Augustine as interpreted by the Pseudo-Dionysius.

There are two major theses of Book I of the *Periphyseon*: (1) God is the first principle;
that is, He is the beginning, the uncaused cause from whom all things are made. He
is the medium through which all things move. And He constitutes the final cause of
all that is in Nature for He is Nature. God is divine transcendence whereby His essence
and existence and His act of creation (of nature) are one and the same. This constitutes
pantheistic monism if Nature is understood in its ordinary sense. Notwithstanding
his use of some misleading examples, Eriugena does not intend to depart from established Christian doctrine, in which there is a real distinction between God and creatures. God is Nature which creates and is not created.

(2) We come to a knowledge of God by both negative and affirmative methods. The
former approaches knowledge by an understanding of what He is not. For example,
we cannot truly predicate of God the ten categories of Aristotle. Nor can anything that
is predicated of purely material things be truly predicated of God. It is via the negative
way that we come to know God by knowing what He is not. We come to know God
by the positive way when we predicate of Him those things which are in the sense
that the cause is manifested in the effect. In other words, we have knowledge of the
effects of God's creation. We can extrapolate upon such effects and by so doing come
to an understanding of what God is. This positive way is Platonic in nature. For
example, we know what wisdom is. There are degrees of (created) wisdom. From this
we come to understand that such knowledge is made possible only if there is Perfect
Wisdom (tantamount to a Platonic Form). Such Perfect Wisdom is not merely an Idea
in the mind of God. It is not something predicated of God as some accident. Rather,
Perfect or Super-Wisdom is part of what God is. Since God's being and essence are
one and the same, Perfect or Super-Wisdom constitutes (part of) the divine being's
essence. But God is not a sum total of parts, He is simply the One, the One who created
but is not created. Such are the ways by which we come to know God.

Nature which is created and creates consists of archetypes or exemplary causes of
creatures existing in the divine mind. They owe their existence to the Word or Logos.
"In the beginning was the Word: the Word was with God and the Word was God"
(John 1:1). The Word is logically prior to the archetypes, and therefore they are not,
strictly speaking, coeternal with Him. Yet He has never existed without them.

Nature which is created and does not create pertains to the world of creatures
existing outside the divine mind. They constitute and embody the personal manifestation of the deity or "theophany". Eriugena calls these creatures *participations*. They
participate in the primordial causes and function below the ultimate Principle and
above their multiple effects. This is most reminiscent of Neoplatonic emanation theory.

Finally, Nature which neither creates nor is created is God qua final cause, the end
and goal of the creative process. This end is the reuniting of the whole of creation with
God. This includes man, the sinner who becomes one with God by being transmuted
and spiritualized. With that the system is complete.

The reading for this chapter was selected from Book II and concerns the nature of
the Trinity. Eriugena follows the Greek (as opposed to the Latin) in his exegesis of the
problem. The Trinity consists of three substances or three persons. Yet they are identical with regard to their essence (*ousia*). It is the identity of essence whereby the Father,
Son, and Holy Ghost are one and the same. Now according to Holy Scripture, man is
created in the image and likeness of God. This can only mean, however, that man's

nature manifested by the operations of his soul is so created. "There are three universal motions of the soul, of which the first is of mind, the second of reason, the third of sense. . . . the soul subsists in her motions and her motions subsist in her. For she is by nature simple and indivisible, and is differentiated only by the substantial differences of her motions." The operations of the soul parallel the personages of the Trinity. Human intellect corresponds to the Father, reason to the Son, and sense to the Holy Spirit.

"ON THE TRINITY" FROM *PERIPHYSEON*

Book II; 561C–579D

Nutritor.[1] So the principal causes of all things are co-eternal with God and with the Beginning in which they were made. For if God does not in any way precede the Beginning, that is, the Word begotten by Himself and from Himself, and the Word itself does not in any way precede the causes of things that are created in it, it follows that all these, I mean, God the Father and the Word and the causes created in it, are co-eternal.

Alumnus. They are not in all respects co-eternal. For while we believe that the Son is in all respects co-eternal with the Father, those things which the Father makes in the Son we call co-eternal with the Son, but not in all respects co-eternal. They are co-eternal in the sense that the Son was never without the primordial causes of natures created in Him, and yet these causes are not in all respects co-eternal with Him in Whom they are created. For (things) made cannot be co-eternal with their maker because the maker precedes the (things) which he makes. For those (things) which are in all respects co-eternal are so united to one another that neither can endure without the other *because they are co-essential. But since the maker and the (thing) made are not co-essential, they are not necessarily co-eternal. They are, however, necessarily correlative and simultaneous, for a maker without a* (thing)

made is not a maker, and a (thing) made without a maker is not a (thing) made. Hence it follows that our reason for saying that the primordial causes of things are co-eternal with God is that they always subsist in God without any beginning in time, (and our reason for saying) that they are not in all respects co-eternal with God is that they receive the beginning of their being not from themselves but from their Creator. But the Creator Himself receives the beginning of His being from no one because He alone is true eternity, without any beginning and any end since He Himself is the Beginning of all things and their End. [For that is not true eternity which receives the beginning of its being from something else, but is a participation of true eternity which is ἄναρχος, that is, without any beginning. But every creature begins to be, because there was (a time) when it was not. It was in its causes when it was not in its effects. Therefore it is not in all respects co-eternal with true eternity].

But if within the very Cause of all causes, I mean in the Trinity, there is understood (to be) some kind of precedence—for the Deity which begets and which sends forth is prior to the Deity which is begotten and the Deity which proceeds from the begetter and the begotten, although it is one indivisible Deity—, is it surprising or incredible that the Cause of all causes should precede all things of which it is the Cause, and (yet) that they have been in it immutably and eternally without any beginning in time? If, then, the Father precedes the ori-

From John Scotus Eriugena, *Periphyseon*, translated by I. P. Sheldon-Williams and revised by John J. O'Meara (Montreal: Éditions Bellarmin, 1987), pp. 163–184. Reprinted by permission of Éditions Bellarmin.

gins of the things which He made in the Son in the way in which a maker precedes (the things) which he has made, and the Word precedes (the things) which the Father has made in it in the way in which the art of the artist precedes those reasons which are created in it by the artist, why should not the Holy Spirit Who is borne above the abyss of the primordial causes which the Father has created in the Word be understood to precede [those (things) above which it is borne]? Therefore the Holy Spirit, by virtue of His eternity, surpasses and precedes the mystical waters which he eternally ferments and fertilizes in Himself.

But if these are resonable answers to the question concerning the creation of the beginnings, I beg you to explain clearly what is the special role, so to say, which seems to be attributable to the Father, what to the Word, what to the Holy Spirit. For although the operation of the three Substances of the Divine Goodness is believed and understood to be one and the same and common (to all), yet it must be said that it is not without any difference (in each) or property (of each). For there are things which are attributed by God's holy word to each of the Persons as though by proper right, examples of which are doubtless known to you [but, to make use of a few examples, let us hear from the mouth of God the property of the Father: "When the fulness of time had come God sent His Son, made of a woman, made under the Law;" the property of the Son: "Who being in the form of God thought it not robbery to be equal to God and yet emptied Himself, receiving the form of a servant", and so forth; the property of the Holy Spirit in administering the Incarnation of the Word is shown in the Gospel when the angel says of the Holy Mother of God, "That which is born in her is of the Holy Spirit"].

N. Your thought seems to me to be pursuing its investigation along right lines. For it does not, in my opinion, deviate from the truth, and therefore I shall attempt an inquiry into that which you ask of me, under the guidance of Him Who enlightens and encourages us to inquire of Him. It seems to me, then, that the divine word attributes to God the Father the property of creating natures in their causes. For it says: "In the Beginning God made heaven and earth," (and) again in another place: "Thou madest all (things) in (Thy) Wisdom," (and) again: "Thou Who madest the world out of unformed matter," and in another place: "All things whatsoever the Lord willed He made in heaven and earth, in the sea and in all the depths," and (there are) a thousand other (instances). But it (also) asserts that it is in the Word that the substantive reasons of things are created, as these [same] passages which have been quoted witness: "In the Beginning God made heaven and earth," and, "Thou madest all things in (Thy) Wisdom." For Beginning is not one thing and Wisdom another and the Word another, but by all these names the only begotten Son of God in Whom and through Whom all things are made by the Father is properly signified. *The Apostle also says*: "In Whom we live and move and have our being" [(and) again: "He is the image of the invisible God, the Firstborn of every creature, in Whom all (things) are created in the heavenly (regions) and on earth, whether visible or invisible, whether Thrones or Dominations or Principalities and Powers. All were created through Him and in Him"]. Finally, the distribution of all the causes which the Father created in His Word generically and essentially we find allotted by the [same] divine word to the Holy Spirit. For if to Him, as the Apostle witnesses, is given the sharing-out and-distribution of divine gifts, why should He not also be given the division of the primordial causes (which are) substantially created in the Word of God? For he says: "To one is given through the Spirit the speaking of wisdom, [to another the speaking of knowledge] according to the same Spirit, to another faith in the same Spirit, but to another the gifts of healing in the same Spirit, but to another the working of miracles, to another prophecies, to another the discerning of spirits, to another (divers) kinds of language, to another interpreta-

tions of *discourses*. But all these are operated by one and the same Spirit, Who dispenses to each as He wills that which is
proper (for each)." This we can also demonstrate from the Book of Genesis where it
is written: "And the Spirit of God fer-
mented the waters." For what is to be understood by the Spirit of God fermenting,
fertilizing (and) nourishing the waters of
the primordial causes except the distribution and ordering of those things which in
the Word are made simply, as of one form
and one (substance), into the differences of
all the genera (and) species and wholes
[and] parts and individuals? [And if no one
of sound faith and right understanding
hesitates to affirm that the spiritual gifts
which the prophet Isaiah prophesied
would rest upon the Head of the Church,
which is Christ, are distributed by no other
than the Holy Spirit upon God the Incarnate Word, what wonder if upon the
Church, which is His Body, the same Spirit
should divide and bestow not only the gifts
of grace through Christ, but also the gifts
of nature through the same Christ?

Moreover upon every creature visible
and invisible He bestows the gift of essence
so that those things which possess only being should be, to living things the gift of
life by which they live, to sentient things
the gift of sense by which they perceive
sensibly, to rational beings the gift of reason by which through the act of reasoning
they inquire into and find out the natures
of things truly and diligently, to intellectual
beings the gift of intellect by which they
revolve in an ineffable motion and marvellous return about their God, about the
Cause, that is, of all gifts, in a manner beyond knowledge and surpassing every
creature.] *For* the symbolic candlestick of
the prophet Zechariah, to say nothing of
that of Moses [which symbolizes the same
thing], signifies the Church. But its lamp
which is placed above it is the Light of the
Father and of truth "which lighteth every
man that cometh into the world", our Lord
Jesus Christ Who, because He was conceived and born and manifested in the
world for us and out of us in the nature of
our flesh, is called the lamp above the
candlestick of the Church; for by nature it
is the substantial Wisdom and Word of
God the Father, upon Whom rest first (of
all), humanly speaking, because He is the
Head of the universal body of the Church,
the gifts of the Holy Spirit, which are usually signified by the number seven.

For the divine gifts which are distributed
through the Holy Spirit to the Church,
since their distribution by the one Spirit
starts from the Church's Head, I mean
Christ, are usually signified by the name of
the Spirit Himself. For by nature He cannot
be called a gift but the Distributor of gifts,
and He is called sevenfold for the reason
that He divides among the Church universally and particularly the plenitude of the
divine gifts to which the number seven refers. And rightly so; for the Spirit Himself
is co-essential with [the Father and] the Son
in respect of His Divinity, upon Whom [I
mean, upon the Son] in His Humanity He
causes the divine gifts which He distributes
to rest. "And," says [the prophet], "the
Spirit of God shall rest upon Him," as
though he said openly: And there shall rest
upon Him the gifts which the Spirit of God
divides: "the spirit of wisdom and understanding; the spirit of counsel and strength;
the spirit of knowledge and piety; and He
shall be filled with the spirit of the fear of
the Lord", and all these spirits, that is to
say, all these gifts of the Spirit, the Head of
the Church, which is Christ, first receives
in His Humanity and then shares through
His Spirit with [His Body] (, that is,) the
Church. But the Holy Spirit Himself, as He
essentially subsists [in] the nature of God
the Father, so also essentially is [in] the nature of the Son since *as substance* He proceeds from the Father through the Son in-
effably born, and therefore the gifts which
He distributes are not only His but the
Father's from Whom He proceeds and the
Son's from Whom and through Whom He
proceeds.

And do not suppose that the manifold
gifts of the Spirit by which the manifold
seeds of sin are expelled from the Church
and utterly destroyed are the only ones dis-

tributed through the Spirit. For wisdom takes away unwisdom, understanding removes stupidity, counsel destroys indiscretion, strength dissolves weakness, science abolishes ignorance, piety drives out impiety and the wickedness of the works (that are wrought) in it, fear banishes the blindness of contempt; *but* also in addition to these gifts of grace by which the Church is purified and edified as well as illuminated and perfected, [the donations] of all good (things) which are both of (the Church's) essence and its natural accidents come, *as none of the faithful doubts*, from no other source than the Cause of all good (things), I mean, from the Father, from Whom are all things; through the Son, in Whom are all things; and [their] distribution *is* [through none other] but the Holy Spirit, Who divides all [among all as He wills].

"Every good gift and every perfect boon", says the theologian, "cometh down from the Father of Lights." What is more explicit, what more obvious? From no other source, he says, than the Father of Lights, that is, from the Father of all good (things), those which are of nature as well as those which are of grace. For well does he call lights all the gifts which come down from the unbegotten Light through the begotten Light, and [through] the proceeding Light to the limits of the capacity [of nature and of the bountifulness of grace] are divided in the substance of every essence, whether general or specific or individual. For that which the Apostle appears to say as though to man alone, "O, man, what hast thou that thou didst not receive?", can be universally addressed to every creature whether visible or invisible. For there is no created nature which has <anything> but that which it has received from the creative <nature>. For [as we said before] if it is, it receives from that its being; if it lives, from that its life; if it is sentient, from that its sensible perception; if it enjoys reason, from that its reason; if it possesses intellect, from that its intellect; and a thousand other things of that kind. If, then, nothing is known to be in the nature of created things except what is given by the Creator, it fol-

lows that the creature, whether in essence or accident, is nothing else but the <gifts and> boons of the Creator. But the divine word reserves the distribution of boons, as a kind of property, to the Holy Spirit. Therefore all things which the Father makes in the Son the Holy Spirit distributes and divides as the property of each as He wills.

Do you then see how the divine word is understood to give to each of the Substances or Persons of the Divine Goodness as it were its (special) property? For to the Father it gives the making of all things, to the Word it gives the coming into being eternally in Him of the primordial causes of things universally, essentially (and) simply, to the [Holy] Spirit it gives the distribution of the primordial causes made in the Son and the fertilization into their effects, that is to say, [into] the genera and species, the individuals and differences, whether of the celestial <and spiritual> essences which (either) are wholly without body or adhere to the very pure and spiritual bodies (which are) made from the simplicity of [the general] elements, or of the sensible (beings) of this visible world, (whether) of the universals or of the particulars which occupy separate places and move through times and are differentiated by quality and quantity. [For one would not unreasonably agree that the primordial causes are without body at all, whether visible or invisible, and without quality or quantity in themselves. But we call an invisible body the simple subsistence of each of the elements of this world, considered in itself, while the celestial essences, that is to say, the angelic powers, although they are not unreasonably regarded as being outside this sensible world by reason of the excellence of their intelligible nature, yet, to go by the opinions of the holy fathers, must not be thought entirely lacking in bodies of a spiritual kind. For they must be believed to be subject to the human senses, to which they often become manifest, in spiritual bodies (which are) not foreign (to themselves) but which are their own and with which they are always associated.]

(It is) not that the operation of the indivisible unity of the divine Substances is divided—for that which the Father does so does the Son and [so] does the Holy Spirit—, but that the divine word appears to distribute to each of Them certain (special) properties [and it is right to understand that they possess them. For in the Holy Trinity while the unity of a common operation is recognized, the property of distinct operations is not excluded. For if there is in (the Trinity) unity of Essence and difference of Substances, I do not see why a common operation and different (operations) should not also be believed and understood (to exist) in it, so that the common operation be attributed to the common Essence without denying threefold action to the Trinity of Substances].

A. I see (this) clearly, and it seems to me probable and to accord with the Divine Oracles. But would you please confirm what has been said about the properties of the divine administration by some similitude taken from our own nature, since it is said to be in the likeness of God.

N. I would not easily believe that you are unaware of the trinity in our own nature.

A. Please tell me what it is.

N. Do you remember the conclusion we reached in our discussion in the preceding book? Did we not decide that there is no nature which is not understood to fall under these three terms which by the Greeks, as we have often said, are called οὐσία, δύναμις, ἐνέργεια, [that is] essence, power, operation?

A. I certainly remember and most firmly have (it in mind).

N. Therefore our nature, which is called human because all men participate in it, consists of essence, power, and operation?

A. I should think that no one of those skilled in theology would have any doubt about that.

N. How does it seem to you? Is not our nature, according to Holy Scripture, created in the image and likeness of God?

A. You must be mocking me. He who doubts this is not a man.

N. Do you think that the God Who created our nature in His image is a body or a spirit?

A. Concerning this too it would be ridiculous to hesitate, for "God is a spirit, and those who worship Him worship in spirit and in truth."

N. Therefore it is not in the body but in the soul that the image of God is stamped on our nature?

A. This also is very true.

N. God is Trinity and Unity, that is, three Substances in one Essence and one Essence in three Substances or Persons. For as the Greeks say μίαν οὐσίαν τρεῖς ὑποστάσεις or τρία πρόσωπα, that is, One Essence three Substances or three Persons, so the Romans (say) unam essentiam tres substantias or tres personas; but [they appear] to differ in that we do not find the Greeks saying μίαν ὑπόστασιν, that is, one Substance, whereas the Latins most frequently say unam substantiam tres personas. <The Greeks say> ὁμοούσιον ὁμοά-γαθον ὁμόθεον, that is, of one essence, of one goodness, of one deity [or one essence, one goodness, one deity. But these terms which among the Greeks signify the indivisibility of the Divine Nature do not go easily into Roman speech, and never do so exactly, I think; and therefore their meaning is only translated in separate words by περίφρασις, so that their sense only is understood while the translation is not word for word].

A. All this the catholic faith of the universal Church professes and as far as possible understands, but where does this lead us?

N. Nowhere else but that we may inquire as best we may how the trinity of our nature expresses [in itself] the image and likeness of the creative Trinity, that is, what [in it] more appropriately applies to the Father, and what to the Son, (and) what to the Holy Spirit. [I say more appropriately because although the whole trinity of our nature is an appropriate image of the whole Divine Trinity, the whole (of it) bearing the image of the Father, the whole (of it) the image of the Son, the whole (of it) the image of the Holy Spirit, yet there is in it (something) that as it were in a more special sense seems, I think, capable of being connected with each Person severally. For even (considered) in itself our trinity is present as a whole in each (of its members). For its essence is both power and operation, its power both essence and operation, its operation both essence and power, in the same way as the Father is both in the Son and the Holy Spirit, the Son both in the Father and the Holy Spirit, the Holy Spirit both in the Father and the Son.]

A. Nothing seems to me more likely than that the essence of our nature is accommodated to the image of the Father, its power (to that) of the Son, its operation (to that) of the Holy Spirit. For the paternal Substance which brought forth from itself the filiated Substance and the proceeding Substance is not unreasonably called the principal Substance—not that the one Essence of the Holy Trinity is [separable]— for it is one and indivisible—, but being one it is yet not without difference of substance. For it is the Deity which begets and the Deity which is begotten and the Deity which proceeds, though He be one indivisible Deity, even though it is not indistinguishable in differences of substance.

Also, the power (of our nature) not inappropriately appertains to God the Son, for He is often called by the divine word the Power of the Father; but to take a single instance out of many, hear the Apostle: "For the invisible things of Him are seen to be understood by means of the things that are made, and so are His everlasting Power and His Eternity;" for in this passage we understand the Power of the Father (to be) the Father's Wisdom [I mean, the Son], while the Eternity (we understand to be) the Holy Spirit, according to the venerable master Maximus. [For that the Holy Spirit is customarily called by the name of Power in the Scriptures the Gospel testifies when the Lord says, as He is healing the woman (who is) αἱμοῤῥοοῦσα, that is, afflicted with an issue of blood: "I perceived power go out of Me," that is, the Holy Spirit which dispenses the gifts of healing].

What should I say of the essential operation of our nature? Does it not most aptly appertain to the Holy Spirit, to Whom is attributed, as His (special) property so to speak, the operation of the powers and the distribution of the divine gifts both universally (to all) and particularly (to each)?

Thus, in the essence of our nature is recognized the property of the paternal Substance; in its power (that of) the Substance of the Son; in its operation (that of) the Substance of the Holy Spirit.

N. I think your reply does not disagree with the truth; but consider: What is your opinion of that very much spoken-of trinity of our nature which is understood (to consist) of intellect and reason and sense? *Is it something different* from the one we have just mentioned or are this and that one and the same, and not two (trinities) in our nature (which is) one and the same? Now by sense I mean not the exterior but the interior. For it is the interior which is co-essential with reason and intellect, while the exterior, although it seems to belong more to the soul [than to the body], yet does not *constitute* the essence of the soul but, as the Greeks say, is a kind of conjunction of soul and body. For when the body perishes and life departs it disappears entirely. For if it remained in the soul and belonged to its substance, then (the soul) would make use of it even without the body, but since in fact without the body it neither does nor can do so, one is left with the conclusion that it neither remains in the body when it perishes nor does it continue with the soul when she ceases to control the body. [For even that definition by which St. Augustine wished to define exterior sense clearly does not (make it) belong to the substantial parts of the soul. "Sense", he says, "is a passion of the body of which the soul as such is not unaware." Also another (definition) according to which "sense is the φαντασία of sensible things assumed through the instruments of the body" similarly does not seem to attach it to the nature of the soul, but makes it a kind of messenger between body and soul.]

And if one examines more carefully the semasiology of the Greek language one will find that the word has two senses. For in that language intellect is called νοῦς, reason λόγος, and sense διάνοια; (but) this (does) not (mean) exterior but interior (sense), and it is of these three that the essential trinity of the soul constituted in the image of God subsists. For (the trinity of the soul) is intellect and reason and the sense that is called interior and essential, while the exterior which we have described as a link between body and soul [is called] αἴσθησις, and the instruments in which it resides (are called) αἰσθητήρια for αἰσθήσεως τήρια, that is, the guardians of sensation, for in them sense is guarded and functions; and they are five in number: sight, hearing, smell, taste, touch. And it ought not to worry you that the fivefold instrument is named after the fivefold sense. For a very frequent usage both in common speech and in Holy Scripture calls the seat of the senses by the names of the senses themselves. For the eye is called sight and the ear hearing and the other senses also have their instruments named after them. But sense is called fivefold not because it is in itself divided into five parts—for it is simple and uniform and resides in the heart as its principal seat—but because it is through the fivefold instrument of the body, as though through the five gates of a city, that it receives within *likenesses* of sensible (things) originating *from the qualities and quantities* of the outside world [and from the other things by which the exterior sensation is formed] and like a gate-keeper and messenger announces to the presiding interior sense whatever it lets in from outside.

A. It does not worry me [that the names of the senses are given to their instruments] nor am I unaware, as I think, of the difference between the two (kinds of) sense which you have clearly distinguished; and with such power of comprehension as my feeble intellect possesses I shall say what I perceive about the aforesaid trinity of our nature.

There seem to be two trinities in which our nature is shown to subsist in so far as it is made in the image of God, but if the truth be consulted they are found to differ from each other not in reality but only in name. For νοῦς and οὐσία, that is, intellect and essence, denote the highest part of our nature [or rather, its highest motion. For, as you yourself understand, it is not one thing for our nature to be and another thing for it to move. For its essence is its motion-in-rest and rest-in-motion about God (and the creature). But when it moves about God, Who surpasses all things, this is called its *highest* motion; while when it turns about the primordial causes which are closest to God and come next after Him, it is understood, as it were, to moderate its motion somewhat; but when it attempts to perceive the effects of the primordial causes, whether visible or invisible, it is recognized to be going through its lowest motion—not because what is the same substantial motion can itself become greater or less, but because it is thought of as being least or moderate or greatest according to the status of the objects about which it turns]. *Therefore* the essence of our soul is the intellect which presides over the totality of human nature [because it is carried about God above every nature (and) beyond knowledge].

But λόγος or δύναμις, that is, reason or power, signifies, as it were, the second part [not unreasonably, since they are carried about the principles of things, which are first after God]. The third part, however, is denoted by the names of διάνοια and ἐνέργεια, that is, sensation and operation, [and occupies, as it were, the lowest place in the human soul; not unreasonably, for it revolves about the effects of the primordial causes, whether they *be* visible or invisible]. So, we should understand that there are not two substantial trinities, but one and the same, created in the likeness of the Creator.

But I wonder why I do see that life-principle which is called by the Greeks θρεπτική and αὐξητική and by our (writers) nutritive and auctive—for it nourishes the body and gives it increase—included by you either as a fourth substantial part of our nature or within the substantial trinity, but as it were wholly omitted as though it did not belong to the constitution of our nature at all.

N. Do not wonder, for it is not without reason that we have done this, since our discourse is not at the moment concerned with the whole of human nature, which is seen to consist, as it were, of five parts, that is, body [and] vital motion, sense and reason, and intellect; but only with that part in which the image and likeness of the Creator is seen, that is, with intellect, reason, and interior sense, or, so to say, with essence, power, (and) operation. For it is in this triad that the image of the most high and holy Trinity is known to be expressed.

For concerning the vital motion [by which the soul] nourishes and unifies and quickens and administers the body as well as giving it increase [and concerning the body itself which occupies the lowest position in the whole creation] there will be a place for discussion elsewhere when <in the fourth book> the discourse will be, under God's guidance, of the sensible natures. For since it is recognized that this part lies outside the property of our intelligible essence in which we are created in the image of God, it has for this reason been ignored by us for the present since it is a certain motion [outside our nature (as it was) primordially created] [subjoined to, and as a penalty for sin added to] our substantial operation which is called, as we have said, interior sense; by which, that is, (by which) motion, it administers those things which have been added to human nature after sin, I mean this body, corruptible and mortal and variable in places and times, divisible into the number of its parts, extended in spaces, susceptible to increases and decreases, subject to diverse qualities and quantities, prone to every irrational motion, the shelter of the soul while it is still carnal (and) involved in all kinds of disasters as punishment for its disobedience and pride, and all the other things which are spoken of and known by experience concerning the unhappiness of human nature thrust from the happiness of paradise into this life.

So the motion by which human nature administers those things which are joined to it in retribution for violation of the divine command—but by retribution I do not mean the vengeance of an angry God but the chastening of a merciful one—is not unreasonably left outside the bounds of our essential trinity. [And do not suppose that we wish by these words to teach that the aforesaid trinity of human nature created in paradise in the image of God was, before it sinned, without any body at all. Far, far be it from us to believe this or in any way think it! For the Creator made our souls and bodies all at once in paradise— by bodies I mean celestial (and) spiritual bodies such as they will be after the resurrection. For it must not be doubted that the puffed up, mortal, and corruptible bodies with which we are now encumbered take their origin not from nature but from sin.]

Therefore, that which has grown on to our nature in consequence of sin, once (our nature) is renewed in Christ [and restored to its former state, it will be without—for that cannot be co-eternal with nature which is attached to it on account of sin—]; and it is not unreasonable, I think, that it should not be counted among the constituent parts of its substance <—not that even that which has been superadded will perish, but it will pass into that which was created in the beginning, and will become one with that, not as two (entities) but an incorruptible and spiritual One, through the grace of God the Word Who had descended not only into that which is of our nature but also into that which was superadded so that He might restore in Himself all that is ours, and so that He Who made both might make the things which are naturally part of us one with those that were, in addition, attached to them from above>.

A. Certainly it is not unreasonable, but in strictest accord with what a rational nature would find by a valid and subtle investigation. But as yet I do not see where this (leads).

N. Be patient. For it is no trivial inquiry that we are embarked upon nor one which can be investigated or brought to a conclusion except by many devious approaches of a most precise reasoning if, indeed, it can ever be wholly concluded. For no mortal sense, however shrewd its inquiry may seem, can give assurance of this without incurring the charge of rashness [because he who undertakes to find the solution by himself surpasses his own powers. For if it is found it is not he who searches but He Who is sought and Who is the Light of our minds Who finds it]. For, unless I am mistaken, we are inquiring how we can argue from the substantial trinity of our nature created in the image of God to that most high Trinity [which is God], and *the distribution to each of the Persons* of their proper operations, so to speak, in created nature.

A. This it is which we are now seeking and nothing else; and the proper procedure requires that we should seek the truth in this way [for it is by arguing from the image that the very truth of which it is the image must be sought], which the more diligently and painstakingly it is sought, the more ardently it is preferred and the more clearly it is revealed. For of what avail is speed if the pure contemplation of truth eludes it, and what harm is there in slowness if it lead to the Divine Countenance?

N. Let us then begin our reasoning from the words of the venerable Maximus, not making use of continuous extracts from the discourses but availing ourselves of their sense.

A. Proceed upon the path of reasoning by whatever means you wish.

N. There are three universal motions of the soul, of which the first is of the mind, the second of the reason, the third of sense. And the first is simple and surpasses the nature of the soul herself and cannot be interpreted [that is, it cannot have knowledge of that about which it moves]; "by this motion the soul moves about the unknown God, but, because of His excellence, she has no kind of knowledge of Him from the things that are" as to what He is [that is to say, she cannot find Him in any essence or substance or in anything which can be uttered or understood; for He surpasses everything that is and that is not, and there

is no way in which He can be defined as to what he is].

The second motion is that by which she "defines the unknown" God "as Cause" of all. For she defines God as being Cause of all things; and this motion is within the nature of the soul, "and by it she moves naturally and takes upon herself by the operation of her science all the natural reasons (which are) formative of all things, which subsist as having been eternally made in Him Who is known only as Cause" [for He is known because He is Cause], that is, she expresses (them) in herself through her knowledge of them, and the knowledge itself is *begotten* by the first motion *in the second*.

The third motion is "composite, (and is that) by which" the soul "comes into contact with that which is outside her as though by certain signs and re-forms within herself the reasons of visible things". It is called composite not because it is not simple in itself as the first and second are simple, but because its first knowledge of the reasons of sensible things does not come from (the things) themselves. *For first* (the soul) receives the phantasies of the things themselves through the exterior sense, (which is) fivefold because of the number of the corporeal instruments in which and through which it operates, and by gathering them to itself (and) sorting them out it sets them in order; then, getting through them to the reasons of the things of which they are the phantasies, she moulds them [I mean the reasons] and shapes them into conformity with herself.

[And let it not trouble you that a little earlier we defined exterior sense as the phantasy of sensible things while now we teach that it is the means by which the phantasies of those same sensible things reach the interior sense. *For* this third motion begins to move as a consequence of being informed of the phantasies of exterior things by means of the exterior sense.

For there are two kinds of phantasies, of which the first is that which is born at first of sensible nature in the instruments of the senses and is properly called the image expressed in the senses; while the second is that which is formed next out of this image, and it is this phantasy which properly bears the customary name of exterior sense. And that (which comes) first is always attached to the body, that (which comes) after to the soul. And the first, although it is in the sense, is not sensible of itself, but the second is both sensible of itself and receives the first.]

But when *this third motion* abandons the phantasies of sensible things and clearly understands the reasons stripped bare of all corporeal imagery and in their own simplicity, it transmits the reasons of visible things freed from every phantasy back to the first motion through the intermediate motion as the simple operation of something which is also (itself) simple, that is to say (it transmits them as) universal reasons by a universal operation. But the first motion itself carries back whatever it perceives from the third through the intermediate, and from that intermediate immediately in the modified forms of created things, to that which, unknown immediately in itself [as to what it is], is yet known by the fact that it is the cause of all things, and to the principles of all things, that is, to the principal causes which are created by it and in it and distributed by it. [That is, he understands that they proceed from God through them into all things that are after them and through them return to Him again.]

Therefore the motion of the soul which is purged by action, illumined by knowledge, perfected by the divine word, (the motion) by which she eternally revolves about the unknown God, and understands that God Himself is beyond both her own nature and that of all things, absolutely distinct from everything which can either be said or understood and everything which cannot be said or understood—and yet which somehow exists—, and denies that He is anything of the things that are or of the things that are not [and] affirms that all things that are predicated of Him are predicated of Him not literally but metaphorically, is called νοῦς by the Greeks but by our writers intellectus or animus or mens;

and it exists substantially, and is understood to be the principal part of the soul. For the essential being of the soul is not other than her substantial motion. *For* the soul subsists in her motions and her motions subsist in her. For she is by nature simple and indivisible, and is differentiated only by the substantial differences of her motions. For if, according to the tradition handed down by the holy fathers, the celestial essences, which the Divine Oracles also call the celestial and angelic powers, are substantially nothing else but intelligible, eternal [and] unceasing motions about the Beginning of all things, from Whom and through Whom and in Whom and towards Whom they move and subsist [for the motion of the celestial powers about their Beginning is circular, that is to say, <it starts> from Him as their Beginning, it passes through Him *by means of the created causes*, (it moves) in Him as in the natural laws which are in Him and beyond which it neither wills (to stray) nor can (stray) nor can will to stray, (and) returns to Him as its end, and such a motion exists in the understanding alone; for they understand that they are from Him and that their intellect *moves* through Him and in Him, and they know for certain that they have no other end than Him], what is to prevent us from understanding in a similar way that human intellects unceasingly revolve about God, seeing that they are from Him and through Him and in Him and for Him [for they revolve in the same intelligible circle], especially as the Divine Oracles declare that man is made in the image of God, which we do not find explicitly said of the angels? <However, we are left to infer this from their intellectual nature.> Also we read that the celestial powers stand in the presence of God and minister to Him, but the Catholic Faith witnesses that human nature became God in the Word of God and sitteth at the right hand of God and reigneth.

But that which the Lord promises to all men generally after the resurrection of all, "They shall be as angels of God in heaven," is to be understood, I think, as a sharing in the same status of nature *and as* an equality of immortality and (as meaning) that they shall lack all corporeal sexuality and every corruptible mode of generation. For it is not unreasonable to believe that man's first state before sin in paradise, that is, in heavenly bliss, was equal and, as it were, of the same nature with (that of) the angels. [For the divine word refers to both these natures, I mean the angelic and the human, when it says: "Who made the heavens in intellect," that is, in order that they might be intelligences in essence and substance.] But since man when he was in honour abandoned his intellect and became equal to the beasts who lack wisdom and was made like them, he withdrew far from his angelic status and fell into the misfortune of this mortal life. But after the Word was made flesh, that is, (after) God was made man, there is fulfilled what is written in the psalm: "What is man that Thou art mindful of him, or the son of man that Thou visitest him?" [marvelling, that is, at the exaltation of the first state of human nature] "Thou madest him" <it says> "a little less than the angels" [that is, Thou hast permitted him to be made less because of his pride, and Thou hast left him of his own proper will to fall into the disgrace of an irrational life. For by a figure of speech God is said to do what He allows to be done]; "Thou hast crowned him with glory and honour and hast set him above the works of Thy hands. Thou hast subjected all things under his feet."

Do you see how deeply human nature has been humiliated in the first man after sin, and how highly, through grace, it has been exalted in the second man, I mean, in Christ? For man is not only restored to the first state of his nature from which he fell, but is even lifted up <in his Head, which is Christ> above all the celestial powers. For where sin was abundant grace was more abundant.

If therefore human nature, renewed in Christ, not only attains the angelic status but is even carried up beyond every creature into God, and if it would be impious to deny that that which was done in the Head will be (done) in the members, what

wonder if human intellects are nothing else but the ineffable and unceasing motions— in those [I mean] who are worthy—about God, in Whom they live and move and have their being? [For they have their being through the reasons by which they exist, they move through the reasons of the powers by which they are able to exist well, they live through the reasons by which they exist eternally. Thus they have being and well being and eternal being in God.]

A. Not only do I admit but I also understand that the most excellent motion of the soul about the unknown God beyond every creature is most rightly called, and is, intellect. But how or in what sense the intellect, while confined to the limits of human nature, can ascend above itself and above every creature so as to be able to perform its substantial motions about the unknown God Who is far removed from every created nature <should, I think, be investigated>.

N. In this part of (our) contemplation which concerns the intellectual and rational substances, when it comes to the question how created nature can ascend beyond itself so as to be able to adhere to the creative Nature, every inquiry of those who study the potentiality of nature fails. For there we see not a reason of nature but the ineffable and incomprehensible excellence of Divine Grace. For in no created substance does there naturally exist the power to surpass the limits of its own nature and directly attain to Very God in Himself. For this is of grace alone, not of any power of nature.

[This is why the Apostle confesses that he does not know how he was rapt into paradise, saying: "I know the man (was) rapt but I do not know how, whether in the body or out of the body." For it is not in the natural motions of the soul that I see in the body or out of the body any power by which I can be rapt into the Third Heaven. <But> only God knows, and it is only by His grace that I know for certain I was rapt. For no nature can of itself ascend into that place of which the Lord says: "Where I am, there (is) my servant also." <Therefore, just as it passes all intellect how the Word

of God descends into man, so it passes all reason how man ascends into God.>]

A. Although your reply is brief it is sufficient <and> clear; so turn your attention to what comes next, the consideration of the second motion of the soul.

N. The second motion of the soul, as we have said, is that which is contained within the bounds of its nature and defines the Very God as Cause, that is, it knows only this about the God Who is unknown as to what He is, (namely), that He is the Cause of all things that are, and that the primordial causes of all (things) are eternally created by Him and in Him; and it impresses the knowledge of those causes, when it has understood them, upon the soul herself, whose motion it is, as far as her capacity allows. [For as from what is below her the soul receives the images of sensible things, which the Greeks call φαντασίαι, so from what is above her, that is, from the primordial causes, she implants within herself the cognitions which are usually called by the Greeks θεοφάνειαι and by the Latins diuinae apparitiones, and through them, through the first causes, I mean, she receives some motion of God]—not that it understands what they are substantially—for this is beyond every motion of the soul—but it has the general knowledge that they are and that they flow forth by an ineffable process into their effects; and this is the motion which is called by the Greeks λόγος or δύναμις, but by our (writers) ratio or uirtus, and it is born of the first motion, which is intellect.

For *just as* a wise artist produces his art from himself in himself and foresees in it the things he is to make, and in a general and causal sense potentially creates their causes before they actually appear, so the intellect *brought forth* from itself and in itself its reason, in which it foreknows and causally pre-creates all things which it desires to make. For we say that a plan is nothing else but a concept in the mind of the artist.

The second motion of the soul, then, is the reason, which is understood as a kind of substantial seeing in the mind and a kind of art begotten of it and in it, in which it

fore*knows* and pre-*creates* the things which it wishes to make; and therefore it is not unreasonably named its form, for (the intellect) in itself is unknown but begins to become manifest both to itself and to others in its form, which is reason. [For just as the Cause of all things cannot in itself be discovered as to what it is either by itself or by anyone else, but somehow comes to be known in its theophanies, so the intellect, which ever revolves about it and is created wholly in its image, cannot be understood as to what it is either by itself or by anyone else, but in the reason which is born of it begins to become manifest. But as to my saying that the Cause of all and the intellect are not understood by themselves [as to what they are], the reason for that will be considered a little later.] Concerning the second motion, what it is and whence it takes its origin, enough has been said, I think.

A. Enough, certainly.

N. There remains, then, the third motion, which functions in the particular reasons of particular things, which are created simply, that is, as a whole, in the primordial causes; and which, although it takes the beginning of its substantial motion from the phantasies of sensible things which are communicated to it through exterior sense, attains, by the most precise discrimination of all things through their proper reasons, to the most general essences and to the less general genera, then to the species and to the most specific species, that is, the individuals, countless and unlimited, but limited by the immutable proportions of their nature; and this is the motion which in Greek is called διάνοια or ἐνέργεια, but in Latin sensus or operation—by sensus *I mean that which* is substantial and interior—, which similarly proceeds from the intellect through the reason. For everything which the intellect by its gnostic view of the primordial causes impresses upon its art, that is, its reason, it distributes through the sense which proceeds from it and is called after its operation, into the particular reasons of individual *things*, which were created in the causes primordially and as a whole.

All essences are one in the reason; in sense they are divided into different essences. Therefore reason receives the most unified knowledge of all the essences from the most unified unity of their principles through the <descending> intellect; but sense separates that unity by means of differences. Similarly, reason knows through intellect the genera of things after a uniform and simple mode in their universal causes and in themselves; but that most universal simplicity *which in itself is indivisible and is liable to no differences and is subject to no accidents and is not extended by spatial intervals and is not composed of any parts and is not varied by any motion through place or time*, sense breaks up *into* the diverse genera and differences *and a thousand other things*. Those things which from the point of view of reason are one in their genera are the same in different forms as those which, on the other hand, by the operation of sense are differentiated from one another by natural distinctions. [That is to say, the intellect itself <through the medium of reason> (and) through the sense which is consubstantial with itself, infallibly investigates and discovers and comprehends by sure rules the manner in which they are divided by their natural motions under the rule and ordinance and administration of Divine Providence into the manifold differences of nature.]

What shall I say of the unlimited number of individuals which, as much as they become multiple by the operation of sense, whether it is in sense itself or in nature (that they are multiple), so much are they one when by the reason they are considered in their forms under a universal and simple mode?

And to sum up: whatever the soul through her first motion, which is the intellect, knows under one form [and as a whole] concerning God and the primordial causes she implants, still [under one form and] as a whole, in her second motion, which is reason; but whatever she receives from the natures that are above her, through the intellect, after it has been formed in the reason, this whole she dis-

tributes through sense into the separated genera, into the diverse species, into the multiple individuals, in the effects below, and, to speak more plainly, whatever the human soul, through her intellect in her reason, knows of God and the principles of things as a unity *she always retains as a unity; but whatever, through the reason, she perceives to subsist in the causes as one and under a uniform mode, this whole, through sense, she understands as multiple and under a multiform mode <in> the effects of the causes.* But she most clearly knows through her intellect that from the one Cause of all things all things start upon their movement towards multiplicity without abandoning the simplicity of the unity by which they subsist in it eternally and immutably, and (move) towards it as the end of their whole movement, and end in it.

The three motions of the soul, that is, intellect which is also called (her) essence, and reason which (is called her) power, and sense which (is called her) operation, have been sufficiently discussed, as I think.

A. Most clearly and abundantly.

N. Contemplate, then, and, dispelling all mist of ambiguity, understand with the sharpness of your mind how clearly, how explicitly the substantial Trinity of the Divine Goodness is revealed in the motions of the human soul to those who study them carefully, and manifests itself to those who seek it piously as though in a most limpid mirror of their own made in its image, and although it is removed from every creature and is unknown to every intellect descends through its image and likeness (to become), as it were, known and comprehensible and in some measure present to [the eyes of] the intellect [and of its own accord cleanses the mirror which reflects it so that it may shine forth from it most brilliantly (as) one essential Goodness in three Substances; for this Unity and Trinity, because it eludes every intellect on account of the infinity of its exceeding brightness, would not appear in itself (and) by itself unless it impressed the traces of knowledge of itself upon its image]. For the likeness of the Father shines forth most clearly in the intellect, that of the

Son in the reason, that of the Holy Spirit in the sense. For as we call the Son the art of the almighty Artist, and not unreasonably, since in Him, as in [His] Wisdom, the almighty Artist, the Father Himself, has made all things whatsoever He desired and preserves (them) eternally and immutably in Him, so also the human intellect, through the act of knowing, creates, by a wonderful operation of its science, whatsoever it most clearly and unambiguously receives from God, and from the principles of all things in its art, as it were, I mean, in its reason, and by means of the memory stores (it) in its most secret recesses. But as whatever the Father, the omnipotent Maker of all things, created at one and the same time primordially, causally, uniformly, universally in His art which is His Wisdom and His Power, in His Word, in His only begotten Son, He divides through the Holy Spirit Who proceeds from Him and from the Son into the innumerable effects of the primordial causes, whether they have flowed forth into intelligible essences and differences which surpass every corporeal sense or into the various and multiple display of this sensible world diversified by the divisions of places and times; so everything which the intellect, that is the principal motion of the soul formed by her gnostic contemplation of intelligible things, creates and stores in the art of its reason, it divides through the interior sense of the soul into the discrete and unconfused knowledge of individual things, whether intelligible or sensible. For everything which the intellect considers in the reason universally it divides into the discrete cognitions and definitions of things through the sense particularly.

NOTES

1. Nutritor is the master. Alumnus is the disciple.

CHAPTER 22

St. Peter Damian

Peter Damian was born at Ravenna in 1007. Little is known of his early life. An elder brother, Damiani, from whom Peter acquired his name, cared for him and sent him to school. Later he studied the liberal arts at Faenza and Parma, after which he taught at Ravenna. It was there that he became attracted to the ascetic life led by several groups of hermits in the area. About 1035 he joined a community of hermits at Fonte Avellana, near Gubbio, in Umbria, becoming its prior around 1040.

This was to remain his base of operations for the rest of his life, even though he was required to spend great periods of time away from the hermitage due to the active leadership role he played in a growing movement of ecclesiastical reform. In 1057 he became cardinal bishop of Ostia. Two years later he was sent on a papal mission to Milan, then to France and Florence in 1063, Germany in 1069, and Ravenna in 1072. He died that year at Faenza.

Peter was eloquent with both the written and spoken word, which undoubtedly played a role in his success as a church reformer as well as a papal emissary. His disciple and biographer, John of Lodi, reports that Peter's sermons would captivate audiences for six hours at a time. The popularity of his writings extended throughout the remainder of the Middle Ages.

Damian was always suspicious of philosophy, seeing it as potentially intentionally misleading and therefore corruptible. Behind every philosophical argument is a potential sophist. Philosophy ought always be kept in its place, principally as the "handmaid" of theology. It would be a mistake, however, to conclude that Damian was an anti-intellectual. Rather, man's intellectual energy ought properly be devoted to the contemplation of God and the salvation of the soul as opposed to the dialectics of philosophy, which result in nothing but useless theories. Clearly, this view is consistent with one who found the ascetic life most rewarding.

St. Peter Damian on Divine Omnipotence

St. Peter Damian directs his attention to St. Jerome's claim that "while God can do all things, he cannot cause a virgin to be restored after she has fallen. He may, indeed, free her from guilt, but he cannot award her the crown of virginity which she lost". The problem here concerning God's omnipotence is that once an event has occurred and therefore become a matter of fact, it would appear it cannot, under any circumstances, be altered. In other words, it is not within God's power to alter facts. It is surely within his power to determine states of affairs, but once so determined then it is beyond God's power to alter that which He, or anybody else, has determined to be the case. Damian interprets this view as one curtailing God's power and therefore as one undermining His omnipotence.

Damian's way of circumventing this apparent problem is based on God's existing in eternal time, which entails that there is for Him no past or future. He exists in a state of eternal present. The understanding of mortals is inextricably tied to a time continuum. Consequently, it does not make sense to us that a virgin can be restored after she has fallen. But there is no "after" relative to God. Since He functions only in an eternal "now," He can (as opposed to could, or could have) restore her virginity. Such restoration does not mean that God has the power to alter facts *after* they have become the states of affairs that they are. By 'can' Damian means that God has the power to cause a virgin to be restored and not to be restored at one and the same time. Thus God's omnipotence entails that He has within His power that of contradiction. Anything less, according to the Saint, would be less than omnipotence, which followers of the faith accept as one of God's immutable attributes.

LETTER ON DIVINE OMNIPOTENCE

(Selections)

I

To lord Desiderius, most reverend rector of the monastery of [Monte] Cassino, and to the entire holy convent [there], Peter the sinner, a monk, [sends you] the kiss of peace in the Holy Spirit. . . .

II

For once, as you can recall, while the two [of us] were sitting around the table, the following [passage] of blessed Jerome came up in our conversation: "I dare say," he says, "although God can do all things, he cannot raise up a virgin after her fall. True, he can free her from punishment, but he cannot crown her [with the crown of virginity] once she has been corrupted."[1] Al-

Translated by Paul Vincent Spade (copyright 1989) from the edition in *Pierre Damien: Lettre sur la toute-puissance divine. Introduction, texte critique, traduction et notes*, edited and translated by André Cantin ("Sources Chrétiennes," vol. 191; Paris: Les Editions du Cerf, 1972). Reprinted by kind permission of Paul Vincent Spade.

though I was terrified, inasmuch as I would not dare to argue about the testimony of so great a man, nevertheless to a father of like mind [with me]—namely, to you—I said exactly what I thought. "This view," I said, "I confess has never been able to satisfy me. For I pay attention to what is said, not to by whom it is said. It seems too much a dishonor that an inability should be ascribed so lightly to him who can do all things, unless sworn to by a higher intelligence."

But you replied, on the contrary, that what was said [by Jerome] was sure and quite authenticated, namely, that God is not able to raise up a virgin after her fall. Then, after running through many [points] with long and wordy arguments, you finally brought the conclusion of your explanation down to this, that you would say that on no other account is God unable [to do] this than because he does not want to.

To this I say, if God can do nothing he does not want [to do], but [rather] he does nothing except what he wants, therefore, he can do nothing at all that he does not do.

And so consequently, to speak freely, God does not [make it] rain today for the reason that he cannot. He does not raise up the feeble for the reason that he cannot. For that reason [too] he does not kill the unjust. For that reason he does not free the blessed from their oppressions. These and many other things God does not do, for the reason that he does not want to. And because he does not want to, he cannot. It follows, therefore, that whatever God does not do, he is altogether incapable of doing. But, really, this seems so absurd and so ridiculous that not only is the assertion incompatible with the omnipotent God, it cannot even be applied to fragile mankind. There are many things, after all, that we do not do and yet are able to do.

Nevertheless, if it should happen that we find some [statement] like this in the mystical and allegorical [passages of] Scripture, it should be taken with caution and reverence rather than broadcast boldly and freely according to its literal sense. For example, what was said by the angel to Lot, [who was] hurrying to Segor. "Hurry up," [the angel] said, "and save [yourself] there, because I will be unable to do anything until you enter in there" (Gen. 19:22). And "I repent of having made man" (Gen. 6:7).[2] And that God, taking warning in advance about the future, is touched within by a sorrow of the heart, and many things of that kind. So if anything like that is found included in the Holy Scriptures, it should not be spread around right away all over the place with insolent and presumptuous, vulgar impudence, but rather under the restrained discipline of sober discourse. For if it should reach the common people that God is asserted to be impotent in some respect (which is a wicked thing to say), the unschooled masses would instantly be confused and the Christian faith would be upset, not without grave danger to souls.

III

Clearly God is said to be unable in the same way that he is said to be ignorant. For instance, whatever is bad, just as he cannot do it, so he does not know how to do it. For he neither can nor knows how to lie or to commit perjury or to do anything unjust, even though he says through the prophet, "I the Lord who forms the light and creates the shadows, who makes peace and creates evil" (Isaiah 45:7).[3] . . .

Many such things are found in the statements of the Scriptures. If we are intent on taking them according to their meaning on the surface, we will be unable to pour out light but rather [only] to give birth to the darkness of shadows.

So the claim that God cannot [do] anything evil, or does not know how to, is not to be referred to ignorance or impossibility, but rather to the rectitude of [his] perpetual will. For because he does not want evil, it is rightly said that he neither knows how nor is able [to do] anything evil. For the rest, whatever he wants he no doubt is able [to do], according to the Scripture, "You however, the master of strength, judge with calm and treat us with great respect. For power is available to you when you want [it]" (Wisdom 12:18).

IV

The will of God is in fact the cause of all things, whether visible or invisible, that they exist, to such an extent that all things [that are] made, before they proceed to the visible appearances of their forms, were living already, truly and essentially, in the will of their maker. "What was made," says John, "in him was life" (John 1:4). And in Revelations, he bears witness that the twenty-four elders said the same thing. "You are worthy, Lord our God, to receive glory and honor and power, because you created all things, and because of your will they were and were created" (Rev. 4:11). First it is said that they "were", and afterwards that "they have been created." For the things that are expressed outwardly, through the making of the product, were already [there] within, in the providence and plan of the maker.

But furthermore, just as the will of God is the cause that what has not yet been made should come to be in the first place, so too is it no less powerful a cause that things that have been lost should return to the rank [appropriate to] their station. "For do I will the death of the impious?, says the Lord. Rather, I will that he be converted and live" (Ez. 18:23).

So, to get back to the point, what prevents God from being able to raise up a virgin after falling? Is he unable to do it because he does not want to? And does he not want to because it is evil, just as it was said that God neither wants nor is able to lie, to commit perjury, or to do anything evil? But heaven forbid that it should be bad for a violated woman to turn into a virgin! Indeed, just as it is evil for a virgin to be violated, so there is no doubt it would be good for her, once violated, to revert to [being a] virgin [again], if the order of the divine plan granted it. . . .

V

To be sure, for a virgin to be "raised up" after falling is understood in two ways, namely, either with respect to the fullness of merit or with respect to the integrity of the flesh. So let us see whether God is strong enough to do both.

Now with respect to merit, the Apostle calls the company of the faithful a "virgin" when he says to the Corinthians, "For I promised you to one man, a chaste virgin to show to Christ" (2 Cor. 11:2). For in that people of God there were not only virgins, but also many women bound in marriage or living continently after losing their virginity.

And the Lord says through the prophet, "If a man puts his wife aside, and she goes off and takes another man, will he ever go back to her? Will not the woman be called defiled and polluted? But you have fornicated with many lovers. Nevertheless, come back to me, says the Lord" (Jer. 3:1).

This coming back to the Lord, as far as the quality of the merit is concerned, is

plainly this, that a corrupted woman should become whole [again], that a virgin be retrieved from prostitution. . . .

Observe that it has been proved, in my opinion, that with respect to merit, God can "raise up" a virgin after falling.

But with respect to the flesh, who can doubt even with an insane mind that he, who restores crushed [spirits], [who] releases those in chains, who cures every weakness and every infirmity, cannot restore the virginal barrier? Oh yes, he who put the body itself together out of the thinnest seminal fluid, who in the human form diversified the species through the various features of the limbs, who made what did not yet exist into the pinnacle of creation— once it existed, he could not get it back when it went bad?

I say it outright, I say without fear of contradiction by scoffing quibbles, I affirm that the omnipotent God is strong enough to make any women, [even one who has been] married many times, a virgin again, and to restore in her flesh the seal of incorruption, just as she emerged from her mother's womb.

I have said these things, not to defame blessed Jerome, who spoke with pious zeal, but to disprove with the unconquerable reason of faith those who take the occasion from his words to assert that God is incapable.

VI

I see I must respond finally to what many people, on the basis of your holiness's [own] judgment, raise as an objection on the topic of this dispute. For they say: If, as you assert, God is omnipotent in all things, can he manage this, that things that have been made were not made? He can certainly destroy all things that have been made, so that they do not exist now. But it cannot be seen how he can bring it about that things that have been made were not made. To be sure, it can come about that from now on and hereafter Rome does not exist; for it can be destoyed. But no opinion can grasp how it can come about that it was not founded long ago. . . .

VII

But what do they want for themselves, these useless men, [these] introducers of sacrilegious doctrine, who, while they contrive the snares of their questions for others, pay no attention to the fact that they themselves have fallen headlong into them first, [who,] while they put the traps of frivolous questioning in the path of simple travelers, tripped themselves up instead on the stumbling-block?

They say, "Is God able to act so that, after something has once happened, it did not happen?"—as if this impossibility should seem to arise for past [times] alone, and is not also found likewise in the case of present and future times. For whatever even now is, as long as it is, no doubt necessarily is.[4] It is not possible, as long as something exists, for it not to be.

Again, it is impossible for what will be not to be going to be, even though there are some things that can equally come about and not come about. For instance, my going riding or not going riding today, seeing or not seeing a friend, its raining or there being fine weather. These things and [others] like them the wise men of this world usually call "indifferent", because they are equally prone to happen and not to happen.

But they are called "indifferent" more in accordance with the variable nature of the things than in accordance with the inference-relations among statements. For according to the natural order of diverse sequences, it can come about that it rains today, and it can also come about that it does not rain. But with respect to inference-relations in discourse, if it will come about that it rains, [then] it is altogether necessary that it rain. Hence it is absolutely impossible that it not rain.

Therefore, what is said about past things follows no less for present and future

things, so that just as for everything that was, it is necessary for it to have been, so too for everything that is, as long as it is, it is necessary for it to be, and for everything that will be, it is necessary for it to be going to be.

And so, with respect to the arrangement of discourse, for whatever was, it is impossible for it not to have been, and for whatever is, it is impossible for it not to be, and for whatever will be, it is impossible for it not to be going to be.

Hence, let the blind thoughtlessness of [these] naive "wise" [men], who inquire about groundless [questions], see that if they boldly apply to God these things that pertain to the art of discourse, they make him altogether impotent and incapable not only in the case of past things, but also for present and future things.

Because they have not yet learned the elementary points about words, they discard the foundation of a clear faith because of the obscure darknesses of their arguments. Still ignorant of what boys treat in school, they hurl the slanders of their complaints at the divine mysteries. Because they have acquired no experience in the rudiments of learning or the humane arts, they upset the study of ecclesiastical purity with the murkiness of their curiosity.

Plainly, these things, which arise from the arguments of logicians or rhetoricians, are not to be easily adapted to the mysteries of divine power. Heaven forbid that these [people] should stubbornly introduce into holy laws things invented so that they might progress in the tools of syllogisms and [in] rhetorical periods, and that they should oppose to divine power the necessities of their inference.

Yet, if skill in the humane art is sometimes used in dealing with Scripture, it should not arrogantly grasp for itself the right of a master, but rather play a certain subordinate role as a servant, like a handmaiden to her mistress, lest it should fall into error if it take the lead, and while following out the consequences of the outwardly [expressed] words, it lose the light of innermost power and the right path to truth.

Who does not plainly see that, if faith has recourse to these arguments, taking their wording as it stands, the divine power would be made to appear impotent at all moments of time? For, according to the contention of this empty line of inquiry, God is not strong enough to act in such a way that things that happened a while ago would not have happened, or on the other hand [in such a way that] things that now are, as long as they are, are not, or things that will be will not be, or contrariwise, [that] things that will not be will be.

The old [authors] who discussed the liberal arts—not only pagans but also partakers of the Christian faith—have treated this question at great length. But none of them has dared to put forward the insanity that would ascribe a mark of incapability to God and would doubt his omnipotence (especially if he was a Christian). Rather they argued about concluding necessity or impossibility with respect to the mere power of the [dialectical] art only, so that they made no mention of God in these disputes. But the people who nowadays take up the old question, eager to know higher things than they [are able to] grasp, instead dull the edge of their mind because they are not afraid to give offense to the author of light himself.

So the question, because it is shown to pertain not to the discussion of the divine majesty's power but rather to skill in dialectical art, not to the power or material of things but rather to the manner and order of speech and to the inferential connection among words, has no place among the mysteries of the Church. [This question] is aired in the schools by secular boys. For it pertains not to the rule of the faith or to the good character of [one's] behavior, but rather to the richness of speech and the dazzle of words.

Therefore, let it suffice for us to defend in [this] brief [treatment] the faith we hold; to the wise men of the present age we concede the things that are theirs. Those who

want may hold on to the letter that kills, provided the life-giving Spirit, through God's mercy, does not withdraw from us. . . .

XVII

. . . we can say without absurdity that God, in that invariable and always most stable eternity of his, can make it so that what was made, with respect to our transience, was not made. That is, so that we may say "God is able to act so that Rome, which was founded in antiquity, was not founded". The expression 'is able', in the present tense, is used appropriately here, as far as the immovable eternity of the omnipotent God is concerned. But with respect to us, for whom there is uninterrupted mobility and continuous movement, we would more properly say 'was able', as we usually do.

Hence we understand the above statement 'God is able [to act] so that Rome was not founded' from the point of view of him, namely, for whom "there is no shifting, or shadow of alteration" (James 1:17). Of course for us this means 'God was able'. For with respect to his eternity, whatever God was able [to do], he also is able [to do] it, because his present never turns into the past, his today does not change into tomorrow or into any alteration of time. Rather, just as he always is what he is, so [too] whatever is present before him is always present before him.

Thus, just as we can properly say 'God was able [to bring it about] that Rome, before it had been founded, was not founded',[5] so can we no less appropriately say 'God is able [to bring it about] that Rome, even after it has been founded, was not founded'. He "was able" with respect to us; he "is able" with respect to himself. For the being able that God had before Rome came to be persists, always unchangeable and immovable, in God's eternity. Hence, whatever thing we can say God "was able" [to do], so no less can we say that God "is able" [to do] it. For his being able, which is of course coeternal with him, is always fixed and immobile. It is only with respect to us that there is a "having been able" for God. With respect to himself, however, there is no having been able, but rather always an unmoved, fixed and invariable being able.

Whatever God was able [to do] no doubt he also is able to do. For him, certainly, just as there is no being and having been, but [only] everlasting being, so [too] as a consequence [there is] no having been able and being able, but [only] an always immobile and everlasting being able.

Just as he does not say "I am who was and am" but rather "I am who am" and "He who is sent me to you" (Ex. 3:14), so there is no doubt that he says as a consequence not "I am who was able and am able" but rather "[I am] who immovably and eternally am able". For that being able that was with God before the ages [still] is today, and that being able that belongs to him today belonged [to him] no less before the ages, and will eternally persist, still fixed and immobile, for all the ages to come.

Therefore, just as God was able, before all things were made, [to bring it about] that they would not be made, so no less is he able even now [to bring it about] that the things that were made had not existed. For the being able that he had then is neither changed nor taken away. Rather, just as he always is what he is, so too God's being able cannot be changed. For it is he who says through the prophet, "I am God, and I am not changed" (Mal. 2:6), and in the Gospel, "Before Abraham came to be, I am" (John 8:58). He is not changed, after the fashion of our [own] condition, from being about to be to being, or from being to having been. Rather, he is always the same, and always is what he is.

Thus, just as one and the same God al-ways is, so being able [to do] all things is present in him, imperishably and without failing. And just as we say truly and without any contradiction that what now and always is God was [also] before the ages, so no less truly do we say that what now and always God is able [to do] he was [also] able [to do] before the ages. Thus, if through all [ages] God is able [to do] whatever he was able [to do] at the beginning, but before the foundation of things he was able [to bring it about] that things that have now been made were not made in any way, therefore he is able [to bring it about] that the made [things] did not exist at all.

In fact, his being able is fixed and eternal, so that anything he was ever able [to do] he always is able [to do]. Neither does the difference of times make any room for change in eternity. Rather, just as he is the same now as he was in the beginning, so too he is able [to do] everything whatsoever that he was able [to do] before the ages.

We must, therefore, put an end to the dispute before us. Accordingly, if being able [to do] all things is coeternal with God, God was able [to bring it about] that things that have been made were not made. Therefore, it is to be asserted steadfastly and faithfully that God, just as he is said [to be] omnipotent, so with absolutely no exception he is truly able [to do] all things, whether with respect to things that have been made or with respect to things that have not been made.

Thus, the passage of Esther may be placed as an inviolable seal at the end of our work: "Lord, omnipotent king, all things are put in your power, and there is no one who can resist your will. For you made heaven and earth and whatever is contained in the circuit of the heaven. You are lord of all; neither is there anyone who resists your majesty" (Esther 13:9–11).

NOTES

1. Jerome, *Epistle 22 ad Eustochium*, 5, in *Select Letters of St. Jerome, with an English Translation by F. A. Wright* ("The Loeb Classical Library"; London: William Heinemann, Ltd., 1933), p. 62.

2. This example and the next one seem to be illustrating a somewhat different point than the earlier example did.
3. Damian goes on to give a number of other examples, which I shall omit.
4. An allusion to Aristotle, *De interpretatione*, 9, 18b8. As you might expect, this perplexing line in Aristotle has occasioned much commentary, both in the Middle Ages and thereafter.
5. This is awkward in Latin too. The sense is: 'God was able, before Rome was founded, to bring it about that it would never be founded'.

CHAPTER 23

St. Anselm

(See Chapter Three for biography.)

St. Anselm on Grace and Free Will

The grace of God plays an important role in Christian theology. In short, man's salvation depends on it. Because human beings are sinners, there needs be an explanation as to how they can reap the benefits of an afterlife in heaven. How can they be saved from eternal damnation? They cannot save themselves. They need help. This help comes by way of God's grace. This issue, however, is slightly more complicated. God also created man with free will for the purpose of his choosing between good and evil. This would appear to be enough for salvation. If a person consistently and on balance chooses good over evil, then this would seem to be enough to warrant an afterlife of heaven rather than hell. Anselm argues that grace is compatible with free choice. His first observation concerning grace, however, is unrelated to free will. He observes that "every creature exists by grace, because by grace he was created". That is, God created the universe and all that therein is. Hence, we owe our existence to him. It is by His grace that we exist at all.

That God created man with free will would seem to be sufficient for him to save himself. After all, all a person needs to do is to exercise his free will and choose good over evil. Anselm does not view the situation as that simple. When a person does choose good over evil, he demonstrates what Anselm calls uprightness-of-will. How does one possess uprightness-of-will? Having the freedom to choose good over evil is not enough to so choose. One needs to be disposed to exercise his free will for the good. This is made possible by uprightness-of-will. But one cannot provide himself with such a disposition; that is, one cannot as an act of free will will that he have uprightness-of-will. Rather, he can will it only if he possesses it. And he possesses it only by the grace of God. Furthermore, the continuation of the possession of uprightness-of-will (whereby one is disposed to choose good over evil) is also made possible by God's grace: ". . . just as no one receives uprightness except by means of grace preceding, so no one keeps uprightness except by means of this same grace following. Assuredly, even though uprightness is kept by free choice, still its being kept must be imputed not so much to free choice as to grace; for free choice possesses and keeps uprightness only by means of prevenient and of subsequent grace." From this one ought not conclude that free will is an insignificant factor in the equation of salvation. Grace only provides for uprightness-of-will. Man must exercise it. This is made possible by free choice. Grace and free choice are both necessary conditions for salvation.

GRACE AND FREE CHOICE

1

It remains now for us to consider grace and free choice—doing so with the assistance of this grace. This controversy arises from the fact that Divine Scripture sometimes speaks in such a way that only grace—and not at all free choice—seems to avail to salvation. On the other hand, it sometimes speaks as if our entire salvation were dependent upon our free will. For, indeed, the Lord says concerning grace: "Without me you can do nothing,"[1] and "No one comes to me unless my father draws him."[2] And the Apostle Paul [asks]: "What do you have that you have not received?"[3] And concerning God [he says]: "He has mercy on whom He wills to, and He hardens whom He wills to."[4] [He says] also: "It is not of him who wills nor of him who runs but of God, who shows mercy."[5] We also read many other texts which seem to ascribe our good works and our salvation to grace alone apart from free choice. Furthermore, there are many people who profess to prove by experience that a man is never at all supported by any free choice. For they feel that countless individuals put forth an enormous effort of mind and body. But because these individuals are burdened by some obstacle—indeed, by some impossibility—they either make no headway, or else after having made much headway they suddenly and irretrievably fail.

But in the following manner Scripture teaches that we do have free choice. God declares through Isaiah: "If you are willing and shall hearken unto me, you shall eat the good things of the land."[6] And David [says]: "Who is the man who wants life, who loves to behold good days? Keep your tongue from evil; and let not your lips

From St. Anselm, *The Harmony of the Foreknowledge, The Predestination, and the Grace of God with Free Choice from Anselm of Canterbury*, Vol. 2, edited and translated by Jasper Hopkins and Herbert Richardson (Toronto and New York: The Edwin Mellen Press, 1976), pp. 198–223. Reprinted by permission of The Edwin Mellen Press.

speak guile. Turn away from evil and do good.'"[7] And the Lord [says] in the Gospel: "Come unto me all of you who are laboring and are heavily laden, and I will give you rest. Take my yoke upon you and learn from me, for I am meek and lowly in heart, and you shall find rest for your souls."[8] Moreover, there are countless other passages which are seen (1) to urge free choice to do good and (2) to reprove it because it spurns their admonitions. Divine Authority would never do this if it knew that there were no freedom-of-will in man. And if no one were to do good or evil by free choice, there would not be any way for God justly to reward good men and evil men according to their respective merits.

Therefore, since we find in Sacred Scripture certain passages which seem to favor grace alone and certain passages which are believed to establish free choice alone, apart from grace: there have been certain arrogant individuals who have thought that the whole efficacy of the virtues depends only upon freedom of choice; and in our day there are many who have completely given up on the idea that there is any freedom of choice. Therefore, in regard to this dispute, my intention will be to show that free choice coexists with grace and cooperates with it in many respects—just as we found it to be compatible with foreknowledge and with predestination.

2

We must recognize that just as this controversy (as I have said above)[9] concerns no other free choice than that without which no one (after he has reached the age of understanding) merits salvation, so it concerns no other grace than that without which no man is saved. For every creature exists by grace, because by grace he was created; moreover, by grace God gives in this life many goods without which a human being can still be saved. Indeed, in the case of infants who die, baptized, before they are able to use their free choice, the harmony which we are seeking does not appear. For in their case grace alone accomplishes salvation apart from their free choice. For the following fact occurs by grace: viz., that to others is given the will to assist, by their faith, these infants. Therefore, the solution we are seeking must be exhibited with regard to those who have reached the age of understanding,[10] because the controversy concerns them alone.

There is no doubt that whoever of these are saved are saved because of justice. For eternal life is promised to the just, because "the just shall live forever, and their reward is with the Lord."[11] Now, Sacred Authority often teaches that justice is uprightness-of-will. It suffices to cite one example of this fact. David said: "The Lord will not cast off His people nor forsake His inheritance until justice is turned into judgment."[12] And after he had said this, then in order to teach us what justice is, he asked: "And who is conformed to justice?" To this he replies, answering himself: "All who are upright in heart"—i.e., all who are upright in will. For although we both believe and understand in our heart,[13] even as we will in our heart, nevertheless the Holy Spirit does not deem to have an upright heart a man who believes rightly or understands rightly but does not will rightly. For this man does not use the uprightness of faith and of understanding for rightly willing; and rightly believing and rightly understanding are given to a rational creature for the sake of rightly willing. For he who does not rightly will in accordance with right understanding ought not to be said to have right understanding. And he who does not rightly will to act in accordance with faith—for this is the reason for which faith is given—is not said to have any faith except a dead faith.[14] Therefore, we correctly understand David to have meant by "the upright in heart" the upright in will. But lest someone think that Divine Authority calls just or upright a man who keeps uprightness-of-will only for the sake of something else, we say that justice is uprightness-of-will kept for its own sake.[15] For he who keeps uprightness only for the sake of

something else does not cherish uprightness but cherishes that thing for whose sake he keeps uprightness. And so he must not be called just, and such uprightness must not be called justice.

When I dealt with foreknowledge and free choice, I showed by an example[16] that uprightness-of-will, which I am calling justice, can coexist with free choice. (By means of this one example it is easy to discern that the same thing holds true in many other instances.) Therefore, if we can show that no creature can obtain uprightness-of-will except by means of grace, the harmony between grace and free choice will be manifest. This is the harmony which we are seeking and whose purpose is man's salvation.

3

Assuredly, there is no doubt that the will wills rightly only because it is upright. For just as sight is not acute because it sees acutely but sees acutely because it is acute, so the will is not upright because it wills rightly but wills rightly because it is upright. Now, when it wills uprightness-of-will, then without doubt it wills rightly. Therefore, it wills uprightness only because it is upright. But for the will to be upright is the same as for it to have uprightness. Therefore, it is evident that it wills uprightness only because it has uprightness. I do not deny that an upright will wills an uprightness which it does not have when it wills more uprightness than it already has. But I maintain that the will is not able to will any uprightness unless it has the uprightness by which to will uprightness.

Let us now consider whether someone who does not have uprightness-of-will can in some way have it from himself. Surely, he could have it from himself only by willing it or without willing it. But, indeed, it is not the case that by willing it someone is able to obtain it by his own efforts, because he is able to will it only if he has it. On the other hand, no one's mind accepts the view that someone who does not have uprightness-of-will can acquire it by himself without willing it. Therefore, a creature can in no way have uprightness from himself. But neither can one creature have it from another creature. For just as one creature cannot save another creature, so one creature cannot give to another creature the necessary means for salvation. Thus, it follows that only by the grace of God does a creature have the uprightness which I have called uprightness-of-will. Now, I have shown that uprightness-of-will can be kept by free choice (as I stated above).[17] Therefore, by the gift of God we have found that His grace harmonizes with free choice in order to save human beings. Thus, as happens in the case of infants, grace alone can save a human being when his free choice can do nothing; and in the case of those with understanding, grace always assists the natural free choice (which apart from grace is of no avail to salvation) by giving to the will the uprightness which it can keep by free choice.

Now, God does not give to everyone; for "He shows mercy to whom He wills to, and He hardens whom He wills to."[18] Nevertheless, He does not give to anyone on the basis of any antecedent merit; for "who has first given to God and it shall be recompensed to him?"[19] But if by free choice the will keeps what it has received and thereby merits either an increment of received justice, or, as well, the power for a good will, or some kind of reward: all of these are the fruits of the first grace, and are "grace for grace."[20] And so, everything must be imputed to grace because "it is not of him who wills" that he wills, "nor of him who runs" that he runs, but, instead, "is of God, who shows mercy."[21] For to all except God alone it is said: "What do you have that you have not received? And if you have received it, why do you glory as if you had not received it?"[22]

4

I deem myself to have shown[23] in my treatise on *Freedom of Choice* how a free will which is keeping its received uprightness is not beset by any necessity to abandon it but is beset by difficulty and yields to this difficulty willingly rather than unwillingly. Since grace assists in many ways, I cannot list all the ways in which grace aids free choice (after free choice has received this uprightness) to keep what it has received. Nonetheless, it will not be useless to say something about this matter. Assuredly, no one keeps this received uprightness except by willing it. But no one can will it unless he possesses it. And he cannot at all possess it except by means of grace. Therefore, just as no one receives uprightness except by means of grace preceding, so no one keeps uprightness except by means of this same grace following. Assuredly, even though uprightness is kept by free choice, still its being kept must be imputed not so much to free choice as to grace; for free choice possesses and keeps uprightness only by means of prevenient and of subsequent grace.

However, grace so follows its own gift that the only time grace ever fails to bestow this gift—whether it is something large or something small—is when free choice by willing something else forsakes the uprightness it has received. For this uprightness is never separated from the will except when the will wills something else which is incompatible with this uprightness—as when someone receives the uprightness of willing sobriety and rejects it by willing the immoderate pleasure of drinking. When a man does this, it is by his own will; and so, through his own fault he loses the grace which he received. For when free choice is under attack to abandon the uprightness it has received, grace even assists free choice—either by mitigating the assailing temptation's appeal, or by completely eliminating its appeal, or by increasing free choice's affection for uprightness. In fact, since everything is subject to the ordinance of God, all of what happens to a man which assists free choice to receive or to keep this uprightness of which I am speaking must be imputed to grace.

I have said[24] that all justice is uprightness-of-will kept for its own sake. Hence, it follows that everyone who has uprightness-of-will has justice and is just (since everyone who has justice is just). But it seems to me that eternal life is promised not to all who are just, but only to those who are just without any injustice. For these are properly and unqualifiedly called just in heart and upright in heart. For [there is a case where] someone is just in some respect and unjust in another respect (for example, a man who is both chaste and envious). The happiness of the just is not promised to such individuals, since even as true happiness exists without any deficiency, so it is given only to him who is just without being at all unjust.[25] The happiness which is promised to the just shall be like unto that of God's angels. Therefore, even as in the good angels there is no injustice, so no one with any injustice will be admitted into their company. But it is not my purpose to show how a man becomes free of all injustice. Nevertheless, we do know that for a Christian this state is attainable by means of holy endeavors and the grace of God.

5

If the points which have been made are considered carefully, one recognizes clearly that when Sacred Scripture says something in favor of grace it does not completely do away with free choice; and when it speaks in favor of free choice, it does not exclude grace. The case is not as if grace alone or free choice alone sufficed to save a man (as it seems to those who are the cause of the present controversy). Indeed, the divine sayings ought to be construed in such way that, with the exception of what I said about infants,[26] neither grace alone nor free choice alone accomplishes man's salvation.

Indeed, when the Lord says: "Without me you can do nothing,"[27] what He means is not "Your free choice is of no avail to you," but "It is of no avail without my grace." And when we read "It is not of him who wills nor of him who runs, but of God, who shows mercy,"[28] Scripture is not denying that free choice is of some use in the case of one who wills or runs; rather, it is

indicating that the fact that he wills and the fact that he runs have to be credited to grace rather than to free choice. For when Scripture says "It is not of him who wills nor of him who runs," we must supply: "The fact that he wills and the fact that he runs." The case is like someone's giving clothes to a naked person to whom he owes nothing and who by himself is unable to obtain a garment. Although the naked person has the ability to use and not to use the clothing he has received, still if he does use it, the fact that he is clothed must be credited not to him but to the one who gave him clothes. Therefore, we can speak as follows: "The fact that he is clothed is not of the one who is clothed but is of the one who shows mercy—i.e., of the one who gives the clothing." Much more would this be said if the one who gave the clothing had also given the ability to keep it and to use it—as when God gives to a man the oft-mentioned uprightness, He also gives the ability to keep and to use it, because He first gave the free choice for keeping and using uprightness. Now, if clothing were not given to this naked person to whom nothing is owed, or if this person were to throw it away after having received it, his state of nakedness would be credited to no one but himself. Similarly, when God gives willing and running to someone conceived and born in sin,[29] to whom He owes nothing except punishment, "it is not of him who wills nor of him who runs but of God, who shows mercy." And as for one who does not receive this grace, or one who rejects it after having received it: the fact that he remains in his obduracy and iniquity is due to him rather than to God.

The same interpretation—viz., that free choice is not ruled out—must be held to in the other passages in which Scripture speaks in favor of grace.

Likewise, when the divine sayings are expressed in such way that they seem to attribute man's salvation to free choice alone, grace ought in no respect to be excluded. Therefore, grace and free choice are not incompatible but cooperate in order to justify and to save a man—even as, although natural functioning procreates an offspring only by means of a mother and not without a father, nevertheless no accurate account excludes either a father or a mother from an offspring's generation.

6

Yet, in regard to those passages in which Scripture is seen to invite free choice to right-willing and right-working, people wonder why it invites a man to will rightly and why it condemns him if he is disobedient, seeing that no one can have or receive uprightness unless grace bestows it. We must note [the following comparison]: Without any cultivation on man's part the earth produces countless herbs and trees by which human beings are not nourished or by which they are even killed. But those herbs and trees which are especially necessary to us for nourishing our lives are not produced by the earth apart from seeds and great labor and a farmer. Similarly, without learning and endeavor human hearts freely germinate, so to speak, thoughts and volitions which are not conducive to salvation or which are even harmful thereto. But without their own kind of seed and without laborious cultivation human hearts do not at all conceive and germinate those thoughts and volitions without which we do not make progress toward our soul's salvation. Hence, those men upon whom such caretaking is bestowed the apostle calls "God's husbandry.[30] Now, the word of God constitutes the seed of this husbandry—or, better, not the word but the meaning which is discerned by means of the word. (For, indeed, without meaning, a word forms[31] nothing in the mind.)[32] And not only does the meaning of the word [of God] constitute a seed of willing rightly but so also does the entire meaning or signification of "uprightness"—which signification the human mind conceives either as a result of hearing or of reading or of reasoning or in whatever other way. For no one is able to will what he does not first conceive in his

mind.[33] Now, to will to believe what ought to be believed is to will rightly. Therefore, no one can will this if he does not know what ought to be believed. For after the apostle had first stated "Whoever shall call upon the name of the Lord shall be saved," he added: "How, then, shall they call upon Him in whom they have not believed? Or how shall they believe Him whom they shall not hear? And how shall they hear without a preacher? And how shall they preach unless they are sent?"[34] And a little later [he said]: "Therefore, faith [comes] by hearing; and hearing [comes] by the word of Christ."

Now, the apostle's statement that faith is derived from hearing must be interpreted to mean that faith is derived from that which the mind conceives as a result of hearing—derived not in such way that the mere mental concept produces faith in a man, but in such way that the concept is a necessary condition of faith. For, indeed, when uprightness-of-willing is added to the concept, faith is produced by grace, because the man believes what he hears. "And hearing comes by the word of Christ"—i.e., by the word of those who preach Christ. But there are no preachers unless they are sent. But the fact that they are sent is a grace. Therefore, preaching is a grace, because what derives from grace is a grace; and hearing is a grace, and the understanding which comes from hearing is a grace, and uprightness-of-willing is a grace. But sending, preaching, hearing, and understanding are worthless unless the will wills what the mind understands. But the will can do this only if it has received uprightness. For, indeed, it wills rightly when it wills what it ought. Thus, what the mind conceives as a result of hearing the word constitutes the seed of the preacher; and uprightness constitutes the growth which God gives—without which growth "neither he who plants nor he who waters is anything, but only God, who gives the growth."[35]

Therefore, just as in the beginning God miraculously—without seeds and without a cultivator—created wheat and other things which grow from the earth for the nourishment of men, so He miraculously—without human teaching—made the Gospels and the hearts of the prophets and apostles to be rich in salutary seeds. From these seeds we receive whatever we beneficially sow, in God's husbandry, for the nourishment of our souls—just as that which we cultivate for the nourishment of our bodies comes to us only from the first seeds of the earth. For, indeed, in our preaching, nothing which Sacred Scripture—made fruitful by the miracle of the Holy Spirit—has not set forth or does not contain is conducive to spiritual salvation. Now, if on the basis of rational considerations we sometimes make a statement which we cannot clearly exhibit in the words of Scripture, or cannot prove by reference to these words, nonetheless in the following way we know by means of Scripture whether the statement ought to be accepted or rejected. If the statement is arrived at by clear reasoning and if Scripture in no respect contradicts it, then (since even as Scripture opposes no truth, so it favors no falsity) by the very fact that Scripture does not deny that which is affirmed on the basis of rational considerations, this affirmation is supported by the authority of Scripture. But if Scripture unquestionably opposes a view of ours, then even though our reasoning seems to us unassailable, this reasoning should not be believed to be supported by any truth. So, then, Sacred Scripture—in that it either clearly affirms them or else does not at all deny them—contains the authority for all rationally derived truths.[36]

Let us now see in terms of examples how the word is the seed. When those to whom it is addressed hear the phrase "If you are willing and will hearken unto me . . ." they understand and conceive of what is called willing and obedience, or hearing. (For he who hears and does not obey is said not to hear.) Now, they cannot obey unless they will to. But to will to obey is to will rightly. And no one can will rightly unless he has uprightness-of-will, which a man has only

by grace. But uprightness-of-willing something is given to no one except to one who understands willing and what he ought to will. Thus, we see (1) that unless uprightness is added, the words "If you are willing and will hearken unto me . . ." are not at all a seed which bears fruit by itself, and (2) that uprightness-of-will is given only by means of seeds.

Likewise, when God says "Be converted to me,"[37] the seed is without germination as long as God does not turn a man's will to willing the conversion which this man thinks when he hears the words "Be converted"; but without this seed no one can will to be converted. Even to those who are already converted the command "Be converted" is addressed—either so that they become still further converted or so that they maintain the fact of their conversion. Now, those who say "Convert us, O God"[38] are already to some extent converted, because in willing to be converted they have an upright will. But because of the fact that they have already received conversion they are praying that their conversion be increased—even as those who were already believers requested: "Increase our faith."[39] It is as if both the former and the latter were saying: "Increase in us what You have given; complete what You have begun."

What I have shown with respect to these cases must be understood [to hold true] in similar cases as well.

So it is not the case that without seeds the earth naturally brings forth those plants which are especially necessary for the health of our bodies. And although God does not give growth to every seed, nevertheless our farmers do not cease to sow in the hope of some small harvest. Similarly, the soil of the human heart does not bring forth the fruit of faith and of justice without the appropriate seeds. And although God does not cause all seeds of this kind to grow, nevertheless He commands His husbandmen to sow His word earnestly and in hope. I have shown, it seems to me, how it is not superfluous to invite men to faith in Christ and to those things which this faith demands, even though they do not all accept this invitation.

7

I said[40] that we can also ask why those who do not accept the word of God are blamed, seeing that they cannot do this unless grace directs their wills. For the Lord says, with reference to the Holy Spirit: "He will accuse the world of sin because they do not believe in me."[41] Although it may be difficult to reply to this question, I ought not to keep to myself what I am able to answer with God's help. We must note that the inability which results from [someone's] guilt does not, as long as the guilt remains, excuse the one who has the inability.[42] Hence, in the case of infants,[43] in whom God demands from human nature the justice which it received in our first parents, together with its receiving the ability to keep justice in all its offspring: the inability to possess justice does not excuse human nature, since human nature fell into this inability blamably. For, indeed, the very fact that human nature does not possess that which it is unable by itself to reacquire [viz., justice] constitutes its inability to have [justice]. Human nature fell into this [condition of] inability because it freely abandoned that which it was able to keep. Therefore, since human nature abandoned justice by sinning, the inability which it brought upon itself by sinning is reckoned to it as sin. And in those who are not baptized, not only the inability to have justice but also the inability to understand it is likewise reckoned as sin, for this latter inability also results from sin.

We can also reasonably maintain the following point: the fact that human nature was corrupted and diminished in relation to the original dignity and strength and beauty of the human condition is reckoned to it as sin. For human nature thereby diminished, as much as it could, the honor

and the praise of God. Indeed, the wisdom of an artisan is praised and proclaimed in accordance with the excellence of his work. Therefore, the more human nature diminished and marred in itself the precious work of God, from which God was supposed to receive glory, the more it dishonored God by its own fault.[44] And this dishonoring is reckoned to it as such a grave sin that it is blotted out only by the death of God.[45]

Indeed, Sacred Authority shows very [clearly] that the following are reckoned as sin: viz., the impulses or appetites to which (as are brute animals) we are subject as a consequence of Adam's sin. The apostle calls these appetites flesh and concupiscence.[46] And when he says[47] "What I hate, that I do" (i.e., "against my will I inordinately desire"), he evidences that against his will he experiences concupiscence. Indeed, the Lord says of merely the impulse to anger, unexpressed in deed or word: "He who is angry with his brother will be held accountable for it at the judgment."[48] When He says this, He shows clearly that this guilt is not light—a guilt from which such grave condemnation (viz., the condemnation of death) follows. It is as if He were to say: "He who does what a man ought not to do, and who would not have done it if he had not sinned, ought to be removed from among men." And Paul says regarding those who against their will experience the flesh, i.e., carnal desires: "There is no condemnation to those who are in Christ Jesus, who do not walk after the flesh"—i.e., who do not freely consent [to the flesh].[49] When he says this, without question he signifies that those who are not in Christ are followed by condemnation as often as they feel carnal desire, even if they do not walk in accordance with it. For man was made in such way that he ought not to feel carnal desire, just as I said regarding anger. Therefore, if anyone considers carefully what I have said, he does not at all doubt that those who cannot—by their own fault—receive the word of God are rightly to be blamed.

8

But as regards those to whom the grace of Christian faith is given: just as in baptism the original injustice with which they are born is forgiven them, so [in baptism] there is forgiven all guilt of inability and of all the corruption which they incurred because of the sin of our first parent—corruption through which God is dishonored. For after baptism they are not blamed for any of the guilt which was in them before baptism,[50] even though the corruption and the appetites which are the penalty for sin are not immediately blotted out in baptism. Moreover, after baptism no transgression is charged to them except that which they commit of their own volition. Hence, it appears that the corruption and the evils which were the penalty for sin and which remain after baptism are not in themselves sins. For, indeed, only injustice is in itself a sin; and until injustice is forgiven, these evil consequences which follow from injustice are, due to their cause, *deemed* to be sins. For if they were [properly] sins, they would be blotted out in baptism, in which all sins are washed away by the blood of Christ. Likewise, if they were properly called sins they would be sins in the case of brute animals, after whose likeness our nature undergoes these evil consequences as a result of sin.

There is something else which can be discerned in human nature's first sin and which must be greatly feared. Since man is a "wind which goes out and does not return":[51] after he freely falls—to speak now only of voluntary sins—he can in no way rise up again unless he is raised up by grace. And unless he is held back by mercy, he is plunged by his own doing from one sin into another, down into the bottomless abyss (i.e., the measureless depth) of sins, in such way that even the good becomes something hateful to him and is for him unto death. Hence, the Lord says to the apostles: "If the world hates you, know that it hated me before hating you."[52] And the apostle [says]: "We are a good odor to God—among some the odor of death unto

death, but among others the odor of life unto life."[53] For this reason Scripture says concerning God: "He shows mercy to whom He wills to, and He hardens whom He wills to."[54] But He is not equally merciful to all to whom He is merciful; and He does not equally harden all whom He hardens.

9

Another question is why in this life the penalty for sin remains in us after the sin has been blotted out. Although I did not plan to deal with this question now, I will say briefly that if the faithful were immediately transformed at baptism or at martyrdom into the state of incorruption, then merit would perish and men would be saved without any merit (except for those first men who would believe without any precedent). Surely [in that case, then,] faith and hope—without which no man who has understanding[55] can merit the Kingdom of God—would vanish. (For faith and hope are directed toward those things which are unseen.) For since men would see those who would be converted to Christ pass over immediately into the state of incorruptibility,[56] there would be no one who would be able even to will to turn away from this very great happiness which he would behold. Therefore, in order that through the merit of faith and of hope we may more gloriously obtain the happiness we desire, we remain—for as long as we are in this life—in this state which is no longer reckoned unto us as sin, even though it has resulted because of sin.

In fact, it is not the case that through baptism and the Christian faith we are assured of the happiness which Adam had in Paradise before sinning. Rather, we are assured of the happiness which he was going to have when the number of men who were to be added to fill up the Heavenly City[57] would be complete. This city is to be filled with angels and men; but in it men will not procreate,[58] as they would have done in Paradise. Therefore, if converts to Christ were immediately to pass over into that state of incorruptibility, there would not remain men from whom this number could be gathered, because no one would be able to keep from rushing toward the happiness he would behold. I think that this is what the apostle means when he says regarding those who through faith have worked justice: "And all of these, approved by the witness of their faith, did not receive the promise, since God is providing something better for us, so that they are not made complete without us."[59] Now, if one asks what better thing God has provided for us from their not having received the promise, I do not see that anything can be replied more suitably than what I said above, viz., the following: If the happiness promised to the just were not delayed for those who have been approved, merit would perish in those who would learn of this fact by experience rather than by faith. Also the process of human procreation from which we are begotten would stop, since all men would run after that incorruptibility which they would see to be present. Therefore, God provided a great good for us when for the saints who have been approved by the witness of their faith He delayed the reception of the promise. [He caused this delay] in order that we would continue to be propagated and that faith would remain—by which faith we would together with them merit the promise and would be made perfect at the same time as they.

There is also another reason why the baptized and the martyrs do not immediately become incorruptible. Suppose that a master severely scourges his servant, whom he had planned to enrich some day with great honors, for a wrong for which the servant is not at all able by himself to make satisfaction. And suppose that after this scourging the master is going to thrust his servant, at a fixed time, into a dreadful prison where he will be afflicted with grievous punishments. Suppose, further, that someone influential with his master makes satisfaction for him and reconciles him. Surely, the stripes which the guilty servant deservedly received prior to the satisfaction and while he was at fault, are not removed; but the graver torments into which he was not yet thrust are averted by the prevening reconciliation. Moreover, as for the honors which, had he not sinned, he was going to receive in due time and of which, had he not been reconciled, he was going to be deprived after his wrongdoing: because of the complete satisfaction these honors are given to him without any alteration, as was originally determined. Indeed, if he had been disinherited of these honors before his reconciliation (just as, had he not been reconciled, he would deservedly and irrecoverably have been disinherited of them after his wrongdoing), there would have been no way for any reconciliation to assist [in their recovery]. But since he could not be disinherited of an honor which he did not yet have and was not required to have, the reconciliation can intervene prior to this disinheritance and can avert it—provided that while lying in the soreness of his stripes until such time as this soreness passes away, the servant pledges in heart and in word fidelity to his master and self-reform, and provided he fulfills his pledge.

The relationship between God and man is analogous to this one. Indeed, when human nature first sinned, it was scourged with the following penalty: (1) it would never by natural means beget offspring except in that state in which we observe infants to be born; (2) after this life it would be forever banished into Hell—banished from the Kingdom of God, for which it was created. [This was to happen] unless someone reconciled human nature—something which human nature was unable to do by itself. But Christ is the only one by whom human nature is able to be reconciled. Therefore, in all infants who are begotten by natural means human nature is born with sin and its penalty. When human nature enters the state of reconciliation, this penalty which it received before reconciliation deservedly remains. But those torments which human nature was going to suffer in Hell are remitted for those whom Christ redeems. And human nature is presented with the Kingdom of God which in due time it was going to receive after its sojourn in the earthly paradise—provided that the redeemed persevere unto the end in the faith which they promise at baptism.

10

Certain individuals think that free choice is proved by experience to be able [to accomplish] nothing; for many people make an enormous effort to live rightly, and yet because of some impossibility (as they call it) which stands in their way, they either make no headway or else after having made some progress they fail irreparably. But the fact [that they think this] does not destroy the point which has been rationally demonstrated: viz., that free choice can [accomplish something] cooperatively with grace. But in my opinion that fact that when they make an effort they either do not make any headway or else after having made some progress they fail, occurs not because of an impossibility but because of an obstacle which is sometimes serious, sometimes easily surmountable.[60] Indeed, we are accustomed to say that something which we are unable to accomplish without difficulty is impossible for us. For if each of us carefully examines his own acts of willing, he will discern that he never abandons uprightness-of-will (which he has received by grace) except by willing something else which he cannot will compatibly [with willing uprightness].[61] Surely, he abandons uprightness-of-will not because the *ability* to keep it fails him (which ability constitutes freedom of choice) but because the *will* to keep it fails him. The will-to-keep-uprightness is not deficient in itself but ceases because another willing expels it (as I said).

11

But since this last consideration concerns the will, I deem it necessary to say in more detail about the will something which shall

not be useless, it seems to me. In our bodies we have five senses and [various] members, each of which, distinctly, is adapted for its own special function. We use these members and senses as instruments. For example, the hands are suited for grasping, the feet for walking, the tongue for speaking, and sight for seeing. Similarly, the soul too has in itself certain powers which it uses as instruments for appropriate functions. For in the soul there is reason, which the soul uses (as its instrument) for reasoning; and there is will, which the soul uses for willing. Neither reason nor will is the whole of the soul; rather, each of them is something within the soul. Therefore, since the distinct instruments have their essence, their aptitudes, and their uses, let us distinguish in the will—in regard to which we are discussing these matters—the instrument, its aptitudes, and its uses.[62] In regard to the will we can call these aptitudes *inclinations (affectiones)*. Indeed, the instrument-for-willing is modified by its own inclinations. Hence, when a man's soul strongly wills something, it is said to be inclined to will that thing, or to will it affectionally.

Assuredly, the will is seen to be spoken of equivocally—in three senses. For (a) the instrument-for-willing, (b) the inclination of this instrument, and (c) the use of this instrument, are distinguishable. The instrument-for-willing is that power-of-the-soul[63] which we use for willing—just as reason is the instrument-for-reasoning, which we use when we reason, and just as sight is the instrument-for-seeing, which we use when we see. The inclination (*affectio*) of the instrument-for-willing is that by which the instrument is so inclined to will some given thing (even when a man is not thinking of that which he wills) that if this thing comes to mind, then the will wills [to have] it either immediately or at the appropriate time. For example, the instrument-for-willing is so inclined to will health (even when a man is not thinking of it) that as soon as health comes to mind, the will wills [to have] it immediately. And the instrument-for-willing is so inclined to will sleep (even when a man is not thinking of this) that when it comes to mind, the will wills [to have] it at the appropriate time. For the will is never inclined in such way that it ever wills sickness or that it wills never to sleep. Likewise, in a just man the instrument-for-willing is so inclined to will justice (even when a man is asleep) that when he thinks of justice he wills [to have] it immediately.

On the other hand, the use of this instrument is something which we have only when we are thinking of the thing which we will.

Now, the word "will" applies to the instrument-for-willing, to the inclination of this instrument, and to the use of this instrument. (1) Indeed, we call the instrument *will* when we say that we direct the will toward various things (e.g., now toward willing to walk, now toward willing to sit, now toward willing something else). A man always possesses this instrument even though he does not always use it. The case is similar to his having sight, in the sense of the instrument-for-seeing, even when he does not use it (e.g., when he is asleep). But when he does use it, he directs it now toward seeing the sky, now toward seeing the earth, now toward seeing something else. Moreover, the case is similar to our always possessing the instrument-for-reasoning, viz., reason, which we do not always use and which, in reasoning, we direct toward various things. (2) But the inclination of the instrument-for-willing is called *will* when we say that a man always possesses the will for his own well-being. For in this case we label as *will* that inclinationn (of the instrument) by which a man wills his own well-being. [The same thing is true] when in this way we say that a saint—even when he is sleeping and is not thinking about living justly—continually has the will to live justly. Moreover, when we say that one person has more of the will to live justly than another person, the only thing we are calling *will* is the instrument's inclination, by which a man wills to live justly. For the instrument itself is not greater in one person and less in another. (3) But the use of the instrument-for-willing

is called *will* when someone says "I now have the will to read" (that is, "I now will to read")—or says, "I now have the will to write" (that is, "I now will to write"). Indeed, seeing is using sight, i.e., using the instrument-for-seeing; and the use of sight is seeing, or sight (in cases, that is, where "sight" signifies the same thing as "seeing," for "sight" also signifies the instrument-for-seeing). Similarly, willing is using the will, i.e., using the instrument-for-willing; and the use of the will is the willing which occurs only when we are thinking of that thing which we will.

Therefore, there is only one will in the sense of the instrument; that is, there is in a man only one instrument-for-willing (even as there is only one reason, i.e., only one instrument-for-reasoning). But the will by which the instrument is modified is twofold. For just as sight has several aptitudes (viz., an aptitude for seeing light, and an aptitude for seeing figures by means of light, and an aptitude for seeing colors by means of figures), so the instrument-for-willing has two aptitudes, which I am calling inclinations. One of these is the inclination to will what is beneficial; the other is the inclination to will what is right.[64] To be sure, the will which is the instrument wills nothing except either a benefit or uprightness. For whatever else it wills, it wills either for the sake of a benefit or for the sake of uprightness; and even if it is mistaken, it regards itself as referring what it wills to these two ends. Indeed, because of the inclination to will what is beneficial, a man always wills happiness and to be happy. On the other hand, because of the inclination to will uprightness, he wills uprightness and to be upright (i.e., to be just). Now, he wills something for the sake of a benefit when, for instance, he wills to plow and to labor in order to have the wherewithal to preserve his life and health, both of which he deems to be benefits. And [he wills something] for the sake of uprightness when, for example, he wills to work at learning in order to know rightly, i.e., to live justly. But the will which is the use of this oft-mentioned instrument is present only when someone is thinking of that thing which he wills, as was already said. The distinctions of this will are multiple; I shall not discuss them now, though perhaps elsewhere I shall.[65]

Indeed, "to will" has equivocal senses, just as does "to see." For just as "to see" is predicated both of the one who uses his sight and of the one who does not use it even though he has the aptitude to see, so "to will" is predicated both of the one who (while he is thinking of the thing he wills) uses the instrument-for-willing and—since he has the inclination (i.e., the aptitude) to will—of the one who does not use it.

From the consideration which follows, we can also recognize that the instrument-for-willing, the inclination of this instrument, and the use of this instrument are different "wills": A just man is said to have—even while he is asleep and is not thinking of anything—the will to live justly. And an unjust man is denied to possess—when he is sleeping—the will to live justly. Now, the same will which is being affirmed of the just man is being denied of the unjust man. But obviously when we deny that the will to live justly is in the unjust man who is sleeping, we are not denying that the will which I have called the instrument is in him; for every man, both while asleep and awake, always has this will. Therefore, since no other will than that will which is absent from the evil man is said thus to be present in the good man: it is not the will-as-instrument which is being signified to be present in the good man; rather [what is being signified is] that will by means of which the instrument is modified. Now, there is no doubt that the will-as-use is not present in a sleeping man (unless he is dreaming). Hence, when the will to live justly is said to be present in a just man who is asleep, the will-as-use is not meant. Therefore, the will-as-inclination is not identical with the will-as-instrument or with the will-as-use. Moreover, everyone knows that the will-as-instrument is not identical with the will-as-use; for when I say that I do not have the will to write, no one interprets this to mean that I do not

have the instrument-for-willing. Consequently, the will-as-instrument, the will-as-inclination, and the will-as-use are not identical.[66]

Indeed, the will-as-instrument moves all the other instruments which we freely use—both those instruments which are a part of us (such as our hands, our tongue, our sight) and those that are independent of us (such as a pen and an ax). Furthermore, it causes all of our voluntary movements; but it moves itself by means of its inclinations. Hence, it can be called an instrument that moves itself. I am saying that the will-as-instrument causes all our voluntary movements. Yet—if we consider the matter carefully—God is more truly said to cause everything that our nature or our will causes, for He causes the nature and the instrument-for-willing, together with the instrument's inclinations, without which the instrument does nothing.

12

A man's every merit, whether good or evil, derives from these two inclinations which I am also calling wills. These two wills also differ in that the one for willing what is beneficial is inseparable, but the one for willing what is upright was (as I have said above)[67] separable, originally, in angels and in our first parents; and it is still separable in those who remain in this life. These two wills also differ in that the one for willing benefit is not this thing which it wills; but the one for willing uprightness is uprightness. Indeed, no one wills uprightness except someone who has uprightness; and no one is able to will uprightness except by means of uprightness. But it is clear that this uprightness belongs to the will considered as instrument. This is the uprightness I am speaking of when I define "justice" as uprightness-of-will kept for its own sake.[68] This uprightness is also the truth of the will wherein the Lord charges the Devil with not having remained steadfastly, as I have stated in the treatise *On Truth*.[69]

We must now consider how men's merits (as I was saying)—whether merits unto salvation or unto condemnation—proceed from the two wills which I am calling aptitudes or inclinations. In itself, to be sure, uprightness is a cause of no evil merit but is the mother of every good merit. For uprightness favors the spirit as it strives against the flesh; and uprightness "delights in the law of God in accordance with the inner man,"[70] i.e., in accordance with the spirit [which strives against the flesh]. However, [even] if evil sometimes seems to follow from uprightness, it does not proceed from uprightness but proceeds from something else. Indeed, because of their uprightness the apostles were a good odor unto God.[71] But the fact that unto certain men the apostles were "the odor of death unto death"[72] did not proceed from their justice but from evil men's wickedness. Now, the will for willing what is beneficial is not always evil, but is evil when it consents to the flesh as it strives against the spirit.[73]

13

But in order to understand this matter more clearly, we must investigate how the will [for what is beneficial] became so corrupt and so prone to evil. For we must not believe that in our first parents God created it prone to evil. Now, when I stated[74] that because of sin human nature became corrupt and acquired appetites similar to those of brute animals, I did not explain how such a will arose in man. Indeed, base appetites are one thing; a corrupt will that assents to these appetites is another thing. Therefore, it seems to me, we must ask about how such a will became the lot of man.

The cause of such a will as this shall readily become apparent to us if we consider the original condition of rational nature. The intention of God was to create rational nature just and happy in order that it would enjoy Him.[75] Now, it was able to be neither just nor happy without the will-for-justice and the will-for-happiness. As-

suredly, the will-for-justice is itself justice; but the will-for-happiness is not happiness because not everyone who has the will-for-happiness has happiness. However, everyone believes that happiness—whether angelic happiness is meant or the happiness which Adam had in Paradise—includes a sufficiency of suitable benefits and excludes all need. For although the happiness of angels is greater than the happiness of man in Paradise, still Adam cannot be denied to have had happiness. For, indeed, nothing prevents Adam from having been happy in Paradise and free of all need, in spite of the fact that angelic happiness was greater than his. (By comparison, an intense heat is free of all cold; and, nevertheless, there can be another more intense heat. And cold is free of all heat, even though there can be a more intense cold.) To be sure, having less of a thing than does another is not always identical with being in need; to be in need is to be deprived of something when it ought to be possessed— a condition which was not true of Adam. Where there is need there is unhappiness. God created rational nature for knowing and loving Him; but it is not the case that He created it unhappy when it had no antecedent guilt. Therefore, God created man happy and in need of nothing. Hence, at one and the same time rational nature received (1) the will-for-happiness, (2) happiness, (3) the will-for-justice (i.e., uprightness which is justice itself), and (4) free choice, without which rational nature could not have kept justice.

Now, God so ordained these two "wills," or inclinations, that (1) the will-as-instrument would use the will-which-is-justice for commanding and governing (though being itself instructed by the spirit, which is also called mind and reason), and that (2) without any detriment it would use the other will to the end of obedience. Indeed, God gave happiness to man—not to speak of the angels—for man's benefit. But He gave man justice for His own honor. [He gave] justice in such way that man was able to abandon it, so that if he did not abandon it but kept it perseveringly, he would merit being elevated to fellowship with the angels. But if man did abandon justice, he would not thereafter be able to regain it by himself; nor would he attain to the happiness of the angels. Rather, he would be deprived of that happiness which he possessed; and falling into the likeness of brute animals, he would be subjected with them to corruption and to the appetites I have often mentioned. Nevertheless, the will-for-happiness would remain in order that by means of man's need for the goods which he had lost he would be justly punished with deep unhappiness. Therefore, since he abandoned justice, he lost happiness. And the will which he received as being good and as being for his own good is fervent with desire for benefits which it is unable to keep from willing. And because it is unable to have the true benefits which are suitable for rational nature but which rational nature has lost, it turns itself to benefits which are false and which pertain to brute animals and which bestial appetites suggest. And thus when the will inordinately wills these benefits it either (1) shuns uprightness, so that it does not accept uprightness when uprightness is offered, or else (2) it casts uprightness away after having received it. But when the will wills these benefits within proper bounds, it neither shuns nor casts away uprightness.

So the will-as-instrument was created good, with respect to the fact that it has being; moreover, it was created just and having the power to keep the justice it received. And in the above manner it was made evil by free choice. [It was made evil] not insofar as it exists but insofar as it was made unjust as a result of the absence of justice, which was freely abandoned and which it was always supposed to have. Moreover, it now became powerless to will the justice it had deserted. For it is not the case that by free choice the will can will justice when it does not have justice—as it is the case that by free choice the will can keep justice when it has justice. Furthermore, the will-for-the-beneficial, a will which was created good insofar as it is something, became evil (i.e., unjust) because it was not subordinate to justice,

without which it ought to will nothing. Therefore, since the will-as-instrument freely became unjust: after having abandoned justice, it remains (as regards its own power) a servant of injustice and unjust by necessity. For it is unable by itself to return to justice; and without justice the will is never free, because without justice the natural freedom of choice is idle. The will was also made the servant of its own inclination for the beneficial, because once justice has been removed, the will is able to will only what this inclination wills.

I predicate "to will" of both the instrument and its inclination; for the instrument is *will*, and the inclination is *will*. And without impropriety "to will" is predicated of both these wills. For the instrument, which wills by means of its inclination, does indeed will; and the inclination, by means of which the instrument wills, also wills. (Similarly, "to see" is predicated both of the man who sees by means of sight and of the sight by which the man sees.) Hence, we can without absurdity say that the inclinations of this will which I have called the soul's instrument are, so to speak, "instruments" of this instrument, because it does something only by means of them. Therefore, when the "instrument"-for-willing-justice (i.e., when uprightness) has been lost, the will-as-instrument cannot at all will justice, unless justice is restored by grace. Therefore, since the will-as-instrument ought to will nothing except justly, whatever it wills without uprightness, it wills unjustly. None of the appetites which the apostle calls the flesh and concupiscence are evil or unjust with respect to the fact that they exist; rather they are called unjust because they are present in a rational nature, where they ought not to be found. For, indeed, they are not evil or unjust in brute animals, because they ought to be present there.

14

From what has already been said above, one can recognize that the reason a man does not always possess justice (which he ought always to have) is that he cannot at all acquire or regain it by himself. It is also clear that God causes good works only by His goodness, since He creates the will with free choice and gives it the justice in accordance with which it is acting. But God causes evil deeds only because of man's fault; for God would not cause these deeds if man did not will to do them.[76] Nevertheless, God causes that which they are [essentially], since He has placed in man the will which man uses without justice. And so, the evil deeds which God causes occur only by man's fault. For it is not the case [that they occur] by the fault of God, who created in man a will with freedom of choice and who conferred justice on it so that it would will nothing except justly. Rather, [they occur] by the fault of man, who abandoned the justice which he could have kept. Therefore, in the case of good works God causes both the fact that they are good with respect to their being and that they are good with respect to their justice. But in the case of evil works God causes only the fact that they are good with respect to their being; He does not cause the fact that they are evil with respect to the absence of required justice—an absence which is not anything. Man, however, in the case of good deeds,

causes the fact that they are not evil, because although he was able to abandon justice and to do evil deeds, he did not abandon it but kept it by means of free choice—[justice] being given and followed up by grace.[77] Now, in the case of evil deeds [man causes] only the fact that they are evil, because he does them by an autonomous will (i.e., by an unjust will).[78]

I think that I can now fittingly conclude this treatise which has dealt with three difficult controversies—a treatise which I undertook in the expectation that God would help me. If I have herein said something which ought to suffice any inquirer, I do not impute it to myself, for it is not my [doing] but is [the work of] God's grace in me. However, I do make the following claim: Had someone given me—when I was asking about these issues and when my mind, perplexed, was seeking in them a rationale—the answers which I have written, I would have been grateful, because he would have satisfied me. Therefore, since what I know about this topic, by God's revelation, was especially pleasing to me: knowing that it would likewise please certain others if I recorded it, I wanted freely to bestow, on those who are seeking, that which I have freely received.

NOTES

1. John 15:5.
2. John 6:44.
3. I Cor. 4:7.
4. Rom. 9:18.
5. Rom. 9:16.
6. Isa. 1:19.
7. Ps. 33:13–15 (34:12–14).
8. Matt. 11:28–29.
9. *De Concordia Praescientiae et Praedestinationis et Gratiae Dei cum Libero Arbitrio* I, 6 (S II, 256:5–7, 9–10).
10. Rom. 9:18.
11. Wisd. of Sol. 5:16.
12. Ps. 93:14–15 (94:14–15).
13. "*Cor*" is broader than the English word "heart"—even in the figurative sense of "heart," viz., the seat of all affections. Indeed, in its figurative sense, "*cor*" signifies the seat of all affections and of all mental activity. Accordingly, it can in some instances—as in the above instance— also be translated as *mind*. N.B. *Cur Deus Homo* II, 4 (S II, 99:8).
14. Regarding dead faith see *Monologion* 78.
15. Note *De Veritate* 12.
16. *De Concordia Praescientiae et Praedestinationis et Gratiae Dei cum Libero Arbitrio* I, 6 (S II, 257:5–24).

17. Loc. cit.
18. Rom. 9:18.
19. Rom. 11:35.
20. John 1:16.
21. Rom. 9:16.
22. I Cor. 4:7.
23. *De Libertate Arbitrii* 5–7.
24. *De Concordia Praescientiae et Praedestinationis et Gratiae Dei cum Libero Arbitrio* III, 2 (S II, 265:14–15).
25. See *Cur Deus Homo* I, 24 (S II, 93:7–9).
26. In the first part of *De Concordia Praescientiae et Praedestinationis et Gratiae Dei cum Libero Arbitrio* III, 2.
27. John 15:5.
28. Rom. 9:16.
29. Ps. 50:7 (51:5).
30. I Cor. 3:9.
31. Cf. *Monologion* 10; *Proslogion* 4; *On Behalf of the Fool* 4; *Ein neues unvollendetes Werk des hl. Anselm von Canterbury* (Philosophical Fragments) 43:5–11.
32. "In the mind," i.e., *in corde*. See n. 15.
33. See n. 15.
34. See Rom. 10:13–15.
35. I Cor. 3:7.
36. Cf. the last paragraph of *De Processione Spiritus Sancti* 14.
37. Isa. 45:22.
38. Ps. 84:5 (85:4).
39. Luke 17:5.
40. At the beginning of *De Concordia Praescientiae et Praedestinationis et Gratiae Dei cum Libero Arbitrio* III, 6.
41. John 16:8–9.
42. See the first portion of *Cur Deus Homo* I, 24. Note *De Conceptu Virginali et de Originali Peccato* 29.
43. See *De Conceptu Virginali et de Originali Peccato* 2 (S II, 142:1–4).
44. Cf. *Cur Deus Homo* I, 15.
45. I.e., by the death of Jesus, who was God.
46. Rom. 7:7–8.
47. Rom. 7:15.
48. Matt. 5:22.
49. Rom. 8:1.
50. Cf. *De Conceptu Virginali et de Originali Peccato* 29.
51. Ps. 77:39 (78:39).
52. John 15:18.
53. II Cor. 2:15–16.
54. Rom. 9:18.
55. I.e., no one who has passed beyond infancy and reached the age of understanding. See n. 10.
56. Cf. the last part of the Teacher's speech in *De Libertate Arbitrii* 9.
57. Note *Cur Deus Homo* I, 16–18.
58. Note *Cur Deus Homo* I, 18 (S II, 83:12–16). Also see *De Casu Diaboli* 5 and 23.
59. Heb. 11:33, 39, 40.
60. Cf. *De Libertate Arbitrii* 6.
61. See *De Casu Diaboli* 3 for Anselm's fuller argument.
62. In *De Libertate Arbitrii* 7 Anselm distinguishes only two wills (or two senses of "will"): the instrument-for-willing and the uses of this instrument.
63. The instrument-for-willing is thus the power-of-willing. Cf. *De Conceptu Virginali et de Originali Peccato* 4 (S II, 143:27–28).
64. Note *De Casu Diaboli* 4 (S I, 241:13, 16).
65. See *Ein neues unvollendetes Werk des hl. Anselm von Canterbury* (Philosophical Fragments) 37 ff., where various distinctions occur. We are not required, however, to infer that this section of *Ein neues unvollendetes Werk des hl. Anselm von Canterbury* was written *later* than *De Concordia Praescientiae et Praedestinationis et Gratiae Dei cum Libero Arbitrio*. Anselm is suggesting that he may publish another work; but portions of it may have been written prior to *De Concordia Praescientiae et Praedestinationis et Gratiae Dei cum Libero Arbitrio*.
66. In *De Libertate Arbitrii* 7 Anselm distinguishes only between will-as-instrument and will-as-use. *De Casu Diaboli* 13–14 discusses the will-as-inclination without designating it by this label. The present treatment is an explicit refinement of the view put forth in *De Casu Diaboli*.
67. *De Concordia Praescientiae et Praedestinationis et Gratiae Dei cum Libero Arbitrio* I, 6 (S II, 256:22–23).

68. *De Concordia Praescientiae et Praedestinationis et Gratiae Dei cum Libero Arbitrio* III, 2 (S II, 265:14–15). Note *De Veritate* 12.

69. *De Veritate* 4.

70. Gal. 5:17.

71. Cf. II Cor. 2:15.

72. II Cor. 2:16.

73. Gal. 5:17.

74. *De Concordia Praescientiae et Praedestinationis et Gratiae Dei cum Libero Arbitrio* III, 7 (S II, 274:3–7). Note *De Casu Diaboli* 23 (S I, 270:1–3); *De Conceptu Virginali et de Originali Peccato* 2 (S II, 141:12–16).

75. See *Cur Deus Homo* II, 1.

76. Note *De Casu Diaboli* 20.

77. Note the first part of *De Concordia Praescientiae et Praedestinationis et Gratiae Dei cum Libero Arbitrio* III, 4.

78. Note *De Concordia Praescientiae et Praedestinationis et Gratiae Dei cum Libero Arbitrio* I, 6 (S II, 256:24); *De Concordia Praescientiae et Praedestinationis et Gratiae Dei cum Libero Arbitrio* I, 7 (S II, 259:26); *De Casu Diaboli* 4 (S I, 242:3–10); *Epistola de Incarnatione Verbi* 10 (S II, 27:1–6); *Cur Deus Homo* II, 9 (S II, 105:22–24).

CHAPTER 24

St. Bonaventure

St. Bonaventure, whose real name was John of Fidanza, was born circa 1217 at Bagnorea in Tuscany (Italy). He was awarded a master of arts degree at Paris, after which he joined the Franciscan friars (probably in 1243) in time to study theology under the masters Alexander of Hales and John of La Rachelle before these two died in 1245. He continued his studies at Paris and in 1248 began lecturing on the Gospel of St. Luke and then on other books of Scripture. He composed his monumental "Commentary of the *Sentences* of Peter Lombard" between 1250 and 1252. Traditionally he is known as the Seraphic Doctor.

It is clear from the writings of Bonaventure that throughout his life he was a devoted Franciscan from an intellectual point of view. That is, he thoroughly embraced the Augustinian tradition, staunchly resisting Aristotelian philosophy, which was avant-garde at the University of Paris at the time. In 1253 he was licensed by the chancellor of that university as regent master of theology, a role in which Bonaventure functioned until 1257. During this period he composed "On Christ's Knowledge," "On the Mystery of the Trinity," and "On Charity and the Last Things". Also during this period (1255) he became embroiled in the controversy between the mendicant friars and the secular masters. This caused a delay in his recognition as a doctor and professor of the university staff. As a result of papal intervention, he was so recognized and readmitted to the university staff in October 1257. This acceptance was of little substantive import to Bonaventure, since earlier that year he had been elected minister general of his order. He subsequently resigned his chair at the university to devote his energies to resolving various disputes which at the time were prevalent within the order itself. He continued to reside at Paris, making it his general headquarters. He never lost touch with the university, where he frequently preached and lectured. Furthermore, Bonaventure encouraged the development of studies within the Franciscan order. He believed that any person destined for the priesthood must study the Scriptures and theology. However, it is impossible to study scholastic theology without a background in philosophy. The study of philosophy is an ongoing process, an everlasting inquiry into the Truth. Consequently, there was a push by Bonaventure toward erudition within the priesthood.

In 1265 Pope Clement IV appointed Bonaventure to the archbishopric of York, which the former rescinded in light of the latter's resistance. In 1273, however, he was made cardinal bishop of Albano by Pope Gregory X, with whom he worked in organizing the Second Ecumenical Council of Lyons, called for the purpose of considering the eastern schism, the condition of the Holy Land, and the abuses in the church. It was at that council in 1274 that he preached on and lobbied for the reunion of the Eastern Church with Rome. On July 15, 1274, shortly before the close of the council, Bonaventure died. He was buried at Lyons in the presence of the pope.

St. Bonaventure on the Trinity

The start of Bonaventure's analysis is Anselm's characterization of God as that being than which nothing greater can be conceived. "He is therefore most excellent in nature and power, in wisdom and goodness, in influence and causality." The unicity of God follows from His possession of these attributes as they are understood as dimensions of His perfection. For example, if omnipotence were the attribute of many, it would follow that one of those beings would have the power to cancel the power of another of those beings. Consequently, many beings cannot (logically) be omnipotent. Such is, and can only be, the attribute of only one God. It is objected, however, that omnipotence entails the highest degree of (possible) power, from which it follows God "can produce something distinct from Himself that would be as great as himself. It is, therefore, consonant with omnipotence that there be a multiplicity of gods." To this objection Bonaventure notes that the sharing of such power among many gods is possible to initiate. However, such sharing would be an affront to the dignity of God acting according to his omnipotence. That is to say, sharing power would not be a worthy attribute of a being than which none greater can be conceived. Hence, there must be only one God that is omnipotent. A similar line of reasoning applies to the other five attributes cited by Bonaventure.

He then addresses the issue as to how God's unicity can exist together with a trinity of persons. At first it would appear that such cannot be the case. For example, ". . . to be one both in substance and in property is more perfect than to be one in only one of these". A trinity, however, entails a plurality of properties. Consequently, a trinity is incompatible with God's unicity. The resolution of this problem lies in understanding that property is twofold; namely, absolute and relative. If property is taken in the absolute sense, there is indeed an incompatibility between God's unicity and the Trinity. However, if property is construed as relative there is no problem "since plurality in terms of a relative property does not posit diversity in the thing or in the nature, neither with respect to the essence nor with respect to existence. . .". In other words, that Christ sits on the right hand of God does not entail that the essence of Christ differs from God, for their essence would remain unaltered were Christ to sit to the left of God. Relational predicates are accidental and therefore do not affect the essence of God or Christ or the Holy Spirit, which are one by virtue of identical essence and existence. Overall, Bonaventure addresses twenty such issues concerning the relationship between the Trinity and God's unicity.

DISPUTED QUESTIONS ON THE MYSTERY OF THE TRINITY

Question II
Whether a Trinity of Persons Can Exist Together with Unity of Nature

Supposing that it is a truth of faith that God is a trinity, it is then asked whether a trinity of persons can exist together with unity of nature. Two questions are raised concerning this matter. The first is whether the divine being is supremely one. The second is whether the highest unity of nature can exist together with a trinity of persons.

Article I
Whether the Divine Being Is Supremely One

Concerning the first question, we will proceed to show that the divine being is supremely one. That this is so is sufficiently proclaimed by faith and by the divine Scriptures, in Exodus 20: "God, your God, is one";[1] and in Deuteronomy 32: "See, therefore, that I alone am God, and there is no other God beside me";[2] and David in the *Psalm*: "There shall be no strange God among you, and you shall not worship any foreign God."[3] The divine Scriptures give sufficient instruction on this matter. It is now our intention to demonstrate the same thing by arguments. For every mind that makes use of reason supposes that God is that than which nothing greater or better can be conceived; He is therefore most excellent in nature and power, in wisdom and goodness, in influence and causality. For if He suffered a defect in any of these, then He would not be the highest, and consequently He would not be God. Therefore these six qualities are supposed as true and most certain.

From St. Bonaventure, *Disputed Questions on the Mystery of the Trinity*, translated by Zachary Hayes, O.F.M., D.Th. (St. Bonaventure, N.Y.: The Franciscan Institute; St. Bonaventure University, 1979), pp. 138–158. Reprinted by permission of The Franciscan Institute.

Arguments in Agreement

1. The argument from sublimity of nature is as follows. That which excels all others is more sublime than that which does not. Therefore, if it is impossible for more than one being to excel all others, then it is impossible and even unintelligible that God should not be one.[4] For if we were to suppose a plurality here, it would follow that one and the same being both excels the others and is excelled by them. Therefore if several beings were God, none would be God. Therefore, either God does not exist, or if He exists, He is one.

2. The argument from omnipotence is the following. A being is truly omnipotent not only if it can do all things, but also if it is the source from which all power is derived. But to be able to do all things and to be the cause of all power can belong only to one being—if it belonged to many, it would belong to none. If, therefore, omnipotence is an attribute of God, it is impossible and unintelligible that God should not be one; because if several beings were omnipotent, each of them could annul the power of the other. Therefore, if several beings are omnipotent, none of them would be omnipotent.[5]

3. The argument from the highest wisdom is as follows. It is proper to the supremely wise being to know all things.[6] Therefore, if there were several gods, either they would be mutually ignorant of each other, and thus neither of them would be supremely wise; indeed, they would be truly foolish; or they would know each other either through a species, or through the other's essence, or through themselves. If one knows the other through a species or through the other's essence, then it would be informed by receiving something from the other. If it knows the other through itself, then it would be the principle of the other; hence one of these would not be

God. Therefore, the highest wisdom does not allow that there be a plurality of gods, nor can we think of such a plurality. For if several gods are throught to exist, their wisdom would be either identical or distinct. If they have distinct wisdoms, then either one of them excels the other or both of them are imperfect. If they have the same wisdom, they would not have different natures, since each of them would be the highest wisdom. Therefore, they would not be two.

4. The argument from the highest good is the following. That which is the highest good is to be loved supremely and for its own sake. Therefore, if there were several supremely good beings, either each of them would love the other for the other's sake, or not. If not, then neither of them would be good. If yes, then each of them beatifies the other; therefore, neither would be the highest. Therefore, it is impossible that the highest good be multiplied. Indeed, this would also be contrary to reason, because each of these would either be or not be the greater good. If not, then one of them is superfluous. If yes, then neither is the highest. Therefore, if a multiplicity of highest goods is thought to exist, they are not understood to be supremely good.[7]

5. The argument from influence is the following. God influences all things in a most perfect manner. Therefore, He confers the whole of being and not a part thereof.[8] But if there were several gods, either one would give nothing, and hence would not be God; or each would give either part of being or nothing at all, and neither would be God; or each would communicate the same being, and then each would be simultaneously in the same effect by way of essence, power, and presence, since this is proper to the highest influence. Therefore, either one would be in the other, or both would be circumscribed, and thus neither would be God.

6. The argument from the highest causality is the following. God is the first, ultimate, and most perfect cause; and hence He is the cause in whom all things come to rest fully in terms of efficient, exemplary, and final causality.[9] Therefore, if there were several gods, one would be reduced to the other, and none would be first, highest, or most perfect. Hence, none would be God.

7. The argument from all the qualities given above is the following. If there were a plurality of gods, either they would be totally identical in all these qualities, or they would differ totally, or they would agree in part and differ in part. If they were totally identical, there would not be a plurality of gods; if they differed entirely, then if one were God the other would not be God. If they agreed in part and differed in part, then they would both be composed of parts. Therefore, neither of them would be simple; hence, neither would be God.

From the above, it is argued that the divine being cannot be multiplied, either in reality or in thought.

Objections

In opposition to this, arguments are raised first of all against the proofs given above.

1. The arguments do not appear to draw a true conclusion. Since the fact that God is one is a matter in which pagans, unbelievers, and heretics have erred, all of whom had the use of reason, not only can it be thought, but it can be judged and believed that there are many gods. Or if the contrary cannot be judged, then it is not an article of faith.

2. Again, the arguments do not seem to draw necessary conclusions because the same arguments can be used to prove that there are not several persons in God. This is clear for anyone who reflects further on it, whether from the sublimity of nature, or of power, or of wisdom, or of goodness, or of influence, or of causality. But if the arguments proceed from the same means to arrive at false conclusions, they do not lead to necessary conclusions.

3. Again, if by means of the arguments given above it is necessarily proved and demonstrated that God is one, then the faith seems to be emptied of merit, since "that faith for which human reason pro-

vides a proof has no merit."[10] Therefore arguments are either weak or useless.

Objections are raised against the proofs from the same attributes.

4. First, from sublimity. It is of greater sublimity to excel things of a similar nature than to excel things of a different nature; and to excel great things rather than to excel small things. Therefore, if the creature is not of like nature with God, and if creation is, as it were, nothing in comparison with God, then God is not understood to be highest and most excellent if He excels created being only. Therefore it seems that it pertains to the divine excellence to posit a plurality of uncreated natures, and then to posit one above the others.

5. From omnipotence, the argument is the following. As Hilary says, "It is proper to perfect power that the nature in which it resides can carry out whatever the speaker has declared."[11] And again, reason dictates that a certain degree of power can accomplish only so much; a greater degree is capable of more; and the highest degree of power is capable of the most. But God is omnipotent in the highest degree. Therefore, since it is possible for us to say that there are many gods, God can bring it about that they should exist. And since He can cause lesser things to be, He can also cause greater things, and even the greatest things. Therefore, He can produce something distinct from Himself that would be as great as Himself. It is, therefore, consonant with omnipotence that there be a multiplicity of gods.

6. From wisdom, it is argued that it is proper to the highest wisdom to know that which is other than itself: and the more perfect the object known, the more perfect is the wisdom. If nothing is entirely perfect except that being which is God, and if divine wisdom eternally knows something distinct from itself with a most perfect knowledge, it seems that from eternity there would be something distinct from God which, nonetheless, would be divine. Therefore, the divine wisdom does not exclude but rather requires several divine essences.

7. From goodness, it is argued: "Good-ness is diffusive to the highest degree";[12] and "many good things are preferable to fewer."[13] Both of these propositions are self-evident truths. Since the highest diffusion of the divine being cannot take place in a creature, it must take place in another uncreated nature. Having posited this, the whole divine essence is better because of the multiplicity of goods. Therefore, if all that is better is to be attributed to God because of His supreme goodness, it seems that the highest goodness does not exclude but rather demands the existence of many divine natures.

8. From the highest influence, it is argued that the perfect influence necessarily demands that such influence not take place without the divine essence, presence, and power. Therefore for the same reason, it cannot be multiplied without the multiplication of essence, power, and presence. Therefore, since there is a plurality of divine influences, there is also a plurality of essences.

9. From causality, the following argument is made. The first cause is the most perfect cause; it is first and immediate, and therefore cause in the proper sense. But if the effect is multiplied, it is necessary that the proximate and proper cause be multiplied. Therefore it is necessary to affirm multiplicity in the first cause, since multiplicity is affirmed and exists in the effects caused by it.

10. Again, from all these properties an objection is raised against all the above; for the most perfect sublimity in nature and power, wisdom and goodness, influence and causality is the reason for positing a multitude in the effects that are caused. Therefore, if the same being is not to be the cause of opposite effects,[14] it seems that these qualities lead us to posit multiplicity rather than unity in the efficient cause; and thus rather than favoring the proposition defended here, they favor the opposite thesis.

Conclusion

That God is one is a truth that is not only believable but also intelligible.
Response. The fact that God is one is a

truth that is not only believable but intelligible as well since it is both necessary and certain not only from the testimony of Scripture and the illumination of grace which is received in faith, but its truth is self-evidently certain from the testimony of creation as well.

It is certain of itself, therefore, because the divine being possesses unity in every way by reason of its singular sublimity and its sublime singularity. Since God has every perfection in Himself, and this in the highest and most excellent degree, He is proved to be one not only from the sublimity of nature and wisdom, power and goodness, influence and causality, but also from all His qualities and from the noble properties which are attributed to Him in the highest way. Therefore, all these qualities attest to the unity of the highest essence.

It is certain also from the testimony of created beings, because every creature is seen to possess unity just as it possesses a natural goodness. "Nothing can exist unless it be one," as Boethius[15] and Augustine[16] say, and as both sense and intellect teach us. As each creature, by reason of its goodness, proclaims that the true and highest goodness is in God, so by reason of its unity, it proclaims that the cause of all things is one in itself.

Nor does the diversity among beings run counter to this testimony. For all the diversity among beings is comprehended within one universe, which in itself is finite and limited, and perfect. But that would not be the case unless that plurality were reduced to some being in which it comes to rest. And therefore it is necessary that all be reduced to one final end and one first principle, otherwise an infinite series would arise. Therefore, the very universe of beings testifies that God is one. Whence, as it is impossible to reasonably think of one circumference except in reference to a single center from which all lines flow and to which all are reduced as to their end, so in the one universe, we should not speak nor think of God except as one alone.

Therefore this is both necessary and evident; and it is known in such a way that no one who has the use of reason can doubt

it if he knows "what it is that is expressed by this name." For if the word *God* signifies the first and highest principle of all things thereby encompassing the entire universe, anyone who understands this affirms as a consequence that God is one. Whence, just as principles are self-evident because they are known immediately in the knowledge of their terms,[17] so for anyone who understands what is signified by the terms, it is clear without doubt that God is one.

However, many have erred concerning the number of the gods, for ignorance of the significate begets deception concerning the supposite, and this leads to the heresy which affirms a plurality of gods. Because men believe that God is that which exceeds human power or human knowledge, when they see that demons can do such things, they believe that demons are gods. And they are led into error and blindness and fall into the worship of idols. This is indeed most absurd, but it is not to be marveled at, since "an error that is small at the beginning becomes great at the end." Philosophy can rescue us from such an error, but the Christian faith does so even more effectively; and both of these agree that the divine being is supremely one. Therefore the arguments which prove this should be conceded, because they arrive at a true conclusion through a necessary middle term.

Replies to the Objections

1. To the objection that the conclusion is false because many men are of the opinion that there are many gods, the response is clear since they use the supposite and the significate of the term *God* in a way that differs from its proper meaning. Therefore, there is no contradiction. While the name *God* has no plural according to its proper meaning, it may have a plural when it is taken in an improper sense. So it should be understood in the present case. And the illumination of faith was necessary because of the blindness of the mind, which frequently accepts as true something which is false. Nonetheless, it can be maintained that reason is capable of proving that God is one in as far as His unity is taken in an absolute sense; but the illumination of faith

is necessary in as far as the unity is related to a plurality of persons.

2. To the objection that the same conclusion can be drawn concerning the persons, it should be said that there is no parallel since in all the persons there is one nature and power and wisdom and goodness and influence and causality. This would not be so if there were different divine natures; therefore a plurality of persons involves no contradiction.

3. To the objection that faith is emptied of its merit, it must be said that this would be true if assent were given only because of the arguments. However, since assent is given because of truth itself and not principally because of the arguments, merit is possible because of the assent of faith. Nothing excludes the possibility that the same matter be both known and believed in terms of different aspects and considerations.

4. To the objection concerning sublimity in relation to great things and things of a similar nature, it should be said that there would be a point to this if something were to accrue to the divine sublimity from the subjection of others. But it is not true, since God is just as sublime in Himself and existing alone as He would be if He ruled over a thousand worlds. Furthermore, it would not add to His sublimity to have something of like nature existing in a servile condition. Thus, even though sublimity of this sort might seem, in a way, to increase His glory, in reality it would decrease it.

5. To the objection concerning power, it must be said that every word must be understood in terms of what is truly possible for a power, for certain possibilities involve weakness rather than sublimity. The possibility of having a nature equal to but different from oneself pertains to the dignity of a limited power, and therefore it is repugnant to omnipotence. Therefore, even though this can be said in words, yet it cannot be attributed to God, for the extent of the divine power is not to be judged according to the degree of this possibility, but rather according to the dignity of its own

proper act which is immense; therefore the power is immense.[18]

6. To the objection from wisdom, namely, that it knows another, it must be said that though God knows eternally that which is other than Himself, and this is in accord with the highest wisdom, nonetheless, it is not fitting for God to know the other through the other but through Himself. But this is not possible unless the other being, which is of such a nature as to proceed from God Himself, is in God as in its causal principle. For even if evil is known by God, this is by means of the idea of the opposite good. Therefore the perfection of divine knowledge does not require that the object of knowledge be an actual being, nor that it be the highest being, since God knows earthly realities in the best and highest manner through Himself. The objection has its place in that sort of knowledge which takes its origin from things, but God does not have that sort of knowledge.

7. To the objection that the highest diffusion and multitude of goods pertains to the highest good, it must be said that, if *highest* is understood absolutely, then the highest communication within is appropriate to the highest good, but not the highest communication to something outside itself. For there ought to be but one highest good which indeed cannot be added to by a multitude of goods. When it is said that the highest good is supremely diffusive, it should be understood that this is true in as far as *highest* refers to that which is diffusive in power and not in act. And when it is said that a multiplicity of goods is better, we reply that this is true in reference to finite goods where one adds something to the other, and where something of the good is lacking to each one and this is supplied for by a good added to it.

8. To the objection concerning influence, namely, that it cannot exist without God and therefore it cannot be multiplied unless God be multiplied, it must be said that this does not hold, and there is no parallel because it pertains to the perfection of the agent that an effect cannot exist without the presence of the agent since the effect de-

pends totally on the agent; and that agent which acts immediately acts in a more noble manner than one which acts through another. However, this is not so in the case of number and multitude. For it does not pertain to the perfection of an agent that it be multiplied in a multiplicity of effects, but quite the contrary, namely, that while remaining one in itself, it is the cause of diverse effects.

9. To the objection that the proximate and immediate cause is multiplied, it must be said that this is true of a cause which operates by way of nature and whose power is limited. Thus it is a cause in the proper sense, but not a universal cause. But in the production of creatures, the first cause acts by way of art and will. For this reason, it is supremely free as a cause and is limited by nothing; and it is simultaneously a proper and universal cause because whatever perfection exists in the creature must necessarily be posited in the creative essence.

10. To the objection that these are means of proving multitude and diversity, it must be said that they prove not just any sort of diversity among creatures, but rather a diversity with order and connection and an inclination to unity; and thus a diversity in unity. And by reason of that unity, they infer a unity in their cause. Moreover, they do not lead to the opposite conclusion because unity in the cause is not contradictory to multiplicity in the effects; as is clear in that sort of unity from which infinite species of numbers proceed. So it is that the supreme wisdom and power and goodness—though they are one—are not sufficiently manifested through one effect. Therefore, they imply a diversity in the effects caused by them. Thus our response to all the objections is clear.

Article II
Whether Unity of Nature Can Exist Together with a Trinity of Persons

Supposing that the divine being is supremely one, it is then asked whether the unity of nature can exist together with a trinity of persons. Their incompatability appears in the following.

Objections

1. To be one both in form and in supposite is more perfect than to be one in only one of these. Therefore, if the divine being is one in form and not in hypostsis, it would seem that it is not supremely one.

2. Again, to be one both in substance and in property is more perfect than to be one in only one of these. But the trinity cannot exist without a plurality of properties. Therefore it necessarily involves some lack of unity. Therefore these two cannot exist simultaneously.

3. Again by reason of the definition of *one*,[19] the more a thing is undivided, the more it is one. Therefore, there must be total lack of division and total lack of distinction in that which is supremely one; and therefore there can be no plurality. Therefore, either there is no trinity there, or the supreme unity is not found there.

4. Again, that which is one both as a real unity and as a unity of reason is more perfect than that which is one only in reality. But a trinity of persons cannot coexist with a unity of reason. Therefore, the highest and most perfect unity is lacking. Therefore, they cannot exist together.

5. Again, there is a rule that "Two things that are equal to a third are equal to each other."[20] If that third being is simply one, it follows that either the divine substance is not supremely one, and the persons do not communicate in it, or one person does not differ from the other. But if either of these is granted, then trinity and unity are incompatible.

6. Again, there is a rule that when two things are so related to each other that what is predicated of one is predicated formally of the other, then if one is multiplied the other is multiplied also; as is apparent in man and animal, and white and color.[21] But formally, person is the essence. Therefore, if there are several persons, there are several essences. And thus the same conclusion follows as above.

7. Again, the syllogistic form does not err in the case of propositions that are self-evidently true and in which no accidental reality is found.[22] But these propositions are self-evidently true, namely, each person is distinct; and each person is the essence. Therefore, the essence is distinguished, and it is therefore numbered. Therefore the essence is not one in a trinity of persons.

8. Again, there is a rule that when the object defined is multiplied, then the definition is multiplied together with its defining elements. But substance and nature are contained in the definition of person. Therefore, if there are many persons, there are many essences, substances, and natures. Therefore, the plurality of persons is incompatible with the highest unity of the divine nature.

9. Again, person is defined either by reason of substance or by reason of relation. If it is defined by reason of relation, then a plurality of persons would be identical with a plurality of relations. If it is defined by reason of substance, then the multiplication of persons is identical with the multiplication of substance and nature. Therefore, unity in nature is incompatible with a trinity of persons.

10. Again, when I say that the person is one and the essence is one, this refers either to the same unity or to a different unity. If it refers to a different unity, then there is a plurality of unities, and therefore, it would not be supremely one. If it refers to the same unity, then if one is multiplied so is the other, and if one is not multiplied, neither is the other. Therefore, trinity and highest unity are incompatible.

11. Again, a person is capable of producing only by reason of its nature; but there is no plurality in God except by reason of production. Therefore, if production multiplies person, in the same way it will multiply the nature. Therefore, in God plurality cannot exist together with the supreme unity of nature.

12. Again, the supreme simplicity of God excludes composition not only in nature but also in person. Therefore, since unity is related to plurality as simplicity is to composition, if the highest unity exists in the divine nature, there can be no plurality, neither in nature nor in person.

13. Again, in the divine being, either there is no distinction or there is the most perfect distinction. But the most perfect distinction is that which exists by reason of the form. Since this cannot exist together with the highest unity,[23] it remains either that the highest unity is not found there, or plurality is not found there.

14. Again, unity and truth are convertible and are attributed to every nature. Therefore, if there is a true plurality in God, then truth is multiplied in God; there are, then, multiple truths in God and therefore a plurality of entities. Therefore there is not true unity. And thus the same conclusion follows as above.

15. Again, that the "Father generates" and that the "Holy Spirit proceeds" are two true statements if there is a trinity in God; therefore there are two truths. Therefore if a plurality of truths is repugnant to the highest unity, so also is a plurality of persons.

16. Again, the trinity is constituted either by the repetition of the same unity or by the addition of diverse unities. If it is the repetition of the same unity,[24] then there is no real plurality; and the result would be a superfluous triviality. If it is by addition of diverse unities, since any multiplication or aggregation of diverse unities is repugnant to the highest unity, it is clear, etc.

17. Again, all plurality can be reduced to unity. But in God nothing should be posited that is reducible to something else. Therefore, etc.

18. Again, many properties existing in many subjects bespeak the highest distinction. Contrariwise, therefore, one property existing in only one subject bespeaks the highest unity. Therefore, if the highest unity is found in God, it follows that there is no plurality.

19. Again, God has nothing that is not of Himself. Therefore, every person that is God has whatever it possesses of itself. But only one person can be of itself. Therefore,

a plurality of persons cannot exist together with the unity of the divine being.

20. Again, where there is plurality, there is diversity. And where there is diversity, there is a lack of identity. And where there is a lack of identity, supreme unity is lacking.[25] Therefore, etc.

But, on the contrary, objections are raised against this from authority and from reason. From authority in the following way.

Arguments in Agreement

1. 1 Jn. 5: "There are three who give testimony in heaven, the Father, the Word, and the Holy Spirit. And these three are one."[26] I call that thing one in an absolute sense to which nothing else is added. Therefore, they are one in an absolute sense. Therefore, trinity does not destroy unity.

2. Again, Bernard to Eugene: "Among all the unities, the unity of the trinity holds first place."[27] But that which holds the highest place among many has being in the highest degree. Therefore, the unity of the trinity is the highest unity. Therefore, a true trinity stands together with the highest unity.

3. Again, a plurality of individuals is not repugnant to the unity of a species; indeed, they coexist. Therefore, if nature designates the common form and person designates the individual or the supposite,[28] a trinity of persons is in no way derogatory to the unity of essence.

4. Again, a plurality of nature is not repugnant to unity of person; indeed they coexist, as is clear in the case of man. Therefore, by reason of a logical conversion a plurality of persons in God is not repugnant to the unity of essence or nature. Therefore they can exist together without diminution.

5. Again, we find one nature in one person, as in the case of the angels; and we find three extremely diverse natures in one person, as in Christ. Therefore, it seems that it is not only possible, but, indeed, very fitting to find a trinity of persons in one nature. And this is the case in God; therefore, etc.[29]

6. Again, that unity which can remain one in many subjects is more excellent than that unity which can maintain its unity only in one person. But the divine unity is the most excellent unity. Therefore it must stand together with a plurality of persons. Therefore, there is no contradiction.

7. Again, as the Philosopher says: "That which generates does not generate another except by means of matter."[30] But in God, there is no matter. Therefore, the one who generates is not distinguished from the one generated. Indeed, moreover, one cannot generate oneself. Therefore, if in God there exists generation without matter, then there exists a plurality of person without the multiplication of form.

8. Again, as Damascene says, "To generate is to produce a similar being from one's own substance."[31] But the divine substance is not capable of division. Therefore, it is necessary that the one who generates gives his entire substance to the one that is generated. Therefore they cannot be distinguished according to substance. And yet they are distinguished. But neither are they distinguished accidentally because in God there is no accident. Therefore they are distinguished in person; for there remains the distinction in person together with total indistinction in nature.

9. Again, that unity is more perfect in which, together with the unity of nature, there remains the unity of love. But "love tends toward the other."[32] Therefore it includes the distinction of the lover and the beloved. Therefore, if the most perfect unity exists in God, it is necessary that He possess an intrinsic plurality for He has nothing outside Himself that is supremely lovable.

10. Again, likeness, equality, and identity include in their concepts both plurality and unity. This is clear because "likeness is the same quality existing in diverse beings."[33] Therefore, since the highest likeness can exist both in reality and in the mind, and since the highest likeness and identity cannot be or be conceived except with unity and plurality, therefore either it is necessary that the highest unity exist together

with true plurality, or else the highest likeness can neither exist nor be conceived. And as a result, no sort of likeness could exist or be conceived. But if these conclusions are impossible, it remains that in God the highest unity coexists with true plurality.

Conclusion

The highest unity and trinity in God are not repugnant to each other, but manifest marvelous concord and harmony.

Response. In God the trinity and the highest unity are not contradictory, but manifest a marvelous concord and harmony, according to what the most saving faith says. And the soul purged and elevated by faith can grasp this to some extent; in general, it is difficult and impossible to understand anything unless one first assents to it.

The Christian faith, therefore, says that the divine nature is one and supremely one, and nevertheless there are three persons, one of whom proceeds from the other and through the other; and therefore they communicate in essence and form while their properties are truly distinct. While to the non-believer these seem to be incompatible, to the believer, they seem to be not only compatible but harmonious. However, two things must be considered if we are to understand this. The first is what person and nature signify; the second is how they are related to production. The first removes any contradiction; the second shows the harmony.

It must be recognized, therefore, as Boethius says in *Concerning Two Natures and One person*,[34] that "nature is the specific difference informing a particular thing"; "person, however, is an individual substance of a rational nature"; or as Richard says, "incommunicable existence."[35] The difference, therefore, is that nature refers to the form itself by which each thing is what it is; while person refers to the individual or incommunicable supposite. Because they were ignorant of these definitions, heretics have said that in Christ there are two persons as there are two natures; others have

said that there is one nature as there is one person. If they had known the difference between these, they would have seen how it is possible for a plurality of natures to exist with a unity of person, as is clear in any human being.[36] Therefore if a plurality of natures of itself is not contradictory to unity of person, for like reason the reverse is not contradictory—namely, the plurality of persons in a unity of nature. If it is not contradictory, then it can exist in God.

Not only do they have a different meaning, but they are related differently to production. Since it is proper to the supposite to act through the form,[37] it is proper not to the nature but to the person to produce and to be produced, while it is proper to the nature to be communicated through production. Therefore, since the divine nature is entirely indivisible and without any matter, therefore it is not multiplied or numbered by division or partition. Therefore it is entirely one in the produced and in the producer. But because no one can produce himself, it is necessary that there be a plurality at the level of person. Since in the emanation of persons, the nature is communicable while the person is that which produces, emanation requires that there be plurality at the level of persons and unity at the level of nature in such a way that there is no contradiction here but rather the highest harmony.

Therefore, since the plurality does not divide the unity, nor does the unity confuse the plurality, it becomes apparent that the divine being is singularly admirable and marvelously singular. And this is proper to it alone because of the highest simplicity which does not allow that the nature have parts nor that it be associated with matter. Therefore this is proper to it alone; and this in a most admirable way because nothing can be found that is entirely similar to this. Therefore to be one in many with no multiplication or diversification of essence is the exclusive property of the divine nature and is its singular privilege. And that which is one in the first and highest degree ought to have this privilege because it is first and highest. Therefore, it is one in such a way that it cannot be formally multiplied; and it is one in such a way that it can be neither limited nor restricted to only one supposite; it is one in a way which does not impede it from being the eternal principle with respect to that which is coequal with itself, and coeternal and most perfect. Hence no man praises the divine unity perfectly unless at the same time he recognizes the trinity, nor does anyone render perfect worship to the one God unless in faith he confesses that God is a trinity. Hence, those arguments that demonstrate this are to be conceded.

Replies to the Objections

1. To the first objection, it must be said that form is twofold. One type of form is multiplied in many supposites,[38] and in such a form perfect unity cannot coexist together with a plurality of supposites. The second type is that kind of form which is not multiplied in a plurality of supposites, and such is the form of the deity. And since such a form is in no way multiplied by reason of the plurality of supposites, therefore in it there exists simultaneously true plurality and highest unity. This is what is expressed in the name *trinity* in which the unity of nature is included with plurality.

2. To the objection that it is more perfect to be one both in substance and in property, etc., it must be said that property is twofold; namely, absolute and relative. If the objection is understood of an absolute property, it is true; but if it is understood of a relative property, it is not true, since plurality in terms of a relative property does not posit diversity in the thing or in the nature, neither with respect to the essence nor with respect to existence; but it asserts only a different relation which is not incompatible with the highest unity, as can be shown by examples in the case of a point and unity.

3. To the objection that the more a thing is undivided, the more it is one, it must be said that the indivisibility in the definition of unity excludes that sort of division which divides a whole into its parts. But the unity of the trinity is not related to the plurality of persons as is a whole to its parts because the entire deity is in each of the persons most fully and perfectly. Therefore, personal distinction does not contradict that sort of indivisibility which is to be found in the highest unity.

4. To the objection that whatever is one both as a real unity and as a unity of reason is more perfect, etc., it must be said that the word *reason* can be understood in two ways. In the first sense, it adds something really distinct from the essence, such as is the case with essential elements of a being. In the second sense, it does not add anything over and above the essence, but adds only a relation. If the proposition is understood in this way, it is not true, because the plurality of such reasons in no way diminishes the highest unity of the essence or nature.

5. To the objection that two things which are equal to a third are equal to each other, it must be said that this is to be understood of identity in the supposite. Hence it is that—though there is in Christ a unity of dignity that is less than the unity of trinity which is in God—nevertheless man is predicated of God, and God of man, by reason of the unity of person. However, Son is not predicated of Father, nor Father of Son, by reason of the unity of nature since the distinction of the supposites stands in the way of this.[39] Or it can be said that this rule is not violated if it is understood of one and the same genus of unity; but if it is applied to different types of unity, the understanding of this rule is neither correct nor sound. For it does not follow that if different things are equal to a third in generic terms that therefore the persons are numerically identical. In this case, therefore, it is to be so understood that even if essence and person are essentially one, yet it does not follow that they are personally one. It suffices that there be an essential unity between them.

6. To the objection that in formal predication when the subject is multiplied, the predicate also is multiplied, it must be said that this is true when the multiplication of the subject takes place by addition or by formal difference. For in that case it is nec-

essary for the multiplication of the subject that the predicate be multiplied. But this is not the case in the present question; for the multiplication of persons is not a formal multiplication nor is it one that takes place by the addition of any absolute quality; but by reason only of origin and the respective emanation.

7. To the objection that the syllogistic form does not err in self-evident propositions, it must be said that even though in God there is nothing accidental inhering in Him, nonetheless, there are various levels of predication used to speak of God, namely, predication in reference to substance and in reference to relation, so that "substance contains unity, and relation unfolds the trinity."[40] From this it follows that each of these modes of speech and predication is extraneous to the other; and this is sufficient to cause that sophism known as the fallacy of accident.

8. To the objection that when the object defined is multiplied, the defining elements are multiplied also, it must be said that this is true concerning those things that fall under the formal definition directly. But nature falls under the definition of person indirectly; and substance—in as far as it falls under the definition of person—is identical with hypostasis, which is multiplied in God without any multiplication of the essence.

9. To the objection that person is defined either by reason of substance or by reason of relation, etc., it must be said that person is nothing other than an "hypostasis distinct by reason of a property."[41] Therefore it is predicated by virtue of an intrinsic relation and by virtue of the substance that is not common but proper. Therefore, it does not follow that there is only a plurality of relations, nor that there is a diversity of natures because of the plurality of the divine persons.

10. To the objection that when person and essence are one, they are such either by the same unity or by diverse unities, it must be said that it is neither absolutely identical nor absolutely diverse; rather it is one and the same according to a real unity,

but diverse because of a distinction introduced by reason, according to what Augustine says, "It is one thing for Him to be God, and another thing for Him to be Father."[42] He is called Father not because there is an essential or real distinction between deity and paternity, but because Father involves a relation to another which is not included in the essence.

11. To the objection that a person is capable of producing only by reason of the nature, it must be said that production involves the person as subject and principle and as object or term. And therefore true production necessarily effects a multiplication of persons. But production involves nature as the principle of production and as the very reality which is communicated by means of the production. And since in that production the whole nature is communicated and nothing is lost in the communications; therefore, even though person is multiplied, yet the nature is not multiplied.

12. To the objection that the highest simplicity excludes composition in nature as well as in person, it must be said that the highest simplicity excludes composition out of diverse elements and with another being; and therefore it can coexist neither with a composition of nature nor with one of person. But the highest unity of nature excludes only essential diversity, and therefore it is not incompatible with a plurality of persons. And thus the two cases are not similar.

13. To the objection that in the divine being there must be either the most perfect distinction or no distinction at all, it must be said that a perfect distinction may be understood in two ways, either intensively or in terms of completion. In the first sense, it should not be predicated of God; in the second sense it is predicated of God because the less a thing deviates from unity the more perfect it is. Therefore because that plurality does not deviate from the highest unity, it follows that such a plurality alone is at the same time true and most perfect.[43]

14. To the objection that unity and truth are convertible, it must be said that this re-

fers to truth in the singular and not in the plural. But when truth and plurality are put in relation to each other, and vice versa, then a single object is related not to another single object but to a plurality. Therefore, in this case the consequence is not necessary. When one speaks of a true plurality in God, the word *true* is nothing else but an expression of the plurality that is in the supposites. But on the contrary, when truth is said to be multiplied, a multiplicity is implied in truth itself and in the divine essence.

15. To the objection that it is one truth for the Father to generate and another for the Holy Spirit to proceed, it must be said that if this is understood to refer to the truth of complex judgments, such as in the truth of prayer and of speech, then there are many truths and many articles of faith. But if this is understood to refer to the truth of simple terms, or to the truth of reality, then to say that the Father generates and that the Son is generated, and that the Holy Spirit proceeds is to say nothing else than that the Father, the Son, and the Holy Spirit exist, and that there is but one act of being in them. Thus, the truth of reality is absolutely one.

16. To the objection that there is either a repetition of the same unity or not, it must be said that it is a repetition of the same unity, not however in the same respect but in different respects. Therefore it is not a superfluity nor an aggregation of unities. Therefore the multiplication which is found here is not incompatible with the highest unity. It is in this sense that the statement of Boethius, *On the Trinity*,[44] is to be understood when he says that "God is a trinity in this sense, as if one were to say three times: sun, sun, sun." There is a similarity because of the repetition of the same unity. There is a dissimilarity because the unity of the trinity is repeated in reference to different subjects whereas the unity of the sun is repeated in reference to the same subject. Therefore, the trinity in God is real while that in the sun is not.

17. To the objection that plurality is reducible to unity it must be said that a plurality which bespeaks a defect in the highest unity is related to that unity as to its principle and cause; and this is reduced to unity by a proper reduction, which is the reduction of an effect to its cause; and there is no such plurality in the divine being. But a plurality which does not bespeak any defect in the highest unity does not need to be reduced in this way since it is itself the highest unity. Nonetheless, in as far as in God the emanation of divine persons is affirmed from the first person as from a principle, in this sense it is not repugnant that there be a reduction to the first person as to the principle from which the others are produced.

18. To the objection that many properties existing in many subjects bespeak highest distinction or diversity, it must be said that even though, in terms of an extrinsic reason, a plurality of nature in a plurality of person seems to be quite repugnant to the highest unity, nonetheless, in reality and in terms of an intrinsic reason, there is greater repugnance in the case of a plurality of natures in one supposite which is constituted by the natures, since the supposite is made into a composite and is less one than if a plurality of natures were found in a plurality of supposites, as is clear in the nature of angels and of man. And therefore, since the highest unity is found in God, therefore unity is to be affirmed of Him in a more noble and more excellent way, as when we affirm one nature which is not multiplied in the plurality of supposites, instead of affirming one nature in only one person.

19. To the objection that whatever God has, He has of Himself, it must be said that this is true because the divine essence cannot be derived from any other principle. But from this it does not follow that whatever a person has it has of itself. Likewise it does not follow that if the essence is not produced therefore the person is not produced. Thus the argument cited does not come to a true conclusion.

20. To the objection that where there is plurality there is diversity, it must be said, as is clear from the above, that a plurality which relates to form, substance, and na-

ture does not lead to diversity in the proper sense of the word. Therefore nothing is lost from the highest unity and identity, which consists in this; namely, that three persons have the highest unity of essence and nature.

NOTES

1. Ex. 20, 2.
2. Dt. 6, 4; 32, 39.
3. Ps. 80, 10.
4. Aristotle, *V Topic.*, c. 3 (c. 5).
5. Rich. of St. Victor, *De Trin. I*, c. 25; *II*, c. 15.
6. Aristotle, *I Metaph.*, c. 2.
7. Rich. of St. Victor, *De Trin. II*, c. 19.
8. *Lib. de Causis*, prop. 1.
9. Aristotle, *II Metaph.*, text. 5 ff.
10. Gregory, *II Homil. in Evang.*, homil. 26, n. 1.
11. *De trin. V*, n. 5.
12. Ps.-Diony., *De Caelest. Hierarch.*, c. 4, p. 1; *De Div. Nom.*, c. 4, p. 1.
13. Aristotle, *III Topic.*, c. 2.
14. Aristotle, *II De Gener. et Corrupt.*, text. 56 (c. 10).
15. *De Consol.*, III, prosa 11.
16. *De Moribus Manich.*, II, c. 6, n. 8.
17. Aristotle, *I Poster.*, c. 3.
18. Rich. of St. Victor, *De Trin. I*, c. 21.
19. Aristotle, *III Phys.*, text. 68 (c. 7).
20. Aristotle, *I Elench.*, c. 5 (c. 6).
21. Aristotle, *IV Topic*, c. 5.
22. Aristotle, *I Prior.*, c. 1 ff.; *I Poster.*, c. 4 ff.
23. Boethius, *De Trin.*, c. 2.
24. Boethius, *De Trin.*, c. 3.
25. Aristotle, *V Metaph.*, text. 16 (IV, c. 9).
26. Verse 7.
27. *De Considerat.*, *V*, c. 8, n. 19.
28. Boethius, *De Persona et Duabus Naturis*, c. 1–3.
29. Bernard, *De Consideratione.* c. 9, n. 20.
30. *VII Metaph.*, text. 28 (VI, c. 8); *II De Anima*, text. 47 (c. 4).
31. *De Fide Orthod.*, *I*, c. 8.
32. Gregory, *I Homil. in Evang.*, homil. 17, n. 1.
33. Boethius, *III De Differentiis Topic.*
34. C. 1 and 3.
35. *De Trin. IV*, c. 18 and 22 ff.
36. Boethius, *De Persona et Duabus Naturis*, c. 4, 5 and 7.
37. Aristotle, *I De Anima*, text. 64 (c. 4).
38. Aristotle, *I Periherm.*, c. 5 (c. 7).
39. Bernard, *V De Consideratione*, c. 8, n. 18 and c. 9, n. 20 ff.
40. Boethius, *De Trin.*, c. 6.
41. Cf. *I Sent.* d. 25, a. 1, q. 2, ad 4 (I, 441).
42. *De Trin.*, *VII*, c. 6, n. 11; *Enarrat. in Ps. 68*, serm. 1, n. 5.
43. Ps.-Dionysius, *De Div. Nom.*, c. 13, p. 2–4.
44. C. 3.

PART V

POLITICAL PHILOSOPHY

CHAPTER 25

Al-Fārābī

Abū Naṣr Muhammad al-Fārābī was born circa 870 of Turkish origin. His name indicates that he came from the district of the city of Fārāb (Turkestan). Al-Fārābī studied under the Nestorian Christian Yuhannā ibn-Haylān, who was a logician of note and must have had a considerable influence on his student as al-Fārābī became celebrated for his own works on logic. His principle instructor, however, was the translator and commentator Abū-Bishr Mattū ibn-Yānus, the most prominent member of the school of Christian Aristotelians in Baghdad. It was here that al-Fārābī studied not only philosophy but mathematics, physics, astronomy, and music as well. He became known as "the Second Master" (Aristotle being the first), a widely respected scholar who commented on many of Aristotle's works and wrote exegeses on the doctrines of Plato and Aristotle. His political theories were very influential in both Muslim and Jewish circles, with Maimonides in particular holding him in high regard. In 942 he was invited to the court of Sayf al Dawlah at Aleppo, where he spent the rest of his life. Although academically trained, he never had an identifiable occupation whereby he could earn a livelihood, which seems to account for his frugal lifestyle, which was often spent in solitude. Some believe he was ascetically inclined. He died circa 950.

Al-Fārābī on the Perfect State

Man cannot provide for the satisfaction of all of his needs by himself. Therefore, to attain his "highest perfections" he must engage in cooperative behavior. This is accomplished by living in communities called societies, some of which are perfect, others not. "There are three kinds of perfect society, great, medium and small. The great one is the union of all the societies in the inhabitable world; the medium one the union of one nation in one part of the inhabitable world; the small one the union of people of a city in the territory of any nation whatsoever. ... the society in which there is a cooperation to acquire felicity is the excellent society." Al-Fārābī draws an analogy between a city and the body of an animal. Each part of the body serves a different function. For a body to be healthy, all the parts, namely, limbs and organs, must cooperate. Yet, the parts of the body are hierarchical in that they are unequal in "excellence". The ruling organ is the heart. So it is with a city. The "excellent" city has a ruler. Immediately below but close to the ruler are those who dispatch the dictates of the ruler. The same applies to the second and third ranks "until eventually parts are reached which perform their actions according to the aim of others, while there do not exist any people who perform their actions according to their aims; these, then, are the people who serve without being served in turn, and who are hence in the lowest rank at the bottom of the scale". The difference between the functioning of the parts of a body and a city is that the former is natural, the latter voluntary.

Few are fit to be a ruler. One must be innately predisposed for the position and possess the attitude and habit of will for rulership. Nor is every discipline suitable for rulership. The various disciplines also constitute a hierarchy. "Some of the arts rule certain (other) arts while serving others at the same time, whereas there are other arts which, not ruling anything at all, only serve." At this point Plato's influence on al-Fārābī's thinking becomes clear. The art at the top of the hierarchy is philosophy, and the ruler of the perfect city is a philosopher-king. Philosophy is the necessary art by which a city is ruled, and "if it happens that no philosopher can be found who will be attached to the actual ruler of the city, then, after a certain interval, this city will undoubtedly perish".

The 'ignorant' city stands in opposition to the excellent city and takes several forms. (1) The city of necessity strives only for satisfaction of animal needs. (2) The city of meanness is only dedicated to the acquisition of wealth and riches. (3) The city of depravity and baseness is hedonistic. (4) The city of honor values only glory and splendor. (5) The city of power seeks to prevail over others. (6) "Another is the 'democratic' city: the aim of its people is to be free, each of them doing what he wishes without restraining his passions in the least." Finally, there is the wicked city: "a city whose views are those of the excellent city; it knows felicity . . . but the actions of its people are the actions of the people of the ignorant cities". Al-Fārābī maintains the view that all cities other than the excellent city are doomed sooner or later.

THE PERFECT STATE

Section V

Chapter 15

Perfect Associations and Perfect Ruler; Faulty Associations

§1. In order to preserve himself and to attain his highest perfections every human being is by his very nature in need of many things which he cannot provide all by himself; he is indeed in need of people who each supply him with some particular need of his. Everybody finds himself in the same relation to everybody in this respect. Therefore man cannot attain the perfection, for the sake of which his inborn nature has been given to him, unless many (societies of) people who co-operate come together

Reprinted from *Al-Fārābī on The Perfect State*, translated by Richard Walzer (Oxford: The Clarendon Press, 1985), pp. 229–259. Reprinted by permission of Oxford University Press.

who each supply everybody else with some particular need of his, so that as a result of the contribution of the whole community all the things are brought together which everybody needs in order to preserve himself and to attain perfection. Therefore human individuals have come to exist in great numbers, and have settled in the inhabitable region of the earth, so that human societies have come to exist in it, some of which are perfect, others imperfect.

§2. There are three kinds of perfect society, great, medium and small. The great one is the union of all the societies in the inhabitable world; the medium one the union of one nation in one part of the inhabitable world; the small one the union of the people of a city in the territory of any nation whatsoever. Imperfect are the union of people in a village, the union of people in a quarter, then the union in a street, eventually the union in a house, the house being the smallest union of all. Quarter and village exist both for the sake of the city, but the relation of the village to the city is one of service whereas the quarter is related to the city as a part of it; the street is a part of the quarter, the house a part of the street. The city is a part of the territory of a nation, the nation a part of all the people of the inhabitable world.

§3. The most excellent good and the utmost perfection is, in the first instance, attained in a city, not in a society which is less complete than it. But since good in its real sense is such as to be attainable through choice and will and evils are also due to will and choice only, a city may be established to enable its people to co-operate in attaining some aims that are evil. Hence felicity is not attainable in every city. The city, then, in which people aim through association at co-operating for the things by which felicity in its real and true sense can be attained, is the excellent city, and the society in which there is a co-operation to acquire felicity is the excellent society; and the nation in which all of its cities co-operate for those things through which felicity is attained is the excellent nation. In the same way, the excellent universal state will arise only when all the nations in it cooperate for the purpose of reaching felicity.

§4. The excellent city resembles the perfect and healthy body, all of whose limbs co-operate to make the life of the animal perfect and to preserve it in this state. Now the limbs and organs of the body are different and their natural endowments and faculties are unequal in excellence, there being among them one ruling organ, namely the heart, and organs which are close in rank to that ruling organ, each having been given by nature a faculty by which it performs its proper function in conformity with the natural aim of that ruling organ. Other organs have by nature faculties by which they perform their functions according to the aims of those organs which have no intermediary between themselves and the ruling organ; they are in the second rank. Other organs, in turn, perform their functions according to the aim of those which are in the second rank, and so on until eventually organs are reached which only serve and do not rule at all. The same holds good in the case of the city. Its parts are different by nature, and their natural dispositions are unequal in excellence: there is in it a man who is the ruler, and there are others whose ranks are close to the ruler, each of them with a disposition and a habit through which he performs an action in conformity with the intention of that ruler; these are the holders of the first ranks. Below them are people who perform their actions in accordance with the aims of those people; they are in the second rank. Below them in turn are people who perform their actions according to the aims of the people mentioned in the second instance, and the parts of the city continue to be arranged in this way, until eventually parts are reached which perform their actions according to the aims of others, while there do not exist any people who perform their actions according to their aims; these, then, are the people who serve without being served in turn, and who are hence in the lowest rank and at the bottom of the scale. But the limbs and organs of the body are natural, and the dispositions which they have are natural faculties, whereas, although the parts of the city are natural, their dispositions and habits, by which they perform their actions in the city, are not natural but voluntary—notwithstanding that the parts of the city are by nature provided with endowments unequal in excellence which enable them to do one thing and not another. But they are not parts of the city by their inborn nature alone but rather by the voluntary habits which they acquire such as the arts and their likes; to the natural faculties which exist in the organs and limbs of the body correspond the voluntary habits and dispositions in the parts of the city.

§5. The ruling organ in the body is by nature the most perfect and most complete of the organs in itself and in its specific qualification, and it also has the best of everything of which another organ has a share as well; beneath it, in turn, are other organs which rule over organs inferior to them, their rule being lower in rank than the rule of the first and indeed subordinate to the rule of the first; they rule and are ruled. In the same way, the ruler of the city is the most perfect part of the city in his specific qualification and has the best of everything which anybody else shares with him; beneath him are people who are ruled by him and rule others.

The heart comes to be first and becomes then the cause of the existence of the other organs and limbs of the body, and the cause of the existence of their faculties in them and of their arrangement in the ranks proper to them, and when one of its organs is out of order, it is the heart which provides the means to remove that disorder. In the same way the ruler of this city must come to be in the first instance, and will subsequently be the cause of the rise of the city and its parts and the cause of the presence of the voluntary habits of its parts and of their arrangement in the ranks proper to them; and when one part is out of order he provides it with the means to remove its disorder.

The parts of the body close to the ruling organ perform of the natural functions, in agreement—by nature—with the aim of the ruler, the most noble ones; the organs beneath them perform those functions which are less noble, and eventually the organs are reached which perform the meanest functions. In the same way the parts of the city which are close in authority to the ruler of the city perform the most noble voluntary actions, and those below them less noble actions, until eventually the parts are reached which perform the most ignoble actions. The inferiority of such actions is sometimes due to the inferiority of their matter, although they may be extremely useful—like the action of the bladder and the action of the lower intestine in the body; sometimes it is due to their being of little use; at other times it is due to their being very easy to perform. This applies equally to the city and equally to every whole which is composed by nature of well ordered coherent parts: they have a ruler whose relation to the other parts is like the one just described.

§6. This applies also to all existents. For the relation of the First Cause to the other existents is like the relation of the king of the excellent city to its other parts. For the ranks of the immaterial existents are close to the First. Beneath them are the heavenly bodies, and beneath the heavenly bodies the material bodies. All these existents act in conformity with the First Cause, follow it, take it as their guide and imitate it; but each existent does that according to its capacity, choosing its aim precisely on the strength of its established rank in the universe: that is to say the last follows the aim of that which is slightly above it in rank, equally the second existent, in turn, follows what is above itself in rank, and in the same way the third existent has an aim which is above it. Eventually existents are reached which are linked with the First Cause without any intermediary whatsoever. In accordance with this order of rank all the existents permanently follow the aim of the First Cause. Those which are from the very outset provided with all the essentials of their existence are made to imitate the First (Cause) and its aim from their very outset, and hence enjoy eternal bliss and hold the highest ranks; but those which are not provided from the outset with all the essentials of their existence, are provided with a faculty by which they move towards the expected attainment of those essentials and will then be able to follow the aim of the First (Cause). The excellent city ought to be arranged in the same way: all its parts ought to imitate in their actions the aim of their first ruler according to their rank.

§7. The ruler of the excellent city cannot just be any man, because rulership requires two conditions: (a) he should be predisposed for it by his inborn nature, (b) he should have acquired the attitude and habit of will for rulership which will develop in a man whose inborn nature is predisposed for it. Nor is every art suitable for rulership, most of the arts, indeed, are rather suited for service within the city, just as most men are by their very nature born to serve. Some of the arts rule certain (other) arts while serving others at the same time, whereas there are other arts which, not ruling anything at all, only serve. Therefore the art of ruling the excellent city cannot just be any chance art, nor due to any chance habit whatever. For just as the first ruler in a genus cannot be ruled by anything in that genus—for instance the ruler of the limbs cannot be ruled by any other limb, and this holds good for any ruler of any composite whole—so the art of the ruler in the excellent city of necessity cannot be a serving art at all and cannot be ruled by any other art, but his art must be an art towards the aim of which all the other arts tend, and for which they strive in all the actions of the excellent city.

§8. That man is a person over whom nobody has any sovereignty whatsoever. He is a man who has reached his perfection and has become actually intellect and actually being thought (intelligized), his representative faculty having by nature reached its utmost perfection in the way stated by us; this faculty of his is predisposed by nature to receive, either in waking life or in sleep, from the Active Intellect the particulars, either as they are or by imitating them, and also the intelligibles, by imitating them. His Passive Intellect will have reached its perfection by [having apprehended] all the intelligibles, so that none of them is kept back from it, and it will have become actually intellect and actually being thought. Indeed any man whose Passive Intellect has thus been perfected by [having apprehended] all the intelligibles and has become actually intellect and actually being thought, so that the intelligible in him has become identical with that which thinks in him, acquires an actual intellect which is superior to the Passive Intellect and more perfect and more separate from matter (immaterial?) than the Passive Intellect. It is called the 'Acquired Intellect' and comes to occupy a middle position between the Passive Intellect and the Active Intellect, nothing else being between it and

the Active Intellect. The Passive Intellect is thus like matter and substratum for the Acquired Intellect, and the Acquired Intellect like matter and substratum for the Active Intellect, and the rational faculty, which is a natural disposition, is a matter underlying the Passive Intellect which is actually intellect.

§9. The first stage, then, through which man becomes man is the coming to be of the receptive natural disposition which is ready to become actually intellect; this disposition is common to all men. Between this disposition and the Active Intellect are two stages, the Passive Intellect which has become actually intellect, and [the rise of] the Acquired Intellect. There are thus two stages between the first stage of being a man and the Active Intellect. When the perfect Passive Intellect and the natural disposition become one thing in the way the compound of matter and form is one—and when the from of the humanity of this man is taken as identical with the Passive Intellect which has become actually intellect, there will be between this man and the Active Intellect only one stage. And when the natural disposition is made the matter of the Passive Intellect which has become actually intellect, and the Passive Intellect the matter of the Acquired Intellect, and the Acquired Intellect the matter of the Active Intellect, and when all this is taken as one and the same thing, then this man is the man on whom the Active Intellect has descended.

§10. When this occurs in both parts of his rational faculty, namely the theoretical and the practical rational faculties, and also in his representative faculty, then it is this man who receives Divine Revelation, and God Almighty grants him Revelation through the mediation of the Active Intellect, so that the emanation from God Almighty to the Active Intellect is passed on to his Passive Intellect through the mediation of the Acquired Intellect, and then to the faculty of representation. Thus he is, through the emanation from the Active Intellect to his Passive Intellect, a wise man and a philosopher and an accomplished thinker who employs an intellect of divine quality, and through the emanation from the Active Intellect to his faculty of representation a visionary prophet: who warns of things to come and tells of particular things which exist at present.

§11. This man holds the most perfect rank of humanity and has reached the highest degree of felicity. His soul is united as it were with the Active Intellect, in the way stated by us.[1]

He is the man who knows every action by which felicity can be reached. This is the first condition for being a ruler. Moreover, he should be a good orator and able to rouse [other people's] imagination by well chosen words. He should be able to lead people well along the right path to felicity and to the actions by which felicity is reached. He should, in addition, be of tough physique, in order to shoulder the tasks of war.

This is the sovereign over whom no other human being has any sovereignty whatsoever; he is the Imām; he is the first sovereign of the excellent city, he is the sovereign of the excellent nation, and the sovereign of the universal state (the *oikumenē*).

§12. But this state can only be reached by a man in whom twelve natural qualities are found together, with which he is endowed by birth. (1) One of them is that he should have limbs and organs which are free from deficiency and strong, and that they will make him fit for the actions which depend on them; when he intends to perform an action with one of them, he accomplishes it with ease. (2) He should by nature be good at understanding and perceiving everything said to him, and grasp it in his mind according to what the speaker intends and what the thing itself demands. (3) He should be good at retaining what he comes to know and see and hear and apprehend in general, and forget almost nothing. (4) He should be well provided with ready intelligence and very bright; when he sees the slightest indication of a thing, he should grasp it in the way indicated. (5) He should have a fine diction, his tongue enabling him

to explain to perfection all that is in the recess of his mind. (6) He should be fond of learning and acquiring knowledge, be devoted to it and grasp things easily, without finding the effort painful, nor feeling discomfort about the toil which it entails. (7) He should by nature be fond of truth and truthful men and hate falsehood and liars. (8) He should by nature not crave for food and drink and sexual intercourse, and have a natural aversion to gambling and hatred of the pleasures which these pursuits provide. (9) He should be proud of spirit [*megalopsychos*] and fond of honour, his soul being by his nature above everything ugly and base, and rising naturally to the most lofty things. (10) Dirham and dīnār and the other worldly pursuits should be of little amount in his view. (11) He should by nature be fond of justice and of just people, and hate oppression and injustice and those who practise them, giving himself and others their due, and urging people to act justly and showing pity to those who are oppressed by injustice; he should lend his support to what he considers to be beautiful and noble and just; he should not be reluctant to give in nor should he be stubborn and obstinate if he is asked to do justice; but he should be reluctant to give in if he is asked to do injustice and evil altogether. (12) He should be strong in setting his mind firmly upon the thing which, in his view, ought to be done, and daringly and bravely carry it out without fear and weak-mindedness.

§13. Now it is difficult to find all these qualities united in one man, and, therefore, men endowed with this nature will be found one at a time only, such men being altogether very rare. Therefore if there exists such a man in the excellent city who, after reaching maturity, fulfils the six aforementioned conditions—or five of them if one excludes the gift of visionary prophecy through the faculty of representation[2]—he will be the sovereign. Now when it happens that, at a given time, no such man is to be found but there was previously an unbroken succession of sovereigns of this kind, the laws and the customs which were introduced will be adopted and eventually firmly established.

The next sovereign, who is the successor of the first sovereigns,[3] will be someone in whom those [twelve] qualities are found together from the time of his birth and his early youth and who will, after reaching his maturity, be distinguished by the following six qualities: (1) He will be a philosopher. (2) He will know and remember the laws and customs (and rules of conduct) with which the first sovereigns had governed the city, conforming in all his actions to all their actions. (3) He will excel in deducing a new law by analogy where no law of his predecessors has been recorded, following for his deductions the principles laid down by the first Imāms. (4) He will be good at deliberating and be powerful in his deductions to meet new situations for which the first sovereigns could not have laid down any law; when doing this he will have in mind the good of the city. (5) He will be good at guiding the people by his speech to fulfil the laws of the first sovereigns as well as those laws which he will have deduced in conformity with their principles after their time. (6) He should be of tough physique in order to shoulder the tasks of war, mastering the serving as well as the ruling military art.

§14. When one single man who fulfils all these conditions cannot be found but there are two, one of whom is a philosopher and the other fulfils the remaining conditions, the two of them will be the sovereigns of this city.

But when all these six qualities exist separately in different men, philosophy in one man and the second quality in another man and so on, and when these men are all in agreement, they should all together be the excellent sovereigns.

But when it happens, at a given time, that philosophy has no share in the government, though every other condition may be present in it, the excellent city will remain without a king, the ruler actually in charge of this city will not be a king, and the city will be on the verge of destruction; and if it happens that no philosopher can be found who will be attached to the actual ruler of the city, then, after a certain interval, this city will undoubtedly perish.

§15. In opposition to the excellent city are the 'ignorant' city, the wicked city, the city which has deliberately changed its character and the city which has missed the right path through faulty judgment. In opposition to it are also the individuals who make up the common people in the various cities.

§16. The 'ignorant' city is the city whose inhabitants do not know true felicity, the thought of it never having occurred to them. Even if they were rightly guided to it they would either not understand it or not believe in it. The only good things they recognise are some of those which are superficially thought of as good among the things which are considered to be the aims in life such as bodily health, wealth, enjoyment of pleasures, freedom to follow one's desires, and being held in honour and esteem. According to the citizens of the ignorant city each of these is a kind of felicity, and the greatest and perfect felicity is the sum total of all of them. Things contrary to these goods are misery such as deficiency of the body, poverty, no enjoyment of pleasures, no freedom to follow one's desires, and not being held in honour.

§17. The ignorant city is divided into a number of cities. One of them is the city of necessity, that is the city whose people strive for no more food, drink, clothes, housing, and sexual intercourse than is necessary for sustaining their bodies, and they co-operate to attain this. Another is the city of meanness; the aim of its people is to co-operate in the acquisition of wealth and riches, not in order to enjoy something else which can be got through wealth, but because they regard wealth as the sole aim in life. Another is the city of depravity and baseness; the aim of its people is the enjoyment of the pleasure connected with food and drink and sexual intercourse, and in general of the pleasures of the senses and of the imagination, and to give preference to entertainment and idle play in every form and in every way. Another is the city of honour; the aim of its people is to co-operate to attain honour and distinction and fame among the nations, to be extolled and treated with respect by word and deed, and to attain (gain, achieve) glory and splendour either in the eyes of other people or amongst themselves, each according to the extent of his love of such distinction or according to the amount of it which he is able to reach. Another is the city of power; the aim of its people is to prevail over others and to prevent others from prevailing over them, their only purpose in life being the enjoyment which they get from power. Another is the 'democratic' city: the aim of its people is to be free, each of them doing what he wishes without restraining his passions in the least.

§18. There are as many kings of ignorant cities as there are cities of this kind, each of them governing the city over which he has authority so that he can indulge in his passion and design.

We have herewith enumerated the designs which may be set up as aims for ignorant cities.

§19. The wicked city is a city whose views are those of the excellent city; it knows felic-ity, God almighty, the existents of the second order, the Active Intellect and everything which as such is to be known and believed in by the people of the excellent city; but the actions of its people are the actions of the people of the ignorant cities.

The city which has deliberately changed is a city whose views and actions were previously the views and actions of the people of the excellent city, but they have been changed and different views have taken their place, and its actions have turned into different actions.

The city which misses the right path (the 'erring' city) is the city which aims at felicity after this life, and holds about God Almighty, the existents of the second order and the Active Intellect pernicious and useless beliefs, even if they are taken as symbols and representations of true felicity. Its first ruler was a man who falsely pretended to be receiving 'revelation'; he produced this wrong impression through falsifications, cheating and deceptions.

§20. The kings of these cities are contrary to the kings of the excellent cities: their ways of governing are contrary to the excellent ways of governing. The same applies to all the other people who live in these cities.

NOTES

1. Cf. Chapter 14 §9.
2. Literally: 'the gift of foreseeing and warning of things to come.'
3. Reading the plural instead of the singular in all the MSS.

CHAPTER 26

John of Salisbury

John of Salisbury was born circa 1115 at Old Sarum (Wiltshire), England. His academic background was somewhat channeled. In 1136 he traveled to France, where he read dialectic first under Abelard and then under Alberic and Robert of Melum. Two years later, it appears, he traveled to Chartres, where he began the study of grammar under Richard of Arranches as well as William of Conches. It was here that he also studied rhetoric. In 1141 he made his way to Paris, where he turned his attention to theology. He eventually became a member of the Roman Curia and in 1148 attended the Council of Rheims. Subsequently, he became secretary and council to Theobald, archbishop of Canterbury. Upon the archbishop's death, he entered the service of Thomas Becket, who followed Theobald as archbishop. John's association and allegiance to him remained firm throughout Becket's strife with King Henry II. John spent some years in exile in France (1163–70), most of which were devoted to working with King Louis VII on behalf of Becket, who was also there in exile. During this period he lived primarily in Rheims. In 1170 both John and Becket returned to Canterbury, England. John was present, most likely in concealment, when the knights following the orders of Henry II murdered Becket in the cathedral. He subsequently worked for Thomas' canonization. In July 1176, at the request of King Louis, John became bishop of Chartres. He died in 1180.

John of Salisbury and *The Policraticus*

It is clear that John considers secular authority to be inferior and subject to that of the church. The prince is the exemplification of secular authority. He is distinguished from a tyrant in that "the prince understands that nothing is permitted to him if it is at variance with justice and equity". There are, however, two standards of justice. A prince can rule by his own justice or the justice of God. It is characteristic of tyrants that they rule by their own standards of justice. A prince rules by the justice of God, "whose justice is justice forever, and his law equity". In one sense, though, the prince is above the law, "not because evil actions are allowed him, but because he should be one who cherishes equity, not from fear of punishment but from the love of justice". Since a prince properly rules by divine justice, it follows that he receives his authority from the Church. He is the servant of the priesthood, discharging "that part of sacred duties which seem unworthy of the hands of the priesthood".

It is here that John draws an analogy between a prince and the head of a family.

The head of the family rules and dispenses justice. Yet he is motivated to do so for the well-being of the members of the family. A prince does likewise. "Let him be, therefore, the father and husband of his subjects, or, if he knows a more tender affection, let him practice it; let him strive to be loved more than he is feared, and let him show himself to them in such a light that out of sheer devotion they may put his life before their own and reckon his safety to be a kind of public life."

THE POLICRATICUS

Book Four

Prologue

The expression of the truth is unquestionably a difficult undertaking, and it is very frequently spoiled by the assault of the darkness of error or by the carelessness of the one who tries to express it. For when things are unknown, who rightly ponders what is true? However, the knowledge of things, in so far as it does not direct the ways of the disdainful, sharpens the stings of justice for the punishment of the transgressor. The first step, therefore, in philosophizing is to discuss the genera and the properties of things,[1] so that one may prudently learn what is true in individual things, and the second step is that each should faithfully follow whatever truth has shone upon him. Now this paved route to those who philosophize is open only to the man who cries out from the realm of falsehood into the liberty[2] by which those whom the truth has delivered are made free[3] and, serving the Spirit,[4] withdraw their necks from the yoke of wickedness and injustice. For "where the Spirit of" God "is, there is liberty,"[5] while the fear which is servile and consents to vices banishes the Holy Spirit. Moreover, it is the Spirit who speaks righteousness[6] in the sight of princes and feels no shame,[7] and who sets

Reprinted from *A Scholastic Miscellany: Anselm to Ockham*, edited and translated by Eugene R. Fairweather (Vol. 10: The Library of Christian Classics). First published in 1955 by SCM Press Ltd., London and the Westminster Press, Philadelphia. Reprinted by permission of Westminster/John Knox Press, Louisville, and SCM Press, London, pp. 247–260.

the poor in spirit[8] above, or at least on a level with, kings,[9] and teaches those whom he makes to cleave to him to speak and do the truth.[10] But he who will not hear or speak the truth is a stranger to the Spirit of truth.[11] But no more of this. Now let us hear in what respect a tyrant differs from a prince.

Chapter I

The Difference Between a Prince and a Tyrant, and What a Prince Is

This, then, is the sole (or at least the greatest) difference between a tyrant and a prince, that the latter conforms to the law, and rules the people, whose servant he believes himself to be, by its judgment. Also, when he performs the dutes of the commonwealth and undergoes its burdens, he claims for himself the first place by privilege of law, and is set before others in so far as universal burdens hang over the prince, while individuals are bound to individual concerns. On this account, the power over all his subjects is rightly conferred on him, so that, in seeking and accomplishing the welfare of each and all, he may be self-sufficient and the state of the human commonwealth may be best disposed, while one is the member of another.[12] In this, indeed, we follow nature, the best guide for living,[13] which arranged all the senses of its microcosm[14]—that is, its little world, man—in the head, and subjected all the members to the latter so that they all are rightly moved, as long as they follow the decision of a sound head. Therefore, the princely crown is exalted and shines with privileges as many and as great as it has believed to be necessary for itself. And this is done rightly, because nothing is more beneficial for the people than for the prince's necessity to be met—when his will is not opposed to justice, to be sure. Therefore (as many define him) the prince is the public ruler and a kind of image of the divine Majesty on earth.[15] Beyond doubt, it is shown that something great in the way of divine power indwells princes, when men submit their necks to their nods and very often fearlessly yield their necks to be smitten, and each for whom he is a matter of dread fears him by divine instigation. I do not think that this could happen, save by the act of the divine pleasure. For all power is from the Lord God,[16] and it has been with him always, and is with him eternally. Therefore, what the prince can do comes from God in such a way that the power does not depart from the Lord, but he exercises it by a hand that is subject to him, and that follows in all things the instruction of his clemency or justice. Thus "he that resisteth the power resisteth the ordinance of God,"[17] with whom rests the authority to confer it and (when he wills) to take it away or lessen it. For when a mighty one decides to rage against his subjects, this involves not just himself but also the divine dispensation, by which those who are subject to it are punished or vexed for God's good pleasure. So, for instance, during the depredations of the Huns, Attila was asked, by the devout bishop of a certain city, who he was, and replied, "I am Attila, the scourge of God." It is written that, when the bishop had reverenced the divine Majesty in him, he said, "Welcome to the servant of God," and, repeating, "Blessed is he that cometh in the name of the Lord,"[18] opened the doors of the church and admitted the persecutor, and through him attained to the palm of martyrdom.[19] For he did not dare to shut out the scourge of God, knowing as he did that it is the beloved son that is scourged,[20] and that the very power of the scourge comes from the Lord alone.[21] If, then, the power is to be

reverenced in this way by the good, even when it brings misfortune to the elect, who will not reverence it? After all, it was instituted by the Lord "for the punishment of evildoers, and for the praise of the good,"[22] and it serves the laws with the readiest devotion. For, as the emperor says,[23] it is a statement worthy of the majesty of the ruler that the prince should acknowledge that he is bound by laws, because the authority of the prince depends on the authority of the law,[24] and it is certainly a greater thing for the realm when sovereignty is set under laws, so that the prince understands that nothing is permitted to him if it is at variance with justice and equity.

Chapter II

What Law Is, and That the Prince, Although He Is Released from the Obligations of Law, Is Still the Bondservant of Law and Equity, and Bears a Public Character, and Sheds Blood Blamelessly

Princes should not think that anything is taken away from them in all this, unless they believe that the statutes of their own justice are to be preferred to the justice of God, whose justice is justice forever, and his law equity.[25] Besides, as legal experts affirm,[26] equity is the fitness of things, which makes everything equal by reason and desires equal laws for unequal things; it is equitable toward all and assigns to each what belongs to him.[27] But law is its interpreter, in so far as the will of equity and justice has been made known to it. Therefore, Chrysippus claimed that law has power over all things human and divine, and on that account is superior to all goods and evils and is the chief and guide of things and men alike. Papinian, a really great expert in the law, and Demosthenes, the powerful orator, seem to uphold the law and to subject the obedience of all men to it, inasmuch as in truth all law is the device and gift of God, the doctrine of wise men, the corrector of inclinations to excess, the settlement of the state, and the banishment of all crime, so that all who are engaged in the whole world of political affairs must live according to it.[28] Thus all are closely bound by the necessity of maintaining the law, unless there may perhaps be someone to whom license seems to have been conceded for wickedness. Nevertheless, the prince is said to be released from legal obligations,[29] not because evil actions are allowed him, but because he should be one who cherishes equity, not from fear of punishment but from love of justice, and in everything puts others' advantage before his personal desires. But who will speak of the desires of the prince in connection with public business, since in this area he is permitted to desire nothing for himself save what law or equity suggests or the nature of the common welfare determines? For in these things his will ought to have the effect of a judgment, and it is quite right that what pleases him in such matters should have the force of law,[30] in so far as his sentence is not in disagreement with the intention of equity. "Let my judgment," the psalmist says, "come forth from thy countenance; let thine eyes behold the thing that is equitable,"[31] for an uncorrupt judge is he whose sentence is the image of equity, because of assiduous contemplation. The prince, then, is the servant of the public welfare and the bondservant of equity, and in that sense plays a public role, because he both avenges the injuries and losses of all and punishes all crimes with impartial justice.[32] Moreover, his rod and staff, applied with wise moderation, bring the agreements and the errors of all into the way of equity, so that the spirit rightly gives thanks to the princely power, when it says, "Thy rod and thy staff, they have comforted me."[33] It is true also that his shield is strong,[34] but it is the shield of the weak and it effectively intercepts the darts aimed at the innocent by the malicious. His function also is of the utmost benefit to those who have the least power, and is most strongly opposed to those who desire to do harm. Therefore, "he beareth not the sword in vain,"[35] when he sheds blood by it, but

blamelessly, so that he is not a man of blood, but often kills men without thereby incurring the name or the guilt of a homicide. For if the great Augustine is to be believed, David was called a "man of blood,"[36] not because of his wars but on account of Uriah.[37] And it is nowhere written that Samuel was a man of blood or a homicide, even though he slew Agag, the very rich king of Amalek.[38] In fact, the princely sword is the "sword of the dove,"[39] which strives without animosity, smites without fury, and, when it goes into combat, conceives no bitterness whatsoever. For, just as the law proceeds against crimes without any hatred of persons, so the prince also punishes offenders most rightly, not by any impulse of anger but by the decision of a mild law. For though the prince may seem to have his own "lictors,"[40] we should believe that in fact he is his only (or his foremost) lictor, but that it is lawful for him to smite by the hand of a substitute. For if we consult the Stoics, who diligently search out the origins of names, we shall learn that he is called a "lictor"— as it were, a "striker of the law"—inasmuch as it pertains to his office to smite him who, in the law's judgment, is to be smitten.[41] On this account also, when the guilty were threatened with the sword, it used to be said in ancient days to the officials by whose hand the judge punished evildoers, "Comply with the decision of the law," or "Fulfill the law," so that the mildness of the words might in fact modify the sadness of the event.

Chapter III

That the Prince Is the Servant of Priests and Beneath Them, and What It Means to Carry Out the Princely Office Faithfully

The prince, therefore, receives this sword from the hand of the Church, even though, to be sure, the latter does not possess the sword of blood.[42] Nevertheless, she does possess it as well, but makes use of it by the hand of the prince, to whom she has conceded the power of keeping bodies under restraint, although she has retained authority in spiritual matters for her pontiffs.[43] Thus the prince is in fact the servant of the priesthood, and exercises that part of the sacred duties which seems unworthy of the hands of the priesthood. For while every duty imposed by the sacred laws is a matter of religion and piety, the function of punishing crimes, which seems to constitute a kind of image of the hangman's office, is lower than others. It was on account of this inferiority that Constantine, the most faithful emperor of the Romans, when he had convoked the council of priests at Nicaea,[44] did not dare to take the first place or mingle with the assemblies of the presbyters, but occupied the lowest seat.[45] Indeed, he reverenced the conclusions which he heard approved by them as if he supposed that they proceeded from the judgment of the divine Majesty.[46] As for the written accusations, stating the offenses of the priests, which they had drawn up against one another and presented to the emperor, he received them and put them away, still unopened, in his bosom.[47] Moreover, when he had recalled the council to charity and concord, he said that it was unlawful for him (as a man, and as one who was subject to the judgment of priests) to consider the cases of the gods, who can be judged by God alone. And he committed the books which he had received to the fire, without looking at them, because he was afraid to disclose the crimes or vices of the Fathers, lest he bring on himself the curse of Ham, the rejected son, who failed to cover what he should have respected in his father.[48] For the same reason, he is said (in the writings of Nicholas, the Roman Pontiff) to have stated: "Truly, if with my own eyes I had seen a priest of God, or anyone who had been clothed in the monastic habit, committing sin, I should have spread out my cloak and covered him, lest he be seen by anyone."[49] Theodosius also, the great emperor, when he was suspended from the use of the regalia and the badges of sovereignty by the bishop of Milan, because of a crime that was real enough, but

not quite that serious, patiently and solemnly did the penance imposed on him for homicide.[50] Certainly, to appeal to the testimony of the doctor of the Gentiles, he who blesses is greater than he who is blessed,[51] and he who possesses the authority to confer a dignity surpasses in the privilege of honor him on whom the dignity itself is conferred. Besides, according to the very nature of law, it pertains to the same person to will and not to will, and it is he who has the right to confer who also has the right to take away.[52] Did not Samuel bring sentence of deposition against Saul on account of his disobedience, and substitute the lowly son of Jesse for him in the highest place in the kingdom?[53] But if he who is set up as prince has faithfully performed the function he received, he is to be shown great honor and great reverence, in proportion to the superiority of the head over all the members of the body. Now he performs his task faithfully when, mindful of his rank, he remembers that he bears in himself the totality of his subjects, and knows that he owes his own life not to himself but to others, and as it were distributes it among them with due charity. He owes his entire self, then, to God, most of himself to his fatherland, much to his kinsfolk and neighbors, and least (but still something) to strangers. He is debtor, then, to the wise and the unwise, to the small and the great.[54] In fact, this concern is common to all who are set over others,[55] both to those who bear the care of spritual things and to those who exercise worldly jurisdiction. On this account we read of Melchizedek, who is the first king and priest referred to in Scripture—not to mention, for the present, the mystery by which he prefigures Christ, who was born in heaven without a mother and on earth without a father[56]—we read, I say, that he had neither father nor mother. It is not that he lacked either, but that flesh and blood do not by their nature bring forth kingship and priesthood, since in the creation of either respect of parents should not carry weight without regard for meritorious virtue, but the wholesome desires of faithful subjects should have priority. Thus, when anyone reaches the pinnacle of either kingship or priesthood, he should forget the affection of the flesh and do only what the welfare of his subjects demands. Let him be, therefore, the father and husband of his subjects, or, if he knows a more tender affection, let him practice it; let him strive to be loved more than he is feared, and let him show himself to them in such a light that out of sheer devotion they may put his life before their own and reckon his safety to be a kind of public life. Then everything will go well with him, and if need be a few guards will prevail by their obedience against countless enemies. For "love is strong as death,"[57] and a wedge which the cords of love hold together is not easily broken.[58]

When the Dorians were about to fight with the Athenians, they consulted oracles about the outcome of the battle. "The reply was that they would win unless they killed the king of the Athenians. When the war began, care for the king was the first order given to the soldiers. At that time Codrus was king of the Athenians. When he learned of the response of the god and the orders of the enemy, he changed his kingly garments and, bearing fagots on his neck, entered the enemy's camp. There in a crowd of his opponents he was slain by a soldier, whom he had struck with his sickle. When the king's body was recognized, the Dorians withdrew without a battle. And in this way the Athenians were delivered from war by the virtue of their chief, who offered himself to death for the preservation of the fatherland."[59]

Again, Lycurgus in his kingdom established decrees which set the people in obedience to their chiefs and the chiefs to the justice of their commanders.[60] "He abolished the use of gold and silver and the source of all crimes."[61] He gave to the senate the care of the laws, and to the people the power of electing the senate.[62] He decreed that a maiden "should be married without a dowry, so that wives and not money should be chosen. He intended that the greatest honor should correspond

closely . . . with the age of the old—nor in fact does old age have a more honored place anywhere on earth."[63] Finally, "in order to give eternity to his laws, he bound the citizens by an oath not to change anything in his laws before he returned. . . . Then he set out for Crete, and lived there as a perpetual exile, and when he was dying he ordered his bones to be thrown into the sea, lest, if they were taken home, the Spartans might think that they were released from the obligation of their oath and might abrogate his laws."[64]

I use these examples more freely, because I find that the apostle Paul made use of them when he preached to the Athenians.[65] The illustrious preacher strove to impress "Jesus Christ, and him crucified"[66] on their minds in such a way that he might teach them, by the example of the Gentiles, that the deliverance of many had come about through the shame of the cross. But he also convinced them that these things came about only by the blood of the just and of those who carried on the magistracy of the people. Besides, no one could be found who was sufficient for the deliverance of all—namely, of Jews and Gentiles—save him to whom the Gentiles were given for an inheritance and for whose possession the whole earth was foreordained.[67] Now he affirmed that this could only be the Son of Almighty God, since apart from God no one has subdued all nations and lands. Therefore, while he preached the shame of the cross, so that little by little the folly of the Gentiles should be made void, he gradually lifted up the word of faith and the language of his preaching to the word of God and the wisdom of God and even to the very throne of the divine Majesty, and, lest the power of the gospel should become worthless through the weakness of the flesh, because of the stumbling block of the Jews and the folly of the Gentiles,[68] he expounded the works of the Crucified, which were also supported by the testimony of public opinion, since it was agreed by all that God alone could do these things. But because public opinion often tells many lies on both sides, he assisted opinion itself, because his disciples did greater things,[69] as, for instance, when the sick were healed from any sickness whatever by the shadow of a disciple.[70] But why many things? He overthrew the subtleties of Aristotle, the acuteness of Chrysippus, and the snares of all the philosophers,[71] when he rose from the dead.

It is in everyone's mouth that the Decii, Roman commanders, devoted themselves for their armies.[72] Julius Caesar also said: "A commander who does not try to be esteemed by his soldiers does not know how to arm a soldier, does not know that the humanity of a general in an army tells against the enemy."[73] Caesar never said to his soldiers, "Go thither," but always said, "Come," for he used to say that labor shared with the commander seems less to soldiers. Moreover, according to the same author, bodily pleasure is to be avoided, for he used to say that men's bodies are wounded by swords in war, by pleasures in peace. For the conqueror of the nations had thought that pleasure could most easily be overcome by flight, because he who had subdued the nations was tied up in the coils of Venus by a shameless woman.[74]

Chapter IV

That It Is Certain, by the Authority of Divine Law, That the Prince Is Subject to the Law of Justice

But why do I appeal to examples borrowed from the Gentiles, even though they are so numerous, when anyone can be urged more suitably by laws than by examples to do what must be done? But lest you suppose that the prince himself is wholly free from laws, listen to the law which the "great king over all the earth,"[75] who is "terrible" and "who taketh away the spirit of princes,"[76] imposes on princes. "When thou art come," he says,[77] "into the land, which the Lord God will give thee, and possessest it, and shalt say: 'I will set a king over me, as all nations have that are round about'; thou shalt set him whom the Lord thy God shall choose out of the number of thy brethren. Thou mayest not make a man of another nation king, that is not thy brother. And when he is made king, he shall not multiply horses to himself, nor lead back the people into Egypt, being lifted up with the number of his horsemen, especially since the Lord hath commanded you to return no more the same way. He shall not have many wives, that may take possession of his mind,[78] nor immense sums of gold and silver. But after he is raised to the throne of his kingdom, he shall copy out to himself the Deuteronomy[79] of this law in a volume, taking the copy of the priests of the Levitical tribe, and he shall have it with him, and shall read it all the days of his life, that he may learn to fear the Lord his God, and keep his words and ceremonies, that are commanded in the law. And that his heart be not lifted up with pride over his brethren, nor decline to the right or to the left, that he and his son[80] may reign a long time over Israel." I ask, is he bound by no law, whom that law restrains? Certainly this is a divine law, and cannot be relaxed with impunity. If they are prudent, each of its words is thunder in the ears of princes. I say nothing of the election and the form required in the creation of a prince; consider with me for a little while the rule of living which is prescribed for him. When, it reads, he who professes himself to be the brother of the whole people by religious worship and charitable affection is set up, he shall not multiply horses to himself, since a large number of these would make him oppressive to his subjects. Now to multiply horses means to gather together more horses than necessity requires, for the sake of vainglory or some other fault. For "much" and "little," if we follow the chief of the Peripatetics,[81] refer to the decrease or excess of legitimate quantity in particular genera of things. Will he, then, be permitted to multiply dogs or birds of prey or savage beasts or any natural monsters whatever, when he is told that the number of horses—which are necessary for warfare and the requirements of the whole life—must be of a legitimate quantity? There was no need for mention to be made in the law of actors and mimes, jesters and prostitutes, procurers and human monsters of this kind (which a prince ought to exterminate, and not to foster); indeed, the law does not simply exclude all these abominations from the prince's court, but also turns them out of the people of God. By the term "horses" we are to understand the necessary use of a complete household and all its equipment; whatever amount of this a concern for necessity or utility demands is legitimate. The useful and the virtuous[82] must, however, be equated, and government be chosen by the virtuous. For already in ancient times it was the view of the philosophers[83] that no opinion was more pernicious than the opinion of those who separate the useful from the virtuous, and that the truest and most beneficial judgment was that the virtuous and the useful are altogether convertible. Plato, as the histories of the Gentiles relate,[84] when he had seen Dionysius, the tyrant of Sicily, surrounded by his bodyguards, said, "What great evil have you done, that you need so many to guard you?" This certainly is unnecessary for a prince, who so attaches the affections of all to himself by his services that any subject will risk his head for him when dangers threaten, since at the urging of nature the members are wont to risk themselves for the head, and "skin for skin and all that a man hath he will" lay down "for his life."[85]

The text [of Deuteronomy] goes on: "Nor lead back the people into Egypt, being lifted up with the number of his horsemen."[86] For everyone who is set in a high place is to exercise the greatest diligence, lest he corrupt his inferiors by his example and his misuse of things, and by way of pride or luxury lead back the people to the darkness of confusion. For it often happens that subjects imitate the vices of their superiors, because the people strive to be conformed to the magistrate, and each and every one readily desires that in which he sees that another is distinguished. There is a celebrated passage of the distinguished poet, in which he states the thoughts and words of Theodosius the Great:

> If you order and decree anything to be
>   held in common,
> First submit to what is ordered; then
>   the people becomes
> More observant of the right, nor does it
>   refuse to accept it,
> When it sees the lawgiver himself obey
>   it. The nation
> Is ordered by the king's example, nor
>   can ordinances
> Affect human inclinations as does the
>   life of a ruler.
> The inconstant multitude always
>   changes with the prince.[87]

Now the means of individuals are far from equal to the resources of all. Each man dips into his own coffers, but the ruler draws on the public chest or treasury; if this by any chance fails, recourse is had to the means of individuals. But it is necessary for each private person to be satisfied with his own. If these prove to have been reduced, he who just now desired the ruler's renown is ashamed of the obscurity of his own disorder, mean as he is in his poverty. On this account thrift in the use of public goods was imposed by decree on the rulers of the Spartans, even though it is permissible by common right to make use of an inheritance or of something acquired by good fortune.

NOTES

1. On "genus" and "property," cf. Aristotle, *Topica*, I, 5–6 ($101^{b}36$–$103^{a}5$); summary in W. D. Ross, *Aristotle* (3d ed., Methuen, London, 1937), 57.

2. Cf. Rom. 8:20 f.

3. Cf. John 8:32.

4. Cf. Rom. 7:6.

5. II Cor. 3:17.

6. Cf. Ps. 51:5 (A.V. 52:3).

7. Cf. Ps. 118:46 (P.B.V., 119:46).

8. Cf. Matt. 5:3.

9. Cf. Luke 1:52.

10. Cf. John 16:13; I John 1:6.

11. Cf. John 14:17; 15:26; 16:13; I John 4:6.

12. Cf. Rom. 12:5.

13. Cf. Cicero, *De amicitia*, 5, 19 (Loeb Classical Library ed., *Cicero: De senectute, De amicitia, De divinatione* [Heinemann, London, 1938], 128).

14. The word *microcosmus* appears in Isidore of Seville, *Orig.*, III, 23 (*PL*, 82, 169); it does not seem to have been used (except as two words: *mikros kosmos*) by the ancient Greeks (cf. C. C. J. Webb's edition of the *Policraticus*, I, 235n.). The term had been used by John of Salisbury's teacher, Bernard of Chartres (on Bernard, cf. Gilson, *History*, 140; 619 f.).

15. On this definition of the *princeps*, cf. Vegetius, *Epitome rei militaris*, II, 5 f. (ed. C. Lang [2d ed., Leipzig, 1885], 38 f.).

16. Cf. Rom. 13:1.

17. Rom. 13:2.

18. Matt. 21:9.

19. Who was the bishop? A similar story is told of Lupus of Troyes (d. 478), but he was not martyred (cf. *Acta Sanctorum*, July, Vol. 7, 78; 82).

20. Cf. Heb. 12:6.

21. Cf. Deut. 32:27; Isa. 10:5–15.

22. Cf. I Peter 2:14.

23. Cf. *Codex Iustinianus*, I, 14:4, in *Corpus Iuris Civilis*, II (ed. P. Krueger, Berlin, 1888), 68.

24. *Ius.*

25. Cf. Ps. 118:142 (P.B.V., 119:142).

26. This definition was current in the Middle Ages, and was cited by Azo, the famous Bolognese legal expert of the thirteenth century (cf. *Policraticus*, ed. C. C. J. Webb, I, 237n.).

27. Cf. *Institutiones Iustiniani*, I, 1:1, ed. P. Krueger, *Corpus Iur. Civ.*, I (Berlin, 1889), 1.

28. On the last two sentences, cf. *Digesta Iustiniani* (= *Pandects*), I, 3:1 f., ed. T. Mommsen, *Corpus Iur. Civ.*, I, 5 (separate pagination for *Digesta*). For Eng. trans. of this and other texts, cf. C. H. Monro, *The Digest of Justinian*, 2 vols. (Cambridge, 1904–1909).

29. Cf. *Digesta*, I, 3:31 (*Corp. Iur. Civ.*, I, 6).

30. Cf. *Digesta*, I, 4:1 (*Corp. Iur. Civ.*, I, 7).

31. Ps. 16:2 (P.B.V., 17:2), quoted almost exactly.

32. Cf. the "Prayer for the Whole State of Christ's Church," in the *Book of Common Prayer*: "That they may truly and indifferently minister justice, to the punishment of wickedness and vice, and to the maintenance of thy true religion, and virtue."

33. Ps. 22:4 (P.B.V., 23:4).

34. II Kings 1:21 (A.V., II Sam. 1:21).

35. Rom. 13:4.

36. Cf. II Kings 16:7 f. (A.V., II Sam. 16:7 f.); I Chron. 22:8.

37. Cf. II Kings, ch. 11 (A.V., II Sam. ch. 11). The closest parallel I can find in Augustine is his statement that "men of blood" are those who hate their brethren (*Enarr. in Ps.* 138, 26 (*PL*, 37, 1801).

38. Cf. I Kings 15:32 f. (A.V., I Sam. 15:32 f.).

39. Jer. 46:16.

40. On "lictors," cf. W. Smith, *Smaller Classical Dictionary* (ed. E. H. Blakeney, Everyman's Library, Dent, London, 1934), 308: "*Lictors*, attendants who carried the *fasces* (rods bound in bundle form, and containing an ax in the middle) before a Roman magistrate."

41. *Lictor* is really derived, not from *legis ictor*, but from *ligare* (to bind together).

42. Cf. *Policraticus*, VI, 8 (ed. Webb, II, 22 f.).

43. In liturgical and other usage, *pontifex* is applied to all bishops, and not simply to the pope (cf. "pontifical mass"). The symbol of the "sword" (cf. Matt. 26:52; John 18:10) and of the "two swords" (cf. Luke 22:38), seems to have been first applied to the authority of the Church by Bernard of Clairvaux in 1149 (*Epist.* 256 [*PL*, 182, 463–465]; cf. *De consider.*, IV, 3 [col. 776]). The *Policraticus* was written perhaps ten years later. On the history of the idea, cf. H. X. Arquillière, "Origines de la théorie des deux glaives," in *Studi Gregoriani*, I (Abbazia di San Paolo, Rome, 1947), 501–521; P. Lecler, "L'argument des deux glaives," *Recherches de science religieuse*, 21 (1931), 293–399; 22 (1932), 151–177, 281–303.

44. I.e., the first Council of Nicaea (A.D. 325).

45. Cf. Cassiodorus, *Hist. tripart.*, II, 5 (*PL*, 69, 924).

46. Cf. ibid., II, 14 (col. 934).
47. Cf. ibid., II, 2 (col. 922); Rufinus, *Hist. eccles.*, I, 2 (*PL*, 21, 468); Gregory the Great, *Epist.* 5, 40 (*PL*, 77, 766); Gratian, *Decret.*, II, 11, q. 1, c. 41 (ed. E. A. Friedberg, *Corpus Iuris Canonici*, I [Leipzig, 1879], 638).
48. Cf. Gen. 9:22 ff.
49. Cf. Nicholas I, *Epist.* 86 (*PL*, 119, 944); Gratian, *Decret.*, I, dist. 96, c. 8 (p. 339).
50. Cf. Ambrose, *De obitu Theodos.*, 24 (*PL*, 16, 1396); Paulinus, *Vita S. Ambrosii*, 24 (*PL*, 14, 35).
51. Cf. Heb. 7:7.
52. Cf. *Digesta Iustin.*, L, 17:3 (*Corp. Iur. Civ.*, I, 868).
53. Cf. I Kings 15:26 to 16:13 (A.V., I Sam. 15:26 to 16:13).
54. Cf. Rom. 1:14.
55. Lit., *praelati* (i.e., those set before others, or "prelates").
56. Cf. Heb. 7:1–3.
57. S. of Sol. 8:6.
58. Cf. Eccl. 4:12.
59. Justinus, *Hist. Philip.*, II, 6:16–21 (Delphin Classics ed., London, 1822, I, 83 f.); quotation practically verbatim.
60. Ibid., III, 2:9 (p. 106).
61. Ibid., III, 2:12 (p. 106, reads "*as* the source").
62. Cf. ibid., III, 3:2 (p. 106).
63. Cf. ibid., III, 3:7–9 (p. 107).
64. Ibid., III, 11 f. (pp. 107 f.).
65. Cf. *Acta Pauli*, in M. R. James, *The Apocryphal New Testament* (Oxford, 1926), 299; *Acta* of Dionysius the Areopagite, in *Acta Sanctorum*, October, Vol 4, 704; Richard of St. Victor, *De verbo incarn.*, 13 (*PL*, 196, 1007).
66. I Cor. 2:2. For the description of Saint Paul as *praedicator egregius*, cf. Gregory the Great, *Epist.* 5, 40 (*PL*, 77, 767).
67. Cf. Ps. 2:8.
68. Cf. I Cor. 1:23.
69. Cf. John 14:12.
70. Cf. Acts 5:15.
71. Cf. Jerome, *Epist.* 57, 12 (CSEL, 54, 526).
72. Cf. Augustine, *De civ. dei*, IV, 20 (CSEL, 40/1, 187).
73. Cf. Caecilius Balbus, *De nugis philosophorum* (ed. E. Wölfflin, Basel, 1855), 32.
74. Scil., Cleopatra.
75. Ps. 46:3 (P.B.V., 47:2).
76. Ps. 75:12 f. (P.B.V., 76:11 f.)
77. Deut. 17:14–20.
78. Vulgate, "allure."
79. So the Vulgate, transliterated from LXX.
80. Vulgate, "sons."
81. The closest approximation to this statement in a work accessible to John of Salisbury is found in Aristotle, *Categ.*, 6 (5^b15–29). It seems certain enough that he could not have read *Metaphysica*, X, 6 (1056^b17–19).
82. On the useful (*utile*) and the virtuous (*honestum*), cf. R. J. Deferrari and M. I. Barry, *A Lexicon of St. Thomas Aquinas* (Catholic University of America, Washington, 1948), 120: "*Bonum honestum*, that good which is fitting, or decent, or strictly in accordance with the nature which seeks it for itself, not as a means to some further good, as opposed to *bonum utile*." The distinction, as John indicates, is classical: cf. Quintilian, *De instit.*, III, 8:13.
83. Cf. Cicero, *De offic.*, III, 3:11 (Loeb Classical Library ed. [Heinemann, London, 1928], 314 ff.).
84. Cf. Caecilius Balbus, *De nugis philos.*, 32.
85. Job. 2:4.
86. Deut. 17:16.
87. Claudian, *De IV⁰ cons. Honorii*, 11. 296–302 (Loeb Classical Library ed. [London, 1922], I, 308).

CHAPTER 27

St. Thomas Aquinas

(See Chapter Five for biography.)

St. Thomas Aquinas on Kingship

The views of Thomas Aquinas concerning the state are eclectic. On the one hand, he agrees with Aristotle that the state is the natural extension of human beings qua sociopolitical animals. Consequently, the raison de d'être of the state is the well-being of its members consistent with the desire of each person to live the good life. On the other hand, consistent with his Christian, otherworldly views, he believes there to be an even greater purpose of existence because "through virtuous living man is further ordained to a higher end, which consists in the enjoyment of God". Here Aquinas establishes a parallel between the universe and the state qua political entity. ". . . whatever is in accord with nature is best, for in all things nature does what is best. Now, every natural governance is governance by one. . . . Among bees there is one king bee and in the whole universe there is One God, Maker and Ruler of all things. . . . it follows that it is best for a human multitude to be ruled by one person." The purpose or guiding principle of a (political) unity or state is peace. Indeed, St. Thomas identifies unity with peace. This identity allows him to conclude that one ruler is most likely to maintain peace because of the unity of his own (numerical) oneness. More than one person sharing power and making political decisions jointly increases the likelihood of instability through disagreement, thereby endangering social peace. Nevertheless, St. Thomas is wary of tyranny, a common by-product of single rule. Consequently, he believes that elective kingship is safer than monarchies based on heredity. And he suggests that the king's power "be so tempered that he cannot easily fall into tyranny". To that end he maintains that "all should take some share in the government"; that is, it is proper that the monarchy be supplemented by aristocratic as well as popular elements of participation in government.

ON KINGSHIP TO THE KING OF CYPRUS

Book One

Chapter I

What Is Meant by the Word 'King'

[2] The first step in our undertaking must be to set forth what is to be understood by the term *king*.

[3] In all things which are ordered towards an end, wherein this or that course may be adopted, some directive principle is needed through which the due end may be reached by the most direct route. A ship, for example, which moves in different directions according to the impulse of the changing winds, would never reach its destination were it not brought to port by the skill of the pilot. Now, man has an end to which his whole life and all his actions are ordered; for man is an intelligent agent, and it is clearly the part of an intelligent agent to act in view of an end. Men also adopt different methods in proceeding towards their proposed end, as the diversity of men's pursuits and actions clearly indicates. Consequently man needs some directive principle to guide him towards his end.

[4] To be sure, the light of reason is placed by nature in every man, to guide him in his acts towards his end. Wherefore, if man were intended to live alone, as many animals do, he would require no other guide to his end. Each man would be a king unto himself, under God, the highest King, inasmuch as he would direct himself in his acts by the light of reason given him from on high. Yet it is natural for man, more than for any other animal,[1] to be a social and political animal,[2] to live in a group.

[5] This is clearly a necessity of man's

nature.[3] For all other animals, nature has prepared food, hair as a covering, teeth, horns, claws as means of defence or at least speed in flight, while man alone was made without any natural provisions for these things. Instead of all these, man was endowed with reason, by the use of which he could procure all these things for himself by the work of his hands.[4] Now, one man alone is not able to procure them all for himself, for one man could not sufficiently provide for life, unassisted. It is therefore natural that man should live in the society of many.

[6] Moreover, all other animals are able to discern, by inborn skill, what is useful and what is injurious, even as the sheep naturally regards the wolf as his enemy. Some animals also recognize by natural skill certain medicinal herbs and other things necessary for their life. Man, on the contrary, has a natural knowledge of the things which are essential for his life only in a general fashion, inasmuch as he is able to attain knowledge of the particular things necessary for human life by reasoning from natural principles. But it is not possible for one man to arrive at a knowledge of all these things by his own individual reason. It is therefore necessary for man to live in a multitude so that each one may assist his fellows, and different men may be occupied in seeking, by their reason, to make different discoveries—one, for example, in medicine, one in this and another in that.

[7] This point is further and most plainly evidenced by the fact that the use of speech is a prerogative proper to man. By this means, one man is able fully to express his conceptions to others. Other animals, it is true, express their feelings to one another in a general way, as a dog may express anger by barking and other animals give vent to other feelings in various fashions. But man communicates with his kind more completely than any other animal known

From Thomas Aquinas, *On Kingship to the King of Cyprus*, translated by Gerald B. Phelan, revised by I. Th. Eschmann, pp. 3–10, 11–13, 23–29, 58–63, by permission of the publisher. Copyright 1949, 1982 by the Pontifical Institute of Medieval Studies, Toronto.

to be gregarious, such as the crane, the ant or the bee.[5]—With this in mind, Solomon says: "It is better that there be two than one; for they have the advantage of their company."[6]

[8] If, then, it is natural for man to live in the society of many, it is necessary that there exist among men some means by which the group may be governed. For where there are many men together and each one is looking after his own interest, the multitude would be broken up and scattered unless there were also an agency to take care of what appertains to the commonweal. In like manner, the body of a man or any other animal would disintegrate unless there were a general ruling force within the body which watches over the common good of all members.—With this in mind, Solomon says: "Where there is no governor, the people shall fall."[7]

[9] Indeed it is reasonable that this should happen, for what is proper and what is common are not identical.[8] Things differ by what is proper to each: they are united by what they have in common. But diversity of effects is due to diversity of causes. Consequently, there must exist something which impels towards the common good of the many, over and above that which impels towards the particular good of each individual. Wherefore also in all things that are ordained towards one end, one thing is found to rule the rest.[9] Thus in the corporeal universe, by the first body, i.e. the celestial body, the other bodies are regulated according to the order of Divine Providence; and all bodies are ruled by a rational creature.[10] So, too, in the individual man, the soul rules the body; and among the parts of the soul, the irascible and the concupiscible parts are ruled by reason.[11] Likewise, among the members of a body, one, such as the heart or the head,[12] is the principal and moves all the others. Therefore in every multitude there must be some governing power.

[10] Now it happens in certain things which are ordained towards an end that one may proceed in a right way and also in a wrong way. So, too, in the government of a multitude there is a distinction between right and wrong.[13] A thing is rightly directed when it is led towards a befitting end; wrongly when it is led towards an unbefitting end. Now the end which befits a multitude of free men is different from that which befits a multitude of slaves, for the free man is one who exists for his own sake, while the slave, as such, exists for the sake of another.[14] If, therefore, a multitude of free men is ordered by the ruler towards the common good of the multitude, that rulership will be right and just, as is suitable to free men. If, on the other hand, a rulership aims, not at the common good of the multitude, but at the private good of the ruler, it will be an unjust and perverted rulership. The Lord, therefore, threatens such rulers, saying by the mouth of Ezechiel:[15] "Woe to the shepherds that feed themselves (seeking, that is, their own interest): should not the flocks be fed by the shepherd?" Shepherds indeed should seek the good of their flocks, and every ruler, the good of the multitude subject to him.

[11] If an unjust government is carried on by one man alone,[16] who seeks his own benefit from his rule and not the good of the multitude subject to him, such a ruler is called a *tyrant*—a word derived from *strength*[17]—because he oppresses by might instead of ruling by justice. Thus among the ancients all powerful men were called tyrants. If an unjust government is carried on, not by one but by several, and if they be few, it is called an *oligarchy*, that is, the rule of a few. This occurs when a few, who differ from the tyrant only by the fact that they are more than one, oppress the people by means of their wealth. If, finally, the bad government is carried on by the multitude, it is called a *democracy*, i.e. control by the populace, which comes about when the plebeian people by force of numbers oppress the rich. In this way the whole people will be as one tyrant.

[12] In like manner we must divide just governments. If the government is administered by many, it is given the name com-

mon to all forms of government, viz. *polity*, as for instance when a group of warriors exercise dominion over a city or province.[18] If it is administered by a few men of virtue, this kind of government is called an *aristocracy*, i.e. noble governance, or governance by noble men, who for this reason are called the *Optimates*.[19] And if a just government is in the hands of one man alone, he is properly called a *king*. Wherefore the Lord says by the mouth of Ezechiel:[20] "My servant, David, shall be king over them and all of them shall have one shepherd."

[13] From this it is clearly shown that the idea of king implies that he be one man who is chief and that he be a shepherd seeking the common good of the multitude and not his own.

[14] Now since man must live in a group, because he is not sufficient unto himself to procure the necessities of life were he to remain solitary, it follows that a society will be the more perfect the more it is sufficient unto itself to procure the necessities of life.[21] There is, to some extent, sufficiency for life in one *family of one household*, namely, insofar as pertains to the natural acts of nourishment and the begetting of offspring and other things of this kind. Self-sufficiency exists, furthermore, in one *street*[22] with regard to those things which belong to the trade of one guild. In a *city*, which is the perfect community, it exists with regard to all the necessities of life. Still more self-sufficiency is found in a *province*[23] because of the need of fighting together and of mutual help against enemies. Hence the man ruling a perfect community, i.e. a city or a province, is antonomastically[24] called *the* king. The ruler of a household is called father, not king, although he bears a certain resemblance to the king,[25] for which reason kings are sometimes called the fathers of their peoples.

[15] It is plain, therefore, from what has been said, that a king is one who rules the people of one city or province, and rules them for the common good. Wherefore Solomon says:[26] "The king ruleth over all the land subject to him."

Chapter II

Whether It Is More Expedient for a City or Province to Be Ruled by One Man or by Many

[16] Having set forth these preliminary points we must now inquire what is better for a province or a city: whether to be ruled by one man or by many.

[17] This question may be considered first from the viewpoint of the purpose of government. The aim of any ruler should be directed towards securing the welfare of that which he undertakes to rule. The duty of the pilot, for instance, is to preserve his ship amidst the perils of the sea and to bring it unharmed to the port of safety. Now the welfare and safety of a multitude formed into a society lies in the preservation of its unity, which is called peace. If this is removed, the benefit of social life is lost and, moreover, the multitude in its disagreement becomes a burden to itself. The chief concern of the ruler of a multitude, therefore, is to procure the unity of peace.[27] It is not even legitimate for him to deliberate whether he shall establish peace in the multitude subject to him, just as a physician does not deliberate whether he shall heal the sick man encharged to him,[28] for no one should deliberate about an end which he is obliged to seek, but only about the means to attain that end. Wherefore the Apostle, having commended the unity of the faithful people, says:[29] "Be ye careful to keep the unity of the spirit in the bond of peace." Thus, the more efficacious a government is in keeping the unity of peace, the more useful it will be. For we call that more useful which leads more directly to the end. Now it is manifest that what is itself one can more efficaciously bring about unity than several[30]—just as the most efficacious cause of heat is that which is by its nature hot. Therefore the rule of one man is more useful than the rule of many.

[18] Furthermore, it is evident that several persons could by no means preserve the stability of the community if they totally disagreed. For union is necessary among them if they are to rule at all: several

men, for instance, could not pull a ship in one direction unless joined together in some fashion. Now several are said to be united according as they come closer to being one. So one man rules better than several who come near being one.[31]

[19] Again, whatever is in accord with nature is best, for in all things nature does what is best. Now, every natural governance is governance by one.[32] In the multitude of bodily members there is one which is the principal mover, namely, the heart; and among the powers of the soul one power presides as chief, namely, the reason. Among bees there is one king bee[33] and in the whole universe there is One God, Maker and Ruler of all things. And there is a reason for this. Every multitude is derived from unity. Wherefore, if artificial things are an imitation of natural things[34] and a work of art is better according as it attains a closer likeness to what is in nature, it follows that it is best for a human multitude to be ruled by one person.

[20] This is also evident from experience. For provinces or cities which are not ruled by one person are torn with dissensions and tossed about without peace, so that the complaint seems to be fulfilled which the Lord uttered through the Prophet:[35] "Many pastors have destroyed my vineyard." On the other hand, provinces and cities which are ruled under one king enjoy peace, flourish in justice, and delight in prosperity. Hence, the Lord by His prophets promises to His people as a great reward that He will give them one head and that "one Prince will be in the midst of them."[36]

Chapter VI

How Provision Might Be Made That the King May Not Fall into Tyranny

[41] Therefore, since the rule of one man, which is the best, is to be preferred, and since it may happen that it be changed into a tyranny, which is the worst (all this is clear from what has been said), a scheme should be carefully worked out which would prevent the multitude ruled by a king from falling into the hands of a tyrant.

[42] First, it is necessary that the man who is raised up to be king by those whom it concerns should be of such condition that it is improbable that he should become a tyrant. Wherefore Daniel,[37] commending the providence of God with respect to the institution of the king says: "The Lord hath sought him a man according to his own heart, and the Lord hath appointed him to be prince over his people." Then, once the king is established, the government of the kingdom must be so arranged that opportunity to tyrannize is removed. At the same time his power should be so tempered that he cannot easily fall into tyranny. How these things may be done we must consider in what follows.

[43] Finally, provision must be made for facing the situation should the king stray into tyranny.[38]

[44] Indeed, if there be not an excess of tyranny it is more expedient to tolerate the milder tyranny for a while than, by acting against the tyrant, to become involved in many perils more grievous than the tyranny itself. For it may happen that those who act against the tyrant are unable to prevail and the tyrant then will rage the more. But should one be able to prevail against the tyrant, from this fact itself very grave dissensions among the people frequently ensue: the multitude may be broken up into factions either during their revolt against the tyrant, or in process of the organization of the government, after the tyrant has been overthrown. Moreover, it sometimes happens that while the multitude is driving out the tyrant by the help of some man, the latter, having received the power, thereupon seizes the tyranny. Then, fearing to suffer from another what he did to his predecessor, he oppresses his subjects with an even more grievous slavery. This is wont to happen in tyranny, namely, that the second becomes more grievous than the one preceding, inasmuch as, without abandoning the previous oppressions, he himself thinks up fresh ones from the malice of his heart. Whence in Syracuse, at

a time when everyone desired the death of Dionysius, a certain old woman kept constantly praying that he might be unharmed and that he might survive her. When the tyrant learned this he asked why she did it. Then she said: "When I was a girl we had a harsh tyrant and I wished for his death; when he was killed, there succeeded him one who was a little harsher. I was very eager to see the end of his dominion also, and we began to have a third ruler still more harsh—that was you. So if you should be taken away, a worse would succeed in your place.[39]

[45] If the excess of tyranny is unbearable, some have been of the opinion that it would be an act of virtue for strong men to slay the tyrant and to expose themselves to the danger of death in order to set the multitude free.[40] An example of this occurs even in the Old Testament, for a certain Aioth slew Eglon, King of Moab, who was oppressing the people of God under harsh slavery, thrusting a dagger into his thigh; and he was made a judge of the people.[41]

[46] But this opinion is not in accord with apostolic teaching. For Peter admonishes us to be reverently subject to our masters, not only to the good and gentle but also the forward: "For if one who suffers unjustly bear his trouble for conscience' sake, this is grace."[42] Wherefore, when many emperors of the Romans tyrannically persecuted the faith of Christ, a great number both of the nobility and the common people were converted to the faith and were praised for patiently bearing death for Christ. They did not resist although they were armed, and this is plainly manifested in the case of the holy Theban legion.[43] Aioth, then, must be considered rather as having slain a foe than assassinated a ruler, however tyrannical, of the people. Hence in the Old Testament we also read that they who killed Joas, the king of Juda, who had fallen away from the worship of God, were slain and their children spared according to the precept of the law.[44]

[47] Should private persons attempt on their own private presumption to kill the rulers, even though tyrants, this would be dangerous for the multitude as well as for their rulers. This is because the wicked usually expose themselves to dangers of this kind more than the good, for the rule of a king, no less than that of a tyrant, is burdensome to them since, according to the words of Solomon:[45] "A wise king scattereth the wicked." Consequently, by presumption of this kind, danger to the people from the loss of a good king would be more probable than relief through the removal of a tyrant.

[48] Furthermore, it seems that to proceed against the cruelty of tyrants is an action to be undertaken, not through the private presumption of a few, but rather by public authority.

[49] If to provide itself with a king belongs to the right of a given multitude, it is not unjust that the king be deposed or have his power restricted by that same multitude if, becoming a tyrant, he abuses the royal power. It must not be thought that such a multitude is acting unfaithfully in deposing the tyrant, even though it had previously subjected itself to him in perpetuity, because he himself has deserved that the covenant with his subjects should not be kept, since, in ruling the multitude, he did not act faithfully as the office of a king demands. Thus did the Romans,[46] who had accepted Tarquin the Proud as their king, cast him out from the kingship on account of his tyranny and the tyranny of his sons; and they set up in their place a lesser power, namely, the consular power. Similarly[47] Domitian, who had succeeded those most moderate emperors, Vespasian, his father, and Titus, his brother, was slain by the Roman senate when he exercised tyranny, and all his wicked deeds were justly and profitably declared null and void by a decree of the senate. Thus it came about that Blessed John the Evangelist, the beloved disciple of God, who had been exiled to the island of Patmos by that very Domitian, was sent back to Ephesus by a decree of the senate.

[50] If, on the other hand, it pertains to the right of a higher authority to provide a king for a certain multitude, a remedy

against the wickedness of a tyrant is to be looked for from him. Thus when Archelaus, who had already begun to reign in Judaea in the place of Herod his father, was imitating his father's wickedness, a complaint against him having been laid before Caesar Augustus by the Jews, his power was at first diminished by depriving him of his title of king and by dividing one-half of his kingdom between his two brothers. Later, since he was not restrained from tyranny even by this means, Tiberius Caesar sent him into exile to Lugdunum, a city in Gaul.[48]

[51] Should no human aid whatsoever against a tyrant be forthcoming, recourse must be had to God, the King of all, Who is a helper in due time in tribulation.[49] For it lies in his power to turn the cruel heart of the tyrant to mildness.[50] According to Solomon:[51] "The heart of the king is in the hand of the Lord, withersoever He will He shall turn it." He it was who turned into mildness the cruelty of King Assuerus, who was preparing death for the Jews.[52] He it was who so filled the cruel king Nabuchodonosor with piety that he became a proclaimer of the divine power. "Therefore," he said,[53] "I, Nabuchodonosor do now praise and magnify and glorify the King of Heaven; because all His works are true and His ways judgments, and they that walk in pride He is able to abase." Those tyrants, however, whom he deems unworthy of coversion, he is able to put out of the way or to degrade, according to the words of the Wise Man:[54] "God hath overturned the thrones of proud princes and hath set up the meek in their stead." He it was who, seeing the affliction of his people in Egypt and hearing their cry, hurled Pharaoh, a tyrant over God's people, with all his army into the sea.[55] He it was who not only banished from his kingly throne the above-mentioned Nabuchodonosor because of his former pride, but also cast him from the fellowship of men and changed him into the likeness of a beast.[56] Indeed, his hand is not shortened that He cannot free His people from tyrants.[57] For by Isaias[58] He promised to give his people rest from their labours and lashings and harsh slavery in which they had formerly served; and by Ezechiel[59] He says: "I will deliver my flock from their mouth," i.e. from the mouth of shepherds who feed themselves.

[52] But to deserve to secure this benefit from God, the people must desist from sin, for it is by divine permission that wicked men receive power to rule as a punishment for sin,[60] as the Lord says by the Prophet Osee:[61] "I will give thee a king in my wrath" and it is said in Job[62] that he "maketh a man that is a hypocrite to reign for the sins of the people." Sin must therefore be done away with in order that the scourge of tyrants may cease.

Book Two

Chapter III

That the Office of Governing the Kingdom Should Be Learned from the Divine Government

[102] Just as the founding of a city or kingdom may suitably be learned from the way in which the world was created, so too the way to govern may be learned from the divine government of the world.

[103] Before going into that, however, we should consider that to govern is to lead the thing governed in a suitable way towards its proper end. Thus a ship is said to be governed when, through the skill of the pilot, it is brought unharmed and by a direct route to harbour. Consequently, if a thing be directed to an end outside itself[63] (as a ship to the harbour), it is the governor's duty, not only to preserve the thing unharmed, but further to guide it towards this end. If, on the contrary, there be a thing whose end is not outside itself, then the governor's endeavours will merely tend to preserve the thing undamaged in its proper perfection.

[104] Nothing of this kind is to be found in reality, except God Himself, Who is the

end of all. However, as concerns the thing which is directed to an end outside itself, care is exercised by different providers in different ways. One might have the task of preserving a thing in its being, another of bringing it to a further perfection. Such is clearly the case in the example of the ship; (the first meaning of the word *gubernator* [governor] is *pilot*). It is the carpenter's business to repair anything which might be broken, while the pilot bears the responsibility of bringing the ship to port. It is the same with man. The doctor sees to it that a man's life is preserved; the tradesman supplies the necessities of life; the teacher takes care that man may learn the truth; and the tutor sees that he lives according to reason.

[105] Now if man were not ordained to another end outside himself, the above-mentioned cares would be sufficient for him. But as long as man's mortal life endures there is an extrinsic good for him, namely, final beatitude which is looked for after death in the enjoyment of God, for as the Apostle[64] says: "As long as we are in the body we are far from the Lord." Consequently the Christian man, for whom that beatitude has been purchased by the blood of Christ, and who, in order to attain it, has received the earnest of the Holy Ghost, needs another and spiritual care to direct him to the harbour of eternal salvation, and this care is provided for the faithful by the ministers of the church of Christ.

[106] Now the same judgment is to be formed about the end of society as a whole as about the end of one man.[65] If, therefore, the ultimate end of man were some good that existed in himself, then the ultimate end of the multitude to be governed would likewise be for the multitude to acquire such good, and persevere in its possession. If such an ultimate end either of an individual man or a multitude were a corporeal one, namely, life and health of body, to govern would then be a physician's charge. If that ultimate end were an abundance of wealth, then knowledge of economics would have the last word in the community's government. If the good of the knowledge of truth were of such a kind

that the multitude might attain to it, the king would have to be a teacher. It is, however, clear that the end of a multitude gathered together is to live virtuously. For men form a group for the purpose of *living well*[66] together, a thing which the individual man living alone could not attain, and *good life* is virtuous life. Therefore, virtuous life is the end for which men gather together. The evidence for this lies in the fact that only those who render mutual assistance to one another in living well form a genuine part of an assembled multitude. If men assembled merely to live, then animals and slaves would form a part of the civil community.[67] Or, if men assembled only to accrue wealth, then all those who traded together would belong to one city. Yet we see that only such are regarded as forming one multitude as are directed by the same laws and the same government to live well.

[107] Yet through virtuous living man is further ordained to a higher end, which consists in the enjoyment of God, as we have said above. Consequently, since society must have the same end as the individual man, it is not the ultimate end of an assembled multitude to live virtuously, but through virtuous living to attain to the possession of God.[68]

[108] If this end could be attained by the power of human nature, then the duty of a king would have to include the direction of men to it. We are supposing, of course, that he is called king to whom the supreme power of governing in human affairs is entrusted. Now the higher the end to which a government is ordained, the loftier that government is. Indeed, we always find that the one to whom it pertains to achieve the final end commands those who execute the things that are ordained to that end.[69] For example, the captain, whose business it is to regulate navigation, tells the shipbuilder what kind of ship he must construct to be suitable for navigation; and the ruler of a city, who makes use of arms, tells the blacksmith what kind of arms to make. But because a man does not attain his end, which is the possession of God, by human power but by divine—according to the words of

the Apostle:[70] "By the grace of God life everlasting"—, therefore the task of leading him to that last end does not pertain to human but to divine government.

[109] Consequently, government of this kind pertains to that king who is not only a man, but also God, namely, our Lord Jesus Christ, Who by making men sons of God brought them to the glory of Heaven. This then is the government which has been delivered to Him and which "shall not be destroyed,"[71] on account of which He is called, in Holy Writ, not Priest only, but King. As Jeremias[72] says: "The king shall reign and he shall be wise." Hence a royal priesthood is derived from Him, and what is more, all those who believe in Christ, in so far as they are His members, are called kings and priests.[73]

[110] Thus, in order that spiritual things might be distinguished from earthly things, the ministry of this kingdom has been entrusted not to earthly kings but to priests, and most of all to the chief priest, the successor of St. Peter, the Vicar of Christ, the Roman Pontiff. To him all the kings of the Christian People[74] are to be subject as to our Lord Jesus Christ Himself. For those to whom pertains the care of intermediate ends should be subject to him to whom pertains the care of the ultimate end, and be directed by his rule.[75]

[111] Because the priesthood of the gentiles and the whole worship of their gods existed merely for the acquisition of temporal goods (which were all ordained to the common goods of the multitude, whose care devolved upon the king), the priests of the gentiles were very properly subject to the kings. Similarly, since in the old law earthly goods were promised to the religious people[76] (not indeed by demons[77] but by the true God), the priests of the old law, we read,[78] were also subject to the kings. But in the new law there is a higher priesthood by which men are guided to heavenly goods. Consequently, in the law of Christ, kings must be subject to priests.

[112] It was therefore also a marvellous disposition of Divine Providence that, in the city of Rome, which God had foreseen would be the principal seat of the Christian priesthood, the custom was gradually established that the rulers of the city should be subject to the priests, for as Valerius Maximus[79] relates: "Our city has always considered that everything should yield precedence to religion, even those things in which it aimed to display the splendour of supreme majesty. We therefore unhesitatingly made the imperial dignity minister to religion, considering that the empire would thus hold control of human affairs if faithfully and constantly it were submissive to the divine power."

[113] And because it was to come to pass that the religion of the Christian priesthood should especially thrive in France, God provided that among the Gauls too their tribal priests, called Druids, should lay down the law of all Gaul, as Julius Caesar[80] relates in the book which he wrote about the Gallic war.

NOTES

1. Aristotle, *Pol.* I, 2: 1253a 8.
2. Aristotle, *Hist. Anim.* I, 1: 488a 7; *Eth. Nic.* I, 5; 1097b 11; ibid. IX, 9: 1169b 18; *Pol.* I, 2: 1253a 3. The Aristotelian formula is always that man is a *political* animal. Unless special reasons suggested to Aquinas the exact textual reproduction of this Aristotelian principle, he generally prefers to say that man is a *social* animal (Seneca, *De Beneficiis* VII, 1, 7). The combination *social and political animal* is also found in *Summa* I–II, 72, 4; *In Periherm.* I, 2.
3. The source of the teaching in §§5–7 is not the Aristotelian Politics but Avicenna, *De Anima* V, 1. See also *In Eth. prol.* 4 where St. Thomas, following more closely the Aristotelian doctrine of *Pol.* I, 2: 1252b 30–1253a 18 no longer believes the Avicennian reasoning to be capable of demonstrating the conclusion that man is a *political* animal. Avicenna's argument is used by Aquinas in 4 *Sent.*, 26, I, 1; *Quodl.* VII, 17; *CG* III, 85 and ibid. 128, 129, 136, 147; *Summa* I–II, 95, 1.
4. Aristotle, *De Partibus Animalium* IV, 10: 687a 19.
5. Aristotle, *Hist. Anim.* I, 1: 488a 9.

6. Ecclesiastes iv, 9.
7. Proverbs xi, 14.
8. Cf. *Summa* I, 96, 4.
9. Aristotle, *Pol.* I, 5: 1254a 28.
10. Cf. *CG* III, 23; ibid., 78.
11. *Summa* I, 81, 3 *ad* 2; I–II, 9, 2 *ad* 3.
12. Aristotle, *Metaph. Delta* 1: 1013a 5.
13. Aristotle, *Pol.* III, 6; 1279a 17; *Eth. Nic.* VIII, 10: 1160a 31.
14. Aristotle, *Metaph. Alpha* 2: 982b 25.
15. xxxiv, 2.
16. The classification of constitutions in §§ 11–12 is owed to Aristotle, *Pol.* III, 7: 1279a 27 ff. The basis of number, however, on which this classification rests, is found inadequate by Aristotle himself ibid. 1279b 38. In later texts, St. Thomas gradually abandoned it; see *In Eth.* VIII, 10; *Summa* I–II, 95, 4. St. Thomas ends up, just as Aristotle did, with a list of constitutions in which each finds its essential characteristic in a certain qualification on account of which political power is awarded: in monarchy and aristocracy, power is given on account of virtue, in oligarchy on account of riches, in democracy on account of liberty.
17. St. Isidore of Seville, *Etymologiae* IX, 19: *PL* 82, 344. St. Augustine, *De Civ. Dei* V, 19.
18. The meaning of this proposition, which is doubtlessly intended to be a reproduction of *Pol.* III, 7: 1279b 1, is not clear. Aristotle says loco cit.: "There is a good reason for the usage [which gives to this form of government the generic name *Polity*.] It is possible for one man, or a few, to be of outstanding excellence, but when it comes to a large number, we can hardly expect a fine edge of all the varieties of excellence. What we can expect is the military kind of excellence, which is the kind that shows itself in a mass" (Transl. Barker.) See *In Pol.* III, 6.
19. Cf. Cicero, *Pro P. Sestio* 45, 36; Id., *De Officiis* II, 23, 80.
20. xxvii, 24.
21. Aristotle *Pol.* I, 2: 1252b 9–30; *In Pol.* I, 1. The Aristotelian doctrine is here adapted to mediaeval realities in almost the same fashion as in some other earlier writings of Aquinas: *In Matth.* XII, 2 (p. 170a); *In Ioan.* XIV, 1, 3 (p. 377a); *In I Cor.* XI, 4 (p. 333a); *In Hebr.* XI, 3 (p. 414a). In the later writings, Aquinas (a) more clearly emphasizes the fact that the Aristotelian city seeks the satisfaction of not only the material but also the moral needs of man: *In Eth. prol.*; *Summa* I–II, 90, 2. Moreover (b) he treats cities and kingdoms not as specifically different communities each having its own essential characteristics, but as formally equal and only materially, i.e., historically different realizations of the same idea of "perfect community". Proof of this is the use of the combination *city or kingdom* in *Summa* II–II, 47, 11.
22. In Latin *vicus*. This is neither here nor *In Pol.* I, 1 the Aristotelian clan-village but the street of the mediaeval town, called *vicus* (*v.g. Vicus Straminis*). In each street, St. Thomas says *In Pol.*, "one craft is exercised, in one the weaver's, in another the smith's." Modern towns still preserve the memory of this mediaeval arrangement in street names such as Shoemaker Row, Cordwainer Street, Comerslane, Butter Row etc.
23. The word is of Roman imperial origin; cf. St. Isidore, *Etymologiae* XIV, 3, 19. It is also used in mediaeval Canon Law; see Gratian's *Decretum* c. 2 C. VI, p. 3: an ecclesiastical province is a territory where there are ten or eleven cities, one king . . . , one metropolitan . . . In St. Albert's cosmography (*De Nat. Locorum* III, 1 ff: IX, 566 ff) Italy "is a province" but it also "contains several provinces", viz., Calabria, Apulia, Romana, Emilia, Tuscia, Lombardia. Likewise, Spain is a province and "has several provinces and kingdoms." See St. Thomas' use of the word in 2 *Sent.*, 10, I, 3 *ad* 3; 4 *Sent.*, 24, III, 2 *sol.* 3; *Summa* II–II, 40, 1.—Nothing is very definite about this notion except that, at any rate, a province is part of a greater and more comprehensive whole. The word is therefore characteristic of a properly mediaeval type of political thinking which still retains the memory of the Roman Empire. It was soon to be cast out of the political vocabulary; see John of Paris *De Pot. Regia et Papali* I, 1; ed. Leclercq 176/7.
24. Antonomasia is the figure of speech by which a generic predicate is used to designate an individual because it belongs to this individual in an eminent degree; for instance: Rome is *the* city (*Summa* II–II, 125, 2); divine truth is *the* truth (*CG* I, 1.)
25. Aristotle, *Eth. Nic.* VIII, 12: 1160b 24; *In Eth.* VIII, 10: 1682.
26. Eccles. v, 8.
27. *CG* I, 42, IV, 76; *Summa* I, 103, 3. This idea is characteristic of Hellenistic political philosophy, according to which the main function of the King-Saviour is considered to be the establishment of order and peace. St. Augustine, *De Civitate Dei* XIX, 12 ff; Dionysius (Ps.-Areopagite), *De Divinis Nominibus* XI: *PG* 3, 935 ff.
28. Aristotle, *Eth. Nic.* III, 5: 1112b 14 (Latin text). *In Eth.* III, 8: 474; *CG* III, 146; *In Matth.* XII, 2: p. 170a. In thus tracing back to Aristotle the idea that peace is the chief social good, St. Thomas was misled by the fact that the Latin text of the Ethics translated the Greek EUNOMIA (good laws well obeyed) by *peace*.
29. Ephes. iv, 3.
30. *CG* IV, 76; *Summa* I, 103, 3.

31. *In Eth.* VIII, 10.
32. See above 9; *CG* I, 42.
33. In popular ancient and mediaeval opinion the chief bee was considered to be a male. Aristotle, *Hist. Anim.* V, 21: 553a 25.
34. Aristotle, *Phys.* II, 2: 194a 21.
35. Jerem. xii, 10.
36. Ezech. xxxiv, 24; Jerem. xxx, 21.
37. I Kings xiii, 14.
38. The considerations of the present chapter should also be read against the background of the history of the Italian Communes in the XIIIth century; see *Cambridge Med. Hist.* VI, 179 ff.
39. Valerius Maximus VI, 2, Ext. 2 (Vincent of Beauvais, *Speculum Historiale* III, 73).
40. Cf. John of Salisbury, *Policraticus* VIII, 18 (788c)–20 (797a).
41. Judges iii, 14 ff. See John of Salisbury, *Policraticus* VIII, 20 (794b).
42. I Petr. ii, 18, 19.
43. *Acta Sanctorum Septembris*, t. VI, 308 ff.
44. IV Kings xiv, 5–6.
45. Prov. xx, 26.
46. Eusebius, *Chronicorum Lib.* II: *PG* 19, 467a, 471b; St. Augustine, *De Civitate Dei* V, 12.
47. Eusebius, *Chronicorum Lib.* II: *PG* 19, 551h; St. Jerome, *De viris illustribus* I, 9: *PL* 23, 655. See also St. Augustine, *De Civitate Dei* V, 21.
48. Flavius Iosephus, *De Bello Iud.* II, 80 ff, 93, 111. Archelaus, however, was not exiled to Lugdunum (Lyons) by Tiberius, but to "Vienna (Vienne), a town in Gaul" by Augustus. St. Thomas was probably misled by the *Glossa Ordinaria, In Matth.* ii, 22: *PL* 114, 78.
49. Psalm ix, 10.
50. Cf. Esther xv, 11.
51. Prov. xxi, 1.
52. See the Book of Esther.
53. Dan. iv, 34.
54. Eccli. x, 17.
55. Exod. xiv, 23–28.
56. Dan. iv, 30.
57. Isaias lix, 1.
58. xiv, 3.
59. xxxiv, 10.
60. St. Gregory, *Moralium L.* 25, 16: *PL* 76, 344; St. Isidore, *Sententiae* 3, 48, 11: *PL* 83, 720.—*2 Sent.*, 33, I, 2 *ad* 5; *Summa* II–II, 108, 4 *ad* 1.
61. xiii, 11.
62. xxxiv, 30.
63. Aristotle, *Metaph. Lambda* 10: 1075a 11 sqq. *In Met.* XII, 12: 2627.
64. II Cor. v, 6.
65. Aristotle, *Pol.* VII, 2: 1324a 4.
66. Aristotle, *Pol.* I, 2: 1252b 30. The source of what follows is again Aristotle, *Pol.* III, 9: 1280a 25–1281a 10. Especially derived from the Stagirite are (a) the definition of "good life" which is "virtuous life" (1280b 5–10), (b) the remark about slaves and animals (1280a 32), (c) the remark that the exchange of material goods does not make a society, i.e., a state (1280a 25, b 23: Aristotle's criticism of Plato.)
67. See *Summa* I–II, 98, 6 *ad* 2.
68. Cf. *Summa* I–II, 6 *prol.*
69. Aristotle, *Eth. Nic.* I, 1: 1094a 10. *In Eth.* I, 1: 16; *CG* III, 64.
70. Rom. vi, 23.
71. Dan. vii, 14.
72. xxiii, 5.
73. *Apoc.* i, 6; v, 10; xx, 6.
74. *Populus Christianus*, i.e., the institutional unity of all Christians, whose head is the Pope "holding the apex of both powers, spiritual and temporal". All-important in Aquinas' political thought, this notion was for the first time criticized by the Dominican John of Paris, A.D. 1302.
75. See above note 69.
76. "As is clear from Levit. xxvi and Deut. xxviii", *In Ep. Ad Rom.* IX, 1; *Summa* I–II, 114, 10 *in* 1.
77. This was taught by the Manicheans and the Waldenses.
78. See the quotations from Holy Scripture in Gregory IX, *Decretales* I, 33, 6 (c. *Solitae Benignitatis*), Friedberg 197.
79. I, 1, 9.
80. *De Bello Gallico* VI, 13, 5.

CHAPTER 28

John of Paris

John of Paris, also known as Jean Quidort, was born at Paris but precisely when is uncertain. We do know that he received his master's degree in theology in 1304, which would most likely place his birth sometime in the 1250s. He was a member of the Dominican order and made important contributions in theology and philosophy, especially political philosophy. A great deal of his life was surrounded by controversy. As a young bachelor of theology he was accused of expounding erroneous doctrines in his lectures on Peter Lombard. This necessitated his defending thirteen propositions taken from his teachings, which he did via his *Apology*. It seems that this temporarily calmed the waters. Later, when Thomas Aquinas was attacked by William de la Mare concerning the *Prima Secundae* of his *Summa Theologiae*, John came to the former's defense, responding with his *Correctorium Corruptorii Thomae* (c. 1282–84).

John wrote his best-known work, *On Royal and Papal Power*, in 1302 or early 1303—a time when King Philip the Fair was in the midst of a dispute with Pope Boniface VIII over the proper extent of secular power. In this work John makes a radical departure from established medieval political theory by arguing for severe limits on papal power in the secular realm. The work, however, is not a wholesale endorsement of the views of Philip, and one cannot help but notice its lack of polemical spirit. Without a historical background, one would never be aware of the raging political controversy between the pope and the French king during this time.

In 1305 John once again became the center of controversy when he proposed an alternative to the theory of transubstantiation to explain the real presence of Christ in the Eucharist. His views were denounced as heretical. Notwithstanding his stated willingness to recant, he was suspended from teaching and preaching. In addition, he was perpetually silenced by an episcopal board. He appealed his case to the papal Curia but to no avail. He was then summoned to Bordeaux to explain his doctrinal position, but he died there on September 22, 1306, while awaiting an answer. All indications are that John was the leading Dominican theologian in Paris at the end of the thirteenth century.

John of Paris on Royal and Papal Power

In 1302 Pope Boniface VIII issued the bull *Unam Sanctam*. Although it affirmed no new doctrine, it expressed in no uncertain terms the extreme and intransigent papalist viewpoint. There is "neither salvation nor remission of sins" outside the "holy catholic and apostolic church"; this "one and only Church" has one body and one head, "not two heads as if it were a monster"; there are but two swords, one spiritual and one temporal, and "both swords are in the power of the church, the one by the hand of the priest, the other by the hand of kings and knights, but at the will and sufferance of the priest". Then, Boniface claims, "One sword, moreover, ought to be under the other, and the temporal authority to be subjected to the spiritual". Each power is to be judged by its superior authority; that is, kings are to be judged by priests if they err. If the highest priest errs, he can only be judged by God alone, not by man. "A spiritual man judges all things, but he himself is judged by no one", because his authority is divine. The bull concludes with the statement "We therefore declare, say, define, and pronounce that it is altogether a necessity of salvation for every human creature to be subject to the Roman Pontiff".

John wrote his best-known work, *On Royal and Papal Power*, in 1302 or early 1303 as a response to the *Unam Sanctam*. Although John of Paris was greatly influenced by Aquinas, this essay is the first of its kind by a theologian to systematically delineate the separation of powers between church and state. So influential was this work that it was used as a reference until as late as the seventeenth century, notwithstanding vociferous criticism by the papalists.

The central thesis of the essay is the natural separation between the soul and the body, which have different needs and dominion. Consistent with Aristotle, John of Paris understands man to be, by nature, a political or civil animal. This is distinct from his also possessing a soul. Thus, he has spiritual needs which make an individual aware that life everlasting is a goal to be achieved beyond those of a temporal nature. Because of these two distinct natures, the temporal and spiritual realms are properly guided by two different leaders, neither of which is to meddle in the affairs of the other. A king is the proper ruler of civil society: ". . . kingship is the rule over a perfect multitude by one man for the sake of the common good". The common good of the multitude cannot be attained by an oligarchy, a tyranny, or a democracy.

It is clear to John of Paris that the church was to be ruled by one person, namely, Jesus Christ. But "since Christ was to deprive His church of His corporeal presence, it was necessary that he institute some ministers". Although there are many priests and a bishop is the leader of a diocese, there is but one ruler of the church at large, the pope. A single spiritual leader is made possible for the whole of Christendom because there is no diversity of spiritual need among people. "The laymen among the faithful, however, are not subject by divine right to one supreme monarch in temporal matters; rather, by a natural instinct, which comes from God, they are inclined to live politically and in a society, and so, in order to live well together, they choose rulers, and choose different ones according to the difference of communities."

From the standpoint of dignity, priestly power is higher than kingly power. This fact, however, constitutes no basis for the spiritual power structure to encroach upon the proper domain of the temporal power. In essence, there is properly a clear separation of the powers of church and state.

ON ROYAL AND PAPAL POWER

Prologue

It happens sometimes that a person wishing to avoid a certain error falls into its opposite. Thus, as we read in Gratian's *Decretum 16, 1*, some maintain that because monks are "dead" to the world, they cannot give penances and spread Christianity, since this is inconsistent with their state as monks. Others,[1] wishing to avoid error or to oppose it strongly, have said that by reason of their having chosen a state of perfection monks ought to hear confessions, give absolution, and impose salutary penances. Sound doctrine is midway between these two errors, and holds that this power is neither improper to monks, nor does it belong to them by virtue of their state. Rather, it can pertain to them if it is committed to them by their ordinaries, to whom this power does belong by right. Similarly, the book *On the Two Natures and One Person of Christ* shows that faith holds the middle position between the two errors of Nestorius and Eutyches.[2]

So, too, the truth about the power of ecclesiastical pontiffs holds a middle position between two errors. For the error of the Waldensians[3] was to deny dominion over temporal things to the successors of the apostles, that is, to the pope and ecclesiastical prelates, and to forbid them to possess temporal wealth. Accordingly, they maintain that the Church of God, the successors of the apostles, and the true prelates of the Church continued only up to the reign of Sylvester. They hold that the Roman Church began afterwards, as a result of the donation made to the Church by the Emperor Constantine. And according to them this is not the Church of God. They claim that the Church of God has already failed except insofar as it is continued in them, or has reappeared through them. To substan-

tiate their view they point to such texts as the following: Matthew 6: "Do not store up for yourselves any treasure on earth";[4] Epistle to Timothy 6: "Having food and clothing, we are content," and "Those who wish to become rich, etc.";[5] Matthew 6: "You cannot serve God and mammon";[6] Matthew 6: "Be not solicitous for your soul what you shall eat, nor for your body, etc.";[7] Matthew 6: "Notice the birds of the air: they do not sow, neither do they reap";[8] Matthew 10, where Christ said to His disciples: "Do not possess gold or silver or money";[9] Luke 14: "Unless a man renounce all his possessions, etc.";[10] and Acts 3: "Gold and silver I have none, etc."[11] They employ these texts in asserting that the prelates of God's Church, the successors of the apostles, ought not to have dominion over temporal wealth.

The other error was that of Herod who, hearing that Christ was born king, believed He was an earthly king.[12] The opinion of certain modern thinkers[13] seems to be derived from this. They react against the abovementioned error by going to the completely opposite extreme, and claim that the lord pope, inasmuch as he stands in the place of Christ[14] on earth, has dominion, cognizance, and jurisdiction over the temporal goods of princes and barons. They also assert that the pope has this power over temporal things more excellently than a prince, because the pope has it by primary authority and immediately from God, while the prince has it mediately from God through the pope. They maintain further that, unlike the prince, the pope does not have immediate execution of this power, except in certain cases noted in *Extra, Qui filii sunt legitimi, per venerabilem.*[15] These men, then, who otherwise have spoken against princes, speak in their favor on this point. Further, if the pope sometimes asserts that he does not have temporal jurisdiction, they maintain that this is to be understood with respect to regular and immediate execution, or because the pope wishes to preserve peace between princes

From John of Paris, *On Royal and Papal Power*, translated by Arthur P. Monahan (New York and London: Columbia University Press, 1974), pp. 1–29. Reprinted by permission of Columbia University Press.

and the Church, or so that prelates not be excessively prone to intrude themselves into matters concerning temporal goods and secular affairs. They say too that the pope has a different relationship to temporal goods than do princes and prelates, because he alone is the only true lord, such that if he wishes he can absolve a usurer from any obligation due to usury, and can take for his own use what otherwise belongs to someone else. And the action of a pope holds, even though he sins and should not act in this way except for a reasonable cause such as the defense of the Church or some such thing. Other prelates and princes, however, are not lords but custodians, procurers, and dispensers.

This opinion concerning dominion over things does not arise solely from the error of Herod, but seems also to infer the error of Vigilantius.[16] For everyone holds, and indeed it must be held, that nothing pertaining to evangelical perfection is repugnant to the lord pope by reason of this state. It is evident, moreover, that if the pope is lord of all things by virtue of his state inasmuch as he is pope and vicar of Christ, renunciation of ownership and rejection of dominion over temporal things is repugnant to him by reason of his state, since the very opposite belongs to him naturally; and therefore, poverty and lack of dominion over external things are not of evangelical perfection. This latter position, however, was what Vigilantius asserted, about whom Augustine stated in the work *On Christian Combat* that there are those who, though Catholics, strive for their own possessions, or who seek for glory from Christ's name itself as heretics, one of whom was Vigilantius, who arose a long time ago in Gaul, which formerly lacked the monstrosities of errors.[17] He presumed to equate the state of poverty with that of wealth, just as long ago in Italy Jovinian[18] seems to have preferred marriage to chastity. And this opinion has something in it of the pride of the Pharisees, who maintained that the people were not bound to pay tax to Caesar on tenths and on the sacrifices they offered to God, asserting such

a position so that they might receive larger shares from these richer holdings, as Jerome says.[19] This opinion also seems dangerous because it would imply for persons converting to the faith that they transfer dominion over things they previously possessed to the supreme pontiff. In such a situation the faith of these persons is less freely given, and their faith is disparaged when the rights of possession are distributed by it, as the Gloss on I Peter: 2 asserts.[20] One ought also to be apprehensive about this view for fear that Christ, stern and angry, would enter while business dealings were being conducted in the Lord's house, and would cleanse His temple even by the use of a whip, transforming it from a den of thieves into a house of prayer, as Chrysostom says [in his commentary] on Matthew.[21]

This is why I consider the truth to be midway between these two such contrary opinions. Everyone recognizes the first of them to be an error, insofar as it is not repugnant for prelates of the Church to have dominion and jurisdiction over temporal things,[22] a point contrary to the first erroneous opinion. Neither, however, does dominion over temporal things belong to prelates by reason of their state and by reason of their being vicars of Christ and successors of the apostles. But it can pertain to them to have such powers as a concession from or with the permission of princes, if something of this kind was conferred by princes out of devotion, or if church prelates possessed it from some other source.

I now declare that I intend to say nothing in any of my statements contrary to faith, good morals, or sound doctrine, or against reverence for the person or state of the supreme pontiff. And if anything of this sort does occur either principally or incidentally in what I have said or will say, I wish it to be held as not having been said. And I wish this disclaimer to hold and be valid as if I were to repeat it individually with respect to each statement that will be made.[23]

The procedure for handling the subject set down for examination will be as follows: chapter 1 will define kingly power, and show from what it has arisen; chapter 2 will do the same things for priesthood; chapter 3 will deal with the order of ministers as they relate to one supreme minister, and will show that it is not as necessary for all princes to be subordinated to one as for ministers of the Church to be subordinated to one supreme authority; chapter 4 will show whether kingship or priesthood is prior in time; chapter 5 will show which of them is prior to the other in dignity; chapter 6 will show that the priesthood is not prior in causality, and it will show first the pope's relationship to external ecclesiastical goods with respect to dominion; chapter 7 will show the pope's relationship to the goods of laymen; chapter 8 will show that the pope does not have jurisdiction over laymen's goods from Christ, because Christ Himself did not have it; chapter 9 will pose arguments to the contrary, namely, that Christ has this power, and will offer replies to these arguments; chapter 10 will grant that Christ has this power, but show that He did not give it to Peter; chapter 11 will present contrary arguments of those who say that the pope has jurisdiction over temporal external goods; chapter 12 will present preliminary remarks for a resolution of these arguments, and material to show what authority over temporal goods the pope has from Christ, and in the first instance will describe the authority given by Christ to Peter and the apostles; chapter 13 will show that, according to this authority, ecclesiastical prelates do not have dominion or jurisdiction over temporal things, and that princes are not, because of this authority, subject to ecclesiastical prelates in temporal matters; chapter 14 will offer replies to the first six of the arguments given [in chapter 11]; chapter 15 will offer replies to the second six [arguments 7–12]; chapter 16 will offer replies to the third six [arguments 13–18]; chapter 17 to the fourth six [arguments 19–24]; chapter 18 to the fifth six [arguments 25–30]; chapter 19 to the sixth six [arguments 31–36]; chapter 20 to the seventh six [arguments 37–42]; chapter 21 will examine first the Donation of Constantine, and will show what powers the pope has through it; chapter 22 will show whether it is licit to dispute with and judge the pope concerning temporal matters; chapter 23 will develop the frivolous arguments of those who say that the pope cannot resign; chapter 24 will show that he can resign; chapter 25 will resolve the previous arguments [of chapter 23].

Chapter 1

What Kingly Rule Is, and from What It Has Arisen

Concerning the first topic, it should be known that kingship[24] properly understood can be defined as rule over a community perfectly ordered to the common good by one person.[25] "Rule" in this definition is taken as the genus; "over a community" is added to "rule" to differentiate it from that by which someone governs himself, whether this latter be by natural instinct, as in the case of brutes, or by reason, as in the case of those who lead a solitary life. "Perfectly" is added to differentiate community from a family group, which is not perfect because it is only sufficient for itself for a short while and not for a whole lifetime; and according to the Philosopher in *Politics 1*, the state is sufficient.[26] "Ordered for the good of the community" is put in the definition to differentiate kingship from oligarchy, tyranny, and democracy.[27] In these, and particularly in a tyranny, the ruler intends only his own good. "By one" is meant to differentiate kingship from aristocracy, that is, preeminence of the best persons or aristocrats, where a few men rule according to virtue. Accordingly, some define aristocracy as rule according to the direction of prudent men or the decisions of a senate. "By one" also differentiates kingship from polity, where the people are ruled by popular ordinances.[28] For there is no king unless he alone is the ruler, as the Lord says through

Ezekiel: "My servant David will be over all, and there will be one shepherd over all of them"[29]

This kind of power derives from the natural law, and from the law of nations. For man is naturally a political or civil animal, as is said in the *Politics 1*,[30] and according to the Philosopher, this is shown by reference to food, clothing, and defense, in respect of which one person alone is not self-sufficient, and from speech, which is directed to another.[31] Therefore, it is necessary for man to live in a community, and in a kind of community self-sufficient for life. A household or village community is not sufficient for this, while that of the state of kingdom[32] is. For all the things needed for food, clothing, and defense and for a full life are not found in the household alone or in the village, while they are found in the state or kingdom. Moreover, every community is scattered when each individual person seeks his own interests, and it is dispersed into different paths unless directed to the common good by some one person whose task it is to be concerned with the common good, just as a man's body decays unless there is some common power in the body directing it to the common good of all its members.[33] Accordingly, Solomon wrote in Proverbs: "Where there is no ruler, the people will be dispersed."[34] This is the more necessary because what is proper to one man is not identical with what is common to all. Men differ according to what is proper; they are united in respect of what is common. Besides, different things have different causes. Therefore, in addition to what promotes the good proper to any individual, there must be something to promote the good common to many.

Moreover, rule over a community by a single person preeminent in virtue is more useful than rule either by many or by several persons who are virtuous. This follows on the one hand from the nature of power, for virtue is more unified and therefore greater when vested in one man than when dispersed among several.[35] It also follows

in respect of what should be the purpose in ruling a community—unity and peace, which exist only when people are united and in concord.[36] Wherefore, if there were any such person possessed of these qualities and possessed of them in a superior way, such a single person exercising leadership through virtue would be the better able to keep the peace, and the peace of the citizens would not be disturbed so easily. If follows further because a single leader intending the common good has an eye for what is more common than would be the case if several persons were also to exercise authority according to virtue. For the more persons who are withdrawn from the multitude the less common is what remains, and the fewer who are withdrawn the more common is what remains. This is why the Philosopher said that the tyrant is the worst among those rulers who seek their own good; for he seeks his own good more, and has greater scorn for the common good.[37] The point follows again, because in a natural government we see the whole authority reduced to a single thing, as one element dominates in a mixed body: in the heterogeneous human body there is one principal member in the whole man, and the soul keeps all the elements together.[38] Even gregarious animals, for which it is natural to live in society, are subject to one king.[39]

From the foregoing it follows that it is necessary and useful for man to live in a community, and above all in a community which can be sufficient for the whole of life, as a state or kingdom is, and particularly that he live under one man called a king, who rules for the sake of the common good. It follows also that his rule is derived from the natural law, from the fact, namely, that man is naturally a civil or political and social animal, inasmuch as before Belus and Ninus, the first men to exercise political authority, men lived unnaturally without rule, not living as men but in the manner of beasts. Orosius describes some men as having lived in this fashion in the first chapter of his book *Against the Pagans*.[40] Tullius also mentioned similar things in the beginning of the *Old Rhetoric*.[41] And in the *Politics* the Philosopher says of such men that they do not live as men but as gods or beasts.[42] Since men of this type could not by common words be called back from the life of beasts to a community life that has been seen to be naturally suited to them, men who were better able to use reason and who had compassion on those who had gone wrong tried by reasoned persuasion to call them back to a common life ordered under some one person, as Tullius says.[43] And when these people had been brought back, they were constrained to live in communities by specific laws. These are the laws which can be called here the law of nations.[44] So it follows that this king of rule is derived from the natural law and the law of nations.

Chapter 2

What the Priesthood Is, and from What It Has Arisen

In addition we must consider that man is not ordered solely to the kind of good which can be acquired through nature, that is, to live according to virtue;[45] he is ordered further to a supernatural end, which is eternal life.[46] In fact, the whole community of men living according to virtue is ordered to this end.[47] Consequently, it is necessary that there be some one person to direct the community to this end. And if indeed this end could be achieved through the power of human nature, it would be necessary that it pertain to the office of a human king to direct men to this end; for we call a "human king" that man to whom is committed ultimate responsibility for direction of human affairs. But because man is not brought to eternal life by human but by divine power—as the Apostle wrote to the Romans: "Eternal life is a gift of God"[48]—it does not belong to a human king but to a divine king[49] to lead men to that end.

Rule of this type, therefore, pertains to a king who is not only man but also God, namely, to Jesus Christ, Who brought men to eternal life making them the sons of God. This is why He is called king, as Jeremiah says: "A king shall reign, and he shall be wise."[50] Moreover, this position is entrusted to Him by God the Father, and it is not to be destroyed. And because it is a king's responsibility to remove obstacles to the attaining of an end, and to provide remedies and aids for reaching it, in offering Himself on the cross to God the Father as both priest and sacrifice, Christ removed by His death the universal obstacle, the obstacle, namely, of the offence against God the Father rooted in the common sin of the human race. This is why, in Hebrews 5, He is said to be a true priest standing in the place of men.[51]

It is true also insofar as a universal cause must be joined to particular effects, particular remedies had to be provided through which the general benefit might be transmitted to us in some way. These particular remedies are the sacraments of the Church, in which the spiritual power of Christ's passion is contained as the agent's power is contained in an instrument.[52] And therefore it was fitting that these sensible things be established, to provide for man according to his condition, which is to be led through sensible things to the possession of spiritual and intelligible realities, as we are told in Romans 1: "The invisible things of God through which they were done, etc.",[53] and that those instruments be proportionate to the Word Incarnate, whose power as principal agent they contain, just as they contain spiritual power under sensible signs.

Moreover, because the physical presence of Christ was withdrawn from His Church, it was necessary for Him to appoint ministers to dispense the sacraments to men. These men are called priests because they are givers of sacred things, or sacred leaders or teachers of sacred things, in all of which functions they mediate between God and men.[54]

Moreover, these ministers had to be men, not angels, possessing spiritual power conferred on them, as the Apostle says: "Every pontiff is taken from among men to serve men, etc.",[55] so that the ministers might be appropriate in respect to both the instrument, in which spiritual power is present under a sensible element, and the principal cause of man's salvation, the Word Incarnate, Who achieves our salvation through His own power and authority inasmuch as He is both God and man.

From what has been said, priesthood can be defined as the spiritual power given by Christ to ministers of the Church for dispensing the sacraments to the faithful.[56]

Chapter 3

Concerning the Order of Ministers to One Supreme Minister, and the Position That It Is Not as Necessary for All Princes to Be Subordinated to One Prince as for Ministers of the Church to Be Subordinated to One Supreme Minister

Further, as the Apostle said in the last verse of II Corinthians,[57] because this power was given to the Church for its establishment, it must endure in the Church as long as the Church has need of establishment—that is, until the end of the world. Hence, in the first instance power was given to Christ's disciples, so that through them it might be passed to others, among whom there must always be some higher and perfect ministers whose function it is to confer the priesthood on others through ordination and consecration. These higher minister are the superintending bishops. And although they do not surpass simple priests in respect of their power of consecrating the true body of Christ, they do surpass them in matters pertaining to jurisdiction over the faithful.[58] For bishops are great and perfect priests inasmuch as they can make other men priests, something simple and lesser priests cannot do. In fact, some matters of difficulty in the care of the faithful are reserved for the action of bishops, by whose authority also priests have the power to perform the tasks committed to them. And in matters where priests act on their own, they employ things consecrated by a bishop: for

example, a chalice, an altar, and altar clothes, as Dionysius said in *On Ecclesiastical Hierarchy*, in the chapter on priestly perfections.[59]

It is clear, however, that although people are separated into different dioceses and cities over which bishops preside in spiritual matters, there is still one Church for all the faithful, and one Christian people. Therefore, just as in every diocese there is one bishop, who is the head of the Church for the people in that diocese, so there is one person supreme in the whole Church and for the whole Christian people. He is the Roman pope, the successor of Peter. The Church Militant[60] is thus patterned in the likeness of the Church Triumphant,[61] in which one person rules over the entire universe. Wherefore Revelation 21 reads "And they shall be His people, and God Himself will be their God for them";[62] Hosea 1 reads "The sons of Judah and the sons of Israel shall be brought together equally, and they shall appoint one head for themselves."[63] Whence, too, in John 10 we read: "There shall be one flock and one shepherd,"[64] which cannot be understood to refer only to Christ, but also to the single minister who presides over all in His place. For after the physical withdrawal of Christ's corporeal presence questions concerning matters relating to the faith do sometimes arise. And the Church, which needs unity of faith for its own unity, might be divided by differing opinions about such matters unless its unity were preserved through the judgment of one man. The one person having authority in this respect is Peter or his successor. And he does not have this power through synodal ordination, but from the mouth of the Lord,[65] Who did not wish His Church to lack whatever was necessary to it. In the last chapter of John, He said specifically to Peter before His ascension: "Feed my sheep";[66] and in Luke 22, before His passion we read: "And do you, when once you have turned again, strengthen your brethren."[67]

This subordination to one supreme authority is found more frequently among ministers of the Church than among secular princes, because ecclesiastical ministers are particularly designated by God as a special kind of person responsible for divine worship. Consequently, the subordination of divine ministers to one minister is by divine ordinance.[68] But it is not the case that the faithful laity are by divine law subservient to one supreme monarch in temporal matters. Rather, they live civilly and in community according to the prompting of a natural inclination which is from God. Accordingly, they choose different types of rulers to oversee the well-being of their communities to correspond with the diversity of these communities. Moreover, the notion that all persons are subject in temporal matters to one supreme authority derives neither from natural inclination nor from divine law; nor is it as suitable in this area as in the case of ecclesiastical ministers.

This is so in the first instance because, just as there is a diversity among men in respect to their bodies but not their souls, all of which latter are constituted of essentially the same type because of the unity of the human species, so too secular power has more diversity in respect to differences of climate and conditions[69] than spiritual power, which varies less in respect of such things. Consequently, it is not necessary that there be as much variation in the latter as in the former.

Secondly, one man alone is not enough to rule the entire world in temporal matters, although one man is adequate to rule in spiritual matters. For spiritual power can easily exercise its censure, which is verbal, on all persons near and far; but the secular power cannot so easily apply its sword, which is manual,[70] to persons who are distant. It is easier to extend a word than a hand.

Thirdly, the temporal goods of laymen do not belong to the community, as will be shown below, but to whoever is master of his own property by virtue of having acquired it through his own efforts.[71] Therefore, temporal goods of the laity do not need a common dispenser; for the person

to whom property belongs is its dispenser as he pleases. Ecclesiastical goods, however, belong to the community. Hence, there must be some one person to preside over the community as common dispenser and common disposer of the goods belonging to all. And there is no more need for a single person to have disposition over the temporal goods of the clergy than there is need for such a person to handle the temporal goods of the laity.

Fourthly, all believers are united in the one Catholic faith, without which there is no salvation. Nevertheless, it happens sometimes that questions arise concerning what pertains to faith in different regions and kingdoms. Accordingly, in order to prevent the unity of the faith being disrupted by a variety of controversies one person, as already noted,[72] must be supreme in spiritual matters, through whose pronouncements controversies of this type will be ended. But this purpose does not require that the faithful be united in any common state. There can be different ways of living and different kinds of state conforming to differences in climate, language, and the conditions of men, with what is suitable for one nation not so for another. The Philosopher makes the same point about individuals in *Ethics 2*, where he says that something is too little for one person and too much for another;[73] just as, for example, the consumption of ten minas or ounces would be too much for a beginner in athletic exercises but too little for Milo of Croton, who used to fell a bull with one blow, as the Commentator says.[74]

Therefore, it is not as necessary for the world to be ruled by one man in respect of temporal matters, as it is necessary for it to be ruled by one man in respect of spiritual matters. In addition it is not so set down in either natural or divine law. Accordingly, the Philosopher shows in the *Politics* that development of individual states and kingdoms is natural,[75] although that of an empire or a monarchy is not. Augustine, too, states in the *City of God* 4, that the state is better and more peacefully ruled when the rule of any one man extends only to the limits of his own territory.[76] He also states that a cause for the expansion of the Roman Empire was its own ambition to dominate, or its provoking foreign states to act unjustly.[77] Accordingly, the natural law does not prescribe that there be one monarch in respect of temporal things as there is in respect of spiritual things. The statement in the *Decretum* 7. 1, "In apibus,"[78] to the effect that one and not several ought to rule, is not contrary to this position. That statement indicates that there is no advantage from several persons exercising authority in such a way that their respective powers are not delineated, and as an illustration it cites the case of Remus and Romulus, who ruled together without their powers being distinguished, the result of which was that one of them killed his brother. The same point is also made there through other examples.

Chapter 4

Whether Kingship or Priesthood Is Prior in Time

Now we must see whether kingship or priesthood was prior in time.[79] To determine this it is necessary to know the proper meaning of kingship. The term designates control not only over a household or district but also over a state, in which is found the greatest sufficiency of the things pertaining to a complete life. If we speak of priesthood properly understood, kingship existed before priesthood. For, as Augustine says in the *City of God* 16. 17, the first kingdom was that of the Assyrians, which began before the Law was given.[80] Belus was the first ruler in Assyria, and he ruled for sixty-five years. And after his death his son, Ninus,[81] extended his rule throughout the whole of Greater Assyria, except for India. Ninus ruled for sixty-six years, and had ruled for forty-three years when Abraham was born. This was about 1,200 years before the founding of Rome. The kingdom of the Sicyonians began in Africa concurrently with that of the Assyrians. In the beginning it was not very large; its first king was Egyaclus, and his son was Europs. At this time the king of Salem, whom the Hebrews called the son of Shem, himself the son of Noah, ruled over the followers of the true God; and he is said to have lived until the time of Isaac.[82]

During this period, moreover, even as they had for a long time previously, true kings existed; but there was as yet no true priesthood. And there was no such thing until Jesus Christ came as mediator between God and men.[83] This is true in that, even though there were persons among the Gentiles called priests, they were not true priests because they did not offer true sacrifices; neither did they offer sacrifices to the true God, but to something thought to be the true God, as Deuteronomy 32 says: "They sacrificed to demons and not to God."[84]

Even though some persons from the Levitical tribe were called priests under the Law of God's people, they still were not true priests but symbols of true priests; their sacrifices were only symbolic, and their sacraments were not true sacraments but only symbolic ones, insofar as they did not cleanse from sin and did not open heaven. Rather, they served as symbols in cleansing certain irregularities and opening a man-made temple, through which was prefigured the opening by Jesus Christ of the temple not made by man. Nor did they promise spiritual things except under the species of temporal things, as the Apostle says to the Hebrews: "The light of future benefits remained in shadow."[85]

Certainly before the Law there was Melchisedech,[86] who was a priest of the most high God, and his priesthood was more perfect and more excellent than the Levitical priesthood. But even this was only a symbolic and not a true priesthood, for he was more perfect because he represented the priesthood of Christ in respect of that in which the priesthood of Christ excelled the priesthood of Aaron. Aaron's priesthood was deficient as a symbol of Christ's priesthood in the matter of uninterrupted continuation, because it is not written in Scripture that Melchisedech had a beginning or an end, just as Christ had neither. There are also many other matters mentioned by the Apostle in the *Epistle to the Hebrews*[87] on which Melchisedech excelled Aaron. Nevertheless, his priesthood was still only symbolic and not a true priesthood, just as the Levitical priesthood was not a true one. Accepting, therefore, the meaning of a true priesthood, there was no priesthood until the coming of Jesus Christ as mediator between God and men; and He made us participators and vicars of this priesthood.

Therefore, since before the birth of Christ kings were found among the Assyrians, the Sicyonians, the Egyptians, and others as far back as the time of Abraham—which according to Methodius[88] means for some two thousand years before Christ, and according to other authorities approximately this long—it follows that there were true kings for a long period of time before there was a true priesthood: kings whose office was to care for the necessities of human civil life. These men were indeed true kings, even though those who were anointed in this respect symbolized Christ in His relationship to God's people.[89]

It must be noted, however, that if priesthood is taken broadly and improperly such that a legal priest or any other person who was a priest symbolically or was thought to be one is called priest, then priesthood and kingship arose and fell concurrently. For Melchisedech was simultaneously king of Salem and priest of the most high God among the worshippers of God; and according to the Jews and the learned author of the *History*,[90] the priesthood was continued through his heirs down to the time of Aaron. Moreover, according to the Jews, Melchisedech begot Arphat two years after the Flood, and from this time until the seventieth year of Abraham's life, when the first promise was made to him, as we read in Genesis 12,[91] there were 370 years on a literal reading or, according to some, 430. Now for others the first kingdom was quite

simply that of the Assyrians, as has been said, and its first king was Belus. His son, Ninus, succeeded to the kingship when the father died, and he constructed the idol called Baal, from which the idols of the other territories take their names, such as Beelphegor, Beelzebuth and such names; and Ninus established priests or priestly officials through whom sacrifices were offered to the idol. It follows clearly from what has been said that true kingship was concurrent with the priesthood as it is understood in this latter sense—namely, as a symbolic priesthood or as what was thought to be priesthood—and that this priesthood had been in existence a long time before the true priesthood.

Chapter 5

Whether Kingship or Priesthood Is Prior in Dignity

From the foregoing it can be proven easily whether kingship or priesthood is prior in dignity.[92] For what is later in time is usually prior in dignity, what is perfect is prior to what is imperfect, and the end is prior to what relates to the end.[93] Therefore, we say that priestly power is greater than kingly power, and excels it in dignity; for we always find that that to which the ultimate end pertains is more perfect, and directs that to which a lesser end pertains. Kingship, however, is ordered to the end that a community be brought together and live together according to virtue, as has been said [chapter 2]. And this in turn is further ordered to a higher end, the enjoyment of God, the direction of which was entrusted to Christ, of Whom priests are the vicars and ministers. Therefore, priestly power is of greater dignity than secular power.

This is commonly conceded: *Decretum 96*, "Duo quippe sunt": "By as much as gold is more precious than lead is the priestly order higher than kingly power."[94] And in *Extra, De majoritate et obedientia*, in the chapter "Solite" it is asserted that just as spiritual things are to be preferred to temporal things, and the sun to the moon,[95] in the same way, etc. Hugh of St. Victor stated in On the Sacraments 2.4: "By as much as spiritual life is more worthy than earthly life, and the spirit more worthy than the body, is spiritual power more excellent in honor and dignity than secular or earthly."[96] And Bernard wrote to Pope Eugene, Book I: "Which seems to you to have the greater dignity, the power of remitting sin or of dividing estates? There is no comparison."[97] This is the same as saying that spiritual power is greater; hence it excels the other in dignity.

However, if the priest is greater than the prince in dignity and absolutely, it is not necessary for him to be superior in all things,[98] for the latter secular power does not relate to the higher spiritual power in such a way that it arises or derives from it.[99] This is how the power of the proconsul relates to the power of the emperor; and the latter is greater in all things because the proconsul's power is derived from the emperor. The relationship, rather, is like that between the power of the head of a family and that of a master of soldiers; one is not derived from the other, but both are derived from some superior power. Therefore, secular power is greater than spiritual power in some things, namely, temporal things; and it is not subject to the spiritual power with reference to them in any way, because secular power does not arise from spiritual power. The two arise directly from a single supreme power; the divine power.[100] Wherefore the inferior is not subject to the superior in all things, but only in those things in respect of which the supreme power made it subordinate to the superior.[101] For who could say that, because a teacher of literature or an instructor in morals orders everyone in a household to a more noble end, namely, to the knowledge of truth, a physician who is concerned with a lesser end, the health of the body, is therefore subject to either of these in the preparation of his medicines? This simply does not follow, since the head of the household, who appointed both to his household, would not for that reason sub-

ordinate the physician to one who has a higher purpose. Hence, the priest is superior principally in spiritual matters; and, conversely, the prince is superior in temporal matters, although the priest is superior absolutely insofar as the spiritual is superior to the temporal.

Examples from previously mentioned authorities show this too. For lead does not come from gold as its cause, even though gold is more precious than lead. The same point also is stated expressly in [Decretum], 2.7, "Nos si incompetenter, Cum David."[102] Nevertheless, it must be understood that what has been said applies to the true priesthood of Christ.[103] For the priesthood of the Gentiles and the entirety of their divine cult were directed to temporal goods ordered to the common good of the multitude, whose care is the responsibility of the king. Accordingly, the priests of the Gentiles were subordinate to kings, and kingship was superior to the priesthood, in the same way as the power whose concern is for the common good is greater and superior to the power whose concern is only for a particular good. Similarly, the priesthood of the Old Law promised only temporal goods immediately, even though these were to be provided for the people by the true God and not by demons. Consequently, the priesthood of the Old Law was also lower in dignity than kingly power, and was subject to it; for the king was not directed by the priest to anything higher than the good of the community, whose care fell to his own charge. The opposite, however, is the case in the New Law.

One must consider, then, how marvellously Divine Providence functioned in the case of Rome, a city God chose to be the principal seat of the Christian priesthood. The custom grew there gradually of the rulers of the city voluntarily submitting themselves to priests more so than in other localities. This occurred even though there was no obligation in justice for the leaders to do this, since absolutely they were greater than priests. They did it as a sign of the exellence of the future priesthood, to whom a greater excellence was to be granted. Valerian says: "Our state always placed all things after religion, even those things in which the honor of the highest majesty wished to show itself. Wherefore the rulers did not hesitate to subordinate civil matters to sacred ones, considering that if they served the divine power well and faithfully, they would retain charge over human affairs."[104] Because it would also happen that in France[105] as in many other places the religion of the Christian priesthood would flourish, it was divinely ordained that there also be priests among the Gallic peoples. They were called druids, and were found throughout the whole of Gaul, as Julius Caesar wrote in his book *On the Gallic War*.[106] Therefore, Christ's priesthood has greater dignity than kingly power.

Chapter 6

That the Priesthood Is Not Prior in Causality,[107] and How the Pope Relates to External Ecclesiastical Goods[108] in Terms of Dominion

Now because some wish to raise the excellence of the priesthood above the kingly rank in order to assert that the priesthood is superior not only in dignity, as has been said [chapter 3], but also in causality,[109] and to asset that secular power is contained within priestly power and is constituted from it, it remains to be seen whether the pope, who holds the highest place among the priests of Christ, does or does not possess this power. Wherefore, first it will be shown how the pope relates to external goods in terms of dominion over things; and secondly, granted that he is not a true lord over external goods but a dispenser of them absolutely or as circumstances warrant, it will be shown how in fact he possesses basic and primary authority as superior, and as a person exercising jurisdiction.

Regarding the first of these points, it must be seen initially how the pope relates to the goods of ecclesiastical persons insofar as they are ecclesiastics. Here it must be understood that ecclesiastical goods, as ec-

clesiastical, are used for communities and not for individual persons. Therefore, no individual person has property rights and dominion over them; but the community alone, like the church at Chartres or of some such place, has dominion and property rights over such goods as belong properly to it.[110] Moreover, an individual person who has a right of use[111] over such things to sustain him according to his need and the decency of his person and status does not have this right as an individual but as a part and member of the community. Nevertheless, a differentiation is to be made here. For one man—for example, a simple canon—is a member as a simple member; and such an individual has only the right just described. Another man, however—for example, a bishop—is a member as principal member and as head of the community. For there would not be one congregation, nor would it be ordered, unless there were one head and principal member. This latter type of person has not only the use of community goods according to the needs of his status in the aforementioned manner, but also the administration and general dispensation of all the goods of the community. He appropriates what belongs to anyone from him, according to a proportional obligation in justice;[112] and he dispenses in good faith for the common good of the community what seems to him to further it. The bishop of any cathedral church is such a person.

This is true not only because any congregation of ecclesiastical men is one in a spiritual unity, but also because all ecclesiastical congregations have a certain general unity insofar as they are one Church, which is connected to a single principal member, the lord pope, to whom falls the charge of the general Church. As the head and supreme member of the universe Church, therefore, he is the universal dispenser[113] generally of all ecclesiastical goods, spiritual and temporal. He is not, however, lord[114] over them. Only the community of the universal Church is lord and proprietor over all goods generally, while communities and churches individually have dominion over the goods appropriate to them. Similarly, while principal members have only the power of dispensing, individual persons still do not have dominion, however this term is taken, except insofar as they produce their own fruits from their own efforts according to the demands of person and status. Or perhaps something might be appropriated to one or other of them by the universal dispenser so deciding and determining in good faith, according as the laws established by the pope distinguish four types of ecclesiastical goods in *Decretum* 12.2.[115]

From what has been said, it appears to be wrong to assert that no individual other than the pope, no group or community, has right and dominion over the goods of the Church. To state that the pope alone has this power, since he is not only the universal administrator and dispenser, but also the true lord and proprietor of the goods of the Church, and that he can order them and distribute them as he pleases, and that he can retain this right even if he sins, unless he makes disposition of it for some sufficient cause, while other prelates and even princes and communities do not have dominion, but are only procurers, keepers, and dispensers of such goods would be false according to what has been said before. The pope is not the lord of all ecclesiastical goods generally, any more than lesser prelates are with respect to the goods of their own group. The pope, however, is the universal dispenser and disposer of goods, and he even makes his own, according to the requirements of his personal status, a richer portion of the fruits from common goods than lesser prelates, who are called to a share in solicitude and not to the plenitude of power.[116]

This is why, when speaking to Boniface about prelates, Augustine includes all of them generally when he says: "If we possess privately what is sufficient for us, these things are not ours; rather we see to the management of these things. Therefore, let us not by a damnable usurpation claim property rights for ourselves."[117] And the Apostle does not exclude Peter or the pope when he says in I Corinthians 4: "Let man see us thus as ministers of Christ and dis-

pensers of God's mysteries."[118] And speaking of temporal goods, Bernard said to Pope Eugene, in book II: "Whatever the reason is for you to be engaged in buying and selling, it is not by apostolic right, since He could not give you what he did not possess. Silver and gold, He said, are not mine, What He had He gave, namely, care over the churches but not domination. Hear Him: Not as dominating, He said to the clergy, but as directing force over the gathered flock."[119] This is what Bernard held.

From this it is evident also that it is not repugnant for clerics as clerics or for monks as monks to have dominion over external goods at least in common, because their vows do not make them incapable of dominion in particular and in common, as is the case with some religious. Where the founders of churches directed that dominion and property rights over the goods they gave transfer firstly and directly to the community of a group, that is, to a given church, for the use of the servants of the Lord and not for the lord pope, it is clear that the community itself has immediate and true dominion over these goods, and neither pope nor any lesser prelate has it. For otherwise the mode of life of clerics would not differ with respect to this kind of exterior goods from the mode of life of the friars minor, who by their own peculiar vows are incapable of dominion over external goods in particular and in common. Friars minor have only the use of work, as Pope Nicholas says.[120] And to prevent the scattering and disordering of the goods collected for them, which are ecclesiastical goods insofar as they are conferred on ecclesiastical persons, the lord pope takes right and dominion over them to himself and to the Church. However, there is no mention that a different situation obtains with respect to external ecclesiastical goods for clergy and for certain types of religious. For Pope Nicholas also states in the same decretal that the monk in the monastery and the servant of the Lord acquire right and dominion in some manner.[121] Therefore, the pope alone is not lord. Rather, he is the general dispenser; and the bishop or abbot is a special and immediate dispenser, while the community has true dominion over goods.

Further, it cannot be said that the pope lacks right and dominion over such goods as a private person, but has them as a public person and vicar of Jesus Christ,[122] to Whom all such goods belong as principal lord, and to the pope as His vicar general. To say this proves nothing, because Christ as God is not lord only over ecclesiastical goods, but over all other goods as well. As man,[123] however, He does not have communication and corporeal conversation with persons who are in the Church. Nor do those who confer goods on the Church intend to transfer right and dominion to Christ either as God, because all things are His in this way, or as man, because He does not have to use those things now. Rather, they transfer right and dominion to Christ's ministers. Hence, these goods belong to the Church by property right, and to prelates as dispensers, as has been said.[124]

From this it follows also that the pope cannot freely appropriate ecclesiastical goods in order to keep whatever he wishes. This would be true if he were God. But since he is the dispenser of the goods of a community, and good faith is required in such a role, the only power he possesses with respect to these goods relates to their being necessary or useful for the Chruch as a whole. Whence it is said in II Corinthians 13 and 10,[125] that God gave to prelates the power to build and not to destroy. Therefore, if he were to appropriate anything freely without having good faith, his action is not binding in law. And not only is he to be held then to punishment for sin as for an abuse of his own possessions, but he acts unfaithfully and is bound to restitution if he still possesses anything from his own inheritance or from what he has taken, since he would be defrauding with respect to things which do not belong to him.[126]

And just as even a monastery can act to depose an abbot, or a particular church can act to depose a bishop, if the abbot or bishop appears to be dissipating the goods of the monastery or the church and disposing of goods unfaithfully and for private

and not for the common good, so too can a pope be deposed,[127] provided he has been admonished and does not make amends, if it appears that he is unfaithfully disposing of the goods of the Church for other than the common good which as the supreme bishop he is charged to maintain. Decretum 11, chapter "Si papa" states: "He who is the judge of all is to be judged by none, unless he be observed to be in error on a matter of faith."[128] On this the Gloss comments: "If he is observed to be at fault in any matter whatsoever, and does not act to correct himself when admonished to do so, and gives scandal to the Church, the same action can be taken."[129] Some argue, however, that this can be done only through a general council: Decretum 21, chapter, "Nunc autem."[130]

And if indeed the pope knows that some men, whether they be ecclesiastics or laymen, are protesting in possible and legitimate ways against him for an unwarranted dispensation, he cannot by rights remove them or take away what belongs to them in any fashion whatsoever, since he does not have authority from God for this kind of action. And those who claim that the pope's will is in such confusion commit an affront to heaven and do injury to the most holy pontiff, our father. For it should be assumed that the will of so great a father is not contrary to rights, and that he will not take what belongs to anyone from him without reasonable cause. For he cannot by rights act otherwise.[131] In fact God does not will to remove or to have removed from anyone what He has given him unless a sin intervenes; for as the Apostle says to the Romans: "The gifts of God are irrevocable."[132] It is because of men's sins that He also says: "I regret that I have made man."[133] It was on account of sin also that He made over the spoils of the Egyptians to the Hebrews.[134] However, He wishes to take nothing from the just man, or to have nothing taken from him: Job 36: "Judgment favors the poor, does not take his eyes from the just man, and places kings on their thrones for eternity."[135] Therefore, even though God gave the dispensation of goods to Peter or the pope in good faith and not contrary to the express will of God, the pope cannot lawfully take away the power of administration which a person has rightly and properly received, without there being a clear fault intervening. This, therefore, is the type of power the pope has in respect of ecclesiastical goods.

Chapter 7

The Relation of the Supreme Pontiff to the Goods of Laymen

From what has been said the relation of the pope to the goods of laymen is clear: he has much less dominion over the external goods of laymen than over those of clerics. He is not even their administrator, except in circumstances of most extreme necessity for the Church; and even here he is still not an administrator but a proclaimer of what is right.

To establish this point one must acknowledge that the external goods of laymen are not given to a community as ecclesiastical goods are. Rather, they are acquired by individual persons through their art, labor, or their own industry; and individual persons as individuals exercise right, power, and true dominion over such goods. As lord over such goods, a person can order, dispose, keep, or transfer what is his as he sees fit, without injury to anyone else. These goods, therefore, have no order and relation among themselves, nor are they ordered or related to any one common head[136] who has them to dispose of and dispense; for everyone can do with his own possessions as he sees fit. Thus, neither prince nor pope has dominion or administration over such things.

Now it sometimes happens that these external goods lead to a disturbance of the general peace, as when someone usurps what belongs to someone else, or when men desire excessively what is theirs and do not share it as the needs or use of the country require. This is the reason why the people name a ruler: to govern, to act as judge of what is just and unjust in such

matters, to punish injustices, and to be the measure in receiving goods from individuals according to a just proportion for the needs and use of the community. Indeed, as general shaper of faith and morals the pope is, as it were, not only head of the clergy but also of all the faithful insofar as they are faithful. And, therefore, in circumstances of extreme necessity[137] with respect to faith and morals, when all the goods of the faithful—even the chalices—belonging to churches are common and to be shared, he has the power to dispense and determine what is to be turned over for the common needs of the faith, which otherwise would be subverted by an invasion of pagans or some such thing. And so great and evident a necessity could exist that he could exact tithes or specified portions of their property from individual members of the faithful, conceding however that this must be done according to a just assessment, so that no person be unreasonably burdened more than others in aid of the common needs of the faith. An order of this kind from the pope would be nothing less than a declaration of right.

The pope can also coerce rebels or dissenters by the use of ecclesiastical censure.[138] And he can even use the same measures in a parish where there are so many new faithful that the old revenue is no longer sufficient to maintain the priest in charge of the parish, and he suddenly finds it necessary to maintain many new chaplains as assistants. In such a situation the pope can require the faithful of that parish to increase contributions from their goods to an amount needed for a sufficient income. And in such circumstances this kind of order is a declaration of right.

Except for cases of this kind, however, where there is the necessity of the common spiritual good involved, the pope has no disposition over goods of the laity, but each individual person disposes of what is his as he sees fit; and in cases of necessity the ruler disposes for the common temporal good. Now in cases where there is no necessity but some spiritual use, or where it happens that material goods of the laity are not collected for such use or necessity, the pope does not have the right to coerce anyone, although he can grant indulgences to the faithful for giv-ing assistance.[139] And in my view nothing else is to be granted to him.

NOTES

1. The controversy over the right of mendicant friars to hear confessions and preach was addressed by Boniface VIII in the bull *Super cathedram* of February 18, 1300, a document John must have had in mind when he chose this contemporary ecclesiastical problem to illustrate the virtues of the *via media* approach to such problems. Boniface's resolution of the controversy in favor of the mendicants was shortly qualified by restrictions imposed on the mendicants' powers to confess by his successor, Benedict XI, in the bull *Inter cunctos* of 1304. Quidort himself took part in the controversy, which erupted in 1304, over this latter papal document. See Leclercq, *Jean de Paris*, p. 8.
2. Boethius, "Liber de persona et duabus naturis," prooemium (*PL* 64. 1341). John is greatly indebted, in the formulation of his position in this first paragraph, to Thomas Aquinas, *Contra impugnantes dei cultum et religionem* 3. 70–77, especially 73–75 (ed. Raymond M. Spiazzi [Turin, 1958], p. 24).
3. The Waldensians, adjudged heretical for their views, were along with the Albigensians one of the greatest sources of disturbance to the twelfth- and early-thirteenth-century Church. Founded about 1176 by Peter Waldo, a wealthy banker from Lyons, they were violently opposed to the clergy and advocated a return to the simplicity of the Apostolic Church and elimination of organizational and bureaucratic structures in the Church. See Philip Hughes, *A History of the Church*, 3 vols. (New York: Sheed and Ward, 1948) 2:336–38.
4. Matt. 6:19. Note: References for biblical citations are from the King James version. The translation is rendered directly from John's text, which was based on the Vulgate text.
5. I Tim. 6:8, 9.
6. Matt. 6:24.
7. Matt. 6:31.
8. Matt. 6:26.
9. Matt. 10:9.
10. Luke 14:33.
11. Acts 3:6.
12. Matt. 2:3.
13. John later specifies only one of these *moderni*, Henry of Cremona. See also Leclercq's careful analysis of these "modern" theocratic advocates: Jean Leclercq, *Jean de Paris et l'écclesiologie du XIIIè siècle* (Paris, 1942), pp. 29–33, and especially Leclercq's comment that although he never refers directly to Aegidius of Rome's work, *De ecclesiastica potestate*, this is the single most useful source for John's enumeration of his opponents' views.
14. Although John refers here to the papalist argument that the pope stands in the place of Christ (*loco Christi*), it is clear that the argument he has in mind is that which designates the pope as "vicar of Christ" (*vicarius Christi*). John is perfectly aware that this had been one of the cornerstones of the papalist claims since Innocent III had formally incorporated it within the canonists' armory. See Walter Ullmann, *The Growth of Papal Government in the Middle Ages, a Study in the Ideological Relation of Clerical to Lay Power*, 2d ed. (London: Methuen, 1964), p. 428, note 4.

    Its use as a title exclusively applicable to the pope came to be adopted as a result of its employment by St. Bernard: cf. Bernard of Clairvaux, "Epistola CCLI" (*PL* 182. 451); "De consideratione" 2. 8. 6, *Sancti Bernardi Opera*, ed. J. Leclercq (Rome, 1961), 3:424; 4. 7. 23, ibid., 3:426.

    The general character of the argument, though not the term *vicarius Christi*, is found as far back as Pope Gelasius and Pope Leo I. John himself frequently employs the term when referring to the pope; he uses it in the following paragraph. He accepts the term, but accepts also the necessity of denying temporal authority to the "vicar of Christ." John was well aware of the need to dismiss the papalist claims resting on the notion of the pope as "vicar of Christ." See Ullmann's application of this necessity to his assessment of the anonymous antipapalist *York Tracts* and the twelfth-century *Liber de unitate ecclesiae conservandi*: Ullmann, *Papal Government*, pp. 394–404.
15. *Decretalium d. Gregorii papae IX* 4, "Per venerabilem." *Corpus iuris canonici* 2. 714.
16. Vigilantius was an early-fifth-century parish priest in Gaul whose views on the cult of martyrs were considered heretical by St. Jerome. None of Vigilantius' own writings are extant, and his doctrines are known only in the incomplete expression given them by Jerome. See below, note 20.
17. Augustine, "De agone christiano" 12 (*PL* 40. 297).
18. Jovinian, an ex-monk and man of the world, maintained that since baptism guaranteed salvation,

mortification of the flesh was absurd. He was excommunicated by Pope Siricius (384–398), and drew written criticisms of his views from Sts. Ambrose and Jerome. See following note.

19. Jerome, "Adversus Vigilantium liber" 1 (*PL* 23. 355). For the argument about ownership being repugnant to the pope by reason of his state and John's response, see Thomas Aquinas, *Contra pestiferum doctrinam retrahentium homines a religionis ingressu*, 1. 735–36, (ed. Raymond M. Spiazzi [Turin, 1961], pp. 159–60.)

20. *Glossa interlinearis in I Petrum* 2:13 (Anvers, 1634), 6:1319.

21. John Chrysostom, "Opus imperfectum in Mattheum, Homilia XXXVIII" (*PG* 56. 841); cited in Thomas Aquinas, *Catena aurea in Mattheum*, 21:12.

22. For John, the general right of clerics to have dominion or jurisdiction over temporal things is restricted to the right, enjoyed by any man, to possess one's own private property—that is, the right based on his own expenditure of labor or money. The only exception to this general principle is stated immediately: viz. some type of specific concession or permission granted to a cleric by a temporal ruler. See chaps. 6 and 7.

23. This disclaimer indicates John's wish to be considered an orthodox Christian. There is no need to raise the issue of whether or not he sees his own position as heterodox, as has been suggested in respect of the more extreme antipapalist position of Marsilius of Padua. See Alan Gewirth, *Marsilius of Padua, the Defender of Peace*, vol. 1, *Marsilius of Padua and Mediaeval Political Philosophy* (New York: Columbia University Press, 1951), pp. 82–84.

24. The term I have chosen to translate *regnum* is "kingship" rather than the more general term "state," although it is clear that John designates the basic unit of political society as a *regnum*. In fact, he concedes that there can be other types of political entity than monarchies, and even his notion of monarchy admits the possibility of other sources of authority within it than the king alone; he speaks frequently of the consent of the people.

For John, however, kingship—one-man rule by a king—is the best form of temporal authority; and his position in discussing the legitimacy of the exercise of temporal authority by a cleric is stated consistently in terms of the contrast between the basic type of authority in temporal matters, kingship, and the basic type of authority in spiritual matters, priesthood. For qualifications and reservations on the one-man character of both these types of authority see the remaining citations for this chapter.

25. This definition of kingship (or state) is basically Aristotelian, although the definition is not found in so many words in Aristotle; cf. Aristotle, *Politics* 1. 2. 1252b27. The definition in its Aristotelian derivation was common to many medieval political thinkers, especially those who followed Aristotle in describing temporal authority and political society as natural to man: Cf. Thomas Aquinas, *De regimine principum* 1. 1; Ptolemy of Lucca, *De regimine principum* 4. 2; Aegidius of Rome, *De regimine principum* 1. 1; James of Viterbo, *De regimine christiano* 2; Englebert of Admont, *Liber de ortu, progressu et fine romano imperii* 13; Dante, *De monarchia* 1. 5; Augustinus Triumphus, *Summa de ecclesiastica potestate* 1. 6; Marsilius of Padua, *Defensor pacis* 1. 4. 1; William of Ockham, *Dialogus*, 3. 2. 2. 5.

26. Aristotle, *Politics*, 1. 2. 1252b33. John's characterization of the kingly state as a "perfect community" is, again, typically medieval and can be seen frequently in this period: Cf. Thomas Aquinas, *De regimine principum* 1. 1; Aegidius of Rome, *De regimine principum* 3. 1. 1; Englebert of Admont, *Liber de ortu, progressu et fine romani imperii* 15; James of Viterbo, *De regimine christiano* 1. 1; Dante, *De monarchia* 1. 3. 5. See also, note below.

The emphasis is on the state viewed from the side of its purpose, end, or final cause as well as its perfection seen from the point of view of completeness. See Aristotle, *Politics* 1. 2. 1252b35. The teleological character of John's definition, while typically medieval, must meet the kind of reservation that can be brought against this method of defining a political society. See Gewirth, *Marsilius of Padua* vol. 2, *Defensor pacis* (1956), pp. xxxviii; li. On the general use of the *Politics* as a source for medieval political theories, see G. von Hertling, "Zur Geschichte der aristotelischen Politik im Mittelalter," *Historische Beitrage zur Geschichte der Philosophie* (Kempten and Munich, 1914), pp. 20–32; M. Grabmann, "Studien uber den Einfluss der aristotelischen Philosophie auf die mittelalterlichen Theorien uber das Verhaltnis von Kirche und Staat," *Sitzungsberichte der Bayerischen Akademie der Wissenschaften*, Phil.-hist. Abt no. 2, (1934): M. Grabmann, "Die mittelalterlichen Kommentare zur Politick des Aristoteles," Ibid. vol. 2, no. 10 (1941); G. Lagarde, *La Naissance de l'esprit laique au déclin du moyen âge*, 3d ed. (Louvain, Editions de l'Institut supérieur de philosophie, 1956).

27. Aristotle, *Politics* 3. 7. 1279a5–10. For similar insistence on the end of political society as the common good, see Thomas Aquinas, *De regimine principum* 1. 1; Aegidius of Rome, *De regimine principum*, 3. 2. 2; *De monarchia* 1. 12; James of Viterbo, *De regimine christiano* 2. 2; John of Jandun, *Questiones in duodecim libros metaphysicae* 1. 18; William of Ockham, *Dialogus* 3. 1. 2. 6; *Octo quaestiones de potestate papae* 3. 4. Contrast Marsilius of Padua, *Defensor pacis* 1. 9. 5, 6, 7. 9.

28. For the distinctions among kingship, aristocracy and polity see Aristotle, *Politics* 3. 7.

29. Ezek. 34:23. This use of a scriptural text to support the Aristotelian preference for one-man rule illustrates the reaction of many medieval users of the Aristotelian *Politics* to the Philosopher's reluctance

to favor a single political authority in a state. Aristotle himself says that this type of rule would be "best" if a single man could be found who was preeminent in virtue. Logically, it would seem, such a person ought to rule, and all other men ought to pay him a willing obedience. However, in practice Aristotle himself despaired of finding such a paragon of virtue, and favored a mixed polity as the best type of government or political society (*Politics* 3. 15–17). Typically, medieval Aristotelians simply ignored Aristotle's practical reservations about finding this maximally virtuous leader, accepted his statements extolling such a single man as the natural embodiment of authority, and suppressed any reference to Aristotle's own declared preference for the mixed polity. John follows such a procedure here, and bolsters the argument in favor of one-man rule by an appeal to scriptural authorities. Later, however, he makes some interesting and important references to the benefits of a mixed polity, and even extends the Aristotelian preference for such a system to the Church.

30. Aristotle, *Politics* 1. 2. 1253a2. The view that man is by nature a political animal is to be found also in Thomas Aquinas, *De regimine principum* 1. 1; Ptolemy of Lucca, *De regimine principum* 4. 2; Aegidius of Rome, *De regimine principum* 3. 1. 4; James of Viterbo, *De regimine christiano*, 1. 1; Dante, *Il convivio*, 4. 4. A little later on in this same chapter, John repeats this principal, adding "social" to the list of natural qualities: "Man is naturally a civil or political and social animal."

31. Aristotle, *Politics*, 1. 2. 1252b15–1253a15. On the point of the relationship between speech and man's social nature as perfected in a community see Thomas Aquinas, *De regimine principum* 1. 1; Ptolemy of Lucca, *De regimine principum* 4. 3; Aegidius of Rome, *De regimine principum*, 2. 1. 1; 3. 1. 4; Marsilius of Padua, *Defensor pacis* 2. 22. 15; G. Lagarde, "Une adaptation de la Politique d'Aristote au XIVè siècle," *Revue historique de droit français et étranger* 4th series, vol. 11 (1932):236–37.

32. In this instance I have translated *regnum* as "kingdom," implying some quality of territorial extent as well as a form of political authority. John does not mention here any form of political authority of larger territorial extent than a kingdom. In the present context this is consistent with his description of the ascending order of perfection among communities, from household to village to kingdom, the last-mentioned being perfect because it is all-providing in terms of its members' needs. In chapter 3, however, John specifically rejects any theory of universal political authority. Note his use of *regnum* here too to designate a territorially limited state. Later, he makes reference to an emperor as a temporal ruler having no superior (chap. 10) and also refers on one occasion to the emperor as having "universal and ubiquitous jurisdiction over temporal affairs" (chap. 13).

33. The analogy between one-man rule in a state, the single common power of soul in organisms, and unity in the governance of the universe is also found in Thomas Aquinas, *De regimine principum*, 1. 2; Ptolemy of Lucca, *De regimine principum* 3. 1; Aegidius of Rome, *De regimine principum* 3. 2. 3; Dante, *De monarchia* 1. 8; James of Viterbo, *De regimine christiano* 2. 5; Marsilius of Padua, *Defensor pacis* 1. 17, 8, 9.

34. Proverbs 11:14. Cf. Thomas Aquinas, *In I politicorum* 1. 31.

35. Kingship is the preferred form of government among all medieval Aristotelians, all of whom tend to view the state from the standpoint of virtues which the ideal king should attempt to foster, and which he himself might personify. See Thomas Aquinas, *De regimine principum* 1; Ptolemy of Lucca, *De regimine principum* 3. 12; Aegidius of Rome, *De regimine principum*, 1. 1. 3; 1. 2. 7; 1. 3. 4; Englebert of Admont, *De ortu, progressu et fine romani imperii* 2. 14, 15; James of Viterbo, *De regimine christiano*, 2. 2, 6, 8; Augustinus Triumphus, *Summa de ecclesiastica potestate*, 44. 1; John of Jandun, *Questiones in duodecim libros metaphysicae*, 1. 1. 18; 1. 2. 11.

36. John's ideal of peace and order as promoted through unity of political authority in the state is the traditional one expressed by medieval political theorists. See John of Salisbury, *Policraticus*, 5. 22 ff; Thomas Aquinas, *In decem libros ethicorum Aristotelis ad Nicomachum expositio*, Lect. 8, n. 474; *Summa theologiae*, 2–2. 183. 2, *ad* 3; *De regimine principum*, 1. 12; Ptolemy of Lucca, *De regimine principum*, 4. 23; Aegidius of Rome, *De regimine principum*, 1. 2. 11; Marsilius of Padua, *Defensor pacis*, 1. 2. 3; 1. 19. 2.

37. Aristotle, *Politics*, 3. 7. 1279b6–10.

38. Aristotle, *Politics* 1. 5. 1254a35. See above note 33.

39. Aristotle, *Politics*, 1. 2. 1253a7.

40. Orosius, *Historiarum*, 1. 1 (*PL* 31, 669).

41. Cicero, *De inventione* 1. 2, ed. and transl. H. M. Hubbell (Cambridge, Mass., 1949), p. 6.

42. Aristotle, *Politics*, 1. 2. 1253a28–9.

43. Cicero, *De inventione* 1. 2, p. 6.

44. John has used the term "law of nations" (*ius gentium*) earlier in this chapter, but this is the first effort he makes at its definition. The "law of nations" is that body of written legislation common to all political societies which embodies basic principles of the "natural law." The ideology is completely derivative from Thomas Aquinas: *Summa theologiae*, 1–2, 95. 4. John's canonist opponents, for the most part, had a completely different notion of "natural law": cf. Walter Ullmann, *Medieval Papalism, the Political Theories of the Medieval Canonists* (London, Methuen, 1949), pp. 38 ff.

45. While the point is implicit in John's earlier remarks about the proper end of a political society, this is

his first explicit comment about the "moral" character of a state's purpose. The purpose of a state, and of its authority, is to make men good, to achieve virtue for its citizens. Again the concept is Aristotelian, and again it is a typically medieval one: Aristotle, *Politics* 3. 9. 1280b1 ff; 6. 13. 1332a4 ff; *Nicomachean Ethics* 2. 4. 1105a29 ff. See also Thomas Aquinas, *Summa theologiae*, 1–2. 96. 2; 1–2. 100. 9; *De regimine principum* 1. 14, 15; Ptolemy of Lucca, *De regimine principum* 3. 3; 4. 24; Godfrey of Fontaines, *Quodlibeta* 1. 6; James of Viterbo, *De regimine christiano* 2. 4; Englebert of Admont, *De ortu, progressu et fine romani imperii*, 7. 8; Durand of St. Pourçain, *De origine et usu jurisdictionum* 2; Alexander of St. Elpidius, *Tractatus de ecclesiastica potestate* 2. 3. 1; John of Jandun, *Questiones in duodecim libros metaphysicae* 1. 1, 18; 2. 11.

46. Here John transcends the Aristotelian framework of argument and basis for his position, adding to the Aristotelian concept of the natural for man the Christian element of the "supernatural." See also Thomas Aquinas, *Summa theologiae* 1. 2. 1–5, esp. 5. 3 and 5. 5.

47. John repeats, in the supernatural order, the same argument, linking unity of end to unity of personal agent to achieve this end, that he employed in advocating a one-man rule in a political society in the previous chapter.

48. Romans 6:23.

49. Reference to God, more specifically to Christ, as "king" has many and long-standing precedents, and was made quite universally by both papalist and anti-papalist commentators. The issue, of course, was to specify what was meant by designating Christ as king. See also, Walter Ullmann, *The Growth of Papal Government in the Middle Ages, a Study in the Ideological Relation of Clerical to Lay Power*, 2d ed. (London: Methuen, 1964), pp. 26 ff.

50. Jeremiah 23:5.

51. Hebrews 5:1. John has now specifically designated Christ as king and priest. This double designation, which John frequently employs, is traditional and reflects the frame of reference normally employed by the papalists. John's acceptance of the terminology, while almost unavoidable, shows again his tendency to turn away from radical rejection of the traditional framework of expression. It is the papalist's interpretation of these traditional formulae to which he takes exception. See chap. 8 and Ullmann, *Papal Government*, pp. 26 ff.

52. This, too, is the traditional concept of the sacraments of the Church: they are means, given to the Church by Christ, to assist men in achieving salvation. Cf. the traditional medieval description of the sacraments in Thomas Aquinas, *Summa theologiae* 3. 60, esp. 60. 4; *In IV Sententiarium*, 1. 1. 1; Peter Lombard, *Sententiae* 4. 1.

53. Romans 1:20.

54. On this definition of priest cf. Thomas Aquinas, *Summa theologiae*, Suppl. 34. 1.

55. Hebrews 5:1.

56. See the purely rationalistic and empirical basis for formulating a definition of the priesthood, its nature and function in Marsilius of Padua, *Defensor pacis*, 1. 5. 10–13; and Alan Gewirth, *Marsilius of Padua, the Defender of Peace*, vol. 1, *Marsilius of Padua and Medieval Political Philosophy* (New York: Columbia University Press, 1951), pp. 43, 83–84; 108–15; 119–25.

57. II Cor. 13:10.

58. The distinction John draws between the power of bishops and the power of ordinary priests on the issues of consecration and jurisdiction is crucial for any doctrine of hierarchical structure in the Christian Church. John argues that bishops, like all priests, have the power to consecrate the bread and wine into the Body and Blood of Christ. All ordained priests, simple priests and bishops (and pope) alike, possess this power to an equal degree. Bishops (and by inference the pope as well), however, have additional powers as "higher and perfect ministers," and these are not possessed by ordinary priests: the power to confer the priesthood on another man and the power to exercise jurisdiction over other priests. The specific character of this episcopal (and papal) power of jurisdiction is the crux of the issue. John's view that the priest receives his jurisdiction from the bishop is traditional: cf. Thomas Aquinas, *Summa theologiae*, Suppl. 40. 4. In point of fact, the first half of John's chapter follows closely the contents of Thomas Aquinas, *Summa contra gentiles*, 4. 76 and *In IV Sent.*, 13. 1. 1. *resp. 2, ad 2*.

59. Pseudo-Dionysius, "De ecclesiastica hierarchia," 4. 3 (*PG* 3. 506). John's reference to the Pseudo-Dionysius marks the introduction of a major authority for the traditional medieval conceptions of unity and order applied to the formultion of political theory. It is the base for all arguments and procedures employed by the papalists in their development of a universalist theologico-political theory subsuming all political authority under the spiritual authority of the papacy, and was also a normal part of the intellectual framework of many antipapalist descriptions of papal authority. Cf. Boniface VIII, *Unam sanctam*, and the commentary on this attributed to Aegidius of Rome, edited by P. de Lapparent, in *Archives d'histoire littéraire et doctrinale du moyen âge* 18 (1940–42):127–45; Aegidius of Rome, *De ecclesiastica potestate* 1. 4; Augustinus Triumphus, *Summa de ecclesiastica potestate* 44. 1; Alexander of St. Elpidius, *Tractatus ecclesiastica potestate* 2. 6. 4; James of Viterbo, *De regimine christiano* 2. 2. 5; Francis of Mayron, *Quaestio de subjectione* 1. 10.

60. The term Church Militant is pseudo-Dionysian in origin, although the notion of the Church and of

Christians as "militant" goes back as far as St. Paul. The conception of the parallel between Church
Militant and Church Triumphant was a strong basis for the papalist position: see Walter Ullmann,
Medieval Papalism, the Political Theories of the Medieval Canonists (London: Methuen, 1949), pp. 159–60.

61. The Church Triumphant is the pseudo-Dionysian correlative of the Church Militant (see Pseudo-
Dionysius, "De ecclesiastica hierarchia," 4. 3 [PG 3. 506]), and this term has had a lengthy history. The
Church Triumphant is the heavenly kingdom, in the literal sense. In heaven Christ rules supreme.
Again, however, the possibilities for interpreting the terminology in such a way as to emphasize some
form of ecclesiastical "triumph" over the whole universe of the temporal world are clearly present,
and they did not go unnoticed by the papalists. See Ullmann, *Medieval Papalism*, pp. 77 ff.

62. Rev. 21:3.

63. Hosea 1:11.

64. John 10:16.

65. John is prepared to accept the view that the unity and supremacy of papal authority derived directly
from Christ, in virtue of the commission to Peter. He does not find it necessary to limit papal authority
by ascribing its origin to any other than a divine source, as Marsilius of Padua does in introducing the
element of popular consent. See Marsilius of Padua, *Defensor pacis*, 1. 13. 7 ff.; 1. 15. 2; 1. 18. 3; 1. 15. 4,
9; Gewirth, *Marsilius of Padua*, 1:167 ff.

66. John 21:17.

67. Luke 22:32. The argument in this chapter parallels Humbert of Rome, "Opus tripartitum," 2. 14, in
Appendix ad fasciculum rerum expetendarum (London, 1690), 2:209.

68. For John, all men and by extension all ecclesiastics are ordered to one supreme spiritual authority
according to "divine ordinance." They are ordered to political authority not by explicit law but by
"natural inclination." This natural inclination toward political society, however, does not extend to a
single person's being the supreme political authority, any more than a universal political society is
imposed by divine law. Accordingly, the character of political authority is multiform, less rigidly
specified than spiritual authority. This point is crucial for John's development of the distinction between the two spheres, temporal and spiritual. It is also the starting point for his rejection of a universal
or world state, a point of great interest in this treatise which is not easily reconcilable with John's
emphasis in chapter 1 on the value of a unified type of political authority. Dante, too, asserts that the
Church was caused by divine ordinance and not by nature, while the state proceeds from the natural
law: Dante, *De monarchia*, 3. 14.

69. The argument that differences of climate and other circumstances justify a diversity of forms of political
authority and society is not peculiar to John: cf. Englebert of Admont, *De ortu, progressu et fine romani
imperii* 16; Dante, *De monarchia* 1. 14. John, however, is more explicit than earlier medieval theorists in
the arguments he advances against a single world state, and anticipates Marsilius of Padua in his
seemingly complete lack of interest in the issue of imperial political authority. John does not mention
the issue of empire here as a possible form of temporal authority, although in chapters 3 and 13 he
does comment very briefly on it. See Walter Ullmann, *The Growth of Papal Government in the Middle
Ages, a Study in the Ideological Relation of Clerical to Lay Power*, 2d ed. (London: Methuen, 1964), p. 457,
note 2.

70. The distinction between the spiritual "sword" as verbal and the temporal "sword" as manual is Bernardine in origin: John's application of it in terms of limiting the extent of a single state's territorial
jurisdiction is not. Quidort echoes here the famous retort of Pierre de Flotte to Boniface VIII: the pope
is concerned with a mystical body and thus works only with words; the king, however, must govern
in the proper sense of that term and hence his power is manual. See Ullmann, *Papal Government*, p.
457.

71. See chap. 7. This emphasis on private property is one that John finds very useful in his limitation of
ecclesiastical authority.

72. See chap. 3.

73. Aristotle, *Nicomachean Ethics* 2. 6. 1106b1.

74. Cf. Thomas Aquinas, *In II ethicorum Nicomachum* 7. 325–26. John's reference to Averroës as a critic of
world government is paralleled later (ch. 19, *ad* 33) by his use of the commentator in support of the
value of popular consent for the exercise of political authority.

75. Aristotle, *Politics* 1. 2. 1253a1.

76. Augustine, *De civitate dei* 4. 15; see also 3–15. John's appeal to the authority of St. Augustine in favor
of a territorial limit to the perfect state is found also in Englebert of Admont, *De ortu, progressu et fine
romani imperii* 16.

77. Augustine, *De civitate de* 4. 15.

78. *Decretum magistri Gratiani* 7, "In apibus," *Corpus iuris canonici* 1. 582.

79. The issue of whether kingship or priesthood came first in time is important for John insofar as a
standard papalist claim was that the priesthood was prior to kingship in history. See Hugh of St.
Victor, *De sacramentis* 2. 2. 7 (PL 176. 420). Curiously enough, John's position that temporal authority

existed historically before spiritual authority was asserted by the canonist, Huguccio, before the opposite position became a dominant feature of the papalist argument: Huguccio, *Summa decretorum* 96, 6, quoted in Walter Ullmann, *Medieval Papalism, the Political Theories of the Medieval Canonists* (London: Methuen), p. 144; cf. ibid., p. 151.

80. Augustine, *De civitate dei* 16. 17.

81. Dante, employing the same basic source of information as John for the history of the foundations of early kingdoms, insists that Ninus was the first man to aspire to world domination, something Dante viewed with much greater equanimity than did John: Dante, *De monarchia* 2. 8. Cf. Augustine, *De civitate dei* 16. 17.

82. John's source for this account of early world history is either Orosius, *Historiarum adversum paganos libri VII* 1. 4, or Augustine, *De civitate dei*, 16. 17.

83. For the view that Christ was the first "true" priest inasmuch as He possessed the complete fullness of the priesthood (*tota sacerdotii plenitudo*) see Thomas Aquinas, *Summa theologiae* 3. 63. 6. Cf. chap. 19, *ad* 31.

84. Deut. 32:17.

85. Heb. 10:1.

86. Reference to Melchisedech as both "king and priest" was standard in papalist texts. See Gen. 14:18; Ps. 109:4; Heb. 7:1–2, 10, 11, 15, 21. It was apparently introduced into papal literature by Leo I, in Epistle 156. 3–5; and may be found in the texts of Gelasius and Isidore. It was given its classic medieval thrust by Innocent III and his followers. See Walter Ullmann, *The Growth of Papal Government in the Middle Ages, a Study in the Ideological Relation of Clerical to Lay Power*, 2d ed. (London: Methuen, 1964), pp. 13, 23–24, 25 (note 2), 29, 317 (note 2), 397–98.

87. Heb. 7–9.

88. Methodius is referred to by John from mention made of him by Peter the Eater, *Historia scholastica, Genesis XLI* (PL 198. 1091).

89. John is careful to point out that his reference to the fact that the Old Testament kings were anointed is not intended to indicate that temporal rulers require anointing in order to exercise their authority. The anointing of these early figures, in his view, indicated their status as prefiguring and symbolizing a spiritual, not a temporal, role: viz. the role of Christ in relation to His people. There can be no doubt that this role of Christ toward His people was not a temporal one.

90. Peter the Eater, *Historia scholastica, Genesis XLVI* (PL 198, 1094).

91. Gen. 12:2.

92. The concept of priority in dignity of the priesthood over kingship also became current through Hugh of St. Victor, *De sacramentis* 2. 2. 7, a text with which John is clearly familiar. (See chap. 4.) It was with Hugh that the concept of a universal Church as a fully autonomous entity having governing principles of its own reached full maturity. See Walter Ullmann, *The Growth of Papal Government in the Middle Ages; a Study in the Ideological Relation of Clerical to Lay Power*, 2d ed. (London: Methuen, 1964), pp. 437–42.

93. The argument involving the ordering of ends to one another, with the ultimate end the most perfect, was another favorite tool in the construction of the papalist edifice. The implication taken and insisted upon by the papalists was that the temporal ruler, whose end or purpose was subordinate to that of the spiritual ruler, was therefore himself fully subordinate to the spiritual authority. It was the responsibility of the temporal ruler, then, to subordinate himself in all things to the higher ruler; and in this way the autonomy of temporal or secular rule is destroyed. See Aegidius of Rome, *De ecclesiastica potestate* 3. 4; Durandus of St. Pourçain, *De jurisdictione ecclesiastica* 3; Ullmann, *Papal Government*, pp. 445–46; *Medieval Papalism, the Political Theories of the Medieval Canonists* (London: Methuen, 1949), pp. 85–86.

94. *Decretum* 96, "Duo sunt quippe," 1. 339.

95. "Decratales" 33, "Solite benignitatis," in *Corpus iuris canonici* 2. 198. The sun and moon argument is also taken from Gregory VII, and like the gold and lead analogy it had become a standard item in the papalist armory. See Gregory VII, *Register* 7. 25, "to the Conqueror," p. 505. The biblical reference is quoted from Ambrosius, that is, "De dignitate sacerdotali" 2 (PL 17. 569–70). This comparison was used later by Thomas à Becket: see D. Knowles, *Episcopal Colleagues of Archbishop Thomas Becket* (Cambridge: University Press, 1951), p. 147; Ullmann, *Papal Government*, pp. 282–83.

96. Hugh of St. Victor, "De sacramentis" 2. 2. 4 (PL 176, 418).

97. Bernard of Clairvaux, *De consideratione* 1. 6. 7, p. 402. The allusion here is to Luke 5:23, and the basis for Bernard's position is I Cor. 6:4. John himself refers frequently to this Bernardine position. See chap. 6.

98. It is at this point that John begins his effort to fracture the monolithic structure of the papalist argument based on unity and hierarchy. For John, in addition to the principle of unity and hierarchy, it is necessary to accept the principle of diversity in hierarchy, or dual hierarchy under a single head, Christ, insofar as Christ possessed two natures, divine (spiritual) and human (temporal).

99. John argues that the spiritual order's superiority in dignity over the temporal does not require that

temoral authority be derived from the spiritual. He employs other arguments to make the same point about the necessity of distinguishing temporal from spiritual authority: to argue that temporal authority is derived from the spiritual absolutely is to destroy the integrity of political authority, which must be held to be intrinsically distinct from the spiritual power. See also Dante, *De monarchia* 3. 16; *Quaestio in utramque partem*, 5; *Quaestio de potestate papae*, pp. 670–78; they parallel the distinction between the divine and the human natures in Christ; chap. 19, *ad* 32. See also *Disputatio inter militem et clericum*, pp. 13–14; *Quaestio in utramque partem* 5, pp. 103, 104; Dante, *De monarchia* 3. 12; they parallel the orders of the theological and the moral virtues, each of which has its own integrity and dignity.

The papalists, for their part, accepted the distinction but interpreted it to mean that the only powers it denied to the pope were those supernatural powers over the whole of creation which belong to God alone: cf. Aegidius of Rome, *De ecclesiastica potestate* 3, 9; James of Viterbo, *De regimine christiano* 2. 9; Alexander of St. Elpidius, *Tractatus de ecclesiastica potestate* 1. 4.

100. The view that secular and spiritual authority both derive from a single, supreme source, God, and not from one another can be found in the Justinian Code, in a passage that has been said to be a kind of common denominator of both papalist and antipapalist doctrines: "Novella VI," *Codex Justiniani*, 1. 4. 34. See Ullmann, *Medieval Papalism*, p. 139. A similar idea is to be found in the old canon law. See *Decretum* 23, "Quesitum est," 1. 924. The famous Gelasian text also can be taken in this sense: Gelasius, *Epistola XII*, 2, p. 351. See Ullmann, *Papal Government*, pp. 19–26.

101. John hangs the basis for differentiating and separating the spheres of spiritual and temporal authority on the intention of the single source for these two orders of authority. They are to be distinguished according to what God intended when He established both. This is not to say, however, that for John the differentiation between the orders of the spiritual and the temporal rests on a pure divine voluntarism; for while he does assert that the order of the spiritual authority rests on "divine law," he is quite explicit that the order of temporal political authority is based on nature and derives from the natural law as inclination (chaps. 1 and 3). It also seems fair to say that his conception of divine law is coordinated with his thomistically inspired doctrine of natural law, and as such relates ultimately to the Divine Intellect rather than the Divine Will. See Thomas Aquinas, *Summa theologiae* 1–2. 90. 1; 91. 1–4. See Dante, *De monarchia* 3. 14. On twelfth-century advocates of the lay thesis see Ullman, *Papal Government*, p. 403. Cf. Henry's efforts to assert the duality of the two spheres: Ullmann, *Papal Government*, pp. 345 ff.

102. *Decretum* "Nos si inconpetenter," 1. 496.

103. For John priority in dignity of the priesthood is a characteristic only of the Christian priesthood. Jewish and Gentile priests are for him not true priests, and subordinate to kings even in dignity.

104. Valerian Maximus, *Factorum dictorumque memorabilium* 1. 1, ed. C. Kempf (Leipzig, 1888), p. 5, note 9. This passage is the only one in John's treatise that contains complimentary remarks about the Roman Empire; these remarks have no significance in respect of the political hegemony or propriety of the Roman Empire. Later, John repudiates arguments extolling the value of the Roman Empire, and cites Scripture as containing at least the suggestion that God willed its collapse. See Thomas Aquinas, *De regimine principum* 1. 14.

105. This is the first specific reference to the kingdom of France.

106. Caesar, *The Gallic War* 6. 13, ed. and transl. H. J. Edwards (Cambridge, Mass.: Harvard U. Press, 1946). Cf. Thomas Aquinas, *De regimine principum* 1. 14.

107. John introduces a third element for measuring the priority of priesthood and kingship, thus expanding the Victorine frame of reference in a way that makes it possible to disagree most strongly with Hugh. See also chaps. 4 and 5.

108. There are two classes of things about which John raises the issue of papal control: (1) external ecclesiastical goods (*bona exteriora ecclesiastica*)—material possessions belonging to clerics or in some way relating to the material possessions of churches; he also uses the term *temporalia* to designate temporal goods belonging to ecclesiastics or the Church in some way; (2) "the goods of laymen" (*bona laicorum*)—material possessions belonging to laymen. Material goods, then, whether relating to priests or laymen are "external goods." "Internal goods" are spiritual goods.

109. I have not found any instance of a papalist argument employing precisely the terminology *causalitate praecedere*, although the idea is common enough. See chaps. 11 (*arg.* 17, 18, 20, 23, 32); Walter Ullmann, *The Growth of Papal Government in the Middle Ages, a Study in the Ideological Relation of Clerical to Lay Power*, 2d ed. (London: Methuen, 1964), pp. 277–89; 413 ff.

110. John makes use of this concept of private property rights in his rejection of papal authority over temporal goods. See below, this chapter, and chaps. 7 and 12. See also Thomas Aquinas, *Summa theologiae*, 2–2. 66. 2. John's treatment of his problem parallels Godfrey of Fontaines, *Quodlibet* 13. 5, pp. 224–28. There is some question about whether the reference here to the church at Chartres is not in actuality to that of Châlons instead. See Leclercq, *Jean de Paris*, p. 14, note 5.

111. The "right of use" is distinguished from the "right of possession" or dominion: cf. Thomas Aquinas, *Summa theologiae*, 2–2, 66. 2.

112. This notion of proportional right of use related to a person's status is also a common feature of the doctrine of material goods John is presenting. It is often referred to as "distributive justice" to distinguish it from "simple justice." The distinction originated with Aristotle, *Nicomachean Ethics* 5. 5, 1132b21 ff; and was developed by Thomas Aquinas, *Summa theologiae* 2–2, 61. 1–2.

113. This formula is the one John employs to describe most succinctly the character of papal authority in respect of all goods: the pope is "universal dispenser" (*universalis dispensator*). The reference here is only to ecclesiastical goods, spiritual and temporal, but in chapter 7 John extends the notion to cover all goods later.

114. This was the designation—lord (*dominus*)—applied by the papalists to describe the pope's relation to all goods. See Aegidius of Rome, *De ecclesiastica potestate* 2. 4; James of Viterbo, *De regimine christiano* 2. 8; William of Cremona, *Reprobatio errorum*, pp. 18–21.

115. *Decretum* 12, "Augusto sedis," 1. 687. John admits the possibility that the pope may decide to appropriate particular goods to an individual ecclesiastic. But this must be done within the general framework of what the pope may legitimately do with ecclesiastical goods. Thus a limit exists concerning what the pope can do even with respect to ecclesiastical goods, and it is not the pope himself who determines this limit. The only exception Quidort admits to this general principle relates to a case of urgent necessity for the Church, over which the pope is admitted to have ultimate jurisdiction. But even here, properly speaking, such an action falls within the legitimate limits of papal authority, and thus is not a genuine exception. See chap. 7.

116. John does not deny the plenitude of power (*plenitudo potestatis*) to the pope. He interprets it to signify jurisdiction, not dominion, over material goods; and as such it is subject to the conditions of jurisdiction legitimate for a "dispenser" rather than an owner.

117. Augustine, "Epistola 185" 9 (*PL* 33. 809).

118. I Cor. 4:1. John, in the preceding argument, has been following Thomas Aquinas, *Summa theologiae* 2–2. 185. 7–8.

119. Bernard of Clairvaux, *De consideratione* 2. 6. 10, p. 417.

120. "Liber sextus decretalium" 7, "Quoniam aliqui," in *Corpus iuris canonici* 2, 971.

121. Ibid. It is interesting to see John making such extensive use of texts from Pope Nicholas I to support his own position; for Nicholas was one of the strongest advocates of the plenitude of papal power, and texts of his contain some of the most pungent expressions of this claim. See Ullmann, *Papal Government*, pp. 190–209.

122. John's rejection of the papalist claims based on the concept of the pope as *vicarius Christi* begins here. See chap. 1.

123. This distinction between Christ as God and Christ as man as a basis for dismissing the papalist claim is used frequently by John. See chaps. 8, 9. The same position can be found in the anonymous tracts: *Disputatio inter clericum et militem*, pp. 13–14; *Quaestio in utramque partem* 5, p. 104; *Quaestio de potestate papae*, pp. 68–69.

124. The two preceding paragraphs parallel Godfrey of Fontaines, *Quodlibet* 8, pp. 224–25.

125. II Cor. 13:10; II Cor. 10:8.

126. This emphasis on the necessity for the pope to make restitution for any misuse or misappropriation of goods is an important facet of John's position that the pope enjoys no papal authority over material goods. See above and chaps. 7, 12, and Prologue.

127. John discusses the issue of papal deposition at greater length elsewhere (chaps. 22–25).

128. *Decretum* 40, "Si papa suae" 1. 146.

129. *Glossa ordinaria decreti* 40. 6 (Lyon, 1618), p. 194.

130. *Decretum* 21, "Nunc autem" 1. 71. John's final position on this matter is that a general council is not necessary for papal deposition, and that it can be achieved by action of the college of cardinals.

131. The pope cannot act contrary to the law. Neither can a king nor any temporal or ecclesiastical power. This conception of limiting a ruler's authority within the specified limits of the law was commonly mentioned among those medieval political thinkers influenced by Aristotle. See Thomas Aquinas, *In VIII libros politicorum Aristotelis commentarium* 1, 10; Ptolemy of Lucca, *De regimine principum* 3. 20; 4. 1, 18; Aegidius of Rome, *De regimine principum* 3. 2. 2; 2. 1. 14; Engelbert of Admont, *De ortu, progressu et fine romani imperii* 16; Marsilius of Padua, *Defensor pacis* 1. 10. 2; 1. 14. 10; 1. 15. 7; 1. 10. 1. Cf. R. W. and G. J. A. Carlyle, *A History of Mediaeval Political Theory in the West*, 2d ed., vol. 3 (New York: Barnes and Noble, 1936), pp. 30–40; 52–59; 125–46.

132. Rom. 11:29.

133. Gen. 6:7.

134. Ex. 12:36.

135. Job 36:7.

136. For John, neither prince nor pope can infringe upon the right of private property. He does admit, however, that this right is not an absolute one: the rights of the community—the common good— have precedence over the individual's property rights as the "needs of use of the country [*patria*]

require." But this is a specification of the nature of the right of private property, not a rejection of the right itself.

137. In detailing his position concerning circumstances of extreme necessity for the Church, John is consistent in retaining the principle that papal action in such circumstances must conform to specifications relating to the nature of the events themselves, rather than being based on any plentitude of power possessed by the pope for application to material goods.

138. What John understands by ecclesiastical censure (*censura ecclesiastica*) is clarified in chap. 13. For the preceding paragraphs see Godfrey of Fontaines, *Quodlibet* 13. 5, pp. 227–29.

139. John provides for the possibility that the papacy may encourage the free granting of material goods to the pope. The pope cannot require that persons cede things to him; but he can encourage them to do so by granting spiritual benefits (indulgences) to them in return for their material generosity. Later he also contends that it is legitimate for churches to grant the possession of prebends to laymen in return for their generosity to the Church.

CHAPTER 29

Marsilius of Padua

Marsilius of Padua (Marsilio dei Mainardi) was born at Padua sometime between 1275 and 1280. He studied medicine and natural philosophy at the University of Padua, where his father worked as a notary. It was during his term as rector of the University of Paris (December 1312 to March 1313) that he came in contact with such leading "secular Aristotelians" as Peter of Albano and John of Jandun. In 1316 Marsilius was promised a canonry at Padua by Pope John XXII and two years later a benefice. After unsuccessfully dabbling in politics, he returned to Paris, where he became acquainted with and influenced by the Spiritual Franciscan Michael of Cesena, who had defended the doctrine of evangelical poverty. It was during these years at Paris that Marsilius wrote *The Defender of Peace*, which he finished on June 24, 1324. He was forced to flee when his authorship of this work became known in 1326. He found refuge at the court of Louis of Bavaria in Nuremberg, as Louis also was at odds with the pope (see biography of William of Ockham). Thereupon, Pope John branded Marsilius a heretic. He remained under the protection of Louis throughout the remainder of his life, assisting him with various imperial expeditions in Italy. He died in 1342.

Marsilius of Padua and the Defender of Peace

Notwithstanding Christ's injunction that there be separation between church and state; to wit, "Render therefore unto Caesar the things which are Caesar's; and unto God the things that are God's" (Matthew 22:21), the papacy had over the centuries extended its power into secular affairs of state, culminating in the papalist claims to "plentitude of power" rigorously advanced and defended by Pope Innocent IV (1243–54) and others in the thirteenth and fourteenth centuries, most notably, Boniface VIII (1294–1303). (See introduction to John of Paris.)

The Defender of Peace was a successful refutation of the papalist position. There are three main themes of Marsilius' theory of the state. The first is derived from the *Politics* of Aristotle, the main theme of which is that man is a "political animal" and therefore it is his nature to form "political" groups. The polis is such a group, and its end is consistent with the telos of human life, which is happiness.

Marsilius argues that the raison d'être of the state, including government, is the contribution it makes to the rational "fulfillment" of men's natural desire for a "sufficient life". In this regard, the proper function of government is regulatory, with the law providing a standard of justice. The priesthood contributes to the "sufficient life" qua our spiritual needs relative to "the future world" rather than the present one.

The second theme concerns the inevitability of conflicts among men and therefore the need for coercive law and government for the purpose of controlling such conflicts. Without such regulation human society will destroy itself. It is the secular government that holds this coercive authority, not the church. Therefore, the church must be, in the final analysis, subordinate to the state.

The third theme of Marsilius' political theory is that the source of political authority resides in the people. It is they who must make laws either directly or through elected representatives. He has powerful arguments for this view. The thrust of the first argument for republicanism is that the collective will is better than any of its parts. The collective will produces laws and government most supportive of the common good rather than special interests. Second, individual freedom can be achieved only through self-legislation. Third, people will only obey laws and government to which they freely give their assent. Fourth, it is only reasonable that that which affects all ought to be subject to approval by all. This third theme obviously undermines the authority of the church since its source does not reside with the people. There is nothing republican about the church unless one is a member of the Curia. Given these views of law and government, it is perfectly understandable that Pope John XXII branded Marsilius a heretic. It should be observed that Marsilius did not advocate participatory democracy. Such would be a gross misrepresentation of his Aristotelian views.

THE DEFENDER OF PEACE

Discourse One

Chapter II

On the First Questions in This Book, and the Distinction of the Various Meanings of the Term "State"

Entering upon our proposed task, we wish first to show what are the tranquillity and intranquillity of the state or city; and first the tranquillity, for if this be not clear, one is necessarily ignorant also of what is intranquillity. Since, however, both of these seem to be dispositions of the city or state (let this be assumed from Cassiodorus), we shall consequently make clear what must be revealed at the very outset; namely, what is the state or city, and why.

From Marsilius of Padua, *The Defender of Peace*, translated by Alan Gewirth (New York: Columbia University Press, 1956), pp. 8–9, 27–55. Reprinted by permission of Columbia University Press.

Through this, the definitions of tranquillity and of its opposite will be more readily apparent.

2. Following the aforesaid order for the definition of the tranquillity of the city or state, we must notice, in order to prevent ambiguity from entering our project, that the term "state" (*regnum*) has many meanings. In one sense it means a number of cities (*civitatum*) or provinces contained under one regime; in which sense a state does not differ from a city with respect to species of polity but rather with respect to quantity. In another sense the term "state" signifies a certain species of temperate polity or regime, which Aristotle calls "temperate monarchy";[1] in this sense a state may consist in a single city as well as in many cities, as was the case around the time of the rise of civil communities, for then there was usually one king in a single

city. The third and most familiar sense of this term is a combination of the first and the second. In its fourth sense it means something common to every species of temperate regime, whether in a single city or in many; it was in this sense that Cassiodorus used it in the passage we quoted at the beginning of this book, and this, too, is the sense in which we shall use the term in our discussions of the matters under inquiry.[2]

3. Now we must define tranquillity and its opposite. Let us assume with Aristotle in his *Politics*, Book I, Chapter 2, and Book V, Chapter 3, that the state is like an animate nature or animal.[3] For just as an animal well disposed in accordance with nature is composed of certain proportioned parts ordered to one another and communicating their functions mutually and for the whole, so too the state is constituted of certain such parts when it is well disposed and established in accordance with reason. The relation, therefore, of the state and its parts to tranquillity will be seen to be similar to the relation of the animal and its parts to health. The trustworthiness of this inference we can accept from what all men comprehend about each of these relations. For they think that health is the best disposition of an animal in accordance with nature, and likewise that tranquillity is the best disposition of a state established in accordance with reason. Health, moreover, as the more experienced physicists describe it, is the good disposition of the animal whereby each of its parts can perfectly perform the operations belonging to its nature; according to which analogy tranquillity will be the good disposition of the city or state whereby each of its parts will be able perfectly to perform the operations belonging to it in accordance with reason and its establishment. And since a good definition consignifies contraries, intranquillity will be the diseased disposition of the city or state, like the illness of an animal, whereby all or some of its parts are impeded from performing the operations belonging to

them, either entirely or to the extent required for complete functioning.

In this analogical way, then, we have defined tranquillity and its opposite, intranquillity.

Chapter VIII

On the Genera of Polities or Regimes, the Temperate and the Diseased, and the Division of Their Species

We must now show with greater certainty what was already shown to some extent above, that the establishment and differentiation of the parts of the state are brought about by an efficient cause which we have previously called the legislator. The same legislator establishes these parts, and differentiates and separates them as nature does with an animal, by first forming or establishing in the state one part which in Chapter V of this discourse we called the ruling or judicial part, and through this the other parts, as will be indicated more fully in Chapter XV of this discourse. Hence we must first say something concerning the nature of this ruling part. For since it is the first part of the state, as will appear below, the appropriate procedure will be to go from the indication of its efficient cause to the indication of the efficient cause which establishes and differentiates the other parts of the state.

2. There are two genera of ruling parts or governments, one well tempered, the other diseased. With Aristotle in the *Politics*, Book III, Chapter 5,[4] I call that genus "well tempered" in which the ruler governs for the common benefit, in accordance with the will of the subjects; while the "diseased" genus is that which is deficient in this respect.[5] Each of these genera, again, is divided into three species: the temperate into kingly monarchy, aristocracy, and polity; the diseased into the three opposite species of tyrannical monarchy, oligarchy, and democracy. And each of these again has sub-

species, the detailed discussion of which is not part of our present task. For Aristotle gave a sufficient account of them in Books III and IV of his *Politics*.

3. To obtain a fuller conception of these species of government, which is necessary for the clear understanding of what follows, let us define each species in accordance with the view of Aristotle. A *kingly monarchy*, then, is a temperate government wherein the ruler is a single man who rules for the common benefit, and in accordance with the will or consent of the subjects. *Tyranny*, its opposite, is a diseased government wherein the ruler is a single man who rules for his own private benefit apart from the will of his subjects. *Aristocracy* is a temperate government in which the honorable class (*honorabilitas*) alone rules in accordance with the will or consent of the subjects and for the common benefit. *Oligarchy*, its opposite, is a diseased government in which some of the wealthier or more powerful rule for their own benefit apart from the will of the subjects. A *polity*, although in one sense it is something common to every genus or species of regime or government, means in another sense a certain species of temperate government, in which every citizen participates in some way in the government or in the deliberative function in turn according to his rank and ability or condition, for the common benefit and with the will or consent of the citizens. *Democracy*, its opposite, is a government in which the masses (*vulgus*) or the multitude of the needy establish the government and rule alone, apart from the will or consent of the other citizens and not entirely for the common benefit according to proper proportion.

4. As to which of the temperate governments is best or which of the diseased governments is worst, and the relative goodness or badness of the other species, the discussion of these points is not part of our present concern.[6] Let it suffice to have said this much about the division of governments into their species and the definition of each.

Chapter IX

On the Methods of Establishing a Kingly Monarchy, and Which Method Is the More Perfect; Also on the Methods of Establishing the Other Kinds of Regime or Polity, Both Temperate and Diseased

Having determined these points, we must now discuss the methods of effecting or establishing the ruling part of the state. For from the better or worse nature of these methods, viewed as actions emerging from that nature to the civil regime, we must infer the efficient cause by which these methods and the ruling part established by them will emerge more advantageously to the polity.

2. In this book we are considering the causes and actions by which the ruling part must in most cases be established. First, however, we wish to indicate the method and cause by which this part has been established in the past, although rarely, in order to distinguish this method or action, and its immediate cause, from those by which the government must regularly and in most cases be established, and which we can prove by human demonstration. For of the former method no certain comprehension can be had through demonstration. This method or action, with its immediate cause, by which the ruling part and other parts of the state, especially the priesthood, were formed in the past, was the divine will commanding this either through the determinate oracle of some individual creature or else perhaps immediately through itself alone. It was by this method that the divine will established the government of the people of Israel in the person of Moses and of certain other judges after him, and also the priesthood in the person of Aaron and his successors. With respect to this cause and its free action, as to why it did or did not operate in one way or another, we can say nothing through demonstration, but we hold it by simple belief apart from reason. There is, however, another method of establishing governments which proceeds immediately from the human mind, although perhaps remotely from God as remote

cause, who grants all earthly rulership, as is said in the nineteenth chapter of John,[7] and as the Apostle clearly states in the thirteenth chapter of the epistle to the Romans,[8] and St. Augustine in *The City of God*, Book V, Chapter 21.[9] However, God does not always act immediately; indeed in most cases, nearly everywhere, he establishes governments by means of human minds, to which he has granted the discretionary will for such establishment. And as for this latter cause, what it is, and by what kind of action it must establish such things, this can be indicated with human certainty from what is better or worse for the polity.

3. Omitting, then, that method of which we cannot attain certain knowledge through demonstration, we wish first to present those methods of establishing governments which are effected immediately by the human will;[10] next we shall show which of these is the more certain and the simpler.[11] Then, from the better nature of that method we shall infer the efficient cause from which alone it must and can emerge. From these points, consequently, will appear the cause which must move to the best establishment and determination of the other parts of the state. Finally we shall discuss the unity of the government, through which it will also be apparent what is the unity of the city or state.

4. In pursuit of this program, then, we shall first enumerate the methods of establishing kingly monarchy, by speaking of their origins. For this species of government seems rather kindred to us, and directly connected with the rule of the family, as is clear from what we said in Chapter III. After the determination of this point, the methods of establishing the other divisions of government will be made clear.

There are five methods of establishing kingly monarchies, according to Aristotle's *Politics*, Book III, Chapter 8.[12] One is when the monarch is appointed for one determinate function with respect to the ruling of the community, such as the leadership of the army, either with hereditary succession or for his own lifetime only. It was by

this method that Agamemnon was made leader of the army by the Greeks. In modern communities this office is called the captaincy or constabulary.[13] This leader of the army had no judicial power in time of peace, but when the army was fighting a war he had the supreme authority to kill or otherwise punish transgressors.

Another method is that whereby certain monarchs rule in Asia; they receive their dominating authority through hereditary succession, and while they rule according to law, this law is like that of despots, being for the monarch's benefit rather than completely for the community's. The inhabitants of that region endure such rule "without protest,"[14] because of their barbaric and slavish nature and the influence of custom. This rule is kingly in that it is native to the country and is over voluntary subjects, because, for example, the monarch's ancestors had been the first inhabitants of the region. But it is also in a sense tyrannical, in that its laws are not completely for the common benefit but for that of the monarch.

A third method of kingly government is when the ruler receives his authority through election rather than hereditary succession, but governs according to a law which is not completely for the common benefit but rather for that of the monarch, like the law of tyrants. Aristotle, therefore, called this species of government an "elective tyranny,"[15] a tyranny because the law was despotic, and elective because it was not over involuntary subjects.

A fourth method is that whereby a ruler is elected with subsequent hereditary succession, and governs according to laws which are completely for the common benefit; this method was used "in heroic days,"[16] as Aristotle says in the chapter previously mentioned. Those days were called "heroic" either because the stars then produced men who were believed to be "heroes," that is, divine, on account of their exceeding virtue; or because such men and not others were named rulers on account of their exceeding virtues and beneficial deeds, in that they brought together a scattered multitude and assembled it into a civil community, or they freed the region of oppressors by fighting and strength of arms, or perhaps they bought the region or acquired it by some other appropriate method and divided it among the subjects. At any rate these men were made rulers with subsequent hereditary succession, because of their bestowal of great benefits or their excess of virtue over the rest of the multitude, as Aristotle also said in the *Politics*, Book V, Chapter 5.[17] Under this species of monarchy, Aristotle perhaps included that in which someone is elected only for his own lifetime or a part of his lifetime; or else he designated it through the combination of this fourth species and the one called elective tyranny, because it shares features of both.

There is and was a fifth method of kingly monarchy, whereby the ruler is made lord (*dominus*) over everything in the community, disposing of things and persons according to his own will, just as the head of a family disposes at will of everything in his own household.[18]

5. To make clearer these concepts of Aristotle, and to summarize all the methods of establishing the other kinds of government, we shall say that every government is over either voluntary or involuntary subjects. The first is the genus of well-tempered governments, the second of diseased governments. Each of these genera is divided into three species or kinds, as was said in Chapter VIII. And since one of the species of well-tempered government, and perhaps of the more perfect, is kingly monarchy, let us resume our previous statements about its various kinds or methods, by saying that the king or monarch either is named by the election of the inhabitants or citizens, or duly obtains the rulership without their election. If without the election of the citizens, this is either because he or his ancestors first inhabited the region, or because he bought the land and jurisdiction, or acquired it by a just war or by some other lawful method, such as by gift made to him for some great service. Each of these

kinds of monarchy participates so much the more in true kingship, the more it is over voluntary subjects and according to law made for the common benefit of the subjects; and it savors so much the more of tyranny the more it departs from these features, that is, the consent of the subjects and law established for their common benefit. Hence it is written in the *Politics*, Book IV, Chapter 8: "These," that is, monarchies, "were kingly because they were according to law, and ruled voluntary subjects; but they were tyrannical because they ruled despotically and in accordance with their," that is, the monarchs', "own judgment."[19] These two features, then, distinguish temperate from diseased government, as is apparent from the clear statement of Aristotle, but absolutely or in greater degree it is the consent of the subjects which is the distinguishing criterion. Now if the ruling monarch is elected by the inhabitants, it is either with all his posterity succeeding him or not. If the latter, this may be in several ways, as he is named either for his own lifetime alone, or for his own lifetime and that of one or more of his successors, or not for the whole lifetime either of himself or of any of his successors but only for some determinate period, such as one or two years, more or less. Again, he is named to exercise either every judicial office, or only one office such as leading the army.

6. The elected and the non-elected kingly monarchs agree in that each rules voluntary subjects. They differ, however, in that the non-elected kings rule less voluntary subjects, and by laws which are less politic for the common benefit, as we said before in the case of the barbarians. The elected kings, on the other hand, rule more voluntary subjects, and by laws which are more politic, in that they are made for the common benefit, as we have said.

7. From these considerations it is clear, and will be even more apparent in the sequel, that the elected kind of government is superior to the non-elected. This is also the view of Aristotle in that passage of the *Politics*, Book III, Chapter 8, which we cited above with reference to those who were

made rulers in the heroic days.[20] Again, this method of establishing governments is more permanent in perfect communities. For at some time or other it becomes necessary to have recourse to this form among all the other methods of establishing governments, but not conversely. For example, if hereditary succession fails, or if for some reason the multitude cannot bear the excessive malice of that family's rule, they must then turn to the method of election, which can never fail so long as the generation of men does not fail. Moreover, by the method of election alone is the best ruler obtained. For it is expedient that the ruler be the best man in the polity, since he must regulate the civil acts of all the rest.[21]

8. The method of establishing the other species of temperate government is usually election; in some cases the ruler is chosen by lot,[22] without subsequent hereditary succession. Diseased governments, on the other hand, are usually established by fraud or force or both.[23]

9. Which of the temperate governments is better, monarchy, or one of the other two species, aristocracy or polity; and again, which of the monarchies is better, the elected or the non-elected; and moreover, which of the elected monarchies, that established with hereditary succession ensuing or that in which one man alone is named without such succession; which in turn is divided into the further alternatives of whether it is better to name the ruler for a whole lifetime, either of himself alone or of some of his successors also, or only for some determinate period, such as one or two years, more or less—in all these questions there is room for inquiry and reasonable doubt. It must be held without doubt, however, in accordance with the truth and the manifest view of Aristotle, that election is the more certain standard of government, as will be more fully shown in Chapters XII, XVI, and XVII of this discourse.

10. We must not overlook, however, that different multitudes in different times and places are inclined toward different kinds of polity and government, as Aristotle says in the *Politics*, Book III, Chapter 9.[24] Legislators

and institutors of governments must hearken to this fact. For just as not every man is inclined toward the best discipline or study, whereupon it is appropriate that he be directed toward the acquisition not of that discipline but of some other good one for which he is more fitted, so too a multitude in some time or place may perhaps not be inclined to accept the best kind of government, and therefore recourse must first be had to that kind of temperate government which is more appropriate to it. For example, before the monarchy of Julius Caesar, the Roman people were for a long time unwilling to accept any definite monarch, either with hereditary succession or even one who was named only for his own lifetime. The reason for this was perhaps that there was a large number of heroic men worthy of rulership among them, both families and individuals.

11. From these conclusions, then, it emerges clearly that those who ask which monarch is better for a city or state, the one who rules through election or the one who rules through hereditary succession, do not put the question in the proper way. What they must correctly ask first is, which monarch is better, the elected or the non-elected. And if the elected, again which, the one who is named with hereditary succession ensuing or the one who is named without hereditary succession. For although a non-elected monarch almost always transmits the rulership to his heir, not every elected monarch does so, but only the one who is named to rule with hereditary succession ensuing.

Let these, then, be our conclusions about the methods of establishing governments, and that the absolutely better method is election.

Chapter X

On the Distinction of the Meanings of the Term "Law," and on the Meaning Which Is Most Proper and Intended by Us

Since we have said that election is the more perfect and better method of establishing governments, we shall do well to inquire as to its efficient cause, wherefrom it has to emerge in its full value; for from this will appear the cause not only of the elected government but also of the other parts of the polity. Now a government has to regulate civil human acts (as we demonstrated in Chapter V of this discourse), and according to a standard (*regulam*) which is and ought to be the form of the ruler, as such. We much, consequently, inquire into this standard, as to whether it exists, what it is, and why. For the efficient cause of this standard is perhaps the same as that of the ruler.

2. The existence of this standard, which is called a "statute" or "custom" and by the common term "law," we assume as almost self-evident by induction in all perfect communities. We shall show first, then, what law is; next we shall indicate its final cause or necessity; and finally we shall demonstrate by what person or persons and by what kind of action the law should be established; which will be to inquire into its legislator or efficient cause, to whom we think it also pertains to elect the government, as we shall show subsequently by demonstration. From these points there will also appear the matter or subject of the aforesaid standard which we have called law. For this matter is the ruling part, whose function it is to regulate the political or civil acts of men according to the law.

3. Following this procedure, then, we must first distinguish the meanings or intentions of this term "law," in order that its many senses may not lead to confusion. For in one sense it means a natural sensitive inclination toward some action or passion. This is the way the Apostle used it when he said in the seventh chapter of the epistle to the Romans: "I see another law in my members, fighting against the law of my mind."[25] In another sense this term "law" means any productive habit and in general every form, existing in the mind, of a producible thing, from which as from an exemplar or measure there emerge the forms of things made by art. This is the way in which the term was used in the forty-third

chapter of Ezekiel: "This is the law of the house. . . . And these are the measurements of the altar."[26] In a third sense "law" means the standard containing admonitions for voluntary human acts according as these are ordered toward glory or punishment in the future world. In this sense the Mosaic law was in part called a law, just as the evangelical law in its entirety is called a law. Hence the Apostle said of these in his epistle to the Hebrews: "Since the priesthood has been changed, it is necessary that there be a change of the law also."[27] In this sense "law" was also used for the evangelic discipline in the first chapter of James: "He who has looked into the perfect law of liberty, and has continued therein . . . this man shall be blessed in his deeds."[28] In this sense of the term law all religions, such as that of Mohammed or of the Persians, are called laws in whole or in part, although among these only the Mosaic and the evangelic, that is, the Christian, contain the truth. So too Aristotle called religions "laws" when he said, in the second book of his *Philosophy*: "The laws show how great is the power of custom";[29] and also in the twelfth book of the same work: "The other doctrines were added as myths to persuade men to obey the laws, and for the sake of expediency."[30] In its fourth and most familiar sense, this term "law" means the science of doctrine or universal judgment of matters of civil justice and benefit, and of their opposites.

4. Taken in this last sense, law may be considered in two ways. In one way it may be considered in itself, as it only shows what is just or unjust, beneficial or harmful; and as such it is called the science or doctrine of right (*juris*). In another way it may be considered according as with regard to its observance there is given a command coercive through punishment or reward to be distributed in the present world, or according as it is handed down by way of such a command; and considered in this way it most properly is called, and is, a law.[31] It was in this sense that Aristotle also defined it in the last book of the *Ethics*, Chapter 8, when he said: "Law has coercive

force, for it is discourse emerging from prudence and understanding."[32] Law, then, is a "discourse" or statement "emerging from prudence and" political "understanding," that is, it is an ordinance made by political prudence, concerning matters of justice and benefit and their opposites, and having "coercive force," that is, concerning whose observance there is given a command which one is compelled to observe, or which is made by way of such a command.

5. Hence not all true cognitions of matters of civil justice and benefit are laws unless a coercive command has been given concerning their observance, or they have been made by way of a command, although such true cognition is necessarily required for a perfect law. Indeed, sometimes false cognitions of the just and the beneficial become laws, when there is given a command to observe them, or they are made by way of a command. An example of this is found in the regions of certain barbarians, who cause it to be observed as just that a murderer be absolved of civil guilt and punishment on payment of a fine. This, however, is absolutely unjust, and consequently the laws of such barbarians are not absolutely perfect. For although they have the proper form, that is, a coercive command of observance, they lack a proper condition, that is, the proper and true ordering of justice.

6. Under this sense of law are included all standards of civil justice and benefit established by human authority, such as customs, statutes, plebiscites, decretals,[33] and all similar rules which are based upon human authority as we have said.

7. We must not overlook, however, that both the evangelical law and the Mosaic, and perhaps the other religions as well, may be considered and compared in different ways in whole or in part, in relation to human acts for the status of the present or the future world. For they sometimes come, or have hitherto come, or will come, under the third sense of law, and sometimes under the last, as will be shown more fully in Chapters VIII and IX of Discourse II. Moreover, some of these laws are true,

while others are false fancies and empty promises.

It is now clear, then, that there exists a standard or law of human civil acts, and what this is.

Chapter XI

On the Necessity for Making Laws (Taken in Their Most Proper Sense); and That No Ruler, However Virtuous or Just, Should Rule Without Laws

Having thus distinguished these various meanings of "law," we wish to show the end or necessity of law in its last and most proper sense. The principal end is civil justice and the common benefit; the secondary end is the security of rulers, especially those with hereditary succession, and the long duration of governments. The primary necessity of the law, then, is as follows: It is necessary to establish in the polity that without which civil judgments cannot be made with complete rightness, and through which these judgments are properly made and preserved from defect so far as it is humanly possible. Such a thing is the law, when the ruler is directed to make civil judgments in accordance with it. Therefore, the establishment of law is necessary in the polity. The major premise of this demonstration is almost self-evident, and is very close to being indemonstrable. Its certainty can and should be grasped from Chapter V, paragraph 7 of this discourse. The minor premise will now be proved in this way: To make a good judgment, there are required a right emotion of the judges and a true knowledge of the matters to be judged; the opposites of which corrupt civil judgments. For if the judge has a perverted emotion, such as hate, love, or avarice, this perverts his desire. But such emotions are kept away from the judgment, and it is preserved from them, when the judge or ruler is directed to make judgments according to the laws, because the law lacks all perverted emotion; for it is not made useful for friend or harmful for foe, but universally for all those who perform civil acts well or badly. For all other things are accidental to the law and are outside it; but they are not similarly outside the judge. Persons involved in a judgment can be friendly or inimical to the judge, helpful or harmful to him, by making him a gift or a promise; and in other ways too they can arouse in the judge a desire which perverts his judgment. Consequently, no judgment, so far as possible, should be entrusted to the discretion of the judge, but rather is should be determined by law and pronounced in accordance with it.

2. This was also the view of the divine Aristotle in the *Politics*, Book III, Chapter 9, where he asks whether it is better for a polity to be ruled by the best man without law or by the best laws; and he replies as follows: "That is better," that is, superior for judging, "which entirely lacks the passionate factor," that is, the emotion which may pervert the judgment , "than that to which passion is natural. But law does not have this," that is, passion or emotion, "while every human soul must necessarily have it";[34] and he said "every," not excepting anyone, however virtuous. He repeats this view in the *Rhetoric*, Book I, Chapter 1: "Most of all" is this required, that is, that nothing be left to the discretion of the judge, to be judged apart from the law, "because the judgment of the legislator," that is, the law, "is not partial," that is, it is not made on account of some one particular man, "but is concerned with future and universal matters. Now the judge and the magistrate judge about present and determinate matters, with which love and hate and private benefit are often involved, so that they cannot sufficiently see the truth, but instead have regard in their judgments to their own private pleasure and displeasure."[35] He also makes this point in Book I, Chapter 2, of the same treatise: "We do not render the same judgments when we are pleased as when we are pained, when we love as when we hate."[36]

3. A judgment is also currupted through the ignorance of the judges even if they be of good emotion or intention. This sin or

defect is removed and remedied by the law, for in the law is determined well-nigh perfectly what is just or unjust, beneficial or harmful, with regard to each human civil act. Such determination cannot be made so adequately by any one man, however intelligent he may be. For no single man, and perhaps not even all the men of one era, could investigate or remember all the civil acts determined in the law; indeed, what was said about them by the first investigators and also by all the men of the same era who observed such acts was meager and imperfect, and attained its completion only subsequently through the additions made by later investigators. This can be sufficiently seen from experience, in the additions, subtractions, and complete changes sometimes made in the laws in different eras, or at different times within the same era.

Aristotle also attests to this in the *Politics*, Book II, Chapter 2, when he says: "We must not ignore that attention must be paid to the long time and many years of the past, in which it would not have remained unknown if these things were good,"[37] that is, the measures which are to be established as laws. He says the same thing in the *Rhetoric*, Book I, Chapter 1: "Laws are made after long study."[38] This is also confirmed by reason, since the making of laws requires prudence, as we saw above from the definition of law, and prudence requires long experience, which, in turn, requires much time. hence it is said in the sixth book of the *Ethics*: "A sign of what has been said is that while youths may become geometers, and be learned and wise in such sciences, they do not seem to become prudent. The cause is that prudence is of singular things which become known through experience; but a youth is not experienced, for experience requires a long time."[39] Consequently, what one man alone can discover or know by himself, both in the science of civil justice and benefit and in the other sciences, is little or nothing. Moreover, what is observed by the men of one era is quite imperfect by comparison with what is observed in many eras, so that Aristotle, discussing the discovery of truth in every art and discipline, wrote as follows in the *Philosophy*, Book II, Chapter 1: "One man," that is, one discoverer of any art or discipline "contributes to it," that is, discovers about it by himself alone, "little or nothing, but by the contributions of all a great deal is accomplished."[40] This passage is clearer in the translation from the Arabic, in which it reads as follows: "Each of them," that is, each of the discoverers of any art or discipline, "comprehends little or nothing about the truth. But when a collection is made from among all who have achieved some comprehension, what is collected will be of considerable quantity." This may especially be seen in the case of astrology.[41]

It is in this way, then, by men's mutual help and the addition of later to earlier discoveries, that all arts and disciplines have been perfected. Aristotle indicated this figuratively with regard to the discovery of music in the same place cited above, when he said: "If there had been no Timotheus, we should be lacking much melody; but if there had been no Phrynes, there would have been no Timotheus";[42] that is, Timotheus would not have been so accomplished in melody if he had not had the melodies previously discovered by Phrynes. Averröes expounds these words as follows in the second book of his *Commentary*: "And what he," that is, Aristotle, "says in this chapter is clear. For no one can discover by himself the larger part of the practical or considerative," that is, theoretic, "sciences, because these are completed only through the assistance which an earlier investigator gives to the one following him."[43] And Aristotle says the same thing in the second book of the *Refutations*, last chapter,[44] concerning the discovery of rhetoric and of all other disciplines, whatever the case may have been with regard to the discovery of logic, whose complete development he ascribed to himself alone without the discovery or assistance of any predecessor; in which he seems to have been unique among men. He also makes the same point in the *Ethics*, Book VIII, Chapter 1: "Two persons are better able to act and

to understand"[45] (supply: than one alone). But if two, then more than two, both simultaneously and successively, can do more than one man alone. And this is what Aristotle says with regard to our present subject in the *Politics*, Book III, Chapter 9: "It will appear most unreasonable if one man should perceive better, judging with only two eyes and two ears and acting with only two hands and feet, than many persons with many such organs."[46]

Since, then, the law is an eye composed of many eyes, that is, the considered comprehension of many comprehenders for avoiding error in civil judgments and for judging rightly, it is safer that these judgments be made according to law than according to the discretion of the judge. For this reason it is necessary to establish the law, if polities are to be ordered for the best with regard to their civil justice and benefit; for through the law, civil judgments are preserved from the ignorance and perverted emotion of the judges. This was the minor premise of the demonstration by which we have tried from the beginning of this chapter to prove the necessity of the laws. As to the method by which a dispute or civil lawsuit is to be decided or judged when it is not determined by law, this will be discussed in Chapter XIV of this discourse. Laws, therefore, are necessary in order to exclude malice and error from the civil judgments or sentences of the judges.

4. For these reasons, Aristotle counseled that no judge or ruler should be granted the discretionary power to give judgments or commands without law, concerning those civil affairs which could be determined by law. Hence he said in the *Ethics*, Book IV, Chapter 5, the treatise on justice: "We must not allow man to rule, but" in accordance with "reason,"[47] that is, law; and Aristotle indicated the cause which we pointed out above, the perverted emotion which can be had by man. In the *Politics*, Book III, Chapter 6, he said: "The first question shows plainly above all that laws rightly made should govern,"[48] that is, that rulers should govern in accordance with laws. Again in the same treatise, Book III, Chapter 9, he

said: "He who orders the mind to rule seems thereby to order God and the laws to rule; but he who orders man to rule," that is, without law, according to his own discretion, "instigates a beast";[49] and shortly thereafter he indicated the ground for this: "Hence the law is reason without desire,"[50] as if to say that the law is reason or knowledge without emotion. He repeated this view also in the *Rhetoric*, Book I, Chapter 1: "It is best, therefore, for rightly made laws to determine as many matters as possible and to entrust as little as possible to the judges";[51] giving the reasons adduced above, the exclusion from civil judgments of the judges' malice and ignorance, which cannot arise in the law as they do in the judge, as we have shown above. And even more clearly Aristotle says in the *Politics*, Book IV, Chapter 4: "Where the laws do not govern," that is, where rulers do not govern in accordance with the laws, "there is no polity," that is, none which is temperate. "For the law should govern all things."[52]

5. It still remains to show another reason why all rulers should govern according to law and not without it, and especially those monarchs who rule with hereditary succession: namely, in order that their governments may be more secure and longer lasting. This was the second reason for the necessity of laws which we indicated at the beginning of this chapter. For when rulers govern according to law, their judgments are preserved from the defect which is caused by ignorance and perverted emotion. Hence the rulers are regulated both in themselves and in relation to their citizen subjects, and they suffer less from sedition and from the consequent destruction of their governments which they would incur if they acted badly according to their own discretion, as Aristotle clearly says in the *Politics*, Book V, Chapter 5: "For a kingdom is destroyed least of all by external forces: its destruction most usually comes from within itself. It is destroyed in two ways: one is when those who share the ruling power quarrel among themselves, the other is when they try to govern tyranni-

cally, by controlling more things, and contrary to the law. Kingdoms no longer occur these days, but if monarchies occur, they are rather tyrannies."[53]

6. Someone will raise an objection about the best man, who lacks ignorance and perverted emotion.[54] As for us, however, we reply that such a man happens very rarely, and that even when he does he is not equal in virtue to the law, as we proved above from Aristotle, from reason, and from sense experience. For every soul sometimes has a vicious emotion. We can readily prove this through the thirteenth chapter of Daniel; for it is there written that "two elders came full of wicked device against Susanna, to put her to death."[55] Now these were old men and priests and judges of the people that year: nevertheless they bore false witness against her because she would not acquiesce to their vicious lust. If, then, old priests, about whom it would least be expected, were corrupted by carnal lust, what should be thought of other men, and how much more will they be corrupted by avarice and other vicious emotions? Certainly no one, however vituous, can be so lacking in perverted passion and ignorance as is the law. Therefore, it is safer that civil judgments be regulated by the law than that they be entrusted to the discretion of a judge, however virtuous he may be.

7. Let us assume, however, although it is most rare or impossible, that there is some ruler so heroic that in him neither passion nor ignorance finds a place. What shall we say of his sons, who are unlike him and who, ruling in accordance with their own discretion, will commit excesses which result in their being deprived of the ruleship? Someone may say that the father, who is the best of men, will not hand over the government to such sons. This reply, however, is not to be granted, for two reasons: first, because it is not in the father's power to deprive his sons of the succession, since the rulership is a hereditary possession of his family, and second, because even if it were in the father's power to transfer the rulership to whomever he wanted, he would not deprive his sons of it no matter how vicious

they were. Hence, Aristotle answers this objection as follows in the *Politics*, Book III, Chapter 9: "It is difficult to believe this," that is, that the father will deprive his sons of the rulership, "as it would require a greater virtue than human nature is capable of."[56] For this reason it is more expedient for rulers that they be regulated and limited by law, than that they make civil judgments according to their own discretion. For when they act according to law, they will do nothing vicious or reprehensible, so that their rule will be made secure and longer lasting.

8. This was the counsel which the distinguished Aristotle gave to all rulers, but to which they pay little heed. As he said in the *Politics*, Book V, Chapter 6: "The fewer things the rulers control," that is, without law, "the longer must every government endure, for they," that is, the rulers, "become less despotic, they are more moderate in their ways and are less hated by their subjects."[57] And then Aristotle adduces the testimony of a certain very prudent king called Theopompus, who gave up some of the power which had been granted to him. We have thought it appropriate to quote Aristotle's words here because of this ruler's uniqueness and his outstanding virtue, almost unheard of in anyone else throughout the ages. This is what Aristotle said: "Theopompus exercised moderation," that is, he lessened his power, which may perhaps have seemed excessive, "among other ways by establishing the office of the ephors: for by diminishing his power he increased his kingdom in time," that is, he made it more durable; "hence in a way he made it not smaller but greater. When his wife asked him whether he was not ashamed to give his children a smaller kingdom than he had received from his father, he replied, 'Not at all, for the power I give to them will be more lasting.' "[58] O heroic voice, proceeding from Theopompus' unheard-of prudence, a voice which should be heeded by all those who wish to wield plenitude of power over their subjects apart from laws! Many rulers, not heeding this voice, have been destroyed.

And we ourselves have seen that from lack of attention to this voice not the least of kingdoms in modern times almost underwent a revolution, when its ruler wished to impose upon his subjects an unusual and illegal tax.[59]

It is clear, then, from what we have said, that laws are necessary in polities if they are to be ordered with entire rightness and their governments are to be longer lasting.

Chapter XII

On the Demonstrable Efficient Cause of Human Laws, and Also on That Cause Which Cannot Be Proved by Demonstration: Which is to Inquire into the Legislator. Whence It Appears also That Whatever It Established by Election Derives Its Authority From Election Alone Apart from Any Other Confirmation

We must next discuss that efficient cause of the laws which is capable of demonstration. For I do not intend to deal here with that method of establishing laws which can be effected by the immediate act or oracle of God apart from the human will, or which has been so effected in the past. It was by this latter method, as we have said, that the Mosaic law was established;[60] but I shall not deal with it here even insofar as it contains commands with regard to civil acts for the status of the present world. I shall discuss the establishment of only those laws and governments which emerge immediately from the decision of the human mind.

2. Let us say, to begin with, that it can pertain to any citizen to discover the law taken materially and in its third sense, as the science of civil justice and benefit.[61] Such inquiry, however, can be carried on more appropriately and be completed better by those men who are able to have leisure, who are older and experienced in practical affairs, and who are called "prudent men,"[62] than by the mechanics who must bend all their efforts to acquiring the necessities of life. But it must be remembered that the true knowledge or discovery

of the just and the beneficial, and of their opposites, is not law taken in its last and most proper sense, whereby it is the measure of human civil acts, unless there is given a coercive command as to its observance, or it is made by way of such a command, by someone through whose authority its transgressors must and can be punished.[63] Hence, we must now say to whom belongs the authority to make such a command and to punish its transgressors. This, indeed, is to inquire into the legislator or the maker of the law.

3. Let us say, then, in accordance with the truth and the counsel of Aristotle in the *Politics*, Book III, Chapter 6,[64] that the legislator, or the primary and proper efficient cause of the law, is the people or the whole body of citizens, or the weightier part thereof, through its election or will expressed by words in the general assembly of the citizens, commanding or determining that something be done or omitted with regard to human civil acts, under a temporal pain or punishment. By the "weightier part" I mean to take into consideration the quantity and the quality of the persons in that community over which the law is made.[65] The aforesaid whole body of citizens or the weightier part thereof is the legislator regardless of whether it makes the law directly by itself or entrusts the making of it to some person or persons, who are not and cannot be the legislator in the absolute sense, but only in a relative sense and for a particular time and in accordance with the authority of the primary legislator. And I say further that the laws and anything else established through election must receive their necessary approval by that same primary authority and no other, whatever be the case with regard to certain ceremonies or solemnities, which are required not for the being of the matters elected but for their well-being, since the election would be no less valid even if these ceremonies were not performed. Moreover, by the same authority must the laws and other things established through election undergo addition, subtraction, complete change, interpretation, or suspension,

insofar as the exigencies of time or place or other circumstances make any such action opportune for the common benefit. And by the same authority, also, must the laws be promulgated or proclaimed after their enactment, so that no citizen or alien who is delinquent in observing them may be excused because of ignorance.

4. A citizen I define in accordance with Aristotle in the *Politics*, Book III, Chapters 1, 3, and 7, as one who participates in the civil community in the government or the deliberative or judicial fuction according to his rank.[66] By this definition, children, slaves, aliens, and women are distinguished from citizens, although in different ways. For the sons of citizens are citizens in proximate potentiality, lacking only in years. The weightier part of the citizens should be viewed in accordance with the honorable custom of polities, or else it should be determined in accordance with the doctrine of Aristotle in the *Politics*, Book VI, Chapter 2.[67]

5. Having thus defined the citizen and the weightier part of the citizens, let us return to our proposed objective, namely, to demonstrate that the human authority to make laws belongs only to the whole body of the citizens or to the weightier part thereof. Our first proof is as follows. The absolutely primary human authority to make or establish human laws belongs only to those men from whom alone the best laws can emerge. But these are the whole body of the citizens, or the weightier part thereof, which represents that whole body; since it is difficult or impossible for all persons to agree upon one decision, because some men have a deformed nature, disagreeing with the common decision through singular malice or ignorance. The common benefit should not, however, be impeded or neglected because of the unreasonable protest or opposition of these men. The authority to make or establish laws, therefore, belongs only to the whole body of the citizens or to the weightier part thereof.

The first proposition of this demonstration is very close to self-evident, although its force and its ultimate certainty can be grasped from Chapter V of this discourse. The second proposition, that the best law is made only through the hearing and command of the entire multitude, I prove by assuming with Aristotle in the *Politics*, Book III, Chapter 7, that the best law is that which is made for the common benefit of the citizens. As Aristotle said: "That is presumably right," that is, in the laws, "which is for the common benefit of the state and the citizens."[68] But that this is best achieved only by the whole body of the citizens or by the weightier part thereof, which is assumed to be the same thing, I show as follows: That at which the entire body of the citizens aims intellectually and emotionally is more certainly judged as to its truth and more diligently noted as to its common utility. For a defect in some proposed law can be better noted by the greater number than by any part thereof, since every whole, or at least every corporeal whole, is greater in mass and in virtue than any part of it taken separately. Moreover, the common utility of a law is better noted by the entire multitude, because no one knowingly harms himself. Anyone can look to see whether a proposed law leans toward the benefit of one or a few persons more than of the others or of the community, and can protest against it. Such, however, would not be the case were the law made by one or a few persons, considering their own private benefit rather than that of the community. This position is also supported by the arguments which we advanced in Chapter XI of this discourse with regard to the necessity of having laws.

6. Another argument to the principal conclusion is as follows. The authority to make the law belongs only to those men whose making of it will cause the law to be better observed or observed at all. Only the whole body of the citizens are such men. To them, therefore, belongs the authority to make the law. The first proposition of this demonstration is very close to self-evident, for a law would be useless unless it were observed. Hence Aristotle said in the *Politics*, Book IV, Chapter 6: "Laws are not well ordered when they are well made but not obeyed."[69] He also said in Book VI, Chapter 5: "Nothing is accomplished by forming opinions about justice and not carrying them out."[70] The second proposition I prove as follows. That law is better observed by every citizen which each one seems to have imposed upon himself. But such is the law which is made through the hearing and command of the entire multitude of the citizens. The first proposition of this prosyllogism is almost self-evident; for since "the state is a community of free men," as is written in the *Politics*, Book III, Chapter 4,[71] every citizen must be free, and not undergo another's despotism, that is, slavish dominion. But this would not be the case if one or a few of the citizens by their own authority made the law over the whole body of citizens. For those who thus made the law would be despots over the others, and hence such a law, however good it was, would be endured only with reluctance, or not at all, by the rest of the citizens, the more ample part. Having suffered contempt, they would protest against it, and not having been called upon to make it, they would not observe it. On the other hand, a law made by the hearing or consent of the whole multitude, even though it were less useful, would be readily observed and endured by every one of the citizens, because then each would seem to have set the law upon himself, and hence would have no protest against it, but would rather tolerate it with equanimity.[72] The second proposition of the first syllogism I also prove in another way, as follows. The power to cause the laws to be observed belongs only to those men to whom belongs coercive force over the transgressors of the laws. But these men are the whole body of citizens or the weightier part thereof. Therefore, to them alone belongs the authority to make the laws.

7. The principal conclusion is also proved as follows. That practical matter whose proper establishment is of greatest importance for the common sufficiency of the citizens in this life, and whose poor establishment threatens harm for the com-

munity, must be established only by the whole body of the citizens. But such a matter is the law. Therefore, the establishment of the law pertains only to the whole body of the citizens. The major premise of this demonstration is almost self-evident, and is grounded in the immediate truths which were set forth in Chapter IV and V of this discourse. For men came together to the civil community in order to attain what was beneficial for sufficiency of life, and to avoid the opposite. Those matters, therefore, which can affect the benefit and harm of all ought to be known and heard by all, in order that they may be able to attain the beneficial and to avoid the opposite. Such matters are the laws, as was assumed in the minor premise. For in the laws being rightly made consists a large part of the whole common sufficiency of men, while under bad laws there arise unbearable slavery, oppression, and misery of the citizens, the final result of which is that the polity is destroyed.

8. Again, and this is an abbreviation and summary of the previous demonstrations: The authority to make laws belongs only to the whole body of the citizens, as we have said, or else it belongs to one or a few men. But it cannot belong to one man alone for the reasons given in Chapter XI and in the first demonstration adduced in the present chapter; for through ignorance or malice or both, this one man could make a bad law, looking more to his own private benefit than to that of the community, so that the law would be tyrannical. For the same reason, the authority to make laws cannot belong to a few; for they too could sin, as above, in making the law for the benefit of a certain few and not for the common benefit, as can be seen in oligarchies. The authority to make the laws belongs, therefore, to the whole body of citizens or to the weightier part thereof, for precisely the opposite reason. For since all the citizens must be measured by the law according to due proportion, and no one knowingly harms or wishes injustice to himself, it follows that all or most wish a law conducing to the common benefit of the citizens.

9. From these same demonstrations it can also be proved, merely by changing the minor term, that the approval, interpretation, and suspension of the laws, and the other matters set forth in paragraph 3 of this chapter, pertain to the authority of the legislator alone. And the same must be thought of everything else which is established by election. For the authority to approve or disapprove rests with those who have the primary authority to elect, or with those to whom they have granted this authority of election. For otherwise, if the part could dissolve by its own authority what had been established by the whole, the part would be greater than the whole, or at least equal to it.

The method of coming together to make the laws will be described in the following chapter.

Chapter XIII

On Some Objections to the Statements Made in the Preceding Chapter, and Their Refutation, Together with a Fuller Exposition of the Proposition

Objections will be made to our above statements, to the effect that the authority to make or establish laws does not belong to the whole body of the citizens. The first objection is that those who for the most part are vicious and undiscerning should not make the law. For these two sins, malice and ignorance, must be excluded from the legislator, and it was to avoid them in civil judgments that we upheld the necessity of law in Chapter XI of this discourse. But the people or the whole body of citizens have these sins; for men for the most part seem to be vicious and stupid: "The number of the stupid is infinite," as it is said in the first chapter of Ecclesiastes.[73] Another objection is that it is very difficult or impossible to harmonize the views of many vicious and unintelligent persons; but such is not the case with the few and virtuous. It is more useful, therefore, that the law be made by the few than by the whole body of the citizens or the exceeding majority of them.

Again, in every civil community the wise and learned are few in comparison with the multitude of the unlearned. Since, therefore, the law is more usefully made by the wise and learned than by the unlearned and uncultivated, it seems that the authority to make laws belongs to the few, not to the many or to all. Furthermore, that which can be done by fewer persons is needlessly done by more. Since, therefore, the law can be made by the wise, who are few, as has been said, the entire multitude or the greater part of it would needlessly be occupied therein. The authority to make the laws does not belong, therefore, to the whole body of the citizens or to the weightier part thereof.

2. From what we assumed above as the principle of all the things to be demonstrated in this book, namely, that all men desire sufficiency of life and avoid the opposite, we demonstrated in Chapter IV the civil association of men, inasmuch as through such association they can attain this sufficiency, and without it they cannot. Hence too Aristotle says in the *Politics*, Book I, Chapter 1: "There is in all men a natural impulse toward such a community,"[74] that is, the civil community. From this truth there necessarily follows another, which is presented in the *Politics*, Book IV, Chapter 10, namely, that "that part of the state which wishes the polity to endure must be weightier than the part which does not wish it."[75] For nothing is desired by the same specific nature in most of its individual members and immediately at the same time as the thing's destruction, since such a desire would be futile. Indeed, those who do not wish the polity to endure are classed among the slaves, not among the citizens, as are certain aliens. Hence Aristotle says in the *Politics*, Book VII, Chapter 13: "Everyone in the country unites with the subjects in the desire to have a revolution," and then he adds: "It is impossible that there be so many persons in the government," that is, rebellious, or not caring to live a civil life, "that they are stronger than all the others,"[76] that is, than those who wish to carry on a political life (*politizare*).

Why this is impossible is obvious; for it would mean that nature errs or is deficient for the most part. If, therefore, the weightier multitude of men wish the state to endure, as seems to have been well said, they also wish that without which the state cannot endure. But this is the standard of the just and the beneficial, handed down with a command, and called the law; for "it is impossible for the best-ruled state," that is, the state governed according to virtue, "not to be well ordered by laws," as is said in the *Politics*, Book IV, Chapter 7,[77] and as we demonstrated in Chapter XI of this discourse. Therefore, the weightier multitude of the state wishes to have law, or else there would occur deformity in nature and art in most cases; the impossibility of which is assumed from natural science.[78]

With these manifest truths I again assume that common conception of the mind, that "every whole is greater than its part," which is true with respect both to magnitude or mass and to practical virtue and action. From this it clearly follows of necessity that the whole body of the citizens, or the weightier multitude thereof, which must be taken for the same thing, can better discern what must be elected and what rejected than any part of it taken separately.

3. Now that we have laid down these obvious truths, it is easy to refute the objections whereby one might try to prove that the making of the law does not pertain to the whole body of the citizens or the weightier multitude thereof but rather to a certain few. As for the first objection, that the authority to make laws does not belong to those who in most cases are vicious and undiscerning, this is granted. But when it is added that the whole body of citizens is such, this must be denied. For most of the citizens are neither vicious nor undiscerning most of the time; all or most of them are of sound mind and reason and have a right desire for the polity and for the things necessary for it to endure, like laws and other statutes or customs, as was shown above. For although not every citizen nor the greater number of the citizens be discoverers of the laws, yet every citizen can

judge of what has been discovered and proposed to him by someone else, and can discern what must be added, subtracted, or changed. Hence in the major premise's reference to the "undiscerning," if what is meant is that because most of the citizens cannot dicover the law by themselves, therefore they ought not to establish the law, this must be denied as manifestly false, as is borne out by sense induction and by Aristotle in the *Politics*, Book III, Chapter 6. By induction we can see that many men judge rightly about the quality of a picture, a house, a ship, and other works of art, even though they would have been unable to discover or produce them. Aristotle also attests to this in the place just cited, answering the proposed objection with these words: "About some things the man who made them is not the only or the best judge."[79] He proves this in many species of arts, and indicates that the same is true for all the others.

4. Nor is this position invalidated by those who say that the wise, who are few, can discern what should be enacted with regard to practical matters better than can the rest of the multitude. For even if this be true, it still does not follow that the wise can discern what should be enacted better than can the whole multitude, in which the wise are included together with the less learned. For every whole is greater than its part both in action and in discernment. This was undoubtedly the view of Artistotle in the *Politics*, Book III, Chapter 6, when he said: "The multitude is justly dominant in the more important matters," that is, the multitude or the whole body of citizens or the weightier part thereof, which he here signifies by the term "multitude," should justly be dominant with respect to the more important matters in the polity; and he gives this reason: "The people is composed of many persons including the council and the judiciary and the honorable class, and all of these together are more ample than any single person or group, including the few rulers who hold high governmental offices."[80] He means that the people, or the multitude composed of all the groups of

the polity or city taken together, is more ample than any part of it taken separately, and consequently its judgment is more secure than that of any such part, whether that part be the common mass, which he here signified by the term "council" (*consilium*), such as the farmers, artisans, and others of that sort; or whether it be the "judiciary," that is, those officials who assist the ruler in judicial functions, as advocates or lawyers and notaries; or whether it be the "honorable class," that is, the group of the best men, who are few, and who alone are appropriately elected to the highest governmental offices; or whether it be any other part of the state taken separately. Moreover, even if we assume what is indeed true, that some of the less learned do not judge about a proposed law or some other practical matter equally as well as do the same number of the learned, still the number of the less learned could be increased to such an extent that they would judge about these matters equally as well as, or even better than, the few who are more learned. Aristotle stated this clearly in the place cited above when he undertook to confirm this view: "If the multitude be not too vile, each member of it will indeed be a worse judge than those who have knowledge; but taken all together they will be better judges, or at least not worse."[81]

As for the passage quoted from the first chapter of Ecclesiastes that "the number of the stupid is infinite," it must be replied that by "stupid" was meant those who are less learned or who do not have leisure for liberal functions, but who nevertheless share in the understanding and judgment of practical matters, although not equally with those who have leisure. Or perhaps the wise author, as Jerome says in his commentary thereon, meant by "stupid" the unbelievers who, however much they may know the worldly sciences, are stupid in an absolute sense, in keeping with the statement of the Apostle in the first epistle to the Corinthians, Chapter 3: "The wisdom of this world is stupidity with God."[82]

5. The second objection carries little weight, for even though it be easier to har-

monize the views of fewer persons than of many, it does not follow that the views of the few, or of the part, are superior to those of the whole multitude, of which the few are a part. For the few would not discern or desire the common benefit equally as well as would the entire multitude of the citizens. Indeed, it would be insecure, as we have already shown, to entrust the making of the law to the discretion of the few. For they would perhaps consult therein their own private benefit, as individuals or as a group, rather than the common benefit, as it quite apparent in those who have made the decretals of the clergy, and as we shall make sufficiently clear in Chapter XXVIII of Discourse II. By this means the way would be opened to oligarchy, just as when the power to make the laws is given to one man alone the opportunity is afforded for tyranny, as we showed above in Chapter XI, paragraph 4, where we quoted from the fourth book of Aristotle's *Ethics*, the treatise on justice.

6. The third objection can be easily refuted from what we have already said: for although the laws can be better made by the wise than by the less learned, it is not therefore to be concluded that they are better made by the wise alone than by the entire multitude of citizens, in which the wise are included. For the assembled multitude of all of these can discern and desire the common justice and benefit to a greater extent than can any part of that multitude taken separately, however prudent that part may be.

7. Hence those do not speak the truth who hold that the less learned multitude impedes the choice and approval of the true or common good; rather, the multitude is of help in this function when it is joined to those who are more learned and more experienced. For although the multitude cannot by itself discover true and useful measures, it can nevertheless discern and judge the measures discovered and proposed to it by others, as to whether they should be added to, or subtracted from, or completely changed, or rejected. For many things which a man would have been un-able to initiate or discover by himself, he can comprehend and bring to completion after they have been explained to him by someone else. For the beginnings of things are the most difficult to discover; as Aristotle says in the second book of the *Refutations*, last chapter: "Most difficult is it to see the beginning,"[83] that is, of the truth proper to each discipline. But when this has been discovered, it is easy to add the remainder or to extend it. Hence, while only the best and most acute minds can discover the principles of the sciences, the arts, and other disciplines, nevertheless when these principles have been discovered, additions can be made to them by men of humbler mind. Nor should the latter be called undiscerning because they cannot discover such principles by themselves; on the contrary, they should be numbered among good men, as Aristotle said in the *Ethics*, Book I, Chapter 2: "That man is best who has achieved an understanding of all things by himself. But he too is good who hearkens to the wise words of another,"[84] that is, by listening to him attentively and not contradicting him without reason.

8. It is hence appropriate and highly useful that the whole body of citizens entrust to those who are prudent and experienced the investigation, discovery, and examination of the standards, the future laws or statutes, concerning civil justice and benefit, common difficulties or burdens, and other similar matters. Either some of these prudent and experienced men may be elected by each of the primary parts of the state enumerated in Chapter V, paragraph 1, according to the proportion of each part; or else all these men may be elected by all the citizens assembled together. And this will be an appropriate and useful method whereby to come together to discover the laws without detriment to the rest of the multitude, that is, the less learned, who would be of little help in the investigation of such standards, and would be disturbed in their performance of the other functions necessary both to themselves and to others, which would be burdensome both to each individual and to the community.

After such standards, the future laws, have been discovered and diligently examined, they must be laid before the assembled whole body of citizens for their approval or disapproval, so that if any citizen thinks that something should be added, subtracted, changed, or completely rejected, he can say so, since by this means the law will be more usefully ordained. For, as we have said, the less learned citizens can sometimes perceive something which must be corrected in a proposed law even though they could not have discovered the law itself. Also, the laws thus made by the hearing and consent of the entire multitude will be better observed, nor will anyone have any protest to make against them.

These standards, the future laws, will thus have been made public, and in the general assembly of the citizens those citizens will have been heard who have wanted to make some reasonable statements with regard to them. Then there must again be elected men of the qualities,

and by the method, indicated above, or else the aforesaid men must be confirmed; and they, representing the position and authority of the whole body of the citizens, will approve or disapprove in whole or in part the afore-mentioned standards which had been investigated and proposed, or else, if it so wishes, the whole body of the citizens or the weightier part thereof will do this same thing by itself. After this approval, the aforesaid standards are laws and deserve to be so called, not before; and after their publication or proclamation, they alone among human commands make transgressors liable to civil guilt and punishment.[85]

We think we have adequately shown, then, that the authority to make or establish the laws, and to give a command with regard to their observance, belongs only to the whole body of the citizens or to the weightier part thereof as efficient cause, or else to the person or persons to whom the aforesaid whole body has granted this authority.

NOTES

1. See Aristotle *Politics* III. 7. 1279a 34.
2. This decision to use the term *regnum* to mean "something common to every species of temperate regime" is unique among the medieval Aristotelians in two respects, for the others use the term in Marsilius' third sense alone, i.e., as signifying a *royal monarchy* composed of a *number of cities*.
3. See *Politics* I. 5. 1254a 31 ff.; v. 3. 1302b 34 ff. Cf. ibid. VI. 4. 1290a 24 ff.
4. Aristotle *Politics* III. 7, 8. 1279a 17 ff.
5. Although the reference to the will or consent of the subjects is not entirely absent in the *Politics*, Marsilius' use of it as a basic and even primary criterion of a just or "well-tempered" government is a departure from Aristotle and from the medieval Aristotelian tradition.
6. On the basis and significance of this indifference as to the relative merits of monarchy, aristocracy, and polity, see below, I. ix. 9.
7. John 19:11.
8. Romans 13:1.
9. St. Augustine *De civitate Dei* V. xxi (PL 41. 167).
10. I. ix. 4–6.
11. I. ix. 7.
12. Aristotle *Politics* III. 14. 1284b 35 ff.
13. Marsilius' terms are *capitaneatus* and *constabiliaria*. The former meant a position of army leadership; for a large number of references to the medieval use of this and cognate terms, see Du Cange, *Glossarium mediae et infimae Latinitatis*, s.v. *capitaneatus, capitaneus*. Du Cange has no entry for *constabiliaria*, but for the seemingly related terms *constabularia* and *contestabiliaria* (the latter found in some MSS of the *Defensor* instead of *constabiliaria*), Du Cange refers to *comes stabuli*, meaning the custodian of the royal stable, and gives a large number of citations, s.v.
14. *Politics* III. 14. 1285a 23. See also Ptolemy of Lucca *De regimine principum* III. xi (*fin.*) (ed. J. Mathis [Turin, 1924], p. 63b).
15. *Politics* III. 14. 1285a 32.
16. Ibid. 1285b 4.

17. Ibid. V. 10. 1310b 10 ff.
18. See ibid. III. 16–17. 1287a I ff.
19. Ibid. IV. 10. 1295a 15.
20. *Politics*. III. 14. 1285b 2; above, para. 4.
21. This is a marked ignoring of the papalist claims of superior virtue.
22. Cf. Aristotle *Politics* II. 6. 1266a 9; VI. 2. 1317b 21, 1318a 2.
23. Cf. ibid. V. 4. 1304b 8.
24. Aristotle *Politics* III. 14. 1284b 39, 1285a 19.
25. Romans 7:23.
26. Ezekiel 43:12–13.
27. Hebrews 7:12.
28. James 1:25.
29. Aristotle *Metaphysics* II. 3. 995a 4.
30. Ibid. XII. 8. 1074b 3.
31. This conception of coerciveness as the essence of law is a noteworthy departure from the medieval tradition's emphasis on reason as the essence of law.
32. Aristotle *Nicomachean Ethics* X 9. 1180a 21.
33. See, however, below, I. xiii. 5.
34. Aristotle *Politics* III. 15. 1286a 17.
35. Aristotle *Rhetoric* I. I. 1354b 4 ff.
36. Ibid. I. 2. 1356a 14.
37. Aristotle *Politics* II. 5. 1264a I.
38. Aristotle *Rhetoric* I. I. 1354b 3.
39. Aristotle *Nicomachean Ethics* VI. 9. 1142a 12.
40. Aristotle *Metaphysics* II. I. 993b 2.
41. Marsilius' special mention of "astrology" here may have been occasioned not only by his long acquaintance with Peter of Abano but also by the work he himself had done in the subject.
42. Aristotle, *Metaphysics* II. I. 993b 15.
43. Averröes *Commentarius in Aristotelis Metaphysicam* Lib. II. cap. i, in *Aristotelis opera*, ed. Manardus (Venice, 1560), Vol. IV, fol. 49r.
44. Aristotle *On Sophistical Refutations* 34. 183b 34 ff.
45. Aristotle *Nicomachean Ethics* VIII. I. 1155a 16.
46. Aristotle *Politics* III. 16. 1287b 26. Aristotle himself uses this consideration as an argument for having many rather than few judges in cases not covered by the law, and not, like Marsilius, as an argument for the determination of judgments by law rather than by the discretion of the judges.
47. Aristotle *Nicomachean Ethics* V. 6. 1134a 35. The expression "in accordance with" (*secundum*) is added by Marsilius. Note his other similar interpolations in this paragraph, all motivated by his literal conception that only man can "rule" or "govern," not reason or law.
48. Aristotle *Politics* III. II. 1282b I.
49. Ibid. III. 16. 1287a 28.
50. Ibid. 1287a 32.
51. Aristotle *Rhetoric* I. I. 1354a 32.
52. Aristotle *Politics* IV. 4. 1292a 32. By "polity" in this passage Aristotle himself means a constitution of any kind, whether "temperate" or "diseased."
53. Ibid. V. 10. 1312b 38.
54. Cf. ibid. III. 13. 1284a 3 ff.; III. 17. 1288a 15 ff. Cf. also Dante *De monarchia* I. xi, xiii.
55. Daniel 13:28.
56. Aristotle *Politics* III. 15. 1286b 26.
57. Ibid. V. II. 1313a 20.
58. Ibid. 1313a 26.
59. This is a reference to the leagues formed in France to protest against Philip the Fair's new taxation in 1314.
60. See above, I. ix. 2.
61. See above, I. x. 3. This is really the first subdivision of the fourth sense of law.
62. This seems to refer both to Aristotle's conception of "prudence" (e.g., *Nicomachean Ethics* VI. 8. 1141b 23 ff.) and to the *prudentes* of the Italian communes.
63. See above, I. x. 4–5.
64. Aristotle *Politics* III. II. 1281a 39ff.
65. The words *personarum et qualitate* were omitted from a younger group of manuscripts and from early printed versions, thereby leading to a mistaken interpretation of Marsilius' position as purely majoritarian.
66. *Politics* III. I. 1275a 22, 1275b 19; III. 3. 1277b 33; III. 13. 1283b 42.

67. *Politics* VI. 3–4. 1318a 3 ff.
68. *Politics* III. 13. 1283b 40.
69. *Politics* IV. 8. 1294a 3.
70. Ibid. VI. 8. 1322a 5.
71. Ibid. III. 6. 1279a 21.
72. The point that those who "have some part in government" will "love" it and will work harder for the common good is made by Thomas Aquinas *S. theol.* II. I. qu. 105. a. I. Resp.; *De regimine principum* I. iv (ed. J. Mathis [Turin, 1924], pp. 6–7); see also Ptolemy of Lucca *De regimine principum* II. viii (ed. J. Mathis [Turin, 1924], p. 90), and John of Paris *De potestate regia et papali* cap. xix (ed. D. J. Leclercq, *Jean de Paris et l'ecclésiologie du xiiie siècle* [Paris, 1942], pp. 236–37). In none of these authors, however, is this point made with Marsilius' insistence that the supreme legislative authority can belong only to the people.
73. Ecclesiastes 1:15.
74. Aristotle *Politics* I. 2. 1253a 29.
75. Ibid. IV. 12. 1296b 14. It will be noted how Marsilius' interpretation of this statement in terms of biological necessity removes the hypothetical character which it has for Aristotle.
76. Ibid. VII. 14. 1332b 29 ff. It will be noted that Marsilius' interpolations are precisely contrary to the meaning of Aristotle. Perhaps he misunderstood the term for "government" (*politeumate*).
77. *Politics* IV. 8. 1293b 42.
78. Cf. Aristotle *Physics* II. 8. 199a 9 ff.; *Nicomachean Ethics* I. 9. 1099b 20–24.
79. Aristotle *Politics* III. II. 1282a 17.
80. Ibid. 1282a 38 ff. Marsilius' misinterpretation of this passage is owing to the fact that he, like the other medieval Aristotelians, interprets *honorabilitas* (William of Moerbeke's translation of Aristotle's τίμημα) to mean "the honorable class," rather than "assessed property." In William of Moerbeke's translation as found in Susemihl (p. 197), there is a full stop after *praetorium* ("judiciary") and no comma after *honorabilitas*, so that, without Marsilius' misinterpretations, the English translation should read: "and the assessed property of all of these together is greater than that of the persons who either as individuals or as members of small groups hold high governmental offices."
81. *Politics* III. 14. 1282a 15 ff.
82. I Corinthians 3:19.
83. Aristotle *On Sophistical Refutations* 34. 183b 24.
84. Aristotle *Nicomachean Ethics* I. 2. 1095b 10, quoting Hesiod *Works and Days* 293.
85. As Previté-Orton points out, the procedure here set forth by Marsilius corresponds well with that of the Italian communes of his day.

CHAPTER 30

William of Ockham

(See Chapter Sixteen for biography.)

William of Ockham on the Power of Popes and Emperors

At the outset it is of utmost importance to understand that Ockham was neither secularist nor anticlerical. However, concerning both sources of power, papal and imperial, he was against absolutism. Absolute authority in theory invariably translates into the "law of force" when put into practice. It is abuse of power, not legitimate papal or civil authority, that most concerns Ockham. In this regard he was not like Marsilius of Padua, who was against the principle of the pope as head of the church. Ockham wants safeguards against corruption and lust for power in both clerical and secular realms. Thus he argues against the concept of "plenitude of power" on the basis that the law of God is the law of liberty. "As Christ did not come into the world in order to take away from men their goods and rights, so Christ's vicar, who is inferior and in no way equal to him in power, has no authority or power to deprive others of their goods and rights." Similarly, "the emperor does not possess a plenitude of power in temporal matters so that he can do everything that is not against divine or natural law. His power, instead, is limited, in that in relation to the free men subject to him and to their possessions, he can do only such things as promote the common utility". What is the source of the power of the pope and the emperor? God is the source. Historically, this had led the papacy to argue that secular power is derived from the divine authority of the church. Ockham argues that although secular power is indeed divine, it is not derived from the papacy. Rather, the source of secular power resides in the people who confer upon the emperor his power to legislate.

AN EXCERPT FROM *EIGHT QUESTIONS ON THE POWER OF THE POPE*

Question II: The Origin of the Supreme Civil Power

Chapter I

In the second place, the question is raised whether the supreme lay power derives the character strictly proper to it immediately from God. On this question there are two contrary opinions. According to one, the supreme lay power does not derive the power strictly proper to it immediately from God, because it derives it from God through the mediation of papal power. For the pope possesses the fullness of power in temporal and spiritual matters alike, and therefore no one possesses any power save from him. The things alleged above [in Question I, Chapter II] can be put forward in support of this opinion, and other reasons can also be offered. For it seems to some that, even though the pope did not have the fullness of power of this sort in temporal matters, it should still be said that the imperium[1] comes from him. From this it can be concluded that the supreme lay power—namely, the imperial power—derives the power proper to it from the pope, and not immediately from God, since it derives the power proper to it from him from whom it receives the imperium.

It remains to be proved, then, that the imperium comes from the pope, and this can be demonstrated in many ways. For the imperium comes from him to whom the keys of heavenly and earthly imperium

Eight Questions on the Power of the Pope from *A Scholastic Miscellany: Anselm to Ockham*, edited and translated by Eugene R. Fairweather (Vol. 10: The Library of Christian Classics). First published in 1955 by SCM Press Ltd., London, and the Westminster Press, Philadelphia. Reprinted by permission of Westminster/John Knox Press, Louisville, and SCM Press, Ltd., London, pp. 437–442; *Dialogus de Potestate Papae et Imperatoris* is reprinted from *Medieval Political Philosophy*, edited by Ralph Lerner and Muhsin Mahdi, New York (The Free Press of Glencoe, 1963), pp. 494–499. Reprinted by permission of Macmillan Publishing Co.

were given; but the keys of heavenly and earthly imperium were given to Peter,[2] and consequently to his successors (distinction twenty-two, chapter one),[3] and therefore imperium comes from the pope. To state the point more fully, imperium comes from him who, by the ordinance of God (in whose power imperium most perfectly lies), is the first head and supreme judge of all mortals. Now by God's ordinance the pope, and not the emperor, is the first head and the judge of all mortals; the imperium, therefore, comes from the pope. Again, the imperium is derived from him who can depose the emperor; but the pope can depose the emperor (XV, question six, chapter *Alius*,[4]) and therefore the imperium comes from the pope. Again, the imperium comes from him who can transfer the imperium from one nation to another; but the pope can do this (Extra, *de electione, Venerabilem*,[5]) and therefore the imperium is derived from the pope. Again, the imperium comes from him by whom the emperor, once elected, is examined, anointed, consecrated, and crowned. Now the emperor is examined, anointed, consecrated, and crowned by the pope (Extra, *de electione, Venerabilem*); therefore, the imperium comes from the pope. Again, the imperium comes from him to whom the emperor takes an oath like a vassal; but the emperor executes an oath of fidelity and subjection to the pope, like a vassal of the latter (distinction sixty-three, *Tibi Domine*,[6]) and therefore the imperium comes from the pope. Again, the imperium comes from him who holds both swords,[7] that is, the material and the spiritual. Now the pope possesses both swords, and therefore the imperium is derived from the pope. This seems to be Innocent IV's meaning when in a certain decretal he asserts that "the two swords of both administrations are held concealed in the bosom of the faithful Church"[8]; for this reason, if anyone is not within that Church, he possesses neither. "Thus," he goes on, "both rights are believed to belong to Peter, since the Lord did not say to him, with reference to the material sword, 'Cast away,' but rather, 'Put up again thy sword into thy scabbard,'[9] meaning, 'Do not employ it by thyself.' " Here he significantly expresses the name of the second, because this power of the material sword is implicit with the Church, but is made explicit by the emperor who receives it.

Again, the imperium is derived from him to whom the emperor stands in the relation of a son to his father, of a disciple to his master, of lead to gold, of the moon to the sun.[10] Now the emperor stands in these relations to the pope (distinction ninety-six, *Si imperator*, and chapter *Quis dubitet*, and chapter *Duo sunt*[11]; Extra, *de maioritate et obedientia, Solitae*);[12] the imperium, therefore, comes from the pope. Again, the imperium is derived from him to whom the emperor is obliged to bow his head; but the emperor is bound to bow his head to the pope (distinction sixty-three, *Valentinianus*; distinction ninety-six, *Numquam*),[13] and therefore the imperium comes from the pope. Again, the imperium comes from him by whom, on his own authority and not by the ordinance of the emperor or of some other man, it ought to be ruled during a vacancy; but the pope does this when the imperium is vacant, and therefore the imperium is derived from the pope.

[Chapters II, III have to do with different forms of the papal theory, Chapters IV to VI with different arguments for the imperial position.]

Chapter VII

Now that the above opinions have been considered,[14] a reply should be made in accordance with them to the arguments alleged on the other side, and first to the points put forward above (in Chapter I) against the view last stated. In answer to these, it is said that the imperium does not come from the pope, since after Christ's advent the imperium was derived from the same person as before; but before Christ's advent the imperium was not derived from the pope (as was alleged above), and therefore it has never afterward come from the pope.

But in reply to the first argument to the contrary, to the effect that, according to Pope Nicholas, Christ gave or committed to blessed Peter the rights of heavenly and earthly imperium together, it is said that Pope Nicholas' words are really to be expounded against the interpretation which at first glance appears to be proper, lest they seem to savor of heresy. The same holds for certain other things said by the same pope in the same chapter—for instance, when he says, "He alone established and founded and erected that Church," namely, the Roman, "on the rock of the faith just springing up," and when he says, "The Roman Church instituted all primates, whether the supreme dignity of any patriarch or the primacies of metropolitan sees, or the chairs of episcopates, or, for that matter, the dignity of churches of any order."[15] Unless these words are somewhat discreetly interpreted, they seem to be contrary to the divine Scriptures and the writings of the holy Fathers, because Christ did not found the Roman Church upon the rock of the faith just springing up, since the Roman Church was not founded at the beginning of the faith, nor did it found all the other Churches. For many churches were founded before the Roman Church, and many were raised up to ecclesiastical dignities even before the foundation of the Roman Church, for before the Roman Church existed blessed Matthias was elected to the dignity of apostleship (Acts, ch. 1).[16] Seven deacons also were chosen by the apostles before the Roman Church began (Acts, ch. 8);[17] also, before the Roman Church existed they "had peace throughout all Judea, and Galilee, and Samaria" (Acts, ch. 9).[18] Before the Roman church existed blessed Paul and Barnabas were raised to the apostolic dignity by God's command (Acts, ch. 13);[19] before the Roman Church had the power of appointing prelates, Paul and Barnabas appointed presbyters throughout the several churches (Acts, ch. 14).[20] Before the Roman Church had any authority, the apostles and elders[21] held a general council (Acts, ch. 15);[22] also, before the Roman Church had the power of instituting prelates, blessed Paul said to the elders[23] whom he had called from Ephesus (as we are told in Acts, ch. 20):[24] "Take heed to yourselves, and to the whole flock, wherein the Holy Ghost hath placed you bishops, to rule the church of God." Before the Roman Church held the primacy, the churches of Antioch were so multiplied that the disciples of Christ were first called Christians there (Acts, ch. 11);[25] for this reason also blessed Peter had his see there before Rome (XXIV, question one, chapter *Rogamus*),[26] and thus he instituted churches and ecclesiastical dignities in the Antiochene church before he did so in the Roman. It is necessary, then, to attach a sound interpretation to the words of Pope Nicholas given above, lest they openly contradict the divine Scriptures. And, likewise, his other statements that follow, concerning the rights of heavenly and earthly imperium alike committed to blessed Peter, must be soundly expounded, lest they seem to savor of manifest heresy. For if they are construed as they sound at first hearing, two errors follow from them.

According to the first error, heavenly imperium comes from the pope, because Pope Nicholas says that Christ committed the rights of heavenly as well as earthly imperium to Peter. But it is certain that heavenly imperium does not come from the pope, particularly in the way in which some say, on account of that authoritative statement of Pope Nicholas, that earthly imperium is derived from the pope—namely, so that he who possesses the earthly imperium holds it as a fief from the pope—since it would be heretical to say that anyone held the heavenly imperium from the pope as a fief. Nor does the heavenly imperium come from the pope as its lord, as they claim that the earthly imperium comes from the pope as its lord, since the pope is merely in some sense the key bearer of the heavenly imperium, and in no sense its lord.

The second error which follows from Nicholas' words, understood as certain people understand them, is to the effect that all kingdoms are derived from the pope. It is recognized that this principle works to the disadvantage of all kings who do not pay homage to the pope for their kingdoms. For the king of France seems to err dangerously in faith when he makes no acknowledgement of a superior in temporal affairs (Extra, *Qui filii sint legitimi, Per venerabilem*).[27]

These[28] say, then, that the aforesaid words of Nicholas are to be interpreted in another way than their sound suggests. Thus they say that, just as according to Gregory, in the homily for the Common of virgins,[29] the "kingdom of heaven" must sometimes be understood to refer to the Church Militant, so also the "heavenly imperium" can be understood to refer to the spiritually good in the Church Militant. Therefore, the spiritually evil in the Church can also be designated by the term, "earthly imperium," and the aforesaid words of Nicholas should be interpreted as meaning that Christ committed to blessed Peter some power over the good and over the evil in the Church. Or else, some say that by the "heavenly imperium" Pope Nicholas understands the "spirituals,"[30] whose "conversation is in heaven,"[31] and by the "earthly imperium" the "seculars," wrapped up in earthly business, and that he means that the pope has power over both.

Or else it is said that Christ committed to Peter the rights of heavenly imperium, in so far as in spiritual things he has power over wayfarers predestined to the heavenly imperium, and that he also committed to him the rights of earthly imperium, in so far as he made him superior in spiritual things to the earthly emperor, whom on occasion he can even coerce. Yet just as no one holds the heavenly imperium from the pope in fief, so also no one holds the earthly imperium in fief from him.

[Chapters VIII to XV continue the detailed reply to the assertions made in Chapter I. Chapter XVI provides a reply from the papal standpoint to the objection raised in the first paragraph of Chapter VII.]

DIALOGUS DE POTESTATE PAPAE ET IMPERATORIS

Part Three, Treatise ii, Book II

Chapter 26

[He inquires here whether the emperor has the plentitude of power in temporal matters to as great an extent as the pope has in spiritual matters, and he cites one opinion, which he supports with five arguments. To these arguments a reply is made later on in Chapter 28][32]

PUPIL: We have already inquired to what degree the emperor has power over some matters in particular, but now I ask the general question whether the emperor has a plentitude of power in temporal affairs in the same way as the pope, according to many, is deemed to have a plentitude of power in spiritual matters.

MASTER: On this point there are conflicting positions, one of which claims that the emperor has such a plentitude of power in temporal matters that he can do all things that are not against divine or natural law, so that in matters of this kind all his subjects are bound to obey him.

PUPIL: Would you try to state some arguments in support of this opinion?

MASTER: Many things can be said on behalf of this opinion:

1. For he who is limited by no human law, but is bound only by the divine and natural laws, can do everything that does not run counter to one of the latter [923] laws. Now the emperor is bound by no human law, but by the divine and natural laws, since (as is said in the *Digest*, I, 3, para. 31, and is reiterated in the gloss to the *Decretals*, i, 2, I in v. *ab omnibus*), the emperor is not subject to the laws, and, therefore, has such a plentitude of power in temporal matters that he can do all things that

are not contrary to the divine and natural laws.

2. Besides, he whose will in temporal matters is endowed by law with the force of law, possesses in these things a plenitude of power. But what pleases the prince (and especially the emperor) has the force of law. Therefore, the emperor possesses in these matters a plenitude of power.

3. Again, he whose very error constitutes law in temporal matters enjoys a plenitude of power over them; hence, the emperor has such a plenitude of power.

4. Furthermore, if somebody subject to the emperor can justly resist an imperial decree in temporal matters—one that runs counter neither to the divine nor to the natural law—it is necessary that he can so resist in accordance with some law, since we can do rightly only that which we can do legally. Either, therefore, he can resist the emperor by divine or natural, or by human law. But not by divine or natural, since, as has been said, the imperial decree is contrary to neither of these laws. Nor by human law, since—as is said in the *Decretum*, D. 8, c. I, and was mentioned earlier—human laws are not contrary to the imperial law "because these human laws themselves God promulgates to the human race through emperors and through the kings of the world." Thus, by the law of the emperor, nobody can resist the imperial decree, since the emperor can do everything in all matters of this [temporal] kind.

5. Besides, that to which human society obliges itself, it is bound to observe. But human society binds itself in general to obey kings, and, therefore, so much the more to obey the emperor. For Augustine says in the second book of the *Confessions* (quoted

in the *Decretum*, D. 8, c. 2), "It is, indeed, a general agreement of human society to obey its kings." The emperor, then, is always to be obeyed in temporal things, for he can do everything that is not against divine and natural law.

Chapter 27

[He cites a second opinion that runs counter to the first.]

PUPIL: State the opposite case.
MASTER: The opposed position is that the emperor does not possess a plenitude of power in temporal matters so that he can do everything that is not against divine or natural law. His power, instead, is limited, in that in relation to the free men subject to him and to their possessions, he can do only such things as promote the common utility.
PUPIL: Would you cite some arguments in support of this position?
MASTER: On behalf of this position it may be argued as follows:
1. That he whose laws must be made, not for a private good, but for the common utility, lacks the plenitude of power by which he could do all things. For if he had a plenitude of power he could establish laws, not only for the common utility, but even for a private good (whether his own or another's), and also for any cause whatever, provided only that it was contrary neither to the divine nor to the natural law. But imperial laws and other [human] laws have to be established not for private convenience but for the common utility—witness Isidore, who says (see *Decretum*, D. 4, c. 2): "The law will be just, honorable, and feasible, in accordance with nature and the custom of the land, appropriate to the place and time, necessary, useful, and clear, too, lest through indistinctness it may contain something improper; and it will be drawn up, not for any private good, but for the common utility of the citizens." The emperor, then, does not have such a plenitude of power that he can do all things, but only

those that contribute to the common welfare.
2. Furthermore, if the emperor has in these matters a plenitude of power, all other kings, princes, and other laymen would be subject to him just as mere slaves. For a lord does not have greater power over slaves than that of being able to order them to do everything that is not against divine or natural law—indeed, it is possible that he does not have that great a power over them. If, therefore, the emperor could do in temporal matters, not only those things that contribute to the common utility, but also any other thing at all that is not against the divine or natural low, then every other person would be subject to him as his very slave.
3. Again, the pope does not possess a plenary power in spiritual matters, for he cannot prescribe to anyone those things that are works of supererogation—such as virginity, fasting on bread and water, entering a religious order, and so forth. So much the more, then, does the emperor lack such plenitude of power in temporal things.
4. Or again, the emperor does not possess in temporal matters a power greater than that which the people had, since he owes his power to the people (as was argued earlier), and the people could not transfer to him a greater jurisdiction or power than it possessed itself. But the people never possessed such a plenitude of power that it could order any of its members to do everything that does not run counter to the divine or the natural law, for it was unable to command those things that necessity did not require to be done. On this matter, note the gloss to the *Decretals*, i, 2, c. 6 in v. *cum omnes*, which says that on those things that are [not] required by necessity, "nothing can be done unless all have given their consent." Thus, if the people orders one of its members to do something that is not required by necessity, he is not bound to do it unless he so wishes; and if this is so, it follows that the emperor does not possess such a plenitude of power.
5. In addition, to falsify, alienate, sell, give, or bequeath [anything that pertains to

his imperial prerogatives] is against neither the divine nor the natural law, and yet the emperor cannot do any of these things. He lacks, therefore, a plenitude of power.

6. Furthermore, the emperor possesses no power that is perilous to the common good. But this plenitude of power would imperil the common good, for it could reduce all subjects to poverty, which would certainly be contrary to the common good.

7. Also, that power, which was established only with a view to the common utility, does not reach beyond those things that are ordained to the common utility, and, as a result, falls short of all those things that are contrary to the divine or natural laws. But the imperial power [924] was established simply to further the common utility and does not, therefore, extend to those things that do not pertain to that common utility. This may be proved by the following argument: That which is not directed to its due end seems to lack ordination, and that which lacks ordination is not to be judged lawful. But the end for which emperors are instituted is the common utility. Anything, therefore, that the emperor does by the imperial authority and does not direct to the common utility lacks ordination and, as a result, is unlawful. And from this one may infer that the emperor, by virtue of his imperial authority, cannot do all things that are not contrary to the divine or natural laws, but only those that conduce to the common utility.

Chapter 28

[He replies here to the arguments set forth in Chapter 26.]

PUPIL: Since this second opinion seems to redound to the benefit of human society and of the common good, on behalf of which we are all obliged to concern ourselves, I should like to know how reply is made to the arguments in support of the opposed opinion. Tell me, then, how one can reply to the first of the arguments set forth above in Chapter 26.

MASTER: Reply may be made to that one by posing a distinction concerning human laws. Some of these are laws of the emperor and of other particular persons and communities subject to the emperor, and these can be called civil laws. Others, however, spring in some fashion from the whole of human society, and these seem to belong to the law of nations (*jus gentium*), since they are to some extent natural and to some extent human or positive—as may be gathered from what has already been said in Chapters 10 and 11 of this part [of the book]. So long as he observes those laws that belong to the law of nations, the emperor is in no way obliged of necessity to live in accordance with his own laws, although it is proper that he should do so. For all nations, and especially those that live in accordance with the dictates of reason, accept this law. The emperor, therefore, is bound to it also, and he is not at liberty to transgress at will those laws that pertain to it, but only in a case in which he perceives them to run counter to the common utility. It would not generally be permissible for him, therefore, to forbid the seizure of thrones, wars, the taking of prisoners, the reduction of men to slavery, reprisals, the promise of immunity to ambassadors, and other matters that seem to belong to the law of nations. Now it pertains to the law of nations that the emperor should lack such a plenitude of power as would enable him to do, in temporal matters, everything that is not contrary to the divine law and the unconditional natural law (which was spoken of above in Chapters 11 and 12 of this [part of the book], just as it is deemed to pertain to the law of nations that some people should be free and not wholly servile. And, because the one follows from the other, it follows that the emperor is bound by this law [of nations]. But this is a human law, since it derives its force as law from the agreement of all men in proscribing the contrary.

PUPIL: How then can one reply to the second argument?

MASTER: To this it is said that what pleases the prince (that is, the emperor), justly and with reason on account of the common good, has—when he clearly states it—the force of law. If, however, something pleases him, not because of the common good but on account of a private good, it does not have the force of law because of this—that is to say, it does not have the force of law justly, but wrongly and unjustly.

PUPIL: This argument, like the opinion set forth in the last chapter, seems to detract from the integrity and authority of the emperors; for, according to what is written above, the emperor can establish no law unless it is a general one that looks to the common good. It follows from this that he cannot concede a privilege to anyone, since privileges are not common or general things, but pertain to private law (*Decretum*, D. 3, *secunda pars Gratiani*, para. I, and D. 3, c. 3). The inability, however, to grant a special privilege to anyone seems to detract from the integrity as well as from the authority of the emperor.

MASTER: To this it is replied that because any private person or particular association (*collegium*) is a part of the whole community, then the good of any private person and of any particular association is the good of the whole community and is capable of being ordained to, and of redounding to, the common good. It follows from this that if the emperor, in granting special privileges to some particular persons or associations, is not misled in his reasoning to the detriment of the common good, then the privileges are just and promote the common good. If, however, he does not intend the common good in this way, but grants the privileges because of personal affection or other less just cause, then these privileges are not just, but

wrong and unjust, and, by granting them, he falls into the vice of favoritism, for which he can scarcely be excused.

PUPIL: Tell me, then, what reply is made to the third argument?

MASTER: It is said that the error of the prince probably makes law, in the sense that others are obliged to obey, unless it appears to them that the error of the prince is contrary to the divine or natural laws, or to the common good. For, if this is the case, the error of the prince does not constitute law.

PUPIL: And to the fourth argument?

MASTER: Reply is made along the lines of what was said above in response to the first argument, for a person can often resist, by virtue of human law, a command of the emperor that is not contrary to the divine or natural laws. This can be done, not, indeed, on the grounds of the civil law, but of the law of nations, just as was said. Against the same argument, it is also said that it speaks of those human laws that are called *civil* and not of the law of nations. Civil laws are the laws of emperors and kings, but the law of nations is not the law of emperors or kings in the sense that they establish it—although it can be in the sense that they may approve and observe it.

PUPIL: What does this opinion maintain concerning the last of those arguments?

MASTER: It maintains this: that human society is in general agreed to submit to its kings in those things that pertain to the common good, and, as a result, that human society is in general obliged to obey the emperor in those things that conduce to the common utility, but not in those things that clearly by no means advance the common good.

NOTES

1. There is no common English equivalent for this term, whose shades of meaning include "empire," "imperial authority," "dominion," etc.
2. Cf. Matt. 16:19.
3. Gratian, *Decretum*, p. 1, d. 22, c. 1 (*Corpus iur. canon.*, ed. Friedberg, I, 73).
4. Ibid., p. 2, causa 15, q. 6, c. 3 (Friedberg, I, 756).

5. *Decretal. Greg. IX*, lib. 1, tit. 6, c. 34 (Friedberg, II, 80). The Latin tags refer to "title" and "chapter" respectively.
6. Gratian, *Decretum*, p. 1, d. 63, c. 33 (Friedberg, I, 246).
7. Cf. Luke 22:38.
8. Cf. E. A. Winkelmann, *Acta imperii inedita saeculi XIII et XIV* (Innsbruck, 1880–1885), II, 698; Augustine, *C. Faust.*, XXII, 77 (*PL*, 42, 450).
9. Matt. 26:52 and John 18:11, conflated.
10. Cf. Bartholomew of Lucca, *Determinatio compendiosa de iurisdictione imperii* (Hanover, 1909), 8.
11. Gratian, *Decretum*, p. 1, d. 96, c. 11; c. 9 (Friedberg, I, 340).
12. *Decretal. Greg. IX*, lib. 1, tit. 33, c. 6 (Friedberg, II, 196).
13. Gratian, *Decretum*, p. 1, d. 63, c. 3; d. 96, c. 12 (Friedberg, I, 235; 341). The bowing of the head here seems to be merely a symbol for submission to authority.
14. I.e., the "imperialist" arguments.
15. Gratian, *Decretum*, p. 1, d. 22, c. 1 (Friedberg, I, 73). The text is really derived from Peter Damiani, *Disceptatio synodalis* (*MGH, Libelli de lite*, I, 78).
16. Cf. Acts 1:15–26.
17. Cf. Acts 6:1–6.
18. Cf. Acts 9:31.
19. Cf. Acts 13:1–3.
20. Cf. Acts 14:22.
21. *Seniores.*
22. Cf. Acts 15:6 ff.
23. *Maioribus natu.*
24. Cf. Acts 20:17, 28.
25. Cf. Acts 11:26.
26. Gratian, *Decretum*, p. 2, causa 24, q. 1, c. 15 (Friedberg, I, 970). The Roman rite has a liturgical commemoration of the *cathedra* of St. Peter at Antioch (Feb. 22).
27. *Decretal. Greg. IX*, lib. 4, tit. 17, c. 13 (Friedberg, II, 714 ff.).
28. I.e., the critics of the "papalist" view.
29. Cf. Gregory the Great, *Homil. in evang.*, XII, I (*PL*, 76, 1119). Patristic passages are included in the lections of the Night Office of the Breviary ("Matins"); hence Ockham's method of citation.
30. Ockham's language here calls to mind his polemic in defense of the Franciscan "spirituals"; cf. P. Böhner, *The Tractatus de Successivis*, 6–9.
31. Phil. 3:20.
32. These introductory synopses that head every chapter in Goldast's text seem to have been added by Ascensius, the editor of the Lyons edition of 1494 (the text of which Goldast reprints), for they are not to be found in the first edition of the *Dialogue* (Paris, July 5, 1476).

PART VI

KNOWLEDGE AND SENSATION

CHAPTER 31

St. Augustine

(See Chapter One for biography.)

St. Augustine on Knowledge

Augustine's theory of knowledge is to a great extent a reaction to the skepticism of the New Academy as represented, for example, by the writings of Cicero. It was Augustine's study of the Neoplatonists that provided him with a positive basis for knowledge. As a consequence, he, more than anyone else during his time, shaped Christian theology by inserting into it Neoplatonic conceptions of reality. Nevertheless, the process by which we acquire knowledge is expressed in a form peculiarly his own.

All knowledge begins with the mind becoming aware of itself. *Si fallor sum*: If I doubt, I exist. That is, my existence is verified by my mental act of doubting that, for example, I exist. This I know for certain, and this knowledge is independent of any data of sense perception. The mind is aware of itself and therefore knows itself because it is incorporeal. In *De Civitate Dei* he says, "We do not discern these ideas through some bodily sense as we apprehend colors, sounds, and tastes; but without any delusive representation of spurious perception or of images I am most certain that I am and that I know this and enjoy it."

Thus the stage is set for a radical dualism in knowledge, and it is clear from the outset that sense perception occupies a secondary position. Truth is reached via ideas of the mind. This, however, does not result in subjectivism. That we are capable of communicating (via the written and spoken word) is evidence that our ideas refer to an independent and objective realism. Reality is the world of ideas.

However, there is but one knowledge. Yet it is expressed in two ways; one lower, one higher. The former is called *Scientia*. This is knowledge of temporal and changing things. This is practical knowledge and is necessary for coping with the vagaries of life. *Sapientia*, or wisdom, is the higher form of knowledge. Its subject matter is ideas. Ideas are eternal and immutable and embody truth. Consequently, the pursuit of wisdom is superior to curiosity about the physical world in which we live and function. One should not conclude, therefore, that there is no connection between the two. The mind forms images of material objects from within itself. This image formation is stimulated by sense experience. Yet an epistemological chasm remains. The mind is incorporeal, whereas the physical world is corporeal. Consequently, the material world which the mind reproduces (via sense experience) must necessarily remain a subject not of knowledge but of belief. This belief is a necessary postulate of practical everyday life. However, the images produced by sense experience are doubly important. They are also the means by which we are able to intellectually understand the eternal Ideas which are immutable. Sense experience helps the mind, as it were, in its understanding of the eternal structure of the world. *Sapientia*, then, is knowledge of Ideas, which is knowledge of the constitutive principles of things as well as of archetypes. Augustine's theory culminates in his doctrine of illumination whereby Ideas are understood to be part and parcel of divine intelligence. A complete understanding of the Ideas cannot be achieved via a purely intellectual approach. Rather, the eternal and immutable Ideas are ultimately found to be revelations of God. Therefore, true wisdom requires religious enlightenment.

DE TRINITATE

Book Ten

Chapter 10

Let not the mind then add another thing to that which it knows itself to be when it hears that it should know itself. For it knows with certainty that these words are said to itself, that is, to itself that is, lives, and understands. But a corpse also is, and a beast also lives, but neither the corpse nor the beast understands. It, therefore, knows that it is, and that it lives in such a manner as the understanding is and lives. Consequently, when the mind, for example, regards itself as air, then it thinks that the air understands, but it knows that itself understands, while it does not know that it is air, but only thinks so.

Let it, therefore, remove that which it thinks itself to be, and consider only that which it knows. Let this remain to it, which not even they have doubted who regarded the mind as this or that kind of a body. For not every mind regards itself as air, but, as I mentioned above, some regard it as fire, others as a brain, and others as this or that kind of a body. All know, however, that they understand and live; they refer what they understand to the understanding, but refer being and life to themselves. And no one doubts that no one understands who does not live, and that no one lives who is

St. Augustine, *The Trinity*, from *The Fathers of the Church: Saint Augustine; The Trinity*, translated by Stephen McKenna, C.S.S.R. (Washington, D.C.: The Catholic University of America Press, 1963), pp. 273–74, 277–78, 301–2, 307–10, 337–38, 344–45, 359–61, 363–68, 411–14, and 480–83. Reprinted by permission of The Catholic University of America Press.

not. Therefore, it follows that whatever understands also is and lives, not as a corpse is which does not live, nor as the soul of a beast lives which does not understand, but in its own proper and more exalted manner.

Moreover, they know that they will, and they likewise know that no one can will, who is not and who does not live; and similarly, they refer the will to something which they will with that will. They also know that they remember, and they know at the same time that no one would remember unless he both was and lived; but we also refer the memory itself to something which we remember with the memory. In two of these three, therefore, in the memory and the understanding, the knowledge and science of many things are contained; but the will is present by which we may enjoy or use them. For we enjoy the things that we know when the will rests by rejoicing in them for their own sake; but we use things by referring them to something else which we are to enjoy. Neither is the life of man vicious nor culpable in any other way than in enjoying things badly and in using them badly. But we shall not enter into a discussion of this subject at the present time.

But since we are investigating the nature of the mind, let us not take into consideration any knowledge that is obtained from without through the senses of the body, and consider more attentively the principle which we have laid down: that every mind knows and is certain concerning itself. For men have doubted whether the power to live, to remember, to understand, to will, to think, to know, and to judge is due to air, to fire, or to the brain, or to the blood, or to atoms, or to a fifth body—I do not know what it is—but it differs from the four customary elements; or whether the combining or the orderly arrangement of the flesh is capable of producing these effects; one endeavors to maintain this opinion, another that opinion.

On the other hand who would doubt that he lives, remembers, understands, wills, knows, and judges? For even if he doubts, he lives; if he doubts, he remembers why he doubts, if he doubts, he understands that he doubts; if he doubts, he wishes to be certain; if he doubts, he thinks; if he doubts, he knows that he does not know; if he doubts, he judges that he ought not to consent rashly. Whoever then doubts about anything else ought never to doubt about all of these; for if they were not, he would be unable to doubt about anything at all.

Those who regard the mind either as a body, or as the combination or harmony of the body, wish all these things to be seen in a subject. Thus the air, the fire, or some other body would be the substance which they call the mind, while the understanding would be in this body as its quality; and so the former would be the subject and the latter in the subject; that is, the mind which they regard as a body is the subject, while the understanding, and the other above-mentioned qualities of which we are certain, would be in the subject. And even those who do not regard the mind as a body, but as the combination or harmony of the body, are pretty nearly of the same opinion. For they differ in this respect: the former say that the mind itself is a substance, wherein the understanding is present as in a subject; but the latter declare that the mind itself is in a subject, that is, in a body of which it is the combination or harmony. Wherefore, can they logically maintain anything else

than that the understanding is also in the same body as in a subject?

All of these men overlook the fact that the mind knows itself, even when it seeks itself, as we have already shown. But we can in no way rightly say that anything is known while its substance is unknown. Wherefore, since the mind knows itself, it knows its own substance. But it is certain about itself, as is clearly shown from what we have already said. But it is by no means certain whether it is air, or fire, or a body, or anything of a body. It is, therefore, none of these things. And it belongs to that whole which is commanded to know itself, to be certain that it is none of those things of which it is uncertain, and to be certain that it alone is the only thing of which it is certain.

For the mind thinks in this way of fire, air, or any other bodily thing of which it thinks. But it can in no way happen that it should think that which itself is, in the same way as it thinks that which itself is not. For it thinks all of these through an imaginary phantasy, whether fire, or air, or this or that body, or that part or combination or harmony of the body; nor is it said to be all of these, but one or the other of them. But if it were any one of them, it would think this one in a different manner than the rest. That is to say, it would not think it through an imaginary phantasy, as absent things or something of the same kind are thought which have been touched by the sense of the body, but it would think it by a kind of inward presence not feigned but real—for there is nothing more present to it than itself; just as it thinks that it lives, and remembes, and understands, and wills. And if it adds nothing from these thoughts to itself, so as to regard itself as something of the kind, then whatever still remains to it of itself, that alone is itself.

Book Fifteen

Chapter 12

First of all, the knowledge itself from which our thought is truly formed, and when we say what we know, of what sort

is it, and how much can a man, even of the most extraordinary skill and learning, acquire? For if we pass over those things which come into the mind through the senses of the body, wherein so many things are different from what they seem, that he, who is too much pressed down by their apparent similarity to the truth, believes himself to be sane, while he is insane—and for this reason the philosophical Academy has so prevailed, that by doubting everything it has fallen into a much more wretched folly—if we, therefore, pass over those things that come from the senses of the body into the mind, how much remains of the things which we so know, as we know that we live? Here, at least, we have no fear of perhaps being deceived by some apparent likeness to the truth, because it is certain that even he who is deceived lives; nor do we know this as we know those objects of sight, which are presented from without, where the eye may be deceived, as it is deceived when it sees the bent oar in the water, and when the navigators see the towers moving, and thousands of other things which are otherwise than they appear, for we do not even see this with the eye of the flesh.

It is an inner knowledge by which we know that we live, where not even the academician can say: 'Perhaps you are sleeping, and you do not know, and you see in dreams.' For who does not know that things seen by those who are asleep are very similar to things seen by those who are awake. But he who is certain about the knowledge of his own life does not say in it: 'I know that I am awake,' but 'I know that I live'; whether he, therefore, sleeps, or whether he is awake, he lives. He cannot be deceived in his knowledge of this even by dreams, because to sleep and to see in dreams is characteristic of one who lives. Nor can the academician argue as follows against his knowledge: 'Perhaps you are insane, and do not know it, because the things seen by the sane are very similar to those seen by the insane, but he who is insane lives'; nor does he make this retort to the academicians: 'I know that I am not insane,' but 'I know that I live.' He can never, therefore be deceived nor lie who says that he knows that he lives. Let a thousand kind of optical illusions be placed before one who says: 'I know that I live'; he will fear none of them, since even he who is deceived, lives.

But if such things alone belong to human knowledge, then they are very few; unless it be that they are so multiplied in each kind that they are not only not few, but are even found to reach an infinite number. For he who says: 'I know that I live,' says that he knows one thing; if he were then to say: 'I know that I know that I live,' there are already two things, but that he knows these two, is to know a third thing; and so he can add a fourth and a fifth, and innumerable more, as long as he is able to do so. But because he cannot comprehend an innumerable number by adding one thing to another, or express a thing innumerable times, he comprehends this very fact and says with absolute certainty that this is both true and so innumerable that he cannot truly comprehend and express its infinite number.

Something similar can also be noted when the will is certain. For who would not regard: 'Perhaps you are deceived,' as an impudent reply to one who says: 'I will to be happy'? And if he were to say: 'I know that I will this, and I know that I know this,' then to these two he can also add a third, that he knows these two, and also a fourth, that he knows that he knows these two, and can likewise continue indefinitely. If someone were also to say: 'I do not will to err,' will it not be true that whether he errs or does not err, yet he does not will to err? Would it not be the height of impudence for anyone to say to this man: 'Perhaps you are deceived,' since no matter in what he may be deceived, he is certainly not deceived in not willing to be deceived? And if he says that he knows this, he adds as many known things as he pleases, and perceives it to be an infinite number. For he who says: 'I do not will to be deceived, and I know that I do not will this, and I know that I know this,' can also continue from here towards an indefinite number, however awkward this manner of expressing it may be. And other things are also found which can be used effectively against the academicians who contend that it is impossible for man to know anything.

But we have to set a limit somewhere,

especially since this is not the purpose for which we have undertaken the present work. There are three books of ours on this subject,[1] which we wrote in the first period of our conversion, and anyone who can and will read, and understand what he reads, will certainly not be moved by the many arguments which they have thought up against the perception of the truth. For since there are two kinds of things which are known: one, the knowledge of those which the mind perceives through the senses of the body, the other of those which it perceives through itself, these philosophers have babbled many things against the senses of the body; but they have been utterly unable to cast doubt upon the most certain perceptions of things that are true, which the mind knows through itself, such as that which I have already mentioned: 'I know that I live.'

But far be it from us to doubt the truth of those things which we have perceived through the senses of the body. For through them we have learned of the heavens and the earth, and those things in them which are known to us insofar as He, who has also created us and them, wanted them to become known to us. Far be it also from us to deny what we have learned from the testimony of others; otherwise, we would not know that there is an ocean; we would not know that there are lands and cities which the most celebrated fame commends; we would not know of the men and their works which we have learned in the reading of history; we would not know the news that is daily brought to us from everywhere, and is confirmed by evidence that is consistent and convincing; finally, we would not know in what places and from what persons we were born; because we have believed all of these things on the testimonies of others. But it is most absurd to deny this, and we must confess that, not only the sense of our own bodies, but also those of other persons have added very much to our knowledge.

The human mind, therefore, knows all these things which it has acquired through itself, through the senses of its body, and through the testimonies of others, and keeps them in the treasure-house of its memory; and from them a true word is begotten when we say what we know, but the word that is anterior to every sound and to every thought of sound. For then the word is most like the thing that is known, and from which its image is also begotten, since the sight of thought arises from the sight of knowledge. This is the word that belongs to no language, the true word about a true thing, having nothing from itself, but everything from that knowledge from which it is born. Nor does it make any difference when he who says what he knows has learned this, for sometimes he speaks as soon as he learns, provided only that it is a true word, that is, born from things that are known.

Book Nine

Chapter 3

The mind cannot love itself unless it also knows itself, for how can it love what it does not know? Or if anyone says that the mind by a general or special knowledge believes that it is such, as he knows from experience that others are, he is speaking in a very foolish manner. For whence does a mind know another mind if it does not know itself? For not as the eye of the body sees other eyes and does not see itself, so does the mind know other minds and does not know itself. For we see bodies through the eyes of the body, because we cannot refract the rays which shine through them and touch whatever we see, and reflect them back into the eyes themselves, except when we are looking into a mirror. But this is a subject that is discussed very subtly and very obscurely, until it can be clearly shown whether it is actually so, or whether it is not so.

But whatever may be the nature of the power by which we see through the eyes, we certainly do not see the power itself, whether it be rays or anything else, with the eyes, but we seek it in the mind; and if it is possible, we also comprehend it in the mind. As the mind itself, therefore, gathers the knowledge of corporeal things through the bodily senses, so it gains the knowledge of incorporeal things through itself, since it is incorporeal. For if it does not know itself, it does not love itself.

Book Nine

Chapter 5

But in these three, when the mind knows itself and loves itself, a trinity remains: the mind, love, and knowledge; and there is no confusion through any commingling, although each is a substance in itself, and all are found mutually in all, whether each one in each two, or each two in each one. Consequently, all are in all. For the mind is certainly in itself, since it is called a mind in respect to itself, although in relation to its knowledge it is spoken of as knowing, as being known, or as knowable; and when referring to the love by which it loves itself, it is also spoken of as loving, as being loved, or as lovable. And knowledge, although it is referred to a mind that either knows or is known, yet in respect to itself it is also spoken of both as known and as knowing, for the knowledge by which the mind itself knows itself is not unknown to itself. And love, although it is referred to the mind that loves, of which it is the love, yet it is likewise love in respect to itself, so that it also exists in itself. For love is also loved, nor can it be loved with anything else except with love, that is, with itself. And so each exists in itself. But they are mutually in each other in such a way that the mind that loves is in the love, and love is in the knowledge of him that loves, and knowledge is in the mind that knows.

And so each one is in each two, because the mind that knows and loves itself is in its own love and knowledge; and the love of the mind that knows and loves itself is in the mind and in its knowledge; and the knowledge of the mind that knows and loves itself is in the mind and in its love; because it loves itself as knowing and knows itself as loving. And for this reason each two are also in each one, because the mind that knows and loves itself is in the love with its knowledge, and in the knowledge with its love, since the love itself and the knowledge are also together in the mind that loves and knows itself. But we have shown above, how all are in all, since the mind loves itself as a whole, and knows itself as a whole, and knows all its love, and loves all its knowledge, when these three are perfect in respect to themselves. These three, therefore, are in a marvelous manner inseparable from one another; and yet each of them is a substance, and all together are one substance or essence, while the terms themselves express a mutual relationship.

Book Ten

Chapter 5

Why, then, was it commanded to know itself? It was, I believe, that it might consider itself and live according to its nature, that is, that it might desire to be ruled according to its nature, namely, under Him to whom it must be brought into subjection, and above those to whom it must be preferred; under Him by whom it must be governed, above those whom it must govern. For it does many things through evil desires, as though it had forgotten itself.

For it sees certain intrinsically beautiful things in that more excellent nature which is God, and it ought to remain steadfast in order to enjoy them. But when it wishes to appropriate these things to itself, and to be like Him but not by Him, but by its own self to be what He is, then it is turned away from Him, is moved, and slips into less and less, which it considers to be more and more. For it is not sufficient to itself, nor is anything at all sufficient to him who departs from Him who is alone sufficient. And, therefore, through its need and want, it becomes excessively intent upon its own actions and the fickle pleasures which it gathers through them, and thus by desiring to seek knowledge from these things that are without, the nature of which it knows and loves and which it feels can be lost unless held fast by devoted care, it loses its security; and it thinks itself so much the less, the more certain it is that it cannot lose itself.

Thus, although it is one thing not to know oneself, and another thing not to think of oneself—for we do not say that a man, skilled in many branches of knowledge, is ignorant of grammar when he is not thinking of it, because he is then thinking of the art of medicine—although it is, therefore, one thing not to know oneself and another thing not to think of oneself, yet the force of love is so great that the mind draws in with itself those things upon which it has long reflected with love, and to which it has become attached by its devoted care, even when it returns in some way to think of itself. And because they are bodies which it has loved outside of itself through the senses of the body, and with which it has become entangled by a kind of daily familiarity, it cannot bring them into itself as though into a country of incorporeal nature, and, therefore, it fastens together their images, which it has made out of itself, and forces them into itself. For in forming them it gives them something of its own essence, but it also keeps something by which it may freely judge of the species of these images; this is what is called more precisely the mind, namely, the rational understanding which is kept in order to pass judgment. For we perceive that we have, in common with the beasts, those parts of the soul that are informed by the images of bodies.

Book Eleven

Chapter 9

In this arrangement, therefore, when we begin with the species of the body, and finally arrive at the species which is formed in the gaze of thought, four species are found; they are born, as it were, step by step, one from the other: the second from the first, the third from the second, and the fourth from the third. For the species of the body, which is perceived, produces the species which arises in the sense of the percipient; this latter gives rise to the species in the memory; finally, the species in the memory produces the species which arises in the gaze of thought. Hence, the will thrice unites, as it were, the parent with its offspring: first of all, the species of the body with which it begets in the sense of the body; and this again with that which arises from it in the memory; and this also thirdly, with that which is born from it in the gaze of thought. But the intermediate combination, which is the second, although nearer to the first, is not as similar to it as the third is.

For there are two visions, one of perception, the other of thought. But in order that this vision of thought may be brought about, something similar to it is wrought for this purpose in the memory from the vision of perception, to which the eye of the mind may turn itself in thinking in the same way, as the glance of the eyes turns itself in perceiving to the body. I have, therefore, chosen to mention two trinities of this kind; one, when the vision of perception is formed by the body, the other, when the vision of thought is formed by the memory. But I did not wish to explain the intermediate one because we usually do not speak of a vision there, since the form which arises in the sense of the one seeing is entrusted to the memory. But the will appears everywhere only as the unifier, so to speak, of the parent and the offspring. And for this reason it cannot be called either the

parent or the offspring, no matter from where it may proceed.

Book Twelve

Chapter 3

That part of us, however, which is thus concerned with the treatment of corporeal and temporal things, in that it is not common to us and beasts, is indeed rational, but is drawn, as it were, out of that rational substance of our minds, by which we depend upon and adhere to the intelligible and unchangeable truth, and which is deputed to handle and to direct the inferior things. For just as among all the beasts, a help like unto himself was not found for man, unless one were taken from himself and formed into his consort, so for our mind, by which we consult the superior and inner things, for such employment of corporeal things as the nature of man re-

quires, no help like unto itself was found in the parts of the soul which we have in common with the beasts.

And, therefore, a certain part of our reason, not separated so as to sever unity, but diverted, as it were, so as to help fellowship, is set aside for the performing of its own proper work. And just as in man and woman there is one flesh of two, so the one nature of the mind embraces our intellect and action, or our council and execution, or our reason and reasonable appetite, or whatever other more significant terms there may be for expressing them, so that as it was said of those: 'They shall be two in one flesh,'[2] so it can be said of these: 'Two in one mind.'

Book Twelve

Chapter 12

Insofar as the Lord grants His help, let us now complete the study that we have undertaken of that part of reason to which science belongs, namely, the cognition of temporal and changeable things that is necessary for managing the affairs of this life. For just as in that visible marriage of the two human beings who were the first to be made, the serpent did not eat of the forbidden tree, but only persuaded to eat; but the woman did not eat alone, but also gave to her husband and both ate together, even though she alone spoke to the serpent, and she alone was seduced by him;[3] so too in that hidden and secret marriage, which also takes place and can be discerned in a single

human being, the carnal, or as I should say, the sensual movement of the soul which is directed to the senses of the body, and which is common to us and to beasts, has been excluded from the reason of wisdom.

For corporeal things are perceived by the sense of the body, but the eternal and unchangeable spiritual things are understood by the reason of wisdom. Yet the reason of science has appetite very near to it, seeing that what is called the science of action reasons about the corporeal things themselves that are perceived by the sense of the body; if well, in order that it may refer that knowledge to the end of its highest good, but if badly, in order that it may rejoice, as it were, in such goods in which it rests in a false happiness.

Book Twelve

Chapter 14

For science, too, has its good measure if that which in it puffs up, or is wont to puff

up, is overcome by the love for eternal things which does not puff up but, as we know, edifies.[4] For without science we cannot even possess the very virtues by which we live rightly and by which this miserable life is so regulated that it may arrive at that eternal life which is truly blessed.

But there is a difference between the contemplation of eternal things and the action by which we use temporal things well; the former is called wisdom, the latter science. For though that which is wisdom can also be called science, as the Apostle also speaks of it where he says: 'Now I know in part; but then I shall know even as I have been known';[5] when he certainly means that science is to be understood as the contemplation of God which will be the supreme reward of the saints; yet where he says: 'To one indeed through the Spirit is given the utterance of wisdom; and to another the utterance of knowledge, according to the same Spirit,'[6] there is no doubt that he is clearly distinguishing between these two things, though he does not explain there what the difference is, and by what means both can be distinguished.

But in examining the manifold riches of the Sacred Scriptures, I find it written in the book of Job, where that same holy man is speaking: 'Behold, piety is wisdom, but to abstain from evil is knowledge.'[7] In this distinction it is to be understood that wisdom pertains to contemplation, science to action. For by piety in this passage he meant the worship of God, which in Greek is called *theosébia*. For this is the word used in this sentence in the Greek codices. And what is there in eternal things more excellent than God, who alone has an unchangeable nature? And what else is the worship of Him if not the love of Him, by which we now desire to see Him and believe that we shall one day see Him; and insofar as we make progress 'we see now through a glass in a dark manner, but then' in the manifestation? For this is what the Apostle calles 'face to face,'[8] and this is what John also says: 'Dearly beloved, now we are the children of God, and it has not yet appeared what we shall be. We know that, when he shall appear, we shall be like to him, for we shall see him just as he is.'[9] The utterance (*sermo*) about these and other subjects of this kind seems to me to be the utterance itself of wisdom.

But to abstain from evil things, which Job called knowledge, undoubtedly belongs to the category of temporal things. For it is in relation to time that we are subject to evil things, and we must abstain from them in order to come to those eternal goods. Wherefore, whatever we do prudently, courageously, temperately, and justly, and whatever knowledge we gather from history, either as furnishing us with examples to guard against or to imitate, and with the necessary proofs respecting any subject that is accommodated to our use, pertain to that science or discipline, wherewith our action is conversant in avoiding evil and in desiring good.

Hence, when the utterance is about these things I hold it to be 'the utterance of knowledge,' to be distinguished from 'the utterance of wisdom,' to which belong those things which neither have been nor shall be, but which are; and on account of that eternity in which they are, it is said of them that they have been, are, and shall be without any changeableness of times. For they have not been in such a way that they have ceased to be, nor shall they be in such a way as if they were not now, but they always had and always will have the selfsame being. But they abide not as bodies fixed in space and place, but as intelligible things in their incorporeal nature they are so present to the gaze of the mind, as those visible and tangible things are present in their places to the senses of the body.

But not only in regard to sensible things established in space do there abide intelligible and incorporeal reasons, apart from local space, but also in regard to the motions that pass by in periods of time, there stand also like reasons, apart from any transit in time, reasons themselves that are certainly intelligible and not sensible. Only a few succeed in arriving at these things with the eye of the mind, and when it does arrive insofar as it can, the one who arrives does not abide in them, but is repulsed by the rebounding, as it were, of the eye itself, and thus a transitory thought is formed of a thing that is not transitory.

And yet this transitory thought is committed to the memory by means of the sciences in which the mind is instructed, so that there may be a place to which the thought that was forced to pass from thence may again return; although if the thought should not return to the memory and find there what it had committed to it, then it would have to be brought to them as an uninstructed person, as it had already once been brought, and would find it where it had found it the first time, namely, in that incorporeal truth from which it would again be written down, as it were, and fixed in the memory. For a man's thought does not abide in the incorporeal and unchangeable reason of a square body, for example, as this incorporeal and unchangeable reason itself abides, if, in fact, it could attain to it without the phantasy of local space. Or if one were to grasp the rhythm of some artificial and musical sound, passing through intervals of time, while it stands apart from time in a kind of secret and sublime silence, then it could at least be conceived as long as that singing could be heard. Yet what the gaze of the mind snatched from it, even though only in passing, and swallowing as it were into a belly, stored it in the memory, over this it will be able in a certain measure to ruminate again by recollection, and transfer what it has thus learned into the respective branch of knowledge. But if it shall have been blotted out by absolute forgetfulness, then under the guidance of doctrine it will again come to that which had completely dropped away, and it will be found such as it was.

Chapter 15

Therefore, that noble philosopher, Plato, endeavored to persuade that the souls of men had lived here even before they had these bodies; and hence, it is that those things which are learned are rather remembered as known, than known as new things. For, he relates how a certain boy, when asked I know not what about geometry, replied in such a way as if he were most proficient in this branch of learning. For when questioned step by step and skillfully, he saw what was to be seen and spoke of what he had seen.[10]

But if this were a recollecting of things previously known, then certainly everyone, or almost everyone, would be unable to do the same thing if questioned in this manner. For not all have been geometricians in their previous life, since there are so few of them in the human race that one can hardly be found. But we ought rather to believe that the nature of the intellectual mind is so formed as to see those things which, according to the disposition of the Creator, are subjoined to intelligible things in the natural order, in a sort of incorporeal light of its own kind, as the eye of the flesh sees the things that lie about it in this corporeal light, of which light it is made to be receptive and to which it is adapted.

For the corporeal eye, too, does not, therefore, distinguish white from black objects without a master, because it had already known these colors before it was created in this flesh. Finally, how can this be done only in regard to intelligible things, so that when anyone is properly questioned he is able to answer according to any branch of learning, even though he is ignorant of it? Why can nobody do this with sensible things, unless he has seen them in this present body, or believed the testimony of those who knew them and communicated them by letters or words? For we should not credit the story of those who say that Pythagoras of Samos recalled some such things that he had experienced when he had already been here in another body, and of others who relate that there were yet some others who experienced something of the kind in their minds.

That these were false recollections, such as those we commonly experience during sleep, when we seem to remember as though we have done or seen something which we have not done or seen at all, and that the minds of those even who are awake were affected in this way by the suggestion of the evil and deceptive spirits, whose care it is to deceive men by confirming or sowing this erroneous opinion about the revolutions of souls, can be conjectured from this, that if those things were truly recalled which they had seen when they had been previously placed here in other bodies, then the same thing would happen to many, nay to almost everyone. For they suppose that as the dead come from the living, so the living come from the dead, as sleepers from those who are awake, and those who are awake from those who sleep, and that this process goes on without cessation.

If, then, this is the correct distinction between wisdom and science, that to wisdom belongs the intellectual cognition of eternal things, but to science the reasonable cognition of temporal things, it is not difficult to decide which is to be preferred to or placed after which. But if we must make use of another distinction for keeping these two things apart, it will doubtless be that which the Apostle teaches when he says: 'To one indeed through the Spirit is given the utterance of wisdom, and to another the utterance of knowledge, according to the same Spirit'; nevertheless, the distinction which we have drawn between these two is also very clear, in that the one is the intellectual cognition of eternal things, the other is the rational cognition of temporal

things, and no one doubts that the former is to be preferred to the latter.

As we, therefore, take leave of these things which pertain to the outer man, and desire to ascend within from those things which we have in common with the beasts before we come to the cognition of the intelligible and the highest things, which are eternal, the rational cognition of temporal things presents itself. Let us, therefore, also find a trinity in this if we can, just as we found it in the sense of the body, and in those things which entered into our soul or spirit in the way of images; so that instead of the corporeal things, placed outside of us, with which we came in contact through the bodily sense, we might now have the likenesses of bodies impressed within on the memory, from which thought might be formed, while the will as a third joined both together; just as in forming the sight of the eyes from without, the will applied it to the visible thing in order that vision might arise, joined both together, and itself also added itself thereto as a third.

But this subject shall not be compressed into this book in order that in the one that follows, if God shall give us His help, we may be able to investigate it properly, and then unfold whatever discoveries we have made.

NOTES

1. *Libri tres contra Academicos.* CSEL vol. 63.3–81.
2. Gen. 2.24.
3. Gen. 3.1–6.
4. Cf. I Cor. 8.1.
5. I Cor. 13.12.
6. Cf. I Cor. 12.8.
7. Cf. Job 28.28.
8. I Cor. 13.12.
9. Cf. I John 3.2.
10. Cicero in the *Tusculan Disputations* I, 24, 57, also refers to this example from Plato's *Meno*.

CHAPTER 32

St. Thomas Aquinas

(See Chapter Five for biography.)

St. Thomas Aquinas on Theory of Knowledge

The beginning point of human knowledge is via sense experience, which is always of particulars. Human beings possess no innate knowledge. Rather, we are born as tabulae rasae upon which sense experience makes impressions. At this level of cognition humans are no different than any other sentient creature. What distinguishes man from beast is his power of abstraction from the particulars he perceives. The objects of such abstraction are phantasms or mental images caused by sense experience (of particulars) and are characteristically particular. Although a phantasm may correspond to a perceived particular, it need not. It may be an abstract particular, an amalgamation of several actual particulars which have been perceived. For example, one may have the phantasm of a horse which does not correspond to any horse the owner of that phantasm has perceived; yet that amalgamated image of the horse is nonetheless particular by virtue of being a horse.

Consequently, any given phantasm is limited by the law of excluded middle. The phantasm as a particular must be characteristic of an Arabian or not, a Tennessee walker or not, a draft horse or not. The phantasm cannot include or be the general idea of a horse which includes all horses as its extension. It is the active intellect that makes possible the intellectual idea of a horse. The active intellect "illumines" the phantasm. "Illumination" is the term Aquinas uses for the process of abstraction. It is the function of the active intellect to abstract the universal element from the particular elements of a given phantasm. It is by means of the active intellect that one develops abstract concepts.

It is of utmost importance to realize that an abstract concept is primarily an instrument of knowledge or understanding. It is only secondarily an object of knowledge. Were abstract concepts primarily objects of knowledge, our knowledge would be knowledge of ideas, rendering St. Thomas a subjective idealist, which he most certainly is not. As principally instruments of knowledge, abstract concepts are vehicles of understanding the external world and how it functions. The object of sense is the sensible particular. Knowledge is different than sensation. The active intellect abstracts the essence or universal from particulars, and it is in this sense that the active intellect has direct knowledge of only universals. In turn, the intellect has within its power to "turn its attention" to the phantasms which are the vehicles by which the intellect was able to apprehend the universals. Phantasms function as a tertium quid between the intellect and the particular things represented by the phantasms. Therefore, the intellect has only indirect knowledge of the particulars of the external world. The primary knowledge the intellect has of a universal is that of the universal apprehended in the particular. Only secondarily is a universal understood *simpliciter*, as the sole object of cognition. As St. Thomas observes, ". . . we apprehend the individual through the sense and the imagination. And, therefore for the intellect to understand actually its proper object, it must of necessity turn to the phantasms in order to perceive the universal nature existing in the individual. But if the proper object of our intellect were a separate form, or if, as the Platonists say, the natures of sensible things subsisted apart from the individual, there would be no need for the intellect to turn to the phantasms whenever it understands".

At this juncture a serious problem arises for St. Thomas, namely, how is knowledge of the immaterial, and specifically God, possible? Given the preceding epistemology, Aquinas realizes that the intellect does not, indeed cannot, apprehend God indirectly. We can only come to an imperfect understanding of Him by way of analogy and by deducing what He is not. The negative approach of the latter in no way renders Him imperfect as when we reason that He is not corporeal. Yet if the sum total of our understanding of God was based on negation, we could have no idea of Him whatsoever. It is via analogy that we are capable of apprehending positive qualities of God. Whereas we cannot comprehend what constitutes infinite wisdom, we do know what wisdom is as a human attribute. By extrapolation based on analogy we develop a semipositive idea of God. But any such characterization of God will, in the end, be sorely inadequate. Man during this lifetime can never know God in any sufficient capacity.

SUMMA THEOLOGICA

Part I
Question LXXXIV
How the Soul While United to the Body
Understands Corporeal Things Beneath It
(*In Eight Articles*)

We now have to consider the acts of the soul in regard to the intellectual and the appetitive powers, for the other powers of the soul do not come directly under the consideration of the theologian. Now the acts of the appetitive part of the soul come under the consideration of the science of morals, and so we shall treat of them in the second part of this work, to which the consideration of moral matters belongs. But of the acts of the intellectual part we shall treat now. In treating of these acts, we shall

Reprinted from the *Basic Writings of Saint Thomas Aquinas*, Volume One, translated by Anton C. Pegis (New York: Random House, 1945), pp. 793, 805–35, and 843–50. Reprinted by permission of The Anton C. Pegis Estate.

proceed in the following order. First, we shall inquire how the soul understands when united to the body; secondly, how it understands when separated from the body.[1]

The former of these inquiries will be threefold: (1) How the soul understands bodies, which are beneath it. (2) How it understands itself and things contained in itself.[2] (3) How it understands immaterial substances, which are above it.[3]

In treating of the knowledge of corporeal things, there are three points to be considered: (1) Through what does the soul know them? (2) How and in what order does it know them?[4] (3) What does it know in them?[5]

Under the first head there are eight points of inquiry: (1) Whether the soul knows bodies through the intellect? (2) Whether it understands them through its essence, or through any species? (3) If through some species, whether the species of all things intelligible are naturally innate in the soul? (4) Whether these species are derived by the soul from certain separate immaterial forms? (5) Whether our soul sees in the eternal exemplars all that it understands? (6) Whether it acquires intellectual knowledge from the senses? (7) Whether the intellect can, through the species of which it is possessed, actually understand, without turning to the phantasms? (8) Whether the judgment of the intellect is hindered by an obstacle in the sensitive powers?

Sixth Article

Whether Intellectual Knowledge Is Derived from Sensible Things?

We proceed thus to the Sixth Article:—

Objection 1. It would seem that intellectual knowledge is not derived from sensible things. For Augustine says that *we cannot expect to acquire the pure truth from the senses of the body.*[6] This he proves in two ways. First, because, *whatever the bodily senses reach is continually being changed; and what is never the same cannot be perceived.* Secondly, because, *whatever we perceive by the body, even when not present to the senses, may be present in their images, as when we are asleep or angry; yet we cannot discern by the senses whether what we perceive be the sensible things themselves, or their deceptive images. Now nothing can be perceived which cannot be distinguished from its counterfeit.* And so he concludes that we cannot expect to learn the truth from the senses. But intellectual knowledge apprehends the truth. Therefore intellectual knowledge cannot be conveyed by the senses.

Obj. 2. Further, Augustine says: *We must not think that the body can make any impression on the spirit, as though the spirit were to subject itself like matter to the body's action; for that which acts is in every way more excellent than that which it acts on.*[7] Whence he concludes that *the body does not cause its image in the spirit, but the spirit itself causes it in itself.* Therefore intellectual knowledge is not derived from sensible things.

Obj. 3. Further, an effect does not surpass the power of its cause. But intellectual knowledge extends beyond sensible things, for we understand some things which cannot be perceived by the senses. Therefore intellectual knowledge is not derived from sensible things.

On the contrary, The Philosopher proves that the origin of knowledge is from the senses.[8]

I answer that, On this point the philosophers held three opinions. For Democritus held that *all knowledge is caused by images issuing from the bodies we think of and entering into our souls*, as Augustine says in his letter to Dioscorus.[9] And Aristotle says that Democritus held that knowledge is caused by a *discharge of images*.[10] And the reason for this opinion was that both Democritus and the other early philosophers did not distinguish between intellect and sense, as Aristotle relates.[11] Consequently, since the sense is immuted by the sensible, they thought that all our knowledge is caused merely by an immutation from sensible things. This immutation Democritus held to be caused by a discharge of images.

Plato, on the other hand, held that the intellect differs from sense, and that it is an immaterial power not making use of a corporeal organ for its action.[12] And since the incorporeal cannot be affected by the corporeal, he held that intellectual knowledge is not brought about by sensible things immuting the intellect, but by the participation in separate intelligible forms by the intellect, as we have said above. Moreover he held that sense is a power operating through itself. Consequently not even the sense itself, since it is a spiritual power, is affected by sensible things; but the sensible organs are affected by the sensible, with the result that the soul is in a way roused to form within itself the species of the sensible. Augustine seems to touch on this opinion where he says that the *body feels not, but the soul through the body, which it makes use of as a kind of messenger, for reproducing within itself what is announced from without.*[13] Thus according to Plato, neither does intellectual knowledge proceed from sensible knowledge, nor does sensible knowledge itself come entirely from sensible things; but these rouse the sensible soul to sensation, and the senses likewise rouse the intellect to the act of understanding.

Aristotle chose a middle course. For with Plato he agreed that intellect and sense are different.[14] But he held that the sense has not its proper operation without the cooperation of the body; so that *to sense is not an act of the soul alone,* but of the *composite.*[15] And he held the same in regard to all the operations of the sensitive part. Since, therefore, it is not incongruous that the sensible things which are outside the soul should produce some effect in the *composite,* Aristotle agreed with Democritus in this, that the operations of the sensitive part are caused by the impression of the sensible on the sense; not indeed by a discharge, as Democritus said, but by some kind of operation. Democritus, it must be remembered, maintained that every action is by way of a discharge of atoms, as we gather from *De Gener.* i.[16] But Aristotle held that the intellect has an operation in which the body does not share.[17] Now nothing corporeal can make an impression on the incorporeal. And therefore, in order to cause the intellectual operation, according to Aristotle, the impression caused by sensible bodies does not suffice, but something more noble is required, *for the agent is more noble than the patient,* as he says.[18] Not, be it observed, in the sense that the intellectual operation is affected in us by the mere impression of some superior beings, as Plato held; but that the higher and more noble agent which he calls the agent intellect, of which we have spoken above,[19] causes the phantasms received from the senses to be actually intelligible, by a process of abstraction.

According to this opinion, then, on the part of the phantasms, intellectual knowledge is caused by the senses. But since the phantasms cannot of themselves immute the possible intellect, but require to be made actually intelligible by the agent intellect, it cannot be said that sensible knowledge is the total and perfect cause of intellectual knowledge, but rather is in a way the matter of the cause.

Reply Obj. 1. These words of Augustine mean that truth is not entirely from the senses. For the light of the agent intellect is needed, through which we know the truth of changeable things unchangeably, and discern things themselves from their likenesses.

Reply Obj. 2. In this passage Augustine speaks not of intellectual but of imaginary knowledge. And since, according to the opinion of Plato, the imagination has an operation which belongs to the soul only, Augustine, in order to show that corporeal images are impressed on the imagination, not by bodies but by the soul, uses the same argument as Aristotle does in proving that the agent intellect must be separate, namely, because *the agent is more noble than the patient.*[20] And without doubt, according to the above opinion, in the imagination there must needs be not only a passive but also an active power. But if we hold, according to the opinion of Aristotle,[21] that the action of the imaginative power is an action of the *composite,* there is no difficulty; because the sensible body is more noble than the organ of the animal, in so far as it is compared to it as a being in act to a being in potentiality; even as the object actually colored is compared to the pupil which is potentially colored. Now, although the first immutation of the imagination is through the agency of the sensible, since *the phantasm is a movement produced in accordance with sensation,*[22] nevertheless, it may be said that there is in man an operation which by division and composition forms images of various things, even of things not perceived by the senses. And Augustine's words may be taken in this sense.

Reply Obj. 3. Sensitive knowledge is not the entire cause of intellectual knowledge. And therefore it is not strange that intellectual knowledge should extend beyond sensitive knowledge.

Seventh Article

Whether the Intellect Can Understand Actually Through the Intelligible Species of Which It Is Possessed, Without Turning to the Phantasms?

We proceed thus to the Seventh Article:—

Objection 1. It would seem that the intellect can understand actually through the intelligible species of which it is possessed, without turning to the phantasms. For the intellect is made actual by the intelligible species by which it is informed. But if the intellect is in act, it understands. Therefore the intelligible species suffices for the intellect to understand actually, without turning to the phantasms.

Obj. 2. Further, the imagination is more dependent on the senses than the intellect on the imagination. But the imagination can actually imagine in the absence of the sensible. Therefore much more can the intellect understand without turning to the phantasms.

Obj. 3. There are no phantasms of incorporeal things, for the imagination does not transcend time and space. If, therefore, our intellect cannot understand anything actually without turning to the phantasms, it follows that it cannot understand anything incorporeal. Which is clearly false, for we understand truth, and God, and the angels.

On the contrary, The Philosopher says that *the soul understands nothing without a phantasm.*[23]

I answer that, In the state of the present life, in which the soul is united to a corruptible body, it is impossible for our intellect to understand anything actually, except by turning to phantasms. And of this there are two indications. First of all because the intellect, being a power that does not make use of a corporeal organ, would in no way be hindered in its act through the lesion of a corporeal organ, if there were not required for its act the act of some power that does make use of a corporeal organ. Now sense, imagination and the other powers belonging to the sensitive part make use of a corporeal organ. Therefore it is clear that for the intellect to understand actually, not only when it acquires new knowledge, but also when it uses knowledge already acquired, there is need for the act of the imagination and of the other powers. For when the act of the imagination is hindered by a lesion of the corporeal organ, for instance, in a case of frenzy, or when the act of the memory is hindered, as in the case of lethargy, we see that a man is hindered from understanding actually even those things of which he had a previous knowledge. Secondly, anyone can experience this of himself, that when he tries to understand something, he forms certain phantasms to serve him by way of examples, in which as it were he examines what he is desirous of understanding. For this reason it is that when we wish to help someone to understand something, we lay examples before him, from which he can form phantasms for the purpose of understanding.

Now the reason for this is that the power of knowledge is proportioned to the thing known. Therefore the proper object of the angelic intellect, which is entirely separate from a body, is an intelligible substance separate from a body. Whereas the proper object of the human intellect, which is united to a body, is the quiddity or nature existing in corporeal matter; and it is through these natures of visible things that it rises to a certain knowledge of things invisible. Now it belongs to such a nature to exist in some individual, and this cannot be apart from corporeal matter; for instance, it belongs to the nature of a stone to be in an individual stone, and to the nature of a horse to be in an individual horse, and so forth. Therefore the nature of a stone or any material thing cannot be known completely and truly, except in as much as it is known as existing in the individual. Now we apprehend the individual through the sense and the imagination. And, therefore, for the intellect to understand actually its proper object, it must of necessity turn to the phantasms in order to perceive the universal nature existing in the individual. But if the proper object of our intellect were a separate form, or if, as the Platonists say, the natures of sensible things subsisted apart from the individual, there would be no need for the intellect to turn to the phantasms whenever it understands.

Reply Obj. 1. The species preserved in the possible intellect exist there habitually when it does not understand them actually, as we have said above.[24] Therefore for us to understand actually, the fact that the species are preserved does not suffice; we need further to make use of them in a manner befitting the things of which they are the species, which things are natures existing in individuals.

Reply Obj. 2. Even the phantasm is the likeness of an individual thing; and so the imagination does not need any further likeness of the individual whereas the intellect does.

Reply Obj. 3. Incorporeal beings, of which there are no phantasms, are known to us by comparison with sensible bodies of which there are phantasms. Thus we understand truth by considering a thing in which we see the truth; and God, as Dionysius says,[25] we know as cause, by way of excess and by way of remotion. Other incorporeal substances we know, in the state of the present life, only by way of remotion or by some comparison to corporeal things. Hence, when we understand something about these beings, we need to turn to the phantasms of bodies, although there are no phantasms of these beings themselves.

Eighth Article

Whether the Judgment of the Intellect Is Hindered Through Suspension of the Sensitive Powers?

We proceed thus to the Eighth Article:—
Objection 1. It would seem that the judg-

ment of the intellect is not hindered by suspension of the sensitive powers. For the superior does not depend on the inferior. But the judgment of the intellect is higher than the senses. Therefore the judgment of the intellect is not hindered through suspension of the senses.

Obj. 2. Further, to syllogize is an act of the intellect. But during sleep the senses are suspended, as is said in *De Somno et Vigilia*,[26] and yet it sometimes happens to us to syllogize while asleep. Therefore the judgment of the intellect is not hindered through suspension of the senses.

On the contrary, What a man does while asleep, against the moral law, is not imputed to him as a sin, as Augustine says.[27] But this would not be the case if man, while asleep, had free use of his reason and intellect. Therefore the judgment of the intellect is hindered by suspension of the senses.

I answer that, As we have said above, our intellect's proper and proportionate object is the nature of a sensible thing. Now a perfect judgment concerning anything cannot be formed, unless all that pertains to that thing be known; especially if that be ignored which is the term and end of judgment. For the Philosopher says that *as the end of practical science is a work, so the end of the science of nature is that which is perceived principally through the senses.*[28] For the smith does not seek the knowledge of a knife except for the purpose of producing this individual knife; and in like manner the natural philosopher does not seek to know the nature of a stone and of a horse, save for the purpose of knowing the essential properties of those things which he perceives with his senses. Now it is clear that a smith cannot judge perfectly of a knife unless he knows what making this particular knife means; and in like manner the natural philosopher cannot judge perfectly of natural things, unless he knows sensible things. But in the present state of life, whatever we understand we know by comparison with natural sensible things. Consequently it is not possible for our intellect to form a perfect judgment while the senses are suspended, through which sensible things are known to us.

Reply Obj. 1. Although the intellect is superior to the senses, nevertheless in a manner it receives from the senses, and its first and principal objects are founded in sensible things. Hence, suspension of the senses necessarily involves a hindrance to the judgment of the intellect.

Reply Obj. 2. The senses are suspended in the sleeper through certain evaporations and the escape of certain exhalations, as we read in *De Somno et Vigilia.*[29] And, therefore, according to the disposition of such evaporation, the senses are more or less suspended. For when the movement of the vapors is very agitated, not only are the senses suspended, but also the imagination, so that there are no phantasms; as happens especially when a man falls asleep after much eating and drinking. If, however, the movement of the vapors be somewhat less violent, phantasms appear, but distorted and without sequence; as hap-

pens in a case of fever. And if the movement be still more attenuated, the phantasms will have a certain sequence; as happens especially towards the end of sleep, and in sober men and those who are gifted with a strong imagination. If the movement be very slight, not only does the imagination retain its freedom, but even the common sense is partly freed; so that sometimes while asleep a man may judge that what he sees is a dream, discerning, as it were, between things and their images. Nevertheless, the common sense remains partly suspended, and therefore, although it discriminates some images from reality, yet it is always deceived in some particular. Therefore, while a man is asleep, according as sense and imagination are free, so is the judgment of his intellect unfettered, though not entirely. Consequently, if a man syllogizes while asleep, when he wakes up he invariably recognizes a flaw in some respect.

Question LXXXV
The Mode and Order of Understanding
(*In Eight Articles*)

We come now to consider the mode and order of understanding. Under this head there are eight points of inquiry: (1) Whether our intellect understands by abstracting species from the phantasms? (2) Whether the intelligible species abstracted from the phantasms are what our intellect understands, or that whereby it understands? (3) Whether our intellect naturally first understands the more universal? (4) Whether our intellect can know many things at the same time? (5) Whether our intellect understands by composition and division? (6) Whether the intellect can err? (7) Whether one intellect can understand the same thing better than another? (8) Whether our intellect understands the indivisible before the divisible?

First Article

Whether Our Intellect Understands Corporeal and Material Things by Abstraction from Phantasms?

We proceed thus to the First Article:—

Objection 1. It would seem that our intellect does not understand corporeal and material things by abstraction from the phantasms. For the intellect is false if it understands a thing otherwise than as it is. Now the forms of material things do not exist in abstraction from the particular things represented by the phantasms. Therefore, if we understand material things by the abstraction of species from phantasms, there will be error in the intellect.

Obj. 2. Further, material things are those

natural things which include matter in their definition. But nothing can be understood apart from that which enters into its definition. Therefore material things cannot be understood apart from matter. Now matter is the principle of individuation. Therefore material things cannot be understood by the abstraction of the universal from the particular; and this is to abstract intelligible species from the phantasm.

Obj. 3. Further, the Philosopher says that the phantasm is to the intellectual soul what color is to the sight.[30] But seeing is not caused by abstraction of species from color, but by color impressing itself on the sight. Therefore neither does the act of understanding take place by the abstraction of something from the phantasms, but by the phantasms impressing themselves on the intellect.

Obj. 4. Further, the Philosopher says that there are two things in the intellectual soul—the possible intellect and the agent intellect.[31] But it does not belong to the possible intellect to abstract the intelligible species from the phantasm, but to receive them already abstracted. Neither does it seem to be the function of the agent intellect, which is related to phantasms as light is to colors; since light does not abstract anything from colors, but rather acts on them. Therefore in no way do we understand by abstraction from phantasms.

Obj. 5. Further, the Philosopher says that *the intellect understands the species in the phantasms*,[32] and not, therefore, by abstraction.

On the contrary, The Philosopher says that *things are intelligible in proportion as they are separable from matter.*[33] Therefore material things must needs be understood according as they are abstracted from matter and from material images, namely, phantasms.

I answer that, As stated above, the object of knowledge is proportionate to the power of knowledge.[34] Now there are three grades of the cognitive powers. For one cognitive power, namely, the sense, is the act of a corporeal organ. And therefore the object of every sensitive power is a form as existing in corporeal matter; and since such matter is the principle of individuation, therefore every power of the sensitive part can have knowledge only of particulars. There is another grade of cognitive power which is neither the act of a corporeal organ, nor in any way connected with corporeal matter. Such is the angelic intellect, the object of whose cognitive power is therefore a form existing apart from matter; for though angels know material things, yet they do not know them save in something immaterial, namely, either in themselves or in God. But the human intellect holds a middle place; for it is not the act of an organ, and yet it is a power of the soul, which is the form of the body, as is clear from what we have said above.[35] And therefore it is proper to it to know a form existing individually in corporeal matter, but not as existing in this individual matter. But to know what is in individual matter, yet not as existing in such matter, is to abstract the form from individual matter which is represented by the phantasms. Therefore we must needs say that our intellect understands material things by abstracting from phantasms; and that through material things thus considered we acquire some knowledge of immaterial things, just as, on the contrary, angels know material things through the immaterial.

But Plato, considering only the immateriality of the human intellect, and not that it is somehow united to the body, held that the objects of the intellect are separate Ideas, and that we understand, not by abstraction, but rather by participating in abstractions, as was stated above.[36]

Reply Obj. 1. Abstraction may occur in two ways. First, by way of composition and division, and thus we may understand that one thing does not exist in some other, or that it is separate from it. Secondly, by way of a simple and absolute consideration; and thus we understand one thing without considering another. Thus, for the intellect to abstract one from another things which are not really abstract from one another, does, in the first mode of abstraction, imply falsehood. But, in the second mode of abstraction, for the intellect to abstract things which are not really abstract from one another, does not involve falsehood, as clearly appears in the case of the senses. For if we said that color is not in a colored body, or that it is separate from it, there would be error in what we thought or said. But if we consider color and its properties, without reference to the apple which is colored, or if we express in word what we thus understand, there is no error in such an opinion or assertion; for an apple is not essential to color, and therefore color can be understood independently of the apple. In the same way, the things which belong to the species of a material thing, such as a stone, or a man, or a horse, can be thought without the individual principles which do not belong to the notion of the species. This is what we mean by abstracting the universal from the particular, or the intelligible species from the phantasm; in other words, this is to consider the nature of the species apart from its individual principles represented by the phantasms. If, therefore, the intellect is said to be false when it understands a thing otherwise than as it is, that is so, if the word *otherwise* refers to the thing understood; for the intellect is false when it understands a thing to be otherwise than as it is. Hence, the intellect would be false if it abstracted the species of a stone from its matter in such a way as to think that the species did not exist in matter, as Plato held.[37] But it is not so, if the word *otherwise* be taken as referring to the one who understands. For it is quite true that the mode of understanding, in one who understands, is not the same as the mode of a thing in being; since the thing understood is immaterially in the one who understands, according to the mode of the intellect, and not materially, according to the mode of a material thing.

Reply Obj. 2. Some have thought that the species of a natural thing is a form only, and that matter is not part of the species.[38]

If that were so, matter would not enter into the definition of natural things. Therefore we must disagree and say that matter is twofold, common and *signate*, or individual: common, such as flesh and bone; individual, such as this flesh and these bones. The intellect therefore abstracts the species of a natural thing from the individual sensible matter, but not from the common sensible matter. For example, it abstracts the species of *man* from *this flesh and these bones*, which do not belong to the species as such, but to the individual,[39] and need not be considered in the species. But the species of man cannot be abstracted by the intellect from *flesh and bones*.

Mathematical species, however, can be abstracted by the intellect not only from individual sensible matter, but also from common sensible matter. But they cannot be abstracted from common intelligible matter, but only from individual intelligible matter. For sensible matter is corporeal matter as subject to sensible qualities, such as being cold or hot, hard or soft, and the like; while intelligible matter is substance as subject to quantity. Now it is manifest that quantity is in substance before sensible qualities are. Hence quantities, such as number, dimension, and figures, which are the terminations of quantity, can be considered apart from sensible qualities, and this is to abstract them from sensible matter. But they cannot be considered without understanding the substance which is subject to the quantity, for that would be to abstract them from common intelligible matter. Yet they can be considered apart from this or that substance, and this is to abstract them from individual intelligible matter.

But some things can be abstracted even from common intelligible matter, such as *being, unity, potency, act*, and the like, all of which can exist without matter, as can be verified in the case of immaterial substances. And because Plato failed to consider the twofold kind of abstraction, as above explained, he held that all those things which we have stated to be abstracted by the intellect, are abstract in reality.[40]

Reply Obj. 3. Colors, as being in individual corporeal matter, have the same mode of being as the power of sight; and therefore they can impress their own image on the eye. But phantasms, since they are images of individuals, and exist in corporeal organs, have not the same mode of being as the human intellect, as is clear from what we have said, and therefore they have not the power of themselves to make an impression on the possible intellect. But through the power of the agent intellect, there results in the possible intellect a certain likeness produced by the turning of the agent intellect toward the phantasms. This likeness represents what is in the phantasms, but includes only the nature of the species. It is thus that the intelligible species is said to be abstracted from the phantasm; not that the identical form which previously was in the phantasm is subsequently in the possible intellect, as a body transferred from one place to another.

Reply Obj. 4. Not only does the agent intellect illumine phantasms, it does more; by its power intelligible species are abstracted from phantasms. It illumines phantasms because, just as the sensitive part acquires a greater power by its conjunction with the intellectual part, so through the power of the agent intellect phantasms are made more fit for the abstraction of intelligible intentions from them. Now the agent intellect abstracts intelligible species from phantasms inasmuch as by its power we are able to take into our consideration the natures of species without individual conditions. It is in accord with their likenesses that the possible intellect is informed.

Reply Obj. 5. Our intellect both abstracts the intelligible species *from* phantasms, inasmuch as it considers the natures of things universally, and yet understands these natures *in* the phantasms, since it cannot understand the things, of which it abstracts the species, without turning to phantasms, as we have said above.[41]

Second Article

Whether the Intelligible Species
Abstracted from Phantasms
Are Related to Our Intellect
as That Which Is Understood?

We proceed thus to the Second Article:—

Objection 1. It would seem that the intelligible species abstracted from phantasms are related to our intellect as that which is understood. For the understood in act is in the one who understands: since the understood in act is the intellect itself in act. But nothing of what is understood is in the actually understanding intellect save the abstracted intelligible species. Therefore this species is what is actually understood.

Obj. 2. Further, what is actually understood must be in something; or else it would be nothing. But it is not in something outside the soul; for, since what is outside the soul is material, nothing therein can be actually understood. Therefore what is actually understood is in the intellect. Consequently it can be nothing else than the aforesaid intelligible species.

Obj. 3. Further, the Philosopher says that *words are signs of the passions in the soul.*[42] But words signify the things understood, for we express by word what we understand. Therefore these passions of the soul, viz., the intelligible species, are what is actually understood.

On the contrary, The intelligible species is to the intellect what the sensible species is to the sense. But the sensible species is not *what* is perceived, but rather that *by which* the sense perceives. Therefore the intelligible species is not what is actually understood, but that *by which* the intellect understands.

I answer that, Some[43] have asserted that our intellectual powers know only the impressions made on them; as, for example, that sense is cognizant only of the impression made on its own organ. According to this theory, the intellect understands only its own impressions, namely, the intelligible species which it has received. This is, however, manifestly false for two reasons. First, because the things we understand are also the objects of science. Therefore, if what we understand is merely the intelligible species in the soul, it would follow that every science would be concerned, not with things outside the soul, but only with the intelligible species within the soul; just as, according to the teaching of the Platonists, all the sciences are about Ideas, which they held to be that which is actually understood.[44] Secondly, it is untrue, because it would lead to the opinion of the ancients who maintained that *whatever seems, is true*,[45] and that consequently contradictories are true simultaneously. For if a power knows only its own impressions, it can judge only of them. Now a thing *seems* according to the impression made on the cognitive power. Consequently the cognitive power will always judge of its own impression as such; and so every judgment will be true. For instance, if taste perceived only its own impression, when anyone with a healthy taste perceives that honey is sweet, he would judge truly, and if anyone with a corrupt taste perceives that honey is bitter, this would be equally true; for each would judge according to the impression on his taste. Thus every opinion, in fact, every sort of apprehension, would be equally true.

Therefore it must be said that the intelligible species is related to the intellect as that by which it understands. Which is proved thus. Now action is twofold, as it is said in *Metaph.* ix:[46] one which remains in the agent (for instance, to see and to understand), and another which passes into an external object (for instance, to heat and to cut). Each of these actions proceeds in virtue of some form. And just as the form from which proceeds an act tending to something external is the likeness of the object of the action, as heat in the heater is a likeness of the thing heated, so the form from which proceeds an action remaining in the agent is a likeness of the object. Hence that by which the sight sees is the likeness of the visible thing; and the likeness of the thing understood, that is, the

intelligible species, is the form by which the intellect understands. But since the intellect reflects upon itself, by such reflection it understands both its own act of understanding, and the species by which it understands. Thus the intelligible species is secondarily that which is understood; but that which is primarily understood is the thing of which the species is the likeness.

This also appears from the opinion of the ancient philosophers, who said that *like is known by like*.[47] For they said that the soul knows the earth outside itself by the earth within itself; and so of the rest. If, therefore, we take the species of the earth instead of the earth, in accord with Aristotle who says *that a stone is not in the soul, but only the likeness of the stone*,[48] it follows that by means of its intelligible species the soul knows the things which are outside it.

Reply Obj. 1. The thing understood is in the knower by its own likeness. It is in this sense that we say that the thing actually understood is the intellect in act, because the likeness of the thing understood is the form of the intellect, just as the likeness of a sensible thing is the form of the sense in act. Hence it does not follow that the abstracted intelligible species is what is actually understood; but rather that it is the likeness thereof.

Reply Obj. 2. In these words *the thing actually understood* there is a double meaning:—the thing which is understood, and the fact that it is understood. In like manner, the words *abstract universal* mean two things, the nature of a thing and its abstraction or universality. Therefore the nature itself which suffers the act of being understood, or the act of being abstracted, or the intention of universality, exists only in individuals; but that it is understood, abstracted or considered as universal is in the intellect. We see something similar to this in the senses. For the sight sees the color of the apple apart from its smell. If therefore it be asked where is the color which is seen apart from the smell, it is quite clear that the color which is seen is only in the apple; but that it be perceived apart from the smell, this is owing to the sight, inasmuch as sight receives the likeness of color and not of smell. In like manner, the humanity which is understood exists only in this or that man; but that humanity be apprehended without the conditions of individuality, that is, that it be abstracted and consequently considered as universal, befalls humanity inasmuch as it is perceived by the intellect, in which there is a likeness of the specific nature, but not of the individual principles.

Reply Obj. 3. There are two operations in the sensitive part. One is limited to immutation, and thus the operation of the senses takes place when the senses are impressed by the sensible. The other is formation, inasmuch as the imagination forms for itself an image of an absent thing, or even of something never seen. Both of these operations are found in the intellect. For in the first place there is the passion of the possible intellect as informed by the intelligible species; and then the possible intellect, as thus informed, then forms a definition, or a division, or a composition, which is expressed by language. And so, the notion signified by a *term* is a definition; and a *proposition* signifies the intellect's division or composition. Words do not therefore signify the intelligible species themselves; but that which the intellect forms for itself for the purpose of judging of external things.

Third Article

Whether the More Universal Is First in Our Intellectual Cognition?

We proceed thus to the Third Article:—
Objection 1. It would seem that the more universal is not first in our intellectual cognition. For what is first and more known in its own nature is secondarily and less known in relation to ourselves. But universals come first as regards their nature, because *that is first which does not involve the existence of its correlative.* Therefore universals are secondarily known by our intellect.

Obj. 2. Further, the composite precedes the simple in relation to us. But universals are the more simple. Therefore they are known secondarily by us.

Obj. 3. Further, the Philosopher says that the object defined comes in our knowledge before the parts of its definition.[49] But the more universal is part of the definition of the less universal, as *animal* is part of the definition of *man*. Therefore universals are secondarily known by us.

Obj. 4. Further, we know causes and principles by their effects. But universals are principles. Therefore universals are secondarily known by us.

On the contrary, We must proceed from the universal to the singular.[50]

I answer that, In our knowledge there are two things to be considered. First, that intellectual knowledge in some degree arises from sensible knowledge. Now because sense has singular and individual things for its object, and intellect has the universal for its object, it follows that our knowledge of the former comes before our knowledge of the latter. Secondly, we must consider that our intellect proceeds from a state of potentiality to a state of actuality; and that every power thus proceeding from potentiality to actuality comes first to an incomplete act, which is intermediate between potentiality and actuality, before accomplishing the perfect act. The perfect act of the intellect is complete knowledge, when the object is distinctly and determinately known; whereas the incomplete act is imperfect knowledge, when the object is known indistinctly, and as it were confusedly. A thing thus imperfectly known is known partly in act and partly in potentiality. Hence the Philosopher says that *what is manifest and certain is known to us at first confusedly; afterwards we know it by distinguishing its principles and elements.*[51] Now it is evident that to know something that comprises many things, without a proper knowledge of each thing contained in it, is to know that thing confusedly. In this way we can have knowledge not only of the universal whole, which contains parts potentially, but also of the integral whole; for each whole can be known confusedly, without its parts being known distinctly. But to know distinctly what is contained in the universal whole is to know the less common; and thus to know *animal* indistinctly is to know it as *animal*, whereas to know *animal* distinctly is to know it as *rational* or *irrational animal*, that is, to know a man or a lion. And so our intellect knows *animal* before it knows man; and the same reason holds in comparing any more universal concept with the less universal.

Moreover, as sense, like the intellect, proceeds from potentiality to act, the same order of knowledge appears in the senses. For by sense we judge of the more common before the less common, in reference both to place and time. In reference to place, when a thing is seen afar off it is seen to be a body before it is seen to be an animal, and to be an animal before it is seen to be a man, and to be a man before it is seen to be Socrates or Plato. The same is true as regards time, for a child can distinguish man from not-man before he distinguishes this man from that, and therefore *children at first call all men fathers, and later on distinguish each one from the others.*[52] The reason of this is clear: he who knows a thing indistinctly is in a state of potentiality as regards its principle of distinction; just as he who knows *genus* is in a state of potentiality as regards *difference*. Thus it is evident that indistinct knowledge is midway between potentiality and act.

We must therefore conclude that knowledge of the singular and individual is prior, as regards us, to the knowledge of the universal, just as sensible knowledge is prior to intellectual knowledge. But in both sense and intellect the knowledge of the more common precedes the knowledge of the less common.

Reply Obj. 1. The universal can be considered in two ways. First, the universal nature may be considered together with the intention of universality. And since the intention of universality—viz., the relation of one and the same to many—is due to in-

tellectual abstraction, the universal thus considered is subsequent in our knowledge. Hence it is said that the *universal animal is either nothing or something subsequent.*[53] But according to Plato, who held that universals are subsistent, the universal considered thus would be prior to the particular, for the latter, according to him, are mere participations in the subsistent universals which he called Ideas.[54]

Secondly, the universal can be considered according to the nature itself (for instance, *animality* or *humanity*) as existing in the individual. And thus we must distinguish two orders of nature: one, by way of generation and time; and thus the imperfect and the potential come first. In this way the more common comes first in the order of nature. This appears clearly in the generation of man and animal; for *the animal is generated before man*, as the Philosopher says.[55] The other order is the order of perfection or of the intention of nature. For instance, act considered absolutely is naturally prior to potentiality, and the perfect to the imperfect; and thus the less common comes naturally before the more common, as man comes before animal. For the intention of nature does not stop at the generation of animal, but aims at the generation of man.

Reply Obj. 2. The more common universal may be compared to the less common as a whole, and as a part. As a whole, inasmuch as in the more universal there is potentially contained not only the less universal, but also other things; as in *animal* is contained not only *man* but also *horse*. As a part, inasmuch as the less common universal contains in its notion not only the more common, but also more; as *man* contains not only *animal* but also *rational*. Therefore *animal* considered in itself is in our knowledge before *man*; but *man* comes before *animal* considered as a part of the notion of man.

Reply Obj. 3. A part can be known in two ways. First, absolutely considered in itself; and thus nothing prevents the parts from being known before the whole, as stones are known before a house is known. Secondly, as belonging to a certain whole; and thus we must needs know the whole before its parts. For we know a house confusedly before we know its different parts. So, likewise, that which defines is known before the thing defined is known; otherwise the thing defined would not be made known by the definition. But as parts of the definition they are known after. For we know man confusedly as man before we know how to distinguish all that belongs to human nature.

Reply Obj. 4. The universal, as understood with the intention of universality, is, in a certain manner, a principle of knowledge, in so far as the intention of universality results from the mode of understanding, which is by way of abstraction. But that which is a principle of knowledge is not of necessity a principle of being, as Plato thought, since at times we know a cause through its effect, and substance through accidents. Therefore the universal thus considered, according to the opinion of Aristotle, is neither a principle of being, nor a substance, as he makes clear.[56] But if we consider the generic or specific nature itself as existing in the singular, thus in a way it has the character of a formal principle in regard to singulars; for the singular is the result of matter, while the nature of the species is from the form. But the generic nature is compared to the specific nature rather after the fashion of a material principle, because the generic nature is taken from that which is material in a thing, while the nature of the species is taken from that which is formal. Thus the notion of animal is taken from the sensitive part, whereas the notion of man is taken from the intellectual part. Thus it is that the ultimate intention of nature is towards the species and not the individual, or the genus; because the form is the end of generation, while matter is for the sake of the form. Neither is it necessary that the knowledge of any cause or principle should be subsequent in relation to us, since through sensible causes we sometimes become acquainted with unknown effects, and sometimes conversely.

Fourth Article

Whether We Can Understand Many Things at the Same Time?

We proceed thus to the Fourth Article:—

Objection 1. It would seem that we can understand many things at the same time. For intellect is above time, whereas the succession of before and after belongs to time. Therefore the intellect does not understand different things in succession, but at the same time.

Obj. 2. Further, there is nothing to prevent different forms not opposed to each other from actually being in the same subject, as, for instance, color and smell are in the apple. But intelligible species are not opposed to each other. Therefore there is nothing to prevent the same intellect from being in act as regards different intelligible species. Thus it can understand many things at the same time.

Obj. 3. Further, the intellect understands a whole at the same time, such as a man or a house. But a whole contains many parts. Therefore the intellect understands many things at the same time.

Obj. 4. Further, we cannot know the difference between two things unless we know both at the same time,[57] and the same is to be said of any other comparison. But our intellect knows the difference between one thing and another. Therefore it knows many things at the same time.

On the contrary, It is said that *understanding is of one thing only, science is of many.*[58]

I answer that, The intellect can, indeed, understand many things as one, but not as many, that is to say, by *one* but not by *many* intelligible species. For the mode of every action follows the form which is the principle of that action. Therefore whatever things the intellect can understand under one species, it can understand together. Hence it is that God sees all things at the same time, because He sees all in one, that is, in His essence. But whatever things the intellect understands under different species, it does not understand at the same time. The reason for this is that it is impossible for one and the same subject to be perfected at the same time by many forms of one genus and diverse species, just as it is impossible for one and the same body at the same time to have different colors or different shapes. Now all intelligible species belong to one genus, because they are the perfections of one intellectual power even though the things which the species represent belong to different genera. Therefore it is impossible for one and the same intellect to be perfected at the same time by different intelligible species so as actually to understand different things.

Reply Obj. 1. The intellect is above that time which is the measure of the movement of corporeal things. But the multitude itself of intelligible species causes a certain succession of intelligible operations, according as one operation is prior to another. And this succession is called time by Augustine, who says that *God moves the spiritual creature through time.*[59]

Reply Obj. 2. Not only is it impossible for opposite forms to exist at the same time in the same subject, but neither can any forms belonging to the same genus, although they be not opposed to one another, as is clear from the examples of colors and shapes.

Reply Obj. 3. Parts can be understood in two ways. First, in a confused way, as existing in the whole; and thus they are known through the one form of the whole, and so are known together. In another way, they are known distinctly; and thus each is known by its species, and hence they are not understood at the same time.

Reply Obj. 4. If the intellect sees the difference or comparison between one thing and another, it knows both in relation to their difference or comparison; just as it knows the parts in the whole, as we said above.

Fifth Article

Whether Our Intellect Understands by Composition and Division?

We proceed thus to the Fifth Article:—
Objection 1. It would seem that our intellect does not understand by composition and division. For composition and division are only of many, whereas the intellect cannot understand many things at the same time. Therefore it cannot understand by composition and division.

Obj. 2. Further, every composition and division implies past, present, or future time. But the intellect abstracts from time, as also from other particular conditions. Therefore the intellect does not understand by composition and division.

Obj. 3. Further, the intellect understands things by an assimilation to them. But composition and division are not in things; for nothing is in things but the thing which is signified by the predicate and the subject, and which is one and the same thing, provided that the composition be true; for *man* is truly what *animal* is. Therefore the intellect does not act by composition and division.

On the contrary, Words signify the conceptions of the intellect, as the Philosopher says.[60] But in words we find composition and division, as appears in affirmative and negative propositions. Therefore the intellect acts by composition and division.

I answer that, The human intellect must of necessity understand by composition and division. For since the intellect passes from potentiality to act, it has a likeness to generable things, which do not attain to perfection all at once but acquire it by degrees. In the same way, the human intellect does not acquire perfect knowledge of a thing by the first apprehension; but it first apprehends something of the thing, such as its quiddity, which is the first and proper object of the intellect; and then it understands the properties, accidents, and various dispositions affecting the essence. Thus it necessarily relates one thing with another by composition or division; and from one composition and division it necessarily proceeds to another, and this is *reasoning*.

But the angelic and the divine intellects, like all incorruptible beings, have their perfection at once from the beginning. Hence the angelic and the divine intellect have the entire knowledge of a thing at once and perfectly; and hence, in knowing the quiddity of a thing, they know at once whatever we can know by composition, division and reasoning. Therefore the human intellect knows by composition, division and reasoning. But the divine and the angelic intellects have a knowledge of composition, division, and reasoning, not by the process itself, but by understanding the simple essence.

Reply Obj. 1. Composition and division of the intellect are made by differentiating and comparing. Hence the intellect knows many things by composition and division, by knowing the difference and comparison of things.

Reply Obj. 2. Although the intellect abstracts from phantasms, it does not understand actually without turning to the phantasms, as we have said.[61] And in so far as the intellect turns to phantasms, composition and division involve time.

Reply Obj. 3. The likeness of a thing is received into the intellect according to the mode of the intellect, not according to the mode of the thing. Hence, although something on the part of the thing corresponds to the composition and division of the intellect, still, it does not exist in the same way in the intellect and in the thing. For the proper object of the human intellect is the quiddity of a material thing, which is apprehended by the senses and the imagination. Now in a material thing there is a twofold composition. First, there is the composition of form with matter. To this corresponds that composition of the intellect whereby the universal whole is predicated of its part: for the genus is derived from common matter, while the difference that completes the species is derived from the form, and the particular from individual matter. The second composition is of accident with subject; and to this composition corresponds that composition of the intellect whereby accident is predicated of subject, as when we say *the man is white*. Nevertheless, the composition of the intellect differs from the composition of things; for the components in the thing are diverse, whereas the composition of the intellect is

a sign of the identity of the components. For the above composition of the intellect was not such as to assert that *man is whiteness*; but the assertion, *the man is white*, means that *the man is something having whiteness*. In other words, *man* is identical in subject with the *being having whiteness*. It is the same with the composition of form and matter. For *animal* signifies that which has a sensitive nature; *rational*, that which has an intellectual nature; *man*, that which has both; and *Socrates*, that which has all these things together with individual matter. And so, according to this kind of identity our intellect composes one thing with another by means of predication.

Sixth Article

Whether the Intellect Can Be False?

We proceed thus to the Sixth Article:—

Objection 1. It would seem that the intellect can be false, for the Philosopher says that *truth* and *falsehood are in the mind*.[62] But the *mind* and *intellect* are the same, as is shown above.[63] Therefore falsehood may be in the intellect.

Obj. 2. Further, opinion and reasoning belong to the intellect. But falsehood exists in both. Therefore falsehood can be in the intellect.

Obj. 3. Further, sin is in the intellectual part. But sin involves falsehood, for *those err that work evil* (*Prov.* xiv. 22). Therefore falsehood can be in the intellect.

On the contrary, Augustine says that *everyone who is deceived, does not rightly understand that wherein he is deceived*.[64] And the Philosopher says that *the intellect is always true*.[65]

I answer that, The Philosopher compares the intellect with the sense on this point.[66] For the sense is not deceived in its proper object (as sight in regard to color), save accidentally, through some hindrance to the sensible organ. For example, the taste of a fever-stricken person judges a sweet thing to be bitter, because his tongue is vitiated by ill humors. The sense, however, may be deceived as regards common sensible objects, as size or figure; as when, for example, it judges the sun to be only a foot in diameter, whereas in reality it exceeds the earth in size. Much more is the sense deceived concerning accidental sensible objects; as when it judges that vinegar is honey because the color is similar. The reason of this is evident. Every power, as such, is essentially directed to its proper object; and things of this kind are always uniform. Hence, so long as the power exists, its judgment concerning its own proper object does not fail. Now the proper object of the intellect is the *quiddity* in a thing. Hence, properly speaking, the intellect is not in error concerning this quiddity; whereas it may go astray as regards the accompaniments of the essence or quiddity in the thing, either in referring one thing to another, in what concerns composition or division, or also in the process of reasoning. That is why it is also true that the intellect cannot err in regard to those propositions which are understood as soon as their terms are understood. Such is the case with first principles, from which there also arises infallible truth in the certitude of science with respect to its conclusions.

The intellect, however, may be accidentally deceived in the quiddity of composite things, not by the defect of its organ, for the intellect is a power that is independent of an organ, but on the part of the composition affecting the definition. This may happen, for instance, when the definition of a thing is false in relation to something else, as the definition of a circle predicated of a triangle; or when a definition is false in itself as involving the composition of things incompatible, as, for instance, to describe anything as *a rational winged animal*. Hence as regards simple things, in whose definitions there is no composition, we cannot be deceived; but if we fail, we fail completely in understanding them, as is said in *Metaph.* ix.[67]

Reply Obj. 1. The Philosopher says that falsehood is in the intellect in regard to composition and division. The same answer applies to the *second objection* concerning opinion and reasoning; as well as to the

third objection, concerning the error of the sinner, who errs in the practical judgment of the appetible object. But in the absolute consideration of the quiddity of a thing, and of those things which are known thereby, the intellect is never deceived. In this sense are to be understood the authorities quoted in proof of the opposite conclusion.

Seventh Article

Whether One Person Can Understand One and the Same Thing Better Than Another Can?

We proceed thus to the Seventh Article:—
Objection 1. It would seem that one person cannot understand one and the same thing better than another can. For Augustine says: *Whoever understand a thing otherwise than as it is, does not understand it at all. Hence it is clear that there is a perfect understanding, than which none other is more perfect; and therefore there are not infinite degrees of understanding a thing, nor can one person understand a thing better than another can.*[68]

Obj. 2. Further, the intellect is true in its act of understanding. But truth, being a certain equality between thought and thing, is not subject to more or less; for a thing cannot be said to be more or less equal. Therefore a thing cannot be more or less understood.

Obj. 3. Further, the intellect is that which most pertains to the form in man. But different forms cause different species. Therefore if one man understands better than another, it would seem that they do not belong to the same species.

On the contrary, Experience shows that some understand more profoundly than do others; as one who carries a conclusion to its first principles and ultimate causes understands it better than the one who reduces it only to its proximate causes.

I answer that, To say that a thing is understood more by one than by another may be taken in two senses. First, so that the word *more* be taken as determining the act of understanding as regards the thing understood; and thus, one cannot understand the same thing more than another, because to understand it otherwise than as it is, either better or worse, would be to be deceived rather than to understand, as Augustine argues. In another sense, the word *more* can be taken as determining the act of understanding on the part of the one who understands. In this way, one may understand the same thing better than someone else, through having a greater power of understanding; just as a man may see a thing better with his bodily sight, whose power is greater, and whose sight is more perfect. The same applies to the intellect in two ways. First, as regards the intellect itself, which is more perfect. For it is plain that the better the disposition of a body, the better the soul allotted to it; which clearly appears in things of different species. The reason for this is that act and form are received into matter according to the capacity of matter; and thus because some men have bodies of better disposition, their souls have a greater power of understanding. Hence, it is said that *those who have soft flesh are of apt mind.*[69] Secondly, this occurs in regard to the lower powers of which the intellect needs its operation; for those in whom the imaginative, cogitative and memorative powers are of better disposition, are better disposed to understand.

The reply to the first objection is clear from the above; and likewise the reply to the second, for the truth of the intellect consists in this, that the intellect understands a thing as it is.

Reply Obj. 3. The difference of form which is due only to the different disposition of matter causes, not a specific, but only a numerical, difference: for different individuals have different forms, diversified according to the diversity of matter.

Eighth Article

Whether the Intellect Understands the Indivisible Before the Divisible?

We proceed thus to the Eighth Article:—
Objection 1. It would seem that the intel-

lect understands the indivisible before the divisible. For the Philosopher says that we *understand and know from the knowledge of principles and elements.*[70] But indivisibles are the principles and elements of divisible things. Therefore the indivisible is known to us before the divisible.

Obj. 2. Further, the definition of a thing contains what is known antecedently, for a definition *proceeds from the first and more known*, as is said in *Topic.* vi.[71] But the indivisible is included in the definition of the divisible, as a point comes into the definition of a line; for, as Euclid says, *a line is length without breadth, the extremities of which are two points.*[72] So, too, unity comes into the definition of number, for *number is multitude measured by one*, as is said in *Metaph.* x.[73] Therefore our intellect understands the indivisible before the divisible.

Obj. 3. Further, *Like is known by like*. But the indivisible is more like to the intellect than is the divisible, because *the intellect is simple.*[74] Therefore our intellect first knows the indivisible.

On the contrary, It is said that *the indivisible is made known as a privation.*[75] But privation is known secondarily. Therefore so is the indivisible.

I answer that, The object of our intellect in its present state is the quiddity of a material thing, which it abstracts from phantasms, as was stated above.[76] And since that which is known first and of itself by our cognitive power is its proper object, we must consider its relationship to that quiddity in order to discover in what order the indivisible is known. Now the indivisible is threefold, as is said in *De Anima* iii.[77] First, the continuous is indivisible, since it is actually undivided, although potentially divisible. This indivisible is known to us before its division, which is a division into parts, becaue confused knowledge is prior to distinct knowledge, as we have said above. Secondly, there is the indivisible in species, as man's nature is something indivisible. This way, also, the indivisible is understood before its division into the parts of the nature, as we have said above; and also before the intellect composes and divides by affirmation and negation. The reason of this priority is that both these kinds of indivisible are understood by the intellect of itself as its proper object. The third kind of indivisible is what is altogether indivisible, as a point and unity, which cannot be divided either actually or potentially. And this indivisible is known secondarily, through the privation of divisibility. Therefore a point is defined by way of privation *as that which has no parts;*[78] and in like manner the notion of *one* is that it is *indivisible*, as is stated in *Metaph.* x. [79] And the reason for this posteriority is that this indivisible has a certain opposition to a corporeal being, the quiddity of which is the primary and proper object of the intellect.

But if our intellect understood by participation in certain separate indivisibles, as the Platonists maintained,[80] it would follow that such an indivisible is prior in the understanding, for, according to the Platonists, it is first in being participated by things.[81]

Reply Obj. 1. In the acquisition of knowledge, principles and elements are not always first; for sometimes from sensible effects we arrive at the knowledge of principles and intelligible causes. But in perfect knowledge, the knowledge of effects always depends on the knowledge of principles and elements; for, as the Philosopher says in the same passage, *Then do we consider that we know, when we can resolve principles into their causes.*[82]

Reply Obj. 2. A point is not included in the definition of a line in general; for it is manifest that in a line of indefinite length, and also in a circular line, there is no point, save potentially. Euclid defines a straight line of definite length, and therefore he includes a point in the definition as the limit in the definition of that which is limited.[83]—Unity, however, is the measure of number: wherefore it is included in the definition of a measured number. But it is not included in the definition of the divisible, but rather conversely.

Reply Obj. 3. The likeness through which we understand is the species of the thing known in the knower. Hence, a thing is prior in being known, not according to the likeness of its nature to the knowing power, but according to its agreement with the proper object of that power. Otherwise, sight would perceive hearing rather than color.

Question LXXXVI
What Our Intellect Knows in Material Things
(*In Four Articles*)

We now have to consider what our intellect knows in material things. Under this head there are four points of inquiry: (1) Whether it knows singulars? (2) Whether it knows infinite things? (3) Whether it knows contingent things? (4) Whether if knows future things?

First Article

Whether Our Intellect Knows Singulars?

We proceed thus to the First Article:—

Objection 1. It would seem that our intellect knows singulars. For whoever knows a composition, knows the terms of composition. But our intellect knows this composition: *Socrates is a man*, for the intellect can form a proposition to this effect. Therefore our intellect knows this singular, *Socrates.*

Obj. 2. Further, the practical intellect directs to action. But action has relation to singular things. Therefore the intellect knows the singular.

Obj. 3. Further, our intellect understands itself. But in itself it is a singular, or otherwise it would have no action of its own; for actions belong to singulars. Therefore our intellect knows singulars.

Obj. 4. Further, a superior power can do whatever is done by an inferior power. But sense knows the singular. Much more, therefore, can the intellect know it.

On the contrary, The Philosopher says that *the universal is known by reason, and the singular is known by sense.*[84]

I answer that, Our intellect cannot know the singular in material things directly and primarily. The reason for this is that the principle of singularity in material things is individual matter; whereas our intellect, as we have said above,[85] understands by abstracting the intelligible species from such matter. Now what is abstracted from individual matter is universal. Hence our intellect knows directly only universals. But indirectly, however, and as it were by a kind of reflexion, it can know the singular, because, as we have said above,[86] even after abstracting the intelligible species, the intellect, in order to understand actually, needs to turn to the phantasms in which it understands the species, as is said in *De Anima* iii.[87] Therefore it understands the universal directly through the intelligible species, and indirectly the singular represented by the phantasm. And thus it forms the proposition, *Socrates is a man.*

Therefore the reply to the first objection is clear.

Reply Obj. 2. The choice of a particular thing to be done is as the conclusion of a syllogism formed by the practical intellect, as is said in *Ethics* vii.[88] But a singular proposition cannot be directly concluded from a universal proposition, except through the medium of a singular proposition. Therefore the universal principle of the practical intellect does not move save through the medium of the particular apprehension of the sensitive part, as is said in *De Anima* iii.[89]

Reply Obj. 3. Intelligibility is incompatible with the singular not as such, but as material; for nothing can be understood otherwise than immaterially. Therefore if there be an immaterial singular such as the intellect, there is no reason why it should not be intelligible.

Reply Obj. 4. The higher power can do what the lower power can, but in a more eminent way. And so, what the sense knows materially and concretely, which is to know the singular directly, the intellect knows immaterially and in the abstract, which is to know the universal.

Second Article

Whether Our Intellect Can Know Infinite Things?

We proceed thus to the Second Article:—

Objection 1. It would seem that our intellect can know the infinite. For God excels all infinite things. But our intellect can know God, as we have said above.[90] Much more, therefore, can our intellect know all other infinite things.

Obj. 2. Further, our intellect can naturally know *genera* and *species*. But there is an infinity of species in some genera, as in number, proportion and figure. Therefore our intellect can know the infinite.

Obj. 3. Further, if one body can coexist with another in the same place, there is nothing to prevent an infinite number of bodies being in one place. But one intelligible species can exist with another in the same intellect, for many things can be habitually known at the same time. Therefore our intellect can have a habitual knowledge of an infinite number of things.

Obj. 4. Further, since the intellect is not a corporeal power, as we have said,[91] it appears to be an infinite power. But an infinite power has a capacity for an infinite number of things. Therefore our intellect can know the infinite.

On the contrary, It is said that the *infinite, considered as such, is unknown.*[92]

I answer that, Since a power is proportioned to its object, the intellect must be related to the infinite in the same way as is its object, which is the quiddity of a material thing. Now in material things the infinite does not exist actually, but only potentially, which is to say, successively, as is said in *Physics* iii.[93] Therefore infinity is potentially in our intellect through its considering successively one thing after another; because never does our intellect understand so many things, that it cannot understand more.

On the other hand, our intellect cannot

understand the infinite either actually or habitually. Not actually, for our intellect can know actually at the same time only what it knows through one species. But the infinite is not represented by one species, for if it were it would be something whole and complete. Consequently it cannot be understood except by a successive consideration for one part after another, as is clear from its definition; for the infinite is that *from which, however much we may take, there always remains something to be taken.*[94] Thus the infinite could not be known actually, unless all its parts were counted; which is impossible.

For the same reason we cannot have habitual knowledge of the infinite: because our habitual knowledge results from actual consideration; since by understanding we acquire knowledge, as is said in *Ethics* ii.[95] Hence, it would not be possible for us to have a habit of an infinity of things distinctly known, unless we had already considered the entire infinity, counting them according to the succession of our knowledge; which is impossible. And so, neither actually or habitually can our intellect know the infinite, but only potentially, as was explained above.

Reply Obj. 1. As we have said above,[96] God is called infinite because He is a form unlimited by matter; whereas in material things, the term *infinite* is applied to that which is deprived of any formal termination. And since form is known in itself, whereas matter cannot be known without form, hence it is that the material infinite is in itself unknown. But the formal infinite, God, is of Himself known; but He is unknown to us by reason of our feeble intellect, which in its present state has a natural aptitude only for material things. Therefore we cannot know God in our present life except through material effects. In the future life this defect of our intellect will be removed by the state of glory, when we shall be able to see the essence of God Himself, but without being able to comprehend Him.

Reply Obj. 2. The nature of our intellect is

to know species abstracted from phantasms; and therefore it cannot know actually or habitually species of numbers or figures that have not been imagined, except in a general way and in universal principles; and this is to know them potentially and confusedly.

Reply Obj. 3. If two or more bodies were in the same place, there would be no need for them to occupy the place successively, in order for the things placed to be counted according to this succession of occupation. On the other hand, the intelligible species enter our intellect successively because many things cannot be actually understood at the same time; and therefore there must be a definite and not an infinite number of species in our intellect.

Reply Obj. 4. In the way in which our intellect is infinite in power, so does it know the infinite. For its power is indeed infinite inasmuch as it is not terminted by corporeal matter. Moreover it can know the universal, which is abstracted from individual matter, and which consequently is not limited to one individual, but, considered in itself, extends to an infinite number of individuals.

Third Article

Whether Our Intellect Can Know Contingent Things?

We proceed thus to the Third Article:—

Objection 1. It would seem that the intellect cannot know contingent things: because, as the Philosopher says, the objects of *understanding, wisdom* and *science* are not contingent, but necessary things.[97]

Obj. 2. Further, as is stated in *Physics* iv., *what sometimes is and sometimes is not, is measured by time.*[98] Now the intellect abstracts from time, and from other material conditions. Therefore, as it is proper to a contingent thing sometime to be and sometime not to be, it seems that contingent things are not known by the intellect.

On the contrary, Every science is in the intellect. But some sciences are of contingent things, as the moral sciences, which consider human actions subject to free choice; and, again, the sciences of nature in as far as they consider things generable and corruptible. Therefore the intellect knows contingent things.

I answer that, Contigent things can be considered in two ways: either as contingent, or as containing some element of necessity. For every contigent thing has in it something necessary. For example, that Socrates runs, is in itself contingent; but the relation of running to motion is necessary, for it is necessary that Socrates move if he runs. Now contingency arises from matter, for contingency is a potentially to be or not to be, and potentially belongs to matter; whereas necessity results from form, because whatever is consequent on form is of necessity in the subject. But matter is the principle of individuation, whereas the universal comes from the abstraction of the form from particular matter. Moreover it was laid down above that the intellect of itself and directly has the universal for its object; while the object of sense is the singular, which in a certain way is the indirect object of the intellect, as we have said above. Therefore the contingent, considered as such, is known directly by sense and indirectly by the intellect; while the universal and necessary principles of contigent things are known by the intellect. Hence if we consider knowable things in their universal principles, then all science is of necessary things. But if we consider the things themselves, thus some sciences are of necessary things, some of the contingent things.

From which the replies to the objections are clear.

Fourth Article

Whether Our Intellect Knows the Future?

We proceed thus to the Fourth Article:—

Objection 1. It would seem that our intellect knows the future. For our intellect knows by means of intelligible species which abstract from the *here* and *now*, and are thus related indifferently to all time. But it can know the present. Therefore it can know the future.

Obj. 2. Further, man, while his senses are in suspension, can know some future things, as in sleep, and in frenzy. But the intellect is freer and more vigorous when removed from sense. Therefore the intellect of its own nature can know the future.

Obj. 3. The intellectual knowledge of man is superior to any knowledge in brutes. But some animals know the future; and thus crows by their frequent cawing foretell rain. Therefore much more can the intellect know the future.

On the contrary, It is written (*Eccles.* viii. 6, 7), *There is great affliction for man, because he is ignorant of things past; and things to come he cannot know by any messenger.*

I answer that, We must apply the same distinction to future things as we applied above to contingent things. For future things considered as subject to time are singular, and the human intellect knows them by reflexion only, as stated above. But the principles of future things may be universal; and thus they may enter the domain of the intellect and become the objects of science.

Speaking, however, of the knowledge of the future in a geneal way, we must observe that the future may be known in two ways: either in itself, or in its cause. The future cannot be known in itself save by God alone, to Whom even that is present which in the course of events is future, inasmuch as from eternity His glance embraces the whole course of time, as we have said above when treating of God's knowledge.[99] But in so far as it exists in its cause, the future can be known also by us. Now if the cause be such as to have a necessary connection with its future result, then the future is known with scientific certitude, just as the astronomer foresees the future eclipse. If, however, the cause be such as to produce a certain result more frequently than not, then the future can be known more or less conjecturally, according as its cause is more or less inclined to produce the effect.

Reply Obj. 1. This argument holds of that knowledge which is drawn from universal causal principles; from these the future may be known, according to the order of the effects to the cause.

Reply Obj. 2. As Augustine says, the soul has a certain power of forecasting, so that by its nature it can know the future;[100] and so, when withdrawn from corporeal sense, and, as it were, concentrated on itself, it shares in the knowledge of the future.— Such an opinion as this would be reasonable if we were to admit that the soul receives knowledge by participating in the Ideas, as the Platonists maintained,[101] because in that case the soul by its nature would know the universal causes of all effects, and would only be impeded in its knowledge by the body; and hence when withdrawn from the corporeal senses it would know the future.

But since it is connatural to our intellect to know things, not thus, but by receiving its knowledge from the senses, it is not natural for the soul to know the future when withdrawn from the senses. Rather does it know the future by the impression of superior spiritual and corporeal causes: of spiritual causes, when by divine power the human intellect is enlightened through the ministry of angels, and the phantasms are directed to the knowlede of future events; or, by the influence of demons, when the imagination is moved regarding the future known to the demons, as was explained above.[102] The soul is naturally more in-

clined to receive these impressions of spiritual causes when it is withdrawn from the senses, as it is then nearer to the spiritual world, and freer from external distractions.—The same may also come from superior corporeal causes. For it is clear that superior bodies influence inferior bodies. Hence, since sensitive powers are the acts of corporeal organs, the influence of the heavenly bodies causes the imagination to be affected, and so, as the heavenly bodies cause many future events, the imagination receives certain signs of some such events. These signs are perceived more at night and while we sleep than in the daytime and while we are awake, because, as is stated in *De Somno et Vigilia* ii., *impressions made by day are evanescent. The night air is calmer, when silence reigns; and hence bodily impressions are made in sleep, when slight internal movements are felt more than in wakefulness, and such movements produce in the imagination images from which the future may be foreseen.*[103]

Reply Obj. 3. Brute animals have no power above the imagination to regulate their images, as man has his reason, and therefore their imagination follows entirely the influence of the heavenly bodies. Thus from such animals' movements some future things, such as rain and the like, may be known rather than from human movements directed by reason. Hence the Philosopher says that *some who are most imprudent are most far-seeing; for their intelligence is not burdened with cares, but is as it were barren and bare of all anxiety, moving at the caprice of whatever is brought to bear on it.*[104]

Question LXXXVIII
How the Human Soul Knows What Is Above Itself
(*In Three Articles*)

We must now consider how the human soul knows what is above itself, viz., immaterial substances. Under this head there are three points of inquiry: (1) Whether the human soul in the present state of life can

understand the immaterial substances, called angels, in themselves? (2) Whether it can arrive at the knowledge thereof by the knowledge of material things? (3) Whether God is the first object of our knowledge?

First Article

Whether the Human Soul in the Present State of Life Can Understand Immaterial Substances in Themselves?

We proceed thus to the First Article:—

Objection 1. It would seem that the human soul in the present state of life can understand immaterial substances in themselves. For Augustine says: *As the mind itself acquires the knowledge of corporeal things by means of the corporeal senses, so it gains through itself the knowledge of incorporeal things.*[105] But these are the immaterial substances. Therefore the human mind understands immaterial substances.

Obj. 2. Further, like is known by like. But the human mind is more akin to immaterial than to material things; since its own nature is immaterial, as is clear from what we have said above.[106] Since then our mind understands material things, much more is it able to understand immaterial things.

Obj. 3. Further, the fact that objects which are in themselves most eminently sensible are not most perceived by us, comes from the fact that sense is corrupted by their very excellence. But the intellect is not subject to such a corrupting influence from the excellence of its object, as is stated in *De Anima* iii.[107] Therefore things which are in themselves in the highest degree of intelligibility are likewise to us most intelligible. Since material things, however, are intelligible only so far as we make them actually so, by abstracting them from material conditions, it is clear that those substances are more intelligible in themselves whose nature is immaterial. Therefore they are much more known to us than are material things.

Obj. 4. Further, the Commentator says that, *nature would be frustrated in its end* were we unable to understand abstract substances, *because it would have made what in itself is naturally intelligible not to be understood at all.*[108] But in nature nothing is idle or purposeless. Therefore immaterial substances can be understood by us.

Obj. 5. Further, as the sense is to the sensible, so is the intellect to the intelligible. But our sight can see all things corporeal, whether superior and incorruptible, or sublunary and corruptible. Therefore our intellect can understand all intelligible substances, including the superior and immaterial.

On the contrary, It is written (*Wis.* ix. 16): *The things that are in heaven who shall search out?* But these substances are said to be in heaven, according to *Matthew* xviii. 10, *Their angels in heaven*, etc. Therefore immaterial substances cannot be known by human investigation.

I answer that, In the opinion of Plato, immaterial substances are not only understood by us, but are also the objects we understand first of all. For Plato taught that immaterial subsisting Forms, which he called *Ideas*, are the proper objects of our intellect, and are thus first and essentially understood by us.[109] Furthermore, material things are known by the soul inasmuch as imagination and sense are joined to the intellect.[110] Hence the purer the intellect is, so much the more clearly does it perceive the intelligible reality of immaterial things.[111]

But in Aristotle's opinion, which experience corroborates, our intellect in its present state of life has a natural relation to the natures of material things;[112] and therefore it can understand only by turning to the phantasms, as we have said above.[113] Thus it clearly appears that immaterial substances, which do not fall under sense and imagination, cannot be known by us first and essentially, according to the mode of knowledge of which we have experience.

Nevertheless Averröes teaches that in this present life man can in the end arrive at the knowledge of separate substances by being joined or united to some separate substance, which he calls the *agent intellect*, and which, being a separate substance itself, can naturally understand separate substances.[114] Hence, when it is perfectly united to us, so that through it we are able to understand perfectly, we too shall be able to understand separate substances; just as in the present life, through the possible intellect united to us, we can understand material things.

Now he said that the agent intellect is united to us as follows.[115] For since we understand by means of both the agent intellect and intelligible objects (as, for instance, we understand conclusions by principles understood), the agent intellect must be compared to the objects understood, either as the principle agent is to the instrument, or as form to matter. For an action is ascribed to two principles in one of these two ways: to a principal agent and to an instrument, as cutting to the workman and the saw; to a form and its subject, as heating to heat and fire. In both these ways the agent intellect can be compared to the intelligible object as perfection is to the perfectible, and as act is to potentiality. Now a subject is made perfect and receives its perfection at one and the same time, as the reception of what is actually visible synchronizes with the reception of light in the eye. Therefore the possible intellect receives the intelligible object and the agent intellect together. And the more numerous the intelligible objects received, so much the nearer do we come to the point of perfect union between ourselves and the agent intellect; so much so, that when we shall have understood all the intelligible objects, the agent intellect will become perfectly united to us, and through it we shall understand all things material and immaterial. In this he makes the ultimate happiness of man to consist.[116] Nor, as regards the present inquiry, does it matter whether the possible intellect in that state of happiness understands separate substances through the agent intellect, as he himself maintains, or whether (as he imputes to Alexander) the possible intellect can never understand separate substances (because according to him it is corruptible), but man understands separate substances through the agent intellect.[117]

All this, however, is untrue. First, because, supposing the agent intellect to be a separate substance, we could not formally understand through it; for the formal medium of an agent's action is its form and act, since every agent acts according to its actuality, as was said of the possible intellect.[118] Secondly, this opinion is untrue because the agent intellect, supposing it to be a separate substance, would not be joined to us in its substance, but only in its light, as participated in what we understood. But this would not extend to the other acts of the agent intellect so as to enable us to understand immaterial substances; just as when we see colors set off by the sun, we are not united to the substance of the sun so as to act like the sun but only its light is united to us, that we may see the colors.

Thirdly, this opinion is untrue because, granted that, as was above explained, the agent intellect were united to us in substance, still it is not said that it is wholly united to us on the basis of one intelligible object, or two; but rather on the basis of all intelligible objects. But all such objects together do not equal the power of the agent intellect, as it is a much greater thing to understand separate substances than to understand all material things. Hence it clearly follows that the knowledge of all material things would not make the agent intellect to be so united to us as to enable us to understand separate substances through it.

Fourthly, this opinion is untrue because it is hardly possible for anyone in this world to understand all material things; and thus no one, or very few, would reach perfect felicity. This is against what the Philosopher says, that happiness is a *kind of common good, communicable to all capable of virtue*.[119] Further, it is against reason that only the few of any species attain to the end of the species.

Fifthly, the Philosopher expressly says that happiness is an *operation according to perfect virtue*,[120] and after enumerating many virtues in the tenth book of the *Ethics*, he concludes that ultimate happiness, consisting in the knowledge of the highest things intelligible, is attained through the virtue of *wisdom*,[121] which in the sixth book he had named as *the chief of the speculative sciences*.[122] Hence Aristotle clearly placed the ultimate felicity of man in that knowledge of separate substances which is obtainable by speculative science; and not in any union with the agent intellect, as some have imagined.

Sixthly, as was shown above,[123] the agent intellect is not a separate substance, but a power of the soul, extending itself actively to the same objects to which the possible intellect extends receptively; because, as Aristotle states, the possible intellect is *all things potentially*, and the agent intellect is *all things in act*.[124] Therefore both intellects, according to the present state of life, extend only to material things, which are made actually intelligible by the agent intellect, and are received in the possible intellect. Hence, in the present state of life, we cannot understand separate immaterial substances in themselves, either by the possible or by the agent intellect.

Reply Obj. 1. Augustine may be taken to mean that the knowledge of incorporeal things in the mind can be gained through the mind itself. This is so true that philosophers also say that the knowledge concerning the soul is a principle for the knowledge of separate substances.[125] For by knowing itself, the soul attains to some knowledge of incorporeal substances, such as is within its compass; not that the knowledge of itself gives it a perfect and absolute knowledge of them.

Reply Obj. 2. The likeness of nature is not a sufficient principle of knowledge. Otherwise, what Empedocles said would be true—that the soul needs to have the nature of all in order to know all.[126] But knowledge requires that the likeness of the thing known be in the knower, as a kind of form in the knower. Now our possible intellect, in the present state of life, is such that it can be informed with the likeness abstracted from phantasms: and therefore it knows material things rather than immaterial substances.

Reply Obj. 3. There must needs be some proportion between the object and the power of knowledge; such as of the active to the passive, and of perfection to the per-

fectible. Hence that sensible objects of great excellence are not grasped by the senses is due not merely to the fact that they corrupt the organ, but also to their not being proportionate to the sensitive powers. And it is thus that immaterial substances are not proportionate to our intellect, in our present state of life, so that it cannot understand them.

Reply Obj. 4. This argument of the Commentator fails in several ways. First, because if separate substances are not understood by us, it does not follow that they are not understood by any intellect; for they are understood by themselves, and by one another.

Secondly, to be understood by us is not the end of separate substances and only that is vain and purposeless which fails to attain its end. It does not follow, therefore, that immaterial substances are purposeless, even if they are not at all understood by us.

Reply Obj. 5. Sense knows bodies, whether superior or inferior, in the same way, that is, by the sensible thing acting on the organ. But we do not understand material and immaterial substances in the same way. The former we understand by abstraction, which is impossible in the case of the latter, for there are not phantasms of what is immaterial.

Second Article

Whether Our Intellect Can Come to Understand Immaterial Substances Through Its Knowledge of Material Things?

We proceed thus to the Second Article:—

Objection 1. It would seem that our intellect can come to know immaterial substances through the knowledge of material things. For Dionysius says that *the human mind cannot be raised up to immaterial contemplation of the heavenly hierarchies, unless it uses thereto material guidance according to its own nature*.[127] Therefore we can be led by material things to know immaterial substances.

Obj. 2. Further, science resides in the intellect. But there are sciences and definitions of immaterial substances; for Damascene defines an angel,[128] and we find angels discussed both in theology and in philosophy. Therefore immaterial substances can be understood by us.

Obj. 3. Further, the human soul belongs to the genus of immaterial substances. But it can be understood by us through its act, by which it understands material things. Therefore other immaterial substances also can be understood by us, through their effects in material things.

Obj. 4. Further, the only cause which cannot be comprehended through its effects is that which infinitely transcends them, and this belongs to God alone. Therefore other created immaterial substances can be understood by us through material things.

On the contrary, Dionysius says that *intelligible things cannot be understood through sensible things, nor composite things through simple, nor incorporeal things through corporeal.*[129]

I answer that, Averröes says that a philosopher named Avempace taught that by the understanding of material substances we can be led, according to true philosophical principles, to the knowledge of immaterial substances.[130] For since the nature of our intellect is to abstract the quiddity of material things from matter, anything material residing in that abstracted quiddity can again be made subject to abstraction; and as the process of abstraction cannot go on forever, it must arrive at length at the understanding of a quiddity that is absolutely without matter; and this would be the understanding of immaterial substance.

Now this opinion would be true, were immaterial substances the forms and species of these material things, as the Platonists supposed.[131] But supposing, on the contrary, that immaterial substances differ altogether from the quiddity of material things, it follows that, however much our intellect may abstract the quiddity of a material thing from matter, if could never arrive at anything like an immaterial substance. Therefore we are not able to understand immaterial substances perfectly through material substances.

Reply Obj. 1. From material things we can rise to some sort of knowledge of immaterial things, but not to a perfect knowledge; for there is no proper and adequate proportion between material and immaterial things, and the likenesses drawn from material things for the understanding of immaterial things are very unlike them, as Dionysius says.[132]

Reply Obj. 2. Science treats of higher things principally by way of remotion. Thus Aristotle explains the heavenly bodies by denying to them the properties of sublunary bodies.[133] Hence it follows that much less can immaterial substance be known by us in such a way as to make us know their quiddity; but we may have a knowledge of them from the sciences by way of negation and by their relation to material things.

Reply Obj. 3. The human soul understands itself through its own act of understanding, which is proper to it, showing perfectly its power and nature. But the power and nature of immaterial substances cannot be perfectly known through such an act, nor through any other and material thing, because there is no proportion between the latter and the power of the former.

Reply Obj. 4. Created immaterial substances are not in the same natural genus as material substances, for they do not agree in power or in matter; but they belong to the same logical genus, because even immaterial substances are in the predicament of substance, since their essence is distinct from their being. But God has no community with material things either in a natural genus or in a logical genus; because God is not in a genus at all, as was stated above.[134] Hence through the likenesses derived from material things we can know something positive concerning the angels, according to some common notion, though not according to their specific nature; whereas we cannot acquire any such knowledge at all about God.

Third Article

Whether God Is the First Object Known by the Human Mind?

We proceed thus to the Third Article:—

Objection 1. It would seem that God is the first object known by the human mind. For that object in which all others are known, and by which we judge others, is the first thing known to us; as light is to the eye, and first principles to the intellect. But we know all things in the light of the first truth, and thereby judge of all things, as Augustine says.[135] Therefore God is the first object known to us.

Obj. 2. Further, whatever causes a thing to be such is more so. But God is the cause of all our knowledge; for He is *the true light which enlighteneth every man that cometh into this world* (*Jo.* i. 9). Therefore God is our first and most known object.

Obj. 3. Further, what is first known in an image is the exemplar to which the image is formed. But in our mind is *the image of God*, as Augustine says.[136] Therefore God is the first object known to our mind.

On the contrary, No man hath seen God at any time (*Jo.* i. 18).

I answer that, Since the human intellect in the present state of life cannot understand immaterial created substances, much less can it understand the essence of the uncreated substance. Hence it must be said absolutely that God is not the first object of our knowledge. Rather do we know God through creatures, according to the Apostle (Rom. i. 20): *the invisible things of God are clearly seen, being understood by the things that are made*. Now the first object of our knowledge in this life is the *quiddity of a material thing*, which is the proper object of our intellect, as appears above in many passages.[137]

Reply Obj. 1. We see and judge of all things in the light of the first truth, insofar as the light itself of our intellect, whether natural or gratuitous, is nothing else than an impression of the first truth upon it, as was stated above.[138] Hence, since the light itself of our intellect is not that which the intellect understands, but the medium whereby it understands, much less can it be said that God is the first thing known by our intellect.

Reply Obj. 2. The axiom, *Whatever causes a thing to be such is more so*, must be understood of things belonging to one and the same order, as was explained above.[139] Other things than God are known because of God, not as if He were the first known object, but because He is the first cause of our power of knowledge.

Reply Obj. 3. If there existed in our souls a perfect image of God, as the Son is the perfect image of the Father, our mind would know God at once. But the image in our mind is imperfect; and hence the argument does not hold.

NOTES

1. Q. 89.
2. Q. 87.
3. Q. 88.
4. Q. 85.
5. Q. 86.
6. *Lib. 83 Quaest.*, q. 9 (PL 40, 13).
7. *De Genesi ad Litt.*, XII, 16 (PL 34, 467).
8. *Metaph.*, I, i (981a 2); *Post. Anal.*, II, 15 (100a 3).
9. *Epist.* CXVIII, 4 (PL 33, 446).
10. *De Divinat.*, II (464a 5).
11. *De An.*, III, 3 (427a 17).
12. Cf. q. 75, a. 3.
13. *De Genesi ad Litt.*, XII, 24 (PL 34, 475).
14. *De An.*, III, 3 (427b 6).
15. *De Somno*, I (454a 7).
16. Aristotle, *De Gener.*, I, 8 (324b 25).
17. *De An.*, III, 4 (429a 24).

18. Op. cit., III, 5 (430a 18).
19. Q. 79, a. 3 and 4.
20. *De An.*, III, 5 (430a 18).
21. Op. cit., I, i (403a 5).
22. Op. cit., III, 3 (429a I).
23. Op. cit., III, 7 (431a 16).
24. Q. 79, a. 6.
25. *De Div. Nom.*, I, 5 (PG 3, 593).
26. Aristotle, *De Somno*, I (454b 13).
27. *De Genesi ad Litt.*, XII, 15 (PL 34, 466).
28. *De Caelo*, III, 7 (306a 16).
29. Aristotle, *De Somno*, III (456b 17).
30. Aristotle, *De An.*, III, 7 (431a 14).
31. Op. cit., III, 5 (430a 14).
32. Op. cit., III, 7 (431b 2).
33. Op. cit., III, 4 (429b 21).
34. Q. 84, a. 7.
35. Q. 76, a. 1.
36. Q. 84, a. 1.
37. Cf., q. 84, a. 4.
38. Averröes, *In Metaph.*, VII, comm. 21 (VIII, 80v; 81r); comm. 34 (VIII, 87r).—Cf. St. Thomas, *In Metaph.*, VII, lect. 9.
39. Aristotle, *Metaph.*, VI, 10 (1035b 28).
40. Cf. 1. 84, a. 1; cf. also q. 50, a. 2.
41. Q. 84, a. 7.
42. *Perih.*, I, i (16a 3).
43. The reference seems to be to Protagoras and to Heraclitus: cf. Aristotle, *Metaph.*, VIII, 3 (1047a 6); III, 3 (1005b 25).
44. Q. 84, a. 1 and 4.
45. Cf. Aristotle, *Metaph.*, III, 5 (1009a 8).
46. Op. cit., VIII, 8 (1050a 23).
47. The opinion of Empedocles, according to Aristotle, *De An.*, I, 3 (409b 26); and of Plato: cf. op. cit., I, 2 (404b 17).
48. Op. cit., III, 8 (431b 29).
49. *Phys.*, I, i (184b 11).
50. Ibid. (184a 23).
51. Ibid. (184a 21).
52. Ibid. (184b 12).
53. Aristotle, *De An.*, I, i (402b 7).
54. Cf. q. 84, a. 1.
55. Aristotle, *De Gener. Anim.*, II, 3 (736b 2).
56. Aristotle, *Metaph.*, VI, 13 (1038b 8).
57. Aristotle, *De An.*, III, 2 (426b 22).
58. Aristotle, *Top.*, II, 10 (114b 34).
59. *De Genesi ad Litt.*, VIII, 20; 22 (PL 34, 388; 389).
60. *Perih.*, I, i (16a 3).
61. A. I; q. 84, a. 7.
62. *Metaph.*, V, 4 (1027b 27).
63. Q. 72.
64. *Lib. 83 Quaest.*, q. 32 (PL 40, 22).
65. *De An.*, III, 10 (433a 26).
66. Op. cit., III, 6 (430b 29).
67. Aristotle, *Metaph.*, VIII, 10 (1052a I).
68. *Lib. 83 Quaest.*, q. 32 (PL 40, 22).
69. Aristotle, *De An.*, II, 9 (421a 25).
70. *Phys.*, I, i (184a 12).
71. Aristotle, *Top.*, VI, 4 (141a 32).
72. *Geometria*, trans. Boethius, I (PL 63, 1307).
73. Aristotle, *Metaph.*, IX, 6 (1057a 3).
74. Aristotle, *De An.*, III, 4 (429a 18; b 23).
75. Op. cit., III, 6 (430b 21).
76. A. I; q. 84, a. 7.
77. Aristotle, *De An.*, III, 6 (430b 6).

78. Euclid, *Geometria*, I (PL 63, 1307).
79. Aristotle, *Metaph.*, IX, I (1052b 16).
80. Cf. q. 84, a. 1 and 4.
81. Cf. *De Causis*, I (p. 161).
82. *Phys.*, I, i (184a 12).
83. *Geometria*, I (PL 63, 1307).
84. *Phys.*, I, 5 (189a 5).
85. Q. 85, a. 1.
86. Q. 84, a. 7.
87. Aristotle, *De An.*, III, 7 (431b 2).
88. Aristotle, *Eth.*, VII, 3 (1147a 28).
89. Aristotle, *De An.*, III, 11 (434a 16).
90. Q. 12, a. 1.
91. Q. 76, a. 1.
92. Aristotle, *Phys.*, I, 4 (187b 7).
93. Op. cit., III, 6 (204a 20).
94. Ibid. (207a 7).
95. Aristotle, *Eth.*, I, i (1103a 33).
96. Q. 7, a. 1.
97. Aristotle, *Eth.*, VI, 6 (1040b 31).
98. Aristotle, *Phys.*, IV, 12 (221b 29).
99. Q. 14, a. 13.
100. Cf. *De Genesi ad Litt.*, XII, 13 (PL 34, 464).
101. Cf. q. 84, a. 1 and 4; q. 87, a. 1.
102. Q. 57, a. 3.
103. Aristotle, *De Divinat.*, II (464a 12).
104. Ibid. (464a 18).
105. *De Trin.*, IX, 3 (PL 42, 963).
106. Q. 76, a. 1.
107. Aristotle, *De An.*, III, 4 (429b 2).
108. *In Metaph.*, II, comm. I (VIII 14v).
109. Cf. q. 84, a. 4.
110. Cf. Macrobius, *In Somn. Scipion.*, I, 12 (pp. 531–532).
111. Cf. Cicero, *Tusc. Disp.*, I, 30 (p. 254).—Cf. also Plato, *Phaedo* (p. 80).
112. *De An.*, III, 7 (431a 16).
113. Q. 84, a. 7.
114. *In De An.*, III, comm. 36, pt. 5 (VI, 178v).
115. Ibid. (VI, 179rv).
116. *De An. Beatitud.*, I (IX, 64ra).—Cf. Avicenna, *De An.*, V, 6 (26va).
117. Averröes, *In De An.*, III, comm. 36, pt. 2 (VI, 176r).
118. Q. 76, a. 1.
119. *Eth.*, I, 9 (1099b 18).
120. Op. cit., I, 10 (1101a 14).
121. Op. cit., X, 7 (1177a 21); 8 (1179a 30).
122. Op. cit., VI, 7 (1141a 20).
123. Q. 79, a. 4.
124. Aristotle, *De An.*, III, 5 (430a 14).
125. Averröes, *In De An.*, I, comm. 2 (VI, 108v); III, comm. 5 (VI, 166r).
126. Cf. Aristotle, *De An.*, I, 2 (404b 11).
127. *De Cael. Hier.*, I, 3 (PG 3, 124).
128. *De Fide Orth.*, II, 3 (PG 94, 865).
129. *De Div. Nom.*, I, i (PG 3, 588).
130. *In De An.*, III, comm. 36, pt. 3 (VI, 177v–178v).
131. Cf. q. 84, a. 1.
132. *De Cael. Hier.*, II, 2 (PG 3, 137).
133. *De Caelo*, I, 3 (269b 18).
134. Q. 3, a. 5.
135. *De Trin.*, XII, 2 (PL 42, 999); *De Vera Relig.*, XXXI (PL 34, 147); *Confess.*, XII, 25 (PL 32, 840).
136. *De Trin.*, XII, 4 (PL 42, 1000).
137. Q. 84, a. 7; q. 85, a. 8; q. 87, a. 2, ad 2.
138. Q. 12, a. II, ad 3; q. 84, a. 5.
139. Q. 87, a. 2, ad 3.

CHAPTER 33

Matthew of Aquasparta

Matthew of Aquasparta, a descendant of the noble and illustrious Bentivenghi family, was born at the small village of Aquasparta near Todi in Umbria circa 1238. In 1254 he entered the Franciscan order, after which he studied theology at the University of Paris, where he was profoundly influenced by the works of Bonaventure. He was awarded the degree of *baccalarius biblicus* in 1268. Remaining at Paris, he commented on the *Sentences* of Peter Lombard between 1270 and 1273. After receiving his doctorate in 1273, he was lector at the Studium Generale at Bologna (1273–74), and in 1276 he became master of theology at Paris. From 1277 to 1279 Matthew held the post of regent master at the Franciscan studium at Paris, and in 1279 he succeeded John Pecham as the official theologian of the pope and of the Roman Curia, a post he held for eight years and which carried with it the prestigious title of *Lector sacri palatii*. In 1287 he was elected minister general of the Franciscan order. During this period the order was fraught with strife due to feuding factions, and Matthew successfully functioned as a moderator and peacemaker. In 1288 he was made cardinal priest by Pope Nicholas IV, and in 1291 he was promoted to the bishopric of Porto and Santa Rufina. Matthew spent the remainder of his life in the service of the Holy See. On behalf of Pope Boniface VIII he acted as a papal legate to Lombardy, Romagna, and Tuscany, a diplomatic role in which he again exerted his abilities as a moderator of conflicts. On October 29, 1302, he died at Rome, where he is buried in the church of Ara Coeli.

Matthew of Aquasparta on the Knowledge of Nothing
by
Warren G. Harbison

Since the earliest days of philosophy, the concept of nothing has been a problem. In Parmenides, for instance, the one path that is closed to thought is the path of what is not, for it neither is nor can be known nor is even intelligible. In the case of fictional beings, for example, unicorns or vampires, one can understand or know what they are even if one is quite certain that there are no things of that sort. In such cases, the essence of the things in question is available to the intellect, whereas the existence of such things is accidental, that is, they may or may not be. In the case of nonbeing, however, things stand quite differently, since the very essence of nonbeing evidently precludes there being anything of the sort (and in this regard the problem of nothing merits comparison with the ontological argument for God's existence, wherein it is argued that His essence entails His existence). But the problem of nonbeing is rendered even more serious by the peculiarity of medieval epistemology. Following Plato and Aristotle, medieval theoreticians of knowledge hold that real knowledge or science occurs on the level of species and, hence, on the level of universals apprehendable by the intellect alone. Consequently, for them it is the knowledge of particular things that is problematic. Yet in the case of nonbeing, it is not clear that there can even be an essence of nonbeing, and this, in turn, renders it questionable whether it is even intelligible.

Matthew attempts to resolve these problems in the traditional Aristotelian manner, according to which things are "said in many ways" (*legetai pollakos*): in one way, nonbeing is intelligible and can be known; in another, not. He admits, however, that a solution provided along those lines is incomplete and requires supplementation by ideas drawn from theology. One intriguing feature of his resulting solution is his contention that the mind that grasps immutable truth has been acted upon or touched by the Divine Mind and, as a result, is "irradiated" or shines. Other fascinating points in Matthew's solution can be found in his arguments for the place of nonbeing in such everyday things as memory or records and making or doing things (creation or action).

DISPUTED QUESTIONS ON FAITH AND KNOWLEDGE

Question I

The question is whether the knowledge of a thing requires the existence of the thing known, or whether non-being [*non-ens*] can be an object of the intellect.

That knowledge does require the existence of the thing known and that non-being cannot be understood is shown thus:

1. Anselm, *On Truth*, says that truth is threefold: there is truth that only makes to be, truth that is only made to be, and truth that both makes to be and is made to be [*efficiens et effecta*]. Truth that only makes to be is first truth; truth that is only made to be is truth in the intellect or in declaration [*enunciatio*]; and truth that makes to be and

Translated especially for this volume by Warren G. Harbison from *Fr. Matthaeus Ab Aquasparta, O. F. M., S. R. E. Cardinalis, Quaestiones Disputatae De Fide et De Cognitione (Bibliotheca Fransciscana Scholastica, Medii Aevi Cura, PP. Collegii Bonaventurae,* Tom. I [pp. 201–22], Quaracchi, Florentiae [1957]).

is made to be is the truth of the thing, which is made to be by first truth and makes truth to be in intellect or in declaration. On the other hand, neither the truth of knowledge nor that of declaration is a cause of truth. But if first truth were not, then, since first truth is the cause of truth in things, there could be no truth in things. Therefore, if there were not truth in the thing, then, since the truth of the thing is the cause of truth in the intellect, there could be no truth in the intellect.

2. Truth is in the intellect, not the thing. The Philosopher says, *Metaphysics* VI, that good and bad are in things but true and false are in the intellect. And this is so because truth states an adequacy [*adaequatio*] that is formally in the intellect and that which is adequate is. Against this, it was objected that adequacy is a relation and that, since nothing can be said to be adequate to itself, it is necessary that it be adequate to something else. If, therefore, truth is adequacy of the thing to the intellect and conversely, then it of necessity requires the

existence of the thing. And if this is so, then, since only the true is understood and the true is in the intellect only if it is in the thing, it follows that knowledge of necessity requires the existence of the thing.

3. Avicenna, *Metaphysics* I, says that since the first thing that is impressed in the intellect is being [*ens*], being is therefore the first impression of the intellect. Therefore, the intellect understands only being, and so non-being cannot be understood.

4. The Philosopher, *Metaphysics* II, says, "As each thing is related to being, so is it related to the true." But the true is the object of the intellect, and, therefore, as it is related to being, so is it related to knowledge. Therefore, what is not is not knowable.

5. Augustine, *On Genesis* XII, says, "The intellect either understands and is true or, if it is not true, then it does not understand." But what is not is not true. Therefore, what is not is not understood.—The proof of the minor premise is found where Augustine says, *Soliloquies* II after the beginning, "The true is that which is."

6. Three things are of necessity demanded for knowledge: a power of knowing, which is the intellect, a medium or reason [*ratio*] of knowing, which is the species of the thing, and the object itself. In the case of a non-existent thing, however, there can be the power of knowing and the reason of knowing, but, I ask, what is the object? If it is a thing existing outside [the intellect], then I have the proposition that non-being is not known. If it is the species or the reason of knowing, then the contrary is the case: the medium or the reason of knowing can in no way [*nullo modo*] be the object in so far as it is the medium, because it is not that which is known, but the reason of knowing. It is not understood, but the reason of understanding. Therefore, it is necessary to posit some being [*ens*] that is the object of the intellect.

7. It is said that since quiddity and being [*esse*] differ in every created thing, the understanding of a quiddity therefore abstracts from being and that, therefore, it is not necessary that there be an existent in act, but only that it be apprehended by the

intellect and that it be represented to the intellect. Against this, it may be objected that when the thing does not exist, nothing remains except what is within the intellect. But whatever is within the intellect has itself in the reason of the medium, in the reason of the species, and since it is neither that which is itself understood nor the object, it is therefore the reason of understanding [*ratio intelligendi*] representing the object. Therefore, it is necessary to posit, as being, the thing that is the object of the intellect. Therefore, non-being is not understood.

8. It is said that while the thing known is better is neither in itself nor in act, it is still in cause or in potentiality. It was objected that if even every created cause were removed, the intellect would still understand the quiddity of man. Therefore, if that quiddity is the object of the intellect, not as it is in the thing, since we are supposing that it is not, nor as it is in the created cause, then it must be as it is in the first and uncreated cause. But the first and uncreated cause can be the object only if it is the beatific object, which cannot be in this life. Or, if it were, it would follow that the intellect by its natural means could attain to a knowledge of the first cause of being, but that is erroneous and one of the articles reproved and excommunicated. Therefore, there must needs be given an object in the thing outside the intellect. Therefore, non-being cannot be understood.

9. If the intellect knows non-being, then it knows it only by a species that the intellect has within itself. In that case, either it knows the thing according to the being [*esse*] that it has in its proper genus or it does not. If it does not, then it does not know it according to its true being, since it has its true being in its proper genus, not in the intellect, and then the intellect could not know truly. If it does know the thing according to the being that it has in its proper genus, then it knows or understands some being in act [*actu ens*], not non-being.

10. According to the Philosopher, there is no knowledge, either speculative or prac-

tical, of accidental being *[ente per accidens]*. And the cause or the reason of this is that accidental being is due to a lack of being *[defectum essendi]* or a lack of entity *[entitatis]*. But it is certain that non-being is further from the reason of being than from accidental being. Therefore, of non-being so much the less can there be speculative or practical knowledge.

11. Each thing is more in its cause than in its effect, but the truth of knowledge is caused by the truth of things in their proper genus. Therefore, truth is more in things than in the intellect or knowledge. Therefore, without the truth of things there cannot remain any truth in knowledge.

12. Augustine, *The City of God* XI, says, "To some it seems wonderful yet it is true that this world could not be known by us if it were not, but if it were not known to God, it could not be." From this it may be gathered that the knowledge of God is the cause of things and does not depend on things but that our knowledge is caused by things and for that reason depends on them. But since things depend on divine knowledge as their cause, it is impossible that things might be if there were no divine knowledge. Therefore, since our knowledge likewise depends on things as its cause, it follows that, if things do not exist, then our knowledge cannot be.

13. As sense is related to what is sensible, so is the intellect related to what is intelligible. But sense can in no way sense a thing, if that sensible thing does not exist. Therefore, the intellect likewise cannot understand, if the intelligible thing is not being in act.

14. I am supposing two theses. The first is that knowledge or science is not without assimilation. And Augustine, *On the Trinity* IX, says that, "All knowledge according to species is like the thing that it knows." The second is that the like is not like itself but like something else. Now in any likeness four things must be posited. There must be two like extremes and two reasons of assimilation. Thus, on the side of *[ex parte]* the intellect, there are the intellect itself and the species through which it is assimilated and,

on the side of the thing known, the quiddity is the reason of assimilation. But the term or the extreme cannot be if there is not a like thing. Therefore, there cannot be a science or knowledge of a thing without its existence.

15. The thesis is confirmed by the fact that an accident cannot be without a subject. Therefore, an accident requires and demands that the thing be. But similarity is an accident and so not without a subject. If, therefore, there is true assimilation or true similarity of the intellect to the thing and of the thing to the intellect, then it is necessary to posit a thing assimilated, in which the assimilation is as in a subject.

16. Between an existent and a superexistent *[superexsistens]* the agreement *[convenientia]* is greater and the distance less than it is between a non-existent and an existent. But since God is absolutely superexistent, according to Dionysius, *On Divine Names*, He is neither knowable nor intelligible. Therefore, much less will the non-existent or non-being be knowable.

17. Since God has the reasons of all things, He knows non-existent things. But the human intellect does not have the reasons of non-existents. Therefore, in no way can it know or understand non-existence.

18. Knowledge and the knowable are said *[dicuntur]* in relation so that there is a real relation on the side of knowledge, which depends on the knowable. But there cannot be a real relation if it is not a relation to a thing really existent. Therefore, if there is not a thing knowable or known, real and in act, then knowledge cannot be. The proof of the minor premise is made apparent by the Philosopher in the *Categories*, where he states that the being *[esse]* of what is in the relation is *to* something else, so that the relation depends not less but all the more, as a relation, on the object than on the subject. Therefore, etc.

19. According to the Philosopher, *De Anima* III, to understand is to suffer something, and it is certain that what is suffered is due to what is understood. I therefore ask whether it is due either to the likeness or to the thing. If the likeness, then it is a

knowledge of concepts only; if the thing or object, it is necessary that the object really be, since, as the Philosopher says, it is impossible for a real property to be, if it is not in that which really is. Therefore etc.

20. According to the Philosopher, spoken words [voces—voices] are signs of those passions that are in the soul, but in the intellect they are signs of things. Yet it is certain that concepts depend on things more than the spoken word [vox] does, since they are more immediately related to them. But if things do not exist, then there can be no true declarations. Therefore, if things do not exist, then so much the more can there be no true understanding or concept of them. The proof of the minor premise is by Boethius, Consolation of Philosophy V, by the Philosopher, Categories, by Anselm, On Truth, all of whom say that it is due to a thing's being or not being that speech is said truly or falsely.

21. Augustine, On the Trinity XV, says that for the truth of the thing it is requisite that it be so both in the thing and in knowledge, and that otherwise, if one or the other is lacking, what is said [verbum] is not true. But in all knowledge what is said is of necessity required. Therefore, the existence of the thing is needed of necessity.

22. The knowable is the measure of knowledge, and so things are the measure of our intellect. It is certain, however, that the measure is more perfect than the measured. But a thing is a measure only by adequacy. Therefore, the reason of adequacy or adequacy itself is more perfect in the thing than in the intellect. Therefore, also truth, for truth is adequacy. Therefore, if the measured cannot be without the measure, then there can be no truth in the intellect without the truth of the thing. Therefore, truth cannot be understood without the existence of the thing.

Against [the thesis that knowledge requires the existence of the thing known and that non-being cannot be understood]

a. Avicenna, *Metaphysics* I, says that it is obvious that if anything is declared [enun-

tiatur] of something, it must in some way have being in the soul. Declarations are about some true thing only by that which has being in the soul, and they are by accident—by that which is in what is external. Therefore, in the same way, conceptions, upon which propositions are founded, are by accident—through that which is in exterior things. But things which are by accident are not necessary to the being of anything. Therefore, there can be true conceptions and true declarations when things do not exist.

b. The Commentator on the *Nicomachean Ethics* VI [Averröes] says that, "As a lower art is related to a higher—as, for example, the art of wood-cutting is to the art of architecture—so is sense related to the intellect." But the lower art is related to the higher art in such a way that once it has supplied the matter then the higher art operates and completes the work in the matter supplied, even if the lower art be deficient. Therefore, in the same way, even if sense and the sensible species are deficient, once the intelligible species have been supplied, the intellect will be able both to operate on them and then to understand by them.

c. Anselm, *Monologium*, says that, "The work which is produced in accordance with any art—not only after it is produced but also before it is produced and even afterwards when it is dissolved—always belongs to that art and no other." Yet it is admitted that the maker in any art foresees and knows beforehand the work to be produced in accordance with that art. But that work does not as yet exist. Therefore, the maker knows non-being. Therefore, etc.

d. The power of the intellect is more effective [efficacior] than that of the imagination. Yet the ability to imagine can, by the image of the thing left in it, truly or adequately imagine what is not. Therefore, so much the more can the intellect understand a non-existent thing by the species that it has within itself. The proof of the minor premise is obvious by experiment, for by the image that I have within myself of men who are not, I imagine them truly and record them.

e. Within our intellect are impressed the eternal and immutable reasons of things, such as "every whole is greater than its part" and "of anything whatever there is either an affirmation or a negation." But such reasons do not depend on things. Therefore, by these reasons the intellect can understand non-existent things.

f. Any proposition is necessary that is necessarily posited in being denied. In this way Augustine, *Soliloquies* II, proves that truth is of necessity, since the denial of truth posits truth: "If truth is not, then it is true that truth is not, and anything that is true is true by truth." Therefore, if there is no truth, then there is truth, and it follows that it is necessary that there is truth. I argue for the proposition thus: if non-being is not intelligible, then it is intelligible that non-being is not intelligible, and therefore the proposition that non-being is intelligible is one that is necessary.

g. According to the Philosopher, the true extends to being and non-being. For just as it is true that what is is, so, too, is it true that what is not is not. But anything that is true is intelligible and can be an object of the intellect. Therefore, etc.

h. The existence or non-existence of a thing is neither necessary in itself nor required for knowledge, except in that case where the intellect, by the existence of a thing, is in one disposition or another. But the intellect is neither changed from one disposition to another nor in different dispositions as a result of the existence or non-existence of things. Therefore, existence or non-existence is not required for the knowledge of a thing.

i. Again, according to the Philosopher, the object of the intellect is the what it is [*quod quid est*—essence]. But that object in no way admits of error, since it is abstracted from place and time, being and non-being [*esse et non esse*]. Therefore, the intellect, regardless of the existence or non-existence of the thing, can understand its object without error. Therefore, for the knowledge of a thing the existence of the thing is not required, and so non-being can be an object of the intellect.

I Respond

The present question is not about the signification of names or spoken words [*voces*]. While there may be a question of whether spoken words signify the same things regardless of the existence or non-existence of those things or regardless of whether names are imposed on things or concepts, that question belongs to logic and therefore does not pertain to the present question. Any spoken word, any name, any circumscribed declaration confronts the difficulty stated in that question.

Therefore, it seems to me that before the question proposed at the outset can be satisfactorily resolved distinctions must be drawn from the side of non-being or being and from the side of the intellect that knows.

Firstly, from the side of non-being I distinguish [*distinguo*]: non-being can be taken in two ways. In the first way, there is non-being simply [*non ens simpliciter*], and this in no way [*nullo modo*] is—neither in itself nor in cause, neither in potentiality nor in act, neither was nor will be, neither is nor is possible to be. In this first way, then, I say simply that non-being can in no way be an object of the intellect. For, as Avicenna says, what first occurs to the intellect and what can first be apprehended by the intellect is being [*ens*]. Therefore, since "nothing" is not intelligible, so, too, is non-being. In the second way, however, non-being can be understood: not non-being simply, but non-being in some other way—not non-being in act, but as being in potentiality; not non-being in itself, but as being in its efficient cause or exemplar. And I say that it is in this second way that non-being is an object of the intellect and is intelligible.

This also appears, firstly, from prophetic illumination and the foresight of futures. If there is no certain knowledge of non-being, then, since the future is non-being, it follows that no future can be known or known in advance, which is contrary to sacred

Scripture and the catholic [or common] faith.

It appears, secondly, from the disposition toward things to be done [rerum fiendarum]. If there were not some knowledge of non-being, then, since nothing is done willingly unless also knowingly, no one would be disposed to do anything. In that case, all dispositions and all operations by art would perish. Augustine, *On the Trinity* IX, shows this best: "In our pronouncements and actions we do nothing by the members of the body that we have not arrived at beforehand by the word [verbo] pronounced within ourselves. No one willingly does [facit] anything if he has not previously said it in his heart," and, *On the Trinity* XV, "Just as it is said of the Word of God that 'all are made by it [Omnia per ipsum facta sunt],' so, too, there are no works of man that are not spoken in the heart beforehand. And the two are alike in that our word can be even if the work does not ensue but the work cannot be if the word does not precede it, just as the Word of God could be even if no creature existed but no creature could truly be, if not by it, by which all were made [per ipsum quo facta sunt omnia]." Therefore, if nothing can be known of non-being or the not actually existent, then there would be no disposition toward things to be done, and men would do all things by chance, which is absurd. Therefore, it is necessary that non-being somehow be understood, but the existence of the thing is not required for the knowledge of it, although in some things knowledge precedes of necessity.

Thirdly, that non-being is an object of the intellect and is intelligible appears from the record of precedents. It is certain that whatever has preceded is not. Therefore, if non-being is in no way known or understood, then there is no memory of things past and no record of them, which is simply false since we do have a record of the day before and what transpired in the course of it.— Again, if there were no record, there would be neither continuation nor order nor connection of words [verbi] nor of things done,

since whoever has no record of what has preceded cannot know where a thing ceased and where it should begin again, as is shown by Augustine, *Confessions X*, *On Genesis* XII, and *On Christian Doctrine* II.

Fourthly, it is apparent from the virtue and operation of the intellect. By its active power, by the light of the agent intellect, the intellect can abstract universals from particulars, intelligible species from sensible species, and quiddities from things actually existing. Yet it is certain that universals, intelligible species, and quiddities do not concern any thing existing in act. They are all related indifferently to the existent and non-existent alike and do not concern place or time. Therefore, existence or non-existence does not have anything to do with this sort of understanding. Therefore, just as the intellect can understand the quiddity of a thing by the intelligible species when the thing does exist, so, too, can it also do so when the thing does not exist.

Secondly, distinctions are to be drawn from the side of the intellect that knows. The intellect is said in two ways, just as there is a double operation of the intellect. There is a simple and absolute intellect that apprehends and conceives the simple quiddities of things, and there is another intellect that is the concrete and composite intellect that understands and apprehends a thing to be in or to be under determinate circumstances of time.

If, therefore, it is asked whether for the knowledge of a thing the existence of the thing is of necessity required, I respond that if we are speaking of that operation or of the way [modus] of understanding by which a thing is understood to be under determinate circumstances of time, then according to the exigency of time the existence of the thing is required of necessity. This is so in order that it be understood to be when it is—to be future when it is future, and to have been when it has been— since otherwise the intellect would be false and so would not be an intellect at all. "The intellect either understands and is true or, if it is not true, then it does not understand," as Augustine says, and as has been touched on in the opposition to the argument. But the truth of the future is founded upon the cause, as in the passage where Augustine says, *Confessions* XI, that nothing is seen except as present: "While the future is said to be seen, it is not itself seen because it is not, but what is seen are signs of it, which now are. Thus, not the future but the present is now seen, and from this is predicted the future conceived by the soul. For example, I intuit *[intueor]* the dawn, and I foretell the future." Yet the truth of the present is founded upon things actually existent. And the truth of the precedent is founded upon the image or species of the thing that remains in the intellect together with the comparison to the thing which was but is not now, just as Augustine says in the same text: "My boyhood, which is not now, is in the time preceding, which also is not now, but, when I recall it and tell of it, I intuit at the present time the image of it, which is still in my intellect." But whether images of future things are presented thus, as causes now existing, he says he does not know.

On the other hand, if we are speaking truly of the intellect as regards that simple, absolute, and pure operation by which it apprehends and conceives the absolute quiddities of things, then I say that for this way of knowledge the existence of things is not required and that the existence or non-existence of the thing makes no difference to it. The reason for this has been touched on in part, and it is apparent from the sides of the quiddity, the intellect, and the intelligible species:

1. From the side of the quiddity because, as Avicenna says in *Metaphysics* V and many other places: in every created thing quiddity and being *[esse]* differ. Being is not included in the understanding of the quiddity, but quiddity is related indifferently to being and non-being. Therefore, the only thing that is required for understanding the quiddity of a thing is that the thing be in act. For example, when I state, "man is an animal" this is the essence or quiddity of man by explicit name. It has nothing to do with the existence or non-existence of men, and so even if no men existed, "man is an animal" would be true.

2. From the side of the intelligible species because neither the intelligible nor even the imaginable species represents a thing to be or not to be. They both represent it simply, as the image sculpted in the wall represents Socrates or Hercules to me but neither existent nor non-existent: if existent only, then it would not represent him dead; if non-existent only, then it could not represent him alive. Yet in fact it does represent him indifferently, alive or dead.

3. From the side of the intellect because, as has been said, the intellect possesses the power to abstract, and so it has an absolute operation that has nothing to do with the being of a thing or non-being but does apprehend the thing or the quiddity of the thing nonetheless—as, for example, it understands man: not this or that man, here or there, yesterday or today, but man as such. Therefore, when it does understand man, then, when men do exist, existent man is not its object because it abstracts from that, and so it can understand man even when men are non-existent. Therefore, it is seen that the difficulty is no greater here than there and, moreover, that it is by that very same power that it divides the conjoined and conjoins the separated, provided they are not incompossible.

But then the difficulty remains, for if non-being does fall within the domain of its operation, then what can the object of the intellect be? And in that case could it be said, as has been said, that non-being simply *[non ens simpliciter]* neither is nor can be an object of the intellect? Yet non-being in act, or that which is not some thing or other, by its very reason pertains not to actual being *[esse]* but to intelligible being, and since it is intelligible being and so admits of apprehension and representation by the intellect, it follows that it is and can be an object of the intellect. When the intellect, therefore, has within itself the species of the quiddity of the human, or that of any quiddity whatever, that species does not represent that quiddity to it as being in act *[ens actu]* or as non-being. It represents it simply, as has been said, and from it the intellect forms for itself a concept and understands the quiddity of man or of anything simply, regardless of being or non-being. And this suffices for the reason of the object. For, the thing not existing, the quiddity as it is in things is the object of the intellect.

The way *[modus]* is philosophical and proper, but I do not think it suffices. It may be that the principles of philosophy are here lacking, and recourse must be had to the principles of theology. And this is apparent thus: if nothing falls under the intellect besides non-being, or species, or some concept, then there would be absolutely no point to understanding, as is seen.

Further, when I understand the defining reason of man or of anything whatever that has a quiddity, then neither do I understand nothing nor do I understand a being that is in potentiality, nor do I understand only some thing that admits of apprehension, but I do understand necessary truth, immutable truth, eternal truth. For as Augustine says, *On the Immortality of the Soul*, nothing "is so eternal as the reason of the circle." And, *On Free Will* II: "That 'seven and three are ten' never was not, never will not be, but always was, always will be." And the Philosopher, *Nicomachean Ethics* VI, says that "knowledge is only of beings that are of necessity and eternal, not of what is contingent." Knowledge is therefore founded upon something. It is not founded upon things, for if all things were to pass away, these truths would remain, and even if not one thing existed, these truths would still be, for when not even a single man exists, it is still true that man is a rational, mortal animal. Nor is knowledge founded upon the created intellect, for every such intellect is mutable, and even when no created intellect exists, these truths still are. Therefore, knowledge is founded only upon the eternal exemplar, where "the origins of mutable things remain immutable, and the reasons of things

transient are not themselves transient," as Augustine says, *Confessions* I.

Furthermore, created truth is nothing else but a certain expression of uncreated truth, and each created truth is true only because it imitates that exemplar. Therefore, if these true immutables *[vera immutabilia]* cannot be understood otherwise than where they are, and even if they are not immutable anywhere else besides art, then it is necessary that they be understood in art.

Further, since the truth of a thing is only an expression and imitation of the eternal art and the likeness of that truth expressing the first exemplar is in our intellect, then it is impossible that I should understand anything truly and with certitude without an application in a certain way and a relation to an external exemplar. Therefore, since we do understand the quiddity of something and its defining reason, it follows that the object of the intellect is neither itself the concept of the mind as such nor the quiddity itself as such, which is not in the nature of things. Nor is the eternal exemplar the reposing and ultimate object *[objectum quietans et terminans]*, since that object is solely the blessed and blessing intellect. But it is the quiddity itself conceived by our intellect yet related to the art or the eternal exemplar that, touching our mind, has itself in the reason of that which is moving it. And from that we conceive the true knowledge of a thing, and once the materials have been prepared from below by the senses, the principles of all the arts flow from it. That is why—contrary to Plato, who said that the arts are brought forth within souls, because the ignorant and unlearned give true responses about them— Augustine, *Retractions* I, maintains that "It is more credible that they should respond truly when they are questioned well about some disciplines although unlearned in them, because there is present to them, when they can grasp it, the light of some eternal reason, by which these true immutables are conspicuous." And in the same book, touching on the same error—as well as the error that to learn is to recollect, since anyone responds truly when questioned in good order—he says: "It can come to pass that one can do this, because there is an intelligible nature and it is connected not only with intelligible but also in truth with immutable things, and it comes to pass in such an order that when one is moved to these things, to which one is connected, or to oneself—to the extent that one does see them—one can respond truly about them." And *Confessions* X: "The beauties that are cast by souls in the hands of artists come from that beauty which is above souls."

I have touched upon these few things, examining them in advance, since the way in which mind sees anything in art or in the eternal reasons will be shown more clearly in the following.

Resolution of the Objections

1. To the first argument against the thesis it is to be said that truth first and in principle, and in things and in the intellect, is from first truth. It is nevertheless by origin from things and in things in respect of the intellect in natural knowledge. But formally it is in the intellect itself, so far as it conceives a thing as it is, since there is then an adequacy of thing and intellect. Yet while truth is caused in the intellect by things in point of origin, it is still not so caused in point of conversation and continuation. On the contrary, when things perish, truth—together with the irradiation [*irradiatione*] produced by the uncreated light—still remains in the intellect.—It was also objected that if first truth were, *per impossible*, to cease to be, then truth could not remain in things, and so forth, but that objection does not hold, because the first cause is the effective and conserving cause, so that, if its influence were removed, nothing at all could remain. But things outside the intellect, while they are the efficient cause of truth in the intellect, are not for all that the conserving cause, since if the influence of second causes is removed, there still remains the influence of the first cause. However, the way in which truth is caused in the intellect by things outside itself will be seen elsewhere.

2. To the second it is to be said that adequacy is a relation and so is *to* another. But the relation between knowledge and the knowable depends on the knowable, and, therefore, from the side of knowledge that relation is according to being [*esse*]. The knowable, however, neither depends on knowledge nor does it posit any thing, and so in the knowable the relation is only according to the reason. Therefore, the knowable need be not according to the thing but only according to the reason, as understood or apprehended by the intellect, with there still being a relation to the first exemplar that contains the reason of immutable quiddity.—And I also say that it [relation to the first exemplar] is adequacy: since the intellect understands the quiddity to involve neither being nor non-being, neither place nor time, nor its own reason, it therefore understands the quiddity the way it is. Therefore, the intellect is not adequate to itself [and so I say that adeqacy is relation to the first exemplar].

3. To the third it is to be said, as Avicenna says, that being is what first occurs to the intellect and so non-being cannot be understood. But since being, as such, is neither in act nor in potentiality, neither present nor future, neither man nor horse, nor any thing of this sort, it is therefore not something determinate and so is above all these. And I say that quiddity is being in the intellect and in the eternal exemplar, while in things it is not being in act, since this also is not involved in the understanding of it.

4. To the fourth the response is patent. The Philosopher does not wish to say more than that in the way in which a thing is, in just that way is it knowable. So if it is in act, then it is knowable in act; if in potentiality, then it is knowable in potentiality; if it is abstracted from act and potentiality and from every difference of being, then it is knowable in that way. And, universally, however often being is said, just that often is the true said [*quoties dicitur ens, toties dicitur verum*], and however often or in however many ways as the true can be said, in just that many ways is it knowable, as has been seen.

5. To the fifth the response is likewise patent. The quiddity of a thing is the proper object of the intellect, and so when it understands it, the intellect understands the true. But the true is not nothing but is what something is [*quod quid est*—essence] or that which the thing is. Therefore, it is properly the true, and the reason of Augustine is properly suited to it. Since I understand what man is, I understand the reality of man, and this is "that which man is" immutably. Nor does Augustine understand by "that which is" being in act, since that being admits of corruption while truth of itself is not corrupted when things are, because the reasons of things remain always.

6. To the sixth the response is patent by what has been said in the principal solution. There I say that something is the object. It is necessary neither that it be something existing in act nor that it be in the reason of the object of the intellect. It suffices that it be represented to the intellect and be apprehended by it.—Or, as has been said, the object is the quiddity itself that is conceived by the intellect, so far as it is related to the eternal exemplar, which is related to the intellect in the reason of that which is moving it.

7. The seventh argument is that if all things are removed, then nothing remains that is not within the intellect. In response, I say that that is false and that the immutable reasons always remain there. It is immutably true that man is an animal, and so forth, but it is in the eternal exemplar that is related to the intellect in the reason of that which is moving it. From that the quiddity, conceived and related to that exemplar, is the object of the intellect.—But when the argument adds that whatever is within the intellect is related in the reason of the medium and in the reason of knowing, it is to be said that that contention is false. For from the species that represents something to it, regardless of whether it be or not be, the intellect forms a concept for itself, and that thing it presents to itself. But that leads not to understanding but to something else. It need be neither in the

thing nor in the reason of the object, and it suffices that it can be in the mind's concept.

8. To the eighth it is to be said that if every created cause is removed, then the immutable reason of the quiddity of the thing still remains, as does the species within the intellect by which it can form for itself a concept of the thing. Thus, while the quiddity itself cannot of itself be the object of the intellect, neither can the concept itself as such, since in that case the intellect, understanding not the thing but only its own concept, would be vain. Nor do I say that the exemplar itself is the intellect's ultimate or reposing object [*objectum terminans aut quietans*]. The argument would proceed in that way, but all these concur in making one perfect reason of the object, as has been explained, and that is the quiddity itself conceived or apprehended by the intellect but only insofar as it is referred to the eternal exemplar, which is related to the intellect in the reason of that which is moving it.

9. To the ninth it is to be said that the intellect knows through species and that, since the thing is not in its proper genus but the intellect does know it truly nonetheless, it follows that it does not know it according to the being that it has in its proper genus. It knows the quiddity, which differs from being, but being is not involved in the understanding of it. The understanding of it abstracts altogether from being, as has repeatedly been said. Yet it knows by referring in the first cause and exemplar that is moving it in this knowledge.

10. To the tenth it is to be said that while there is no knowledge of accidental being, this is not due to some lack of entity. It is instead due to a lack of determination in that whatever has accidental being has neither a determinate cause nor any one way of being. It is possible that it occurs as if by infinite causes and in infinite ways, and so it can be known by natural knowledge neither in itself nor in its causes. Yet since being in act is not involved in the reasons of the quiddities of things, they do not have it yet do retain immutable truth nonethe-

less, according to Augustine and the Philosopher.

11. To the eleventh it is to be said that truth is not in things and in the intellect in the same way. Truth is in things by origin and by cause with respect to the intellect, but it is in the intellect formally, as was said above. And since it is not in the same way that it is in things and in the intellect—causally it is more in things, but formally it is more in the intellect—it follows that they cannot be uniformly compared.

12. To the twelfth it is to be said that the way in which God is the cause of things is different from the way in which things are the cause of our knowledge. God is the total and only cause of things and, moreover, is the cause of the whole of things, which is why things depend on His providence. But since God could imprint on our intellect species of things by which we might [directly] know, as he imparts them to angels, it follows that things are not a necessary cause of our knowledge. Moreover, things are not the total and sole cause of our knowledge but also stand in need of the light of our agent intellect and divine light. Therefore, even if things are in some way the original cause, nonetheless they neither are the conserving cause nor does our knowledge depend on them for its conservation.

13. To the thirteenth it is to be said that there is no likeness in that case. Sense does not have the power to conserve sensible species, but the intellect does have the power to conserve intelligible species. It is for this reason that the senses cannot sense if the thing to be sensed is not present but the intellect can understand even if the thing has been destroyed. And it is because we have intelligible species within the intellect but no sensible species within sense that the Philosopher says, *De Anima* II, that we understand at will but do not sense thus.

14. To the fourteenth it is to be said, as has been said above, that there can be no relation of the knowable to knowledge if it is not according to the reason. Therefore, assimilation, too, can be only according to

the reason. It is due to this that it is necessary to posit that something according to the thing exists from the side of the intelligible—but solely in apprehension. Nor is it inconsistent that something be referred to non-being according to the reason. I see that between some things there is a relation according to being from the side of either extreme—namely, when the extremes depend upon each other and the relation posits something in either extreme, as between father and son.—Between other things there is a relation from the side of one of the extremes according to being, but from the side of the other according to the reason, and so from the side of the latter extreme the relation posits nothing. The relation between knowledge and the knowable is precisely of this sort.—Between still other things there is a relation from the side of both extremes according to the reason, as between God and creatures from eternity. From eternity there were in God ideas of the things to be made *[ideae rerum fiendarum]*, which they call a relation to things according to the reason because the relation does not posit any thing either on the part of the divine essence or on the part of things, which were not. Therefore, wherever there is a relation or an assimilation according to the reason, it is not necessary to posit extremes except according to the reason.

15. To the fifteenth the response is patent. It has been said that likeness posits nothing on the side of the knowable according to the thing but only according to the reason, and so it is not necessary to posit the thing on that account. Moreover, it has been said that likeness is a true accident on the part of the other, and so it is necessary to posit the subject according to the truth of the thing. But because from the other side [the knowable] likeness is solely an accident according to the reason, it is therefore not necessary to posit a subject if it is not according to the reason.—If it be asked, as it was in the case of quiddity, whether it is something or nothing, then this must be the response: if it is something—regardless of whether it be accident, or substance, or

creature, or creator—then I say that it is not nothing but something. But since the division of things existing in act is such that they are either substance or accident, either this or that, then, since likeness is not something in act, it follows that it is neither substance nor accident, neither this nor that. As was said above, the understanding of the quiddity abstracts from all being.

16. To the sixteenth it is to be said that "the superexistent" is both intelligible and knowable. While Dionysius does pronounce God to be neither knowable nor intelligible, that pronouncement is to be understood in the following manner. Since God is comprehensible to Himself alone, He is knowable and by a comprehensive knowledge, and so He is fully knowable and intelligible to Himself alone. Yet He is also knowable—but not fully and perfectly—by a notice that apprehends [notitia apprehensiva] what He is and why He is.

17. To the seventeenth it is to be said that since God has the practical and exemplary reason of the things to be made [res fiendas], He knows them. But the human intellect cannot know any future that does not have causes in nature except in the case of divine revelation, which contains the reasons of that which is to be made. Yet once things do exist, the intellect acquires for itself the species of those things, and so while it does not have the reasons that make, it does have the reasons that have been made. Therefore, if the things perish, the intellect knows those things by the species nonetheless.

18. To the eighteenth a response can be made from those given above. From the side of the knowable there is relation according to what is said or according to the reason, but from the side of knowledge there is relation according to being [esse]. Therefore, the knowable must be posited in the reason, not in being.—But from the side of what is said it is clear that a real relation can be only to a thing and that, since the being of relations is to something else, it depends more on the object than on the subject. In view of this I say that, insofar as a relation states an accident, it depends more

upon the subject in which it is, but, insofar as it is a relation to something or a disposition [habitudo], it depends more on the object because it is a relation to it. And I add that a real relation is to a thing—to the thing as it is, but to the thing according to the way and exigency of the thing. And it does not belong to the reason of it either that it be in act or that it have being but only that it admit of apprehension, be conceived by the intellect and be related to the first exemplar. Therefore, to such a thing the reality of relation is such.

19. To the nineteenth I say that to understand is, at the beginning of understanding, to suffer something, but, in its completion, to understand is to act. To receive is to suffer, but to judge and discern is to act. At first, then, the intellect suffers—in the way in which receiving is suffering—the things from which it receives, or from phantasms, but later it acts. Therefore, it is not necessary that the intellect be always active—unless, perhaps, we were to say, as has been said, that it suffers in that it is moved by the eternal reasons.

20. To the twentieth it is to be said that the cases are not at all alike as regards declaration and knowledge or conception. Declaration always declares that something is or is not. Therefore, it is true only when it declares what is to be or what is not not to be. And in a similar way, our intellect, by an operation related to the existence of things under determinate circumstances of time, is true only when it conceives or apprehends what is to be or what is not not to be. Yet, as has been said, the intellect also has a simple and absolute operation that abstracts from these altogether. Therefore, it does not depend on the being or non-being of things.

21. To the twenty-first it is to be said that it is true of the operation of the intellect that has to do with the existence of things but that it is not true of that operation that abstracts from it.—Or it can be said that since the quiddity is in the thing as it is in knowledge, it follows that when the intellect apprehends the simple quiddity of a thing, then it conceives a true word [verbum]. The

quiddity states some thing, of which the reason or intention pertains neither to being nor to non-being, and the intellect understands it thus. Therefore, it understands it as it is, and it is because of this that the word is true.

22. To the twenty-second it is to be said that the knowable is the measure of knowledge and that things are the measure of our intellect. This is according to the saying that science and knowledge are true when they are adequate to things, and that is when knowledge knows the thing as it is and the way it is. Therefore, the reason of adequacy or truth is by origin from things but formally in the understanding and, as exemplar, in God. And since there are diverse ways of being [*diversi modi essendi*], there is no uniform comparison that might apply to all and there is always the fallacy of inferring from a statement qualified in respect of a way of being to a statement about being absolutely. Yet it is certain that whatever is in God simply is more perfectly.—And in response to the objection that the measured depends on the measure, it is to be said that here it is the knowable thing that is the measure. But *is*, I say, not in act, but in the conception of the mind and in the eternal exemplar, and this suffices for the reason of the measure.

CHAPTER 34

Nicolaus of Autrecourt

Nicolaus of Autrecourt, also called Nicolaus of Uttracuria, was born circa 1300 at Autrecourt in the diocese of Verdun. He studied at the Sorbonne between 1320 and 1327, presumably completing the arts program. In 1338 he was made a canon of the cathedral of Metz. With this position went a stipend or prebend for advanced studies. Ultimately, he earned a bachelor's degree in laws and became a licentiate in theology. Advanced study of theology required completion of a commentary on the *Sentences* of Peter Lombard. Over time, Nicolaus lectured not only on the *Sentences* but on Aristotle's *Politics* as well.

In his introductory lecture on the *Sentences* he demonstrated a radical departure from the "party line" characteristic of his predecessors. His arguments, based on construing certain "famous propositions," literally led to what were construed by the powers of the church as "pernicious subtleties". In 1340 Pope Benedict XII sent a letter to the bishop of Paris in which he summoned Nicolaus, together with certain other offenders, to appear at Avignon to answer charges of heresy and error. The unexpected death of the pope led to a delay until after the coronation in 1342 of his successor Clement VI. Under the direction of Cardinal William Curti, the works of Nicolaus were scrutinized in light of a personal defense before the pope by Nicolaus. When it became clear that he was fighting a losing battle, Nicolaus fled from Avignon and purportedly took refuge at the court of Ludwig of Bavaria.

In 1346 the formal trial was conducted, and Nicolaus was sentenced to publicly burn his writing at Paris and to recant many of his published statements, which he did on November 25, 1347. In addition, his degrees were rescinded and he was expelled from the faculty of the University of Paris, being declared unworthy to continue teaching. Subsequently, Nicolaus slipped into obscurity. It is known that on August 6, 1350, he became a deacon at the cathedral of Metz. When he died after that is unknown.

Nicolaus of Autrecourt on Skepticism

These two extant letters of Nicolaus of Autrecourt to Bernard of Arezzo demonstrate a hard-minded approach to knowledge of the external world. In the first letter he argues that we can only be certain of our perceptions and the nature of perception is such that from them we can, strictly speaking, conclude nothing concerning the external world. We can make no inferences (a) that objects exist independently of our perceptions and (b) that such objects were the cause of our perceptions or were the cause of anything else; that is, we have no grounds for asserting that A caused B. Past experience leads us to believe that A caused B based on the constant conjunction of B following upon A. Such a belief pertains only to our perceptions from which we can conclude nothing of a factual causal nature because the only evidence we have for making such claims is itself based solely on our perceptions. This analysis has resulted in Nicolaus being characterized as "the medieval Hume".

In his second letter Nicolaus argues that the first principle of reasoning is the law of noncontradiction. This principle is the only basis of certitude. Any other principle purporting certitude either is reducible to the principle of noncontradiction or it merely appears certain when, in fact, it is not. From this four important points follow: (1) nothing of an existential nature follows from the first principle; (2) the conclusion of a syllogistic argument is certain only if it is reducible to the first principle; (3) all genuinely certain propositions possess the same degree of certainty regardless of whether they follow immediately or mediately from the first principle; and (4) not even God can deprive the first principle of its certainty.

TWO LETTERS TO BERNARD OF AREZZO

I. The First Letter to Bernard

With all the reverence which I am obligated to show to you, most amiable Father Bernard, by reason of the worthiness of the Friars, I wish in this present communication to explain some doubts—indeed, as it seems to some of us, some obvious contradictions—which appear to follow from the things you say, so that, by their resolution, the truth may be more clearly revealed to me and to others. For I read, in a certain book on which you lectured in the Franciscan school, the following propositions which you conceded, to whoever wished to uphold them, as true. The first, which is set forth by you in the first book of the *Sentences*, Dist. 3, Qu. 4, is this: *"Clear intuitive cognition is that by which we judge a thing to exist, whether it exists or does not exist.* Your second proposition, which is set forth in the same place as above, is of this sort: *The in-*

ference, 'An object does not exist, therefore it is not seen' *is not valid; nor does this hold,* 'This is seen, therefore this exists'; *indeed both are invalid, just as these inferences,* 'Caesar is thought of, therefore Caesar exists,' 'Caesar does not exist, therefore he is not thought of.' The third proposition, stated in that same place, is this: *Intuitive cognition does not necessarily require the existing thing."* [1]

From these propositions I infer a fourth, that every awareness which we have of the existence of objects outside our minds, can be false; since, according to you it [the awareness] can exist whether or not the object exists. And I infer another fifth proposition, which is this: By natural cognitive means [*in lumine naturali*] we cannot be certain when our awareness of the existence of external objects is true or false; because, as you say, it represents the thing as existing, whether or not it exists. And thus, since whoever admits the antecedent must concede the consequent which is inferred from that antecedent by a formal consequence, it follows that you do not have evident certitude of the existence of external

Translation and notes by Professor Ernest A. Moody of the University of California at Los Angeles. The translation is from the text edited by J. Lappe, *Beiträge zur Geschichte der Philosophie des Mittelalters.* Bd. VI, Hft. 2, Münster i.-W. 1908, pp. 2–14. Reprinted by permission of the Ernest A. Moody estate.

objects.[2] And likewise you must concede all the things which follow from this. But it is clear that you do not have evident certitude of the existence of objects of the senses, because no one has certitude of any consequent through an inference which manifestly involves a fallacy. But such is the case here; for according to you, this is a fallacy, "Whiteness is seen, therefore whiteness exists."

But you will perhaps say, as I think you wished to suggest in a certain disputation over at the Preaching Friars', that although from the fact of seeing it cannot be inferred, when that seeing is produced or conserved by a supernatural cause, that the seen object exists, nevertheless when it is produced precisely by natural causes—with only the general concurrence of the First Agent—then it can be inferred.

But to the contrary: When from some antecedent, if produced by some agent, a certain consequent cannot be inferred by a formal and evident inference, then from that antecedent, no matter by what thing it be produced, that consequent cannot be inferred. This proposition is clear, by example and by reason. By example in this way: If, whiteness being posited as existing by the agency of A, it could not be formally inferred "Whiteness exists, therefore color exists," then this could not be inferred no matter by what agency the whiteness be posited as existing. It is also clear by reason, because the antecedent is not in itself modified by whatever it is that causes it to be—nor is the fact which is signified by that antecedent.

Further, since from that antecedent it cannot be inferred evidently by way of intuitive cognition, "therefore whiteness exists," we must then add something to that antecedent—namely, what you suggested above, that the [vision of] whiteness is not produced or conserved in existence supernaturally. But from this my contention is clearly established. For when a person is not certain of some consequent, unless in virtue of some antecedent of which he is not evidently certain whether or not the case is as it states it to be—because it is not

known by the meaning of its terms, nor by experience, nor is it inferred from such knowledge, but is only believed—such a person is not evidently certain of the consequent. It is clear that this is so, if that antecedent is considered together with its condition: therefore etc.[3] On the other hand, according to your position, whoever makes the inference from that antecedent without adding that condition, makes an invalid inference as was the case with the philosophers, and Aristotle, and other people who did not add this condition to the antecedent, because they did not believe that God could impede the effects of natural causes.

Again, I ask you if you are acquainted with all natural causes, and know which of them exist and which are possible, and how much they can do. And I ask how you know evidently, by evidence reducible to that of the law of contradiction, that there is anything such that its coming to pass does not involve contradiction and which nevertheless can only be brought to pass by God? On these questions I would gladly be given certitude of the kind indicated.

Again, you say that an imperfect intuitive cognition can be had in natural manner, of a non-existent thing.[4] I now ask how you are certain (with the certitude defined above) when your intuitive cognition is of a sufficiently perfect degree such that it cannot naturally be of a non-existent thing? And I would gladly be instructed about this.

Thus, it is clear, it seems to me, that as a consequence of your statements you have to say that you are not certain of the existence of the objects of the five senses. But what is even harder to uphold, you must say that you are not certain of your own actions—e.g., that you are seeing, or hearing—indeed you must say that you are not sure that anything is perceived by you, or has been perceived by you. For, in the *Sentences, Book 1, Dist. 3,* in the place above cited, you say that your intellect does not have intuitive cognition of your actions. And you prove it by this argument: Every intuitive cognition is clear; but the cognition which your intellect has of your acts, is not clear; therefore etc. Now, on this assumption, I argue thus: The intellect which is not certain of the existence of things of which it has the clearest cognition, will not be certain concerning those things of which it has a less clear cognition. But, as was said, you are not certain of the existence of objects of which you have a clearer cognition than you have of your own acts; therefore etc.

And if you say that sometimes some abstractive cognition[5] is as clear as an intuitive cognition—e.g., that every whole is greater than its part—this will not help you, because you explicitly say that the cognition which we have of our own acts is not as clear as intuitive cognition; and yet intuitive cognition, at least that which is imperfect, is not naturally of evident certainty. This is clear from what you say. And thus it follows evidently, that you are not certain of what appears evident to you, and consequently you are not certain whether anything appears to you.

And it also follows that you are not certain whether any proposition is true or false, because you are not evidently certain whether any proposition exists, or has existed. Indeed it follows that if you were asked whether or not you believed some articles of the Faith, you would have to say, "I do not know," because according to your position, you could not be certain of your own act of believing. And I confirm this, because, if you were certain of your act of believing, this would either be from that very act itself, in which case the direct and reflective act would be identical[6]—which you will not admit—or else it would be by some other act, and in that case, according to your position, you would in the same way be uncertain, because there would then be no more contradiction than that the seeing of whiteness existed and the whiteness did not exist, etc.

And so, bringing all these statements together, it seems that you must say that you are not certain of those things which are outside of you. And thus you do not know if you are in the heavens or on the earth, in fire or in water; and consequently you do not know whether today's sky is the same one as yesterday's, because you do not know whether the sky exists. Just as you do not know whether the Chancellor or the Pope exists, and whether, if they exist, they are different in each moment of time. Similarly, you do not know the things within you—as, whether or not you have a beard, a head, hair, and so forth. And a fortiori it follows from this that you are not certain of the things which occurred in the past—as, whether you have been reading, or seeing, or hearing. Further, your position seems to lead to the destruction of social and political affairs, because if witnesses testify of what they have seen, it does not follow, "We have seen it, therefore it happened." Again, I ask how, on this view, the Apostles were certain that Christ suffered on the cross, and that He rose from the dead, and so with all the rest?

I wish that your mind would express itself on all these questions, and I wonder very much how you can say that you are evidently certain of various conclusions which are more obscure—such as concern the existence of the Prime Mover, and the like—when you are not certain about these things which I have mentioned. Again, it is strange how, on your assumptions, you believe that you have shown that a cognition is distinct from what is cognized, when you are not certain, according to your position, that any cognition exists or that any propositions exist, and consequently that any contradictory propositions exist; since, as I have shown, you do not have certainty of the existence of your own acts, or of your own mind, and do not know whether it exists. And, as it seems to me the absurdities which follow on the position of the Academics, follow on your position. And so, in order to avoid such absurdities, I maintained in my disputation at the Sorbonne, that I am evidently certain of the objects of the five senses, and of my own acts.

I think of these objections, and of so many others, that there is no end to them, against what you say. I pray you, Father, to instruct me who, however stupid, am nevertheless desirous of reaching knowledge of the truth. May you abide in Him, who is the light, and in whom there is no darkness.

II. The Second Letter to Bernard

Reverend Father Bernard, the depth of your subtlety would truly bring forth the admiration of my mind, if I were to know that you possess evident knowledge of the separated substances[7]—the more so if I know this, but even if I had in my mind a slight belief. And not only, if I should think that you possess true cognition of the separated substances, but even of those conjoined to matter. And so to you, Father, who assert that you have evident cognition of such lofty objects of knowledge, I wish to lay bare my doubtful and anxious mind, so that you may have the materials for leading me and other people toward acquaintance with such great things.

And the first point is, that at the foundation of discourse this principle is primary: Contradictories cannot be simultaneously true. And with respect to this, two things hold: the first is, that this is the first principle, taken negatively as that than which nothing is more primary. The second is, that this is first, taken positively, as that which is prior to every other principle.

These two statements are proved by argument, as follows: Every certitude possessed by us reduces to this principle, and it in turn is not reduced to any other in the way that a conclusion is reduced to its premise; it therefore follows that this principle is first, with the twofold primacy indicated. This consequence is known from the meaning of the term "first," according to each of the expositions given. The antecedent is proved with respect to both of its parts. And first, with respect to its first part, namely that every certitude possessed by us, short of this certitude, reduces to this principle of which you say you are certain, I set forth this consequence: It is possible, without any contradiction being implied, that something will appear to you to be so, and yet that it will not be so; therefore you are not evidently certain that it is so. It is

clear to me that if I were to admit this antecedent to be true, I would concede the consequent to be true; and therefore I would not be evidently and unqualifiedly certain of that of which I was saying that I was certain.[8]

From this it is clear that every one of our certitudes is resolved into our said principle, and that it is not resolved into another, as a conclusion into its premise. From this it is plain that all certitudes are resolved into this one, as was said, and that this consequence is valid: If this is prior to everything other than itself, then nothing is prior to it. And thus it is first, with the twofold primacy above stated.

The third point is, that a contradiction is the affirmation and negation of the same (predicate) of the same (subject). etc., as is commonly said.

From these things I infer a corollary—namely, that the certitude of evidence which we have in the natural light, is certitude in the unqualified sense; for it is the certitude which is possessed in virtue of the first principle, which neither is nor can be contradicted by any true law. And hence whatever is demonstrated in the natural light of reason, is demonstrated without qualification; and, just as there is no power which can make contradictories simultaneously true, so there is no power by which it can come to pass that the opposite of the consequent is compatible with the antecedent.

The second corollary which I infer, with regard to this, is that the certitude of evidence has no degrees. Thus, if there are two conclusions, of each of which we are evidently certain, we are not more certain of one than of the other. For as was said, every certitude is resolved into the same first principle. Either, then, those first conclusions are reduced with equal immediacy to the same first principle—in which case there is no ground for our being more certain of one than of the other; or else one is reduced mediately, and the other immediately. But this makes no difference, because, once the reduction to the first principle has been made, we are certain of the one equally with the other—just as the geometrician says that he is as certain of a second conclusion as of the first, and similarly of the third and so on, even though in his first consideration, because of the plurality of the deductions, he cannot be as certain of the fourth or third as of the first.

The third corollary which I infer, in connection with what has been said, is that with the exception of the certitude of faith, there is no other certitude except the certitude of the first principle, or the certitude which can be resolved into the first principle. For there is no certitude except that in which there is no falsity; because, if there were any in which falsity could exist, let it be supposed that falsity does exist in it—then, since the certitude itself remains, it follows that someone is certain of something whose contradictory is true, without contradiction.[9]

The fourth corollary is this: that a syllogistic form is immediately reducible to the first principle; because, by its demonstration, the conclusion is either immediately reduced (in which case the thesis holds), or else mediately; and if mediately, then either the regress will be infinite, or else it must arrive at some conclusion which reduces immediately to the first principle.

The fifth corollary: In every consequence which reduces immediately to the first principle, the consequent, and the antecedent either as a whole or in part, are really identical; because, if this were not so, then it would not be immediately evident that the antecedent and the opposite of the consequent cannot both be true.[10]

The sixth corollary is this: In every evident consequence reducible to the first principle by as many intermediates as you please, the consequent is really identical with the antecedent or with part of what is signified by the antecedent. This is shown because, if we suppose some conclusion to be reduced to the certitude of the first principle by three intermediates, the consequent will be really identical with its (immediate) antecedent or with part of what is signified by that antecedent, by the fifth corollary; and similarly in the second consequence, by the same reason; and thus, since in the first consequence the consequent is really identical with the antecedent or with part of what is signified by the antecedent, and likewise in the second one, and likewise in the third, it follows that in these consequences, ordered from first to last, the last consequent will be really identical with the first antecedent or with a part of what is signified by that antecedent.

On the basis of these statements, I laid down, along with other conclusions, one which was this: From the fact that some thing is known to exist, it cannot be evidently inferred, by evidence reduced to the first principle or to the certitude of the first principle, that some other thing exists.

Aside from many other arguments, I brought forth this argument. In such a consequence, in which from one thing another thing is inferred, the consequent would not be really identical with the antecedent or with part of what is signified by the antecedent; therefore it follows that such a consequence would not be evidently known with the said evidence of the first principle. The antecedent is conceded and posited by my opponent; the consequence is plain from the description of "contradiction," which is affirmation and negation of the same of the same, etc. Since therefore in this case the consequent is not really identical with the antecedent or its part, it is evident that if the opposite of the consequent, and the antecedent, be simultaneously true, this would not be a case of one thing being affirmed and denied of the same thing, etc.

But Bernard replies, saying that although in this case there is not a formal contradiction, for the reason given, yet there is a virtual contradiction; he calls a contradiction virtual, however, if from it a formal contradiction can be evidently inferred.

But against this we can argue manifestly, from the fifth and sixth of the above corollaries. For it has been shown that in every consequence reducible either immediately or mediately to the certitude of the first principle, it is necessary that the consequent—whether the first one or the last—be really identical with the first antecedent or with a part of it.

Again, we may argue conclusively from another premise. For he says that, although in a consequence in which from one thing another thing is inferred, there is not a formal contradiction,[11] there is nevertheless a virtual one from which a formal one can be evidently inferred. Then let there be, for example, the following consequence propounded: "A exists, therefore A exists." If, then, from the propositions, "B exists," "B does not exist," a formal contradiction could be evidently inferred, this would be through a consequent of one of these propositions, or through a consequent of each of them. But whichever way it is, the thesis is not established. For these consequents would either be really identical with their antecedents, or they would not. If identical, then there will not be a formal contradiction between those consequents, since there will not then be an affirmation and a negation of the same predicate of the same subject, and hence not between the antecedents either. Just as it is not a formal contradiction to say that a rational animal exists and that a neighing animal does not exist; and for the same reason. But if it be said that these consequents differ from their antecedents, we argue the same way as before, that this is not a consequence evidently reduced to the certitude of the first principle, since the opposite of the consequent is compatible with whatever is signified by the antecedent, without contradiction. And if it be said that there is a virtual contradiction, from which a formal one can be inferred, we argue as before, either there is a regress without end, or else we must say that in a consequence evident without qualification the consequent is identical in its signification with the antecedent, or with part of what is signified by the antecedent.

And it is true that the reverend Father

has said, with regard to this question, that it would not be true to say that in a consequence evident without qualification it is required that the opposite of the consequent, and the antecedent, cannot simultaneously be false, and that they are therefore not opposed as contradictories. But in actual fact this does not in any way prevent what I am maintaining. For I do not wish to say that the opposite of the consequent must be the contradictory of the antecedent—for in many consequences the antecedent can signify more than does the consequent, though the consequent signifies a part of what is signified by the antecedent—as in this consequence, "A house exists, therefore a wall exists." And on this account the opposite of the consequent, and the antecedent, can both be false. But I wish to say that in an evident consequence the opposite of the consequent, and the antecedent or a part of what it signifies, are opposed as contradictories. It is plain that this is the case in every valid syllogism; for since no term occurs in the conclusion which did not occur in the premises, the opposite of the conclusion, and something signified by the premises, are opposed as contradictories. And so it must be in every valid inference, because an enthymeme is only valid in virtue of a proposition presupposed—so that it is a kind of incomplete syllogism.[12]

Further, I offer this argument for my main conclusion: Never, in virtue of any inference, can there be inferred a greater identity of the extreme term, than that of which is between the extreme term and the middle term, because the former is only inferred in virtue of the latter. But the opposite of this will occur, if from the fact that one thing is a being, it could evidently be inferred that something else is a being; because the predicate of the conclusion, and the subject, signify what is really identical, whereas they are not really identical with the middle term which is posited as another thing.[13]

But Bernard objects to this proposed rule, because it follows evidently, with an evidence reduced to the certitude of the first principle, "Whiteness exists, therefore something else exists"—because whiteness cannot exist unless some subject maintains it in existence. Likewise it follows, "Whiteness is not a being in the primary sense, therefore some other thing exists." Or likewise, "Fire is brought into contact with the fuel, and there is no impediment, therefore there will be heat."

To these objections I have elsewhere given many answers. But for the present I say that if a thousand such objections were adduced, either it must be said that they are irrelevant, or, if relevant, that they conclude nothing, against my position. Because in these consequences which he states, if the consequent is really identical in its signification with the antecedent as a whole or with a part of the antecedent, then the argument is not to the point, because in that case I would concede the consequences to be evident, and nothing against my position would be adduced. But if it be said that the consequent is not identical with the antecedent or part of it, then, if I concede the opposite of the consequent, and the antecedent, to be simultaneously true, it is plain that I am not conceding there to be contradictories, since contradictories are of the same predicate of the same subject, etc. And thus such a consequence is not evident by the evidence of the first principle, because the evidence of the first principle was understood to be had when, if it were conceded that the opposite of the consequent is compatible with the antecedent, contradictories would be admitted as simultaneously true. For though one might concede, with respect to this consequence "A house exists, therefore a wall exists," that a house exists and a wall does not exist, he does not thereby concede contradictories to be simultaneously true, because these propositions are not contradictories, "A house exists," "A wall does not exist," since both of them may be false; yet he does concede contradictories on another ground, because to signify that a house exists is to signify that a wall exists, and then it is a contradiction that a house exists and that a wall does not exist.

From this rule, so explained to anyone having the grasp of it, I infer that Aristotle never possessed an evident cognition concerning any substance other than his own soul—taking "substance" as a thing other than the objects of the five senses, and other than our formal experiences. And this is so, because he would have had a cognition of such a thing prior to every inference—which is not true, since they (substances) are not perceived intuitively, and since (if they were) rustics would know that such things exist; nor are they known by inference, namely as inferred from things perceived to exist antecedently to discursive thought—because from one thing it cannot be inferred that another thing exists, as the above conclusion states.

And if he did not have evident cognition of conjoined (material) substances, much less did he have it of abstract substances.[14] From which it follows, whether you like it or not, and not because I make it so but because reason determines it, that Aristotle in his whole natural philosophy and metaphysics had such certitude of scarcely two conclusions, and perhaps not even of one. And Father Bernard, who is not greater than Aristotle, has an equal amount of certitudes, or much less.

And not only did Aristotle not have evident cognition (of these things)—indeed, though I do not assert this, I have an argument which I cannot refute, to prove that he did not have probable knowledge. For a person does not have probable knowledge of any consequent, in virtue of some antecedent, when he is not evidently certain whether the consequent will at some time be true together with the antecedent. For let anyone really consider well the nature of probable knowledge—as for example that because it was at one time evident to me that when I put my hand in the fire I was hot, therefore it is probable to me that if I should put it there now I would be hot. But from the rule stated above, it follows that it was never evident to anyone that, given these things which are apparent without inference, there would exist certain other things—namely those others which are called substances. It therefore follows that of their existence we do not have probable knowledge. I do not assert this conclusion; but let this argument be resolved, for a solution will surely occur.[15]

And that we do not possess certitude concerning any substance conjoined to matter, other than our own soul, is plain— because, pointing to a piece of wood, or a stone, this conclusion will be most clearly deduced from a belief accepted at the same time. For by the divine power it can happen, with these things which appear prior to all inference, that no substance is there; therefore in the natural light of reason it is not evidently inferred from these appear-

ances that a substance is there. This consequence is plain from what we explained above. For it was said that a consequence is evident only if it is a contradiction for it to occur, through any power, that the opposite of the consequent is true along with the antecedent. And if it is said that the consequence is evident, if to the antecedent we add "God is not performing a miracle," this is disproved by what we have said on this point in our first letter to Bernard.

I ask, Father, that you take up these doubts and give counsel to my stupidity; and I promise that I will not be stubborn in evading the truth, to which I adhere with all my strength.

NOTES

1. Bernard's definition of "clear intuitive cognition," as that by which we judge a thing to exist, whether or not it does in fact exist, is not the definition given by William of Ockham, though a number of historians have failed to appreciate this point. Ockham defines intuitive cognition in the following way: "Intuitive cognition of a thing is cognition that enables us to know whether the thing exists or does not exist, in such a way that, if the thing exists, then the intellect immediately judges that it exists and evidently knows that it exists, unless the judgment happens to be impeded through the imperfection of this cognition. And in the same way, if the divine power were to conserve a perfect intuitive cognition of a thing no longer existent, in virtue of this non-complex knowledge the intellect would know evidently that this thing does not exist." (Translation from Ockham's *Ordinatio*, Prologue, Qu. 1, by Philotheus Boehner, *Ockham: Philosophical Writings*, Edinburgh, 1957, p. 23.) Whereas Bernard of Arezzo defines intuitive cognition in such manner that it can yield a false judgment, Ockham defines it in such a way that it cannot yield a false judgment; thus Ockham's definition does not entail the skeptical consequences that Nicolaus of Autrecourt finds in the definition of Bernard.
2. In fourteenth-century logic, a *consequence* is a conditional proposition of the form "If p, then q" (or, alternatively, "p, therefore q"); the protasis of the conditional was called the *antecedent*, and the apodasis the *consequent* (not the *consequence*, which designates the conditional as a whole). The medieval logic of *consequentiae*, corresponding to the modern sentential calculus, but normally interpreted in terms of entailment rather than in terms of truth-functions, is used regularly by Nicolaus of Autrecourt in his arguments against Bernard of Arezzo in these letters. Cf. Ernest A. Moody, *Truth and Consequence in Mediaeval Logic*, Amsterdam, 1953, for a detailed exposition of the structure and terminology of this branch of medieval logic.
3. Bernard has argued that the inference "A is seen, therefore A exists" is valid on the assumption that God is not interfering with the natural causal relation between existing visible objects and acts of seeing them. But since we can never know, in any particular case, whether God is or is not interfering with the course of nature, Nicolaus argues that the above inference is never valid. Given three propositions, p, q, and r, we may concede the statement "If p, then if q then r," but if we cannot know whether p is true or false, we cannot know whether "if q then r" is valid or invalid.
4. The distinction between "imperfect intuitive cognition" and "clear intuitive cognition" is equivalent to the distinction between memory and direct perception. Ockham held that direct perception (or "clear intuitive cognition") was infallible, but admitted that memory (or "imperfect intuitive cognition") might be mistaken.
5. Abstractive cognition is defined by Ockham (and presumably by Bernard and Nicolaus as well) as "that knowledge by which it cannot be evidently known whether a contingent fact exists or does not exist" (Ph. Boehner, op. cit., p. 23). All judgments not based on immediate perception, including all general or "universal" statements, were held to be based on abstractive cognition; though ultimately abstractive cognitions arise from intuitive cognitions.
6. The distinction between the "direct act" (*actus rectus*) and the "reflective act" (*actus reflexus*), corresponds to the distinction between the act of knowing or believing expressed in the sentence "A is B," and the

act of knowing or believing expressed in the sentence "I know (or I believe) that A is B." Ockham, and most fourteenth-century philosophers (as well as St. Thomas Aquinas), held that the direct and the reflective act are not identical and do not have the same objects.

7. The "separated substances" are immaterial substances, such as angels, or God, or Aristotle's "intelligences" associated with the celestial spheres were thought to be. Material bodies were called "conjoined" or "composite" substances, their forms being determinations of matter, and not capable of existing separately from matter.

8. This appears to be an argument ad hominem against Bernard's simultaneous claims that he is certain of the law of contradiction, and that it is possible for something to appear to him to be so, when it is not so. Nicolaus argues that if Bernard's second claim is conceded—namely that one can be certain of something that is not so—then it follows that he is conceding that contradictories can be simultaneously true; for he admits that that of which he is certain (the law of contradiction) is something of which he is uncertain.

9. This is a similar argument to the previous one—namely, that if one can be certain of something which is false, he would be certain of something whose contradictory is true; and if this is possible, it follows that it is not self-contradictory to be certain of that whose contradictory is true. Hence Bernard cannot be certain of the law of contradiction, as he claims.

10. The statement that in every evident consequence whose evidence is based on the law of contradiction, the antecedent and consequent are "really identical," appears to refer to the type of consequence which was known as "simple material consequence." In such conditionals, the consequential relation is determined by what is now called "analytic necessity," or necessity due to inclusion of what one term signifies in what the other term signifies. For example, in the conditional "If a man walks, an animal walks," what is signified by the term "man" is included in what is signified by the term "animal"; hence the consequence holds by reason of the identity of the things designated by the subject-term of the antecedent, with things (or with part of the things) designated by the subject-term of the consequent. This identity is expressed by the additional proposition (needed to convert the above conditional into a formally valid syllogism), "Every man is an animal." Cf. E. A. Moody, *Truth and Consequence in Mediaeval Logic*, pp. 73–79.

11. The meaning is obviously that it would not involve a formal contradiction to affirm the existence of one thing and to deny the existence of another thing—since the affirmation and negation of the same predicate would not be of the same subject. If A and B are distinct things, the conjunctive statement "A exists and B does not exist" is not logically impossible; consequently the conditional "If A exists, then B exists" is not logically necessary. And the reason for this, according to Nicolaus of Autrecourt, is simply the fact that A is not identical with B.

12. The type of consequence which was called a "material consequence" in fourteenth-century logic was assimilated to what Aristotle called an enthymeme or incomplete syllogism, because the validity of the material consequence depends on an identity of *designata* of the subject terms of the antecedent and consequent, which is made explicit by a "suppressed premise" which, if introduced as an additional antecedent, reduces the material consequence to a formally valid syllogism.

13. Given a statement of the form "A exists," Nicolaus argues that another term B, designating something other than A, could not serve as a middle term through which the predicate "exists" (or "is a being") could be demonstrated of A; for if the conclusion "A is a being" is true, then the predicate "is a being" denotes what is denoted by the subject-term "A," whereas the alleged middle term "B," denoting something other than A, does not denote what is identical with A or with the being which is A. The subsequent argument applies this principle as follows: if a sensible quality such as a particular whiteness, is not identical with the substance that is said to be white or to have whiteness, one cannot validly infer from the sentence "Whiteness exists," the sentence, "A substance, in which whiteness inheres, exists." Since Bernard of Arezzo maintained that a sensible quality is an entity distinct from the substance to which it is attributed, Nicolaus here argues that inference from the existence of such a quality, to the existence of an underlying substance, is invalid; for the existence of one thing does not formally imply the existence of another distinct thing. And on the assumption that Aristotle also considered that sensible qualities are entities distinct from substances (which is perhaps a questionable assumption), Nicolaus argues that Aristotle never had evident knowledge of the existence of any material substance. Not by direct perception, since the direct objects of perception are qualities; and not by any valid inference from direct perception, because from the existence of one thing the existence of another distinct thing cannot be validly inferred. This is, of course, Hume's well-known argument against the possibility of establishing the existence of substances either by experience or by reason.

14. The "abstract substances" in question are those elsewhere called "separated substances," these being immaterial beings such as angels, God, Aristotle's "separated intelligences," and presumably rational souls. Of these direct perception (except possibly in the case of one's own soul) was not admitted by any of the Aristotelian philosophers of the Middle Ages; and since such abstract substances were not considered to have any sensible qualities inhering in them, even the inference from the existence of a

perceived quality, to the substance underlying it, would not be applicable. And since this sort of infer- ence has been shown by Nicolaus to be invalid, in the case of material substances with sensible accidents, a fortiori any inferential knowledge of the abstract substances is invalid or impossible.

15. The distinction between certain and probable knowledge is here assimilated to the distinction between a *consequentia simplex* (or consequence valid without qualification), and a *consequentia ut nunc*, valid for a particular time. Cf. E. A. Moody, *Truth and Consequence in Mediaeval Logic*, pp. 74–75 and 79. Thus, during the time when my hand is in the fire, the consequence "If my hand is in the fire, my hand feels hot" is valid; but it is not necessary, though probable, that the consequence holds for any time in the future. The point here made by Nicolaus is that if at no time one can validly infer from the existence of a sensible quality, that a substance exists, such an inference cannot be even probable, because a probable inference is one which, on the basis of repeated evident experimental judgments in particular cases at particular times, asserts that the same connection will hold for all similar cases at other times. For a very full discussion of the arguments of these letters of Nicolaus of Autrecourt, see the book by Julius Weinberg, *Nicolaus of Autrecourt*, Princeton University Press, Princeton, N.J., 1948.

CHAPTER 35

Jean Buridan

Jean Buridan, or Joannes Buridanus, was probably born at Béthune, France, circa 1295. The first documentary mention of him is found in the records of the University of Paris dated 1328. It is there that he studied philosophy with William of Ockham and remained there, becoming both a most distinguished professor of natural philosophy and a highly influential member of the faculty. He was appointed rector of that university in 1328 and again in 1340.

Buridan was a secular cleric and master of arts. Since he never obtained a theological degree, he was forbidden to write on theology. It is not surprising, therefore, that he concentrated on natural philosophy and he deserves credit for laying the groundwork for much of the modern scientific tradition. Just as important, his work on logic and semantics demonstrate him to be unusually "modern" in his thinking. It is here that he could circumvent his prohibition against theological commentary.

As a logician he believed himself justified to criticize arguments regardless of their subject matter. The lion's share of his work, however, is concerned with detailed questions of logic, ethics, and natural philosophy. Extant are his logical treatises: *Summulae de dialectica* (Law of Dialectic), *Consequentiae* (Consequences), and an advanced work on logical problems, *Sophismata*. Most of his works are literal commentaries and collections of Questions on the works of Aristotle.

Records indicate that Buridan was the recipient of revenues from benefices and by 1349 appears to have been prosperous. The last known date in his life is 1358, according to a document he signed at the University of Paris. It is generally assumed that he died of the plague that same year. He left a sizable bequest, including a house, to the university.

Jean Buridan on Sensation
by Peter Sobol

As accidental forms inhering in subjects, qualities such as color and odor can act on surrounding substances in various ways, including their contribution to the process of sensation. Aristotle divided sensible qualities into three categories: proper, common, and accidental. Proper sensibles were those qualities that could only be detected by a single sense, as color can only be detected by vision. Common sensibles were aspects of bodies that were detectable by more than one sense, as shape, size, and motion can be detected by vision, touch, and hearing. Aristotle used the term "accidental sensible" in two ways, both of which entailed a judgment about a substance that displayed certain proper and common sensible qualities. According to Aristotle, only accidents are sensible, substance is not. In his words, "the percipient is not acted upon by the thing perceived as such." We sense colors, shapes, sizes, sounds, and smells, and we believe we have sensed the presence of, for example, a person. But sense is not equipped to ensure that certain qualities reliably indicate the presence of certain substances, so our identification of those qualities with those substances is accidental. Our willingness to assert such an identification leads us to say that we can see sweet or hear hot, because we associate certain sensible qualities with others when they are commonly found together. Aristotle knew that this association is not infallible. To use Buridan's example, seeing yellow with bile, but it can also lead us to "see" sweetness if we associate yellow with honey. Buridan referred to substances as sensible *per accidens*, and to proper and common sensibles as sensible per se. But he did not mean by this division to suggest that our awareness of per se sensibles is infallible. In the eleventh question of Book II, Buridan showed that we can err about proper sensibles, while at the same time defending Aristotle's remark that, where proper sensibles are concerned, "error is impossible."

Aristotle said little about how per se sensible qualities affected sense organs. In vision, he wrote, the colored body acted upon the medium and the medium in turn acted upon the eye. In another place he wrote that sense receives the form from sensible objects without their matter, in the way that soft clay receives the impression of a signet ring without receiving any of the matter of the ring. But these vague statements failed to adequately explain how our eyes acquire an image of a distant object. In the fifth century B.C., Democritus had proposed that the eye and the object acted upon the medium to produce an image which in turn acted upon the eye. Later atomists proposed that we see because material films peel off visible objects and move through media to our eyes. But then, why do the films not interfere? How can the whole film from a distant mountain penetrate our tiny pupils? If, on the other hand, as others proposed, we see because something is emitted from our eyes, then that emission must cover the distance between the eye and an object as distant as a star instantaneously, and must not interfere with the emission from other observers viewing the same scene.

Islamic scholars addressed these problems by drawing on a worldview in which all objects radiated something of their nature into their environment. The nature of the radiation was such that interference did not occur. The physician Alhazen proposed that each point on a visible object radiated its form in all directions, hence all observers would receive radiation from each point of the visible object.

Scholars in the Latin West referred to the radiation as "sensible species." Most authors referred to species as having "intentional" rather than real being, thereby explaining its rapid propagation across media and its failure to interfere. The science of *perspectiva* treated the existence of sensible species in the medium, in the eye, and on into the brain. In a book entitled *On the Multiplication of Species*, Roger Bacon carried out his century's most thorough study of sensible species. For Bacon, species was the means of influence between agents and patients. He pondered its nature, its means of propagation across media, its interactions in media, and the reasons why species rapidly dissipate when its source is removed.

Buridan too inquired into the nature of species. He devoted the lengthy eighteenth question of Book II to a defense of sensible species by calling upon phenomena of sensation and upon other natural effects that he felt were inexplicable if species did not exist. The questions translated here show Buridan's reliance on species and his attempt to discover how the soul makes use of species to learn about the material world.

I have incorporated in the following translation several changes and references suggested by Jack Zupko, for whose careful reading I am deeply grateful.

COMMENTARY ON ARISTOTLE'S *DE ANIMA*

Book II

Question 9

[The question is asked] whether sense is a passive ability. One can argue that [it is] not, because it is [a property] of matter to be acted upon, and it is [a property] of form to act, for an agent acts according to how much it is actualized, and a recipient receives insofar as it is in a potential state, as is clear in the third book of the *Physics*[1] and in the first book of *On Generation* [*and Corruption*][2] and wherever Aristotle speaks about this topic. But sense is form and not matter, therefore [sense is an active ability].

Furthermore, Aristotle proposes in the second book of *De anima*[3] that the soul is the cause of the body according to three types of cause, namely formal, final and efficient.[4] The principal sense is the soul itself, thus sense is an active power and body is a passive [power]. Averroës, expounding this claim, says that the soul is the cause moving the body "according to all the kinds of motion . . . both the true and the so-called."[5] It seems that, by these so-called kinds, he meant sensing and thinking. And it is clear that when Aristotle wants to say that the soul is the cause of the body as agent and mover, he calls [the soul] the cause of nutrition and growth and sensation,[6] which would not be to the point unless [the soul] was an active ability as far as sensation [is concerned], for which rea-

Translated especially for this volume by Peter G. Sobol from Jean Buridan's *Commentary on Aristotle's* De Anima.

son the soul is called sense. Thus it must be said that sense is an active ability.

Furthermore, to sense is to act, therefore the sensitive virtue is an active virtue. The consequent holds by the topic from *conjugates* [*per locum a coniugatis*].[7] The antecedent is proved because the verb "to sense" belongs to an active genus, and because the grammatical modes of signifying must be taken from the properties of things and [must] agree with them; otherwise they would be fictitious or false, which is wrong, and there would be no agreement in the proposed [claim, that is, that sense is not a passive ability,] if to sense were to be acted upon and not to act.

This is confirmed, furthermore, because everyone thinks of sensation and thinking as immanent actions.[8] And if sensation is an act, it would follow *per locum a coniugatis* that to sense is to act.[9] Nor would there be any reason why [sensation] should be called an immanent act [any] more than building [should be called an immanent act], unless [sensation] remained in its agent.[10] [Sensation] does remain in sense; thus sense is the agent of sensation, thus [sense] is an active ability.

Furthermore, in Book III [of *De anima*] it says that the things that cause local motion in an animal are sense and appetite,[11] or intellect and appetite.[12] A mover, however, is an active virtue, therefore sense and intellect and appetite are active virtues.

Furthermore, if sense were a passive power and not an active [power,] it would follow that the vegetative power would be nobler than the sensitive power, which is false. The consequent holds because the vegetative power is active, and to act is nobler than to be acted upon. But the nobility of a power is argued from the nobility of what it does, hence [sense is active].

Furthermore, it would follow [if sense were passive] that the sensible object would be nobler than [the power of] sense. For example, color [would be nobler] than vision, which is false. And the consequent appears [to hold] as before, because [the visible object's] function would be nobler [than that of vision] because to act is nobler than to be acted upon. And the sensible object would cause sensation, to which [the power of] sense would relate only as a recipient. Hence [sense is active].

Furthermore, some argue from experience that a menstruating woman stains a mirror by [her] vision,[13] and that a basilisk kills a man by [its] vision,[14] which could occur only if vision were an active power.

Aristotle, however, states the opposite [view] in the second[15] book of *De anima* and [speaks] in a similar way about the intellect [i.e., that it is passive] in the third book.[16] Something ought to be said about the terms that we use in this and the following question. Note that "sensible" means the same thing as "able to be sensed" and "sensitive" [means] the same thing as "able to sense."

The first doubtful point is whether the species of color produced in the air or in the eye should be called sensible. I judge that [the species is] not [sensible] according to the proper meaning [of "sensible"], because I judge that it cannot be sensed.[17] Yet according to an attributive way of speaking, we call [species] sensible because, by means of [species], the object of which it is the species is sensed, just as [an animal's] urine is called healthy not according to the proper meaning of health but because it means that the animal [that passed the urine] is healthy.

The second doubtful point is what [kind of thing] we may refer to as "sensitive," whether the animal [as a whole] or the

[sense] organ, that is, body [as] subject of soul or soul itself. I say that Aristotle, in the first[18] book of this work, concluded that, properly speaking, the animal senses or can sense. So [the animal,] properly speaking, is referred to as sensitive, for he says, "it is better perhaps not to say that the soul feels pity or learns or understands, but to say that the man or the animal [does so by means of soul]."[19] Thus the animal senses as the whole sensitive [entity]. But it should not be denied that the soul may sense as a partial sensitive [entity] and that even the body or the organ may sense as a partial sensitive [entity]. Thus even Aristotle often calls the organ sensitive and even more often calls the power of the soul, which is the soul itself, sensitive.

The third doubtful point is what may be called "sense." I say that sometimes "sense" is taken for "sensation," but properly "sense" means the sensitive soul. For not every sensitive [entity], that is, not everything able to sense, is called sense, nor is an animal, properly speaking, called sense, nor is a body. Thus we take "sense" to mean the soul that is able to sense.

The fourth doubtful point is what is properly meant by "to sense." It seems to me that "to sense" does not mean the same thing, properly speaking, as "to have in oneself the species of this sensible object," because then the air would sense, that is to say, it would see, smell and hear.[20] Nor does it correctly mean "to produce this species," because then color would see and sound would hear. Nor does it correctly mean "sensation," because God produces [sensation] and all other things that are produced, and He does not sense. He would be able to produce [sensation] without any contributing agent, and yet, [if He did so,] He would not sense, but would understand.[21]

Furthermore, ["to sense"] does not seem correctly to mean the same thing as "to receive sensation," because although a form, when it is produced, is received in the subject in which it is produced, yet when the form is made, and remains [in the subject], it is neither made nor received nor produced any longer (insofar as "to do" means the same thing as "to produce"), and yet "to sense" continues. Thus it seems that "to sense" sometimes means that a thing is not acting or being acted upon (taking "to act" to mean "to produce" and "to be acted upon" to mean "to receive"). But when sensation occurs, "to sense" is indeed to be acted upon and also to act. And when this is completed, it is true to say that to sense was to be acted upon and to act. For to sense is sensing and to act [is] acting. While sensation occurs, however, sense—sensing—is acting and being acted upon, and when [sensation] is done and remains [in the subject], sense *is* [still] sensing and *was* acting and being acted upon. Thus, finally, it seems to me that "to sense" correctly means the same thing as "to have sensation inhering in oneself." And thus if we propose that the animal, the soul and the organ or body have sensation inhering in them, then it was well said before that any one of them senses.

Now I propose the conclusions. The first is that sense, that is, the sensitive soul, is [both] an active ability and a passive ability. I say [that it is] an active ability because the vegetative power and the power of moving according to place are active abilities and because [sense] acts in order to produce sensation, as I will argue below [in Question 10]. I say further that it is [also] passive because it receives sensation, as I will say below [in Question 10].

The second conclusion is that [1] the organ—the subject of the soul—relates passively to the sensible species in sensation, that is, in receiving the species, and [2] the [sensible] object [relates] actively in producing [sensation], because either the soul or the organ relates to [sensation] passively, but not the soul, as I will argue below [in Question 10], thus [it must be] the organ [that relates passively to sensation]. Similarly, either the [sensible] object or the soul relates to sensation actively. But not the soul, as I argue below [in Question 10], thus [it must be] the object. Whether, however, sense, that is, the sensitive soul, may relate to sensation actively, and in what

way the sensible species may relate to each other in sensation, I will treat in another question.[22]

But now we must see in what way sense is a passive ability and how it is prepared [to function]. We must also see in what way [sense] relates to sensible species and whether it relates passively to sensation.

I thus propose a third conclusion: that the soul does not act to produce sensible species in the organ of the exterior sense—for example, in the eye or the ear. You may be convinced of this conclusion because *lumen*[23] and the species of color seem to be made the same way in the medium and in the organ. Transparency is required no more in one case than in the other.[24] But everyone agrees that *lumen* or the species of color are actively made in the medium—that is, in the air—from a shining or from a colored body, and that air relates in a passive way only in this [process]. Neither air nor its substantial form contributes anything. [The case] of *lumen*, which is the species of *lux*, is similar in the sensitive organ, [as is the case] of the species of color.

Furthermore, *lux* and color, together with the principal agent, which is God, suffice actively to produce their species in the transparent subject sufficiently available to them, and this they do no matter what substantial form inheres in the transparent [medium]; They even do it if no substantial form inheres, as in a celestial body.[25] Thus it does not follow that the substantial form of a transparent body is either a soul or another form that does something actively to produce the sensible species in the sensitive organ.

A fourth conclusion appears probable to me: that the soul does nothing passively toward the reception of sensible species in the sensitive organ, nor does the substantial form of the medium,—air, for example—toward the reception of *lumen* or the species of color. Moreover, reception occurs passively in *matter alone*, insofar as it is disposed to transparency, or [in] a body [that is the] subject of transparency where there is no matter or substantial form, as in the heavens. To be convinced of this conclusion, one should note that if diverse forms are received in the same subject one after the other and remain at the same time in this subject, it does not follow that the one that arrives first receives the one that arrives later so that [the second] becomes [the first's] subject, from the potency of which the first is drawn. If heat makes a thing black or blackness makes a thing hot, it does not follow that blackness is the subject of heat, nor [that heat is the subject of blackness]. For if heat were the subject of blackness, it would follow that, when the heat was destroyed, the blackness would be destroyed, which is false. The consequent is clear because an accident does not go from the subject from whose potency it arose into another subject. Moreover, it does not follow that if a substantial and an accidental form were together at the same time in the same matter, that the latter would be the subject of the former, or vice versa. For example, the coldness of water is not the subject of the substantial form of water, namely, that in which this substantial form [of water] inheres, because [cold] can be destroyed and heat can be generated, with the substantial form remaining. And then another cold, which was not the subject of the form of the water because it came later, can be generated in the same water. Thus neither was the first cold its subject. But also neither is the substantial form of the water the subject of the cold— [the thing] from the potency of which it emerged—because this cold was in the matter *before* the substantial form of water was received in it. In order to receive the form of water, it is necessary that matter be predisposed by wet and cold. And it does not follow that these predispositions are destroyed [by the advent of the substantial form of water] because the constituent qualities remain the same in the generated and destroyed, as can be seen in the second book of *On Generation* [*and Corruption*].[26] Thus, if the water warms and then cools, it does not follow because of this that the heat or the cold is received in the substantial form of water as in a subject, but [it is received in] the matter that is the subject of the substantial form.

So we can say similarly that, if *lumen* or the species of color is received in a living [sense] organ, it does not follow for this reason that the species is received in the soul as in a subject, but in the matter [that is] the subject of the soul. That this is so is proved as follows. Heat would remain the same constituent if air were made into water. Hence neither of these substantial forms [that is, the substantial forms of air and water] can be called the subject of this heat, from the potency of which it emerged. In the same way, if a horse is killed, and transparency remains in the dead eye, *lumen* or the species of color will remain in it just as before if a bright or colored body remains present.[27] Thus the soul was not the subject of this *lumen* or of the species of color, and the substantial form seems to do nothing at all toward receiving it, because there would be reception of this kind in the same way however much the substantial forms were changed, if the subject remained transparent. Moreover we should admit that if there were some amount of transparent matter that, by divine power, lacked substantial form, it would still, as it does now, receive *lumen* and the species of color. Thus the soul does nothing toward [receiving] sensible species, neither actively nor passively.

A fifth principal conclusion is proposed: that it is the organ, the subject of the soul— that is, matter—that receives sensation, so that sensation is drawn from the potency of that matter, and that sensation is act or form extended in the extent of the organ and matter. In this way sense and intellect differ in man. Each form in a material organ is coextended with matter, and it is reasonable that [the form] is drawn from the potency of the matter and inheres in it, thus [sense and intellect differ].[28] Furthermore, because we propose that only the soul in man is indivisible and unextended, it follows that sensation is either drawn from the potency of matter or is only drawn from the potency of the indivisible intellective soul. If the first way [is true], then what I proposed is true. The second way seems to lead to an impossibility, namely, that what is drawn only from the potency of an indivisible and unextended subject would be divisible and extended. And yet sensation is divisible and extended in us, just as we must say if [sensation] is to differ from understanding.

A probable sixth conclusion is proposed: that not only does sensation have a material organ, that is, matter as subject, from the potency of which it is drawn, but so does the sensitive soul, because, if it did not, it would follow that matter would more properly sense and recognize than the soul, and this everyone refuses to admit. The consequent holds because Aristotle often says that to sense is to be acted upon, and it was said above that to sense is to have sensation inhering in oneself. If, then, the soul neither was acted upon nor received sensation but only produced it in matter, and matter was acted upon and received it, it is clear that the soul would properly neither sense nor recognize.

Furthermore, the subject of an accident, from the potency of which that accident is drawn, so that it is not drawn from the potency of another [thing] as subject, must receive principally some kind of denomination from this accident. And you may expound this major premise in a weaker sense, that is, a name from a name. But, as your opponent may say, matter and not the soul thus receives sensation. So matter must receive principally some denomination from sensation, which does not appear true unless [matter] may be called principally the sensing [thing] (which everyone disdains to say), and principally the sensitive[29] [thing], which is false, because, if I see a color, I neither see, therefore, nor do I sense or recognize, matter in that thing. Furthermore, there is a persuasive [argument] for the same conclusion: that no intellect understands unless by means of its essence in a formal way or by means of the understanding inherent in itself. Furthermore, one senses only through his essence or the sensation inherent in him.[30]

It is true that a great difficulty arises if we posit a single soul in man. For it follows that this [one soul] is capable of understanding and is indivisible, not extended in any way by the extension of matter or [its]

subject. And then this unextended soul is [also] the sensitive and vegetative soul. In what way, then, when sensation is proposed [to be] extended by the extension of the organ and matter, will [sensation] be able to be in an inherently indivisible subject and drawn from its potency? This seems miraculous because the only extension that a form may have is the extension of its subject. And in what way will a divisible and extended thing inhere in an indivisible and unextended thing? This seems miraculous. And, indeed, I answer that it is miraculous, because the human soul inheres in the human body in a miraculous and supernatural way, neither extended nor drawn from the potency of the subject in which it inheres, and yet it inheres in the whole body and in every part of it. This is truly miraculous and supernatural.[31]

So we must respond to the consequent, [that is, to the claim that matter senses because matter is the subject of sensation.] We may say that sensation is not drawn only from the potency of matter nor only from the potency of the soul but at the same time from the potency of the composite, both because of the whole composite and because of each of its parts, whether in a horse or in a man. Because [sensation] is drawn from the potency of the soul, and because the soul acts on itself, the soul recognizes. Because [sensation] is drawn from the potency of matter, it is extended by the extension of matter. Nor can anyone object that [sensation] is in an indivisible subject, namely in the intellective soul, because the intellective soul is *not* indivisible because, as is imagined about a point, it has a location in a continuum. [It is indivisible in] that the soul is indifferently in any part of the body whatever the extent [of the part]. Just as it is not wrong for a thing indivisible [in such a way] to exist in a whole extended body, thus neither is it wrong that such an extended species be in such a whole, indivisible subject.

But then it is certainly worth doubting whether the matter of a horse senses and whether my matter understands. For because the sensation of a horse inheres in the matter of the horse and is drawn from its potency, what stands in the way of matter sensing the sensation, just as the subject in which whiteness inheres is white? And similarly: if my intellect inheres in my soul, and my soul inheres in my matter, it follows that understanding inheres in matter. What would stand in the way of my matter understanding by means of this act of intellect? We can answer to this that we propose that many accidents, such as heat, cold, whiteness and blackness and the like, inhere in prime matter immediately, that is, not through a mediating substantial form. And yet, in referring to matter, the common speaker, because of his ignorance of matter, does not attribute this accident to matter, but to the whole composite known to him. For he does not say that the matter of water is hot or cold, but [that] the water [is hot or cold]. And yet, in fact, matter is hot or cold. Whence if the substantial form of water were removed by divine power from the water, leaving other things as they are, the matter would be hot or cold because of the heat or the cold inhering in it. And it is no less warm if the substantial form [of water] inheres in it with the heat. For this [reason,] heat is proposed to inhere [in the matter of water] directly.

But we need not concede in the proposition that, just as a wall is white because of the whiteness inherent in it, matter is alive because the soul is a form inhering in it. Granted that [whiteness] is not an essential feature of the wall, just as neither is the soul an essential feature of matter, yet the common speaker does not usually say that prime matter is alive, but [that] an animal or plant [is alive]. Either one is alive in many ways. For a plant is alive because of a soul that is part of its essence. Matter, however, is alive because of a soul inhering in it. Now, concerning sensation, we may say that sensation inheres not only in matter, nor is it drawn only from the potency of prime matter, but it inheres in the composite of matter and soul, and is drawn from its potency because of either one, and more principally and immediately because of the soul. And so neither the soul nor

matter is said to sense as the whole subject of sensation. This is what Aristotle meant in the first book of this work [by] saying, "To say that the soul is angry is similar to someone saying that the soul weaves or builds. It is better, perhaps, not to say that the soul feels pity or learns or understands, but [that] man [does so by means of soul]."[32] Then it does not appear wrong to me to say that the soul senses and is angered as the partial subject of functions or passions of this kind, and also that the matter or the body, [as] subject of the soul, in a similar way, is angered or senses as a partial subject, and yet less properly than the soul, because the soul is proposed [to be] more principal and more immediate to the sensation and understanding of the subject than the body. Yet neither matter without soul nor soul without matter would sense, because from neither could the sensitive power be sufficiently drawn out, unless God in a miraculous way wished to preserve a sensation without a subject from the potency of which it was drawn.

Concerning understanding, however, in the passage cited, Aristotle proposes that we more properly say that a man understands than [that his] soul [does], yet it is more proper to say that the soul understands than [to say] that it senses, and it is less proper to say that the body understands than [to say] that it senses, because, although understanding inheres in the whole composite and in every part, yet, like the intellective soul itself, it is drawn only from the potency of the soul and not from the potency of matter.

Then it is clear that we need not resolve the arguments that were made in the beginning of the question, because we willingly admit—and it is admitted also in another question—that the sensitive power, which is the sensitive and vegetative soul, is an active power. Moreover, it is a power active in sensation. And this does not prevent its also being a passive power, that is, receptive of sensation. Thus although the arguments, or some of them, that were made [at the beginning of the question] are not entirely true, yet they do not contradict the proposition [that sense is active and receptive] because they conclude only that [sense] is an active power.

But, according to what has been said, there still remains one doubtful point, namely, whether it should be admitted that sense is acted upon by the sensible. And it is clear that Aristotle often says that this is so. But the opposite is clearly seen from what has been said. For it seems that the sensible object produces nothing in the soul, which is sense, because the sensible produces only sensible species, and it is not the soul but only the organ that receives [species.] So sense is not acted upon by the sensible. Similarly, I also believe that, properly speaking, the sensible produces nothing in sense. So, too, sense, that is, the sensitive soul, is not acted upon by the sensible. Indeed, even though the soul and life are destroyed by an extreme heat, yet it is not the soul that is acted upon, but matter. For it is the subject—that in which the form is produced or from which it is removed—that, properly speaking, is acted upon. The form that is thus produced or removed *is* the action or being acted upon. Whence to be created or to be destroyed as a subject is to be acted upon. But to be created or to be destroyed *as a term*[33] is not to be acted upon, unless according to an improper way of speaking which we often use anyway. But I propose that the sensible is proportioned so that there may be sensible species and sensation made in the animal without any destruction. Still, the soul, properly speaking, is not acted upon by the sensible, but is said to be acted upon by it according to an incorrect way of speaking and attributing, namely, because the [soul's] subject, namely the organ, *is* acted upon by the sensible (just as is exemplified [in] that we sometimes say that the jar goes sour [when we mean] that the wine in it goes sour), or [the soul is said to be acted upon] by the intention, because the sensible species that the sensible object produces necessarily contributes as an active or passive disposition toward the formation of the sensation that is received in the soul.

I little realized that the aforementioned doubtful points were to receive such special treatment, so it is difficult for me to do them justice, but perhaps these are principles that will move others to ponder and better to doubt about what has been said.[34] To doubt single points is not without its uses.

Question 10

[The question is asked] whether an agent sense is necessary for sensing.[35] It seems [that this is] so because, just as intellect [relates] to understandable things, so sense [relates] to sensible things, as it says in the third book of *De anima*.[36] And it appears that the relationship [between sense and intellect] is correct. But an agent intellect is necessary for understanding, as appears in the third[37] book of this work, hence [an agent sense is necessary for sensing].

The opposite view is argued because, if there were an agent sense, Aristotle would be found lacking and [his authority] diminished because he did not clearly address this [matter], because this [agent sense], if there were such a thing, would be nobler than the passive or receptive sense, just as Aristotle[38] proposed that the agent intellect is nobler than the receptive intellect.

There are many different opinions concerning this question. To many it is clear that, in what is proposed, sense and intellect are to be spoken of as related, because wherever Aristotle discussed the agent intellect, he proposed a structure [*ratio*] common to sense and intellect, saying that, in every nature—that is, where a new effect is found—there must be two principles, namely, active and receptive,[39] and that it is always the case that the agent is superior to the recipient. And it does not seem that, from this principle, we must always conclude [that there exists] an agent intellect beyond the receptive. The people [who held an agent sense] used such an argument as if it were a certain demonstration. For they supposed that [1] the nobility of a power can be argued only from the nobility of its function or of the way it functions.

Secondly, they supposed that [2] sensation is a nobler function than vegetation [that is, the powers of nutrition, growth and reproduction] because it is by virtue of this function that grades of animals are higher [on the scale of perfection] than plants. Thus they concluded that sensation is the noblest work of the sensitive, non-intellective soul.

Thirdly, they supposed that [3] the sensitive soul is also nobler in animals, as in the horse or the dog, than any other form or disposition of an inanimate thing such as a stone, iron, water or air.

Fourthly, they supposed that [4] the agent must always be more honorable than the recipient, as stated in the third book of this work.[40] This appears true if there is a principal agent, not merely something used by the principal agent. [They] also [supposed] that [5] the recipient may not have a function nobler than being acted upon by the agent.

If these arguments hold up, it does not appear that there should be any instance against this rule of Aristotle's, because the nobility of the subject and of the power can be argued only from the nobility of the function, as the first assumption states.

Then, from these [arguments], we argue as follows. Either the sensitive soul produces sensation, or it does not, but only is acted upon and receives it. If [the soul] produces [sensation,] then [the soul] must be called the agent sense and the proposition is proved, namely, that there is an agent sense involved in sensation. If it is said that [the soul] does not produce [sensation] but only is acted upon and receives it, then we would have to say that the [sensible] object produces [sensation], even as principal agent. The greater nobility of the sensitive soul can be argued only from sensation, because this is its most noble function, as the second assumption states. And yet, in this case, the agent must be nobler than the recipient, as the fourth assumption states. Thus it follows that an inanimate object such as a stone is nobler than the sensitive soul, which is false, as was said in the third assumption. So it is false to say that the sensitive soul does not produce sensation.

The conclusion is confirmed because it does not appear that, by means of another way of arguing, Aristotle's case for [the existence of] the agent intellect in the third book of this work would hold.[41] Although this case is well ordered and evident, some argue against it in two ways. Firstly because it does not appear that, in animals, sensation is nobler than nutrition or procreation, because sensation is only an accident[42] and nutrition is the conversion of nutriment into the subject[43] of the nourished, and thus is substantial generation, which is substance—indeed, which is the sensitive soul—and this is nobler than any accident. Moreover, although sensation is given to us to serve the intellect in understanding, yet it seems to be given to animals only for nutrition or growth or procreation, and entirely for performing and securing the necessities of life, for which [reason] sensation was not given to plants, because plants are sufficiently nourished by the food immediately available to them, and can procreate without sensation. To some animals only the sense of touch has been given, because this suffices for their nutrition and their necessities of life. To animals needing to seek their food from a distance, however, other senses [that are] needed for this have been given, because of which, nutrition and procreation seem to be the end of sensation in them, and the end is nobler than what is ordained for that end. And so, although we would say that the sensitive soul relates in a purely passive way to sensation, and that the [sensible] object contributes to sensation in a nobler way than does the sensitive soul, yet it does not follow that [the object] is nobler, because the sensitive soul—in which we include the vegetative soul—has a nobler function than any function of the inanimate sensible object. Nor, because of this, does it follow that the soul of a horse would not have a nobler operation than the soul of a plant, because the nutrition of the horse is much nobler than the nutrition of the plant, just as the horse is nobler than the plant.

A second criticism would come from speaking as we did about what is generated from decay, because [1] it is necessary that the generating principle be nobler than what is generated, or at least of equal nobility, because [2] the agent cannot by its own ability give more than it has, and because there appears to be no corporeal agent in the generation of a frog that is nobler than the frog, because all bodies involved in the generation are inanimate.[44] For the celestial body contributes only by means of a power that it sends into the air or water containing the matter of the generation of the frog. And yet, because it is only an accident, this power is not nobler than the substance of the frog, that is, than the sensitive soul, because of which it follows that another more principal agent, nobler and incorporeal, contributes to the generation of the frog, which Avicenna calls "The Giver of Forms,"[45] which is blessed God, from whom, either alone or as principal agent, everything that is made is made in matter properly prepared. And then it could be said that sense and intellect receive sensible and intelligible species from sensible and intelligible objects, by means of which they are prepared to receive sensations and understanding, which the Giver of Forms produces in the things so prepared without any other agent. And this [Giver of Forms] is the agent intellect, which Aristotle establishes in the third book of this work, [and] which he praises, saying, "And here the intellect, separable and unchangeable and unmixed, is a substance in act, and more honorable,"[46] that is, than our receptive intellect. Right away he says of [the agent intellect,] "Knowledge in act is the same as the thing [known]."[47] For this [agent intellect] understands each thing according to its simple essence, without any added understanding or knowledge. Thus an agent intellect is needed, not only for the formation of our intellect but also for the formation of sensation and, universally, for the production of every other thing. But it does not follow that there is an agent sense, because the Creator of Forms, although He knows all things by means of His simple essence (and in doing so makes use of no corporeal organ), should not be called "sense," but is [instead] understanding and a pure act of the intellect. This is

the opinion of some, and it is not improbable.

Others, however, explained the agent intellect as a part or as a power of the human soul, [yet] not proposing an agent sense. For they said that the agent intellect was required for abstracting intelligible species from phantasms,[48] or universals from singulars, which does not require that sense occur, because [sense] does not recognize in a universal way. We shall see this again in Book III.[49]

I myself believe and judge [it] demonstrable that, for our understanding and for every other thing that is produced, a first agent intellect who gives being and life to all things, to some more clearly, to some less, as Aristotle says in the first book of *On the Heavens*,[50] must actively contribute, indeed [must] principally act.

Furthermore, it is my opinion that our soul is an active power for understanding and that, as such, it should be called an agent intellect. It is also my opinion that the sensitive soul, whether in us or in animals, acts toward sensation of the sentient by producing, and that thus it should be called an agent sense.

It should be noted that, although the agent that is God can do anything determinately without any other determinate, yet that would be called not a natural but a miraculous act. In natural acts, it is necessary that, in addition to the universal agent, particular, determined agents contribute, in order that one thing is more able to be made than another, as fire [as] agent determines that fire and not water is made or produced, and horse semen contributes in order that a horse and not a goat is produced.

Now it is established that, with these things contributing, our intellect freely can form an affirmative proposition or a negative proposition. For thus I can form in my mind that "this is an ass," just as "this is not an ass," and that "man is not an animal" just as that "man is an animal." Neither the object nor the phantasm determines that I form an affirmative [proposition]. Thus our soul acts in this case as a particular and determining agent.

But further: not only the intellect, but also sense—even in a horse or dog—puts together and separates [sense images]. For [a dog] judges that what it sees and that what calls it is its master, and goes to him. And if it sees that the straight path is a bad one, it judges that he cannot be reached by that [path] and seeks another. And just as Aristotle says later,[51] the common sense discerns that a sweet [thing] is the same or different from a white [thing]. There must be another particular determining agent besides a universal agent for putting together and separating [sense images], and the sensible object does not suffice for this. We must conclude that the soul does it. And again, just as Avicenna and the other expositors of Aristotle say, the estimative power, even in animals, draws forth from the sensible intentions [provided] by the exterior senses [other intentions that are] not sensed,[52] as a sheep [draws forth] from the sight of a wolf the intention of malice, and from the sight of the shepherd the intention of kindness. Exterior sensibles are not sufficient to the drawing forth and forming of such [intentions]. Therefore the soul does it.

[Along] with these arguments, others are proposed that were touched [upon] and posited earlier as probable and persuasive.[53] Such arguments suffice in this matter, for accuracy is not to be expected in all things.[54] So I admit the agent sense, which, I believe, forms sensation actively in itself.

But then there is a doubt: in what way is it possible that the same thing acts upon itself, and is acted upon by itself? Aristotle seems to deny this in many places. I say that this must be examined elsewhere.[55] I will only say that [Aristotle's arguments] prove that it is not possible for the same thing to act on itself in a case in which another [agent] does not contribute, either actively or passively or as a principal or preparing [agent]. For example, when a heavy thing or the form of weight or weight itself moves itself down, and another thing, such as a *generans* and *removens prohibens*,[56] which is not any one of them, contributes as an agent, and something receptive,

which is not any one of them, such as matter or a medium [contributes as a recipient, then weight has not acted on itself alone], as can be seen in the eighth book of the *Physics.*[57]

Drawing upon what has been said here and in the preceding question, something can be said about the doubt that remained in the preceding question, namely, in what way does the sensible species relate to sensation? For if the things said in that question and in this one are true, it follows clearly that sensation differs from the sensible species, because the sensible species is not drawn from the potency of the soul but only [from the potency] of the organ or matter, nor is it received in the soul as subject. Sensation, however, *is* drawn from the potency of the soul and is received in it as subject, although not as in the whole subject, as was said in the other question.[58]

Furthermore, the soul does not act in the production of sensible species. It does act in the production of sensation, as was just said, thus [there is an agent sense.] A persuasive argument [for the existence of an agent sense] can be [made from the fact] that sensible species is perceived in the organ of imagination and [in the organ of] memory, yet no cognition occurs in them. Aristotle in the second book of this work asks whether someone not smelling and not seeing is acted upon by odor and color by receiving their species:[59] "What is it to smell other than to be acted upon by odor?"[60] And he responds that to smell is to sense or to recognize odor, as if to say that smelling is an *act* of sensing occurring after the reception from the odor, namely after the reception of the species of odor from the odor [itself].

Secondly, it is clear that the sensible species relates to sensation as a necessary preparation [or] prerequisite for sensation, because we observe that sensation only occurs when the organ receives, from an exterior sensible object, a representation of the object, which we call the sensible species. And this is why, as Aristotle says,[61] an animal cannot see or hear with any part whatever of its body, as with its feet, even though soul is there. This is because the object cannot cause its species—that is, the species of sound or color, which is a prerequisite for the formation of sensation—in the foot or in the hand.

But then there is a serious doubt whether the [sensible] species is required in order to prepare a recipient to receive sensation, or in order to prepare an agent to produce sensation. It appears likely to me that, just as the soul uses heat as an instrument for carrying out [the functions of] nutrition, so it uses the sensible or the intelligible [thing] for producing sensation or understanding. Whence, just as fire, although it is able to heat and burn other things in and of itself, is not sufficiently in act to do this without heat, just so the soul, although in and of itself it is the principle formative [agent] of sensation after God, yet it is not sufficiently in act to do this without the sensible species. But the combination of it and the sensible species is sufficiently in act to do this, just as will be said in the third book, on the intellect. For what exists in the first act,[62] with the preparations appropriate to it, can put itself into [its] second act, if nothing prevents it. And this is what Aristotle seems to have meant in the second book[63] where he posed this question: Why is there no sensation without an exterior object, even though sensible qualities, namely, the species of heat, cold, wet and dry, are joined to sense in its organ, [and] the organ is never deprived [of them]? He responds [by] saying that the cause of this [failure to sense the qualities inhering in a sense organ] is that the sensitive [power] is not in act, but only in potency. In other words, although sense is very much in potency to receiving sensation, yet it is not in sufficient act without sensible species to do this, and the species must be made by an exterior agent.

Having considered these things, we can respond to this argument, namely: if there were an agent sense, Aristotle would be very much diminished because he said nothing about it. I say that he said enough about it because he said that the soul is a cause according to three types of cause.[64]

He then stated this concerning the agent cause: he said that it is the principle of motion, both in terms of local motion and in terms of nutrition and growth,[65] and also of alteration,[66] which is sense, that is, sensation. He thus expressed well enough that the soul is the agent of sensation, and not only a recipient. But because the agent sense and receiving sense are not different things but are the same soul and in the same organ, "producing sensation" and "receiving" sufficed to distinguish [1] the organs in which sensations were produced and [2] the objects from which sensible species were produced. And in these organs, by means of these species, the soul exercises the functions of sensing.

What remains to be said concerns the agent sense [and] its relationship to the agent intellect. Thus when Aristotle deals with the agent intellect in the third book of this work,[67] he believes, because of the relationship, that this declaration, along with those things that were said about it in the second book, suffices concerning the agent sense. And in truth, this is sufficient, as will appear when we turn to the agent intellect in the third book of this [commentary].[68]

Question 11

[The question is asked] whether sense can be deceived concerning its proper sensible.[69] That it can [be deceived] is proved because [1] intellect is a far more powerful and more certain ability than sense, but [2] it can err about its proper object. Thus all the more so can sense. The consequent holds by the topic of the lesser [*per locum a minori*].[70] For it seems less likely that a more powerful and more certain ability should be deceived than [that] a less certain power or ability [should be deceived]. The first proposition [1] is clear because the intellect, by means of reason, corrects the judgments of sense, as [for example] concerning the size of the sun,[71] which it would not do if it were not a more excellent and more certain ability. The second proposition also appears [correct] because God, the intelligences, and all universals are the proper objects of the intellect, because they are known by no other ability. And yet, in many questions and doubts and opinions concerning these things, even the intellects of the wisest are deficient and err.

Furthermore, color and *lux*[72] are the proper objects of vision because they are sensed by no other sense, and yet vision is deceived about them in many ways, because it judges differently from near and far. Even with a [fixed] distance, and with the same color in place, a thing upon which a ray of *lumen* falls appears white, while a thing in shadow appears black. Sometimes *lumen* so intense falls on a black, polished object and is reflected to the eye that the black thing appears white. In the third book of [his] *Meteorology*,[73] [Aristotle] says that the middle colors, [when placed] next to black, appear whiter, and [when placed] next to white, [appear] blacker. Thus it is clear that, in these ways, vision is deceived about colors.

It is deceived in yet another way, because the sun in rising appears red. Thus redness is judged [to be present], although no [real] redness is seen. And if two pieces of glass are placed one on top of the other, one blue or azure, and the other yellow, what is seen through them will appear entirely green. Thus greenness is judged [to be present], although no [real] greenness is seen.

The same thing happens with touch, because a person getting into a bath judges the water to be very hot. Later, after he has been in the bath for a while, he will judge that [the bath] is not so hot. Similarly with taste, for, to a sick person, things that taste sweet and good often seem bitter, and people that eat garlic cannot detect an odor of garlic.

We conclude many things about objects that glow at night, which we could not do if they did not glow, because they would not affect sense. And yet, during the day, no matter how well prepared the medium, we judge that they do not glow. And when the rainbow appears to us, we judge [that] many different colors [are present], although no real color is seen. This appears

[true] because, if there were a color, then, if we were nearer, we would see it [better], because we see better when nearer than from afar. And yet we find no color there at the place where the rainbow appears to us [to be]. [A final example of visual fallibility:] Darkness seems to be a color because it appears black, yet it is not a color but only a transparent medium devoid of *lumen*.

Aristotle says the opposite, [that is, that the senses are not deceived about their proper objects]. Describing a sensible object, he says, ''I call a proper sensible that which cannot be sensed by another sense, and about which there can be no mistake.''[74] And he says the same thing when discussing imagination,[75] thereby positing a difference between imagination and sense.[76]

The main difficulty is in what way this famous authoritative statement [that is, that the senses are not deceived about their proper objects] should be understood, because the arguments just mentioned show that the senses *are* much deceived concerning their proper objects. Aristotle himself seems to comment on this statement [by] saying that any one of the senses judges concerning these sensibles, that is, the proper [sensibles], and is not deceived about [e.g.] color nor sound, but [can be deceived about] what is colored or where [it is], or what sounds or where [it is].[77] But still the explanation seems imperfect to some, firstly because this property of proper sensibles seems to have been proposed to [establish] a difference [between proper and] common sensibles. And yet, explained in this way, [that is, we can err about what is red or where, but not about seeing red] common sensibles are not different from proper sensibles.[78] For we judge of size and motion, and we are not deceived that [we detect] motion or size. For example, if someone in a boat moving on a river judges that a tree on the shore moves, he errs in judging where the motion is or what is moved. But he does not err in judging that there is motion, because there truly is motion, but of the boat, not of the tree. And it could be said of this observer in this instance that the required condition for differentiating common sensibles did not exist, but [that the requisite conditions] for differentiating sensibles *per accidens* [did exist].[79]

But still it follows [that the senses are deceived,] because, if vision is not deceived concerning color, as far as a general judgment that a color [is seen], yet it is certainly deceived as far as special judgments, that white, black or red or green or greenness [is seen]. For, just as was argued [above], people seeing the sun in the morning judge that it is red, but there is no [real] redness [in the sun]. And [looking] through these two pieces of glass, [one yellow, one blue,] we judge greenness, and there is no [real] greenness [seen]. And also, observing the heavens with the air as pure as it can be, we judge the sky to be a most beautiful blue or azure, although there is [really] no such color as we see there because the sky has no color. And it is clear that, even from nearby, although a wall may be completely white, yet at night, while you study, it appears black to you outside the candle's ray, that is, in shadow. And so you judge white to be black. Thus you are deceived, either concerning white insofar as it is white, or black insofar as it is black, because you judge white to be not-white, and not-black to be black.

Clearly, we are much deceived about proper sensibles as far as the level of intention and remission[80] is concerned, because it is clear that a color appears more pale in stronger light and less pale in weaker light. And to a person entering a bath the heat appears quite intense, and perhaps he cannot bear it. Later, when he is warmed, [the bath] seems less warm to him and he wants it warmer.

Based on these [observations] I say that proper sensibles do not differ from sensibles *per accidens* in terms of this property [that is, the property of being infallibly sensible in the general but not the special case] so understood, because we do not seem to be deceived in general judgment concerning the sensible *per accidens*, but [we do] in

special [judgment], just as we said about proper sensibles. For we are not deceived when we see a color by judging that the colored thing is something or somewhere. But in special judgment we are deceived by judging that it is wood or stone, that it is in that place or this.

There is also a serious doubt whether we are deceived about proper sensibles also as far as general judgements are concerned, for example about color [and] about sound. For sound or odor can be so weak that we judge that there is no sound, but silence; no odor, but an odorless thing. And also, regarding the sight of the rainbow, we judge that there is a color when there is no color but only refraction of solar *lumen* from little drops of rain to our vision.[81] And yet neither is the *lux* of the sun a color, nor [is] *lumen*, nor is there color in the drop of water. For water and air are transparent [and] without color, receptive of all species of different colors, and if perhaps there is a color in them, it is so weak that it is not noticeable to vision. Similarly, if it is dark inside [a house,] without much *lumen*, and outside, where an observer stands, there is strong *lumen*, the observer, standing outside the house and looking in through a window, judges that there is blackness in or beyond the window. By judging blackness, he judges that there is a color, although [in the window] and beyond there is no color but pure [and] dark transparency, without *lumen*. For this reason, painters, wishing to represent open windows in a wall, paint black there. We judge color, although there is no color. Thus, through vision, we are deceived when judging that color [is present].

Themistius[82] gives such an explanation: that, from the indisposition of the organ, we are very much deceived about proper sensibles. For a person having an infected tongue does not judge flavors well. We are deceived also because of the impurity of the medium. The sun appears red to us in the morning because of black fumes risen above the earth. And all things seen through red glass appear red. We are also deceived because of too great a distance.

But we are not deceived if the distance is right, the medium pure, and the sense organ well disposed.

One may object right away against this explanation because it does not propose a difference between proper and common sensibles, because we are also not deceived about size or shape [given Themistius's conditions]. And if we are deceived about motion because of great slowness or little velocity—if we judge that a moving thing is at rest—so, without doubt, are we deceived if we judge silence where there is sound, if the sound is quite weak, and if we judge that there is no odor where the odor is very weak. And perhaps Themistius would have done well to admit that [his explanation of sense fallibility] proposed no difference between common and proper sensibles, but [did so] between sensibles per se and sensibles *per accidens.*[83]

One may argue further against Themistius that, if the indisposition of the organ or the impurity of the medium were to remove the certitude of judgment, it would follow that we could never judge about sensibles with perfect certitude, which is false. And the consequent is clear because our organs are never extremely well disposed, unless perhaps in one moment, for the reason that our complexion[84] always changes, so that there is never a duration of time in which there is a perfectly temperate complexion. And also, there is never perfectly pure air—which is the medium of seeing and hearing—around us, for there are always mixed with it some fumes or vapors risen from the earth or from water. I believe that Themistius was right when he said that, [even] without the highest purity of the medium or the most perfect disposition of the organ, we certainly and without any defect judge that this is white and that black, that sweet and that bitter. But never, however much the organ is well disposed and the medium pure, can we distinguish point by point the level of intention and remission. For we cannot discern the level of difference between two white things not similar point for point but similar enough, because of the infinity of division [of levels of intention] and the finitude of the visual power.

The Commentator,[85] however, explains that sense does not err concerning proper sensibles "in the greater part," or in large degree, although it can err in small degree. Aristotle gives this explanation at the end of the second book of this work, saying, "[The sensation] of the proper ones," that is, [the proper] senses, "is true or has little that is false."[86] And this explanation is true and perfect, if the appropriate conditions that Themistius proposed apply, namely, that the distance is right and [that] the medium and the organ [are] in good shape and well disposed.

So when Aristotle said that the proper sensible is "that which is not sensed by another sense,"[87] he meant thereby [to signify] the difference between proper and common sensibles. And when he said, "and about which there is no error,"[88] he meant [to signify] the difference between "proper sensible" and "sensible *per accidens,*" about which we can err not only a little or in part but regarding the whole, by judging [e.g.] that honey is bile, or that gold is copper, or the like.[89]

So it seems that the opening arguments are resolved. To the first [argument] we say that the intellect cannot err about some things, namely about principles of demonstrative knowledge, by dissenting to them and assenting to their opposites. And many doubtful matters that sense cannot prove can be cleared up and proven by thinking. For in many matters and concerning many matters, the intellect can be more deceived than sense about proper sensibles, because intellect understands the intelligible things in their absence by means of preserved species and intentions, when the things outside have been changed or perhaps corrupted. Sense does not sense proper sensibles unless they are present.[90]

To the next [argument] we admit that vision can be deceived in many ways because of distance and indisposition [of the visual organ], and because it[91] is in shadow because of the indisposition of the medium which is not sufficiently illuminated. And if a highly polished black object, from which much *lumen* is reflected to the eye, appears white, this is because of indisposition of the organ because the organ is filled with too much *lumen*, which represents more strongly the *white-appearing lux* than the species of the color [white represents] that color. That [vision is fallible] also [is shown because] the same thing appears blacker next to white and whiter next to black. This is especially true if the distance is great. This, too, argues only for deception in degree and in small measure.

[In response] to the next [argument] we say that the sun appears red in the morning because of the impurity of the medium, in which there are black fumes risen from the earth. Now a bright body, such as the sun, that appears white through a pure medium, appears under a middle color, namely red, if it is seen through a black body or mixed up with a black body. Thus charcoal, when burning, appears red; extinguished, it clearly appears black. Furthermore, because green is halfway between yellow and blue, when these [colors are] seen at once mixed up together or one through the other, they appear green. A colored medium is not a good medium for judging well about exterior color.

But then someone says, "if a yellow glass is near the eye and a blue glass is further away, why does one not judge correctly about [the presence of] yellow? What prevents him from doing so?" I say that the organ is not well prepared, because, if the eye is to judge well of something, it should be well prepared by the species of the color [it is judging], and should not, at the same place [in the organ], be prepared in a confused way by the species of another color. In the preceding case, however, vision is prepared in a confused way and not only according to the same place [in the organ] but also by the species of the color yellow [more] than by the species of blue. Thus it can judge with certainty of neither, but, because of the confusion of species, judges the median of these colors, [green, to be present.]

Concerning what we said about touch and taste, it seems that this happens because of different dispositions of the organ.

[In response] to the next [argument], we say that the difference between *lux* and color is great. For *lux* has the innate ability to move a dark, transparent medium and to illuminate it by its *lumen*. Color, however, does not [have such an innate ability] without another *lumen* falling on it. And so a medium not illuminated by any other *lumen* is a good medium for seeing *lux*. Thus weak lights are not seen well during the day, but [are seen well] at night. For this [reason], the stars are not seen during the day, nor [are] things emitting flames, nor other things having weak *lumen*, unless they are seen as having their color and not as having their *lux*.

To the next [argument we respond as follows:] it is clear that the determination about the rainbow should be carried out in the third book of [Aristotle's] *Meteorology*.[92] But for now it should be said that *lux*, although it is not, properly speaking, called a color, is commonly called the color white when taken as a color. Whence the sun appears white, although it has no other color than *lux*. So shining whiteness may be called *lux*, and whiteness not shining may, properly speaking, be called color. Whence some call whiteness a distinct *lux*, and say that whiteness differs from blackness because whiteness participates more in *lux* and less in opacity, blackness [more in opacity and less in *lux*], and because the middle colors arise from a mixture of extremes, in the way determined in [Aristotle's] *On Sense and Sensible Objects*.[93] Thus, from the mixture of *lux* with an opaque or black or dark body according to different proportions, a different color will appear to us. And so in a similar way, if *lumen* from a bright body crosses a black or dark body, or is reflected from a black or dark body, it will be judged to be one color or another because of the weakening of *lumen* and its confusion in the eye with the species of other visible things having a share in opacity or darkness, just as was said before about the different pieces of glass.

[In response] to the final [argument], we

admit that we are deceived from far away [in vision,] and that we judge shadows to be blackness. In a place completely dark, we judge nothing seen, but, by an interior ability, we judge darkness.[94] Looking with eyes open, we see nothing by means of exterior vision, which, we conclude, occurs because of lack of *lumen*. It is true that, sometimes, improperly, we call darkness blackness or opacity, for the reason that darkness is privation of *lux* or *lumen*, and *lux* appears white. Thus we say that darkness is a privation of whiteness, and with blackness there is always a privation of whiteness. In doing so we use these terms "darkness" and "blackness," "shadowy" and "black," improperly in an imprecise way. And so the question appears well resolved.

ABBREVIATIONS

AO   *Aristotelis opera cum Averrois commentariis.* 12 vols. Venice, 1562–74.

DA   Aristotle, *De Anima*

Sobol   John Buridan on the soul and sensation: An edition of Book II of his commentary on Aristotle's book on the soul with an introduction and a translation of question 18 on sensible species [by] Peter G. Sobol. Dissertation at Indiana University, 1984.

Sourcebook   Edward Grant (ed.), *A Sourcebook in Medieval Science,* Cambridge: Harvard U. Press, 1974.

NOTES

1. III.3, 202a15–20.
2. I.7, esp. 324a10–24.
3. II.4, 415b9–13.
4. Aristotle distinguished four types of cause: material, formal, efficient and final. In one exposition (*Physics* 2.3) he used the example of a statue to elucidate the four types of causes. The statue is made of something (bronze), hence has a material cause. It has shape and size, hence has a formal cause. It was made by an agent, hence has an efficient cause, and was made for a reason, hence has a final cause. The soul provides all causes for the living creature except the material.
5. DA, 2.37. AO 69D.
6. 415b22–27. AO 68E.
7. Buridan here drew on the study of probable arguments that Aristotle had called *topoi* and that came to be called topics. The topic use here is the topic from conjugates, which assumes that words that are derived from the same root have similar meanings. Given that to sense is to act and given, by the topic from conjugates, that "to sense" means much the same as "sensitive ability" and that "to act" means much the same as "active ability," Buridan concluded that the sensitive ability is an active ability. He will, however, refute this argument toward the end of the question. See Cicero, *Topica* sec. 12. Loeb, p. 390; Boethius, *De differentiis topicis,* Bk III, esp. Migne, 64:1197B.
8. That is, actions that inhere in their subjects.
9. That is, "sensation" and "to sense" are joined by sharing the same root. Hence what is true of one will be true of the other.
10. Cf. DA, II.5, 417b8.
11. "Sense" here refers not to any of the five external senses, but to the internal sensitive power of imagination. 432b19–20.
12. 433a10. At 432a21, Aristotle claims that mind without desire cannot cause motion.
13. That a menstruating woman could stain a highly polished bronze mirror by looking at it was a standard opening argument used to set up a defense of the intromission theory of vision. Disputants did not deny the effect (learned from Aristotle, *On Dreams* 2, 459b28–30) but denied that the visual process was responsible for it.
14. The basilisk appears in medieval bestiaries as a winged serpent. Wilma George and Brunsdon Yapp,

The Naming of the Beasts (London: Duckworth, 1991), p. 199, believe that the basilisk may derive from the cobra, and the basilisk's fatal glance from the cobra's ability to spit its venom.

15. DA, 2:5, 416b33–35.
16. DA, 3:4, 429a20–21.
17. The species itself is not sensed. The color from which the species arose or which initiated the propagation of species is sensed by means of its species.
18. DA, 1.1, 403a3–b15.
19. DA, 1.4, 408b14–15. The insertion "by means of soul" comes from the Greek text of *De anima* and from the Latin texts in AO, 32E–F.
20. As a medium for the species of color, odor and sound, air contains the species, yet does not perceive the qualities that they represent.
21. In this and the following paragraph, Buridan strives to distinguish "to sense" from the reception of species and the form that they bear. He argues that "to produce sensation" is not the same as "to sense," because God can do the former without doing the latter. In the following paragraph, he claims that "to sense" continues after sensation—the reception of species and form—is complete.
22. This may be a reference to II.18.
23. Buridan and others used *lux* to mean the source of light and *lumen* to mean the species of *lux* in the medium. See David C. Lindberg, *Theories of Vision from al-Kindi to Kepler* (Chicago: University of Chicago Press, 1976), pp. 133–35.
24. That is, both medium and eye must be transparent. After reception in the eye, however, both the requirement of transparency and the limitation of rectilinear propagation are lifted so that the species can pass through the optic nerve to the brain.
25. JB denied the existence of celestial matter on the grounds that matter served as substrate for change, yet no change occurs in the heavens, hence celestial matter would have no purpose. See Edward Grant, "Celestial Matter: A Medieval and Galilea," JMRS, 1983, 13(2):178–82.
26. 2.1, 329a30. The problem of how elements persisted in a compound was of major concern to medieval natural philosophers. See the selections from Thomas Aquinas and Albert of Saxony in Edward Grant (ed.), *A Sourcebook in Medieval Science* (Cambridge: Harvard University Press, 1974), pp. 603–14.
27. The substantial form leaving the matter of the horse is the soul. The substantial form arriving is the substantial form of the dead body.
28. Because intellect has no organ and hence is unextended. Cf. DA, III.4, esp. 429a21–26.
29. The manuscripts all agree on "sensitive." Buridan's claim that when he sees a color he does not sense matter seems better directed against the claim that matter is principally sensible, something everyone denied, than the claim that matter is principally sensitive. Toward the end of the question, Buridan admits that the matter of his sense organs plays some role in this ability to sense.
30. Buridan here relies on the popular analogy between sense and intellect evoked at the beginning of Question 10.
31. In the seventh question of Book II—whether the soul is in every part of the living body—Buridan concluded that the unextended human soul made use of extended "instrumental potentials" in the organs of sense and digestion. Only when faced with the problem of how sensation begins in an extended organ and finishes in an unextended soul was he forced to admit the miraculous nature of the union between body and soul. See Jack Zupko, "How Are Souls Related to Bodies? A Study of John Buridan," *Review of Metaphysics*, 1993, 46(3):575–99.
32. 1.4, 408b11–15.
33. See the example of the jar of wine, toward the end of the paragraph.
34. Here JB may have anticipated the indignation of students who objected to any departure from the narrowest demands of the curriculum. He made a similar plea for mercy at the end of his long excursus on the nature of sensible species in II18. "These things have been said about the species of proper sensibles as a kind of digression. But it does not strike me as useless. The arguments raised at the beginning of the question have been resolved according to what has been established here and elsewhere. The authorities have been glossed according to the established requirements, just as anyone might wish." (Translated from Sobol, p. 321.)

    Note also the emphasis on doubt as opposed to an emphasis on the discovery of truth. Medieval natural philosophers may have used the language of nature to explore the science of disputation as much as they used disputation to explore nature.
35. As the text will make clear, the question of an "agent sense" arises in part from Aristotle's contention that every change requires something that acts and something that is acted upon, and in part from the problem of what to do about the apparent passivity of sense, despite its obviously higher position than the active vegetative power.
36. III.4, 429a16, III.8, 431b20 ff.
37. III.5, esp. 430a14.
38. III.5, 430a17.

39. 430a10–14. Cf. AO 160D.

40. III.5, 430a18, AO 161F.

41. If Aristotle's case of the agent intellect holds, so does the case for the agent sense. The agent intellect exists, so Aristotle's case for it must be correct, hence an agent sense also exists.

42. An animal that never sensed would still be an animal. Sensation changes nothing about the animal, while nutrition which involves changing the substance of food to the substance of the body, entails substantial change.

43. See 2.4, esp. 416b3 ff.

44. Buridan here assumes the spontaneous generation of frogs. Aristotle had proposed that certain simple animals such as shellfish arose from earth and from water (*Generation of Animals*, III. 11, 762a8–763b15). Belief in the ability of the simplest animals to spontaneously generate was not abandoned until the nineteenth century.

45. Avicenna referred to the Giver or Author of Forms at S. Van Riet (ed.) *Liber tertius naturalium de generatione et corruptione*, ch. 14, 139:45–49.

46. 3.5, 430a16. Cf. AO 161F.

47. 3.5, 430a20. Cf. AO 161F–162A.

48. "Phantasm" was the name given to the image of a sensible object in the brain. It was composed of sensible species and hence retained traces of the individuality and materiality that marked the original object. In order for the intellect to recognize what kind of object it was, an intelligible species had to be extracted from the phantasm. See Edward P. Mahoney, "Sense, Intellect and Imagination in Albert, Thomas, and Siger," in N. Kretzmann, A. Kenny, J. Pinborg (eds.), *Cambridge History of Later Medieval Philosophy* (Cambridge: Cambridge University Press, 1982), pp. 602–22.

49. III.10.

50. 1.9, 279a28.

51. 3.2, 426b13 ff.

52. The *estimativa* was one of several internal senses proposed by Islamic scholars and adopted by Latin commentators. The number, names, locations and functions of the internal senses varied from one author to another and sometimes varied over one author's lifetime (Albert the Great, for example, on whom see Nicholas H. Steneck, "Albert on the Psychology of Sense Perception," in James A. Weisheipl, O.P. (ed.), *Albertus Magnus and the Sciences* (Toronto: PIMS, 1980, pp. 263–90). Avicenna proposed the *estimativa* to explain instinctive and learned behavior in animals and human infants. See S. Van Riet (ed.), *Liber De anima seu Sextus de naturalibus*, IV.3, pp. 34–40, and Deborah Black, "Estimation (*Wahm*) in Avicenna: The Logical and Psychological Dimensions," *Dialogue*, 1993, 32(2):219–58. The *estimativa* allowed animals to discern the value of a perceived object at first glance, hence, as in the traditional example that Buridan goes on to cite, the sheep's ability to recognize danger in the first wolf that it has ever seen.

53. Above, pp. 501–02.

54. Buridan here paraphrases Aristotle's *Nicomachean Ethics*, I.3, 1094b12. I thank Jack Zupko for this reference.

55. Buridan may have had in mind the first question of the ninth book of his commentary on Aristotle's *Metaphysics*. See f. 56rb–vb of the Paris 1518 edition. I thank Jack Zupko for this reference.

56. On *generans*, creator, and *removens prohibens*, removal of an obstacle, as causes of motion, see the examples from Thomas Aquinas in Grant, *Sourcebook*, p. 265.

57. Cf. 8.4, 255b14–256a5.

58. Question 9, pp. 496–97.

59. JB here reads species back into Aristotle. Species theory is an invention of the 13th century that is Aristotelian only insofar as it does not contradict any Aristotelian tenet. It fills the gap in theory left by Aristotle's weak explanation of how objects affect the senses.

60. 2.12, 424b16. AO 116B–C.

61. II.8, 420a6.

62. At 417a21, Aristotle distinguished three stages of act. The first, the stage at which someone can acquire knowledge, was trivial for Buridan's purposes here and he ignored it. The second is the stage, which Buridan called "first act," achieved by someone who has acquired knowledge but is not exercising that knowledge. By exercising that knowledge, such a person can achieve what Buridan called "second act," if nothing external prevents the person from doing so.

63. 2.5, 417a2–7, b24–25. AO 76E–F.

64. II.4, 415b9–13.

65. On nutrition and growth as types of motion, see 1.3, 406a13.

66. On alteration as distinct from generation and destruction, see II.5, esp. 417a21 et seq.

67. 3.5.

68. In this case Buridan exonerated Aristotle for failure to mention the agent sense by claiming, as had Averroës, that the mention is implicit in his discussion of the agent intellect. In Question II.23 he ex-

onerated Aristotle for failure to anticipate all the internal senses by denying that they are in fact distinct. Sobol, p. 387.

69. This question addresses Aristotle's claim at 418a11 that each sense has a particular quality that it alone can detect, and that it cannot err when perceiving that quality. Aristotle qualified the claim slightly at III.3, 428b18–19.

70. See JB, *Compendium totius logicae*, sig. q[6]. "Locus a minori tenet constructive ut comes potest expugnare castrum ergo et rex. Maxima: quod minus potest hoc maius potest." An ability not had by a greater power cannot be had by a lesser power. If the greater power of intellect is not infallible, Buridan argued, then neither is the lesser power of sense.

71. Aristotle used this example at 3.3, 428b3–5.

72. On *lux* and *lumen* see note 23.

73. III.4, esp. 375a25.

74. 2.6, 418a10 AO 82B–C.

75. 3.3, 428a13.

76. Cf. also *De sensu*, 4, 442b8 on common vs. proper sensibles.

77. DA, II.6, 418a14–17. Cf. *De somniis*, 3, 461a29.

78. If the claim of infallibility of proper sensation is thus weakened, the same claim could apply to common sensibles: I may be deceived that the tabletop is oval, but I am not deceived in detecting an oval shape.

79. The observer in the boat can correctly sense the accidentally sensible tree and boat, but cannot correctly distinguish motion of one from motion of the other.

80. Medieval scholars recognized that qualities could change in intensity and they referred to this as intention and remission of forms, graphically represented by Buridan's famous pupil, Nicole Oresme. See Marshall Clagett, *The Science of Mechanics in the Middle Ages* (Madison: University of Wisconsin Press, 1959), pp. 331–418, and his *Nicole Oresme and the Geometry of Qualities and Motions* (Madison: University of Wisconsin Press, 1968).

81. Theodoric of Freiburg (ca. 1250–1310) showed that the positions of the primary and secondary bow resulted from refraction and internal reflection in spherical droplets. See Grant, *Sourcebook*, pp. 435–41. See also Carl B. Boyer, *The Rainbow: From Myth to Mathematics* (New York: Thomas Yoseloff, 1959).

82. G. Verbeke (ed.), *Thémistius: Commentaire sur le traité de l'âne d'Aristote* (Louvain, 1957), 164:55–165:61.

83. Per se judgment of color does not entail any assertion about any quality of an observed thing. *Per accidens* judgment entails assertions about the subject of the color. In general, we can be sure that a color belongs to a substance and that the substance is in a place, but we easily err if we conclude that we recognize the particular substance or its exact place.

84. Medieval physicians used the term *complexio* to mean the proportion of the four Galenic humors that compose the human body. That proportion was believed to remain in flux even in healthy people. Hence any single complexion optimal for sensation would last only briefly. Illness resulted if the proportion became too out of balance, as when phlegm predominates to an unhealthy degree in head colds. Most medieval pharmacology strove to restore the proper balance of humors.

85. DA, 2.63. Crawford 225:29–30. AO 82E

86. 3.3, 428b18. AO 134B.

87. 2.6, 418a11. AO 82B–C.

88. *Ib.*, a12. AO *ib.*

89. These errors would occur if a sentient associated yellow in honey with bile, or yellow in gold with copper.

90. JB means that the intellect's judgment about sensible things may be false at the time when the judgment is made because the objects from which species were transmitted or propagated to the sense and then to the intellect may have changed or been destroyed in the time between emitting species and the time a judgment is made. NB strictly speaking the same caveat applies to even proper senses, because the multiplication of species from object to sense organ is not instantaneous. Cf. 2.18, Sobol pp. 253–54, 169–72.

91. "It" must be the visible object because JB allows that an eye in the dark can see an illuminated object through a dark medium. In fact an illuminated eye and illuminated medium are insufficient for seeing an object unless it too is illuminated. 2.15, Sobol, pp. 218–19.

92. 3.4.

93. 3, 439b19–440a6.

94. The common sense allows us to (1) associate sight with sounds, (2) sense that we sense, and (3) detect absence of proper sensible qualities. Cf. DA, 3.2.

CHAPTER 36

Nicole Oresme

Very little is known about the early life of Nicole Oresme. He was born circa 1320, by all estimates in the village of Allemagne near the city of Căen in Normandy. During the mid-1340s he entered the University of Paris, where he most likely studied under the celebrated Jean Buridan. Records indicate that by November 1348 he was already a master of arts and a theology student at the College of Navarre. In 1355 or 1356 he received the mastership in theology, and while teaching theology at the College of Navarre he became its grand master in 1356.

Thereafter he rose steadily in the church hierarchy, first as archdeacon of Bayeux in 1361, which he resigned the same year because it conflicted with the grand mastership. In November 1362 he was appointed to the position of canon of Rouen, then as canon of Ste. Chapelle (February 1363), after which he became dean of the cathedral of Rouen (March 1364) and finally bishop of Lisieux (1377). This meteoric rise was undoubtedly enhanced by his faithful service to the royal family of France, with whom he was brought into contact no later than 1356. He first served John II and then his son the Dauphin, Charles, who was regent during his father's imprisonment by the English, and who became king in 1364. The bishopric of Lisieux was given by Charles as a reward for services rendered between 1369 and 1377, during which time Oresme translated four of Aristotle's treatises from Latin into French (*Ethics, Politics, Economics,* and *On the Heavens*). In addition he provided commentaries on each. He remained bishop of Lisieux until his death in 1382.

Oresme was a scholar of enormous range manifested by the numerous commentaries and treatises he wrote on theology, physical science, politics, and economics. Of central importance to him were physical and mathematical problems, and few, if any, medieval natural philosophers are his equal in his range and originality. In an age that lacked scientific sophistication and was rife with superstition, Oresme doggedly pursued and applied his principle thesis, namely, that supposedly marvelous phenomena do, in fact, have natural causes. A lack of knowledge of them is no basis for concluding that they do not exist, and indeed one can discover precisely what they are if one is persistent enough. Many of these supposed marvels are attributable to errors of sensation or to explainable variations in other bodily operations.

Nicole Oresme on the Causes of Marvels Involving Vision

The primary focus of Nicole Oresme's treatise *De causis mirabilium* is on the psychology and physiology of sensation. In Chapter One, "On the Causes of Marvels Involving Vision", he claims, "For perfect seeing eight things are needed: light, distance, position, size, solidity, transparency, proper time and healthy vision". At the end of Chapter Two, "On Apparent Marvels in the Hearing of Sound", he adds to these factors three more fundamental things, namely the soul or internal faculty, the act of paying attention, and the species of a thing. In order to fully appreciate Oresme's analysis, one must understand the doctrine of multiplication of species.

The doctrine of multiplication of species was exploited by Robert Grosseteste in his quest to explain the transmission of species (derived from the Greek εἶδος as utilized by Aristotle) by way of light rays. Take, for example, gazing at the moon. In so doing one does not see the moon directly, yet one does perceive something. The moon emits sensible species projected from it along lines in all directions. These species are non-physical representational forms or likenesses of the object perceived. In a similar vein all other material things emit sensible species of their own, the result being a dynamic world of interacting species. This notion gets expanded by subsequent theorists (a) to include all so-called intangible notions and change, an example being that of the causes and effects of human emotion and (b) to explain the phenomenon of sensation and in the process account for perceptual errors. As the doctrine of multiplication of species gets refined, it explains, for example, vision as a two-way street. On the one hand, an object emits its species via light rays. Such species would not, however, be perceived were it not for one possessing the power to see. There must be some visual apparatus referred to by Oresme as the soul or internal faculty. Yet more is needed. One must also pay attention in order to perceive species. If for some reason there is an aberration regarding one or more of the conditions cited in the first paragraph above, perceptual errors can occur. "And so when a fearful man, thinking about someone dead, enters or leaves a room and sees a shadow or some such thing, he will judge and it will appear that it is [the dead man] etc., just as also from the movement of a mouse at night or the movement of the door by wind a fearful man will judge and it will appear to him that he sees and hears a thief or etc."

DE CAUSIS MIRABILIUM

Prologue

Here begin the quodlibeta annexed to the preceding *Questio [contra divinatores]*.

In order to set people's minds at rest to some extent, I propose here, although it goes beyond what was intended, to show the causes of some effects which seem to be marvels and to show that the effects occur

naturally, as do the others at which we commonly do not marvel. There is no reason to take recourse to the heavens, the last refuge of the weak, or demons, or to our glorious God as if He would produce these effects directly, more so than those effects whose causes we believe are well known to us.

One thing I would note here is that we should properly assign to particular effects particular causes, but this is very difficult unless a person looks at effects one at a time and their particular circumstances.

Consequently, it will suffice for me to show that the things mentioned occur naturally, as I just said, and that no illogicality is involved. Why Sortes is poor and Plato[1] is rich, why an animal died at such a time, why pepper in small quantities is a laxative and a diuretic in large quantities, why scammony is the opposite (as Aristotle says in the first part of the *Problems*), why the crop failed in this field, why Sortes heard such a voice or saw such a marvel—how could we render their particular and direct causes and how could we know their particular circumstances? As I have said, then, I shall only show in a general manner that such things occur naturally, as do successful physicians who compose general rules in medicine and leave specific cases to practising physicians. For no physician would know how to say—if Sortes were ill—what kind of illness he has and how it will be cured, except by seeing him and considering the particulars. Similarly, successful moral philosophers like Aristotle and the rest wrote only general principles and no law exists, as Aristotle said in the *Politics*, that does not need to be changed at some time.[2]

In the first chapter we will see: 1. that one thing can appear to our sight as two or more; 2. that two or more can appear to the sight as one; 3. that a thing can appear to our sight as larger or smaller than it is; 4. that a thing at rest can appear to be moving or vice-versa; 5. that a thing can appear to the sight to be a different colour than it is; 6. that it can appear to be something else than it is.

In the second chapter we will show that it is possible for people to seem to hear what in fact they do not hear, for example, to hear speaking, etc.

Chapter One:
On the Causes of Marvels Involving Vision

1. For the clarification of these matters, note first that Alhazen says, *Perspectiva*, Book 2, that an external sense has no knowledge by itself, but that an internal sense, i.e. the cognitive faculty, is needed.[3]

2. Note that, according to Witelo, *Perspectiva*, Book 4, Proposition 2, "it is impossible for sight to apprehend any one of the [corporeal] forms alone" since it is impossible, as he said, for any one of the corporeal forms which sight apprehends to exist by itself; colour, for example, does not exist without size, or size without shape, or shape without position, etc. Consequently sight cannot apprehend one form alone etc.[4]

3. Note, according to Alhazen,[5] *Perspectiva*, Book 2, and Witelo[6] says it too, that the more a thing is known in detail, the more points of detail and the more time it requires; the more general our knowledge, the less time required. For example, we know sooner and more easily that a wall has colour than that it has the colour white, and that it is white than of a certain degree [of intensity] etc.

4. Note, according to Witelo, *Perspectiva*, Book 4, Proposition 1, that "from an unbalanced ratio of the circumstances of the visible forms there arises deception in seeing, not only in the sight itself, but also in the distinguishing faculty of the soul." For perfect seeing eight things are needed: light, distance, position, size, solidity, transparency, proper time, and healthy vision. Sight varies as a result of the variation of these. For example, as light varies in intensity, things take on another colour etc.; similarly with distance etc.; and with solidity, and so even the same thing, when solid like ice, or non-solid like water, takes on another colour etc.

5. Note, as Witelo says in Book 4, Proposition 3, that "a thing is not seen under every possible angle," since an angle can well be too small or acute. And other things being equal, a thing seen under a greater angle seems that much larger, and that much smaller under a smaller angle. And so, according to Alhazen and Witelo every thing seen is seen in a triangle of which the thing seen is the base and conical lines are extended from it to the eye and the vertex of this triangle is in the eye. For example:

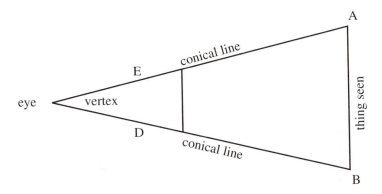

Figure 36.1

6. Note, according to Witelo in Book 4, Proposition 19, that "all things seen under the same angle, if the distance between them is not taken into account, seem equal." And in Proposition 27 he said that "true quantity is not apprehended by sight except by the aid of the distinguishing faculty." And in Proposition 28 he explains how error arises from an imbalance of the things mentioned in the fourth *notabile,* and says that because of the short time, when a glowing ember is moved rapidly, "the whole interval seems ignited since the amount of time is not taken into account."[7] That one thing can appear as two he shows in Proposition 28.[8] And that a moving thing appears to be still, or a round one oblong, or a red one of another colour he explains in the same Book 4.[9]

These and all the things said are demonstrated by Witelo and Alhazen in their *Perspectivas.*

7. Note that species of sensibles remain in the sense [even] in the absence of the objects, as Aristotle shows in the second chapter of the second tract of *De somno et vigilia.*[10] And in the second chapter of the first tract Aristotle says that judgment does not take place in an external sense,[11] and hence we sometimes do not perceive things passed before our eyes even though their species may then be in our sight.[12] And so, in the same place he says that when the internal sense is cut off, the external senses cannot sense, with the result that there is no vision, hearing, etc.; but with the exter-

nal senses cut off the internal common sense can still do its work.[13] For example, with eyes closed it still appears to me that I see my father, and so on. And in the second chapter of the second tract Aristotle explains that those suffering the passions, like those afraid and so on, are easily deceived as to the senses. And he explains in the same place how in crossing the fingers one thing appears to be two although the opposite is patent to the sight.[14]

8. Note, according to Aristotle in *De motu animalium,* Chapter 6, that the soul's faculties which move animals are intellect, sense, fantasy or judgment, choice, will and appetite. And in Chapter 7 he says that members of the body are moved when these faculties are altered, as is clear in fear, anger, shame, and so on. And in the same [book] that thoughts alter members as is clear in intercourse, where merely from thinking etc. And so, Aristotle says in the same place that species received in sensitive organs alter and change the organs, just as the sun by means of light alters the air by illuminating it, upon which illumination (as he says, and it is also clear) other alterations follow, like heating, etc. And in this manner also, organs receiving the species of sensibles are altered in some spiritual way; but that alteration is followed by others, as in fear the limbs become cold, and in anger there is heat and so on, and on account of something imagined the stomach is moved to vomit, and so on. And Aristotle says that from a small movement

of the cause there can arise a large and different movement, as is clear in the rudder of a ship. From which he wants to establish how species received in etc. [viz. organs] move the members.[15] And in the last chapter he asserts, and it is shown there, that the heart and genitals are especially susceptible to involuntary movements.

9. Note finally that vision sometimes occurs via a straight line, sometimes via a refracted line (as is clear from the penny at the bottom of a [water-filled] vase), and sometimes via a reflected line (as is clear in mirrors.)[16] And Antiphon thus saw his own image; it is clear in the *Meteora*, Book 3.[17] That every medium is variably reflective is known from mirrors of water, and from air else we would not see light. Alhazen explains these things in Book [4].[18]

With these *notabilia* presupposed it is easy to see the things set forth at the beginning of the chapter. And many of them are explained and demonstrated by Witelo and Alhazen and are clear as well to the senses. For example, everyone experiences that one thing appears as two on account of placing a finger next to or above the angle of the eye and that a thing at rest appears to be moved on account of moving the eye with a finger. And also should a man move or be turned around vigorously in a circle, all things would seem to him to be moved in circles. Also a thing seen through a red medium appears red, and likewise if there should be in the eye a red humour, namely blood. But if in the pupil or etc. there is yellow bile, then all things appear yellow; and if there is a thick humour in the middle of the pupil, all things appear perforated; and if there is a black humour in etc. [viz. the eye], then there appear flies or something. All these facts are patent to the senses and are also explained by Avicenna, Galen, and other medical men.

And the fact that something which is moved might appear to be at rest is apparent from the heavens, the sun, and the stars, [which seem to be at rest] unless you consider them for a long time, and from the case of a man seen at a distance [approach-

ing] along a straight line. And the fact that he appears larger or equal in size to a tower or a tree is also clear in the above figure—provided that the distance between lines DE and AB is not taken into account. For then line DE, namely the man or another thing, will appear equal to AB even though AB is a tower; and this also is apparent by experience. And that a man even sometimes appears to be a tree or other thing, or the reverse, is known experientially and on any day you want. And the cause of the aforesaid is that sometimes there is an error in the internal judging faculty without which seeing cannot take place, as is clear from the stick partly in the water which is judged broken;[19] and sometimes the error is in the organ, namely the pupil; and sometimes in the medium; and sometimes in other factors, as is shown in the fourth *notabile*.

Therefore, if it should be said that such and such a man, say. Antiphon, constantly sees a man in front of him, one must not marvel at it since it is possible that the reflection by the air is sufficient for his sight, just as for me a mirror reflects etc.[20]

And if it should be said, "In his chamber Sortes has seen his dead father or etc.," I respond that this is possible, I mean the appearance is, since he has the species of his father or someone else in the internal faculty and is thinking intently about him then and is not paying attention to what is present or passing before his eyes, and in this way, from a stick or shadow together with the fact that he is thinking intently about his father, it appears to him that it is etc. It happens in sleep, why can it not happen also when he is awake? And if you should say that he does see some things but his sight is impeded concerning them, I say, as I have said before, that it is possible that on account of strong imagining he does not attend to the things before him, wherefore etc. And so, we see from the evidence of our senses that any person when he withdraws himself can somehow make it appear to him that in his mind he sees Peter or a fortress or something. And so, we see that some people imagine and cogitate so strongly on something that they talk to themselves and it seems to them that they are in the place or with the persons about whom they are thinking.

And so when a fearful man, thinking about someone dead, enters or leaves a room and sees a shadow or some such thing, he will judge and it will appear that it is [the dead man] etc., just as also from the movement of a mouse at night or the movement of the door by wind a fearful man will judge and it will appear to him that he sees and hears a thief or etc.[21] The basis and ground of our reply to points like these is touched on in the sixth, seventh, and eighth *notabilia* with the help of the first and second too: namely that, since species of things are in the [common] sense (which judges and knows), why could it not appear to them etc. [viz. that the dead man or thief is present], since, if you think about it, the case of dreams is even more marvelous, where a man carries on an argument, sees things, etc. And this happens because of retained species and because the interior judging faculty, sometimes on account of a strong passion, according to Aristotle, as was said in the eighth *notabile*, might sometimes err in judgment.

One must not wonder that we often see that, even without passion (like fear, anger, etc.), many judge badly, so that sometimes out of ten men five will judge that a thing is larger or a different colour or shape than the other five and so on. Therefore I say that just as a man—because of the length of distance or the indisposition of the medium or the eye or on account of the weakness of the judging faculty—sometimes judges that a person is an ass or bird or something (as is known to anyone), so I say it is possible that such things all happen to Sortes while he stays in his room. And also just as a person is sometimes angry and becomes heated because of vigorous imagining, or because of what he imagined will also by chance be afraid, and so on, so I say in this matter that it is possible that etc., and the manner and cause are evident to anyone

sufficiently considering the aforesaid. And so, also because of a humour or movement in the eyes it sometimes appears that light[22] is seen at night.[23] Therefore (as is clear from the aforesaid) since [1] a colour can appear other than it is, as is evident in silk capes or etc. [and] in a rainbow; and [2] one thing [can appear as] two, and two as one, and the large as small, and the thing at rest as moved, and so on; and [3] in darkness it can appear, from movement or a humour in the eye, that there is light (as I just said) and so on; I say then that a thing can appear other [than it is] and that error can sometimes arise in either the external or the internal instrument or etc. And so, if there are three men, Sortes and Plato and Martin, the man they are looking at, it is possible that Sortes paying attention and judging correctly sees Martin; but Plato—on account of vigorous imagining and perhaps because some vapour in his eyes impede him or etc.—it will appear to him to be someone else.

And so, the whole solution lies in the fact that so many things can happen to Sortes in his room, both in his internal faculty and in his eye and the medium, or perhaps in one of these or perhaps in two or etc., that it will appear to him differently or as something else than it is, as is exemplified by these things and in other things. And that such an error would arise on the part of the organ and of the internal faculty (namely, the error that to Sortes as he stays in his room or remains out of doors there would appear a man long dead or the devil or etc.) is a warning sign because commonly such people are not much later ill and are as in a trance for some days since the humours and bad vapours are moved irregularly. Just as marvels appear to a man in frenzy and to a melancholic man (i.e. being in a melancholic passion) and to a man verging on epilepsy or other diseases etc., so too it is possible that these experiences can happen to a man for a brief period, like an attack of epilepsy, and then he becomes calm. And so a small humour or passion or vapour in the principal members (especially where the cognitive faculties are) causes marvelous movements and appearances, as is clear in the eighth *notabile*. Rarely however do such things befall people prudent and of good complexion, rather those who are melancholic, impassioned, and of strong imagination, as fearful people or etc.; and this happens on account of diverse vapours and humours etc. and on account of strong passion as in certain lunatics or etc. And so, usually such people are ill, or have been, or are near to being ill, or are children, or are women, or similar to the aforementioned in some ways etc. Also it could be said, as of Antiphon,[24] that it is possible that it would also appear so to someone sometimes in twilight or in etc. And so, you being in a healthy condition judge that the colours you see in the clouds or even in your house (since it can so happen there too) are truly in the rainbow; and you judge that a stick seen half-in and half-out of water is broken;[25] and by putting your finger near to your eyes you judge one thing to be two (or sometimes the reverse); and you judge a whole space to be ignited because of the rapid motion of a [glowing] coal in the air;[26] and you judge from afar that Sortes is Plato etc.; and you judge that such a cape is one colour but in another position you judge it to be another colour and so on. I ask therefore why you cannot imagine that even other errors arise at times, and for various reasons.

People marvel at such things only because they rarely happen; but the causes for these are as apparent as for others, as has been said. For example, at night a fearful man who sees a wolf in the fields, or a cat in his room, will immediately assert and judge that it is an enemy or a devil or etc. because he fixes his imagination on these and fears them. And a person devout and rapt [in ecstasy] will judge that it is an angel or etc.[27] A vigorous imagining of a retained species, then, together with a small external appearance or with an imbalance of some internal disposition (as stated in the fourth *notabile*), produces marvelous appearances in healthy as well as in sick people; and the more that the imbalances

of the said dispositions concur, the more error there is in judging, and the fewer the less etc. And this statement is the whole root of the solution to the preceding questions.

To see a person or a horse, then, is to receive in the eye not only the species of colour (as has been said often), but also size, shape, substance, motion, etc. which are apprehended and judged by an internal faculty—and then seeing is completely achieved. And so, these things are required for complete, perfect, and proper vision. Sometimes one or more are lacking etc., but the more basic needs are both a retained species and the cognitive faculty's judgment or attention to it etc., since it is not a species alone received in the eye that makes for seeing, whether it is a single and simple species of colour or light, or comes with other intentions or forms of other factors, namely size, shape, etc. From this it is evident that when Sortes is in the fields or elsewhere and it appears to him that he sees Plato who is recently dead etc., this happens because the judging, cognitive faculty errs etc. since it [or, he] does not attend to these things which it [or, he] ought before judging that the log or rock which by chance he sees is his father or etc. What are these things? I have often said it; and it is known what they are. And why does it [or, he] not attend to them? This has also been said before; it is either that he is thinking deeply about etc., or that moving vapours or humours or etc. impede it. Do you not see that owing to wine a man errs like this in judging, since what earlier he judged to be good he afterwards judged to be bad, and what is still he judges to be moving and what he used to fear he later dares etc.[28]

Therefore many things come together for seeing. What are these? And how does error arise with respect to them? Think about it from the things said above, and the matter will be quite clear. For instance, people believe that to see (taking "see" in its proper sense) is nothing but receiving the species of the colour of the thing seen; and in this [belief] they are deceived, as I have already said. I have posed these and other similar examples in order that it should be clear and obvious that it is not impossible for one thing to appear other than it is, etc.

From the *notabilia* presented above can be concluded the reasons why those who see such things and those to whom such visions appear are deceived. Sometimes it also happens to them because their limbs or neck or etc. are twisted or blackened. And, as I have said, this is caused by a vigorous movement of bad humours which sometimes begins readily and sometimes not, etc. Readily: as in the case where Sortes riding along the road is by chance startled at the flight of a lark perhaps, or recalls what he heard said about that place, namely that in such a place souls or spirits are wont to appear, and then begins to think excitedly about such things; and in this way a small movement is enough to stupefy him and [for something] to appear to him etc. Not readily: since perhaps he sees some men or a man and does not recognize them or him and does not pay attention to where they go nor to what befalls them, and perhaps in addition he is melancholic and has bad humours in his head etc., and perhaps in addition he has bad eyes which are quickly blurred by a small motion or by fear—and thus he will err in etc. Often have I seen some people sleeping near others, half-way between being awake and asleep so that they somehow heard the other people speaking and yet in such a trance it appeared to them that they were somewhere else, or saw etc., and for three or four hours did not know whether they really had seen or heard or etc., even asking "Was so-and-so here or have I been dreaming?" And I have seen soundly sleeping men rise and go and speak and respond to questions and still their eyes were closed. Hence marvels occur and marvelous appearances can happen when species are retained and strongly impressed and the imaginative faculty is strongly paying attention and actively considering and the organs are disposed.

The notions of what and where the said species are; and what, how, and how many are the internal faculties; and how they are moved with respect to objects; and how they move etc.—these I assume from *De anima* and *De memoria* and *De [sensu et] sensato* and *De somno et vigilia*. And the notions of how vision occurs, what things are required, and what the visibles are, and when one colour is altered merely from its position, and how error arises—these I take from the *Perspectiva* of Alhazen in the first, second, and third books, and also [from the *Perspectiva*] of Witelo, in the first four books, where they treat these matters exquisitely.[29] Let him who cares look there.

NOTES

1. For Oresme this is a *general* not a *particular* case because these names indicate only indefinite persons (like our "John Doe") in hypothetical cases. *Martin* and *Peter* are also used a few times in this treatise. No reference to the ancient thinkers is intended. The manuscripts often have *Sor* and one cannot know whether this is an alternative usage or merely a scribal abbreviation. *Sortes* itself probably derived from an abbreviation of Socrates, but it seems that here *Sortes* has achieved the status of an independent name. The Latin text of this edition preserves a reading of *Sor* only when it stands in the nominative case. The translation uses *Sortes*.

   There are many precedents for this use of these names. For example, in the Latin *Liber de anima* (or *Sextus naturalium*) of Avicenna, which Oresme cites frequently, *Socrates* is substituted for the Arabic name *Zayd*, and *Plato* for *'Amr* (ed. Van Riet, 4–5, p. 45n.). In the Renaissance translation of Averroës's epitome of Aristotle's *De generatione* made from the Hebrew by Vital Nissus, the name *Zaid* is rendered by *Plato* (e.g. in Junta edition of Aristotle [1562–1574], Vol. 5, fol. 396va). In many of the scholastic writings on maxima and minima studied by Wilson (*William Heytesbury*) and in logic texts generally, the names Socrates (or Sortes) and Plato are the standard examples.

2. The notion that particulars are matters for practical men like physicians and moral philosophers seems to derive from Aristotle's *Ethics* 2.2 (1104a5–11). Oresme makes the same point in his gloss on this passage in his French version. *Le livre de ethiques* (ed. Menut, p. 149).

That moral philosophers can proclaim only generalities is indeed argued in Aristotle's *Politics*. The discussion occurs in 2.8 of the Greek text (1269a9–29); in 2.8 of the so-called *translatio imperfecta* by William of Moerbeke (ed. Michaud-Quantin, p. 46); and in 2.15 of Oresme's own glossed French translation, *Le livre de politiques* (ed. Menut, pp. 98–99). Aristotle notes that laws are framed in general terms and he raises the issue of how, when, and by whom laws may be changed. He allows that some laws sometimes need to be changed and then puts the inquiry off to another time. He definitely does not say here what Oresme seems to attribute to him. I have found no modern editor or translator of this passage who indicates that Aristotle did take this up elsewhere. Neither Aquinas's commentary nor Oresme's French version even hints at the position assigned to Aristotle here; but see *Ethics* 5.10 (1137b10–25).

3. The medieval Latin version of Alhazen's *Perspectiva* was published by Risner in the *Opticae thesaurus* in 1572. All citations in these notes are to the book, proposition, and page number of that edition. Of course Alhazen is discussing only the sense of sight, not all senses as Oresme implies. The importance of Alhazen's work for Oresme's analyses within the *De causis*, which extends beyond the specific citations made by Oresme and identified whenever possible in these notes, is indicated by the following remarks which open a major reanalysis of the theory of perception found in Alhazen's work: "Alhazen's theory of visual perception occupies a considerable part of his *Optics*, itself a large work in seven books averaging about forty-three thousand words each. . . . Book II, on the objects of vision and the manner of their apprehension, contains the core of the theory of perception. Book III is on the errors of direct vision and deals, among other things, with errors of 'pure sensation,' of recognition, and of perceptual inferences. The errors of vision through reflection from mirrors of various types are the subject of Book VI, and the last chapter of Book VII is concerned with errors due to refraction" (Sabra, "Sensation and Inference," p. 160). Setting medieval writings on *perspectiva* into the context of theories of visual cognition is the aim of Smith's "Getting the Big Picture in Perspectivist Optics." As Smith's article appeared as the present study was going to press, many of the implications of his analysis could not be taken into account in the notes which follow; but consider Smith's summary of his argument: "The ulterior concern of the perspectivists was epistemology and . . . *perspectiva* should be understood as the science not of visual perception alone, but of visual *cognition*. To support this thesis, I place the perspectivist theory within the broader context of the medieval theory of 'cognition by abstraction' and show how, within that context, vision was effectively reduced to a coherent succession of stages through which we forge a mental passage to objective reality" ("Getting the Big Picture," p. 569). This analysis seems to accord well with the way Oresme, at least in the *De causis*, uses epistemological and psychological and perspectivist notions in an integrated fashion without attention to their origins in distinct disciplines.

4. Witelo's *Perspectiva* was published along with Alhazen's by Risner in the *Opticae thesaurus* in 1572. It follows Alhazen's work with new pagination. (A new edition of Witelo's work is presently being published by the Polish Academy of Sciences. All citations in these notes are to the book, proposition, and page number of the Risner edition. Witelo 4.2 (p. 118): "Impossibile est visum unam intentionum visibilium per se solam comprehendere."

5. This seems to refer to Alhazen 2.72 (p. 72). "Generales visibilis species citius percipiuntur singularibus," even though Alhazen does not posit a proportionality, as Oresme does. It could also derive from Alhazen 2.74 (p. 73), "Tempus obtutus pro specierum visibilium varietate variat."

6. Witelo compares the time for perceiving the characters of the individual and of the species (rather than of the species and the genus): and he posits no proportionality. Witelo 4.71 (p. 116): "Visus in formis individualibus minori tempore comprehendit intentiones speciales quam individuales." For another statement on the time needed for seeing, see Witelo 3.56 (p. 110).

7. In Chapter Two Oresme makes a similar argument (following Boethius) regarding the fact that sounds—which are discrete, but rapid, vibrations—are perceived as continuous due to the short time intervals of silence which pass too quickly to be perceived. This parallel would seem to support my interpretation of Oresme's position, namely that insufficiency of judgment is the reason for the phenomenon of the glowing circle. In such arguments one must be careful to state that the short time intervals, when there is no sound or when the moving ember is not present at any given point, are not perceived, rather than to claim that they are not perceivable. Oresme's statement in the *Questions on the Meteora* ("propter . . . mutacionem . . . insensibilem") seems careless in this regard and is thus in direct opposition to Aristotle's lengthy argument in *De sensu* 8 (448a20–448b18) that there is no such thing as imperceptible time.

8. This is not found in Witelo 4.28 (or 4.16). This particular illusion is mentioned above in the Prologue. See Oresme's explanation of it below in this chapter.

9. I have not found these examples in Witelo's Book 4.

10. Actually in Chapter 2 of Aristotle's *De insomniis* (460b1–3) ed. Drossaart Lulofs, medieval Latin text on p. 17 of Part 2. Of course Aristotle's explanation does not utilize the (medieval) notion of *species*. In the medieval Latin translations, the *De insomniis* circulated as the second tract or second book of the *De somno et vigilia*; and the *De divinatione per somnum* was regarded as Book 3. For all three of these works,

Drossaart Lulofs has edited the Greek text along with the two medieval Latin translations, *De somno et vigilia liber* (= Book 1 in the medieval arrangement) in 1943 and *De insomniis et De divinatione per somnum* (= Books 2 and 3 of *De somno* in the medieval arrangement) in 1947.

11. Aristotle, *De somno* (455a16–23) ed. Drossaart Lulofs, medieval Latin text on p. 4.

12. This example is found in Aristotle, *De sensu et sensato*, 447a15–20, not in the *De somno*.

13. Aristotle, *De somno* (455b10–13) ed. Drossaart Lulofs, medieval Latin text on p. 5.

14. Oresme uses this example repeatedly without citing Aristotle each time. The case itself is mentioned or discussed by Aristotle in many places: in *De insomniis* (cited here by Oresme as the second tract of *De somno*; see n. 10 shortly above), in the *Metaphysics*, at least three times in the *Problems* (cited once by Oresme), and perhaps elsewhere. Some of these Aristotelian texts are quoted in this note. Both in Oresme's sentence and in the traditional Aristotle texts, it is not very clear just why an object held in between two crossed fingers should cause the perception of two objects rather than just one. The point seems to be that the object touches simultaneously the *outer* sides of the two fingers thus producing sensations which normally only two objects could produce. See *De insomniis* (460b1–27) ed. Drossaart Lulofs; the passage cited here, in the medieval Latin translation used by Oresme, is on pp. 17 and 19 of Part 2.

15. These ideas of Aristotle are found in Chapters 7, 8, and 11 of *De motu animalium* (also in part in *De anima*, *De caelo*, and *De insomniis*). The notion that a small cause can have a great effect is one of the main themes throughout Oresme's *Contra divinatores* and *De causis*. Aristotle expresses this idea in *De caelo* and in *De insomniis* 2 (460a23–24).

16. This distinction of straight, reflected, and refracted rays—a common view—is also expressed by Oresme in Question 12 in Book 3 of his *Questions on the Meteora* (ed. McCluskey, pp. 136–137). But as McCluskey notes, Oresme adds a fourth category of mixed reflected and refracted rays in a later discussion in Question 20 of Book 3 as well as in his *De visione stellarum* (ibid., pp. 50, 266–267, 408, 442–443). Viewing a penny at the bottom of a vase is commonly employed as an example of two different phenomena: either (a) that the penny seems larger when the vase is filled with water or (b) that the penny can be seen from farther to the side when water is present than when the vase is empty. The first case is found in Ptolemy's *Almagest* 1.3 and in John of Sacrobosco's popular *De sphaera* 1 (cf. Thorndike, *The Sphere of Sacrobosco*, and Grant, *A Source Book*, p. 444). The second phenomenon is described and the first is mentioned briefly by Oresme in the third conclusion of Question 12 in Book 3 of his *Questions on the Meteora* (ed. McCluskey, pp. 142–145); McCluskey (p. 409) gives references to earlier discussions by Alhazen, Witelo, Pecham, Bacon, and Albertus Magnus. Ockham mentions this in his *Questions on the Sentences (Reportatio)* 3.2, ed. Kelley and Etzkorn, pp. 78 and 95. Question 53 of the *Tabula problematum* asks, "Why is a penny at the bottom of a water-filled vase seen from farther away than in an empty vase?"

17. Aristotle, *Meteora* 3 (373b1 ff.; Latin translation in Aquinas's *Expositio*, ed. Spiazzi, p. 624). Here Aristotle gives the example of a man with weak sight who always sees an image in front of him and facing him. The reason (assuming the extramission theory of vision) is that for weak enough sight even air acts as a mirror and reflects the man's image back to him. Oresme cites this example below and always designates this man with weak sight Antiphon. In the *Meteora* itself Aristotle does not name this man, but Oresme's Antiphon seems clearly an error for Antipheron, a name which Oresme could have taken from either Aquinas's *Expositio Meteorologicorum* 3, lect. 5 (ed. Spiazzi, p. 625) or from the commentary of Alexander of Aphrodisias (Aquinas's source?), which was translated into Latin by William of Moerbeke in 1260 (ed. Smet, p. 233). Alexander identified this man with Antipheron of Oreus, whom Aristotle named in the *De memoria* (451a9) as a lunatic who takes his fantasies for realities. McCluskey ("Oresme on Light," p. 430) notes that Antiphon can be found instead of Antipheron in the variant readings of Peter of Auvergne's *Commentary* and in the *Questions* of Albert of Saxony and Themon Judei, and he suggests that the misreading of Antiphon for Antipheron "would be reinforced by considering the name as not referring to a historical personage, but to those who see themselves antiphonally reflected in the medium." See also 1.107–109 and n. 20 shortly below for more information on Antiphon.

18. I believe that Oresme's brief statement means that if not for atmospheric reflection we would see only bright objects and dark shadows.

19. The example of the stick which appears bent or broken is a common one in writings both of perspectivist science and of philosophical skepticism. McCluskey ("Oresme on Light," pp. 410–411) reviews this history and gives references to a number of instances within each tradition: to Cicero, Augustine, Tertullian, Lucretius, Sextus Empiricus, and Seneca for discussions of the bent stick's skeptical implications, and to Geminos, Ptolemy, Bacon, and Pecham for perspectivist analyses. Readers of Oresme's quodlibetal *De causis* may find interest in McCluskey's further comments: "Since Bacon diverges from both traditions, we cannot be absolutely certain of his source. . . . He may have been aware of both traditions, since he cited Ptolemy frequently on optical matters and Cicero's *Academica* on the causes of errors (*Opus majus*, part 1, cap. 2, vol. 1, p. 5, [ed. Bridges]). It is also possible that the problem was already discussed in these terms among [Bacon's] contemporaries, as in both the *Perspectiva* and the *Opus ter-*

tium . . . Bacon chides the common philosophers and artists who speak of this in quodlibetal questions when they are ignorant of the principles of perspective and particularly of the laws of refraction. I have not found the discussion to which Bacon refers, as it does not appear in the quodlibets of his usual opponent, Albertus Magnus, nor does a likely place for such a discussion appear in any quodlibetal questions dated earlier than 1267 (the date of the composition of the *Perspectiva*) that are listed in Glorieux, *La Littérature quodlibétique*" (p. 411).

20. This very brief statement that air can reflect sufficiently to cause Antiphon's seeing his reflection seems to be in agreement with an opinion expressed by Oresme in Question 15 in Book 3 of his *Questions on the Meteora* (McCluskey, "Oresme on Light," pp. 218–221) but in opposition to the much more extended argument he makes in Question 19 of Book 3, where it is suggested that Antiphon's view of himself is due to humours in the eyes, the fantasy, or the common sense interfering with his judgment (ibid., pp. 228–259, esp. 248–251, and the notes on pp. 430 and 437–438). This latter argument is similar to some of the explanations Oresme gives in the next few paragraphs of the *De causis*.

21. For the remainder of this first chapter, Oresme cites numerous cases of hallucinations and of things misperceived on account of the interference of a strong image, desire, or other mental obstruction; and the issue recurs in Chapter Three for the sayings of maniacs (3.911–958) and in Chapter Four regarding passions distorting judgments (4.899–1105). Melancholy humours are explicitly cited as a possible natural cause for such phenomena throughout the *De causis*. In Oresme's *Questions on the Meteora* 3.19 (ed. in McCluskey, "Oresme on Light," pp. 248–249) such humours serve as an explanation for Antiphon seeing his own image. In *De configurationibus* 2.34 (ed. Clagett, pp. 370–371), Oresme briefly mentions movement of "corporeal spirits or fumes" as the cause of visions among melancholics and frenetics; he discusses visions resulting from illness or damaged interior organs in 2.29 (pp. 344–349). Aristotle had explained, in *De memoria* 2 (453a15–30), how melancholics are especially affected by mental pictures on account of movements of moisture about the sensitive region. Oresme's commonplace examples also reappear in more elegant form in Shakespeare's *A Midsummer Night's Dream* 5.1:

> The lunatic, the lover, and the poet.
> Are of imagination all compact:
> One sees more devils than vast hell can hold.
> That is, the madman; the lover, all as frantic.
> See Helen's beauty in a brow in Egypt:
> The poet's eye, in a fine frenzy rolling
> Doth glance from heaven to earth, from earth to heaven:
> And, as imagination bodies forth
> The forms of things unknown, the poet's pen
> Turns them to shapes, and gives to airy nothing
> A local habitation and a name.
> Such tricks hath strong imagination.
> That, if it would but apprehend some joy,
> It comprehends some bringer of that joy:
> Or, in the night, imagining some fear.
> How easy is a bush suppos'd a bear!

22. Although *lux* and *lumen* have distinct technical meanings in the perspectivist literature of the fourteenth century, they are both translated simply as "light" throughout this book because the distinction between them is never made part of the argument in the *De causis*. The distinction is acknowledged, even if not employed in the argument, at certain points with phrases like "lux et lumen" and "lux vel lumen." For an explanation of the technical meanings, see Lindberg, "The Science of Optics," pp. 356–357: Lindberg also notes that the distinction was often ignored and that Bacon claimed to have used the words interchangeably (ibid., p. 367). McCluskey examines the ways Oresme uses these terms in the *Questions on the Geometry of Euclid*, the *De configurationibus*, and the *Questions on the Meteora*, and shows that Oresme closely follows the distinction as set out in Part 1, Chap. 1, of Bacon's *De multiplicatione specierum* (in *Opus majus* ed. Bridges, Vol. 2, p. 409), except where "it is clear from the context that Oresme has abandoned the distinction" (McCluskey, "Oresme on Light," pp. 415–416).

23. Aristotle discussed this in passing in his critique of a theory which made vision consist of the element fire (*De sensu* 2, especially at 437a20–b15).

24. Regarding Antiphon see nn. 17 and 20 shortly above.

25. See n. 19 shortly above.

26. See n. 7 above in this chapter.

27. Similar examples are found in Aristotle's *De insomniis* 2 (460b1–10), namely that "the sensation still remains perceptible even after the external object perceived has gone, and moreover that we are easily deceived about our perceptions when we are in emotional states . . . , e.g., the coward in his fear, the

lover in his love; so that even from a very faint resemblance the coward thinks that he sees his enemy, and the lover his loved one; and in proportion to his excitement, his imagination is stimulated by a more remote resemblance" (tr. Hett in *Parva naturalia*, pp. 358–361).

28. Book 3 of Aristotle's *Problems* deals with the effects of drinking wine and drunkenness. The examples here seem to come from Problems 9, 10, and 20.

29. In his analysis of Oresme's treatment of optics and vision (*Theories of Vision*, pp. 135–137), Lindberg quotes this concluding paragraph of the chapter to show how "Oresme spells out the nature of his attempts to integrate the ideas of Aristotle with those of Alhazen and Witelo."

PART VII

UNIVERSALS

CHAPTER 37

Peter Abelard

(See Chapter Nine for biography.)

Abelard on Universals

In the *Isagoge* Porphyry raises three questions concerning the nature of universals: (1) Do genera and species (e.g., the universals animal and man) possess independent existence, or are they mental constructs? (2) If universals do, in fact, possess independent existence, are they corporeal or incorporeal? (3) Do universals exist apart from sensible things, or do they exist in sensible objects? To these Abelard adds a fourth question: (4) If the referent of a universal term were to cease to exist (as would be the case for the word 'rose' if all roses ceased to exist), could the universal term still carry with it mental significance (that is, meaning)?

In developing his theory of universals with the goal of answering these questions, Abelard insists that a universal is not a thing (e.g., a Platonic Form). Were it such, as the (extreme) realist maintains, there would ultimately be no way to distinguish between instances of it. Not only would Socrates and Plato be identical by virtue of possessing the essence man, such identity would also occur between individuals possessing contrary or incompatible qualities (e.g., a rational animal becomes identical to an irrational one by virtue of both possessing the essence animal). Such a consequence is obviously unacceptable.

To avoid the problems of both (extreme) realism and nominalism Abelard develops a theory of abstraction. The mind is capable of distinguishing between matter and form although the two never, in fact, exist in isolation. Such is the power of abstraction. The process of abstraction is such that it allows one to concentrate on one or another aspect of a particular. This mental power to focus has a parallel to sense perception. If one perceives an object composed partly of gold and partly of silver, he can concentrate his attention at one moment on the gold and at another instant on the silver. This attention to different aspects of the composite object in no way leads one to conclude with respect to that specific perception that the two aspects, gold and silver, are separate from the object being perceived. So too with abstraction one does not conclude that the quality that is the subject of concentration is something separate from the substance it qualifies. Universals, then, are the products of abstraction. Universals are *sermones*, concepts. On this basis Abelard has very often been judged a conceptualist. Such a conclusion, however, would be hasty.

He also refers to universal terms as *sermones*. They are that which are predicable of many. There is a real basis justifying predication. In other words, objects, as a matter of fact, possess (real) characteristics. This reality, consisting of both matter and form, also provides the subject matter for abstraction. Consequently, one can safely argue that Abelard is a moderate realist.

How, then, does Abelard answer Porphyry's questions? To the first he says that contrary to the nominalist claim that universal *terms* refer to nothing at all, they do refer to reality, namely, real aspects of particulars. Nevertheless, *universals* are the products of abstraction and as such are only thought "objects". As to the second question, the answer depends on one's interpretation. On the one hand, universals are corporeal in that their referents are real qualities. On the other hand, they are incorporeal by virtue of the way in which they are conceived. The answer to the third question follows from the answers to the first two. It is threefold: (1) Universals may exist only in sensible objects (e.g., the mind). (2) They may subsist in sensible things, such as the color whiteness subsists in those particulars which are white. (3) The divine spirit and the soul are incorporeal and exist unto themselves apart from sensible objects. Finally, he answers his own question. If all the things named by a universal word were to cease existing, the word would nevertheless retain its meaning, as would be the case if all roses ceased to exist. Otherwise, observes Abelard, "There is no rose" would not be a proposition.

GLOSSES ON PORPHYRY FROM *LOGICA INGREDIENTIBUS* "ON UNIVERSALS"

Porphyry, as Boethius points out [in his Commentary on the *Isagoge*], raises three profitable questions whose answers are shrouded in mystery and though not a few philosophers have attempted to solve them, few have succeeded in doing so. The first is: Do genera and species really exist or are they simply something in the mind? It is as if [Porphyry] were asking whether their existence is a fact or merely a matter of opinion. The second is: Granting they do exist, are they corporeal or incorporeal? The third is: Do they exist apart from sensible things or only in them? For there are two types of incorporeal things. Some, like God or the soul, can subsist in their incorporeality apart from anything sensible. Others are unable to exist apart from the sensible objects in which they are found. A line, for example, is unable to exist apart from some bodily subject.

Reprinted with the permission of The Free Press, an imprint of Simon & Schuster from *Medieval Philosophy: From St. Augustine to Nicholas of Cusa* by John F. Wippel and Allan B. Wolter. Copyright 1969 by The Free Press, pp. 190–203.

Porphyry sidesteps answering them with the remark: "For the present I refuse to be drawn into a discussion as to whether genus and species exist in reality or solely and simply in thought; or if they do exist whether they are corporeal or incorporeal, or whether, on the admission they are incorporeal, they are separated from sensibles or exist only in and dependent upon sensible things, and other things of this sort."

"Other things of this sort" can be interpreted in various ways. We could take him to mean: "I refuse to discuss these three questions and other related matters." For other relevant questions could be raised that pose similar problems. For instance, what is the common basis or reason for applying universal names to things, which boils down to explaining to what extent different things agree; or how should one understand those universal names wherein one seems to conceive of nothing, where the universal term in a word seems to have no referent? And there are many other difficult points. By understanding "other things of this sort" in this way, we can add a fourth question: Do genera and species, as long as they remain such, require that the subject they name have some reality or, if all the things they designate were destroyed, could the universal consist simply in its significance for the mind, as would be the case with the name "rose" when no roses are in bloom which it could designate in general? . . .[1]

Since genera and species are obviously instances of universals and in mentioning them Porphyry touches on the nature of universals in general, we may distinguish the properties common to universals by studying them in these samples. Let us inquire then whether they apply only to *words* or to *things* as well.

Aristotle[2] defines the universal as "that which is of such a nature as to be predicated of many." Porphyry, on the other hand, goes on to define the singular or individual as "that which is predicated of a single individual."[3]

Authorities then seem to apply "universal" to things as much as they do to words. Aristotle himself does this, declaring by way of preface to his definition of the universal, that "some things are universal, others individual. Now by 'universal' I mean that which is of such a nature as to be predicated of many, whereas 'individual' is not something of this kind."[4] Porphyry too, having stated that the species is composed of a genus and difference, proceeds to locate it in the nature of things. From this it is clear that things themselves fall under a universal noun.

Nouns too are called universals. That is why Aristotle says: "The genus specifies the quality with reference to substance, for it signifies what sort of thing it is."[5]

"It seems then that things as well as words are called universals. . . ."[6]

However, things taken either singly or collectively cannot be called universals, because they are not predicable of many. Consequently it remains to ascribe this form of universality to words alone. Just as grammarians call certain nouns proper and

other appellative, so dialecticians call certain simple words particulars, that is, individuals, and other universals. A universal word is one which is able to be predicated of many by reason of its intention, such as the noun "man," which can be joined with the names of particular men by reason of the nature of the subject on which they are imposed. A particular word, however, is one which is predicable only of a single subject, as *Socrates* when it is taken as the name of but one individual. For if you take it equivocally, you give it the signification not of one word but of many. For according to Priscian, many nouns can obviously be brought together in a single word.[7] When a universal then is described as "that which is predicable of many," *that which* indicates not only the simplicity of the word as a discrete expression, but also the unity of signification lacking in an equivocal term. . . .[8]

Now that we have defined "universal" and "particular" in regard to words, let us investigate in particular the properties of those which are universal. For questions have been raised about universals, since serious doubts existed as to their meaning because there seemed to be no subject to which they referred. Neither did they express the sense of any one thing. These universal terms then appeared to be imposed on nothing, since it is clear that all things subsisting in themselves are individuals and, as has been shown, they do not share in some one thing by virtue of which a universal name could be given to them. Since it is certain then that (a) universals are not imposed on things by reason of their individual differences, for then they would not be common but singular, (b) nor can they designate things which share in some identical entity, for it is not a thing in which they agree, there seems to be nothing from which universals might derive their meaning, particularly since their sense is not restricted to any one thing. . . . Since "man" is imposed on individuals for an identical reason, viz. because each is a rational, mortal animal, the very generality of the designation prevents one from understanding the term of just one man in the way, for example, that one understands by Socrates just one unique person, which is why it is called a particular. But the common term "man" does not mean just Socrates, or any other man. Neither does it designate a collection, nor does it, as some think, mean just Socrates insofar as he is man. For even if Socrates alone were sitting in this house and because of that the proposition "A man sits in this house" is true, still by the name "man," there is no way of getting to Socrates except insofar as he too is a man. Otherwise, from the proposition itself, "sitting" would be understood to inhere in Socrates, so that from "A man sits in this house," one could infer "Socrates sits in this house." And the same applies to any other individual man. Neither can "A man sits in this house" be understood of a collection, since the proposition can be true if only one man is there. Consequently, there is not a single thing that "man" or any other universal term seems to signify, since there is not a single thing whose sense the term seems to express. Neither does it seem there could be any sense if no subject is thought of. Universals then appear to be totally devoid of meaning.

And yet this is not the case. For universals do signify distinct individuals to the extent of giving names to them, but this significative function does not require that one grasps a sense which arises out of them and which belongs to each of them. "Man," for example, does name individual things, but for the common reason that they are all men. That is why it is called a universal. Also there is a certain sense—common, not proper—that is applicable to those individuals which one conceives to be alike.

But let us look carefully now into some matters we have touched on only briefly, viz. (a) what is the common reason for imposing a universal name on things, (b) what is this intellectual conception of a common likeness, and (c) is a word said to be common because of some common cause by virtue of which all the things it designates are alike, or is it merely because

we have a common concept for all of them, or is it for both of these reasons?

Let us consider first the question of the common cause. As we noted earlier, each individual man is a discrete subject since he has as proper to himself not only an essence but also whatever forms [or qualifications] that essence may have. Nevertheless, they agree in this that they are all men. Since there is no man who is not a discrete or distinct individual thing, I do not say they agree "in man," but "in being a man." Now if you consider the matter carefully, man or any other thing is not the same as "to be a man," even as "not to be in a subject" is not a thing, nor is there anything which is "not to undergo contrariety" or "not to be subject to greater or lesser degrees," and still Aristotle says these are points in which all substances agree. Since there is no *thing* in which things could possibly agree, if there is any agreement among certain things, this must not be taken to be some *thing*. Just as Socrates and Plato are alike in being men, so a horse and donkey are alike in not being men. It is for this reason that they are called "nonmen." Different individuals then agree either in being the same or in not being the same, e.g. in being men or white, or in not being men or being white.

Still this agreement among things (which itself is not a thing) must not be regarded as a case of bringing together things which are real on the basis of nothing. In point of fact we do speak of this agreeing with that to the extent of their having the same status, that of man, i.e. the two agree in that they are men. But what we perceive is merely that they are men, and there is not the slightest difference between them, I say, in their being men, even thought we may not call this an essence. But "being a man" (which is not a thing) we do call "the status of man" and we have also called it "the common cause for imposing on individuals a universal name." For we frequently give the name "cause" to some characteristic that is not itself a thing as when one says "He was beaten because he did not wish to appear in court." His not wishing to appear in court, cited here as a cause is not a [constitutive] essence [of his being beaten].

We can also designate as "the status of man" those things themselves in a man's nature which the one who imposed the word conceives according to a common likeness.

Having shown how universals signify, namely by functioning as names of things, and having presented what the reason for imposing such general names is, let us indicate just what these universal meanings consist of.

To begin with, let us point out the distinguishing features of all intellectual conception or understanding. Though sense perception as well as intellectual conception are both functions of the soul, there is a difference between the two. Bodies and what inhere in them are objects of sensory knowledge, e.g. a tower or its sensory qualities. In the exercise of this function, however, the soul makes use of corporeal instruments. In understanding or conceiving something intellectually, the soul needs no corporeal organ and consequently no bodily subject in which the thought object inheres is required. It is enough that the mind constructs for itself a likeness of these things and the action called intellection is concerned with this [cognitive content]. Hence, if the tower is removed or destroyed, the sense perception that dealt with it perishes, but the intellectual conception of the tower remains in the likeness preserved in the mind. As the act of sense perception is not the sensed thing itself, so the act of the intellect is not itself the form understood or conceived intellectually. Understanding is an activity of the soul by virtue of which it is said to understand, but the form toward which understanding is directed is a kind of image or construct (res ficta) which the mind fashions for itself at will, like those imaginary cities seen in dreams or the form of a projected building which the architect conceives after the manner of a blueprint. This construct is not

something one can call either substance or accident.

Nevertheless, there are those who simply identify it with the act itself through which it is understood or conceived. Thus they speak of the tower building itself, which I think of when the tower is not there and which I conceive to be lofty, square, and situated in a spacious plain, as being the same as thinking of a tower. But we prefer to call the [conceptual] image as such the likeness of the thing.

There is of course nothing to prevent the act of understanding itself from being called in some sense a "likeness" because it obviously conceives what is, properly speaking, a likeness of the thing. Still, as we have said—and rightly so—the two are not the same. For, I ask: "Does the squareness or loftiness represent the actual form or quality possessed by the act of understanding itself when one thinks of the height and the way the tower is put together?" Surely the actual squareness and height are present only in bodies and from an imagined quality no act of understanding or any other real essence can be constructed. What remains then but that the substance, like the quality of which it is the subject, is also fictive? Perhaps one could say that a mirror or reflected image is not itself a true "thing," since there often appears on the whitish surface of the mirror a color of contrary quality. . . .[9]

Having treated in general the nature of understanding, let us consider how a universal and a particular conception differ. The conception associated with a universal name is an image that is general and indiscriminate [imago communis et confusa], whereas the image associated with a singular word represents the proper and characteristic form, as it were, of a single thing, i.e. it applies to one and only one person. When I hear the word "man," for instance, a certain likeness arises in my mind which is so related to individual men that it is proper to none but common to all. But when I hear "Socrates," a certain form arises in my mind which is the likeness of a particular person. . . . Hence it is correct to say "man" does not rightly signify Socrates or any other man, since by virtue of this name no one in particular is identified; yet it is a name of particular things. "Socrates," on the other hand, must not only name a particular thing, but it must also determine just what thing is its subject. . . . To show what pertains to the nature of all lions, a picture can be constructed which represents nothing that is the peculiar property of only one of them. On the other hand, a picture suited to distinguish any one of them can be drawn by depicting something proper to the one in question, for example, by painting it as limping, maimed, or wounded by the spear of Hercules. Just as one can paint one figure that is general and another that is particular, so too can one form one conception of things that is common and another conception that is proper.

There is some question, however, and not without reason, whether or not this [universal] name also signifies this conceptual form to which the understanding is directed. Both authority and reason, however, seem to be unanimous in affirming that it does.

For Priscian, after first showing how universals were applied commonly to individuals, seemed to introduce another meaning they had, namely the common form. He states that "the general and special forms of things which were given intelligibility in the divine mind before being produced in bodies could be used to reveal what the natural genera and species of things are."[10] In this passage he views God after the fashion of an artist who first conceives in his mind a [model or] exemplar form of what he is to fashion and who works according to the likeness of this form, which form is said to be embodied when a real thing is constructed in its likeness.

It may be all right to ascribe such a common conception to God, but not to man. For those works of God like a man, a soul, or a stone represent general or special states of nature, whereas those of a human artisan like a house or a sword do not. For "house"

and "sword" do not pertain to nature as the other terms do. They are the names not of a substance but of something accidental and therefore they are neither genera nor ultimate species. Conceptions by abstraction [of the true nature of things] may well be ascribed to the divine mind but may not be ascribed to that of man, because men, who know things only through the medium of their senses, scarcely ever arrive at such an ideal understanding and never conceive the [underlying] natures of things in their purity. But God knew all things he created for what they were and this even before they actually existed. He can discriminate between these individual states as they are in themselves; senses are no hindrance to him who alone has true understanding of things. Of those things which men have not experienced through the senses, they happen to have opinions rather than understanding, as we learn from experience. For having thought of some city before seeing it, we find on arriving there that it is quite different than we had thought.

And so I believe we have only an opinion about those forms like rationality, mortality, paternity, or what is within. Names for what we experience, however, produce understanding to the extent they can do so, for the one who coined the terms intended that they be imposed in accord with the [true] nature or properties of things, even though he himself was unable to do justice in thought to the nature or property of the thing. It is these common concepts, however, which Priscian calls general and special [i.e. generic and specific], that these general names or the names of species bring to the mind. He says that the universals function as proper names with regard to such conceptions, and although these names refer to the essences named only in an indiscriminate fashion, they direct the mind of the hearer immediately to that common conception in the same way that proper names direct attention to the one thing that they signify.

Porphyry too, in distinguishing between things constituted only in the likeness of matter and form and those actually composed of matter and form, seems to understand this common conception by the former. Boethius also, when he calls the conception gathered from a likeness of many things a genus or a species, seems to have in mind this same common conception. Some think that Plato subscribed to this view, i.e. to these common ideas—which he located in the *nous*—he gave the names of genus and species. On this point, perhaps, Boethius indicates some disagreement between Plato and Aristotle, where he speaks of Plato claiming not only that genera, species, and the rest should be understood to be universals, but also that they also have true existence and subsistence apart from bodies, as if to say that Plato understood these common concepts, which he assumed to exist in a bodiless form in the *nous*, to be universals. He means here by universal "a common likeness of many things" perhaps, rather than "predicable of many" as Aristotle understood the term. For this conception [itself] does not seem to be predicated of many in the way that a name is able to be applied to each of many things.

But his [i.e. Boethius'] statement that Plato thinks universals subsist apart from sensibles can be interpreted in another way, so that there is no disagreement between the philosophers. For Aristotle's statements about universals always subsisting in sensibles is to be understood of the way they actually do exist, because the animal nature (which the universal name "animal" designates and which is called a kind of universal in a transferred sense of the term) is never found to exist in anything which is not sensible. Plato, however, thinks this nature has such a natural subsistence in itself that it would retain its existence if it were not subject to sense [i.e. if it were not clothed with sensible accidents]. Hence what Aristotle denies to be actually the case, Plato, the investigator of the nature, ascribes to a natural capacity. Consequently there is no real disagreement between them.

Reason too seems to agree with these authorities in their apparent claim that the universal names designate these common concepts or forms. For what else does to conceive of them by name mean but that names signify them? But since we hold that these forms conceived are not simply the same as the acts of knowing them, there is in addition to the real thing and the act of understanding a third factor, viz. the signification or meaning of the name. Now while there is no authority for holding this, still it is not contrary to reason.

At this point, let us give an answer to the question we promised earlier to settle, namely whether the ability of universal words to refer to things in general is due to the fact that there is in them a common cause for imposing the words on them, or whether it is due to the fact that a common concept of them exists, or whether it is for both of these reasons. Now there seems to be no ground why it should not be for both of these reasons, but if we understand "common cause" as involving something of the nature of the things, then this seems to be the stronger of the two reasons.

Another point we must clarify is the one noted earlier, namely that these universal conceptions are formed by abstraction, and we must show how one can speak of them as isolated, naked, and pure without their being empty. But first about abstraction. Here we must remember that while matter and form are always fused together, the rational power of the mind is such that it can consider matter alone or form alone or both together. The first two are considerations by way of abstraction, since in order to study its precise nature, they abstract one thing from what does not exist alone. The third type of consideration is by way of synthesis. The substance of man, for instance, is a body, an animal, a man; it is invested with no end of forms. But when I turn my attention exclusively to the material essence of a substance, disregarding all its additional forms or qualifications, my understanding takes the form of a concept by abstraction. If I direct my attention, however, to nothing more than the corporeity of this substance, the resulting concept, though it represents a synthesis when compared with the previous concept (that of substance alone), is still formed by abstraction from the forms other than corporeity, such as animation, sensitivity, rationality, or whiteness, none of which I consider.

Such conceptions by abstraction might appear to be false or empty, perhaps, since they look to the thing in a way other than that in which it exists. For since they consider matter or form exclusively, and neither of these subsists separately, they clearly represent a conception of the thing otherwise than the way it is. Consequently, they seem to be vacuous, yet this is not really the case. For it is only when a thing is considered to have some property or nature which it does not actually possess that the conception which represents the thing otherwise than it is, is indeed empty. But this is not what happens in abstraction. For when I consider this man only in his nature as a substance or a body, but not as an animal, a man, or a grammarian, certainly I do not think of anything that is not in that nature, and still I do not attend to all that it has. And when I say that I attend only to what is in it, "only" refers to my attention and not to the way this characteristic exists, for otherwise my conception would be empty. For the thing does not have this, but I only consider it as having this. And while I do consider it in some sense to be otherwise than it actually is, I do not consider it to be in a state or condition other than that in which it is, as was pointed out earlier. "Otherwise" means merely that the mode of thought is other than the mode of existing. For the thing in question is thought of not as separated, but separately from the other, even though it does not exist separately. Matter is perceived purely, form simply, even though the former does not exist purely nor the latter simply. Purity and simplicity, in a word, are features of our understanding, not of existence; they are characteristic of the way we think, not of the way things exist. Even the senses often function discriminatively where composite objects are concerned. If a statue is half

gold, half silver, I can look separately at the gold and silver combined there, studying first the gold, then the silver exclusively, thus viewing piecemeal what is actually joined together, and yet I do not perceive to be divided what is not divided. In much the same way "understanding by way of abstraction" means "considering separately" but not "considering [it] as separated." Otherwise such understanding would be vacuous. . . .[11]

But let us return to our *universal* conceptions, which must always be produced by way of abstraction. For when I hear "man" or "whiteness" or "white," I do not recall in virtue of the name all the natures or properties in those subjects to which the name refers. "Man" gives rise to the conception, indiscriminate, not discrete, of animal, rational and mortal only, but not of the additional accidents as well. Conceptions of individuals also can be formed by abstraction, as happens for example when one speaks of "this substance," "this body," "this animal," "this white," or "this whiteness." For by "this man," though I consider just man's nature, I do so as related to a certain subject, whereas by "man" I regard this nature simply in itself and not in relation to some one man. That is why a universal concept is correctly described as being *isolated, bare*, and *pure*: i.e. "isolated from sense," because it is not a perception of the thing as sensory; "bare," because it is abstracted from some or from all forms; "pure," because it is unadulterated by any reference to any single individual, since there is not just one thing, be it the matter or the form, to which it points, as we explained earlier when we described such a conception as indiscriminate.

Now that we have considered these matters, let us proceed to answer the questions posed by Porphyry about genera and species. This we can easily do now that we have clarified the nature of universals in general. The point of the first question was whether genera and species exist. More precisely, are they signs of something which really exists or of something that merely exists in thought, i.e. are they simply vacuous, devoid of any real reference, as is the case with words like "chimera" or "goat-stag," which fail to produce any coherent meaning? To this one has to reply that as a matter of fact they do serve to name things that actually exist and therefore are not the subjects of purely empty thoughts. But what they name are the selfsame things named by singular names. And still, there is a sense in which they exist as isolated, bare, and pure only in the mind, as we have just explained. . . .

The second question, viz. "Are they corporeal or incorporeal?" can be taken in the same way, that is, "Granting that they are signs of existing things, are these things corporeal or incorporeal?" For surely everything that exists, as Boethius puts it, is either corporeal or incorporeal, regardless of whether these words mean respectively: (1) a bodily or a bodiless substance, (2) something perceptible to the senses like man, wood, and whiteness, or something imperceptible in this way like justice or the soul. (3) "Corporeal" can also have the meaning of something discrete or individual, so that the question boils down to asking whether genera and species signify discrete individuals or not. A thoroughgoing investigator of truth considers not only what can be factually stated but also such possible opinions as might be proposed. Consequently, even though one is quite certain that only individuals are real, in view of the fact that someone might be of the opinion that there are other things that exist, it is justifiable to inquire about them. Now this third meaning of "corporeal" makes better sense of our question, reducing it to an inquiry as to whether it is discrete individuals or not that are signified. On the other hand, since nothing existing is incorporeal, i.e. nonindividual, "incorporeal" would seem to be superfluous in Boethius' statement that everything existing is either corporeal or incorporeal. Here the order of the questions, it seems, suggests nothing that would be of help except perhaps that corporeal and incorporeal, taken in another sense, do represent divisions of whatever exists and that this might

also be the case here. The inquirer in this case would seem to be asking, in effect: "Since I see that some existing things are called corporeal and others incorporeal, I would like to know which of these names we should use for what universals signify?" The answer to this would be: "To some extent, 'corporeal' would be appropriate, since the *significata* are in essence discrete individuals. 'Incorporeal' would be a better description, however, of the way a universal term names things, for it does not point to them in an individual and specific fashion but points only in an indiscriminate way, as we have adequately explained above." Hence universal names are described both as corporeal (because of the nature of the things they point to) and as incorporeal (because of the way these things are signified, for although they name discrete individuals, universals do not name them individually or properly).

The third question ("Do they exist apart from or only in sensible things?") arises from the admission that they are incorporeal, since, as we noted [in the opening paragraph], there is a certain sense in which "existing in the sensible" and "not existing in the sensible" represent a division of the incorporeal. Now universals are said to exist in sensible things to the extent that they signify the inner substance of something which is sensible by reason of its external forms. While they signify this same substance actually existing in sensible garb, they point to what is by its nature something distinct from the sensible thing [i.e. as substance it is other than its accidental garb], as we said above in our reinterpretation of Plato. That is why Boethius does not claim that genera and species exist apart from sensible things, but only that they are understood apart from them, to the extent namely that the things conceived generically or specifically are viewed with reference to their nature in a rational fashion rather than in a sensory way, and they could indeed subsist in themselves [i.e. as individual substances] even if stripped of the exterior or [accidental] forms by which they come to the attention of the senses. For we admit that all genera and species exist in things perceptible to the senses. Since our understanding of them has always been described as something apart from the senses, however, they appeared not to be in sensible things in any way. There was every reason, then, to ask whether they could be in sensibles. And to this question, the answer is that some of them are, but only to the extent, as was explained, that they represent the enduring substrate that lies beneath the sensible.

We can take corporeal and incorporeal in this second question as equivalent to sensible and insensible, so that the sequence of questions becomes more orderly. And since our understanding of universals is derived solely from sense perceptions, as has been said, one could appropriately ask whether universals were sensible or insensible. Now the answer is that some of them are sensible (we refer here to the nature of those things classed as sensible) and the same time not sensible (we refer here to the way they are signified). For while it is sensible things that these universals name, they do not designate these things in the way they are perceived by the senses, i.e. as distinct individuals, and when things are designated only in universal terms the senses cannot pick them out. Hence the question arose: "Do universals designate only sensible things, or is there something else they signify?" And the answer to this is that they signify both the sensible things themselves and also that common concept which Priscian ascribes above all to the divine mind.

As for the fourth question we added to the others, our solution is this. We do not want to speak of there being universal *names*[12] when the things they name have perished and they can no longer be predicated of many and are not common names of anything, as would be the case when all the roses were gone. Nevertheless, "rose" would still have meaning for the mind even though it names nothing. Otherwise, "There is no rose" would not be a proposition.[13]

NOTES

1. *Peter Abaelards philosophische Schriften*, ed. B. Geyer in *Beiträge zur Geschichte der Philosophie des Mittelalters* XXI (Münster: Aschendorff, 1933), 7–8.
2. Aristotle, *De interpretatione*, chap. 7 (17a 38).
3. Cf. Boethius, *In Isagogen Porphyrii commenta*, ed. G. Schepss and S. Brandt, *Corpus Scriptorum Ecclesiasticorum Latinorum*, Vol. 48 (Vienna: Tempsky, 1906), 148.
4. Aristotle, loc. cit.
5. Aristotle, *Categoriae*, chap. 5 (3b 20).
6. Abelard, op. cit., 9–10.
7. Priscian, *Institutiones grammaticae*, XVII, in H. Keil, *Grammatici latini*. Vol. 3 (Lipsiae: in aedibus B. G. Teubneri, 1858), 145.22.
8. Abelard, op. cit., 16.
9. Ibid., 18–21.
10. Priscian, op. cit., 135.
11. Abelard, op. cit., 21–26.
12. When Abelard speaks of "there being universal names," he has in mind terms that have actual reference; he distinguishes in a word between signification in the sense of having meaning or sense and denominating, i.e. actually naming or referring to existing things.
13. Abelard, op. cit., 27–30.

CHAPTER 38

John of Salisbury

(See Chapter Twenty-six for biography.)

John of Salisbury on Universals

John of Salisbury is a moderate realist in the tradition of Aristotle. Universals are genera and species and as such do not possess an ontological status independent of particulars. This is not to say, however, that universals are ontologically the same as particulars. Salisbury established the foundation of his position by observing that we have the mental capacity to distinguish between form and matter. For example, one can observe a piece of chalk and concentrate on its form being cylindrical, or one can concentrate on its content being chalk. Although this process of abstraction is clearly possible, no one can conceive of form as existing apart from matter. He applies this reasoning mutatis mutandis to genera and species versus particulars. One can concentrate on those characteristics that determine a particular to be what it is. What a particular is is by virtue of being some type of thing or other.

Alternatively, one can concentrate on the content (i.e., substance) of a particular. Nevertheless, "a particular thing cannot possess substance or be known by us, unless it is a [certain] species or genus, that is, unless it is some [sort of] thing, or is known as this or that. Thus, in a way, the form exists through the matter, while conversely the matter is determined by the form. Consequently, genera and species are not things that are really and by nature unrelated to individual things. Rather, they are mental representations of actual, natural things, intellectual images of the mutual likenesses of real things, reflected, as it were, in the mirror of the soul's native purity." Here, Salisbury's choice of mental representation is unfortunate since it connotes an actual mental image the content of which consists solely of the essential characteristics by which a particular qualifies as the type of thing that it is. Two devastating problems arise were this the case: (1) the mental representation which is presumably the universal is, in fact, a particular, and (2) as George Berkeley observed, no one ever has or is capable of having such mental representations. Fortunately, Salisbury attempts to clarify this notion by suggesting that the significata of predicative terms are simply species or genera. Upon hearing the word 'man,' for example, one does not (mentally) picture a particular man or other. Nor does he mentally run through all men. Rather, the term 'man' signifies a certain kind of thing, and that is what one thinks of upon hearing the word 'man'.

THE METALOGICON

Book II

Chapter 17

In What a Pernicious Manner Logic is Sometimes Taught; and the Ideas of Moderns About [the Nature of] Genera and Species.[1]

To show off their knowledge, our contemporaries dispense their instruction in such a way that their listeners are at a loss to understand them. They seem to have the impression that every letter of the alphabet is pregnant with the secrets of Minerva.[2] They analyze and press upon tender ears everything that anyone has ever said or done. Falling into the error condemned by Cicero, they frequently come to be unintelligible to their hearers more because of the multiplicity than the profundity of their statements. "It is indeed useful and advantageous for disputants," as Aristotle observes,[3] "to take cognizance of several opinions on a topic." From the mutual disagreement thus brought into relief, what is seen to be poorly stated may be disproved or modified. Instruction in elementary logic does not, however, constitute the proper occasion for such procedure. Simplicity, brevity, and easy subject matter are, so far as is possible, appropriate in introductory studies. This is so true that it is permissible to expound many difficult points in a simpler way than their nature strictly requires. Thus, much that we have learned in our youth must later be amended in more advanced philosophical studies. Nevertheless, at present, all are here [in introductory logical studies] declaiming on the nature of universals, and attempting to explain, contrary to the intention of the author,[4] what is really a most profound question, and a matter [that should be reserved] for more advanced studies. One holds that

From *The Metalogicon of John of Salisbury*, translated with an introduction and notes by Daniel D. McGarry (Berkeley and Los Angeles: University of California Press, 1955), pp. 111–141. Reprinted by kind permission of Daniel D. McGarry.

universals are merely word sounds,[5] although this opinion, along with its author Roscelin, has already almost completely passed into oblivion.[6] Another maintains that universals are word concepts,[7] and twists to support his thesis everything that he can remember to have ever been written on the subject.[8] Our Peripatetic of Pallet, Abelard, was ensnared in this opinion. He left many, and still has, to this day, some followers and proponents of his doctrine. They are friends of mine, although they often so torture the helpless[9] letter that even the hardest heart is filled with compassion for the latter. They hold that it is preposterous to predicate a thing concerning a thing, although Aristotle is author of this monstrosity. For Aristotle frequently asserts that a thing is predicated concerning a thing,[10] as is evident to anyone who is really familiar with his teaching. Another is wrapped up in a consideration of acts of the [intuitive] understanding,[11] and says that genera and species are nothing more than the latter.[12] Proponents of this view take their cue[13] from Cicero[14] and Boethius,[15] who cite Aristotle as saying that universals should be regarded as and called "notions."[16] "A notion," they tell us, "is the cognition of something, derived from its previously perceived form, and in need of unravelment."[17] Or again [they say]: "A notion is an act of the [intuitive] understanding, a simple mental comprehension."[18] They accordingly distort everything written, with an eye to making acts of [intuitive] understanding or "notions" include the universality of universals. Those who adhere to the view that universals are things,[19] have various and sundry opinions. One, reasoning from the fact that everything which exists is singular in number,[20] concludes that either the universal is numerically one, or it is non-existent. But since it is impossible for things that are substantial[21] to be non-existent, if those things for which they are substantial exist, they further conclude that universals must be essentially one with particular things. Accordingly, following Walter of Mortagne,[22] they distinguish [various] states [of existence],[23] and say that Plato is an individual in so far as he is Plato; a species in so far as he is a man; a genus of a subaltern [subordinate] kind in so far as he is an animal; and a most general genus in so far as he is a substance. Although this opinion formerly had some proponents, it has been a long time since anyone has asserted it. Walter[24] now upholds [the doctrine of] ideas, emulating Plato and imitating Bernard of Chartres,[25] and maintains that genus and species are nothing more nor less than these, namely, ideas. "An idea," according to Seneca's definition,[26] "is an eternal exemplar of those things which come to be as a result of[27] nature." And since universals are not subject to corruption, and are not altered by the changes[28] that transform particular things and cause them to come and go, succeeding one another almost momentarily, ideas are properly and correctly called "universals." Indeed, particular things are deemed incapable of supporting the substantive verb,[29] [i.e., of being said "to be"], since they are not at all stable, and disappear without even waiting to receive names. For they vary so much in their qualities, time, location, and numerous different properties, that their whole existence seems to be more a mutable transition than a stable status. In contrast, Boethius declares:[30] "We say that things 'are' when they may neither be increased nor diminished, but always continue as they are, firmly sustained by the foundations of their own nature." These [foundations] include their quantities, qualities, relations, places, times, conditions, and whatever is found in a way united with bodies. Although these adjuncts of bodies may seem to be changed, they remain immutable in their own nature. In like manner, although individuals [of species] may change, species remain the same. The waves of a stream wash on, yet the same flow of water continues, and we refer to the stream as the same river. Whence the statement of Seneca,[31] which,

in fact, he has borrowed from another:[32] "In one sense it is true that we may descend twice into the same river, although in another sense this is not so."[33] These "ideas," or "exemplary forms," are the original plans[34] of all things. They may neither be decreased nor augmented; and they are so permanent and perpetual, that even if the whole world were to come to an end, they could not perish. They include all things, and, as Augustine seems to maintain in his book *On Free Will*,[35] their number neither increases nor diminishes, because the ideas always continue on, even when it happens that [particular] temporal things cease to exist. What these men promise is wonderful, and familiar to philosophers who rise to the contemplation of higher things. But, as Boethius[36] and numerous other authors testify, it is utterly foreign to the mind of Aristotle. For Aristotle very frequently opposes this view, as is clear from his books. Bernard of Chartres and his followers[37] labored strenuously to compose the differences between Aristotle and Plato.[38] But I opine that they arrived on the scene too late, so that their efforts to reconcile two dead men, who disagree as long as they were alive and could do so were in vain. Still another, in his endeavor to explain Aristotle, places universality in "native forms,"[39] as does Gilbert, Bishop of Poitiers,[40] who labors to prove that "native forms" and universals are identical.[41] A "native form" is an example of an original [exemplar].[42] It [the native form, unlike the original] inheres in created things, instead of subsisting in the divine mind. In Greek it is called the *idos*,[43] since it stands in relation to the idea as the example does to its exemplar. The native form is sensible in things that are perceptible by the senses; but insensible as conceived in the mind. It is singular in individuals, but universal in all [of a kind]. Another, with Joscelin, Bishop of Soissons,[44] attributes universality to collections of things,[45] while denying it to things as individuals. When Joscelin tries to explain the authorities, he has his troubles and is hard put, for in many places he cannot bear the gaping astonishment[46] of the indignant letter.[47] Still another takes refuge in a new tongue, since he does not have sufficient command of Latin. When he hears the words "genus" and "species," at one time he says they should be understood as universals, and at another that they refer to the *maneries*[48] of things. I know not in which of the authors he has found this term or this distinction, unless perhaps he has dug it out of lists of abstruse and obsolete words,[49] or it is an item of jargon [in the baggage] of present-day[50] doctors. I am further at a loss to see what it can mean here, unless it refers to collections of things, which would be the same as Joscelin's view, or to a universal thing, which, however, could hardly be called a *maneries*. For a *maneries* may be interpreted as referring to both [collections and universals], since a number of things, or the status[51] in which a thing of such and such a type continues to exist[52] may be called a *maneries*. Finally, there are some who fix their attention on the status of things, and say that genera and species consist in the latter.

Chapter 18

That Men Always Alter the Opinions of Their Predecessors.

It would take too long, and [also] be entirely foreign to my purpose, to propound the opinions and errors of everyone. The saying of the comic poet that "There are as many opinions as heads,"[53] has almost come to hold true. Rarely, if ever, do we find a teacher who is content to follow in the footsteps of his master. Each, to make a name for himself, coins his own special error. Wherewith, while promising to correct his master, he sets himself up as a target for correction and condemnation by his own disciples as well as by posterity. I recognize that the same rule threatens to apply in my own case. By disagreeing with others and committing my dissent to writing, I am, in fact, laying myself open to be criticized by many. He who speaks is judged merely by one or a few persons;

whereas he who writes thereby exposes himself to criticism by all, and appears before the tribunal of the whole world and every age. However, not to be overly harsh with the doctors, I must observe that, very often, many of them seem to be wrangling over words, rather than disputing about facts. Nonetheless there is nothing that is less appropriate for a professor of this art [of logic], since such procedure ill befits a serious man. As Aristotle declares, "To dispute in this wise over a word is utterly abhorrent in dialectic, unless it be the sole possible way in which a proposition may be discussed."[54] Of a truth, on points where they seem to be in profound disagreement, such [professors of logic] admit one another's interpretations, even though they may maintain that the latter are inadequate. They are mutually condemning, not the meaning, but the words of one another's statements.

Chapter 19

Wherein Teachers of This Kind Are Not to Be Forgiven.

I do not criticize their opinions, which [probably] do not actually disagree, as would be shown if it were possible to compare their meanings.[55] Still, they are guilty of certain offenses which, in my opinion, should not be overlooked. In the first place, they load "insupportable burdens" on the frail shoulders of their students.[56] Second, they pay no attention to proper order in teaching, and diligently take care lest "All things be suitably arranged, each in its own place."[57] Thus they, so to speak, read[58] the whole art[59] into its title. With them, Porphyry practically teaches beforehand the contents of the *Topics*, the *Analytics*, and the *Elenchi*.[60] Finally, they go against the mind of the author, and comb, as it were, in the wrong direction. For the [supposed] purpose of simplifying Aristotle, they teach the doctrine of Plato, or [perhaps even] some false opinion, which differs with equal error from the views[61] of both Aristotle and

Plato. At the same time, they all profess to be followers of Aristotle.

Chapter 20

Aristotle's Opinion Concerning Genera and Species, Supported by Numerous Confirmatory Reasons and References to Written Works.

Aristotle stated that genera and species do not exist [as such], but are only understood.[62] What is the point, then, in inquiring as to what genus is, when Aristotle has definitely asserted that it does not exist? Is it not inane to try to determine the nature, quantity, and quality of something that has no existence? If substance be lacking, then none of these other attributes can be present. If Aristotle, who says that genera and species do not exist [as such], is right, then the labors of the foregoing inquiry as to their substance, quantity, quality, or origin, are futile. We cannot describe the quality or quantity of something that lacks substance. Neither can we give the reason why something that does not exist is one thing or another, and of this or that size or kind. Wherefore, unless one wants to break with Aristotle, by granting that universals exist, he must reject opinions which would identify universals with word sounds,[63] word concepts,[64] sensible things,[65] ideas,[66] native forms,[67] or collections.[68] For all of the latter doubtless exist. In short, one who maintains that universals exist,[69] contradicts Aristotle. We should not, however, fear that our understanding[70] is empty when it perceives universals as abstracted from particular things, although the former have no [actual] existence apart from the latter. Our understanding [has two different modes of operation:] at times [it] looks directly at the simple essence of things, apart from composition,[71] as when it conceives of "man" per se, or "stone" per se,[72] in which operation it is simple. But at times it proceeds gradually, step by step,[73] as when it considers a man as white, or a horse as running,[74] in which case its operation is com-

posite. A simple act of the understanding at times considers a thing as it is, as when it considers Plato; but at other times it conceives of a thing as otherwise. Sometimes it combines things that are [in actual life] uncombined, at other times it separates things that cannot [in reality] be dissociated. One who imagines a goat-stag[75] or a centaur,[76] conceives of a combination of man and beast that is alien to nature, or a combination of two species of animals. On the other hand, one who considers line or surface apart from a given mass, dissociates form from matter by the keen blade of his contemplative insight,[77] although, actually, it is impossible for them to exist apart from each other. However, the abstracting intellect does not in this case conceive of form as existing apart from matter. If it did, its operation would be composite. Rather, it simply contemplates the form, without considering the matter, even though in fact the former cannot exist apart from the latter. Such an operation agrees with the intellect's simplicity, which comes into sharper relief in proportion as it considers simpler things in themselves, namely, apart from composition with other things. Nor is this procedure contrary to the order of nature, which has bestowed on the [human] intellect this faculty of distinguishing things that are combined, and putting together things that exist separately, in order to facilitate its investigation of nature itself. The combining process of the intellect, whereby things that are not united are copulated, lacks objectivity;[78] but its abstracting process is both accurate and true to reality. The latter constitutes, as it were, the common factory of all the arts. While things possess but one manner of existence which they have received from nature, they may nevertheless be understood or signified in more than one way. Although a man who is not a specific man cannot exist, "man" may still be conceived mentally and represented in such a way that no given individual man is thought of or denoted. Therefore genera and species may be conceived by the abstracting intellect in order to signify things [as considered] apart from composition.[79] But if one were, ever so diligently, to search for the latter in nature, dissociated from sensible things, he would be wasting his time, and laboring in vain, as nature does not count anything of the sort among her brood. Reason, on considering the substantial mutual resemblances of certain individual things, has discerned genera and species. Thus it has, as Boethius tells us,[80] defined the general concept: "Rational mortal animal," which it has, on reflection, concluded from the mutual conformity existing among men, even though such a "rational mortal animal" [actually] exists only in individual cases. Consequently, genera and species are not things that are really and by their nature unrelated to individual things. Rather, they are mental representations[81] of actual, natural things, intellectual images of the mutual likenesses of real things, reflected, as it were, in the mirror of the soul's native purity.[82] These concepts the Greek call *ennoyas*[83] or *yconoyfanas*,[84] that is to say images of things clearly discernible by the mind. For the soul, as it were by the reflected ray[85] of its own contemplation, finds in itself what it defines. The exemplar[86] of what is defined exists in the mind, while the example[87] exists among actual things. A similar condition maintains when we say in grammar: "Names which have such and such an ending are feminine or neuter."[88] A general rule is laid down, which provides, so to speak, an exemplar for many declinable words. The examples, in turn, are to be found in all the words with a given termination. In like manner, certain exemplars are mentally conceived after their examples have been formed and presented to the senses by nature. According to Aristotle, these exemplars are conceptual, and are, as it were, images and shadows of things that really exist. But if one attempts to lay hold of them, supposing them to have an existence of their own, apart from particular things, they vanish [into thin air] as do dreams. "For they are representations,"[89] apparent only to the intellect. When universals are said to be sub-

stantial for individual things, reference is made to causality in the cognitive order, and to the nature of individual things. It is clear in particular cases that subordinate things[90] cannot exist or be understood without superior ones.[91] Thus the non-existence of animals would preclude the existence of man [a particular kind of animal]. And we must understand what an "animal" is, in order to understand what "man" is. For man is a certain kind of animal. In the same way "man" is in Plato, as Plato both exists and is understood, though Plato actually is a particular given man. While the idea and existence of animal are postulated by the idea and existence of man, this proposition is not convertible, as the concept and existence of man are not postulated by those of animal. For although the concept of man includes that of animal, the concept of animal does not include that of man. Since, therefore, both essentially and in the order of cognition, a species requires its genus, but is not itself required by its genus, the latter [genus] is said to be substantial for the former [species]. The same [general principle] holds true for individual things, which require [their] species and genus, but are not themselves necessitated by their species and genus. A particular thing cannot possess substance or be known by us, unless it is a [certain] species or genus, that is unless it is some [sort of] thing, or is known as this or that. Despite the fact that universals are called things, and are frequently spoken of as existing, without [any] qualification, neither the physical mass of bodies, nor the tenuity of spirits, nor the distinct essence of particular things is for this reason to be found in them. In a similar way, although matters that are the subject of affirmation or negation are called "things," and we very often say that what is true "is," still we do not classify such as substances or accidents. Neither do we refer to them as "Creator" or "creature." In the mart of the various branches of knowledge, free mutual exchange of words between one discipline and another ought to prevail, as observes Ulger, venerable Bishop of Angers.[92] Liberality reigns in the market place of philosophers,[93] where words may be borrowed without restriction or charge.[94] Accordingly, even if it were granted that universals "exist" and are "things," to please the obstinate, still it would not, on this account, follow that the [total] number of things would be increased or diminished by adding or subtracting universals. If one examines universals, he will find that, while they can be numbered, this number cannot be added to the number of individual things. As with corporate colleges or other bodies, the number of heads cannot be added to that of the bodies, or vice versa, so with universals and particular things, the number of universals cannot be added to that of particular things, or vice versa. Only things of the same sort, which are by nature distinct in each given kind of things, can be numbered together with one another. Nothing can be universal unless it is found in particular things. Despite this, many have sought to find the universal, in itself, apart from individual things. But at the end of their search, they have all come out empty handed. For the universal, apart from particular things, is not an entity, unless perhaps in the sense that truths and like meanings of combined words are entities. It does not make any difference that particular material things are examples of universal immaterial things, as every mode of activity (according to Augustine) is immaterial and insensible, although what is done, together with the act whereby it is done,[95] is generally perceptible by the senses. That which is understood in a general way by the mind, as pertaining equally to many particular things, and that which is signified in a general way by a word,[96] as referring equally to several beings, is beyond doubt universal. But even the terms "that which is understood," and "that which is signified," must be accepted in a broad manner, and cannot be subjected either to the narrow straits of disputation or to the subtle analysis of the grammatical art. The latter, of its nature, does not allow demonstrative expressions to be unlimited in application, except after one has sought

and obtained such permission. Neither does it tolerate relative expressions that are vague. It requires, rather, that the meaning of such expressions be fixed by determining the person, or [his] act, or the action of another. A relative expression is, in fact, one which designates something as the subject of foregoing speech or thought. In the saying: "Wise and happy is the man who has recognized goodness,[97] and has faithfully conformed his actions to this," the relative words "who" and "this,"[98] even though they do not designate the specific person [and act], are nevertheless in a way limited, and freed of their indefiniteness, by specification as to how they are to be recognized. There must be someone who corresponds to the statement, someone who, recognizing what is right, has acted accordingly, and is consequently happy. Only in cases where there is a mistake or a figure does it happen that there is nothing sure and definite to which a relative expression refers. Whence if a horse in general [in a generic manner] is promised, and the one to whom the promise was made says: "The horse which is promised to me is either healthy or sickly,[99] since every horse is either healthy or sickly," he is clearly quibbling. For there is no horse that was promised to him. I do not say "There is no horse" because the horse does not or will not exist. Even that which does not exist, such as Arethusa's giving birth to child,[100] may be the subject of a very definite promissory obligation. Rather, I say, "There is no horse," because the promise of a general kind of thing [a generic promise] does not involve the promise of the specific, that is a distinct thing. For when I say "That which is promised," "That which is signified," "That which is understood," and the like, some definite thing is promised or meant if the relation is proper.[101] However, there are also relations that are general [generic], which, if they are to remain true and are to be properly understood, cannot be tied down to some particular subject [the specific]. Examples of such are provided by the sayings: "A woman, both saved [us], and damned

[us]"; "A tree both bore the cause of our death, and that of our life"; "The green leaves, which the freezing north wind bears off, the mild west wind restores."[102] In the instances which I have just mentioned, I believe that these relative expressions should not be conceived as descending to the specific, and pointing out some particular person or thing, but rather that they should be understood as remaining general [generic]. In brief, what is signified by the noun "man" is a species, because man is signified, and man is a special kind[103] of animal. What is signified by the word "animal" is a genus, as an animal is signified, and an animal is a general [generic] kind of thing.[104] For what is signified by a word is that to which it directly refers, or that which the mind reasonably conceives on hearing the word. When one hears the word "man," one does not mentally run through all men, for this would be a task both endless and impossible. Neither does he restrict his concept to one particular man, for this would be inadequate, and would not really correspond to the meaning of the term.[105] Likewise, when one defines an animal as a substance possessing life and the power of sensation, one is not simply describing a single particular animal, lest his definition be incomplete. Neither is he trying to give a description of every animal, lest his labor be endless. Each of these universals signifies or defines, not merely "what,"[106] but rather "what kind of what,"[107] not merely a given [particular] thing,[108] but rather a certain kind of thing.[109] Thus Galen, in his Techne,[110] defines medicine as "the science of healthful, unhealthful, and intermediate[111] things." He does not say "the science of everything," since this would be infinite. Neither does he say "the science of certain [particular] things," since this would be inadequate for the definition of an art. Rather, he defines medicine as the science of a given kind of things.[112] Aristotle tells us:[113] "Genera and species determine the kind[114] of a substance. They do not merely designate 'what,' but, in a way, 'what kind of a thing.' " In like vein, Aristotle declares in

his Elenchi:[115] "General terms, such as 'man,' do not denote some particular thing, but rather a certain kind of thing, or [a thing in] some sort of relation to something, or something like this."[116] A little further on he says: "It is evident that a general, universal predication [concerning things of a class] is not to be understood as referring to some particular thing, but rather as signifying quality, relation, quantity, or something of the sort."[117] In fact, what is not a particular thing cannot be described in detail.[118] Real things[119] have from nature certain limitations, and are distinguished from one another by their properties, even though frequently our knowledge of them is not very definite, and our concept of them rather vague. The well known principle that what common names mean and what they name are not identical, does not militate against what has just been said. For their meaning is universal, even though they name particular things. Evidently, if one looks only for a simple general relationship, he will have no trouble understanding the foregoing, but if he insists on trying to find the precise determination of some individual thing, he may well be at a loss to put his finger on anything of the sort. There is a rule that[120] "Demonstrative expressions provide primary cognition, relative expressions knowledge of a secondary kind."[121] In fact [our] cognition, in apprehending something, circumscribes and defines the latter for itself by a certain [comprehensive] capacity of the mind, so that if a thing presents itself to the mind as absolutely unlimited in every respect, neither primary nor secondary cognition can proceed. All knowledge or cognition possessed by creatures is limited. Infinite knowledge belongs solely to God, because of His infinite nature.[122] However limitless things may be, they are at the same time most certainly circumscribed by His infinite immensity, and defined by His boundless knowledge and wisdom, which cannot be counted and have no limit.[123] But we are imprisoned within the petty dimensions of our human capacity, wherefore we attain neither primary, nor secondary, nor tertiary, nor any distinction of knowledge of what is infinite, save the realization that it is unknown because it is infinite. Accordingly, all demonstrative and relative expressions must refer to a specific, definite subject if they are correctly posited. Otherwise they will miss their mark. For cognition naturally seeks or possesses certitude as its object. However, language is often conscripted to serve in extraordinary senses,[124] and frequently incorrect expressions are used as a matter of convenience. Thus the axiom that "All men love themselves,"[125] is generally accepted, not merely to provide material for the pedantic bickering of those who are content to chatter on any sort of topic that permits disputation, but also to convey knowledge of a truth to hearers who are in good faith. However, if one analyzes this principle according to the strict and proper meaning of a relative expression, one will perhaps charge that it is improperly stated and false. For it is evident that all men do not love all men. Neither do all men love any given man. So whether the expression: "all men," be understood collectively or distributively, the relative pronoun "themselves," which follows, cannot correctly be understood as referring either to every man or to any one man. The relation [here] is accordingly not a strict one. Begging, as it were, indulgent forgiveness from its own rule, it refutes the reliability of the universal with reference to the truth of particular things. While it is true in individual cases that everyone loves himself, and this is affirmed of all men in general in a distributive sense by the saying that "all men love themselves," the relation is to be understood in a broad and free way. It should not be taken in a narrow, grammatical sense, whereby it would either compass all men, or single out some particular individual from this universality. Hence, according to those who always seize upon difficulties and subtleties, and decline to use good faith as their principle in [interpreting] conversation or reading, this is "a form of statement" rather than "a statement of regular form." They also assert the same

whenever a pronoun refers to a common noun, since a pronoun, which is always demonstrative or relative, stands in the place of a proper noun, at least when it correctly fulfills the purpose for which it was originally invented. For occasionally, by indulgence, pronouns have a wider meaning.[126] Thus, when it is said that "If a being is a man, it[127] is also an animal," we have not so much a consequence in a hypothetical statement, as a form of a consequence when something is expressed in a hypothetical manner. For the word "it," according to the strict laws of disputation,[128] does not refer to a man. Nor can we see any definite thing to which it may be referred. Whence come many meaningless and vexatious objections, raised by such as delight in harassing the ignorant and those of a more liberal and less petty disposition. Such tireless wranglers, who refuse to desist from their stubborn objections [must] do so out of either ignorance, or perversity, or greed. Just as cognition seeks certitude, so demonstrative and relative expressions, which convey either primary or other cognition, depend on certain and definite subjects, which such expressions, when they are properly employed, present to our mind as particular things. Let us suppose that common names signify some general status (for I have already declared[129] that I side with the Academicians in regard to things that are doubtful to a wise man, and that I do not care for contentious argumentation). Although I can somehow dream of a status wherein particular things are united, yet [wherein] no particular thing exists, I am still at a loss to see how this can be reconciled with the opinion of Aristotle, who contends that universals do not exist. Even the designations "incorporeal" and "insensible," which, as I have previously mentioned, are appropriate for universals, are only privative[130] with reference to them. They do not attribute to universals any properties whereby the nature of the latter may be ascertained. For a universal is not an incorporeal or insensible thing. Something that is incorporeal is either a spirit or the property of a body or spirit. As universals are neither of these, they cannot strictly be called incorporeal. What incorporeal thing is not a substance created by God, or something united with a substance created by God? If universals were incorporeal [things], they would either be substances, that is, bodies or spirits, or things in composition with the same. They would depend on the Creator as the cause of their existence and the originator and support[131] of their substance. For they would bid farewell and vanish, were they not subject to Him. "By Him, all things were made"[132] to be what they are called from their qualities or effects, whether they are the subjects of forms or the forms of subjects. If a substance is a substance made by the Creator, it must have a certain size, kind, and existence relative to something else, in a given place at a specific time. It must also possess, do, or undergo something, with Him as author through Whom exists every substance and property of a substance, every part or combination of parts. Substantial and accidental forms alike receive from Him their existence and power to produce certain effects in their subjects. If anything exists, it is [necessarily] dependent on Him. The Stoics suppose that matter is coeternal with God, and maintain that form had no beginning. They posit three principles: matter, form, and God, saying that the latter is not indeed the Creator, but only the conciliator of the aforesaid.[133] Others, who, although they profess and affect to be philosophers, by no means attain full cognition of the truth, falsely maintain that there are even more principles. Notwithstanding, there is but one principle of all things, from Whom has proceeded everything that is correctly considered and called something. As Augustine says,[134] "God has created matter possessing [given] form."[135] Although matter is sometimes spoken of as "formless,"[136] it has never existed utterly destitute of form. Reason is subservient to inquiry rather than to actuality. *Ylen*,[137] which neither exists, nor can exist, nor can be fully understood without form, is, by our intellect, relentlessly divested, so to speak, of the forms wherewith it is attired,

and stripped down to its own particular nudity and deficiency. But the strength of reason seemingly melts when confronted by the [first] principles of things.[138] Hence it is that Boethius, defining "nature" in his book *Against Nestorius and Eutyches*, says that it "pertains to things, which, since they exist, may, at least in some way, be understood by the intellect."[139] Explaining the force of the expression "at least in some way,"[140] used in his definition, Boethius states that this qualification is included because of God and matter, since in the investigation of the latter the human intellect is deficient. Indeed, God made matter from nothing, while form, likewise simultaneously created from nothing, is united[141] with this matter, in such a way that, just as the privilege of determination is granted to the form, so that of existence is accorded to the matter. Thus, in a way, the form exists through the matter, while conversely the matter is determined by the form. Neither does the form exist of itself,[142] nor would the matter be determinate without the form. Chaos would reign, or rather the sensible world would come to an end, if nature did not compose the figures of things by means of forms. To the point here is what Boethius says in the first part of his work *On the Trinity*:[143] "Every existence is the result of a form." This proposition he clarifies by examples. "A statue," he points out, "is so called, not because of the bronze,[144] the matter whereof it is made, but because of the form of Hector or Achilles, into which the bronze has been molded. The bronze itself is called bronze, not from the earth, which is its matter, but from the forms allotted it by nature. Even earth itself obtains its name, not from *poutou yle*, its matter, but from dryness and weight, its forms." To its form everything, accordingly, owes the fact that it is what it is, possesses such and such qualities, and has this or that quantity. Just as matter has the potentiality of becoming something of a certain size and kind, so forms have from their Creator the power of making this or that, for example, an animal or a tree, or something of a given size and kind. It is true that mathematics, which deals theoretically[145] with abstractions, and in its subtle analysis separates things that are united in nature, treats matter and form apart from one another, so that the nature of what is composite may be more accurately and definitely understood. Still, the one cannot exist apart from the other, as [in this case] either matter would be without form, or form would lack a subject and hence be ineffective. "Even so the one requires the assistance of the other, and they work together in friendly fashion."[146] It is recorded[147] that in[148] the beginning, heaven and earth were created, and then their[149] various embellishments were created and interposed between the fire and water, which God had, so to speak, established as the first foundations of the world's body. In this account, reference is made to species. I do not refer here to the sort of "species" which logicians have dreamt of as being independent of the Creator. I speak rather of the forms in which things have been born, first in their own essence, and subsequently in our human understanding. The very fact that we call something "heaven" or "earth"[150] is due to its form. It is likewise said that "The earth brought forth the green grass and the various kinds of trees."[151] This shows that forms are united to matter, and also teaches that God is the author, not only of the grass, but also of its greenness. "Without Him, nothing was made."[152] And verily whatever comes from the one principle, not only is one in number, but also is itself good, yea, "exceedingly good."[153] For it proceeds from the supreme good. God willed to make all things similar to Himself, so far as the nature of each was, by His divinely established order, receptive of goodness.[154] And so, in the approving judgment of the Divine Artisan, all the things which He had made were "exceedingly good."[155] If genera and species do not proceed from God, they are nothing. But if each of them does proceed from Him, it is certainly one, and likewise good. And if a thing is numerically one, it is forthwith singular. The fact that some people call a thing "one" simply because it unites several things by expressing

their conformity, although it is not one in itself, does not contradict our point. In the latter case, what is called "one" is neither immediately nor adequately one. If it were, it would be singular. However similar God's works may be, they are singular and distinct, one from another. Such is the arrangement decreed by Him, Who has created all things in number for their differentiation, in "weight"[156] for their generic value,[157] and in measure for their quantitative determination,[158] all the while reserving to Himself universal authority. All things other than God are finite. Every substance is subject to number because it has just so many, and no more accidents. Every accident and every form is likewise subject to number, although in this case because of the singular nature of its subject, rather than a participation of accidents or forms. Everything also has its own "weight," either according to the respect due its form, if it is a substance, or according to the worth of its effects, if it is a form. Hence it is that, in comparing substances, we place man above the brute animals, out of esteem for his form, which is rational, as we deem external appearance[159] less important than rationality, which provides the ability to reason. Measure, for its part, consists in the fact that everything has no more than a certain quantity. An accident or form cannot exceed the limits of its subject, and the subject itself cannot be greater than its accidents or form allow. The "color" of a body is both diffused throughout the whole body, and bounded by the external surfaces of the latter. On the other hand, the body itself extends only as far as its "color," neither going beyond, nor stopping short of the latter. In like manner, every subject is considered to extend as far as its accidents, while every accident which pertains to an entire subject exists complete throughout its whole subject, or if it pertains only to a part of the subject, it exists solely in that part. I do not hesitate to affirm that either genera and species are from God, or they are nothing at all; and I would do so even if the whole world were to hold the opposite. Dionysius the Areopagite makes clear that he holds the same view, and says that the number whereby all things are distinguished, the "weight" wherein they are established, and the measure wherewith they are limited, image God.[160] For, of a truth, God is number innumerable, weight incalculable, and measure inestimable. And in Him alone all things that have been made in number, in "weight," and in measure, have been created.[161] Whence Augustine says: "the invisible differences of invisible things are determinable only by Him, Who has ordained all things in [their] number, weight, and measure, and in Him, Who is measure, fixing the extent of all things; number, giving everything its specific existence;[162] and "weight," drawing each entity to a stable existence, or, in other words, delimiting, forming, and ordering all things.[163] In the account of the works of the six days [of creation], although we read that all good things were created, each according to its own kind, we find no allusion whatsoever to universals.[164] Nor could there properly be such, if universals are essentially united with particular things, or [even] if the Platonic doctrine[165] is correct. Furthermore, I cannot remember ever having read anywhere whence universals have derived existence, or when they have originated. According to Aristotle, universals are only understood, and there is no actual thing that is universal. These representations[166] have licitly, and for instructional purposes,[167] been given names that denote the way in which they are understood. It is true that every man is this or that [particular] man, that is to say, an individual. But "man" can be understood in such a way that neither this nor that [given] man, nor any being that is one in the singularity of its essence, is understood. And by means of this concept we can reason about man in general,[168] that is man in general can be actually represented because of the general nature of the intellect. Accordingly, something that can be so understood, even though it may not be [at a given time actually] understood by anyone, is said to be general.[169] For [certain] things resemble

one another, and our intellect, abstracting from consideration of the [particular] things themselves, considers this conformity. One man has the same form as another, inasmuch as they are both men, even though they [assuredly] differ in their personal qualities. Man also has in common with the horse (from which he differs completely in species, that is, in the whole form of his nature, and so to speak, in his entire appearance)[170] that they both live and have sensation, or, in other words, that they are both animals. That in which men, who are alike in the form of their nature, and distinct only in number (whereby so and so is one, and so and so another man), correspond, is called their "species." And that which is, so to speak, a general image of various forms, is known as "genus." Therefore, in Aristotle's judgment,[171] genera and species are not merely "what" [things are], but also are, in a way, conceptions of "what kind of what"[172] [they are]. They are, as it were, fictions, employed by [human] reason as it delves deeper[173] in its investigation and explanation of things. Reason does this validly, for, whenever there is need, it can point to a manifest example in the world of reality to substantiate its concepts. Civil law does likewise, and has its own fictions. So, in fact, do all branches of learning, which unhesitatingly devise fictions to expedite their investigations. Each of them even, in a way, prides itself on its own special figments. "We may dispense with forms,"[174] says Aristotle[175] "for they are representations (or, according to a new translation:[176] chatter)[177] and even if they did exist, they would have no bearing on our discussion." Although Aristotle may be understood as referring here to Platonic ideas, genera and species may still both, not without reason, be said to "exist," if one bears in mind the diverse meanings of which "being" and "existence" are susceptible when applied to various subjects. For our reason prompts us to say that things exist, when we can see that they are exemplified by particular instances, of whose existence no one can doubt. It is not because genera and species are exemplary forms in the Platonic sense, "and existed as concepts in the Divine mind before they emanated into entities of the external physical world,"[178] that they are said to be exemplars of particular things. It is rather because, when one looks for an example of what is represented in a general way by [e.g.] the word "man" and what is defined when we say [e.g.] that "man is a mortal rational animal," forthwith Plato or some other particular man can be pointed out, in order firmly to establish the general meaning or definition. Genera and species may be called "representations," because on the one hand they represent particular things, and, on the other, they are represented by the latter. Things are made manifest sometimes by what is prior, sometimes by what is posterior. More general things are, in themselves, prior, for they are also understood in other things; while particular things are posterior. Frequently, however, things which are naturally prior, and of themselves more properly objects of knowledge, are actually less known by us. The more solidly substantial things are, the more readily we can recognize them with our senses; the more subtle they become, the more difficult it is to perceive them. As Aristotle observes, "The point is prior to, and in itself more evident than the line. The same may be said of the line relative to the plane surface, and of the plane surface with reference to the solid. It is likewise true of unity in relation to plurality, for which unity is the principle. This also holds in regard to the letter relative to the syllable." The foregoing list could be extended. [Aristotle continues:] "The reserve, however, sometimes occurs in the case of our knowledge. Generally the average mind more readily perceives what is posterior, whereas the comprehension of what is prior is reserved to the more profound and learned intellect."[179] Whence, even though it is true that what is posterior is best defined by what is prior, and this is always more scientific,[180] still, frequently, of necessity, and to provide subject matter within the ken of our senses,[181] what is prior is actually explained by what is posterior. A

point is thus said to be the end of a line; a line, the edge of a surface; a surface, the side of a solid. In like manner, unity is said to be the elementary principle of number, the moment that of time, the letter that of speech. Genera and species are accordingly exemplars of particular things, but rather as instruments of learning[182] than as essential causes of particular things. And this representative[183] (to use the term with considerable license) contemplation of fictions even goes to the extent of completely dispensing with[184] the consideration of individual things. Since every substance is comprised of its own properties, the same collection of which is not found in any other substance, the abstracting intellect proceeds to consider each thing as it is in itself.[185] Although Plato could not exist without form, and divorced from place or time, reason regards him as, so to speak, "nude," stripped of his quantity, quality, and other accidents. It thus gives the individual a [common] name.[186] This, it must be admitted, is a fiction, designed to expedite learning and deeper inquiry.[187] No such thing [as "man" in general] can actually be found. Still, the concept of "man" in general is a valid act of understanding. This is perhaps why, in the *Analytics*, we find the statement: "Aristomenes is always intelligible, even though Aristomenes does not always exist, as he must one day disintegrate."[188] What is uniquely individual can only, according to some, be predicated of a certain subject.[189] Plato, [as] the son of Aristides,[190] is individual neither in quantity, as an atom, nor by solidity, as a diamond, nor even, so they say, by predication. I, personally, neither strongly oppose nor sponsor this opinion. Nor do I think that it is a matter of moment, since I advocate recognition of the fact that words may be used in various senses.[191] This is, I believe, an indispensable condition, if one is accurately to understand what authors mean. What is there to forbid lest, just as a genus may, with truth, be predicated of its species, so this particular Plato, perceptible by the senses, may, with truth, be predicated of the son of Aristides, if he is Aristides' only son. Then, just as man is an animal, so the son of Aristides[192] is Plato. Some believe that this was what Aristotle meant when he said in his *Analytics*: "Of all the things that exist, some[193] are such that they cannot be predicated of anything else with true universality. Such is the case, for example, with Cleon and Callias, as well as with whatever is singular and perceptible by the senses. However, other things may be predicated of them, as each [Cleon, Callias] is both a man and an animal. Some things are themselves predicated of other things, but other things that are prior are not predicated of them. With certain things, however, it is true that both they themselves are predicated of other things, and other things are predicated of them. Thus, for example, man is predicated of Callias, while, in turn, animal is predicated of man. Certain things which exist are clearly fated by their nature not to be predicated of anything. Almost all sensible things fall in this category, and cannot be predicated of anything save as accidents, as when we say, 'That white figure is Socrates'; and 'That object approaching [in the distance] is Callias.' "[194] This distribution would seem entirely out of place if a sensible thing could not be predicated. But while the latter is predicated of something else, it is predicated only as an accident. If it could not be predicated as an accident concerning itself or something else, what Aristotle says would be false, and his example would be pointless. And if a sensible thing could not be made the subject of a predication, then, doubtless, Aristotle would be either lying or talking nonsense. Here, as elsewhere, Aristotle has proceeded in the manner which one should use in teaching the liberal arts, and has discussed his subject in a greatly simplified fashion,[195] so that he may [more easily] be understood. Accordingly, he has not introduced into genera and species a difficulty which the doctors themselves are unable to understand, much less to explain to others. The statement found in the *Topics* that "In the case of animals, all differences must be either species or individuals, since every animal is either a species or an individual,[196] ex-

emplifies the sovereignty of this principle of simplicity. Similar simplification is found in the statement of Boethius that "Every species is its own genus."[197] For every man is an animal, and all whiteness is color. By the same token what prevents sensible things being predicated, or made the subject of predications, in like extended sense? I do not believe that the authors have so done violence to words as to tie them down to a single meaning in all contexts. Rather, I am confident that they express their teachings so as always to serve understanding, which is highly adaptable [to varying meanings], and which reason requires should be here the first and foremost consideration. Predication has several different meanings, which vary according to the context. Still it probably everywhere denotes some sort of conformity or intrinsic connection. For when a word shows an aptness to be joined with another word in the terms of a true affirmation, and when a word is said to be predicated of a thing, it is evident that such an appellation must suit it. At times, to predicate something about a thing denotes that the latter is such and such, as when we say that Plato is a man. At other times, such predication denotes that the subject partakes of something, as for instance that a subject has a certain accident. I do not have any misgivings about declaring that a thing may be predicated of a thing in a proposition, even though the thing is not [explicitly stated] in the proposition. For a thing may be signified by the predicate term of a true affirmation, in whose subject some [given] thing is involved or signified. In fine, instead of fighting against what is written,[198] I believe that we should accept [and try to understand] it in a friendly manner. Our policy should be to admit the liberal interpretation of words that are susceptible of more than one meaning.[199] It is unbefitting a reader or listener to snap like a dog[200] at every figure of speech,[201] or employment[202] of what is deemed poor diction.[203] "Become used to what is hard to bear, and you will bear it."[204] Certainly one is rash, ungrateful, and imprudent if he contradicts his teacher at every turn, and refuses to agree with him on any point. Let us fall [gracefully] into step, therefore, with the figurative speech used by the authors, and let us weigh whatever they say in the light of the causes behind their saying it.[205] In this way we will arrive at an accurate understanding of what they have written. Thus the word "thing" may admit of a wider extension, whereby it may apply to universals, even though Aristotle says that the latter are to be understood as abstracted from particular things in such a way that they would have no existence in the absence of the aforesaid. But those who maintain that genus is numerically one assert the independent existence of universals, according to Aristotle.[206] This they do who suppose the [separate] existence of forms, that is to say "ideas." Aristotle vigorously opposed this doctrine, together with its author, Plato, whenever he had the opportunity. It is true that a great host of philosophers, including not only Augustine,[207] but also several of our contemporaries,[208] have [adopted and] championed Plato's doctrine of ideas. Still we by no means follow Plato in his analysis of the nature of universals. On this question we acknowledge Aristotle, the prince of the Peripatetics,[209] as the master. To judge between the opinions of such great men is a tremendous matter, a task which Boethius in his second commentary on Porphyry,[210] declares to be beyond his abilities.[211] But one embarking upon a study of the works of the Peripatetics, should accept the judgment of Aristotle, if not because it is truer, then certainly because it will serve him better in his studies. Those who declare that genera and species are merely word sounds or word concepts, as well as those who are led astray by other of the aforesaid opinions in their investigations, have all alike obviously strayed far afield from Aristotle's teaching. Indeed, they diverge from his views even more childishly and stupidly than do the followers of Plato, whose opinion[212] they will not even deign to recognize. I believe that what we have said should suffice to show that those who review every opinion that has ever been advanced concerning genera and species, in order to disagree with all of them, and at length establish some plausibility for their own [pet] notion, are neither [really] trying to explain Porphyry with accuracy, nor treating what is introductory in a suitable manner. Such a procedure, entirely foreign to the mind of the author, dulls the mental faculties of students, and usurps time that ought to be given to the study of other points whose knowledge is equally necessary.

END OF BOOK TWO

NOTES

1. Compare, with the present chapter, Abelard's *Fragm. Sangermanense de generibus et speciebus* (in *Ouvr. Inédit. d'Abelard*, ed. V. Cousin, pp. 507–550).
2. *secretis Minerue* here evidently means hidden gems of wisdom, although it refers to Ovid, *Met.*, ii, 749.
3. Reference may be made to Aristotle, *Top.*, i, 2, 101 a, 30 ff., where Aristotle, however, does not use the exact equivalent of John's present wording. Neither does the translation which goes under the name of Boethius. John may here be following a version other than the latter.
4. Aristotle.
5. *uocibus*, physical, spoken, or audible word sounds.
6. Cf. John of Salisbury, *Policraticus*, vii, 12.
7. *sermones*, words as predicated or as signifying concepts, word concepts. This distinction between *uoces* and *sermones* John probably obtained from Abelard. Cf. J. G. Sikes, *Peter Abailard* (Cambridge, England, 1932), pp. 104, 88–112 passim, in addition to the references there cited by Sikes. According to Abelard, *uox* is the mere physical, audible, spoken word; *sermo*, the word considered in relation to its meaning as a mental concept.
8. Cf. *Policraticus*, vii, 12.
9. Literally: captive.
10. See Boethius, *Comm. II in Arist. de Interpr.*, V, II (in Migne, *P.L.*, LXIV, 568, and ed. Meiser, II, 352).
11. *intellectibus*.
12. Cf. *Policraticus*, vii, 12.

13. Literally, take occasion from.
14. Cicero, *Top.*, 7, §31.
15. Boethius, *Comm. in Top. Cic.*, iii (in Migne, *P.L.*, LXIV, 1105–1106).
16. *notiones*.
17. Cicero, *Top.*, §7, 31.
18. Boethius, op. cit., iii.
19. *qui rebus inherent*; again cf. *Policraticus*, vii, 12.
20. Cf. Boethius, *Comm. in Porph.*, iii (in Migne, *P.L.*, LXIV, 110).
21. Or essential.
22. Concerning *Gauterus de Mauritania*, see *Gallia Christiana*, IX, 533. Walter was consecrated Bishop of Laon in 1155, and died in 1174.
23. *status*.
24. Literally: "that one," evidently Walter of Mortagne, who apparently was subsequently converted to the opinion of Plato and Bernard of Chartres.
25. See *Met.*, i, 24, and note.
26. Seneca, *Ep.*, 58, §19.
27. Or: by.
28. *motibus*, movements, forces, changes.
29. *uerbi substantiui*, the substantive verb: *esse*, to be.
30. Boethius, *Arithm.*, i, I (p. 8, lines 1–4, in Friedlein's edition).
31. Seneca, *Ep.*, 58, §23.
32. Heraclitus.
33. Literally: go down twice into the same river, yet into a different river.
34. *rationes*.
35. Augustine, *De Lib. Arbit.*, ii, 17 (in Migne, *P.L.*, LXIV, 1106).
36. Boethius, for example, in his *Comm. in Top. Cic.*, iii (in Migne, *P.L.*, LXIV, 1106).
37. Literally: his hearers.
38. Boethius also declares that he himself tried "to reconcile the opinions of Aristotle and Plato in some way": see Boethius, *Comm. II in Arist. de Interpr.*, ii, 3 (ed. Meiser, II, 79, and in Migne, *P.L.*, LXIV, 79–80).
39. *formis natiuis*; see Gilbert of Poitiers, *In Boeth. de Trin. Comm.*, and his *Comm. in Boeth. lib de Duabus Naturis* (in Migne, *P.L.*, LXIV, 1267 and 1366).
40. Gilbert became Bishop of Poitiers in 1142, and died in 1154. Commentaries written by him on the theological works of Boethius, and his famous *De Sex principiis*, which editors used to append to Aristotle's *Organon*, are extant.
41. *in earum conformitate laborat*.
42. *originalis*, namely, of the original exemplar in the mind of God.
43. See Seneca, *Ep.*, 58 § 20.
44. *Gausleno*, Joscelin; also called *Joslenus*, *Johelinus*, and *Jocelinus*. He was Bishop of Soissons 1126–1152. Some small extant works of his are to be found in Migne's *P.L.*, CLXXVI, but there is nothing in them about universals.
45. Literally: to things collected together.
46. *rictum*, literally: the opening of the mouth.
47. That is, the letter or writing which is opposed to his view, and is, as it were, violated.
48. *maneries*, ways, modes, manners, ways of handling.
49. *in glosematibus*.
50. *modernorum*, modern or present-day.
51. *status*.
52. *permanet*, as though *maneries* would be said to be derived from *manendum*, "remaining."
53. Terence in his *Phorm.*, ii, 4, 14.
54. Aristotle, *Top.*, i, 18, 108 a, 35.
55. Literally: were it possible to superimpose them [their opinions], one on another, for comparison.
56. Cf. Matthew, xxiii, 4.
57. Horace, *A.P.*, 92.
58. *legunt*, they read, or perhaps they lecture or teach.
59. *finem . . . artis*, the end or completion of an art [namely, this art of logic].
60. Of Aristotle.
61. *sententia*, judgment, authoritative opinion, view.
62. See Boethius, *Comm. in Porph.*, i (in Migne, *P.L.*, LXIV, 82–86).
63. *uocibus*; with Roscelin, as explained above (ii, 17).
64. *sermonibus*; with Abelard, ibid.
65. *sensibilibus rebus*; with Walter of Mortagne, ibid.

66. *ideis*; with Walter, after his conversion to the view of Plato and Bernard of Chartres, ibid.
67. *formis natiuis*; with Gilbert of Poitiers, ibid.
68. *collectionibus*; with Joscelin of Soissons, ibid.
69. Or: that universals are these things.
70. *intellectus*, our [intuitive] understanding, intellect, or mind, or the mental concept or idea conceived by the former.
71. *simpliciter*, simply, without admixture.
72. *per se*, of or in himself or itself.
73. *gradatim suis incedit passibus.*
74. See Aristotle, *De Interpr.*, i, as well as the commentary thereon by Boethius.
75. *hircoceruum*, a fabled combination of goat and stag: from Aristotle, *De Interpr.*, i, 16 a, 16.
76. *centaurum*, an imaginary monster half man and half horse.
77. Literally: by the eye of his contemplation.
78. Literally: is empty.
79. *ad significationem incomplexorum.*
80. Boethius, *Comm. in Arist. de Interpr.*, I, i, 5 (ed. Meiser, pp. 72, 26 ff.); cf. I, i, 2 (54, 16) and II, ii, 5 (101, 15).
81. *notiones*, concepts, ideas, semblances.
82. The comma in the Webb text between *speculo* and *natiue* should be omitted. Cf. MSS A, B, and C, and the sense.
83. *ennoyas*; see Cicero, *Top.*, 7, § 31; cf. *Tusc. Disp.*, i, 24, § 57.
84. *yconoyfanas*: MSS C, B, and A have in their margin the gloss: *"ykos: imago; nois: mens; phanos: apparens,"* indicating the etymology of the word as "image appearing to the mind."
85. *reuerberata acie.*
86. *exemplar*, the image, exemplar.
87. *exemplum*, the instance, example.
88. Cf. Priscian, *Inst. Gram.*, v, 3 ff. (Keil, *G.L.*, II, 142 ff.).
89. *monstra*. This may also be translated, monstrosities, things out of the ordinary course of nature, marvels. I have translated it as "prepresentations," in view of John's later discussion of *monstra* in this chapter: cf. below. Here John follows the translation of Aristotle's *An. Post.*, i, 22, 83 a, 33, concerning Platonic ideas, which is attributed to Boethius, *Post. Anal. Interpr.*, chap. 18 (in Migne, *P.L.*, LXIV, 733). See below concerning the "new translation," which more correctly gave *cicadationes*, chatter, or mere sounds without sense. See in this chapter, n. 177.
90. *inferiora*, subordinate, of less wide application.
91. *superioribus*, superior: of wider application.
92. *Ulgerius* or Ulger was consecrated Bishop of Angers in 1125, and died in 1149. No writings of his are known to be extant, save certain testaments and letters (in Migne, *P.L.*, CLXXX, 1641 ff.). Concerning Ulger, cf. St. Bernard's *Ep.*, 200 to the former, where he says: "the great name of master Ulger"; as also Bernard's *Ep.*, 340 to Pope Innocent II, on behalf of Ulger, "whose old age is made venerble both by his life and his knowledge." Also cf. Sikes, *Peter Abailard*, p. 265; and J. F. E. Raby, *Secular Latin Poetry* (Oxford 1934), ii, 42.
93. *philosophantium*, those philosophizing, those who seek wisdom.
94. *distrahuntur ad gratiam.*
95. *illud . . . quod geritur et actus quo geritur*, the thing done and the act of doing, the object of the activity and the activity itself. Thus the food I eat and the eating of it can be seen; but "eating," as a kind of behavior, is a universal, neither material nor sensible.
96. For example, a common noun.
97. Literally: good things.
98. *qui et ea.*
99. The semicolon after *est* in Webb's edition should evidently be changed to a comma.
100. *partus Arethuse*; see Ovid, *Met.*, v, 577 ff.
101. Proper, particular, special.
102. A woman, namely, Mary, brought about human salvation, but another, namely, Eve, occasioned human damnation. A tree, namely, the tree of knowledge, gave us the cause of death, yet another, the cross of Christ, bore for us the source of life. The cold north wind takes away green leaves in winter, the warm west wind restores green leaves in the springtime.
103. Literally: a species.
104. Literally: a genus of things.
105. *doctrinam*, the teaching, meaning, sense, or messsage intended; the instruction.
106. *non simpliciter quid.*
107. *quale quid.*
108. *non simpliciter hoc.*

109. *quid tale.*
110. *Galienus in Tegni,* namely, Galen in his Τέχνηιατρική or *Ars Medica.* See Galen, *Ars medica,* chaps. 1–2 (ed. Kuhn, *Med. graec. op.,* I, 307–313).
111. *neutroum,* neutral, intermediate, neither healthy nor unhealthy.
112. *quorum qualium.*
113. Aristotle, *Cat.,* 5, 3 b, 20.
114. *qualitatem,* quality, kind, or nature.
115. Aristotle, *Soph. El.,* chap. 22, 178 b, 37 ff.
116. Webb's text should read here read: *sed quale quid, uel ad aliquid aliquo modo uel huiusmodi quid significat.* Cf. MSS C, B, and A.
117. Aristotle, *Soph. El.,* chap. 22, 179 a, 8 ff.
118. Literally: cannot be explained by express signification.
119. Literally: existing things.
120. *Regulariter proditum est,* It is stated as a rule (of grammar); it is a (grammatical) rule.
121. Priscian, *Inst.,* xii, 4 (Keil, G.L., II, 579). *secundam . . . cognitionem,* secondary cognition, knowledge of a secondary or indirect kind.
122. Cf. Augustine, *De C.D.,* xii, 19.
123. See Psalms, cxlvi, 5.
124. *Frequens tamen est usurpatio,* There is frequent abuse, misuse, or forcible conscription of language . . .
125. *omnis homo diliget se.*
126. Priscian, Inst., xii, 3 (Keil, *G.L.,* II, 578).
127. *illud,* that.
128. *ex angustia disputandi.*
129. In *Policraticus,* vii, 2.
130. *priuatiua,* privative, negative.
131. *quodam . . . contactu.*
132. John, i, 3.
133. See Seneca, *Ep.,* 65.
134. See Augustine, *De Gen. ad Litt.,* i, 15 (in Migne, *P.L.,* XXXIV, 257).
135. *informatam,* having form.
136. *informis,* lacking form, without form. Cf. Wisdom, xi, 18.
137. *ylen* (from the Greek ὕλη), matter, prime matter.
138. *rerum principia.*
139. Boethius, *Lib. contra Nestorium et Euticen,* chap. i (ed. Peiper, p. 189).
140. *quoquo modo.*
141. *concreta,* grown together, joined, united.
142. *per se.*
143. Boethius, *De Trin.,* chap. 2 (ed. Peiper, pp. 152, 153).
144. *ere: aere,* bronze, or copper; here apparently bronze.
145. *doctrinaliter,* in doctrine, teaching, or theory. Isidore in his *Etym.,* ii, 24, §14, says: "A science which considers abstract quantity is called doctrinal," and lists Arithmetic, Geometry, Astronomy; and Music, namely the Quadrivium, as the *doctrinales scientie.*
146. Horace, *A.P.,* 410, 411.
147. Genesis, i.
148. Literally: from.
149. *tam eorum quam illorum,* literally: both of these and of those.
150. *aliquid celum aut terra.*
151. Genesis, i, 12; cf. Augustine, *De Gen. ad Litt.,* ii, 12, for wording (*protulit, produxit*).
152. John, i, 3.
153. Genesis, i, 31.
154. Cf. Plato, *Tim.,* 29 E, in the version of Chalcidius.
155. Genesis, i, 31.
156. *pondere,* weight, force, value. From what is said later, John seems to regard *pondus* or weight in its more general sense, including value.
157. *ad generis dignitatem,* for the dignity or value of their kind or genus.
158. Cf. Wisdom, xi, 21.
159. *colori,* color, complexion, general aspect.
160. *Dionisius Ariopagita;* see *De Div. Nomin.,* chap. 4, §4, in the version of John Scotus.
161. Cf. Augustine, *De Gen. ad Litt.,* iv, 3, 4, 5 (in Migne, *P.L.,* XXXIV, 299, 300).
162. *speciem,* species, individual existence.
163. Cf. Augustine, loc. cit.
164. Cf. Genesis, i.

165. According to which universals are eternal.

166. *figuralia.*

167. *doctrinaliter*, in the interests of teaching and learning.

168. Literally: "the subject," which in view of the foregoing, is man in general.

169. *communis*, general, common, universal.

170. *facie.*

171. Aristotle, *Cat.*, 5, 3 b, 20.

172. *non omnino quid sit, sed quale quid.*

173. *subtilius.*

174. *species*, forms: said of the Platonic forms or ideas: *species* and *forma* are renderings of the same Greek word, *eidos.*

175. Aristotle, *An. Post.*, i, 22, 83 a, 33.

176. *nouam translationem*; see Webb's Prolegomena to his edition of the *Policraticus*, pp. xxiii–xxvii. Cf. V. Rose, "Die Lücke im Diogenes Laertius und der alte Uebersetzer," *Hermes*, i, p. 383; C. H. Haskins, *Mediaeval Science*, p. 236.

177. *cicadationes*, literally: the shrill noises of the cicadae (large insects common in southern countries); hence, chatter or sounds without sense.

178. Priscian, *Inst. Gram.*, xvii, §44 (Keil, *G.L.*, III, 135). Cf. Abelard, *Introd. ad Theol.*, ii (in *Opp.*, ed. Cousin, II, p. 109; cf. II, p. 14).

179. Aristotle, *Top.*, vi, 4, 141b, 5 ff.

180. *disciplinabilius.*

181. Literally: because of the impotence of our senses.

182. Literally: for "doctrinal purposes."

183. *monstruosa*, see *monstra* (n. 89, above), to which reference is evidently made.

184. *uentilationem*, literally airing, winnowing, minute analysis, elimination.

185. This may also be translated: The activity of the abstracting intellect contemplates each thing in general, namely, the essences of things.

186. Namely, in the case of Plato, the name "man."

187. *subtilioris agitationis*, of more subtle or intensive (mental) application or investigation.

188. In other words, Aristomenes, as an object of thought, is eternal; but Aristomenes himself is not eternal, since he is perishable. Aristotle, *An. Prior.*, i, 33, 47 b, 21 ff.

189. *Et hoc quidem est singulariter indiuiduum, quod solum quidam aiunt posse de aliquo predicari.* The translator is not absolutely certain of the sense of this.

190. This should be Ariston (*Aristonis*).

191. *indifferentiam in uicissitudine sermonum.*

192. Literally: that man (the son of Aristides, or Ariston).

193. Literally: these.

194. Aristotle, *An. Prior.*, i, 27, 43 a, 25 ff.

195. *Minerua pinguiora*, literally: Minerva being lazy, wisdom lagging; hence, with simplicity, without subtlety; cf. Cicero, *De Amic.*, 5, § 19.

196. Aristotle, *Top.*, vi, 6, 144b, I ff.

197. Boethius frequently teaches this; e.g., *In Porph. Dial.*, i (in Migne, *P.L.*, LXIV, 39).

198. *littere*, the letter, things written.

199. *licentioris uerbi indifferentia.*

200. *dentem exercere caninum*; cf. Jerome, *Ep.*, I, § 1. This may also be translated: to gnash his teeth.

201. *translationem*, transfer (of meaning), figure of speech, metaphor.

202. *usurpationem.*

203. *discole.*

204. Ovid., *Art. Am.*, ii, 647.

205. Cf. Hilary, *De Trin.*, iv, 14. Also see *Met.*, i, 19 (47, 8); and iii, 2 (125, 16).

206. John may here be confusing Aristotle with Boethius, *Comm. in Porph.*, i (in Migne, *P.L.*, LXIV, 83).

207. Augustine, *De Div. Quaest.*, lxxxiii, 46 (in Migne, *P.L.*, XL, 29 ff.).

208. *nostrorum*, of ours: of our contemporaries, or of our fellow Christians.

209. *Peripateticorum principem Aristotilem*, Aristotle is so called by Boethius, *Comm. in Arist. de Interpr.*, iii, 9 (ed. Meiser, p. 193).

210. Namely, toward the end of the first book (Migne, *P.L.*, LXIV, 86).

211. Literally: too difficult or trying.

212. That is, the opinion of Plato, as above.

CHAPTER 39

St. Thomas Aquinas

(See Chapter Five for biography.)

St. Thomas Aquinas on Being and Essence

Aquinas flatly rejected the extreme realist theory which supposes that because one can correctly use the same word to refer to any number of particulars that there must be only one thing corresponding to that word. For example, one can say that Peter is a man and that John is a man. From this it does not follow that there is one universal "thing" present in both Peter and John.

For Thomas essences are universals. Essences are what determine a particular to be the type of thing that it is. Here it is crucial not to confuse essence with form. Form and matter are inextricably tied to one another, for one cannot exist without the other although humans can make an intellectual distinction between them by way of abstraction. However, the essence of say, man, is not simply identical to the form man because essential to man (or any sensible object) is matter. Part of what it is to be a man is to possess the substance characteristic of a man as opposed to, say, a rock which has as its essence a different sort of matter. Consequently, essence entails both matter and form. Essences are real and grounded in the sensible world. We identify essences via sense experience. It is our power of abstraction that makes it possible for essences to become the subject of ideas resulting, for example, in the universal idea of man. We have, however, the power by way of abstraction to conjure ideas of things whose essences are not exemplified. For example, one can conceive of a mermaid without that conception entailing exemplification. Therefore, the exemplified existence of a sensible object cannot be caused by the essence of that thing, otherwise such a thing would bring itself into existence. That this is the case requires the existence of a first cause which would needs be such that its essence and existence are identical. There is only one such being, namely God.

CONCERNING BEING AND ESSENCE

Introduction

Because a small error in the beginning is a great one in the end, according to the Philosopher [i.e., Aristotle] in the first book of the *De Caelo et Mundo*,[1] and since being and essence are what are first conceived by the intellect, as Avicenna says in the first book of his *Metaphysics*,[2] therefore, lest error befall from ignorance of them (being and essence), in order to reveal their difficulty it should be said what is signified by the names being and essence, and how they are found in diverse things and how they are disposed with respect to *(se habeant ad)* logical intentions, namely, genus, species, and difference.

Chapter 1

Because indeed we must receive knowledge of the simple from the composite and arrive at what is prior from what is posterior, in order that beginning with the less difficult instruction may be made more suitably, we should proceed from the meaning of being to the meaning of essence.

Therefore one should know, as the Philosopher says in the fifth of the *Metaphysics*,[3] that being by itself *(ens per se)* is said to be taken in two modes: in the one mode, that it is divided into ten genera; in the other, that it signifies the truth of propositions. Moreover the difference between these is that in the second mode everything can be called being concerning which an affirmative proposition can be formed, even if it posits nothing in the thing *(in re)*; by virtue of this mode privations and negations are likewise called beings, for we say that affirmation is the opposite of ne-

From St. Thomas Aquinas, *Concerning Being and Essence*, translated by George G. Leckie (New York & London: Appleton-Century-Crofts, Inc., 1937, renewed 1965), pp. 3–27. Reprinted by permission of Prentice-Hall, Englewood Cliffs, New Jersey.

gation, and that blindness is in the eye. But in the first mode only what posits something in the thing can be called being; consequently, according to the first mode blindness and such are not beings. The name essence, therefore, is not taken from being in the second mode, for in this mode some things are said to have essence which have not being, as is evident in privations. But essence is taken from being only in the first mode; whence the Commentator [i.e., Averroës] says in the same place that[4] "being in the first mode is said to be what signifies the essence of the thing." And because, as has been said, being in this mode is divided into ten genera, it follows that essence signifies something common to all natures by which diverse beings are disposed in different genera and species, as for instance humanity is the essence of man and so for others. And because that by means of which the thing is constituted in its proper genus or species is that which is signified by the definition indicating what the thing is, hence it is that the name essence has been changed by philosophers into the name quiddity. And this is what the Philosopher frequently calls *"quod quid erat esse,"*[5] that is, that by virtue of which a thing (anything) has to be what it is (something). And indeed it is called form according as by means of form the certitude of any single thing is signified, as Avicenna remarks in the second part of his *Metaphysics*.[6] This is called by another name, nature, accepting nature according to the first of the four modes assigned by Boethius in his book *De Duabus Naturis*,[7] namely, according as nature is said to be all that which can be comprehended by the intellect in any mode whatsoever; for a thing is not intelligible except by virtue of its definition and essence. And thus also the Philosopher in the Fourth book of his *Metaphysics*[8] says that every substance is a nature. But the name nature taken in this sense is seen to signify the essence of a thing inasmuch as it has a disposition *(ordinem)* towards an operation proper to the thing, since no thing is lacking in its proper operation. Indeed the name quiddity is taken from that which signifies the definition; but it is called essence according as by virtue of it and in it being has existence (*esse*).

But because being is asserted absolutely and primarily of substances and secondarily and as if in a certain respect (*secundum quid*) of accidents, hence it is that essence also exists truly and properly in substances, but exists in accidents in a certain mode and in a certain respect. Some substances indeed are simple and others are composite, and in both there is an essence. But essence is possessed by simple substances in a truer and more noble mode according as simple substances have a more exalted existence, for they are the cause of those which are composite,—at least the primary substance, which is God, is. But since the essences of these substances are more concealed from us, therefore we must begin from the essences of composite substances in order that instruction may be made more suitably from what is easier.

Chapter 2

In composite substances, therefore, matter and form are noted, as for instance in man soul and body are noted. Moreover it cannot be said that either of these alone is called essence. For it is evident that matter alone is not the essence of the thing, because it is by means of its essence that the thing is both known and ordered in its species and genus. But matter is not the principle of cognition, nor is anything determined as regards genus and species according to it (matter), but according to that by means of which something is in act. And furthermore neither can form alone be called the essence of composite substance, however much some attempt to assert this. From what has been said it is clear that essence is what is signified by the definition of the thing. But the definition of natural substances contains not only form but also matter; for otherwise natural definitions and mathematical definitions would not

differ. Nor can it be said that matter is posited in the definition of a natural substance as an addition to its essence or as a being outside of its essence (*extra essentiam*), since this mode of definition is more proper to accidents which do not have a perfect essence; whence it follows that they must admit the subject into their definition, which (subject) is outside of their genus. It is clear, therefore, that essence comprehends matter and form. But it cannot be said that essence signifies a relation which is between matter and form, or that it is something superadded to them, since something superadded would of necessity be accidental or extraneous to the thing, nor could the thing be conceived by means of it, for everything is appropriate to its essence. For by the form, which is the actuality of matter, matter is made being in act and a this somewhat. Whence that which is superadded does not give existence (*esse*) in act simply to matter, but existence in act of such sort as likewise accidents make, as for instance whiteness makes something white in act. Wherefore whenever such form is acquired it is not said to be generated simply but in a certain respect (*secundum quid*). Hence it follows that in composite substances the name of essence signifies that which is composed of matter and form. And this agrees also with the opinion of Boethius in his commentary *Predicamentorum*,[9] where he says that *ousia* signifies a composite. For *ousia* according to the Greeks is the same as essence according to us, as Boethius himself remarks in his book *De Duabus Naturis*.[10] Avicenna also says[11] that the quiddity of composite substances is itself a composition of matter and form. The Commentator also says concerning the seventh book of the *Metaphysics*:[12] "The nature which species have in things capable of generation is something intermediate that is composed of matter and form." Reason also accords with this, because the existence of a composite substance is not the existence of form only, nor the existence of matter only, but of the composite itself; and indeed essence is that according to which a thing is said to exist. Whence it follows that the essence by virtue of which a thing is called being is not form alone, nor matter alone, but both; although in its mode the form is the cause of its existence. We discover it indeed thus in other things which are constituted from more than one principle, since a thing is not named from one of those principles alone, but from that which unites both. It appears thus in the case of tastes, because sweetness is caused from the action of warmth dissolving moisture, and although in this mode the warmth is the cause of the sweetness, yet a body is not called sweet from its warmth but from the taste which unites both the warmth and the moisture.

But because the principle of individuation is matter, it perhaps seems to follow from this that essence which unites in itself both matter and form would be only particular and not universal. From this it would follow that universals do not have definition, if essence is what is signified by means of the definition. One should therefore understand that matter in any mode whatsoever is not taken to be the principle of individuation, but only signated matter *(materia signata)*. And I call signated matter that which is considered as under determinate dimensions. But now this matter is not posited in the definition of man inasmuch as he is man, but it would be posited in the definition of Socrates if Socrates were to have a definition. But in the definition of man non-signated matter is posited; for in the definition of man this certain flesh and this certain bone are not posited, but bone and flesh absolutely, which are the non-signated matter of man. Accordingly, it is clear that the essence of Socrates and the essence of man do not differ except according to signate and non-signate. Whence the Commentator remarks upon the seventh of the *Metaphysics:*[13] "Socrates is nothing other than animality and rationality which are his quiddity." Thus also the essence of genus and of species differ according to signate and non-signate, although there is a different mode of designation for each of them, because the designation of the individual with respect to species is by means of matter determined by dimensions, whereas the designation of species in respect to genus is by means of the constitutive difference which is taken from the form of the thing.

This determination or designation, however, which is in the species in respect to genus is not by means of something existing in the essence of species, which is in no mode in the essence of genus; nay, whatever is in species is in genus as something undetermined. For if animal is not the whole of man, but part of him, it is not predicated of him, since no integral part is predicated of its whole.

But how this is related can be seen if one observes how body differs according as animal is posited as part or as genus; for it cannot be genus in the same mode in which it is an integral part. This name body, therefore, is taken in several senses. For body according as it is in the genus of substance is asserted of that which has a nature such that three dimensions can be designated in it; in truth the three designated dimensions themselves are body which is in the genus of quantity. But it happens in things that what has one perfection may also aim at further perfection; as for instance is clear in the case of man, since he has both a sensitive nature and further, intellectual nature. Likewise indeed beyond this perfection which is to have such a form that three dimensions can be designated in it, another perfection can be added, as life or something of this sort. This name body, therefore, can signify a certain thing which has a form such that from it follows the possibility of designating three dimensions in it, with this limitation, namely, that from that form no further perfection may follow, but if anything else is added it is beyond the significance of body thus spoken of. And in this mode body is an integral and material part of animal, because the soul will be beyond what is signified by the name body and will be something added to (excelling) body itself in such wise that from these two, that is, from soul and body, the animal is constituted as from its parts. This name body can also be taken so as to signify a certain thing which has a form such that from the form three dimensions can be designated in it, whatsoever that form may be, and whether any further perfection can issue from it or not. And in this mode body is the genus of animal, because in animal nothing is taken which is not contained implicitly in body; for soul is not a form different from that by means of which three dimensions can be designated in that thing. And therefore when it was said that body is what has a form such that from the form three dimensions can be designated in the body, it was to be understood of whatever the form might be, whether animality or lapidity or any other. And so the form of animal is contained implicitly in the form of body, according as body is its genus. And such too is the habitude (relation) of animal to man. For if animal denoted only a certain thing which has a perfection such that it can feel and be moved by virtue of a principle existing in itself, to the exclusion of any further perfections, then whatever further perfection supervened to the thing, would be disposed in respect to *(haberet se ad)* animal by means of the partitive mode *(modum partis)* and not as if implicitly beneath (included in) the principle of animal, and thus animal would not be a genus. But animal is a genus according as it signifies a certain thing from the form of which can issue feeling and motion, whatsoever this form may be, whether it be the sensible soul alone or the sensible and rational together. Thus, therefore, genus signifies indeterminately all that which is in species, for it does not signify matter alone. Similarly, difference signifies the whole, but it does not signify form alone. And definition likewise signifies a whole, and also species does. But yet in diverse ways: because genus signifies a whole as a certain determination determining what is material in a thing, without the determination of the proper form. Whence genus is taken from matter, although it is not matter, as is evident in the instance of what is called body because it has a perfection such that three dimensions can be designated in it, which certain perfection is materially dis-

posed towards further perfection. In truth, on the contrary, difference is taken determinately as a certain determination by form, for the reason that determined matter is involved in the primary conception of it, as appears when it is called animate or that which has soul; for what it is, whether body or something else, is not determined. Whence Avicenna says[14] that genus is not intellected in difference as a part of essence, but only as a being beyond its essence *(extra essentiam)*, just as a subject is in regard to the intellection of the passions. And therefore, likewise, speaking per se, genus is not predicated concerning difference, as the Philosopher remarks in the third of the *Metaphysics*[15] and the fourth of the *Topics*, unless perchance as a subject is predicated of passion. But definition or species comprehends both, namely, determinate matter which the name of genus designates, and determinate form which the name of difference designates.

And from this the reason is clear why genus and species and difference are proportionally disposed towards *(se habeant ad)* matter and form and the composite in nature, although they are not the same as nature, since genus is not matter but taken from matter as signifying the whole, nor is difference form but taken from form as signifying the whole. Wherefore we call man a rational animal, not from the composite of animal and rational, as we say that he is composed of body and soul: for man is said to be composed of soul and body, just as from two things a third thing is truly constituted, which is neither of the two; for man is neither soul nor body. But if man can be said to be composed in some manner of animal and rational, it is not as a third thing from two things but as a third concept from two concepts; for the concept of animal is one expressing, without the determination of a special form, the nature of a thing, by that which is material in respect to its ultimate perfection. The concept, however, of the difference rational consists in the determination of a special form. And from the two concepts (animal and rational) is constituted the concept of the species or definition. And therefore just as a thing constituted from other things does not take the predication of those things, thus neither does the concept take the predication of those concepts from which it is constituted, for we do not say that the definition is genus or difference.

But, although genus signifies the whole essence of species, yet it does not follow that there is one essence of different species which have the same genus, because the unity of the genus proceeds from its very indetermination and indifference; not, however, because that which is signified by genus is one nature by number in different species to which supervenes something else which is the difference determining it, as for instance form determines matter which is numerically one; but because genus signifies some form, though not determinately this or that (form) which difference expresses determinately, which is none other than that (form) which is signified indeterminately through genus. And therefore the Commentator says in the twelfth book of the *Metaphysics*[16] that prime matter is called one through the remotion of all forms (scil. pure potentiality in the order of substance), but genus is called one through the community of its signified form. Whence it is clear that by means of the addition of difference, which removes the indetermination which was the cause of the unity of genus, species remain different by virtue of essence.

And because, as has been said, the nature of species is indeterminate in respect to the individual, just as the nature of genus is indeterminate with respect to species, hence it is that, just as that which is genus according as it is predicated concerning species implies in its signification, although indistinctly, all that is determinate in species, thus likewise it follows that what is species, according as it is predicated of the individual, signifies all that which is in the individual essentially although indistinctly. And in this mode the essence of Socrates is signified by the name of man, and as a consequence man is predicated of Socrates. But if the nature of the species be

signified with the exclusion of designated matter, which is the principle of individuation, it will thus be disposed *(se habebit)* as a part (by means of the partitive mode). And in this mode it is signified by the name humanity, for humanity signifies that in virtue of which man is man. But designated matter is not that in virtue of which man is man; and, therefore, in no mode is it contained among those things from which man possesses manness. Since therefore humanity includes in its concept only those things from which man possesses manness, it is clear that designated matter is excluded from or cut off from its signification. And since the part is not predicated of the whole, hence it is that humanity is not predicated either of man or of Socrates. Wherefore Avicenna says[17] that the quiddity of a composite is not the composite itself of which it is the quiddity, although the quiddity itself is composite: as for instance humanity, although it is composite, still is not man. Nay rather, it must be received in something which is designated matter. But since, as has been said, the designation of species in respect to genus is by virtue of form, whereas the designation of the individual in respect to species is by virtue of matter, it follows therefore that the name signifying that whence the nature of genus is taken, with the exclusion of the determinate form perfecting the species, should signify the material part of the whole itself, as the body is the material part of man. But the name signifying that whence the nature of species is taken, with the exclusion of designated matter, signifies the formal part. And therefore humanity is signified as a certain form, and is spoken of as that which is the form of the whole; not indeed as if it were superadded to the essential parts, namely, to form and matter, as for instance the form of a house is superadded to its integral parts; but rather it is form that is the whole, that is, embracing form and matter, yet with the exclusion of those things by means of which matter is found to be designated. So, therefore, it is clear that the name man and the name humanity signify the essence of man, but in different modes, as has been said, since the name man signifies it as a whole, inasmuch as it does not exclude the designation of matter but contains it implicitly and indistinctly, as for instance it has been said that the genus contains the difference. And therefore the name man is predicated of individuals. But the name humanity signifies the essence as a part, since it does not contain in its signification anything except what is of man inasmuch as he is man, and because it excludes all designation of matter; whence it is not predicated of individual man. And for this reason likewise the name essence sometimes is found predicated of a thing, for Socrates is said to be an essence, and sometimes it is denied, as for instance it is said that the essence of Socrates is not Socrates.

Chapter 3

Having seen, therefore, what is signified by the name of essence in composite substances, we should see in what mode it is disposed towards *(se habeat ad)* the ratio of genus, species, and difference. Since, however, that to which the ratio of genus or species or difference applies is predicated concerning this signate singular, it is impossible that the ratio of the universal, namely, that of genus and of species, should apply to essence according as it is signified by means of the partitive mode, as for instance by the name humanity or animality. And therefore Avicenna says[18] that rationality is not the difference, but the principle of difference. And for the same reason humanity is not species nor is animality genus. Similarly, also, it cannot be said that the ratio of genus or of species applies to essence according as essence is a certain thing existing apart from singulars, as the Platonists were accustomed to assert, since thus genus and species would not be predicated of this individual. For it cannot be said that Socrates is what is separated from him, nor again that the separated conduces to the cognition of a singular. And therefore it follows that the ratio of genus

or species applies to essence according as it is signified in the mode of a whole, as for instance by the name of man or animal, according as it contains implicitly and indistinctly all that is in the individual.

But nature or essence taken thus can be considered in two ways. In one mode according to its proper ratio, and this is the absolute consideration of it, and in this mode nothing is true concerning it except what applies to it according to this mode, whence whatever else is attributed to it is a false attribution. For example, to man inasmuch as he is man rational and animal applies and the other things which fall within his definition. White or black, however, and whatsoever of this mode, which is not of the ratio of humanity, does not apply to man inasmuch as he is man. Accordingly, if it were asked whether this nature thus considered can be said to be one or more than one, neither ought to be conceded, because each is outside the concept of humanity, and either one can happen to it *(accidere)*. For if plurality were to belong to the concept of humanity, it could never be one although nevertheless it is one according as it is in Socrates. Similarly, if unity were to belong to its ratio, then would it be one and the same of Socrates and of Plato, nor could it be multiplied *(plurificari)* in many. It is considered in another mode according to the existence *(esse)* which it has in this or that, and in this mode something is predicated concerning it by means of accident *(per accidens)*, by reason of that in which it is, as for instance it is said that man is white because Socrates is white, although this does not apply to man inasmuch as he is man.

But this nature has a twofold existence: having one existence in singulars and another in the soul, and according to both of the two, accident follows upon the nature spoken of, and in singulars also it has a manifold existence according to the diversity of the singulars. And nevertheless to this very nature according to its primary consideration, that is to say, its absolute one, none of these (existences) ought to belong. For it is false to say that the essence of man, inasmuch as he is man, has existence in this singular, because if existence in this singular applied to man as man, then (man) would never exist outside of this singular. Similarly, also, if it applied to man as man not to exist in this singular, (man) would never exist in it. But it is true to say that man as man does not have to be in this singular or in that or in the soul. Therefore it is clear that the nature of man absolutely considered abstracts from any sort of existence, yet in such wise that it does not exclude any of them. And this nature so considered is what is predicated of all individuals. Still it cannot be said that the ratio of universal applies to nature thus considered, because unity and community belong to the principle of the universal, whereas to human nature neither of these (two) applies according to its absolute consideration. For if community belonged to the concept of man, then in whatsoever humanity were found community would be found. And this is false because in Socrates there is not found any community, but whatever is in him is individuated. Similarly, also, it cannot be said that the ratio of genus or of species belongs to human nature according to the existence which it has in individuals, because human nature is not found in individuals according to its unity so that it is a one appropriate to all, which the ratio of the universal demands. It follows, therefore, that the ratio of species applies to human nature according to that existence (esse) which it has in the intellect. For human nature itself has an existence in the intellect abstracted from all individuations, and therefore it has a uniform ratio to all individuals which are outside the soul, according as it is equally the likeness (similitudo) of all and leads to the understanding of all inasmuch as they are men. And because it has such a relation to all individuals, the intellect discovers the ratio of species and attributes it to it (human nature). Whence the Commentator observes in the first book of the De Anima[19] that intellect is what actuates (agit) universality in things. Avicenna also says this in his Metaphysics.[20] Whence, although this intellectual nature has the ratio of universal according as it is compared to things which are outside of the soul because it is a single likeness of all, nevertheless according as it has existence in this intellect or that it is a certain particular intellected species. And therefore the error of the Commentator in book three of the De Anima[21] is clear, seeing that he wished to conclude from the universality of the intellected form to the unity of the intellect in all men; because there is no universality of that form according to the existence which it has in the intellect, but according as it is referred to things as a likeness of things. Thus, too, if there were a single corporeal statue representing many men, it is clear that the image or species of the statue would have an existence singular and proper according as it existed in this matter, but it would have a ratio of community according as it were a common thing representing many. And because to human nature according to its absolute consideration belongs what is predicated of Socrates, and since the ratio of species does not belong to it according to its absolute consideration, but follows from accidents which issue from it according to the existence which it has in the intellect, therefore the name of species is not predicated of Socrates so that it is said that Socrates is a species, which would necessarily happen if the ratio of species belonged to man according to the existence which he has in Socrates, or according to man's absolute consideration, namely, inasmuch as he is man; for whatever applies to man inasmuch as he is man is predicated of Socrates. Yet to be predicated applies to genus by virtue of itself (per se), since it is posited in its definition. For predication is a certain thing which is perfected by means of the action of the intellect composing and dividing, having in the very thing as its foundation the unity of those things of which one is asserted of the other. Whence the ratio of predicability can be included in the ratio of this mode of intention which is genus, which, similarly, is perfected by means of an act of the intellect. Yet, nevertheless, that to which the intellect attrib-

utes the intention of predication, composing the one with the other, is not the very
intention of genus but rather that to which
the intellect attributes the intention of genus, as for instance what is signified by the
name animal. Thus, therefore, it is clear
how essence or nature is disposed towards
(se habet ad) the ratio of species, because the
ratio of species does not belong to those
things which are appropriate to it according to its absolute consideration, nor likewise does it belong to the accidents which
issue from it according to the existence
which it has outside the soul, as whiteness
or blackness. But it does belong to the accidents which issue from it according to the
existence which it has in the intellect. And
it is according to this mode that the ratio of
genus and of difference also applies to it.

Chapter 4

Now it remains to see through what
mode essence exists in separate substances,
namely, in the soul, in intelligences and in
the first cause. But although all grant the
simplicity of the first cause, yet certain ones
strive to introduce a composition of form
and matter in intelligences and in the soul.
The author of this position appears to have
been Avicebron, the writer of the book *Fons
Vitae*.[22] But this is opposed to what is commonly said by philosophers, seeing that
they call them substances separated from
matter and prove them to be devoid of all
matter. The most powerful reason for the
assertion is (taken) from the power (*virtute*)
of understanding which is in them (separate substances). For we see that forms are
not intelligible in act except according as
they are separated from matter and its conditions, nor are they made intelligible in act
except by the power (*per virtutem*) of intelligent substance, inasmuch as they are received in it and inasmuch as they are actuated by virtue of it. Whence it is
necessary that in any intelligent substance
there be entire immunity from matter in
such wise that they neither have a material

part to them nor yet exist as a form impressed in matter, as is the case respecting
material forms. Nor can anyone say that intelligibility is not impeded by any sort of
matter, but only by corporeal matter. For if
this impediment were by reason of corporeal matter alone, since matter is not spoken of as corporeal except inasmuch as it
stands under corporeal form, then it would
follow necessarily that matter would impede intelligibility by means of its corporeal form. And this cannot be, because the
very corporeal form also is intelligible in
act, just as other forms are, inasmuch as it
is abstracted from matter. Wherefore in the
soul or in an intelligence there is in no way
a composition of matter and form so that
essence might be taken in them in the mode
in which it is taken in corporeal substances.
But there is there (in them) a composition
of form and existence; whence it is said in
the comment on the ninth proposition of
the book *De Causis*[23] that intelligence is
having form and existence; and form is
taken there for the very quiddity or simple
nature.

But it is easy to see how this is. For whatever things are disposed towards (*se habent
ad*) one another in such wise that one is the
cause of the existence of the other, that
which has the ratio of cause can possess existence without the other, but not conversely. But such is found to be the habitude of matter and form, because form
gives existence to matter, and therefore it
is impossible for matter to be without some
form, yet it is not impossible for any form
to exist without matter, for form inasmuch
as it is form does not depend on matter. But
if any forms should be discovered which
cannot exist save in matter, this happens to
them inasmuch as they are distant from the
first principle which is the first and pure
act. Whence those forms which have the
greatest propinquity to the first principle
are forms subsisting by virtue of themselves (per se) without matter. For form
does not require matter according to its entire genus, as has been said, and forms of
this sort are intelligences. And therefore it

is not necessary that the essences or quiddities of these substances be anything save the very form. Therefore the essence of a composite substance and the essence of a simple substance differ in that the essence of a composite substance is not form alone but embraces form and matter, whereas the essence of a simple substance is form alone. And from this two other differences are derived. One is that the essence of a composite substance can be signified as a whole or as a part, which happens according to the designation of the matter, as has been stated. And therefore the essence of a composite thing is not predicated in any mode whatsoever of the composite thing itself; for it cannot be said that man is his quiddity. But the essence of a simple thing, which is its form, cannot be signified except as a whole, since there is nothing there except the form as form receiving, and, therefore, in whatever mode the essence of a simple substance is taken it is predicated of the substance. Whence Avicenna says[24] that the quiddity of a simple (substance) is itself simple, because there is not anything else receptive of the quiddity. The second difference is that the essences of composite things, seeing that they are received in designated matter, are multiplied according to its division, whence it results that some things are the same in species and diverse numerically. But since the essence of simple substance is not received in matter, there cannot be there any such multiplication. And therefore it follows necessarily that in these substances more than one individual of the same species are not found, but however many individuals there are, just so many are the species, as Avicenna expressly says[25] (scil. "A species of this mode is one in number.").

And indeed substances of this sort, although they are forms alone without matter, still do not have an entire simplicity of nature so that they are pure act; on the contrary, they have a mixture of potency, which is evident thus: for whatsoever does not belong to the concept of essence or quiddity is something accruing from without and effecting a composition with the essence, since no essence can be conceived without those things which are parts of essence. But every essence or quiddity can be conceived aside from the condition that something be known concerning its existence, for I can conceive what a man or phoenix is and still not know whether it has existence in the nature of things. Therefore it is clear that existence is something other than essence or quiddity, unless perhaps there be something the quiddity of which is its very existence. And this thing can only be one and primary, because it is impossible that a multiplication of anything should be effected except by virtue of the addition of some difference, as the nature of genus is multiplied into species either by virtue of this, that the form is received in diverse matters, just as the nature of species is multiplied in diverse individuals, or by virtue of this, that it is one thing absolutely but another as received in something, as for instance if there were a certain separated heat it would be other than a non-separated heat from its very separation. But if some thing is posited which is existence alone such that the existence itself is subsisting, this existence does not receive an addition of difference, since then it would not be existence only but existence and beyond that some form; and much less does it receive an addition of matter because then it would be not a subsisting existence but a material existence. Wherefore it is clear that a thing such that it is its own existence cannot be except as one (unique). Whence it follows necessarily that in anything whatsoever except this (the unique) its existence must be one thing and its quiddity or nature or form another. Accordingly, in intelligences there is an existence over and beyond form, and therefore it has been said that an intelligence is form and existence.

But all that belongs to anything is either caused from principles of its nature, as for instance risibility in man, or accrues to it through some extrinsic principle, as for instance light in air from the influence of the sun. But it cannot be that existence itself should be caused by the form or quiddity of the thing, caused, I say, as by means of an efficient cause, because thus something would be the cause of itself and would bring its very self into existence, which is impossible. Therefore it follows that everything such that its existence is other than its nature has existence from another *(ab alio)*. And because everything which exists by virtue of another is reduced to that which exists in virtue of itself (per se), as to its first cause, it follows that there must be something which is the cause of the existence *(causa essendi)* of all things, because it is very existence alone; otherwise the causes would proceed to infinity, since everything which is not existence alone would have a cause of its existence, as has been said. It is clear, therefore, that an intelligence is form and existence, and that it has its existence from the first being which is existence alone, and this is the first cause which is God. But everything which receives something from something *(aliquid ab aliquo)* is in potency in respect to that, and what is received in it is its act. Therefore it follows that the very quiddity or form which is the intelligence is in potency in respect to the existence which it receives from God, and that existence is received according to the mode of act. And thus potency and act are found in intelligences, yet not form and matter, except equivocally. Whence, too, to suffer, to receive, to be a subject and all things of this kind which are seen to belong to things by reason of matter, belong equivocally to intellectual substances and to corporeal substances, as the Commentator says in the third book of the *De Anima*.[26] And because, as has been said, the quiddity of an intelligence is the intelligence itself, therefore its quiddity or essence is the same thing as itself, and its existence, received from God, is that by means of which it subsists in the nature of things. And for this reason substances of this sort are said by some to be composed of that by virtue of which it is *(quo est)* and that which it is *(quod est),* or of that which it is and existence, as Boethius says.[27]

And since potency and act are posited in intelligences it will not be difficult to find a multitude of intelligences, which would be impossible if there were no potency in them. Whence the Commentator says in the third book of the *De Anima*,[28] that if the nature of the possible intellect were unknown we should not be able to discover multiplicity in separate substances. Therefore the distinction of these in regard to one another is according to their grade (measure) of potency and act, so that a superior intelligence which is more proximate to the first (being) has more of act and less of potency, and so for others. And this is fulfilled in the human soul which holds the lowest grade among intellectual substances. Whence its possible intellect is disposed towards *(se habet ad)* intelligible forms just as first matter, which holds the lowest grade in sensible existence, is disposed towards sensible forms, as the Commentator remarks in book three of the *De Anima*.[29] And therefore the Philosopher[30] compares it to a tablet upon which nothing is written, and for this reason among other intelligible substances it has more potency. Accordingly, it is made to be so close to material things that the material thing is drawn to participate in its existence, so that from soul and body results one existence in one composite, although that existence according as it pertains to soul is not dependent upon the body. And therefore after that form which is in the soul are discovered other forms having more potency and more propinquity to matter. In these, too, is found order *(ordo)* and grade (measure: *gradus*) all the way through to the first forms of elements which are in the greatest propinquity to matter. Accordingly, they do not have any operation except according to the exigency of active and passive qualities, and of the others by which matter is disposed to form.

NOTES

1. Aristotle, *De Caelo et Mundo*, A, 271 b 8–13.
2. Avicenna, *Metaphysics*, Tr. I, Cap. 6, f. 72 b A.
3. Aristotle, *Metaphysics*, △, 1017 a 22–35; also *Met.*, E, b 17–35.
4. Averroës, *In Met.* L.V., comm. 14, f. 55 a 56.
5. Aristotle, *An. Post.* I, 22, 82 b 38; *De An.* III, 6, 430 b 28; *Met.*, Z, 1028 b 34.
6. Avicenna, perhaps *Met.* III, 5, f. 80 b; *certitudo*: essence.
7. Boethius, *De Persona et Duabus Nat.*, c. I, PL, t. 64, col. 1341BC.
8. Aristotle, *Metaphysics*, △, 1014 b. 35.
9. In Cat. I, *De Substantia*, PL, t. 64, col. 184 A.
10. *De Persona et Duabus*, Nat., PL, t. 64, col. 1344 C.D.
11. Avicenna, *Met.*, V, 5, f. 90 a F.
12. Averroës, *In Met.*, VII, c. 7, comm. 27, f. 83 a 41.
13. Averroës, *In Met.*, VII, 5, comm. 20, f. 80 a 23.
14. *Met.*, V, 6, f. 90 a BC.
15. Aristotle, *Met.*, B, 998 b 24.
16. Averroës, *In Met.*, XII, c. 14, f. 141 a 53 b 18.
17. Avicenna, *Met.*, V, c. 5, f. 90 a F.
18. Avicenna, *Met.*, V, 6, f. 90 b A.
19. Averroës, *In De An.*, I, com. 8, f. 4.
20. Avicenna, *Met.*, V, i, f., 87 b E, 87 a C–b D.
21. Averroës, *In De An.*, III, com. 5, f. 117.
22. Cf. Baeumker, Avencebrolis (Solomon Ibn Gabirol), *Fons Vitae*, Münster, 1895.
23. Cf. Bardenhewer, "Die pseudo-aristotelische Schrift Über das Reine Gute" bekannt unter dem Namen "Liber de Causis," Fibourg-en-Bas, 1882, No. 8, p. 173.
24. Avicenna, *Met.*, V, 5, f. 90 a F.
25. Avicenna, *Met.*, V, 2, f. 87 a A.
26. Averroës, *In De An.*, III, com. 14, f. 123.
27. Boethius, *De Hebd.*, PL, t. 64, col. 1311 C.
28. Averroës, *In De An.*, III, com. 5, f. 118.
29. Averroës, *In De An.*, III, com. 5, f. 113.
30. Aristotle, *De An.*, III, 430 a I.

CHAPTER 40

John Duns Scotus

(See Chapter Six for biography.)

Duns Scotus on Individuation

Scotus relied heavily on the doctrine of the formal distinction. This doctrine states that there is a legitimate distinction that lies between the real distinction and the virtual or conceptual distinction. There is a real distinction between two or more individual things, such as between a dog and a house. A conceptual distinction pertains to different descriptions of the same thing. For example, the terms 'morning star' and 'evening star' refer to the same entity, namely, Venus. A formal distinction is one in which the mind can distinguish between two or more logically distinct characteristics (formalitates) that in reality are inseparable from one another.

Scotus employs the formal distinction to explain the nature of universals. He argues that the form-content distinction is a real distinction, because matter and form can undergo real separation: matter can manifest itself in different forms, although it cannot possess two different forms at the same time. This is not the case concerning the nature and the "thisness" (haecceity) of a thing. The thisness or individuality of a concrete entity cannot in reality be separated from its nature, although the two are formally distinct. For example, Socrates is an individual (thing) distinct from Plato. Each possesses the characteristic (nature) of humanness, which is in reality inseparable from each. However, the mind can distinguish between the individual and the nature that necessarily characterizes both Socrates and Plato. In other words, the haecceity of both Socrates and Plato are formally distinct from their nature.

The nature of a thing does not constitute a universal, for then there would be as many universals as there are individuals who possess that characteristic and thus universals would not be universal, but particulars. Rather, Scotus chooses to speak of universal judgments we make about individuals. Universal judgments about particulars are made possible by the objective nature of the characteristics possessed by individuals. Consequently, Scotus is not a realist in the sense of holding that universals possess a reality unto themselves such as classes (viz., Aristotle). Nor is he a conceptualist. For him, particulars are what they are by their very nature. As he says, "horseness is simply horseness". Consequently, Scotus is a particularist, and this accounts for the fact that he conceives the problem to be one of individuation rather than one concerning universals.

THE PRINCIPLE OF INDIVIDUATION

Question One:
Is a Material Substance of Its Nature 'This,' That Is, Singular and Individual?

1. Concerning the third distinction (which treats of the personality of the angels) the first question raised is about the singularity in material substances. For it is on the basis of the divergent views about the cause of individuation in material substance that their proponents think differently about the personality of the angels, and about their personality or unity in one species. The first question then is whether a material substance by its very nature is a 'this,' that is, singular and individual. And here 'singularity' is not understood as a second intention corresponding to 'universality' as its opposite, but the question concerns the material substance itself. Is a material substance of its very nature numerically one, incapable of division into several individuals?

Initial Arguments Pro and Con

2. [AFFIRMATIVE] It seems that it is according to the Philosopher (VII *Metaphysics*: ch. 13) who asserts that a universal is not a substance (against Plato). Thus he says: "The substance of each thing is that which is peculiar to it and does not belong to many things"; but a universal does belong to many things; therefore, a universal is not a substance. But if the substance of anything is peculiar or proper to that thing in which it is and is not to be found in many things, then this is something due to its nature, something it has naturally. Another argument he makes in the same place is that "substance is not predicable of a subject, but the universal is always predicable of some subject." The inference drawn from this is that a material substance is of itself a 'this,' for otherwise it would of itself be predicated of a subject.

Reprinted from Duns Scotus' *Early Oxford Lecture on Individuation*, translated by Allan B. Wolter, O.F.M. (Santa Barbara, Calif.: Old Mission Santa Barbara, 1992), pp. 3–103.

3. [NEGATIVE] On the contrary:
What pertains to something of itself also pertains to it in anything where it may be found; if it were the nature of stone to be just this individual, then it would be the self-same individual in anything that was stone, and hence there could not be several stones.

4. Also, whatever pertains of itself to one of polar-opposites, is diametrically opposed to its opposite; if then to be this singular pertained to the nature of stone, a multitude in the same species would be diametrically opposed to the nature of stone.

I. To the Question
A. The Opinion of Others

5. [EXPLANATION OF THE OPINION] Some[1] say to this question that there is no intervening cause between the nature of a thing and its singularity. One should not look for any further reason between the nature and its singularity, but those causes of a thing which give existence to its nature also account for its singularity (and these are the concurrent causes of a thing: agent, matter and form, and final cause).

6. Now they give this reason: A thing, apart from all else, has the status of a singular. Only through an operation of the intellect does it take on the character of a universal. And from this they argue: When characteristics pertain to a thing in different ways, one in an unqualified, the other in a qualified sense, while what belongs to it in this second way, may be due to another, what follows simply from the existence of a thing pertains to it of itself and does not stem from another. Since 'to be a universal,' therefore, is only 'to be' in a qualified sense, it will pertain to a thing because of the intellect, whereas 'to be singular' is 'to be' in an unqualified sense; hence it will pertain to a thing of itself, of its very nature.

7. Thus if you ask them for the cause of singularity, they reply there is nothing between the nature and its singularity that is the cause of individuation. Rather that which is the cause of the nature of the thing

in question is also that by which it is individuated; and in this sense the nature of itself is singular.[2]

8. [REFUTATION OF THIS VIEW] I argue against this opinion in two ways: The first is this: The object of the intellect is prior by nature to the act by which it is understood, for the object is the cause of the act, according to what was explained in Bk. I—or if it is not cause of the act, all admit that it precedes the knowledge of itself. Consequently, a stone, as it first presents itself as object to the intellect, is prior to knowing it, but in that [ontologically] prior status, stone—on this view—is singular of itself [qua stone]. Understanding stone in its universal aspects, therefore, is to grasp it under an objective aspect that is opposed to the way it is and exists as object; therefore, any understanding of a thing qua universal is an intellection opposed to the proper notion of the object.

9. I also argue in a second way. Anything whose proper unity is less than numerical unity, is not a numerical unity; but the unity of the stone-nature is of itself less than a numerical unity; therefore the unity of the stone-nature, which stone has of itself, is not a numerical unity.

10. The major is sufficiently obvious, because a lesser unity is consistent with the opposite of a greater unity; therefore a numerical multitude, the opposite of numerical unity, is consistent or compatible with a unity that is less than numerical unity; now the same thing is not consistent with the opposite of itself; therefore, this unity less than numerical unity is not itself a numerical unity.

11. But the minor is also true. The unity of the stone-nature in this stone is less than the numerical unity of this-stone, because if this unity characteristic of the nature [of stone] were not less than a numerical unity, there would be no 'real unity' less than numerical unity; the consequent is false, however, therefore the antecedent is also.

12. Proof of the implication: Consider any unity other than the unity of nature

that is also less than numerical unity (for example, generic unity or that of analogy). Now if this unity of the nature is not a lesser unity than numerical unity, then no unity whatsoever is less than numerical unity. But this consequent is false, and its falsity is proved in many ways.

13. The first way is this:

The Philosopher says in X *Metaphysics*, [ch. 1] that 'In every genus, there is a first unit that is the measure of all that follows in that genus.'

14. This first, however, qua measure of the rest, has its own unity, as is clear from what he says there. ('One,' which is the measure in numbers, as a unit, has unity, and from this [the notion of *unit*] is transferred to other things.) The unity it possesses is also real; this follows because others share it, for it is not nothing, but some one thing that they share. From this it follows that a real unity characterizes that 'first' in any genus.

15. But this unity of the first in any genus is not a numerical unity, but a lesser unity, for otherwise, that first, which is the measure of the others, would be one in number, which is patently false. First, it contradicts what the Philosopher says in that same book X [ch. 2] about the first species in the genus being the measure of the others (as 'whiteness' is for the other species of color). Second, it contradicts what the Philosopher asserts in III *Metaphysics* [ch. 3] that 'among individuals of the same species there is no priority or posteriority.'

16. Hence the Commentator interprets this badly in claiming that no priority or posteriority among things of the same species is to be understood of the prior as constituting the posterior. For this is not the mind of the Philosopher, for then there would be no order of species of the same genus, since one is not a constitutive part of the other. But Plato is the one Aristotle is attacking,—Plato, who postulated a 'man' apart to be the measure and the essence of these inferiors which are of the same species as it. And against the [theory of the Platonic Ideas] Aristotle declared this is not possible, because in those things

which are of the same species, there is no prior or posterior. Therefore, that which is the measure in any genus is not something that is numerically one which measures all in that genus; for then it would be the measure of individuals in that species, and would be the first among them—something the Philosopher denies.

17. This unity of nature therefore is less than numerical unity.

18. The falsity of this consequent [¶ 12] is also proved in a second way.

According to the Philosopher in VII *Physics* [ch. 4] the unity of a genus is to be distinguished from that of a species, since a comparison is to be made according to the atomic or elementary species and not according to the genus, because the elementary species refers to one nature, but the genus, in which 'many equivocations are latent,' does not.

19. From this it is argued as follows: Both the genus and the species have but one concept in the intellect; if then the species has such a special sort of unity that comparison can be made on the basis of its unity but not on the basis of the unity a genus has, it must be because the unity of the species is more than just a unity of concept. Hence the unity of the most special species is a real unity, and yet is not a numerical unity, because there is no comparison according to numerical unity as is clear from the context [in VII *Physics*]. Since the unity on the basis of which the comparison is made is neither the same nor greater than numerical unity, it follows that there is another real unity less than numerical unity.

20. The major [viz. that the genus has one, not many concepts, in the intellect] is evident. For in the agent intellect there is one numerical object designated by one intention. For unless there were in the intellect an object that was numerically one according to its intelligible being, an object designated by the generic intention, when the genus is predicated of the diverse species, it would not be a predication [of something common] of what falls under it, but a predication of the same thing of itself. Consequently, the concept of the genus is

one numerically just as the concept of the species is. Thus the act grasping that object is numerically one just as the act of understanding the species is numerically one (this is the mind of the Philosopher in VII *Physics*). And the comparison is to be made according to one concept. There is then some real unity which is not numerical unity but less than numerical unity.

21. The falsity of this same consequent [¶ 12] is shown also in a third way.

In the chapter 'On Relation' in V *Metaphysics* [ch. 15] the Philosopher says that the relations based on 'oneness' are similarity, identity and equality. Now similarity is a real relationship, and as such it requires a real foundation, so there is something real at the basis of similarity—something really one that serves as the proximate foundation for the relation. (For if the foundation were only conceptually one, there would be no foundation unless it were produced by an act of the mind and thus the relation of similarity would be only a mental or conceptual relation. Hence if the relation of similarity is real, its foundation must be real.) Now the oneness that serves as the foundation cannot be numerical unity, for nothing is similar to itself; therefore, the unity of this foundation must be both real and other than numerical unity.

22. There is also a fourth argument for the same.

In any opposition there are two primary extremes, both of which are real if the opposition is real. Now contrariety represents a real opposition, for heat destroys cold apart from any thinking about it. Each of the opposite extremes, therefore, is something real and is one by a real unity. This real unity, however, is not numerical unity, because then there would be as many primary contrarieties as there are individual contrary extremes; therefore there must be some unity in the extremes that is real in itself that is other than numerical unity.

23. There is also a fifth argument for the same.

One act of sense perception such as seeing requires an object with some unity. But the unity under which something is an object of vision is not numerical unity; therefore there is some real unity other than numerical unity.

24. Proof of the minor: if vision were to see *this* white object [rather than *a* white object] first, then vision could discriminate between this white and all which did not have this [white's individuality or] unity, which is false, for if God were to make two whitenesses, each with its own proper unity [and haecceity], vision, apart from any other clues, would be able to pick out one from the other, which is not true. And if you say positing [miraculous] power is no viable proposal, you can not deny or ignore the case of the sun's rays. For the sun moves continuously and its rays are continuously changed, so that where there is one now there will already be another. Nevertheless vision does not discriminate one sun ray from another. But if vision did apprehend its object under its numerical unity [or unique individuality] it would discriminate its object from any other that did not have its numerical unity [or individuality].

25. Furthermore, if no mind existed, fire would produce fire by a univocal[3] type of generation; but in univocal generation the begotten is similar in form and nature to the begetter; therefore, there is a real unity they possess which is not numerical; consequently, some real unity besides numerical unity exists.

26. Likewise, if every real unity were precisely numerical, then all real diversity would be precisely numerical. Therefore, all things would be equally diverse, and so Socrates would differ just as much from a line as he would from Plato. And in addition this would follow: From Plato and Socrates the intellect could no more abstract something one [e.g. human being] than from Socrates and a line, and every such abstraction would be a mere figment [of the mind].

27. The first implication is clear, first according to I *Topics* [ch. 15] where two opposites [like one-many, same-diverse] are concerned, as many meanings as one of the opposites bears, so many meanings has the other. Similarly X *Metaphysics* [ch. 3]: For every unity there is a proportionate diversity and its diversity corresponds proportionately to the opposite [unity].

B. Scotus' Own Opinion

28. Admitting the validity of these arguments, we must say that it is not a unity of singularity that characterizes stone as stone, for then it could not be thought of under the aspect of universality except by conceiving it under an aspect opposed to its proper essence, as the first argument infers.

29. And also, if it were singular of itself, there would be no real unity other than numerical unity, which is false as the second argument shows.

30. I say, then, according to Avicenna in Bk. V of his *Metaphysics*, 'Equinity is just equinity; of itself it is neither one nor many, universal nor singular.'

31. Consequently, just as it is not only singular or only universal in the mind, so also in the extramental world of nature it is neither one nor many of itself. Hence, nature of itself includes neither this nor that numerical unity.

32. Just as stone is first presented to the intellect as something in its own right and not as universal or singular, neither is stone first grasped through a second intention,[4] nor is universality a part of the meaning of the concept, but the mind understands the nature of stone for what it is in itself and not as universal or as particular or singular,—so in its extramental existence stone is primarily neither one nor many numerically, yet it has its own proper unity which is less than the unity pertaining to a singular. And this is the essential being of the stone and the universal aspect according to which stone is defined, and propositions predicating this being or nature are true in the first mode of essential predication. According to its nature, then, stone in this prior state where it is not determined to be in this or that individual, has whatever is predicated of it essentially, to which as such is added the notion of being in this or in that.

33. An objection to this [i.e. ¶¶. 31–32]. If in addition to numerical unity there were some other real unity in a thing according to which it would pertain to numerically diverse individuals, then something which is a real thing would be of itself universal. But that universality is in things or that a thing of itself is universal contradicts what Averröes says.

34. I reply that the unity in the thing is the sort of unity to which 'to be universal' is not repugnant, but that there is nothing here that is formally universal, for 'the universal is one in many and predicated of many.' Hence, the universal according to one numerical aspect is predicated of many, because the intelligible content is numerically one that is predicated of Socrates and Plato, but this does not mean there is only one numerical being in both. The nature which is in Socrates, then, considered in itself is neither determined to be in this or in that or to be universal; nevertheless it always has one or the other of these modes of existence. Just as color per se is not of itself determined to compress [the medium] of vision [as does black color] or to dilate it [as does white color], though color will do one or the other,[5] and so it is here with the nature in its own right; and as such, nature is the proximate foundation of universality.

35. Another objection to what we have said [¶¶. 31–32] is drawn from Damascene [De fide orthodoxa] Bk. I, chapter 8, where he says that there is a difference between what is universal in the divine and in material things, because in the divine what is common is numerically one, whereas in creatures what is common is only one in thought and diverse in reality.

36. I say that as in the divine there is real unity, so in material things there is only a unity in thought, for there [in God] is a unity of maximal singularity, which is not the case in creatures, but that which is numerically one [among creatures] is only one conceptually according to the intelligible being it has in the intellect. Nevertheless, in the extramental thing there is some real unity, less than numerical unity.

C. To the Argument for the Other Opinion

37. To the argument for the other opinion I say that it holds what is false, because nature is only a being with its own unity, and this is less than the unity that is numerical. And the nature's unity is something it has of itself, but it is not numerical unity.

II. Reply to the Initial Argument

38. To the argument at the beginning [¶. 2], we must say that it only holds good against Plato, who assumed the universal to be a separate substance, one in number, and that it is the essence of this and that, such as Socrates and Plato. For if the universal were this sort of thing, then the argument of the Philosopher would hold that 'the substance of each thing is that which is peculiar to it, and does not belong to many things.' But such a universal [as Plato had in mind] could not be peculiar to Socrates. Also one could not appropriate to Socrates what in itself was wholly in Plato—which was also Plato's view. And therefore it follows that no universal of this sort could be a substance.

Question Two:
Is a Material Substance Individual by Something Positive and Intrinsic?

39. Because of another opinion on the aforesaid question about the cause of individuation, it is asked whether a material substance is individual by reason of something positive and intrinsic to it.

Initial Arguments Pro and Con

40. [NEGATIVE] It seems not: 'One' only asserts a double negation, namely lack of division within itself and a division [or separation] from everything else (for, if 'one' were to signify something positive the expression 'one being' would be repetitious; therefore, 'unity' formally expresses only a negation); hence a material substance will not be numerically one and individual by anything positive, but by a negation.

41. [AFFIRMATIVE] On the contrary: First substance [i.e. the individual] is what is generated per se according to VII *Metaphysics*, and first substance is what functions per se (according to I *Metaphysics*); but these attributes pertain to first substance only because of something positive; therefore, first substance is individual and one numerically by something positive.

I. To the Question
A. What the Question Means

42. First I explain how I understand the question. For when it is asked whether a material substance is singular, and one, and individual, the question is not about singularity as a second intention (for in this way something is said to be singular by an act of the intellect). Neither is the query about unity as a principle of number (for a thing is said to be one with this unity through that which falls formally into the category of quantity). But what we ask is whether the proximate reason for the individuation of a material substance as such is something positive or privative (I don't mean to ask whether 'one' means merely a privation or negation or affirmation). Whether it does or not, the understanding is that a material substance has such an indivisibility that it is repugnant to it to be divided into several things each of which is like a subjective part[6] of its whole.

B. The Opinion of Henry of Ghent

43. [EXPLANATION OF HIS VIEW] Some say then that a material substance is individual and this and singular by a double negation (and not by anything positive): a singular supposit[7] has one negation as regards anything under it, for there is nothing into which it could be divided. It has another negation with regard to what is beside it, in virtue of which it is not the same as that. And this [combination] is nothing else than 'an indivision of a thing in itself and its division from all else.'[8]

44. That this represents his mind is clear from what he says elsewhere, when he assumes the angel knows the singular by an innate species of universals, because the singular adds nothing beyond the species of the nature and so requires no other principle for knowing it.[9] There is nothing then in an individual besides the nature of the species except this twofold negation.

45. [REJECTION OF THIS VIEW] Against this view:

Everything that is repugnant to anything's entity is repugnant to it because of something positive it has. But to be divided into subjective parts is repugnant to an individual material substance. Therefore, it is repugnant to it because of something positive it has, and hence not repugnant because of some negation in it.

46. The major is evident. For the cause of any formal repugnance is not to be found in the fact that a negation follows and we have another negation. Though a proximate potency may be removed by a negation (as the proximate potency to see is removed by no object to be seen, and the proximate potency for division is removed by the lack of quantity), still the reason for a 'formal repugnance' has to be something positive. Hence if the negations were removed *per impossibile* it would still be necessary to postulate something positive as the cause of the repugnance. It is not because of any double negation then that it is repugnant for any individual material nature to be divided into several, but there must be something positive in it that is the basis for its formal repugnance to such a division.

47. Furthermore, it is only because of some perfection that what is of imperfection can be repugnant to a thing. But to be divided into many is a matter of imperfection. Therefore, this is not repugnant to an individual material substance except because of some perfection in it. But a negation is not some perfection. Therefore, etc.

48. Furthermore, the aforesaid answer [in ¶. 43] does not resolve the question [in ¶. 39], because it does not really respond to the per se question, 'Why can the material individual not be divided—according to the nature in it—into several of

the same nature?' You say: 'Because of the twofold negation, namely the indivision in itself and its division from all else.' But the other question (raised above [¶. 42]) remains: Whence the double negation that is in it? Hence, the aforesaid answer does not assign any reason for individuation.

49. Furthermore, the singular receives the per se predication of what is common to a singular; but there is no per se predication by reason of a negation; therefore, such predication requires something positive in the singular. But if there is nothing positive in it except the nature qua nature, then there could be no common predication in regard to instances of such, but [a nature] could only be predicated of itself.

50. Furthermore, entity is never constituted by a negation, for a negation always presupposes something positive in which it is rooted. If a first substance then has only a nature and a double negation, and this negation adds no perfection over and above the nature, it follows that a 'first substance' implies no greater perfection than does a 'second substance' [i.e., genus and species]—which is false, because—according to the *Categories* [ch. 5]—"It is the first [i.e. the individual] which is properly and especially called 'substance.'"

51. Furthermore, this double negation is the same in this as in that. Only because of something positive is it contradictory for this to be that. Hence the question still remains why this double negation can be multiplied or divided into many things similar to it.

C. Scotus' Own Solution

52. The reason for the individuation of a material substance into subjective parts, therefore, cannot be [this double negation] but some affirmative reason must be given—which I concede.

But just what this is will become clear later [¶¶. 164–172].

II. Answer to the Initial Argument

53. To the argument at the beginning [¶. 40], one should say it is false to claim that 'one' asserts only a negation. (Whether or not there is a negation will be made clear elsewhere.) But the position that says there is only a double negation still leaves a question of just what is the positive cause of this double negation. Hence, one must cite something positive for this twofold negation.

Question Three:
Is It Through Actual Existence That a Material Substance Is This and Singular?

54. Because of a third opinion about the individuation of a material substance, the question is asked: Is material substance this and singular through actual existence?

I. The View of Others

55. Certain people say it is, because—according to VII *Metaphysics*, [ch. 13]—it is the function of act to distinguish. Therefore, the last distinction stems from what is the ultimate actual; but the ultimate actual is the being of existence, because all that precedes is as it were in potency to existence; therefore supposits[10] of the same species to which this last distinction accrues, are distinguished hypostatically and thus are constituted through the being of existence.

II. Rejection of This View

56. On the contrary:
Actual existence does not have per se differences, but only varies according to the quidditative[11] being; therefore, actual existence is not of itself distinctive, and as a consequence it cannot be the primary reason for any distinction.

57. Furthermore, actual existence is of the same sort in this or that, just as is the nature in this and that; therefore, if the nature is not of itself *this* (for the reasons given in the first question [¶¶. 28–29]), then neither is this something that pertains to it precisely by reason of the being of existence.

58. Furthermore, in every essentially ordered categorical hierarchy one can find

whatever pertains to this hierarchy, apart from and to the exclusion of anything not of this hierarchy. But the being of existence does not pertain to the hierarchy of substances, neither as a species nor as a difference nor as a genus; therefore in the categorical hierarchy of substances, one can think of anything of this hierarchy without thinking of its existential being. Therefore, just as genus and species are in the categorical hierarchy before their actual existence is thought of, so the individuals of this category will be in this hierarchy before their actual existence is thought of.

III. To the Arguments for This View

59. Since I concede the conclusion that follows from these reasons against this view, it is clear how to reply to the argument cited in its favor [¶. 55].

When it is said that 'act distinguishes,' this is true in the sense that in the manner in which it is act, in that same manner it distinguishes.

60. And when it is said that 'the last distinction stems from what is the ultimate actual in this hierarchy,' this 'ultimate' is not the being of existence. Just what it is, however, will be evident later [¶¶. 164–172]. Hence actual existence is not the ultimate intrinsic actual feature, but it follows the distinction of things in a categorical hierarchy. Hence the distinction that stems from actual existence is somehow [extrinsic] and arises from a thing's relationship to an agent. Therefore, this distinction pertains to a thing as it relates to its extrinsic causes, and a thing is not in potency to actual existence in the way that it is to other sorts of essential being within the categorical hierarchy.

Question Four:
Is Quantity That Positive Characteristic Whereby a Material Substance Is This Singular and Indivisible into Subjective Parts?

61. Because of a fourth opinion as to the cause of the individuation of a material

substance, the question is raised whether quantity is that positive something whereby material substance is a 'this' and singular and indivisible into many subjective parts.[12]

Initial Arguments Pro and Con

62. [AFFIRMATIVE] It seems so:
Boethius at the beginning of *De Trinitate* says 'accidents make for a numerical difference, and if you take all of them away, at least you cannot take away place—why numerically diverse things are in diverse places'; but it is only through quantity that they are in diverse places: therefore etc.

63. Furthermore, Damascene in his *Elementarium,* chapter 5 also says that 'everything by which things differ hypostatically,[13] is an accident.'

64. Furthermore, Avicenna in chapter 2 of V *Metaphysics* says: "To a nature requiring matter in order to exist, accidents accrue whereby it is individuated."

65. [NEGATIVE] To the contrary: The first substance is what is first generated and functions primarily; but 'a being *per accidens*' is not what is first generated, according VI *Metaphysics* [ch. 2], neither is it functional, for 'it is close to non-being,' as is clear from what is also said there. A composite of substance and an accident (such as quantity) however is a being *per accidens.* Therefore, it will not be what is first generated or functions. Therefore, neither is a material substance a first substance and singular through quantity.

I. To the Question
A. The Opinion of Others
1. Explanation of the Opinion

66. To this question some say[14] that quantity is that positive something whereby a material substance is this and singular.

67. They give these proofs:
First, from the Philosopher's statement in V *Metaphysics* [ch. 13] that " 'Quantum' means that which is divided into those [constituent parts] that are in it, each of which is suited to be a 'something' and 'this

something.' " And they take this to mean that the function of dividing things into parts of the same kind pertains primarily to quantity. Then it is argued: What pertains to something primarily, pertains to everything of that same sort. Therefore, since to be divided into parts of the same sort pertains primarily to quantity, divisibility of this sort will pertain to everything by reason of quantity. But the division of a species into individuals is a division into parts of the same sort, for this is what distinguishes the division of a species into individuals from the division of a genus into species; therefore individuals of the same species are distinguished by quantity—and as a consequence, material substance becomes singular through quantity.

68. Furthermore, this material substance is other than that material substance—as one fire from another—only because one form is different from another form; but the form of this fire is different from the form of that only because it is received in other matter (for it is not by reason of form that they are distinguished, because all distinction of form based exclusively on form is specific; therefore form is only diversified because it exists in other matter). But matter is not divided or multiplied except through quantity (viz. because another part of matter is the subject of another part of quantity); therefore, quantity is the primary cause why individuals are distinguished and multiplied.

69. This argument is confirmed by the Philosopher's statement in VII *Metaphysics* [ch. 8] that the producer generates another because of matter, since the matter of what is produced is other than that of the producer. But the matter cannot be other except it be quantified and other in quantity. For it is primarily required to be quantified, because a natural agent only acts on something quantified. That it be quantified by another quantity is also required, because otherwise the matter would not be other; therefore the distinction of producer and what is generated stems primarily from their quantity.

70. For this opinion arguments from au-

thoritative statements about this question are adduced.

2. Refutation of This Opinion

71. Before examining this opinion I preface one remark about how the question is to be understood. We are not looking for the cause of individuality as something indefinite, in the sense that 'one in number' can be abstracted from this or that unit by reason of each one's numerical unity, something they have in common. What we are looking for is the reason why a material substance is singular by this determinate or unique singularity that is the reason why a stone is just *this* stone and could not be any other stone.

72. Understanding the question in this way, then, I show four ways in which it is impossible that quantity could be that through which a material substance is this and singular and one numerically in the way this opinion explains it. Three of these apply to all accidents and show that no accident can be the reason why a material substance is a 'this.'

a. First Way: From the Nature of Singularity

73. The first way is based on the singularity and the notion of numerical unity. It goes in this way:

An existing material substance that is numerically one and singular cannot, while remaining the same [in substance], lose its singularity and cease to be this without being corrupted, annihilated or substantially changed in any way. For this truth is self-evident: from the fact that something is not changed substantially, it remains the same substance numerically in its unique singularity; otherwise the same thing numerically is numerically many. But remaining a material substance in actuality, unchanged in any way substantially, it need not have quantity or any other accidents, as we will prove. Therefore, no material substance is this and singular through some accident.

74. Proof of the minor: without any contradiction this material substance can exist

and this quantity no longer be in it and another could be in it. Hence if it is by this quantity inhering in it that a material substance would be 'this' and singular, it would follow that, after being this substance, it could cease to be this substance without undergoing any substantial change, which is false.

75. You may object that God could miraculously make many things happen not permitted by nature.

76. [I say] No! God could not do anything that includes a contradiction; but it is a contradiction that this material substance become not-this and that it lose its singularity without a substantial change; nevertheless this would follow if quantity were the cause of this singular or if any accident were.

77. Furthermore, there is an argument involving no miracle: that in the case of rarefaction, according to what one Doctor says [viz. Godfrey of Fontaines] who better than [Giles of Rome] explains many points about the author of this opinion.[15] In rarefaction the same numerical quantity does not remain, but the former perishes entirely. (His opinion is touched on in the problem of how charity is augmented.) Therefore, the same substance remains in the case of rarefaction whereas the quantity is changed (or at least—according to all, the entire quantity no longer remains in the condensed state). Therefore, if the singularity of the substance stemmed from its quantity, it would follow that it remained the same substance numerically, without having the same singularity, and thus it would not be the same substance in number nor the same individual substance as before—which is false. And it would follow further that if the rarified quantity were later condensed, the same numerical quantity would return. If the material substance derived its singularity from quantity, it would follow that it would pass from a state of not having this singularity to having this singularity without a substantial change—all of which is impossible.

78. Furthermore, two substantial changes or productions, not simultaneous, could not have as their identical primary term this same numerical substance. Proof: if the first sufficed to produce this substance, it would have its total being from this production, and the other production is not simultaneous with this. Hence, if that substance were to have another production sufficient to produce it, this also would embrace its entire being and give it anew what it already had, so that it would receive its being twice. Yet this follows if a material substance has its singularity through quantity, since bread will be produced and later transubstantiated;[16] and since its quantity remains per se, other bread will be created that is affected by this quantity. Both productions, then, would have as their primary term 'this substance' with the same singularity, since the same singularity of an indivisible substance cannot be in two substances, for then the same individual singular would be two individuals and two singular things.

b. Second Way: From the Manner Substance Is Ordered to Accident

79. Furthermore, I argue against the aforesaid opinion in a second way, derived from the way substance is ordered to quantity and other accidents; according to the Philosopher (VII *Metaphysics*, [ch. 1]), substance is prior to quantity and every other accident, and this 'priority' refers to the nature of substance and its whole coordination [or substantial concatenation].[17] It does not refer—as the Commentator incorrectly claims—to matter which is prior to all quantity or God who precedes all quantity. For this is not the mind of the Philosopher. What he wishes to prove is that to determine the whole of being, it suffices to determine it in regard to substance which is the first division of being, because once a knowledge of substance in itself is had, insofar as it divides being from other things, a knowledge of anything other can be had. But such would not suffice if you prove only that substance precedes an accident of whatever sort only by reason of matter or as God. (God is not in the category of substance which divides being from acci-

dent.)[18] For [the Philosopher] intends it to hold good of the whole order of substance, insofar as substance is what first divides being and thus precedes every accident. If therefore the entire order of substance is prior to every accident, therefore, nothing posterior to substance can be the reason why something is in this coordination [or substantial concatenation]—and as a consequence an individual in the category of substance will not be individual and singular within that genus by quantity.

80. You may say perhaps that substance according its whole coordination [or substantial concatenation] is prior to every accident in regard to being, but not in regard to its being divided,—just as substance is prior to quantity, and still quantity is prior so far as 'division into parts of the same sort' goes, because this pertains to substance only by reason of its quantity; hence quantity is first divided into parts of the same kind and substance is divided through quantity.[19]

81. To the contrary: This reply has destroyed this opinion at the outset [¶. 66], because if substance according its whole coordination [or substantial concatenation], is prior to quantity then everything to the extent it pertains to that coordination—is prior to quantity; hence an individual in the category of substance will not have its indivisible[20] being primarily by reason of its quantity.

82. Furthermore, if any substance is prior to quantity in being and nothing 'exists in actuality' unless it is something determinate;[21] then its determinate character as a material substance is prior to its being marked by quantity, and consequently it is not a particular individual because it is marked by quantity.

83. Furthermore, the reply is not relevant. Substance is prior to quantity in the support-way that substance is the subject of quantity, because, inasmuch as it is the subject of quantity, it enters into its definition—and that of 'accident' generally—as a something added;[22] but to the extent that it is a subject for quantity and enters into its definition, substance is a cause[23] of it;

and in every generic type of cause it is a singular cause that is prior to the effect; therefore substance qua subject and as a 'this' is prior to quantity.

84. There is another reply that some offer.[24] It states that quantity is not the formal principle whereby substance or matter is singular, but quantity leaves a certain modification in the substance which is really not something other than the subject, and this mode that it leaves is the substance's singularity. They give the example of quantity, which is primarily divisible itself into parts of the same sort, and when it affects matter, it leaves a certain impression in matter whereby matter has its own divisibility into parts of the same sort, so that if one assumes that quantity were to be separated from matter, the latter would still have the particularity proper to it by reason of this affection that is left behind.

85. To the contrary:

It is even more impossible that something naturally prior should have something really identical with itself from what is naturally posterior than that it have some sort of being from such, as will be proved [in ¶. 86]. But this answer [in ¶. 84] assumes that a substance acquires a characteristic left by quantity, which is nothing other than the substance itself. Thus it postulates that a substance would have something the same as itself from quantity which is naturally posterior to substance. This answer, then, is even more absurd than the one before which only assumed that the substance had some being, namely that of being indivisible, from the quantity.

86. Proof of the major: When something is really and truly the same as anything, this cannot exist without what is really the same as it, since it includes such by identity, though perhaps not formally. Hence if it could exist without that which is really the same as itself, then the same thing could really be and not be. But it is clear that what is prior (such as substance) can be without the posterior quantity, as they concede. But if the posterior could cease to be while the prior continues to exist, then

all the more so could what is left behind by the posterior cease to exist while that which is prior by nature continues to be. Therefore, that which is left behind is not really the same as the prior.

87. Furthermore, it is impossible that a cause derives a necessary condition for its causing from its effect, for then the cause would be naturally posterior to its effect since, qua cause, it would stem from its effect. But that demarcation [namely its singularity or individuation] would necessarily pertain to the substance insofar as it is the cause of the accident, since it can only cause the accident insofar as it is something singular. And therefore [Giles of Rome] avoids this by postulating that this 'formal demarcation' does not stem formally from quantity, for then the singular would be a being *per accidens*, which is false. Hence if substance were to be separated from quantity, he would still assume it to be singular. Therefore, substance does not acquire its demarcation from quantity by something this leaves behind.

88. Furthermore, I ask: Just what is this act of 'leaving behind'? Is it an effect caused by the quantity, or does it follow from another form which causes this demarcation? If it were assumed to be an effect (like something that is said of the divine),[25] where you postulate that, if quantity did not exist, matter would still retain the particularity it left, this could not be any effect caused by quantity, since quantity is not an active form. On the other hand, if it followed from some form other than quantity that caused the singularity, then there is no reason to postulate quantity, because I would argue that a natural agent would have made that form and then quantity would be like applying an ell or measure, which does nothing toward making a thing singular.

89. Also, if quantity were to leave something behind in the matter, by the same token whiteness in perfecting the surface would leave some alteration behind in the surface—which is false.[26]

90. Furthermore, the aforesaid conclusion [¶. 66] is challenged in another way.

According to the Philosopher substance is temporally prior to every accident (VII *Metaphysics* [ch. 1]). According to the better interpretation, this is to be understood as follows. Substance is prior by nature to any accident, and what is prior by nature can exist without the posterior with no contradiction, since if such is prior by its nature to the other, in its being we find no imperfection by assuming it to exist without the other. There is nothing inconsistent, then, about a singular substance existing for a time without quantity. But this would be impossible if it were singular because of its quantity.

c. The Third Way: From the Nature of a Categorical Hierarchy

91. Furthermore, a third way of arguing against the aforesaid opinion stems from the [nature of the essential] order that obtains within a category or predicament.[27] In every such precise coordination all that pertains to that concatenation can be found there apart from any other ordered arrangement.—Furthermore, each item of one ordered set is different from those of the other ordered set. Therefore in the predicamental order of substance, everything required is there apart from anything contributed from another category. But just as any predicamental order requires a highest term, so also it essentially requires a lower term, and eventually an ultimate one. Therefore apart from anything from another category [such as quantity], there will be something ultimate in the category of substance (intrinsic to this genus). And this is the singular of this genus; therefore, etc.

92. Furthermore, the lowest or ultimate in any coordination requires that what is higher in that order be predicable of it per se. But an accidental being does not receive essentially any per se predication of something in a higher genus. Hence it follows that the lowest or ultimate in any essentially ordered set does not include anything from diverse coordinations.

93. Furthermore, the species in any genus is a species according to the essential notion of that genus. But it pertains to the

essential notion of a species that it be predicable of several, or at least of one. Therefore, apart from any other genus, that species still has some subject of which it is predicable, and this is the singular. Hence this singular, apart from any accident, is in the category of substance.

94. Furthermore, when something pertains to anything by reason of some precise characteristic—anything essentially possessing such a characteristic will have as well whatever pertains to that characteristic (as is evident inductively). In the ordered hierarchy or coordination of substance, however, 'being universal' does pertain in this way [to any substance], just by reason of the absolute nature of this genus, [substance].[28] To whatever this stark, unconcretized,[29] nature pertains, will be itself a universal in that ordered hierarchy. But insofar as one assumes some subject is contracted [i.e., qualified] by a thing belonging to a category other than substance, one admits nothing whatsoever contracts that subject qua substance. For instance, if one posits that Socrates is contracted by [the accidental quality of] whiteness, he would not be substantially or essentially qualified any more than he was before. Therefore, if one were to assume that something is contracted in its nature qua substance by something from another category [i.e., one of the nine accidents], the thing would be simultaneously singular and universal.

d. The Fourth Way: From the Part of Quantity

95. Furthermore, the aforesaid opinion is challenged in a fourth way specifically on the basis of quantity.—For the three preceding ways refer universally to the impossibility of any accident being the cause of singularity. But this fourth way argues particularly against quantity. For if quantity were the cause of singularity, that quantity would have to be either a definite or indefinite quantity. But it is not a definite quantity, because that follows the existence of the form (for quantity has a certain terminus), since the form perfects matter.[30]

Hence, since that [i.e., its quantity] follows as an effect, it cannot be the cause of the singularity. Neither can indeterminate quantity be the cause of the individuation, because according to the proponents of this theory—this remains the same in what is generated and what perishes. Therefore, if indeterminate quantity were the cause of singularity, the thing that perishes and that which is produced from it would be the same singular and the same 'this,' because it would have the same basis or reason for singularity.

96. You may object that this does not follow, because quantity cannot be the cause of the individuation of some individual save in the same species, and what is generated and perishes are not of the same species.

97. I counter: Fire is assumed to be generated from water and afterwards perishes in becoming water again where the same quantity is involved. Now the indeterminate quantity remains the same and is in the same species; therefore it will be the same singular thing and consequently the corrupted thing will return numerically the same after having perished from natural causes.

98. Furthermore, no nature—qua such a nature—is of itself this (as was proved above in question 1 of this distinction [¶¶. 8–27]). For anything that is of itself just 'this' cannot be grasped by the intellect under the aspect of a universal, and similarly there would in such a case be no real unity less than numerical unity (as was inferred there). But quantity of its nature does have such an indifference [towards being just this] just as flesh does. Therefore, just as flesh is not of itself just this, so neither is quantity insofar as it is quantity of itself this, for quantity is of the same sort in this quantity as in that quantity, just as flesh is of the same sort in this flesh or that flesh. But nothing can be the primary reason why something is just this, to which it is repugnant to be just this. Therefore, quantity cannot be the cause of singularity, in virtue of which something is a 'this' as regards some nature.

99. He [i.e., Thomas Aquinas] says that quantity is this by its situation or position [*situs*].

100. To the contrary: Position or situation is either a per se category or something which pertains to the category of quantity. If it pertains to the category of quantity, then it is a [specific] difference of that genus. If it is a category in its own right, then it is posterior to quantity. Therefore quantity is not contracted or specified thereby. Furthermore, situation is the same sort of thing in this or in that.—Hence this, 'situation,' is a generic term, and one can argue as before.

101. Furthermore, here is where their Achilles' [heel] is vulnerable, viz. their claim that 'all difference in form is specific.' Now quantity is a form. Hence, the diversity of this quantity from that is specific; therefore, within the same species no two quantities could differ.

e. Counterarguments to the Reasons for This Opinion

102. Furthermore, there are counterarguments to the reasons given for this opinion [in ¶¶. 67–69]. For when it is argued that quantity is the formal ground for divisibility into parts of the same sort, and therefore the specific material substance cannot be divided except by means of quantity, the objection would be this. That which is the formal reason for the divisibility of anything has to be something in the thing which is divided by this sort of division (otherwise you would not be dividing that thing). But quantity is not formally intrinsic to the specific nature. Therefore, it is not the formal reason for the specific nature's divisibility into its parts.

103. Hence their reason is based upon a false picture of the situation,—as if the division of some quantum into its parts would be a division of a specific nature into its subjective parts [i.e., into the individuals that are of that species]. This is false, because 'an integral part' is never its 'whole,' whereas a subjective 'part' is its 'whole' [i.e., an individual man is a whole man]. Hence, when a whole is divided through

quantity, the part is not the divided whole, and therefore one can never infer a division of the specific nature from a division of a continuum.

104. Furthermore, this argument [in ¶. 67] proceeds from a false understanding of the text. For the Philosopher says that "quantity is divided into those things [i.e., constituent parts] which are in it, each of which is suited to be a 'something' and 'this-something.'" From the fact that he says "it is divided into those things which are in it," new [or actually separated] parts that arise when the division is made are excluded. And by saying "each is suited to be something," he understands that each is suited to be a per se existent. And by saying "it is apt to be 'this-something,'" he excludes the division of a genus [into species]. How then does one get the idea from this that quantity is divisible into parts of the same sort? This meaning just isn't there! For if one assumes the number six consists of two *three's* and three *two's* or of *four* plus *two*, and that it may be divided into such— and this is the division of quantity "into those things which are in it, each of which is apt to be a 'something' and 'this-something,'" then the parts are not of the same sort. Hence the division of a quantum can be into parts of different sorts, but not by reason of quantity.—It is as if a man were divided into a heart and a head. This would not be a division into parts of the same sort. Hence, quantity permits division of substance into parts of different sorts, although such a division would not happen through quantity.

105. Also, nothing relevant to our topic lies in that text, for 'quantum' is divided "into those things which are in it" refers to what is integral to whole. But the specific nature is not this sort of integrated whole made up of the natures of individuals; and therefore the statement that quantity may be divided into parts of the same sort that are in it, contributes nothing to our problem. Hence that argument is completely without value.

106. Furthermore, against the other argument—when it is argued that 'the producer generates another because of the

matter,' I argue: The producer is distinguished from what is produced (apart from everything else), because nothing begets itself. But the producer does not generate by virtue of quantity but by virtue of its proper form, because quantity is not an active form. Therefore it cannot be the reason for generating nor the term of the generation. Hence quantity contributes nothing to the distinction between producer and the thing produced.

B. Scotus' Own Conclusion

107. I concede therefore, because of the reasons cited [in ¶¶. 72–106], that 'this water' that underlies quantity is inconsistent with its being 'not this,' given that this water remains such and no substantial change occurs in its regard; and therefore through the quantity that is posterior to it [qua water], it cannot be singular. But what this is [whereby water is made singular in this way] will become clear later.

II. To the Reasons for the Other Opinion

108. As for the arguments, the answer to the first [¶. 67] is evident from what has been said, first because the argument is wholly irrelevant to our problem, since the division of a quantum is not a division of a nature into its subjective parts;[31] second, it is accidental that sometimes the division is into quantitative parts that are subjective, as is the case with a homogeneous whole. This is not so, however, when the whole is heterogeneous.

109. To the other reason, when it is said that 'form is not distinguished from form, except by reason of being in other matter' [¶. 68] this is simply not true. For just as form is prior in being to matter, so also is it prior in giving matter a being that is one (hence form is that from which some entity is one entity). Although the form is prior, it still concurs (with matter) to constitute the composite a kind of partial cause.

110. And when it is said that 'every distinction that is in the form, is specific,' the answer is clear from book I.

111. What is more, the proposition they accept, viz. 'Matter is only a 'this' through quantity,' is false, for it is already 'this matter' before quantity accrues to it, although it only has factual existence as quantified-being.[32]—Also it would not have a divisibility[33] [i.e., into integral parts, each in a distinct place] other than what stems from its quantity.

112. And when it is said that 'matter is neither divided nor multiplied except by being under this quantity and that quantity,' this is true,—but here quantity is a sine qua non [i.e., a necessary condition] for the multiplication of individuals.[34] But if it is only a sine qua non with respect to the division of matter, all the more so is it only a sine qua non with respect to what is produced.[35] But this does not imply that it is the 'formal reason' for division into parts of the same sort [i.e., individuals of the same species].

113. Hence it does not follow 'the producer generates another because of matter, and matter is not other unless it is under another part of quantity, therefore quantity is the formal reason for division into parts of the same sort' [¶. 69]. For it only follows [from the two-premised antecedent] that quantity is necessary for production or generation as something sine qua non. But from this one cannot infer that it is the formal ground required for generation.[36]

114. If you were to say that quantity precedes generation, because the producer can only generate another by acting on a quantum,[37] hence quantity precedes the individuation of the product (as was said, this does not follow of course!), then I would reply: It is true that quantity—and also the other accidents in that thing that perished [i.e., the thing from which the new product was formed] did precede the generation [of the new product], but in the product itself quantity is subsequent to the substance of that product.

115. But you may still insist that it seems that quantity precedes generation not only in what perished but also in what is generated, for it precedes, at the instant of generation, the induction of the form into the matter. But it is qua quantity of the matter in that instant, that it precedes by nature both the form and the individuation of the

thing produced, for otherwise it would be produced from something unquantified and so something quantified would come from something unquantified.

116. But these [opponents] ought not to argue in this way, because they claim (contrary to what the Commentator says) that no form remains the same in both the product generated and the thing that perished (i.e. they admit no corporeal form that remains the same). Consequently, since the substantial form, not the quantity, is the first perfection of the matter—according to him [i.e. Godfrey],[38] it follows that quantity does not remain the same and thus follows the induction of the substantial form. Therefore, I reply to the argument [in ¶. 115] that no quantity would precede the induction of the substantial form in matter (for then quantity would perfect matter before the substantial form would). Quantity, however, naturally follows the induction of the form and thus follows the existence of the composite [of matter and form].

117. And when it is argued [in ¶. 115] that 'then something quantified would come from what is unquantified,' I say that if one understood this to mean that from something preexisting with no quantity something quantified was formed, then in this sense it would be impossible, (as it would be impossible to get something divisible from a point). To the extent that the generated comes to be from what perishes, therefore, it comes to be from something quantified as well. For before the instant of generation a quantum continued to exist, but in that instant that the generation took place both the preceding form and its quantity perished and the following form was induced, and at the same instant the quantity which extended it followed. But if the arguer meant that from some non-quantum there came a quantum in the sense that something was generated from an essential part of it [i.e., of the material substance], then in this sense it is necessary, because matter is first perfected by form, from which matter the composite is generated, and the quantity that extends it follows.

118. But you may ask: How is it possible that a natural agent, since it always acts on a body, immediately contacts the essence of matter (for it seems that it does not do so immediately, but only insofar as matter is corporeal)?—I reply: I do not know whence came this philosophy that claims a natural agent does not contact the essence of matter. For if a natural agent is to induce a substantial form into the matter, it must necessarily reach the matter insofar as it is perfectible by form. Hence this must not be understood to mean that matter may have one tunic (such as quantity) and by means of this tunic it may receive the form.

III. Reply to the Initial Arguments

119. To the arguments at the beginning:
To the argument from Boethius [¶. 62], which is more cogent than the other, I say that Boethius wished to show there that the Father, Son and Holy Spirit are three Persons, but only one God, and that there are not three individuals with substances that differ numerically, because in a substance the variety of accidents makes for a numerical difference; but in the Father and Son, etc. there can be no accidental variation, since—as he says later, 'a simple form cannot be a subject.' Now I claim that this meaning Boethius had in mind can be preserved, if one assumes that accidents are only a sine qua non for numerical difference, and then argues that 'without accidental variety there cannot be a numerical difference; but in the Father and Son there is no such variety; therefore etc.'—So much for the intent of Boethius—which can be salvaged even though accidents would not be the formal cause of numerical difference.

120. But what may we say about Boethius' intent in itself, since he claims that in substance 'there cannot be numerical difference without accidental variety'? I say this authoritative statement must be understood literally as it sounds. For accidents account for some difference in a substance, not a specific one, therefore a numerical difference. Hence, in the manner

that they exist, in that manner do they make for a difference. And just as these accidents differ numerically, so they make for a numerical difference—but not the primary numerical difference, neither is it this difference alone. And hence there is a fallacy of the consequent when it is argued that 'they make for a numerical difference in substances, therefore they make the first numerical difference and this is all they make.'

121. But you may object that variety in accidents is not the primary cause of numerical difference, but it is a consequence of the primary difference, therefore, since the prior could remain apart from the posterior, it would follow that although there is no variety of accidents in the divine, still there is numerical difference there. And thus Boethius does not make his point.

122. I say that Boethius showed that there is no numerical difference in God and he argued in this way: 'A variety of accidents makes for numerical difference; but there are no accidents in God, because a simple form [like the divine essence] cannot be [their] subject; therefore, etc.' I say that he argued from effect to what necessarily accompanies such in the cause, for a variety of accidents is a necessary concomitant of a numerical difference;[39]—and this is true. Therefore, if in God there is no such variety, then it follows there is no numerical difference there either.

123. To Damascene [¶. 63] it must be said that this statement is explained away by what he says at the end of that same chapter: 'Whatever is only adventitious to the same species, is an accident,' i.e., any such are accidents of that species. And it is not because of accidents [that the divine persons differ], as is evident from what that same person writes in [*The Orthodox Faith*], Bk. I, ch. 8, where he says: "But more than all [the accidental characteristics whereby created persons differ], they do not exist in one another but are separate." But he says this because the persons in the deity do exist in one another.[40]

124. To Avicenna [¶. 64] I say that he speaks as a metaphysician should speak,

calling—according to his way of speaking—an 'accident' anything that falls outside the definition of the essence: and in this sense unity is an accident of a thing's entity and essence. And because all things whereby individuals are distinguished, lie outside a specific nature that needs matter, it follows that such 'accidents' are called such not because they fall into any accidental category, but because they lie outside the specific nature in the way we speak, for instance, of the 'fallacy of accident' when the middle term is extraneous to the extremes (for instance, 'rational' is only accidental to 'animal' and thus is extrinsic[41] to that notion).

Question Five: Does Matter Individuate a Material Substance?

125. From all that has been said, the question arises: Is a material substance individuated by matter?

Arguments Pro and Con

126. [AFFIRMATIVE] It seems so:
V *Metaphysics*, in the chapter 'On the One': "Those things are numerically one whose matter is one." Therefore matter is the cause of numerical unity.

127. [NEGATIVE] To the contrary: "At the foundation of nature, there is nothing distinct" (from V *Metaphysics* [ch. 4]), and this refers to [primary] matter; hence matter according to him is indistinct in itself and therefore, cannot be the cause of distinction.

I. The Opinion of Others

128. [EXPLANATION OF THIS VIEW] Some[42] are wont to reply to this question saying matter is why a material substance is individual, and form only becomes such because it is received into this or that matter, so that the entire singularity of a material substance stems from its matter.

129. They[43] prove this from VII *Metaphysics* [ch. 8]: 'The producer begets another because of the matter, but of the same species because of the form.' Thus the nu-

merical difference stems from the matter and the specific unity from the form.

130. Also, VII *Metaphysics*, [ch. 11], 'On the Parts of Definition' near the end, we read that 'in things conceived with matter, the essence [or what-something-is] and the one whose essence it is are not the same— but they are same in things without matter (e.g., curvature, if it were apart from matter).' And in ch. [3] of VIII *Metaphysics* 'We should not fail to notice,' he says, 'that the essence of the soul and a soul are not the same, if a soul is an animal.' Because in things thought to have matter the essence or 'what it is' and the one whose it is are not the same as they are in the case of things without matter, these persons conclude that matter is the cause of the individuation. For if it were not, one could abstract from this and that matter something akin to form, and hence the abstract from this composite and that would be identical with itself just as is the abstract in things with no matter.

131. Likewise, the Philosopher in XII *Metaphysics* [ch. 8] proves there are not several heavens, because then there would be several first movers; wherefore they would have matter. Hence, according to his way of thinking numerical distinction is not possible apart from matter.[44]

132. Also in *De caelo et mundo* [ch. 9]: 'When someone speaks of heaven he is speaking of form, and when he talks about this heaven, he is talking about matter.' Hence, singularity stems from the matter.[45]

133. [REFUTATION OF THIS VIEW] On the contrary:

If one could abstract 'matter' from this and that matter, and 'man' from this or that man, then matter would not pertain [to the essence of matter or man]; but this is false, as is clear from VII *Metaphysics*, ch. [11] ('On the parts of a definition'), where several authorities assert the contrary; therefore it must be that 'matter' can be abstracted from this and that matter, just as 'form' or 'composite' can. Hence, matter cannot be the cause of individuation, for it is a general rule that what is indifferent to several things of the same sort cannot be

itself the cause of distinctness. It is fitting then to look for a cause of the individuation and singularity of the matter, just as it is appropriate to do so for the composite.

134. Furthermore, this is what the Philosopher has in mind in XII *Metaphysics* ch. [5], where he is looking for the unity of the principles of genera, and says that they are the same in an analogous sense to those things that are one by analogy, and that they are generically the same as those things which are one generically and are of the same species as those things that are specifically one, just as my matter and yours are one specifically and therefore matter is abstractable from each and cannot be the cause of individuation.

135. Furthermore, if matter were the cause of individuation and singularity, since the matter remains the same when fire perishes to become water, then the singularity will remain the same, and thus it will be the same singular.

136. If you say this is not so, because the species does not remain the same (as some above would answer), I say: No, and argue as above. If fire turned to water, but the water perishes again to become fire, then what has perished will return numerically the same in virtue of the nature!

137. If it be said that matter continuing to exist as it does under the same accident remains the same and this is the cause of individuation, then you make perdurance in time, and not the nature of matter the cause. And I concede matter is not the cause of individuation.

138. The answers to the arguments will be made clear after the solution of the following question [¶¶. 189–95].

Question Six:
Is a Material Substance Individual Through Some Positive Entity Restricting the Nature to be Just This Individual Substance?

139. Is a material substance individual through some positive entity restricting the nature to be just this individual substance?

Arguments Pro and Con

140. It seems not:

If a material substance or a specific nature were determined to singularity through some other positive entity, this would be related to the specific nature as act to potency; but act and potency make one composite; therefore every individual would be a composite, one part of which would be the specific nature and the other some positive nature,—and thus no individual could be assumed to exist unless it had a greater composition than its specific nature has, which seems incongruous.

141. And if this is not regarded as absurd, I argue in another way that this is incongruous; for that which would determine [the specific nature] in this way could be neither the matter nor the form of that nature, for these pertain to the specific nature; therefore, if it be other than the specific nature, it would follow that if it were matter or form (act or potency), then matter is added to matter or form to form.

142. Also, if the individual were such a composite in a material substance, then this composite would be intelligible per se, since it would have in itself a specific nature and something else—which is a quasi-act—making up something that is per se one. Thus it would be another sort of thing. But this seems to be false, since according to the Philosopher, the singular is not per se intelligible.

143. Likewise, if the singular as such had another nature in addition to its specific nature, then it could be defined by means of that nature plus this other, which definition would express this singular nature, and this definition would represent an addition to the definition of the species just as the individual adds to the species.

144. And then there could be a science of the singular just as there could be a definition, and it would be distinct as the singular adds a distinct nature over and above specific nature.

145. To the contrary:

Everything special adds something over and above what is common in it, otherwise it would not be 'less common.' But what is added in this way forms a per se unit with the nature, otherwise the singular would not be one per se, an alternative disproved above. But the species falls under the species, and therefore something is added whereby the specific nature is contracted to this singularity.

A. To the Question
1. The View of Others

146. [EXPLANATION OF THEIR OPINION] To this question some[46] say that the specific nature of itself is individual, but since what is of itself individual exists in several only through quantity, it follows that a material substance, though individual of itself, owes its presence in several individuals to its quantity.

147. They prove the first point [that the specific nature of itself is individual] as follows:

The nature of a stone itself is elementary or atomic (from VII *Physics);* therefore it is individual of itself.

148. Also Porphyry says: "In the descent from the most general, Plato bids one halt at the most special." But one who descends in this way would not halt there, if the specific nature were further divisible; therefore the specific is of itself individual.

149. Boethius, likewise, in his book *On Division* assumes no division of the species into individuals, since he has adequately specified the divisions, both per se and *per accidens,* without such.

150. Furthermore, if the nature of stone could be divided such that the result of the division would be this and that singular, then the nature would not express the complete essence of the individual, but there would be something in the individual beyond what is essential to its specific nature whereby it would be contracted and divided.

151. The second point [that it is several by virtue of quantity] is explained thus. Although division of something quantified is not a division into subjective parts, nevertheless a whole is never divided into quantitative parts unless the nature is also di-

vided. Consequently, whatever suffices for division of something into quantitative parts is also a sufficient reason for its division into subjective parts. Now quantity is the reason for the first division; therefore it also explains the second division. But that by reason of which the whole is divided is also that by which the resulting parts are really distinguished from one another, and hence they are subjective parts of some specific nature and these are nevertheless distinguished by quantity.

152. An example from I *Physics* [to show the compatibility of these two aspects]. The Philosopher states that 'substance is indivisible of itself,' and nevertheless it can be partitioned in some way by being extended through quantity. And so too in this case. Though the nature is individual of itself, still through quantity it can become this or that and have this or that singularity.

153. [REFUTATION OF THIS OPINION] Against this view it is argued:

Only two interpretations can be given to this opinion. First, that there is but one specific nature (for instance that of a stone) and it is of itself individual, and while remaining this individual, the nature receives this or that quantity, and while receiving this quantity or that, it still possesses in itself this same singularity qua distinct from quantity. Now this interpretation would make for diverse simultaneous wholes [or combinations of this nature with different quantities] (since he who holds this assumes the nature is not formally singular through quantity),—and the nature, qua distinct from quantity, would have the self-same singularity under diverse quantities. Another interpretation could be that when the nature receives this quantity or that, there are several singularities in the category of substance, although quantity is a sine qua non condition for this. There can be two ways then to understand the aforesaid opinion. Either there are at the same time several wholes containing the same substance with the same singularity, but with different quantities,—or the substance does not retain the same singularity under diverse quantities.

154. The first interpretation leads to many absurdities in theology, metaphysics, mathematics and physics or natural philosophy.

155. First in theology, for according to this first interpretation, the nature of stone with the same singularity will be in this stone and that stone, but under diverse quantities, and this would mean that for one nature to be in several supposits would no longer be something proper to the divine essence (and though this is not something that has to be understood as defined, it is commonly assumed to be possible only where the supposits are relative [as in the case of the divine persons and not absolutes as is the case with individual stones or quantities]).

156. A second incongruity that would follow in theology is that it would not be possible for some wine to be transubstantiated unless all the wine in the world were transubstantiated, for according to this opinion the self-same singular wine-substance would be in all the world's wine. Just as the same soul-substance is in the right and left hand, so—on this view—the same substance will be in this and that quantity.

157. Absurdities in metaphysics also follow.

To begin with we face a greater incongruity than the Platonic Idea. For Plato's idea (as ascribed to him) is only that there is some numerically one substance with no accidents which is the essence of all sensible substances here on earth and is predicated of all *in quid*. But an equal—or even greater—absurdity is postulated here, because this opinion claims that this wood does not differ from that wood except in quantity and both pieces have the same substance.

158. Another metaphysical absurdity follows, for the advocates of this view regard it as incongruous that several absolute accidents of the same species should coexist in the same thing, for then the thing in question would be both in potency and act, which is contrary to metaphysical principles. Yet this absurdity would follow if the same singular substance were present under this quantity and that quantity.[47]

159. Also this mathematical absurdity of

the same thing being actuated by two quantities would follow.

160. For natural philosophy also there is this incongruity. No material substance can be generated or perish. It cannot be generated, since this wood can only come to be in some quantity, according to this view. Neither can it perish, for then all wood would perish, hence only the quantity perishes.

161. If the second interpretation is taken, where the material substance is individual of itself, but—with the advent of actual quantity—it is distinguished according to diverse singularities as the quantity is divided, so that the substance has one singularity under one quantitative part and another singularity under another part, then those who propose this view affirm what they deny. For nothing that is of itself individual or this, while remaining such, can become of itself not-this. If then a material substance or specific nature is of itself this, it cannot become not-this by means of quantity.

162. And if you say 'Does not the example cited above show this is no absurdity, for to be divisible does not pertain of itself to substance, which is indivisible, but it is divided through its quantity? (and so it is here),' I reply. Those who cite this illustration commit a fallacy of the consequent, for this does not follow: 'This is not of itself divisible, therefore it is of itself non-divisible or indivisible.' For it is not repugnant that a substance, which of itself [i.e., qua substance] is indivisible, be extended through its quantity (as is the case with material substance). But that substance which of itself is not divisible, like the soul or an angel, cannot be divided. Hence, if a material substance were of itself indivisible, it could not be extended through quantity and so if it were this of itself, it could not become not-this through quantity and be these several singularities.

163. Hence an atomic specific nature is not of itself individual. There is nothing absurd then about its being divided into several singular instances, but it is not formally through quantity that this occurs. If then a specific nature were indeed this of

itself (i.e., by its nature), then this singular would be distinguished from that by its nature and not by quantity, for whatever constitutes a thing in itself also distinguishes it from everything else. And if they deny this, they have to deny metaphysical principles, for the source of a thing's 'being' [esse] and 'being one' [esse unum] are identical.

2. Scotus' Personal View

164. I reply then to this (sixth) question that a material substance is determined to being this singularity by something positive and to other diverse singularities by diverse positives [i.e., by other haecceities].

165. This I show first by arguments and afterwards I shall explain what this positive thing is and how it functions.

166. My first point then is to show that the specific nature is contracted to this singularity by something positive. All unity follows upon some entity,—and just as 'one' in general follows upon 'being' in general, so analogously with what is special. Hence the unity characteristic of singularity, which excludes any sort of division, will have some analogous entity as its base. But such unity does not stem from the entity of the nature. For, as was shown above [¶¶. 9–25], the unity of nature is less than this singularity that is numerical unity. That is why the unity characteristic of nature can stand in opposition to this [numerical] unity and is not a sufficient reason for such. Hence this must stem formally from some extra entity besides what is essential to the specific entity.—This unity then does not follow from the specific entity. Nevertheless that entity [or haecceity] from which it does stem, forms a per se unity with the specific nature, because the individual—as was proved above [¶¶. 65, 72–76, 87, 91–93]—is a per se unity and not through unity of another genus [such as that of quantity]. It follows then that the specific nature is determined to be this individual by something positive.

167. Furthermore, things that differ are 'other-same things';[48] but Socrates and Plato differ, hence there must be something whereby they differ, the ultimate basis of their difference. But the nature in the one

and the other is not primarily the cause of their difference, but their agreement. Though the nature in one is not the nature in the other, nature and nature are not that whereby the two differ primarily, but that whereby they agree (for they do not differ just of themselves—otherwise there would be no real agreement between them), hence there must be something else whereby they differ. But this is not quantity, nor existence, nor a negation, as was established in the preceding questions [¶¶. 153–163]; therefore, it must be something positive in the category of substance, contracting the specific nature.

168. This last point can also be inferred from the above. It was shown above that the specific nature is not of itself *this;* therefore, it becomes *this* through something positive; not through quantity and the same with the other [accidents], hence it must have something in the substance-category.

169. Now what is this positive something assumed to individuate the specific nature? It is explained by comparison and analogy with specific difference, for a species can be compared with what falls below it [i.e., individuals], to what lies above it [i.e., the genus], or what is along side it [i.e., other species of the same genus].

170. If a specific nature is compared in the first way [to what can fall under it], then it is the specific difference that is the ultimate reason why that nature has its own unity and cannot be divided [like a genus] into several specific natures, and this impossibility stems primarily from the specific indivisibility of the specific difference, which renders the nature atomic or elementary. And just as indivisibility characterizes this difference, so too is it a mark of the nature from which the difference derives. Consider for example the nature of whiteness according to that perfection from which the notion of its difference is derived. That sort of whiteness defies division into several further whitenesses. And this occurs analogously in the case of the individual, for here there is a certain entity, from which—as from one perfection—the notion of the individual difference [or haecceity] is derived, something to which it is simply repugnant to be divided [into further individuals of the same sort], and in this it differs from a specific difference, which excludes division into parts of another nature, but not into those of the same nature. And this individual entity has a unity proper to itself, which is singularity. If one assumes that to a nature from which the notion of the genus[49] is derived [e.g. animal nature common to man and brute] corresponds a proper unity of its own [i.e., generic unity], then all the more so should some proper entity correspond to that maximal unity, singularity,—even as there is a proper entity corresponding to unity of the genus and a proper entity corresponding to the specific unity. There is no good reason for denying this to the greater unity [singularity] and conceding it for the lesser unity [the generic and specific].

171. Secondly, also, our proposed thesis is evident if you compare the species and individual to what is above each. For not only is the concept of the genus determined by a concept of the difference [in the case of the species], but that reality [or formality] from which the generic notion is derived, is naturally prior to that reality from which the intention of the difference is derived, and the reality from which the genus is derived, is determinable and able to be contracted through the reality of the difference. And so it is with what we propose. The specific nature is determinable and able to be contracted through the reality from which the individual difference is derived. As there are diverse formal perfections or formal entities, then, in one and the same thing (such as whiteness) from which a generic intention can be derived (such as the intention of color), and another formal entity from which the intention of the difference (white) is derived—as we said in Bk. I [*Lectura* d. 3]—so too in the same thing there is a positive entity from which the specific nature is derived, and an entity formally other from which the ultimate individual difference is derived, one which is completely a 'this,' to which any sort of di-

vision is abhorrent. As the generic reality is in potency to the reality of the difference, so the reality of the nature qua nature is in potency to the reality from which the individual difference is derived. But there is a dissimilarity, for the difference with the generic nature constitutes quidditative [or essential] being—called formal being—whereas the individual difference is not constitutive with the nature of quidditative being. For it lies beyond the quidditative characteristics and therefore does not constitute [an individual] in its formal or constitutive being. Rather it pertains to its material being, insofar as 'material' is opposed to 'formal' being, in the aforesaid meaning of 'formal being' [viz. namely, constitutive of its essence]. For it is in this sense that the Philosopher calls 'form' the 'what-the-something-was-to-be' [i.e. the essence or quiddity].[50]

172. The third way [of clarifying our view] is by comparing the specific difference with what is on a par with it, namely that by which a species is distinguished through a difference that specifies [cf. ¶. 169]. There is clearly something similar to this in a difference that individuates. For although the specific differences which are derived from the nature as a whole can have something in common predicated of them *in quid* [i.e. if they are not ultimate specifying differences], nevertheless those which are derived from ultimate perfections, do not have anything predicable of them *in quid* as was said in I [*Lectura*, d. 3].[51] And this is so in the case of individual differences whose concepts are derived from the ultimate perfection which is in a thing and in nature, and hence individual differences are primarily diverse, not having anything said of them *in quid*[52] (neither 'being' nor anything else), as was pointed out in Bk I. Consequently, it is just through such primarily diverse differences, as regards which natures are in potency and able to be contracted, that things are individuated and become singular.

173. [OBJECTIONS] You may object: If individual differences are primarily diverse; then one cannot abstract any 'one' from

them. Hence the things constituted through such differences would be primarily diverse.

174. Furthermore, the unity of nature in an individual, such as Socrates, either is numerically 'one' or not. If not, then the same numerical thing [i.e., humanity] will be in several diverse things. If it is numerically one in this same [Socrates]; then there will be no basis for distinguishing in this [Socrates] any unity other than numerical unity, which is assumed to be the ultimate.

175. [ANSWER TO THE OBJECTIONS] To the first of these, the response must be that, if the meaning is this: 'Where the differences are primarily diverse, what is constituted thereby is also primarily diverse, i.e., they are incompossibles'—then this is true. For the differences of whiteness and blackness are primarily diverse, and thus whiteness and blackness are primarily incompossibles. On the other hand, if the meaning is this: 'If the constitutive differences are primarily diverse, then the things constituted thereby are [so] primarily diverse that they agree in nothing,' then this is false. For the things so constituted also have a nature, in which nature they primarily agree. But this is not the case with their differences, as is clear from the case where species are constituted by ultimate specific differences, which agree in nothing.

176. To the other [in ¶. 174] it must be admitted that in Socrates that unity proper to his nature qua nature is other than his numerical [or individual] unity. For this [Socrates' nature] has its own unity which is less than numerical unity, as was said earlier. Hence, just as in whiteness the unity of that nature from which the intention of the genus [i.e., color] is taken is other than the unity of nature from which is taken the intention of the difference [its being white], so too [Socrates' human] nature is other than his individual difference [i.e. his Socratic haecceity].

177. And when one asks: 'How does that unity [characteristic of human nature in Socrates] who is one in number, become such numerically,' one must say that it is numerically one by denominative predi-

cation, but it is not so by formal predication for formally speaking, it has another sort of unity.

B. Reply to the Initial Arguments

178. To the first argument at the beginning [¶. 140], when it is argued that then every individual would be composed of a nature and something positive, we must admit that this is true of that composition which takes this unity into consideration. For there is a threefold unity: [i] one, based on a composition resulting from diverse things (like the composite of matter and form); [ii] another is the unity of what are distinguished according to their formal reasons, but which are still such that one—according to its total formal reason—includes the other by identity, though not formally. (Thus essence and paternity, and the attributes are interrelated in God, so that although the meaning [*ratio*] of paternity is other than the essence and vice versa, because [the Father] 'is not father by the same [characteristic] that he is God,' nevertheless the [divine] essence according to its formal meaning [*ratio*] includes by identity the [paternal] relation and [divine] attributes. Hence it is not potential or contractible by these [relations and attributes], and that is why they do not make for any composition.) [iii] But there is an intermediate unity and distinction in one and the same thing which has diverse perfections and diverse formal entities but in such a way that one formal reality does not include another; neither is it of itself formally the other [i.e. by identity as in the deity], and therefore one formal reality is perfectible and determinable by another—such is the composition in a simple thing having a genus and difference (as in whiteness). For it has one formal reality from which the generic intention is taken, and this reality has nothing that includes the formal reality from which the difference is derived, any more indeed than if it were another thing entirely distinct from the other. Now the composition of specific nature and individual difference, through which that nature is contracted and determined, is of this sort.

179. To the other [¶. 141], where it is argued that [a positive individuating difference] would have to be either form or matter, I admit that it is the same thing but is another formal perfection. Hence there is matter and this matter, for matter in itself is indifferent and is contracted by that formal individual perfection. It is similar with the form where this form adds some formal entity over and above the form [as determinable and indifferent].—And thus in an individual there is a nature and this nature, and the individual adds to the nature considered absolutely that formal reality whereby it has its own proper unity and singularity.—And this holds universally of every created nature and of everything that is indifferent and of the same sort. Each such can be contracted and has such a perfection whereby it can be contracted.

180. And when it is argued [in ¶. 142] that [on my theory] the singular would be intelligible per se by a species other than the nature-species, just as the latter species is intelligible by a likeness other than that of the genus, for as the species adds to the genus, so the singular would add to the species,—to all this I say that the singular is not grasped [intellectually] when the species is understood; and that the singular is understood per se by an intellect that is able to understand all intelligibles (such as God's intellect or that of an angel). That it is not understood per se by our intellect, then, is not due to anything on the side of the singular but stems from the imperfection of our intellect—just as the inability of the owl to see the sun is on the part of the owl, not of the sun.

181. As for the other [¶. 143] where it is argued 'then the singular would be defined per se,' I say: No! According to the Philosopher in I *Topics* [ch. 5], 'a definition is completely expressive of the what-the-thing-was-to-be [ie., the quiddity or essence].' But the entity of singularity is of another sort than that of the quiddity, as should be clear from the preceding remarks [¶¶. 170–172], and hence it has no definition other than that of the species.

182. And that is also why it has no other

attribute than what is attributed to the species; hence it has neither any proper attribute or proper means [of demonstrating an attribute of it]; and therefore there is no science of it [¶. 144].

C. To the Arguments for the Other Opinion

183. As for the arguments for the other opinion, when it is argued that the most special species is atomic [¶. 147], I grant it is atomic and indivisible so far as that divisibility goes which allows for further division into diverse natures, but it is not completely elementary or atomic. As a matter of fact, consistent with its indivisibility is its capacity to be divided into parts of the same sort [i.e. individuals of the same species].

184. As for the other [¶. 148] where it is argued from Porphyry's statement: 'in the descent from the most general, Plato bids one halt at what is most special,' I say there are two reasons why division is said 'to halt with the most special species': one, because individuals are infinite, and such infinites "should be left alone" by art (that is why art and science do not go beyond the most special species);—another reason is because individuals have no proper attributes or definitions or means [whereby anything can be demonstrated of them, as one demonstrates attributes of a subject by means of its essence]. Hence, artistic and scientific knowledge must halt at the level of the most special species. Still consistent with this, however, is the fact that a specific nature is potentially divisible into an infinity [of individuals of that species] as there is an infinity of potential entities to contract it.

185. To the other [¶. 149], when it is argued that Boethius postulates no division of the species into individuals, I say this is because a proper division is into parts which bear some proportion to what is divided, so that taken together they exhaust the divided. For according to Boethius in that same [*Liber de divisione*]: 'Except for lack of words, every division immediately would be into two.' Then, if each may be

further divided, their members, as with the first, would include the divided (such would be the case if a genus were divided into two species immediately and these in turn into others). But this is not the situation in our case [where a species is divided into individuals], for here is no division into two, each of which is subject to a further primary division. Instead the specific nature is divided immediately into an infinity [of potential individuals], and this would not be properly a division [in the Boethian sense]. Nevertheless, speaking of division in more general terms, insofar as that into which something is divided represents something of the thing divided, then it is true that the specific nature is divided into individuals by individual differences.—And so this division could be brought reductively under his heading of a generic division, to which it has a greater affinity—as is evident from what he says [there about the properties of a generic division].

186. As for the other [¶. 150], where it is argued that according to Boethius in his *Liber de divisione*, 'The species predicates the whole being [*esse*] of the individual,' I say that Boethius doesn't say this but says something quite different to the effect that 'the species is the whole being of the individual.' And then I say that 'being' [*esse*] here means the quiddity, just as it does in the case of Porphyry's statement in the chapter 'On the difference': "The being of anything is not subject to intensification or remission." (He takes 'being' [*esse*] here for the essence, as the Philosopher is wont to do. Individuality[53] however has no quiddity (it is not the quiddity of a species) for the entity which it adds is not quidditative or formal entity, as was said. Hence it does not add essential entity to the species in the way the species does to the genus. And that is why it is said that 'the species expresses the whole being of the individual.' The genus, however, does not predicate the whole quiddity of the species in this way, but the species[54] adds more quiddity.

187. As for the last [¶. 151], it is argued that 'although subjective parts are not parts

of quantity, nor are quantitative parts subjective parts, nevertheless when a thing is divided into quantitative parts there is a sufficient division into subjective parts; therefore a division according to quantitative parts is the cause of division into subjective parts; but the principle[55] of a division is the principle of the distinction of its parts; therefore, etc.' To this argument one must reply that granted that when there is a division into quantitative parts, then there is a division into subjective parts (as happens at times when the divided whole is homogeneous). On the other hand, when the divided parts refer to diverse things in it, namely, they are parts of quantity and of substance, then these divisions are of two wholes [namely, a 'quantitative whole' and a 'whole' that is a universal],—and given the division into quantitative parts it is only *per accidens* that a division into subjective parts [i.e. individual substances] occurs.

188. And when it is said that 'the principle of a division is the principle of the distinction of its parts' [¶. 187], we have to say this is false. It is not because the concept of the genus is divided into species, that is the principle of the distinction. Consequently, the 'whole as having parts' is the principle of the distinction.[56]

II. To the Arguments for the Other View in Question Five

189. To the first argument of the preceding question, when it is argued [¶. 126] from V *Metaphysics* that 'those things are numerically one whose matter is one,' I reply: The Philosopher frequently—in the *Metaphysics* and elsewhere—takes 'form' for the quiddity and 'matter' for anything that contracts quiddity. (Hence he says in Bk. VIII that 'forms are like numbers'— where, by 'forms' he understands quiddities and definitions.) Those things are one in number, then, whose quiddity has been contracted by an entity that is one in number, and it is this he understands by 'matter.'

190. Similarly [¶. 132] when he says, in I *De caelo:* 'When someone speaks of heaven

he is speaking of form, and when he talks about this heaven, he is talking about matter,' he takes 'form' as 'quiddity' and 'this heaven' for 'having quiddity.'

191. To the other [¶. 131] argument that 'if there were several [first] movers, they would have matter, wherefore there could be no numerical difference except through matter,' I say that it is necessary that everything in the same species have 'matter' in the aforesaid sense [¶. 189], namely that they have some entity contracting the quiddity. If there were several [prime] movers, then, they would need to have this 'matter' through which they would differ, and in this sense there is 'matter' in every created simple thing.

192. To the other argument [¶. 130] that 'in things conceived to have matter, the essence [or what-something-is] and the one whose essence it is are not the same,' it must be granted that each thing having a quiddity, in the manner in which it has that quiddity, is identical with its quiddity. But the first question to ask is not "Is the quiddity the same as that of which it is the quiddity?" but "Does it have a quiddity?" And since 'white man' has no quiddity, therefore its quiddity is not the same as it. But in everything that has quiddity, the quiddity is the same as that to which it pertains. The Philosopher uses this same sort of solution in Bk. VII [ch. 6]: "For nothing is other than its substance,"—and from the many things said there, this is clear. Therefore in things conceived to have matter (i.e., with an entity contracting the nature), the quiddity is not the same as that to which it pertains, because they do not have quiddity primarily, for what-something-is primarily pertains to the species. And since matter-concepts of this sort add something over and above the specific nature, and do not have just that nature but some entity contracting it, therefore, things conceived to have matter are not precisely the same as the quiddity which they could have.

193. But so understood, in the case of things separated from matter the quiddity and that of which it is the quiddity are identical, because—according to the mind

of the Philosopher—everything which he assumes to be formally necessary, is of itself a 'this,' and thus does not have any contracting matter. His argument is that if that which is formally necessary, were not of itself singular, then its nature would be contractible and in potency; hence that nature—insofar as it is of itself—would be in potency to an infinity of supposits[57] to which it could be contracted. And whatever in its form can be, must exist—according to him. Therefore, the nature would exist in infinite [singulars]. Thus he does not look for any contracting entity in natures separated from matter, and hence he assumes that whatever lacks a matter-part in itself, has no 'this' (i.e., matter) contracting it. That is why things conceived to have matter are not precisely the same as the quiddity that they can have, whereas in things separated from matter the quiddity is the same as that to which it pertains, and there is but one such in one species.

194. To the other argument [¶. 129] that 'the producer begets another because of the matter, (namely, 'diverse in number because of the matter, but of the same species because of the form'),' I say that the Philosopher claims there that to explain generation of an assumption of Ideas[58] is unnecessary. For one individual suffices to produce another since it has what both distinguish it from, and yet makes it like, the begotten product, for it resembles the product by reason of unity of form. For form and nature in the producer and the produced are the same by a real identity, which is still less than numerical unity, (as said above [¶¶. 9–25]). Thus the producer produces something similar to itself not through the form 'qua this,' but through the form 'qua form,' having a unity less than numerical unity. Similarly, the producer has that which distinguishes it and allows it to generate something distinct from itself, because the producer intends through generation to perfect matter, and he cannot perfect his own matter, since that

is already informed. Hence he does not beget from his matter, but from that of another. Hence, it is in the other matter that he induces the form of the product that is similar to his own.

195. Why then does the Philosopher claim that producer and produced are diverse because of matter, but the same in species and form? I say that producer and product are distinct both because of matter and because of form; but more because of form than because of matter. But for all that, the Philosopher can say appropriately that matter distinguishes producer and produced, whereas it is their form that makes them similar. The reason is this. Though the producer is more this through the form than through the matter, and thus more distinct, it may nevertheless be distinguished through the matter. Just as there is present here *matter* and *this matter* (namely, that entity contracting the nature), so too there is *form* and *this form*; and hence it is the form (and also the matter) considered absolutely that is the source of the similarity—more appropriately, however, this stems from the form, because for similarity we look to the *quale* [or sortal feature], which pertains more to form than to matter. As for the distinction, however, this is due more to *this* form rather than to *this* matter, just as a thing is more [producing or being produced) because of *this* form rather than *this* matter. And still the Philosopher appropriately assigns the distinguishing factor to matter, both because similarity is not appropriated to matter, and because the distinction according to matter—precisely on account of its otherness from the matter of the product—is presupposed for generation. Hence a distinction of matter from which the product may be generated from the producer is presupposed, but in a way that distinct form is not presupposed. Consequently, the Philosopher says fittingly that 'producer and produced are diverse because of matter.'

NOTES

1. The editors of the Vatican edition attribute this view to the Franciscan Masters Roger Marston and Peter of Falco.

2. "Individuation," Roger Marston wrote, "is from the efficient [cause] generating or giving existence, from the matter as providing the occasion, from the form as constituting it formally; this gives being formally and as a consequence being that is distinct and is one." (*Quodl.* I, q. 3) And again: "A thing cannot be something that is one and 'this' through a negation, but just as it has being or existence through its principles, so too does it have unitary being and individual being. . . . Effectively, however, individuation is from the one creating and generating, and formally it is from the individual's own principles. . . . Consequently individuation does not stem from some accident, but from the principles of the substance." (*Quodl.* II, q. 30)

3. A univocal cause is one that produces an effect specifically like itself, e.g., fire. An equivocal cause does not, its effect being unlike and less perfect than itself; e.g., an artist. Generation of offspring is considered to be a type of univocal causality.

4. When Avicenna's works were translated into Latin *ma'na* was consistently rendered as "intention" (*intentio*) with the meaning of a "natural sign in the soul." Just as Porphyry had distinguished between words of first and second imposition, Avicenna differentiated concepts or notions as either first or second intentions, indicating that while first intentions referred to things, second intentions (i.e., abstract notions like *genus* or *species*) referred to first intentions.

5. According to Aristotle's theory of color, borrowed from Plato (*Timaeus* 67E), fine particles penetrate and dilate the diaphanous medium whereas large particles compress it, producing white and black color respectively. Color understood generically or in general can be considered indifferent to producing either.

6. Subjective parts are contrasted with essential parts (like matter and form) or integral parts (whether they differ in kind or are of the same sort); subjective or extensional parts refer to the members of a class, such as the species that fall under genera, or the individuals that fall under a species.

7. *Supposit* (Latin *suppositum*) is the general designation for any fully subsistent individual, whether it is rational, and therefore a person, or non-rational, such as a stone, a plant, an animal. Historically the Latin *suppositum* is a literal translation of the Greek term *hypostatis*, the name Greek theologians used to designate a divine person in the Trinity.

8. Henry of Ghent, *Summa quaestionum ordinariarum* art. 39, ad 2; q. 4 ad 5; art 53, q. 3; *Quodl.* V, q. 8.

9. Ibidem, *Quodl.* V, qq. 14–15.

10. See note 7.

11. Webster's *Third New International Dictionary* defines "quidditative" as "constituting the essential nature of something." The term "quiddity" (or essence) is so called because an essential definition (consisting of a genus and specific difference) is the most fundamental or basic answer one can give to the question: *What* is it? (*Quid* est?).

12. See note 6.

13. Namely, as supposits. See note 7.

14. This view is obviously an attempt on Scotus' part to synthesize the essential position of a number of theologians whose views he was familiar with. The editors of the Vatican edition indicate it was held with minor variations by Thomas Aquinas (*Sum. theol.* I, q. 50, art. 2; III, q. 77, a. 2; *Contra Gent.* II, c. 50, arg. 1; IV, c. 65); Giles of Rome, (*Quodl.* I, q. 11), Thomas Sutton, (*Quodl.* I, q. 21) and Godfrey of Fontaines, (*Quodl.* VII, q. 5; VI, q. 16).

15. Namely, Thomas Aquinas, see paragraph 66.

16. Scotus' point is to show that the theory of individuation by quantity is inconsistent with the Church's understanding of transubstantiation as explained by theologians at the Fourth Lateran Council in 1215 and the Second Council of Lyons in 1274.

    When the priest, in the person of Christ, consecrates the bread with the words: "*This* is my body . . . ," the substance of this individual piece of bread is annihilated, to be replaced with the glorified body of Christ. Though the substance of bread ceases to exist, its primary material accident (quantity or extension) as the support of all the other accidental characteristics of bread, remains, miraculously sustained without the original substance.

    Scotus' argument assumes that while it is possible for an absolute accident like quantity to be miraculously separated from the substance of bread (or wine), since the material substance and its quantity are two really distinct things, the cause of the bread-substance's singularity cannot continue to exist unless it is individuating bread-substance.

    If the original bread-substance is annihilated while its quantity as the principle-individuating-bread remains (for transubstantiation leaves the accidents of bread unchanged), then other bread-substance must be co-created to replace the original bread that was annihilated. Since the numerically identical quantity remains, however, this newly created bread-substance will still be the same individual piece of bread as the bread-substance annihilated. This contradicts the principle that two temporally distinct productions of bread have the same singular substance as their effect.

In revising the argument for the *Ordinatio* II, d. 3, ¶. 81 (7, 429) he added further consequences he considered to be logically absurd. "It follows that the term of [new] creation will be 'this bread,' identical with the bread that was the term of [the original] generation, because that bread was 'this' by the same singularity by which this bread will be 'this'; and it follows further that 'this bread' is both transubstantiated and not transubstantiated. What is more, it follows that no bread is transubstantiated. Surely no universal-bread,—nor this singular bread, because (on their view)—this bread remains if the quantity by which it is formally 'this' is unchanged. Therefore nothing is transubstantiated into the body of Christ, which is to assert heresy."

17. Webster's *Third New International Dictionary* defines *coordination* as an "arrangement in the same order, class, rank or dignity." Scotus applies the term to the arrangement that holds between genera, species and individuals within any Aristotelian category, here that of substance. These are arranged in a chain-like or concatenated fashion according to what Scotus elsewhere refers to as an "essential order" where each lower member presupposes each higher class member, but not vice versa. See "Tree of Porphyry" (in Webster's) as it applies to an individual human being. At the apex of the tree is the most general genus (viz., "substance" as a cateogy). As one descends through the branches, there follows "body," "living thing," "animal," "man," and at the lowest level, "Socrates," "Plato" and "other Individuals."

What differentiates any lower member in the hierarchy from any higher, Scotus argues, is not an accidental difference but something that characterizes it per se or substantially. If the specific difference of "rational" (that sets human animality apart from that of the brute) pertains to the category of substance, so too must the individuating difference that makes each individual unique and uncommon. Each individual differs from another by some positive per se characteristic that pertains to the category of substance.

18. The ten Aristotelian categories represent a division of finite being, therefore substance as a category is finite. One can give the word an extended or transcendental meaning, however, in the sense of any being, whether infinite or finite, that exists in itself (*ens in se*, in contrast to an accident as an *ens in alio*). In this sense, God is a divine substance. See my *The Transcendentals and Their Function in the Metaphysics of Duns Scotus* (St. Bonaventure, NY: The Franciscan Institute, 1946), p. 152.

19. The opinion of Godfrey of Fontaines in *Quodl.* VII, q. 5.

20. "Indivisible being" refers to the fact that the positive entity associated with the individuating principle as the principle of "indivisibility into subjective parts" (see note 6) invests the substantial entity itself with this sort of "indivisibility."

21. 'Signatus' has the meaning here of being *determined, designated* or *marked* in a specific or unique way. Hence, *signatio* can be translated as *marked character* or *demarcation*. One of the essential or defining marks of a material substance is the fact that it is composed of integral parts that are spatially extended. But *extension* (defined as 'having spatially distinctive or distinguishable parts') is a form of quantity. This suggests to the proponents of quantitative individuation theory that since it is the quantity or extension of a material body that allows it to be divided into 'parts,' each of which is identical in kind or species with the others, then the divisibility of a species into individuals must be similar. Scotus is arguing that what specifies a substance as material is by its nature prior to its quantity or how much or little it extends in space. For increase or decrease in quantity—according to Aristotle—is only an accidental, not a substantial change. Since Scotus believes individuation results simply from a further logical determination or limitation analogous to that which specifies substance as material, rather than spiritual or immaterial, John argues that an individual is already something determinate or 'signed' prior to the fact that it has a certain quantity or extension and therefore it is not extension or divisibility that makes it individual. In fact, as he will argue later, 'extended' or 'divisible' are general or universal characteristics in a way that 'haecceity' is not.

22. "*as something added*"—Aristotle distinguishes two ways in which a term enters into the definition of anything. One is the way the genus and specific difference enter into a definition of the essence of a specific substance, e.g., the Aristotelian definition of the essence of a human being as 'rational animal.' Here the common or generic term, 'animal,' and the specific difference, 'rational,' are mutually exclusive terms. This ideal form of definition, for Aristotle, applies to any reality that has an essence, i.e., that can be analyzed in terms of two mutually exclusive notions, one the genus, the other the specific difference.

The other is the way the proper subject of an irreducibly simple or logically primitive attribute enters into a description or quasi-definition of that attribute. (See my *Transcendentals and Their Function* pp. 88–89.) Aristotle cites as examples, 'odd or even' as a disjunctive attribute of number, or 'male or female' as an attribute of animal. An animal need not be female, hence femaleness adds something over and above what is essential to the notion of 'animal' understood as a sexual being, just as maleness does. It makes sense, therefore, to speak of a male animal or a female animal. Yet 'animal' enters into the quasi-definition or description of either 'male' or 'female' as a difference. Unlike the ideal definition of an essence in terms of genus and difference, however, the quasi-generic term 'animal,' and the quasi-differential term expressing the sex of the animal are not mutually exclusive terms, for 'animal' has to be *added* to the description of 'female' or to that of 'male.' These terms do not designate an essence, says Aristotle. For there will be an inevitable repetition or tautology involved in any quasi-definition we give them. For if X = animal and Y = female, and we define female essentially as 'an X that is Y' or simply 'an XY,' then a female animal would be 'an XXY.' "What I mean, then 'by addition,' " Aristotle explains, "is that it turns out that we are saying the same thing twice as in such expressions." (*Metaphysics* VII, ch. 5 1031a 4).

With this in mind consider Scotus' argument. His point is that just as 'animal' needs to be introduced into the definition of 'male' or 'female' *as an addition*, so the notion of substance as the first of Aristotle's ten categories enters somehow into the description or quasi-definition of any of the nine accidental categories (quantity, quality, relation, etc.), but it does so *as something added*. In such a case the logical relationship between the subject [here the individuated substance] and the attribute [here its quantity] is one of essential priority and posteriority. The attribute presupposes the subject, but the subject does not presuppose any particular attribute. This logical relationship of their definitions mirrors the real existential relationship that exists between them. Quantity depends essentially and existentially on the individual substance, not vice versa. For Aristotle, however, such existential dependency is expressed in causal terms, where 'cause' may be any one of the four classical causal principles upon which an effect essentially depends (viz. material cause, formal cause, efficient cause or final cause).

23. That is, a 'material cause' in the Aristotelian sense with respect to quantity as an accidental 'form.'

24. The interpretation of Giles of Rome in his *Quodlibet* I, q. 11: "Just as matter is not of itself extended, but is extended through quantity (nevertheless the extension of matter is other than the extension of quantity), so that even though matter is individuated and signed with quantity and this marked character [*signatio*] and individuation of substance stems from that of quantity, the marked character and the individuation of substance is other than that of its quantity. Therefore, just as matter does not have parts except through quantity, although the parts of matter are other than the parts of quantity (nevertheless, matter's parts do not assert something other than matter, to the extent that each part of matter is itself matter), so too this same situation obtains here. For even though the marked character in substance stems from its quantity, it is nevertheless other than the marked character of quantity. Inasmuch as the marked character of substance, however, does not assert something other than substance, it expresses only a certain relationship substance has because it is perfected by quantity [or extension]. Therefore it is evident how individuation takes place, and why individuation does not withdraw things from their proper categories."

25. Scotus refers to a theory of Henry of Ghent, who claims that in the divine Trinity, the Son's power to spirate the Holy Spirit (which power is proper to the Father) is "something left behind in the Son by the act of generation, as a property shared with the Father." (*Vis spirative est quod derelictum in Filio per actum generationis, ut proprium cum Patre*). See Henry of Ghent, *Summa* a. 60, q. 8 (II, f. 170 M).

26. The argument here seems to be that it is more likely that a dynamic quality (like whiteness, which dilates the translucent medium) than an accident like quantity should produce an effect, for some qualities (e.g., acquired habits) do exercise efficient causality.

27. The "Tree of Porphyry" (see note 17) illustrates the essential order that obtains within the category of substance.

28. The argument here is that anything which can generically be classified as a substance is potentially universal, that is to say, there is no reason why there cannot be more than one of its kind. Even 'individual substance' (Scotus' indefinite individual or *individuum vagum*, see ¶. 71) as the lowest logical class of substances has many members and "to be universal" pertains to it as a subclass of the class of substance. If nothing further is added to specify it per se as singular in an unqualified sense, it will remain a universal. Quantity as an accident cannot specify as substance per se but only *per accidens*.

29. We have translated the adjectival phrase *absoluta et non contracta* (literally, a nature "taken absolutely without [any logical] contraction") as "stark and unconcretized."

30. Scotus argues especially against the position defended by Giles of Rome, who holds that before a material thing is specified by some substantial form, (e.g., as a distinct kind of mineral, plant, animal, etc.) no definite quantity can be assigned to it, but if one specifies the sort of material thing it is, the quantity characteristic of that species will fall within definite limits. Giles, *Quodl.* II q. 11 ". . . quantitas indeterminata praecedit formam substantialem, terminata sequitur."

31. Re 'subjective parts,' see note 6.

32. It is not clear just how 'esse' is to be interpreted in the hyphenated expression 'esse-quantum.' Since Scotus does not regard the existing being to be a real composition of essence and existence (see my *Transcendentals and Their Function*, pp. 66–71), 'esse' does not have any further existential connotation here than that associated with a 'real being' i.e., one capable of existing extramentally in a way a chimera or a mental fiction [an *ens rationis*] is not.

33. Scotus' main purpose is to clarify some of the logical ambiguities that are inherent in the quantitative

theory of individuation. One is the ambiguity the term 'divisibility' has when applied to continuous or discrete quantity,—and in regard to discrete quantity, whether this 'divisibility' refers to 'subjective parts' (see note 6 above) or to the fact that matter is potentially divisible into discrete parts by reason of its extension as a continuum. (This seems to be what Scotus is admitting here in ¶. 111 and in the following two paragraphs).

34. Matter is essentially defined as a subject of form and the distinguishing characteristics of any material substance are rooted either in the substantial form or the accidents of the composite of matter and form. Consequently, if matter were to exist miraculously apart from any form—as Scotus believes it can (see my article "The Ockhamist Critique," in *The Concept of Matter*, ed. Ernan Mcmullin (Notre Dame, IN: University of Notre Dame, 1963), pp. 151–152—it would still be divisible into distinct portions qua matter. And, if it existed as it does in nature with some elementary or composite substantial form, it could be divided. Take for example a definite amount of some elementary substance like earth or water, which consists of primary matter and one of the four elementary substantial forms. Material of this sort could be divided and each portion of the earth or water into which it was divided would have its own quantity. Some distinct quantity would accompany any factual existence earth or water would have and as such would be a sine qua non condition of its normal state of existence, but it would not be the reason why earth qua earth is divisible, or why water is a substance that can be divided into integral parts. This is something characteristic of earth or water as the sort of material substances that are continua in their normal state of existence.

35. This like the preceding paragraphs is an answer to what is said in paragraph 68. There the proponents of the matter/quantity theory of individuation are obviously confusing the various senses of divisibility referred to above in note 33. Matter qua matter is not distinguishable qualitatively, they argue, but only quantitatively. But how is distinguishable quantitatively to be understood? Is it because one is discrete from another numerically, or is it because the amount (of continuous matter) differs with respect to the nature of a substantial form? According to the Aristotelian doctrine, the substantial form determines what 'amount' of matter is required for that form. The amount of matter in a flea is not the amount required for an elephant. The precise meaning of quantity becomes even more ambiguous if one is dealing with an elementary substance like fire, as is the case in paragraph 68. Recall that this account of Scotus represents an attempt to synthesize the views of several of his contemporaries. The Dominican, Thomas Sutton was certainly one of these. See infra note 37.

The ambiguities are multiplied when an example of univocal causality is introduced (as is the case in ¶. 68). Fire produces fire as its effect. Here—interpreted hylomorphically—cause and effect have the same kind of substantial form (that of the element fire). Cause and effect are really distinct, and hence are numerically different as well, each—according to Scotus—has its own haecceity. The fire form does not owe its haecceity to the particular matter it is informing, nor does the particular matter it informs owe its haecceity to the accident of quantity, viz. its actual extension in space. Furthermore, inasmuch as the matter in any material substance has its own substantial entity, according to Scotus, it too requires a principle of individuating distinct from that of form.

36. The reason given in ¶. 69 why matter must be quantified is that "a natural agent only acts on something quantified." Inasmuch as having their materially distinct parts extended is a necessary condition for an agent acting on a patient, natural agents of whatever sort only exercise their causality when they are spatially extended and juxtaposed. But the causality of any material agent is based on its active potencies, and these—according to Scotus—are powers rooted in the singular substance and are only formally distinct from its substantial form which requires haecceity to exist, since only what exists can act. That its parts be actually extended in space, and have certain dimensions may be an accident, but this is certainly "not the formal ground for generation." Furthermore, there is the additional confusion where the natural agent is a univocal cause like fire. The fire form generates a second fire numerically distinct from itself only because it acts on wood and induces in the wood or other flammable material the substantial form of fire. Other matter does not get its numerical distinctness from quantity, but from the fact that it has a distinct haecceity as combustible material. The reason Scotus speaks of quantity as a sine qua non condition of the natural agent producing its effect is that he believes for one burning substance to ignite a second burning substance, the two must be spatially juxtaposed.

37. The editors of the Vatican edition ascribe this view specifically to Thomas Sutton, the Dominican contemporary of Scotus at Oxford.

38. Godfrey of Fontaines, *Quodl.* XI, q. 3.

39. Scotus' point seems to be that where we have two numerically distinct things, their accidents (at least their spatial properties) will be different as well. This spatial difference would be a sine qua non condition of natural existence. Scotus admits that in practice we distinguish things other than our selves, by their accidental differences, since we do not perceive the haecceity of extramental things immediately. This was the point of the argument in ¶. 24.

40. A reference to the theological doctrine of circumincession.

41. Though 'rational' is the specific difference in the Aristotelian definition of 'man' as a 'rational animal'

and hence expresses a substantial or essential qualification, it is logically related only *per accidens* to 'animal,' otherwise there could be no brute or irrational animal.

42. This view again is meant as a synthesis of the essential position of several theologians whose views Scotus was familiar with. The editors of the Vatican edition cite the following as probable sources: Thomas Aquinas (*Sum. theol.* I, q. 7, art. 3; III, q. 77, a. 2; *Contra Gent.* II, c. 75, arg. 1; c. 83, arg. 20; c. 93, arg. 2; III, c. 65, arg. 3; IV, c. 63); Giles of Rome, (*Quodl.* I, q. 11); Godfrey of Fontaines, (*Quodl.* VII, q. 5 in *Les Philosophes Belges* III [Louvain, 1914], 324–326).

43. This seems largely a reference to Aquinas, *Metaph.* VII, lect. 11.

44. Aquinas, *Metaph.* XII, lect. 10.

45. Aquinas, *De caelo* I, lect. 19, ¶. 4–6.

46. Godfrey of Fontaines, *Quodl.* VII, q. 5 (III, 319, 324–325).

47. Quantity is one of the absolute accidents.

48. According to Aristotle, *different* things vary from those that are *diverse* in that they have something that is the same and something diverse, whereas diverse things are radically or irreducibly disparate.

49. The Vienna MS has the better reading here, viz. "ratio generis." The species, not the "specific difference," has a proper unity, just as the genus and the individual have. The "difference" may be the ultimate reason why the unity characteristic of the respective subject of which it is the difference is different, but it is the respective subject that has the unity. That the species has a unity proper to itself is not in question, but Scotus' argument here seems to be that the unity of genus is not as great as that of the species; but if it has a proper unity, a fortiori the individual has a unity which is even more circumscribed than that of the species.

50. A literal translation of Aristotle's designation for the essence or quiddity of anything, *tò tí ēn eínai*. See note 11.

51. Scotus is concerned with those specific differences that are primitive or 'simply simple,' namely, those that are essentially *qualia* and have nothing predicable of them *in quid*. On the distinction between specific differences of which being is predicable *in quid* and those which are ultimate or primitive, see my *Transcendentals and Their Function*, pp. 84–85.

52. *In quid* predication predicates something in the nominative case of the subject, as opposed to *in quale* or *in quantum* predication where what is predicated is an adjectival term that is qualitative or quantitative respectively.

53. Scotus understands "Individual" (*individuum*) abstractly. As the editors of the Vatican edition indicate, it refers to the individuating difference.

54. The *Ordinatio* II, d. 3, ¶. 197 (7, 489) expresses this more clearly. It reads: "Non sic autem genus dicit totum esse speciei, quia species superaddit entitatem quidditativam."

55. *Principle* was not mentioned in the original argument in ¶. 151; but Scotus introduces it here as equivalent in meaning to "a sufficient reason for." As the subsequent paragraph indicates, the concept of the genus (that is, something predicable of one or more species) is the principle for its divisibility into parts, for the fact that the genus is common suffices to explain why it could be divided (or predicated of subjective parts), but its commonness does not explain why the factual partitions are distinct, since the difference, not the genus, is the basis for the distinction of one species from another. See the parallel passage in the *Ordinatio* II in the following note.

56. This obscure argument is clarified in the parallel passage of the *Ordinatio* II, d. 3, ¶. 189 (7, 489): "Dico quod illa propositio est falsa 'idem est principium divisibilitatis et distinctionis dividentium'; conceptus quidem secundum se communis speciebus est ratio divisibilitatis eius in species, sed non est ratio distinguendi species ab invicem, sed haec species ab illa distinguitur per differentiam. In quantitativa autem divisione, tota quantitas, ut confuse continet omnes partes, est ratio divisibilitatis in toto quanto,—non sic autem est ratio distinctionis partium ab invicem, sed in quantum 'haec quantitas' distincte in actu non est 'illa' in actu quae est in toto."

   Webster defines "genus" as "a class, kind, or group marked by common characteristics or by one common characteristic." In the *Ordinatio* Scotus is arguing that the reason the genus is divisible into subjective parts is because it expresses the one characteristic that is common to the species into which it is divided. In the *Lectura* he expresses this principle of division simply as *quia conceptus generis dividitur in species* ("because the concept of the genus is divided into species"). But this is not why the species are distinct from one another. The *Ordinatio* indicates it is because of their specific differences that species are distinct. In the *Lectura* he expresses this principle of distinction as *totum ut habet partes* ("the whole as having parts"). That is to say, it is because this whole is a group of [subjective] parts, each with its specific difference, that is the principle of the distinction.

   In the *Ordinatio*, he goes on to show the principle of quantitative division is that any given quantity is a whole whose potential parts are still fused and are indistinct. They become actually distinct when they are no longer fused, but actually divided. Here again, the principle they claim does not hold up. The basis for division is not that of distinction.

57. See note 7 above re "supposit."

58. A reference to Plato's theory of ideas.

CHAPTER 41

William of Ockham

(See Chapter Sixteen for biography.)

Ockham on Universals

If universals carry with them any sort of independent status, then they must be particulars, which is contradictory. Therefore, realism of any variety is untenable. Only particulars exist in re. To understand the nature of universals one must consider how one thinks of and refers to particulars. Consider the word 'man.' Ockham distinguishes both the spoken and written word from that which he calls the natural sign of the word which is its meaning. In other words, universals are not just *flatus voci.* Rather, they constitute an essential element of mental language which is ontologically prior to spoken language. This is so by virtue of the fact that speech is a mere extension of thinking. Universals therefore are the common terms of mental language. The word 'man' is ambiguous. It can refer to either particular men or to the species of man. When 'man' is used to refer to a particular man it is a term of first intention. When 'man' is used to refer to the species of man it is a term of second intention. Second intentions are natural signs of first intentions. Terms of second intention refer to features of particulars abstracted for special investigation.

Here Ockham employs another important expression, that of *suppositio*, which means "standing for." He classifies terms under three types of *suppositio*, namely *personalis*, *materialis*, and *simplex*. When the term 'man' stands for a precise individual, it is an instance of *suppositio personalis*. When the word 'man' is mentioned (as opposed to used), that is an instance of *suppositio materialis*. When the word 'man' stands for all men, namely the species, such is an instance of *suppositio simplex*.

It is *suppositiones simplices* that stand for universals. Universals are second intentions of the simple order, that is, the significata (i.e., referents) of species words. The significatum of a species word is its meaning. Universals do not refer to any realities. Ockham says, "no universal is anything existing in any way outside the soul; but everything which is predicable of many things is of its nature in the mind, whether subjectively or objectively; and no universal belongs to the essence or quiddity of any substance whatsoever". Universals are natural signs standing for characteristics individually possessed by two or more particulars. *Suppositiones simplices* arise because (1) two or more particulars possess similarities in varying degrees, and (2) the human intellect is capable of understanding (1). In other words, Socrates and Plato do not share a common characteristic or nature. Rather, the nature that is Socrates and the nature that is Plato resemble each other. A universal is the natural sign standing for such a resemblance. This is the consummate expression of nominalism.

SUMMA LOGICAE

Part I

Chapter 14

Since such a general knowledge of terms[1] is not enough for a logician, but rather he must know about terms in a more special way [too], therefore after the general divisions of terms have been treated, we must follow up [by treating] certain of the contents under some of those divisions.

Now first we must treat terms of second intention, [and] second terms of first intention. It has been said [already][2] that terms of second intention are ones like 'universal', 'genus', 'species', etc. Therefore, we must now speak about [the terms] that are posited [as] the five universals.[3] But first, we have to speak about the common [term] 'universal', which is predicated of every universal, and about 'singular', which is opposed to it.

Now first, you have to know that 'singular' is taken in two senses. In one sense, the name 'singular' signifies everything that is one and not several. In this sense, those who hold that a universal is a certain mental quality predicable of several [things], yet not for itself but for those several [things], have to say that every universal is truly and really a singular. For, just as any utterance, no matter how common [it is] through institution, is truly and really singular and numerically one, because it is one and not several, so [too] an intention of the soul, signifying several external things, is truly and really singular and numerically one, because it is one and not several things, even though it signifies several things.

In another sense the name 'singular' is taken for everything that is one and not several, and is not apt to be a sign of several [things]. Taking 'singular' in this way, no

From William of Ockham, *Summa logicae*, Part I, Chapters 14–17; Quodlibet 4, Question 35, and Quodlibet 5, Questions 12 and 13, translated by Paul Vincent Spade, copyright 1989. Reprinted by kind permission of Paul Vincent Spade.

universal is a singular, because every universal is apt to be a sign of several [things] and apt to be predicated of several [things].

Hence, calling "universal" something that is not numerically one (which is the sense many [people] attribute to 'universal'),[4] I say that nothing is a universal, unless perhaps you abuse the word by saying that a "people" is a universal, because it is not one but many. But that is childish.

Therefore, it must be said that every universal is one singular thing, and is therefore not universal except by signification, [this is,] because it is a sign of several [things]. This is what Avicenna says, *Metaphysics*, V:[5] "One form before the intellect is related to a multitude, and in this respect is a universal, because it is an intention in the intellect the comparison of which is not changed to [just] anything you pick." And it follows:[6] "This form, even though in comparison to individuals it is universal, nevertheless in comparison to the singular soul in which it is impressed, it is individual. For it is one from among the forms that are in the intellect."

He means to say that a universal is a singular intention of the soul itself, apt to be predicated of several [things], so that insofar as it is apt to be predicated of several [things], not for itself but for those several [things], it is called universal. But insofar as it is one form, existing really in the intellect, it is called singular.

So 'singular' said in the first sense is predicated of a universal, but not said in the second sense. In [the same] manner, we say that the sun is a universal cause, and yet it is truly a particular and singular thing, and consequently is truly a singular and particular cause. For the sun is called a universal cause because it is the cause of several [things], namely, of all these generable and corruptible [things here] below. But it called a particular cause because it is one cause and not several causes. So [too] an intention of the soul is called universal because it is a sign predicable of several [things]. And it is also called singular because it is one thing and not several things.

Nevertheless, you should know that there are two kinds of universal. One kind is a universal naturally, namely, one that is naturally a sign predicable of several [things], in the way (analogously) in which smoke naturally signifies fire, and the groans of the sick [signify] pain, and a laugh signifies inner delight. Such a universal is nothing but an intention of the soul, so that no substance outside the soul, or any accident outside the soul, is such a universal. I will be speaking about this kind of universal in the following chapters.

There is another [kind of] universal, through a voluntary institution. In this way a spoken utterance, which is truly numerically one quality, is universal, because, namely, it is a sign voluntarily instituted to signifying several [things]. Hence, just as an utterance is called "common", so it can be called "universal". But it does not have this from the nature of the thing, but rather only from the choice of those who institute [it].

Chapter 15

Since it is not enough [just] to recite these [claims] if they are not proven by plain reason, therefore I shall set out some reasons in favor of what was said above, and will confirm [my claim] by authorities.[7]

For it can be evidently proven that no universal is any substance existing outside the soul. First, as follows: No universal is a singular, numerically one substance. For if it were said that it is, it would follow that Socrates would be a universal. For there is no greater reason why a universal should be one singular substance rather than [any] other.

Therefore, no singular substance is any universal. Rather, every substance is numerically one and singular, because every substance is either (a) one thing and not several, or else it is (b) several things.

If it is (a) one and not several, it is nu-

merically one. For that is what everyone calls [being] numerically one. But if some substance is (b) several things, either it is (i) several singular things or else (ii) several universal things.

If (i) is granted, it follows that some substance would be several singular substance, and consequently, by the same reasoning, some substance would be several men. In that case, even though the universal would be distinguished from one particular, nevertheless it would not be distinguished from particulars.

But if (ii) some substance were several universal things, [then] I take one of these universal things and ask: Is it (1) several things or (2) one and not several? If (2) is granted, it follows that it is singular. If (1) is granted, [then] I ask: Is it several singular things or several universal things? And so either there will be an infinite regress, or else it will be established that no substance is universal in such a way that [it is] not singular. As a result, the only remaining alternative is that no substance is universal.

Again, if some universal were one substance existing in singular substances [and] distinct from them, it would follow that it could exist without them. For every thing naturally prior to another can, [at least] by divine power, exist without that [other]. But the consequent is absurd.

Again, if this view were true,[8] no individual could be created if any individual pre-existed. For it would not take its whole being from nothing if the universal that is in it was in something else earlier. For the same reason, it would also follow that God could not annihilate one individual substance unless he were to destroy the other individuals. For if he were to annihilate some individual, he would destroy all that belongs to the essence of the individual. Consequently, he would destroy the universal that is in it and in other [individuals]. Consequently, the others would not remain, since they could not remain without their part, as the universal is claimed to be.

Again, such a universal could not be posited as something completely outside the essence of the individual. Therefore, it would belong to the essence of the individual. Consequently, the individual would be put together out of universals, and so the individual would not be any more singular than [it is] universal.

Again, it would follow that something belonging to the essence of Christ would be wretched and damned, because the common nature really existing in Christ and in a damned [person] would be damned, because [it is damned] in Judas. But this is absurd.

Many other reasons could be added, which I pass over for the sake of brevity.

[Now] I confirm the same conclusion through authorities.

First, from Aristotle, *Metaphysics*, VII,[9] where with an aim to treat the question whether the universal is a substance, he demonstrates that no universal is a substance. Thus, he says: "It is impossible for a substance to be anything that is said universally."

Again, *Metaphysics*, X,[10] he says: "And so, if none of the universals can be a substance, as was said in our discussions of substance and being,[11] [and] neither [can] this itself[12] [be] a substance as a one beyond the many."

From these [passages] it is clear that, according to Aristotle's meaning, no universal is a substance, even though it supposits for substances.

Again, the Commentator, *Metaphysics*, VII, comment 44:[13] "In an individual there is no substance except the matter and the particular form from which it is put together."

Again, in the same place, comment 45:[14] "Let us say, therefore, that it is impossible for [any] one of what are called universals to be the substance of any thing, even though it reveals the substances of things."

Again, in the same place, comment 47:[15] "It is impossible for these to be parts of substances that exist through themselves."

Again, *Metaphysics*, VIII, comment 2:[16] "The universal is not a substance or a genus."

Again, *Metaphysics*, X, comment 6:[17] "Since universals are not substances, it is

plain that common being is not a substance existing outside the soul."

From the authorities cited above, and from several others, it can be gathered that no universal is a substance, however it is considered. Hence, the consideration of the intellect does not make something be a substance or not be a substance, even though the signification of a term makes the name 'substance' be predicated, or not predicated, of it ([but] not for itself). For example, if the term 'dog' in the proposition 'A dog is an animal' stands for the animal that can bark, [then the proposition] is true, [but] if it [stands] for the star in the heavens,[18] it is false.[19] Nevertheless, it is impossible for the same thing to be a substance on account of one consideration and not a substance on account of another.

Therefore, it is to be simply granted that no universal is a substance, however it is considered. Rather every universal is an intention of the soul, which according to one likely opinion does not differ from the act of understanding.[20] Hence, they say[21] that the intellection by which I understand a man is a natural sign of men, just as natural [a sign] as a groan is a [natural] sign of sickness or sadness or pain. It is such a sign that it can stand for men in mental propositions, just as an utterance can stand for things in spoken propositions.

For Avicenna [states] quite expressly that the universal is an intention of the soul, *Metaphysics*, V, where he says:[22] "I say therefore that 'universal' is said in three senses. For (a) 'universal' is said according to the fact that it is predicated in act of many [things], like 'man'. And (b) an intention that can be predicated of many [things] is called a universal." And there follows: "Also, an intention that nothing prevents being thought to be predicated of many is called a universal."

From these and many other [passages], it is clear that a universal is an intention of the soul apt to be predicated of many.

This can be confirmed by reason too. For every universal, according to everyone, is predicable of many. But only an intention of the soul or a voluntarily instituted sign, and not any substance, is apt to be predicated. Therefore, only an intention of the soul or a voluntarily instituted sign is a universal. But I am not now using 'universal' for a voluntarily instituted sign, but rather for what is naturally a universal.

For it is clear that a substance is not apt to be predicated, because if it were, it would follow that a proposition would be put together out of particular substances. Consequently, the subject might be in Rome and the predicate in England, which is absurd.

Again, there is no proposition except in the mind, in speech, or in writing. Therefore, its parts are only in the mind, in speech, or in writing. But particular substances are not like this. Therefore, it is clear that no proposition can be put together out of substances. But a proposition is composed out of universals. Therefore, universals are not in any way substances.

Chapter 16

Although it is plain to many [people] that the universal is not some substance outside the soul, existing individuals [and] really distinct from them, nevertheless it seems to some [people][23] that the universal is in some way outside the soul in individuals, not to be sure really distinct from them, but only formally distinct from them. Hence they say that in Socrates there is human nature, which is contracted to Socrates by an individual difference that is not really but formally distinguished from the nature. Thus they are not two things, and yet the one is not formally the other.

But this opinion seems altogether unlikely to me. First, because in creatures no distinction of any kind can ever be outside the soul except where there are distinct things. Therefore, if between this nature and this difference there is any kind of distinction, they have to be really distinct things. The assumption I prove in syllogistic form, as follows: This nature is not formally from this nature; this individual difference is formally from this nature.

Therefore, this individual difference is not this nature.

Again, the same thing is not [both] common and proper. But, according to them, the individual difference is proper, whereas the universal is common. Therefore, no universal is the same thing as an individual difference.

Again, opposites cannot belong to the same created thing. But "common" and "proper" are opposites. Therefore, the same thing is not [both] common and proper. Yet that would follow if the individual difference and the common nature were the same thing.

Again, if the common nature were really the same as the individual difference, therefore there would really be as many common natures as there are individual differences. Consequently, none of them would be common, but rather each would be proper to the difference with which it is really the same.

Again, each thing, either by itself or through something intrinsic to it, is distinguished from whatever it is distinguished from. But Socrates' humanity is other than Plato's. Therefore, they are distinguished by themselves. Therefore, [they are] not [distinguished] through added differences.

Again, according to Aristotle's view,[24] whatever [entities] differ specifically differ [also] numerically. But the nature of a man and the nature of an ass are specifically distinguished by themselves. Therefore, by themselves they are numerically distinguished. Therefore, each of them by itself is numerically one.

Again, what cannot through any power belong to several, is not through any power [made] predicable of several. But such a nature, if it is really the same as the individual difference, cannot through any power belong to several, because in no way can it pertain to another individual. Therefore, through no power can it be [made] predicable of several. Consequently, through no power can it be [made] a universal.

Again, I take this individual difference and the nature it contracts, and ask: Is there a greater distinction between them than [there is] between two individuals, or [is there] a lesser one? Not a greater [distinction], because they are not really different, whereas individuals are really different. Neither [is there] a lesser [distinction], because in that case they would be of the same kind, just as two individuals are of the same kind. Consequently, if the one is of itself numerically one, the other will also be of itself numerically one.

Again, I ask: Is the nature the individual difference or not? If it is, [then] I argue syllogistically as follows: This individual difference is proper and not common. This individual difference is the nature. Therefore, the nature is proper and not common. [And] that is the point.

Likewise, I argue syllogistically as follows: This individual difference is not formally distinct from the individual difference. This individual difference is the nature. Therefore, the nature is not formally distinct from the individual difference.

But if it is given that this individual difference is not the nature, I have my point. For it follows: The individual difference is not the nature; therefore, the individual difference is not really the nature. For from the opposite of the consequent there follows the opposite of the antecedent, arguing as follows: The individual difference is really the nature; therefore, the individual difference is the nature. The inference is clear, because there is a good inference from a determinable, taken with a determination [that is] not destructive or diminishing, to the determinable taken by itself. Now 'really' is not a destructive or diminishing determination. Therefore, it follows: The individual difference is really the nature; therefore, the individual difference is the nature.

It has to be said, therefore, that in creatures there is no such formal distinction. Rather, whatever [entities] are distinct among creatures are really distinct, and are distinct things if each of them is a true thing. Hence, just as in the case of creatures such ways of arguing as the following should never be denied: "This is a; this is

b; therefore, b is a," or the following: "This is not a; this is b; therefore, b is not a," so it should never be denied in the case of creatures that whenever contradictories are verified of some [entities], they are distinct—unless some determination or some syncategoremata is the cause of such verification, which should not be maintained in the present case.

Therefore, we ought to say with the philosophers that in a particular substance there is nothing substantial at all except the particular form and the particular matter or something put together out of them. Therefore, it is not to be imagined that in Socrates there is a humanity or a human nature distinct from Socrates in any way, to which an individual difference that contracts that nature is added. Rather anything substantial imaginable that exists in Socrates is either a particular matter or a particular form or something put together out of them. Therefore, every essence and quiddity, and whatever belongs to a substance, if it is really outside the soul, is simply and absolutely either matter or form or put together out of them, or else an immaterial, abstract substance, according to the teaching of the Peripatetics.

Chapter 17

Because the solution of doubts is the manifestation of truth, therefore some objections should be set out against what has been said, in order that they be solved. For it seems to many [people] of no little authority that the universal is somehow outside the soul and belongs to the essence of particulars. To prove this they bring forth some reasons and authorities.

(1) Hence, they say[25] that when some [entities] really agree and [also] really differ, they agree through one [entity] and differ through another. But Socrates and Plato really agree and really differ. Therefore, they agree and differ in distinct [entities]. But they agree in humanity, and also in matter and form. Therefore, they include some [entities] besides these, by which they

are distinguished. These they call "individual differences".

(2) Again, Socrates and Plato agree more than [do] Socrates and an ass. Therefore, Socrates and Plato agree in something in which Socrates and an ass do not agree. But they do not agree in anything numerically one. Therefore, that in which they agree is not numerically one. Therefore, it is something common.

(3) Again, *Metaphysics*, X:[26] In every genus there is something first that is the measure of all the other [entities] in that genus. But no singular is the measure of all others, because [it is] not [even the measure] of all individuals of the same species. Therefore, there is something besides the individual.

(4) Again, everything superior belongs to the essence of [its] inferior. Therefore, the universal belongs to the essence of a substance. But non-substance does not belong to the essence of substance. Therefore, some universal is a substance.

(5) Again, if no universal were a substance, therefore all universals would be accidents. Consequently, all categories would be accidents, and so the category of substance would be an accident. Consequently, some accident would be by itself superior to substance. Indeed, it would follow that the same [entity] would be superior to itself. For those universals could not be put [anywhere] except in the genus of quality, if they are accidents. Consequently, the category of quality would be common to all universals. Therefore, it would be common to the universal that is the category of quality.

Innumerable other reasons and authorities are brought forth in favor of this opinion, which I omit at present for the sake of brevity, [although] I will say [something] about them in various places below.[27]

I reply to these:

To (1), I grant that Socrates and Plato really agree and really differ. For they really agree specifically, and really differ numerically. And they specifically agree and numerically differ through the same [entity],

just as the others[28] have to say that the individual difference really agrees with the nature and formally differs [from it] through the same [entity].

If you say that the same [entity] is not the cause of agreement and difference, it is to be said that it is true that the same [entity] is not the cause of an agreement and a difference opposed to that agreement. [But] that is not [what happens] in the case at hand. For there is no opposition at all between specific agreement and numerical difference. Therefore, it is to be granted that Socrates, through the same [entity], agrees specifically with Plato and differs numerically from him.

The second argument, (2), does not work either. For it does not follow: "Socrates and Plato agree more than [do] Socrates and an ass; therefore, they agree more in something." Rather, it is enough that they agree more in themselves. Thus, I say that Socrates through his intellective soul agrees more with Plato than [he does] with an ass, and by himself as a whole he agrees more with Plato than [he does] with an ass. Hence, literally it should not be granted that Socrates and Plato agree by something that belongs to their essence. Rather, it should be granted that they agree by some [entities],[29] because [they agree] by their forms and by themselves—even though if, by a contradiction, there were one nature in them, they would agree in that, just as if, by a contradiction, God were foolish, he would rule the world badly.

To (3), the other [argument], it is to be said that, even though one individual is not the measure of all individuals of the same genus or of the same most specific species, nevertheless the same individual can be the measure of individuals of another species, or of many individuals of the same species. And that is enough for Aristotle's meaning.

To (4), the other [argument], it is to be said that, speaking literally and according to proper speech, it should be granted that no universal belongs to the essence of any substance whatever. For every universal is an intention of the soul, or else [is] some voluntarily instituted sign. But no such [entity] belongs to the essence of a substance. Therefore, no genus or species or universal belongs to the essence of any substance whatever. Rather, more properly speaking, it should be said that the universal expresses or explicates the nature of a substance—that is, the nature that is a substance.

This is what the Commentator says, *Metaphysics*, VII,[30] that "it is impossible for any of what are called universals to be the substance of any thing, even though they reveal the substances of things." Thus, all the authorities who say that universals belong to the essence of substances, or that they are in substances or are the parts of substances, should be understood [in the sense] that the authors mean only that such universals reveal, express, explicate, and convey the substances of things.

Suppose you say: Common names— such as, say, 'man', 'animal', and the like— signify some substantial things. And they do not signify singular substances, because in that case 'man' would signify all men, which seems false. Therefore, such names signify some substances besides singular substances.

It must be said [to this] that such names signify precisely singular things. Hence, the name 'man' signifies no thing except one that is a singular man. Therefore, it never supposits for a substance except when it supposits for a particular man. Therefore, one has to grant that the name 'man' equally primarily signifies all particular men. Yet it does not follow because of this that the name 'man' is an equivocal utterance. This is because, even though it signifies several [things] equally primarily, nevertheless it signifies them by a single imposition, and it is subordinated in signifying those several [things] to only one concept and not to several. Because of this it is univocally predicated of them.

To (5), the last [argument], those who maintain that intentions of the soul are qualities of the mind have to say that all universals are accidents. Yet not all universals are signs of accidents. Rather, some are

signs of substances only. Those that are only signs of substances constitute the category of substance, [whereas] the others constitute the other categories. Therefore, it is to be granted that the category of substance is an accident, even though it reveals substances and not accidents. Therefore, it must be granted that some accident— namely, one that is a sign only of substances—is by itself superior to substance. This is no more a problem than saying that some utterance is a name of many substances.

But is the same [thing] superior to itself? It can be said that [it is] not, because in order for something to be superior to [something] else, a distinction between them is required. So it can be said that not all universals are by themselves inferior to the common [term] 'quality', even though all universals are qualities. For the common [term] 'quality' is a quality, but it is not inferior to that [term]—rather, it *is* that [term].

Suppose it is said: The same [thing] is not predicated of diverse categories; therefore, quality is not common to diverse categories.

It must be said [to this] that, whether the same [thing] is predicated of diverse categories when they stand significatively or not, nevertheless when the categories stand and supposit not significatively, it is not incongruous for the same [thing] to be predicated of diverse categories. Hence, if in 'Substance is a quality', the subject stands materially or simply for the intention, [the proposition] is true. In the same way 'Quantity is a quality' is true, if 'quantity' does not stand significatively. So the same [thing] is predicated of diverse categories. For example, the two [propositions] 'Substance is an utterance' [and] 'Quantity is an utterance' are true if the subjects supposit materially and not significatively.

Suppose you say: Spiritual quality is in more than any category [is], insofar as it is predicated of several [categories]. For it is predicated of all categories, and no category is predicated of all categories.

It must be said that spiritual quality is not predicated of all categories taken significatively, but only taken for signs. For this reason it does not follow that it is in more than any category [is]. For superiority and inferiority among [things] is taken from the fact that the one taken significatively is predicated of more than the other taken significatively [is predicated]. Hence, the difficulty here is like the one about the name 'word'. For this name is one of the contents under 'name'. For the name 'word' is a name, and not every name is the name 'word'. Nevertheless, the name 'word' is in a certain way superior to all names, and to the name 'name'. For every name is a word, but not every word is a name.

And so it seems that the same [thing] is superior and inferior with respect to the same [thing]. This can be solved by saying that the argument would be conclusive if in all the propositions from which the conclusion is proved the terms supposited uniformly. Now, however, it is otherwise in the present case. Yet if that is called "inferior" of which, suppositing in some way, [something] else is predicated and [is predicated] of more [besides], even though if it supposited otherwise [that something else] would not be predicated of it taken universally, [then] it can be granted that the same [thing] is superior and inferior with respect to the same [thing]. But in that case 'superior' and 'inferior' are not opposites but [only] disparate.

Quodlibet 4, Question 35
Whether first and second intentions are really distinguished

No. For beings of reason are not really distinguished. But both first and second intentions are only beings of reason. Therefore, etc.

To the contrary: First and second intentions are things. And they are not the same thing. Therefore, they are distinct things. Consequently, they are really distinguished.

Here first it has to be seen what a first intention is and what a second intention [is]. Second, [I shall speak] to the question.

Article 1

First intention

On the first point, I say that both first intention and second [intention] can be taken in two senses, namely, broadly and strictly. In the broad sense, every intentional sign existing in the soul, which does not precisely signify intentions or concepts in the soul, or other signs, is called a first intention. And I say this whether 'sign' is taken for what can supposit in a proposition and be a part of a proposition (as categoremata are) or whether 'sign' is taken for what cannot supposit or be an extreme of a proposition when it is taken significatively (as are syncategoremata).

In this sense, not only mental categoremata that signify things that are not signs, but even mental syncategoremata and verbs and conjunctions and the like are called first intentions. For example: In this sense, not only are the concept of man, which signifies all singular men (who signify nothing) and can supposit for them and be a part of a proposition, and the concept of whiteness and the concept of color, etc., called first intentions, but syncategorematic concepts like 'it', 'nevertheless', 'not', 'while', and 'is', 'runs', 'reads' and the like are [also] called first intentions. This is because while, taken by themselves, they do not supposit for things, nevertheless when conjoined with other [terms] they make them supposit for things in different ways. For example, 'every' makes 'man' supposit and be distributed for all men in the proposition 'Every man runs'. Yet the sign 'every' by itself signifies nothing, because [it] does not [signify] either an external thing or an intention of the soul.

But in the strict sense, precisely a mental name [that is] apt to be an extreme of a proposition and to supposit for a thing that is not a sign is called a first intention. For example, the concept of man, animal, substance, body—and in short, all the mental names that naturally signify things that are not signs.

Second intention

Likewise, taken in the broad sense, a concept of the soul is called a second intention if it signifies not only intentions of the soul that are natural signs of things (as first intentions are, taken strictly), but also can signify mental signs signifying by convention—say, mental syncategoremata. In this sense, perhaps, we have only a spoken [term] corresponding to a second intention.[31]

But taken strictly, a concept is called a second intention if it precisely signifies first intentions that signify naturally, like 'genus', 'species', 'difference', and others like that. For, just as the concept of man is predicated of all men, by saying 'This man is a man', 'That man is a man', and so on, so [too] a common concept that is a second intention is predicated of first intentions that supposits for things, by saying 'Man is a species', 'Ass is a species', 'Whiteness is a species', 'Animal is a genus', 'Body is a genus', 'Quality is a genus', in the way that one 'name' is predicated of different names by saying 'Man is a name', [and] 'Whiteness is a name'.[32] And so a second intention naturally signifies first intentions, and can supposit for them in a proposition, just as much as a first intention naturally signifies external things and can supposit for them.

Article 2

On the second point, some people say[33] that first and second intentions are certain fictive entities that are only objectively in the mind and [are] nowhere subjectively.

To the contrary:[34] When a proposition is verified for things, if two things suffice for its truth, it is superfluous to posit another, third thing. But all propositions like 'Man is understood', 'Man is a subject' 'Man is a predicate', 'Man is a species', 'Animal is a genus' and the like, on account of which such fictive being is posited, are verified for things. And two things suffice—at least, [two] things truly and really existing suffice—for verifying all [of them]. Therefore, etc. The assumption is clear. For, positing the cognition of man in the intellect, it is impossible for 'Man is understood' to be false. Likewise, positing the intention of man is general and the intention of subject in general, and if the mental proposition 'Man is a subject' is formed, in which the one intention is predicated of the other, [then] it is necessary for the proposition 'Man is a subject' to be true—[even] without any fictum. Therefore, etc.

Moreover, such a fictum will get in the way of the cognition of the thing. Therefore, it is not to be posited on account of [that] cognition. The assumption is clear. For [the fictum] is not the cognition or the external cognized whiteness or both together, but rather a certain third [entity] midway between the cognition and the thing. In that case, when I form the mental proposition 'God is three and one', I do not understand God in himself but rather the fictum, which seems absurd.

Moreover, by the same reasoning [that leads to this view], God in understanding other [things] would understand such ficta. And so, from eternity, there was an arrangement of as many fictive beings as there can be different intelligible beings. These [fictive beings] are so necessary that God could not destroy them, which seems false.

Moreover, such a fictum is not to be posited in order to have a subject and a predicate in a universal proposition, because the act of understanding is enough for that. For the fictive being is just as singular, both in being and in representing, as is the act [of understanding].

This is clear from the fact that a fictum can be destroyed, while the other [entity]—the act—remains. For either the fictum depends essentially on the act or it does not. If it does, then when one act stops, the fictum is destroyed. Yet the fictum remains in another act. Consequently, there are two singular ficta, just as [there are] two acts. If it does not depend on this singular act, [then] neither consequently does it depend essentially on any [other] act of the same kind. And so the fictum will remain in objective being without any act, which is impossible.

Moreover, it is not a contradiction for God to make a universal cognition without such a fictum. For the cognition does not depend essentially on such a fictum. But it is a contradiction for an intellection to be posited in an intellect without anything that is understood. Therefore, [such a fic-

tum] is not to be posited on account of a common intellection.

Ockham's reply

Therefore, I say that both first intention and second intention are truly acts of understanding. For whatever can be saved by means of the fictum can be saved by means of the act, insofar as the act is a likeness of the object, can signify and supposit for external things, can be a subject and a predicate in a proposition, can be a genus, a species, etc., just as a fictum [can].

From this it is clear that first and second intention are really distinguished. For a first intention is an act of understanding that signifies things that are not signs. A second intention is an act of signifying first intentions. Therefore, they are distinguished.

To the main argument, it is clear from what has been said that both first and second intentions are truly real beings. For they are truly qualities existing subjectively in the intellect.

Quodlibet 5
Question 12
Whether the universal is singular

No. For every universal is predicated of several. A singular is predicated of one only. Therefore, etc.

To the contrary: Everything that is is singular. The universal is. Therefore, it is singular.

Here I first distinguish [the senses of the term] 'singular'. Second, I will speak to the question.

Article 1

On the first point, I say that according to the philosopher[35] 'singular', 'individual', [and] 'suppositum' are convertible names. I say this with respect to logicians, although according to theolo-

gians a suppositum is found only among substances, [whereas] the individual and the singular [are found] among accidents [too].

But speaking logically now, 'singular', and 'individual', are taken in three senses: (a) In one sense, that is called a singular which is numerically one thing and not several things. (b) In another sense, a thing outside the soul, which [thing] is one and not several and is not a sign of anything, is called a singular. (c) In a third sense, a sign proper to one [thing] is called a singular. This [last] is [also] called a "discrete term".

This division is plain as far as its first two branches are concerned. The third branch is proved [as follows]: For Porphyry[36] says that the individual is predicated of one only. This cannot be understood about a thing existing outside the soul—say, about Socrates—since a thing outside the soul is not in predicate position or in subject position, as is shown in another *Quodlibet*.[37] Consequently, it is understood about some proper sign that it is predicated of one only, not for itself but for the thing.

Moreover, logicians[38] say that the supposita of a common term are of two kinds: some per se, some by accident. For example: The per se supposita of the common term 'white' are this white [thing] and that white [thing]. The supposita by accident are Socrates and Plato. This cannot be understood about the Socrates who is outside the soul, because he is the sign of nothing. Because a thing outside the soul cannot be a suppositum of a common term, either per se or by accident, therefore 'suppositum' has to be taken for a term proper to one [thing only], which is called a "suppositum" because the common term is predicated of it, not for itself but for its significate.

In that case, there are two kinds of supposita for a common term: One kind per se—namely, demonstrative pronouns taken with the common term. For example, the per se supposita of the common term 'white' are 'this white' [and] 'that white'.

The supposita by accident are proper names—say, the name 'Socrates' and 'Plato.'

There is a big difference between these [kinds of] supposita. For it is impossible for one contrary to be truly predicated of a per se suppositum of another contrary. For example, 'This white is black' is impossible. But it can quite well be predicated of a suppositum by accident, even though not while[39] it is a suppositum of it. For example, if Socrates is white, still 'Socrates is black' is possible. This is because the same [thing] can be a suppositum by accident of two contraries, although not a suppositum per se. Therefore, etc.

Article 2

On the second point, I say that the universal is a singular and an individual in sense (a), because it is truly a singular quality of the mind, and is not several qualities. But in sense (b) it is not a singular, because in no way is any thing whatever outside the soul a universal. Likewise, the universal is not a singular in sense (c), because the universal is a natural or voluntary sign [that is] common to several and not only to one.

[The reply] to the main argument is clear from [these] statements.

Question 13
Whether every universal is a quality of the mind

No. For the substance that is a most general genus is not a quality of the mind. Therefore, not every universal is a quality of the mind. The assumption is clear, because it is predicated univocally and *in quid* of a substance. Therefore, it is not a quality.

To the contrary: The universal is only in the soul. And not objectively, as was shown earlier.[40] Therefore, subjectively. Therefore, it is a quality of the mind.

To this question, I say: Yes. The reason for this is that, as will be clear,[41] the universal is not anything outside the soul. And it is certain that it is not nothing. Therefore, it is something in the soul. Not just objectively, as was proved earlier.[42] Therefore, subjectively. Consequently, it is a quality of the mind.

Objection 1[43]

But to the contrary: Given this, then all categories would be accidents. Consequently, some accident would be superior to substance.

Objection 2

Moreover, the same [thing] is not predicated of diverse categories. Consequently, quality is not common to all the categories.

Objection 3

Moreover, it follows that the same [thing] is superior to itself. For all universals are in the genus of quality, according to this opinion, as [are] species and individuals. Consequently, the category of quality is common to all unviersals. Consequently, the category of quality is common to itself. And so the same [thing] is superior to itself.

Objection 4

Moreover, given this, one has to grant that the same [thing] signifies itself and supposits for itself. For in the proposition 'Every universal is a being', 'being' supposits personally for all universals. Consequently, it supposits for the universal that is 'being'. So 'being' supposits for itself.

Likewise, [taken] as it supposits personally, it supposits only for its significates and it supposits for itself. For otherwise the universal proposition 'Every universal is a being' would be false, because it would have a false singular. Therefore, the same [thing] signifies itself.

Objection 5

Moreover, it follows that the same [thing] is superior and inferior with respect to the same [thing]. For the universal 'being' is superior to the categories. And it is inferior, because it is one individual in the genus of quality. Therefore, etc.

To Objection 1

To the first of these, I grant[44] that all universals are accidents. Yet not all [of them] are signs of accidents. Rather some universals are signs of substances only. And those accidents constitute the category of substance, [while] the other accidents constitute the other categories. I grant further that some accident that is only a sign of substances is per se superior to any substance. That is no more of a problem than saying that some utterance is a name of many substances, or signifies many substances.

To Objection 2

To the other [objection], I say[45] that the same [thing] is not predicated of diverse categories when the categories stand personally and significatively. But when they supposit materially or simply, it is not incongruous for the same [thing] to be predicated of diverse categories. Hence, if in the proposition 'Substance is a quality' the subject supposits materially or simply, [the proposition] is true. Likewise 'Quantity is a quality'. But if [the subjects] supposit materially, then [the propositions] are not true. Hence, just as the two propositions 'Substances is an utterance' [and] 'Quantity is an utterance' are true if the subjects supposit materially and simply and not significatively, so it is in the present case [too].

To Objection 3

To the other [objection], I say[46] that the same [thing] is not superior and inferior to itself. For in order for something to be superior to another, a distinction between them is required, [and it is also required] that the superior signify more than the inferior [does]. Therefore, I say that not all universals are per se inferior to the common [term] 'quality', even though all universals are qualities. For the universal 'quality' is a quality. Yet it is not inferior to 'quality'—rather it *is* that.

Suppose you say:[47] It follows at least that spiritual quality of the mind is in more than, and superior to, any category. For it is predicated of all categories, and no category is predicated of all categories. Therefore, etc.

I reply:[48] A spiritual quality of the mind is not predicated of all categories taken significatively and personally, but only taken for signs. Therefore, it does not follow that quality is in more than, or superior to, any category. For superiority and inferiority between [things] is taken from the fact that the one taken significatively is predicated of more than the other taken significatively [is]. And this is not so for every spiritual quality that is universal. Nevertheless, some [such quality], like the concept of being, is predicated of more than any category [is].

To Objection 4

To the other [objection], I say[49] that the conclusion is to be granted, that the same [thing] signifies itself, that the same [thing] supposits for itself, that the same [thing] is predicated univocally of itself. For example, in the proposition 'Every utterance is a being', the subject supposits for every utterance, and so it supposits for the utterance 'utterance', and it signifies it and is predicated univocally of it.

To Objection 5

To the other [objection], I say [50]that there is the same difficulty here as with the name 'word' and the name 'name'. For the name 'word' is one of the contents under 'name', because the name 'word' is a name, and not every name is the name 'word'. Nevertheless, the name 'word' is in a certain way superior to all names, and consequently to the name 'name'. For the name 'name' is a word. But not every word is a name. And so the same [thing], with respect to the same [thing], is [both] inferior and superior.

Therefore, I say for both cases that the argument would be conclusive if in all the propositions from which the conclusion is predicated,[51] the terms supposited uniformly. But that is not so in the case at hand. For 'being', when it is predicated of the categories, supposits personally, not simply or materially. But [taken] as it is an individual [in the category of] quality, it supposits materially and simply.

But we are taking both 'being' and 'quality' significatively. In that case, 'being' is simply superior, because it signifies more. And in that sense it is not inferior to quality and [is] not an individual in [that category]. Nevertheless, if that is called "inferior" of which, suppositing in some way, there is predicated [something] else that is also predicated of several [other things], even though it would not be predicated of it if supposited otherwise—especially if it is taken universally—in that case it can be granted that the same [thing], with respect to the same [thing], is [both] superior and inferior. But in that case 'superior' and 'inferior' are not opposites but [only] disparate.

[The reply] to the main argument is clear from what has already been stated.

NOTES

1. such . . . terms: That is, the general account given in the preceding chapters of the *Summa logicae*.
2. Ockham, *Summa logicae*, I, 11–12.
3. That is, the five treated in Porphyry's *Isagoge*.
4. See Scotus, *Opus Oxoniense*, II, d. 3, q. 1, n. 8 (VI, 360 f.).
5. Avicenna, Metaphysics, 5, 1 (87rb).
6. That is, it follows in Avicenna's text.

7. The following arguments are roughly the same as those found in Henry of Harclay (Gál, ed.) and in Richard of Campsall's *Contra ponentes naturam* (9–17).

8. Namely, that a universal is a substance existing in but distinct from singular substances.

9. Aristotle, *Metaphysics* 7, 13 (1038b 8–9).

10. Ibid. 10, 2 (1053b 17–19).

11. Ibid. 7, 13 (1038b 8–9).

12. That is, being.

13. Averroes, *In Aristot. Metaph.* 7, t. 44 (VIII, 92vb).

14. Ibid. t. 45 (93ra).

15. Ibid. t. 47 (93va). There 'that exist' refers to 'parts' and not, as here, to 'substances'.

16. Ibid. 8, t. 2 (99ra).

17. Ibid. 10, t. 6 (120rb).

18. star . . . heavens: The star Canis major, the "dog star".

19. The example does not give an instance of the point, but rather presents an analogue to it.

20. As stated in *Summa logicae*, I, 12. See the following note.

21. Ockham himself says this in *Summa logicae*, I, 12.29–39: "But what is it in the soul that is such a sign? It must be said that with respect to this article [of the question], there are different opinions. Some say that it is nothing but a certain [something] contrived by the soul. Others [say] that it is a certain quality subjectively existing in the soul, [and] distinct from the act of understanding. Others say that it is the act of understanding. Reason is on the side of these last, because 'What can be done through fewer [things] is done in vain through more.' But all [the things] that are saved by positing something distinct from the act of understanding can be saved without that distinct [something], insofar as suppositing for [something] else and signifying [something] else can belong to an act of understanding just as much as to [any] other sign. Therefore, besides the act of understanding, one does not have to posit anything else."

22. Avicenna, *Metaphysics* 5, 1 (86va).

23. This is Scotus' view. See Scotus, *Opus Oxoniense*, II, d. 3, qq. 1–6 (VI, 334–421).

24. See Aristotle, *Metaphysics* 5, 9, and 10, 3 (1018a 12–15 and 1054b 27–1055a 2).

25. See Scotus, *Ordinatio*, I, d. 2, p. 2, qq. 1–4, ¶ 398 (Vatican ed., II, 354 f.).

26. Aristotle, *Metaphysics* 10, 1 (1052b 31–32).

27. See Ockham, *Summa logicae*, II, 2.

28. That is, the Scotists.

29. The point is that they agree not in something, in the singular, but in some entities, in the plural.

30. Averröes, *In Aristot. Metaph.* 7, t. 45 (VIII, 93ra).

31. I can make no sense of the last part of this paragraph. According to what Ockham usually says, mental syncategoremata certainly do *not* signify by convention. And the last sentence of the paragraph seems completely unmotivated. The editor of the Latin text (ed. line 49) notes that for 'only' (non . . . nisi) one manuscript has 'name', yielding: "we do not have a spoken name corresponding to a second intention'. This perhaps makes better sense. Two other manuscripts omit the 'nisi', resulting in pretty much the same meaning.

32. The point of the simile is not clear. Perhaps it is simply that both the cases of second intentions and the case of 'name' involve propositions in which the subjects are not in personal supposition.

33. The following arguments are like those given by Walter Chatton, *Reportatio*, I, Prol., q. 2 (O'Callaghan ed., 241), and d. 3, q. 2, a. 1 (Gál ed., 201–202).

34. See Ockham himself, *Scriptum*, I, d. 2, q. 8 (271.14–272.2); *Summa logicae*, I, 12.29–31; *Expositio in lib. Perihermenias Aristot.*, I, Prooem. sects. 7 and 10 (359.1–360.29, and 370.1–14). Henry of Harclay, *Quaestiones disputate*, q. 3 (Gál ed., 225–227); Peter Auriol, *Scriptum*, I, d. 9, a. 1 (320bC–323b).

35. This presumably does not refer here to Aristotle, but to "the typical philosopher'. The editor of the Latin text (ed., line 10) gives no reference.

36. Porphyry, *Isagoge*, Busse ed., p. 3, line 15.

37. Ockham, *Quodlibet* III, q. 12.19–59.

38. See Aristotle, *Posterior Analytics*, I, 22 (83a 1–20); Ockham, *Scriptum*, d. 2, q. 3 (95.4–96.18).

39. not while: Reading 'non dum' for the edition's 'nondum' (ed. lines 45–46).

40. Above, *Quodlibet* IV, q. 35.

41. The point is discussed in many places in *Quodlibets* V–VII. See also *Quodlibet* V, q. 12, above; *Summa logicae*, I, 15; *Scriptum*, d. 2, qq. 4–8.

42. *Quodlibet* IV, q. 35.

43. For these objections, except for the fourth, see Ockham's *Summa logicae*, I, 17 lines 25–32, 110–112, and 136.

44. See Ockham, *Summa logicae*, I, 17.93–103.

45. Ibid., lines 111–120.

46. Ibid., lines 104–109.

47. Ibid., lines 121–124.
48. Ibid., lines 125–13; also ibid., 18.85–87.
49. Ibid., 38.28–32.
50. Ibid., 17.130–143.
51. predicated.

CHAPTER 42

Walter Burley

Walter Burley (also spelled Burleigh) was an English scholar and diplomat. Born circa 1275, he was educated at Oxford (master of arts by 1301) and Paris (doctor of theology by 1324). He taught at both universities and was a member of the Franciscan Order of Friars. During his career it was necessary for him to function in the wake of the Paris condemnation of Aristotelianism of 1277. Two hundred nineteen propositions positing the unity of the intellect, the necessity of events, the eternity of the world, as well as numerous limitations on the divine power and knowledge were condemned. Far from stifling intellectual activity, the condemnation generated a period of fecundity to which the writings of fourteenth-century scholars attest, including the many works of Burley.

No fewer than fifty distinct topics are explored in the eighty-three of his extant works. Curiously enough, his theological writings are missing yet were necessary for him to be awarded the degree of doctor of theology. Of particular philosophical significance are his works on logic, science, and the problem of Averroism.

Burley also had a political life. In 1327 he became an attaché to the Avignon papacy for Edward III. In his decade of service he also functioned in the capacity of tutor to the king's heir, Edward of Woodstock (later the Black Prince). We also know that he was for some time under the patronage of Richard de Bury, a bibliophile of note. He seems to have spent his last years in southern France and northern Italy. He died sometime after June 1344.

Walter Burley on Universals

Walter Burley was a traditionalist of the Aristotelian school of thought, and this clearly manifests itself regarding his analysis of universals. As such, he is considered the principal opponent of Ockham. By rejecting the *supositio simplex*, Burley repudiated Ockham's contention that all general terms are nothing but purely mental phenomena called meanings. He argued that universals have being in reality, that they exist independently of the mind. A universal is part of its singular (i.e., individual thing) yet not identical to the particular of which it is a part. In the process of his discussion, Burley reiterates Aristotle's criticisms of universals qua Platonic Forms. He then addresses the Neoplatonism of Augustine by demonstrating that essences cast in the form of ideas must be different from the divine essence and therefore different from the being of God since His essence and being are identical. Nevertheless, universals exist independently of the mind. Given Burley's Aristotelian views, it is not surprising that we come to know universals through particulars. That is, the intellect comprehends a particular via sense experience. As Burley says, ". . . every intellective cognition has [its] origin from sense, . . .". The (active) intellect comes to an understanding of the universal by reflection, specifically by directing our imaginative faculty to a true understanding of perceived particulars.

"ON UNIVERSALS"

Porphyry's Text

. . . ABSTAINING FROM THE HIGHER QUESTIONS, BUT INTERPRETING THE SIMPLER ONES STRAIGHTFORWARDLY. NOW I SHALL BEG OFF SAYING [ANYTHING] ABOUT THE [QUESTION] WHETHER GENERA AND SPECIES SUBSIST OR ARE PLACED IN SOLE, BARE AND PURE[1] UNDERSTANDINGS, OR WHETHER, SUBSISTING, THEY ARE CORPOREAL OR INCORPOREAL, AND WHETHER THEY ARE SEPARATED FROM SENSIBLES OR PLACED IN THOSE VERY SENSIBLES AND STAND IN CONNECTION WITH THEM. FOR THAT BELONGS TO A VERY EXALTED BUSINESS, AND REQUIRES A GREATER INVESTIGATION. BUT I SHALL NOW TRY TO SHOW YOU HOW THE ANCIENTS, AND THE PERIPATETICS AMONG THEM MOST OF ALL, PLAUSIBLY TREATED THESE [THINGS][2] AND THE [OTHERS] BEFORE US.[3]

Burley's Commentary

Explanation of Porphyry's Questions

The questions irrelevant to this science, which he eliminates from his consideration, are four. (1) First, whether universals are (1a) subsistents outside the soul or [are] (1b) in the understanding only.

Then the second question follows. It has three parts: For assuming (1b) that universals are in the understanding only, then there is the question whether universals are (2a) in sole understandings, or (2b) in bare understandings, or (2c) in pure understandings.

He understands by these three [terms] three operations of the understanding. For by 'sole understanding' he understands an operation of the understanding to which there corresponds nothing in reality. Thus,

From Walter Burley, *Burlei super artem veterem Porphirii et Aristotelis*, Venice: Otinus (de Luna) Papiensis, 11 May 1497, fols. 3rb–7rb (HCR 4133, Goff B-1313). Translated by Paul Vincent Spade, copyright 1994. Reprinted by kind permission of Paul Vincent Spade.

the operation of the understanding by which a chimera is understood is called a "sole understanding". And he understands by 'bare understanding' an operation of the understanding by which matter is apprehended when form is not apprehended. By 'pure understanding' [he understands] an operation of the understanding by which a form is apprehended when matter is not apprehended. Assuming that universals have [their] being through the sole operation of the understanding,[4] there is a question (2a) whether they are in the sole operation of the understanding in such a way that nothing corresponds to them in reality, or (2b) [whether] they are in the operation of the understanding after the fashion of matter apprehended without form, or (2c) [whether] they are in the operation of the understanding like a form apprehended without matter—that is, whether it is apprehended like matter or like form.

Yet some [people] do not understand by 'understanding' the *operations* of the understanding, but rather the *substance* of the understanding. In that case, by 'sole understanding' they understand the divine understanding, which [is the] sole [thing that] is called an understanding primarily and principally. It is "sole", because it is unique. There neither is nor can be any other equal to it. By 'pure understanding' they understand an angelic understanding, which is pure, without [any] union with a body as if it were the form of a body. By 'bare understanding' they understand the human understanding, which in the beginning is like a blank and bare slate[5] on which nothing is drawn, according to the Philosopher, *On the Soul*, III. Hence the human understanding, taken by itself, is bare and denuded of every material form and of every species of a material thing.

Assuming (1a) that universals are existents outside the soul, there are two questions:

(3) The first [question], and [this] is the third in order: If universals are outside the soul, whether universals are corporeal or incorporeal. That is, whether they are extended, like a body, or unextended.

(4) The other question, and it is the fourth in order, is: Assuming that universals are incorporeal, whether universals are separated from singulars or sensibles, or placed in the sensibles themselves.

The author says he wants to abstain from these questions that arise, because they do not pertain to the logician but rather to the metaphysician. And he says that in this work he wants to pursue the plausible statements of the ancients about these universals, insofar as they are relevant to the logician. And he says that he wants to pursue the Peripatetics' statements in this work more than [those] of other ancients.

The Usefulness of the *Isagoge*

Here a doubt arises, how the knowledge of the five universals[6] is useful for the above four [tasks],[7] namely, (a) for the science handed down in the book *Categories*, (b) for assigning definitions, and (c) for making divisions and (d) demonstrations.

[To (a)] You should know that the science of the five universals is useful for knowing the ten categories. For in every category there are genera and species and differences. Therefore, the knowledge of those three is useful for the knowledge of the ten categories.

Likewise, all [the things] in the nine categories other than substance are accidents. And among accidents, one kind is common and another is proper. Therefore, for knowing the nine categories that are accidents, the knowledge both of common and of proper accident is useful. So it is clear that the knowledge of those five universals is useful for the science that is in the ten categories.

[To (b)] It is useful for assigning definitions. For only species is defined. And every definition consists of genus and difference. Accident or property should not be included in a definition in the absolute sense. Therefore, the knowledge of these five universals is useful for assigning definitions. For the knowledge of the species is useful, since it alone is defined. The knowledge of the genus and difference is useful, since genus and difference are included in the definition. The knowledge of property and accident is useful, not insofar as they are included[8] in a definition but rather insofar as they are eliminated from a definition.

[To (c)] The knowledge of the five universals is also useful for making divisions. For sometimes the division of a genus into species is made by essential difference, and sometimes by accidental differences. An accidental difference is of two kinds: One kind is common, another is proper. Therefore, for making both essential and accidental divisions, the knowledge of those five universals is useful.

[To (d)] It is also very useful for the art of demonstrating. For by a demonstration a property is concluded of the species of which it is a property through the definition of the species, as through a middle [term]. And the definition consists of genus and difference. Therefore, the knowledge of those four (namely, genus, species, property and difference) is useful for the art of demonstrating. And because common accident does not enter into demonstration, therefore the knowledge of accident is useful for the art of demonstrating, insofar as it is eliminated from a demonstration.

Doubts About Universals

There are doubts concerning universals, and not a few of them either.[9]

(I) The first is: Whether universals exist in reality or not.

(II) Secondly, assuming that they do exist in reality, the second doubt is: Whether they have a being separate from singulars or exist in their singulars.

(III) The third doubt: Whether entirely the same thing is in singulars, or diverse [things].

(IV) Assuming that they are separated from singulars, there is a fourth doubt: Whether they are in the understanding or outside the understanding.

(V) Assuming that they are outside the understanding, there is a fifth doubt: Whether they exist in God, as [those maintain who] posit ideas in the divine mind representing the species of created things, or do they exist by themselves outside the divine mind.

Discussion of Doubt I

In solving the first doubt—namely, whether universals exist in reality or not—almost everyone grants the statement that science is about universals. Now about the subject of a science, one should know what it is. But there is no science about a non-being, as is said in *Posterior Analytics*, I. Therefore, universals have to have being in reality.

Again, universals like genera and species are in a category, since in every category there is a most general genus and a most specific species and intermediate genera that are genera and species with respect to

different [things], as is clear from Porphyry. But everything in a real category is a real being. Therefore, genera and species, taking them not for simple things but for what they denominate, are real too.

But there is another opinion, which maintains that no universal by predication exists in reality, but only that it has a being according to the understanding. This opinion will be discussed at the end.[10]

Discussion of Doubt II

There are [various] opinions on the second doubt. For some say that universals are in singulars, and some say that they are outside singulars.

Those who say that universals are in [their] singulars have authorities in their favor:

(1) First, because Aristotle says in the *Categories* that second substances are in first [substances]. But second substances are universals and first substances are singulars. Therefore, universals are in their singulars.

(2) And Aristotle, *Posterior Analytics*, I, says that universals are everywhere and always. The Lincolnite[11] explains the first part [of this] as follows: Universals are everywhere, that is, universals are in each of their places. For the places of universals are singulars, as he says. Hence a universal is everywhere, that is, a universal is in each of its singulars. So it is clear that a universal has being in its singulars.

There are two [arguments from] reason in favor of affirming this opinion:

(1)The first is that a quiddity is not separated from that of which it is the quiddity. For a quiddity is the same as that of which it is the quiddity, as is clear from *Metaphysics*, VII. And [what is] the same cannot be separated from itself. But the universal is the quiddity of a singular. Therefore, etc.

The minor [premise] of this reasoning is argued: For the universal is predicated *in quid* of its singular, as is clear through Porphyry, who defines the species as follows,

"Species is what is predicated," etc. And whatever is predicated *in quid* of something is its quiddity. Therefore, etc.

(2) Again, the part is not separated from the whole of which it is a part. But [what is] per se superior is a part of [what is] per se inferior to it, as is clear from *Metaphysics*, VII. But a universal is per se superior to [its] singular. Therefore, the universal is a part of its singular. Consequently, a universal is not separated from its singulars.

Discussion of Doubt III

The Theory That Universals are the Same as Their Individuals

Assuming this, some people say to this doubt[12] that the universal is the same thing as its singular, and differs [from it] only according to concept. For the same thing while it is under singular and material conditions is a singular, and while it is abstracted by the understanding from [its] singular conditions is a universal. And so while it is understood under a common concept, it is a universal. This is what Boethius says on Porphyry, that [the thing] is a singular while it is sensed, but a universal while it is understood.

Hence, [these people] say that man and animal are entirely the same things, yet they differ by reason or concept. For the concept of Socrates insofar as he is Socrates is one [concept], and the concept of Socrates insofar as he is a man is another, and the concept of Socrates insofar as he is an animal is [yet] another.

But it is argued against this opinion:

(1) The singular is not defined, according to the Philosopher, *Metaphysics*, VII. But a species is defined. Therefore, the species is another thing than the singular.

If it is said that the singular is not defined under a singular concept but rather under a universal concept, and the same [thing] is defined under one concept and not defined under another concept, [then] to the contrary: A definition is convertible with the defined, as is clear from *Topics*, I, and *Posterior Analytics*, II. But the definition of man is not converted with any singular man. For Socrates and mortal rational animal are not converted, because if they were convertibles, then 'Every mortal rational animal is Socrates' would be true. For a convertible is predicated of [its] convertibles. But this [proposition] is false. Therefore, no singular or individual man is defined by the definition 'mortal and rational animal'.

Suppose it is said: "I grant that no singular is defined under its own concept. Yet the singular is quite well defined under a common concept." Then, to the contrary: If this were true, then Socrates under a common concept is converted with the definition 'mortal rational animal'. Consequently, 'Every mortal rational animal is Socrates under a common concept' would be true. Therefore, Socrates would be Plato under a common concept.

Suppose it is said that the singular is not defined, but a name common to all singulars of the same species is defined, and the same name is convertible with [what is] defined. But, to the contrary: Every name and every concept is an accident. But, according to the Philosopher, *Metaphysics*, VII, no accident has a simple definition. Rather, only substance is defined by a definition simply so called. Therefore, I take a substance—say, the substance of man—that is defined by a definition simply so called. Now that substance cannot be a singular substance, like Socrates and Plato. For no singular substance is convertible with the definition 'mortal and rational animal', as was proven [above], [and] therefore a singular substance is not defined [by that definition]. On the other hand,[13] no accident is predicated *in quid* of substance, as is clear in the book *Categories*. But what is defined by the definition 'mortal rational animal' is predicated of Socrates and Plato *in quid*. Therefore, what is defined by the definition 'mortal and rational animal' is not an accident. Consequently, it is neither a name nor a concept.

Likewise, suppose it is said, alternatively, that the definition and the *name* of the defined are converted, but the defined itself and its definition are not converted. Hence the singular is defined, and a name common to all singulars of the same species is converted with the definition. To the contrary: One utterance is not converted with another utterance. Hence, when it is said that the name of the defined is converted with the definition, and that the defined itself is not converted with it—that is to make impossible statements.

(2) Again, what is converted with the definition [is that] of which an attribute is demonstrated in the strongest [kind of] demonstration. For in the strongest [kind of] demonstration, the extremes and the middle [term] are convertible, as is clear from *Posterior Analytics*, I. But the attribute in the strongest [kind of] demonstration is not demonstrated of any singular. For, according to the Philosopher, *Posterior Analytics*, I, it is a mistake to say that the attribute of the species inheres primarily in any singular. Therefore, since the attribute is demonstrated of some thing, and it is not demonstrated of any singular, there has to be some thing (where "thing" is contrasted with "sign"), other than a singular thing, of which the attribute is demonstrated. And that thing is convertible with the definition.

This reasoning is confirmed, because sciences and demonstrations are about entirely the same subject. For science is acquired through demonstration, by demonstrating the attribute of the subject the science is about. But a real science—like metaphysics and natural physics—is not about names. Therefore, demonstrations in the real sciences are about things. But demonstrations are not made about singular things, as is clear from the Philosopher in *Physics*, I. Therefore, the things about which demonstrations are made are things other than singulars. Consequently, the singular and the universal are not the same thing.

If it is said that demonstration is about the singular thing under a common concept, [then] to the contrary: The extremes in the strongest [kind of] demonstration are converted with the middle [term]. There-

fore, a singular under a common concept is converted with the definition, which was disproved above.

(3) Again, about the subject of a science, it should be known what it is and that it is, according to the Philosopher, *Posterior Analytics*, I. But natural science is about substance or about mobile body, as about [its] subject. I ask then whether the mobile body that is the subject in natural philosophy is a singular thing or a thing other than a singular. If the latter is granted, the point is established, namely, that the universal the science is about is a thing other than a singular. If it is granted that it is the same as the singular thing, then some singular mobile body is the subject in natural philosophy. And, by the same reasoning, every other [one will be too]. Therefore, every peasant in India would be the subject in natural philosophy. Consequently, one could not have natural scientific knowledge unless he knew of every peasant that he exists, which is a big problem. The inference is clear. For it is necessary for one having scientific knowledge of a subject to know what it is and that it is.

(4) Again, definition is the principle of distinctly and perfectly knowing the defined, as is clear from *Topics*, VII, and *Physics*, I. I ask, then: Is what is defined by the definition 'rational and mortal animal' a singular thing, namely, some individual man, or is it a universal thing? If the latter is granted, the point is established. If the former is granted, [then] since there is no greater reason in the case of one individual that the one individual man is defined by this definition than [there is in the case of any] other, consequently, one cannot know or have this definition unless he were to know every individual perfectly and rightly.

(5) Again, there is no greater identity between the universal and the individual in external things than between the universal and the individual in the concept. For the universal is predicated just as essentially and *in quid* of the individual in the case of concepts as in the case of external things. But in the case of concepts, a universal con-

cept and an individual concept, or a superior concept and an inferior concept, are not the same. Therefore, neither in the case of things will the universal and the individual, or the superior and the inferior, be the same.

The major is plain. The minor is proved: For a concept abstracted from two concepts is another concept than either of the ones from which it is abstracted, as is clear. For the concept of a genus is other than the concept of the species from which it is abstracted. So it is clear that in the case of concepts, the universal and the singular are not the same, and the superior and the inferior in the case of concepts are not the same. Consequently, neither in the case of things are superior and inferior the same things.

(6) Again, everyone agrees on the fact that the universal is abstracted by the understanding from singulars and from material conditions. For the Commentator, *On the Soul*, I, says that the understanding makes universality in things. From this it is argued as follows: What is abstracted by the understanding from material conditions and accidents is really under them. For otherwise those who abstract would be lying, which is contrary to the Philosopher, *Physics*, II. Therefore, a universal abstracted from accidents [and] really existing under them is another[14] thing than a singular. So in the case of things, the universal and the singular or individual are not the same thing.

Let these statements, therefore, be enough for the present concerning the opinion that maintains the universal is a thing outside the soul completely the same on the part of reality with the singular thing.

The Theory That Universals are Distinct from Their Individuals

There is another opinion, which maintains that a universal has subjective being in its singulars, and that a universal is as a whole in each of its singulars. These [people] say that one kind of universal has being in the soul only, another kind has being outside the soul only, and [yet] another

kind of universal has being both in the soul and outside the soul.

For example, one kind of universal—like science, art, prudence, and the like—only has singulars existing in the soul. In that case the universal is in the soul [only]. Another kind of universal only has singulars existing outside the soul, as stone has, [and] wood, and the like. In that case, the universal is only outside the soul. And [yet] another kind is a universal that has certain [singulars] in the soul and certain ones outside the soul.

For example, the common [entity] quality and the common [entity] state[15] have certain singulars in the soul and certain ones outside the soul. For one kind of quality—like grammar [and] music—is in the soul, and another kind of quality is outside the soul—like whiteness, blackness, and the like. Likewise, one kind of state is in the soul, like the moral and theological virtues, and another kind of state is outside the soul, like bodily states such as strength [and] health. They say, therefore, that universals of this [last] kind have some singulars in the soul and some outside the soul.

Those who maintain this say that the universal, both the kind that is in the soul and the kind that is outside the soul, is some thing distinct from the singular thing from which it is extracted, which is contrary to the opinion described immediately above.

This is proved[16] through the fact that two contradictories are not verified of altogether the same thing. This is clear from *Metaphysics*, IV, where the Philosopher says that the first principle or the truest and best known concept is that, for anything, there is [either] an affirmation or a negation, but for nothing [is there] both of them. And in *Physics*, VII, he says that in order to know whether [things] are the same or diverse, one must see whether [this or] that is affirmed of the one and denied of the other, and in that case they are not the same but rather diverse. If nothing is affirmed of the one that is denied of any other, then they are the same. And in the *Categories*, the Philsopher proves that being blind and blindness are not the same. For being blind is truly affirmed of something of which blindness is not affirmed. For of some man it is truly said that he is blind, and it is not said that he is blindness.

From all these [texts], the truth of the basis for this opinion is apparent, and [that basis] is this, namely, that of what is entirely the same on the side of reality, the same [thing] is not truly [both] affirmed and denied.

On this foundation, it is proved that a singular and a universal are not the same, because of the many contradictories that are verified of them. Thus, I construct the following line of reasoning, based on the foundation: Of [what is] entirely the same, the same [thing] is not [truly both] affirmed and denied. But something is truly affirmed of a universal that is truly denied of each of its singulars, and something is affirmed of a singular that is denied of [its] universal. Therefore, the singular and the universal are not the same.

The major is clear from the truest and most known complex principle [mentioned above]. The minor is proved in many ways.

(1) First, as follows: Every universal is in many. No singular is in many, as is clear from the book *On Interpretation*. Therefore, something is truly affirmed of a universal that is denied of each of its singulars.

(2) Second, as follows: The universal is defined. But no singular is defined, as is clear from *Metaphysics*, VII. Therefore, etc.

(3) Again, the universal and the genus are divided by contrary differences, like animal by rational and irrational. But no singular is divided by such differences. Therefore, etc.

Suppose it is said to these arguments that the same [thing] is not affirmed and denied of the same [thing] under the same concept. But the same [thing] can be affirmed and denied of the same [thing] under one concept and another. Hence, Socrates under a common concept is defined, but under a proper concept he is not defined.

To the contrary: When it is said that the same [thing] is affirmed and denied of [what is] entirely the same [thing, but un-

der different concepts, I deny that]. For example, 'Socrates under a common concept is defined', [and] 'Socrates under a proper concept is not defined'. In these propositions the same predicate is not affirmed and denied of the same subject. For in 'Socrates is defined under a common concept', this whole, namely, 'Socrates under a common concept' is the subject. And[17] in 'Socrates under a proper concept is not defined', this whole, namely, 'Socrates under a proper concept' is the subject. And so the aggregate [expressions]—the subjects of the propositions—are not entirely the same.

For example, [the same point can be made] in other cases, as in the following propositions: 'Socrates the grammarian is known by you', 'Socrates who is coming is not known by you'. Here the same [thing] is not affirmed and denied of [what is] entirely the same, and therefore they can be true together. For I can know that Socrates is a grammarian, yet without knowing that he is coming.

If it is said perhaps that these determinations 'under a common concept' and 'under a proper concept' belong on the side of the predicate, [then] to the contrary: It follows from this that in these [propositions]—namely, 'Socrates under a common concept is defined' and 'Socrates under a proper concept is not defined'—the same predicate is not affirmed and denied of the same [thing]. For 'to be defined under a common concept' and[18] 'to be defined under a proper concept' are not the same terms, and the same thing is not assigned by these terms.

This is confirmed as follows: If a universal and a singular, like the species man and Socrates, are entirely the same on the side of reality, then there is just as much identity between the species man and Socrates on the side of reality as there is between Socrates and Socrates. But 'Socrates is defined' and 'Socrates is not defined' are incompatible, because they are two contradictories. For the same predicate is affirmed and denied of entirely the same subject. Therefore, 'The species is defined' and 'Socrates is not defined' will be incompatible too. For there is the same cause of the inconsistency in either case, namely, the identity between the things predicated and the identity between the things for which [the subjects] supposit.

Again, the reasoning about identity under different concepts does not solve the argument constructed about the division of genus into species by contrary differences. For it is certain that no one singular thing, [either] under a common concept or under a proper concept, is divided by [the differences] rational and irrational, because in that case the singular thing would be [both] rational and irrational.

If it is said that the division of animal by [the differences] rational and irrational is not a division of a thing into things, but rather is a division of a general concept into specific concepts, [then] it follows that it is a division of an accident into accidents. This is contrary to Boethius in the book *On Division*. He says that the division of a genus into species by differences is division per se, and the division of a subject into [its] accidents is division by accident.

(4) Again, just as in the genera of accidents there are genera and species and differences that belong by themselves to some genus, so all the more in the genus of substance there are genera and species and differences, through which differences the genera descend into their species. But nothing is by itself in the genus of substance except a substance. Therefore, animal, which is a subalternate genus in the genus substance, is a substance, and the species into which it descends and the differences by which it descends into its species belong to substance.

(5) Again, [it is argued] that the individual and the universal are not the same things. For if they were, [then] since the most general genus in the genus substance is substance, as this opinion maintains, it follows that the most general genus in the category[19] substance would be some singular thing, like Socrates or Plato. And for whatever reason one individual or singular would be the same thing as the most gen-

eral genus, for the same reason every other singular in the genus substance would be the most general genus in the genus substance. This seems a problem, both because, (a) in accordance with this, there would be several most general genera in the genus substance. For there would be as many most general [genera] as there would be individuals in the genus substance. Also, because (b) Socrates would by himself be superior to an ass.

(6) Again, according to this opinion[20] there would be no aspect common to two individuals of the same species. For every thing outside the soul is singular. And no singular thing is common to two individuals of the same species. Therefore, no thing, etc. But this is false, as is proved in two ways.

(a) First, as follows: [Even] if there were no intellect, two stones would still agree more than one stone [would] with an ass. But every agreement is [an agreement] in something one. For every agreement is a unity founded on a multitude, because whatever [things] agree agree in something one. Therefore, there is some common thing outside the soul in which two stones agree, and in which a stone and an ass do not agree.

[This] is confirmed as follows: Whatever [things] are really compared are compared in something one, as greater and less, or as equal. For if a and b are compared to one another as greater and less, they are not compared in what belongs only to a or in what belongs only to b, but rather in something that belongs to both. For example, if a is more white than b, [then] a and b are not compared in the whiteness of a itself, or in the whiteness of b itself. For 'a is more white by the whiteness of a itself than b [is white] by the whiteness of a itself' is false. Likewise, 'b is less white by the whiteness of b^{21} itself than a^{22} [is white] by the whiteness of b itself' is false. Therefore, that in which they are compared has to belong to both. But no singular belongs to both. Therefore, there is some universal thing in which they are really compared to one another.

(b) Second, it is proved that there is something common to two individuals of the same species, which [thing] is not singular. For otherwise, two individuals of different species would not differ any more than two individuals of the same species [do], because nothing that is in the one singular of the one species would be in the other singular of the same species. For no singular thing is the same in two such [individuals], and there is no other [kind of] thing outside the soul, according to this opinion. Rather one individual of the one species differs from another individual of the same species through something that is in it and not in the other. And so Socrates differs from Plato through something that is in him [but not in Plato]. But something cannot differ from something else through [anything] more than through something that is in it [and not in the other]. So Socrates does not differ more from a stone than [he does] from Plato.

Because of these reasons and infinitely many others, it is maintained that a universal is in each of its singulars, whether it is a universal being in the soul or whether it is a universal being outside the soul.

Objections

There are some apparent reasons against this opinion.

(1) First, according to this reasoning[23] it follows that the same [thing] is in heaven and in hell. For man, which is in Socrates, is in each individual. Therefore, it is in the individual which is in hell and in that one which is in heaven. And so the same man will have the greatest joy and the greatest pain.

If it is said that it is not a problem for contraries to be in the same [thing] according to species, in the sense that the universal man is one according to species and not according to number, [then] to the contrary: What is the same as something in such a way that [it is] in no way diverse [from it] and there is no diversity between

them, that is numerically one with it? But there is no diversity between the [universal] man existing in heaven and the [universal] man existing in hell. Therefore, the [universal] man who is in hell and the [universal] man who is in heaven are numerically the same man.

Again, it would follow numerically the same man would simultaneously be moved and be at rest. For when something is moved, everything in it is moved, and when something is at rest, everything in it is at rest. Therefore, when Socrates is moved, the specific nature that is in Plato is not moved, assuming that Socrates is moved and Plato is at rest. In that case, it follows that the specific nature of man, which is numerically one in Socrates and Plato, is simultaneously moved and at rest.

If it is said that the nature is not numerically one, [then] to the contrary: (1a) Same and different are the first differences of being, as is clear in the fourth and tenth [books of the *Metaphysics*]. Therefore, if the specific nature is not[24] numerically [one] in Socrates and Plato, it follows that it will be numerically diverse in them. And so there will be as many specific natures, according to specific nature, as there are individuals, which is a problem. And so it follows that Socrates and Plato are not in numerically the same species, because Socrates is in the species that is in Socrates, and Plato is in the species that is in Plato.

(2) Again, the specific nature that is in Socrates, according to you, is a substance. Therefore, either it is a corporeal substance or an incorporeal one. But it is not an incorporeal substance, because if it were, [then] Socrates would be contained under incorporeal substance. For whatever the species is contained under, the individual of the same species is contained under the same [thing]. But this is false, namely, that Socrates is contained under incorporeal substance. It remains, therefore, that the specific nature of man is a corporeal substance. If [it is] a corporeal substance, either [it is] animate or inanimate. Not inanimate, certainly. Therefore, animate. Therefore, ei-

ther [it is] a sensitive substance or an insensitive one. Not insensitive, as was said.[25] Therefore, it is an animate sensitive substance. Consequently, it is an animal. Therefore, either [it is] rational or irrational. Not irrational. Therefore, rational. Consequently, the specific nature of man is a man. And every man either is Socrates or is Plato, and so on for singular [men]. Consequently, the specific nature of man does not differ from the individual nature, which was the point.

(3) Again, it follows from this opinion that there are two suns, namely, the universal sun and the individual sun.

(4) It follows also that in Socrates there is a man other than Socrates, namely, the universal man. Proof: Let Socrates be a and the universal man b. Then a and b agree, because a and b are two men, [and] therefore a and b agree in the human nature common[26] to them. That nature common to them is other than a and other than b. For, according to you, a common nature is another thing than those to which it is common. Therefore, let that third nature be c. And then a, b, [and] c are three men. Therefore, they really agree in the common nature of man. And let that be d. Thus, there will be an infinite regress in the categories predicated *in quid*. There will also be an infinite [number of] men, as is clear through the deduction [just] constructed.

(5) Again, according to this opinion God could not annihilate Socrates unless he annihilated every man, which seems a problem. The inference is proved: For annihilation is the destruction of something with respect to everything that is in it. If, therefore, God annihilated Socrates, he would have to destroy the common nature that is in Socrates, namely, the specific nature of man. But when the species is destroyed, every individual of the same species is destroyed. Therefore, God could not destroy Socrates unless he destroyed every man. That is unheard of.

Suppose it is said that the annihilation of something is [its] destruction with respect to all its parts. But the species is not a part

of the individual. Therefore, when the individual is annihilated, the species does not have to be annihilated.

(5a) To the contrary: Whatever is the case for the species and the individual, according to this opinion, there is the genus. But the genus is a part of the species. Therefore, it follows that [God] cannot annihilate the species man unless the genus animal, and even the most general genus substance, is destroyed. But when the genus is destroyed, all the species of that genus are destroyed. Therefore, God could not destroy the species man unless he destroyed every species belonging to the genus substance, which is a problem. The inference is clear. For when the most general genus is destroyed, all the inferiors of that genus are destroyed.

Replies to the Objections

Because these arguments do not conclude anything that goes against the truth of [this] opinion in itself, [therefore] we must reply to (1), the first argument. When it is said that numerically the same [thing] would be in heaven and on earth and in hell, it must be said that 'numerically the same' is taken in two senses, namely, broadly and strictly.

[What is] numerically the same, taken broadly, is that which, together with [something] else, can make a number or constitute a number, in such a way that of this and of the other it is true to say that they are two. In this sense I grant that the nature of man is numerically one. For it and the specific nature of an ass are two natures.

But [what is] numerically one, taken strictly, is only that which is distinguished as against [what is] specifically one and generically one. The Philosopher speaks about the numerically one in this way in *Metaphysics*, V and VII.

There is the same division about [what is] numerically the same.[27] For [what is] numerically the same in one sense is what, together with [something] else, makes a number. In another sense it is what is distinguished as against [what is] specifically the same and generically the same, as is clear from *Topics*, I.

Therefore, I say that taking 'numerically the same' in the broad sense, for all that constitutes a number together with [something] else, there is no problem with numerically the same [thing's] being simultaneously in heaven and in hell, and [its] being simultaneously moved and at rest. And [I say] that ['numerically the same'] said in this sense is superior to 'numerically the same' taken strictly, and to 'specifically one' and 'generically one'. Also, it is common to every being, and has the same generality[28] as 'being'.

And when it is said [in objection (1)], "Numerically the same [man] would have the greatest joy and the greatest sadness," I say that [this] does not follow as [it did in the argument] about [what is] numerically the same in heaven and on earth. For acts and operations like this belong to singulars, according to the Philosopher, *Metaphysics*, I. Thus, just as running is by itself only in singulars, so [too for] being joyful and being sad.

Nevertheless, it can be said that operations like this belong to universals by accident, as the Philosopher says, *Metaphysics*, I, that man heals or is healed by accident, and this man heals or is healed by himself. In this sense, it could be granted that, taking 'numerically one' in a broad sense, [what is] numerically one is [both] supremely sad and joyful by accident, because for the universal to be joyful or to be sad is nothing else but for its individual to be joyful or to be sad by itself.

Hence, just as there is no problem about contraries' being in the same [thing] according to species, so there is no problem about contraries' being in the same [thing] according to number, speaking in the broad sense, at least by accident. Indeed it follows that if contraries are in [what is] specifically the same, therefore contraries are also in [what is] numerically the same,

speaking about [what is] numerically the same in the broad sense. The inference is clear, because it argues from an inferior to its superior, as was said.

But taking 'numerically one' strictly, according as it is distinguished as against [what is] specifically one and generically one, in that sense [what is] numerically one is distinguished as against everything common. And in that sense [what is] numerically one and the same is the same as the individual, with the concept of which it is inconsistent for it to be represented[29] in several, like Socrates or Plato.

In this sense, no universal is numerically one. Taking 'numerically one' in this sense, it is impossible for [what is] numerically one to be in heaven and in hell [simultaneously], or that it be simultaneously moved and at rest, and so on.

'Numerically one', said in this sense, is inferior to 'generically one' and 'specifically one', as the Philosopher says in *Topics*, I, and *Metaphysics*, VII, where he says that whatever [things] are specifically one are [also] numerically one, but not conversely.

When it is said [in (1a)] that the specific nature either is numerically one in Socrates (taking 'numerically one' strictly) or else [it is numerically] diverse, it must be said that [it is] neither the one nor the other. Hence, although same and diverse [are] applied to anything whatever, [but] only in the aspect according to which they are the first differences of being (for everything that is is [either] the same [as] or diverse from Socrates), nevertheless, same and diverse *by a specific nature* or [same and diverse *as*] *contracted through some determinate subject* are not the immediate differences of being.[30] [For example,] although 'same as Socrates' and 'diverse from Socrates' divide being, nevertheless 'same ass as Socrates' and 'diverse ass from Socrates' do not divide being immediately. For not every being is the same ass as Socrates or a diverse ass from Socrates.

Or take the example of Browny [the ass]. For, even though everything that is is [either] the same as Browny or diverse from

Browny, nevertheless not everything that is is the same ass as Browny or a diverse ass from Browny.

The same thing must be said about the numerically same and diverse. For even though the specific nature of man is the same as Socrates or diverse from Socrates, nevertheless it is not numerically the same [as] or numerically diverse from Socrates, taking 'numerically the same' strictly.

To (2), the other [argument], when it is asked whether the specific nature of man that is in Socrates is corporeal substance or incorporeal [substance], I reply by distinguishing the [proposition] 'The species of man is corporeal substance', insofar as the predicate can have (a) general or (b) special simple supposition. This only applies in the case of a common term containing [both] species and individuals under it. For (a) when such a term has general simple supposition, it then supposits for the genus itself, namely, for its primary significate, which is the genus. But (b) when it has special simple supposition, it then supposits for the species contained under that genus. Therefore, I say that 'The species of man is corporeal substance' is false according as the predicate has general supposition. For that is the way Porphyry is speaking when he says that substance is a genus in such a way that it is not a species. For in that sense 'substance' supposits for the common [category] substance, and not for any content inferior to that. But if ['substance'] has special simple supposition, it then supposits for its species, and in that sense 'The species of man is corporeal substance' is true, and so on descending down to the lowest genus.

Hence, I grant 'The species of man is animal', [but only] according as the predicate has special simple supposition. For each of the following is false: 'The species of man is some corporeal substance', 'The species of man is some animal', because a particular sign[31] added to a common term that is per se in a genus makes it stand personally for individuals and [for] species that have personal supposition. For according to this

kind of supposition, the genus standing personally is verified of them.

Hence, 'Some substance is a species' is false, and yet the subject supposits both for species and for individuals, since it is common to both. For since the subject supposits personally, it does not supposit for species unless species are taken according to the supposition according to which [the subject] is verified of them. And it is not verified of them unless the species supposits personally. For 'Man is some substance' is not true except according as the subject supposits personally. Therefore, 'Some substance is a species' is false, despite the fact that the subject supposits personally for species that supposit personally. For each of the following is false: 'Man is a species', 'Ox is a species', when the subject supposits personally.

Suppose it is said that 'Some being is a species' is true, taking the subject personally. From this it follows that some substance is a species or some quantity [is a species], and so on for its other species.[32]

It must be said that the following inference is not valid: "Some being is a species; therefore, some substance is a species, [or some quantity is a species, etc.]".[33] But it does correctly follow: "Some being is a species; therefore, some substance, or substance, is a species, [or] some quantity, or quantity, is a species, [etc.]", where, [for each category], the name of the genus in the first occurrence supposits personally, and in the second occurrence simply—and this indifferently according to simple or personal supposition.[34]

Hence, you should know that it belongs to the notion of a transcendental [term] that, when it supposits personally, it supposits for all its inferiors, under whatever [kind of] supposition it is possible that they be taken,[35] whether materially or simply or personally. But this is not so for a term [that is] per se in a genus. For such a term, suppositing personally or taken with a sign that makes it stand personally, only supposits personally for individuals. Therefore, under a transcendental term suppositing personally and disjunctively, it is not right to descend under a disjunction[36] to its inferior supposita [taken] personally only. Rather the descent should be made from it to its inferior supposita [taken] both personally and simply[37] under a disjunction, as was said.

To (3), the other argument, it must be said that it does not follow from [this] opinion that there are two suns. On this [point], you must know that just as a universal sign[38] added to a common term having individuals under it distributes that [term] for the individuals, so [too] a numeral added to a common term—namely, to a genus or species—numbers it for individuals and makes it supposit for individuals. Therefore, it is the same [thing] to say 'There are two suns' and to say 'There are two individual suns'. Thus, just as the universal sun and the particular sun are not two individual suns, so [too] there are not two suns. Nevertheless, there are two *things*, because a transcendental term—like the term 'thing', which is a transcendental term—is numerical[39] among all [its] inferiors, whether they are individual or common, [and] so is distributable for each of its inferiors, whether it be individual or common.

To (5), the other [argument], it is to be said that it does not follow from this opinion that God could not annihilate Socrates unless he annihilated every man. And when it is said that if God annihilated Socrates, then he would annihilate the species of man, I say that [this] does not follow, as was said. For the species is not a part of the individual, as is clear from the Philosopher, *Physics*, II, and *Metaphysics*, V. He says that there are particular causes of particular effects and universal causes of universal effects. Therefore, Socrates, who is a particular effect, is put together only out of particular causes, namely, out of this matter and this form.

When it is argued to the contrary [in (5a)]—when it is said that at least there would follow the problem that God could not annihilate the species of man unless he

annihilated the whole genus of substance—it must be said that that does not follow. For annihilation is the destruction of the thing as far as everything that is proper to it is concerned, not as far as everything common to it and to other [things] is concerned. Therefore, a species can be annihilated without the annihilation of the genus. For the genus is not a proper part of the species, but rather common to it and to others. Hence, if God destroys [the universal] intellective soul and [the universal] human body too, then he would annihilate [the species] man, because soul and human body are proper parts of man.

To (4), the immediately preceding argument, the one that proves an infinite regress if it is claimed that the universal is a thing other than singulars, it must be said that if '*a*' is a sign for an individual—say, Socrates—and '*b*' [a sign for] the species of man, then '*a* and *b* are two men' is false, as was said earlier about the sun. Neither is it true that *a* and *b* agree in a third human nature [distinct] from them. Indeed, the one of them is contained under the other (namely, *a* under *b*) as an individual under a species. But *a* and *b* do not agree in a third most specific species [that is] common to them, since the one of them is the most specific species of the other.

Discussion of Doubt V

Plato's Theory

There is yet another opinion, which maintains that universals are outside the soul [and] separated in being from singulars. This was Plato's opinion, according to [what] Aristotle attributes to him. There are two motives for this opinion, as Aristotle reports in *Metaphysics*, VII. One was to have scientific knowledge of sensible things, and the other motive was [to account] for the generation of [things] that come about by putrefaction, like many [kinds of] worms.

The first motive is based on the fact that there is scientific knowledge of natural or sensible things, and there is no scientific knowledge about individuals that have being in sensible matter. Therefore, besides sensible individuals, one must posit universals separated from sensible matter. Natural science is about them.

Now the reason there is no scientific knowledge of sensibles is that, when the sensibles withdraw from the sense, it is not known whether they [continue to] exist or do not [continue to] exist. Therefore, since they are transmutable and variable, there can be no certain knowledge about them.

The second motive is based on the fact that nothing is generated except from [something] like it in species. But [things] generated by putrefaction do not have [anything] similar to them in species existing in the nature from which they are generated. For a fly [generated from putrefied matter] does not have another substantial fly like himself [in that matter], from which he is generated. Therefore, in the case of things generated by putrefaction, one must posit [something] similar in species [and] separated from matter, from which they are generated. And that [entity], separated from sensible matter, is claimed by Plato to be the universal.

So it is clear that there are two motives for maintaining that universals are separated from sensibles, namely: one [to account] for scientific knowledge, and the other [to account] for generation.

The Philosopher argues against this opinion in *Metaphysics*, III and VII. He assumes that everything whatever that exists by itself and separately is a singular or individual. From this, it is argued as follows: The universal existing by itself and separately from individuals is an individual. Consequently, the universal sun and the particular or singular sun are two individual suns. And there will be two suns and even two worlds—namely the universal world and the particular world—each of which exists by itself. Consequently, each is singular and individual.

Likewise, it follows that two bodies are in the same place, namely, the universal body[40] and the particular or singular body.

If it is said that universal body is not in a place, [then] to the contrary: From this there follows the problem that some body is without a place.

Again, that one does not have to posit separated universals in order to have scientific knowledge is proved as follows: For that of which scientific knowledge is had has a definition. But a separated universal does not have a definition, since it is singular and no singular is defined, as is proved in *Metaphysics*, VII. Therefore, if a separated universal is posited, there is no scientific knowledge of it.

Again, the separated universal is less known to us than are sensible singulars. But scientific knowledge of the more known is not had through the less known. Therefore, one does not have to posit a separated universal, since it is unknown to us, in order to have scientific knowledge about singulars [that are] known to us.

Hence Aristotle, in opposing Plato in *On the Soul*, I, says that the universal is nothing, or else it is posterior. That is, the universal separated from sensible singulars, as Plato claimed, is either nothing in reality or else, assuming that it is in reality, it is posterior with respect to cognition. For it is less known to us, and posterior to sensible singulars.

Again, the corporeal and the incorporeal are not in the same species. For the universal man, since he is incorporeal, will not be in the same species with a particular man— for example, with Socrates. Consequently, scientific knowledge of particular sensible men will not be had through the fact that scientific knowledge is had of the universal man. So one does not have to posit a separated universal in order to have scientific knowledge of singulars.

The Philosopher destroys the other motive for positing universals separated from singulars, through the fact that the agent that induces the form transmutes and disposes the matter for the induction of the form. Therefore, what does not transmute the matter does not induce the form. But in [things] generated by putrefaction, the separated universal does not transmute the matter. Therefore, it does not induce the form. Therefore, in the generation of a fly, the universal fly is not the generator of the particular fly.

Thus, the proposition 'The same agent transmutes the matter and induces the form' is universally known in the case of the induction of a material form, by which [induction] such a form is drawn out from the potency of matter, and consequently [is drawn out] by an agent transmuting the matter. (This is the case, for example, with the intellective soul. For it is not drawn out from its [own] potency.) Consequently, [the agent that induces the form] is different from a separated agent, as is clear in *On Animals*, XVI.

Hence, you should know, according to Aristotle, in the book *On the Generation of Animals*, that some [things] are generated by propagation, and they are generated from seed. Some are generated from putrefaction, and they are not generated from seed, but rather from a similar power caused in matter by the sun. Thus, in the putrid matter from which a fly is generated there is caused by the sun some power, similar to the power of seed, which acts in the generation of a fly like seed in the case of [things] generated by propagation. Aristotle calls this power a "divine power," according to [what] the Commentator says on *Metaphysics*, II.

Further, [things] generated by propagation are of two kinds. For some are generated by [what is] similar in most specific species, as man from man, and [some] from [what is] similar in closest genus. (There is no name given to that.) Hence, the proposition on which Plato was based is not universally true, namely, that everything that is generated is generated from [what is] like it in species. For heat is generated from a motion that is not similar to it in species. And fire [is generated] from the striking or collision of solid bodies against one another. And a worm is generated from the action of the sun.

It is true, according to Aristotle in the book *On the Generation of Animals*, that in general [what is] generated from seed and [what is] generated without seed differ according to species, no matter how much they are alike in [their] acts. For example, suppose that some rat is generated without seed—say, from earth. Such a rat afterwards generates, by his seed, another rat. No matter how much these rats would be alike in their acts, nevertheless they differ according to species. For the one is generated with seed and the other without seed.

Nevertheless, Avicenna maintained the opposite of this. He holds that the same [things] according to species could be generated from seed and [could also be generated] without seed. Thus, he maintained, [at least] as the Commentator attributed [it] to him, that man can be generated without seed, from an extreme commingling of the elements.[41]

Again, you must know that one kind of generation is univocal. That [kind of] generation is [the generation] of the similar by [what is] similar [to it] in species. Another kind is equivocal generation, which is the generation of something from [what is] dissimilar to it in species. This dichotomy is maintained both by philosophers and by theologians.

Augustine's Theory

Now that we have seen Plato's opinion about ideas, we must look at the opinion of Saint Augustine and other theologians about ideas.

It should be known that the divine essence represents from eternity all the [things] that are to be made. Thus, God, before he made things, knew them. Otherwise he would be ignorant of what he was about to do. Therefore, Augustine maintains, in his book *On Eighty-Three Questions*, that from eternity there were exemplars representing things to be made, and those exemplars he calls "ideas".

Thus, he says that from eternity there were ideas in the divine essence, after the examples of which things were going to be made. About those ideas, he says three things that appear difficult, namely, that the ideas in the divine mind are (1) eternal and (2) immutable and are (3) diverse. For, as he says, man was established by one reason,[42] and horse was established by another reason.

But there is a big doubt about this. For I ask: Is an idea the divine essence or another thing? If it is the same [as the divine essence], then there will not be several ideas. For in God there is not any plurality. If the idea is another thing than the divine essence, problems follow: (a) that there was [something] other than God from eternity, namely, the idea of man. And it follows (b) that [something] other than God is immutable, which is a problem. For everything other than God is transmutable by the divine power, and can revert to nothing. Likewise, (c) from the fact that God is supremely simple, everything that is in God is the same as the divine essence. Therefore, it cannot be maintained that an idea is another thing than the divine essence.

On these doubts and many others, there is one way of talking, [namely], that some [things] are really the same and [yet] diverse with respect to what they connote. By this means, one replies to difficulties about the [divine] attributes. For they say that in God to know is the same as to will, or to know about is the same as to will. Nevertheless, God knows about the evil of sin and does not love or will the evil of sin. In this way, contradictories are attributed to [what is] really the same, by reason of what they connote. And so [too] for ideas, namely, the idea of man and the idea of horse are really the same, since they are the same in the divine essence, and yet are diverse with respect to what they connote.

But to the contrary: The idea of man either is a thing signified by the utterance[43] ['man'] or else it is the utterance signifying the thing signified by the utterance. If, [in either case,] a is the thing signified by 'the divine knowing', and b is the thing signified by 'the divine loving', then a and b are entirely the same thing, because in God knowing and loving are the same. If, therefore, a and b are entirely the same thing, it cannot be said that a connotes something unless b connotes the same [thing]. For this

diversity of connotations cannot be on the side of the things connoted. And if it is said that it is on the side of the utterances, then this kind of diverse connotation makes no difference to the case at hand. For there is no difficulty about the identity or diversity of the utterances, but only about the identity or diversity of the thing.

Keeping to[44] the question and to [this] famous opinion [about it], we can say that the connotatum[45] included in the total significate of a name is either signified in an oblique case or in the nominative. What is signified in the nominative is said to be signified principally. For example, the utterance 'divine essence representing man', as far as the part of the utterance that is in the nominative is concerned, signifies the divine essence. Yet through the other part of the utterance, which is in an oblique case,[46] it signifies the thing represented by the divine essence, namely, man. Therefore, the principal significate is signified in the nominative, and the connotatum is signified in an oblique case. Therefore, when it is said that the idea or name of a [divine] attribute connotes, the connotation is [indeed] on the side of the defined utterance [even] when it is on the side of the things signified by the utterance.

Thus, when it is said [that "the term] 'idea' connotes [something] other than the divine essence", it is understood here that the name 'idea' includes more [things] in its total significate than [does] the name 'divine essence'. And then the question arises about the thing signified by the utterance, insofar as it is signified by it. When it is asked whether the idea is the same as the divine [essence] or not, I say that the idea, with respect to the principal significate in it, is the same. But with respect to the connotatum, it is not the divine essence but [something] else.

Thus, Blessed Augustine grants that there are several ideas, with respect to [their] connotata—that is, with respect to [their] ideata. For there are several [things] ideated or connoted by the divine essence. But there are not several ideas with respect to what is principally conveyed by the name 'idea', because that is the divine essence only.

But there is a doubt. For Blessed Augustine says that the ideas are immutable reasons,[47] and he is speaking [there] in personal supposition about the same [things] of which he says 'eternal essence'. But the connotata and ideata are not eternal. Therefore, a plurality must be attributed to other [things] than to the ideata. So, from eternity there was a plurality in the divine essence.

It must be said that the ideata were objectively eternal in the divine essence. That is, from eternity they were represented and understood by God. Thus, one should not grant absolutely that man, or a quantity of man,[48] was from eternity. For in this [proposition] the verb predicates as an "adjacent second".[49] For the determination 'from eternity' is not a predicate but rather a determination of the verb. Thus, for nothing other than God should there be granted a predication of the verb ['is'] in the past tense, or the present, together with the determination 'from eternity' or 'eternally', according as [the verb] predicates as an "adjacent second". Yet, according as [the verb 'is'] predicates as an "adjacent third", many affirmative propositions with the determination 'from eternity' can correctly be granted of [something] other than God.

For instance, 'Man was from eternity' is not to be granted. Neither was the proposition 'Man is' true from eternity. For in these [propositions] the verb 'is' predicates as an adjacent second. Yet in another way, propositions in which the verb 'is' predicates affirmatively as an adjacent third are to be granted with the determination 'from eternity'. Thus 'Man, or a quantity of man, was understood by God from eternity and was creatable by God from eternity' is true.

And so it is for ideas. For what is connoted by 'the idea of man' was represented from eternity by the divine essence. Hence, Augustine says that the ideas are eternal reasons. The author's meaning is that an idea, with respect to [its] connotata, is eternally represented according as it was from eternity objectively in the divine essence.

That is plain enough. For it is certain that God is an agent and cause through [his] cognition, and therefore all that God creates now and anew[50] he earlier and from eternity knew was going to be created. So a thing that is made by God was understood from eternity by the divine intellect.

From these [considerations] it can be made clear that certain [people] are mistaken. They say that all the things understood by God from eternity are the same as the divine essence. For it is manifest that Antichrist, who wil be created, is not God himself. For if numerically the same [thing] that is Antichrist, who will be created, were numerically the same as the divine essence, it would follow that Antichrist was already created, and he would be the same as the divine essence, which is false.

Thus, one can argue as follows: Nothing that is the divine essence will be created. Antichrist will be created. Therefore, Antichrist is not the divine essence. The premises are true. Therefore, etc.

Suppose it is said that (a) everything that is in the divine essence is the same as the divine essence. But a thing that will be made was never in the divine essence. Therefore, such a thing was never the divine essence.

(b) Again, if Antichrist, who will be created, is not the same as the divine essence, therefore he is other than the divine essence. But the same and other are differences of being. Therefore, if Antichrist, who will be created, was other than God, it follows that Antichrist, who will be created, is a being.

(c) [This] is confirmed as follows: 'Other' conveys a relation, but only between things.

To (a), it is to be said that for something to be in the divine essence happens in two ways: either (i) essentially, or (ii) objectively or representatively. I say then that everything that is in the divine essence essentially is the same as the divine essence. And the proposition [in objection (a)] should be understood in this sense. Nevertheless, not everything that is in the divine essence objectively or representatively is the same as the divine essence.

If it is said that God understands nothing outside himself, according to the Commentator, *Metaphysics*, XII, [and] therefore whatever God understands is the same as God, [then] it must be said that God understands nothing outside himself primary. Rather he understands himself first, and in understanding himself understands all other [things].

Likewise, God understands nothing outside himself through a reception from external things, as our intellect understands by receiving species from external things. But God, in understanding himself, understands all other [things], because the divine essence is a sufficient representative of all other [things].

The common slogan from the Commentator, namely, that in the case of [things] separated from matter, the intelligible is the same as the understood, should be understood in this sense, [namely,] understanding by 'understood' that through which the separated intellect understands.[51] In [things] separated from matter, the intelligible is the same as that through which [the intellect] understands.[52]

Thus, according to the Commentator, no substance separated from matter understands through a received species, but only through its essence. Rather this is proper to an intellect conjoined to matter, namely, to understand through a species received from the understood thing.

To (b), I grant that a thing that is going to be created is other than God, taking 'other' insofar as it is a difference of the transcendental 'being', as was noted. And ['being', in this sense, is] maximally transcendental, because 'being', so said, is convertible with the common [term] 'intelligible'. Therefore, just as the thing that is going to be created was from eternity intelligible, so from eternity it was a being, taking 'being' insofar as it is a name. Nevertheless, it should not be granted that the thing that is going to be created was from eternity, because in this [proposition] 'be-

ing' is predicated as a participle, because the verb 'was' is predicated in it as an adjacent second.

To (c), when it is said that otherness is a relation, and a relation [is only between things], I say that [otherness] is a transcendental relation. For in every category there is found an otherness between things in that category[53] and in another. Such a relation can quite well be between a nonbeing and a being. Hence the understanding is related to the understood, as is clear from *Metaphysics*, V, and yet [there is sometimes] something understood [that] is not a being.

There is another [way] of dividing [questions] about ideas, which is really the same as the one described earlier. It is that 'idea' can be taken either for what it signifies or for what it denominates. In the first sense, there are several ideas, because the name 'idea' not only signifies the divine essence but also the divine essence representing the ideatum. Hence 'idea of man' signifies the same as the expression 'divine essence representing man', and 'idea of a horse' signifies the divine essence representing a horse. And it is certain that not only the divine essence belongs to the significate of the whole expression, but also the ideatum—namely, man or horse. So it is clear that the idea of man signifies one thing, and the idea of horse signifies another.

But if 'idea' is taken for what it denominates, then only the divine essence is an idea. For 'The divine essence is the idea of man' is true, and is a denominative predication, like 'The divine essence is representing man'.

But then there is a doubt in which way of taking 'idea' is it to be granted [both] that the ideas are eternal and that there are several ideas. For taking 'idea' for what it denominates, there is no plurality there, and taking 'idea' for what is signifies, there is no eternity there. For the ideatum belongs to the significate of the idea, and the ideatum is not eternal.

It must be said that expert statements must be taken in the sense in which they are made, and not in the sense they make. I say that, literally, it is false that the ideas are several and eternal. But the author's meaning is true, and it is that the ideata are several, and that they are objectively represented or drawn out by the divine essence from eternity. And that is true.

Or let it be said that the plurality is referred to one [thing], and the eternity is referred to [something] else, according to Augustine's meaning. For the plurality is referred to things, and the eternity[54] [is referred] to what [the term 'idea'] denominates, namely, to the divine essence. So [too] the division, (that a term can be taken for what it signifies and for what it denominates) can be applied to the matter, namely, about eternity and in eternity.[55]

For the Doctors maintain three kinds of measure for the duration of things: (a) time, which is claimed to be the measure of mutable and corruptible [things]; (b) everlastingness,[56] according to the duration or measure of angels. And there is maintained (c) another [kind of] measure, which is called eternity, [and] which is posited, according to imagination, to be the measure of God. Nevertheless, this common claim about the different kinds of duration cannot be understood in the sense that there are three simple measures of duration. Indeed, every measure of duration is time. For duration cannot be understood without earlier and later. But only time is the measure of earlier and later in duration. Thus, an angel does not have a measure of [its] duration that is another thing than the essence of the angel. For by the same reasoning, that other thing would have [yet] another measure, and there would be an infinite regress. Neither[57] does God have some measure of his duration, which [measure] is another thing from God himself.

Thus, ['everlastingness' or] 'eternity' can be taken principally for what it conveys, and that is what it denominates, like the essence of an angel or of God, or else it can be taken for what it signifies. In the first sense, everlastingness is the same as the essence of an angel, and eternity is the

same as the divine essence. In the second sense, [everlastingness] is the same as what the expression 'angelic essence coexisting with time' signifies, and eternity is the same as [what the expression] 'God's essence coexisting with eternal time, true or imaginative' [signifies]. Thus, that is eternal which coexists with eternal time, if there were to have been time from [all] eternity.

So, therefore, I say that, taking 'everlastingness' or 'eternity' for what it signifies, in that sense each is other than time, because it conveys more—namely, the essence of the angel or of God. But taking 'everlastingness' or 'eternity' for what it denominates,[58] in that sense everlastingness is nothing but the essence of the angel, and eternity is nothing but the essence of God.

If it is said that the name 'eternity' cannot be denominative, since it is abstract by an ultimate abstraction,[59] it is to be said that [something] can be called "denominative" [in the sense of] (a) what is denominative in itself, and that is not abstract by an ultimate abstraction, or else (b) it can be called "denominative" in its equivalent. 'Eternity' is like the latter, because it is the same as 'coexisting with the whole of eternal time, if [time] should be [eternal]'. But now my phrase 'coexisting with the whole of eternal time' is also in a certain way denominative.[60] In this way, therefore, it appears that the measure of the duration of an angel is not some thing besides the nature or essence of the angel and besides the time with which the angel coexists. Neither is eternity another thing than God and than the infinite time, if there should be [such a thing], with which God coexists.

You should know that the [notion of] a concrete term is divided [as follows]: One kind is concrete by a concretion of the subject, another kind by a concretion of the suppositum. To be concrete by a concretion of the subject is to be[61] what conveys a form and [along with that] the subject of the form, whether it signifies adjectivally or substantivally. For example: adjectivally, like 'white,' 'black,' and the like. Substantivally, like 'master,' 'servant,' and the like—and in general, all the names of offices and of positions of dignity or subservience.

A concrete [term] by a concretion of the suppositum is what conveys a thing existing by itself. In this sense, 'man,' 'ass,' and the like, are said to be concretes by a concretion of the suppositum. Such [concrete terms] are called concrete subjectively. Of this kind, there are some that indicate a substantial form inhering in the suppositum with which they are concerned, like 'man' and 'ass.' There are others that indicate a form inhering in [something] other than that with which they are concerned, like the words 'human,' 'forged'[62] and the like. For these indicate a form inhering in [something] else extrinsic to that of which they are predicated. For a house is called "human" not from [any] humanity that is in the house but rather from the humanity that is in the man, and a [produced] work is called "forged" not from [any] art of forging that is in the work but rather from the art of forging that is in the smithy.

In the same way, it can be said about the [notion of an] abstract [term] that one kind is abstract by an abstraction of an accidental form from a suppositum in which it finally inheres, like 'whiteness,' 'blackness,' etc. Another kind is abstract by an abstraction of a substantial form [from a suppositum][63] in which it really inheres or [which] it denominates in any way whatever. In this sense 'humanity' is said to be abstracted from 'man,' or from a suppositum in which [humanity] really inheres. It is also called abstract with respect to 'human,' which is denominated from humanity.

Thus, with respect to 'human,' 'man' is called a kind of abstract [term]. For although 'man' is concrete with respect to 'humanity,' nevertheless it is abstract with respect to 'human,' which is more concrete than 'man,' because it concerns and conveys more [things]. For it signifies human nature and conveys and denominates another, extrinsic thing—say, a work or a possession of a man.

Thus, it is to be known that when some-

thing includes or signifies a greater composition, to that extent it is called more concrete. On account of this, what signifies the simplest concept of some form is called "abstract by an ultimate abstraction," and what signifies a maximally composite concept is said to be "a most remote concrete"—namely, [most remote] from matter.

Hence 'humanity' is abstract by an ultimate abstraction, because there is no [concept] before the intellect simpler in [the case of] human nature than is the name 'humanity.' And 'human' is concrete by an ultimate concretion, because there can be no concept before the intellect signified by the name 'man' more composite than what is signified by the name 'human.' But 'man' is in a certain way concrete and in a certain way abstract. For it is concrete with respect to 'humanity' and abstract with respect to 'human.' But 'humanity' is not concrete with respect to anything, and 'human' is not abstract with respect to anything. For a [term] abstract by an ultimate abstraction signifies whatever form [it does] with precision from every other thing whatever. This is why Avicenna says in his *Metaphysics*, V, "Entity is entity only." That is, the name 'entity' indicates such and such a form with precision from every other thing whatever. But this is not so for a concrete [term]. For every concrete [term] indicates something besides the form conveyed by the common name.

Continuation of the Discussion of Doubt I: The Fictum-Theory

Now that we have seen the opinions that maintain that universals have being in reality, one more opinion can be maintained, [namely,] that universals are not existents in reality, either in the soul or outside the soul. Rather they only have objective being in the intellect. Hence this opinion maintains two things: The first is that universals have objective being in the intellect. The second is that they do not have the being of existence. Neither do they have [any] other kind of being than the objective [being] of the intellect.

By 'objective being' I understand being cognized, and "the objective being of the intellect" is the same as being intelligible. Thus, some things have being in effect[64] and also object-being.[65] For example, things that exist in reality and are also known by the intellect, like things existing outside the soul that, together with the fact that they are outside the soul, are known by the intellect. Other things have only object-being in the intellect, as a chimera [and] a golden mountain have only object-being in the intellect. And [yet] other things that appear to sense to be existing[66] in reality have only object-being in the sense and in a superior power.

This is clear in the case of the number of candles and the sun. For if an eye is stretched up or pressed down beyond its normal position, one candle will appear as two candles, and one sun will appear as two suns. Such duality is not anything in nature, but only in sensory appearance or in the apparent cognition of the sense.

Likewise, if an undamaged stick is put one-half in water, it will appear to sight that the stick is broken. But this break only has being in appearance, or in the apparent cognition of sight. And as is the case for vision,[67] so is the case [too] for the other senses.

Such an appearance occurs also in the interior sensible powers and even in the intellect, because whatever is known by an inferior power is known by a superior power. For whatever is known by an exterior [sense-] power is known by the common sense,[68] and not conversely, and so on climbing right up to the intellect.

Therefore, I[69] say that a universal has only object-being in the intellect. This is proved as follows: For the universal is known by the intellect, as is clear. For the intellect can have a knowledge of ass or lion in general without having a knowledge of any particular ass or singular lion. So it is clear that the universal has object-being only in the intellect.

That the universal does not have [any] other [kind of] being outside the [mental]

object is clear. For it does not have the being of existence in the soul or outside the soul, as the above arguments prove against both opinions, the one of which maintains that universals are concepts in the soul and the other maintains that universals are things existing outside the soul.[70] Thus it follows that the universal has only[71] object-being in the soul.

This is what Boethius says on Porphyry, that universals are understood as existing things, and are not such things.

Against this[72] opinion it is argued as follows:

(1) When the singular is posited, the universal is posited. For it follows: "Socrates is; therefore, man is," and not conversely. [Thus] this inference is good: "The singular exists; therefore, the universal exists." The antecedent is true. Therefore, the consequent [is] too. Consequently, the universal has the being of existence and not only objective being.

(2) Again, when the superior is destroyed, the inferior is destroyed. Therefore, if universals do not exist, singulars do not exist. The consequent is false. Therefore, etc.

(3) Again, what does not have [any] other kind of being than as an object in the soul has being as a figment. For figments of the intellect, like a chimera, have object-being. Therefore, if the universal does not have [any] other kind of being than object-being in the soul, it follows that universals are figments, which is false.

(4) Again, science is about universals, as is clear from *Posterior Analytics*, I. But about the subject of a science it must be assumed that it is. Therefore, the universal has true being.

To (1), it is said that from an inferior to its superior is a good inference according as the superior has personal supposition, and not according as it has simple supposition. Thus it correctly follows: "Socrates is; therefore, some man exists." But it does not follow: "Socrates is; therefore,[73] man is," according to this way [of viewing universals]. Neither does it follow: "The singular is; therefore, the universal is."

In the same way, I say [to objection (2)]

that when a superior is destroyed taken personally, the inferior is destroyed. For it follows: "No man is; therefore, Socrates is not." But when the superior is destroyed simply [taken], the inferior is not destroyed on that account.

To (3), the other [argument], it is said that what has object-being in the soul [both] according to itself and [also] according to all its singulars has only being as a figment, as is clear in the case of a chimera. For both chimera in general and this chimera only have being in the soul as an object. But what in itself only has object-being in the soul, such as man, and [yet has] singulars existing outside the soul, does not have being as a figment.

But there is a doubt about cases that neither in themselves nor in their singulars have being [outside the soul]. How can they have object-being in the soul? For nothing is in the intellect except what was previously under a sense [-power]. And every intellective cognition has [its] origin from sense, as is clear from *Posterior Analytics*, I.

You must know that a chimera and such ficta have a concept in the soul, which [concept] is a true being in the soul, because it is a quality of the soul. But the concept is not efficiently caused by that of which it is a concept. Rather it is caused by the parts of such a fictum, and by the soul that puts the concepts of the parts together with one another. For instance, the intellect has the concept of a mountain, and it has the concept of gold. These concepts are caused by a mountain and by gold. With those concepts existing in the intellect, the intellect puts those concepts together with one another and makes one composite concept that represents a golden mountain, which is a certain fictive being.

It is the same way for a chimera. For the intellect has a concept of a man's head and of a lion's body and of other things, and from those concepts it makes a composite concept that represents a chimera.[74]

NOTES

1. and pure: Reading 'purisque' for the edition's 'plurisque'. In the Indiana University copy, the word has been corrected by hand.
2. these things: That is, genus and species, the *topics* of the three questions above. Porphyry has just stated that he is not going to try to *answer* those three questions.
3. That is, difference, property and accident, the remaining three predicables.
4. sole operation of the understanding: Thus in the edition. But since this notion has just been defined in a technical sense, perhaps it is a mistake for 'operation of the understanding only'. See the statement of question (1), above.
5. blank and bare slate: *tabula rasa et nuda*.
6. That is, the five "predicables" discussed in Porphyry's *Isagoge*.
7. four tasks: Tasks discussed earlier in Burley's commentary on Porphyry.
8. they are included: Reading 'ponantur' for the edition's 'ponatur'.
9. The discussion in the remainder of the treatise will be clearer if you notice the structure of the five questions listed here:

(I) Do universals exist in reality or not? (p. 622, ¶ 3)
    (Ia) Yes (p. 622, Discussion of Doubt I)
        (II) Separate from singulars or in them? (p. 622, ¶ 4)
            (IIa) In them. (pp. 622–23, Discussion of Doubt II)
                (III) Distinct from individuals or the same? (p. 622, ¶ 5)
                    (IIIa) The same. (pp. 623–25)
                    (IIIb) Distinct. (pp. 625–28)
        (IIb) Separate.
    (IV) In the understanding or outside? (p. 622)
                (IVa) In the understanding.
                (IVb) Outside.
                    (V) In God or existing in themselves? (p. 622)
                        (Va) Existing in themselves. (Plato's theory.) (pp. 632–34)
    (Ib) No. (The fictum-theory.) (pp. 639–40)
The discussion is complicated, however, by the following factors:

(a) Question (III) is asked in the form "Whether entirely the same thing is in singulars, or diverse things?" That is, is there one humanity common to Socrates and Plato, or does Socrates have his own humanity and Plato a distinct humanity of his own? But, although the question is asked in this form, it is discussed in a different form: Is the universal distinct from its individuals or the same as them? The connection between these two formulations seems to be as follows: If one humanity is common to Socrates and Plato, then presumably that one humanity cannot be the same as those two numerically distinct individuals. (Note that the converse connection is weaker. If Socrates and Plato each has his own distinct humanity, it need not follow that Socrates is *identical* with his humanity and Plato with his.)

(b) Question (IV), although announced in the list of questions here, is never explicitly discussed at all.

10. See below, the section "Continuation of the Discussion of Doubt I: The Fictum-Theory".
11. the Lincolnite: Robert Grosseteste, bishop of Lincoln.
12. The abrupt 'this doubt' suggest that the reference is to Doubt (II). But in fact this passage marks the transition to Doubt (III).
13. On the other hand: The edition has 'ergo' (= 'therefore'), which seems to be inappropriate here.
14. Reading 'alia' for the edition's 'aliqua'.
15. state: *habitus*-like quality, one of the Aristotelian categories.
16. This is proved: Reading 'Quod probatur' for the edition's 'Quod probat'. Another possibility is to read 'Quod probant' (= 'They prove this').
17. And: Reading 'et' for the edition's 'est'.
18. The edition adds a 'not' to the quoted expression that follows. This must surely be deleted for sense. The quoted expression is supposed to be *denied*. Hence, if the expression contained the word 'not', then denying it of a subject would result in a sentence with a double negation. This is not what Burley has in mind.
19. category: Reading 'praedicamento' for the edition's 'praedicato'.
20. That is, the opinion that the individual and the universal are the same things, the opinion being argued against here.
21. *b*: The edition has '*a*'. See the next note.
22. *a*: The edition has '*b*'. The edition seems to have switched the '*a*' and the '*b*' here. See the preceding note.
23. reasoning: *rationem*. I suspect this is an error for '*opinionem*' (= 'opinion'), but either one will make sense.
24. There is plainly a lacuna in the text here. The Latin, which spans fols. 4vb–5ra of the edition, reads: "ut patet ex quarto et decimo nu-(5ra)-mero in Sorte et Platone, sequitur quod erit" etc.
25. He has not said this, but the point is plain anyway.
26. common: Reading 'communis' for the edition's 'cum'. The emendation is confirmed by the next sentence.
27. The text here seems to suppose that the division just given was of two senses of 'numerically *one*', so that now Burley goes on to give the same two senses for 'numerically *the same*'. In fact, however, the previous division was introduced as a division of 'numerically *the same*', and it is not until we get to the second half of the division that the term 'numerically *one*' appears.
28. generality: Tentatively reading 'communitatis' for the edition's 'communiter'. The emendation is very speculative, but I can make no sense of the text as it stands in the edition.
29. represented: Not in the sense of "picturing", but in the sense of "being duplicated", as a universal is represented in its particulars.
30. I suspect the Latin is corrupt for this sentence. It reads: "Unde quamvis idem vel diversum cuicumque comparata in ratione tantum ad quam sunt primae differentiae entis, omne enim quod est est idem Sorti vel diversum a Sorte, tamen idem vel diversum natura specifica seu contracta per aliquod determinatum subjectum non sunt immediate differentiae entis." My translation is accordingly extremely tentative. Fortunately, the examples make the point clear enough.
31. particular sign: That is, the sign of particularity, the existential quantifier 'some'.
32. species: This is surprising. We are presumably *not* to understand this as if substance, quantity, etc., were the species of being. For that would make being a genus, and it is well known that Aristotle denied that being is a genus. On the contrary, substance, quantity, etc., are categories, which is to say that they are the most general genera; they are not the species of anything. I take it that the word 'species' in the text here (if it is not an outright mistake in the edition) must be taken in a metaphysically innocuous sense, so that it means something like "divisions". In any event, the word is surprising.
33. The addition seems to be implied by the context. See the preceding paragraph, and also the next sentence of the text. As it stands, the inference is fallacious in the same way as 'Some animal is an ox; therefore, some man is an ox' is fallacious. The invalidity Burley is here concerned to point out is presumably not of this trivial kind.

34. and . . . supposition: The import of this is not clear. Perhaps it only serves to reiterate the alternative kinds of supposition in the consequent of the inference.
35. they be taken: Reading 'accipiantur' for the edition's 'accipaiatur'. The rest of the paragraph suggests that the subject of the verb here must be 'inferiors', not 'transcendental term'.
36. under a disjunction: Reading 'sub disjunctione' for the edition's 'subdisjunctive. The emendation is confirmed by the next sentence of the text.
37. What happened to material supposition? It is explicitly included in the first sentence of the paragraph, but no mention is made of it here or in the example in the preceding paragraph.
38. universal sign: The universal quantifier 'every'.
39. numerical: *numeralis*. I am not familiar with this usage, but the sense can be gathered from the context. The point is to contrast the case of transcendental terms like 'thing' or 'being' with other terms, like 'animal'. One can say that Socrates is an animal, and man is an animal too. But Socrates and man (the common nature) are not *two* animals; they cannot be counted together when counting animals. On the other hand, Socrates is a being, and man is a being too. And in this case it does follow that they are two beings; they can be counted together when counting beings.
40. universal body: The Latin reads '*corpus in universale*'. I have deleted the '*in*' as an error. The emendation is confirmed by the next sentence of the text.
41. extreme . . . elements: maxima commixtione elementorum. I do not know the doctrine being cited here.
42. reason: *ratio*. Here, a "divine reason" or divine idea. This was a standard idiom.
43. utterance: *vox*. The word is surprising here. Certainly, Burley is not talking about spoken words here. By 'utterance', he seems to mean the actual divine thought, so that the distinction made here is between the idea as the divine act of thinking and the idea as the *object* of that act. If thinking is regarded as a kind of "mental language" (as was common in Burley's day), then perhaps '*vox*' here simply means "word"—that is, *term*—of mental language. It is still surprising, however; '*vox*' almost always refers to speech. (We get 'voice' from it, after all.) The usual term for the mental or divine "word" is '*verbum*'.
44. keeping to: Reading 'sustinentes' for the edition's 'sustinente'. I take the word to agree with 'possumus' later in the sentence.
45. connotatum: Reading 'connotatum' for the edition's 'connotari'.
46. 'Man' is in the accusative case in the Latin.
47. The point here seems to be the fact that Augustine speaks in the plural.
48. quantity of man: *quantitas hominis*. This could refer to a man's size. But I suspect that it just means "a certain number of men."
49. adjacent second: *secundum adjacens*. This is a standard piece of terminology. The verb 'is' (and its various tenses), when it serves as the copula in a subject-predicate proposition of the form *S is P*, is said to be an "adjacent third" (*tertium adjacens*). But when it serves as the predicate in a proposition of the form *S is*, it is said to be an "adjacent second." The latter case is sometimes analyzed as *S is a being*, thus reducing propositions *secundum adjacens* to propositions *tertium adjacens*.
50. anew: *de novo*. Creation *de novo* is creation now, after the original six days of creation. For istance, the creation of individual human souls during the development of the fetus is a creation *de novo*. Human souls, it was generally agreed at this time, did not pre-exist in some celestial warehouse from which they would then be taken and implanted in suitably prepared matter. No, they were created on the occasion.
51. understands: Tentatively reading 'intelligit' for the edition's 'intelligitur'.
52. The Latin for these last two sentences is: "Et sic debet intelligi illud commune dictum Commentatoris, scilicet, quod in separatis a materia idem est intelligibile et intellectum, intelligendo per intellectum illud per quod intellectus separatus intelligit (*ed.*, intelligitur) et in separatis a materia idem est intelligible et illud per quod intelligit." In this paragraph, an "intelligible" is an object of understanding, the external object, whereas "the understood" is the *means* through which the intellect reaches that object. The point is that, in immaterial cases, the distinction vanishes.
53. category: Reading 'praedicamenti' for the edition's 'praesenti'.
54. eternity: Reading 'aeternitas' for the edition's 'idea'. The emendation seems required by the context.
55. The end of this sentence is gibberish, as far as I can make out. I suspect some textual problems here. The Latin is: "Ita divisio, scilicet, quod terminus potest accipi pro eo quod significat et pro eo quod denominat potest applicari materiae, scilicet, de aeternitate et in aeternitate." The textual problems continue for the next three paragraphs.
56. everlastingness: *aevum*.
57. Neither: Reading 'Nec'for the edition's 'Nam', which seems to make little sense in the context.
58. The edition adds '*vel quasi*', which seems unintelligible in the context.
59. abstract by an ultimate abstraction: This notion is explained in the following paragraphs.
60. Namely, in sense (a) above.
61. to be: Reading 'esse' for the edition's 'omne'. Palaeographically, this is not at all implausible. The parallel sentence at the beginning of the next paragraph offers no help here.

62. forged: *fabrile*. The edition has 'fabule' here. The correct reading is clear from the example given later. The word does not mean "forged" in the sense of "faked," but rather in the sense of being produced by a forge or furnace.

63. from a suppositum: These words are added in the translation not just to make the English clearer. I suspect there is an omission in the Latin text. The Latin is "Et quoddam est abstractum abstractione formae substantialis cui realiter inhaeret vel quomodocumque denominat." See also the following sentence.

64. in effect: *in effectu*. This is a characteristic Arabism. It means "in actuality," "as a result of its causes."

65. object-being: The Latin here is *'esse objectum'*, not *'esse objectivum'* as one finds in other discussions of the topic. The sense appears to be "being a [thought-] object", or "being a [mental-] object".

66. to be existing: Reading 'esse existentia' for the edition's 'et existentia'. The emendation is tentative, but in virtue of the *'only* object-being in the sense' later on in the sentence, it is clear that the 'et' must be wrong.

67. And . . . vision: Reading 'et sicut est de visu' for the edition's 'et sic est diversa', which makes no sense here.

68. common sense: Not common practical wisdom, but the "*sensus communis*" in the sense of Aristotle's *On the Soul*, III, 2.

69. I: That is, one who holds the fictum-theory. Burley's own theory appears to be more realist than this. See also the following note.

70. This is puzzling. In fact, the theory that universals are concepts has never been explicitly addressed in the above discussion, even though it plainly belongs under Doubt (IV). On the other hand, the arguments given above in favor of the two forms of realism considered under Doubt (III) may, I suppose, be considered as arguments *against* the theory of universals as concepts. As for arguments against realism, we may count the six (unanswered) arguments, above, against the theory that the universal is the same as its singulars (so that the universal is *not* the same thing in each of its singulars), and the five arguments given against the theory that the universal is not the same as its singulars (and so *is* the same thing in each of its singulars). Burley answered the five latter arguments, which lends credence to the view that he is not speaking for himself in the present paragraph.

71. has only: Reading 'solum habet' for the edition's 'non solum habet'. The 'non' must be deleted for sense.

72. this: Reading 'illam' (or 'istam') for the edition's 'aliam'. It is plain that the following arguments are directed to the view just described.

73. The edition adds *'omnis'* (= 'every') here. This is surely a mistake, since quantifiers like this force the following term into personal supposition, not simple.

74. Objection (4) above remains unanswered. Note that objection (4) is virtually the same as the argument given at the beginning of the discussion of Doubt (I).

PART VIII

LOGIC AND THE PHILOSOPHY OF LANGUAGE

CHAPTER 43

Boethius

(See Chapter Thirteen for biography.)

Boethius on Division

Boethius and Augustine constitute the main philosophical sources for the early Scholastics. The former wrote five theological treatises, several works on logic including *On Division*, as well as two treatises on mathematics and one on music. In addition, he translated most of Aristotle's logical works and provided commentaries for them. *On Division* is significant for several reasons. (1) It demonstrates the intimate relationship between logic and language. Language is the medium by which one thinks, and logic is the science of sound thinking. Consequently, one must be aware of the division of an utterance into its significations as well as the division of a genus. He notes that an utterance may signify many things and therefore may be equivocal, after which he discusses the three ways of dividing an utterance. (2) The division of a genus is thoroughly analyzed. "A genus is what is predicated of more than one thing differing in species in respect of what it is. A species, on the other hand, is what we gather together under a genus; a differentia, that by means of which we present one thing as standing apart from another." The dimensions of a genus are numerous. Boethius details these divisions and explores the logical relations between that which is divided and its dividing elements.

ON DIVISION

Preface

The book on division published by Andronicus, a most painstaking ancient, teaches what great benefits the science of dividing confers on those who study it, and in what great honor this knowledge has always been held in the Peripatetic school. The same point is also confirmed by Plotinus (*Enneads*, II, 6), that most profound philosopher, and is reinforced by Porphyry in his commentaries on Plato's *Sophist* as well as by the highly valued usefulness of his *Isagoge* to Aristotle's *Categories* (Ia 2–5). For he says that a practical knowledge of genus, species, differentia, proprium, and accident will be necessary not only for many other purposes but also for the incomparably great usefulness of distributing things into their parts.

Therefore, because it is of the greatest possible use and instruction in it is especially easy, I also have written this down by way of an introduction, passing on to

Reprinted from *The Cambridge Translations of Medieval Philosophical Texts*: Vol. 1, edited by Norman Kretzmann and Eleonore Stump (Cambridge: Cambridge University Press, 1988), pp. 12–38. Reprinted by permission of Norman Kretzmann, Eleonore Stump, and Cambridge University Press.

Roman ears almost everything included in the subject with appropriate, detailed discussion, and with moderate brevity, so that my readers' minds might not be afflicted with the frustration that accompanies a truncated discourse and an unfinished line of thought. Nor should anyone who is ignorant of the subject, unsophisticated, and disdainful of everything new imagine that my hearers' minds will be subjected to pointless verbiage. And let no malice, with its hostile, vicious attacks of disparagement, vilify this digest of material both difficult by nature and unknown to our times which I have made with a great deal of effort and for the use of my readers. Let them give way to these studies—sometimes forgivingly, sometimes even approvingly—rather than reining in the beneficial arts while repudiating with shameless obstinacy whatever is novel. For who does not see what a dearth of beneficial arts there could be if men's minds were never beset with the desperation of dissatisfaction?

But enough of that for now.

I. The Types of Division

1a. Introduction

To begin with, the name of division itself has to be divided. (And the distinctive characteristics and parts of any subject matter have to be conveyed under absolutely any designation of it.)

'Division' is used in many ways, of course. There is the division of a genus into its species; there is also division when a whole is divided into its proper parts; and there is another division when an utterance that signifies many things is split into its proper significations. In addition to those three there is another division, one that is said to be carried out in connection with accidents. But it occurs in three ways: first, when we separate a subject into its accidents; second, when we divide an accident into its subjects; third, when we split an accident into accidents (which is done if both of them appear to be in the same subject).

We have to provide examples of all these [divisions], however, until the organization of division as a whole becomes clear.

1b. Type I: The Division of a Genus into Its Species

We divide a genus into its species when we say of animals that some are rational, others irrational; or that of the rational ones some are mortal, others immortal; or when we say of colors that one is white, another black, another intermediate. Every division of a genus into its species has to be made into two or more parts, but there cannot be infinitely many or fewer than two species belonging to a genus. (The reason of this result will have to be shown later.)

1c. Type II: The Division of a Whole into Its Parts

A whole is divided into its parts whenever we resolve anything into the things of which it is composed, as when I say that one thing that belongs to a house is the roof, another is a wall, and another is the foundation; or when I say that a man is joined together out of a soul and a body; and when we say that the parts of *man* are Cato, Virgil, Cicero, and the individuals who, because they are *particulars*, are joined together and make up the quantity of *man* as a whole. For *man* is not a genus, and individual men are not species; they are instead the parts out of which *man* as a whole is joined together.

1d. Type III: The Division of an Utterance into Its Significations

Now a division of an utterance into its proper significations is made whenever a single utterance that signifies many things is opened up and the plurality of its significations is disclosed, as when I say of 'dog' that it is a name and designates this four-footed thing capable of barking, as well as the heavenly body that twinkles near the disease-bearing foot of Orion. (There is also the sea-dog, which grows to an enormous size and is called *Caeruleus*.)

There are, however, two varieties of this division, since either a single name or an expression already made up of names and verbs may signify many things. A name signifies many things in the way I pointed out just above, but an expression designates many things as in 'I declare that you, Aeacides, the Romans can conquer.' The division of a name through its proper significations is named a partition of equivocation, while the distribution of an expression into its proper significations is a discrimination of ambiguity, which the Greeks call *amphibolia*. So let a name that signifies many things be called equivocal but an expression that designates many things be called amphibolous and ambiguous.

1e. Type IVa: The Division of a Subject into Its Accidents

Now of things that are divided in connection with accidents, the division of a subject into its accidents occurs when we say of all men that some are black, some white, and some of an intermediate color; for these are accidents for men, not species of men, and *man* is the subject for them, not their genus.

1f. Type IVb: The Division of an Accident into Its Subjects

But the splitting of an accident into its subjects happens as in the case of all things that are sought after: Some are situated in the soul, others in the body. For, indeed, what is sought after is an accident, not a genus, for the soul and for the body; and the soul and the body are not the species but the subjects of a good that is situated in them.

1g. Type IVc: The Division of an Accident into Accidents

There is [also] a division of an accident into accidents, however, as in the case of all white things: Some are hard, such as a pearl, and others liquid, such as milk. For liquidity, whiteness, and hardness are accidents here, but white is separated into hard and liquid. Therefore, when we speak in that way we separate an accident into other accidents.

But this sort of division is always transformed in turn into one or the other of the two [preceding divisions in connection with accidents]. For we can say of things that are hard that some are black and others white and, again, of things that are liquid that some are white and others black. But we divide these again the other way around: Of those that are black, some are liquid and others hard; and of those that are white, some are liquid but others hard.

This sort of division differs from all those that were discussed above, however. For we cannot partition a signification into utterances when an utterance is distinguished into its proper significations. Nor are parts divided into a whole even though a whole is separated into its parts, and species are not split into genera although a genus is divided into species.

What was said above—that this division is made if both [accidents] should happen to be in the same subject—is clear if it is examined more closely. For when we say of things that are hard that some are white and others black, such as stone and ebony, it is obvious that both hardness and blackness are in the ebony. (A careful reader will find this in connection with the others, too.)

2. Differentiating the Types of Division

2a. Introduction

Now in connection with things for which we seek truth's highest work, it is essential to understand first the distinguishing characteristic of all those things taken together, and the differentiae by which they are singly set apart from one another. For every division of an utterance, of a genus, and of a whole is called division per se, whereas the remaining three are located in the distribution of accident.

2b. Differentiating Type I from Type III

Of division per se, however, there is a differentia of this sort. For the division of a genus differs from the division of an utterance in that an utterance is of course separated into its proper significations, whereas a genus is disjoined not into significations but into certain things that are in some sense generations descending from it.

Also, genus is a whole relative to its proper species, as being more universal in nature; but an equivocation, more universal as far as signification is concerned, is called a whole in utterance, not a whole in nature as well.

[The division of a genus] is divided from the distribution of an utterance in this way also: The things that are under the utterance have nothing in common besides the name alone; the things that are gathered together under a genus, on the other hand, take on both the name and the definition of the genus.

Furthermore, the distribution of an utterance is not the same for all; although many significations of the name 'dog' occur in the Roman language, what is called 'dog' by us may be expressed simply in a barbarian language, since the things we name by means of one name, they may signify by means of more than one name. [On the other hand,] the division and distribution of a genus remain the same for all. And so the division of an utterance pertains to the imposition [of the utterance] and to convention, whereas the division of a genus pertains to nature; for what is the same for all has to do with nature, whereas what varies from group to group has to do with convention.

These are the differentiae of the distribution of a genus and of an utterance.

2c. Differentiating Type I from Type II

The splitting of a genus is disjoined also from the distribution of a whole in that the division of a whole is made in respect of quantity; for the parts making up a whole substance either actually or conceptually are separated in mind (*animo/animi*) and thought. The distribution of a genus, on the other hand, is carried out in respect of quality; for when I have located *man* under *animal*, a division has been made in respect of

quality because man is a sort of animal in that it gets a form from a quality. That is why someone answering the question 'What sort of animal is man?' will reply 'Rational,' or at least 'Mortal.'

Furthermore, every genus is naturally prior to its proper species, but a whole is [naturally] posterior to its proper parts. The parts that make up a whole precede the completion of their composite sometimes only naturally, sometimes also temporally. That is why we resolve a genus into things posterior but a whole into things prior to it. It is for this reason also that it is truly said that if a genus is destroyed its species perish immediately, [but] if a species has been destroyed, its genus is not prevented from subsisting naturally. The very opposite happens in connection with a whole; for if a part of a whole perishes, the whole of which that one part was destroyed will not exist, whereas if the whole perishes, its distributed parts remain. For example, if someone takes the roof off a complete house, he breaks up the whole that existed before, but when the whole has been destroyed [in that way], the walls and foundation will continue to exist.

Furthermore, a genus is the matter for its species. For, just as the bronze passes over into the statue when it has taken on the form, so the genus passes over into the species when it has taken on the differentia. In the case of a whole, on the other hand, the plurality of the parts is the matter, whereas the composition of those same parts is the form. For just as a species consists of a genus and a differentia, so does a whole consist of parts. That is why the difference between a whole and any one of its parts lies in the very composition of those parts, whereas the difference between a species and a genus lies in the conjunction of a differentia.

Furthermore, a species is always the same as its genus. For example, *man* is the same as *animal, virtue* the same as *habit.* A part, on the other hand, is not always the same as its whole; for a hand is not the same as the man, nor is a wall the same as the house. This is obvious in the case of things that have parts that are not alike, but it is otherwise in the case of things that have parts that are alike. For example, in the case of a rod of bronze, because its parts are continuous and of the same bronze, the parts appear to be the same as the whole is—but that is a mistake. For the parts may be the same [as the whole] as regards the sort of substance, but not also in quantity.

2d. Differentiating Type II from Type III

The differentiae between the distributions of an utterance and of a whole have not yet been given. [Those distributions] differ in that a whole consists of its parts but an utterance does not consist of the things it signifies, and a whole is divided into its parts but an utterance is divided not into its parts but into the things it signifies. That is why a whole perishes when a single part has been taken away, but an utterance designating many things remains when a single thing signified by that utterance has been taken away.

3. The Division of a Genus

3a. Genera, Species, and Differentiae

Now that the differentiae in division per se have been presented, we have to explore the distribution of genus. First we have to define what a genus is. A genus is what is predicated of more than one thing differing in species in respect of what it is. A species, on the other hand, is what we gather together under a genus; a differentia, that by means of which (*qua/quia*) we present one thing as standing apart from another.

Genus is indeed also what is appropriately given in reply to anyone asking what any thing is; the differentia is what is most correctly given in reply to an inquiry into what sort it is. For when anyone asks 'What is man?', the correct answer is 'Animal'; to the question 'What sort [of animal] is man?', one answers appropriately 'Rational.'

3b. Division into Species and into Differentiae

Now a genus is divided sometimes into the species, sometimes—if the species through which the genus is properly divided lack names—into the differentiae. For example, when I say 'Of animals some are rational, others irrational,' *rational* and *irrational* are differentiae. But since there is no single name of the species *rational animal*, we put the differentia in place of the species and connect it to the higher genus, because every differentia produces a species when it comes to its proper genus. That is why the genus is a kind of matter, the differentia a form. When species are called (*appellantur/appellatur*) by their own names, however, the correct division of a genus is not into the differentiae but into the species.

3c. Division and Definition

It is for that reason that a definition is put together out of several terms; for if all species were called by their own names, every definition would be made up of only two terms. When I say 'What is man?', for example, why would it be necessary for me to say that *mortal rational animal* completes the definition of *man* with soundest reasoning and full conclusiveness if *rational animal* had been picked out with its own name and joined with the remaining differentia *mortal*? As things are, however, division is necessary for full definitions of species. And perhaps the essential nature of division and of definition have to do with the same thing, since a single definition is made up of divisions joined together.

But some things are equivocal and others univocal, and we split those that are univocal into genera whereas for those that are equivocal there is only a division of signification. And so we first have to see what is equivocal and what is univocal so that we do not resolve an equivocal name into significant [components] as if they were species when we have been deceived [about the equivocal and the univocal]. And that is why definition is necessary for division, for by means of definition we collect together whatever is equivocal, whatever is univocal.

3d. Differentiae Suited to Definition and the Division of Genus

Now some differentiae are per se and others are *per accidens*, and some of the latter regularly follow along with [their subjects] whereas others are regularly left behind. Those that are left behind are of this sort: being asleep, being seated, standing, being awake; but those that follow along with [the subject] are, for example, curly hair (if it has not been acquired with a curling iron) and bright eyes (if they have not been affected by some extraneous disability). But these [differentiae *per accidens*] are not to be used for the division of a genus. They are not suitable for definitions either, for everything that is appropriate to the division of a genus we quite properly bring together for definitions. It is only those [differentiae] per se that are appropriate to the division of a genus, for they complete and give form to the substance of anything whatever, in the way rationality and mortality do [for the substance] of *man*.

But the way we can test whether [differentiae] are the sort that are regularly left behind, the sort that follow along [with the subject], or the sort that remain in the substance has to be seen along these lines (for it is not enough to know which ones we use in division unless we also know how to recognize very precisely those that are to be used and those that are to be rejected). Therefore, we have to see, first of all, whether the proposed differentia can be in every subject and at all times; if it is [ever] severed [from any subject] either actually or conceptually, it must be kept away from the division of a genus. For if [the differentiae] are often severed [from subjects] both actually and conceptually, they are the sort that are regularly left behind—*being seated*, for example, which is very often separated and actually divided from the subject itself. But those that are divided from the subject only conceptually belong to the differentiae that follow along with [the subject]—as when we conceptually sever *having bright eyes* from the subject. When I say, for example, 'There is an animal with bright eyes—e.g., any man whatever,' if this [or that] individual were not of that sort, no actual fact would prevent him from being a man.

On the other hand, there is another sort of differentia that cannot be conceptually separated [from its subject], because if it is separated, the species is destroyed. There is an example of this sort when we say that it inheres in man that he alone can use numbers or learn geometry: if that possibility is severed from man, man himself does not remain. But these are not regularly included among the differentiae that inhere in a substance; for [an animal] is a man not because it can do those things but because it is rational and mortal.

Therefore, the differentiae by means of which a species is constituted are gathered together both in the definition of a species such as *man* and in the division of the genus that contains a species such as *man*. And we have to say in general that all differentiae that are of such a sort that there can be no species without them but only in virtue of them [are the ones that] must be used either in the division of the genus or in the definition of the species.

But there are [features] that do differ which [nevertheless] must not be set against each other in division—e.g., *rational* and *two-footed* in connection with *animal* (for no one says, 'Of animals some are rational while others have two feet'). And so even though *rational* and *two-footed* differ, they are not severed from each other in respect of any opposition. [But] it is undisputed that only [features] that differ from each other in respect of some opposition can disjoin a genus, and they alone are placed under that genus as differentiae.

3e. Excursus on Opposition

3e(i). The Four Oppositions

Now there are four oppositions: either [—first—] contraries, as good to evil, or [—second—] possession and privation, as sight and blindness. (There are cases, however, in which it is hard to tell whether they have to be classified as contraries or as privation and possession—e.g., motion, rest; health, sickness; wakefulness, sleep; light, darkness. But those must be discussed another time; now we have to speak of the remaining oppositions.) The third opposition has to do with affirmation and negation—e.g., Socrates is alive, Socrates is not alive; the fourth, with relationship—e.g., father, child; master, slave.

We have to show in an altogether appropriate rational order which of these four oppositions the division of a genus is, for it is evident that there are four oppositions and that genera and species are separated by means of opposites. And so now we have to tell in which way or in accordance with which of these four oppositions it is appropriate to disjoin a species from a genus.

3e(ii). Affirmation and Negation

First there is the opposition of contradiction. (I call the opposition put forward in connection with affirmation and negation the opposition of contradiction.)

The negation in that opposition produces no species on its own. When I say 'man' or 'horse' or anything of that sort, they are species; but whatever a person mentions using a negation fails to express a species. *Not being man* is [not] a species; for every species is an ordering of being, but negation disjoins being from something that is, no matter what it presents. For example, when I say 'man,' I have spoken as if there is something; but when I say 'non-man,' with the negation I have destroyed the substance of *man*. In that respect, therefore, considered in itself, the division of a genus into species has nothing to do with negation.

All the same, it is often necessary to use negation in constructing a species when we want to use a simple name to assign a species to something that is not picked out by any word. This happens when, for example, I say 'Of odd numbers some are prime—e.g., three, five, seven,—others

non-prime—e.g., nine'; and, again. 'Of figures some are rectilinear (*rectissimae*), [others non-rectilinear]'; and 'Of colors some are white, others black, others neither white nor black.' Therefore, when no single name has been applied to species, we have to designate them by means of negation; thus it is [our] need, not nature, that sometimes requires this.

So whenever we use negation to split something, it is the affirmation or the simple name that is to be said first—as in 'Of numbers some are prime, others non-prime'—because if the negation is said first there will be a delay in a person's understanding of the thing we are presenting. For when you say first that some numbers are prime (once you have taught by example or by definition which sort are prime and which sort are not prime), your listener understands at once. But if you do it the other way around, he will learn (*coqnoscet/ coqnosces*) neither one right away, or both more slowly; and a division, which is sought after in order to reveal a genus as much as possible, must instead be reduced to the things that are more understandable.

Furthermore, affirmation is prior and negation posterior, and what is first ought also to be given first place in a division. It is always necessary, too, that finite things be prior to non-finite things—the equal to the unequal, virtue to the vices, the certain to the uncertain, the stable and fixed to the unstable and mutable. But all the things that are expressed by a part of speech that is definite or by an affirmation are more finite than a name with a negative particle or a complete negation. For that reason a division ought to be carried out with what is finite rather than with what is non-finite.

(But if anyone should be troubled by these things, or if they may be more obscure than he would like, it is not my business to promise easy learning. We put forward these [elements] of the whole art [of divison] to be read and learned, not for beginners, but for the initiates, and for those who are just about to move ahead to a more advanced level. But I have carefully explained the scheme of this art—i.e., the dialectician's art—since it had to be told to me in accordance with the scheme of the Peripatetic discipline.)

3e(iii). Possession and Privation

The preceding remarks were made regarding the opposition constituted by affirmation and negation. But the opposition formed on the basis of possession and privation also seems to be a great deal like the preceding one, since privation is in a way the negation of possession. It differs, however, in that negation can always occur, but privation not always—only when it is possible to have possession. (The *Categories* have already taught us that, though [c. 10, 12a26–b16].) And so a privation is understood to be a kind of form, since it not only deprives but also classifies in respect of the privation each thing affected by the privation. Blindness, for instance, not only deprives the eye of light but also classifies according to the privation the one deprived of light; for he is called blind relative to the privation in such a way that it is as if he were classified and affected [in that way]. (Aristotle, too, takes this position in the *Physics* [V2, 226b15].) That is why we often use a differentia associated with a privation for the division of a genus.

But we have to proceed here just as we did in connection with contradiction; for the possession, the analogue to the affirmation, must be put first, but the privation, analogous to the negation, after it. Still, certain privations are sometimes expressed by means of a word associated with possession—e.g., 'orphaned,' 'blind,' 'widowed'—sometimes with a privative particle, as when we say 'finite,' 'infinite'; 'equal,' 'unequal.' But in those cases [the words like] 'equal' and 'finite' should be put first in the division, the privations second.

And let these remarks about the opposition of privation and possession suffice.

3e(iv). Contraries

One might be uncertain whether the opposition of contraries such as white and

black seems to be a case of privation and possession, whether white is indeed the privation of black, [or] black of white; but that will have to be considered another time. For the present, we have to treat [contrariety] as if it were another genus of opposition, as it is classified by Aristotle himself in the *Categories* (c. 10, 11b17–19; 33ff.).

Much of the division of genera occurs in connection with contraries, for we bring almost all differentiae down to contraries. But since some contraries lack an intermediate and others have intermediates, division has to be carried out accordingly—as in the case of colors, for instance: some are black, others are white, others neither.

Every definition and every division would be accomplished by means of two terms, however, if it were not for the fact (discussed above) that want of a name, which often occurs, prevents it. It will be evident in the following way how both [definition and division] would be accomplished by means of two terms. When we say 'Of animals some are rational, others irrational,' *rational animal* aims at the definition of *man*. But since there is no single name for *rational animal*, let us give it the letter *A* as a name. Then: 'Of *A* (i.e., *rational animal*) some are mortal, others immortal.' Therefore, when we want to provide the definition of *man*, we will say 'Man is a mortal *A*.' For if the definition of *man* is *mortal rational animal*, but *rational animal* is signified by *A*, one reacts to 'mortal *A*' just as if 'mortal rational animal' had been said (for, as we said, *A* signifies *rational animal*). And so in that way the definition of *man* is made out of the two terms 'mortal' and '*A*.' But if names were found in connection with all things, a complete definition would always be made of two terms. So would division, if names had been imposed [on all things]. For we always split [things] into two terms, it is clear, if we impose a name on the genus and differentia when a name is lacking—as when we say 'Of figures that (*quae/quaedam*) are three-sided some are equilateral, others have two sides equal, and others are all unequal.' If that tripartite division were put forward, therefore, it would be made twofold: 'Of figures that are three-sided some are equal and others are unequal; of those that are unequal there are some with only two sides equal, and others with three (i.e., all) sides unequal.' And when we say 'Of all things some are good, others are bad, and others indifferent (i.e., those that are neither good nor bad),' if we were to speak in that way, a paired division would be produced: 'Of all things some are differentiated [in respect of goodness and badness] and others are indifferent; of those that are differentiated some are good and others bad.' In that way, then, every division would be split into pairs, if words for species and differentiae were not lacking.

3e(v). Relationship

We mentioned a fourth opposition, however, which occurs in accordance with relationship—e.g., father, child; master, slave; double, half; sense object, sense. These [opposed things], then, have no substantial differentia by which they diverge from each other. On the contrary, they have a natural association by which they are referred to each other, and they cannot exist without each other. That is why the division of a genus must not be made into relative parts. Rather, this way of splitting things must be kept entirely separate from genus; for of *man* there is no species *slave* or *master*, nor of *number* [is there a species] *half* or *double*.

Therefore, although differentiae are to be drawn from the four oppositions of affirmation and negation, of privation and possession, of contraries, [and of relationship,] unless it is necessary, a division associated with relationship is always to be rejected. Contrariety, on the other hand, is especially to be applied in connection with differentiae. And privation as well, because one sort of contrary—such as *finite* and *infinite*—seems to be opposed to possession, for although *infinite* is a privation, it is formed on the basis of an image of the contrary since (as was said above) it is a kind of form.

3f. More on Division into Species and Differentiae

It is worth inquiring whether genera are correctly divided into species or into differentiae. Because the definition of division is, indeed, the distribution of a genus into its proximate species, therefore, in accordance with the nature of division and its definition, the dissection of a genus must always be made into its proper species. But sometimes this cannot be done, for the reason we gave above; there are many species for which there are no names.

(Some genera are first, others last, and others intermediate. *Substance*, for example, is a first genus; *animal*, a last genus; *body*, an intermediate genus. For *body* is the genus of *animal*; *substance*, of *body*. But just as one can find nothing above *substance* that can be assigned the role of a genus, so neither is there anything of that sort under *animal*; for *man* is a species, not a genus.)

And so the division into species will appear preferable, if there is no lack of names; but if we are not very well supplied with names for all things, it is appropriate to separate the first genera down to the last genera into differentiae. Now that is done in the following way: we dissect the first genus into its own and not into subsequent differentiae; and, again, we dissect a subsequent genus into its own and not into subsequent differentiae. For the differentiae of *body* are not the same as those of *animal*. If someone says 'Of substance one sort is corporeal, another incorporeal,' he has made the division correctly because those differentiae are indeed proper to *substance*. But if someone says 'Of substances some are animate, others inanimate,' he has not set the substantial differentiae apart correctly; for those are differentiae of *body*, not of *substance*—i.e., of a second genus, not of a first. And so it is clear that the division of prior genera must be made in accordance with their own differentiae and not in accordance with those of a subsequent genus.

But whenever a genus is resolved into differentiae or into species, definitions or examples should be supplied as soon as the division has been made. If a person is not very well supplied with definitions, however, it is enough to add examples. When, for instance, we say 'Of bodies some are animate,' we may add'—such as men or beasts; others inanimate—such as stones.'

3g. Conversion in Division

A division, like a term, must be neither too narrow nor too broad. One must introduce neither more nor fewer species than are under the genus, so that the division converts with itself, as a term does. For a term converts in this way: 'Virtue is the mind's best habit'; again, 'The mind's best habit is virtue.' Division also converts, in this way: 'Every genus will be one of those that are [its] species'; again, 'Each species is [its] proximate genus.'

3h. Multiple Divisions

The division of one and the same genus is made in many ways, like the division of all bodies and of any things having any magnitude. For we distribute a circle into semicircles and into the things the Greeks call *tōmeis* (we can call them divisions), and we sometimes separate a rectangle into triangles by means of a diagonal beginning from an angle, sometimes into parallelograms, and sometimes into rectangles. We also do the same sort of thing with a genus, as when we say 'Of numbers some are even, others odd' and, again. '[Of numbers] some are prime, others non-prime'; 'Of triangles some are equilateral, others have only two sides equal, and others are unequal on all sides' and, again, 'Of triangles some have a right angle, others have three acute angles, and others have one obtuse angle.' And so the division of a single genus is in that way multiple.

3i. Genus, Species, and Differentia Again

It is very useful to know that a genus is in a certain respect the likeness of many species, a likeness that brings out the substantial agreement of all of them. And it is for that reason that the genus is collective

of the many species, but the species are disjunctive of the single genus. Since the species are given their form by the differentiae (as was said above), there cannot be fewer than two species under a single genus; for every differentia consists in a plurality of differences.

4. Definition

4a. Transition from Division of Genus to Definition

We have now said a great deal about the division of genus and species, and so those who follow along this path have access to a more skillful technique for defining species via the division of genus. But we must undertake not only to learn about the differentiae we use in definition, but also to comprehend with painstaking understanding the art of definition itself. I am not going to consider whether any definition can be demonstrated, or how a definition can be found by means of demonstration, or any of the issues regarding definition that Aristotle handled with precision in the *Posterior Analytics* (II 10, 93b29–94a19). I merely want to provide a thorough treatment of no more than the rule of defining.

4b. Definition Confined to Intermediate Things

Of things some are higher, others lower, and others intermediate. Certainly no definition encompasses the higher things, for no genera higher than they are can be found. On the other hand, however, the lower things, such as individuals, lack specifying differentiae; for that reason they too are excluded from definition. Therefore, it is the intermediate things, those that have genera and that are predicated of the others—of genera, of species, or of individual—that can fall under definition.

4c. Constructing Definitions

Therefore, when I have been given a species of the sort that both has a genus and is predicated of subsequent things, I first take up its genus, I divide the differentiae of that genus, I join a differentia to the genus, and I see whether that differentia joined to the genus can be equal to the species I have undertaken to circumscribe with a definition. If the species turns out narrower, then, again, the differentia we applied to the genus a moment ago is taken up by us as if it were a genus, and we separate it into other differentiae of its own, and, again, we conjoin those two differentiae with the higher genus. If it has succeeded in equaling the species, it will be said to be the definition of the species; but if [the species] is narrower, we again separate that second differentia into others. We conjoin all of them with the genus, and again we look to see if all the differentiae together with that genus are equal to the species that is defined. Finally, we distribute differentiae under differentiae as often as we must until all of them joined to the genus describe the species in a definition that is equal to it.

But examples will provide a clearer conception of this operation, in the following way. Suppose it is our job to define *name*. The word 'name' is predicated of many names, and in some sense [they are] species containing individuals under themselves. And so I define *name* in this way: I take up its genus, which is *utterance*, and I divide it: 'Of utterances some are significant, but others are not.' A nonsignificant utterance has nothing to do with a name because, of course, a name signifies. And so I take up the differentia *significant*, and I join it to the genus *utterance*, and I say 'significant utterance'; then I look to see whether this genus and differentia are equal to *name*.

But they are not equal yet, because an utterance can be significant without being a name; for there are certain utterances that indicate pain [naturally] and others that indicate passions of the mind naturally that are not names—e.g., interjections. I again divide *significant utterance* into other differentiae: 'Of significant utterances some are significant in accordance with men's imposition of them, others are naturally significant.' And a naturally significant utterance certainly has nothing to do with a name, but an utterance that is significant in accordance with men's imposition of it does fit a name. And so I join the two differentiae *significant* and *in accordance with imposition* to *utterance*—i.e., to the genus—and I say 'A name is an utterance significant by convention.'

But in my view this is still not equated to *name*; for of course verbs too are utterances significant in accordance with imposition, and so that is not a definition of *name* alone. I again distribute the differentia *in accordance with imposition*, and I say 'Of utterances significant in accordance with imposition some are significant with a tense, others without a tense.' And of course the differentia *with a tense* is not conjoined to *name*, because it belongs to verbs but not to names to consignify times. The result is that the differentia *without a tense* is appropriate. Therefore, I join those three differentiae to the genus, and I say 'A name is an utterance significant by convention without a tense.'

But in my view the definition is still not completely finished; for an utterance can be significant, in accordance with imposition, and without a tense, and yet be not a single name but names joined together—i.e., an expression (*oratio/ratio*). For example, 'Socrates together with Plato and his disciples' is an expression, even though it is of course incomplete. For that reason the last differentia, *without a tense*, must again be divided into other differentiae. And we will say 'Of utterances significant in accordance with imposition without a tense there are some having a part that signifies something independently (this pertains to an expression), others having no part that signifies anything independently.' This pertains to a name, for a part of a name signifies nothing independently. And so the definition is made in this way: A name is an utterance significant by convention, without a tense, having no part that signifies anything independently when separated.

Do you see, then, how a correct definition is constructed? For by saying 'utterance' I disjoined a name from other sounds; by adding 'significant' I separated a name from nonsignificant utterances; with 'by convention' and 'without a tense' the distinctive character of a name was disjoined from naturally significant utterances and from verbs; by proposing that its parts signify nothing independently I disjoined it from an expression, the separated parts of which do signify independently. That is why anything that is a name is included in that definition, and wherever the expression of that definition fits, you will be in no doubt whether the thing in question is a name.

4d. Wholes and Parts in Definition and Division

It must also be pointed out that a genus is a whole in division but a part in definition. In definition it is as if parts join together to make a kind of whole, and in division it is as if a whole is resolved into its parts; the division of a genus is like the division of a whole, definition like the composition of a whole. For in the division of the genus, *animal* is the whole belonging to *man* because it encompasses *man* within itself; in the definition, however, it is a part, since the genus joined together with the various differentiae makes up the species (*speciem/specie*). For example, when I say 'Of animals some are rational, others irrational' and, again, 'Of rational [animals] some are mortal, others immortal,' *animal* is the whole belonging to *rational* and, again, *rational* is the whole belonging to *mortal* (*mortalis/mortale*), and those three are [the whole] belonging to *man*. But if in the definition I say 'Man is a mortal rational animal,' those three join together to make the single thing that is *man*. For that reason both the genus and the differentia are ascertained to be part of *man* itself.

In division, therefore, the genus is in that way a whole and the species a part; in the same way the differentiae are also a whole, whereas the species into which they are divided are parts. In definition, on the other hand, both the genus and the differentiae are parts, whereas the species defined is the whole.

But that is enough regarding these matters.

5. The Division of a Whole

5a. Introduction

Now let us discuss the division of a whole into its parts, since that was the second division after the division of a genus. What we call a whole we signify in various ways. For a whole is what is continuous, such as a body, a line, or something of that sort. We also call what is not continuous a whole—e.g., 'the whole crowd.' 'the whole population,' 'the whole army.' We also call what is universal a whole, such as *man*, or *horse*; for they are the wholes belonging to their parts—i.e., to men, or to horses. (That is also why we call each single man a *particular*.) We also call what consists of certain powers a whole. Of the soul, for example, there is one capacity for understanding, another for sensing, and another for living; they are parts, but not species [of the soul]. Therefore, the division of a whole is to be made in as many different ways as the ways in which 'whole' is used.

5b. Divisions of a Continuous Whole

First, indeed, if [a whole] is continuous, [it is to be divided] into the parts it is observed to consist of; otherwise no division is made. For that is how you will divide a man's body into its parts; the head, the hands, the trunk, and the feet. (The division is also correct if it is made in accordance with proper parts in some other way.)

Of things whose composition is multiple, however, the division is also multiple. An animal, for instance, is of course separated into parts that have parts like themselves—into flesh and bone—[or,] on the other hand, into those that do not have parts like themselves—into hands and feet. The same applies to a ship and to a house. We resolve a book, too, into lines, the lines into words, the words into syllables, and the syllables into letters. It is in that way that the syllables, letters, names, and lines are seen to be some sort of parts of the whole book; taken in another way, however, they are not parts of the whole but parts of parts.

Not all things must be viewed as if they divide in fact, but [some things are to be viewed] as if [they divide] mentally and conceptually. Wine mixed with water, for example, we divide into [quantities of] wine mixed with water (*aqua/aquae*), and we do that in fact; [but] we also divide it into the wine and the water from which it was mixed, and we do that conceptually, because once those things are mixed, they cannot be separated in fact.

But the division of a whole is [also] made into matter and form. For in one way a statue consists of its parts, and in another of [its] matter and form—i.e., of the bronze and the image.

5c. Divisions of Discontinuous and Universal Wholes

Likewise, wholes that are not continuous and those that are universal must be divided in the same way. Of men, for example, some are in Europe, others in Africa, and others in Asia.

5d. Divisions of Wholes Consisting of Powers

The division of a whole that consists of powers is also to be made in this way: Of the soul, one part is in plants, the other in animals; and, on the other hand, of the one that is in animals one part is rational, the other sensitive; and those are dispersed in turn under other divisions. Of these, however, soul is not the genus but the whole; and yet they are parts of soul not in respect of quantity but in respect of a certain capacity and power, because it is out of those capacities that the substance of soul is joined together. And that is why this sort of division bears a certain resemblance to the division of a genus and of a whole. For the fact that each part of which *soul* is predicated is associated with soul is traced back

to the division of a genus: Whenever a species of [a genus] occurs, it is directly associated with the genus itself. On the other hand, the fact that not every soul is joined together out of all the parts (but some [souls] out of these, and others out of those) must be traced back to the nature of a whole.

6. The Division of an Utterance

6a. Three Ways of Dividing an Utterance

We still have to discuss the division of an utterance into its significations. The division of an utterance is made in three ways. It is divided into more than one signification either [1] as an equivocal utterance or [2] as an ambiguous utterance; for [1] a single name, such as 'dog,' signifies more than one thing, and [2] so does a single expression, as when I say that the Greeks the Trojans have conquered. But [the division of an utterance] is made in the other way [3] in accord with manner; these utterances signify not more than one thing but [one thing] in several different manners.

When we say 'infinite,' for example, it does indeed signify a single thing—one whose limit cannot be discovered—but we call it that in respect of measure, of plurality, or of species. In respect of measure, as in 'infinite is the universe' (because we are saying that it is infinite in size); in respect of plurality, as in 'infinite is the division of bodies' (because we are signifying that the plurality of [those] divisions is infinite); and, again, in respect of species, as when we call figures infinite (because there are infinitely many species of figures). We also call something infinite in respect of time. For example, we call the world infinite [because] no limit in respect of time can be found for it, and in the same way we call God infinite [because] for his supreme life no limit in respect of time can be found. And so in itself the utterance ['infinite'] does not signify more than one thing; rather, signifying only one thing itself, it is predicated of individuals in several different manners.

6b. Determinations of Signification

But another way [of dividing an utterance occurs] in accord with determination; for whenever any utterance is used without a determination, it produces uncertainty in the understanding. 'Man' is of that sort, for that utterance signifies many things because when no definition confines it the hearer's understanding is carried away on many different currents and misled by errors. For what does any hearer understand when the speaker does not confine what he says by means of some determination? Unless the person who is speaking defines [the utterance 'man'] in this way: 'Every man is walking' (or at least 'Some man is walking'), and designates this by a name, if it can be done in that way, the hearer's understanding has nothing it understands with good reason.

There are other determinations, too. For example, if someone says "Give me it," no one understands what he is supposed to give unless the understanding and definite reason associated with a determination are added. Or if someone says 'Come to me,' we know where we are to come or when we are to come only in virtue of a determination.

Although everything ambiguous is uncertain, not everything uncertain is ambiguous; for the things we have [just] been discussing are indeed uncertain although not ambiguous. Where ambiguities are concerned, the hearer thinks, reasonably enough, that he has understood one or the other [of the significations]. For example, when someone says 'I hear that the Greeks the Trojans conquered,' one person thinks that the Greeks conquered the Trojans, another that the Trojans conquered the Greeks; and both understand those things with good reason on the basis of the words themselves (*ipsis/ipsius*). On the other hand, when I say 'Give me it,' no hearer understands with good reason on the basis of the words themselves what you are supposed to give; for instead of seeing clearly, with

some reason, what was not said before, he will conjecture about what I did not say.

6c. Distinguishing Among Signified Things

Therefore, since the division of an utterance is made in all these ways—by meanings (*significantias*), by the manner of significations, or by determinations—in connection with those that are divided in accord with meaning, it is not only that the signified things are to be divided; we must also show by definition that there are various things that are signified. Aristotle painstakingly taught these things in the *Topics* (II 9, 114b16–24), e.g., that among things that are called good, some are good—those that possess the quality of goodness—[while] others are called [good] with no quality [of goodness] itself but because they bring about a good thing.

6d. Sophistry and the Art of Division

Now one must practice this art [of division] especially against sophistical tricks, as Aristotle himself says (*Soph. el.* 5, 166b29–36). For if there is no subject thing that the utterance signifies, it is not said to be designative; if there is one thing the utterance signifies, it is called simple; if more than one, multiple—i.e., signifying many things. And so these things must be correctly divided so that we may avoid being caught in some syllogism.

But if an expression is amphibolous—i.e., ambiguous—it sometimes turns out that things that are signified in each of the two ways are possible. What I said above is an example of this, for that the Greeks conquered the Trojans could happen, likewise that the Trojans overcame the Greeks. There are others, however, that are impossible, as when I say that the man the bread is eating. That does indeed signify that the man is eating the bread and, on the other hand, that the bread is eating the man—but that is impossible. And so when it comes to controversy, the possibilities and impossibilities have to be divided. When truth is at issue, the impossibilities are to be left to one side while only the possibilities are to be expressed.

6e. Equivocation and Ambiguity

Because there is more than one species of utterances that signify more than one thing, it is important to point out that some of them have their signification of multiplicity in a small part, others in the complete expression. As for those that have it in a small part, the part itself is called equivocal, whereas the complete expression [of which it is a part] is multiple in accordance with the equivocation. On the other hand, an utterance that possesses its multiplicity of signification in the complete expression is named ambiguous, as was said above.

Now the significations of equivocals or of expressions [multiple] in accordance with equivocations are sometimes divided by means of definition. For example, when I say 'The man is alive,' one understands both a real and a painted man. But it is divided in this way: 'The mortal rational animal is alive' (which is true); 'The image of a mortal rational animal is alive' (which is false). There is also division by means of any addition that determines [the utterance], whether [the addition] belongs to gender, to case, or to an article. For example, when I say 'Canna was fouled with the Romans' blood.' ['Canna'] points to both the reed and the river. But we divide it in the following ways: by an article, as when we say 'The Canna (*hic Canna*) was fouled with the Romans' blood'; by gender, as in 'Canna was full (*plenus*) of the Romans' blood'; or by case; or by number (for in connection with the one of them only the singular occurs, but with the other, the plural [as well]). And we deal in the same way with other examples.

But there are other [divisions] in accordance with accent, and still others in accordance with spelling. In accordance with accent, '*pone*' and '*ponè*'; in accordance with spelling, '*queror*' and '*quaeror*', having to do with inquiry and complaint [in reverse order]. The latter [two] are also divided again in accordance with spelling, or in accord-

ance with action and passion, since the '*quaeror*' associated with inquiry is passive, whereas the '*queror*' associated with complaint belongs to an agent.

The division of ambiguous expressions, on the other hand, is to be made by addition ('I hear that the Trojans are conquered, that the Greeks have conquered'), by subtraction ('I hear that the Greeks have conquered'), by division ('The Greeks have conquered; the Trojans have been conquered'), or by some rearrangement (e.g., when some one says 'I hear the Trojans the Greeks have conquered', we may say 'I hear that the Greeks have conquered the Trojans'). This ambiguity is resolved in any of these ways.

6f. A Difference Between Divisions of Utterance and of Genus

Nevertheless, not every signification of utterances is to be divided as if it were [a division] of a genus. For in a genus all the species are enumerated, but in connection with ambiguity it is enough to provide as many significations as can be useful for the discourse that one or another expression contains.

7. Divisions *per accidens*

7a. Transition from Divisions per se

We have said enough about the division of utterance, and we have also presented and explained the division of a genus and of a whole. And so we have very carefully considered all the per se partitionings. Now we will say something about divisions that are made *per accidens*.

7b. General Rules of Division per accidens

It is a general rule regarding them that anything that belongs to these [divisions] and is divided is dissected into opposites. For example, when we divide a subject in connection with accidents we do not say 'Of bodies some are white, others sweet' ([because white and sweet] are not opposed), but 'Of bodies some are white, some black, others neither.' We must also divide in the same way in other divisions *per accidens*.

And notice in particular that we must say neither too much nor too little, just as in the division of a genus. For no accident may be left out of the opposition [so] that there is something in the subject that is not expressed in the division; but neither may anything be added that cannot be in the subject.

7c. Peripatetics on Division *per se* and *per accidens*

The later school of Peripatetic scholarship examined the differences among division with especially careful reasoning, and it disjoined division per se from division *per accidens*, distributing them relative to each other. The older [Peripatetics] treated them in an undifferentiated way, however, using an accident for a genus, and using accidents for species or differentiae. And so setting forth the features common to the divisions and dissecting them by means of their own differentiae struck us as having considerable practical value.

8. Conclusion

And so regarding every division, indeed, we have presented with care as much as the brevity of an introduction would permit.

CHAPTER 44

William of Sherwood

Very little is known of the life of William of Sherwood or Shyreswood. He was an English logician born between 1200 and 1210. There is evidence that he taught logic at the University of Paris from about 1235 to about 1250, during which time he directly influenced Peter of Spain, Lambert of Auxerre, Albert the Great, and Thomas Aquinas. He was a master at Oxford in 1252 and in 1254 became treasurer of the cathedral church of Lincoln. He also held the position of rector of Aylesbury and of Attleborough. He died sometime between 1266 and 1271.

The medievals referred to their contributions to logic as the *logica moderna* to distinguish them from strictly Aristotelian logic. The *logica moderna* can be seen in the writing of, for example, Abelard. However, the works by William, namely, *Introductiones in Logicam, Syncategoremata, De Insolubilibus* (on paradoxes of self-reference), *Obligationes* (on rules of argument for formal disputation), and *Petitiones Contrariorum* (on logical puzzles arising from hidden contrariety in premises) are the earliest systematic and complete presentation of the *logica moderna*.

William of Sherwood on the Properties of Terms

Although the theory the *proprietates terminorum* most likely originated with Abelard, the first known published account of it appears in William of Sherwood's *Introduction to Logic*. The theory of the properties of terms is an analysis of the various roles words or phrases play as terms in propositions. Initially, the theory concentrated on general terms such as 'animal'. It was understood that syncategorematic words such as 'a', 'the' and 'with' do not count as terms. First and foremost, a term must possess signification (*significatio*), that is, the property of being a meaningful linguistic expression. However, signification is independent of how a term is used in a proposition. For example, the term 'animal' can function as either a subject or a predicate. In other words, syntax is inevitably involved in any theory of terms by adding a dimension to terms beyond signification. This is called a term's supposition (*suppositio*). It pertains to what a given term stands for in terms of its signification dictated by the syntax of the proposition in which the term plays a role. Simply stated, supposition is a term's reference and is a property principally of nouns and pronouns. The reference of a term is determined by the syntax or sentence structure in which a term participates.

The first division of supposition is that of the formal versus the material. This roughly corresponds to the use-mention distinction. A term materially supposits when it is mentioned. A term formally supposits when it is used, that is, when a word supposits what it signifies. Formal supposition has two divisions, simple and personal. There is a difference between 'man is a species' and 'a man is running'. The latter is personal, for it signifies some individual. The former supposits simply in that 'man' stands for the referent of that common term, namely, that which is common to all individual men. Here it is significant to note that William is a realist in that he believes that general terms signify universals, namely, those characteristics that two or more particulars have in common. Copulation (*copulatio*), in essence, is the supposition of verbs, adjectives, and participles. Finally, appellation (*appellatio*) is "the present correct application of a term" and is a property only of nouns, adjectives, and participles. For example, in 1994 San Francisco is an appellation of 'city' but Nineveh is not.

The supposition theory of William was very influential regarding subsequent medieval logicians and language theorists. It was discussed and modified by Peter of Spain, William of Ockham, Walter Burley, and the Spanish Dominican friar St. Vincent Ferrer.

INTRODUCTION TO LOGIC

Chapter Five
Properties of Terms

1. Signification, Supposition, Copulation, and Appellation[1]

There are four properties of terms that we intend to distinguish now, since an understanding of them will contribute to the understanding of the term and thus to the understanding of the statement and the proposition. These properties are signification, supposition, copulation, and appellation.

Signification, then, is a presentation of the form of something to the understanding[2] (*presentatio alicuius forme ad intellectum*). Supposition, however, is an ordering of the understanding of something under something else (*ordinatio alicuius intellectus sub alio*); and copulation is an ordering of

Reprinted from *William of Sherwood's Introduction to Logic*, translated by Norman Kretzmann (Minneapolis: University of Minnesota Press, 1966), pp. 105–131. Reprinted by permission of the University of Minnesota Press.

the understanding of something over something else (*ordinatio alicuius intellectus supra alium*).[3]

Note that 'supposition' and 'copulation,' like many names of this sort, are used in two ways: either with respect to an actual occurrence (*secundum actum*) or with respect to the capacity for such an occurrence (*secundum habitum*). The above definitions of supposition and copulation are with respect to what they are in actual occurrence. With respect to what they are in capacity, however, supposition is called a signification of something as subsisting (*significatio alicuius ut subsistentis*) (for what is of that sort is naturally suited to be ordered under something else), and copulation is called a signification of something as adjoining (*adiacentis*) (for what is of that sort is naturally suited to be ordered over something else).

Appellation, finally, is the present correct application (*presens convenientia*)[4] of a term—i.e., the property with respect to which what the term signifies can be [truly] said of something through the use of the verb 'is.'[5]

From these [definitions] it is clear that there is signification[6] in every word or part of speech, whereas there is supposition only in a substantive name, or a pronoun, or a substantive word[7] (for these signify a thing as subsisting and capable of being ordered under something else). There is copulation, however, in all adjectives, participles, and verbs. Finally, there is appellation in all substantives, adjectives, and participles, but not in pronouns (since they do not signify a form, but only a substance)[8] and not in verbs (since a verb does not signify something that is attached [to something else] by means of the substantive verb,[9] because if it did so [the verb] would be beyond itself)[10] (*aliquid quod apponitur per verbum substantivum, quia sic esset extra ipsum*). Moreover, none of these three—supposition, copulation, appellation—is in the indeclinable parts of speech (since no indeclinable part signifies a substance or anything in a substance).[11]

Let us set signification aside and consider the other three properties.

2. The Division of Supposition

To begin with, [let us consider] supposition: first, as such; afterwards,[12] [with respect to] the rules given for it. And since we already have the definition, let us look at the division of it.[13]

Supposition, then, is on the one hand material, on the other hand formal. It is called material[14] when a word itself supposits either [A] for the very utterance itself or [B] for the word itself, composed of the utterance and the signification—as if we were to say [A] 'man is a monosyllable' or [B] 'man is a name.' It is formal when a word supposits what it signifies.

Formal supposition is divided into simple and personal supposition. It is simple[15] when a word supposits what it signifies *for*

what it signifies[16] (*supponit significatum pro significato*), as in 'man is a species.' It is personal, however, when a word supposits what it signifies, but for a thing that is subordinate [to what it signifies], as in 'a man is running' (*homo currit*); for running is in man because of some individual[17] (*Cursus enim inest homini gratia alicuius singularis*).

There is also another division of formal supposition—viz., into common and discrete. Common supposition is that which occurs through a common term, as in 'a man is running'; discrete, that which occurs through a discrete term, as in 'Socrates is running' or 'that man is running'[18] (*ut Sortes currit vel iste*).

Note that both these divisions are completely exhaustive of what I call formal supposition; for every suppositing word is either common or discrete, and [every formally suppositing word] is taken either for the signified form (in which case it is simple supposition) or for a thing bearing the form (in which case, personal).

Personal supposition is divided as follows: on the one hand determinate, on the other hand confused. Confused supposition is divided into merely confused and distributive confused supposition, the latter being divided into mobile and immobile distributive confused supposition.

Personal supposition is determinate when the locution can be expounded by means of some single thing[19] (*exponi . . . per aliquod unum*), which is the case when the word supposits for some single thing, as when I say 'a man is running.' Therefore it can be true for anyone running.

[Personal supposition is] confused, on the other hand, when the word supposits for many, and distributive when it supposits for many in such a way as to supposit for any—e.g., the word 'man' when I say 'every man is an animal.' It is merely confused, [however, when it supposits as does] the word 'animal' [in that statement]. [Distributive confused supposition is] mobile when a descent can be made, as in the term 'man' in the example above.[20] It is immobile when a descent cannot be made, as here: 'only every man is running' (for one cannot infer 'therefore only Socrates is running').[21]

3. A Doubt Regarding the Division Mobile/Immobile

But it seems a descent can be made in every case of distributive supposition, for a word supposits distributively that supposits for many in such a way as to supposit for any; therefore a descent can be made to any. And it must be said that a descent *can* be made in every case of distributive supposition considered in itself[22] (*quantum est de se*); nevertheless, the descent can be impeded by means of an adjunct, as by means of the word 'only' in the example above.

4. A Doubt [Regarding the Division Material/Formal]

There is some doubt (*Dubitatur*) regarding the first division of supposition, for it seems that [material and formal supposition] are not different ways of suppositing but rather of signifying, since signification is a presentation of the form of something to the understanding. Therefore, [where there is] a different presentation [there is] a different signification. Now when a word supposits materially it presents either itself or its utterance; but when it supposits formally it presents what it signifies. Therefore it presents something different; therefore it signifies something different.

This is not true, however, because words considered in themselves (*quantum de se est*) always present what they signify; and if they present their utterance they do so not in themselves but as a result of adjunction to a [certain] predicate. For one predicate is disposed to have reference to (*vult respicere*) only the utterance or the word but another to what is signified.[23] But this does not produce a different signification, for just as a word is a word before it is arranged [with other words] in an expression, so it has [its]

signification beforehand, not as a result of being arranged together with something else.[24]

5. A Doubt [Regarding the Relation Between the Divisions Simple/Personal and Common/Discrete]

There is some doubt regarding [the relation between] the second and third divisions, for some maintain that the division into simple and personal is a division [only] of common supposition, since that difference does not occur within discrete supposition.[25] This is because it is never anything but personal, since in discrete supposition an individual is always supposited.

We must point out, however, that it is not the fact that an individual is supposited that produces personal supposition, but the fact that a thing bearing the form signified by the name is supposited, and this can occur in a proper name when it signifies a substance together with a quality.[26] Thus when I say 'Socrates is running' it is with respect to his real being (*respicitur pro sua re*); when I say 'Socrates is predicable of one only'[27] it is with respect to the form signified by the name.

6. A Doubt [Regarding the Division Simple/Personal]

There is likewise some doubt regarding the division into simple and personal supposition, for this division seems to produce equivocation, since when a name supposits simply it presents to the understanding the form signified by the name, but when it supposits personally it presents a thing bearing the form.

We can respond to this just as to [the doubt regarding the division material/formal], or we can say that [in formal supposition a word] always supposits the same thing—viz., what it signifies—but in two ways: either *for* what it signifies (in which case it supposits simply) or for a thing signified[28] (in which case, personally).

7. A Note on the Three Modes of Simple Supposition

It should also be noted that simple supposition can occur in three ways, because there are three ways in which a word can be posited (*potest poni*) for its significatum[29]—[A] without any connection with things, or [B] for the significatum connected with things insofar as it is actually preserved in every single thing and is predicable of it, or [C] for the significatum connected with things insofar as it is related to anything generally, in an unfixed way, and is not identified with anything in a determinate way.

7.1. 'Man Is a Species'

The first mode occurs as follows: 'man is a species.' It is often said that this is manerial supposition, because ['man' here] supposits for the specific character in itself[30] (*suppositio manerialis, quia supponit pro ipsa manerie speciei*).

7.2. 'Man Is the Noblest of Creatures'

The second mode occurs as follows: 'man is the noblest of creatures.' This is unlike the preceding supposition since the predicate is not ascribed to the abstract species itself but to the species insofar as it is in things. Thus such a predicate can be ascribed to any of the things belonging to the species insofar as it shares the nature of the species; and so one can say 'this man, insofar as he is a man, is the noblest of creatures.' This [mode of simple] supposition occurs whenever the things belonging to a species acquire some predicate only with [that kind of] reduplication of the species and in no other way. Thus if I say 'man is an animal,' ['man' has] *personal* supposition, since the individuals acquire this predication without reduplication of the species.[31]

7.3. 'Pepper Is Sold Here and in Rome'

The third mode occurs as follows: 'pepper is sold here and in Rome.' This supposition is unlike the first, since the species itself is not sold, and unlike the second, since 'pepper' is not used here [for everything belonging to the species] insofar as it is pepper. Instead, 'pepper' here supposits for its significatum [as] related in a general, unfixed way to the things belonging to it. Thus it is often said that this is unfixed (*vaga*) supposition. [A term having this third mode of simple supposition] supposits for a species insofar as [it does so] through individuals belonging to the species, but undesignated (*non signata*). It is as if someone asked 'what animal is useful for plowing?' and one answered 'the ox'; in answering one does not intend to speak of a particular ox, but simply of *ox*. Likewise, whoever says 'pepper is sold here and in Rome' does not intend to speak of some pepper in particular, but simply of *pepper*.[32]

8. Question: [Whether Simple Supposition Is a Property of Predicates]

Suppose someone asks whether or not a word that occurs as a predicate predicates a form only and thus stands simply.[33] It seems it does not, for if that were the case one would truly say 'some species is a man' just as one says 'man is a species.'

We must point out, however, that this does not follow; for *every* name signifies a form only—not separately (*absolute*), but insofar as it informs a substance bearing it and thus in some way makes the substance intelligible. I maintain, therefore, that a name *in the predicate* makes a form intelligible to the extent to which it is the form of the substance of the subject;[34] and so, since that substance is understood in the subject, it is not understood a second time in the predicate. So the predicate does predicate (*dicit*) a form only.

Nevertheless, it is not true to say 'a species is a man,' since the word 'man' signifies humanity to the extent to which it is the form of [certain] individuals.[35] Therefore it is not predicated of the species, since it is not the form of the substance of the species. Note, moreover, that because a predicate is said to be in a subject, a form is always predicated to the extent to which it inheres in and informs [the substance of the subject].

A subject, on the other hand, sometimes supposits a form separately and sometimes does not, depending on what the predicate demands, in accordance with the following [principle]: *Subjects are of such sorts as the predicates may have allowed (talia sunt subiecta, qualia permiserint predicata).*

(It should be pointed out, however, that the authoritative opinion of Boethius is as follows: *Predicates are of such sorts as the subjects may have allowed, and not vice versa;* and his example in the same passage is 'a man is just; God is just,' the word 'just' being taken differently in the two cases, depending on what the subject demands.)[36]

9. Simple Supposition and Singular, Indefinite, or Particular Propositions

It seems that propositions such as 'man is a species' are singular since the subject is the proper name of a species.

We must point out, however, that this is not the case, for a common name is common just because it is a proper [name] of one form, and so to be proper in that respect is to be common. But if such propositions are indefinite, then it seems [A] they can be made definite through the application of a sign[37]—for example, one might say 'some man is a species.' And this seems right also because [B] particular and indefinite propositions are interchangeable.[38]

With respect to [A] we must point out that that procedure is to be understood [as applying only] to an indefinite proposition in which the supposition is particular;[39] in this case, however, it is applied to an indefinite proposition taken indefinitely (*indefinite sumpta*). Singular propositions taken indefinitely[40] are also of this sort, as are certain singulars taken universally— e.g., 'all (*totus*) Socrates is white.'[41]

With respect to [B] we must point out that particular and indefinite propositions are interchangeable not as regards the truth but as regards syllogistic procedure. This is

because anything that follows [syllogistically] from some proposition together with an indefinite proposition follows from that same proposition together with a particular proposition, and vice versa.

10. Question: [Whether Expressions Such as 'This Plant Grows Here and in My Garden Can Be True]

It is also asked whether these expressions can be true: [A] 'this plant grows here and in my garden';[42] [B] 'woman, who has damned us, has also saved us'[43] (*mulier que damnavit salvavit*). And it seems they cannot. This is because a demonstrative pronoun [as in [A]] indicates (*demonstrat*) something under such conditions as can be seen with one's own eyes; therefore it points out an individual. But [A] is false regarding an individual plant; therefore it is absolutely (*simpliciter*) false. Likewise, the purpose of a relative pronoun [as in [B]] is to bind the succeeding part of the sentence to the same suppositum with which the sentence began (*Item relativum ad hoc est, ut continet sequentem sermonem ad idem suppositum, de quo processit sermo*). But [if 'woman' is replaced] by the name of one and the same suppositum,[44] [B] is false (*Sed de nomine eiusdem suppositi est secundus sermo falsus*); therefore it is absolutely false.

In response to this we must point out that the term occurring with the demonstrative pronoun in [A] and the term occurring with the relative pronoun in [B] are suppositing simply in the third mode[45] (*in hiis sermonibus est demonstratio simpliciter et similiter relatio tertio modo*); for [the demonstrative pronoun] in [A] indicates *plant* insofar as it is related to more than one individual, which is also the way the relative pronoun functions in [B].

11. A Doubt [Regarding the Division Determinate/Confused]

There is some doubt regarding the division of personal into determinate and confused supposition, for it seems that when I say 'a man is running' the term 'man' does not supposit determinately, since [A] the proposition is indefinite, and [B] it is uncertain for whom the term 'man' supposits. Therefore it supposits [A] indefinitely and [B] uncertainly; therefore indeterminately.

In response we must point out that there is a respect in which determinateness is opposed to uncertainty, and in that respect we can say that 'man' supposits indeterminately, as the objection has it. There is, however, another respect in which determinateness is opposed to plurality (*multitudini*) and whatever is single is determinate; and in this respect 'man' does stand determinately. For the sentence 'a man is running' means that the predicate is in some one individual, not in many, even though the predicate *is* in many—for [a sentence] sometimes *permits* this but does not *signify* it[46] (*Vis enim huius sermonis vult predicatum inesse alicui uni et non multis, licet predicatum insit multis. Hoc enim patitur aliquando, sed non significat*). And therefore 'man' supposits determinately, not confusedly, since by virtue of the expression (*de virtute locutionis*)[47] [in which it occurs] it supposits for one and not for many.

12. A Note on Confused Supposition

Note that a word has confused supposition whenever it supposits either for many things or for one thing taken repeatedly with the capacity of keeping one and the same thing [constant] for many things (*pro uno multotiens sumpto cum potentia ibidem tenendi pro multis*)—e.g., 'if everyone sees only Socrates, then every man sees a man.' Here [the second occurrence of] 'man' does not supposit for many things, but for one thing taken repeatedly with the capacity of keeping one and the same thing [constant] for many things. Understand, moreover, that [that occurrence of] the word 'man' supposits virtually as many times as [there are individuals] that can be descended to in the subject (*ly hominem totiens supponit virtualiter, quotiens potest descendi in sub-*

iecto).[48] It is therefore important to know that every case of confused supposition is the result of (*omnis confusio est ab*) some distribution or something having the force of distribution.[49]

But suppose someone says 'every man sees Socrates.' Here 'Socrates,' although it supposits repeatedly, cannot be picked out separately (*cerni*) for many things. Therefore it does not stand confusedly.[50]

13. Rules Regarding Confused and Determinate Supposition[51]

13.1. Rule I

It is, then, considered to be a rule that [A] *every distributive sign confuses the term immediately adjoining it confusedly and distributively.* But [B] *an affirmative [distributive] sign confuses the remote term merely confusedly.* Finally, [C] *a negative [distributive][52] sign confuses the remote term confusedly and distributively.*

Thus this follows: 'no man is an ass; therefore no man is this ass.' But this does not follow: 'every man is an animal; therefore every man is this animal.'

13.2. Rule II

An argument from merely confused supposition to distributive confused supposition does not follow.

Thus when every man sees only himself this does not follow: 'every man a man does not see; therefore every man does not see a man.'[53]

13.3. Rule III

An argument from many cases of determinate supposition to one of determinate supposition does not follow, but [only] to one of confused supposition.

Thus when every man sees only himself this does not follow: 'a man is seen by Socrates, and by Plato (and so on with respect to [all] individual [men]); therefore a man is seen by every man.'[54] But this does follow: '. . . therefore by every man a man is seen,' for a distribution has force in a succeeding phrase but not in a preceding phrase (*in consequens et non in antecedens*).

13.4. Rule IV

An argument from determinate supposition to distributive confused supposition does follow, but not from merely confused supposition.

Thus this does not follow: 'a man is not seen by Socrates (*hominem non videt Sortes*);[55] therefore Socrates does not see a man'—as if there is only one he might see (*ut si videat unum solum*). But this follows correctly: 'a man is seen by every man; therefore every man sees a man.'

13.5. Rule V

An argument from distributive confused supposition to determinate supposition does follow, but not from merely confused supposition.

Thus this follows: 'Socrates does not see a man; therefore a man is not seen by Socrates.'[56] But this does not: 'every man sees a man (e.g., every man sees only himself); therefore a man is seen by every man.'[57]

Sometimes, however, distribution remains immobile, as in 'not every man is running,' 'only every man is running,' and other cases of that sort. It is called immobile, however, not because we cannot *ascend* in the subject but because we cannot *descend*.[58] This is due to the fact that distribution is of the supposita themselves,[59] and therefore when we cannot descend to one of them[60] (*ad hoc*) it is a case of what is properly called immobile distribution.[61]

Supposition is called immobile for a similar reason, viz., that we cannot descend to the supposita; for supposition is for a suppositum.[62]

14. Copulation[63]

As to copulation, it should be known that none of the following divisions applies to it: [A] material/formal, [B] common/discrete, [C] simple/personal. The reasons are as follows:[64] [A] if a copulating word[65] is posited (*ponitur*) *materially* it is said to sup-

posit and not to copulate; [B] every copulating word is the name of an accident, but every name of an accient is common; therefore no copulation is *discrete*; [C] every copulating word signifies in adjunction to a substantive (*in adiacentia ad substantivam*)[66] and thus is copulated *personally* [if at all].

We do, however, find the following divisions in copulation: determinate/confused (determinate as in 'a man is white,' confused as in 'every man is white'); merely confused/distributive confused (merely confused as in the last example, distributive confused as in 'no man is white'). Distributive confused copulation occurs in connection with signs distributive of the copulata, such as 'of every sort' (*qualislibet*), 'of every amount'[67] (*quantuslibet*), and the like. Note that signs of that kind distribute the copulata in respect of their substantives; it is for this reason that the kind of copulation they give rise to (*unde sua copulatio*) is distributive. On the other hand, their substantives have merely confused supposition.[68] For example, when I say 'a man of every sort is running' the copulation is distributed; I can therefore descend to the specific copulata (*copulata specialia*) as follows: 'a man of every sort is running; therefore a white man is running, and a black [man is running], (and so on).' But the word 'man' [in the premiss] supposits merely confusedly, since we cannot descend as follows: 'a man of every sort ... therefore Socrates ...'[69] A sign such as 'of every sort' signifies some accident and distributes it in respect of its substantive.[70]

We also find immobile distributive copulation, as in 'not every sort of ...'

Note also that where the inference does not hold (*ubi non tenet processus*) from the supposition to a suppositum it does not hold from the copulation to a copulatum.[71]

15. Appellation

We have yet to examine appellation, which has already been defined.[72]

The difference between it and supposition is clear from its definition—i.e., supposition is in a term insofar as it is under another, but appellation is in a term insofar as it is [truly] predicable of the things subordinate to it (*predicabilis de suis rebus*) through the use of the verb 'is.' [The difference between appellation] and copulation [is likewise clear from the definition of appellation], because copulation is never lacking in a term when it is as such capable of being ordered over something else (*et ad copulationem, quia ipsa nunquam, cum est secundum se ordinabilis supra aliud, [non] inest termino*).[73]

Accordingly some say[74] that a term serving as a subject (*ex parte subiecti*) supposits and that it appellates when it serves as a predicate. And it is true that a term serving as a subject supposits in accordance with both definitions of supposition,[75] while a term serving as a predicate supposits [only] in accordance with the [second] definition of supposition [as a signification of something as subsisting] (*secundum habitualem suam diffinitionem*).

It is also true, however, that a term serving as a subject appellates the things subordinate to it, but not as a result of its being a subject. A term serving as a predicate, on the other hand, does appellate as a result of its being a predicate, [because a predicate] is related to its subject through some of the things subordinate to it, and in that capacity it appellates.

16. A Rule Regarding Supposition and Appellation

Notice that sometimes a suppositum of a term is something that exists and at other times something that does not exist. An appellatum, on the other hand, is simply something that exists. Thus a suppositum and an appellatum are sometimes the same and at other times not; and the following rule is given for the purpose of determining when they are and when they are not the same: *An unrestricted common term, having*

sufficient appellata and suppositing in connection with a present-tense verb that has no ampliating force, supposits only for those [things subordinate to it] that do exist.[76]

16.1. "Unrestricted"

The reason for adding the word "unrestricted" is that if a common term is restricted it can supposit for something that does not exist—e.g., a man who has been [but is not now] is something that does not exist. Understand that to restrict something is, strictly speaking, to force it to exist in a smaller space than it is naturally suited for (*quam sue nature competit*). Because of its resemblance [to restriction in the strict sense], a relative clause (*implicatio*)[77] is also called [restriction]. [Finally,] an adjectival word is likewise said to restrict a common term.[78]

Thus the word "unrestricted" here is to be understood [as ruling out those] three kinds of restriction and not [the kind that occurs] in connection with a verb. [A verb,] however, may sometimes restrict, as in 'a man runs.'[79] The term 'man' as such can supposit for past, present, and future men, but here it is confined to present men by the verb in the present tense.[80]

16.2. "Having Sufficient Appellata"

The reason for adding the phrase "having sufficient appellata" is that if [a common term] does not have sufficient appellata it can supposit for something that does not exist. And notice that sufficient appellata amount to at least three; therefore if there are not that many appellata a term can supposit for something that does not exist—e.g., if there are only two men 'every man exists' is false.

Proof: The sign 'every' is imposed for the purpose of distributing for the greatest plurality and the sign 'both' for the least. Therefore since the least plurality is in a pair, the sign 'both' distributes only for two. But the greater plurality is in a group of three or more; therefore the sign 'every' distributes for at least three.[81] Therefore, since in the example above there are two supposita existing and the sentence means (*et vult iste sermo*) that the predicate is in [at least] three, it means that it is in something that does not exist. And so 'every man exists' is false and its contradictory, 'some man does not exist,' is true. Therefore a man does not exist. But nonexistence is not predicated of something that exists; therefore 'man' supposits for something that does not exist.

But [suppose someone says that] on the contrary 'every animal exists' is true and therefore 'every man exists' is true, for the term 'animal' has enough appellata.

[In that case] we must point out that in the case [in which there are only two men] this does not follow: 'every animal exists; therefore every man exists,' because the term 'animal' does have sufficient appellata, and so supposits only for what exists, while 'man' does not, and so supposits for something that does not exist. And by the same reasoning this does not hold: 'a man does not exist; therefore an animal does not exist.'

But again, consider this counterargument: 'every animal is, every man is an animal; therefore every man is.'[82] The first premiss is true, and the second is necessary, since the genus is predicated of a species.

[In response to this] we must point out that the argument is not valid (*non valet*), for when one says 'every animal is' one predicates *actual* being (*esse actuale*)—i.e., existence. But when I say 'every man is an animal' *relational* being (*esse habituale*) is predicated, and insofar as it is necessary it has the force of this conditional: 'if it is a man it is an animal' (*Si homo est, animal est*). For when 'is' is placed as a kind of means between the extremes 'a man' and 'an animal' it declares an interrelation between the two (*dicit habitudinem mediam inter hec duo*). Thus it is clear that the signification of 'is' in the first proposition differs from that in the second. Therefore the conclusion 'every man is' does not follow.

Nevertheless it may seem that 'every man is' is true because Aristotle says that the principle of *dici de omni* applies

whenever there is nothing . . . etc.[83] But nothing is to be found under this subject . . . etc., since there exist only two men of whom the predicate is asserted. Therefore this is an instance of *dici de omni*.

But we must point out that the term 'man' [in our example] does supposit for a nonexistent man, and that therefore there is something nonexistent under the term, to which the predicate does not apply. Therefore this is not an instance of *dici de omni*.

16.3. "Suppositing in Connection with a Present-Tense Verb"

The reason for adding the phrase "suppositing in connection with a present-tense verb" is that if the common term were to supposit in connection with a past-tense or future-tense verb it could supposit for something that does not exist. 'A man has run,'[84] for example, is true for Caesar.

[In this connection] it is customary to call attention to the following rule: *A common term suppositing in connection with a past-tense verb supposits for present things as well as for past things; likewise a common term suppositing in connection with a future-tense verb supposits for present things as well as for future things.*[85]

But [suppose someone says that] on the contrary the verb through its consignification of time *restricts* what the term supposits, and therefore a past-tense verb restricts it to past things and a future-tense verb to future things.[86]

Then we must point out that sentences such as 'a man has run,'[87] in which a past-tense (or future-tense) verb is predicated, have two senses (*sunt duplices*); for this sentence can be said to be either compounded or divided[88] (*dici compositus vel divisus*).

If compounded, it must be pronounced with continuity (*continue proferri*), and the continuity of the subject with the predicate signifies that the supposition [of the subject] must be strictly indicated (*discerni*) by the predicate.[89] In that case 'man' [in 'a man has run'] supposits for past [men] and not for present [men] except insofar as they are past.[90]

If divided, it must be pronounced with

discontinuity (as in 'a man has run'),[91] and the discontinuity of the expression signifies that the supposition [of the subject] is not strictly indicated by the predicate.[92]

That is how [this] rule is to be understood. Thus this does not follow: 'something white was seen by Socrates; therefore Socrates has seen something white,' as, for example, if a shield is white now but was black when it was seen by Socrates. I maintain that it does not follow if the premiss (*antecedens*) is divided. It does follow, however, if the premiss is compounded.[93]

And [the portion of this rule] having to do with a future-tense verb is to be understood as follows: A common term [suppositing in connection with a future-tense verb] with reference to [things existing] before [the time of utterance] supposits for present or future things through composition and division, but with reference to [things existing] after [the time of utterance it supposits] only for future things (*Et sic intelligendum est de verbo de futuro scilicet quod terminus communis ex parte ante supponit pro presentibus vel futuribus per compositionem et divisionem, ex parte autem post solum pro futuris*).[94]

16.4. "That Has No Ampliating Force"

The reason for adding the phrase "that has no ampliating force" is that if the verb is an ampliating verb the subject can supposit for something that does not exist. 'A man is praised,' for example, is true for Caesar. An ampliating verb is one that signifies a condition that can occur in something that does not exist[95] (*cuius res potest inesse non enti*).

But [suppose someone says that] on the contrary a verb *restricts* the supposition of a term. Therefore it does so either through its signification or through its consignification. If through its signification, then, as-suming that [at least] three men exist,[96] 'every man is running' is true, which is false (*ergo tribus hominibus existentibus hec est vera: omnis homo currit. Quod falsum est.*).[97] If through its consignification, it will not be through any [consignification] other than its consignification of time. Therefore

every present-tense verb restricts [the supposition of the subject] to present things. Therefore when I say 'a man is praised' the term 'man' supposits [only] for present things.

[In response to this] we must point out that a verb does not restrict exclusively through its signification or through its consignification but through both. Therefore a present-tense verb forces (*cogit*) a term to supposit[98] for those things in which the condition it signifies (*sua res*) can occur [at present]. Thus, since the condition signified by the verb 'is praised' occurs at present in things that do not exist, the verb will ampliate to the extent of including [within the supposition of 'man'] something that does not exist. (The verb 'can' and others like it[99] are to be similarly treated.)

Thus it is clear why (assuming [at least] three men exist) 'every man exists' is true, but (assuming [at least] three men are running) 'every man is running' is false. It is because 'to exist' (*ly esse*) cannot occur at present in things that do not exist but is actually in all things that do exist, while 'to run' cannot occur at present in things that [do exist but] are not running.[100]

When all these conditions are observed the suppositum will be the same as the appellatum.[101]

Or, putting it another way, if we want to speak strictly we say that a term supposits on its own (*de se*) for present things and if it supposits for other things it will be because of what is adjoined to it—i.e., an ampliating verb or a past-tense verb or future-tense verb. And the ampliation will not be the result exclusively of the signification or of the consignification [of the verb] but will occur by virtue of both.

Thus when I say 'a man is running,' 'man' supposits on its own for present [men] and is not drawn away from that supposition by the predicate (*ad predicatum*). But if someone says 'a man is running or can run,' the supposition [of 'man'] is already drawn away in the sense of what I call composition to [men] that do not exist.[102]

Therefore, speaking strictly, we must say that the verb 'can' and others like it ampliate the supposition of a term while the verb 'is running' and others like it do not restrict [the supposition of] a term since a term supposits on its own for present things. And I say that the term 'man' does supposit on its own for present [men] because it signifies a form in relation to the

things subordinate to the form; but that relation is preserved only in [men] that exist and, speaking strictly, it is for those [men] that exist that the term supposits on its own.

Let these remarks on the properties of terms suffice.

NOTES

1. On this chapter generally, see Kneale, *The Development of Logic* (Oxford: The Clarendon Press, 1962), pp. 246–265.
2. Cf. John of Salisbury, *Metalogicon* (tr. McGarry), pp. 125–128 and 134, for passages illustrating the twelfth-century background of this doctrine of signification and of the (then implicit) distinction between signification and other properties of terms.
3. These initial definitions seem unnecessarily vague and play no important part in the remainder of the chapter. Supposition is discussed in detail in the sections immediately following. On copulation see p. 670. Cf. also the somewhat different definitions of supposition, copulation, and appellation on pp. 670–71.
4. I.e., everything with which the term "goes together" (*convenit*) at the present time. See n. 73 and 74, this chapter.
5. On appellation see pp. 670–71.
6. G (Grabmann's edition of Sherwood's *Introduction to Logic*) has '*significatio non est*' (with no indication that the '*non*' is an emendation); '*significatio est*' in manuscript.
7. By 'substantive word' (*dictio*) as distinct from 'substantive name' Sherwood probably means substantive expressions, such as definite descriptions—'the father of the bride,' 'this man over here.'
8. Note the discrepancy between this claim about pronouns and the claims on pp. 664–65 that signification is the presentation of a form and that every part of speech has signification. Cf. n. 11, this chapter.
9. Viz., the verb 'to be.'
10. The basis for this restriction is the traditional classification of the verb and the participle as distinct parts of speech, the participle "participating" in the characters of both the verb and the name (substantive or adjective). Evidently in 'Socrates is white' the adjective 'white' signifies something—whiteness—attached to something else and does so by means of the substantive verb, while in 'Socrates runs' the verb 'runs' does not by means of the substantive verb signify running as something attached to something else. As Aristotle and the medievals (including Sherwood) recognized, however, 'Socrates runs' may be analyzed into 'Socrates is running,' which does employ a participle and the substantive verb. Sherwood evidently would allow that in such a case the participle does signify by means of the substantive verb something attached to something else.
11. As this sentence suggests, the supposition, copulation, and appellation of a term are functions of its signification. It is evidently for this reason that Sherwood believes that he can treat the four properties of terms without providing a specific treatment of signification.
12. See pp. 669–70 ff.
13. Among several twelfth-century sources for the doctrine of supposition, the doctrine of univocation has many instructive parallels, in its "divisions" as well as in the central notion. See, e.g., the anonymous twelfth-century *Fallacie parvipontane* (ed. De Rijk, *Logica modernorum*, Vol. I), p. 562: "Univocation is the varied supposition of a name, the signification remaining the same; for although supposition varies, signification remains the same." The treatise goes on to discuss three kinds of univocation. The first includes *both* 'master' in 'master is a noun' and 'man' in 'man is a species'. The second includes *both* 'man' in 'man is the noblest of creatures' and 'pepper' in 'pepper is sold here and in Rome.' The third introduces the notions of ampliation and restriction. (See De Rijk, *Logica modernorum*, Vol. I, pp. 561–571 and 51–56.) Sherwood discusses these (or very similar) examples and introduces the notions of ampliation and restriction later in this chapter.
14. Some insight into the origin of this division and its terminology may be found in John of Salisbury's *Metalogicon* (tr. McGarry), p. 175.
15. Cf. John of Salisbury's *Metalogicon* (tr. McGarry), p. 119: "Our understanding at times looks directly at the simple essence of things, simply, as when it conceives of *man* as such, or *stone* as such, in which operation it is simple."
16. It seems that the first occurrence of 'what it signifies' is intended to distinguish simple supposition (as

a division of formal supposition) from the kind just discussed (material), in which a word supposited something other than what it signified. The second occurrence of 'what it signifies' indicates that in simple supposition the suppositum is *a form* which, on p. 664, was said to be the significatum of every word.

17. The force of this observation might be made plainer by adopting the ordinarily unnatural translation 'man runs' (rather than 'a man is running') for the example *'homo currit.'*

18. Cf. William of Sherwood's *Introduction to Logic* (tr. Kretzmann), p. 51.

19. Expounding the location seems tantamount to answering the question 'which one?' or attaching a namely-rider to a case of determinate supposition—'a man, namely Socrates, is running.' Cf. Geach, *Reference*, p. 64.

20. Sherwood's notion of a logical descent is quite stringent as compared, say, with Ockham's (see *Philosophical Writings*, tr. Boehner, pp. 71–74). It seems clear from this and other passages—e.g., p. 666 and p. 670—that Sherwood means by 'descent' a valid inference from an original proposition whose subject is a common term to a single singular proposition whose subject is a discrete term under the original common term in the "predicamental line." Thus where Ockham will descend from 'every man is running' to the exhaustive conjunction 'man$_1$ is running and man$_2$ is running and . . . and man$_n$ is running,' which Ockham seems to have considered equivalent to the original proposition, Sherwood's descent is unquestionably irreversible—'therefore this man is running.' (Cf., however, his descent in the case of "distributive copulation," on p. 670.)

21. For a further discussion of "immobility," see p. 670 below. Cf. also Sherwood's *Syncategoremata*, where such examples are frequently discussed. Of course one cannot infer the exhaustive conjunction of singular propositions here, but in accordance with Ockham's notion of descent it seems correct to infer a proposition the subject of which is an exhaustive conjunction of discrete terms under the original common term. 'Only every man is running; therefore only man$_1$ and man$_2$ and . . . and man$_n$ are running.' As far as I know, Ockham does not, however, produce this result. Cf. Geach's discussion of "conjunctive supposition," *Reference*, p. 72.

22. I.e., a case of distributive supposition that is not embedded in another syntactic context. Cf. Sherwood's remarks about supposition *de se,* or *secundum se,* William of Sherwood's *Introduction to Logic* (tr. Kretzmann), pp. 130–131.

23. E.g., the predicates *'est nomen'* and *'est species'* respectively, when attached to *'homo.'*

24. This sentence seems to contain a clue to the motivation behind supposition theory. The *definition* is supposed to provide the fixed signification—e.g., 'man' considered in itself always does or should present the form *mortal rational animal*. But there are countless legitimate uses of the word 'man' that cannot be explained if we are provided with no other account of its meaning than the simple, rigid signification presented in the definition. That supplementary account of the meaning of a term as a function of its various uses is provided in supposition theory.

25. Peter of Spain divides supposition first into discrete and common, common supposition into natural and accidental, and accidental (common) supposition into simple and personal (*Sum. log.*, ed. Bocheński, p. 58), thus taking the position opposed here by Sherwood. Ockham, on the other hand, considers the division common/discrete to be a division only of *personal* supposition (*Summa logicae*, tr. Boehner in *Philosophical Writings*, p. 70).

26. Priscian (*Inst. gram.*, 1.55) says that *every* name signifies a substance together with a quality. Cf. Abelard, *Dialectica* (ed. De Rijk), p. 93, lines 5–6. Sherwood's use of this doctrine to support the division of discrete (as well as common) supposition into simple and personal seems quite unusual, as does his arrangement of those divisions.

27. See p. 668, on singular propositions "taken indefinitely." See also n. 69, this chapter.

28. This must be elliptical for 'or for a thing bearing the form signified.'

29. The translation 'what it signifies' for *'significatum'* seems clumsy in the context of this note and is therefore temporarily abandoned.

30. G has *'suppositio materialis'*; *'suppositio manerialis'* in manuscript. Cf. Kneale, *Development*, p. 255. On the notion of *maneries*, apparently a twelfth-century innovation, see John of Salisbury, *Metalogicon* (tr. McGarry), p. 116; also De Rijk, *Logica modernorum*, Vol. I, p. 139.

31. If 'man is the noblest of creatures' were a case of personal supposition, the following descent would be valid: 'therefore this man is the noblest of creatures, or that man . . .' The reduplication of the species is the insertion of the phrase 'insofar as he is a man,' which validates the descent to 'therefore this man, insofar as he is a man, is the noblest of creatures, and that man . . .' But the need for reduplication in the descent marks this as simple rather than personal. Ockham attacks this kind of treatment of this example and claims that 'man' here has *personal* supposition but that the proposition is false "taken literally as it stands" (*de virtute sermonis*) (*Summa logicae*, 1.66).

32. Ockham likewise opposes the treatment of this example as an instance of simple supposition. Again he thinks the statement is false "taken literally as it stands" and that it must be analyzed into 'pepper is sold here and pepper is sold in Rome,' as a result of which analysis it becomes interpretable as two

distinct instances of *personal* supposition (*Summa logicae* 1.66). (For another treatment of this example see n. 13, this chapter.) Sherwood's point in the ox example might be described (anachronistically) as an observation that not only mass nouns such as 'pepper' but also count nouns such as 'ox' admit of "unfixed supposition"—e.g., 'The ox has been domesticated for centuries in Europe and Asia.'

33. Reading '*et sic stet simpliciter*' for '*et si stet simpliciter.*' Sherwood sometimes, as here, uses 'stands' where he ordinarily uses 'supposits'; cf. pp. 669–70.
34. Making a form intelligible by supplying an instantiation of it.
35. Cf. p. 674.
36. At this point Grabmann supplies a reference to Boethius's *Introductio ad syllogismos categoricos* (Migne, *P.L.*, 64.768). Neither the principle as Sherwood cites it nor the examples he quotes appear there. In 768B Boethius does indicate that a singular subject has a certain effect over its predicate, and he introduces the verb '*suppono*' in an interesting way: "in singular propositions an individual is always supposited by the predicate term, as in 'Socrates is wise,' for Socrates is singular and individual . . ." The nearest approach to the principle in column 768 appears at 768C: "A subject is that which supports the expression (*dictionem*) of the predicate . . ." There is at least a suggestion of the example Sherwood cites in 780C–781A, but the passage is badly confused, and it is difficult to know exactly what Boethius intended to illustrate by means of it.
37. I.e., a word such as 'every,' 'some,' or 'no'.
38. Cf. William of Sherwood's *Introduction to Logic* (tr. Kretzmann), p. 30.
39. I.e., *determinate* supposition, as in the indefinite proposition 'a man is running' (*homo currit*).
40. See p. 666—'Socrates is predicable of one thing only.'
41. Cf. Sherwood's *Syncategoremata* (ed. O'Donnell), p. 54.
42. Cf. Ockham's discussion of this example (*Philosophical Writings*, tr. Boehner, pp. 70–71).
43. An allusion to Eve, on the one hand, and Mary on the other. Cf. John of Salisbury, *Metalogicon* (tr. McGarry), pp. 124–125: "However, there are also relations that are general, which, if they are to remain true and are to be properly understood, cannot be tied down to some particular subject. Examples of such are provided by the sayings: 'A woman both saved us and damned us'; 'A tree both bore the cause of our death, and that of our life'; 'The green leaves, which the freezing north wind bears off, the mild west wind restores.' In the instances which I have just mentioned, I believe that these relative expressions should not be conceived as descending to the specific and pointing out some particular person or thing, but rather that they should be understood as remaining general . . ." Cf. also *Secundum Magistrum Petrum Sententie*, XXIV (*Abaelardiana inedita*, ed. Minio-Paluello, p. 118): "When we say 'woman, who has damned us, has also saved us,' [we are speaking] not of one and the same person but of the nature of the female sex . . . for Eve damned us and Mary saved us. Neither does Priscian treat a construction of this kind as related to a person—viz., where he discusses the word '*sui*' " (Cf. Priscian, *Inst. gram.*, 12.1–3).
44. I.e., both 'Eve, who has damned us, has saved us' and 'Mary, who has damned us, has saved us' are false, and, a fortiori, so are all other such instances.
45. Although '*suppositio*' is not used in this passage, the reference is obviously to the third mode of simple supposition (see p. 667). The phrase '*demonstratio simpliciter*' is usually used to designate a logical demonstration which simply confirms a truth as distinguished from argumentative demonstrations such as ad hominem or *ad contradicendum*. Here, however, it must be a variant of '*demonstratio simplex*,' which might be read 'simple supposition in connection with a demonstrative pronoun.' Aquinas distinguishes *demonstratio simplex* and *demonstratio personalis* on the same grounds as are used to distinguish simple and personal supposition (see Deferrari, *Lexicon*, "*demonstratio*").
46. Cf. Peter of Spain, *Sum. log.* (ed. Bocheński), p. 59: "Determinate supposition is the acceptance of a common term taken indefinitely or together with a particular sign—e.g., 'a man is running,' or 'some man is running.' Each of these is called determinate since the term 'man' in each of them may legitimately supposit for every man, not running as well as running. Nevertheless these propositions are true for any single running man; for it is one thing to supposit and another to render an expression true for something in predicates (*reddere locutionem veram pro aliquo in praedicatis*). In fact, as has been said, the term 'man' supposits for all [men], not running as well as running, but it renders the expression true only for one that is running."
47. Cf. Ockham's frequent use of '*de virtute sermonis*' in *Summa logicae* (ed. Boehner), 1.66 ff. Cf. n. 31, this chapter.
48. The example under discussion is '*si quilibet videat Sortem tantum, tunc omnis homo videt hominem,*' and Sherwood's first remark on this example begins "*Hic homo non supponit pro multis . . .*" This wording might suggest that he intends this remark to apply to the *subject* of the consequent rather than the inflected form '*hominem*,' but the kind of confused supposition he describes can scarcely be considered a property of the subject. In his second remark on this example he does talk explicitly about the occurrence of '*hominem*,' but notice that when he does so he introduces it with '*ly*'. This medieval particle (frequently written '*li*') seems simply to indicate that one is referring to a particular *occurrence*

of the word in question, so that 'ly' (or 'li') might be viewed as a precursor of quotation marks employed to distinguish between "mentioning" a word and "using" it. Thus in discussing the example in the paragraph just below Sherwood says "hic Sortes licet supponit multotiens . . ." although the proper name occurs in the example in the inflected form 'Sortem.'

The second remark on the example seems to mean that we may infer from 'if everyone sees only Socrates, then every man sees a man' that if everyone sees only Socrates, then Plato sees a man, and Aristotle sees a man, and so on, and that in each conjunct in this descent 'man' supposits once for Socrates, now as the object of Plato's sight, now as the object of Aristotle's, and so on.

49. The word 'not', for example, although it is not a distributive sign, may count as "something having the force of distribution." See n. 52, this chapter.

50. I.e., it does not supposit confusedly (see n. 33, this chapter) but determinately (and discretely). (This paragraph occurs in the original between the second and third sentences of the preceding paragraph.)

51. On these rules, see Kneale, *Development*, pp. 258–259.

52. Part A of Rule I and the two examples following part C support the interpolation of the word 'distributive' in part C. Sherwood may, however, intend part C to apply also to such negative signs as 'not' (non), since the predicate term of the particular negative—'some man is not a philosopher'—would probably also be said to have distributive confused supposition. See also the conclusion of the inference illustrating Rule II, where an occurrence of 'not' is evidently taken to produce distributive confused supposition in the predicate term of a universal affirmative proposition.

53. The premiss of this example—'omnis homo hominem non videt'—seems correctly analyzable as 'for every man there is at least one man whom he does not see,' and on that analysis the premiss is true under the stated assumption that every man sees only himself. The conclusion—'omnis homo non videt hominem'—is intended to be equivalent to 'no man sees a man,' as is clear from Sherwood's discussion of equipollent signs in Chapter One. Thus the second occurrence of 'man' in the premiss has merely confused supposition while the second occurrence of 'man' in the conclusion has distributive confused supposition as the predicate of a universal negative proposition. (See Rule I, part C.)

54. The premiss as it stands is a single proposition with what might be described as a conjunction of discrete terms in the predicate, but taken as it stands the premiss is false under the stated condition and the inference is valid. Evidently Sherwood intended a conjunction of propositions as the premiss— viz., 'a man is seen by Socrates, and a man is seen by Plato, and . . .'—otherwise he would not even have his "many cases of determinate supposition" in the premiss.

55. Here as elsewhere Latin active constructions must be translated into English passive constructions in order to avoid ambiguity.

56. G has 'hominem videt Sortes'; 'hominem non videt Sortes' in manuscript.

57. "In effect the fourth of the rules . . . provides that a doubly general proposition with an existential quantifier in front of a universal quantifier implies the corresponding doubly general proposition with quantifiers transposed, while the fifth rightly rejects the converse implication" (Kneale, *Development*, p. 259).

58. On immobile distributive supposition and logical descent see p. 666. Sherwood's notion of a logical ascent is probably that of a valid inference from a single singular proposition whose subject is a discrete term to a proposition whose subject is a common term over that discrete term in the predicamental line. His remark and examples here are evidently intended to show that since logical ascent is possible in *some* of these cases—e.g., his first example here—it is the general impossibility of logical descent despite the occurrence of a universal sign that is the criterion of immobility. (In the first of these examples Ockham's notion of logical descent would produce 'it is not the case that every man is running; therefore either it is not the case that man_1 is running, or it is not the case that man_2 is running, or . . . or it is not the case than man_n is running,' where the alternation is exhaustive. But for Ockham this descent would indicate that 'man' in 'not every man is running' had *determinate* supposition. See *Philosophical Writings*, tr. Boehner, p. 71.)

59. Since the discussion here is only of varieties of *personal* supposition, the supposita are the individuals of which a given common term may be truly predicated.

60. I.e., despite the occurrence of a universal sign.

61. Note that Sherwood is speaking of distribution, not of distributive supposition, and that he goes on to make similar remarks about (distributive) supposition in the next paragraph. Distribution does not seem to be a thoroughly distinct or carefully developed notion in Sherwood's book, but Peter of Spain devotes an entire chapter (Tractatus XII) to "Distribution," beginning with the following definition: "Distribution is the multiplication of a common term accomplished by means of a universal sign— e.g., when one says 'every man is running,' the term 'man' is distributed or confused for any of its inferiors by means of the sign 'every,' and so there is multiplication there" (Sum. log., ed. Bocheński, p. 112). (Incidentally, passages such as this contradict Geach's claim, on p. 63 of *Reference*, that "the expression 'distributed term' is in fact a muddled memory of the medieval '[suppositio confusa et] distributiva'." The distinction between distribution and distributive supposition as well as the expres-

sion 'distributed term' are themselves medieval, though they do seem muddled.) I can see no clear difference between the notions of distribution and distributive supposition in Sherwood unless it is that distribution emphasizes considerations of syntax and distributive supposition has more to do with semantical considerations. But even that is not an especially clear difference.

62. There may be some clue to Sherwood's basis for distinguishing distribution from distributive supposition in the fact that he says that distribution is *of* the supposita themselves (*ipsorum suppositorum*) whereas supposition is *for* a supposition (*pro supposito*).

63. On the nature of copulation cf. pp. 664–65 and p. 670. Sherwood's notion of copulation as a property of terms is obscure and apparently different from the notions of copulation discussed by other medieval logicians. Peter of Spain, for example, has nothing on copulation in his *Summulae logicales* except the following remark in the chapter on supposition: "Copulation is the acceptance of an adjectival term for something" (ed. Bocheński, p. 58), having said a few lines earlier that "substantival names are said to supposit, while adjectival names as well as verbs are said to copulate" (p. 57). Lambert of Auxerre defines copulation as "the acceptance of a term [as] representing a dependent thing"—i.e., not a substance—and says that adjectives never supposit but only copulate (in Prantl, *Geschichte*, 3.31.127). By the time Walter Burleigh wrote his *De puritate artis logicae tractatus longior* (hereafter cited as *De puritate artis logicae*) (between 1325 and 1328) copulation apparently had lost its connection with supposition theory and was defined simply as "the union or composition of a predicate with a subject" (Boehner ed., p. 54). Cf. Mullally on this notion and its probable source in Boethius and Abelard in his partial edition and translation of the *Summulae logicales* of Peter of Spain, pp. xliv–xlv.

64. The order of explanations here is revised from the original order so as to conform to the order of the divisions in the preceding sentence.

65. Evidently a copulating word is (a) the name of an accident, (b) a word joined to a subject term somehow, especially by means of an occurrence of 'is' or 'are', the copula. But not every such word has copulation. E.g., "the last word in the sentence is 'white'," where 'white' is a copulating word that has material supposition rather than copulation.

66. See p. 664. Reading "*substantivam*" for "*substantiam.*"

67. Just as '*quilibet*,' ordinarily translated 'anyone', must frequently be translated 'everyone' when found in medieval texts, so here the ordinary translations 'of any sort whatever' and 'of any amount whatever' must be altered. See Sherwood's example of distributive copulation in this paragraph. Cf. his treatment of '*qualelibet*', introduced as a sign distributive of copulata, in his *Syncategoremata* (ed. O'Donnell), pp. 55–56.

68. "The copulata" are instances of the accident(s) signified by the copulating word(s); "their substantives" are the common terms occurring as subjects in connection with the copulating words. The individuals, or substances, are the supposita of the substantives, and the accidents said to inhere in them are the copulata of the copulating words. Since "distribution is of the supposita themselves" (p. 670), and since accidents do not occur except as inhering in individuals, distributive copulation must distribute the copulata as inhering in the supposita for which the substantive in the proposition is suppositing. Nevertheless, the substantive itself will have merely confused (rather than distributive confused) supposition in cases where the copulating word has distributive copulation. (This seems to be the gist of Sherwood's doctrine here.)

69. On logical descent, see n. 20, this chapter. Here Sherwood refuses to take the discrete term 'Socrates' as naming a *sort* of man, but cf. p. 666.

70. 'Of every sort' ('*qualislibet*') thus combines the roles of copulating word and distributive sign into one word in Latin although the roles are played by separate words in the English translation.

71. A medieval note in the margin of the manuscript at this point reads: "He says this because the rules given for supposition on the preceding page [pp. 669–70] hold likewise for copulation." Whether or not those rules do hold for copulation, the passage does not seem to have the purpose assigned it in this note, since those rules govern inferences from one kind of supposition to another kind of supposition, not "from the supposition to a suppositum." That phrase is certainly ambiguous, but it does suggest the sort of inference involved in Sherwood's notion of descent. He may, then, be pointing out that descent is blocked in copulation just as in supposition, an interpretation rendered more plausible by the fact that this passage immediately follows his remarks on *immobile* distributive copulation.

72. On pp. 664–65.

73. I have inserted the word '*non*' before '*inest termino*' because the sense of the passage seems to demand it. Without this interpolation the English would read "because copulation is never in a term when . . ." With this interpolation the passage presents the distinction between copulation and appellation as based on the fact that copulation is a permanent property of such terms as it belongs to at all whereas the question of whether or not a term has appellation depends on the present existence of individuals bearing the form signified by the term. On pp. 664–65 copulation is said to occur in adjectives, participles, and *verbs* while appellation is a property only of adjectives, participles, and *substantives*. Evidently this distinction is intended to apply only to adjectives and participles.

74. I do not know which of Sherwood's contemporaries or predecessors maintained this distinction. Walter Burleigh, whose book was written about eighty years *after* Sherwood's, says "just as supposition strictly speaking is a property of the subject in so far as it is related to the predicate, so appellation is a property of the predicate related to the subject or to what is subordinate" (*De puritate artis logicae,* ed. Boehner, p. 47).

75. A medieval note in the margin of the manuscript at this point reads: "Given above at the beginning of the third folio before this one"—i.e., on p. 664.

76. G has '*suppositiones*'; '*supponens*' in manuscript. Pp. 671–74 contain a detailed explanation and discussion of the various conditions laid down in this rule, as the inserted subsection headings will indicate. On this rule and Sherwood's explication of it, see Kneale, *Development,* pp. 260–262.

77. Reading '*implicatio*' for '*inplicatio.*' On this technical sense of the word see Sherwood's *Syncategoremata* (ed. O'Donnell), pp. 50–51.

78. The text is unusually compressed here and quite possibly corrupt. At the beginning of the next paragraph Sherwood refers to three kinds of restriction, which are evidently supposed to have been introduced in this paragraph, and distinguishes them from a fourth. It seems highly plausible that the intended distinctions are analogous to those developed in Tractatus XI, "On Restrictions," in the *Summulae logicales* of Peter of Spain (ed. Bocheński, p. 104): "Restriction is the contraction of a common term from a greater to a lesser supposition. . . . One kind of restriction occurs as a result of an [*adjectival*] *name,* as when someone says 'white man', the term 'man' does not supposit for black men nor for those colored with any color in between [black and white], but is restricted to white men. A [second] kind occurs as a result of a *verb,* as when someone says 'a man runs', the term 'man' supposits for, or is restricted [to], presently existing men. A [third] kind occurs as a result of a *participle,* as in 'a running man argues'; the term 'man' is restricted to running men. A [fourth] kind occurs as a result of a relative clause (*implicationem*), as when someone says 'a man who is white is running', the relative clause 'who is white' restricts the term 'man' to white men (*restringit homines ad albos*)." Peter's second kind is explicitly treated by Sherwood in the next paragraph, and the fourth and first kinds seem to have been mentioned by name in this paragraph. If there *is* a third kind of restriction mentioned in this paragraph, I suppose it could be Peter's third kind, although the description of restriction "strictly speaking" more nearly resembles the kind of general description with which Peter begins his account.

79. '*Homo currit*' is not translated as 'a man is running' here only in order to retain the distinction between restriction by a verb and restriction by a participle.

80. Sherwood seems thus to have explained that "unrestricted" in the rule is intended only to rule out such restrictions as may occur within the subject term itself—'a white man', 'a running man', 'a man who is white'; a *further* condition laid down in the rule is intended to cover the effect of *verbs* on supposition and appellation. (See Section 16.3 below.)

81. Cf. Sherwood's *Syncategoremata* (ed. O'Donnell), pp. 49–50, where he develops this point and cites Aristotle (*De caelo,* 268a16: "Of two things, or men, we say 'both,' but not 'all': three is the first number to which the term 'all' has been appropriated"). In the discussion in the *Syncategoremata* Sherwood drops the unfortunate example 'every man exists' in favor of 'every man is colored'.

82. '*Omne animal est*' and '*omnis homo est*', which have been translated above as 'every animal exists' and 'every man exists', are translated otherwise here to suit the argument.

83. See William of Sherwood's *Introduction to Logic* (tr. Kretzmann), Chapter One, n. 22.

84. G has '*currit*'; '*cucurrit*' in manuscript. Cf. Kneale, *Development,* p. 261, n. 2.

85. The immediate purpose of this rule and the accompanying explication of it is evidently to justify the use of 'could' rather than 'would' in the preceding paragraph—"it *could* supposit for something that does not exist. . . ."

86. This objection acquires special force from Sherwood's admission (at the end of Section 16.1 above) that verbs do sometimes restrict supposition, and thus it also provides the opportunity for stipulating conditions under which such restriction does (or does not) occur.

87. G has '*currit*'; '*cucurrit*' in manuscript.

88. Distinctions between compounded and divided sentences or compounded and divided senses of sentences underlie the well-known fallacies of composition and division and occur in several different contexts in medieval logic. (See, e.g., Paul of Pergula (d. 1451), *Tractatus de sensu composito et diviso,* ed. Brown; Bocheński, *History,* pp. 184–187.) Sherwood's use of such a distinction here may be characterized as an attempt to specify the scope of a tense operator. Thus the *compounded* sense of 'a man has run' might be analyzed into 'it has been the case that there is at least one individual such that it is a man and it is running', while the *divided* sense might be analyzed into 'there is at least one individual such that it is a man and it has been the case that it is running'. In these analyzed versions the phrase 'it has been the case that . . .' serves as a tense operator, making explicit "the consignification of time" in the past-tense verb 'has run'. The distinction between compounded and divided senses and the associated notion of the scope of various operators is of primary importance in Sherwood's *Syncategoremata.* Cf. also p. 673 below.

89. Evidently a difference in intonation patterns marks the difference between compounded and divided senses, and since a *continuous* pattern marks the *compounded* sense and a *discontinuous* pattern marks the *divided* sense (see next paragraph), there is some suggestion that the character of the pattern gives rise to the designation of the sense.

90. What does it mean to pronounce 'a man has run' ('*homo cucurrit*') "with continuity"? It seems it must mean at least to pronounce it without any pause or unusual stress—i.e., in the ordinary way. Sherwood appears to be claiming that it ought then to be understood in this sense: 'something that was a man (regardless of whether or not it still is so) has run'; or, disregarding the anachronistic mode of analysis: 'it has been the case that there is at least one individual such that it is a man and it is running'. Such an account of the ordinary sense of 'a man has run' does seem substantially correct.

91. G has '*currit*'; '*cucurrit*' in manuscript. Of course a mere reiteration of the original sentence cannot help to make the distinction clear. It seems likely that some indication of stress, probably on the verb— '*homo cucurrit*'—has been omitted.

92. It is difficult to see what might be meant by a discontinuous pronunciation of 'a man has run' other than a pronunciation involving a slight pause after 'man' and an unusual stress on 'has' (or on the first syllable of '*cucurrit*', the syllable distinguishing this past-tense form from the present-tense '*currit*'). Perhaps the example is not well chosen for this purpose, but it does not seem that such an intonation pattern (in English or in Latin) would convey the speaker's intention to have his utterance of the sentence understood in its divided sense. The divided sense, as Sherwood might have expressed it, is evidently this: 'something that is now a man has run'; or, 'there is at least one individual such that it is a man and it has been the case that it is running'. On *this* analysis, as Sherwood remarks, the past tense of the verb does *not* restrict the supposition of the subject to past individuals bearing the form signified by the subject. On the analysis of the sentence as *compounded*, the past tense of the verb does have a restrictive effect, but even in that case present individuals are included among the supposita of the subject insofar as they acted in the past.

93. The different senses of the premiss may be presented in this way (see n. 88, this chapter). Compounded: 'it has been the case that there is at least one individual such that it is white and it is seen by Socrates'; divided: 'there is at least one individual such that it is white and it has been the case that it is seen by Socrates'. The divided sense as presented here follows Sherwood's illustration of the newly painted shield, but his point could have been made as well on this analysis of the divided sense: 'there is at least one individual such that it has been the case that it is white and it has been the case that it is seen by Socrates'. The two periods of past time indicated in this analysis need not, of course, coincide.

94. Among the crucial difficulties in this very difficult passage are the phrases '*ex parte ante*' and '*ex parte post*'. The interpretations suggested for them stem from their use in such technical medieval phrases as '*infinitus ex parte ante*' ('infinite with respect to what went before'—i.e., without beginning) and '*infinitus ex parte post*' ('infinite with respect to what will come after'—i.e., without end). Consider the example 'a man will stand on the moon'. The analyzed versions of the two senses may be presented as follows. Divided: 'there is at least one individual such that it is a man and it will be the case that it is standing on the moon'; compounded: 'it will be the case that there is at least one individual such that it is a man and it is standing on the moon'. The *ex parte ante* case seems to be associated with the divided sense and the *ex parte post* case with the compounded sense, but there are difficulties with these apparent associations. For one thing, the phrase "through composition and division" seems totally out of place, and no plausible emendation suggests itself. For another, the supposition in the *ex parte ante* case should evidently be only for present things, not "for present or future things", and the supposition in the *ex parte post* case should be extended to present things insofar as they are future (on the model of the discussion of the compounded sense on p. 672). On the other hand, those apparent associations suggest another interpretation (tempting but evidently farfetched) for the phrases '*ex parte ante*' and '*ex parte post*', stemming from the different *positions* of the temporal operator in the analyses supplied in the notes (but not in the text)—i.e., the common term ('man') occurs *ex parte ante* when it occurs *before* the temporal operator ('it will be the case that . . .') in the analysis and *ex parte post* when it occurs *after*. The difficulties are no doubt partly the result of a corrupt text, but the choice among possible emendations is not a clear one.

95. On ampliation see Peter of Spain, *Sum. log.*, Tr. IX, "On Ampliations" (ed. Bocheński, pp. 100–101); Kneale, *Development*, pp. 261–262; De Rijk, *Logica modernorum*, Vol. I, pp. 567–571.

96. See p. 671.

97. The response to this objection on p. 673 below suggests that a line has been omitted from the Latin, which probably should be emended to read: *ergo tribus hominibus existentibus hec est vera:* [*omnis homo est; tribus hominibus autem currentibus:*] *omnis homo currit, quod falsum est.* In that case the translation would read: "then assuming that [at least] three men exist ['every man exists' is true; but assuming that (at least) three men are running] 'every man is running' is false". The objection, however, seems to make some sense as it stands. The possibility that verbs restrict supposition through their signification is taken up here only to be dismissed, and it seems to be dismissed in the passage as it stands

because of the absurd consequence that the present-tense verb 'is running' would then restrict the supposition of 'man' in 'every man is running' to *running* men, thereby rendering this statement and all other affirmative categoricals analytically true—'every (running) man is running'.

98. G has "*suppositione*'; '*supponere*' in manuscript.

99. I.e., other modal operators. See pp. 673–74. Cf. Peter of Spain, *Sum. log.* (ed. Bocheński), pp. 100–101.

100. See n. 97, this chapter.

101. Although this sentence seems to announce the end of Sherwood's explication of the rule regarding supposition and appellation, the sentences immediately following seem to present some afterthoughts on the subject of ampliation.

102. Divided: 'there is at least one individual such that it is a man and either it is running or it is possible that it is running'. Compounded: 'it is possible that there is at least one individual such that it is a man and either it is running or it is running'—i.e., 'it is possible that there is at least one individual such that it is a man and it is running'. In the *divided* sense the supposition of 'man' is presently existing men. In the *compounded* sense the supposition of 'man' is ampliated (by the modality) to include possible, nonexistent men—e.g., future men.

CHAPTER 45

Peter of Spain

Peter of Spain, born Petrus Juliani, was born at Lisbon sometime between 1210 and 1220. He engaged in his preliminary studies at the cathedral school of Lisbon, after which he attended the University of Paris. There he studied logic under William of Sherwood, metaphysics under Albert the Great, and theology under John of Parma. It is most likely that his noteworthy logical works *Summulae Logicales*, *Syncategoremata*, and *Tractatus Maiorum Fallaciarum* were written before he left Paris in 1245 for the University of Siena, at which he was a member of the faculty of medicine from 1246 to 1250. Sometime before 1261 he wrote his most important philosophical work, the *Scientia Libri de Anima*. It was during that year that he became dean of the cathedral of Lisbon. It was as arch-deacon of the diocese of Braga that he probably met Teoboldi Visconti, who, after becoming Pope Gregory X, appointed Peter as his personal physician in 1272. Within a year Peter became archbishop of Braga and the cardinal of Tusculum.

Pope Gregory X died in January 1276. He was succeeded by Pope Innocent V and Pope Hadrian V, both of whom had untimely deaths that same year. In September 1276, Peter was elected Pope, choosing the name John XXI. In an effort to continue his scholastic perscrutations, he directed a private study be added to the papal palace at Viterbo. On May 20, 1277, Peter died of injuries he sustained when the ceiling of his new study collapsed on him.

Peter of Spain on Distributions

It is interesting to note that of all the elaborate logicosemantic schemata devised by medieval logicians, that which has survived into modern times is the doctrine of *distributio terminorum* or distribution. In the case of Peter of Spain it pertains to the use of a universal quantifier. His "Treatise on Distributions" is an analysis of the various uses of the universal quantifier and its negation for the purpose of eliminating the obscurities surrounding its use. He says, "Distribution is the multiplication of a common term produced by a universal sign; e.g., when it is said 'Every man is running,' the term man is distributed for each of its inferiors by the sign 'every,' and so there is multiplication in that case." For example, the proposition 'Every man has ten fingers' is said to be confused, for the term following the universal quantifier stands for all of its individual values in such a way that its reduction to singular propositions results in a conjunctive set, namely, Joseph has ten fingers and Alex has ten fingers and Mark has ten fingers and. . . . This is also a case of confused supposition. It is confused for the individual values are strictly speaking unknown, that is, Joseph, Alex, and Mark and. . . . It is also a matter of *suppositio*. The term 'supposition' means to stand for, namely, the term 'man' stands for those individuals constituting that class.

Although it may appear at the outset that the use of the universal quantifier in syllogistic reasoning is straightforward, Peter admirably demonstrates that there are many pitfalls attendant to its use. He accomplishes this by discussing numerous sophisms and their solutions.

Because his *Summulae logicales* is clear, concise, and unencumbered by philosophical problems, it served as *the* introductory logic text for three hundred years.

"TREATISE ON DISTRIBUTIONS" FROM *SUMMULAE LOGICALES*

Distribution is the extension of a general term effected by a universal sign; as when one says "every man," the term "man" is distributed or referred indeterminately to any of its particulars by virtue of the sign "every," and in this fashion extension occurs. I say "of a general term" because a singular term cannot be distributed. Hence, such expressions as "every Sortes," "every Plato," and so forth are incongruous, for they constitute solecisms.

Some universal signs are distributive of substance, such as "every," "none"; others are distributive of accident, such as "such a kind," "such a size." A sign distributive of substance distributes things essentially related, such as "every," "none," as when one says "every whiteness," "every blackness." But substance is taken in the broader sense to include things of any genus whatsoever when one says "A sign distributive of substance." A sign distributive of accident is one which distributes things related by a mode of accident, such as quality or quantity, for example, "any kind whatever," "any size whatever."

Some signs distributive of substance are distributive of integral parts, such as "the

Reprinted from *The* Summulae Logicales *of Peter of Spain*, translated by Joseph P. Mullally (Notre Dame, Ind.: The University of Notre Dame Press, 1945), pp. 63–103. Reprinted by permission of the University of Notre Dame Press.

whole"; others are distributive of subjective parts, such as "every" (*omnis*),[1] "none." Further, some signs distributive of subjective parts are distributive of two parts, such as "either of two," "neither of the two"; others are distributive of many parts, such as "every," "none," and the like. Of these signs, we must first treat those distributive of substance and, among these, primarily the sign "every."

It must be known that every (*omnis*) is taken in the plural in a twofold sense: in one way collectively, as in the statement: "All the apostles of God are twelve"—it does not follow: "Therefore these apostles of God are twelve," some of them being pointed to; in another way it is taken distributively, as in the statement: "All men naturally desire to know."

The next question is what does the sign "every" signify. It appears to signify nothing, because every thing is either universal or particular; but the sign "every" does not signify a universal thing or a particular thing; therefore, it signifies no thing.

Furthermore, on the same point, "every" is neither predicable of one nor of many; therefore it is neither universal nor particular; so it signifies nothing.

Yet, on the contrary, from the fact that a thing is or is not, a statement is said to be true or false. Therefore, if "every" signifies nothing, the truth or falsity of a proposition will not be caused by its presence or absence. But this statement is true: "An animal is a man"; and therefore [if the presence or absence of "every" does not affect the truth of statements] this is also true: "Every animal is a man." But this is false. Hence the first statement is false, namely, that "every" signifies nothing.

The solution of the problem follows: It is said that "every" does not signify a universal but signifies universally, because it makes the general term which it qualifies stand for all its particulars, as "Every man runs." In this way, "every" signifies something. But "thing" is taken in two senses, because in one sense a thing is that which can be a subject or a predicate, as man, animal, runs, argues, and so forth, and in this case it is true that "every" signifies nothing, because any such thing is either universal or particular; [and] there is another thing which is a disposition of that thing which is a subject or a predicate, and the sign "every" signifies such a thing. But the truth or falsity of a proposition is caused by both things.

However, it is objected that "every" does not signify a disposition of a subject thing, because the middle term of a syllogism must be repeated with its dispositions in the minor premise. Therefore we should syllogize in the following fashion: "Every man is an animal; Sortes is every man; therefore, Sortes is an animal," because "every" is a disposition in the major premise and therefore must be repeated in the minor premise. But this is false. Therefore, "every" is not a disposition of a subject.

The solution follows: Just as "father" connotes two things, namely, that thing which is the father and the father insofar as he is a father, so "subject" connotes two things, namely, the thing which is the subject and the subject insofar as it is a subject. According to this, the subject has a twofold disposition, for one is a disposition of that thing which is the subject, as white, black, and such similar accidental dispositions, and these dispositions should be repeated with the middle term in the minor premiss;

the other is a disposition of the subject insofar as it is a subject, that is, in relation to the predicate, as "every," "none," and all signs both general and particular, and such a disposition should not be repeated with the middle term in the minor premiss because it is relative, since it distributes the subject in relation to the predicate. For example, when one says: "Every white man runs," that disposition "white" should be repeated with the middle term in the minor premiss because it is an absolute disposition of that which is the subject; but that disposition "every" should not be repeated because it is a sign of a relation of the subject to the predicate and so is a disposition of the subject insofar as it is the subject. Consequently, we should say: "Every white man runs; Sortes is a white man; therefore, Sortes runs"; and not: "Sortes is every white man".

Having discussed how this sign "every" signifies things and their dispositions, the question naturally follows as to whether "every" requires three things named. This would seem to be so, because every perfection occurs in threes, as is held in the first book of the De Caelo et Mundi[2]; and thus all that is perfect occurs in threes. But the all and the perfect are the same, as is held in the same passage. Therefore, all occurs in threes. Hence "every" requires three things named.

Aristotle, speaking on the same point in the same passage, says that we do not predicate "all" of two men but we do predicate it of three men; wherefore, "every" requires three things named.

To the contrary: There are universal propositions in any demonstration; but demonstrations can be formed involving the sun and the moon; therefore we must say "every sun," "every moon"; but "sun" has only one denotation and so also "moon"; therefore "every" does not require three things named.

On this same point: "Every [object] deprived of light by the interposition of the earth is eclipsed." This proposition is conceded since it is held by the authorities. But

"Every [object] deprived of light by the interposition of the earth" has only one denotation, namely, the individual moon. Therefore "every" does not demand three things named.

Again, the sign "every" signifies quantity universally. But "quantity universally" is a proper universal mode. However, a property is diversified according to the diversity of its subject, so that if "man" is of less extension, "capable of laughter" is of less extension; and if a man is dead, what is capable of laughter is dead. But the universal is sometimes preserved in many things, such as "man" and "horse"; sometimes in one thing alone, as "sun" and "moon." Hence "every" sometimes requires three things named and sometimes not; indeed, at times, only one.

On the same point, form can be taken in a twofold manner, because one form is the form of matter, as the soul is the form of the body, and this form is a part of but is not predicated of that of which it is a part; the other is predicable form, and thus all the higher [predicables]—as genera, species, and differentia—are said to be the forms of the particulars included under them, for example, "man," "horse," and so forth, and the individuals included under the predicable form are its matter. Therefore, since form, in neither of the aforementioned modes, exceeds its matter nor is exceeded by it, no universal exceeds the individuals included under it nor are the individuals exceeded by it.

Therefore, since "every" bespeaks adequation of the universals with their particulars, as "every man," it follows that "sun" has only one denotation so that one can truly say "every sun." We grant this in affirming that the aforementioned statements are true and that "every" does not always require three things named. Nay rather, when it is joined to a general term denoting many things, it requires many things named; but when it is joined to a term denoting one thing only, it requires only one thing named.

To the first objection, that all perfections occur in threes, we still say that the statement is true; and these three are the substance of the thing, its potency, and its operation. Aristotle briefly touches upon these three when he says: "Nature, being so constituted, acts this way."[3] When Aristotle says "nature," he touches upon the substance of a thing; when he says "being so constituted", he touches upon its potency; and when he says "acts this way", he touches upon the operation proper to it. In like manner, this sign "every" has the substance of a universal sign, the potency to distribute, and its operation or act when it distributes. Its perfection lies in these three things.

With regard to the second objection, it must be said that "man" and "men" differ because "man" asserts that species as such which is predicable of many; but "men," in the plural, does not assert species as such but species multiplied in act according to the matter diversified in the number of individuals. Whence "every," in the plural, by reason of the multitude represented, effects distribution by reason of the diversified matters and requires three things named. But "every," in the singular, embraces the species as such but not the matter of the individuals; and it requires an essence naturally predicable of many, whether it actually belongs to one or to many. Hence "every" requires three things named, or only one, depending on the nature of the universal to which it is conjoined.

However, some say that "every" requires at least three things named and they assign the following reason. Whenever a universal sign is added to a general term lacking sufficient things named, it refers to a non-being, as when one says: "Every Phoenix is," the term "Phoenix" refers to non-existent Phoenices because it denotes only one thing. Consequently, when one says: "Every Phoenix is," the meaning is "The one Phoenix, which is, is" and "The two Phoenices, which are not, are." Hence, they say these two propositions are false: "Some Phoenix is not" and "Every Phoenix is," but they are not contradictories because the Phoenix, which is, is taken for granted in the negative proposition and the two Phoenices, which are not, are taken for granted in the affirmative proposition; from this point of view the propositions do not have the same subject. However, their argument can be disproved in many ways since the difficulty arises from their begging the question in assuming that "every" always requires three things named, an assumption previously shown false.

Besides, Aristotle thinks that a proposition which has a distributed universal as the subject of any predicate, contradicts that negative proposition in which the universal, undistributed, is subject of the same predicate.[4] But the aforementioned propositions are such: "Every Phoenix is," "Some Phoenix is not"; therefore they are contradictories. But this is what these people deny. Therefore, their rule is false.

On the same point, another rule is as follows: a general term which occurs as subject or predicate with a verb in the present tense which is taken simply and which does not have the power of amplification, either intrinsically or extrinsically, is restricted to the denotation of those things of the nature signified by the denoting general term, which are existing. Therefore, when one says: "Every Phoenix is", the term "Phoenix" is restricted to the denotation of that Phoenix alone which is, since it denotes only one thing. Therefore, utilizing the rule just given, if a universal sign is added to it, it only distributes it in relation to the one thing denoted [by the term]. Consequently, the rule of those other people is false and rests on a fallacy. This we grant.

With reference to the foregoing, the sophism arises: "Every man is and whatever differs from him is not-man." Proof: This is a copulative [proposition] each of whose parts is true; therefore the copulative is true.

Disproof: "Every man is and whatever differs from him is not-man; Sortes is a man; therefore, whatever differs from Sortes is not-man," which is false, because this is a copulative proposition one of whose parts is false; consequently, the whole is false.

Solution: The initial statement is absolutely true and the disproof is guilty of the fallacy of the consequent because the phrase "different from every man" is less in extent than "different from Sortes" because "different from every man" only denotes things other than man but "different from Sortes" denotes these and all men other than Sortes as well. Therefore the following is a valid inference: "Different from every man; therefore different from Sortes"; and this is a topical argument from the subjective part to its whole. But if a [universal] sign is added to the statement: "Different from every man," there will be, simultaneously with distribution, an inference from the particular to the general. Thus the [disproof] is guilty of the fallacy of the consequent according to one process of reasoning, for there is a twofold process of reasoning in the disproof because the following is a valid inference: "Every man is; therefore, Sortes is," and it is a topical argument from a quantitative whole to its part; but this is not a valid inference: "This is different from every man; therefore it is different from Sortes," but a fallacy of the consequent just as "Every man is; therefore every animal is."

Let us now examine the sophism: "Every man and another man are." Proof: Sortes and another man are; Plato and another man are, and so on; therefore, every man and another man are.

Disproof: "Another" is a relative of diversity of substance; therefore it denotes a thing different from man. But there is not another man distinct from every man. Therefore, the initial statement is false.

Solution: The initial statement is absolutely false and the proof is guilty of the fallacy of figure of speech in arguing from several determinate suppositions to one determinate supposition, because that term "other" has determinate supposition in the premises and in the conclusion.

Again, the proof is guilty of the fallacy of accident, because although "Sortes and

Plato and so on" makes an inference to every man as such, nevertheless every man cannot be inferred from the conjunction "Every and another man", as when one says: "Every man and another man are"; just as I know Coriscus, as such, nevertheless I do not know him under this accident of coming.

Wherefore, the following rule is offered: whenever something follows another, convertibly or not, if something belongs to one which does not belong to the other, and if through that to which it belongs, an inference is made concerning that to which it does not belong, there is always a fallacy of accident. For example: "Man is; therefore substance is." But species belongs to man and not to substance. Therefore, if through man species is inferred of substance, there is a fallacy of accident, as "Man is a species; therefore substance is a species." Likewise in the case of "Risible is a property; therefore man is a property." However, of things which are logically related, some are related convertibly, as "man" and "risible"; but others are not, as "man" and "substance."

Having dealt with this sophism, we now discuss another: "Every man is every man." Proof: Sortes is Sortes; Plato is Plato and so on; therefore, every man is every man.

And, as Boethius thinks, no proposition is more true than the one in which the same thing is predicated of itself.[5] But the proposition in question is such, because "every man" is predicated of "every man." Therefore, no proposition is more true than that; and consequently it is true.

Disproof: The contradictory of this proposition is true, viz., "Some man is not every man." Therefore, the proposition is false.

On the same point: Every man is every man; but Sortes is man; therefore, Sortes is every man. This is a syllogism of the type Darii. The conclusion is false; therefore, one of the premises. Not the minor; therefore the major. But the major is the sophism; therefore, this sophism is false.

Solution: The initial statement is absolutely false and the proof is guilty of the fallacy of the consequent due to an insufficient enumeration of the particulars, because along with those which it includes, it should include in the subject: "Sortes is every man; Plato is every man and so on," and it certainly should include in the predicate: "Every man is Sortes; every man is Plato and so on"; which things it fails to do. Thus it is guilty of the fallacy of the consequent from an insufficient enumeration of the particulars. With regard to the other point, it is said that in this case the same thing is not predicated of itself but "every man" is predicated of "every man" taken in extension.

We now treat of the sign "no" (nullus) which signifies a universally negative quantity. Hence it signifies the same thing as the sign "every" with the negative placed after it; therefore "every not" and "no" (or "none") are equipollent.

We submit the following rule concerning "none": whenever the sign "no" is immediately added to a general term, it distributes the term movably and distributively, and it does the same for the general term which is mediately added to it, as "No man is an ass." Hence an inference can be made to the particulars included under the subject in the following way: "Therefore, Sortes is not an ass, nor Plato and so on"; and also under the predicate.

In this connection, we have the sophism: "No man is every man." It is proved thus: Sortes is not every man; Plato is not every man and so on; therefore, the sophism is true. Or in the following fashion: Its contradictory is false, viz., "Some man is every man"; therefore, the sophism is true.

To the contrary: In the sophism, a thing is predicated of its opposite; therefore, the statement is false.

Solution: The initial statement is true. As to the disproof, it is overruled because in the proposition a thing is not predicated of its opposite, but rather "every man" is denied of "every man" taken as distributed; and this is true.

We now discuss the term "nothing" which signifies the same thing as "no" but which includes in itself the term it distributes, for "nothing" is a universal sign with a negation and "thing" is the term it distributes.

From what has been said, the problem of the sophism arises: "Seeing nothing is seeing something". It is proved thus: Not seeing this thing is seeing something, because not seeing Sortes is seeing Plato: not seeing that thing is seeing something and so on; therefore, seeing nothing is seeing something. Therefore, the sophism is true.

To the contrary: In this case a thing is predicated of its opposite; therefore the statement is false. Some observe that in the proposition: *"Nihil videns est aliquid videns"*, the word "nothing" (*nihil*) can be in the accusative case and the meaning is: "Seeing nothing is seeing something", or it can be in the nominative case and the meaning is: "Nothing seeing is something seeing"; and in this manner they posit amphibology by reason of case. But this does not solve the problem, for in each sense the sophism is false.

Again, others observe in the proposition: "Seeing nothing is seeing something," that the negation included in the term "nothing" can deny the first participle and the meaning is: "Seeing no thing is seeing something"—and in this way the proposition is taken in the divided sense; or it can deny the verb "is" and the meaning is: "Seeing anything whatever is not seeing something"—and in this way the proposition is taken in the composite sense.[6] But this does not solve the problem because the proposition is false in each sense in that opposites are predicated of the same thing.

Solution: One must say that the sophism is absolutely false and the proof is guilty of the fallacy of figure of speech in reasoning from a determinate many to a determinate one with regard to this term "seeing," because in the premises, and likewise in the conclusion, it has determinate supposition. Or it is guilty of the fallacy of accident, because although "seeing" is predicable of all, as among themselves, nevertheless it is not predicable of all insofar as they are united in the whole "seeing nothing"; as a result, the whole belongs to the part and the being of "seeing something" is assigned to be in each.

It should be understood that the premisses of the proof are ambiguous because the negation can determine the verb or the participle, as was stated above. On this account, the ancients reckoned the premisses ambiguous in the light of the following rule which they offered: whenever negation and distribution are included in one term, to whatever one is referred, the other is also. From this it follows that since distribution, posited in the accusative case, cannot affect the verb in the previous statement, neither can the negation. The same opinion holds concerning the following sophisms: "Having no head is having some head", "Different from no man is different from some man", etc.

We now discuss signs distributive of two things, as "neither" and "both" [taken separately]. They differ from the terms discussed previously, because "every," "no," and the like, distribute all individuals included under the general term, while "both" and "neither" distribute only two such as may be pointed to, as "both of them," "neither of them." With reference to this, we have the sophism: "What is stated by both of them is true". Posit that Sortes says "God is"; Plato says "Man is an animal"; and both simultaneously say "Man is an ass"; and suppose that those two are indicated by the pronoun "of them." Proof: What is stated by Sortes is true; what is stated by Plato is true; therefore, what is stated by both of them is true.

To the contrary: What is stated by both of them is true; but nothing is stated by both of them except "Man is an ass"; therefore "Man is an ass" is true. But this is false.

Solution: The initial statement is true but the proof is guilty of the fallacy of accident. As it is held by Aristotle, the following proposition is posited as true: "There is the same science of all opposites."[7] Nevertheless there is no particular science of all opposites, for in this case "science" is taken distributively. Consequently, the fallacy of accident occurs in the following: There is the same science of all opposites; but there is no science apart from this science or that science and so on; therefore, this or that science is the same for all opposites. But this is false. In like manner: Man is a species; but no one is man apart from Sortes or Plato and so on; therefore, Sortes is a species or Plato and so on. Hence there is the fallacy of accident in the sophism, because the expression "what is stated" and the word "true" are each taken for what they signify generically, and in this way "What is stated by both of them is true." It follows from this that "what is stated" does not stand for a particular statement by both. Consequently, "what is stated by both of them" in the particular sense is accidentally related to "what is stated" in the generic sense, just as a particular included under a general term is accidentally related to that general term; and "true" is said to belong to both. Here, general refers to all that is greater, whether essential or accidental.

However, some say that the sophism is absolutely false. They say that "what is stated" is taken for a particular statement by both and similarly "true" for a particular truth; and that the proof is guilty of the fallacy of figure of speech in arguing from a determined many to a determined one with respect to both the term "what is stated" and the term "true." But the first solution is the better and the more subtle.

We now treat of the sign "neither" which means the same as "both" with a negation placed before it. Just as "no" intrinsically distributes and negates, so also does "neither." But "neither" is only distributive of two.

Now the question of this sophism arises: "Having neither eye, you can see." Proof: Not having the right eye, you can see; not having the left eye, you can see; therefore, the sophism is true.

To the contrary: Having neither eye, you can see; therefore, having neither eye or while you have neither eye, you can see. But this is false. The consequence is obvi-

ous, for gerunds ending in do have to be resolved by "while," "if," or "because." But in each case it is false. Therefore the sophism is false.

Solution: The sophism is false and the proof is guilty of the fallacy of accident because the ability to see is proper to the parts as such, that is to say, separately, but it is not proper to the parts taken together as a whole. Hence it is evident from a former rule that since the whole follows after the parts, the power of seeing is proper to the parts and not to the whole. Therefore, there is a fallacy of accident if the parts are inferred from the whole.

Having treated signs distributive of subjective parts, the question next arises as to whether negation has the power of distributing or of rendering indeterminate. It seems that it does, because Aristotle, in the first book of the De Interpretatione, says that these are contradictory: "Man is just," "Not man is just."[8] Hence, one of them is universal, since it has a general term as subject; but it can only be this one: "Not man is just"; therefore the term "man" is distributed. But there is nothing by which it is distributed except the negation. Therefore, it is distributed by the negation.

To the contrary: If negation has the capacity to render indeterminate, then just as "Every Sortes runs" is incongruous, so "Not Sortes runs" is incongruous. But this is false, because although a distributive sign cannot be added to a singular term, nevertheless negation can.

Secondly, wherever distribution takes place, a general term is taken universally. Wherefore, it is necessary that there be a word signifying quantity universally. But only a universal sign signifies quantity universally, for negation does not. Therefore, negation does not have the power to distribute. This we grant, maintaining that negation does not render indeterminate but denies that which follows it. From which it follows that when negation is added to a general term, it denies the general term. But in the case of the negation of the more general, the negation of any inferior included under it follows from the fact that when the more general is nullified, any particular whatever included under it is nullified. Consequently, negation does not render indeterminate but denies what follows after it, be it universal or particular.

The solution to the objection is obvious, because the fact that the proposition: "Not man is just" is a universal, is not due to the nature of distribution existing in the negation but rather because man in general is denied; and this being denied, any of its particulars whatsoever is denied.

Again, it is customary to posit a certain "distribution of aptitude," as "Every man fears the sea," that is, man is born apt to fear the sea. Or again, it is customary to posit "befitting distribution," as "Heaven touches all things apart from itself" and "God created all things apart from Himself." But these two kinds of distribution are not as proper as the other.

We now discuss the sign "whole" which is distributive of integral parts, as in the proposition: "Sortes as a whole is white." The sense is: "Sortes according to any one whatsoever of his parts, is white." From this it follows: "Any part whatever of Sortes is white." Proof: In the proposition, "Sortes as a whole is white", Sortes as such is the subject of whiteness, and his parts are not white by reason of themselves but according as they are in the whole of Sortes or under the form of the whole. Therefore they are not the subject of whiteness except through the whole. Hence, this proposition follows first in order, "Sortes, according to any one whatsoever of his parts, is white"; and then there follows this proposition: "Any part whatever of Sortes is white."

Further, in the proposition: "Sortes as a whole is white," the whole is the subject of whiteness directly; but the parts indirectly, because the parts are understood indirectly in that which is the whole and the whole is understood indirectly in that which is the part. This is evident from a division of the whole, as a house is constructed of wall, roof, and foundation and Sortes is constituted by his parts. Therefore the whole causes us to understand the parts indirectly. Consequently, from the proposition: "Sortes as a whole is white," there follows immediately the proposition: "Sortes, according to any one whatsoever of his parts, is white"; and mediately the proposition: "Any part whatever of Sortes is white."

Again, on the same point, that which is the part, has being only from that which is the whole because it derives its perfection only from the whole. Therefore it is the subject of something only through the whole. Consequently, the whole is the primary subject. Therefore, from the proposition: "Sortes as a whole is white" immediately follows: "Sortes, according to any one whatsoever of his parts, is white"; and mediately "Any part whatever of Sortes is white."

In reference to what has been said, we have the sophism: "Sortes as a whole is less than Sortes." Proof: Any part whatever of Sortes is less than Sortes, and Sortes, according to any one whatsoever of his parts, is less than Sortes; therefore, Sortes as a whole is less than Sortes.

It is argued to the contrary: Sortes as a whole is less than Sortes; therefore, Sortes is less than Sortes.

Solution: The initial statement is true, viz., "Sortes as a whole is less than Sortes," but the proof is guilty of the fallacy of accident because in the proposition: "Sortes as a whole is less than Sortes," the predicate is attributed to the parts to which it truly belongs; but it does not belong to Sortes; therefore, the proposition: "Sortes is less than Sortes," is absolutely false. On that account, if one infers that the parts are less than Sortes as a whole *or as Sortes*, there will be a fallacy of accident by virtue of the previously mentioned rule. Hence Sortes as a whole is the subject thing, Sortes belongs accidentally to it, and "to be less than Sortes" is ascribed to both.

In like manner, the disproof is guilty of the fallacy of confusion of absolute and qualified statement (*secundum quid ad simpliciter*), because the proposition: "Sortes as a whole is less than Sortes," does not posit

Sortes as such but according to his parts. Therefore, it asserts that Sortes in a qualified sense is less than Sortes without qualification. So when one makes the unqualified inference: "Therefore, Sortes is less than Sortes," there is the fallacy of confusion of absolute and qualified statement, as in the case: "Sortes qua foot is less than Sortes; therefore, Sortes is less than Sortes."

Furthermore, in some cases it follows: "Sortes as a whole; therefore Sortes," as "Sortes as a whole is white; therefore Sortes is white"; in other cases it does not follow. We may ask in which cases it follows and in which cases it does not follow. It must be said that there are some accidents which belong to the part and to the whole indifferently, as white, black, hot, cold, growth and shrinkage, and in such cases, "Sortes as a whole; therefore Sortes" logically follows; there are other accidents which belong to the part and not to the whole and conversely to the whole and not to a part or parts, as totality, minority, smallness and, in such cases, "Sortes as a whole; therefore Sortes" does not follow.

We now discuss signs distributive of accidents among which we first treat those distributive of quality. A sign distributive of quality is said to be one which distributes things related through a qualitative mode, as "such a sort as you please" whose particular is "some one sort as you please."

But it is objected that if an accident is multiplied when the subject is multiplied, it necessarily follows that since signs distributive of substance distribute or multiply the subject, they necessarily multiply or distribute the accident itself. Consequently, signs distributive of accidents are superfluous.

To this it must be said that the multiplication of accidents is twofold, because one is the multiplication of accident according to number and is effected through a sign distributive of substance, as "Every white man runs"; the other is multiplication according to species and is effected through a sign distributive of accident, as "Such a sort as you please runs," which is equivalent to the proposition: "A thing, having any quality whatever, runs."

In connection with the foregoing, this sophism is discussed: "Everything of whichever kind you please, knows, concerning that kind, that it is what it is." Let it be supposed that Sortes knows grammar, logic and rhetoric, and Plato and Cicero likewise, and that they know themselves to possess these; and suppose that there are three other men of whom one knows logic, another grammar, and the third rhetoric, and that these do not know themselves to possess these sciences, and that they know nothing of the other men, whereas the others know about themselves and also of these three; and suppose that there exist no other men and no other qualities. Proof: This "whichever kind you please" knows, concerning that kind, that it is what it is. Similarly with the second and the third; and there are not any more "whichever kind you please." Therefore, "every thing of whichever kind you please, knows, concerning that kind, that it is what it is."

To the contrary: Everything of whichever kind you please, [knows, concerning that kind, that it is what it is]; therefore, every grammatical thing knows, concerning that kind of thing, that it is what it is.[9]

The first solution is true, and the disproof is guilty of the fallacy of the consequent in reasoning from the inferior to the superior with the distribution of the superior. For "of whichever kind you please" stands only for three [men], namely, for the first three; but "grammarian" stands for these and also for someone who possesses grammar only, and thus "grammatical thing" stands for more things than does "of whichever kind you please." Hence, if the universal distributive sign is placed before it, as in saying "Everything of whichever kind you please", et cetera, therefore "everything grammatical," there arises a consequence like this one: "Every man; therefore every animal." And the same occurs in the later expression, when it is said "concerning that kind", as if [we argued] "Concerning everything of whichever kind; therefore concerning everything grammatical."

We turn our attention to signs distributive of quantity and they are signs which distribute things related through a mode of quantity, as, for instance, "as often as," "as much as".

In this relation we have the sophism: "As often as you were at Paris, so often you have been a man." Proof: At one time you were at Paris and at that time you were a man; at another time you were at Paris and at that time you were a man, and so on; therefore, as often as you were at Paris, so often you were a man.

Disproof: As often as you have been at Paris, so often you have been a man; but twice you have been at Paris; therefore, twice you have been a man. This is false, because the word "twice" introduces the interruption of the act to which it is joined but the act of being man was not interrupted in you.

Solution: The initial statement is false. The proof is to be answered by destroying it, because the second part of the copulative is false, viz., "at that time you were a man," for as yet you have not been a man even once, because of the fact that life has not yet been terminated in such manner that you might once again begin to live and afterwards have your life terminated, which is required in order that you be a man twice; the same as a race must be begun and terminated twice in order that anyone run twice. Note that "twice" does not involve interruption of time but only the termination of that act to which it is joined; but interruption follows a termination. If, however, the paralogism were formed in the following fashion: "Whenever you have been at Paris, you have been a man; but twice you have been at Paris; therefore, twice you have been a man," the initial statement would be true and the disproof would be guilty of the fallacy of figure of speech due to a change in category, because "whenever" is in the category of time and "twice" is in the category of quantity, for it is a member of the genus of discrete quantity.

We now discuss the sign "infinite" which is spoken of in five ways. In the first way, "infinite" is said to be that which is incapable of being gone through, as the voice is said to be invisible because of the fact that it is not its nature to be seen. In a second way, "infinite" is said to be that which has incomplete transition by reason of the fact that it has not yet been terminated, although it is its nature to be terminated, as while someone is crossing a space and has not yet arrived at its end. In a third way, we speak of the "infinite" in the sense of addition, as augmentable number is infinite by the addition of unity or another number. In a fourth way, "infinite" is spoken of in relation to division, as in the case of a continuum. But every continuum is infinitely divisible. Hence Aristotle defines it thus in the fourth book of the *Physics*: "The continuum is divisible ad infinitum."[10] In the fifth way, "infinite" is spoken of in both ways, viz., according to addition and division, as in the case of time; for since time is a continuum, it is divisible ad infinitum and since one time follows another, it is infinite through the addition of one time to another. With regard to the last three significations, "infinite" is defined thus: "Infinite is that whose quantity is such that we can always take a part outside what has been already taken";[11] as if another part were taken after the last part of the line, and after this, a third, and [since] the end of the line could never be attained, the line is said to be infinite.

It is customary to assert that "infinite" is sometimes taken for a universal term, in which case the proposition: "Infinites are finite" is equivalent to the proposition: "Some infinites are finite"; and at other times it is taken as a distributive sign, in which case the proposition, as far as distribution is concerned, is equivalent to the proposition: "More than whatever number you please, is finite." And it is proved thus: More than one is finite; more than two is finite; more than three is finite and so on; therefore, more than whatever number you please, is finite. In this fashion there is said to be an interrupted or discontinuous distribution within the numerical scale, because this word "more" in the first proposition stands for two, in the second for three, and in like manner, step by step, in the ascending numerical scale. So the expression "More than whatever number you please" effects distribution within the numerical scale, because the expression "than whatever number you please" stands for some [numbers] and "more" stands for other [numbers] according to increasing number, as was said above.

In reference to what has been said, this sophism arises: "Infinites are finite." Proof: Two is finite; three is finite and so on ad infinitum; therefore, infinites are finite.

Disproof: Here an opposite is predicated of its opposite: therefore, the statement is impossible.

It also can be proved thus: More than whatever number you please, is finite; therefore, infinites are finite.

Solution: Some distinguish by reason of the fact that "infinite" is equivocal as regards what is infinite with respect to us and what is infinite in the absolute sense. Wherefore, if we take what is infinite with respect to us, the initial statement can be true and an opposite is not predicated of an opposite, for the stars and the sands of the sea, which are not absolutely infinite, are infinite with respect to us. But if we take what is infinite in the absolute sense, the initial statement is absolutely false and an opposite is predicated of an opposite. But others make a distinction by reason of the fact that "infinite" can be a universal term and thus the initial statement is false; or it can be a syncategorematic word, implying in itself distribution, as has been said, and in this way they consider the statement to be true.

But neither of these solutions has value, because if the distinction in each is denied and "infinite" is taken absolutely and as a universal term, the proof and the disproof of the sophism still remain. Wherefore, it must be said that the initial statement is absolutely false, and the proof is guilty of the fallacy of confusion of absolute and qualified statement because "infinite" in succession is infinite in a qualified sense and not absolutely. Wherefore, when the parts of number are taken in succession, as two and three, we do not grasp the infinite absolutely but in a certain fashion or a qualified sense; hence infinite in the absolute sense cannot be inferred from these.

NOTES

1. "Omnis" means "every" and "all" in the singular but only "all" in the plural. However, the customary translation is "every" in the singular and "all" in the plural.
2. Aristotle, *De Caelo et Mundi*, I, 1, 268a, 12 sqq.
3. Exact citation not located. Possible source: *Metaphysica*, V, 4, 1015a, 14 sqq.
4. Aristotle, *De Interpretatione*, 7, 17b, 16–19.
5. Possible source: Boethius, *In Librum Aristotelis De Interpretatione, Editio Prima*, Liber II, col. 387 (J. P. Migne, P.L., LXIV).
6. The traditional distinction between *sensus divisus* and *sensus compositus* usually relates to the two senses of modal terms in modal propositions. Any modal proposition which is understood as if the modal term functioned as predicate, whether it actually functions as predicate or it functions as an adverb modifying the copula (the only two ways in which modal terms enter into propositions), is taken in the composite sense. Otherwise, it is taken in the divided sense. Here, Peter of Spain applies this distinction to the two ways in which the negation in the sophism can be understood, either as internal to the participial phrase *"nihil videns"* in the divided sense or as negating the predicate *"aliquid videns"* in the composite sense.
7. Aristotle, *Metaphysica*, IV, 2, 1004a, 9–10.
8. Aristotle, *De Interpretatione*, 10, 19b, 25 sqq.
9. Interpolate [But this is false. Therefore, the sophism is false.]. This consequence is offered as proving the falsity of the sophism, since it appears to conclude a false consequent—for, on the hypothesis, it is false that the grammarian among the three "other men" knows himself and the first three men to be grammarians.
10. Perhaps this refers to *Physica*, IV, 12, 220a, 30. However, the language and context suggest rather *Physica*, III, 7, 207b, 15.
11. Aristotle, *Physica*, III, 6, 207a, 8.

CHAPTER 46

Robert Kilwardby

The Englishman Robert Kilwardby was born circa 1215. He studied at Paris during the 1230s, after which he taught arts there from about 1237 to about 1245. He then returned to England, whereupon he entered the Dominican order. Robert then pursued studies in theology at Oxford, where he was regent master in the late 1250s. He was elected prior provincial of the English Dominicans in 1261, and in 1272 he was consecrated Archbishop of Canterbury, a position he held for the better part of five years.

Within the church at this time there was feuding between the Augustinians and Aristotelians. The lion's share of Aristotle's works were translated from the Greek into Latin in the mid-1200s. It did not take long for certain Christian theologians, as well as numerous members of the church hierarchy, to become deeply suspicious of the physical and metaphysical theses of Aristotle and his Muslim interpreters. Many of Aristotle's doctrines contradicted Scripture. The University of Paris was the center of the controversy, and on three separate occasions (1210, 1215, and 1231) the teaching there of select Aristotelian works was prohibited by bishop, cardinal, and pope, respectively. These attempts at censorship were a failure as these works continued to be read privately, and the prohibitions seem to have been forgotten by the 1240s. The controversy was far from dead, however. By 1267 Bonaventure became noticeably vocal in his attacks on philosophical inquiry, pushing new boundaries and by so doing encroaching on established church doctrine. Even Aquinas did not escape criticism during the following decade. On March 7, 1277, Étienne Tempier, bishop of Paris, condemned 219 propositions concerning the eternity of the world, the necessity of events, namely, divine action, the unity of the intellect and the scope and limits of philosophy. On March 18, 1277, Archbishop Kilwardby, apparently taking his cue from Tempier, condemned thirty articles on logic, grammar, and natural philosophy, forbidding their teaching at Oxford.

In 1278 Kilwardby was named cardinal bishop of Porto. He died the following year at Viterbo.

Robert Kilwardby on the Nature of Logic

Drawing heavily on the various books of Aristotle's *Organon* Kilwardby begins by noting that the Greek word 'logos' is equivocal. It signifies both speech and reason. Consequently, logic is both the science of discourse and the science of reason. Kilwardby is principally concerned with logic in the latter sense. "Regarding philosophical questions that are to be settled, one can reason on the basis of specific considerations as well as on the basis of common considerations." The first pertains to argumentation pertaining to science and "to which the question to be settled belongs". This is properly called demonstrative logic. The second type of reasoning deals with argumentation, the subject matter of which involves "things belonging to every science and that can be suited to all sciences, and not only to the conclusions but to the principles of all of them". This is properly understood as dialectic. Both these forms of reasoning, demonstration and dialectic, utilize syllogisms, yet they differ in the types of syllogisms they use. Syllogisms of demonstration are "based on the first principles of the thing to be concluded, principles that are true, [known] per se, universal, immediate causes, and the like; . . . . " Syllogisms of dialectic are ones "in which an opinion is diligently sought after by the inquiry of two people" and involve only what is readily believable. To Kilwardby's way of thinking, dialectic is always preparatory to demonstration.

Now, since "reasoning, both demonstrative and dialectical, is the source of recognizing and discovering truth, and a careless person can be deceived in connection with either, logic must determine the deceptions that can occur in either of them so that they can be avoided and one may thus come to the truth more expeditiously and recognize it more confidently". Kilwardby refers to defective demonstrative syllogisms as syllogisms of ignorance and to fallacious dialectical syllogisms as sophistical reasoning. Both forms of reasoning, when sound, contribute to the sciences. In fact, all the sciences are established and developed by demonstration. However, dialectic proves indispensable to science when the science at hand has exhausted all demonstrative arguments at its disposal. In that case dialectic provides science with readily believable arguments. Notwithstanding this benefit, dialectical reasoning cannot establish or otherwise determine knowledge in any of the sciences.

"THE NATURE OF LOGIC"
FROM *DE ORTU SCIENTIARUM*

Chapter LIII. The Name of Logic, Its Origin, Adequacy, Subject Matter, End, and Definition.

Regarding logic, it is important to know that its very name is equivocal. For, as Hugh of St. Victor says in his *Didascalion* (i, II, ed. Buttimer, pp. 20–21), the name ['logic'] is taken from the Greek name '*logos*,' which among the Greeks signifies both

Reprinted from *The Cambridge Translations of Medieval Philosophical Texts*: Vol. 1, edited by Norman Kretzmann and Eleonore Stump (Cambridge: Cambridge University Press, 1988), pp. 264–282. Reprinted by permission of Norman Kretzmann, Eleonore Stump, and Cambridge University Press.

speech and reason and so is equivocal among them. And so among us logic is in one sense a science of discourse, and in that sense it includes grammar, rhetoric, and logic properly so-called; in the other sense it is a science of reason, and in that sense it is a science belonging to the trivium, distinguished from grammar and rhetoric. It is our present intention to discuss logic in this latter sense.

Regarding logic in that sense, it is important to know that it is called a science of reason not because it considers things belonging to reason as they occur in reason alone, since in that case it would not properly be called a science of discourse, but because it teaches the method of reasoning that applies not only within the mind but also in discourse, and because it considers the things belonging to reason as well as the reasons why things set forth in discourse can be reasoned about by the mind. It is for this reason that a syllogism is called an expression in which a conclusion follows of necessity when certain things have been asserted. It is, therefore, a ratiocinative science, or science of reason, because it teaches one how to use the process of reasoning systematically, and a science of discourse because it teaches one how to put it into discourse systematically.

The origin of this science, as was mentioned before, was as follows. Since in connection with philosophical matters there were many contrary opinions and thus many errors (because contraries are not true at the same time regarding the same thing), thoughtful people saw that this stemmed from a lack of training in reasoning, and that there could be no certainty in knowledge without training in reasoning. And so they studied the process of reasoning in order to reduce it to an art, and they established this science by means of which they completed and organized both this [science] itself and all others; and it is the science of the method of reasoning on all [subject] matters.

For in the *Prior Analytics* there is a treatment of the form of reasoning not only in dialectical and demonstrative [syllogisms] but also in rhetorical [syllogisms], and generally in every art, and wherever belief occurs, as Aristotle declares toward the end of the *Prior Analytics*, in the chapter on induction (II 23, 68b9–13). Nevertheless, the form suited to the universal, scientific matters considered by philosophers, who deal with theses, properly belongs to the business of logic, while the form that is suited to the singular, sensible things considered by orators, who are connected with hypotheses, belongs to the business of rhetoric.

Therefore, in order that we might see the adequacy of logic with equal depth in the methods of reasoning and in the parts of logic, we should note that, regarding philosophical questions that are to be settled, one can reason on the basis of specific considerations as well as on the basis of common considerations.

[We reason] on the basis of specific considerations, I maintain, when the argumentation is based on the things that belong and are considered as belonging to the science to which the question to be settled belongs—as, for example, when one concludes that the three angles of a triangle are equal to two right angles in virtue of an exterior angle that is equipollent to the two opposite interior angles, and when one concludes that the moon when diametrically opposed to the sun is eclipsed in virtue of the interposed shadow of the earth, and other cases of that sort. For middles of that sort are the specific causes of such conclusions.

[We reason] on the basis of common considerations, I maintain, when the argumentation is drawn from things that occur commonly in the things belonging to every science and that can be suited to all sciences, and not only to the conclusions but to the principles of all of them. For dialectic 'has the way to the principles of all methods,' as Aristotle teaches in *Topics* I (2, 101b3–4). Common considerations of this sort are reasons belonging to whole and part, to a contrary, to a similar, and to an associated accident and things of that sort, from which dialectical Topics can be drawn. For example, one can show that a triangle has three angles equal to two right angles in virtue of the fact that every per se accident is in its per se subject and that having three angles is a per se accident of a triangle; and one can show that the moon when opposed to the sun is eclipsed because it is hidden from its light source, or that the sun is eclipsed because it is hidden from our sight, and other things of that sort. For in the cases just discussed the middle is drawn from associated accidents. And it can be suited to other conclusions and sciences as well as to those just discussed.

Now, the reason we argue to scientific conclusions both on the basis of specific considerations and on the basis of common considerations, and even to principles on the basis of common considerations, is that the truth is often hidden from us, and our cognition begins from the more universal and tends to the more specific. And so at first we reason by means of common, readily believable middles until an opinion is formed, and then we penetrate to the specific causes; and in that way genuine science comes about, provided that they are comprehended as specific causes. Therefore, because one must unquestionably have one method of finding, judging, proposing, and disputing as regards the specific considerations belonging to any discipline, and another method as regards the common considerations (since in the former one is to find only a readily believable middle, in the latter a necessary middle, the first of which is carried out in many ways and the second in one way, or a few, to the same conclusion); and because in the one case it must be proposed with a question and disputed on the basis of a common consideration with the respondent's consent, in the other case [it is proposed] without a question and must be disputed unhesitatingly to the conclusion even if the respondent does not consent, as Aristotle teaches in *Topics* VIII (1, 155b3–28) and in *Sophistici Elenchi* I (2, 165a38–b11)—for that reason it is the business of logic, which is the method of the sciences and must teach the method of finding the truth in them, to transmit the art of reasoning on the basis of specific considerations and on the basis of common considerations. And the logic that teaches us how to reason on the basis of specific considerations is called demonstrative logic and is transmitted in Aristotle's *Posterior Analytics*, whereas that which teaches us how to reason on the basis of common considerations is called dialectic and is transmitted in Aristotle's *Topics*.

Again, because those differentiae of reasonings on the basis of specific considerations and on the basis of common consid-

erations are drawn from the [subject] matter (since they are drawn from the things and the middles about which the reasonings are carried out), although the form of reasoning is the same as regards every [subject] matter, logic had to offer a treatment of the method of reasoning in general insofar as it abstracts from all matter, specific or common, which both the demonstrator and the dialectician who want to reason would of course have in view. For syllogistic form is the same in every [sort of] matter, the necessary and the readily believable.

Notice, however, that that form is not abstracted in such a way that it is determined on its own, without matter of any sort; for that could not happen. Instead, just as mathematics is abstracted from physical matter only and yet has its own intelligible matter (as we showed in preceding discussions), so syllogistic and ratiocinative form of every sort is abstracted from matter both common and specific—i.e., both readily believable and necessary. Nevertheless, it carries a kind of simpler matter along with it, which is between both those mentioned— namely, the three terms: the two extremes and the one middle out of which the two propositions [or premises] are put together.

Syllogistic and ratiocinative form of every sort is established in Aristotle's *Prior Analytics* (I 4, 25b32ff.), where we are always given three terms constituting two propositions [or premises], but [terms] that abstract from both readily believable and necessary matter. And we are taught in how many and which moods and in how many and which figures true reasoning can be carried out in connection with those [terms] in every [sort of] matter in such a way that both the demonstrator and the dialectician take the form of reasoning from it. Therefore, in the *Prior Analytics* Aristotle teaches a method of reasoning by way of all sorts of possible combinations of all sorts of propositions, and he does this in three figures, showing that there is no other figure or true combination [of propositions] than those he presents. [He] also [shows] what sort of middle [term] there must be and how it is to be found. Finally, toward the end of the book, he teaches other methods of reasoning that evidently have none of the reasoning power of syllogism except as a result of syllogism and on the basis of the figures and moods predetermined there; and he shows this regarding induction, example, deduction, counterinstance, and enthymeme.

Then in the *Posterior Analytics* he teaches a method of reasoning on the basis of specific considerations belonging to a particular scientific subject in order to construct a demonstrative syllogism and seek diligently after true science. And he does this not by establishing a syllogistic form different from the earlier one or by reproducing the same one; instead he establishes certain material conditions of syllogism in virtue of which syllogism, [which has been considered] unconditionally, is restricted to demonstration. [He does it in such a way] that demonstration most strictly speaking must be based on the first principles of the thing to be concluded, principles that are true, [known] per se, universal, immediate causes, and the like; but by extension [a demonstration] can sometimes be made on the basis of conclusions that have been concluded in virtue of true principles, sometimes on the basis of an effect, sometimes on the basis of a particular cause, and the like. He also teaches how many and what sorts of questions there are to which the demonstrator attends, what sort of thing a demonstrative middle must be, and how it is to be found.

And those two books belong to a single sequence, as is clear from the general preface at the beginning of the *Prior Analytics* (I 1, 24b12–14), where the aim of the *Posterior Analytics* is stated, and from the general epilogue toward the end of the *Posterior Analytics* (II 19, 99b15–17), where there is a brief summation of both books. And for that reason they are called [books of] examination, or the *Prior* and *Posterior Analytics*. Now the reason for this sequential arrangement may be that the demonstrative is the preeminent method of syllogistic

reasoning, the one that is principally and finally aimed at, and the one the possession of which brings human inquiry to rest. For dialectical and sophistical [syllogistic reasoning] are not principally aimed at in their own right, as will soon be clear, but on account of the science that is to be acquired in the end by means of demonstrative [syllogistic reasoning]. And it is for that reason that the method of demonstrating is transmitted in the same unbroken sequence with the form of syllogism considered unconditionally.

Another reason may be that much judgment must be brought to bear in connection with syllogism considered unconditionally as well as with demonstrative syllogism. For in connection with syllogism considered unconditionally one must judge regarding the terms and the conjoining of them, regarding figure, [and] regarding mood, which consists in the arrangement of the propositions, each one of which occurs in many ways, as is clear throughout almost the whole book of the *Prior Analytics*. It is also a requirement of demonstration that one consider whether or not the principles that are set down to begin with are causes and, if they are, whether they are mediate or immediate, universal or particular, and many other things, as is taught in *Posterior Analytics* I. And so there is a great deal to do with judgment as regards both [syllogism considered unconditionally and demonstration]. And both books are called [books of] analysis or examination because when a syllogism has been made, one judges it on the basis of an examination of it. But there is a little in both as regards discovery in respect of judgment, as is clear in *Prior Analytics* I, where Aristotle teaches how to discover a syllogistic middle, and in *Posterior Analytics* II, where he teaches how to discover a demonstrative middle.

In the *Topics*, however, he teaches the method of reasoning from common considerations to all sciences—viz., from things readily believable to the construction of a dialectical syllogism, in which an opinion is diligently sought after by the inquiry of two people, the one opposing and the other responding—not in order to come to a stop with it, but in order that by means of that opinion a complete and easier access to trustworthy knowledge might be gained. And in that book he teaches us how (by means of certain conditions pertaining to the [subject] matter) to restrict the syllogistic form considered unconditionally to the dialectical syllogism. And because dialectic is good for three things—for the philosophical disciplines (so that truth may be found in them), for opposing someone, and for [intellectual] exercise—he establishes it in respect of all three of its ends. First, up to Book Eight, [he establishes] its principal end, by which it is directed to the recognition of the truth in the sciences, distinguishing four kinds of problems in connection with four kinds of predicates—the essential interchangeable and noninterchangeable [predicates], and the accidental interchangeable and noninterchangeable [predicates]—teaching how to produce syllogisms on the basis of readily believable things on both sides of any problem whatever.

In connection with these things it should be noted that he does not teach us how to determine whether a genus, proprium, or definition inheres or does not inhere unconditionally, but whether anything inheres as a genus, as a proprium, or as a definition. And so the problem of genus occurs not when one asks about that which is the genus, but when on asks whether something inheres as a genus (and likewise, I maintain, as regards proprium and definition); for those three problems are recognizable by the fact that they ask only about the mode of inhering. The problem of accident, on the other hand, is recognized in two forms: if one asks whether something inheres unconditionally, and if one asks whether it inheres with a mode—i.e., whether it inheres as an accident. Thus, when one asks about the unconditional inherence of any predicate whatever, it is always a problem of accident; or every question of that sort reduces to a determination of accident, both because it is a proprium of accident to inhere, and because when

something can inhere both unconditionally and in a certain respect, both of those modes of inhering are found in accident, while in the other [predicables] only unconditional inherence is to be found. For that reason a question of unconditional inherence is associated with accident rather than with the others.

In *Topics* VIII (1, 156a6ff., and 5, 159a25ff.), however, dialectic for opposing and dialectic for exercising are established. And, if I am not mistaken, these two exist not in their own right, but for the sake of dialectic as an inquiry into truth, so that we might become more adept at it. Aristotle does not expressly say this, although his words toward the beginning of the *Topics* suggest it (I 2, 101a25–b4). On the basis of these remarks it is clear that the three books we have been discussing are both necessary and sufficient for logic.

But since among the things opposed to the principles none must be better known [than the principles], as Aristotle says in the *Posterior Analytics* (I 2, 72a37–b3), and reasoning, both demonstrative and dialectical, is the source of recognizing and discovering truth, and a careless person can be deceived in connection with either, logic must determine the deceptions that can occur in either of them so that they can be avoided and one may thus come to the truth more expeditiously and recognize it more confidently. Deceptive reasoning is called sophistic because it appears to produce knowledge in some way when it does not do so. If it takes place in connection with a demonstrative syllogism having to do with specific considerations belonging to some subject, it is called a paralogism of a discipline (because it produces a paralogism on the basis of specific considerations belonging to some discipline or other) or a syllogism of ignorance (because it brings about a dispositional ignorance, which is a wrong state of mind opposed to knowledge, as Aristotle teaches in *Posterior Analytics* I (12, 77b19–22). Some also call it a syllogism deceptive with regard to a cause (*propter quid*), a name Aristotle uses in *Sophistici Elenchi* I (11, 171b7–12), because it does not indicate the cause it seems to indicate, and so is deceptive. And according to Aristotle in *Topics* I (1, 101a5–8) and *Posterior Analytics* I (16–17, 79a23–81a37ff.), this paralogism draws its conclusion from a false premise—one or the other or both—but it reasons on the basis of specific considerations and in specific terms and draws its conclusions necessarily. For it does not err as regards syllogistic form but as regards the definition of demonstration, which must always proceed on the basis of truths. (Aristotle discusses this in the same book in which he discusses demonstration—viz., *Posterior Analytics* I.)

But the deceptive reasoning that occurs in connection with dialectical syllogism having to do with things common to all subjects is called the contentious syllogism in the *Topics* and *Sophistici Elenchi*, and the *Sophistici Elenchi* is about it. And it occurs in many different ways indeed; for either it does what it should not do, or it does not do what it should. It does what it should not do when it introduces a false premise or conclusion to produce a wrong state of mind, something reasoning should not do. And that occurs in three different ways, according to Aristotle in *Topics* I (1, 100b23–101a18).

[A] It errs as regards form alone (when the consequence does not hold good, as in 'Every man is an animal, a donkey is not a man; therefore, it is not an animal').

[B] It errs as regards matter alone (when the consequence is good but at least one of the premises is false and not readily believable even though it appears to be readily believable, as in 'Every statue is natural, the figure of Hercules is a statue; therefore, it is natural'; the first [premise], which is false and not readily believable, can appear acceptable in virtue of the fallacy of accident: 'Every statue is bronze, and all bronze is natural; therefore, every statue is natural').

[C] It errs as regards both matter and form (as in 'Every man is an animal, what is risible is not a man; therefore, it is not an animal', the minor premise is false and not readily believable, but it can seem readily believable to someone in virtue of the fal-

lacy of accident in this way: 'No property is a man, risible is a property; therefore, it is not a man'; and that reasoning erred also in form because it argued from the destruction of the antecedent).

These ways are discussed in the *Sophistici Elenchi*. The one that errs in form is discussed in the section that discusses verbal and extra-verbal sophistical Topics, for it is there that the specious syllogism is discussed, and that is the sort that errs as regards form. But in the chapter of *Sophistici Elenchi* I that begins 'But since we have . . .' (8, 169b18ff.), I think Aristotle gives his view on the [syllogism] that errs as regards matter, which in that same place he calls sophistical, as he himself explains. As a result of these considerations we have sufficiently discussed the syllogism that errs as regards matter and as regards form.

On the other hand, the sophistical syllogism that does not do what it should do is the one that is based on readily believable things and concludes necessarily, and yet deceives in virtue of the fact that it promises to yield a conclusion producing knowledge on the basis of specific considerations and concludes on the basis of common considerations that can produce only belief. Bryson's syllogism on the squaring of the circle was of this sort, it is said: In any genus in which one can find a greater and a lesser than something, one can find what is equal; but in the genus of squares one can find a greater and a lesser than a circle; therefore, one can also find a square equal to a circle. This syllogism is sophistical not because the consequence is false, and not because it produces a syllogism on the basis of apparently readily believable things—for it concludes necessarily and on the basis of what is readily believable. Instead, it is called sophistical and contentious because it is based on common considerations and is dialectical when it should be based on specific considerations and is dialectical when it should be based on specific considerations and be demonstrative (*demonstrativus/demonstrativis*). It is for that reason that Aristotle in *Sophistici Elenchi* I (11, 171b17–18) says that the circle is squared in Bryson's inference, but because it is not squared in reality, [the syllogism] is sophistical. And this syllogism is the third of the sorts of false inference Aristotle presents in *Topics* VIII (12, 162b8–10)—viz., when the inference yields what was sought but not in its proper discipline, which occurs when what is not medical is presented as medical, or what is not geometrical is presented as geometrical. It seems to me that it is this sort of contentious syllogism that is discussed in *Sophistici Elenchi* I in the chapter [beginning] 'And a contentious and sophistical syllogism is one that indeed appears . . .' (11, 171b7–9). Someone might also think that it is the same as the one that Aristotle calls deceptive with regard to a cause (in the chapter soon after the beginning) (11, 171b10–12), because it is deceptive in virtue of the fact that it is based on common considerations although it should present the cause of the thing and bring about knowledge based on the cause.

The contentious syllogism, therefore, occurs in the ways that have been mentioned, and *Sophistici Elenchi* deals with it in all those different ways. For since dialectic is based on common considerations regarding all the arts and the contentious syllogism is deceptive regarding common considerations and is based on common considerations, dealing with the contentious syllogism will be altogether the business of the dialectician, as dealing with a paralogism of a discipline is the business of the demonstrator, since one and the same discipline deals with opposites. And so the book of the *Topics* and the *Sophistici Elenchi* is one continuous treatise regarding common considerations having to do with all the arts and sciences, pertaining altogether to dialectic, which is traditionally called by almost everyone the art of discovery because in it one must find a great deal and judge very little. For in connection with arguing on the affirmative or negative side of a dialectical problem one can think up a middle in innumerable different ways, in none of which is there any need to judge further than that a readily believable middle has been found and that it concludes

correctly. For in *Topics* VIII (12, 162b24–30) Aristotle teaches that as regards a dialectical judgment the first thing to consider is whether the inference yields a conclusion; second, whether it is true or false, third, what sort of things it is based on. For one that concludes on the basis of false though readily believable things is better than one that concludes on the basis of true things that are not readily believable; but the worst is the one that is based on things that are false and not readily believable. In connection with the contentious syllogism, on the other hand, the discovery is carried out in as many ways as [the syllogism] is made. As far as the opponent is concerned, however, the only judgment is whether [his argument] has the semblance [of good reasoning] in its matter, its form, or both. As far as the respondent is concerned, [judgment is made] in as many ways as there are causes of the semblance, as is clear in *Sophistici Elenchi* II.

On this basis it is clear, then, why the *Topics* and *Sophistici Elenchi* are traditionally said to be the art of discovery, the *Prior* and *Posterior Analytics* the art of judgment. For the designation comes from the greater part [of the treaties], even though in the details there is something about discovery and something about judgment [in all of them], but more or less as necessity and the suitability of the matter require.

It is also clear that the whole treatise on the dialectical and contentious syllogism pertains to dialectic, both because each of them is based on common considerations and because one and the same discipline deals with opposites. And Aristotle shows this clearly in *Sophistici Elenchi* I, in the chapter [beginning] 'But in accordance with the things they argue about, those who use refutations . . .' (9, 170a20ff.). And the continuity of the whole treatise testifies to this, because a general preamble is put at the beginning of the *Topics* (I 1, 100a18–25) and a general epilogue follows at the end of the *Sophistici Elenchi* (34, 183a27–b15). On this basis it is also clear that those who say that the *Sophistici Elenchi* is about the sophistical syllogism in all its generality are mistaken. The sophistical [syllogism] that produces a paralogism on the basis of specific considerations belonging to some discipline concerns not the dialectician but the demonstrator, as Aristotle shows in the cited chapter of *Sophistici Elenchi* I, 'But in accordance with the things they argue about . . .' (9, 170a36–39), and so it is dealt with in the *Posterior Analytics*.

On the basis of things said so far we can assess, in a way, the general adequacy of the ways of reasoning Aristotle establishes in four books of his logic: *Prior* and *Posterior Analytics*, *Topics*, and *Sophistici Elenchi*.

But because reasoning is an inquiry of reason advancing from one term to another through a middle—the sort of thing that cannot happen unless it first puts the terms together with the middle, or puts the one together with it and divides the other from it, so that in this way it follows (*consequatur/ consequantur*) the composition of terms with one another or the division of them from one another—one must be in possession of the art of compounding and dividing terms before one is taught the art of reasoning. And because composition and division are species of proposition or of statement, Aristotle had to deal with statement and its species and their nature. And for that purpose he produced the book *Perihermenias* [or *De interpretatione*].

Again, because the composition and division that thought brings about must have reference to the being and not-being of things outside thought (since in statements one must consider the true and the false on the basis of which the reasoning founded on those statements seeks the true and the false that are unknown, and statements are true or false only in virtue of a relationship to the being or not-being of things outside thought), the logician has to have some knowledge of things and learn their nature to the extent to which it is appropriate to their capacity for being compounded and divided by thought. And for that purpose Aristotle produced the *Categories*.

On the basis of these considerations the entire general adequacy of the books and parts of Aristotle's logic can now be seen. For, since reasoning is the task of the reason

compounding and dividing in itself in accordance with what is outside it in real things, in order that this may be carried out systematically, one needs first of all an understanding of things that have the capacity to be compounded and divided, which is transmitted in the *Categories*: second, the systematic composition and division of them, which is transmitted in the other books.

But because reasoning is not just any composition and division belonging to reason, but the sort that is of extremes via a single middle, for the science of reasoning one must, first of all, know how any sort of composition and division of two terms is systematically brought about by means of reason and, second, how the composition or division of extremes is brought about via a middle. For the first lies before the second, and reason runs through the first into the second; for from the premises reason advances to the conclusion. The first is transmitted in the *Perihermenias*, the second in the other books.

But because the composition and division of extremes via a middle can occur via a middle unconditionally, abstracting from every restriction having to do with matter—and I mean by matter in connection with this sort [of middle] what is readily believable or necessary (om. ⟨*medium*⟩) whether common to all sciences or specific to any one of them—or via a middle that is restricted to some matter, one must first teach the art of reasoning unconditionally, common to every matter, both common and specific, both readily believable and necessary, in connection with terms and propositions not significant of but applicable to every matter and capable of standing for everything, such as 'A', 'B', 'C'; and that is done in the *Prior Analytics*. Second, [one must teach] the art of reasoning specifically in connection with both kinds of matter, and that is done in the other books.

And because reasoning that is based on things necessary and specific to any science produces cognition that is knowledge, and reasoning that is based on things readily believable and common to every science produces cognition that is opinion (of which the first is more powerful and the one that is ultimately aimed at by those who reason), the first is taught in the first place in the *Posterior Analytics* and is called demonstration, and the second is taught in the second place in the *Topics* and is called dialectical syllogism. And because ambiguity and deception occur in connection with both of these reasonings, [ambiguity and deception] which must be known so as to be avoided, the paralogism of a discipline, which is deceptive in connection with demonstration, is dealt with in the *Posterior Analytics*, and the contentious syllogism, which is deceptive in connection with dialectic, is discussed in the *Sophistici Elenchi*. And so the art of reasoning has been adequately dealt with.

On the basis of these considerations one can easily consider the subject of logic as well as its end and definition. For its subject is reasoning, since it is to reasoning that all the things treated in logic are traced back as subjective or integral parts, or in some

such way. Those who claim that its subject is syllogism return to that same thing; for all modes of reasoning, as Aristotle teaches in the *Prior Analytics* (II 23, 68b8–37), draw their force from syllogism and are traced back to it. Thus, those who claim that its subject is reasoning propose that which is commonly predicated of every mode of reasoning, and those who claim that it is syllogism propose the most powerful reasoning, to which all modes of reasoning are traced back. Now, the end of logic is the investigation of unknown truth, especially in connection with theses that pertain to philosophical consideration. From these observations one can infer a definition of the following sort: Logic is the science of reasoning, teaching the way of investigating unknown truth in connection with a thesis or in connection with a philosophical question. From the things already said one can in one way or another infer briefly a reasoned explanation for the name of logic, its origin, adequacy, subject matter, end, and definition.

"DIALECTIC AND DEMONSTRATION"

Chapter LVII. A Comparison of Dialectic and Demonstration: Their Difference and Their Agreement.

We are still faced with a difficult question regarding dialectic and demonstration, which are parts of logic: How do they differ? For demonstration teaches us how to reveal the characteristic proper to the species to which it belongs, and that is the same as revealing the proprium. Again, it often teaches us how to reveal a definition, since what is material is revealed by way of the formal in that form is the cause of matter; for example, the inflammation of the blood around the heart is demonstrated by a desire for misfortune for one's opponent—which are the two definitions of anger. But dialectic also teaches us how to reveal both the proprium and the definition. Again, demonstration uses cause and definition as a middle [term]—but so does di-

alectic. For dialectic argues on the basis of the Topic *from a cause* and on the basis of the Topic *from definition*. Again, demonstration occasionally reveals a cause by means of an effect, as when it reveals that the stars are near because they do not twinkle; but dialectic also argues *from an effect*. Therefore, since they use the same middle [terms] and [argue] to the same conclusions, we ask how they differ.

At the same time we also ask in what different ways they serve as auxiliaries, for each of them can be considered both in itself and as an auxiliary. (For on that basis even the whole science of reasoning can be considered in two different ways.)

In reply to the first question we have to say that demonstration and dialectic differ in their revealing both a proprium and a definition, [and] first in respect of the middle [term]. For dialectic reasons on the basis of many intrinsic, extrinsic, and intermediate Topics to a solution that is to be given to every sort of problem, and it does so on either side [of any problem] and on the basis of readily believable things and common considerations only. For the Topics *from a cause, from definition, from the whole,* or [any others] of that sort, as considered by the dialectician, provide a middle [term], sometimes for a problem involving accident, sometimes for a problem involving genus, and similarly as regards the other [predicables]. Also, they sometimes give us an argument in ethics, sometimes in physics, sometimes in logic.

Demonstration, on the other hand, does not use such a large number of middle [terms]; but, if it is demonstration of the preeminent sort, it is demonstration on the basis of the proximate and immediate cause, and it is so exclusively. But, by an extension [from] things drawn from the proximate and immediate cause, [it demonstrates] also on the basis of a remote and mediate cause, and sometimes even from the effect. But the fact that it reveals things via definition is a result of the fact that a definition indicates a cause when it is based on prior things, a result of the fact that it indicates an effect if it happens to be a definition expressed on the basis of posterior things. Demonstration is made up of these ways [of revealing and indicating]. Nor does it adduce proof for both sides of a contradiction, but for the true side only; and it does so by means of considerations that are true, necessary, and specific. For it does not consider cause, effect, or definition in its common character, but in its specific and essential character, in virtue of which one thing is the specific cause (or effect, or definition) of another, and essentially indicative of that very thing. And so, as far as the demonstrator is concerned, a Topic common to many is not under consideration; rather, his Topic is specific for a particular conclusion, as well as for things that derive from a primary and specific conclusion by means of a particular demonstration.

They differ, in the second place, in respect of the conclusion. For dialectic uses the art of reasoning for determining many kinds of propria, of which some are assigned as complex and others as noncomplex, as is clear from *Topics* V (1, 128b14–129a16); for as far as the dialectician is concerned, every accidental and interchangeable predicate is called a proprium. Demonstration, on the other hand, tries to demonstrate a specific characteristic that is said of the subject per se in the second way; and that is a noncomplex proprium. And it applies to every [thing in the subject], and only [to every such thing], and always, and also in respect of what it is, if the demonstration is based on immediate [causes].

Similarly, dialectic also argues in order to determine every kind of definition, whether it is made up of integral or of essential parts. Definition, similarly, is also assigned in virtue of all sorts of causes; for [Aristotle] calls definition 'every essential interchangeable predicate' [cf. *Topics* I 4, 101b20–21, VII 3, 153a15–23]. Demonstration, on the other hand, does not reveal a definition unless there is some other cause of it; so that the definition that is the middle [term] is the specific and essential cause of the revealed definition. Therefore, although both [dialectic and demonstration] reveal a proprium and a definition, the difference [between them] is clearly great.

Again, although both argue by means of definition and cause and effect, they are very dissimilar. For the dialectician considers his middle [term] as readily believable and possibly otherwise than it is, and so by its means he acquires only opinion, which is cognition that can change. The demonstrator, however, considers his middle [term] as necessary and essential, and as not possible otherwise than it is; and so he acquires knowledge, which is certain cognition that cannot change.

Thus, it should be noted that the same person can have first opinion and then knowledge by means of numerically the same middle [term] and regarding numerically the same thing, or that at the same time on person can have opinion regarding something and another have knowledge regarding the same thing by means of the same middle [term], as Aristotle teaches near the end of *Posterior Analytics* I (33, 89a11–b6). For there he teaches that, just as there can be true and false opinion regarding the same thing in reality, differentiated reason alone, so likewise, regarding something that is the same in reality but differentiated in reason and [considered] by means of a middle [term] that is the same in reality and differentiated in reason alone, there can be both knowledge and opinion. And he teaches that the differentiation in reason comes to this: That anyone who knows a conclusion by its essence and in accordance with pure truth, and perceives that it could not be otherwise, and judges that the middle [term] by means of which he knows it could likewise not be otherwise, does not have opinion but truly knows. On the other hand, anyone who considers the conclusion and the middle [term] associated with it as possibly being otherwise has opinion and does not truly know. For example, anyone who knows that the moon when opposite to the sun is eclipsed in virtue of falling into the earth's shadow and thinks that this could be otherwise (because, perhaps, he imagines that it can be eclipsed otherwise than by the earth's shadow—e.g., by the shadow of a cloud or some other body, or by the rotation of the moon's globe, according to those who imagine that part of it is bright and part of it dark, and that by the rotation of various parts it appears to us to be waxing and waning)—[such a person] has opinion and not knowledge. On the other hand, anyone who has seen clearly that the earth's shadow is the true essential cause of the eclipse of the moon, and that it could not be otherwise, has knowledge. In this way, then, the dialectician and the demonstrator use the same middle [terms], but in different ways, as was said.

And the demonstrator uses no middle [terms] other than definition and cause, since one cannot properly know otherwise than by means of the cause, and the definition indicates the cause—except that sometimes he uses an effect, and in that case the effect must be interchangeable with and better known than the cause, as [Aristotle] teaches in *Posterior Analytics* I (13, 78a26). The dialectician, on the other hand, uses many other middle [terms] and uses those already mentioned in more ways than the demonstrator does, since a person can acquire an opinion in very many different ways.

In reply to the second question, we have to say that the demonstration taught in the *Posterior Analytics* is auxiliary to other sciences in virtue of setting them up and expanding those that have been set up; for a science is acquired in the first place by demonstration and expanded by that means once it has been acquired. The dialectic taught in the *Topics*, however, is auxiliary to other sciences only in moving reason forward to a variable degree of cognition short of knowledge (which is invariable), a cognition by means of which the way is opened to true knowledge (which is the possession of the conclusions), up to understanding (which is called the possession of the principles). And that is why Aristotle says in *Topics* I (14, 105b19–26, 30–31) that although there are three kinds of propositions and problems—viz., ethical (e.g., whether one should obey one's parents or the laws if they disagree), physical (e.g., whether the world is eternal), and logical (e.g., whether opposites belong to the same discipline)—all of them are the business of philosophical consideration, which is called demonstration as far as truth is concerned but dialectic as regards opinion.

But dialectic might be called auxiliary rather than (and in a way more correctly than) demonstration, because (in the first place) to be an auxiliary is to give part of the support and not to provide all of it, and dialectic contributes something toward knowledge but does not establish it, whereas demonstration effects and completes it; and because (in the second place) in all the parts of philosophy—ethics, physics, and logic—readily believable arguments are easily found, although in all likelihood demonstrations are not. For in ethics, demonstration is either not easy or altogether impossible, and similarly in some natural [sciences] (as was said above, where we explained how the practical sciences are parts of philosophy).

All the same, the demonstrative science taught in logic is called an auxiliary to other sciences, because all of them are established, expanded, and completed by means of it, and [because] it begins by offering one or only a few conclusions, [and] then many on the basis of those. And I say 'all' only to the extent to which entities have the possibility of being the subjects of sciences; for we cannot find equal necessity (or perhaps necessity at all) in connection with all things [whatsoever].

And we should take note of the fact that when the parts of philosophy are said to be physics, ethics, and logic, by 'physics' we understand the entire speculative science that has to do with divine matters; for it speculates regarding the natures of all entities, and it includes physics properly so-called as well as mathematics and metaphysics. And by 'logic' we understand the entire science belonging to the trivium, so-called from 'logos,' which is speech. But mechanics falls outside this division because philosophers traditionally do not trouble themselves much about it. Or perhaps it can be traced back to ethics as its handmaiden, or to physics, since mechanics is subordinated in a way to physics, commonly so-called because of the physical things with which it deals or because of its mode of operation (as was said above where the comparison of the speculative and practical sciences was sorted out).

On the basis of these considerations, then, the difference between dialectic and demonstration is clear, both in themselves and in their role as auxiliaries. But there is no need to inquire now into the way in which syllogistic and reasoning in general serve as auxiliaries to all the sciences, since it is clear that in its species, dialectic and demonstration, it does provide auxiliaries, as long as they serve as auxiliaries to the sciences. Nor can it be otherwise, as is clear per se. For [reasoning] does not stoop to contributing to any science except when there is reasoning either by means of common considerations and readily believable things—in which case it is dialectic—or by means of specific considerations and necessary things—in which case it is demonstration.

CHAPTER 47

Jean Buridan

(See Chapter Thirty-five for biography.)

Jean Buridan On Sophisms

The term 'sophism,' in the medieval sense of the word, is intentionally ambiguous. On the one hand, it means a sentence that is problematic. The broader sense of the term, however, entails the arguments for and against such a problematic proposition with the expectation of learning from the dialectical interplay, namely, the entire discussion surrounding the sophism in question. Throughout the *Sophismata* Buridan uses both senses of the term.

In chapter 8 of this very significant work Buridan discusses twenty sophisms which naturally fall into four main categories. (A) The first six constitute a miscellaneous group of problems which are concerned with self-reference. These, however, do not involve insolubles proper. He uses them to "set up" subsequent arguments, and it should be noted that they are principally concerned with the nature of propositions and the conditions of the validity of inferences. (B) The second set of sophisms (7–12) constitute discussions of Liar-type paradoxes. Sophism 11 is the Liar paradox itself and reads:

> It is posited that I say nothing except this proposition, "I speak falsely." Then, it is asked whether my proposition is true or false.
> If you say that it is true, then it is not as my proposition signifies. Thus, it follows that it is not true but false.
> And if you say that it is false, then it follows that it is as it signifies. Hence, it is true.

The Liar paradox is the classic case of self-reference whereby the referred proposition is true if it is false and false if it is true. Central to the paradox is that it asserts a proposition that contains an expression that refers to itself.

(C) Sophisms 13–15 are epistemic paradoxes. That is, they are predicated on the notions truth and falsity, knowing and doubting. (D) The last five sophisms (16–20) pertain to propositional attitudes such as wishing.

It is evident from Chapter 8 of his *Sophismata* that Buridan was an astute thinker. He clearly ranks as one of the most noteworthy philosophers of the fourteenth century.

SOPHISMATA

Chapter VIII: Insolubles

The eighth chapter will be about propositions having reflection on themselves, due to the significations of their terms, in which chapter are contained the so-called insolubles. And starting from the easier, this sophism is stated:

A. Sophism

(1) Every proposition is affirmative, so none is negative.

It is proved, first, by the argument from contraries, for just as it follows that if every man is ill, then no man is healthy, because it is impossible for the same person to be both healthy and ill, so it follows in the proposed [case] that it is impossible for the same proposition to be both affirmative and negative at once.

Likewise, an enthymematic consequence is valid if by the addition of a necessary proposition, one could complete a syllogism of valid form. For by such additions are we accustomed to prove our enthymematic consequences. For example, we say that this consequence is valid: the ass flies, so the ass has wings, because this [proposition] is necessary: "Every flying [thing] has wings." And if it is made the major premiss, the syllogism will be valid in the third mood of the first figure. But so also in the proposed [case], this is necessary: "No affirmative proposition is negative." And if this is made the major premiss in the preceding enthymeme, it will be a valid syllogism in the second mood of the first figure.

Again, from the opposite of the consequent, there follows the opposite of the antecedent. Therefore, the consequence is

From *John Buridan, Sophisms on Meaning and Truth*, translated by Theodore Kermit Scott (New York: Appleton-Century-Crofts, 1966), pp. 180–223. Reprinted by kind permission of Theodore Kermit Scott.

valid. This rule is not common to every valid consequence. But the antecedent is clear, since it manifestly follows that if a certain proposition is negative, then not every proposition is affirmative.

The opposite is argued, because from a possible proposition there does not follow an impossible. And yet the first proposition is possible, namely, "Every proposition is affirmative." For God could destroy all negatives, leaving the affirmatives. Thus, every proposition would be affirmative. But the other is impossible, namely, "None is negative," for in no case could it be true. For whenever it is not, it is neither true nor false, and whenever it is, then some [proposition] is negative, namely, it. Hence, it is false to say that none is negative.

Likewise, a consequence is not valid, if the antecedent could be true without the truth of the consequent. But so it is in the proposed case, since from the fact that the antecedent could be true and the consequent could not be true, it is apparent that the antecedent could be true without the truth of the consequent. And this is clear also because this is true: "Every proposition is affirmative," granting that God should destroy negatives. And then that consequent would not be true, because it would not be. Hence, it is manifest that the antecedent could be true without the consequent. So the consequence is not valid.

But I answer that a consequence is not said to be valid because the antecedent could not be true without the consequence or without the necessity of the consequent, but because it could not be true without the truth of the consequent formed at the same time as [the antecedent]. But this is not the case in the proposed consequence.

The contrary is argued, because if a consequence were called valid for this reason, it would follow that this consequence would be valid: No proposition is affirmative, so a stick is in the corner, since it is impossible for the antecedent, formed at the same time as the consequent, to be true. And if it could not be true, it follows that it could not be true without the consequent.

Likewise, those are not good consequences in which the consequent, if it should be stated with a true antecedent, would falsify that antecedent. For such a consequent seems to have more conflict,[1] than agreement[2] with such an antecedent. And yet this is so in the proposed case. For positing that this is true: "Every proposition is affirmative," then if this: "No proposition is negative" should be stated with it, it will be false. Hence, it is not a valid consequence.

I answer that the consequence is valid, as is well proved. But then it is difficult to say whence the consequent ought to be called true or false. And concerning this, I posit briefly some conclusions.

B. Conclusions

(1) The *first conclusion* is that a consequence is valid of which the antecedent could be true without the truth of the consequent and without the consequent. For this consequence is valid: a man runs, so an animal runs, and yet the first could be true although the second should not be true and should be destroyed.

(2) The *second conclusion* is that in a valid consequence, the antecedent could be true and the consequent could be not true. This is clear in the proposed case, for this could be true: "Every proposition is affirmative," and this could not be true: "No proposition is negative." And yet the latter follows from the former. And it must be similar in many other [cases], such as: every syllable is of many letters, so no syllable is of one letter.[3]

(3) The *third conclusion* is that some proposition is possible which could not be true. It is proved, because from a possible antecedent, there never follows an impossible consequent, as I suppose from the first book of the *Prior Analytics*.[4] And yet from this which is possible: "Every proposition is affirmative," there follows this: "No

proposition is negative." Hence, this is possible, and yet it could not be true. And so it is manifest that a proposition is not called possible because it can be true, nor impossible because it cannot be true. But it is called possible because as it signifies, so it can be, taking these words in a good sense, according to that use which they were said to have in the second chapter, and impossible when it could not be so, etc.

(4) The *fourth conclusion* is that it is impossible for the antecedent of a valid consequence to be true and the consequent to be false. For thus ought to be understood the statement that a false statement cannot follow from a true, as is said in the *Prior Analytics*.[5] And so indeed it is true that of every valid consequence, it is impossible for the antecedent to be true without the truth of the consequent formed at the same time as it. Hence, without denying this, it is to be conceded that from a true proposition, there can follow a false. For we could posit that this proposition is true: "Every proposition is affirmative." Then there could follow from this a false proposition, namely, "None is negative." But when this is concluded, namely, "None is negative," then the first is no longer true, but false.

(5) The *fifth conclusion* is that it is not sufficient for a consequence to be valid that it is impossible for the antecedent to be true without the consequent formed at the same time as it, as has been well argued previously, concerning a stick in the corner. And this is apparent in another example, for it does not follow that no proposition is negative, so no proposition is affirmative. Which should be clear, because from the opposite of the consequent, there does not follow the opposite of the antecedent. And yet the first could not be true without the truth of the second, which could not be true. So more is required, namely, that it could not be as the antecedent signifies, unless it were as is signified by the consequent. But concerning this conclusion, it has been said earlier that these words are not proper, but we use them to convey the meanings otherwise given. For we cannot express in one general statement, concern-

ing all true propositions, why they are true, nor concerning false ones, why they are false, as has been said elsewhere.

C. Solution of Sophism

(1) And by these remarks are solved the arguments refuting the sophism. To the first argument, it is said that this is possible: "No proposition is negative," although it could not be true. To the second, it is clear from the preceding what the answer is. To the third, it is to be said that those propositions are indeed in conflict with regard to being true, but they are not in conflict with regard to the case being as they signify, speaking always in the proper sense. Rather, they are in this way in agreement. For it is necessary that if the case is as the first signifies, so also it is as the second signifies.

D. Sophisms

(2) No proposition is negative; hence, a certain proposition is negative.

I prove it, assuming that from any proposition it follows that it is true. This seems to be expressed by Aristotle in the chapter of the *Categories* on the term "prior."[6] For it follows that if man is, then this is true: "Man is," and conversely. And he says the same of others. Then it is argued: it follows that if no proposition is negative, then this is true: "No proposition is negative." And it follows that if this is true, then it is. And it follows that if it is, then some proposition is negative. Hence, it follows, from the first to the last, that if no proposition is negative, then a certain proposition is negative.

Likewise, it is not possible for it to be as the first signifies, unless it is as the second signifies. Hence, the consequence is valid. The consequence seems manifest, because in the preceding sophism, we said a consequence to be valid for this reason, and no other reason could be given why a consequence is called valid. But I prove the an-

tecedent, because it follows that if it is as it signifies, then it signifies, and it follows that if it signifies, then it is; and if it is, then it is as the second proposition signifies.

The opposite is argued by that which was said in the preceding sophism, for it could be as it is signified to be by the first and yet not be as the second signifies. For it could be thus if every negative proposition should be destroyed. Hence, the consequence is not valid.

Likewise, from a possible proposition, its contradictory does not follow. But the first is possible, and its contradictory is the second. Therefore, etc.

I say briefly that the sophism is false, for that was not a valid consequence, as was well proved. And I answer to the first argument that the second proposition, as it is stated, is not true, properly speaking,[7] namely, that from any proposition, it follows that it is true. Thus, it does not follow: man is, so this is true: "Man is." For a man could be, even if there were no proposition. For it is possible for it to be as this proposition "Man is" signifies or could signify, even if the case stated by this proposition "This is true: 'Man is' " were without existence. For it could be as the first signifies, if a man should be and no proposition should be. But you could ask how that rule of Aristotle should be understood. I say that it should be understood as assuming the existence of the proposition, so that from every conjunction composed of some proposition and the statement that it is, it follows that it is true. For example, it follows that if man is and the proposition "Man is" is, then that proposition is true. For it could not be as that copulative signifies unless it were as is signified by the conclusion, speaking always in the proper sense.

Concerning the second argument, which seems to be difficult, I say, first, that a conclusion is never either true or false unless it is. And in order for the conclusion to be valid or true, it is necessary that both its antecedent and consequent are. And then, this rule is given, that the consequence is valid if it is impossible for it to be as is signified by the antecedent, unless it is as is signified by the consequent.

And this rule can be understood in two ways. One way is that it is a proposition of impossibility in the composite sense, in which way it is commonly stated. And the sense is that a consequence is valid if it is impossible to say "It is as is signified by an existing antecedent, and it is not as is signified by an existing consequent." And this rule is not valid, since according to this rule, it would follow that the sophism is true. And the argument proceeded according to this false rule.

In another way, it is understood that it is a proposition of impossibility in the divided sense, so that it has the sense that a consequent is valid if howsoever it is signified by the antecedent, it is impossible that it is so unless howsoever the consequent signifies, so it is. And it appears that it could not be argued by this rule that the sophism is true. For howsoever this signifies: "No proposition is negative," it is possible that it is so, even though it is not as the other signifies, because it would be thus, if, affirmatives remaining, every negative should be destroyed, which is possible.

(3) If every man runs, then an ass runs.

The third sophism is determined from the following. And it is this: I posit that every man is an ass. It follows that if every man runs, then an ass runs.

This is proved by syllogizing in the first mood of the first figure, as follows: every man runs, every ass is a man, by the case; hence, an ass runs. Hence, a syllogism to an impossible conclusion could be thus, namely, by taking the position of the opponent with some true proposition. And so we could infer the conclusion by a valid consequence, although that conclusion should be impossible. Thus also, in the proposed case, the consequence is valid. Likewise, as it is stated, it could not be as that antecedent signifies, unless it were as that consequent signifies. Therefore, from that

antecedent, with another assumption, there follows that consequent.

The opposite is argued, for the rule is posited in logic that every false consequence is impossible, and every true consequence is necessary. But an impossible proposition cannot be made necessary by positing any case. Hence, whatever case is posited or removed, conceded or not conceded, a false consequence cannot be made true. But it is certain that this consequence is false, for it is not necessary, namely, this: every man runs, so every ass runs. hence, whatever case is posited, it never follows that every man runs, so an ass runs.

The solution to this sophism is easy. For you voluntarily say or posit or assert whatever proposition you please. And never because of such an act could a necessary consequence be made not necessary, or conversely. Thus, as the sophism is stated, it is false. But still because of the arguments, it is to be known that some proposition can be uttered or posited or conceded simply as a proposition taken by itself. And then nothing follows from this proposition taken by itself. And then nothing follows from this proposition concerning other propositions or consequences, whether they are true or false. In another way, one might posit a proposition as the antecedent or a part of the antecedent, in order to infer something. And then it is indeed necessary to see whether or not the proposed conclusion follows from that statement, together with other statements. For example, in positing, if you should posit simply that every man is an ass, the consequence stated in the sophism is not made better or worse because of this. But if you posit in the manner of an antecedent, in order to infer some other conclusion, that every man is an ass, immediately I say that it does indeed follow that every man is an ass. And if you should propose that aforesaid proposition in the manner of a part of the antecedent, together with this other part "Every man runs," then I say that it does indeed follow: "Hence, an ass runs." And so the arguments proceed.

(4) I say that a man is an ass.

And it is asked concerning this sophism whether, in so speaking, one speaks truly or falsely.

And it is argued that one speaks falsely, for one says that a man is an ass and this is false; hence, etc.

But it is argued that he speaks truly, for his whole proposition was this: "I say that a man is an ass," and that was true, since he actually uttered that whole. Likewise, his proposition was affirmative, so it was true, because the subject and the predicate stood for the same thing. Hence, his proposition which he uttered was true. But that the subject and predicate stood for the same thing is clear, for if the copula is explicated, the proposition will be this: "I am saying that a man is an ass," and it is manifest that the term "I" and the term "saying that a man is an ass" stand for the same.

Concerning this sophism, many answer that he speaks both truly and falsely, since he utters the whole proposition "I say that a man is an ass" and this is true; hence, he speaks truly. But in so uttering that whole proposition, he utters each part of it. Hence, he says that a man is an ass, and in this he speaks falsely.

But this solution seems to me very dubious, for this solution supposes that a part of a proposition is a proposition, which I do not believe. The psalmist David, in speaking prophetically by the Holy Spirit, says nothing false, and yet he utters this whole proposition "He begins to say in his heart that God is not." Therefore, the psalmist utters the expression "God is not," and if this should be a proposition, he would be speaking falsely and heretically. Hence, it was not a proposition so expressed, but a part of this proposition. But that foolish one sinned who uttered such an expression alone as a proposition. And similarly, the half of a worm is not an animal, as long as it is part of an animal. But separated from the other part, it is an animal.

And concerning this proposition, I have said enough in the first chapter of the first tract of the *Summula de dialectica*. Therefore, it seems to me that in saying "I say that a man is an ass," one speaks truly, properly speaking. It is to be said also that he does not speak falsely. And when it is objected that he says that a man is an ass, I say that he does indeed utter such an expression, but not alone, as a proposition. Thus, that expression was neither true nor false.

But you reply strongly that from this position, it would follow that one would lie who said that this proposition "A man is an animal" is true. It is proved because his whole proposition is affirmative, and the subject stands for nothing. For this expression "A man is an animal" is not a proposition, but part of a proposition. And so that whole subject "this proposition 'Man is an animal' " stands for nothing, just as it would be if, pointing at a stone, I should say "This man is a substance." The subject would stand for nothing and the proposition would be false.

I answer that one must know what you indicate by the pronoun "this." For if you are indicating this expression "A man is an animal," which you say in your proposition, I say that your proposition is false, as was well argued. But if you should indicate another similar expression, taken and stated in itself, then the proposition would be true and its subject would stand for something, namely, for that expression which is by itself a false proposition. So in this sense, such propositions ought to be understood and conceded, and not in the other sense, except perhaps conditionally, namely, that proposition "Man is an animal" is true, that is, this expression "Man is an animal," if it should be stated by itself, would be a true proposition. And it appears that the whole thing is resolved in the same way.

The fifth sophism is solved in a similar way.

(5) Whatever Socrates hears Plato says.

The case is posited that Plato says this proposition "No man is an ass," and Socrates does not hear the first word but hears the rest, namely, "Man is an ass," and he hears nothing else.

Then the sophism is proved, for Socrates hears this expression "Man is an ass" and nothing else. And Plato utters that expression with another expression. Hence, whatever Socrates hears Plato says.

The opposite is argued, for Plato did not speak falsely, but truly. But Socrates heard a false proposition, namely, "Man is an ass." Hence, he hears what Plato does not say.

Likewise, by a syllogism with an impossible conclusion, it is argued thus: whatever Socrates hears Plato says, and Socrates hears a false proposition; hence, Plato says a false proposition. But this conclusion is false, for Plato says a most true proposition, namely, "No man is an ass," and it can be condemned for no falsity.

I answer that the sophism is true. Concerning the arguments for the opposite, I say that Socrates does not hear a true proposition or a false proposition, for he hears no proposition, but he hears only a part of a true proposition. Indeed, I believe that Plato said nothing false, but something true which implies no falsity. Yet he did indeed say something which was not true, namely, part of a true proposition.

But you will say against this that that expression is false which, when heard, causes a false mental proposition in the mind. But that expression which Socrates hears causes in Socrates a false mental proposition, whence Socrates, in the given case, believes that Plato is speaking falsely. Therefore, that expression is false.

I answer that he who speaks truly speaks neither badly nor falsely because of those badly hearing and receiving his proposition. Hence, it is certain that often someone utters a proposition, and another hearing it badly, believes that he utters another. And then that proposition causes in the hearer not the mental proposition which it signifies, but the mental proposition which that proposition which one believes he hears would signify. And in such a case, the spoken proposition is not false for the hearer. But that would be false which he believes

he hears. But every proposition would be false to a hearer which, when perfectly heard by one who also perfectly understands its signification, causes, according to those significations, a false mental proposition in the hearer.

So in our case, Socrates does not hear any proposition. But he believes that he hears one. Hence, that expression which Socrates hears does not make in him the sense which it signifies, for that is not the sense of the proposition, but it makes in him the sense which that proposition makes which he believes himself to hear. And from this it follows only that that proposition which he believes himself to hear would be false.

(6) It is true to say a man to be animal.

It is asked concerning this sophism whether in saying a proposition such as "It is true to say a man to be an animal," one speaks the truth. I posit that it is said. And I note that in these sophisms, I intend to speak of absolutely nothing as true or false, except as they pertain to differences in propositions. For I do not intend to ask whether God is true and the first truth, and whether man is false or a coin is false. But I want to speak of true and false according as they establish contradictions, as is said in the sixth of the *Metaphysics*,[8] for the logician is not concerned about the true and the false.

Therefore, I argue that one does not speak the truth in that. For this predicate "to say a man to be an animal" is taken either materially or significatively. If significatively, then to say a man to be an animal is the same as saying a man to be an animal, as I suppose from the *Metaphysics*.[9] And saying man to be an animal is one which is neither true nor false, because it is not a proposition nor a part of a contradiction. And if it is taken materially, it appears that it does not stand for any proposition. For if it should stand for itself or for something similar in expression, it is manifest that this expression "to say a man to be an animal" or something similar is not a proposition nor a complete sentence. Thus, it is neither true nor false. And if it is said that it does not stand for itself nor for any similar expression, but for another sentence formed under the indicative mood—just as this expression "man to run" ordinarily stands for an expression such as "Man runs," which is a proposition—then it is manifest that it does not stand for a proposition, but for a part of a proposition. For although "man to be good" could stand for that proposition "Man is good," still "to be good" does not stand for that proposition, but for an expression such as "is good," which is not a proposition. And so it is in this case. For although this expression "someone to say a man to be an animal" should stand for an expression such as "Someone says that a man is an animal," still this expression "to say a man to be an animal" could stand only for an expression such as "says a man to be an animal," which is not a proposition, nor is it either true or false. Thus, the sophism was false, but it is true to say "man to be animal."

The opposite is argued, because it is true that a man is an animal, and yet this expression "a man to be an animal" and this expression "A man is an animal" are materially equivalent, and one is taken for the other. Therefore, it is true to say a man to be an animal.

Likewise, to affirm a true proposition is true, just as to deny a true proposition is false. But to say a man to be an animal is to affirm a true proposition, namely, "A man is an animal." Therefore, to say a man to be an animal is true. And then the proposition may be converted, and it is the sophism.

I answer that the sophism is false, properly speaking. Yet some, speaking properly, substitute such expressions for others which could be true. For example, this is true: "One speaks the truth saying 'a man to be an animal,' " i.e., saying such an expression itself as "A man is an animal." Similarly, this is true: "To say 'a man to be an animal' is to say the truth." Similarly, this is true: "It is true 'man to be an animal.' " And yet the sophism, properly speaking, was false, as was well proved.

Then concerning the arguments. To the first, I say that this is false: "true to say that man is an animal." But this is true: "It is true that man is an animal." But "a man to be an animal" and "to say a man to be an animal" are greatly different.

To the second, I deny that to affirm or to deny any proposition is true or false. For to affirm or to deny is nothing other than the one affirming or denying. And this is a man, who is neither true nor false. And if "to affirm a proposition" should stand materially, then it is the same to say "to affirm a proposition" and to say "affirms a proposition," and this not a proposition but an incomplete sentence, as Vergil reads.[10]

(7) Every proposition is false.

The seventh sophism is this so-called insoluble: "Every proposition is false."

I posit the case that all true propositions should be destroyed and false ones remain. And then Socrates utters only this proposition: "Every proposition is false." Then it is asked whether his proposition is true or false.

And it is argued that it is not true, for I assume that it is impossible for the same proposition to be both true and false at the same time stated in the same language and received by all hearers. Thus if the proposition is true, it follows that not every proposition is false, for a certain one is true, and this contradicts that proposition. Hence, it is false, indeed, impossible, for every proposition is impossible from which its contradictory follows.

Furthermore, it is proved that it is not false, but true, for it is a universal proposition having no exception, neither in itself nor in another, according to the case. Therefore, it is true.

Likewise, if it is false, its subject and predicate do not stand for the same universally. Thus, since it is affirmative, it follows that it is true.

Again, if it is false, then howsoever it signifies, so it is. For it signifies only that every proposition is false, and so it is. Therefore, it is true.

Concerning this sophism, there are difficult doubts to be considered. The first is whether this proposition, in the given case, is true or false. The second is how it is possible to assign to it a contradictory or an equivalent.

And to the first, I say that retaining and conceding the aforesaid case, still with that it can be posited that it is true, which is apparent by what was said in the second sophism and in the third sophism of the seventh chapter, where it was said that we can use one time for another time. For we say truly in some time that Socrates sits, in which time he does not sit. For by the time known and by this verb "sits," we do not understand the time which now coexists with the proposition, but another time. And so generally the case is conceded that for the whole first hour of this day, no proposition is true, but every one is false. And let us posit that after the end of that hour Socrates says that every proposition is false, and that he speaks not for the time at which he speaks, but for the time of that first hour. Thus, his proposition would be true, for an induction would be sufficient which would take account of the propositions of the first hour.

But this solution, although it is true in that case, still does not remove the difficulty of the sophism in another case, namely, that he speaks for that time in which he speaks. And some, wanting to escape, say that terms which are of a nature to stand for propositions are not placed in propositions to stand for those propositions in which they are placed, but for others. Thus, they say that Socrates' proposition was true, because that term "proposition" in Socrates' proposition did not stand for that proposition, but for all others, and all those were false.

But it is clear that this solution is not correct. For one can speak of what one understands but by the concept from which this name "proposition" is taken, one understands indifferently every proposition, present, past, and future, his as well as another. Thus, he can speak of all proposi-

tions. So, it is manifest that I can say that the proposition which I now actually utter is affirmative, and it can be my intention to speak of it. Thus, that term stood for that proposition in which it was placed.

Likewise, in no way does this evasion avoid the difficulty, for I state that Socrates utters that proposition, and similarly Plato utters another similar proposition. And then by what reason one could call one true, by the same reason the other. And so of the false. Thus, either one should call both true or one should call both false. I ask then whether Socrates speaks truth. If you say he does, then since he speaks of the proposition of Plato, although not of his own, it follows that Plato's proposition is false. And consequently, for the same reason, Socrates' proposition is false. And if one says that either is false, it follows that both are true, for the case is as they assert it to be. For they assert that every proposition is false, and it is so. And because also, if they are false, then their subjects and predicates stand for the same. Hence, they are true, because they are affirmative, and also because they are universal propositions, among the singulars of which there is no exception.

Others have said that such a proposition is both true and false at once. But this is unsuitable, as is clear; for if its contradictory were true, both contradictories would be true. And if it were false, both would be false, and each of these is impossible. Therefore.

Then also there is a doubt how a contradictory can be given. I posit the case that there are only two propositions, one that a man is an ass, and the other the aforesaid proposition of Socrates. Then, I show that a contradictory cannot be given. For the terms of the contradictories ought to stand for the same thing or things, not in one contradictory for more than in the other. Now in the proposition of Socrates, the subject stands for two propositions, namely, for itself, according to the case, and for this proposition "A man is an ass." Now if you wish to give the contradictory, namely,

"Some proposition is not false," immediately in that, the subject would stand for more, namely, for three—itself, and the other two. Therefore, it could not contradict that proposition of Socrates.

But this doubt is solved by that which was said in the second and third sophisms of the seventh chapter. For that proposition contradicting the proposition of Socrates could be formed and not for the time in which it is formed, but for the time in which the proposition of Socrates was made. Thus, that third proposition would stand only for those for which Socrates' proposition would stand, and it would not stand for itself, since it was not of this time.

Now we must look into the truth and falsity of these propositions. And briefly, I believe that that proposition would be false. For it would be either false or not false. If it is false, I have my conclusion, and if it is not false, it follows that it is true, from which also it is. And if it is true, it follows also that it is false, as was previously argued. Hence, I have my conclusion, namely, that it is false.

But then it is difficult to respond to the sophism. For concerning the arguments, some have said, and so it formerly seemed to me, that although the proposition, according to the significations of its terms, signifies or affirms only that every proposition is false, still since every proposition, because of its form, signifies or asserts itself to be true, so every proposition asserting itself to be false, whether directly or indirectly, is false. For although howsoever it signifies the case to be, so it is, insofar as it signifies itself to be false, still it is not the case that how it signifies to be, so it is, insofar as it signifies itself to be true. Thus, it is false and not true, because for its truth, it is required, not only that how it signifies the case to be, so it is, but howsoever it signifies the case to be, so it is.

This response does not seem to me to be valid, properly speaking. And I do not object for now to this way of speaking: howsoever it signifies the case to be, so it is. For enough has been said about this. But I show that that which was said is not true,

namely, that every proposition signifies or asserts itself to be true. For you take that expression "itself to be true" either significatively or materially. If materially, then this proposition "A man is an animal" does not assert itself or signify itself to be true, for its sense would be that it would signify this proposition " 'A man is an animal' is true," which is false. For that second proposition is of second intention, and the first, since it is of first intention, could not signify these second intentions. But if someone should say that that expression "itself to be true" is taken significatively, then that proposition "A man is an ass" does not signify itself to be true. For just as man-being-ass is nothing, since man could not be an ass, so this proposition " 'Man is an ass' to be true" is nothing, nor could it be, since it could not be true. Now concerning that which could not be or is not, it is not true to say that it is signified or understood or asserted, as has been sufficiently said elsewhere. For if you say this proposition " 'A man is an ass' being true" is signified or understood or asserted, then you speak falsely, since the proposition is false, for it is affirmative and its subject stands for nothing. And so it is in the proposed case, that a proposition such as "Every proposition is false" cannot be true, so it-being-true neither is nor could be. Thus, it is not signified or understood. So it does not signify itself to be true.

Thus, it is otherwise said, nearer the truth, that every proposition virtually implies another proposition, so that of the subject standing for it, there is affirmed this predicate "true." I say it implies virtually just as an antecedent implies that which follows from it. Thus, any proposition is not true, if in this consequent affirmation, the subject and predicate do not stand for the same. For example, we could posit that this proposition of Socrates "No proposition is true" is properly called by the name "C." And then it follows that no proposition is true; therefore C is not true. And thus, unless it is as is signified by this consequent, it follows that the predicate in the given proposition was virtually implied in that proposition. The proposition is not true. For it does not suffice for a proposition to be true that it is as it signifies according to formal significations. Rather, it is required that it is as is signified by the consequent which was virtually implied. Hence, because of this, it will be said that when a proposition has or can have reflection on itself, it does not suffice for the truth of an affirmative that the terms stand for the same, as is said elsewhere. But it is required that in such a consequent, the terms stand for the same. And then it is necessary, given this, for the proposition to be true. And by this the arguments are easily solved.

To the first argument, it could be said that it is indeed universal, but the objection is not in itself against its formal signification, but against that which it implies as consequent.

To the other, it could be said that the subject and predicate of the said consequence do not stand for the same, that, however, for the truth of a proposition, this is required, whatever that proposition should be. To the last, it could be said similarly that it is not howsoever that implied consequent signifies, even if this way of speaking is employed in the proper sense.

But this solution, although it is near the truth, as I think, yet is still not complete. For it assumes falsely that from any proposition that consequent follows. For given that this proposition "A horse runs" is properly called by the name "B," then it does not follow that a horse runs, so B is true, as was said in the second sophism of this chapter. And so for completing this solution, we ought to say that from every proposition, together with the condition that it is, there follows the conclusion that it is true. So in the aforesaid case, namely, that this proposition "A horse runs" is properly called by the name "B," it follows that a horse runs and B is, so B is true.

Now in our proposition which is the present sophism, it seems that this proposition is added by the case. For it was stated that Socrates uttered this proposition "No proposition is true." Hence, it is posited

that it is true, and so from this proposition and the case, or from a proposition explaining the case, it follows that it is true, which is false. Therefore, either it is false or the case is false. Hence, if the case is taken as true, it is necessary to say that this proposition is false.

But then, it is necessary to solve the arguments.

The first argument, even with that addition, has not been sufficiently solved. For when it is said that it is a universal having no exceptions, I say also that although there is not an exception opposed to it according to its precise formal significations, still there would be opposed that exception which is implied by way of the consequent in it, together with the case. And this suffices to falsify it, if the posited case is true. And so are solved the other arguments.

But then it is doubted whether such a proportion is possible, namely, "Every proposition is false." And I say that it is possible, although it could not be true. For it could be as it signifies if God should destroy all propositions except these two: "God is an ass" and "A horse is a goat." For then every proposition would be false. And I would say that the copulative from this and the case would be impossible. For an impossible proposition would follow, namely, that it is both true and false.

(8) Plato speaks falsely.

There is an eighth sophism and it seems more difficult. And it is this: "Plato speaks falsely."

I posit the case that Socrates utters this proposition "Plato speaks falsely" and he utters no other. And conversely, Plato utters this proposition "Socrates speaks falsely," and not another. Then it is asked whether Socrates' proposition, which is the sophism is true or false.

And it is argued that it is true, for there is no reason why Socrates' proposition should be more true or false than Plato's proposition, or conversely. For they are related to each other in exactly the same way. Thus, if one is true, the other is true. And if one is false, the other is false. This I assume. So if you say that Socrates' proposition is not true but false, then also Plato speaks falsely for the same reason. And Socrates affirms this and nothing else. So he affirms what is, so his proposition is true. Also his proposition is affirmative and the terms stand for the same, namely, Plato and the one speaking falsely. From which we assert that Plato speaks falsely. Hence, it is a true proposition.

Likewise, I posit that with Socrates, Robert also says that Plato speaks falsely. And I posit also that Socrates and Robert utter these propositions according to similar intentions, and they believe that they speak the truth, because they believe that Plato utters the proposition "God is not." Hence, it appears that Socrates' proposition and Robert's proposition are absolutely similar in sound and intention, to the hearer as well as to the speaker. And yet Robert's proposition is true, because we posit that Plato speaks falsely. Hence, similarly, Socrates' proposition is true.

Again, we posit that Robert wants to contradict Socrates, by saying that Plato does not speak falsely. Then it appears that this proposition is false, because we posit that Plato speaks falsely; hence, only Socrates' proposition was true, unless you say that both contradictories are at once false, which is impossible.

The opposite is argued, because if Socrates speaks truly, then for the same reason, Plato speaks truly. And if Plato speaks truly, since he says that Socrates speaks falsely, it follows that Socrates speaks falsely. Thus, the proposition of Socrates is false and not true.

It is to be said briefly that Socrates' proposition is false and not true, because every proposition is false, from which, together with some true proposition, there follows a false one. But from this, together with a true proposition, there follows a false one. Hence, it is false. The major is an infallible rule. And the minor is proved, for since the case is possible, I suppose the positing of the case to be true. Now from the case and the proposition of Socrates, it follows that

Socrates' proposition is true and that it is false. And consequently, the whole is false and impossible. Hence, it appears that from Socrates' proposition, together with a true proposition, there follows a false one.

Now, therefore, it remains to show in what way from the proposition of Socrates and the case, it follows that that proposition is both true and false. And first it is proved that it is true, because the case posits that that proposition of Socrates is. And yet it has been said that from any proposition, together with the statement that it is, it follows that it is true. But also it appears that it is false, as was argued. For if it were true, it would be necessary for Plato's proposition to be true, from which it would follow that Socrates' proposition would be false. And similarly, for the same reason, it is to be said that Plato's proposition is false.

Thus, it is necessary only to answer the arguments that are very difficult, and the reader is referred to that which was said in the preceding sophism.

To the first, it is said that although it is as Socrates' proposition signifies according to its formal signification, still it is not as the proposition following from it and the case signifies. For it follows that it is true, and it is not so.

Similarly, concerning the second, it is said that when a proposition can have reflection on itself, whether mediately or immediately, according to which reflection it follows that it is false, it is not sufficient for the truth of an affirmative that the subject and predicate stand for the same. But it is also necessary that the subject and predicate of that consequent, namely, that it is true, stand for the same, as was said earlier.

But the third and fourth arguments are difficult. And I say, concerning the third without doubt that Socrates' proposition and Robert's proposition are consimilar, according to expression and intention, of the speakers as well as the hearers. But they are not equivalent, because Plato's proposition, concerning which both spoke, has reflection on Socrates' proposition and not on Robert's proposition. Thus, from the propositions of Socrates and Plato, together with the case, it follows that Socrates' proposition is false. And this does not follow from Robert's proposition. Rather, it is true.

Then it is doubted how one can take equivalent propositions in another than the aforesaid way. Concerning this, I say that if a proposition is of a nature to reflect on itself because its terms stand for propositions, then it is also required that an equivalent proposition be of a nature to reflect on it. For example, there is first a proposition A, and secondly B. And if B should be equivalent to A, it is necessary that in whatever case A reflects on itself, so B reflects on A, since it is necessary in every case that if one is true, then the other is true. Now the second does not have reflection on the first except in asserting that consequent which is implied by asserting the first, namely, that A is true. But if this second is posited, then it is equivalent to the first. Thus should it be the proposition of Socrates that Plato speaks falsely, then Robert's proposition will be equivalent to "Plato speaks falsely and A is true," positing that Socrates' proposition is called A. For this proposition of Robert's adds nothing which is not implied indirectly in the case in which the proposition of Socrates is. And we posit this case in positing that they are neither equivalent nor contradictory. For if they are not, then they are neither equivalent nor contradictory. And generally, from every proposition and the statement of its existence, there can be taken an equivalence, for example, that if those statements exist, then they are equivalent. Namely, Socrates' proposition, which is properly named B, could be that a man runs, and Robert's equivalent proposition could be that a man runs, and B is true. But it is not necessary to add the other statement when the proposition is not of a nature to reflect on itself. But when it can, it is necessary to add this. For if there is reflection on the first, then there is reflection on the second.

And something similar, I believe, must be said about the fourth argument. For Socrates' proposition and Robert's proposition are both false and do not contradict. For it is possible for there to be reflection on one, from which it follows that it is false, although there be no reflection on the other, as it is in the case posited. Thus, in contradicting Socrates' proposition, it is necessary to contradict the copulative composed of it and the consequent implied in it, namely, that which was stated to be equivalent to it. For example, Robert may say that Plato does not speak falsely or A is not true. For in no way could those two be at the same time either true or false. Nor also is it hostile if more of other terms are applied in one than in the other. For whatever terms are explicitly expressed in one are implicitly and equivalently contained in the other.

But again, it is doubted, for if those propositions of Socrates and Robert were contradictories, then positing that they would always remain by divine power, it is certain that never by a change in other things could they be at the same time true or false. Then I posit that the case concerning Plato is changed, so that Plato does not utter the proposition "Socrates speaks falsely," but he utters the proposition "Robert speaks falsely." Then it is asked concerning each of those propositions, namely, Socrates', Robert's, and Plato's, which is true or false. And I say that Plato's proposition is false, because it follows from it immediately and according to the case that it is false. For if it should be held to be true, it would follow that Robert's proposition is false. And if Robert's proposition is false, this is either because Plato speaks falsely or because Socrates' proposition is true. And from both it follows that Plato's proposition is false. And then, it likewise follows that Robert's proposition is false and Socrates' proposition is true. For Socrates asserts only that Plato speaks falsely, and so it is. Nor is there reflection from Plato to Socrates, because of which it does not follow that Socrates' proposition is false. Thus, it is true, and Robert's proposition contradicting it is false, because it is a disjunctive of which each part is false.

(9) Socrates speaks truly.

The ninth sophism is related to the preceding, namely, "Socrates speaks truly."

The case may be posited that Socrates utters only this [proposition] "Plato speaks falsely" and Plato, conversely, only this proposition "Socrates speaks truly." Then it is asked whether that proposition of Plato is true or false. And similarly also, it could be asked concerning Socrates' proposition.

It is argued that Plato speaks truly, because he speaks either falsely or truly. If truly, we have the conclusion. If falsely, still it follows that he speaks truly. Hence, whatever is given, it follows that he speaks truly. Then I demonstrate the assumption, that is, the antecedent, namely, that if Plato speaks falsely, then he speaks truly. And if he speaks falsely, then Socrates does not speak truly. And if Socrates does not speak truly, then Plato speaks truly, and so we have the conclusion as it was proved above, namely, that Socrates speaks truly.

Next, it is disproved similarly. For either Plato speaks truly or he speaks falsely. If he speaks falsely, I have the conclusion. If he speaks truly, still it follows that he speaks falsely, and again I have the statement. I prove, then, the assumption, namely, that it follows that if Plato speaks truly, Socrates speaks falsely. For if he speaks truly, it follows that Socrates speaks truly. And if Socrates speaks truly, it follows that Plato speaks falsely.

It is to be said briefly, as before, that each proposition is false, because I assume it to be as it is supposed to be in the case, since this is possible, and so the proposition expressing the case is true. Hence, every proposition is false from which, together with the statement given in the case, a falsehood follows, since the false does not follow from the true. But from each, together with the case, the false follows. Therefore, etc.

I prove that from each, together with the case, the false follows. For it follows that the same proposition is both true and false without equivocation, and this is false. First, therefore, it is demonstrated that

from Plato's proposition, together with the case, it follows that the same proposition, namely, itself, is both true and false. For it is posited in the case that it is, and it has been said earlier that from every proposition, together with another stating that it is, it follows that it is true. And yet it follows finally, that if it is true, then it is false. Therefore, it follows that it is false. And so it would be argued concerning the other.

But then it is doubted whether these are impossible. It seems that they are, for from a possible there follows only a possible. And yet from these there follows an impossible, namely, that the same is both true and false.

The contrary is stated, because a proposition is possible which, when it is true, could be false, because of a change in the things signified. But Plato's proposition, namely, that Socrates speaks truly, could be true if we posit that Socrates says that proposition "God is." Hence, it is possible or not impossible. And so it is argued that Socrates' proposition could be possible, for it could be true if Plato should say that a man is an ass.

Concerning the argument, I say that an impossible follows from neither, but from each and the case posited, an impossible follows. Thus, I concede that the copulative constituted of these and the case is impossible. And this is often the case, namely, that a copulative is impossible of which each part is possible. For instance, if I say "Every running thing is a horse and a man is running," there follows from this an impossible, namely, that a man is a horse. So also, this is impossible: "Socrates runs and Socrates does not run," although either part is possible.

Then it is answered concerning the argument which held that Plato's proposition could be true. When it is asked whether it is true or false, I agree that it is false. And when it is said that if it is false, then it is true, I deny the consequent. And when it is proved because if Plato speaks falsely, it follows that Socrates does not speak truly, I concede. And when it is further said that if Socrates speaks falsely, it follows that

Plato speaks truly, I deny the consequent. For Socrates' proposition is not said to be false because it is other than it signifies according to its formal significations, for thus it signifies that Plato speaks falsely and so it is. But it is called false because the consequent implied by it and the case, which is true, is false. Thus, it is consistent that A is a true proposition, for it is posited that Socrates' proposition is properly named A. And it is not the case that it is not true because it is not true.

And if it is argued that Socrates' proposition, stating that Plato speaks falsely is true, because the terms stand for the same, and because howsoever it signifies, so it is, and because its equivalent, which Robert utters, is true, or because its contradictory, which John utters, is false, it is to be replied to all these arguments as we did in the preceding sophism.

(10) There are just as many true propositions as there are false propositions.

There is a tenth sophism, and it is similar in force, namely, "There are just as many true propositions as there are false propositions."

The case may be posited that there are only four propositions. The first is "God is," the second "A man is an animal," the third "A horse is a goat," the fourth the stated sophism. With it so being, I ask whether the sophism is true or false.

It is argued first that it is not true, for then it would not be as it signifies, rather, there would be more true than false, since there would be three true and one false.

Next, it is argued that it is not false, for if it were false, then it would be as it signifies, since with two true and two false, it is true.

I say that the sophism is false, because from it and the case, it follows that it is false and that it is true. And the argument for the opposite is answered, since it is not false because it is other than it signifies according to formal significations, but because it is not as that proposition signifies which is virtually implied by it and the

case, as the consequent [is implied] by its antecedent. For this is implied by it: "A is true," positing the case that that sophism is properly named A. And it is not as this signifies: "A is true."

But it is asked whether the sophism is possible and whether it could be true. And I immediately answer that it is possible, since it could be that there were as many true as there were false as for instance, if there were only these four: "God is," "God is good," "A man is an ass," and "A horse is a goat." I say also that it could be true in the case that we do not take the time consignified by the verb for the present time in which we form it, but for the time in which there were only those four immediately aforesaid. Indeed, also, in this way, this could be true: "Every proposition is negative," but it could not be true if we take the time consignified by the verb for the time in which it is formed. Nor also could the present sophism be true, but still if the case posited in the sophism is as it is posted, some man, coming in, could truly say that for the time of this case, precisely as many were true as were false. But for a verb of the present, some man could not truly say this, except as was said, namely, using the time of the verb for a time other than that which precisely coexists with his proposition.

(11) I speak falsely.

The eleventh sophism is of similar force—"I speak falsely."

It is posited that I say nothing except this proposition "I speak falsely." Then, it is asked whether my proposition is true or false.

If you say that it is true, then it is not as my proposition signifies. Thus, it follows that it is not true but false.

And if you say that it is false, then it follows that it is as it signifies. Hence, it is true.

Also, since then the terms stand for the same and it is affirmative, it follows clearly that if it is false, it is true. And then from this, it follows that it is necessary to concede that it is true and false, since whoever concedes the antecedent ought to concede the consequent. And it is necessary to concede either that it was true or that it was false. And then it follows that if it is true, it is false, and if it is false, it is true. Hence, it is necessary to concede both. But again, to concede this is inconsistent, since then its contradictory would be true, and so two contradictories would be true at the same time. And if it is false, then the two contradictories would be false at the same time. And all these are impossible.

Next, also, it is doubted in what way the contradictory of the sophism is to be taken and whether it is possible or impossible.

I answer that the sophism is false, because from it and the proposition expressing the case, a false proposition follows. Yet since this proposition expressing the case is said to be true, and that false, what thus follows is that the sophism is both true and false at once. But a proposition is false, from which, together with its truth, a false proposition follows.

And the arguments for the opposite are answered, according to what was said earlier. For it is said that if it were false, it would follow that it is true. I deny that consequent. And you prove it because if it is false, then it is as it signifies. I agree, with respect to the formal signification. But this is not sufficient because it reflects on itself. For because of this it is not true, for it is not as the consequent of it and of the case signifies. For that consequent is that A is true, positing that my proposition is properly named A. And it is not as this signifies: "A is true." And similarly, it is said, concerning this, that the terms stand for the same.

But still you can object, arguing that it follows that if it is false, then it is true, because if it is false, it follows that it is, and so it is. And from its being so and the fact that it is, it follows that it is true. Hence, it follows that if it is false, then it is true. And whoever concedes that antecedent ought to concede the consequent. Therefore, we ought to concede that it is true.

I answer that it does not follow that if it is false, then it is true. But I do indeed agree that it follows that if it is false, then it is. I

concede also that from it and the fact that it is, it follows that it is true. But I do not concede the antecedent. Rather, I deny the antecedent, because the antecedent was composed of it and its being. And I deny it, so I also deny the consequent, namely, that it is true.

But there is a doubt in what way you can contradict me. Hence, if you speak negatively concerning a similar subject, according to expression, as by saying "I do not speak falsely," you do not contradict me, because in a contradiction, the terms of one ought to stand for the same things as the terms of the other. And this would not be here, for in my proposition, this term "I" stands for me, but in yours it stands for you. And if you say negatively, changing that term "I" to that term "you," namely, saying to me "You do not speak falsely," it is apparent that you do not indeed contradict me. For a contradictory ought to be of the same subject and predicate, and it is not sufficient that there are different predicates standing for the same. Likewise, my proposition is false, and yours is also false. Therefore, they do not contradict.

For solution, I say that it is not necessary for contradictories to be exactly alike in words. For first it is necessary for them to be dissimilar according to affirmation and negation. Secondly, they can be dissimilar according to what they signify or according to their manners [of supposition]. For instance, these contradict: "Every man runs" and "Some man does not run." And similarly these two: "It is possible that Socrates runs" and "It is necessary that Socrates does not run." But also sometimes, we can change the verbal predicate, on account of relative terms. For instance, if you say "Every man having a horse sees that [horse]," if we should have to contradict that other than by asserting the negation of the whole proposition, it will be necessary to change the wording of the predicate. For this is not its contradictory: "Some man having a horse does not see that [horse]," since both can be true at once in the case in which every man should have one horse which he sees and another which he does not see. Hence, it seems that its contradictory is this: "Some man having a horse does not see the horse which he has." But this will be discussed in particular elsewhere.

But still, just as was said in the eighth sophism, because of the reflection which a proposition has on itself, or is of a nature to have, it is necessary in contradicting it to express it in other words, in accordance with the sense of the consequent implied by the first proposition. And also if someone speaks of himself in the first person, it will be necessary for another, in contradicting him, to speak in the second person and not in the first. For instance, if Socrates says "I am running," Plato does not contradict him by saying "I am not running," but by saying "You are not running." It is necessary, therefore, principally to inspect the intention, since we use words only to express intentions. Thus, if we cannot express a mental contradictory without changing the words, it is necessary to change them. So, therefore, it seems that you contradict me in saying "You are not speaking falsely," yet with the additions mentioned in the prior sophisms. Hence, if you wish to state a proposition equivalent to mine, you say "You are speaking falsely, and A is true," positing the case that my proposition is properly named A. And then the contradictory would be "You are not speaking falsely, or A is not true," and this disjunctive is true.

(12) God is and some copulative is false.

Let us posit that that proposition is written on a wall, and that there is no proposition besides it and its parts. Then it is asked whether it is true or false.

And it is argued as before. For if it is true, it follows that it is false. And if it is false, it seems to follow that it is true, for it would be as it signifies, since its contradictory would be false, namely, this: "God is not or no copulative is false."

It is to be said that it is false. And the arguments are solved as before. Granted that it would be as it signifies according to its formal signification, still it would not be as would be signified by the consequent implied in it and the case posited. I assume that it is properly named A, and its contradictory would be "No God is, or no copulative is false, or A is not true." Similarly also, sophisms can be made from disjunctive propositions, such as "A man is an ass, or a disjunctive is false," positing that there is no other disjunctive. Similarly also, concerning exceptives, such as "Every proposition except an exceptive is true," positing that there are no other propositions except the aforesaid exceptive and two others, namely, "God is" and "A man is an animal." So also concerning an exclusive, such as if Socrates says "God is" and Plato says "Only Socrates speaks truly," and no one else says anything.

Other sophisms can also be formed from that which is a proposition of doubt or no doubt, of knowing or not knowing, of belief or unbelief.

(13) Socrates knows the proposition written on the wall to be doubted by him.

I posit the case that only the aforesaid proposition is written on the wall, and that Socrates sees it, examines it, and doubts whether it is true or false, and that he knows himself to doubt it. It is asked whether it is true or false.

And it is argued that it is true. For the case is posited that Socrates truly knows that proposition to be doubted by him, and this is what the proposition signifies. Hence, it is true. Likewise, of similar propositions, if one is true, the other is true. But whoever should utter a proposition similar to this one would speak the truth. Hence, it is true.

The opposite is argued. A proposition is false from which an impossible follows, namely, that Socrates knows and doubts the same proposition. For according to the case, he doubts it, and yet he knows it, because he knows it to be as it signifies, since he knows that it is doubted by him. Indeed, it is also possible that he knows himself to know that it is doubted by him. And that proposition signifies nothing more. But to know that it is as a proposition signifies is to know the proposition. For you know the proposition "A man is an animal," from the fact that you know that it is indeed so.

It is confirmed that if he gives it heed, he knows that proposition to be true, since if you should utter a similar one, he will know that you are speaking the truth. Hence, for the same reason, he would know it to be true.

And similarly, if you utter the contradictory, he will know that you speak falsely. But whoever knows one contradictory to be false knows the other to be true, if he gives it attention, and he knows those to be contradictories. Therefore, etc.

Some people respond concerning that sophism that there is a twofold proposition written on the wall, according to the case, namely, one whole one, that Socrates knows that the proposition written on the wall is doubted by him. And there is another partial one, which is a part of that, namely, that the proposition written on the wall is doubted by him. Now, therefore, Socrates indeed knows this partial one, namely, that the proposition written on the wall is doubted by him, but he does not know the whole, rather, that is doubted by him. And this is not impossible, so it is conceded that the proposition is true.

But this solution does not appear to me to remove the doubt. First, because it is not true according to the case that there is a twofold proposition written on the wall, because it was said elsewhere that no part of a proposition is a proposition, as long as it is a part of a proposition. And likewise, the case did not posit a proposition concerning which it was asserted that it was written on the wall, but a proposition such as "Socrates knows the proposition written on the wall to be doubted by him." But that expression of the infinitive mood "proposition written, etc." is not a proposition. And even if it should stand for a proposition, still it would be only for this whole, since nothing else is written on the wall. Thus, if he knows the proposition written on the wall, he knows this whole.

Likewise, it was posited that he not only knows that it is doubted by him, but rather

he knows himself to know this. We could posit, therefore, that it is possible. So Socrates knows not only that that proposition is doubted by him, but he knows that Socrates knows that proposition to be doubted by him. And so it seems to follow that he knows a whole proposition and not only a partial one. Thus, I say otherwise, conceding that that written on the wall is doubted by him and that he knows with certainty that it is doubted by him, indeed, he knows that he knows this. And then there is a doubt whether he knows that proposition.

For the purpose of resolving these doubts, it is to be noted that the concept is in more than knowledge.[11] For the concept can be without complexion and it can be without enunciation. And it is required for knowledge that a man assents to a true enunciation. And this kind of enunciation, to which we thus assent with certitude and evidence, we say to be known, and that we have knowledge of it. Indeed also, concerning things themselves signified by terms, we thus distinguish a twofold knowledge, namely, one primary and immediate which is that enunciation, to which we assent in the aforesaid way. The other is a remotely known thing or remotely known things, namely, the things signified by the terms of the enunciation known in the first way.

But it is impossible that a proposition is doubted by you and known by you as a thing primarily known. For you do not assent with certitude and evidence to a proposition doubted by you. And yet you assent to the proposition thus primarily known. Hence, it is necessary that that proposition written on the wall is not known by Socrates by the primary way of knowing, since it is doubted by him, and he does not know whether it is true or false. But I say that it is known by Socrates by the remote way of knowing, since Socrates forms in his mind a mental proposition such as "The proposition written on the wall is doubted by me." And he assents to that mental proposition with certitude and evidence, because of which that mental proposition is known by him by the primary way of knowing. And since the subject of that mental proposition stands for the proposition written on the wall, it follows that Socrates has knowledge of that proposition written on the wall as a remotely known thing.

But again, I say that if Plato should utter the proposition "Socrates knows the proposition written on the wall to be doubted by him," and if Socrates should hear and understand Plato well, immediately Socrates will know Plato's proposition also by the primary way of knowing. For Socrates would assent to Plato's proposition with certitude and evidence as true and not doubted by him. Indeed also, if on a paper is written a proposition exactly like the one written on the wall, Socrates, seeing and reading it, would know it to be true, nor will he have doubt concerning it.

Then it will be doubted how this is possible, namely, that there are two absolutely consimilar propositions and that a man is certain of one and doubts the other, since he still notices them and knows them to be consimilar. And I say that this is indeed possible, since one observes that that which is written on the wall reflects on itself. Thus, the doubt is that because of this reflection it could be false, as happened in the preceding sophisms. But also he observes that Plato's proposition or also that written on paper does not reflect on itself, so there is no doubt whether it is true. But also, when it is argued that if Plato utters the contradictory, namely, this: "Socrates does not know the proposition written on the wall to be doubted by him," immediately Socrates knows that Plato's proposition is false, I agree. And you conclude, therefore, he should know that that proposition written on the wall is true, since it is its contradictory. I say that this does not follow, for he does not know that they are contradictories. For one could doubt whether the reflection which the proposition written on the wall has on itself impedes the contradiction.

Finally, it is doubted whether this proposition written on the wall is true or false. And I say that it is true, since the reflection which it has on itself does not determine

that it is false, but only that it is doubted, from which it does not follow that it is false. And when it is argued that from it an impossible follows, I deny it, for it does not follow that it is known except by the remote way of knowing. But you prove that Socrates knows it to be as it signifies. This is conceded. And you conclude, therefore, that there is no doubt whether it is true, if one heeds this. I say that this does not follow. For Socrates sees in the solution of the preceding sophisms that many propositions were false by the reflection which they had on themselves, although it was as they signified. Thus, because of this ignorance, it is necessary to opine that this is also false, because it is seen to reflect on itself, or at least he may have doubt concerning it.

But still there is a doubt concerning that sophism, whether that proposition is true or false, adding to the case posited before that Socrates is most wise. And I say that the case is impossible, since because Socrates is most learned in the art and he observes as far as he can concerning that proposition, it follows that if it is true, then he knows it to be true, and if it is false, then he knows it to be false. And yet with neither of these is it consistent that it is doubted by him. But if that clause is removed from the case, namely, that it is doubted by him, it is asked whether it is true or false for him. And I say that it is false, and that Socrates knows it to be false, and not to be doubted by him.

(14) Socrates sits, or the disjunctive written on the wall is doubted by Plato.

Let us posit the case that this proposition is written on the wall and that Plato sees it and gives full consideration to whether it is true or false. And I posit also that Plato is in every art most trained and most learned in knowledge, but yet that Plato does not see Socrates and does not know whether he stands or sits. And so he doubts that proposition "Socrates sits." Then, therefore, it is asked how Plato is related to that whole proposition, which is a disjunctive, namely, whether he knows it to be true or he knows it to be false or he doubts it.

And it is argued first that Plato does not know it to be true, for he must know either part to be true, since it is required for the truth of a disjunctive that either part be true. But yet by the case, he does not know the first part to be true, namely, that Socrates sits. And similarly, he does not know the second part to be true, since from this it would follow that that second part would be true and false, which is impossible. I prove the conclusion. For first it would follow that that could be true, since nothing is known to be true except the true. Secondly, it would also follow that it would be false, since if he should know it to be true, he would know the disjunctive to be true, since for the truth of a disjunctive, it suffices that one part is true. Therefore, he would not doubt it, and consequently, that second part would be false, since it says that disjunctive to be doubted by Plato.

Next, it is also argued that Plato does not know that disjunctive to be false, since in order to know a disjunctive to be false, one must know each part to be false. And it is posited that Plato does not know whether the first is true or false. Likewise, if he should know the disjunctive to be false, he would know its contradictory to be true, if he should pay it heed. For he is stated to be most learned in every art. But the consequent is false, for its contradictory is this: "Socrates does not sit, and no disjunctive written on the wall is doubted by Plato." But this copulative Plato does not know to be true, for he does not know concerning the first part whether it is true or false. For he doubts it.

Next, it is argued that this disjunctive is not doubted by Plato, for if it is doubted by him, he knows it. Indeed, even if a person with little learning should attend to any proposition, he would know well whether he doubts it. But if he knows that to be doubted by him, he knows the second of its parts to be true, which says this. And if he knows that second part to be true, he knows the disjunctive to be true, from which it follows that he does not doubt it.

I answer that Plato does not know that disjunctive to be true and that he does not know it to be false, as the reasons concerning this argued. Thus, it remains that he doubts it, and he knows that he doubts it. Which is also proved. For the second part of that disjunctive is false, as is proved. And Plato well knows this, since he is posited to be most learned in every art. Thus, he knows that the disjunctive is false if the first part is false, and that it is true if the first part is true. Since he thus knows that he doubts the first part, he knows that he doubts the whole disjunctive.

Now, therefore, it is necessary to show that this second part of the disjunctive is false. This is proved thus: since that proposition is false from which, together with some true proposition, a false one follows. But so it is concerning this. So it is false. Then I prove the minor, because since the whole case is possible, I suppose that the proposition stating the case is true; and because from the case and the second part, a false proposition follows, indeed an impossible proposition. For it follows that that disjunctive is doubted by Plato and not doubted. First, that it is doubted, because this is stated by the second part. Second, that it is not doubted, as was earlier argued. This is clear also, because from the second part and the case, it follows that it is both true and false. First, that it is true, because by the case it is posited to be, and it was often said that from any proposition and another stating that it is, it follows that it is true. But again, also, it follows that it is false, because if it is true, then Plato knows this, since he is assumed to be most learned, and who knows the truth either doubts concerning that disjunctive or not. And if he knows it to be true, then he does not doubt. And consequently, that second part is false.

Then, it is responded concerning the arguments in opposition that although Plato knows it to be as it is signified by that second part according to formal signification, still he does not know it to be true, but false, for he knows that it reflects on itself, from which it follows, together with the statement that the case is true, that it is false. And he also knows every such proposition to be false.

But perhaps there is a reply against the statement, since if that disjunctive is doubted by Plato,[12] it is necessary that its contradictory also be doubted, and yet this is false. For the contradictory is that Socrates does not sit and no proposition written on the wall is doubted by Plato. And Plato does not doubt that, since he knows it to be false, for it is a copulative whose second part is false. It follows, therefore, that Plato ought not to doubt the proposition written on the wall, but to know it to be true.

For solution, I say that the contradictory is not sufficiently taken, because it reflects on itself. Thus, it is necessary to explain the consequent implied by the second disjunct and the case. So that if that disjunctive written on the wall is properly named A, the equivalent of it will be this: "Socrates sits, or the disjunctive written on the wall is doubted by Plato, and A is true." And then the contradictory will be this: "Socrates does not sit, and no disjunctive written on the wall is doubted by Plato, or A is not true." And then I say that this is doubted by Plato, since it is a disjunctive composed of a copulative which is known to be false and a categorical which is doubted. Thus, the whole is doubted.

(15) To someone is proposed a proposition doubted by him.

And I posit the case that only the aforesaid proposition is proposed to you and that you do not know that any other is proposed to someone else. And I posit also that you are most learned in the art and that you seek, as far as you can, to discover whether that proposition is true or false. And then it is asked whether you know it to be true, or you know it to be false, or it is doubted by you.

It is argued first that you do not know it to be false, since you could not know that to be false, unless you know that to no man is proposed a proposition which he doubts. For it is known that it could be true if in Rome a proposition were proposed to Robert that was doubted by him. And you could not know whether it is so, so you could not know it to be false. Or it is argued thus: if you knew it to be false, you would also know its contradictory to be true, if it should be proposed to you, since you are most learned in the art. But this is impossible, namely, that you should know this to be true: "No doubted proposition is proposed to anybody." Therefore, etc.

Next, it is argued that you do not know that to be true. For you do not know concerning other men whether or not any proposition which is doubted is proposed to anybody. Hence, you do not know that there is proposed any proposition which is doubted by someone, unless you know this one which is proposed to you to be doubted by you. But it is impossible that you know that to be true and that you know it to be doubted by you. For it would follow that that would not be doubted by you, because you know it to be doubted by you.

Next, it is argued that this could not be doubted by you, for if it were doubted by you, then you would know that it was doubted by you. Then, you would know that to someone is proposed a proposition doubted by him, namely, you. And so you would know it to be as that proposition signifies. Thus, you would know that to be true for you, from which it follows that it would not be doubted by you. It follows, therefore, that that would neither be known by you to be true, nor known to be false nor doubted by you. And this is impossible in the case posited, namely, that you should consider it as far as you can and that you should be sufficiently learned for the consideration.

I say that this proposition could be doubted by you and that you could know it to be doubted by you, since you could not know that it would be false, as was well argued. Nor could you know that it would be true, as was also well argued. Thus, it remains that you doubt it. And the cause of this is that if to someone else is proposed another proposition doubted by him, then it is simply true. If, however, to no one else is proposed a proposition doubted by him, it will be false; which I prove, because that is false from which, together with a true, a false follows. And so it would be in the given case. I prove this, because I suppose the aforesaid case to be true, for it is possible. And yet from that proposition and the case, it follows that that is both true and false, which is impossible. I assert, first, that from it and the case, it follows that it is true. For the case posits that it is and yet it has often been said that from any proposition, together with another stating that it is, it follows that it is true. Next, it is shown that from it and the case, it follows that it is false. For you know that it is doubted by you, and you know that this is signified by its formal significations. Hence, you know that it is as it signifies, with regard to its formal significations. Now you who are most learned know well that every proposition is true if it is as it signifies in its formal signification, unless it has reflection on itself, because of which it follows that it is false. Therefore, you ought to conclude that you know this disjunctive: "Either it is true or it has reflection on itself, because of which it is false." Now, finally, you who are most learned should know whether in any such case a proposition can reflect on itself or not. And if you know that it cannot, then you know it to be true, which is false, as has been said. Therefore, you know that in some case, it can have such reflection, and yet you well know that this could not be if to another should be proposed a proposition doubted by him. For you know that in some case it would be true. Hence, it remains that you know that the reflection would be such that from it, it follows that it is false, if no other doubted proposition should be stated. Therefore, it would be false. And so it is clear that from it and the true case posited earlier, namely, that no other doubted proposition is proposed, it follows that it is false. And this is what we wanted to prove. So, therefore, it has been explained that it is true if to another should be proposed a doubted proposition, and

that it is false if to no other should be proposed another doubted proposition. And you do not know whether another doubted proposition is proposed to another person or not. So it is necessary that you doubt whether it is true or false.

Concerning the arguments in opposition, it is to be said that you do indeed know that it is doubted by you and that it is as it signifies according to formal signification. But from this it does not follow that you know it to be true nor that it is true. For it can have reflection on itself such that it is false, and you do not know whether it has.

However, someone replies that of contradictory propositions proposed to you, if one is known by you to be false, it is necessary if you give heed and are learned, that you know the other to be true. But it is established that if the contradictory of the sophism is stated, namely, this: "No proposition doubted by him is proposed to anybody," you know that it will be false. For you know that there is an exception in your case, since you know that a proposition doubted by you has been proposed to you. Hence, it follows that you know the sophism to be true. Again, more strongly, it is argued that you do not doubt this sophism. Indeed, you know it to be true, since I could argue thus: a proposition doubted by you is proposed to you, and you are someone; hence, a proposition doubted by someone is proposed to him. This syllogism is valid and formal, because it is expository. And yet, you know the premises to be true, and hence, if you pay heed and are learned, you know the conclusion[13] to be true, since you well know that a false proposition does not follow from a true. And yet that conclusion is the sophism. Therefore, you know it to be true. So it was badly said that it was doubted by you.

Concerning the first of these objections, it seems that the contradictory was not sufficiently taken, because it can have reflection on itself, from which it follows that it is false. The contradictory is to be taken from a copulative composed of it and that which is implied in it and the case, namely, that it is true. So that if the given proposition is properly named A, it will be equivalent to this affirmative proposition "To someone is proposed a proposition doubted by him, and A is true." Thus, the contradictory will be "No proposition doubted by him is proposed to anybody, or A is not true." And it is clear that this would be doubted by you, just as would the preceding. For the first part of this disjunctive you know to be false. And concerning the second part, you do not know whether it is true or false.

Concerning the second objection, I say that that argument was valid: to you is proposed a proposition doubted by you, and you are someone; hence, to someone is proposed a proposition doubted by him. And I say that you know the argument is valid and that the premises are true, and consequently, that you know that the conclusion is true. But the conclusion is not the sophism. Rather it is another similar to it, which is known to be true, because its terms stand for a sophism which you know to be doubted. Nor is it equivalent to the sophism, as it was earlier stated to be. Rather, to make it equivalent, it would be necessary to say that to someone is proposed a doubted proposition, and A is true, positing as before that the sophism is properly named A. But then, this does not follow from those given premises.

Therefore, it is to be noted well that if someone first proposes this to you: "A doubted proposition is proposed to you," you will doubt it and you will consider whether it is true or false. But granting this, whoever, coming in, should say to you that to someone is proposed a doubted proposition, you will know that he speaks truly and that his proposition is true, not for itself, but for that first one.

But then you will posit another case, namely, that Socrates and Plato are coming at the same time, and each utters a proposition such as "A doubted proposition is proposed to someone," and one does not speak sooner than the other, and you give

heed equally to them. Then [it is asked] whether both propositions will be doubted by you or one doubted and the other known to be true.

I say that both will be doubted by you, because you could know neither to be true for the other. Because for the same reason that you would know one to be true for the other, for the same reason conversely. And so you would know both to be true, which is false. For they are perhaps false in the case in which to no one is proposed a proposition doubted by him. For in that case, if you should know them to be true, you would not doubt them. Thus, nothing would be doubted by anybody, of which the opposite would be signified by those propositions. Thus, they would be false. But doubts not existing, whatever doubtful proposition comes to you, signifying something to be doubted by someone, it would be known by you to be true, not for itself, but for that which you then doubted.

Finally, concerning this sophism, someone can ask how it would be if it should not be posited in the case that you should be learned. And I say that perhaps because of your ignorance you would indeed not doubt. Rather, perhaps because of some reasons, you could believe it to be true without doubt, although it should perhaps be false. Or perhaps, because of other reasons, you will believe it to be false, also without any doubt. For it happens that one doubts nothing concerning that which he falsely opines. Hence, Aristotle says in the seventh of the *Ethics* that some, in a state of opinion, do not doubt, but opine.[14] Certainly, some believe in what they opine no less than others in what they know.

(16) You will answer negatively.

The sixteenth sophism concerning combinations of answers to questions is this: "You will answer negatively."

And this is proposed to you, and you are obligated that concerning what is proposed to you, you ought to respond directly that it is so or that it is not so. For you ought to admit this obligation, since whatever proposition is proposed is either true or not true, and since by "to be so" we signify that it is true and by "not to be so" we signify that it is not true. Therefore, concerning any, we can truly answer either that it is so or that it is not so. Hence, you ought to accept the obligation that you will so respond. Then, therefore, I ask that you respond to the stated proposition which is proposed to you, namely, this: "You will answer negatively."

If then, you respond that it is so, I shall argue against you, since you respond falsely. For you concede that you respond negatively and yet it is not so, for you respond affirmatively. But if you respond that it is not so, again I shall argue against you, that you answer falsely. For you deny that you respond negatively, and yet, as a matter of fact, you do respond negatively. Therefore, etc.

I say that according to the aforesaid obligation, you could not respond truly. But without that obligation, you could respond well, saying to him who proposes that he proposes falsely, or that his proposition was false. Or also, you can truly respond saying that he does not propose falsely to you. Hence, I say that you ought not to admit that obligation except under the condition that a proposition proposed to you could not consignify your response, because of which signification, your response would reflect on itself, from which it follows that it is false.

When, therefore, it is argued that you ought to admit the obligation because whatever proposition is proposed to you, it will be either true or false, I agree. But that proposition which was proposed to you was either true or false, since if you respond nothing, it was false. And if you respond that it is so, it was also false. And also your response was false, because it affirms that which was false to be true. But if you answer that it is not so, then that is true and your response is false, since it denies that which is true. Therefore, when it is said that concerning every true proposition, we ought to answer that it is so, and concerning every false proposition that it is not so,

I concede, unless the response should have reflection on itself, because of which it would follow that it is false. But in this case, one ought to change the response.

In the same way, if someone wishes to obligate you to respond precisely concerning a proposition which he proposes to you, that it is true or it is not, you ought not to accept the obligation. First, because you do not know whether a proposition doubted by you will be proposed. But also, if one wishes to obligate you to respond either that it is true or that it is false or doubtful, still you ought not to accept the obligation, unless under the aforesaid condition. Hence, to that proposition "You will respond negatively," you ought not to respond that it is true, nor that it is not true, nor that you doubt it. But you could respond that it is false.

But someone has replied that these are contradictories: "You have spoken truly" and "You have not spoken truly." But to whichever of these you should respond to him who proposes to you the given sophism, your response will be false. Therefore, both contradictories will be false, which is impossible.

To this, I say that to whichever of these you respond without the other, it will be false. Nor from this does it follow that the two contradictories are at the same time false, since they are not at the same time. But if you should respond to both at once, then you will respond negatively and affirmatively at once. And if you should respond negatively and verify the sophism, then your affirmative response would be true, and the negative false. Thus, both contradictories would still not be false at the same time. It would be the same, if we should posit that A signifies every man responding or going to respond negatively and nothing else, just as "man" signifies every man and nothing else, and that an opponent proposes to you that you are A. And then he asks whether it is so or is not so, for this is similar as to a proposal that you will answer or are going to answer negatively. And then it could be asked whether it is so or not so. Thus, you could not answer well by saying directly that it is so or not so, because of reflection. But you could truly answer, saying that the proposition was false, or answering that the proposition was not false but true.

(17) You will throw me in the water.

The seventeenth sophism is about some conditional promises or vows. And this is the sophism: "You will throw me in the water."

I posit the case that Plato guards a bridge with much assistance, so that none can cross without his assent. And then Socrates comes asking Plato with great supplication that he allow him to cross. Then Plato angrily vows and swears, saying "Surely, Socrates, if in the first proposition which you utter, you speak the truth, I will permit you to cross. But surely, if you speak falsely, I shall throw you in the water." Then Socrates will say to Plato the aforesaid sophism, namely, "You will throw me in the water." Thus, it is asked then what Plato ought to do, according to his promise.

If you say that he will throw Socrates in the water, this is against the promise, since then Socrates spoke truly. Thus, Plato ought to allow him to cross. And if you say that he will allow him to cross, it appears that this is again against the promise and the oath, since then Socrates speaks falsely, in which case Plato ought to throw him in the water.

It is to be answered that concerning this sophism, many questions can be raised. The first is whether Socrates' proposition is true, which was stated for the sophism. The second is whether Plato's proposition, which was the promise or vow, was true or false. The third is what Plato ought to do, keeping the promise or the vow.

Concerning the first, I say that Socrates' proposition is about a future contingent. Thus, I cannot determinately know whether it is true or false, until I see what will be concerning that future act. Hence, it is in Plato's power whether it is true or false. For if he throws him in the water, the proposition is true, and if he permits him to cross, it is false.

Concerning the second question, I say that Plato's proposition was a conditional, which according to the proper sense, could not be true. For the antecedent could be true without the consequent. For it was possible that Socrates should have said a great truth, as that God is, and that Plato yet should not have permitted him to cross. But still a promissive conditional in a less proper sense is conceded in the case that, the condition being fulfilled, the promise is fulfilled. For instance, if I say "If you will come to me, I will give you a horse," then if, you coming to me, I give you a horse, all would believe that I had spoken truly. And so speaking, I say that Plato does not speak truly, since Socrates has not fulfilled the condition. For he utters a proposition which had to be true or false, although not determinately true or determinately false, until the future act has followed, as ought to be seen in the *De Interpretatione*.[15] And yet, given this, Plato cannot fulfill the promise, since because of Socrates' proposition, Plato's promise reflects on itself, from which it follows that it is false.

When, therefore, it was asked on the third question what Plato ought to do, keeping the promise, I say that he ought not to keep the promise, for he could not or ought not so to promise except with an exception, namely, unless Socrates should utter a proposition having reflection on the promise, because of which it would follow that the promise could not be verified.

(18) Socrates wishes to eat.

The case may be posited that Socrates wishes to eat if Plato wishes to eat and not otherwise, for men often wish so to have company in eating, so that without company, they do not wish to eat. Next, it may also be posited, conversely, that Plato does not wish to eat if Socrates wishes to eat. For he is angry with Socrates, so he does not wish to eat with him. Then it is asked whether the sophism is true or false. For these are contradictories: "Socrates wishes to eat" and "Socrates does not wish to eat." So it is necessary for one to be true and the other false, whatever case is posited.

Thus, if you say that Socrates wishes to eat, the opposite follows, since it follows that Plato does not wish to eat, from which it also follows that Socrates does not wish to eat.

And if you say that Socrates does not wish to eat, the opposite follows. For it follows that Plato wishes to eat, from which it also follows that Socrates wishes to eat.

I respond that the case, as it is posited, is impossible, properly speaking. For this is a conditional: "Socrates wishes to eat if Plato wishes to eat," and it is not a valid consequence from the antecedent to the consequent. For it is possible that when Plato wishes to eat, Socrates does not wish to eat. But still, as conditionals are usually conceded in our promissive acts or vows or desires, this case is possible: Socrates desires to make true this proposition (or desires it to be as it signifies): "If Plato eats here, I will eat with him, and if not neither will I." And Plato, conversely, desires to verify this: "If Socrates eats here, I will not eat, and if he does not eat, I will eat." But I say that it is impossible for both to fulfill their wishes. But you ask whether, therefore, Socrates wishes to eat or not. I say unless Socrates and Plato have other acts of willing than the preceding, neither wishes to eat here, since the will is determined to that which one wills. And the will of neither of them is determined to eating. Hence, it does not follow: I wish to go to Rome if Socrates goes; hence, I wish to go to Rome. But you say it follows that if Socrates does not wish to eat here, then Plato wishes to eat here. I deny it, because that conditional was false and not to be admitted. But that categorical is indeed to be admitted, that Socrates desires the case to be as is signified by this proposition "If Plato eats here, I will eat with him." And Plato has an aversion to this being the case, so he intends the contrary. And from this, nothing impossible follows.

(19) Socrates curses Plato.

The case may be posited that Socrates says "Plato should be cursed if he curses me, and not otherwise." And Plato says, on the contrary, "Socrates should be cursed if he does not curse me, and not otherwise." Then it is asked concerning the truth of the sophism whether Socrates curses Plato.

If you say that he does, there follows an inconsistency, namely, that Plato curses Socrates and does not curse Socrates. And if you say that he does not, the opposite follows, since it follows that Plato curses Socrates, and consequently Socrates curses Plato.

I say that you posit here, to express the case, a proposition such as "Socrates says that Plato should be cursed if he.curses Socrates." I say that that proposition can be understood as a conditional, namely, in a sense such as "If Plato curses Socrates, Socrates says that Plato should be cursed." And that proposition is false and impossible and not to be admitted. For it does not follow that if Plato curses Socrates, then Socrates says Plato should be cursed. Rather, whether Plato curses Socrates or not, Socrates says what he says, or also, does not say what he does not say.

In another way, it can be understood that that proposition is a categorical in this sense: "Socrates utters a sentence such as 'Plato should be cursed, if, etc.'" And this ought to be conceded. For it is possible that Socrates utters such a proposition.

In the same way ought to be distinguished the proposition which the case posits, that if Plato says, etc.

Then a question is asked, whether thus speaking, Socrates and Plato curse each other. And I answer that to curse someone is to say, under a verb of the optative mode, that that person should come by some evil. Hence, I understand the same in saying "Plato should be cursed" as in saying "Plato should come by evil." And then, furthermore, I say that such cursing sentences are absolute curses without the addition of a condition, as if I say "Plato should be cursed." And sometimes there are conditioned curses, as if I say "Plato should be cursed if he goes into the fields." And then since names can signify conventionally, if you wish to call both simply curses, I say both cursed each other, although not absolutely.

But you argue against this, since it follows that if Socrates curses Plato, then Plato does not curse Socrates. I deny this consequence for I did not admit the proposition directly as a conditional. But granting that Plato uttered such a proposition, and that it is true that he uttered it, then he cursed Socrates by a conditional curse, whether Socrates cursed or not. However, if you do not wish to call a conditional curse simply a curse, then I say that neither curses the other. Nor does it follow that if Socrates does not curse Plato, then Plato curses him. For it follows only that Plato says that he said it, and this was only a conditioned curse.

In order to fill out more the preceding sophism, because verbal abuse is seen to designate a desire that someone come to evil, there is still one sophism posited.

(20) Socrates wishes Plato evil.

I posit that Socrates conditionally wishes Plato evil, namely, if Plato wishes Socrates evil. And conversely, Plato wishes Socrates evil, if Socrates does not wish Plato evil. Then it is asked concerning this sophism whether Socrates wishes Plato evil or not.

And it could be argued as it was argued concerning curses.

And I answer as before, that the propositions expressing the case can be taken as conditionals. And then they are not to be admitted, since it does not follow that if Plato wishes Socrates evil, then Socrates wishes Plato evil.

In another way, they can be taken and received as categoricals, so that Socrates wishes it to be as is signified by this sentence "May Plato come to evil if he wishes Socrates evil." And then when it is asked whether Socrates wishes Plato evil, I say that he does, according to a conditional wish, but not absolutely.

And so leaving the curses behind, may God, who is praised through all time, bless us.

AMEN

NOTES

1. *repugnantiam.*
2. *convenientiam.*
3. *omnis syllaba est plures littere, ergo nulla syllaba est unica littera.*
4. Aristotle, *Prior Analytics* i. 13. 32a 17–27.
5. Aristotle, *Prior Analytics* ii. 2. 53b 7–8.
6. Aristotle, *Categories* 12. 14b 14–16.
7. *de virtute sermonis.*
8. Cf., Aristotle, *Metaphysics* vi. 4. 1027b 17–25.
9. Aristotle, *Metaphysics* v. 7. 1017a 25–30.
10. This appears to be only a point of grammar, but it is interesting to note that Buridan was familiar with Vergil and assumed that his readers were as well.
11. *conceptus est in plus quam scientia.*
12. Reading *Platoni* instead of *Sorti.*
13. Reading *conclusionem* instead of *contradictionem.*
14. Aristotle, *Nicomachean Ethics* vii. 3. 1146b 25–36.
15. Aristotle, *De Interpretatione* 9. 19a 27–29.

CHAPTER 48

Paul of Venice

Paul of Venice was born at Udine, Italy, circa 1369. He studied at Padua after entering the Augustinian convent of Stephano in Venice. In 1390 he was assigned to Oxford University, where he remained at least three years. Records indicate that by May 1408 he was a lector in philosophy at the University of Padua, having achieved the status of doctor of arts and theology.

Biographical data on Paul are incomplete. However, it is known that he was active in the political and religious arenas as well as in academia. He was a skilled diplomat, frequently serving as ambassador of Venice to foreign rulers. Throughout his adult life he held positions of leadership within his order. For the years 1409–10 he was its rector and vicar general. He served as the prior provincial of Siena, (1420) and of Marche Tarvisine (1420–21); in 1421 he became regent of the Siena convent.

Within academia he enjoyed international recognition as a philosopher, lecturing at several universities, including Padua, Bologna, and Siena. At the latter he held the position of rector in 1428. He died on June 15, 1429.

Paul of Venice on Entailment Propositions

Entailment propositions are molecular inferences consisting of an antecedent and a consequent joined together by an entailment sign most typically expressed by the terms 'hence' and 'therefore'. (Note: entailment and conditional propositions are not identical.) Paul's first observation is that "some inferences—and this applies both to affirmative and to negative ones—are valid, and some are invalid or defective". The conditions determining validity and invalidity are explored in detail. "Just as every valid inference is necessary per se or without qualification, so every invalid inference is per se false and impossible."

His second main observation is that "some valid inferences are formally valid and some are materially valid". Formal validity obtains by virtue of (a) neither the antecedent nor the consequent entailing a contradiction or (b) the entailment not being per se impossible. What Paul calls 'per se impossible' "is a proposition which has a significate which, naturally or supernaturally, neither is nor was nor will be able to be true". In contrast, "a *materially valid* inference . . . may be defined as one in which the contradictory of its conclusion . . . would be materially incompatible within the premise of that inference; . . . And I call things *materially incompatible* when a conjunction formed from them would be per se impossible but would not be so if the conjuncts were assumed to be purely contingent".

Paul's third main observation is that the validity of an inference is a function of form in some cases and a function of its content in other cases. "An inference which is *valid because of its form* may be defined as one where every inference of the same form is valid. . . . An inference which is *valid because of its matter* may be defined as one where not every inference of the same form is valid." From this two theses follow: (1) form is unaffected by the interchangeability of content, and (2) truth and falsity affect only matter, not form.

"ON ENTAILMENT PROPOSITIONS" FROM *LOGICA MAGNA*

I now turn to discuss entailment propositions.

[1]

What I have said up to now has not completely clarified the topic of conditionals, so in order to have a full grasp of it we must finally turn our attention to entailment propositions. What I have to say here runs parallel to what I said earlier on: an entailment proposition is a molecular statement which implicitly or explicitly joins two propositions together by an entailment sign, which is commonly expressed as 'hence' or 'therefore'. Examples are:

You are running, hence you are moving; You are a human being, therefore you are an animal.

The proof that an entailment is a molecular proposition runs as follows:

Every complex that is to be accepted or denied or doubted is a proposition; every entailment is of this kind; therefore every entailment is a proposition. Then the next step is: Every entailment is a proposition; but no entailment is a categorical proposition; therefore every entailment is a molecular proposition.

Reprinted by permission from Paul of Venice: Logica Magna, Part II, Fascicule 4, *Capitula de Conditionali et de Rationali*, edited with an English translation and notes by G. E. Hughes. (Copyright by The British Academy, 1990.) Pp. 79–122.

A second argument is this: Every statement which has as its principal parts two complete categoricals joined together by a sign that does not presuppose anything else, is a molecular proposition; but an entailment statement is of this kind; therefore etc.

And a third argument is this: A conditional is a molecular proposition, therefore so is an entailment. This inference holds because there is no reason which applies more to the one case than to the other; and its premiss was demonstrated earlier on.

It should be noted in this connection that some entailment propositions are affirmative and some are negative. The affirmative ones are those in which the entailment sign is affirmed, such as

You are a human being, therefore you are an animal;

the negative ones are those in which the sign is negated, such as

It is not the case that (you are a human being, therefore you are running).[1]

However, since the word 'entailment' can be replaced by 'inference', I shall now stop using it and in this chapter I shall adopt this alternative terminology which other people use.

The *first main observation* is this:

⟨1⟩ Some inferences—and this applies both to affirmative and to negative ones—are valid, and some are invalid or defective.

A *valid* inference which signifies in accordance with the composition of its elements may be defined as one in which the contradictory of its conclusion would be incompatible with the premiss of that inference, given that these signify as they do; and by 'as they do' I refer to what they customarily signify. Thus in

You are a human being, therefore you are an animal

the contradictory of 'You are an animal', namely

You are not an animal

is incompatible with

You are a human being.

Or alternatively: A valid inference which signifies in accordance with the composition of its elements may be defined as one whose premiss is naturally suited to be incompatible with the contradictory of the conclusion of that inference. Thus in

You are running, therefore you are moving,

even if we were to suppose there was no opposite of its conclusion in existence, nevertheless the premiss would be no less suited to be incompatible with it.

Moreover, I call two things incompatible with each other when the conjunction formed from them is per se impossible.[2] For example, these two,

You are a human being

and

You are not an animal,

are incompatible, since a conjunction formed from them is per se impossible and, given its customary signification, could never be made true, either naturally or even supernaturally. Similarly, these two,

You are a donkey

and

You are running

are incompatible, since a conjunction formed from them is per se impossible in virtue of its first conjunct.

And note that I say 'per se impossible', for it can happen that two propositions form a conjunction which is accidentally impossible but whose conjuncts are not incompatible with each other. This is clearly so with

Adam did not exist

and

You are running.

For quite certainly a conjunction formed from these is accidentally impossible, in virtue of its first conjunct; yet they are not incompatible, because at one time they could have been true together (with their customary signification), as was explained in another chapter.

Note, too, that when I speak of what is per se impossible or per se necessary, I do not mean to speak theologically, but only from the point of view of logic or natural science. Thus I use 'per se impossible' to denote anything whose adequate significate neither is nor was nor will be able to be made true naturally or by any natural hypothesis. Examples are

A human being is a donkey,
The heavens are at rest,
The sun is not moving.

And I use 'per se necessary' to denote anything whose primary significate neither is nor was nor will be able to be made false by any natural hypothesis. Examples are

A human being is an animal,
The heavens are in motion.

For if one wanted to speak theologically, one would have to say that

A human being is a donkey

is possible and that

A human being is an animal

is contingent.[3]

A valid inference which does not signify in accordance with the composition of its elements can be defined as one which is immediately subordinable to a valid one. This is clear in the case of

> You are a human being, therefore you are a non-animal,

on the assumption that it signifies that you are a human being, therefore you are an animal.[4] For the opposite of the conclusion is consistent with the premiss, and yet the inference is valid because it is subordinated to a valid one, namely

> You are a human being, therefore you are an animal.

The same clearly applies to the second conjunct in

> You are moving, therefore you are running, and conversely.

This is a valid inference, and yet the opposite of its conclusion cannot be incompatible with its premiss, because it cannot have a premiss or a conclusion or an inference sign. It is, however, enough that it is subordinate to an inference that is valid.

An invalid inference which signifies in accordance with the composition of its elements may be defined as one in which the contradictory of its conclusion would not be incompatible with the premiss of that inference, given that these signify in the customary way. Obvious examples are

> You are a human being, therefore you are running,
> Adam did not exist, therefore you do not exist;

for it is quite clear that the contradictory opposites of their conclusions are not incompatible with the premisses, since the two conjunctions formed from them are not per se impossible.

Or alternatively: An invalid inference which signifies in accordance with the composition of its elements is one in which

the premiss is not naturally suited to be incompatible with the contradictory opposite of its conclusion; for example

> This (indicating your soul) does not exist, therefore a stick is standing in the corner.

An invalid inference which does not signify in accordance with the composition of its elements may be defined as one which is subordinable to an invalid one. A clear case is

> You are a human being, therefore you are an animal,

on the assumption that it adequately signifies as

> You are a human being, therefore you are a donkey

does. For in spite of the fact that the opposite of its conclusion is incompatible with its premiss, it is nevertheless invalid; and the reason is that it does not signify in accordance with the composition of its own elements, but in accordance with the composition of those of a different, and invalid, inference, with which it is interchangeable or to which it is subordinated. The same can be said about the second conjunct in

> You are running, therefore you are moving, and conversely.

These rules have been stated for affirmative inferences, but from them we can derive the corresponding rules for negative ones, as we showed in the case of conditionals.[5]

These points lead to a number of theses:

Thesis 1: The following form of argumentation is not valid:
Inference A is valid, therefore the contradictory of its conclusion is incompatible with its premiss.

The reason is that the conclusion may exist but have no contradictory; or else, as was mentioned above, A may be an inference which does not have a premiss or a conclusion or an inference sign.

Thesis 2: This inference is not valid:
It cannot be the case that the premiss of a certain inference is true unless its conclusion is also true (when they signify in the customary way), therefore the inference is valid.

This is clear in the case of

Adam did not exist, therefore you are a donkey[6]

and

This (indicating your soul) does not exist, therefore God does not exist.[7]

And according to one commonly held view it is also clear in the case of

No proposition is true, therefore no God exists,

for what is maintained is that it is impossible for its premiss (with its customary signification) to be true at all.[8]

Thesis 3: This argument is not valid:
A is a valid inference, therefore if things are as its premiss signifies that they are, then they are as its conclusion signifies that they are.

This is because it may be that A does not have a premiss or a conclusion; and even if it does have them, it may be that it does not signify in accordance with their composition. But we *can* argue correctly like this:

A is a valid inference which signifies in accordance with the composition of its premiss and conclusion, and things are as its premiss signifies that they are, therefore things are as its conclusion signifies that they are.

And if someone advances as a counterexample,

Only a being exists, therefore a chimera does not exist,

in the belief that things are not as its conclusion signifies that they are, then I maintain that this is not a genuine counterexample; for in fact it *is* the case that a

chimera does not exist, since it is true that a chimera does not exist.

Thesis 4: This argument is not valid:
A is a valid inference which signifies precisely in accordance with the composition of its terms, therefore if you are thinking that things are as its premiss signifies that they are, then you are also thinking that things are as its conclusion signifies that they are.

For

A human being is running, therefore something that can laugh is running

is a valid inference, but it is not the case that if you are thinking that a human being is running, then you are thinking that something that can laugh is running.[9]

Thesis 5: The following inference is valid:
A is a valid inference which signifies precisely in accordance with the composition of its terms, and its conclusion is per se impossible, therefore so is its premiss; moreover, if its premiss is per se necessary, so is its conclusion.

This makes it clear that the inference

God exists, therefore Adam existed

is not a valid one, in spite of the fact that its conclusion is necessary; for its conclusion is only accidentally necessary.[10]

Thesis 6: Just as every valid inference is necessary per se or without qualification, so every invalid inference is per se false and impossible. This should be clear from what has already been said.

There are some arguments against the foregoing, designed to prove that there are no invalid inferences.
⟨1-0b1⟩ Suppose there is some invalid inference. Call it 'A'. Then the argument runs: A is an inference, therefore A is a logical following. (This holds because 'logical following' and 'inference' are synonymous terms, like 'dagger' and 'poniard'.[11] We

next have: A is a logical following, therefore it is a logical following of something that follows—just as we can argue,

Fatherhood is a relation, therefore it is a relation of something that is related.

We next have

A is a logical following of something that follows, therefore A is a logical following of something that follows from something else.

This is clear from the similar case:

Fatherhood is a relation of something that is related, therefore fatherhood is a relation of something that is related to something else.

Finally we have

A is a logical following of something that follows from something else, therefore in A (i.e. in the 'following') the thing that follows does follow from that other thing.

But if that is so, then inference A is valid.

⟨1-0b2⟩ A second argument is this: Suppose that A is an invalid inference, that B is its premiss and that C is its conclusion. Then the argument runs: C is a conclusion, therefore it is derived from something other than itself; but there does not seem to be anything from which it is derived except B; therefore it is derived from B, and as a result it follows from B. But if so, then inference A is valid. Analogously, we can argue: B is a premiss, therefore it yields something other than itself; but there does not seem to be anything which it yields except C; therefore it does yield C—and if so, then A is a valid inference.

To be able to reply to these arguments we should note that 'A's being an inference' can be understood in two ways. In one sense, what it means is that A is a proposition in which, implicitly or explicitly, there are joined together two propositions, one of which actually does follow from the other; and in that sense I agree that all inferences are valid and none are invalid. That, however, is not the sense which those

who say that some inferences are invalid have in mind. The second way in which it can be understood is that A is a proposition in which, implicitly or explicitly, there are joined together two propositions, one of which is *claimed* to follow from the other; and it is in this sense that I hold that some inferences are invalid.[12] This, moreover, is the sense which all who discuss this topic have in mind.[13] So the position is that if there is any such affirmative entailment proposition—one in which one thing is claimed to follow from another—then if in fact it does follow, the inference will be valid, and if it does not, the inference will be invalid.

I want similarly to say that 'B's being a premiss' can be understood in two ways. In one sense it means that B is a proposition which does yield something other than itself; and in that sense I shall say that no false affirmative conditional or entailment proposition has an antecedent or a premiss at all. The other sense is that B is a proposition which is *claimed* to yield something other than itself; and in that sense I hold that some false affirmative entailment propositions or conditionals do have premisses or antecedents. The same sort of thing can be said about C. Now this is the mode of speaking that I adopt throughout this book; and in the light of it I now reply to the arguments.

⟨1-0b1R⟩ In reply to the first, I reject the inference which runs

A is an inference, therefore A is a logical following.

And these terms are not synonymous, except in the first of the two senses; but we are not speaking in that way.

⟨1-0b2R⟩ In reply to the second, I maintain that B *is* a premiss and C a conclusion. But from this it does not follow

Therefore C is derived from something other than itself.

What we ought to deduce is rather,

Therefore C is derived from something other than itself, or it is claimed to be derived from something other than itself.

Here I accept both the inference and its conclusion. But then, since C is claimed to be derived from B and it is not in fact so derived, A is a false and invalid inference. Therefore etc.

[2]

The *second main observation* is this:

⟨2⟩ Some valid inferences are formally valid and some are materially valid.[14]

A *formally valid* inference which signifies precisely in accordance with the composition of its terms may be defined as one in which the contradictory of its conclusion, when it signifies primarily in the customary way, would be formally incompatible with the premiss of that inference; or alternatively, as one in which the premiss is naturally suited to be formally incompatible with the contradictory of the conclusion of that inference. An example is

An animal exists, therefore something exists;

for

Nothing exists

and

An animal exists

are formally incompatible. And in this context I call two things formally incompatible when either (a) even assuming that each was purely contingent,[15] a conjunction formed from them (with their customary signification) would be per se impossible,[16] or (b) one of the pair in fact formally entails a contradiction.[17] An example of (a) is

Something exists and nothing exists,

since, even if we assume that 'Something exists' and 'Nothing exists' are both purely contingent, nevertheless their conjunction is per se impossible, just like the conjunction of 'You are a human being' and 'You are not an animal'. For an example of (b), take

You are other than yourself[18]

and

A stick is standing in the corner.

Note that what I call 'purely contingent' is a proposition which has a significate that can be true and can be false indifferently, both naturally and supernaturally. And what I call 'per se impossible' is a proposition which has a significate which, naturally or supernaturally, neither is nor was nor will be able to be true, such as

Someone who is sitting is running.

But more of this later on when we come to deal with the truth of propositions.[19]

It follows from all this that the inference

This man believes precisely[20] that some man is mistaken, therefore some man is mistaken

is formally valid, since

This man believes . . .

and

No man is mistaken

are formally incompatible. The proof is that from their conjunction there follows something that is per se impossible, namely

Some man is mistaken and no man is mistaken,

since each conjunct in this conclusion follows formally from some conjunct in the premiss which is referred to by the other one, as will become clear to anyone who reflects on the matter.[21]

In this connection, in order to reconcile the points of view of natural scientists, theologians and metaphysicians, who are apt to react in different ways to one and the same inference, I want to draw attention to a certain classification of formally valid inferences. This is that some formally valid inferences are *merely formally valid*, others are *more than merely formally valid*, and yet others are *formally valid in the highest degree* (or *formally formally valid*).

A *merely formally valid* inference (which signifies precisely in accordance with the composition of its elements) may be defined as one in which the contradictory of its conclusion (signifying primarily in the customary way) would be merely formally incompatible with the premiss of that inference. (Or we could express this in the alternative way mentioned earlier.) Examples are

You are sitting, therefore you are not running;
You are white, therefore you are not black.

And two things are *merely formally incompatible* when, even assuming that each is contingent, a conjunction formed from them would be per se impossible, but only naturally, in the way that

You are sitting and you are running

and

You are white and you are black

are. For neither of these conjunctions could be made true by any natural means, though this could well happen by some supernatural means.[22]

A *more than merely formally valid* inference (which signifies precisely in accordance with the composition of its elements) may be defined as one in which the contradictory of its conclusion (signifying in the customary way) would be more than merely formally incompatible with the premiss of that inference. (Or we could use the other formulation given earlier.)[23] For example,

You are a human being, therefore you are able to laugh.

And I call things *more than merely formally incompatible* when, even assuming that each is contingent, a conjunction formed from them would be in actuality[24] per se impossible, supernaturally as well as naturally. It is in this way that

You are a human being

and

You are not able to laugh

are incompatible; for no power whatsoever could make a subject without its proper attribute.[25] In this sense, however, the inference

You are sitting, therefore you are not running

is not valid, since by the divine power

You are sitting

and

You are running

could be true at the same time. This could be brought about by a divisive multiplication.

An inference that is *formally valid in the highest degree*, or *formally formally valid* (when it signifies precisely in accordance with the composition of its terms) may be defined as one in which the contradictory of its conclusion (signifying primarily in the customary way) would be in the highest degree incompatible with the premiss of that inference. (Or alternatively, we could define it as we did before, in terms of the premiss, as one whose premiss is naturally suited to be incompatible etc.) For example,

You are a human being, therefore you are an animal.

And I call two things mutually *incompatible in the highest degree* when one of them cannot without contradiction be understood or imagined along with the other (given that they signify in the customary way). This is the case with

You are a human being

and

You are not an animal,

for it is not possible without contradiction to understand a logically posterior term without its logically prior one.[26] In this sense, however, the inference

> You are a human being, therefore you are able to laugh

would not be valid (taking 'able to laugh' not in an ampliative way but as referring to the actual possession of the proper attribute of a human being, which is the ability to laugh).[27] For although it is not possible for you to be a human being and not be able to laugh, yet one could think about the former without the latter, without any possible contradiction being involved.

A *materially valid* inference which signifies precisely in accordance with the composition of its terms may be defined as one in which the contradictory of its conclusion, when it signifies primarily in the customary way, would be materially incompatible with the premiss of that inference; or, alternatively, as one in which the premiss is naturally suited to be materially incompatible with the contradictory of the conclusion of that inference. Examples are

> No God exists, therefore a stick is standing in the corner;
> You are running, therefore God exists.

And I call things *materially incompatible* when a conjunction formed from them would be per se impossible but would not be so if the conjuncts were assumed to be purely contingent. Now a conjunction formed from

> You are running

and

> No God exists

would always be per se impossible, because of the per se impossibility of one of its conjuncts. But if

> No God exists

were purely contingent, the conjunction would not be impossible but would itself be contingent. Therefore etc.[28]

We can easily work out from the foregoing the conditions of the formal or material validity of inferences that do not sig-nify in accordance with the composition of their terms. These are that such an inference is said to be formally or materially valid in virtue of its being subordinable to a mental inference satisfying the relevant conditions described above.

In the light of what we have said, we can now state two rules about materially valid inferences:

Rule 1: If we have an affirmative inference which adequately signifies in accordance with the composition of its terms, which is not based on any rule for formally valid inferences, and whose conclusion is per se necessary, then that inference is materially valid.

An example is

> You are running, therefore God exists.

Note that I say 'not based on any rule for formally valid inferences'. For the inference

> A human being is a human being, therefore a human being is an animal

is *formally* valid, even though its conclusion is necessary. What makes it valid, however, is not the fact that its conclusion is necessary, but the fact that the argument proceeds from an inferior to a superior term etc.[29]

Rule 2: If we have an inference of the kind described, and its premiss is impossible but does not contain a contradiction, then that inference is materially valid.

Examples are

> The heavens are motionless, therefore you are running;
> No God exists, therefore this instant used to exist.

Note that I say 'does not contain a contradiction'; for if the premiss did contain a contradiction, anything and everything would follow *formally* from it, as I shall prove in a moment.

To understand this rule more clearly, however, it is important to realise that 'to imply (*or* to contain) a contradiction' can be understood in either of two ways. In one sense, 'to contain a contradiction' means 'to assert a contradiction'; in the other sense, 'to contain a contradiction' means 'to be a premiss from which a contradiction follows'. If we understand the expression in the first way, no proposition implies a contradiction unless a contradiction follows formally from it, as it does from

You are other than yourself.

But in the second sense every proposition that is per se impossible contains a contradiction, since a contradiction follows from any such proposition. Now the phrase in the rule has to be understood in the first of these ways. So to avoid any confusion about the matter, let us accept 'formally contain a contradiction' for the first sense, and 'materially imply a contradiction' for the second. Thus 'A formally implies a contradiction' will mean the same as 'A contradiction follows formally from A', and 'B materially contains a contradiction' will mean the same as 'A contradiction follows materially from B'.

It follows from this that some propositions contain formal contradictions but do not formally contain any contradictions. A clear example is

No God exists,

from which there follows[30] the formal contradiction

You exist and you do not exist.

⟨3⟩ I shall now prove that from an impossible proposition which formally implies a contradiction, anything whatsoever (i.e. any proposition whatsoever) follows formally.[31]

(a) From

You are other than yourself

it follows formally that a stick is standing in the corner; but there is no more reason why this should follow rather than anything else; therefore everything else follows from it as well. This inference holds. And its premiss can be proved as follows:

(1) The inference

You are other than yourself, therefore you are yourself and you are not yourself

is formally valid.

(The proof is this: The conclusion is a conjunction whose second conjunct is the negative exponent of the premiss and whose first conjunct follows formally from its first or second exponent;[32] therefore the whole conjunction follows from the categorical proposition which is the premiss. This inference holds, and so does its major premiss. The proof of the minor premiss is that

You exist, therefore you are yourself

is formally valid, since the contradictory of its conclusion is incompatible with its premiss. So we have the result that the conjunction follows from the categorical.)

(2) Next, the inference

You are yourself and you are not yourself; therefore either you are yourself or a stick is standing in the corner, and you are not yourself

is valid: for its conclusion is a conjunction—that at least is how I intend it[33]—whose first conjunct follows formally from the first conjunct in the premiss (by an argument from one disjunct to the whole disjunction), and whose second conjunct is identical or interchangeable with the second conjunct in the premiss; therefore the whole conjunction which forms the conclusion (because it signifies only in accordance with the composition of its elements) follows formally from the conjunction which forms the premiss.

(3) Finally, the inference

Either you are yourself or a stick is standing in the corner, and you are not yourself; therefore a stick is standing in the corner

is formally valid, since it argues from a disjunction, together with the denial of one disjunct, to the other disjunct.

(b) I shall now run through the proof with

You are a donkey.

(1) From this it follows formally that you are not a human being, and that you are a human being.

(The proof is this: It is obvious that the first conjunct follows, since the contradictory of the conclusion is formally incompatible with the premiss, as has been said already. And here is a proof that the second conjunct also follows: The inference

You are a donkey, therefore you exist

is formally valid, since it proceeds from a third to a second component in the absence of any impediment. And

You exist, therefore you are yourself

is also valid, since the opposite of its conclusion is formally incompatible with its premiss. Furthermore,

You are yourself, therefore you are a human being

is valid, since it argues from an inferior to a superior term.[34] This makes it clear how the whole conjunction follows from the original premiss.)

(2) Then from this conjunction one can draw any conclusion one pleases, e.g. that no God exists. The argument will run: The inference

You are a human being and you are not a human being; therefore, either you are a human being or no God exists, and you are not a human being

is valid, for the reason given earlier; and from this it follows that no God exists, by an argument from a disjunction together with the denial etc. So, going from the first to the last,

You are a donkey, therefore no God exists

is formally valid.

(If I have said the opposite of these things anywhere else, it should be understood that this was only in expounding the views of others.)

(c) I shall now argue that

A human being is a non-human-being

entails any and every other proposition. For

A human being is a non-human-being, therefore a human being is not a human being

is valid, since it proceeds from an affirmative proposition with an infinite predicate to a negative one with a finite predicate.[35] Moreover,

A human being is a non-human-being, therefore a human being exists is formally valid, since it is an argument from a third to a second component; and from the latter it follows formally that every human being is a human being. We have thus obtained the contradiction

A human being is not a human being and every human being is a human being,[36]

and we can then easily derive the conclusions that a human being is a donkey by arguing as follows:

Every human being is a human being and a human being is not a human being; therefore either every human being is a human being or a human being is a donkey, and a human being is not a human being

—from which it follows that a human being is a donkey. So, going from the first to the last,

A human being is a non-human-being

entails

A human being is a donkey.

⟨3-0b⟩ But a doubt has been expressed about this, on the ground that

A human being is a donkey

does not seem to imply a contradiction formally.[37] The argument is this: A proposition which formally implies a contradiction cannot (given its customary signification) be made true either by any natural power or by any supernatural power. Now

You are other than yourself

is like that; but according to the theologians,

A human being is a donkey

(with its customary signification) is possible and could be made true by the power of God. This proved as follows: We say that God is a human being because he is something in which human nature inheres in a dependent way, just as Socrates is white because he is something in which whiteness inheres in a dependent way;[38] but God is just as capable of being something in which asinine nature inheres in a dependent way as he is in the case of human nature; therefore God could be a donkey by assuming asinine nature, as he now is a human being by assuming human nature. Let us suppose, then, that God does assume asinine nature, without relinquishing humanity; it will then follow, by the joining together of distinct natures, that a human being is a donkey, for we can argue

This is a human being, and this is a donkey (indicating God); therefore a human being is a donkey.

⟨3-0bR⟩ My reply to this is that I laid it down at the outset that I did not wish to speak about divine, but only about natural, possibility or impossibility; and what I call *impossible and formally implying a contradiction* is anything from which a contradiction formally follows and this cannot be avoided by any natural means.[39] For there are many things which are possible for God but which imply a contradiction as far as nature is concerned. Thus

Someone who is sitting is running

is naturally impossible, and yet it is possible through a supernatural power. For let us suppose that God were to multiply you so that you are in two places at once, and that you are running in one of them and sitting in the other, white in one and black in the other, hot in one and cold in the other. This would immediately give us the truth of

Someone who is sitting is running;
Something that is white is black;
Something that is hot is cold;

and thus the following inferences would not be valid in the eyes of a theologian,

A human being is a donkey, therefore a human being is a non-human-being;
Something that is white is black, therefore something that is white is non-white;
Something that is hot is cold, therefore something that is hot is non-hot.

Since, however, these things violate the principles of logic and natural science, they ought to be ignored in our present discipline.[40]

Nevertheless, although a theologian would maintain that

A human being is a donkey

is possible, he would never admit that

You are a donkey

(indicating a created being)[41] is possible. The reason is this: Just as every accident is something that can be rendered determinate by a substantial nature, so every complete created substance is able to be assumed by God. But just as one accident cannot determine the nature of another accident, so one complete substance cannot be the basis of another complete nature.[42] As a result, you cannot be a donkey by a joining together of distinct natures, as God can; for a created substance is related to him as an accident is related to a substance (though it is not in him as in a subject, in the way that an accident is in a substance).

But now, since these matters are irrelevant to our present business, let us leave them and go back to our proper concerns.

A number of theses follow from the foregoing.

Thesis 1: Every proposition which formally contains a contradiction is formally incompatible with every other proposition.

The proof is this: As we have already

shown, every proposition which formally contains a contradiction formally entails every other proposition; but every proposition—so I am assuming—has a contradictory; therefore every proposition other than the one that contains a contradiction is formally incompatible with it. This influence is obvious in the light of what was said earlier.[43]

An even better proof is this: Let A and B be contradictory propositions, and let C be a proposition which formally contains a contradiction. Then the argument runs: C formally entails A, and B exists; therefore B is formally incompatible with C. This inference is self-evident. We then argue similarly that A is formally incompatible with C: C formally entails B, and A exists; therefore A is formally incompatible with C. And we could give just the same sort of argument for any other propositions as we have given for A and B.

Thesis 2: Every proposition which is impossible but only materially contains a contradiction is incompatible with every other proposition, formally incompatible with some of them but only materially incompatible with others.

The proof is this: Every impossible proposition which does not formally contain a contradiction entails every other proposition, and every proposition has a contradictory, therefore every proposition is incompatible with the impossible one in question. But since some propositions are entailed formally and others only materially, some are incompatible with it formally and others only materially. For example, the proposition

Nothing exists

entails these two,

You exist

and

You do not exist

the former materially and the latter for-

mally; therefore the opposite of the former is incompatible with it only materially, but the opposite of the latter is incompatible with it formally. This inference is self-evident in that

Nothing exists

and

You exist

are formally incompatible, but

Nothing exists

and

You do not exist

are materially incompatible; therefore etc.

Thesis 3: Every per se impossible proposition is incompatible with itself, in some cases formally and in other cases only materially.

The proof is this: Let A be the proposition

You are other than yourself,

and let B be one that is interchangeable with it.[44] Then the argument runs: Whatever is incompatible with B is incompatible with A, since A and B are interchangeable with each other; but A is incompatible with B, since it entails its opposite; therefore A is incompatible with A itself (since this single A, I am assuming, is every A). Now it is clear that A is *formally* incompatible with B; therefore it is formally incompatible with itself.

Next, I shall prove that

No God exists

is incompatible with itself, but materially so. The proof is this: It is incompatible with

No first cause exists,

since it entails the opposite of this.[45] Now whatever is incompatible with one of a pair of interchangeable propositions is also incompatible with the other; but each of these is incompatible with the other; therefore each is incompatible with itself. Neither, however, entails its affirmative contradictory formally; so each is incompatible with itself only materially.

Thesis 4: To every per se impossible proposition every other proposition is relevant.

This is obvious. For every other proposition both follows from any such proposition and also is incompatible with it; therefore etc. This inference clearly holds, since everything that is relevant is either relevant and following or relevant and incompatible, and vice versa.

[3]

The *third main observation* is this:

⟨4⟩ some valid inferences are valid because of their form, and others are valid because of their matter.[46]

An inference which is *valid because of its form* may be defined as one where every inference of the same form is valid. An example is

A human being is running, therefore an animal is running.

An inference which is *valid because of its matter* may be defined as one where not every inference of the same form is valid; for example,

Only a father exists, therefore not only a father exists.

This is valid because of its matter, since not every inference of the same form is valid; for

Only something exists, therefore not only something exists

is not valid.

To reach an understanding of what the form of an inference is, or what sameness of form consists in, we must first take note of what the matter or the form of a categorical proposition in general is. What I have to say about this is that the matter of a proposition is its term or terms, whereas its form is the arrangement or relationship of its parts. This is like the way in which the matter of a house is stones, timber and other necessary materials, whereas the form of the house is the relationship of these things to one another. So, for two

propositions to have the same form, nothing that is relevant to form must be found in one unless something just like it is found in the other. Thus

A human being is an animal

and

A donkey is a substance

have the same form; for it is quite clear that an exactly similar relationship of the various parts is found in each of them, since in each a superior term is related to one of its inferiors and the two are linked by a simple copula. It is therefore not correct to argue

In one of the propositions what is predicated is a term of the highest generality,[47] and in the other a less general one, therefore the form is not the same,

for the fact that one term is more general than another does not change the form, but only the matter; just as we cannot argue

This house is built of marble and pear wood, and another one is built of bricks and walnut, etc., therefore they do not have the same form.[48]

These, however, do not have the same form,

A human being is an animal

and

A human being is not an animal,

since in one of them, but not in the other, there is a negation, and this changes the form. Nor do

Every human being is running

and

   Only a human being is running

have the same form, because they have different kinds of signs of quantity, and these change the form. Similarly,

   This is a human being

and

   A human being is a human being

or

   A human being is an animal

do not have the same form, since the presence of a singular term changes the form.

What I want to say, then, is that the sameness of form of two propositions consists in this: that if one is of a certain quantity,[49] the other is also of that quantity; if one is of a certain quality,[50] the other is also of that quality; if one is not quantified in a certain respect, the other is not quantified in that respect either; if one is categorical or molecular, so is the other. In this we are to pay no attention to the relationship of the terms to one another in respect of their being superior or inferior, or being interchangeable or non-interchangeable; but we *are* to have regard to whether the elements of the propositions are similar in the following respects: that if the subject or the predicate in one is a singular term, so it is in the other; if it is a common term, so it is in the other; if it is a simple term, so it is in the other; and if it has a certain kind of complexity, so it has in the other.

As a result, the following do not have the same form,

   A human being is running

and

   A white human being is running;

nor do these,

   Socrates and Plato are arguing

and

   Either Socrates or Plato is not arguing,

since in one of them the subject is a con-

junctive complex term and in the other it is a disjunctive one, and it is quite clear that the difference between conjunction and disjunction affects the form or a proposition.

A number of theses follow from the foregoing.

Thesis 1: The inferiority or superiority of the terms in a proposition, and their identity, interchangeability or non-interchangeability, do not effect its form but are relevant only to its matter.

This is so because

   An animal is white

and

   An animal is a body

have the same form, in spite of the fact that in one of them a superior term is predicated of one of its inferiors, and this is not so in the other. Similarly, these two,

   A human being is a human being

and

   A human being is a donkey,

have the same form, and so do

   A human being is able to laugh

and

   A human being is able to bray,

in spite of the fact that in one a term is predicated either of that very same term or of one that is interchangeable with it, and this is not so in the other.[51] Therefore etc.

Thesis 2: The possibility or impossibility of a proposition, its truth or falsity, and its necessity or contingency, do not affect its form, but only its matter.

This is clear because

   A human being is a human being

and

   A human being is a donkey

have the same form, but one is necessary and the other is impossible.

Thesis 3: In the case of conjunctions and disjunctions, whether one clause entails or is entailed by the other, or whether they are incompatible or consistent with each other, makes no difference to the form of the conjunction or disjunction, but relates only to its matter.

This is clear, since the two conjunctions,

Socrates is running and moving

and

Socrates is running and arguing

have the same form, and yet there is an entailment in the former but not in the latter.[52] And it is clear that these do have the same form, for this reason: For two conjunctions to have the same form it is sufficient that their principal parts should have the same form,[53] and also that their logical particles and their modifiers (if in fact they have any) should be the same. Now in the present examples the parts do have the same form, and they are conjoined; so they satisfy the stated conditions.

Note that I have mentioned modifiers. For

Necessarily Socrates is running and Socrates is moving

and

Socrates is running and Socrates is moving

do not have the same form, since there is a necessity modifier in the former but not in the latter. Similarly,

Necessarily a king is sitting and no king is sitting

and

Perhaps a pope is sleeping and no pope is sleeping

do not have the same form, since a necessity modifier occurs in the former but a contingency modifier in the latter.

Again,

A king is sitting and no king is sitting

and

A king is sitting and no pope is sleeping

have the same form, in spite of the fact that there is an incompatibility and a mutual inconsistency in the former but not in the latter.

The same sorts of things can also be said about disjunctions.

A conditional proposition or an inference, however, not merely joins its clauses together but also indicates that there is an entailment relation between them, and this is relevant to its form. Hence for two conditionals or inferences to have the same form, it is necessary, not only that their premises and conclusions should have the same form, but also that there should be the same simple mode of arguing in a formal inference. For example,

Every animal is running, therefore every human being is running

and

Every animal is arguing, therefore every donkey is arguing have the same form, since their premises and their conclusions have the same form and in each there is the same simple mode of arguing, namely from a superior term to one of its inferiors.[54] But

A human being is running, therefore an animal is running

and

A human being is running, therefore a log is running

do not have the same form, since, although their premises and their conclusions have the same form, the simple mode of arguing is not the same, because in the former the argument proceeds from an inferior term to one of its superiors, but not in the latter.

To get a clearer understanding of this, we have to note that some modes of arguing in a formal inference are simple, whereas others are mixed and express the matter of a proposition.[55]

Simple ones are ones like these: arguing from an inferior term to one of its superiors, or vice versa; from an expounded proposition to one or other of its exponents, or vice versa; from a conjunction to one or other of its conjuncts, or vice versa; from one disjunct to a whole disjunction, or vice versa.

Mixed modes are ones like these: arguing from an inferior term to one which is per se or accidentally one of its superiors, or vice versa; from an indefinite proposition to the corresponding universal in the case of substantial terms in direct predication;[56] from one conjunct, when this entails the other one, to the whole conjunction; from a disjunction to one of its disjuncts, when this is entailed by the other disjunct; and so forth. All such modes are called *mixed* because they express the matter of propositions which is not relevant to their form or to a simple mode of arguing. It is quite clear that entailing or being entailed per se or accidentally, or being constructed from such and such terms, is related to matter, not form, as was said earlier on.

What I maintain, then, is that simple modes of arguing in a formal inference are relevant to the form of conditionals and inferences, but that mixed ones are not. For it is undeniable that

A human being is an animal, therefore every human being is an animal

and

A human being is running, therefore every human being is running have the same form, since their premises and their conclusions have the same form, and there is the same simple mode of arguing, namely from an indefinite proposition to the corresponding universal. And we cannot validly argue,

In the first inference the argument proceeds with substantial terms, and in the second with accidental ones, therefore they do not have the same form;[57]

for arguing with substantial or with accidental terms makes no difference to the form of an inference—only a simple mode of arguing does that.

To make things clearer, I shall now deduce some conclusions from all this.

Thesis 1: Every valid syllogism is an inference which is valid because of its form.

This is clear, because every inference which has the same form as it does is valid. And two syllogisms have the same form when their premises and their conclusions have the same form and there is the same simple mode of arguing, namely being in such and such a mood or in such and such a figure to be reduced to such and such a mood or to such and such a figure.[58]

It follows from this that we cannot validly argue,

Syllogisms A and B are in the same mood of such and such a figure, therefore they have the same form;

for their premises or their conclusions may happen not to have the same form, as in

Every human being is running, you are a human being, therefore you are running

and

Every animal is running, a human being is an animal, therefore a human being is running.

Clearly both of these syllogisms are in *Darii*, but they differ in form on account of their second premises and conclusions.[59]

Another thing that follows is that this argument will be valid:

A and B are two syllogisms of which one is in a certain mood or figure but the other is not, therefore they differ in form.[60]

Thesis 2: An inference from a conjunction to either of its conjuncts, or from one disjunct to a whole disjunction, is both formally valid and valid because of its form.

This is clear, because every influence with the same form is valid.

It follows from this that an inference from one conjunct to a whole conjunction is not valid because of its form. For even though

A human being is running, therefore a human being is running and an animal is running

is formally valid, it is nevertheless not valid because of its form, since the following inference, which has the same form, is not valid,

A human being is running, therefore a human being is running and a log is running.

Secondly, it follows that an argument from a whole disjunction to one of its disjuncts is not valid because of its form, in spite of the fact that the inference

Either you are a human being or you are an animal, therefore you are an animal

is formally valid; for

Either you are a human being or you are a log, therefore you are a log

is not valid.

Thesis 3: Without exception, an argument from an expounded proposition to each of its exponents, or from one ground of truth to a proposition of which it is such a ground, is valid because of its form.[61]

An argument in the reverse direction can indeed be valid, but not because of its form, as in these cases,

A human being is a donkey, therefore every human being is a donkey

and

Not only a human being is a donkey, therefore something other than a human being is a donkey.[62]

The first of these holds because its premiss is per se impossible, and the second because its conclusion is per se necessary.

Thesis 4: An inference from an inferior term to one of its superiors, in the case

of affirmative propositions and in the absence of any impediment, is both formally valid and valid because of its form; and the reverse holds when negations are prefixed.

For

A human being is running, therefore an animal is running

is valid formally and because of its form, since every inference with the same form as it has is valid. And so too is

No animal is running, therefore no human being is running.

It follows from this that an argument from an inferior term, together with an appropriate mediating premiss, to one of its superiors, when negations come after them, is not valid because of its form. An example is

Socrates is not running, and Socrates is a human being, therefore a human being is not running,

because the following inference, which has the same form, is not valid,

Socrates is not running, and Plato is a human being, therefore a human being is not running.

The proof that it has the same form is that the premisses and the conclusions have the same form, and that there is the same simple mode of arguing, namely from an inferior term to one of its superiors; therefore etc.

It follows, secondly, that an argument from a superior term, together with an appropriate mediating premiss, to one of its inferiors, where the terms are distributed and the propositions are affirmative, is not valid because of its form, even though the inference is formally valid. An example is

Every animal is running, every human being is an animal, therefore every human being is running,

because the following is not valid,

Every human being is running, every Plato is a human being, therefore every Socrates is running.

(I say all this on the understanding that such inferences are based on a category; for if they are based on a syllogism they are not merely formally valid but also valid because of their form.)[63]

It follows, thirdly, that an inference from a superior term to one of its inferiors is sometimes valid formally but not because of its form. For

A human being is an animal, therefore a human being is a human being

is formally valid, for the following reason:

A human being is an animal, therefore a human being exists is formally valid; and so is

A human being exists, therefore a human being is a human being, since the opposite of its conclusion is formally incompatible with its premiss; hence, going from the first to the last,

A human being is an animal, therefore a human being is a human being

is formally valid. It is not, however, valid because of its form, since

A human being is an animal, therefore a human being is a donkey, where there is the same mode of arguing, is not valid.

Similarly, an inference from an inferior term to one of its superiors is sometimes valid formally but not because of its form. For

This human being is not a human being, therefore this human being is not an animal

is formally valid, since the contradictory of its conclusion is formally incompatible with its premiss; but the parallel inference

This donkey is not a human being, therefore this donkey is not an animal

is not valid.

Thesis 5: An argument from a universal proposition to the corresponding indefi-

nite or particular proposition is always valid both formally and because of its form; and the converse holds for 'second component' propositions.

For the inferences

Every human being is running, therefore a human being is running

and

A human being exists, therefore every human being exists

are valid because of their form, since in each case every inference with the same form is also valid. This can be seen by running through all the relevant cases, both affirmative and negative.

From this thesis it follows that an argument from a 'third component' indefinite proposition to the corresponding universal is not valid because of its form, no matter what its terms may be, even though it may be a formally valid inference. An example is

A human being is a human being, therefore every human being is a human being.

This is formally valid, but is not valid because of its form since

A human being is Socrates, therefore every human being is Socrates

is not valid. Similarly,

A human being is an animal, therefore every human being is an animal

is not valid because of its form, since

A human being is running, therefore every human being is running is not valid.

It follows in the second place that the following inferences are not valid because of their form:

A human being exists, therefore a human being is a human being;
A human being exists, therefore every human being is a human being;

A white thing is a non-human-being; therefore every white thing is white.

This is because there are inferences which have the same forms as these do but are not valid; for example,

> A human being exists, therefore a human being is a donkey;
> A human being exists, therefore every human being is a goat;
> A white thing is a non-human-being, therefore every white thing is black.

It should be clear that the premisses and the conclusions have the same form; and there does not seem to be any simple mode of arguing on which an inference in the first group might be based unless some inference in the second group could also be based on it or on one just like it.

Thesis 6: No inference which is only materially valid holds because of its form.

This is clear because every such inference holds either because its premiss is impossible or because its conclusion is necessary.

It follows from this thesis that some inferences with impossible premisses are valid because of their form. A clear case is

> You are other than yourself, therefore a stick is standing in the corner.

It is quite certain that every inference with the same form as this has is valid. And if someone objects that

> You are other than this (indicating a donkey), therefore a stick is standing in the corner

is not valid, then I agree. But if the argument proceeds, 'And this has the same form as the original inference, therefore etc.', then I reject the minor premiss. For the original inference does not hold in virtue of the fact that its premiss is impossible, but by the simple mode of arguing in a formal inference which consists in proceeding from the first step to the last.[64]

It follows in the second place that every proposition which formally implies a contradiction entails every other proposition,

both formally and because of its form. This should be clear because there is no greater reason why it should do so in any one case than in any other.[65]

From these and earlier remarks it clearly follows that there are many inferences which are formally valid and hold formally, but are not valid because of their form but only because of their matter. Among them are

> You believe precisely that some human being is mistaken, therefore some human being is mistaken

and

> You believe that every human being is mistaken, therefore you are mistaken.

Each of these is formally valid, since the contradictory of its conclusion is formally incompatible with its premiss, but neither of them is valid because of its form. This is clear because

> You believe precisely that some donkey is mistaken, therefore some donkey is mistaken

is not valid; nor is

> You believe that every human being is running, therefore you are running;

nor—to use the terms in the original example—is

> This being believes that every human being is mistaken (indicating some intelligence), therefore this being is mistaken.

And in this way we could use many other examples to illustrate the truth of our thesis.

Arguments against the foregoing

⟨4-0b1⟩ The inference, or syllogism,

> Every A is B, every C is A, therefore every C is B

is valid, yet it holds only because of its matter; therefore etc.[66] This inference holds. So does its major premiss, because the syllogism is in *Barbara*. And the proof of the minor premiss is that terms occur in it which refer precisely to its matter, since they are not significative terms.[67]

⟨4-0b2⟩ A second argument is this: An inference in the mind does not have any matter, because if it had any matter it would be a substance and a composite body. Hence there cannot be in the mind any inference which is valid materially or because of its matter; and therefore there cannot be any that is valid formally or because of its form either, since all form presupposes matter.

⟨4-0b3⟩ A third argument is this: It is quite possible for an inference to be valid formally and because of its form, even though no other inference with the same form exists. Therefore the account which was given of how to recognize an inference that is valid because of its form cannot be correct.

⟨4-0b4⟩ A fourth argument is this: In other things, qualities and quantities are said to be accidental forms. This is what the author of the *Six Principles*[68] says, and so does the Philosopher in many places. So if being affirmative and being negative are qualities of propositions, they must be accidental forms of them. But in that case one accident will be based directly on another accident and will directly refer to it, since spoken and mental propositions are accidents.

I now reply to these arguments.

⟨4-0b1R⟩ There are two ways of replying to the first. One of these is by claiming that a form of arguing of this kind is not an intelligible one, since it is constructed from non-significative terms.[69] Alternatively, we can accept the inference—the syllogism— and deny that there is no form in it. And then when it is said

'The terms A, B and C are not significative terms',

we can deny this on the following grounds: Although they are not significative of things distinct from themselves and other terms equiform with them, as the term 'human being' is, yet they do signify themselves and other equiform terms and stand for these (unless there is some fresh impo-

sition of meaning). If, then, it is posited that these terms correspond in the mind to some common terms which occur in a syllogism and signify things distinct from themselves and any equiform terms, though no more definite certification is given, then I accept, as before, that the syllogism is valid because of its form, even though I do not understand it because I do not understand its premisses or its conclusion. This is like the way in which I can know something to be true, and know many Greek propositions to be false, although I do not understand them. For as I mentioned earlier, I know that the conjunction

This exists and this does not exist

is impossible, and that the disjunction which is its opposite is necessary, given merely that I know that its clauses contradict each other; and yet I do not understand either of these clauses, because for a proposition to be understood, each separate part of it must be understood. In the same way,

This is not this

can be denied, given that it is certified that the same thing is being referred to each time, and

This is this

can be accepted.

It follows, therefore, that in making a correct response you can accept or deny a proposition which you do not understand, provided that it is established for you, by a certification, that it is true, or established for you, by a certification, that it is false. On the other hand, if no such certification is given, and the proposition

This is this,

is proposed to me, I shall not respond either by accepting it or by denying it or by doubting it, until I am informed what is referred to by 'this'.[70] And the reason we should not doubt it is this: To doubt is to consider a proposition but, because of various reasons for or against it, neither to believe firmly that it is true nor to believe firmly that it is false; thus every proposition to which someone gives sufficient consideration, and which he understands but neither believes to be true nor believes to be false, is doubtful to that person; wherefore etc.

⟨4-0b2R⟩ The reply to the second argument is that the word 'matter' is ambiguous and can be taken in different ways, either literally or metaphorically. In the literal sense it refers to a purely passive principle, which is not itself active but has an unlimited capacity for receiving an unlimited number of forms, and is a necessary constituent in the coming into being of anything that can come into being and pass away, though without itself coming into being or passing away.[71] It is of matter in this sense that the Philosopher speaks in Book I of the *Physics*. But secondly, 'matter' can be taken metaphorically, to refer to anything that is required for the formation of anything new. In this sense the stuff from which artefacts are made is called 'matter', and so is the intellective soul which receives the indivisible forms. Now it is in this latter sense that the terms in a proposition can be called its matter; so it is obvious that we cannot validly argue

This has matter, therefore it is a composite being of a substantial kind.[72]

⟨4-0b3R⟩ In reply to the third argument, I accept its premiss but deny the validity of the inference. The reason is that in what I

say on this topic I speak conditionally and with a certain presupposition, i.e. in the following sense:

If there comes to be any valid inference, and if every inference of the same form that either will be or could be constructed (signifying in the customary way) will or would also be valid, then the inference in question will be valid because of its form; and if it is valid, but not every inference of the same form (signifying in the customary way) would be valid, then it is not valid because of its form.

Therefore etc.

⟨4-0b4R⟩ In reply to the fourth argument, I reject the inference, for this reason: Being affirmative or being negative is said to be a quality of a proposition, and whiteness or blackness is said to be a quality of a human being, only in a metaphorical or equivocal way. For it is clear that whiteness and other qualities in a human being are accidents inhering in a human being and do not belong to his essence. But it is not in this way that being affirmative or negative is a quality of a proposition, since this is a part of, or of the essence of, the proposition itself. It is said to be a quality simply because when the question is asked 'Of what quality is this proposition?' the answer is either 'Affirmative' or 'Negative'. Analogous things can be said about quantity as well.[73] Therefore etc.

NOTES

1. The Latin version is produced by simply prefixing *non* ('not') to the Latin equivalent of 'You are a human being, therefore you are running', but it does not seem possible to imitate this construction closely in English.

2. Per se impossibility is contrasted with accidental impossibility. An accidentally impossible proposition is one which could once have been true but cannot now, or at any time in the future, come to be true; false propositions about the past are typically of this kind. By contrast, a per se impossible proposition is one which could not be, or have been, true at any time, past, present or future. Paul draws an analogous distinction between per se and accidental necessity. He also distinguishes three degrees of per se impossibility at pp. 740–42.

3. This point is elaborated below on pp. 91 f and 99–101.

4. What is posited is not that 'non-animal' is to signify what 'animal' normally does, or even that 'You are a non-animal' is to signify what 'You are an animal' usually does, but solely that the whole inference is to signify in the way indicated, without any abnormal attribution of meaning to either of its causes or any of its terms taken separately. If this and nothing else were posited and admitted in an obligation exercise, the respondent would be committed to accepting 'You are a human being', accepting 'You are a human being, therefore you are a non-animal' but denying 'You are a non-animal'. Cf. Paul's treatment of the example 'You are a human being, therefore you are an animal' p. 737 second column.

5. The fact that 'negative inferences' count as valid or true if and only if their conclusions do *not* follow from their premises may make it seem strange that Paul should wish to call them inferences at all, and

not all medieval logicians would have done so. Venator, for example, explicitly denies that they are inferences or entailment propositions, and similarly argues that there are no negative conditionals. However, the matter seems to be little more than one of terminology, and in any case Paul has no more to say about negative inferences in this chapter. From here on, when he speaks of inferences, it is only affirmative ones he is referring to.

6. The argument is this: Assuming (with Paul) that Adam did in fact exist, it cannot (now) be the case that Adam did not exist; this, however, is only an accidental impossibility, and hence 'Adam did not exist and you are not a donkey' is only accidentally, not per se, impossible.

7. According to Paul, your soul might never have come into existence, but now that it does exist, it cannot be destroyed by any natural means. Thus 'This does not exist' (indicating your soul) is accidentally, but not per se impossible.

8. I take the 'commonly held view' referred to here to be one which holds that the proposition 'No proposition is true' is not impossible, not even accidentally impossible, but that it cannot be *true*: not impossible, since what it asserts to be so would in fact be so if the only propositions that existed were, say '2 + 3 = 7' and 'A human being is a donkey'; but not possibly true, since for it to be true it must exist, and if it exists and is true it provides a counter-instance to itself. This view was certainly well known in Paul's day; cf., e.g., the treatment of 'No proposition is negative' and 'Every proposition is false' in Buridan's *Sophismata*, ch. VIII, Sophismata 1 and 7 respectively.

9. Cf. Paul's remarks on pp. 744 f below.

10. According to Paul (and most other logicians of his time) 'God exists' is per se necessary. Part of his point in giving this example may have been to underline the theological belief that God is completely free to create or not to create any kind of world he chooses: nothing about the course of the world, not even its existence, follows logically from the mere existence of God.

11. The two Latin words in this example both mean 'sword', but I cannot think of any English synonym of 'sword'.

12. A similar ambiguity exists in English. We sometimes say, e.g. that q cannot be inferred from p, and yet that many people do infer q from p.

13. If this is intended as a generalization about all fourteenth century logicians it is not correct. Buridan, in his *Consequentiae* (Book I, ch. 3) defines an inference (*consequentia*) in such a way that what is usually called an invalid inference does not count as an inference at all, though he acknowledges that this is an arbitrary stipulation on his part.

14. In the long passage which runs from here to p. 755 Paul's main aim is to classify valid inferences into various types. He draws two main distinctions. The first, introduced here, is between inferences which are formally valid and those which are (merely) materially valid. The second, introduced on p. 747, is between inferences which are valid because of their form (*de forma*) and those that are valid (merely) because of their matter (*de materia*). It is important not to confuse these two distinctions. All merely materially valid inferences are valid because of their matter, and none are valid because of their form; but formally valid inferences are divided into those that are valid because of their form and those that are valid because of their matter.

   The first of these distinctions is complicated by the fact that Paul recognises three grades of formal validity (pp. 740–42); thus this distinction is in effect a fourfold, not merely a twofold one. In each case the validity of 'p, therefore q' is defined as the impossibility of 'p and not-q', and the distinctions are spelled out in terms of different kinds of impossibility.

15. The phrase Paul uses here, *contingentibus simpliciter assignatis* (literally, 'simply contingent propositions having been assigned'), is somewhat obscure, but I base the interpretation expressed in the translation on his treatment of the example he gives a few lines later, viz. 'Something exists and nothing exists', and of 'No God exists' on p. 742. The notion of assuming an impossible or necessary proposition to be contingent has its difficulties; but perhaps all that he means is that in the cases he has in mind we can show 'p and not-q' to be impossible without making any appeal to the modal status either of p or of q taken separately.

16. 'Per se' is important here. According to Paul, if the conjunction is merely accidentally impossible, the inference in question is not valid at all, not even materially valid.

17. 'Formally' is crucial here. Paul classifies per se impossible propositions into those which formally entail a contradiction and those which do not; and 'formally' is critical to this distinction because he holds that *every* per se impossible proposition entails any and every proposition (and therefore entails, *inter alia*, a contradiction), though in some cases it does so only materially. The upshot of clause (b) here, taken together with what is said later about materially valid inferences (pp. 742 ff), is that if a proposition p formally entails a contradiction, then 'p, therefore q' is formally valid, no matter what proposition q may be; but that if p is per se impossible but does not formally entail a contradiction, and if q has no 'connection of content' with p, then 'p, therefore q' is valid, but only materially.

18. Paul's proof that 'You are other than yourself' formally entails a contradiction is given on pp. 743–44.

19. In the chapter *On the Truth and Falsity of Propositions* (in *L.M.* II, 6).

20. 'Precisely': i.e., the man in question has no other belief than the one mentioned.
21. This is not as clear to me as Paul seems to think it ought to be. The premiss is the conjunctive proposition

(i) This man believes that some man is mistaken and (ii) no man is mistaken,

and the conclusion is

(iii) Some man is mistaken and (iv) no man is mistaken.

Presumably (iv) is obtained from (ii) on the ground that they are equiform. The most straightforward way of obtaining (iii) would seem to be to argue that, given (ii), the belief that some man is mistaken is false; therefore, given (i), this man has a false belief, and hence some man—namely he—is mistaken. But this would seem to be better described as a derivation of (iii) from (i) and (ii) jointly than in the way Paul describes it.

This example, in the form 'You believe precisely that some man is mistaken, therefore some man is mistaken', is discussed in detail in the *Consequentiae* of Richard Feribrigge, with whose work Paul was certainly familiar (see *L.M.* II, 6). Feribrigge, however, unlike Paul, thinks that the inference is invalid. His argument is this: Posit a case in which no one other than yourself is mistaken and you believe precisely that some man is mistaken. Then manifestly the premiss is true. But the conclusion is false, for this reason: Since by hypothesis no one else is mistaken, the only person who might be mistaken is yourself. Suppose then that you are mistaken. Then, since you are a man, some man is mistaken. But that is precisely what you believe, so your belief is correct, and therefore you are not mistaken after all. Thus no one at all is mistaken, and so the conclusion of the inference is false.

22. The sort of thing Paul has in mind here is that God might bring it about that you were in two places at once, sitting in one of them and running in the other. (See the reference to 'divisive multiplication' in the next paragraph, and the elaboration of this point on pp. 744–45). This, he holds, would violate the settled order of nature, but not be beyond the divine power. Note that Paul regards the *natural* impossibility of '*p* and not-*q*' (assuming the contingency of *p* and *q* themselves) as sufficient for the formal validity of '*p*, therefore *q*' from a *logical* point of view. Cf. his use of the phrase 'from the point of view of logic or natural science' (*logice vel physice*) on p. 736.

23. I.e. a formulation in terms of 'is naturally suited to . . .'

24. 'In actuality' (*realiter*): this term is intended to mark the difference between the kind of impossibility discussed here and the kind to be mentioned in the next paragraph, where we have an impossibility at the level of thought.

25. The ability to laugh (*risibilitas*) is a standard medieval example of a *proprium* of human beings, i.e. a characteristic which necessarily belongs to every human being (and to nothing else). According to this account, a being incapable of laughing, no matter what else it might be like, would not be a human being. It is therefore no limitation on God's power that he cannot create a human being without the ability to laugh.

26. The meaning of the logically prior term 'animal' is part of the very meaning of the logically posterior term 'human being'. By contrast, the ability to laugh, though it necessarily belongs to every human being, is not part of what 'human being' means.

27. Paul here is distinguishing between a wider and a narrower way in which '*risibilis*' ('able to laugh') can be understood. If this term is taken in the wider sense (*ampliative*), '*A* is *risibilis*' means merely that *A* *would be* able to laugh (if he existed), and makes no claim about whether *A* in fact exists or not; if it is taken in the narrower sense (*concretive*), the sentence means that *A* actually does possess the ability to laugh. Thus Antichrist (to use the favourite example) is *risibilis* in the former sense, but not in the latter. But it is only in the latter sense that *risibilitas* is a *proprium* of human beings, for it is only in the latter sense that from '*A* is *risibilis*' we can infer '*A* is (i.e. is now) a human being'. (Cf. note 25 above.) Paul makes this distinction more explicitly, though using a somewhat different terminology, later in *L.M.*, at f. 148ᵛᵃ, 11.42–9 and 60–6.

28. It will turn out that materially valid inferences for Paul are precisely those in which either the premiss or the negation of the conclusion is per se impossible but does not formally entail a contradiction, and which have no other claim to validity than this. Note that he defines 'formally valid' and 'materially valid' in such a way that no inference can be both formally and materially valid. Some other medieval logicians made formally valid inferences a sub-class of materially valid ones, and thus spoke of materially valid ones in Paul's sense as *merely* materially valid (as Paul too sometimes does—unnecessarily, in view of his own definitions, but perhaps to make matters clearer for his readers).

29. The term 'human being' is a species-term which falls under the genus-term 'animal'. In Paul's view this is enough to make 'An x is a human being, therefore an x is an animal' formally valid, no matter what (common) term we put for 'x'.

30. I.e. *materially* follows.

31. Paul's method of proof is to deduce an arbitrary proposition from each of three sample impossible propositions. In each case the argument falls into two stages: (a) he deduces an explicit self-contradiction from the initial proposition; and then (b) he deduces an arbitrary proposition from that self-contradiction. Stage (b) is the same in all three examples: it consists in moving from 'p and not-p' to '(p or q) and not-p' by the principle that any proposition entails a disjunction in which it is one disjunct, and then from this to q by disjunctive syllogism. Essentially the same proof is given by many other medieval logicians, e.g. by Buridan (*Consequentiae*, Bk. I, ch. 8 conclusion 7) and by Pseudo-Scotus (see Kneale [1961], pp. 281–2); and its restatement by C. I. Lewis in Lewis and Langford [1932], pp. 250–1, has given rise to much debate in more recent times.

    Stage (b) is in fact all that Paul needs in order to prove his thesis (3) as he formulates it here, but his discussion of his three separate examples is of interest as illustrating the variety of the propositions which he believes entail self-contradictions. It is important that he should be able to claim that each step in each deduction is *formally* valid.

32. The exponents of a proposition of the form 'A is other than B' are 'A exists', 'B exists' and 'A is not B'.

33. I.e. as '(Either you are yourself or a stick is standing in the corner) and (you are not yourself)'. Grammatically, it could be construed either in this way or as 'Either (you are yourself) or (a stick is standing in the corner and you are not yourself)'.

34. The rationale of this seems to be that since 'you' (or 'yourself') is a purely singular term which on any given occasion simply denotes the individual addressed, it is inferior to the term designating the species to which that individual belongs. In the present example it is being assumed that the argument is addressed to a human being.

35. I.e. it proceeds, by what was later called obversion, from 'Some A is a non-B' to 'Some A is not a B'. (An 'infinite' term is simply a negative term, a 'finite' term a non-negative one). The converse implication was usually held by medieval logicians not to be unrestrictedly valid, because of the doctrine that affirmative propositions have existential import but negative ones do not.

36. This proposition is not explicitly of the form 'p and not-p', but counts as a self-contradiction because 'An A is not a B' (or 'Some A is not a B') is the standard contradictory of 'Every A is a B'.

37. 'A human being is a donkey' was not in fact an example which Paul used in his argument, though he does not press this point in reply to the objection.

38. The argument is that, according to the Christian doctrine of the Incarnation, God 'assumed human nature' in the person of Jesus of Nazareth, and in this sense 'God is a human being' is true. The phase 'in a dependent way' means that being a human being is not, however, essential to the divine nature as it is to, say, Socrates. For Socrates not to be a human being would be for him not to be Socrates at all; but God would have had the same essential nature even if the Incarnation had never taken place— in which case, of course, 'God is a human being' would have been false. The relation of human nature to God, it is being claimed, is more analogous to that of an accident, such as whiteness, to an ordinary substance, such as Socrates; for Socrates could still be Socrates even if he were not white.

    The rest of the argument is to the effect that if it is within God's power to become a human being, it must also be within his power to become a donkey; and if he were to do so, there would be a valid syllogism with true premises yielding the conclusion that a human being is a donkey. So this proposition could be true, and therefore cannot formally entail a contradiction.

39. Paul is accusing the objector of ignoring the distinction drawn on pp. 740–42 between merely formally valid and more than merely formally valid inferences.

40. Nevertheless Paul cannot resist the temptation to go on to discuss them.

41. Other than a donkey, presumably.

42. Note that God is not thought of as a substance. The locus classicus for the view that God is not a substance is Aquinas, *Summa Theologiae*, I, Q. 3, Art.

43. Presumably 'what was said earlier' refers to the definition of formal incompatibility given on p. 740. But then there is a puzzle; for Paul said there that two propositions are formally incompatible whenever either of them on its own formally entails a contradiction, and Thesis 1 follows immediately from this without the need of any further proof.

    Be that as it may, his first proof of the thesis, which is somewhat obscurely stated, seems to be this: Suppose that p formally contains a contradiction, and let q be any arbitrary proposition. By 3 above, p formally entails every proposition and in particular it formally entails not-q. Therefore p must be formally incompatible with the contradictory of not-q, i.e. q itself.

44. I.e. logically equivalent to it.

45. Since 'No God exists' is per se impossible but does not formally entail a contradiction, it entails, at least materially, any and every proposition, and therefore, *inter alia*, 'A first cause exists'.

46. This is the second of the two main distinctions referred to in note 14, and as was mentioned there, the two should not be confused: in particular, some *formally* valid inferences are valid because of their form (*de forma*), but others are valid only because of their matter (*de materia*). Presumably, though Paul does not explicitly say so, the present distinction is meant to apply within all three grades of formal validity

described on pp. 740–42.

A valid inference, Paul tells us, is valid because of its form if every inference of that same form is valid; otherwise it is valid because of its matter. This immediately raises the question, what is it for two inferences to have the same form? His answer, in outline, is that two conditions have to be satisfied: (a) the corresponding premisses and conclusions must have the same form, and (b) the conclusions must be derived from their premisses in the same way. Thus the first question to be considered is what it is for two *propositions* to have the same form; and this resolves itself into the question, what features of a proposition are relevant to its form, and what features are relevant to its matter? He deals with this question immediately, on pp. 747–49, and then turns to consider condition (b).

47. I.e. the term 'substance', which, unlike 'animal', is held not to fall under any more general term.

48. This, however, does not seem to be a helpful analogy to illustrate the irrelevance of degrees of generality.

49. I.e., is universal or particular or singular.

50. I.e., is affirmative or negative.

51. Paul regards 'human being' and 'able to laugh' as interchangeable or logically equivalent terms; see note 25. He regards 'donkey' and 'able to bray' similarly. It is noteworthy that he does not regard the repetition of a term in a proposition, as in 'A human being is a human being' as a formal feature of that proposition.

52. I.e., 'Socrates is running' entails 'Socrates is moving' but does not entail 'Socrates is arguing'.

53. I.e. that each conjunct in one should have the same form as one of the conjuncts in the other.

54. I.e., in each case the conclusion is obtained from the premiss by replacing a more general (superior) term by a less general (inferior) one which falls under it.

55. This paragraph and the next three—I shall call them, for convenience, (a), (b), (c) and (d) respectively— contain a number of perplexities. Certain things are clear: It is clear that Paul wishes to divide modes of arguing (rules or patterns of inference) into two kinds, which he calls *simple* and *mixed* respectively, and that he wants to maintain that two inferences have the same form whenever, in addition to having premisses and conclusions of the same form, they exhibit the same *simple* mode of arguing. It is also clear that his criterion of an inference's being valid because of its form is that every inference in which the premiss(es) and the conclusion have the same form as those in the original and which exhibit the same *simple* mode of arguing as it does, it also valid. It is not sufficient that every inference which exhibits the same mixed mode of arguing should be valid. For example, the inference

    (1) Socrates is running, therefore Socrates is running and Socrates is moving

is valid, it exhibits the mode of arguing 'From *p* to infer *p*-and-*q* where *p* entails *q*', and every inference which exhibits this mode of arguing is valid. But, Paul tells us, this mode of arguing is a mixed one: the *simple* mode exhibited by (1) is not this, but 'From *p* to infer *p*-and-*q*', and manifestly many inferences of this form are invalid; therefore (1), though valid, and even formally valid, is not valid because of its form.

It is clear, finally, that by a 'mode of arguing in a formal inference' he does not mean a *valid* mode of arguing, in the sense of a rule of inference all of whose instances are valid (in spite of the fact that '*consequentia formalis*' sometimes means 'formally valid inference'). Several of the examples he gives both of simple modes in paragraph (b) and of mixed modes in paragraph (c) are patently invalid, and so is the mode he illustrates in paragraph (d). Two inferences can have the same form, but one be valid and the other not; and two inferences can be valid precisely because they both commit the same formal fallacy.

What is not clear, however, is how the distinction between simple and mixed modes is to be drawn. The explanation given in paragraph (a) and repeated in paragraph (c), that certain modes are called *mixed* 'because they express the matter of propositions' suggests that a mode is *simple* if its formulation makes reference only to the forms of premisses and conclusions and not at all to their matter (as form and matter were distinguished on pp. 747–49), and mixed if its formulation refers to their matter as well. This would fit in admirably with some of Paul's examples: thus, arguing 'from one conjunct, when this entails the other one, to the whole conjunction' is, he says here, a mixed mode; and in Thesis 3 on p. 749 he assured us that the entailment of one conjunct by the other relates only to the matter, not the form, of the conjunction. However, we are then left with a problem about his first example of a simple mode, viz. 'arguing from an inferior term to one of its superiors, or vice versa'; for in Thesis 1 on p. 748 we were told that the inferiority or superiority of terms in a proposition affects only the matter of that proposition, not its form. He may, of course, want to maintain that when one term is superior to another, their occurrence in the same (categorical) *proposition* does not affect the form of that proposition, but their occurrence in the same *inference* does affect the form of that inference; but if so, he does not tell us this explicitly, and one would like to know what the rationale of such a view might be.

A further problem is how to reconcile this same example of a simple mode with the claim made in paragraph (c) that arguing 'from an inferior term to one which is per se or accidentally one of its superiors, or vice versa' is a *mixed* mode. It is difficult to suppose that the presence of this example in

(b) is a mere slip or oversight, since arguing from a superior to an inferior term was also explicitly claimed as a simple mode, and illustrated, on p. 749. Nevertheless the text is perhaps corrupt *somewhere* in this passage, and the possibility that this is so is heightened by the fact that E omits all the examples in paragraph (b) and reads as if all those in (c) were simple modes, which is certainly incorrect.

56. 'In the case of substantial terms' means that both the subject and the predicate are in the category of substance, like 'human being' and 'animal' in the example given below. Predication is said to be *direct* when the subject and the predicate either are inferior and superior terms respectively, or else are equivalent terms; *indirect* in all other cases.

57. Paul's argument is that although the first inference is indeed an instance of arguing 'from an indefinite proposition to the corresponding universal in a case of substantial terms in direct predication' and the second is not, yet this mode of arguing is a mixed one; hence the fact that the inferences do not both instantiate it does not show that they have different forms.

58. The text appears to be corrupt here, since neither in M nor in E do we even have a grammatical sentence. I do not know how to suggest an amendment, and have translated by an approximately equivalent ungrammatical piece of English. 'To be reduced' translates a passive infinitive (*reduci*), not a gerundive.

59. In the first syllogism the second premiss and the conclusion are singular propositions, while in the second they are indefinite ones (equivalent to particulars), and Paul explained on pp. 747f that this difference affects the form of a proposition.

60. This point, together with the preceding one, makes it clear that according to Paul there are more syllogistic forms of inference than there are syllogistic moods.

61. The connection between the two notions, namely, *exposition* and *grounds of truth* to which Paul is alluding here, is this: If q and r are the exponents of p, p is equivalent to q-and-r. Hence not-p is equivalent to either-not-q-or-not-r, and thus not-q and not-r are grounds of truth of not-p.

62. The exponents of 'Every A is a B' are 'An A (*or* some A) is a B' and 'Nothing is an A unless it is a B'; hence the first inference is one which deduces a proposition from only one of its exponents. The exponents of 'Only an A is a B' are 'Some A is a B' and 'Nothing other than an A is a B'; hence, as explained in the preceding note, 'No A is a B' and 'Something other than an A is a B' are grounds of truth of 'Not only an A is a B'. Thus the second inference argues from a proposition to only one of its grounds of truth. Inferences of these kinds are in general invalid, but Paul is pointing out that they can be valid in special cases.

63. This parenthetical remark contains the important idea, which, however, Paul does not develop, that a given inference may be an instance of two or more simple modes of arguing, and may satisfy the requirements for being valid because of its form with respect to some of these modes but not others. If he had developed this idea he would have had to modify his account of validity because of form, e.g. by relativizing it to various simple modes of arguing, or by defining an inference valid because of its form as one which exemplifies at least one simple mode of arguing such that all inferences with formally similar premisses and conclusions which exemplify that mode are valid.

64. 'Proceeding from the first step to the last' means arguing by the transitivity of entailment. Paul cannot mean, however, that every inference obtained by transitivity of entailment is valid because of its form, irrespective of the validity, or kind of validity, of the intermediate steps. Perhaps what he says here is meant as a condensed way of saying that the first of the two cited inferences can be established, as on pp. 743–44, by applying transitivity of entailment to a chain of inferences each of which is valid because of its form, but that the second one cannot.

65. This seems (and I think in fact is) a lame reason. It is easy to see, by reflection on the argument given on p. 743f, why an inference from an explicit self-contradiction to an arbitrary proposition should be held to be valid because of its form. But the first stage in the overall deduction consists in deriving an explicit self-contradiction from the original proposition by a formally valid inference; and it is not clear that *that* inference will always be valid because of its form.

66. I.e., therefore Thesis 1 (p. 750) is incorrect.

67. This argument is obscurely stated, but Paul's second reply to it below (4-0b1R) suggests that he understands it in the following way: The terms 'A', 'B' and 'C' are non-significant; therefore the inference does not have a form; therefore it cannot be valid because of its form; therefore, since it is valid, it must be valid because of its matter.

68. An anonymous 12th century work dealing with some of the Aristotelian categories, frequently commented on by medieval logicians.

69. I.e., there is strictly speaking no inference here at all, and therefore no counter-example to Thesis 1.

70. But, according to what Paul said in the previous paragraph, all I need to be told is that the same thing is being referred to by each occurrence of 'this', not what that thing is.

71. I.e. Aristotelian 'prime matter' (at least on one common interpretation of Aristotle).

72. I.e. an individual substance composed of matter and form.

73. The quantity of a proposition is its being universal or particular or singular. Paul's point is that in this context the terms 'quality' and 'quantity' are being used simply as logicians' terms of art, not in a metaphysical sense.

PART IX

PHYSICS

CHAPTER 49

Robert Grosseteste

Robert Grosseteste was born at Stradbroke in Suffolk, England, circa 1168 of a peasant background. Precise details of his life are sketchy, and, unfortunately, much of his work remains unpublished. It is believed that he studied law, medicine, and theology at Oxford and perhaps at Paris as well. It was at one or the other that he had become *magister in artibus* by 1190. Sometime during the succeeding eight years he rendered service to William de Vere, bishop of Hereford, by becoming a member of his household. During this time he may have taught in the Hereford schools.

Subsequent to the bishop's death in 1198, Grosseteste became a member of the arts faculty at Oxford. This was during the reign of King John, a period of some turmoil. One side effect of the king's difficulties was the *suspendium clericorum* whereby the schools were closed between 1209 and 1214. It is likely that Grosseteste studied theology at Paris during those years.

Upon the reopening of the schools, he returned to Oxford and became chancellor of that university sometime around 1221, the first to hold that post. In 1224 the Franciscans came to Oxford, whereupon Grosseteste became their teacher. Although he remained a member of the secular clergy, he acted as master of the Franciscan House of Studies from 1229 to 1235. It is an understatement to say that he had great influence upon Franciscan thought and its subsequent development.

He left this post in 1235 when he became bishop of Lincoln, then the largest single diocese in England. During the subsequent eighteen years until his death, Grosseteste was a vigorous defender of papal authority, especially as it related to church and state reform, a key issue associated with the signing of the Magna Charta by King John at which Grosseteste had been present in 1215. During his tenure as bishop of Lincoln, his disputes with Henry III, King John's successor, were not uncommon. Outspoken and energetic, Grosseteste stands out as one of the most constructive and influential men of the English Middle Ages. He died in 1253.

Robert Grosseteste on Light

Robert Grosseteste was one of the first medieval scientists. He wrote on the generation (i.e., efficient causation) of the stars, of sound, the tides, of rainbows and of comets to mention only a few. Grosseteste is to be credited with two fundamental milestones: (1) He was among the first of the Scholastics to adopt Aristotle's conception of scientific method—that of reasoning from particulars to universal principles from which a greater understanding of particulars is thence made possible. Grosseteste called this the process of resolution and composition. (2) He considered mathematics crucial to an understanding of the natural sciences. Central to the natural sciences is the study of the causes of natural effects. It is mathematics that provides for complete and certain demonstration of those causes. This is made clear in his essay *On Light*. Light is the source of all generation and motion. Fundamental to light are configurations of lines and points. Consequently, the workings of the universe can ultimately be explained via mathematics.

According to Grosseteste, God created light *(lux)* as both the first corporeal form and unextended matter. This light instantaneously multiplied itself in every direction. The initial point of light and unextended matter were joined of necessity due to the impossibility of matter and form existing separately. The expansion of light with matter formed a spherical universe extremely rare at the periphery (the firmament) yet dense and opaque near the center. Grosseteste reasons that this universe must be finite since unextended, namely, simple matter, regardless of its multiplicity, must remain finite. The universe thus created, light reflected back from the periphery to the center, where it gathered together the mass within and therefore below the firmament, creating a sphere smaller than the first. This process continued until thirteen spheres were formed, four of which being the elements of earth, air, fire, and water. At the periphery, matter exists in a state of total actualization. It is thus stable, incapable of change. Toward the center, however, matter is less actualized, thus providing matter the potential of acquiring a variety of forms. Light, the first form, is the source of generation of all subsequent forms. It is the source of both the essential and accidental characteristics which makes prime matter identifiable as some "thing" and in that sense is the source of existence. What something is is a function of its qualities. This is both a physical and a metaphysical issue.

As the source of motion, light also brings to matter the potentiality to actualize various forms, hence it is a second source of existence. Motion qua causation has physical and metaphysical dimensions. Light is the point of intersection between physics and metaphysics. Rarely does a philosopher attempt to, much less succeed in, isolating such a point. To that end, credit is due to Robert Grosseteste.

ON LIGHT

The first corporeal form which some call corporeity[1] is in my opinion light. For light of its very nature diffuses itself in every direction in such a way that a point of light will produce instantaneously a sphere of light of any size whatsoever, unless some opaque object stands in the way. Now the extension of matter in three dimensions is a necessary concomitant of corporeity, and this despite the fact that both corporeity and matter are in themselves simple substances lacking all dimension. But a form that is in itself simple and without dimension could not introduce dimension in every direction into matter, which is likewise simple and without dimension, except by multiplying itself and diffusing itself instantaneously in every direction and thus extending matter in its own diffusion. For the form cannot desert matter, because it is

From Robert Grosseteste, *On Light*, translated by Clare C. Riedl (Milwaukee, Wis.: Marquette University Press, 1942, 1978), pp. 10–17. Reprinted by permission of Marquette University Press.

inseparable from it, and matter itself cannot be deprived of form.—But I have proposed that it is light which possesses of its very nature the function of multiplying itself and diffusing itself instantaneously in all directions. Whatever performs this operation is either light or some other agent that acts in virtue of its participation in light to which this operation belongs essentially. Corporeity, therefore, is either light itself or the agent which performs the aforementioned operation and introduces dimensions into matter in virtue of its participation in light, and acts through the power of this same light. But the first form cannot introduce dimensions into matter through the power of a subsequent form. Therefore light is not a form subsequent to corporeity, but it is corporeity itself.

Furthermore, the first corporeal form is, in the opinion of the philosophers, more exalted and of a nobler and more excellent essence than all the forms that come after it. It bears, also, a closer resemblance to the forms that exist apart from matter. But light is more exalted and of a nobler and more excellent essence than all corporeal things. It has, moreover, greater similarity than all bodies to the forms that exist apart from matter, namely, the intelligences. Light therefore is the first corporeal form.

Thus light, which is the first form created in first matter, multiplied itself by its very nature an infinite number of times on all sides and spread itself out uniformly in every direction. In this way it proceeded in the beginning of time to extend matter which it could not leave behind, by drawing it out along with itself into a mass the size of the material universe. This extension of matter could not be brought about through a finite multiplication of light, because the multiplication of a simple being a finite number of times does not produce a quantity, as Aristotle shows in the *De Caelo et Mundo*.[2] However, the multiplication of a simple being an infinite number of times must produce a finite quantity, because a product which is the result of an infinite multiplication exceeds infinitely that through the multiplication of which it

is produced. Now one simple being cannot exceed another simple being infinitely, but only a finite quantity infinitely exceeds a simple being. For an infinite quantity exceeds a simple being by infinity times infinity. Therefore, when light, which is in itself simple, is multiplied an infinite number of times, it must extend matter, which is likewise simple, into finite dimensions.

It is possible, however, that an infinite sum of number is related to an infinite sum in every proportion, numerical and non-numerical. And some infinites are larger than other infinites, and some are smaller. Thus the sum of all numbers both even and odd is infinite. It is at the same time greater than the sum of all the even numbers although this is likewise infinite, for it exceeds it by the sum of all the odd numbers. The sum, too, of all numbers starting with one and continuing by doubling each successive number is infinite, and similarly the sum of all the halves corresponding to the doubles is infinite. The sum of these halves must be half of the sum of their doubles. In the same way the sum of all numbers starting with one and multiplying by three successively is three times the sum of all the thirds corresponding to these triples. It is likewise clear in regard to all kinds of numerical proportion that there can be a proportion of finite to infinite according to each of them.

But if we posit an infinite sum of all doubles starting with one, and an infinite sum of all the halves corresponding to these doubles, and if one, or some other finite number, be subtracted from the sum of the halves, then, as soon as this subtraction is made, there will no longer be a two to one proportion between the first sum and what is left of the second sum. Indeed there will not be any numerical proportion, because if a second numerical proportion is to be left from the first as the result of subtraction from the lesser member of the proportion, then what is subtracted must be an aliquot[3] part or aliquot parts of an aliquot part of that from which it is subtracted. But a finite number cannot be an aliquot part or aliquot parts of an aliquot part of an infinite number. Therefore when we subtract a number from an infinite sum of halves there will not remain a numerical proportion between the infinite sum of doubles and what is left from the infinite sum of halves.

Since this is so, it is clear that light through the infinite multiplication of itself extends matter into finite dimensions that are smaller and larger according to certain proportions that they have to one another, namely, numerical and non-numerical. For if light through the infinite multiplication of itself extends matter into a dimension of two cubits, by the doubling of this same infinite multiplication it extends it into a dimension of four cubits, and by the dividing in half of this infinite multiplication, it extends it into a dimension of one cubit. Thus it proceeds according to numerical and non-numerical proportions.

It is my opinion that this was the meaning of the theory of those philosophers who held that everything is composed of atoms, and said that bodies are composed of surfaces, and surfaces of lines, and lines of points.[4] This opinion does not contradict the theory that a magnitude is composed only of magnitudes, because for every meaning of the word whole, there is a corresponding meaning of the word part. Thus we say that a half is part of a whole, because two halves make a whole. We say, too, that a side is part of a diameter,[5] but in a different sense, because no matter how many times a side is taken it does not make a diameter, but is always less than the diameter. Again we say that an angle of contingence[6] is part of a right angle because there is an infinite number of angles of contingence in a right angle, and yet when an angle of contingence is subtracted from a right angle a finite number of times the latter becomes smaller. It is in a different sense, however, that a point is said to be part of a line in which it is contained an infinite number of times, for when a point is taken away from a line a finite number of times this does not shorten the line.

To return therefore to my theme, I say that light through the infinite multiplication of itself equally in all directions extends matter on all sides equally into the form of a sphere and, as a necessary consequence of this extension, the outermost parts of matter are more extended and more rarefied than those within, which are close to the center. And since the outermost parts will be rarefied to the highest degree, the inner parts will have the possibility of further rarefaction.

In this way light, by extending first matter into the form of a sphere, and by rarefying its outermost parts to the highest degree, actualized completely in the outermost sphere the potentiality of matter, and left this matter without any potency to further impression. And thus the first body in the outermost part of the sphere, the body which is called the firmament, is perfect, because it has nothing in its composition but first matter and first form. It is therefore the simplest of all bodies with respect to the parts that constitute its essence and with respect to its quantity which is the greatest possible in extent. It differs from the genus body only in this respect, that in it the matter is completely actualized through the first form alone. But the genus body, which is in this and in other bodies and has in its essence first matter and first form, abstracts from the complete actualization of matter through the first form and from the diminution[7] of matter through the first form.

When the first body, which is the firmament, has in this way been completely actualized, it diffuses its light (lumen) from every part of itself to the center of the universe. For since light (lux) is the perfection of the first body and naturally multiplies itself from the first body, it is necessarily diffused to the center of the universe. And since this light (lux) is a form entirely inseparable from matter in its diffusion from the first body, it extends along with itself the spirituality of the matter of the first body. Thus there proceeds from the first body light (lumen), which is a spiritual body, or if you prefer, a bodily spirit. This light (lumen) in its passing does not divide the body through which it passes, and thus it passes instantaneously from the body of the first heaven to the center of the universe. Furthermore, its passing is not to be understood in the sense of something numerically one passing instantaneously from that heaven to the center of the universe, for this is perhaps impossible, but its passing takes place through the multiplication of itself and the infinite generation of light (lumen). This light (lumen), expanded and brought together from the first body toward the center of the universe, gathered together the mass existing below the first body; and since the first body could no longer be lessened on account of its being completely actualized and unchangeable, and since, too, there could not be a space that was empty, it was necessary that in the very gathering together of this mass the outermost parts should be drawn out and expanded. Thus the inner parts of the aforesaid mass came to be more dense and the outer parts more rarefied; and so great was the power of this light (lumen) gathering together—and in the very act of gathering, separating—that the outermost parts of the mass contained below the first body were drawn out and rarefied to the highest degree. Thus in the outermost parts of the mass in question, the second sphere came into being, completely actualized and susceptible of no further impression. The completeness of actualization and the perfection of the second sphere consist in this that light (lumen) is begotten from the first sphere and that light (lux) which is simple in the first sphere is doubled in the second.

Just as the light (lumen) begotten from the first body completed the actualization of the second sphere and left a denser mass below the second sphere, so the light (lumen) begotten from the second sphere completed the actualization of the third sphere, and through its gathering left below this third sphere a mass of even greater density. This process of simultaneously gathering together and separating continued in this way until the nine heavenly spheres were completely actualized and there was gathered together below the ninth and lowest sphere the dense mass which constitutes the matter of the four elements. But the lowest sphere, the sphere of the moon,

which also gives forth light (lumen) from itself, by its light (lumen) gathered together the mass contained below itself and, by gathering it together, thinned out and expanded its outermost parts. The power of this light (lumen), however, was not so great that by drawing together it could expand the outermost parts of this mass to the highest degree. On this account every part of the mass was left imperfect and capable of being gathered together and expanded. The highest part of this mass was expanded, although not to the greatest possible extent. Nevertheless by its expansion it became fire, although remaining still the matter of the elements. This element giving forth light from itself and drawing together the mass contained below it expanded its outermost parts, but not to as great an extent as the fire was expanded, and in this way it produced air. Air, also, in bringing forth from itself, a spiritual body or a bodily spirit, and drawing together what is contained within itself, and by drawing together, expanding its outer parts, produced water and earth. But because water retained more of the power of drawing together than of the power of expanding, water as well as earth was left with the attribute of weight.

In this way, therefore, the thirteen spheres of this sensible world were brought into being. Nine of them, the heavenly spheres, are not subject to change, increase, generation or corruption because they are completely actualized. The other four spheres have the opposite mode of being, that is, they are subject to change, increase, generation and corruption, because they are not completely actualized. It is clear that every higher body, in virtue of the light (lumen) which proceeds from it, is the form (species) and perfection of the body that comes after it. And just as unity is potentially every number that comes after it, so the first body, through the multiplication of its light, is every body that comes after it.

Earth is all the higher bodies because all the higher lights come together in it. For this reason earth is called Pan by the poets, that is "the whole," and it is also given the name Cybele, which is almost like *cubile*, from cube *(cubus)* that is, a solid.[8] The reason for this is that earth, that is to say, Cybele, the mother of all the gods, is the most compact of all bodies, because, although the higher lights are gathered together in it, nevertheless they do not have their source in the earth through its own operations, but the light *(lumen)* of any sphere whatever can be educed from it into act and operation. Thus every one of the gods will be begotten from it as from a kind of mother. The intermediate bodies have a twofold relationship. Towards lower bodies they have the same relation as the first heaven has to all other things, and they are related to the higher bodies as earth is related to all other things. And thus in a certain sense each thing contains all other things.[9]

The form *(species)* and perfection of all bodies is light, but in the higher bodies it is more spiritual and simple, whereas in the lower bodies it is more corporeal and multiplied. Furthermore, all bodies are not of the same form *(species)* even though they all proceed from light, whether simple or multiplied, just as all numbers are not the same in form *(species)* despite the fact that they are all derived from unity by a greater or lesser multiplication.

This discussion may perhaps clarify the meaning of those who say that "all things are one by the perfection of one light" and also the meaning of those who say that "things which are many are many through the multiplication of light itself in different degrees."[10]

But since lower bodies participate in the form of the higher bodies, the lower body because it participates in the same form as the higher body, receives its motion from the same incorporeal moving power by which the higher body is moved. For this reason the incorporeal power of intelligence or soul, which moves the first and highest sphere with a diurnal motion, moves all the lower heavenly spheres with this same diurnal motion. But in proportion as these spheres are lower they receive

this motion in a more weakened state, because in proportion as a sphere is lower the purity and strength of the first corporeal light is lessened in it.

But although the elements participate in the form of the first heaven, nevertheless they are not moved by the mover of the first heaven with a diurnal motion. Although they participate in that first light, they are not subject to the first moving power since that light in them is impure, weak, and far removed from the purity which it has in the first body, and also because they possess the denseness of matter which is the principle of resistance and stubbornness. Nevertheless, there are some who think that the sphere of fire rotates with a diurnal motion, and they take the rotating motion of comets to be an indication of this. They say also that this motion extends even to the waters of the sea, in such a way that the tide of the seas proceeds from it. But all sound philosophers say that the earth is free from this motion.

In this same way, too, the spheres that come after the second sphere, which is usually called the eighth when we compute from the earth upward, all share in the motion of this second sphere because they participate in its form. Indeed this motion is proper to each of them in addition to the diurnal motion.

But because the heavenly spheres are completely actualized and are not receptive of rarefaction or condensation, light *(lux)* in them does not incline the parts of matter either away from the center so as to rarefy them, or toward the center to condense them. On this account the heavenly spheres are not receptive of up or down motion but only of circular motion by an intellectual moving power, which by directing its glance upon them in a corporeal way revolves the spheres themselves in a circular corporeal motion. But because the elements are incompletely actualized and subject to rarefaction and condensation, the light *(lumen)* which is in them inclines them away from the center so as to rarefy them, or toward the center so as to condense them. And on this account they are naturally capable of being moved in an upward or downward motion.

The highest body, which is the simplest of all bodies, contains four constituents, namely form, matter, composition and the composite. Now the form being the simplest holds the position of unity. But matter on account of its twofold potency, namely its susceptibility to impressions and its receptiveness of them, and also on account of its denseness which belongs fundamentally to matter but which is primarily and principally characteristic of a thing which is a duality, is rightly allotted the nature of a duality. But composition has a trinity in itself because there appears in it informed matter and materialized form and that which is distinctive of the composition, which is found in every composite as a third constituent distinct from matter and form. And that which is the composite proper, over and above these three constituents, is classed as a quaternary. There is, therefore, in the first body, in which all other bodies exist virtually, a quaternary and therefore the number of the remaining bodies is basically not more than ten. For the unity of the form, the duality of the matter, the trinity of the composition and the quaternity of the composite when they are added make a total of ten. On this account ten is the number of the bodies of the spheres of the world, because the sphere of the elements, although it is divided into four, is nevertheless one by its participation in earthly corruptible nature.

From these considerations it is clear that ten is the perfect number in the universe, because every perfect whole has something in it corresponding to form and unity, and something corresponding to matter and duality, something corresponding to composition and trinity, and something corresponding to the composite and quaternity. Nor is it possible to add a fifth to these four. For this reason every perfect whole is ten.

On this account it is manifest that only five proportions found in these four numbers, one, two, three, four, are suited to composition and to the harmony that gives stability to every composite. For this reason these five proportions are the only ones that produce harmony in musical melodies, in bodily movements, and in rhythmic measures.

This is the end of the treatise on light of the Bishop of Lincoln.

NOTES

1. According to Father Leo W. Keeler the reference here would seem to be to Philip the Chancellor, who was the first to use the 'form of corporeity' in the technical sense in which it appears here and throughout the *De Luce*. This, Philip, according to Father Keeler's thesis, was one of Grosseteste's teachers at Paris. Cf. "The Dependence of R. Grosseteste's *De Anima* on the *Summa* of Philip the Chancellor," *The New Scholasticism*, XI (1937), 218.
2. Throughout the *De Caelo et Mundo*, Aristotle is at pains to show that a quantity cannot be produced by combining things which are without quantity. Thus it would be impossible, if two parts of a thing have no weight, that the two together should have weight (III, 1, 299 a 25–30). Grosseteste, however, interprets Aristotle to mean only that a *finite* multiplication of the simple will *not* produce a quantity, thereby leaving the way open for Grosseteste's own notion that an *infinite* multiplication of the simple *will* produce a quantity. Cf. also *De Caelo et Mundo*, I, 5–7, 271b1–276a17.
3. The part of a number that divides the given number without a remainder. (Editor's note.)
4. Aristotle in the *De Caelo et Mundo*, III, 1, 299a2–300a19, attributes this theory to Plato in the *Timaeus* (54d–55b), although he may also have had in mind the Pythagoreans whom he mentions immediately after. In fact, Diogenes Laertius, *Lives of Eminent Philosophers*, VIII, 25, attributes the theory directly to Pythagoras. Grosseteste seems to be aware of Aristotle's criticism of the theory, for he tries in the next sentence to reconcile it with Aristotle's dictum that a magnitude is composed only of magnitudes. Cf. note 2 above.
5. The reference would seem to be to one of the two shorter sides of a right triangle inscribed in a semicircle, the diameter of which is the hypotenuse of the triangle. No matter how much either of these sides is extended it will never equal the diameter until it becomes identical with it, in which case there is no longer a triangle.

6. Grosseteste explains what an 'angle of contingence' is in his *De Lineis, Angulis, et Figuris*. It is the infinitesimal angle between the circumference of a sphere and its tangent.
7. The first form is said to 'diminish' matter when instead of rarefying it and extending it to the full it leaves it more dense, as with the inner parts of the sphere. Cf. Grosseteste, *De Motu Corporali et Luce*.
8. Cf. Aristotle, *De Caelo et Mundo*, III, 8, 307 a 8–9, where this doctrine of the earth as cube is attributed to Plato in the *Timaeus* (55d–e).
9. This principle Grosseteste could have found in Pseudo-Dionysius, *De Divinis Nominibus*, IV, 7. Dionysius took it over from Proclus, *Elements of Theology*, prop. 103. Cf. the illuminating history of this formula in Greek philosophy, in Dodds, *Proclus, the Elements of Theology* (Oxford: Clarendon Press, 1933), p. 254.
10. I have not been able to find the source of these quotations. They have, however, a decidedly Neoplatonic savor. Cf. in particular Pseudo-Dionysius, *De Divinis Nominibus*, IV, 4–6.

CHAPTER 50

Peter Peregrinus of Maricourt

Practically nothing is known of Peter Peregrinus of Maricourt save for his famous letter to his "*amicorum intimus*" (the dearest of friends) Sigerus de Foucaucourt dated August 8, 1269. The content of this letter is the first great milestone concerning the nature of magnetism. Peter derives his surname from the village of Maricourt in Picardy (the present-day administrative districts of Somme, Calais, Oise, and Aisne, all north of Paris). It is known that during the early part of his life he studied at the University of Paris, where he graduated with highest scholastic honors. The appellation Peregrinus, or Pilgrim, he acquired as a result of traveling to the Holy Land as a member of one of the Crusades. However, there are no known records of his date of birth or death.

Peter Peregrinus of Maricourt on the Magnet

The following letter by Peter of Maricourt was written on August 8, 1269, to a hometown friend. At the time Peter was in the engineering corps of the French army, then laying siege to Lucera in southern Italy, a city which had revolted from the authority of Charles of Aujou, its French master. Oddly enough, this letter lay unnoticed in the libraries of Europe for the better part of three centuries until 1562, when it was plagiarized by one Jean Taisnier, a Belgian who as a result gained considerable celebrity. Peter's observations concerning magnetism are noteworthy. His letter is divided into two parts. Part I consists of ten chapters detailing the properties of the lodestone (natural magnet). Part II contains three chapters detailing the construction of a compass and a perpetual motion machine. At the outset, Peter provides a guide to choosing a lodestone. "Its color should be ironlike, pale, slightly bluish or indigo, just as polished iron becomes when exposed to the corroding atmosphere." Next, he details two methods for determining the poles of a magnet and then proceeds to provide a way of determining the north and south poles of it. These are such that unlike poles attract each other whereas like poles repel one another. Furthermore, the fragments resulting from the splitting of a lodestone into pieces are themselves complete magnets. And he demonstrated the effects of one lodestone on another; that is, of two magnets of unequal strength, the pole of the stronger magnet can neutralize the pole of the same name of the weaker magnet, if not reverse its polarity altogether. It is clear that Peter was no mere theorizer. In his works we see the seeds of modern scientific method whereby the theory is formulated to fit the facts rather than facts the theory.

LETTER TO SIGERUS DE FOUCAUCOURT
ON THE MAGNET

Part I

Chapter I
Purpose of This Work

Dearest of friends:

At your earnest request, I will now make known to you, in an unpolished narrative, the undoubted though hidden virtue of the lodestone, concerning which philosophers up to the present time give us no information, because it is characteristic of good things to be hidden in darkness until they are brought to light by application to public utility. Out of affection for you, I will write in a simple style about things entirely unknown to the ordinary individual. Nevertheless I will speak only of the manifest properties of the lodestone, because this tract will form part of a work on the construction of philosophical instruments. The disclosing of the hidden properties of this stone is like the art of the sculptor by which he brings figures and seals into existence. Although I may call the matters about which you inquire evident and of inestimable value, they are considered by common folk to be illusions and mere creations of the imagination. But the things that are hidden from the multitude will become clear to astrologers and students of nature, and will constitute their delight, as they will also be of great help to those that are old and more learned.

Chapter II
Qualifications of the Experimenter

You must know, my dear friend, that whoever wishes to experiment, should be

Reprinted from *The Letter of Petrus Peregrinus on the Magnet, A.D. 1269*, translated by Brother Arnold, M.Sc. (New York: McGraw Publishing Co., 1904), pp. 3–34.

acquainted with the nature of things, and should not be ignorant of the motion of the celestial bodies. He must also be skilful in manipulation in order that, by means of this stone, he may produce these marvelous effects. Through his own industry he can, to some extent, indeed, correct the errors that a mathematician would inevitably make if he were lacking in dexterity. Besides, in such occult experimentation, great skill is required, for very frequently without it the desired result cannot be obtained, because there are many things in the domain of reason which demand this manual dexterity.

Chapter III
Characteristics of a Good Lodestone

The lodestone selected must be distinguished by four marks—its color, homogeneity, weight and strength. Its color should be ironlike, pale, slightly bluish or indigo, just as polished iron becomes when exposed to the corroding atmosphere. I have never yet seen a stone of such description which did not produce wonderful effects. Such stones are found most frequently in northern countries, as is attested by sailors who frequent places on the northern seas, notably in Normandy, Flanders and Picardy. This stone should also be of homogeneous material; one having reddish spots and small holes in it should not be chosen; yet a lodestone is hardly ever found entirely free from such blemishes. On account of uniformity in its composition and the compactness of its innermost parts, such a stone is heavy and therefore more valuable. Its strength is known by its vigorous attraction for a large mass of iron; further on I will explain the nature of this attraction. If you chance to see a stone with all these characteristics, secure it if you can.

Chapter IV
How to Distinguish the Poles of a Lodestone

I wish to inform you that this stone bears in itself the likeness of the heavens, as I will now clearly demonstrate. There are in the heavens two points more important than all others, because on them, as on pivots, the celestial sphere revolves: these points are called, one the arctic or north pole, the other the antarctic or south pole. Similarly you must fully realize that in this stone there are two points styled respectively the north pole and the south pole. If you are very careful, you can discover these two points in a general way. One method for doing so is the following: With an instrument with which crystals and other stones are rounded let a lodestone be made into a globe and then polished. A needle or an elongated piece of iron is then placed on top of the lodestone and a line is drawn in the direction of the needle or iron, thus dividing the stone into two equal parts. The needle is next placed on another part of the stone and a second median line drawn. If desired, this operation may be performed on many different parts, and undoubtedly all these lines will meet in two points just as all meridian or azimuth circles meet in the two opposite poles of the globe. One of these is the north pole, the other the south pole. Proof of this will be found in a subsequent chapter of this tract.

A second method for determining these important points is this: Note the place on the above-mentioned spherical lodestone where the point of the needle clings most frequently and most strongly; for this will be one of the poles as discovered by the previous method. In order to determine this point exactly, break off a small piece of the needle or iron so as to obtain a fragment about the length of two fingernails; then put it on the spot which was found to

be the pole by the former operation. If the fragment stands perpendicular to the stone, then that is, unquestionably, the pole sought; if not, then move the iron fragment about until it becomes so; mark this point carefully; on the opposite end another point may be found in a similar manner. If all this has been done rightly, and if the stone is homogeneous throughout and a choice specimen, these two points will be diametrically opposite, like the poles of a sphere.

Chapter V
How to Discover the Poles of a Lodestone and How to Tell Which Is North and Which South

The poles of a lodestone having been located in a general way, you will determine which is north and which south in the following manner: Take a wooden vessel rounded like a platter or dish, and in it place the stone in such a way that the two poles will be equidistant from the edge of the vessel; then place the dish in another and larger vessel full of water, so that the stone in the first-mentioned dish may be like a sailor in a boat. The second vessel should be of considerable size so that the first may resemble a ship floating in a river or on the sea. I insist upon the larger size of the second vessel in order that the natural tendency of the lodestone may not be impeded by contact of one vessel against the sides of the other. When the stone has been thus placed, it will turn the dish round until the north pole lies in the direction of the north pole of the heavens, and the south pole of the stone points to the south pole of the heavens. Even if the stone be moved a thousand times away from its position, it will return thereto a thousand times, as by natural instinct. Since the north and south parts of the heavens are known, these same points will then be easily recognized in the stone because each part of the lodestone will turn to the corresponding one of the heavens.

Chapter VI
How One Lodestone Attracts Another

When you have discovered the north and the south pole in your lodestone, mark them both carefully, so that by means of these indentations they may be distinguished whenever necessary. Should you wish to see how one lodestone attracts another, then, with two lodestones selected and prepared as mentioned in the preceding chapter, proceed as follows: Place one in its dish that it may float about as a sailor in a skiff, and let its poles which have already been determined be equidistant from the horizon, i.e., from the edge of the vessel. Taking the other stone in your hand, approach its north pole to the south pole of the lodestone floating in the vessel; the latter will follow the stone in your hand as if longing to cling to it. If, conversely, you bring the south end of the lodestone in your hand toward the north end of the floating lodestone, the same phenomenon will occur; namely, the floating lodestone will follow the one in your hand. Know then that this is the law: the north pole of one lodestone attracts the south pole of another, while the south pole attracts the north. Should you proceed otherwise and bring the north pole of one near the north pole of another, the one you hold in your hand will seem to put the floating one to flight. If the south pole of one is brought near the south pole of another, the same will happen. This is because the north pole of one seeks the south pole of the other, and therefore repels the north pole. A proof of this is that finally the north pole becomes united with the south pole. Likewise if the south pole is stretched out towards the south pole of the floating lodestone, you will observe the latter to be repelled, which does not occur, as said before, when the north pole is extended towards the south. Hence the silliness of certain persons is manifest, who claim that just as scammony attracts jaundice on account of a similarity between them, so one lodestone attracts another even more strongly than it does iron, a fact which they suppose to be false although really true as shown by experiment.

Chapter VII
How Iron Touched by a Lodestone Turns Towards the Poles of the World

It is well known to all who have made the experiment, that when an elongated piece of iron has touched a lodestone and is then fastened to a light block of wood or to a straw and made float on water, one end will turn to the star which has been called the Sailor's star because it is near the pole; the truth is, however, that it does not point to the star but to the pole itself. A proof of this will be furnished in a following chapter. The other end of the iron will point in an opposite direction. But as to which end of the iron will turn towards the north and which to the south, you will observe that that part of the iron which has touched the south pole of the lodestone will point to the north and conversely, that part which had been in contact with the north pole will turn to the south. Though this appears marvelous to the uninitiated, yet it is known with certainty to those who have tried the experiment.

Chapter VIII
How a Lodestone Attracts Iron

If you wish the stone, according to its natural desire, to attract iron, proceed as follows: Mark the north end of the iron and towards this end approach the south pole of the stone, when it will be found to follow the latter. Or, on the contrary, to the south part of the iron present the north pole of the stone and the latter will attract it without any difficulty. Should you, however, do the opposite, namely, if you bring the north end of the stone towards the north pole of the iron, you will notice the iron turn round until its south pole unites with the north end of the lodestone. The same thing will occur when the south end of the lodestone is brought near the south pole of the iron.

Should force be exerted at either pole, so that when the south pole of the iron is made touch the south end of the stone, then the virtue in the iron will be easily altered in such a manner that what was before the south end will now become the north and conversely. The cause is that the last impression acts, confounds, or counteracts and alters the force of the original movement.

Chapter IX
Why the North Pole of One Lodestone Attracts the South Pole of Another and Vice Versa

As already stated, the north pole of one lodestone attracts the south pole of another and conversely; in this case the virtue of the stronger becomes active, whilst that of the weaker becomes obedient or passive. I consider the following to be the cause of this phenomenon: the active agent requires a passive subject, not merely to be joined to it, but also to be united with it, so that the two make but one by nature. In the case of this wonderful lodestone this may be shown in the following manner: Take a lodestone which you may call $A D$, in which A is the north pole and D the south; cut this stone into two parts, so that you may have two distinct stones; place the stone having the pole A so that it may float on water and you will observe that A turns towards the north as before; the breaking did not destroy the properties of the parts of the stone, since it is homogeneous; hence it follows that the part of the stone at the point of fracture, which may be marked B, must be a south pole; this broken part of which we are now speaking may be called $A B$. The other, which contains D, should then be placed so as to float on water, when you will see D point towards the south because it is a south pole; but the other end at the point of fracture, lettered C, will be a north pole; this stone may now be named $C D$. If we consider the first stone as the active agent, then the second, or $C D$, will be the passive subject. You will also notice

that the ends of the two stones which before their separation were together, after breaking will become one a north pole and the other a south pole. If now these same broken portions are brought near each other, one will attract the other, so that they will again be joined at the points B and C, where the fracture occurred. Thus, by natural instinct, one single stone will be formed as before. This may be demonstrated fully by cementing the parts together, when the same effects will be produced as before the stone was broken. As you will perceive from this experiment, the active agent desires to become one with the passive subject because of the similarity that exists between them. Hence C, being a north pole, must be brought close to B, so that the agent and its subject may form one and the same straight line in the order $A B$, $C D$ and B and C being at the same point. In this union the identity of the extreme parts is retained and preserved just as they were at first; for A is the north pole in the entire line as it was in the divided one; so also D is the south pole as it was in the divided passive subject, but B and C have been made effectually into one. In the same way it happens that if A be joined to D so as to make the two lines one, in virtue of this union due to attraction in the order C $D A B$, then A and D will constitute but one point, the identity of the extreme parts will remain unchanged just as they were before being brought together, for C is a north pole and B a south, as during their separation. If you proceed in a different fashion, this identity or similarity of parts will not be preserved; for you will perceive that if C, a north pole, be joined to A, a north pole, contrary to the demonstrated truth, and from these two lines a single one, $B A C D$, is formed, as D was a south pole before the parts were united, it is then necessary that the other extremity should be a north pole, and as B is a south pole, the identity of the parts of the former similarity is destroyed. If you make B the south pole as it was before they united, then D must become north, though it was south in the original stone; in this way neither the identity nor similarity of parts is preserved. It is becoming that when the two are united into one, they should bear the same likeness as the agent, otherwise nature would be called upon to do what is impossible. The same incongruity would occur if you were to join B with D so as to make the line A B D C, as is plain to any person who reflects a moment. Nature, therefore, aims at being and also at acting in the best manner possible; it selects the former motion and order rather than the second because the identity is better preserved. From all this it is evident why the north pole attracts the south and conversely, and also why the south pole does not attract the south pole and the north pole does not attract the north.

Chapter X
An Inquiry into the Cause of the Natural Virtue of the Lodestone

Certain persons who were but poor investigators of nature held the opinion that the force with which a lodestone draws iron, is found in the mineral veins themselves from which the stone is obtained; whence they claim that the iron turns towards the poles of the earth, only because of the numerous iron mines found there. But such persons are ignorant of the fact that in many different parts of the globe the lodestone is found; from which it would follow that the iron needle should turn in different directions according to the locality; but this is contrary to experience. Secondly, these individuals do not seem to know that the places under the poles are uninhabitable because there one-half the year is day and the other half night. Hence it is most silly to imagine that the lodestone should come to us from such places. Since the lodestone points to the south as well as to the north, it is evident from the foregoing chapters that we must conclude that not only from the north pole but also from the south pole rather than from the veins of the mines virtue flows into the poles of the lodestone. This fol-

lows from the consideration that wherever a man may be, he finds the stone pointing to the heavens in accordance with the position of the meridian; but all meridians meet in the poles of the world; hence it is manifest that from the poles of the world, the poles of the lodestone receive their virtue. Another necessary consequence of this is that the needle does not point to the pole star, since the meridians do not intersect in that star but in the poles of the world. In every region, the pole star is always found outside the meridian except twice in each complete revolution of the heavens. From all these considerations, it is clear that the poles of the lodestone derive their virtue from the poles of the heavens. As regards the other parts of the stone, the right conclusion is, that they obtain their virtue from the other parts of the heavens, so that we may infer that not only the poles of the stone receive their virtue and influence from the poles of the world, but likewise also the other parts, or the entire stone from the entire heavens. You may test this in the following manner: A round lodestone on which the poles are marked is placed on two sharp styles as pivots having one pivot under each pole so that the lodestone may easily revolve on these pivots. Having done this, make sure that it is equally balanced and that it turns smoothly on the pivots. Repeat this several times at different hours of the day and always with the utmost care. Then place the stone with its axis in the meridian, the poles resting on the pivots. Let it be moved after the manner of bracelets so that the elevation and depression of the poles may equal the elevation and depressions of the poles of the heavens of the place in which you are experimenting. If now the stone be moved according to the motion of the heavens, you will be delighted in having discovered such a wonderful secret; but if not, ascribe the failure to your own lack of skill rather than to a defect in nature. Moreover, in this position I consider the strength of the lodestone to be best preserved. When it is placed differently, i.e., not in the meridian, I think its virtue is weakened or obscured rather than maintained. With such an instrument you will need no timepiece, for by it you can know the ascendant at any hour you please, as well as all other dispositions of the heavens which are sought for by astrologers.

<h1 style="text-align:center">Part II</h1>

Chapter I
The Construction of an Instrument for Measuring the Azimuth of the Sun the Moon or Any Star on the Horizon

Having fully examined all the properties of the lodestone and the phenomena connected therewith, let us now come to those instruments which depend for their operation on the knowledge of those facts. Take a rounded lodestone, and after determining its poles in the manner already mentioned, file its two sides so that it becomes elongated at its poles and occupies less space. The lodestone prepared in this wise is then enclosed within two capsules after the fashion of a mirror. Let these capsules be so joined together that they cannot be separated and that water cannot enter; they should be made of light wood and fastened with cement suited to the purpose. Having done this, place them in a large vessel of water on the edges of which the two parts of the world, i.e., the north and south points, have been found and marked. These points may be united by a thread stretched across from north and south. Then float the capsules and place a smooth strip of wood over them in the manner of a diameter. Move the strip until it is equally distant from the meridian-line, previously determined and marked by a thread, or else until it coincides therewith. Then mark a line on the capsules according to the position of the strip, and this will indicate forever the meridian of that place. Let this line be divided at its middle by another cutting it at right angles, which will give the east and west line; thus the four cardinal points will be determined and indicated on the edge of the capsules. Each quarter is to be subdivided into 90 parts, making 360 in the circumference of the capsules. Engrave these divisions on them as usually done on the back of an astrolabe. On the top or edge

of the capsules thus marked place a thin ruler like the pointer on the back of the astrolabe; instead of the sights attach two perpendicular pins, one at each end. If, therefore, you desire to take the azimuth of the sun, place the capsules in water and let them move freely until they come to rest in their natural position. Hold them firmly in one hand, while with the other you move the ruler until the shadow of the pins falls along the length of the ruler; then the end of the ruler which is towards the sun will indicate the azimuth of the sun. Should it be windy, let the capsules be covered with a suitable vessel until they have taken their position north and south. The same method, namely, by sighting, may be followed at night for determining the azimuth of the moon and stars; move the ruler until the ends of the pins are in the same line with the moon or star; the end of the ruler will then indicate the azimuth just as in the case of the sun. By means of the azimuth may then be determined the hour of the day, the ascendant, and all those other things usually determined by the astrolabe. A form of the instrument is shown in the following figure.

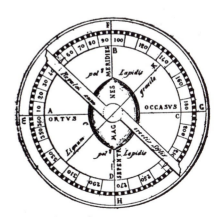

Figure 50.1 Azimuth compass

Chapter II
The Construction of a Better Instrument for the Same Purpose

In this chapter I will describe the construction of a better and more efficient instrument. Select a vessel of wood, brass or any solid material you like, circular in shape, moderate in size, shallow but of sufficient width, with a cover of some transparent substance, such as glass or crystal; it would be even better to have both the vessel and the cover transparent. At the centre of this vessel fasten a thin axis of brass or silver, having its extremities in the cover above and the vessel below. At the middle of this axis let there be two apertures at right angles to each other; through one of them pass an iron stylus or needle, through the other a silver or brass needle crossing the iron one at right angles. Divide the cover first into four parts and subdivide these into 90 parts, as was mentioned in describing the former instrument. Mark the parts north, south, east and west. Add thereto a ruler of transparent material with pins at each end. After this bring either the north or the south pole of a lodestone near the cover so that the needle may be attracted and receive its virtue from the lodestone. Then turn the vessel until the needle stands in the north and south line already marked on the instrument; after which turn the ruler towards the sun if day-time, and towards the moon and stars at night, as described in the preceding chapter. By means of this instrument you can direct your course towards cities and islands and any other place wherever you may wish to go by land or sea, provided the latitude and

Figure 50.2 Double-pivoted needle

longitude of the places are known to you. How iron remains suspended in air by virtue of the lodestone, I will explain in my book on the action of mirrors. Such, then, is the description of the instrument illustrated in Figures 50.2 and 50.3.

Chapter III
The Art of Making a Wheel of Perpetual Motion

In this chapter I will make known to you the construction of a wheel which in a remarkable manner moves continuously. I have seen many persons vainly busy themselves and even becoming exhausted with much labor in their endeavors to invent such a wheel. But these invariably failed to notice that by means of the virtue or power of the lodestone all difficulty can be overcome. For the construction of such a wheel, take a silver capsule like that of a concave mirror, and worked on the outside with fine carving and perforations, not only for the sake of beauty, but also for the purpose of diminishing its weight. You should manage also that the eye of the unskilled may not perceive what is cunningly placed inside. Within let there be iron nails or teeth of equal weight fastened to the periphery of the wheel in a slanting direction, close to one another so that their distance apart may not be more than the thickness of a bean or a pea; the wheel itself must be of uniform weight throughout. Fasten the middle of the axis about which the wheel revolves so that the said axis may always remain immovable. Add thereto a silver bar, and at its extremity affix a lodestone placed between two capsules and prepared in the following way: When it has been rounded and its poles marked as said before, let it be shaped like an egg; leaving the poles untouched, file down the intervening parts so that thus flattened and occupying less space, it may not touch the sides of the capsules when the wheel revolves. Thus prepared, let it be attached to the silver rod just as a precious stone is placed in a ring; let the north pole be then

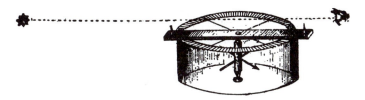

Figure 50.3 Pivoted compass

turned towards the teeth or cogs of the wheel somewhat slantingly so that the virtue of the stone may not flow diametrically into the iron teeth, but at a certain angle; consequently when one of the teeth comes near the north pole and owing to the impetus of the wheel passes it, it then approaches the south pole from which it is rather driven away than attracted, as is evident from the law given in a preceding chapter. Therefore such a tooth would be constantly attracted and constantly repelled. In order that the wheel may do its work more speedily, place within the box a small rounded weight made of brass or silver of such a size that it may be caught between each pair of teeth; consequently as the movement of the wheel is continuous in one direction, so the fall of the weight will be continuous in the other. Being caught between the teeth of a wheel which is continuously revolving, it seeks the centre of the earth in virtue of its own weight, thereby aiding the motion of the teeth and preventing them from coming to rest in a direct line with the lodestone. Let the places between the teeth be suitably hollowed out so that they may easily catch the

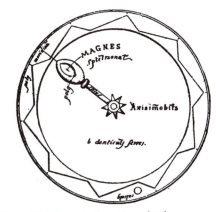

Figure 50.4 Perpetual motion wheel

body in its fall, as shown in the diagram above. (Figure 50.4.)

Farewell: finished in camp at the siege of Lucera on the eighth day of August, Anno Domini MCCLXIX.

CHAPTER 51

Roger Bacon

Roger Bacon was born circa 1213, probably at Oxford, England, to a family of minor nobility. He studied the liberal arts first at Oxford and then at Paris. As regent master of the latter (c. 1237) he was one of the first to lecture on the *Libri naturales* and the *Metaphysics* of Aristotle after the ban on these works had been lifted, and he continued to do so until at least 1247. This was the early period of his Scholastic writings, which include his *Summa Grammatica, Summulae Dialectics, Questiones* on Aristotle's *Physics* and *Metaphysics*, and *Questiones* on the pseudo-Aristotelian *De plantis* and *Liber de causis*, to name only a few.

Around 1247 he left Paris and returned to Oxford, where he was introduced to the works of Robert Grosseteste. For the next two decades Bacon tells us that he studied languages and the sciences. By 1257 he had probably become a member of the Franciscan order to which Grosseteste had bequeathed his library. During this period Bacon became embittered by the lack of support that his Franciscan brothers showed for his scientific work by not providing him with either the experimental equipment or the freedom he deemed necessary to fully pursue his work. He lashed out at them for being narrow-minded, and his association with the extremist followers of Joachim of Floris (a twelfth-century Cistercian mystic with an apocalyptic interpretation of history) made his views suspect. As punishment, he was sent to Paris, where he was forbidden to circulate his writings outside the order.

Fortunately, his situation changed for the better. Pope Clement IV, while still only a cardinal, had become aware of Bacon's proposal to revise the entirety of human science so as to better serve the interests of theology. Upon becoming pope in 1265, he wrote to Bacon requesting a copy, not realizing that it was still in the planning stage. Thus stimulated, Bacon composed his *Opus Majus* in only eighteen months. His *Opus Minor* (the Lesser Work) and *Opus Tertium* (the Third Work) followed shortly thereafter.

By the end of 1268 Bacon probably returned to Oxford, where he completed his *Communia Mathematica, Communia Naturalium,* and *Compendium Studii Philosophiae*. This last work brought trouble once again to Bacon, for in it he bitterly attacked the Dominicans and Franciscans, the two teaching orders, for neglecting subjects he believed essential to the curriculum. The Franciscan minister-general, Jerome of Ascoli (later Pope Nicholas IV), brought charges against Bacon's teachings because of "certain suspect novelties", and Bacon was subsequently imprisoned, most likely from 1277 to 1279. It was clearly a political move because there was nothing in Bacon's writings that had not been endorsed by many reputable theologians of the day. His outspoken views on the morals of secular masters gained him many enemies. He died in 1292 before completing his *Compendium Studii Theologiae*. It is clear from this work that he had not lost his zeal and power of invective.

━━━━━━━━━━━━━━━

Roger Bacon on Mathematics

In the first section of Part IV of his *Opus Majus*, Roger Bacon argues for the fundamental importance of mathematics, viewing it as the foundation of our knowledge of physical causes. Specifically, he was of the belief that knowledge of astronomy would yield knowledge of events on earth and mathematics is crucial to an understanding of the functioning of the heavenly bodies. He argued vigorously that the categories, such as quality, relation, place, and time, are reducible to that of quantity and ". . . the category of quantity cannot be known without mathematics. Hence it is clear that it should be studied first, that through it we may advance to all the later sciences."

He attaches particular importance to geometry. It is via geometry that one gains knowledge of physical causes, especially of efficient or generating causes. Here we see the influence of Grosseteste on Bacon. The former argued that all physical force and specifically light is transmitted in pulses like sound waves. The latter's theory of the propagation of force along straight lines is an extension and modification of Grosseteste's views. Bacon was unparalleled in his knowledge of parabolic mirrors and convex lenses. His principal contribution to scientific theory was his research in optics and his application of it to the theory of vision and the working of the eye. This functioned as a pivotal point of departure from the Middle Ages to scientific developments in the seventeenth century. To his great credit, Bacon saw the practical applications of science, as manifested by his prediction of the invention of automobiles, aircraft, and motorboats.

Bacon utilizes the doctrine of sensible species. That doctrine is discussed on p. 515.

OPUS MAJUS

Part Four of This Plea
In which is shown the power of mathematics in the sciences and in the affairs and occupations of this world.

First Distinction
In three chapters

Chapter I

After making it clear that many famous roots of knowledge depend on the mastery of the languages through which there is an entrance into knowledge on the part of the Latins, I now wish to consider the foun-

Reprinted from *The Opus Majus of Roger Bacon*, translated by Robert Belle Burke, Vol. I, pp. 116–147. (Philadelphia: University of Pennsylvania Press, 1928).

dations of this same knowledge as regards the great sciences, in which there is a special power in respect to the other sciences and the affairs of this world. There are four great sciences, without which the other sciences cannot be known nor a knowledge of things secured. If these are known any one can make glorious progress in the power of knowledge without difficulty and labor, not only in human sciences, but in that which is divine. The virtue of each of these sciences will be touched upon not only on account of knowledge itself, but in respect to the other matters aforesaid. Of these sciences the gate and key is mathematics, which the saints discovered at the beginning of the world, as I shall show, and which has always been used by all the saints and sages more than all other sciences. Neglect of this branch now for thirty or forty years has destroyed the whole system of study of the Latins. Since he who is ignorant of this cannot know the other sciences nor the affairs of this world, as I shall prove. And what is worse men ignorant of this do not perceive their own ignorance, and therefore do not seek a remedy. And on the contrary the knowledge of this science prepares the mind and elevates it to a certain knowledge of all things, so that if one learns the root of knowledge placed about it and rightly applies them to the knowledge of the other sciences and matter, he will then be able to know all that follows without error and doubt, easily and effectually. For without these neither what precedes nor what follows can be known; whence they perfect what precedes and regulate it, even as the end perfects those things pertaining to it, and they arrange and open the way to what follows. This I now intend to intimate through authority and reason; and in the first place I intend to do so in the human sciences and in the matters of this world, and then in divine knowledge, and lastly according as they are related to the Church and the other three purposes.

Chapter II
In which it is proved by authority that every science requires mathematics.

As regards authority I so proceed. Boetius says in the second prologue to his Arithmetic, "If an inquirer lacks the four parts of mathematics, he has very little ability to discover truth." And again, "Without this theory no one can have a correct insight into truth." And he says also, "I warn the man who spurns these paths of knowledge that he cannot philosophize correctly." And again, "It is clear that whosoever passes these by, has lost the knowledge of all learning." He confirms this by the opinion of all men of weight say-

ing, "Among all the men of influence in the past, who have flourished under the leadership of Pythagoras with a finer mental grasp, it is an evident fact that no one reaches the summit of perfection in philosophical studies, unless he examines the noble quality of such wisdom with the help of the so-called quadrivium." And in particular Ptolemy and Boetius himself are illustrations of this fact. For since there are three essential parts of philosophy, as Aristotle says in the sixth book of the Metaphysics, mathematical, natural, and divine, the mathematical is of no small importance in grasping the knowledge of the other two parts, as Ptolemy teaches in the first chapter of the Almagest, which statement he also explains further in that place. And since the divine part is twofold, as is clear from the first book of the Metaphysics, namely, the first philosophy, which shows that God exists, whose exalted properties it investigates, and civil science, which determines divine worship, and explains many matters concerning God as far as man can receive them. Ptolemy likewise asserts and declares that mathematics is potent in regard to both of these branches. Hence Boetius asserts at the end of his Arithmetic that the mathematical means are discovered in civil polity. For he says that an arithmetic mean is comparable to a state that is ruled by a few, for this reason, that in its lesser terms is the greater proportion; but he states that there is a harmonic mean in an aristocratic state for the reason that in the greater terms the greater proportionality is found. The geometrical mean is comparable to a democratic state equalized in some manner; for whether in their lesser or greater terms they are composed of an equal proportion of all. For there is among all a certain parity of mean preserving a law of equality in their relations. Aristotle and his expositors teach in the morals in many places that a state cannot be ruled without these means. Concerning these means an exposition will be given with an application to divine truths. Since all the essential parts of philosophy, which are more than forty sciences distinct in their turn, may be reduced to these three, it suffices now that the value of mathematics has been established by the authorities mentioned.

Now the accidental parts of philosophy are grammar and logic. Alpharabius makes it clear in his book on the sciences that grammar and logic cannot be known without mathematics. For although grammar furnishes children with the facts relating to speech and its properties in prose, meter, and rhythm, nevertheless it does so in a puerile way by means of statement and not through causes or reasons. For it is the function of another science to give the reasons for these things, namely, of that science, which must consider fully the nature of tones, and this alone is music, of which there are numerous varieties and parts. For one deals with prose, a second with meter, a third with rhythm, and a fourth with music in singing. And besides these it has more parts. The part dealing with prose teaches the reasons for all elevations of the voice in prose, as regards differences of accents and as regards colons, commas, periods, and the like. The metrical part teaches all the reasons and causes for feet and meters. The part on rhythm teaches about every modulation and sweet relation in rhythms, because all those are certain kinds of singing, although not so treated as in ordinary singing. For it is called "accent" since it is, as it were, song [*accantus*] for *accino, accinis*. Hence these subjects pertain to music as Cassiodorus teaches in music, and Censorinus in his book on Accent, and so too in those on other topics. Authorities on music bear witness to this fact as well as do their books on that science. And Alpharabius agrees with them in his book on the Division of the Sciences. Therefore grammar depends causatively on music.

In the same way logic. For the purpose of logic is the composition of arguments that stir the active intellect to faith and to a love of virtue and future felicity, as we have already shown, which arguments are handed down in the books of Aristotle on these arguments, as has been stated. But these arguments must have a maximum amount of beauty, so that the mind of man may be drawn to the truths of salvation suddenly and without previous consideration, as we are taught in those books. And Alpharabius especially teaches this in regard to the poetic argument, the statements of which should be sublime and beautiful, and therefore accompanied with notable adornment in prose, meter, and rhythm, as befits place, time, personages, and subject for which the plea is made. And thus Aristotle taught in his book on the Poetic Argument, which Hermannus did not venture to translate into Latin on account of the difficulty of the meters, which he did not understand, as he himself states in the prologue to the commentary of Averroës on that book. And therefore the end of logic depends upon music. But the end of everything is its noblest part in every matter and imposes necessity on what is related to it, as Aristotle states in the second book of the Physics; nor have those things any utility of their own which are naturally formed for the end, except when they are related to their end, as is clear in individual cases. And therefore the whole utility of logic is drawn from the relation of all logical arguments to arguments of this kind, and therefore since they depend on the arguments of music, necessarily logic must depend on the power of music. All these facts are in accordance with the opinion of Alpharabius in his book on the Sciences, and they are likewise clearly stated by Aristotle and Averroës in their books, although these are not used by the Latins. But not only does a knowledge of logic depend on mathematics because of its end, but because of its middle and heart, which is the book of Posterior Analytics, for that book teaches the art of demonstration. But neither can the fundamental principles of demonstration, nor conclusions, nor the subject as a whole be learned or made clear except in the realm of mathematics, because there alone is there true and forceful demonstration, as all know and as we shall explain later. Therefore of necessity logic depends on mathematics.

What has been said is applicable likewise because of its beginning and not only because of its middle and end. For the book of Categories is the first book of logic according to Aristotle. But it is clear that the category of quantity cannot be known without mathematics. For the knowledge of quantity belongs to mathematics. Connected with quantity are the categories of when and where. For when has to do with time, and where arises from place. The category of habit cannot be known without the category of place, as Averroës teaches in the fifth book of the Metaphysics. But the greater part of the category of quality contains the attributes and properties of quantities, because all things that are in the fourth class of quality are called qualities in quantities. And all the attributes of these which are absolutely essential to them are qualities, with which a large part of geometry and arithmetic is concerned, such as straight and curved and other essential qualities of the line, and triangularity and other figures belonging to surface or to a solid body; and the prime and non-factorable in numbers, as Aristotle teaches in the fifth book of the Metaphysics, as well as other essential attributes of numbers. Moreover, whatever is worthy of consideration in the category of relation is the property of quantity, such as proportions and proportionalities, and geometrical, arithmetical, and harmonic means, and the kinds of greater and lesser inequality. Moreover, spiritual substances are known by philosophy only through the medium of the corporeal, and especially the heavenly bodies, as Aristotle teaches in the eleventh book of the Metaphysics. Nor are inferior things known except through superior ones, because the heavenly bodies are the causes of things that are lower. But the heavenly bodies are known only through quantity, as is clear from astronomy. Therefore all the categories depend on a knowledge of quantity of which mathematics treats, and therefore the whole excellence of logic depends on mathematics.

Chapter III
In which it is proved by reason that every science requires mathematics.

What has been shown as regards mathematics as a whole through authority, can now be shown likewise by reason. And I make this statement in the first place, because other sciences use mathematical examples, but examples are given to make clear the subjects treated by the sciences; wherefore ignorance of the examples involves an ignorance of the subjects for the understanding of which the examples are adduced. For since change in natural objects is not found without some augmentation and diminution nor do these latter take place without change; Aristotle was not able to make clear without complications the difference between augmentation and change by any natural example, because augmentation and diminution go together always with change in some way; wherefore he gave the mathematical example of the rectangle which augmented by a gnomon increases in magnitude and is not altered in shape. This example cannot be understood before the twenty-second proposition of the sixth book of the Elements. For in that proposition of the sixth book it is proved that a smaller rectangle is similar in every particular to a larger one and therefore a smaller one is not altered in shape, although it becomes larger by the addition of the gnomon.

Secondly, because comprehension of mathematical truths is innate, as it were, in us. For a small boy, as Tullius states in the first book of the Tusculan Disputations, when questioned by Socrates on geometrical truths, replied as though he had learned geometry. And this experiment has been tried in many cases, and does not hold in other sciences, as will appear more clearly from what follows. Wherefore since this knowledge is almost innate, and as it were precedes discovery and learning, or at least is less in need of them than other sciences, it will be first among sciences and will precede others disposing us toward them; since what is innate or almost so disposes toward what is acquired.

Thirdly, because this science of all the parts of philosophy was the earliest discovered. For this was first discovered at the beginning of the human race. Since it was discovered before the flood and then later by the sons of Adam, and by Noah and his sons, as is clear from the prologue to the Construction of the Astrolabe according to Ptolemy, and from Albumazar in the larger introduction to astronomy, and from the first book of the Antiquities, and this is true as regards all its parts, geometry, arithmetic, music, astronomy. But this would not have been the case except for the fact that this science is earlier than the others and naturally precedes them. Hence it is clear that it should be studied first, that through it we may advance to all the later sciences.

Fourthly, because the natural road for us is from what is easy to that which is more difficult. But this science is the easiest. This is clearly proved by the fact that mathematics is not beyond the intellectual grasp of any one. For the people at large and those wholly illiterate know how to draw figures and compute and sing, all of which are mathematical operations. But we must begin first with what is common to the laity and to the educated; and it is not only hurtful to the clergy, but disgraceful and abominable that they are ignorant of what the laity knows well and profitably. Fifthly, we see that the clergy, even the most ignorant, are able to grasp mathematical truths, although they are unable to attain to the other sciences. Besides a man by listening once or twice can learn more about this science with certainty and reality without error, than he can by listening ten times about the other parts of philosophy, as is clear to one making the experiment. Sixthly, since the natural road for us is to begin with things which befit the state and nature of childhood, because children begin with facts that are better known by us and that must be acquired first. But of this nature is mathematics, since children are first taught to sing, and in the same way they can learn the method of making figures and of counting, and it would be far easier and more necessary for them to know about numbers before singing, because in the relations of numbers in music the whole theory of numbers is set forth by example, just as the authors on music teach, both in ecclesias-

tical music and in philosophy. But the theory of numbers depends on figures, since numbers relating to lines, surfaces, solids, squares, cubes, pentagons, hexagons, and other figures, are known from lines, figures, and angles. For it has been found that children learn mathematical truths better and more quickly, as is clear in singing, and we also know by experience that children learn and acquire mathematical truths better than the other parts of philosophy. For Aristotle says in the sixth book of the Ethics that youths are able to grasp mathematical truths quickly, not so matters pertaining to nature, metaphysics, and morals. Wherefore the mind must be trained first through the former rather than through these latter sciences. Seventhly, where the same things are not known to us and to nature, there the natural road for us is from the things better known to us to those better known to nature, or known more simply; and more easily do we grasp what is better known to ourselves, and with great difficulty we arrive at a knowledge of those things which are better known to nature. And the things known to nature are erroneously and imperfectly known by us, because our intellect bears the same relation to what is so clear to nature, as the eye of the bat to the light of the sun, as Aristotle maintains in the second book of the Metaphysics; such, for example, are especially God and the angels, and future life and heavenly things, and creatures nobler than others, because the nobler they are the less known are they to us. And these are called things known to nature and known simply. Therefore, on the contrary, where the same things are known both to us and to nature, we make much progress in regard to what is known to nature and in regard to all that is there included, and we are able to attain a perfect knowledge of them. But in mathematics only, as Averroës says in the first book of the Physics and in the seventh of the Metaphysics and in his commentary on the third book of the Heavens and the World, are the same things known to us and to nature or simply. Therefore as in mathematics we touch upon what is known fully to us, so also do we touch upon what is known to nature and known simply. Therefore we are able to reach directly an intimate knowledge of that science. Since, therefore, we have not this ability in other sciences, clearly mathematics is better known. Therefore the acquisition of this subject is the beginning of our knowledge.

Likewise, eighthly, because every doubt gives place to certainty and every error is cleared away by unshaken truth. But in mathematics we are able to arrive at the full truth without error, and at a certainty of all points involved without doubt; since in this subject demonstration by means of a proper and necessary cause can be given. Demonstration causes the truth to be known. And likewise in this subject it is possible to have for all things an example that may be perceived by the senses, and a test perceptible to the senses in drawing figures and in counting, so that all may be clear to the sense. For this reason there can be no doubt in this science. But in other sciences, the assistance of mathematics being excluded, there are so many doubts, so many opinions, so many errors on the part of man, that these sciences cannot be unfolded, as is clear since demonstration by means of a proper and necessary cause does not exist in them from their own nature because in natural phenomena, owing to the genesis and destruction of their proper causes as well as of the effects, there is no such thing as necessity. In metaphysics there can be no demonstration except through effect, since spiritual facts are discovered through corporeal effects and the creator through the creature, as is clear in that science. In morals there cannot be demonstrations from proper causes, as Aristotle teaches. And likewise neither in matters pertaining to logic nor in grammar, as is clear, can there be very convincing demonstrations because of the weak nature of the material concerning which those sciences treat. And therefore in mathematics alone are there demonstrations of the most convincing kind through a necessary cause. And therefore here alone can a man arrive

at the truth from the nature of this science. Likewise in the other sciences there are doubts and opinions and contradictions on our part, so that we scarcely agree on the most trifling question or in a single sophism; for in these sciences there are from their nature no processes of drawing figures and of reckonings, by which all things must be proved true. And therefore in mathematics alone is there certainty without doubt.

Wherefore it is evident that if in other sciences we should arrive at certainty without doubt and truth without error, it behooves us to place the foundations of knowledge in mathematics, in so far as disposed through it we are able to reach certainty in other sciences and truth by the exclusion of error. This reasoning can be made clearer by comparison, and the principle is stated in the ninth book of Euclid. The same holds true here as in the relation of the knowledge of the conclusion to the knowledge of the premises, so that if there is error and doubt in these, the truth cannot be arrived at through these premises in regard to the conclusion, nor can there be certainty, because doubt is not verified by doubt, nor is truth proved by falsehood, although it is possible for us to reason from false premises, our reasoning in that case drawing an inference and not furnishing a proof; the same is true with respect to sciences as a whole; those in which there are strong and numerous doubts and opinions and errors, I say at least on our part, should have doubts of this kind and false statements cleared away by some science definitely known to us, and in which we have neither doubts nor errors. For since the conclusions and principles belonging to them are parts of the sciences as a whole, just as part is related to part, as conclusion to premises, so is science related to science, so that a science which is full of doubts and besprinkled with opinions and obscurities, cannot be rendered certain, nor made clear, nor verified except by some other science known and verified, certain and plain to us, as in the case of a conclusion reached through premises. But mathematics alone, as was shown above, remains fixed and verified for us with the utmost certainty and verification. Therefore by means of this science all other sciences must be known and verified.

Since we have now shown by the peculiar property of that science that mathematics is prior to other sciences, and is useful and necessary to them, we now proceed to show this by considerations taken from its subject matter. And in the first place we so conclude, because the natural road for us is from sense perception to the intellect, since if sense perception is lacking, the knowledge related to that sense perception is lacking also, according to the statement in the first book of the Posterior Analytics, since as sense perception proceeds so does the human intellect. But quantity is especially a matter of sense perception, because it pertains to the common sense and is perceived by the other senses, and nothing can be perceived without quantity, wherefore the intellect is especially able to make progress as respects quantity. In the second place, because the very act of intelligence in itself is not completed without continuous quantity, since Aristotle states in his book on Memory and Recollection that our whole intellect is associated with continuity and time. Hence we grasp quantities and bodies by a direct perception of the intellect, because their forms are present in the intellect. But the forms of incorporeal things are not so perceived by our intellect; or if such forms are produced in it, according to Avicenna's statement in the third book of the Metaphysics, we, however, do not perceive this fact owing to the more vigorous occupation of our intellect in respect to bodies and quantities. And therefore by means of argumentation and attention to corporeal things and quantities we investigate the idea of incorporeal things, as Aristotle does in the eleventh book of the Metaphysics. Wherefore the intellect will make progress especially as regards quantity itself for this reason, that quantities and bodies as far as they are such belong peculiarly to the human intellect as respects the common condition of understanding.

Each and every thing exists as an antecedent for some result, and this is true in higher degree of that which has just been stated.[1]

Moreover, for full confirmation the last reason can be drawn from the experience of men of science; for all scientists in ancient times labored in mathematics, in order that they might know all things, just as we have seen in the case of men of our own times, and have heard in the case of others who by means of mathematics, of which they had an excellent knowledge, have learned all science. For very illustrious men have been found, like Bishop Robert of Lincoln and Friar Adam de Marisco, and many others, who by the power of mathematics have learned to explain the causes of all things, and expound adequately things human and divine. Moreover, the sure proof of this matter is found in the writings of those men, as, for example, on impressions such as the rainbow, comets, generation of heat, investigation of localities on the earth and other matters, of which both theology and philosophy make use. Wherefore it is clear that mathematics is absolutely necessary and useful to other sciences.

These reasons are general ones, but in particular this point can be shown by a survey of all the parts of philosophy disclosing how all things are known by the application of mathematics. This amounts to showing that the other sciences are not to be known by means of dialectical and sophistical argument as commonly introduced, but by means of mathematical demonstrations entering into the truths and activities of other sciences and regulating them, without which they cannot be understood, nor made clear, nor taught, nor learned. If any one in particular should proceed by applying the power of mathematics to the separate sciences, he would see that nothing of supreme moment can be known in them without mathematics. But this simply amounts to establishing definite methods of dealing with all sciences, and by means of mathematics verifying all things necessary to the other sciences. But this matter does not come within the limits of the present survey.

Second Distinction
In which it is shown that the matters of this world require mathematics. The distinction has three chapters.

Chapter I
In the first chapter it is shown in general that celestial and terrestrial things require mathematics.

What has just been shown in regard to the sciences can be made clear in regard to things. For the things of this world cannot be made known without a knowledge of mathematics. For this is an assured fact in regard to celestial things, since two important sciences of mathematics treat of them, namely theoretical astrology and practical astrology. The first considers the quantities of all that is included in celestial things, and all things which are reduced to quantity discontinuous as well as continuous. For it gives us definite information as to the number of the heavens and of the stars, whose size can be comprehended by means of instruments, and the shapes of all and their magnitudes and distances from the earth and thicknesses and number, and greatness and smallness, the rising and setting of the signs of the stars, and the motion of the heavens and the stars, and the numbers and varieties of the eclipses. It likewise treats of the size and shape of the habitable earth and of all great divisions which are called climes, and it shows the difference in horizons and days and nights in the different climes. These matters, therefore, are determined by this branch of the subject as well as many things connected with them. Practical astrology enables us to know every hour the positions of the planets and stars, and their aspects and actions, and all the changes that take place in the heavenly bodies; and it treats of those things that happen in the air, such as comets and rainbows and the other changing phenomena there, in order that we may know their positions, altitudes, magnitudes, forms, and

many things that must be considered in them. All this information is secured by means of instruments suitable for these purposes, and by tables and by canons, that is, rules invented for the verification of these matters, to the end that a way may be prepared for the judgments that can be formed in accordance with the power of philosophy, not only in the things of nature, but in those which take their tendency from nature and freely follow celestial direction; and not only for judgments in regard to present, past, and future, but for wonderful works, so that all things prosperous in this world may be advanced, and things adverse may be repressed, in a useful and glorious way. Nor are these matters doubtful. For the patriarchs and prophets from the beginning of the world had full information respecting these matters as well as all others. Aristotle restored the knowledge of the ancients and brought it to light. All those informed in great subjects agree in this, and experience teaches it. But concerning these matters an exposition will be given in the proper place.

It is plain, therefore, that celestial things are known by means of mathematics, and that a way is prepared by it to things that are lower. That, moreover, these terrestrial things cannot be learned without mathematics, is clear from the fact that we know things only through causes, if knowledge is to be properly acquired, as Aristotle says. But celestial things are the causes of terrestrial. Therefore these terrestrial things will not be known without a knowledge of the celestial, and the latter cannot be known without mathematics. Therefore a knowledge of these terrestrial things must depend on the same science. In the second place, we can see from their properties that no one of these lower or higher things can be known without the power of mathematics. For everything in nature is brought into being by an efficient cause and the material on which it works, for these two are concurrent at first. For the active cause by its own force moves and alters the matter, so that it becomes a thing. But the efficacy of the efficient cause and of the material cannot be known without the great power of mathematics even as the effects produced cannot be known without it. There are then these three, the efficient cause, the matter, and the effect. In celestial things there is a reciprocal influence of forces, as of light and other agents, and a change takes place in them without, however, any tendency toward their destruction. And so it can be shown that nothing within the range of things can be known without the power of geometry. We learn from this line of reasoning that in like manner the other parts of mathematics are necessary; and they are so for the same reason that holds in the case of geometry; and without doubt they are far more necessary, because they are nobler. If, therefore, the proposition be demonstrated in the case of geometry, it is not necessary in this plea that mention be made of the other parts.

In the first place, I shall demonstrate a proposition in geometry in respect to the efficient causes. For every efficient cause acts by its own force which it produces on the matter subject to it, as the light of the sun produces its own force in the air, and this force is light diffused through the whole world from the solar light. This force is called likeness, image, species, and by many other names, and it is produced by substance as well as accident and by spiritual substance as well as corporeal. Substance is more productive of it than accident, and spiritual substance than corporeal. This species causes every action in this world; for it acts on sense, on intellect, and all the matter in the world for the production of things, because one and the same thing is done by a natural agent on whatsoever it acts, because it has no freedom of choice; and therefore it performs the same act on whatever it meets. But if it acts on the sense and the intellect, it becomes a species, as all know. Accordingly, on the other hand, if it acts on matter it also becomes a species. In those beings that have reason and intellect, although they do many things with deliberation and freedom of will, yet this action, namely, a production of species, is natural in them, just

as it is in other things. Hence the substance of the soul multiplies its own force in the body and outside of the body, and any body outside of itself produces its own force, and the angels move the world by means of forces of this kind. But God produces forces out of nothing, which he multiplies in things; created agents do not do so, but in another way about which we need not concern ourselves at the present time. Forces of this kind belonging to agents produce every action in this world. But there are two things now to be noted respecting these forces; one is the multiplication itself of the species and of force from the place of its production; and the other is the varied action in this world due to the production and destruction of things. The second cannot be known without the first. Therefore it is necessary that the multiplication itself be first described.

Chapter II
In which the canons of the multiplication of the forces of agents as respects lines and angles are explained.

Every multiplication is either with respect to lines, or angles, or figures. While the species travels in a medium of one rarity, as in what is wholly sky, and wholly fire, and wholly air, or wholly water, it is propagated in straight paths, because Aristotle says in the fifth book of the Metaphysics that nature works in the shorter way possible, and the straight line is the shortest of all. This fact is also made evident by the twentieth proposition of the first book of Euclid, which states that in every triangle two sides are longer than the third.

But when the second body is of another rarity and density, so that it is not wholly dense, but changes in some way the passage of the species, like water, which in one way is rare, and in another dense, and crystal similarly, and glass and the like, through the media of which we are able to see, then the species either impinges upon the second body perpendicularly, and still travels along the straight line as in the first medium; or if it does not fall perpendicularly, then of necessity it changes its straight path, and makes an angel on entering the second body, and its declination from the straight path is called refraction of the ray and the species. This is because the perpendicular is the stronger and shorter, and therefore nature works in a better way on it, as geometrical demonstrations show, of which mention will be made later more particularly in the proper place. But this refraction is twofold, since if the second body is denser, as is the case in descending from the sky to these lower objects, all the forces of the stars that do not fall perpendicularly on the globe of elements, are broken between the straight path and the perpendicular drawn from the place of refraction. If the second body is rarer, as is the case in ascending from water into the air, the straight path falls between the refracted ray and the perpendicular drawn from the place of refraction. And this is a wonderful diversity in the action of nature, but it is not strange, when countless wonders are performed by nature in accordance with the laws of these refractions; and by means of art aiding nature those things can be done which the world cannot receive, as I shall explain in perspective science. But it will be driven by these means in the times of Antichrist to those things which it will itself wish for in great part.

That, moreover, these things are true authorities teach, and all experts know, and instruments can be made so that we may sensibly see propagations of this kind; but until we have instruments we can prove this by natural effect without contradiction, as Figure 51.1 shows. Let us take then a hemisphere of crystal or a glass vessel, the lower part of which is round and full of water. When, therefore, rays come from the center of the sun to the body of crystal, or of glass, which is denser than the air, those that are not perpendicular to such a body (and these are the ones that do not pass through its center, as is clear from geometric principles) are refracted between the straight path and the perpendicular drawn from the point of refraction, as is the ray *ac*, which after passing through the whole

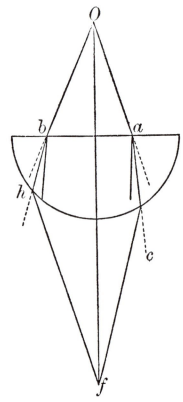

Figure 51.1

body of the vessel, comes obliquely to the air which is of less density. Of necessity, therefore, it so travels that the straight path is between the path of the ray and the perpendicular drawn to the point of refraction, and therefore the ray will not travel to *c*, but bends to *f*, on the principal perpendicular, which comes from the sun, that is, ray *Of*. And in the same way at any other point, owing to the double refraction, *hf* will pass through the same point *f* on the ray *Of*. But an infinite number of rays come forth from every point on the sun to the body; therefore an infinite number will meet in this same point by means of the double refraction. But a convergence of rays is the cause of heat. Therefore a burning heat will be produced at this point. And this is a fact, as is clear to the sense; for if a combustible be placed at this point, as wool, silk, or a piece of rag, it will be consumed. Since,

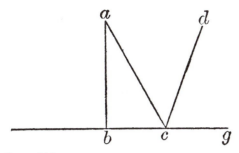

Figure 51.2

therefore, there is combustion at this point and this cannot happen except through a convergence of rays, and the rays cannot assemble except through a double refraction, because a single refraction would not suffice and a third refraction is not required, therefore we must assume this kind of refraction, a wonderful thing in the eyes of men of science. For why is it that nature so acts? Surely nothing is pleasing to nature, or to her will, except what is remade by change; but the causes are hidden. We need not now investigate the causes, since we know this marvel by means of a very certain test, and in what follows other tests will be added.

When, however, the second body is so dense as in no way to permit the passage of the species,—I am speaking of a passage appreciated by human vision,—we say that the species is reflected. Yet according to Aristotle and Boetius the vision of the lynx penetrates walls. Therefore the species does actually pass through as a matter of fact; but human vision forms no judgment concerning this, but does concerning the reflection which of necessity takes place. For on account of the difficulty of passage through the dense medium, since in the air from which it came it finds an easy road, it multiplies itself more abundantly in the direction from which it came. And this in the first place can happen in general in two ways; for either the ray falls perpendicularly on the dense body and then returns upon itself wholly by the same path by which it came, and a ray is generated in the same place, as for example the ray *ab* (in

Figure 51.2) falls perpendicularly, and this is in planes at right angles, as is shown in the eleventh book of geometry, just as in spherical shaped bodies when the ray passes through the center. And the reason for this is that the angles of incidence and reflection are always equal, as a manifold demonstration shows, and authorities maintain, and instruments made for this purpose make clear to the eye. But there are only two right angles at the dense body in the case of *ab*. Therefore by these same angles the reflex ray will return upon itself and therefore in the same place. But the line *ac* which falls at oblique angles and not perpendicularly, does not return upon itself, but passes to *d*, because of the equality of the angles of incidence and reflection. Whenever the ray falls at oblique angles, the acute angle is called the angle of incident; and from the obtuse angle an angle equal to the angle of incidence is cut off by the reflected line. The angle so formed is contained between the reflected line and the dense body, as is the angle *dcg*, and it is called the angle of reflection, which of necessity must equal the acute angle on the other side, and we prove this to the sight in mirrors. For we cannot see things, unless the eye is in the line of reflection, as if the eye be at *d* it will see *a*; and if not, it will not see by means of that reflected ray. These are known facts, and tests will be given adequately concerning this matter in what follows.

Moreover, an infinite number of rays can be assembled by reflection, just as by multiplication, so that strong combustions take place. But from a plain surface rays cannot converge to one point, because one goes to one point, another to another point. Nor can they do so from a convex mirror; but they can converge from a concave spherical mirror, or from one column-shaped, or pyramidal, or ring-shaped, or oval, and so too from others. If, therefore, a concave spherical mirror be exposed to the sun, an infinite number of rays will converge to one point by means of reflection. And therefore of necessity fire is kindled when a concave mirror is exposed to the sun, as is stated in the last proposition of the book on Mirrors, and the demonstration is there given. But an instrument might very well have been made for this purpose, and the phenomenon would then be visible to the eye, as we stated before in the case of refraction. Hence if a mirror should be made of good steel, or of silver, the combustion would occur more easily; but a combustion does not take place by all rays falling on a mirror, but by those only which fall on the circumference of a circle around the axis of the mirror, because all that fall in one circumference fall at equal angles, and therefore are reflected to a point on the axis, because the angles of the reflected rays are equal, and those that fall in another circle are reflected to another point, and those in a third circle to a third point, and the same statement may be made of an infinite number of circles imagined around the axis of the mirror; for of necessity rays falling on different circumferences travel to different points, because they do not fall at equal angles. Those falling in a smaller circle are reflected higher, and those in the greatest circle are reflected to the lowest point, namely to the pole of the sphere, or to the end of the axis. But neither nature nor art is content with combustion of this kind, nay, they wish so to fashion bodies that all the rays falling on the whole surface of the mirror may converge to a single point; and what is more at every distance we desire. This is the ultimate which the power of geometry can do. For this mirror would burn fiercely everything on which it could be focused. We are to believe that Antichrist will use these mirrors to burn up cities and camps and armies. Since if a moderate convergence of rays by refraction or by a concave mirror burns perceptibly, how much more so without limit, when rays without number converge by means of this mirror. Scientists reckon that this is a necessary consequence. And an author in a book on burning mirrors shows how this instrument is made, but without sufficient reason hid in that book much respecting the artifice, and states that he has placed the lacking information in another book, which has

not been translated by the Latins. But there are Latins who because of the ill favor of that author in concealing the perfection of his knowledge, have studied this wonderful secret nature, because that author stimulates greatly men skilled in science to perfect what is lacking, and he shows that the mirror must be nearly ring-shaped or oval, as if the cones of an egg were cut off, the figure would be ring-shaped; if, however, one cone remains, it is oval. Now in such a figure properly constructed all the rays falling on the whole surface must fall at equal angles, and therefore they must be reflected at like angles, and for this reason to one point. Moreover, the most skillful of the Latins is busily engaged on the construction of this mirror, and the glory of your Magnificence will be able to order him to complete it when he is known to you. This triple multiplication is said to be a principal one, because it comes from the agent itself.

But the fourth kind is more necessary to the world, although it is called accidental multiplication. For light is called accidental with respect to the principal light coming from an object, since it does not come from an agent, but from principal multiplications, as in a house the principal multiplication falls through the window from the sun, but in a corner of the house the accidental light comes from the ray of the window. Moreover, the bodies of mortals would not be able to be exposed always to principal species without destruction, and for this reason God has tempered all things by means of accidental species of this kind.

The fifth kind is different from the others, for it does not follow the common laws of nature, but claims for itself a special privilege. This multiplication does not take place except in an animated medium, as in the nerves of the senses; for the species follows the tortuous course of the nerve, and pays no attention to the straight path. This happens through the force of the vital principle regulating the path of the species, as the actions of an animated being require. Concerning this propagation something will be said in the truth of perspective. The first four in respect to which nature delights to work are common to the inanimate things of the world; the fifth is known to pertain to sensation.

Chapter III
In which multiplication is given as respects figures.

We must next consider how multiplication takes place with respect to figures. Multiplication of necessity takes place in the form of a sphere. For the agent multiplies itself equally in every direction, and with respect to all diameters, and all difference of position, namely, above, below, before, behind, to the right, and to the left. Therefore everywhere the lines go forth in every direction from the agent as from a center: but lines traveling everywhere from one place cannot terminate except on the concave surface of a sphere. And this is clear, because the eye sees only by means of the coming species, but if an infinite number of eyes were placed everywhere, all would see the same thing; therefore the species goes forth by means of an infinite number of lines; but an infinite number of lines terminate only on a spherical surface. If it should be said that light entering through a large triangular opening or through one of another polygonal figure does not fall in spherical form, but does so when it enters through a small opening, we must state that the sides of the small opening are not far apart and therefore the light in a short distance is able to regain its figure, but when it passes through a large figure, it cannot do so easily, but it will do so at some sufficient distance, if obstacles are removed. This principle is made evident by the fourteenth and fifteenth propositions of the first book of the elements of Euclid, as Figure 51.3 shows. For let the rays be drawn as far from the intersection as from the intersection to the sun, by the propositions mentioned the bases of the triangles must be equal. But those bases are the diameters of the lights. Therefore the diameter of the species is necessarily equal to the diameter of the sun at some one distance,

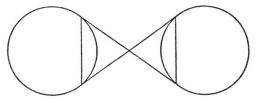

Figure 51.3

and consequently the multiplication will be an equal spherical one, and can be varied according to difference of distance, but it will always be of spherical form. Nor is the light of fire a case in point, which ascends in the form of a pyramid; because this is not a multiplication from the proper nature of light, but is owing to the motion of the body of the fire itself, of which light is an accident, and the accident moves in accordance with the motion of its subject, like the light of the sun in the sun. Now fire must ascend in pyramidal form, since the interior parts are removed from the surrounding cold, and therefore they are less impeded and extricate themselves more quickly than the parts on the outside, and for this reason rise higher, and the remaining parts the nearer they are to these, the more quickly do they extricate themselves, and they attach themselves to the ones in the interior, failing somewhat to reach the height of the inmost parts, and so in regular gradation the remoter ones reach a lesser height, because they are more impeded by the contrary force surrounding them; and therefore a pyramid must necessarily be formed. But in the sphere all regular figures can be inscribed, as is clear from the fifteenth book of the elements of Euclid, among which figures is the pyramid.

And although according to the principle of inscribing geometrical figures irregular ones cannot be inscribed, nor round figures, nevertheless all figures can be produced and marked on the sphere. And therefore not only in spherical multiplication shall we find pyramids with sides, which can be inscribed in a sphere, but also round[2] pyramids, which can be marked and drawn in spherical multiplication. And it is this figure that nature especially selects in every multiplication and action, and not any pyramid at all, but that one whose base is the surface of the agent and whose vertex falls on some point of the surface acted on, because in this way can the species of the agent come to each point of the surface acted on by means of an infinite number of separate pyramids, as is clear in Figure 51.4.

For from each point of the surface acted on there are an infinite number of rays and therefore they can be combined infinitely to form an infinite number of round pyramids with one common base, namely, the surface of the whole agent; and to every part of the surface acted on there comes an apex of a pyramid, so that force comes from the whole agent to each point of the surface acted on, and not from some limited part, to the end that the force may come complete and as a whole, not partial and imperfect, so that the action may be complete, because nature acts in accordance with what is better.

Third Distinction
In which the difference of natural action is made clear by means of geometry. This distinction has three chapters.

Chapter I

After considering these facts in regard to multiplication, we must take up some matters in regard to ulterior action. For light by means of its multiplication makes a luminous image, and this action is called univocal, because the effect is univocal, and of one kind and conformable to the agent. But there is another equivocal multiplication, as light generates heat, heat generates putrefaction, putrefaction death, and wine inebriates, and so of every agent, because it produces many effects besides its own species and force univocal to itself. And so the sun and stars cause all things here below, and the angels move the heavens and the stars, and the soul its own body; the force, however, of the agent does all those things, and this is complete action of the agent and of its force and the one desired finally by nature. Concerning this action therefore

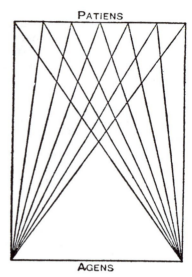

PATIENS

AGENS

Figure 51.4

some canons or rules must be considered. These rules relate chiefly to this action, and yet they have place in a univocal action and contain truth in regard to it.

Nature, therefore, as has been said, works more effectively in a straight line than in a curve, because the former is shorter, and causes the surface acted on to be less distant from the agent, and therefore it receives more of the force of the agent, as he who is near a fire is warmer than one farther away. But the equal is better than the unequal, as Boetius states in the practical part of his Geometry. But in the straight line there is equality. Likewise every united force is of stronger action, as is stated in the book on Causes. But uniformity and unity are greater in the straight line, as Aristotle states in the fifth book of the Metaphysics. For in the curve is an angle, which causes dispersion and irregularity in form and resists unity. Therefore nature acts with more force in the straight line than in the broken or reflected one. But the straight line, which falls at equal angles and perpendicularly either on planes or on spherical bodies, is the one on which nature chooses to work both on account of its equality and greater uniformity, and on account of its shortness. For by the nineteenth

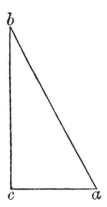

Figure 51.5

proposition of the first book of the elements of Euclid, in every triangle the greater side is opposite the greater angle. But from the seventeenth proposition of the same book, the greater angle in a triangle is the right angle, namely *acb* in Figure 51.5. Therefore the greatest side, *ab*, is opposite this angle. But this line does not fall perpendicularly. Therefore the perpendicular is shorter; wherefore the force coming along it will act more strongly. Moreover, the effectiveness of a perpendicular force is shown not only by demonstration, but also by experience, whence a stone falling from a height perpendicularly strikes with more force; and if a man falls from a height perpendicularly he is hurt more: for should any one divert from the perpendicular path a man falling from a height, he would not be injured, provided he was near the ground. If this help is not given he will die from the perpendicular fall, and will be shattered completely.

And we must consider that if from different points of the agent rays come to the same thing, one perpendicular to the agent and another not perpendicular to it, the perpendicular will always be the shorter. Let *ac* (in Figure 51.6) represent the agent, then *ab* is shorter than *cb*, and therefore stronger for this reason. And although *cb* falls on *ed*, a surface acted on at right angles, and *ab* does not, so that *cb* will be strengthened for this reason, nevertheless it will not reach the strength of *ab*, because

ab is shorter, and because the point *b* of *ed* is likewise a point of another line, as *fg*, to which *ab* is perpendicular, and so the explanation of a body acted on is applicable in its main point to *b*. And the action in particular is most complete on a spherical body, since the force does not fall there at some angle, but passes through the surface and the spherical body, and there is no difference or difformity and completeness of action is there found. For unless circles be marked on the sphere, there is no angle there; but when they are marked the angles of the perpendicular line will be equal, just as in planes, and the action will be complete. But, however, they are not right angles, but obtuse, as is clear from geometry.

In the second place, we must know that nature works on broken lines more strongly than on reflected ones, because refraction is in the direction of the straight path, but reflection advances in the opposite direction, and contrary to the natural path which the nature of the advancing force seeks in continuity and direction unless it is impeded, and therefore reflection weakens greatly the species and the force, and much more so than refraction. But this is to be understood of refraction and reflection as regards the peculiar property of forward motion in them. If, however, we consider that reflection takes place in the same medium, and refraction in different ones, of necessity the double medium impedes more than the single, and this is the case at least when reflection takes place in a rare

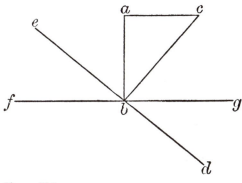

Figure 51.6

medium and the refraction in a second denser medium, as in a glass vessel. For if rays should be assembled from a burning mirror and behind a burning glass, the combustion is of necessity greater, as will be explained below in the proper places. Refraction which takes place in a second denser body weakens less than in a second rarer body. For the perpendicular advance is the strongest, and therefore that which approaches nearer to the perpendicular is the stronger. But refraction in a second denser body is deflected toward the perpendicular, which is erected at the same point at which the refraction takes place, as is clear above in Figure 51.6, both in planes and in spheres, and therefore that kind weakens less. In the case of reflection at right angles, although the ray is accidentally doubled, and thus the action becomes stronger, yet it is in accordance with the nature of that reflection that by repeating itself it weakens the species more; for it is wholly opposed to the natural effort of the species itself, since the species returns by the same line by which it came. But when the reflection takes place at oblique angles, it is not wholly in the opposite direction, but to the side, and therefore this reflection does not weaken so much as the other. I am speaking in reference to the nature of the reflection, but owing to the doubling of the force in the same place and owing to the equality of the angles and the conditions of the perpendicular, the action is stronger. And yet we must here consider that by the falling of rays at oblique angles more rays can be assembled by intersection than by rays falling at right angles, not only from the property of mirrors, as has been said, but because of rays meeting in infinite numbers in accordance with the law of incidence and reflection at oblique angles, just as happens in the air, because owing to the falling of rays of this kind and their reflection the rays intersect one another at every point in infinite number, and heat is produced. For few rays are incident perpendicularly on any body, because from a point of the agent only one perpendicular ray falls to a point of the surface acted on,

and therefore few are reflected. But an infinite number of non-perpendicular rays proceed from each point of the agent, and an infinite number corresponding to these are reflected. Then by the perpendicular falling only two are united at the same point in the air, namely, the incident ray and its equal reflected ray. But by the falling at oblique angles an infinite number intersect one another at every point in the air. And likewise incident rays penetrate reflected ones that do not belong to them, and reflected rays penetrate reflected ones in countless numbers. For at every point of the earth rays in infinite number are incident, and from the same point infinite numbers are reflected, and therefore a stronger action is produced in this way accidentally from the incident and the reflected rays at oblique angles than at right angles. Art, moreover, is able to aid nature in bringing about the action; for it can form mirrors in such a way that a great convergence of forces is produced by means of concave mirrors, and especially by those of oval shape, just as has been stated. But the principal force, namely, the straight refracted and reflected one, is stronger than the accidental, because the accidental one does not come from the agent, but from the species of the agent, and it is the species of a species, and for this reason is weaker.

Chapter II
In which the strength of action according to figures is considered.

And since the pyramid, as has been said, is required for the action of nature, we must consider that the apex of the shorter pyramid acts more strongly, both because it is less distant from the agent, and because the rays conterminal around the apex of the shorter pyramid are in closer proximity, and proximity of rays and convergence act more strongly; and this is shown in Figure 51.7. For by the thirteenth proposition of the first book of the elements of Euclid, all the angles around a single point in a surface are equal to only four right angles, therefore the four angles at the apex of the shorter pyramid equal the remaining four

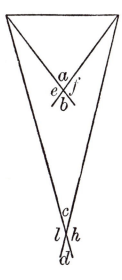

Figure 51.7

at the apex of the longer pyramid. But by the twenty-first proposition of the same book, the angle in the apex of the shorter pyramid is greater than the angle in the apex of the longer pyramid, namely, *a* is greater than *c*; and by the fifteenth proposition of the same book, angles placed opposite are equal, namely, *a* and *b*, likewise *c* and *d*; therefore *c* and *d* taken together are less than *a* and *b* taken together; therefore since the four taken together equal the other four so taken by the thirteenth proposition, of necessity *h* and *l* are greater than *f* and *e*. Wherefore the rays containing *e* are in greater proximity than the rays containing *h*. And in the same way the rays containing *f* are nearer than the rays containing *l*, and so of an infinite number of rays conterminal in the shorter pyramid, and of necessity all of them are in closer proximity than the rays conterminal in the apex of the longer pyramid. But proximity of forces is the cause of stronger action. But, however, since the forward motion of perpendicular rays is the strongest, and every deflection toward perpendiculars is stronger than deflection away from them, the rays of the longer pyramid, since they deflect more toward the perpendicular *ac, bd* will be stronger (viz. Figure 51.8). Likewise as many rays come to the apex of the longer

pyramid as to the apex of the shorter, since they are infinite in number on both sides. But the apex of the longer pyramid has the more acute angle by proposition XXI. Therefore its rays are the more united. Therefore they will burn more strongly. And we must state that these reasons are demonstrations for both conditions, but they are stronger for the first condition, and therefore they outweigh the other. Whence, as far as the last reasons can, so far do they draw conclusions, but there are other more potent ones and more effective in action.

Chapter III
Explaining how much of the surface acted on is changed and how much of the agent produces the change.

To these statements we must add that in equal spherical bodies the half of each receives the force of the other, because the extreme rays touch those bodies, and therefore they pass through the ends of the diameters, and no ray reaches any part of the other half. (See Figure 51.9.) But the lesser body receives the force of the greater in its own larger portion, because the extreme rays are not equidistant always, but converge and are able to embrace more than half of the smaller. For the diameter of the greater sphere is greater than the diameter of the smaller; and therefore rays coming from the ends of the diameter of the greater body are able to pass beyond the diameter

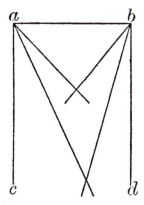

Figure 51.8

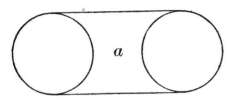

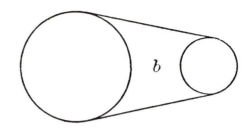

Figure 51.9

of the smaller body so as to embrace the larger portion of it; and on the contrary the smaller portion of the larger body receives the force from the smaller body, because the diameter of the smaller body does not equal the diameter of the larger, but equals some chord of the smaller portion of the larger body. And no point of a spherical body can exert a force from it except to the space which is separated from it by a line touching that body in that point from which the force acts; since from the point *a* no other line can fall between the tangent line and the spherical body, as is proved in the fifteenth proposition of the third book of the elements of Euclid. And therefore the space which is in the angle of tangency, as well as that back of the whole tangent line on the side of the body, will not receive the force from the point *a*, but all the space beyond the tangent line, in which are the points *bcde* will receive the force. (See Figure 51.10.) And all rays coming forth from the surface of the spherical body, whose direction falls to the center of that body, are perpendicular to it and such lines come forth everywhere in infinite numbers, as is shown in the figure. And yet from the same point on the surface of a body, at which the ray is perpendicular, there are an infinite number of rays on the same body, as is shown at the point *a*, and this is true of all points; but only one ray, namely, *ab*, is perpendicular to that body, because, it alone, if produced continuously and in a straight line, passes through the center of the body, and therefore it is the strongest and possesses more force by far. And those perpendicular rays, because they meet at the center of the body, are not equidistant; yet

the eye can be so far distant from the body that it does not perceive their meeting, and judges such rays to be equidistant, as we experience in the case of rays from the sun and stars, and therefore we judge the shadows of different things equidistant when they are opposite to the sun, but we do not do so in accordance with the fact. For we think that many things are equidistant, because we do not perceive their meeting, as the walls of any house seem equidistant to our sense, but they are not so, because everything with weight tends naturally to the center, and therefore the house would fall if the walls were absolutely equidistant. And the meridian circles of different states seem to be equidistant, and the meridian lines, because we do not perceive their meeting, and yet they do meet at the pole of the earth.

We should also know that rays falling to the center of the spherical body from which they come are the ones by which we judge when we consider the stars through the

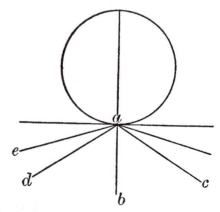

Figure 51.10

openings of instruments. Hence the astronomer and the man working with perspective, who examine matters of this kind,
make use of those rays, because they are
perceived by the senses and are strong. For
although from some portion of a spherical
body opposite to the thing acted on there
comes a pyramid with infinite rays, which
are from the individual points of that portion, and all rays converge at the apex of
the pyramid with the perpendicular ray,
yet one alone is perpendicular in a pyramid, and that perpendicular is superior in
strength, and is the axis of the pyramid and
the whole pyramid is named from it by ex-
perimenters, and it is called the ray of the
acting body, as is shown in Figure 51.11.
For let *a* be the center, and *dc* the portion
of the sun opposite to the earth, and *b* the
apex of the pyramid falling upon the earth;
it is evident that the ray *eb* falls to the center
of the sun, and no others that are of the
body of the pyramid, although they are infinite in number. For *gb* diverges from the
center of the sun, as is clear, and so do all
the others, *fb*, *cb*. And therefore it is per-

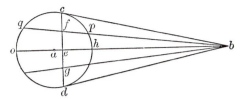

Figure 51.11

pendicular to the sun's body, and is the axis
of the pyramid, and therefore is stronger
and has more force, since force comes by
this ray from the whole depth of the sun,
which is not the case in the others. For the
diameter *ho* is longer than *pq*, and longer
than all lines falling in the circle to the side
of the diameter, and therefore receives
more of the sun's substance, and therefore
has more force. And the line *hb* is shorter
than *cb* and all other lines descending from
the portion of the sun to the earth, wherefore it has more force according to the statements made. And that which has now been
said is clear from the eighth proposition of
the third book of the elements of Euclid.

NOTES

1. The Latin of this sentence is obscure.
2. Bacon's expression for a cone.

CHAPTER 52

John Pecham

It is not certain when or precisely where John Pecham was born. The best guess is that he was born in the early or mid-1230s in the English village of Patcham near Brighton in the county of Sussex. It is most likely that his earliest education was attained at the priory of Lewes. He was then trained in the liberal arts at the Universities of Paris and Oxford. It was during his studies at Oxford that he joined the Franciscans sometime during the 1250s. Subsequently he returned to Paris to study theology, probably between 1257 and 1259. In 1269 he was awarded the doctorate in theology, after which he served for two years as regent master in theology and lector to the Franciscan friary in Paris. In 1272 he returned to Oxford to assume the position of eleventh lecturer to the Franciscan school, a post which he resigned in 1275 to assume the provincial ministership of the Franciscan order. Two years later he was appointed master in theology to the papal Curia. This appointment of Pecham to the papal court indicates the high degree of respect he had acquired to that point in his career. Theologically he stood squarely in the Augustinian camp, and he persistently fought to counteract the influence that Aristotle had exerted on Christian doctrine. Pecham was a staunch supporter of the condemnation of 1277 whereby 219 propositions were condemned as heretical to the Christian faith. These propositions were ones of Aristotelian influence.

As a consequence of the elevation of Robert Kilwardby, archbishop of Canterbury, to the College of Cardinals in 1278, Pope Nicholas III nominated Pecham for the vacated post, and on the fourth Sunday of Lent, 1279, he was consecrated archbishop of Canterbury. He went about his duties as archbishop with vigor, believing that the clergy must be above reproach. In that vein he instituted a campaign against clerical abuses. He remained archbishop until his death on December 8, 1292.

John Pecham on Vision by Reflected Rays

Part II of Pecham's *Perspectiva communis* is an analysis of the reflection of rays. In the first half, consisting of propositions 1–18, he sets forth the properties and law of reflection. It should be noted that on the one hand he endows rays with an innate property of self-diffusion, namely, self-multiplication that demands expression: ". . . the power of radiating and the onward flow of rays are not brought to an end by the opposition of a dense body of negligible transparency". In other words, if rays are obstructed in one direction, their power is such that they will diffuse themselves in another direction. On the other hand, Pecham offers a mechanistic account of reflection, and by so doing formulates the law of reflection, namely, that a "ray recoils in the same mode as that in which it would be transmitted [if it were not deflected by a reflecting surface], and consequently it must rebound at an equal angle [to the angle of incidence]". In this section of propositions, Pecham also offers data concerning the process of reflection and the nature of mirrors (e.g., there are seven types of regular reflecting surfaces, and "Nothing is seen in glass mirrors from which the lead has been scraped"). Before turning to the remaining propositions he is eager to dispel a long-standing belief that images are (somehow) impressed in mirrors. This simply cannot be the case: ". . . if a thing were impressed into the mirror, it would diffuse itself from the mirror in all directions and could be seen [in the mirror] from every direction relative to the mirror" (II.19).

In the second half of Part II Pecham concentrates on the geometry of image formation. Propositions 20 to 27 detail image formation by reflection. Propositions 28 to 54 concentrate on the perceptual errors occurring in vision by reflected rays. The subject of proposition 55 is burning mirrors, and proposition 56 discusses the twinkling of stars.

PERSPECTIVA COMMUNIS

Part II
Reflection

Preface

The investigation of mirrors is threefold: first, understanding the nature of and differences between mirrors and the manner and place of reflection; second, locating images; third, investigating the differences between [various] errors of reflection and the differences between mirrors.

The first part of this threefold investigation is consigned to the fourth, the second part to the fifth, and the third part to the sixth [book of Alhazen].

[Proposition] 1. Primary and pure secondary light and unmixed colors rebound from the surfaces of dense bodies.[1]

This is evident from experience with mirrors of iron and other materials. Moreover, because rays are reflected from the surface of the earth, heat is more intense near the

Reprinted from *John Pecham and the Science of Optics,* translated by David C. Lindberg (Madison, Milwaukee, and London: The University of Wisconsin Press, 1970), pp. 157–211. Reprinted by permission of The University of Wisconsin Press.

earth than in the middle interstice of the air[2] and [is also intense] in valleys to which rays are reflected by the density of the mountains on both sides. The reason for this is that rays of light and color are so constituted as to proceed through a transparent body, and the power of radiating and the onward flow of rays are not brought to an end by the opposition of a dense body of negligible transparency. Since the rays cannot continue in a straight line—when opposed not only by opaque and terrestrial bodies, but also by transparent bodies having a weaker kind of transparency, such as water and glass—the impulse to diffuse produces reflection.[3] Therefore, as to its nobler purity, a solar ray is reflected from water; nevertheless, some part of it enters and illuminates water. Therefore a person situated in water would be able to see the sun and moon.

[Proposition] 2. Only reflection from regular surfaces is discerned by the eye.[4]

I call those surfaces regular that are of uniform disposition in all their parts, as plane, concave, convex, and so forth. The surfaces of rough bodies are irregular, and light incident upon them is dispersed and scattered so that it cannot fall on the eye in a regular fashion. However, light is reflected from regular surfaces in the form of radiant pyramids in the same order as that in which it is received. Therefore, since sight occurs only through radiant pyramids, observation [by reflection] occurs only through such [regular] surfaces and not through others; for just as the rays, if extended in straight lines, would exhibit to the eye the object to which they belong, so they exhibit it when they have been reflected, although in a different way,[5] for it is essential to rays to manifest the bodies of which they are the likenesses.

[Proposition] 3. Reflected light or color is weaker than that which is radiated directly.[6]

This is caused not only by the separation [of the light or color] from its source, but also (and more significantly) by the weakness that results from bending. Since straightness is naturally associated with the propagation of light (as well as with every other action of nature), it arranges and orders nature, for every action is strong in proportion to its straightness; consequently, when straightness is lacking, strength must be decreased. That is why light from the sun passing through colored glass causes the color [of the glass] to radiate sensibly and to bathe facing opaque bodies in color, i.e., because rays are strong when they radiate nearly in a straight line. However, a ray reflected from a dense body cannot cause the glass to radiate sensibly, since the light must be strong enough to excite not only the color itself, but also the medium along with it; the strength of the [solar] ray penetrating the glass exceeds this [requirement] even though it is slightly refracted.

[Proposition] 4. Reflections from strongly colored surfaces affect vision slightly or not at all.[7]

As shown in the preceding proposition, the reason for this is that direct light and color are stronger than reflected light and color. However, if the [reflecting] surface is regular and highly polished, objects will be visible in it, not as they really are but vested with the color of the mirror.

[Proposition] 5. Light and color reflected from mirrors manifest to the eye the objects of which they are the species.[8]

This is evident, because a species produced by a visible object has the essential property of manifesting the object of which it is the likeness; for since the species has no permanent being in itself, it necessarily reveals the object of which it is the species. Therefore, even though it is reflected, it maintains its essence and thereby reveals the object—albeit in another position, the reason for which will be evident below.[9]

[Proposition] 6. The angles of incidence and reflection are equal, and the incident and reflected rays are in the same plane as the line erected [perpendicularly] at the point of reflection.[10]

The angle formed by the incident ray and either the surface of the mirror (on one side) or the imaginary line erected [perpendicularly] at the point of reflection (on the other side) is called the angle of incidence; the angle formed by these [i.e., the surface of the mirror and the imaginary perpendicular] and the reflected ray is called the angle of reflection. Equality of the angles is gathered from experience and proved by reason in any of several ways; for if an incident ray could advance into the depth of a mirror, it would form (with the perpendicular extended into the depth [of the mirror] at the point of reflection) an angle equal to the angle of incidence because, according to Euclid, vertical angles are equal.[11] Therefore the ray recoils in the same mode as that in which it would be transmitted [if it were not deflected by a reflecting surface], and consequently it must rebound at an equal angle [to the angle of incidence]. Accordingly, if it is incident on the mirror perpendicularly, it is reflected back on itself; if it is incident obliquely, it is reflected obliquely toward the other side. The same thing is evident in the motion of a body, since a heavy body descending vertically onto a solid body or projected perpendicularly along a line is driven back along the same line; if projected obliquely, it rebounds along a similar line on the other side.[12]

Furthermore, the perpendicular ray is stronger than [all] others, not only because of the absolute nature of the ray but also because of the mode of incidence on the object, as the exposition of Proposition 15, Part I, makes clear. Therefore the strength of the incident ray varies with the size of the angle of incidence, and the strength of the reflected ray varies with the strength of the incident ray; consequently the mode of reflection follows the mode of incidence.

It is evident also that the three lines [i.e., the incident ray, the reflected ray, and the perpendicular] are in the same plane, because a ray conforms as closely as possible to a rectilinear path, since straightness is natural to light. However, if a ray were to forsake that plane, it would be departing doubly from straightness, both by rebound and by deviation.

[Proposition] 7. Transparency is not essential to mirrors, but may be conferred on them as an accident.

For if (as is now evident) an object is exhibited in a mirror by reflected rays, transparency, through which a species proceeds into the depth of the mirror, obstructs rather than aids sight, since reflection occurs at a dense body because of its density. Therefore common glass mirrors are coated with lead. But if, as some say, transparency were essential to mirrors, mirrors would not be made of iron and steel—so far removed from transparency—nor of polished marble; but the contrary is true. Yet observation [of objects by reflection] is not efficacious in iron and such materials because of the intensity of their blackness. Nevertheless, observation [by reflection] is clearer in certain stones of weak color than in glass.

[Proposition] 8. Nothing is seen in glass mirrors from which the lead has been scraped.

The reason for this is that, although some reflection can occur from a glass surface, direct light passes through when the glass is not shaded on the other side, and its strength overcomes the reflected light, as Proposition 3 of this part makes clear. But if a dark, black cloth or something of that kind is applied [behind the mirror], the reflected light can be seen because nothing is transmitted directly through the glass, which is then of great efficacy in radiating.

[Proposition] 9. Regular reflecting surfaces are of seven types.[13]

Indeed, mirrors are plane, spherically concave or convex, pyramidal and polished either inside or outside, or columnar and polished either inside or outside. As will be evident, individual things vary in appearance according to the following seven different types [of mirrors]: plane, spherically concave and convex, pyramidal inside and outside, and columnar inside and outside. However, some surfaces are irregular, i.e., partly plane and partly convex or concave; even though such surfaces are polished, figures appear distorted in them because of irregular reflection resulting from variations in the surface.

[Proposition] 10. The matter of mirrors is intense smoothness, the form perfect polishing.[14]

By "smoothness" is meant great continuity of parts altogether free from sensible pores; therefore wood and such bodies cannot be mirrors. By "polishing" we understand the removal of all roughness. Consequently, if a body is very smooth and highly polished, it is essentially a mirror. However, so that the mirror may represent visible things clearly, it must not be sensibly colored. It is required also that it should not be covered with dust, breath, or moisture, and for this reason they say that a mirror must be wiped clean.

[Proposition] 11. Objects always appear dimmer in mirrors than by direct vision.[15]

As Proposition 3 shows, the explanation of this is that reflected forms are weaker and therefore represent [the object] more weakly. Consequently they act [on sight] weakly, for which reason a man remembers his own appearance with difficulty.[16] Furthermore, the color of the mirror is mingled with the reflected light and obscures it, and as a result the face appears tinted. Moreover, blemishes of the face remain hidden because of the weakness of reflection.

[Proposition] 12. When a luminous object is present, two pyramids of light are terminated at every point of a mirror, one incident and the other reflected.[17]

The first part of this is evident from Proposition 4 of Part I. And since light is reflected from a polished surface, the second part of the proposition follows, for thus [it follows that] a pyramid is also reflected from every point.

[Proposition] 13. A ray from every point of a luminous body is incident on every point of a facing mirror.[18]

This follows from Proposition 3 of Part I.

[Proposition] 14. A pyramid is extended from every point of a luminous body to occupy the whole surface of a facing mirror.[19]

This follows from Proposition 6 of Part I.

[Proposition] 15. From the surface of a mirror there are an infinite number of complete reflections of the form of the visible object.

This is evident from the foregoing.[20] For instance, let there be a flat object and a plane mirror. The whole species of the visible object is received not only by the whole surface of the mirror but by every part of it; and although the parts from which reflection can occur are finite in number, nevertheless they are infinite by various combinations with other parts.[21] Therefore, since reflection occurs according to the mode of incidence, an infinite number of reflections must take place from every mirror, for there is a different pyramid corresponding to each point [of the mirror] through which sight occurs. But nevertheless, the reflections are not thereby actually infinite, since they all form one body of light. Now complete reflections are those that present the entire object.

[Proposition] 16. A ray perpendicularly incident on a mirror is reflected back on itself.[22]

This follows from Proposition 6 of this part, since, if the ray were reflected along any other line, it would recoil through an angle smaller [than the angle of incidence], and the angles of incidence and reflection would not be equal.

[Proposition] 17. By aggregation reflected light becomes stronger than [directly] incident light.[23]

[This follows] because every united power is stronger[24] and because rays are weakened when dispersed and strengthened when brought together and because reflected rays that have been brought together suffice better for the production of any effect than do direct rays that have been dispersed. That is why fire can be kindled in spherical concave mirrors facing the sun; for if the mirror directly faces solar rays, all those rays converge partially on a point and partially on a line.[25] [This follows] because all rays reflected from the same circle must converge on one point, since equal angles of incidence [for all rays incident on one circle] lead to equal angles of reflection. Therefore direct light does not generate fire, because solar rays cannot converge unless refracted or reflected.

[Proposition] 18. Light is incident on and reflected from a mirror along natural lines.[26]

[This is so] because a radiant line is natural, and the essence of a ray cannot be preserved except in some width. And since the appearance [of an object] in a mirror varies with the shape of the mirror, it is clear that reflection does not occur from a mathematical point since a mathematical point has no diversity of surface.

[Proposition] 19. Forms appearing in mirrors are not seen by means of impressions made in the mirrors.[27]

Some people believe that objects appear in mirrors by means of images that are impressed in the mirrors and that the objects appear, as it were, in the images, even though the images themselves are seen first. This error has been compounded, for some say that the image is impressed into the mirror itself and exists there and acts on sight.[28] This is shown to be false in various ways, for objects are seen in iron and adamantine mirrors in which there is no transparency capable of receiving the impression. Besides, if a thing were impressed into the mirror, it would diffuse itself from the mirror in all directions and could be seen [in the mirror] from every direction relative to the mirror. [But] this is false, since the object is seen only if the eye is located in the same plane as the visible point and the point of reflection and if the angles of incidence and reflection are equal. Furthermore, [if the image were impressed into the mirror,] its size would never exceed the size of the mirror, which is false. Moreover, if an image were impressed into the mirror, it would appear there and not beyond, which is false, for the image appears at the imaginary intersection of the ray and the perpendicular. In addition, transparency of itself is not essential to mirrors, as was taught above in Proposition 7 of this part.

Therefore other people maintain that the image is impressed not into the mirror but [into the matter] at the place where the image appears, i.e., at the intersection of the ray with the perpendicular, behind the mirror. [But] this is false, since a tower [seen] in water appears to extend as far into the earth as it [actually] extends into the air. And if it is assumed that a mound of

bronze is located at the place of its image, [it should be noted that] it appears as transparent as if air or water were located there. Consequently [it is evident that] nothing is impressed there.

What then is an image? I say that it is merely the appearance of an object outside its place. For example, sometimes the eye judges one thing to be two, as was evident above,[29] because the object appears not only in its true place but also outside it. So in the present case, it is the object that is really seen in a mirror, although it is misapprehended in position and sometimes in number, as will be seen below.[30]

[Proposition] 20. In plane mirrors, and for the most part in others, the images appear at the intersection of the ray and the cathetus.[31]

The cathetus is the line dropped perpendicularly from the visible object to the surface of the mirror, whether plane or spherical. Indeed, that which is seen in a mirror appears to be located at the imaginary intersection of the ray under which the object is seen and the perpendicular dropped from the object to the surface of the mirror. This can be explained by reference to Proposition 67 of Part I, since [by that proposition] the lengths of rays are perceived by the eye. But because the reflected part of the ray acts directly on sight and sight occupies itself with that part, through its mediation the part of the ray incident on the mirror is so perceived that the whole ray is apprehended by the eye as though proceeding without interruption in a straight line; for reflection cannot be discerned by the eye, which perceives nothing except the part of the ray that [actually] conveys the qualities [of the visible object] to sight. Therefore an object seen in a mirror, if above the mirror, must appear beneath it at the imaginary intersection of the ray and the cathetus.

For example, let *ABG* [Figure 52.1] be the mirror, *CK* the visible object, and *D* the eye of the observer. Rays *KA* and *CB* fall from the visible object and are reflected to the eye along rays *AD* and *BD*. Consequently

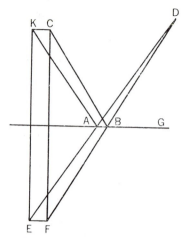

Figure 52.1

KA appears to be the [direct] continuation of *AD*, and *CB* of *BD*; it follows that *KA* and *CB* seem to be directed behind the mirror under the same angles at which they are reflected because vertical angles are equal, and *DA* falls to *E* and *DB* to *F*. Furthermore, the object appears on the aforementioned perpendicular, i.e., the cathetus, exactly as in its true location. I say "in plane mirrors" because the appearance [of images] is more faithful there [than in curved mirrors]. And this is the explanation of the Author in Book 5, Chapter 2.[32]

[Proposition] 21. Altitudes appear inverted in mirrors placed beneath them.[33]

This is evident from the previous proposition; nevertheless it is relevant [here], since in plane mirrors the visible object appears to extend as far below the mirror as it actually projects above. This is demonstrated as follows. Let the cathetus *CEF* [Figure 52.2] fall from the visible point *C*, let *BGF* be the ray under which *C* is seen, and let *CG* be the ray falling from the visible object. It is certain, then, that sides *EG* and *GC* are equal to sides *GE* and *GF* in triangles *CEG* and *FEG*, as the previous proposition shows, and that angle *CGE* is equal to angle *EGF* because vertical angles are equal and angles of incidence are equal to angles of reflection. Therefore base *CE* is

equal to base *EF*; consequently the object appears as far beyond or below the mirror as it actually is above. The same thing would occur if the eye should look at itself, even though the ray would [then] be incident perpendicularly, because (as has been said)[34] the ray itself is perceived. Moreover the ray is not [exactly] perpendicular in its natural state of being but only in the imagination. Therefore in truth it inclines, and the demonstration proceeds as above. The case is different for other [than plane] mirrors, however, as will be evident below.[35]

[Proposition] 22. In plane mirrors directly opposite, figures appear turned around, and right appears opposite left and vice versa.[36]

The first part of this proposition is evident from the foregoing; for it follows that the higher appears lower, from which it follows that the front appears at the rear. Furthermore, the second part follows because an object appears opposite itself in a mirror, and the object and image have right opposite left and vice versa. But the reason why the image should, on this account, appear opposite is that the part of the ray acting on the eye is directed to the opposite side, and therefore the entire ray is received as though extended in that direction. Consequently the object appears at its extremity.

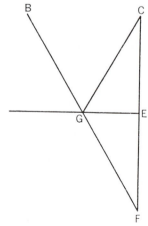

Figure 52.2

[Proposition] 23. Only one image [of a single object] appears in a plane mirror.

Let *A* [Figure 52.3] be an object visible in mirror *BEG*, let *F* be the eye, and let sight occur by means of incident ray *AE* and reflected ray *EF*. I say that point *A* cannot be reflected to point *F* by any point on the mirror other than *E*; if it could, let that point be the one onto which ray *AC* falls. Then since reflection [of this latter ray] will be at an angle equal [to its angle of incidence] and since the angle of incidence [at] *C* is greater than the angle of incidence [at] *E* because the former is the angle exterior to *E* in triangle *AEC*, the angle of reflection associated with *C* will be greater than the angle of reflection [at] *E*.[37] Therefore it is impossible for rays *CK* and *EF* to intersect at a point on the side of the mirror toward *K* and *F*, for angle *BEF* and angle *GEF* have a sum equal to two right angles; therefore angle *BEF* and angle *GCK* (which is larger than angle *GEF*) have a sum larger than two right angles. Consequently lines *FE* and *KC* intersect beyond the mirror and not on the near side, by the fourth postulate of the first book of Euclid.[38] Furthermore, if the point of reflection is other than *E*, [by virtue of a shift of the point] not lengthwise (as assumed) but in breadth,[39] it would be possible to drop a perpendicular from the eye [to this new point of reflection] parallel to the perpendicular erected at the other point; thus there would be more than one perpendicular leading from a single point [to a plane surface], which is impossible. And this demonstration concerning reflection holds for one eye.[40]

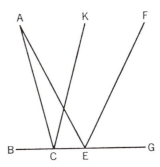

Figure 52.3

[Proposition] 24. When the parts of a broken mirror have been shifted from their positions, several images appear.[41]

Experience makes this evident, because if the parts of a broken mirror are fitted together in the same positions they occupied before breaking, the images will be no more numerous in the broken than in an unbroken mirror. Indeed multiplication of images is not the result of breaking but of alteration of the positions of the parts, for several images appear in an unbroken concave mirror, as will be evident below.[42] But since, as Propositions 12 and 15 have taught, reflection occurs at every point of a mirror and, [if the mirror is broken,] in various directions through alteration of the positions of the broken parts, it is possible for the reflected rays to converge at the same place so that the various images appear simultaneously, manifesting not several things but one. Furthermore, it is for a similar reason that several images of one luminous body appear when a mirror is placed in water, for reflection occurs at the surface of the water, [and] since light rays proceed into the depth of the water, they must [also] be reflected when they encounter the mirror; because of the diversity of the position and surface of the mirror [relative to the water surface] another image of the same luminous body must appear. Therefore I do not believe, as it seems to many and as it has sometimes erroneously seemed to me, that a star appears along with the sun; rather, separate images of the sun are produced because of the difference [in position] between the surface of the water and that of the mirror. However, only a very strong light produces several images in this way, since light is weakened by entering the water and becomes still weaker after reflection from the mirror; consequently it can scarcely generate a sensible impression unless it was originally very strong.

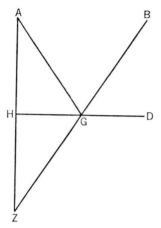

Figure 52.4

[Proposition] 25. The image seen in a plane mirror by two eyes is single.[43]

The explanation of this is that, although the points at which reflection [from one object] takes place are different for each eye, nevertheless the planes of reflection[44] intersect in the cathetus, and the sight of both eyes is terminated at the same thing, as can be seen by applying the demonstration of Proposition 20 to each eye.

[Proposition] 26. There are four principal points in every plane of reflection and what is outside that plane cannot be seen.[45]

These four points are the center of the eye, the point perceived, the end of the axis (i.e., of the perpendicular [to all the tunics of the eye] dropped from the center of the eye to the mirror),[46] and the point of reflection. And what is outside that surface is not seen, as is evident from Proposition 23.

[Proposition] 27. To find the point of reflection in a plane mirror.[47]

Let A [Figure 52.4] be the visible point, B the center of the eye, and DGH the mirror. Let cathetus AH be drawn and extended to Z, as far behind the mirror as A is in front of it, and let straight line BZ be drawn through point G of the mirror. I say that G is the point of reflection. Thus draw ray

AG; now angle ZGH and angle DGB are equal because they are [vertically] opposite each other. Likewise angles ZGH and HGA are equal because triangles HZG and HGA are equal, as was shown above.[48] Consequently angles HGA and DGB are equal, and reflection takes place at point G and no other. Nevertheless one object can appear as two in a plane mirror because of the elongation of the visible object from the axis, as was shown above to happen with an object visible directly.[49]

[Proposition] 28. In plane mirrors, the true shapes and sizes [of objects] appear.[50]

Let FLR [Figure 52.5] be a plane mirror, above which is situated length ZH; draw rays ZL and HR reflected to the eye E, and draw perpendiculars ZS and HK from points Z and H. Since the perpendiculars are parallel, the image at their [lower] extremities will be of the same size as ZH. Thus the size appears the same as [when seen] directly. The shape also [appears] the same because any part appears as far below the mirror as it is above the mirror, as was shown previously.[51] Therefore the parts [of an object] must retain the same relative order as they have in reality. Nevertheless, in plane mirrors a body appears smaller than its true size for the same reason as [that which operates] in direct vision, namely,

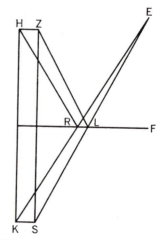

Figure 52.5

distance.[52] It is true, therefore, that a slight error does occur in plane mirrors, but merely in position and in those things that are common to all mirrors, as shown above in Propositions 3 and 4 of this part and in others.

[Proposition] 29. All errors that occur in plane mirrors occur [also] in convex spherical mirrors.[53]

Indeed the causes of error are common [to both kinds of mirrors]: sometimes that light is weakened by reflection and sometimes that the object appears outside its true place and opposite itself, as was seen above.[54] But more errors occur [in convex spherical mirrors] than in plane mirrors, as will be evident [below].[55]

[Proposition] 30. In convex spherical mirrors the image appears at the intersection of the ray and the cathetus, i.e., the line dropped [from the object] to the center of the sphere.[56]

This can be proved by experience and [can be shown to result] from natural causes, as it was for plane mirrors above.[57] Nevertheless plane mirrors and convex spherical mirrors differ in that an object always appears as far below a plane mirror as it actually is above it, whereas in a convex spherical mirror the image appears sometimes on the surface of the mirror, sometimes inside the mirror, and sometimes outside it.[58] For example, let E [Figure 52.6] be the visible point, G the eye, N the point of reflection, and D the center of the sphere. It is clear that the image is located at K. However if the visible object should be placed at B, the image would appear at O; if the visible object should be placed still closer to the sphere, the image would appear outside the sphere, as will be evident by careful investigation.[59]

The point of reflection is easy to find in these [mirrors] when the eye and the visible object are at exactly equal distances from the sphere.[60] Otherwise the length [of time required] to find the point is greater than the difficulty or utility, as can be seen

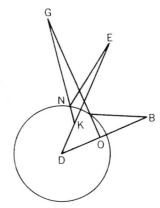

Figure 52.6

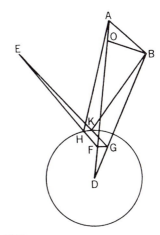

Figure 52.7

by examining the section [in Alhazen's *Perspectiva*] on images.[61] From that section also it is apparent that the image in convex spherical mirrors is nearer the mirror than is the visible object, [a relationship] which is in contrast to [that for] plane mirrors as shown above.[62]

[Proposition] 31. In convex spherical mirrors the parts of an object appear ordered as they actually are.[63]

For example, let the visible object be AB [Figure 52.7], the center of the mirror D, and the eye E. It is clear that ray EH inter-

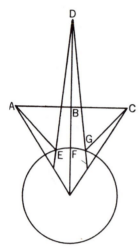

Figure 52.8 The manuscripts err unanimously in drawing this figure, confusing incident rays *AE* and *CG* with the perpendiculars to the surface of the mirror. I have not drawn the image of *ABC* or indicated the location of the image of point *B*, since these do not appear in the manuscripts, and it is not certain that Pecham was capable of establishing their exact location.

sects the perpendicular [from *A*] at point *F* and that ray *EK* [intersects the perpendicular from *B*] at point *G*. Therefore the image *GF* will indeed be smaller than the visible object; nevertheless, the parts [of the object] appear distinct and in order.[64] But if the visible object were placed in the same location, with its diameter [aligned] like *OB*, the same judgment would hold, as is evident because the lines have been drawn to *OB* exactly as to *AB*.[65]

[Proposition] 32. Straight things usually appear curved in convex spherical mirrors.[66]

This curving is to be understood not as a bending in toward the center of the mirror but as a turning away from the mirror.[67] For example, let *ABC* [Figure 52.8] be the visible object and *D* the eye, which is not in the same plane as the visible object [and the center of the mirror]; and let the object be reflected to the eye through [rays] *DE*, *DF*, and *DG*. Consequently the object appears curved, [a fact] which cannot be dem-

onstrated to the mind in a plane but will easily appear to the investigator in a solid figure. The explanation of this is that, for all mirrors, the shape of the image follows the shape of the reflecting surface, for reflection takes place at the surface according to its shape. And since the visible object appears, it is necessary also that curvature of the object should appear not as a bending back toward the mirror but as a turning away from it; and this is applicable when the eye is not in the same plane as the visible line and the center of the sphere.[68] It is through action of the same cause that faces appear monstrous in irregular surfaces such as certain mirrors full of shallow depressions. Nevertheless in the aforesaid mirrors straight things sometimes appear straight,[69] namely, if the visible line and the center of the sphere are in the same plane as the eye. For example, let *LM* [Figure 52.9] be the visible object, *N* the eye, and *O* and *P* the points of reflection; it is clear that the image will be straight line *QR*.

[Proposition] 33. In convex spherical mirrors the images are usually smaller than the visible objects.[70]

The explanation of this is twofold. First, as was seen above, the intersection of the rays with the perpendicular is closer to the eye than it is in plane mirrors.[71] However, as the length of rays proceeding from the

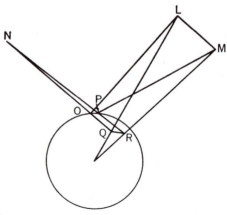

Figure 52.9

same point is greater, so also is the separation between their ends; and conversely, as the rays are shorter, the separation between their ends is smaller. Therefore from the same demonstration that showed the image and visible object to be of equal size in plane mirrors, it follows that the image is smaller than the visible object in convex spherical mirrors. Second, I maintain that reflection occurs from a larger surface area in plane than in convex spherical mirrors, as the author of the book *De speculis* proves.[72] The reason for this is that rays reflected from convex surfaces are more widely dispersed than those reflected from plane surfaces because of the declination of the circle from which reflection occurs. Therefore, in order that the rays may impinge on the eye, reflection must take place from a smaller surface, and consequently the object appears smaller. This is the theory of the author of the book *De speculis*.

These things are to be understood as the more usual case, since in convex spherical mirrors there are positions in which the object appears according to its true size and other positions in which it appears larger, as is proved in Book 6 of the *Perspectiva*,[73] namely, when the image is not parallel to the visible object and forms an acute angle with a ray falling very close to the center [of the mirror]; for then the image can be equal to or larger than [the object]. This was unknown to the author of the book *De speculis*. Indeed, since the object is oriented obliquely with respect to the mirror, one ray is shorter than the other; thus, because of the oblique approach [of its rays], the image can be equal to or larger than the object.[74]

[Proposition] 34. The smaller a convex [spherical] mirror is, the smaller is the image that appears in it.

The reason for this is clear, since, as a sphere becomes smaller, the intersection [of a ray] with the perpendicular is closer to the center, and the place occupied by the image is narrower because it is seen to be met by a shorter radius.

[Proposition] 35. The same errors occur in convex columnar mirrors as in plane and spherical mirrors.[75]

This discussion concerns round columns, which conform to planes in longitude and to spheres in roundness; therefore they participate in the errors of both.

[Proposition] 36. There are three modes of reflection in [convex] columnar mirrors.[76]

Reflection can occur from the longitude of the column, from a transverse section, or from an oblique section intermediate between the other two.[77] When reflection occurs from the longitude as in plane mirrors, i.e., when the visible line is parallel to the axis of the column, the image is located at the intersection of the ray with the perpendicular dropped [from the object] to the axis of the column; and the object appears exactly as in plane mirrors, with the exception that, since reflection occurs from a natural line, the object must appear curved, as was seen above in connection with convex [spherical] mirrors.[78] But if reflection takes place from a transverse section of the column, i.e., from a circular line parallel to the base of the column, the image is located in the plane of the circle of reflection;[79] and the appearance is somewhat similar to that in [convex] spherical mirrors, as described above,[80] so that the image can be located within the circle, outside it, or on it. Nevertheless the object appears smaller than in [convex] spherical mirrors. Furthermore, when reflection occurs in the intermediate fashion, the size [of the image] varies as the section approaches more closely the latitude or longitude of the column; and again the image can be located outside, inside, or on [the surface of] the mirror.[81]

[Proposition] 37. Reflections are multiplied in convex pyramidal mirrors just as in columnar mirrors.[82]

This is evident, since reflection can occur from the longitude of the pyramid, from its latitude, or in an intermediate mode, and the images are correspondingly diverse, just as in columnar mirrors. The location and shape of the images vary in the same way.[83] However, pyramidal mirrors differ in that the object appears pyramidal in them for the same reason as that for which it appears columnar in a column. Nevertheless reflection of one object from one point to one place occurs as in columnar and other convex mirrors.

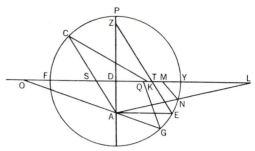

Figure 52.10

[Proposition] 38. In pyramidal mirrors the image becomes smaller as the place of reflection approaches the vertex.

This is apparent from what was said about convex spherical mirrors above in Proposition 34.

[Proposition] 39. Since it is possible for a ray not to intersect the perpendicular in concave spherical mirrors, the location of the image must be different from the foregoing.[84]

For example, let *FPY* [Figure 52.10] be a concave mirror with its center at *D*. Draw diameter *DA* and let *A* be the eye. Draw another diameter *YF* intersecting the first one perpendicularly, draw *AE* parallel to it, and mark points *M*, *T*, *K*, and *Q* on diameter *YF*; it is clear, then, that *AE* does not intersect the perpendicular [*YF*].[85] *M* is reflected from point *N*, and [the extension of the ray incident on the eye] intersects the perpendicular outside the mirror at point *L*. *T* is reflected from *E* and does not intersect the perpendicular.[86] *K* is reflected from point *C* and intersects the perpendicular at point *S*.[87] *Q* is reflected from point *G* and intersects [the perpendicular] at point *O*. However, if we consider point *Z* on diameter *DA*, it also can be reflected from point *E*, and ray *AE* intersects perpendicular *ZD* only in the eye itself.[88]

Therefore the image of point *M* is located beyond the mirror at *L*, the image of *K* behind the eye at *S*,[89] the image of *Q* behind the mirror at *O*,[90] [the image of] *Z* in the eye itself,[91] and the image of *T* in the mirror. Since *T* is a divisible point,[92] it should appear beyond the mirror according to its

higher part, but within the mirror according to its lower part.[93] However, since form is one, it must appear in the intermediate place, namely, on the mirror itself at point *E*. Nevertheless, in these various appearances, the truth of the image is not perceived except when the image is located beyond the mirror or between the eye and the mirror.[94] Thus those images that appear in the eye itself or behind the head do not have their appearance certified as does an object [directly] visible, because it is not natural for sight to perceive forms unless they are opposite the face.

[Proposition] 40. Objects located at the center of a concave mirror are not seen.

[Such an object] cannot be seen by reflection, since its rays fall perpendicularly on the surface of the mirror. Consequently they return on themselves and so turn aside to no point outside the center; and since the eye is outside the center, it cannot see that which is in the center.

[Proposition] 41. An eye located at the center of a concave spherical mirror sees only itself.[95]

This follows indirectly from the foregoing, since rays from an object located outside the center fall obliquely onto the surface of the mirror. It follows that the rays are reflected to the opposite side and not into the center, for the angles of incidence and reflection are equal.

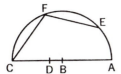

Figure 52.11

[Proposition] 42. An eye situated on the radius of a concave spherical mirror sees [by reflection] nothing situated on that radius.[96]

Let *ABC* [Figure 52.11] be the diameter, and let the eye be at point *D* on side *BC* of the diameter. I say that it is impossible for [a ray from] any point on line *BC* to return [by reflection] to *D*. But if it could, [let the point be *C* and] let [its ray] fall [onto the mirror] along line *CF*. It is clear that it will be reflected at an angle equal [to the angle of incidence], and consequently the reflected line will be a chord of equal length, such as *EF*, which cannot be on the same side [of the diameter as *D*]. Therefore it must be reflected to the other side.

[Proposition] 43. The image can be located at any point on the diameter of a concave mirror, however far that diameter may be extended.[97]

For example, let *AMG* [Figure 52.12] be a circle, *AG* its diameter, and *D* its center. Let another diameter, *ME*, be taken, and let *E* be the eye. Clearly *L* is seen at *Z* if angle *DTL* equals angle *DTE*. Similarly point *C* is reflected from *B* to *E* and is seen at *L*.[98] Therefore according to the various positions of the visible object, the image can be seen in [any] part of the diameter, extended however far, so long as it is not out of all proportion to the size of the mirror.

[Proposition] 44. It is possible for a visible point, reflected from several [different] points in a spherical concave mirror, to have a single image.[99]

Although reflection occurs at several places at the same time, it is not therefore

necessary for different images to appear, since all the visual rays in such observation intersect the cathetus at the same point; this is true when the center of the eye and the visible object are situated on the same diameter, for then it is possible for a single image to exist even though reflection occurs from any point on the [great] circle [whose plane is perpendicular to that diameter]. For example, let *ABZG* [Figure 52.13] be a mirror and *AZ* the diameter on which the visible object *H* and the center of the eye *E* are located. I say that reflection

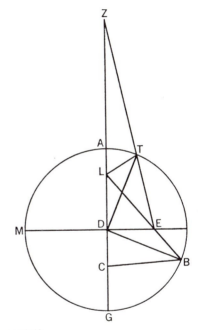

Figure 52.12

Figure 52.13

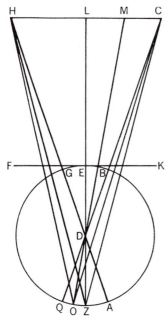

Figure 52.14

occurs at point G because triangle HGD equals triangle DGE, as is evident from [the equality of] the sides and angles that are above D; [therefore] the image is located at point E. Reflection occurs at point B for the same reason, and the image is located in the same place. Indeed reflection occurs in like manner from the whole circle represented by line BG; nevertheless there is but a single image, namely, at E. By "the circle" I mean that which is described if point G is moved circularly while diameter AZ is regarded as stationary.[100]

[Proposition] 45. When the visible object and the eye are located outside the sphere on separate diameters, reflection occurs at one point only.[101]

For example, let C [Figure 52.14] be the visible object, H the center of the eye, D the center of the sphere, and draw lines HD and CD. It is clear that plane HDC cuts the sphere of the concave mirror along circle EBAG. Therefore C is reflected to H only by some point on this circle, as is evident from Proposition 26, above.[102] It is certain that

reflection does not occur from arc GB because the line dropped from H falls on its exterior rather than on its interior. Therefore it will be reflected from arc QA, at the extremities of which CD and HD are terminated. Nevertheless there is only one point on this arc from which reflection can occur, namely, Z, which is the end of line LD, which divides angle HDC into equal parts; draw lines CZ and HZ. It follows, then, if HD and CD are equal, that triangle DCZ is equal to triangle HDZ; consequently angles HZD and DZC are equal.

But if HD were smaller than CD, or vice versa, so that the object of vision and the eye were unequally distant [from the sphere], it would make no difference, for if tangent KF is drawn (or else a line cutting through the circle and reducing those lines [HD and CD] to equality), the same thing follows. And reflection can occur at no other point [than Z] of arc QA; for if it could, let that point be O and draw lines HO and CO. It is clear that ZC is smaller than CO since [the latter] is nearer the center, and HO is smaller than HZ for the same reason. Assume line ODM dividing angle HOC into equal parts;[103] then since HZL and CZL are similar triangles, the proportion of CZ and HZ will be the same as that of CL to HL. Also the proportion of CO to HO will be as CM to HM, and that is impossible.[104] Therefore that from which it follows [is also impossible], namely, that reflection occurs at point O. However, these demonstrations hold [only] when the two points, namely, the visible object and the center of the eye, are outside the sphere and beyond the tangent drawn at the end of the line dividing the angle of the diameters [GDB] into equal parts.[105]

[Proposition] 46. It is possible for one object to have two images in a concave mirror.[106]

It should be understood that there are two requirements for an object to have two images. The first requirement is for reflection to the eye to occur from several parts of the mirror. The second is that the image be located at different places for different

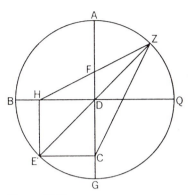

Figure 52.15

reflections; I say "different places" [meaning places separated] by a sensible distance. Therefore, depending on its position relative to the mirror, an object can have two, three, or four images, but no more. For instance, let *BDQ* and *ADG* [Figure 52.15] be two diameters of the mirror intersecting perpendicularly. Also draw a third diameter *EDZ* dividing angle *BDG* into equal parts, and from point *E*, the end of this intermediate diameter, draw two perpendiculars *EC* and *EH* to the first two diameters; triangles *ECD* and *EHD* will then be equal. Now if the eye should be placed at *H* and the object of vision at *C*, the form of *C* would be reflected from point *E* to *H*, and the image would be located at *E* because *EH* and *CD* are parallel.[107] *C* can also be reflected from point *Z* because triangles *CDZ* and *HDZ* are equal, as can easily be proved because *DZ* is common and vertical angles are equal; furthermore angle *QDA* is divided into equal parts [by diameter *EDZ*]. However, [when the object and the eye are] in this position, reflection cannot occur from any other parts of the mirror, as is evident by a repetition of the demonstration of the preceding proposition. At any rate, the second image is located at *F*.

[Proposition] 47. It is possible for one object to have three images in a concave mirror.[108]

Assuming this is so, take two points[109] on different diameters, one inside the cir-

cle[110] and the other on the circumference of the circle or outside. And if a [second] circle is drawn including these two points along with the center of the mirror, then if the [second] circle intersects the circle of the mirror in one place,[111] reflection will take place from one arc only; if intersection occurs in two places, reflection can take place from one point of the arc interposed between the diameters or from two or from three or sometimes from four.[112]

[Proposition] 48. It is possible for one object to have four images in a concave mirror.

For example, let *ABGQ* [Figure 52.16] be a mirror as above, and let *D* be the center; assume two diameters, *AG* and *QB*, and let *EZ* be a third diameter dividing the angle contained by the first two into equal parts. Assume point *C* on diameter *QB* closer to the circumference than point *C* was assumed to be in that [proposition] concerning two images, and assume *AH* on *AG* equal to *QC*. I say then that *C* is reflected from points *E* and *Z*, as is evident from the above.[113] Furthermore, it is reflected also by two other points. For instance, draw a perpendicular from point *C*, which necessarily intersects *ZE* outside the sphere at point *O* because angle *DCE*, which reaches the most remote part of the sphere, is acute; therefore the perpendicular line must be incident [on *ZE*] outside the sphere. Thus draw circle *DCH*, which necessarily passes

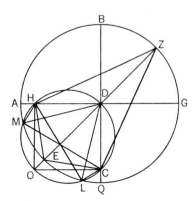

Figure 52.16

through O; since this smaller circle cuts the larger at two points, M and L, draw lines HM, DM, CM, CL, DL, and HL. Now angles CLD and DLH are equal because they intercept equal arcs of the smaller circle, namely, fourths;[114] therefore C can be reflected from L [to the eye at H]. For the same reason angles DMH and DMC are equal; consequently C can be reflected from point M [to the eye at H]. And so point C will have four images.

[Proposition] 49. Things are of confused and doubtful appearance only in concave mirrors.

The reason for this is that only in these mirrors does a thing appear in or behind the eye. But the eye is not designed to receive the forms of things unless they are opposite the face. Therefore things that appear otherwise must be of confused and doubtful appearance.[115]

[Proposition] 50. In concave [spherical] mirrors things sometimes appear reversed and sometimes inverted.[116]

This is easily demonstrated from the book *De speculis*,[117] since rays converge in one place and not in another. When they intersect, however, those objects that are before the place of intersection of the rays appear inverted: those that are beyond appear as they are [in reality].[118] For example, ray BA [Figure 52.17] is reflected to E and ray BG to D.[119] Since the rays intersect at point Z, objects located before that intersection must appear different from those that are beyond, for those that are before appear inverted as in plane mirrors and for the same reason, while those that are beyond appear as they are [in reality]. This is demonstrated [in *De speculis*] according to the principle that things seen under higher rays appear higher. For although the image at the intersection of EO and DQ appears inverted,[120] nevertheless the disposition of the rays that excite the eye is more effective

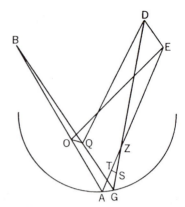

Figure 52.17

in altering sight than is the disposition of the perpendiculars, since the latter are imaginary lines.[121] But if the author of the book *De speculis* has not comprehended this, I believe he has erred. However, if a more lengthy demonstration would please anyone, he should consult the sixth book of the *Perspectiva*.[122] But if the lower part of ST, which is between the place of intersection [and the mirror], is seen by means of a higher ray, and vice versa, it obviously appears inverted, and the inversion is easily evident by extension of the perpendiculars somewhere beyond the mirror.[123]

[Proposition] 51. In concave [spherical] mirrors, objects sometimes appear equal [to their true size], sometimes larger, and sometimes smaller.

This is demonstrated laboriously and at length in Book 6 of the *Perspectiva*.[124] However, it may be gathered briefly from previous considerations, for those things that are before the intersection of the rays appear larger than they actually are, while those that are beyond, according to different positions, can appear larger, smaller, or equal, depending on whether they are farther from or closer to the intersection. From this it is apparent also that [images] are larger as they are more remote from the mirror.[125]

[Proposition] 52. In concave mirrors objects sometimes appear straight, sometimes concave,[126] and sometimes convex according to different positions.

This was unknown to the author of the book *De speculis*, who attributed a curved appearance to images in all positions.[127] However, the opposite conclusion is amply demonstrated in Book 6, Chapter 7 [of the *Perspectiva* of Alhazen].[128] Moreover, the truth of this proposition is evident by the converse of that which was said in Propositions 32 and 33 of this part.[129]

[Proposition] 53. The same errors occur in concave cylindrical mirrors as in concave spherical mirrors.

This is amply demonstrated in Book 6, Chapter 8 [of the *Perspectiva* of Alhazen],[130] but since [its truth] is highly probable, it is unnecessary to labor [here] in its demonstration. This is true of all the aforesaid errors—of the number of images, of position, and of the straightness and curvature of images.

[Proposition] 54. All errors that occur in concave cylindrical mirrors occur [also] in concave pyramidal mirrors.

This [follows] from Book 6, Chapter 9 [of the *Perspectiva*][131] and is clearly evident from the foregoing.

[Proposition] 55. Fire is kindled in concave mirrors facing the sun.[132]

If the mirror is a portion of a sphere and faces the sun directly, fire is kindled in its center at the intersection of the reflected rays and the incident rays. This is not so, however, in mirrors that are concave but of irregular shape, fabricated by the method taught in the book *De speculis comburentibus*;[133] for in such mirrors all rays are reflected outside the place of incidence [on the reflecting surface], near or far according as the mirror is more or less concave. All the rays reflected from such a mirror converge at one point so as to rarefy and ignite the air. In concave mirrors of spherical shape, on the other hand, reflection of all rays to one point occurs only from a single circle, and therefore concave spherical mirrors kindle fire weakly.[134]

[Proposition] 56. Certain stars appear to twinkle because they reflect solar rays.[135]

For since stars are solid bodies of uniform surface, their surfaces must be reflective, and consequently they reflect solar rays. But since celestial bodies are continually moved, the angle of incidence is continually varied, and the resulting sensible variation in reflection produces a certain appearance of vibration. The author of the *Perspectiva*, however, does not mention this; nevertheless it does not seem to me that the whole cause of twinkling should be attributed to a defect of the eyes; nor, apparently, can any effort or straining of the rays[136] effect this by itself, since we see a gilded surface opposite the sun glitter, and since things that the eye perceives with the greatest ease seem to sparkle when bathed in an intense and very clear light. Moreover, sight is as defective in the perception of some of the planets as in the perception of other stars, [and yet the planets do not twinkle]. Furthermore, Canis Minor and certain other fixed stars are seen more clearly than the others even though there is no greater exertion by sight nor greater reflection [of solar rays] than with the others. Therefore, although a defect in sight could contribute to this [twinkling], it does not suffice.

But perhaps you will argue that, if stars are mirrors, then in seeing stars we should see the sun. For the same reason, [you say,] planets ought to twinkle. To the first remark I reply that, even if the whole sky were a mirror, an eye located at the center would see only itself, as is evident from Proposition 41 of this part. Therefore since the angles of incidence and reflection are equal, a solar ray falling on a star is reflected either back on itself, if it is perpendicular, or to the other side, if it is not perpendicular, and consequently not to the earth. To the second assertion I reply that planets do not twinkle, because they are nearby, for a solar ray falling on the body of a fixed star has a large angle of incidence, because of the remoteness of the star, and consequently a large angle of reflection.[137] Therefore because of the elongation of the ray from the star, sight is somehow capable of perceiving the difference between stellar light and solar light reflected from a star.

Conversely, the angle formed by the incident and reflected rays at the surfaces of planetary bodies is smaller because they are nearby; consequently our sight does not distinguish between light of the [planetary] star itself and solar light reflected from that star.

Here Ends Part II

Referred Propositions Part I and Cited Texts

[*Proposition*] 3 {3}. *Any point of a luminous or illuminated object simultaneously illuminates the whole medium adjacent to it.*

This is proved by an effect, for any point of a luminous or colored object is visible in any part whatsoever of the adjacent medium. But the point is seen only by making an impression on the eye. Therefore the point makes an impression on every part of the medium. {This will be more clearly evident below, where it is proved that any point of an object seen in a mirror fills the whole surface of the mirror with its species.}

[*Proposition*] 4 {4}. *The pyramid of light originating from the whole luminous or illuminated object terminates at any point of the medium.*

This is proved as follows. If any point of a luminous object illuminates any point of the medium, then the whole luminous object illuminates every point [individually]. [But] this can be true only if light falls to the point in the form of a pyramid, under which the object can be seen.

[*Proposition*] 6. *Radiant pyramids proceeding from the same or different surfaces differ in effective strength and weakness at different points in the medium.*

{Although, contrary to this, it should be known that all the pyramids in a single body of illumination constitute essentially one light, nevertheless they differ virtually,

i.e., in efficacy. In the same way, when a stone is thrown into water, distinct circles are generated, which nevertheless do not differentiate the water; hence in a sense the water is not of all [different] sorts. Light departs powerfully from any point on a luminous body, and the more nearly perpendicular, the stronger it is; therefore as pyramids proceed more obliquely from the surface of a luminous body, they are without doubt correspondingly weaker, and as they are more nearly perpendicular, they are correspondingly stronger. This is why without cultivation the diversity of earthly plants is so great, so that now a nettle springs up and then, almost in the middle, an herb of a contrary species. Therefore what Rabbi Moses [Maimonides] says— that individual stars in heaven correspond to individual plants on the earth—is unnecessary, since different crops can be produced by the power of the same star according to the diversity of pyramids, i.e., by the star's second, third, or fourth degree from the sun or Mars, with the concurring influence of other bright stars.}

[*Proposition*] 15 {30}. *A ray of light or color, when obliquely incident on a denser medium, is refracted toward the perpendicular.*

Although this is taught in the seventh book of the *Perspectiva*, I consider it necessary to examine it here. The universal cause of refraction is variation in transparency, for greater transparency has less resistance to light {than does the lesser transparency

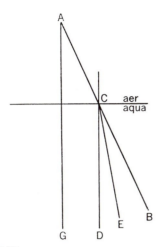

Figure 52.18

the other hand, a ray perpendicularly incident on any medium is unrefracted because it is not weakened by the interposition of the transparent body, for every ray is more suited to perpendicular than to oblique motion. For example, perpendicular *AG* falls from the luminous body *A* through air onto water and is not refracted at all. [Ray] *AC*, which would proceed to *B* if the [second] medium were of the same transparency [as the first], falls obliquely and is refracted toward perpendicular *DC*, falling to *E*.

[Proposition] 19 {17}. Shorter pyramids, because of their shortness, are in some respects stronger and in other respects weaker than pyramids proceeding farther from the same base.

of a denser medium}. Therefore, since there is variation in the ease with which media may be traversed, it will necessarily be found that the direction of the ray in the second medium (the one farther from the luminous object) is proportioned to its direction in the first medium as the resistance of the second medium to the resistance of the first. Traversal [of the medium] is strongest, however, for rays that enter or emerge perpendicularly, and traversal by a nonperpendicular ray is weaker as it diverges from the perpendicular and stronger as it approaches the perpendicular. Therefore a ray meeting a denser and more resistant medium must assume a stronger position, closer to the direct path. Consequently, in order that traversal of the second medium should be commensurate with traversal of the first, the [refracted] ray bends toward the perpendicular erected at the point of incidence on the second medium. Wherefore, it is evident that the strongest position is the perpendicular—i.e., perpendicular incidence on the medium, not perpendicular emergence from the luminous body. Also, it should not be thought that the ray bends toward the stronger position as by choice, but rather that traversal of the first medium impels a proportional traversal of the second, as is evident in the figure [Figure 52.18]. On

Indeed, shorter pyramids are necessarily more obtuse because they are shorter, as the first book of Euclid makes clear. But in obtuse pyramids, as the angle of the vertex becomes more obtuse, the rays that intersect to form vertices approach more closely the opposite sides of the pyramid. For example, let *ABC* [Figure 52.19] be an obtuse pyramid, and let side *AC* be extended to *D* and *BC* to *E*. Then, since angle *ACB* equals angle *ECD* because they are vertically opposite, these two angles necessarily become larger as the remaining two angles [*ACE* and *BCD*] become smaller; and as the former [two angles] become larger, the alternate rays approach each other. Thus ray *CD* approaches ray *BC*, and vice versa, with the enlargement of angle *DCE*. However, light has the property of gaining

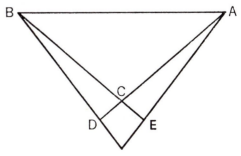

Figure 52.19

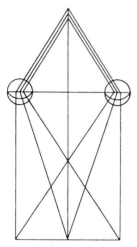

Figure 52.20

strength by approach to another light. Therefore shorter pyramids are stronger by nature and not merely by the cause assigned in Proposition 18. On the other hand, light is more nearly united in a long pyramid than in a shorter one, except at the vertex; and in this respect the longer pyramid exceeds the shorter [in strength]. Nevertheless, the absolute strength of shorter pyramids is greater [than that of longer pyramids]. Thus mountains are naturally warmer, although they may be cooled accidentally in accordance with their approach to the middle interstice [of the air].

[*Proposition*] *32 {35}. The duality of the eyes must be reduced to unity.*

The benevolence of the Creator has provided that there should be two eyes so that if an injury befalls one, the other remains. However, their source is as follows. Two hollow nerves originate in the anterior part of the cerebrum and are directed toward the face. At first these are joined and form a single nerve, but then they branch into two [nerves] at the two hollow openings beneath the forehead; here they are spread apart, and on the ends of these nerves the eyes are formed. Accordingly, the species of visible things are received by both eyes so that, if the species were not united, one

thing would appear as two. This is evident also when a finger is placed under the eye and one eye is elevated from its [customary] position: one thing [then] looks like two because the species received through the two eyes are not joined in the common nerve. Therefore [if vision is to be single,] species must be brought together in the common nerve and united there.

[*Proposition*] *35 {38}. It is necessary for only one of all the rays incident on the eye to pass through unrefracted.*

The explanation of this is that it is impossible for more than one line to be perpendicular to [each of several] eccentric spheres. Therefore with the exception of the line passing through all the centers, called the axis, the entire pyramid of radiation under which an object is seen is refracted upon entrance into the interior glacial humor.

[*Proposition*] *67 {70}. The lengths of rays can be perceived by sight.*

This is evident from experience with mirrors, wherein the object is believed to be at the end of radial lines, which are all judged to be extended continuously and rectiline-

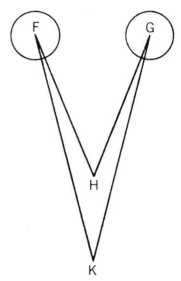

Figure 52.21

arly and through which one examines the part [of the object] that acts on sight. For this reason the species acting on the eye exhibits to the eye not only the object but also the ray serving as intermediary, the end of which is the species itself; [this is true] even though sight cannot be fixed on the ray because the entire ray is the likeness of something else. Nevertheless, a very strong argument for the emission of rays [from the eye] can be drawn from this proposition.

[*Proposition*] *80 {84}. An object appears double when it has a sensibly different position relative to the two axes.*

If the visible object is to the right of one axis and to the left of the other, the object appears double because of the sensible difference. For example, if the axes of the eyes *F* and *G* [Figure 52.21] are fixed on point *H* with a steady gaze, *K* will appear double—and similarly *H* [will appear double when the gaze is fixed on *K*]—because each is to the right of one axis and to the left of the other. Furthermore, if a point is on the same side of both axes but has a large dec-

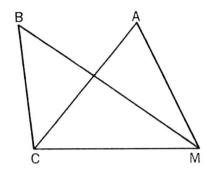

Figure 52.22

lination with respect to one, there is a sensible variation between the angles formed by the axes and the rays under which the object is seen; as before, the single object appears double. For example, point *M* [Figure 52.22] is on the same side of both axis *AC* and axis *BC*. Nevertheless, because of the great difference between angles *MAC* and *MBC*, there is diversity of position in the eye, and one object is seen as two. An object can appear double in other ways also, as was shown above.

ABBREVIATIONS

For works cited frequently in the notes, the abbreviations that follow have been used. Citations of proposition numbers unaccompanied by the name of the author or work (e.g., "Proposition II.20") refer to the present edition of the *Perspectiva communis*.

Alhazen, *Opt. thes.*	*Opticae thesaurus Alhazeni Arabis libri septem, nunc primum editi a Federico Risnero* (Basel, 1572).
Bacon, *De mult. spec.*	Roger Bacon, *De multiplicatione specierum* , included in vol. 2 of *The "Opus Majus" of Roger Bacon*, ed. J. H. Bridges (3 vols.; London, 1900). (No volume number is given in references to *De mult. spec.*, vol. 2 being understood.)
Bacon, *Opus maius*	*The "Opus Majus" of Roger Bacon*, ed. J. H. Bridges (3 vols.; London, 1900).
BGPM	*Beiträge zur Geschichte der Philosophie des Mittelalters.*
Björnbo and Vogl	Axel Anthon Björnbo and Sebastian Vogl, "Alkindi, Tideus, und Pseudo-Euklid. Drei optische Werke," *Abhandlung zur Geschichte der mathematischen Wissenschaften*, vol. 26, pt. 3 (1912), pp. 1–176.
Grosseteste, *Phil. Werke*	*Die philosphiscen Werke des Robert Grosseteste*, ed. Ludwig Baur (*BGPM*, vol. 9 [Münster, 1912]).
Reg. epist.	*Registrum epistolarum fratris Johannis Peckham archiepiscopi Cantuariensis*, ed. Charles T. Martin (3 vols.; London, 1882–85).

Witelo, *Optica*   *Vitellonis Thuringopoloni opticae libri decem. Instaurati, figuris novis illus-*
trati atque aucti: infinitisque erroribus, quibus antea scatebant, expurgati a
Federico Risnero (Basel, 1572). (Bound with the *Opticae thesaurus* of
Alhazen.)

NOTES

1. On reflection, see Pseudo-Euclid, *De speculis*, in Björnbo and Vogl, pp. 97–101, 104–05; Alkindi, *De aspectibus*, ibid., pp. 28–36; Alhazen, *Opt. thes.*, bks. 4–6, pp. 102–230; Grosseteste, *De lineis*, in *Phil. Werke*, pp. 61–63; Bacon, *Opus maius*, pt. V.iii, dist. 1 (ed. Bridges, vol. 2, pp. 130–46); Bacon, *De mult. spec.*, bk. 2, pp. 463–64, 478–91; Witelo, *Optica*, bks. 5–9, pp. 189–403.
2. Cf. Proposition I.19{17}.
3. Rays of light and color are reflected, Pecham explains, because it is their nature to diffuse themselves only through transparent media. When rays of light and color encounter bodies possessing little or no transparency, they are unable to continue in a straight line and so diffuse themselves back through the transparent medium at angles equal to the angles of incidence. When rays of light and color proceeding through air encounter a medium, such as water, with a lower degree of transparency than air, the rays diffuse themselves in two directions: they penetrate the interface and illuminate the water, but they are also reflected at equal angles. Thus Pecham endows rays with an innate property of self-diffusion or self-multiplication that requires expression; if diffusion is obstructed in one direction, it immediately assumes another.

   However, there are remarks in the *Perspectiva communis* suggestive of a more mechanistic explanation of reflection. After describing how rays are reflected perpendicularly or obliquely depending on their mode of incidence, Pecham writes, "The same thing is evident in the motion of a body, since a heavy body descending vertically onto a solid body or projected perpendicularly along a line is driven back along the same line; if projected obliquely, it rebounds along a similar line on the other side." However, the claim is not that light rays are reflected by virtue of the same causes that operate in the rebound of a heavy body, but only that both are reflected with the same equality of angles; the analogy is intended to elucidate only the geometry of reflection, not the causes of reflection or the nature of the reflected entity.
4. Cf. Grosseteste, *De lineis*, in *Phil. Werke*, pp. 62–63; Bacon, *Opus maius*, pt. V.iii, dist. 1, chap. 1 (ed. Bridges, vol. 2, pp. 130–31).
5. I.e., altered in position.
6. Cf. Alhazen, *Opt. thes.*, bk. 4, sec. 4, p. 103; Grosseteste, *De lineis*, in *Phil. Werke*, pp. 62–63.
7. Cf. Alhazen, *Opt. thes.*, bk. 4, sec. 3, p. 103.
8. Cf. Proposition I.67{70}; Bacon, *De mult. spec.*, bk. 1, chap. 2, p. 431.
9. Proposition II.20.
10. Cf. Hero, *Catoptrica*, in *Opera*, vol. 2, fasc. I, pp. 324–30; Pseudo-Euclid, *De speculis*, in Björnbo and Vogl, p. 100; Alkindi, *De aspectibus*, ibid., pp. 29–31; Ptolemy, *Optica*, bk. 3 (ed. Lejeune, p. 88); Alhazen, *Opt. thes.*, bk. 4, secs. 10–13, pp. 108–09; Grosseteste, *De lineis*, in *Phil. Werke*, p. 62; Bacon, *Opus maius*, pt. V.iii, dist. 1, chap. 1 (ed. Bridges, vol. 2, pp. 131–32); Bacon, *De mult. spec.*, bk. 2, chap. 6, pp. 481–86; Witelo, *Optica*, bk. 5, secs. 10–17, pp. 195–98.
11. Euclid, *Elements*, I.15, trans. Heath, vol. I, pp. 277–79.
12. It appears that the mechanical analogy presented here is meant to explain the equality of angles in the reflection of light, not the causes of reflection or the nature of the reflected entity. See n. 3 to this part, just above.
13. Cf. Bacon, *Opus maius*, pt. V.iii, dist. 1, chap. 2 (ed. Bridges, vol. 2, pp. 134–35).
14. Cf. Alhazen, *Opt. thes.*, bk. 4, sec. 6, p. 104.
15. Cf. ibid., bk. 6, sec. 1, p. 188.
16. Cf. James 1:23–24.
17. Cf. Alhazen, *Opt. thes.*, bk. 4, sec. 14, p. 111.
18. Cf. ibid.
19. Cf. ibid.
20. Propositions II.12–II.14.
21. The number of individual points from which reflection can occur is finite, since sight takes place through "natural lines" having breadth (Proposition II.18) and thereby requiring a point of finite area for reflection. However, when Pecham claims that "the parts from which reflection can occur . . . are infinite by various combinations with other parts," he appears to mean that, although a finite number of points (or small areas) exhausts the surface area of the mirror, those small areas can be defined in

an infinite number of ways. Such reasoning is consistent with the argument later in the proposition that all the pyramids through which reflection occurs constitute a single body of light.

22. Cf. Alhazen, *Opt. thes.*, bk. 4, sec. 11, p. 108.
23. Cf. Pseudo-Euclid, *De speculis*, in Björnbo and Vogl, pp. 104–05; Grosseteste, *De lineis*, in *Phil. Werke*, p. 63; Bacon, *Opus maius*, pt. IV, dist. 2, chap. 2 (ed. Bridges, vol. 1, pp. 115–17); Bacon, *De mult. spec.*, bk. 2, chap. 7, pp. 486–91; Witelo, *Optica*, bk. 9, pp. 392–403; *Perspectiva communis*, Proposition II.55.
24. "*plus infinita.*" I have rendered this expression freely.
25. I.e., all rays incident on a given circle of the mirror converge to a point, and the collection of all such points constitutes a line. The inability of a spherical concave mirror to focus all the incident solar rays on a single point was understood also by Bacon and Witelo (see references in n. 23, just above). Alhazen does not make this point in his *Perspectiva*, but Pecham may have learned it from his *De speculis comburentibus*; see H. J. J. Winter and W. Arafat, "Ibn al-Haitham on the Paraboloidal Focussing Mirror," *Journal Royal Asiatic Society of Bengal*, Ser. 3, vol. 15, nos. 1–2 (Calcutta, 1949), pp. 25–40. Cf. Pseudo-Euclid, *De speculis*, in Björnbo and Vogl, pp. 104–05.
26. Cf. Alhazen, *Opt. thes.*, bk. 4, sec. 16, p. 112; Bacon, *De mult. spec.*, bk. 2, chap. 1, pp. 459–60; Witelo, *Optica*, bk. 2, sec. 3, pp. 63–64.
27. Cf. Alhazen, *Opt. thes.*, bk. 4, sec. 20, pp. 113–14; Bacon, *Opus maius*, pt. V.iii, dist. 1, chap. 2 (ed. Bridges, vol. 2, pp. 132–33). An elaborate analysis of image formation by reflection dominates Part II of the *Perspectiva communis*. But before proceeding to the geometry of image formation, Pecham finds it expedient to offer a causal account. He argues forcefully that forms or images are not seen in mirrors by virtue of having been impressed in the mirrors. In the first place, objects are seen by reflection in hard mirrors possessing no transparency capable of receiving an impression. Second, if an impression were made in the matter of the mirror, it could be seen from every direction and not just from that direction satisfying the law of reflection. Third, images are often larger than the mirror. Finally, images are located not in the plane of the mirror, but behind it. This final objection suggests an alternative account of reflection: the image is impressed in the matter where it appears to be situated, i.e., behind the mirror at the intersection of the cathetus and the rectilinear extension of the reflected ray. But this cannot be true either, since a tower or mountain may appear extended into the earth, which is obviously incapable of receiving such an impression.
28. This and the preceding sentence are somewhat obscure. The question at issue seems to be: What acts on sight, the object or the image? The view described in the first sentence is that the object acts on sight through the mediation of the image; in the second sentence, that the image alone acts on sight.
29. Propositions I.32{35} and I.80{84}.
30. Propositions II.20–II.22, II.24, and II.46–II.48.
31. Cf. Alhazen, *Opt. thes.*, bk. 5, chap. 2, pp. 125–31. Bacon, *Opus maius*, pt. V.iii, dist. 1, chap. 3 (ed. Bridges, vol. 2, pp. 134–36), admits the truth of the principle only for plane mirrors. On this principle, see Turbayne, "Ancient Optical Principle." Although the principle was demonstrated to be inexact as early as the seventeenth century, it continues to be taught in modern texts on *geometrical* optics; its fault is that it ignores the psychological factors in sight.
32. Alhazen, *Opt. thes.*, pp. 125–88.
33. Cf. ibid., bk. 5, sec. 11, pp. 131–32.
34. Proposition I.67{70}.
35. Propositions II.30, II.36, and II.39.
36. "*Facies*" could be translated "faces" as well as "figures"; cf. Proposition II.9.
37. By Euclid, *Elements*, I.16, trans. Heath, vol. 1, pp. 279–81.
38. This is the fourth postulate of *Preclarissimus liber elementorum Euclidis perspicacissimi: in artem Geometrie incipit quam foelicissime*, trans. Adelard of Bath, ed. John Campanus (Venice, 1482), but the fifth postulate of Heath's English translation.
39. By this Pecham means a shift of point C (in Figure 52.3) through a distance perpendicular to the plane of the paper on which the figure is printed.
40. I.e., for monocular vision. Roughly half the manuscripts read "*circuli*" for "*oculi*," but with that reading the statement becomes unintelligible.
41. Cf. Bacon, *Opus maius*, pt. V.iii, dist. 1, chap. 4 (ed. Bridges, vol. 2, pp. 144–46).
42. Propositions II.46–II.48.
43. Cf. Alhazen, *Opt. thes.*, bk. 5, sec. 15, pp. 133–34.
44. There is a plane of reflection for each eye, formed by the incident ray, reflected ray, and perpendicular.
45. Cf. Alhazen, *Opt. thes.*, bk. 4, sec. 23, p. 115. The "plane of reflection" is defined in n. 44, just above.
46. The axis is defined in Proposition I.35{38}. The syntax at this point implies that the axis is perpendicular to the mirror, but Pecham means that the axis is perpendicular to the tunics and humors of the eye.
47. Cf. Alhazen, *Opt. thes.*, bk. 5, sec. 12, p. 132.
48. Proposition II.21.
49. Proposition I.80{84}.

50. It is evident that Pecham is comparing the absolute size of the object and image, rather than the angles subtended at the observer's eye. This concern with absolute sizes characterizes his treatment of reflection and distinguishes it from his treatment of refraction. Pecham follows Alhazen in this peculiarity; see Alhazen, *Opt. thes.*, bk. 6, sec. 2, p. 189. But see n. 125, below.

51. Proposition II.21.

52. I.e., the image, though as large as the object in a plane mirror, is more remote from the observer than is the object and therefore subtends a smaller angle.

53. A more literal translation would be "spherical mirrors polished on the outside," but elsewhere (e.g., Proposition II.9) Pecham refers to such mirrors as *convex*, and the circumlocution seems to have no point. Cf. Alhazen, *Opt. thes.*, bk. 6, chap. 4, pp. 189–205.

54. Propositions II.3, II.11, II.20, and II.22.

55. Propositions II.46–II.52.

56. Cf. Alhazen, *Opt. thes.*, bk. 5, sec. 16, p. 134; Bacon, *Opus maius*, pt. V.iii, dist. 1, chap. 3 (ed. Bridges, vol. 2, pp. 135–36); Euclid, *Catoptrica*, trans. Ver Eecke, p. 99, definitions 2 and 5. On this principle, see n. 31 to this part, just above.

57. Proposition II.20.

58. Although it is impossible for the image to be located anywhere except *behind* a convex mirror, it is true as Pecham asserts that the image may be inside, outside, or on the surface. As Figure 52.23 below illustrates, when the image is outside or on the surface of the mirror, it is nevertheless *behind* that surface of the mirror closest to the observer (i.e., over the "horizon"). In the figure, E is the eye, O the object, I the image, and C the center of the mirror.

59. Moving the object closer to a spherical mirror will not necessarily move the image outside the sphere as Pecham implies, since the position of the image is a function not solely of the distance between the object and the mirror but also of the angular separation between the object and observer (as measured from the center of the sphere). However, moving the object closer to the mirror reduces the angular separation between the object and observer required to produce an image outside the mirror.

60. Cf. Alhazen, *Opt. thes.*, bk. 5, sec. 31, p. 142.

61. Ibid., sec. 39, pp. 150–51.

62. Proposition II.21. Pecham's conclusion is correct.

63. Cf. Alhazen, *Opt. thes.*, bk. 6, secs. 4–5, pp. 189–90.

64. In spherical mirrors (according to Pecham) the image of any point is located on the perpendicular dropped from the point to the center of the sphere (Proposition II.31). Since the perpendiculars maintain a fixed order, points on the image are ordered exactly as the corresponding points on the object.

65. Since the same lines serve as perpendiculars (see n. 64) for both AB and OB, the argument establishing a similar order for points of the object and image of AB applies also to OB.

66. Cf. Alhazen, *Opt. thes.*, bk. 6, secs. 11–23, pp. 199–205; Bacon, *Opus maius*, pt. V.iii, dist. 1, chap. 3 (ed. Bridges, vol. 2, pp. 135–37). Here, as on a number of other occasions, Pecham writes "*spericus*" when he means spherically convex.

67. The two alternatives, bending in toward the center of the mirror and turning away from the mirror, the former of which is denied while the latter is affirmed, seem to describe identical states of affairs, since the image in convex mirrors is always between the reflecting surface and its center of curvature. It is probable that Pecham has misstated an idea that he correctly states later in the proposition: "it is necessary . . . that curvature of the object should appear not as a bending back toward the mirror but as a turning away from it." On the other hand, it is possible that Pecham is here simply stating that the *cause* of curvature is associated not with the center but with the surface of the mirror.

68. Cf. Alhazen, *Opt. thes.*, bk. 6, sec. 12, pp. 199–200.

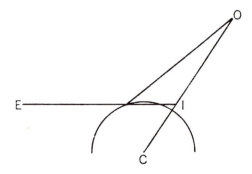

Figure 52.23

69. The manuscripts read "straight things sometimes appear *bent*," but emendation is clearly required. Cf. Alhazen, *Opt. thes.*, bk. 6, sec. 18, p. 202.
70. Pecham has in mind the absolute sizes of object and image, in which case the image is *always* smaller than the object; see n. 50, just above. See also Alhazen, *Opt. thes.*, bk. 6, secs. 5–6, pp. 190–97. Here, as on a number of other occasions Pecham writes "*spericus*," when he means spherically convex.
71. Proposition II.30.
72. The closest approach to this idea that I can locate is in the Pseudo-Euclidean *Catoptrica*, Proposition 4, trans. Ver Eecke, pp. 102–03.
73. Alhazen, *Opt. thes.*, bk. 6, secs. 5–6, pp. 190–97.
74. Pecham errs in thinking that the image (considered absolutely) can be equal to or larger than the object in a convex spherical mirror. The simplest case, in which the object directly faces the mirror, is illustrated in Figure 52.24 (below). This is the case for which Pecham correctly asserts that the image is smaller than the object. However, Pecham believes that, if the object should be oriented obliquely with respect to the mirror, the image might be of equal or greater size. Figure 52.25 (p. 826), in which the image is of greater length than the object, illustrates what he had in mind. However, *CD* is larger than *AB* in Figure 52.20 only because the figure is carelessly drawn; if care is taken to make the angles of incidence and reflection equal, the obliquely situated object will always have an image smaller than itself, as illustrated in Figure 52.26 (p. 826). Had Pecham been referring to the sizes of the object and image as seen by an observer, i.e., the ratio of angles subtended at the eye, his statement would be entirely correct, but it is evident from the form of the proposition that this is not what he had in mind. In each of Figures 52.24–26, *E* is the eye, *AB* the object, and *CD* the image.
75. On the errors of convex columnar mirrors, see Alhazen, *Opt. thes.*, bk. 6, chap. 5, pp. 205–09.
76. Here, as in the discussion of spherical mirrors, the convexity of the mirrors is not explicitly stated, but understood.
77. I.e., an elliptical section.
78. Proposition II.32; see also Proposition II.18.
79. "in . . . reflection." I have emended the text, which otherwise reads, "at the center of the circle of reflection." Pecham could not have intended the latter, since it is clearly contradicted by the rest of the sentence and by Proposition II.30. My emendation not only makes Pecham's statement true and consistent with what follows, but recalls his own argument of Proposition II.26.
80. Propositions II.30 and II.32.
81. For a discussion of this statement, see the n. 58, just above; the argument is identical for convex spherical and convex columnar mirrors.
82. Cf. Alhazen, *Opt. thes.*, bk. 6, secs. 30–31, pp. 209–11.
83. I.e., in the manner described in Proposition II.36.
84. Cf. Alhazen, *Opt. thes.*, bk. 5, sec. 60, p. 162; Bacon, *Opus maius*, pt. V.iii, dist. 1, chap. 4 (ed. Bridges, vol. 2, pp. 137–39).
85. Because *AE* and *YF* are parallel. It is evident from the context that the perpendicular Pecham has in mind is *YF*, which is the perpendicular to the surface of the mirror passing through points *M, T, K,* and *Q*.
86. I.e., the reflected ray, *AE*, corresponding to incident ray *TE*, does not intersect perpendicular *YF*.
87. A ray from point *K* is also reflected between *E* and *G*. Pecham has followed Alhazen in the awkward step of considering the reflection at *C*, which produces a reflected ray incident on the back of the head (since the eye is facing in the general direction of *E*) and hence not perceived. This neglect of even the

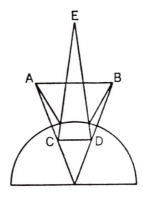

Figure 52.24

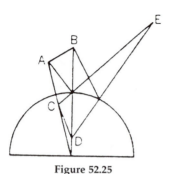

Figure 52.25

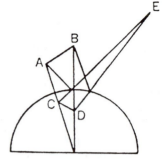

Figure 52.26

most fundamental physiological factors illustrates how purely geometrical was their approach to problems of reflection.

88. Note that the perpendicular to the surface of the mirror from point Z is line ZDA rather than line FDY.
89. But the image of K is invisible for the reasons presented in n. 87, just above. If the head were turned around, the image would be perceived at S.
90. Judged by his own concept of image formation, which is also the basis for most modern discussions of *geometrical* optics, Pecham has reached the correct conclusion. However, the presence of an observer greatly complicates the situation, introducing physiological and psychological factors, which neither Pecham nor modern geometrical optics takes into account. In fact, no observer ever has the impression that the image he is perceiving is located behind his head; rather, the image of Q would be perceived outside the mirror in the general direction of L, its precise position being determined by a number of psychological factors. On this problem, see Vasco Ronchi, *Optics: The Science of Vision*, trans. Edward Rosen (New York, 1957), pp. 135–38.
91. As is true for Q, psychological factors interfere with the principles of geometrical optics and produce an image of Z appearing somewhere beyond the mirror. See n. 90.
92. I.e., it has magnitude, as any *visible* point must. Cf. Proposition II.18.
93. The "higher part" of the point is the part closer to M, the "lower part" closer to Q. Pecham recognizes that T constitutes a transition between images formed as is the image of M and those formed as is the image of Q, and consequently he considers each half of T as producing its image differently; expressed in modern terms, T is at the focal point of the mirror. Continuing to exhibit remarkable insight, Pecham argues that, since T is a unity, its two halves cannot be perceived as two distinct entities. Thus far, Pecham's conclusions are fully correct. But when he concludes that, since the two halves of T cannot be separately perceived, T must be perceived as a whole at an intermediate position, he errs. The theory of modern *geometrical* optics predicts that an observer will perceive an infinitely large image of T located in the direction of L at an infinite distance. In fact, however, psychological and physiological factors determine that the image will be perceived at only a short distance beyond the mirror, in the direction of L. See Ronchi, *Optics: the Science of Vision*, pp. 131–34; for a more popular presentation of the argument, see Vasco Ronchi, "Twenty Embarrassing Questions," trans. Edward Rosen, *Atti della Fondazione Giorgio Ronchi*, vol. 13 (1958), pp. 86–87.
94. Here Pecham recognizes the awkwardness, from a geometrical and physiological standpoint, of an image located in or behind the eye, though he was unaware of the compensating psychological factors mentioned above in nn. 90 and 93. However, his conclusion appears to run counter to his own theory of vision, since rays from an object at Z should assume the same order on the surface of the glacial humor as the points on the object from which they originated, just as do rays from an object at M. Yet, Pecham asserts, the object at M is clearly perceived while the object at Z is not.
95. Cf. Alhazen, *Opt. thes.*, bk. 5, sec. 62, p. 163.
96. Except *itself*, of course. Cf. ibid., sec. 63, p. 163.
97. Cf. ibid., sec. 68, pp. 165–66.
98. See n. 90, above.
99. Cf. Alhazen, *Opt. thes.*, bk. 5, secs. 65, 69, pp. 164, 166–67.
100. I.e., the great circle passing through B and G (Figure 52.13) and perpendicular to diameter AZ. Pecham correctly affirms the truth of Alhazen's claim that reflection from the visible point to the eye may occur from any point of the great circle, but Alhazen and Pecham are wrong in supposing that the observer perceives an image as though situated within his eye; see n. 90, above.
101. Cf. Alhazen, *Opt. thes.*, bk. 5, sec. 70, pp. 167–68.

102. "Proposition 26." I have emended the text, the manuscripts reading "Proposition 18." Yet Pecham's statement, which does not follow at all from Proposition II.18, does not follow directly from Proposition II.26. In general terms, however, Proposition II.26 asserts that the plane of reflection, containing the eye, the object, and the point of reflection, is perpendicular to the reflecting surface, a condition fulfilled by circle *EBAG* referred to in Proposition II.45. Thus circle *EBAG* must coincide with the plane of reflection and consequently must contain the point of reflection.

103. Line *ODM* (Figure 52.14) obviously fails to divide angle *HOC* into equal parts, but, as Pecham realized (following Alhazen), the line bisecting angle *HOC* must pass through the center of the sphere, for otherwise it would not be perpendicular to the reflecting surface at the point of reflection. The demonstration proceeding from this construction is valid.

104. Since *ODM* (Figure 52.14) passes through the center of the sphere, if *O* is to the left of *Z*, *M* must be to the right of *L*. Consequently it is impossible that *CO/HO* = *CM/HM*, since *CO* is greater than *HO* while *CM* is smaller than *HM*.

105. Pecham insists that the object and the eye be outside the sphere, since, if they were not, reflection could occur at two points (as demonstrated in Proposition II.46), contrary to the proposition being demonstrated. However, there is no reason why the object and eye must be outside the tangent line.

106. Cf. Alhazen, *Opt. thes.*, bk. 5, sec. 71, p. 168.

107. The image would be located at *E* (Figure 52.15) by the reasoning of Proposition II.39.

108. Cf. Alhazen, *Opt. thes.*, bk. 5, sec. 86, pp. 179–81; Witelo, *Optica*, bk. 8, sec. 40, pp. 342–44.

109. The point seen and the center of the eye.

110. I.e., the mirror.

111. Pecham does not mean that there is only one point of intersection between the two circles considered in their entirety, for that would be true only if they were tangent. He means that there is but one point of intersection along the arc intercepted by the two diameters; see n. 112, just below.

112. This proposition seems to be a somewhat garbled version of Alhazen's demonstration in the passage cited in n. 108. Briefly summarized, Alhazen argues that when one of the two points (*A*) is inside mirror *BDNL* (Figure 52.27) and the other point (*B*) is on the circumference, the circle (*BGA*) passing through these two points and the center of the mirror intersects are *BL* at a single point *T*. With this arrangement, there will be either three or four reflections and the same number of images: one or two from arc *TB*, one from arc *LT*, and one from arc *ND*. However, when both points *A* and *B* are within the circle of the mirror (as in Fig. 52.28), the circle passing through them and the center of the mirror intersects *ML* at two points, *T* and *H*. Under these circumstances there will also be three or four reflections: two or three from arc *LM* and one from arc *ND*. See Witelo (reference in n. 108) for a more elaborate demonstration of the same thing.

113. Proposition II.46. *H* is the eye.

114. By Euclid, *Elements*, III.21, trans. Heath, vol. 2, pp. 49–51.

115. See nn. 90 and 93, above.

116. It is evident from the context that Pecham has spherical mirrors in mind, though the demonstration would hold as well for cylindrical mirrors.

117. Pseudo-Euclid, *Catoptrica*, Proposition 12, trans. Ver Eecke, pp. 107–08; cf. Witelo, *Optica*, bk. 8, sec. 53, p. 355; Bacon, *Opus maius*, pt. V.iii, dist. 1, chap. 4 (ed. Bridges, vol. 2, pp. 139–41).

118. The "intersection of the rays" is point *Z* (Figure 52.17). "Before the place of intersection" means before *Z* from the standpoint of the observer, as object *TS*. Pecham could not mean before intersection *Z* from the standpoint of the object, since it is the object he is trying to locate. "Beyond the intersection" means beyond *Z* from the standpoint of the observer, as object *DE*.

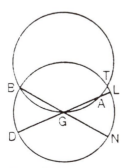

Figure 52.27

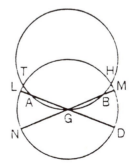

Figure 52.28

119. Since B is the eye, this is the language of the visual ray theory. The theory of visual rays also underlies Pecham's description of the location of objects before or beyond the intersection of the rays, as discussed in n. 118. That Pecham's source for this demonstration was the medieval version of the Pseudo-Euclidean *Catoptrica* is clearly indicated both by this use of the visual ray theory and by the great similarity between Pecham's demonstration and that of the Greek text of Pseudo-Euclid. It is surprising that Pecham did not translate this proposition into the language of luminous rays, as did Witelo; Bacon, in his demonstration of this same proposition, speaks in terms of both luminous rays and visual rays.

120. The intersection of EO and DQ is the center of curvature of the mirror, and no image is located there. Perhaps Pecham means the image OQ of line DE.

121. The meaning of this sentence is obscure. An examination of the particular version of *De speculis* available to Pecham might shed light on it.

122. Alhazen, *Opt. thes.*, bk. 6, secs. 41–44, pp. 216–18.

123. This proposition can be clarified by reference to the corresponding demonstration in Witelo's *Perspectiva* and its accompanying figure, reproduced here as Figure 52.29. Rays from the endpoints of object DE are reflected at points A and G to the eye at B. The image of DE is located at LN, where the rays incident on the eye intersect perpendiculars (to the mirror) DM and EM, dropped from the object through the center of the mirror, M. Since N, the uppermost point of the image, corresponds to E, the lowest point of the object, it is evident that the image is inverted with respect to the object. Consider a second object CK, so drawn as to be visible by means of the same rays as object DE. The image of CK is located at SF, where the rays incident on the eye intersect perpendiculars MC and MK dropped from the object to the surface of the mirror. It is evident from the figure that there is not inversion or reversal of this image, since corresponding points on CK and SF are directly opposite one another.

   Pecham's statement of this proposition is exceedingly obscure. In the first place, he refers several times to "the place of intersection of the rays," by which he evidently means points Z (in Fig. 52.29). He correctly identifies this as the point separating objects that have an inverted image from those that do not. (In Fig. 52.29, DE has an inverted image, but CK does not.) This point of intersection, Z, will have a different location for different objects and different observers, but the collection of all such points constitutes a surface that corresponds in position and function to the modern focal plane of the mirror, located (for spherical mirrors) about halfway between the mirror and its center of curvature.

   But a point requiring even more clarification is Pecham's conception of image inversion and image reversal. In the technical sense in which these terms are employed in modern optics, they denote only a lack of correspondence between points directly opposite each other on the object and image, i.e., the case in which the image has been flipped end for end relative to the object; inversion and reversal are geometrically indistinguishable, except that the former applies to phenomena in a vertical plane and the latter to phenomena in a horizontal plane. Thus LN (Fig. 52.29) is a reversed or inverted image of

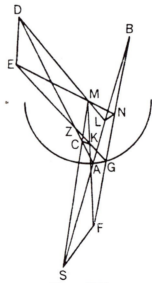

Figure 52.29

DE, while *SF* is an erect image of *CK*. According to this precise usage, then, there is neither reversal nor inversion in plane or convex mirrors. In concave mirrors, the image is reversed and inverted when the object is more than a focal length from the mirror, but unreversed and erect when the object is between the mirror and the focal plane.

Yet there is another sense in which we employ the terms "inversion" and "reversal." When a person observes himself in a plane mirror, we speak of the reversal of his image, since he is right-handed while his image is left-handed, even though corresponding points of the person and the image remain directly opposite each other. Again, a person standing on a plane mirror placed in a horizontal plane is said to have an inverted image, even though there is a direct correspondence between opposite points on the person and his image.

It is in this latter, less technical sense that Pecham employs the terms "inversion" and "reversal." This is evident from Propositions II.21 and II.22, where he refers to inversion in plane mirrors; for according to the more technical usage described above, images are inverted only in concave mirrors. In Proposition II.50, Pecham claims that objects located before the intersection of the rays, i.e., between *Z* and the mirror, "appear inverted as in plane mirrors and for the same reason." This statement is entirely correct according to Pecham's nontechnical usage of the term "inversion," though false if inversion is taken in our more technical sense. For unexplained reasons Pecham did not draw the image of such objects in his diagram, but in the final line of the proposition he refers to the advantages of so doing; such an image is included, however, in the corresponding figures of Witelo and Bacon. (Bacon refers to the incorrect figure contained in *De speculis*, and it is possible that Pecham's incomplete figure is to be explained thus; see Bacon, *Opus maius*, pt. V.iii, dist. 1, chap. 4 [ed. Bridges, vol. 2, pp. 139–41]. Note, however, that the figure appearing in Bridge's edition of Bacon's *Opus maius* is also incorrect, the error, it would seem, being due to Bridges rather than Bacon.) On the other hand, objects located beyond the intersection of the rays, Pecham says, do not appear inverted. This statement is false, for image *LN* of object *DE* (Fig. 52.29) and image *OQ* of object *DE* (Fig. 52.17) are inverted according to either the technical or nontechnical sense of inversion, as the figures reveal. Pecham's entire discussion may be obscure, but this seems to be its only outright error.

124. Alhazen, *Opt. thes.*, bk. 6, secs. 38–44, pp. 214–18.
125. Actually, for an object between the center of the mirror and the point of reflection, the absolute size of the image is greater than the absolute size of the object; for an object beyond the center, the image is smaller than the object. Apparently Pecham is here concerned with the ratio between the angles subtended at the eye of the observer by the object and the image (an exception to my earlier generalization regarding his approach to image formation by reflection—see n. 50); thus the observer's position and the obliquity of the object and image relative to the line of sight must be introduced, greatly complicating the problem and discouraging generalization.
126. The text reads "curved," but "concave" appears to be a more appropriate translation in this context.
127. Cf. Pseudo-Euclid, *Catoptrica*, Proposition 23, trans. Ver Eecke, pp. 115–16.
128. *Opt. thes.*, bk. 6, secs. 45–50, pp. 218–25.
129. Proposition 33 is not directly relevant to the topic under discussion.
130. *Opt. thes.*, bk. 6, chap. 8, pp. 225–29.
131. Ibid., chap. 9, pp. 229–30.
132. Cf. Pseudo-Euclid, *De speculis*, in Björnbo and Vogl, pp. 104–05; Bacon, *Opus maius*, pt. IV, dist. 2, chap. 2 (ed. Bridges, vol. 1, pp. 115–17); Bacon, *De mult. spec.*, bk. 1, chap. 7, pp. 486–91; Witelo, *Optica*, bk. 10, secs. 36–44, pp. 392–403.
133. Pecham is apparently referring to parabolic mirrors, undoubtedly as described in the *De speculis comburentibus* of Alhazen. See J. L. Heiberg and Eilhard Wiedemann, "Ibn al Haitams Schrift öber parabolische Hohlspiegel," *Bibliotheca Mathematica*, Ser. 3, vol. 10 (1910), pp. 201–37; Winter and 'Arafat, "Ibn al-Haitham on the Paraboloidal Focussing Mirror." On the translation of this work into Latin see Eilhard Wiedemann, "Zur Geschichte der Brennspiegel," *Annalen der Physik und Chemie*, N.S., vol. 39 (1890), pp. 126–27.
134. Cf. Proposition II.17.
135. Cf. Bacon, *Opus maius*, pt. V.ii, dist. 3, chap. 7 (ed. Bridges, vol. 2, pp. 120–26); Witelo, *Optica*, bk. 10, sec. 55, p. 449. Pecham's conclusion agrees with neither Bacon's nor Witelo's.
136. Cf. Bacon, *Opus maius*, pt. V.ii, dist. 3, chap. 7 (ed. Bridges, vol. 2, pp. 122–24). Bacon seems to use the term "*involutio*" in the sense of "straining," and I have interpreted Pecham similarly.
137. Pecham is measuring the angles with respect to the reflecting surface rather than the perpendicular to the reflecting surface; cf. Proposition II.6.

CHAPTER 53

Jean Buridan

(See Chapter Thirty-five for biography.)

Jean Buridan on Physics

From this reading it is clear that Buridan set the stage for (a) modern scientific method and (b) the physics of Galileo and Newton. He was neither impressed by nor interested in the presumed supernatural powers of God traditionally used to mask a general ignorance of physics. Furthermore, he believed it was not essential that scientific hypotheses be known with certainty. They are inductive generalizations; that is, particular principles observed to be true in many instances and false in none.

He offers his impetus theory as an alternative to the flawed analysis of Aristotle whereby the upward motion of an object required an external motive power in continuous contact with it. For example, air functions as the motive power relative to the upward motion of a stone. Buridan correctly observed that air does not contribute to the movement of projectiles, rather it inhibits it. *Experientie*, that is experiences qua experiment, verifies ". . . that impetus is continually decreased (*remittitur*) by the resisting air and by the gravity of the stone, which inclines it in a direction contrary to that in which the impetus was naturally predisposed to move it". Furthermore, if air contributed to the movement of an object with respect to its impetus, it would follow that it would move a light object (e.g., a feather) faster and farther than a heavy one (e.g., a stone). Again, experience demonstrates otherwise.

Concerning the free fall of bodies and contradicting Aristotle and Averroës, bodies closer to their natural place of earth do not accelerate or fall faster than those at a greater distance from earth. Rather, they fall at the same rate. The amount of air beneath a body does not affect the relative velocities of a body falling farther away from earth than one closer to it. The solution is "that the natural gravity of this stone remains always the same and similar before the movement, after the movement, and during the movement".

Buridan explored the possibility that the earth rotates daily from west to east on its axis. Interestingly enough, it was experimentation that led him to reject this possibility. Presupposing such rotation, an arrow shot straight up should fall noticeably to the west of its launching site. However, such is not the case. Underlying Buridan's faulty conclusion was the presumption that the earth's surface relative to its speed of rotation was much smaller than it actually is. Nevertheless, it is clear that Buridan was unusually "modern" in his thinking.

"THE IMPETUS THEORY OF PROJECTILE MOTION"
FROM *QUESTIONS ON THE EIGHT BOOKS OF*
THE PHYSICS OF ARISTOTLE

1. Book VIII, Question 12. It is sought whether a projectile after leaving the hand of the projector is moved by the air, or by what it is moved.

It is argued that it is not moved by the air, because the air seems rather to resist, since it is necessary that it be divided. Furthermore, if you say that the projector in the beginning moved the projectile and the ambient air along with it, and then that air, having been moved, moves the projectile further to such and such a distance, the doubt will return as to by what the air is moved after the projectile ceases to move. For there is just as much difficulty regarding this (the air) as there is regarding the stone which is thrown.

Aristotle takes the opposite position in the eighth [book] of this work (the *Physics*) thus: "Projectiles are moved further after the projectors are no longer in contact with them, either by antiperistasis, as some say, or by the fact that the air having been pushed, pushes with a movement swifter than the movement of impulsion by which it (the body) is carried towards its own [natural] place." He determines the same thing in the seventh and eighth [books] of this work (the *Physics*) and in the third [book] of the *De caelo*.

2. This question I judge to be very difficult because Aristotle, as it seems to me, has not solved it well. For he touches on two opinions. The first one, which he calls "antiperistasis," holds that the projectile swiftly leaves the place in which it was, and nature, not permitting a vacuum, rapidly sends air in behind to fill up the vacuum. The air moved swiftly in this way and impinging upon the projectile impels it along

Reprinted from *The Science of Mechanics in the Middle Ages*, edited by Marshall Clagett (Madison: The University of Wisconsin Press, 1959), pp. 532–38, 557–62, 594–98. Reprinted by permission of The University of Wisconsin Press.

further. This is repeated continually up to a certain distance. . . . But such a solution notwithstanding, it seems to me that this method of proceeding was without value because of many experiences *(experientie)*.

The first experience concerns the top *(trocus)* and the smith's mill (i.e. wheel—*mola fabri*) which are moved for a long time and yet do not leave their places. Hence, it is not necessary for the air to follow along to fill up the place of departure of a top of this kind and a smith's mill. So it cannot be said [that the top and the smith's mill are moved by the air] in this manner.

The second experience is this: A lance having a conical posterior as sharp as its anterior would be moved after projection just as swiftly as it would be without a sharp conical posterior. But surely the air following could not push a sharp end in this way, because the air would be easily divided by the sharpness.

The third experience is this: a ship drawn swiftly in the river even against the flow of the river, after the drawing has ceased, cannot be stopped quickly, but continues to move for a long time. And yet a sailor on deck does not feel any air from behind pushing him. He feels only the air from the front resisting [him]. Again, suppose that the said ship were loaded with grain or wood and a man were situated to the rear of the cargo. Then if the air were of such an impetus that it could push the ship along so strongly, the man would be pressed very violently between that cargo and the air following it. Experience shows this to be false. Or, at least, if the ship were loaded with grain or straw, the air following and pushing would fold over *(plico)* the stalks which were in the rear. This is all false.

3. Another opinion, which Aristotle seems to approve, is that the projector moves the air adjacent to the projectile [simultaneously] with the projectile and that

air moved swiftly has the power of moving the projectile. He does not mean by this that the same air is moved from the place of projection to the place where the projectile stops, but rather that the air joined to the projector is moved by the projector and that air having been moved moves another part of the air next to it, and that [part] moves another (i.e., the next) up to a certain distance. Hence the first air moves the projectile into the second air, and the second [air moves it] into the third air, and so on. Aristotle says, therefore, that there is not one mover but many in turn. Hence he also concludes that the movement is not continuous but consists of succeeding or contiguous entities.

But this opinion and method certainly seems to me equally as impossible as the opinion and method of the preceding view. For this method cannot solve the problem of how the top or smith's mill is turned after the hand [which sets them into motion] has been removed. Because, if you cut off the air on all sides near the smith's mill by a cloth (linteamine), the mill does not on this account stop but continues to move for a long time. Therefore it is not moved by the air.

Also a ship drawn swiftly is moved a long time after the haulers have stopped pulling it. The surrounding air does not move it, because if it were covered by a cloth and the cloth with the ambient air were withdrawn, the ship would not stop its motion on this account. And even if the ship were loaded with grain or straw and were moved by the ambient air, then that air ought to blow exterior stalks toward the front. But the contrary is evident, for the stalks are blown rather to the rear because of the resisting ambient air.

Again, the air, regardless of how fast it moves, is easily divisible. Hence it is not evident as to how it would sustain a stone of weight of one thousand pounds projected in a sling or in a machine.

Furthermore, you could, by pushing your hand, move the adjacent air, if there is nothing in your hand, just as fast or faster than if you were holding in your hand a stone which you wish to project. If, therefore, that air by reason of the velocity of its motion is of a great enough impetus to move the stone swiftly, it seems that if I were to impel air toward you equally as fast, the air ought to push you impetuously and with sensible strength. [Yet] we would not perceive this.

Also, it follows that you would throw a feather farther than a stone and something less heavy farther than something heavier, assuming equal magnitudes and shapes. Experience shows this to be false. The consequence is manifest, for the air having been moved ought to sustain or carry or move a feather more easiiy than something heavier. . . .

4. Thus we can and ought to say that in the stone or other projectile there is impressed something which is the motive force (virtus motiva) of that projectile. And this is evidently better than falling back on the statement that the air continues to move that projectile. For the air appears rather to resist. Therefore, it seems to me that it ought to be said that the motor in moving a moving body impresses (imprimit) in it a certain impetus (impetus) or a certain motive force (vis motiva) of the moving body, [which impetus acts] in the direction toward which the mover was moving the moving body, either up or down, or laterally, or circularly. And by the amount the motor moves that moving body more swiftly, by the same amount it will impress in it a stronger impetus.[1] It is by that impetus that the stone is moved after the projector ceases to move. But that impetus is continually decreased (remittitur) by the resisting air and by the gravity of the stone, which inclines it in a direction contrary to that in which the impetus was naturally predisposed to move it. Thus the movement of the stone continually becomes slower, and finally that impetus is so diminished or corrupted that the gravity of the stone wins out over it and moves the stone down to its natural place.

This method, it appears to me, ought to be supported because the other methods do not appear to be true and also because all the appearances *(apparentia)* are in harmony with this method.

5. For if anyone seeks why I project a stone farther than a feather, and iron or lead fitted to my hand farther than just as much wood, I answer that the cause of this is that the reception of all forms and natural dispositions is in matter and by reason of matter. *Hence by the amount more there is of matter, by that amount can the body receive more of that impetus and more intensely* (intensius). *Now in a dense and heavy body, other things being equal, there is more of prime matter than in a rare and light one. Hence a dense and heavy body receives more of that impetus and more intensely, just as iron can receive more calidity than wood or water of the same quantity.* Moreover, a feather receives such an impetus so weakly *(remisse)* that such an impetus is immediately destroyed by the resisting air. *And so also if light wood and heavy iron of the same volume and of the same shape are moved equally fast by a projector, the iron will be moved farther because there is impressed in it a more intense impetus, which is not so quickly corrupted as the lesser impetus would be corrupted. This also is the reason why it is more difficult to bring to rest a large smith's mill which is moving swiftly than a small one, evidently because in the large one, other things being equal, there is more impetus.* And for this reason you could throw a stone of one-half or one pound weight farther than you could a thousandth part of it. For the impetus in that thousandth part is so small that it is overcome immediately by the resisting air.

6. From this theory also appears the cause of why the natural motion of a heavy body downward is continually accelerated *(continue velocitatur).* For from the beginning only the gravity was moving it. Therefore, it moved more slowly, but in moving it impressed in the heavy body an impetus. This impetus now [acting] together with its gravity moves it. Therefore, the motion becomes faster; and by the amount it is faster, so the impetus becomes more intense. Therefore, the movement evidently becomes continually faster.

[The impetus then also explains why] one who wishes to jump a long distance drops back a way in order to run faster, so that by running he might acquire an impetus which would carry him a longer distance in the jump. Whence the person so running and jumping does not feel the air moving him, but [rather] feels the air in front strongly resisting him.

Also, since the Bible does not state that appropriate intelligences move the celestial bodies, it could be said that it does not appear necessary to posit intelligences of this kind, because it would be answered that God, when He created the world, moved each of the celestial orbs as He pleased, and in moving them He impressed in them impetuses which moved them without His having to move them any more except by the method of general influence whereby He concurs as a co-agent in all things which take place; "for thus on the seventh day He rested from all work which He had executed by committing to others the actions and the passions in turn." And these impetuses which He impressed in the celestial bodies were not decreased nor corrupted afterwards, because there was no inclination of the celestial bodies for other movements. Nor was there resistance which would be corruptive or repressive of that impetus. But this I do not say assertively, but [rather tentatively] so that I might seek from the theological masters what they might teach me in these matters as to how these things take place. . . .

7. The first [conclusion] is that that impetus is not the very local motion in which the projectile is moved, because that impetus moves the projectile and the mover produces motion. Therefore, the impetus produces that motion, and the same thing cannot produce itself. Therefore, etc.

Also since every motion arises from a motor being present and existing simultaneously with that which is moved, if the impetus were the motion, it would be necessary to assign some other motor from which that motion would arise. And the principal difficulty would return. Hence there would be no gain in positing such an impetus. But others cavil when they say that the prior part of the motion which produces the projection produces another part of the motion which is related successively and that produces another part and so on up to the cessation of the whole movement. But this is not probable, because the "producing something" ought to exist when the something is made, but the prior part of the motion does not exist when the posterior part exists, as was elsewhere stated. Hence, neither does the prior exist when the posterior is made. This consequence is obvious from this reasoning. For it was said elsewhere that motion is nothing else than "the very being produced" (ipsum fieri) and the "very being corrupted" (ipsum corumpi). Hence motion does not result when it *has been* produced (factus est) but when it *is being* produced (fit).

8. The second conclusion is that that impetus is not a purely successive thing (res), because motion is just such a thing and the definition of motion [as a successive thing] is fitting to it, as was stated elsewhere. And now it has just been affirmed that that impetus is not the local motion.

Also, since a purely successive thing is continually corrupted and produced, it continually demands a producer. But there cannot be assigned a producer of that impetus which would continue to be simultaneous with it.

9. The third conclusion is that that impetus is a thing of permanent nature (res nature permanentis), distinct from the local motion in which the projectile is moved. This is evident from the two aforesaid conclusions and from the preceding [statements]. And it is probable (verisimile) that that impetus is a quality naturally present and predisposed for moving a body in which it is impressed, just as it is said that a quality impressed in iron by a magnet moves the iron to the magnet. And it also is probable that just as that quality (the impetus) is impressed in the moving body along with the motion by the motor; so with the motion it is remitted, corrupted,

or impeded by resistance or a contrary inclination.

10. And in the same way that a luminant generating light generates light reflexively because of an obstacle, so that impetus because of an obstacle acts reflexively. It is true, however, that other causes aptly concur with that impetus for greater or longer reflection. For example, the ball which we bounce with the palm in falling to earth is reflected higher than a stone, although the stone falls more swiftly and more impetuously (impetuosius) to the earth. This is because many things are curvable or intracompressible by violence which are innately disposed to return swiftly and by themselves to their correct position or to the disposition natural to them. In thus returning, they can impetuously rush or draw something conjunct to them, as is evident in the case of the bow (arcus). Hence in this way the ball thrown to the hard ground is compressed into itself by the impetus of its motion; and immediately after striking, it returns swiftly to its sphericity by elevating itself upward. From this elevation it acquires to itself an impetus which moves it upward a long distance.

Also, it is this way with a cither cord which, put under strong tension and percussion, remains a long time in a certain vibration (tremulatio) from which its sound continues a notable time. And this takes place as follows: As a result of striking [the chord] swiftly, it is bent violently in one direction, and so it returns swiftly toward its normal straight position. But on account of the impetus, it crosses beyond the normal straight position in the contrary direction and then again returns. It does this many times. For a similar reason a bell (campana), after the ringer ceases to draw [the chord], is moved a long time, first in one direction, now in another. And it cannot be easily and quickly brought to rest.

This, then, is the exposition of the question. I would be delighted if someone would discover a more probable way of answering it. And this is the end.

"ON THE FREE FALL OF BODIES"
FROM *QUESTIONS ON THE FOUR BOOKS ON THE HEAVENS AND THE WORLD OF ARISTOTLE*

1. Book II, Question 12. Whether natural motion ought to be swifter in the end than the beginning. . . . With respect to this question it ought to be said that it is a conclusion not to be doubted factually *(quia est)*, for, as it has been said, all people perceive that the motion of a heavy body downward is continually accelerated *(magis ac magis velocitatur)*, it having been posited that it falls through a uniform medium. For everybody perceives that by the amount that a stone descends over a greater distance and falls on a man, by that amount does it more seriously injure him.

2. But the great difficulty *(dubitatio)* in this question is why this [acceleration] is so. Concerning this matter there have been many different opinions. The Commentator (Averroës) in the second book [of his commentary on the *De caelo*] ventures some obscure statements on it, declaring that a heavy body approaching the end is moved more swiftly because of a great desire for the end and because of the heating action *(calefactionem)* of its motion. From these statements two opinions have sprouted.

3. The first opinion was that motion produces heat, as it is said in the second book of this [work, the *De caelo*], and, therefore, a heavy body descending swiftly through the air makes that air hot, and consequently it (the air) becomes rarefied. The air, thus rarefied, is more easily divisible and less resistant. Now, if the resistance is diminished, it is reasonable that the movement becomes swifter.

But this argument is insufficient. In the first place, because the air in the summer is noticeably hotter than in the winter, and yet the same stone falling an equal distance in the summer and in the winter is not moved with appreciably greater speed in the summer than in the winter; nor does it strike harder. Furthermore, the air does not become hot through movement unless it is previously moved and divided. Therefore, since the air resists before there has been movement or division, the resistance is not diminished by its heating. Furthermore, a man moves his hand just as swiftly as a stone falls toward the beginning of its movement. This is apparent, because striking another person hurts him more than the falling stone, even if the stone is harder. And yet a man so moving his hand does not heat the air sensibly, since he would perceive that heating. Therefore, in the same way the stone, at least from the beginning of the case, does not thus sensibly heat the air to the extent that it ought to produce so manifest an acceleration *(velocitatio)* as is apparent at the end of the movement.

4. The other opinion which originated from the statements of the Commentator is this: Place is related to the thing placed as a final cause, as Aristotle implies and the Commentator explains in the fourth book of the *Physics*. And some say, in addition to this, that place is the cause moving the heavy body by a method of attraction, just as a magnet attracts iron. By whichever of these methods it takes place, it seems reasonable that the heavy body is moved more swiftly by the same amount that it is nearer to its natural place. This is because, if place is the moving cause, then it can move that body more strongly when the body is nearer to it, for an agent acts more strongly on something near to it than on something far away from it. And if place were nothing but the final cause which the heavy body seeks naturally and for the attainment of which the body is moved, then it seems reasonable that that natural appetite *(appetitus)* for that end is increased more from it as that end is nearer. And so it seems in every way reasonable that a heavy body is moved more swiftly by the amount that it is nearer to [its] downward place. But in

descending continually it ought to be moved more and more swiftly.

But this opinion cannot stand up. In the first place, it is against Aristotle and against the Commentator in the first book of the *De caelo*, where they assert that, if there were several worlds, the earth or the other world would be moved to the middle of this world. . . .

Furthermore, this opinion is against manifest experience, for you can lift the same stone near the earth just as easily as you can in a high place if that stone were there, for example, at the top of a tower. This would not be so if it had a stronger inclination toward the downward place when it was low than when it was high. It is responded that actually there is a greater inclination when the stone is low than when it is high, but it is not great enough for the senses to perceive. This response is not valid, because if that stone falls continually from the top of the tower to the earth, a double or triple velocity and a double or triple injury would be sensed near the earth than would be sensed higher up near the beginning of the movement. Hence, there is a double or triple cause of the velocity. And so it follows that that inclination which you posit not to be sensible or notable is not the cause of such an increase of velocity.

Again, let a stone begin to fall from a high place to the earth and another similar stone begin to fall from a low place to the earth. Then these stones, when they should be at a distance of one foot from the earth, ought to be moved equally fast and one ought not to be swifter than the other if the greater velocity should arise only from nearness to [their] natural place, because they should be equally near to [their] natural place. Yet it is manifest to the senses that the body which should fall from the high point would be moved much more quickly than that which should fall from the low point, and it would kill a man while the other stone [falling from the low point] would not hurt him.

Again, if a stone falls from an exceedingly high place through a space of ten feet

and then encountering there an obstacle comes to rest, and if a similar stone descends from a low point to the earth, also through a distance of ten feet, neither of these movements will appear to be any swifter than the other, even though one is nearer to the natural place of earth than the other.

I conclude, therefore, that the accelerated natural movements of heavy and light bodies do not arise from greater proximity to [their] natural place, but from something else that is either near or far, but which is varied by reason of the length of the motion (*ratione longitudinis motus*). Nor is the case of the magnet and the iron similar, because if the iron is nearer to the magnet, it immediately will begin to be moved more swiftly than if it were farther away. But such is not the case with a heavy body in relation to its natural place.

5. The third opinion was that the more the heavy body descends, by so much less is there air beneath it, and the less air then can resist less. And if the resistance is decreased and the moving gravity remains the same, it follows that the heavy body ought to be moved more swiftly.

But this opinion falls into the same inconsistency as the preceding one, because, as was said before, if two bodies similar throughout begin to fall, one from an exceedingly high place and the other from a low place such as a distance of ten feet from the earth, those bodies in the beginning of their motion are moved equally fast, notwithstanding the fact that one of them has a great deal of air beneath it and the other has only a little. Hence, throughout, the greater velocity does not arise from greater proximity to the earth or because the body has less air beneath it, but from the fact that that moving body is moved from a longer distance and through a longer space.

Again, it is not true that the less air in the aforementioned case resists less. This is because, when a stone is near the earth, there is still just as much air laterally as if it were farther from the earth. Hence, it is just as difficult for the divided air to give way and flee laterally [near the earth] as it was when the stone was farther from the earth. And, in addition, it is equally difficult or more difficult, when the stone is nearer the earth, for the air underneath to give way in a straight line, because the earth, which is more resistant than the air, is in the way. Hence, the imagined solution (*imaginatio*) is not valid.

6. With the [foregoing] methods of solving this question set aside, there remains, it seems to me, one necessary solution (*imaginatio*). It is my supposition that the natural gravity of this stone remains always the same and similar before the movement, after the movement, and during the movement. Hence the stone is found to be equally heavy after the movement as it was before it. I suppose also that the resistance which arises from the medium remains the same or is similar, since, as I have said, it does not appear to me that the air lower and near to the earth should be less resistant than the superior air. Rather the superior air perhaps ought to be less resistant because it is more subtle. Third, I suppose that if the moving body is the same, the total mover is the same, and the resistance also is the same or similar, the movement will remain equally swift, since the proportion of mover to moving body and to the resistance will remain [the same]. Then I add that in the movement downward of the heavy body the movement does not remain equally fast but continually becomes swifter.

From these [suppositions] it is concluded that another moving force (*movens*) concurs in that movement beyond the natural gravity which was moving [the body] from the beginning and which remains always the same. Then finally I say that this other mover is not the place which attracts the heavy body as the magnet does the iron; nor is it some force (*virtus*) existing in the place and arising either from the heavens or from something else, because it would immediately follow that the same heavy body would begin to be moved more swiftly from a low place than from a high one, and we experience the contrary of this conclusion. . . .

From these [reasons] it follows that one must imagine that a heavy body not only acquires motion unto itself from its principal mover, i.e., its gravity, but that it also acquires unto itself a certain impetus with that motion. This impetus has the power of moving the heavy body in conjunction with the permanent natural gravity. And because that impetus is acquired in common with motion, hence the swifter the motion is, the greater and stronger the impetus is. So, therefore, from the beginning the heavy body is moved by its natural gravity only; hence it is moved slowly. Afterwards it is moved by that same gravity and by the impetus acquired at the same time; consequently, it is moved more swiftly; and because the movement becomes swifter, therefore the impetus also becomes greater and stronger, and thus the heavy body is moved by its natural gravity and by that greater impetus simultaneously, and so it will again be moved faster; and thus it will always and continually be accelerated to the end. And just as the impetus is acquired in common with motion, so it is decreased or becomes deficient in common with the decrease and deficiency of the motion.

And you have an experiment [to support this position]: If you cause a large and very heavy smith's mill [i.e., a wheel] to rotate and you then cease to move it, it will still move a while longer by this impetus it has acquired. Nay, you cannot immediately bring it to rest, but on account of the resistance from the gravity of the mill, the impetus would be continually diminished until the mill would cease to move. And if the mill would last forever without some diminution or alteration of it, and there were no resistance corrupting the impetus, perhaps the mill would be moved perpetually by that impetus.

7. And thus one could imagine that it is unnecessary to posit intelligences as the movers of celestial bodies since the Holy Scriptures do not inform us that intelligences must be posited. For it could be said that when God created the celestial spheres, He began to move each of them as

He wished, and they are still moved by the impetus which He gave to them because, there being no resistance, the impetus is neither corrupted nor diminished.

You should note that some people have called that impetus "accidental gravity" and they do so aptly, because names are for felicity of expression. Whence this [name] appears to be harmonious with Aristotle and the Commentator in the first [book] of this [work, the *De caelo*] where they say that gravity would be infinite if a heavy body were moved infinitely, because by the amount that it is moved more, by that same amount is it moved more swiftly; and by the amount that it is moved more swiftly, by that amount is the gravity greater. If this is true, therefore, it is necessary that a heavy body in moving acquires continually more gravity, and that gravity is not of the same constitution (*ratio*) or nature as the first natural gravity, because the first gravity remains always even with the movement stopped, while the acquired gravity does not remain. All of these statements will appear more to be true and necessary when the violent movements of projectiles and other things are investigated. . . .

"ON THE DIURNAL ROTATION OF THE EARTH" FROM *QUESTIONS ON THE FOUR BOOKS ON THE HEAVENS AND THE WORLD OF ARISTOTLE*

1. Book II, Question 22. It is sought consequently whether the earth always is at rest in the center of the universe. . . .

This question is difficult. For in the first place there is a significant doubt as to whether the earth is directly in the middle of the universe so that its center coincides with the center of the universe. Furthermore, there is a strong doubt as to whether it is not sometimes moved rectilinearly as a whole, since we do not doubt that often many of its parts are moved, for this is apparent to us through our senses. There is also another difficult doubt as to whether the following conclusion of Aristotle is sound, namely, if the heaven is by necessity to be moved circularly forever, then it is necessary that the earth be at rest forever in the middle. There is also a fourth doubt whether in positing that the earth is moved circularly around its own center and about its own poles, all the phenomena that are apparent to us can be saved (*possent salvari omnia nobis apparentia*). Concerning this last doubt let us now speak.

2. It should be known that many people have held as probable that it is not contradictory to appearances for the earth to be moved circularly in the aforesaid manner, and that on any given natural day it makes a complete rotation from west to east by returning again to the west—that is, if some part of the earth were designated [as the part to observe]. Then it is necessary to posit that the stellar sphere would be at rest, and then night and day would take place through such a motion of the earth, so that that motion of the earth would be a diurnal motion (*motus diurnus*). The following is an example of this [kind of thing]: If anyone is moved in a ship and he imagines that he is at rest, then, should he see another ship which is truly at rest, it will appear to him that the other ship is moved. This is so because his eye would be completely in the same relationship to the other ship regardless of whether his own ship is at rest and the other moved, or the contrary situation prevailed. And so we also posit that the sphere of the sun is everywhere at rest and the earth in carrying us would be rotated. Since, however, we imagine that we are at rest, just as the man located on the ship which is moving swiftly does not perceive his own motion nor the motion of the ship, then it is certain that the sun would appear to us to rise and then to set, just as it does when it is moved and we are at rest.

3. It is true, however, that if the stellar

sphere is at rest, it is necessary to concede generally that the spheres of the planets are moving, since otherwise the planets would not change their positions relative to each other and to the fixed stars. And, therefore, this opinion imagines that any of the spheres of the planets moved evidently like the earth from west to east, but since the earth has a lesser circle, hence it makes its rotation (circulatio) in less time. Consequently, the moon makes its rotation in less time than the sun. And this is universally true, so that the earth completes its rotation in a natural day, the moon in a month, and the sun in a year, etc.

4. It is undoubtedly true that, if the situation were just as this position posits, all the celestial phenomena would appear to us just as they now appear. We should know likewise that those persons wishing to sustain this opinion, perhaps for reason of disputation, posit for it certain persuasions. . . . The third persuasion is this: To celestial bodies ought to be attributed the nobler conditions, and to the highest sphere, the noblest. But it is nobler and more perfect to be at rest than to be moved. Therefore, the highest sphere ought to be at rest.

The last persuasion is this: Just as it is better to save the appearances through fewer causes then [sic] through many, if this is possible, so it is better to save [them] by an easier way than by one more difficult. Now it is easier to move a small thing than a large one. Hence it is better to say that the earth, which is very small, is moved most swiftly and the highest sphere is at rest than to say the opposite.

5. But still this opinion is not to be followed. In the first place because it is against the authority of Aristotle and of all the astronomers (astrologi). But these people respond that authority does not demonstrate, and that it suffices astronomers that they posit a method by which appearances are saved, whether or not it is so in actuality. Appearances can be saved in either way; hence they posit the method which is more pleasing to them.

6. Others argue [against the theory of the earth's diurnal rotation] by many appearances (apparentiis). One of these is that the stars sensibly appear to us to be moved from the east to the west. But they solve this [by saying] that it would appear the same if the stars were at rest and the earth were moved from west to east.

7. Another appearance is this: If anyone were moving very swiftly on horseback, he would feel the air resisting him. Therefore, similarly, with the very swift motion of the earth in motion, we ought to feel the air noticeably resisting us. But these [supporters of the opinion] respond that the earth, the water, and the air in the lower region are moved simultaneously with diurnal motion. Consequently there is no air resisting us.

8. Another appearance is this: Since local motion heats, and therefore since we and the earth are moved so swiftly, we should be made hot. But these [supporters] respond that motion does not produce heat except by the friction (confricatio), rubbing, or separation of bodies. These [causes] would not be applicable there, since the air, water, and earth would be moved together.

9. But the last appearance which Aristotle notes is more demonstrative in the question at hand. This is that an arrow projected from a bow directly upward falls again in the same spot of the earth from which it was projected. This would not be so if the earth were moved with such velocity. Rather before the arrow falls, the part of the earth from which the arrow was projected would be a league's distance away. But still the supporters would respond that it happens so because the air, moved with the earth, carries the arrow, although the arrow appears to us to be moved simply in a straight line motion because it is being carried along with us. Therefore, we do not perceive that motion by which it is carried with the air. But this evasion is not sufficient because the violent impetus of the arrow in ascending would resist the lateral motion of the air so that it would not be moved as much as the air. This is similar to the occasion when the air

is moved by a high wind. For then an arrow projected upward is not moved as much laterally as the wind is moved, although it would be moved somewhat.

10. Then I come to the other doubts. One would be whether the earth is situated directly in the middle of the universe. It should be answered in the affirmative. For we suppose that the place [designated] absolutely (simpliciter) as "upward," insofar as one looks at this lower world, is the concave [surface] of the orb of the moon. This is so because something absolutely light, i.e., fire, is moved toward it. For since fire appears to ascend in the air, it follows that fire naturally seeks a place above the air, and this place above the air is at the concave [surface] of the orb of the moon; because no other element appears to be so swiftly moved upward as fire. Now the place downward ought to be the maximum distance from the place upward, since they are contrary places. Now that which is the maximum distance from the heaven is the middle of the universe. Therefore the middle of the universe is absolutely downward. But that which is absolutely heavy—and earth is of this sort—ought to be situated absolutely downward. Therefore, the earth naturally ought to be in the middle of the universe or be the middle of the universe.

11. But it is a significant difficulty as to whether the center of magnitude in the earth is the same as the center of gravity (medium gravitatis). It seems according to some statements that it is not. This is because if a large region of the earth is not covered with waters due to the habitation of animals and plants, and the opposite part is covered with waters, it is clear that the air which is naturally hot, and the sun, make hot the noncovered part, and thus they make it to some degree more subtle, rarer, and lighter. The covered part remains more compact and heavier. Now if one body in one part is lighter and in an opposite part heavier, the center of gravity will not be the center of magnitude. Rather with the center of gravity given, the greater magnitude will be in the lighter part, just

as in the case of balances if on one side a stone is placed and on the other side wool [and they balance], the wool will be of a much greater magnitude.

12. With this understood, it ought to be seen which of those centers is the center of the universe. It should be answered immediately that the center of the universe is the center of gravity of the earth. This is because, as Aristotle says, all parts tend toward the center of the universe through their gravity, and a part which is heavier would displace another, and thus finally it is necessary that the center of the universe coincide with the center of gravity. From these arguments it follows that the earth is nearer to the heaven in the part not covered with waters than in the covered part, and thus at the covered part there is greater declivity, and so the waters flow to that part. So, therefore, the earth, with respect to its magnitude, is not directly in the center of the universe. We commonly say, however, that it is in the center of the universe, because its center of gravity is the center of the universe.

13. By this another doubt is solved, evidently, whether the earth is sometimes moved according to its whole in a straight line. We can answer in the affirmative because from this higher [part of] the earth many parts of the earth (i.e., debris) continually flow along with the rivers to the bottom of the sea, and thus the earth is augmented in the covered part and is diminished in the uncovered part. Consequently, the center of gravity does not remain the same as it was before. Now, therefore, with the center of gravity changed, that which has newly become the center of gravity is moved so that it will coincide with the center of the universe, and that point which was the center of gravity before ascends and recedes, and thus the whole earth is elevated toward the uncovered part so that the center of gravity might always become the center of the universe. And just as I have said elsewhere, it is not apparent how it could be saved unless the mountains were consumed and destroyed sometimes, nay infinite times, if time were

eternal. Nor is any other way apparent by which such mountains could be generated. This was spoken of elsewhere, so I shall now desist. . . .

NOTES

1. The italics here and elsewhere are those of the translator.

CHAPTER 54

Nicholas of Cusa

Nicholas of Cusa, also known as Nicholas Krebs or Kryfts and as Nicholas Cusanus, was born at Kues (Cusa) on the Moselle River between Trier and Koblenz (Germany) in 1401. He attended the school of the Brothers of the Common Life in Deventer, Holland, after which he studied philosophy at Heidelberg (1416), canon law at Padua (1417–23), and theology at Cologne (1425). He received the doctorate in canon law in 1423. Records indicate that he taught for a few years at Cologne after 1425. His active presence at the Council of Basel (1431) was greatly enhanced by publication of his *De concordantia catholica*, in which he recommended a prodigious program for reform of the church and the empire, defending the superiority of a general council over the pope. As time wore on, however, he became disillusioned with the prospects of conciliar reform of the church. He changed his position upon concluding that the unity of the church could only be assured via the papacy.

Subsequently Cusa carried out several missions for Pope Eugenius IV in an effort to unify and reform the church. In 1437–38 he was a member of the commission sent to Constantinople to negotiate with the Greek Church for reunion with Rome. Between 1436 and 1440 he became a priest and was created a cardinal in 1448. He was consecrated Bishop of Brixen in 1450, the same year he was sent to Germany as a papal legate to carry out church reforms. This mission lasted sixteen months, after which he took possession of his diocese. He died at Todi, Austria, in 1464.

Given his academic background, it is not surprising that Cusa contributed a substantial number of writings to the areas of philosophy, theology, political theory, and science. His most well known philosophical work is *De docta ignorantia*, or *On Learned Ignorance*, the central thesis of which is that wisdom is a function of one's being aware of the limits of the mind in knowing the truth. Knowledge, in essence, is learned ignorance. There is no certain knowledge. Conviction that there is certain knowledge is manifest ignorance.

Nicholas of Cusa Concerning Experiments in Weight

One gets the impression from this essay that Cusa was in agreement with Roger Bacon that quantity is the most basic of the categories. And although it is somewhat of an exaggeration, one can detect the seeds of that branch of chemistry called quantitative analysis in his writings. Cusa's central thesis is the desirability of compiling "a table of exact, experimentally verified differences of weights". Such a table would be practically invaluable. It would have medical application. "Then by comparing the weights of the herbs to the weight of blood or urine [the physician] might know by the likeness or difference of the medicines what dose to prescribe, and he might make many startling prognoses and by static experiments more precisely conjecture whatever is known." The physics of buoyancy is determined by weight, which has applications in shipbuilding. Metallurgy relies on quantitative measurement. For example, a workman "could determine [the amount of mercury and sulphur contained in every metal] by the concord and difference of weights; also the elements of quicksilver, by the diversity of its weight in air, metal, and oil compared to oil, water, and ashes of the same greatness weighed against it; and similarly with sulphur. Through these methods man may come to a true conjecture of the elements of all metals and stones and the weights of those elements". Also harmonics is to a great extent determined by weights. Astronomy involves weights, and "knowledge of weights is very profitable, for anything concerning geometry".

CONCERNING EXPERIMENTS IN WEIGHT

Author: A Roman Orator often sought the company of a Citizen to hear the man's ideas which he always welcomed. Once when the Orator commended the balance-scale, the rule of justice, as an instrument necessary for the common good, the citizen replied:

Citizen: Although nothing in the world is absolutely precise yet experience demonstrates that the judgment of the balance-scale is one of the truest measurements we have; and so it is in demand everywhere. But please tell me, seeing different things of like volume cannot have the same weight, has anyone yet compiled a table of exact, experimentally verified differences of weights?

Orator: Not to my knowledge.

Citizen: I wish that someone would compile such a table; I would regard it more highly than many volumes of other books.

Orator: I feel no one could do it any

Reprinted from *Unity and Reform, Selected Writings of Nicholas de Cusa*, edited by John Patrick Dolan (Notre Dame: University of Notre Dame Press, 1962), pp. 239–260. Reprinted by permission of the University of Notre Dame Press.

better than you, yourself, if you would undertake the task.

Citizen: Anyone could easily do it; but for my part I haven't the time.

Orator: Tell me what profit there would be in it and how to do it; and I'll see whether I, myself, or someone else whom I ask can do it.

Citizen: I think that by knowing the differences in the weights of things we can more surely understand them and that many more probable conjectures can be made about things.

Orator: What you say is true; for I recall that a certain prophet says (Prov. 16:11) weight and the balance are the judgments of the hand who created (Wisd. II, 17) all things in number, weight, and measure; who (Prov. 8:28) weighed the oceans and the greatness of the Earth in a balance, as the wise man says.

Citizen: If therefore water from one source is not of the same weight as a like volume of water from another source, certainly a balance will better indicate the difference between the natures of the two than any other instrument.

Orator: That's right and Vitruvius,

writing on architecture, tells us to choose for a dwelling a place which has light and airy waters and to avoid places where the waters are heavy and earthly.

Citizen: Just as waters from the same source seem to be of the same weight and nature so, too, waters from different sources seem to be of different weights and natures.

Orator: You say *seem to be* as though they are necessarily so.

Citizen: I confess that time may alter them though not perceptibly; for no doubt water has different weights at different seasons just as there is one weight of water near the source or head and another farther off. But their differences being scarcely noticeable are regarded as being of no account.

Orator: Do you think that what you say about water is also true of all other things?

Citizen: Yes, I do, because different things of the same volume never have the same weight. Therefore, if there is one weight for blood, another for urine, and for each of these one weight in a healthy man and another weight in a sick man, one in an old man, another in a young man, one in a German, another in an African. Wouldn't it be convenient for a physician to have a table of these differences?

Orator: I should say so; and, what is more, by having their weights noted down, one might make himself more respected.

Citizen: I think that a physician might make a more accurate judgment of urine by both weight and color than by color alone which may be misleading.

Orator: Yes, certainly.

Citizen: The same can be said of the roots of herbs, stocks, leaves, fruits, seeds, and juices having their own weights. Now if the weights of all herbs were noted down, with the different places they come from, the physician might better reach the nature of them all with the various phases of their origin, by their weight and smell, rather than by their taste which is misleading.

Orator: That is very true.

Citizen: Then by comparing the weights of the herbs to the weight of blood or urine he might know by the likeness or difference of the medicines what dose to prescribe, and he might make many startling prognoses and by static experiments more precisely conjecture whatever is known.

Orator: One wonders a good deal at the fact that even with so much painstaking research all men have been so neglectful of the designation of weights.

Citizen: If one had an hour glass filled with water and out of a straight, narrow hole in it allowed water to run into a basin while counting the pulse of a healthy young man to one hundred and if one did the same thing with a sick man, don't you think that there would be a great deal of difference between the weights of the two volumes of water?

Orator: Without a doubt.

Citizen: By the weight of water, therefore, one could arrive at the difference in pulse between a young man and an old man, a sick man and a sound man; consequently one could arrive at a better understanding of the disease since there must be one weight for one disease and another weight for another disease. And so there might be given a more perfect judgment by such an experimental difference of the pulses and weight of the urine than by merely the touch of one and the color of the other.

Orator: You are quite right.

Citizen: If furthermore one should observe particularly the frequency of breathing, using the above method, wouldn't one give a more precise judgment?

Orator: I believe he would.

Citizen: For if, while the water is running out of the hour glass, one could observe a child breathing one hundred times and do the same for an old man, it is not possible for the weights of the two volumes of water to be the same? The same holds true for different ages and complexions. If then a physician were correctly informed of the weight of the breathing of a healthy man or a child or a young man or the like, all of whom were sick with different illnesses, without a doubt by such an experiment he could more surely arrive at an understanding of health and sickness and so to the administration of remedies.

Orator: Yes, one could even conjecture about matters of time.

Citizen: You are so right. For if he should find in a young man a weight associated with an old, decrepit man, he might more certainly predict the time of his death. And he might make many other admirable conjectures. Moreover, in the case of fevers, if he would similarly register hot and cold paroxysms by the difference in the weights of volumes of water, couldn't he more truly determine the seriousness of the disease and the best remedy for it?

Orator: Certainly he could, for he would then have learned the volume of one quality over another, of heat over cold or vice versa; and according to the result he might apply a remedy.

Citizen: Furthermore, I would say that in different nations, regions, and times these things would be different, even though in the same age. Therefore, even though it might be difficult, yet it would be highly profitable for the differences in weights to be designated in accordance with all these circumstances.

Orator: What you say is true.

Citizen: On the other hand it seems to me that the weight of anything is to be considered as the average of the different weights of a thing in the average climate, I mean in different climates. Thus if we would consider the weight of a man as compared with some other living weight then we must consider a man not as inhabiting such a latitude as to be termed a northerner or a southerner, where there may be excess on both sides, but rather as inhabiting the average climate.

Orator: You are right. The ancients called that climate Dia Rhodon because it extends itself from the East to the West through the Rhodes Islands. But tell me, if you should seek the weight of a man in comparison to some other living creature, how would you go about it?

Citizen: I would put the man onto one side of the scale and the same weight of some other thing onto the other side of the scale to fix the exact weight of the man. Then I would put the man into water and weigh him again when he came out, noting the difference in the two weights. I would do the same with the other living creature, and by the difference in weights I would note that which I sought. Then I would look to the difference of the weight of the man and the other weight, out of the water, and according to this I would moderate the weight found and write it down.

Orator: I do not understand this moderation.

Citizen: I will demonstrate.

Orator: Then the Citizen took a light piece of wood having a weight of three, and such that five would be the weight of an equivalent volume of water; he divided the wood into two unequal parts, one representing one third of the volume of the wood, the other, two thirds; he put them both into a deep flagon; and holding them down with a stick, he poured water on them; then pulling away the stick, he allowed the two pieces of wood to rise to the top of the water; and the larger piece reached the top before the smaller. Then he said:

Citizen: You see now that the difference in the motion is in proportion to this extent, that in light wood the greater the volume of the wood the more buoyancy there is in it.

Orator: I see that, and I am well pleased.

Citizen: That is what I mean; for that reason moderation should be made; for if a man should have more weight and be heavier than the other living creature, only for his great size, then he will necessarily sink faster into water than the other. Wherefore it is necessary that diminishing the moderation of the known difference be done proportionately according to the excess.

Orator: I understand now. But tell me, how does the water keep the wood from sinking?

Citizen: As a greater heaviness resists a lesser; for if you press a round piece of wood into wax and then pull it out again and fill the depression with water and then weigh both water and wood, you will find that if the weight of the wood exceeds the weight of the water then the wood will sink; if not, the wood will float; and a proportionate part of the wood will be above the water according to the extent to which the weight of the water exceeds the weight of the wood.

Orator: Why do you speak of a round piece of wood?

Citizen: Because if it were a broad piece, it would float more easily because it occupies more of the water; thus ships in shallow waters need broader bottoms.

Orator: Contrive in your original purpose, whether the weight of animals might be determined in another way.

Citizen: I think they might. First one should fill to the top a large vessel full of water and then pour that out into a still larger vessel and then weigh some man out of water. Then have the man step into the first vessel and pour over him from the second vessel enough water to fill the first vessel to the top. Finally, weigh the water which is left over. Proceed in like manner with another man, beast, or any other thing. By the difference in weights one can, by subtle inquiry, find what he is seeking.

Orator: You proceed with a great deal of subtlety and I have heard that in the same way the difference of metals has been found and that some have noted how much the fusion of an ounce of wax gathers of gold, silver, copper, and thus of all metals.

Citizen: Certainly he is much to be commended who by the fusion of wax understood the greatness, for he saw that if an ounce of gold filled the place of an ounce of wax that then it must weigh just as much as an ounce of wax and the same must be true with other metals; for it is most certain that there is one weight of gold and another

of silver, and another of other things all having the same volume, and that something has one weight in air, another in water, another in oil or some other liquid. And if one had a table of these weights he would readily know how much more one metal weighs than the other in air and in water. Thus, given any volume of metal knowing its weight in air and in water, one would know of what metal and what mixture the volume is. And what I have said of air and water may also be said of oil or any other liquid with which the experiment may be conducted.

Orator: So, indeed, without mixing the volume of metal, or separation of the metals one could know the mixture; and this method would work with money to know how much copper there is in gold and silver.

Citizen: What you say is true and it would work in determining how far short of the truth the alchemist comes in his sophistic science.

Orator: If anyone would propose to write a book of weights he must, it seems, note the variety of every metal; for Hungarian gold is of one weight and fine gold, which is called aurum obryzum, of another, and so of all the metals.

Citizen: By what has been said it seems that as in fountains so in minerals there are found differences in weight yet gold, wherever it is found, is always heavier than any other metal even though the species may be found to vary with a certain latitude, and this is true of other metals also.

Orator: But couldn't the characteristic or proportion of the value of metals be found out, by the characteristic or proportion of their weights?

Citizen: Lead is the closest to gold in weight, but not in perfection; therefore, we must not consider one weight only, but every kind of weight; for if one looks at the weight of the heat of fusion of gold and lead; he finds that lead comes not as near to gold as other metals do. And if one looks to the weight of the heat in the melting of iron, he finds that iron comes closer to gold than any other metal, even though the heaviness of iron does not come so close. Therefore, we must look at all of the weights and not the weight of heaviness only, and so we find that silver is next to gold.

Orator: Vitruvius says that in speaking of the natural heaviness of gold, it alone sinks in quicksilver even though other metals of greater weight and greater bulk float.

Citizen: Quicksilver is naturally conjugible to all the metals because of something which it has in common with them; but it more readily clings and adheres to gold, as that which is imperfect to its own most perfect nature. For this cause, the Alchemists strive to tame quicksilver in the fire until it not only jumps from the fire itself but clings to all other metals to which it is joined. And not only to this extent but until it also compacts them all into the weight of gold and colors them with a fixed permanent color while their own fluxion and moisture still remain.

Orator: But do you think that through these means they can fulfill their purpose?

Citizen: Precision is always hard to see, but the balance will show how much they accomplish; without the balance nothing is certain. For through the judgment of the fire and the balance the truth of this question must be resolved.

Orator: Couldn't all precious stones be weighed in the same manner?

Citizen: No doubt of it, they might all be one by the same device, for a diamond has no weight in respect to the magnitude of lead as does neither a sapphire. And by this diversity, the habitude of proportion of lead to either weight may be known and, therefore, it was very good to have these weights written down, by the way of a static experiment with their differences known of these originals, that if there were any sophistication done with Beryl or colored crystal, they might be known and found.

Orator: Yes, and furthermore, there being one weight of a stone in air, another in water, and another in oil, it is good to have these diversities that without any habitude to lead or any third thing, the difference of the weights might be known.

Citizen: That is very true.

Orator: Tell me, do you have any device through which the virtues of stones may be weighed?

Citizen: I think the virtue of the lodestone might be weighed, if putting some iron on one scale, and a lodestone on the other, until the balance became even, then taking away the lodestone and putting something else of the same weight on that scale, then by holding the lodestone over the iron so that the scale would begin to rise; by reason of the lodestone's attraction to the iron. Now by taking weight off of the other scale until equilibrium is again achieved, I believe that the weight of what was taken out of the contrary scale would be proportional to the weight of the virtue of power of the lodestone. And in a similar manner, the virtue of a diamond may be found since they say it hinders the attraction of the lodestone to the iron, and so other virtues of other stones could be found always considering the greatness of the bodies because in a greater body there is a greater power and virtue.

Orator: Couldn't a workman also use these means to determine the amount of mercury and sulphur contained in every metal?

Citizen: Certainly he could determine such things by the concord and difference of weights; also the elements of quicksilver, by the diversity of its weight in air, water, and oil compared to oil, water, and ashes of the same greatness weighed against it; and similarly with sulphur. Through these methods man may come to a true conjecture of the elements of all metals and stones and the weights of those elements.

Orator: This is fine, but couldn't the same be done with woods, herbs, flesh, living creatures and humans?

Citizen: I believe it could be done in all things, for in weighing a piece of wood and then burning it thoroughly and thus weighing its ashes it is known how much water is in the wood, for there is nothing that has a heavy weight but water and earth. It is known, moreover, by the various weights of wood in air, water, and oil how much water in the wood is heavier or lighter than clean spring water, and so how much air is in it. Thus by the various weights of the ashes the amount of fire in them and the elements may be even more closely determined, though precision is always unattainable. And as I have so described for wood so it can also be done with herbs, flesh and other things.

Orator: There is a saying that there is no pure element; how is this proved by the balance?

Citizen: If a man should put a hundred weight of earth into a great earthen pot, then taking some herbs and seeds, weigh them, and plant or sow them in that pot, then let them grow there until they weigh one hundred weight, he would find the earth very little diminished when he weighed it again. From this he may gather that all the herbs received their weight from water. Therefore, the waters being impregnated in the earth attracted a terrestreity, and by the operation of the Sun was condensed into the herb. If these herbs are then burned to ashes, couldn't one guess by the diversity of all the weights how much more earth was found than one hundred weight and then conclude that the water brought all of it? For the elements are convertible one into another by parts as we see by placing a glass of water in snow and watching the air condense into water and flow into the glass. So we find by experience that some water is turned into stones, some into ice, and there is in some fountains a hardening and petrifying power which it is reported turns things put into them into stone. It is reported, there is a certain water fountain found in Hungary which through the power of the virtue which is in it turns iron into copper, by such powers and virtues it is evident that the waters are not purely elementary but

elemented, and so it would be very nice to have weights of all these waters of such various virtues that by the diversity of these weights in air and oil one might come nearer to a value of their virtues.

Orator: Couldn't one also do it with the soil?

Citizen: Yes, even with the soil, because one soil is fertile, another barren; in one there are found stones and minerals and not in another; therefore, for the searching into the secrets of nature it would be very helpful to know the various weights of the soil, in water, air, and oil; so that by the difference of weights of wines, waxes, oils, gums, alums, onions, leeks, garlics, and all such things, I think that the virtues that are different in them might in some manner be determined, and we might give a close estimate of the weight of the whole earth: for the circumference and the diameter are both known from which may be gotten the capacity and the contents and the number of miles, therefore numbering even one solid inch of earth, the weight of the whole capacity may be easily determined.

Orator: These things could hardly be written in one huge volume.

Citizen: Experimental knowledge requires many volumes, for the more there are the easier we may arrive at answers in experiments from the knowledge contained in them.

Orator: Perhaps in time a man may even determine the weight of air.

Citizen: If any man would put a great deal of hard packed dry wool in one pan of a balance and stones to counterbalance it in the other, he would then find by experience that when the air condenses the weight of the wool would increase; and when the air becomes arid, it would decrease; and by these differences he might weigh the air and might give predictions of the change of the times and weather. So if any man should desire to know the various strength of the sun in different climates, he should take and weigh a thousand grains, either of wheat or barley from the most fertile field of the one and the other, by the difference of the weights, he might determine the various powers of the sun, for if the number and field be similarly fruitful in any place, the difference has to be in the sun. So you may also determine the different powers of the sun in the mountains and the valleys, and also the same when it is rising and setting.

Orator: Couldn't a man by letting a stone fall from a high tower and during the time of fall let water run out of a narrow hole into a basin; and then by weighing the water that had run out and then doing the same with wood of the same size, determine the weight of the air by the difference of the weights of the water, wood and stone?

Citizen: If a man should do this in different towers of equal height and at different times, he might come near to a likely estimate. But he could determine the weight of air sooner by different figures or shapes of things of equal heaviness. For if I would drop one pound of lead which was round in shape from a high tower and weigh the water that ran out of the hour glass in that time, and then do the same with an equal weight of lead which was broad; I might by the different weights of the waters, determine the weight of the air. For we know from experience that birds are more still when they spread their wings because they take up more air; just as also something which is heavy will sink faster in water if it is round than if it is square. And possibly the air may yet be more easily weighed: as if equal bellows were equally filled, in different times and places, for by the motion of those equal bellows, and the measurement of these motions by dripping water through an hour glass of equal height during the time of motion and by comparing the weights of the waters, the weight of air might easily be known. For the proportion of the two waters will be the same as the proportion of the air in the two bellows. But the best way of all is to take an empty glass full of air, suppose the glass weighs just a pound, then filling the hole

with wax, put it under water, then if a one pound weight exactly will hold it under water, then you could say that the air in the glass is of the lightness of two pounds. So in this method one may know the proportion of the lightness of one air to another in different places, times, and regions. One can also weigh smoke and wind by using a bellows: for by pressing out the air from a bellows and filling it with smoke which you can weigh the same as for the air, you can then determine whether smoke or air is lighter and by how much. And so also can you do it with wind. And you may also by the motion of the smoke while so many drops of water distill in the hour glass and the motion of fire during the distilling of so many drops determine the lightness of fire, above smoke or air.

Citizen: And it can be done with a piece of lead, made in the shape of a crescent such that one end is heavier than the other, and on the light end fasten an apple or some other light thing. When such an instrument is thrown into water the heavier end will reach the bottom first, then having reached the bottom the apple is freed and will again return to the surface, provided you first have the knowledge of how long the lead will be sinking, and the apple is rising in a water of a known depth; for then by the difference of the weights of the water, or sand of the hour glass, from the time the lead was thrown in and the apple's return in various waters, you may find what you are looking for.

Orator: I believe that the depth of the water may be searched both by this and by other means. But tell me, can it not also be guessed at, by the way ships do it at sea?

Citizen: How do you say?

Orator: By throwing an apple as far as one can out from the prow or fore part of the ship and then letting the water run from the hour glass until the ship comes up to the apple and comparing the weight of the water at one time with the weight of it at another time.

Citizen: It can be done that way and

also by shooting an arrow from a cross bow and weighing the water when the ship comes up to the arrow.

Orator: The knowledge of the strength of the bows and other engines, it seems, are proportional to the water which flowed out of the hour glass, from the time when the shaft is shot upwards and returns again to the earth, provided that in various engines the shafts are always equal.

Citizen: Not only the strength of the bows and engines but of the winds also, the flying of the birds, the running of men and beasts and whatever is similar may be determined by the static experiments and the running of water from an hour glass.

Orator: How may the strength of a man be known by this method?

Citizen: Using a pair of even scales let a man hold on to one of them and in the other put as much weight as he can lift until the balance is even: (it will be more exact if the man has something to hold his feet against) then take the weight of that which he has lifted and deduct it from the weight of the man himself, the remainder being proportional to his strength.

Orator: Couldn't the breath of a man also be weighed?

Citizen: The weight of man is different when he draws in a breath and when he breathes out; and it is also different while he is living and while he is dead. This is true of all living things. Therefore, it would be good to have these differences noted in various living things, various men, and of various ages of men, so that one might determine the weight of the vital spirits.

Orator: Couldn't man determine the heat and cold, and the dryness and moisture of the weather?

Citizen: Certainly, for if in frosty weather you would note the weight of the water before and after it is frozen you shall find it different: since ice floats in water we know it to be lighter than water: and therefore, according to the intensity of the cold, there is a greater difference of the weight; or if you would weigh green wood and af-

ter a time find the difference in weight you would know the excess of heat and cold, moisture and drought.

Orator: Couldn't the time of day be also weighed?

Citizen: If you would let the water run out of an hour glass from sunrise of one day and let it run until the sunrise of the next day, and then let it run for another day beginning at sunrise, by the proportion of water that has run on this day to that which ran out on the first day, you may determine the hour and time of day.

Orator: From this could he also determine the time of the year?

Citizen: Yes, if for an entire year you would run water through an hour glass every day from sunrise to sunset and observe the weight, you may give a close guess by the balance at any time, to the day of the month and the hour of the day, although on shorter days the difference will be less certain than on others.

Orator: I see that by this invention one may determine even the motion of the heavenly bodies, as Nimrod is said to have done, and Hipparchus to have written.

Citizen: What you say is true, though in this case there is a great need for an explanation: for if any man noting a fixed star in the meridian line, would gather and note the water running from an hour glass, until the return of the same star to the same place and do the same for the sun from its rising until its rising again on the next day, he might find the motion of the sun to the east by the change of the decrease of the water's weight, of the star's motion from the meridian line to its return to the same place, respectively, to the motion of the sun from its rising to its rising; for it is determined by the difference of weight in comparison to the weight as a whole if the motion is in order to the equinoctial circle, not to the Zodiac, which is not described upon the poles of the world, but its own. So if any man would determine how much the sun was moved in fifteen minutes in relation to the same star, he might do it in the same manner, different distance of the sun's rising respectively to the place of that star on the meridian line. As for example, if today the distance of the place of that star, in the line from the sun's rising is found in some proportion by the hour glass, and fifteen minutes later it is found in another proportion, by the difference of those proportions the motion might be proved, so it is always in the equinoctial.

Orator: May the motion in the Zodiac be also found in this manner?

Citizen: Certainly, by the motion of the sun from noon to noon, and from the East to the East, and from the East to the West; for by these differences the declination of the Zodiac from the equinoctial might be reached.

Orator: And what may be done concerning the variety of the motion, which is said to be caused by the Eccentric?

Citizen: That also may be determined, when in a year you shall find the inequality of the Zodiac, in equal days: for the sun moves in the summertime from the equinoctial, and does not return to the equinoctial again in the same number of days in winter, for in winter it returns sooner; for it would not be found to have spent the same number of days in going from Libra to Aries as from Aries to Libra. By this difference one would get the eccentric, or little circle of the spica, by the difference of the motion.

Orator: And what about the size of the sun's body?

Citizen: By the weight of the water that runs in the hour glass, in the equinoctial, from the beginning of the rising of the sun until it is far above the horizon, in the position of the water of the star's revolution, is known the size of the sun's body. But one may also determine the size of the sun's body by the eclipses of the sun.

Orator: How?

Citizen: First we would determine the motion of the moon as we have of the sun. Then by the eclipse and its motion through the shadow of the earth, we determine the size of the moon in proportion to the different shadow of the earth, by which

we conclude the average proportion to be the proportion of the moon's size to that of the earth. Then by the motion of the moon, and the eclipse of the sun, we determine the sun's distance from the earth and its size; and although it be a subtle way of determining, it is still conjecture.

Orator: From what you have already said, it seems that all the differences of motions, and eclipses of the sun and moon, yes the progresses of all the planets, their stations, retrogradations, directions, and eccentricities may be determined by the same means, that of the hour glass.

Citizen: You may do it yourself, if you work at collecting the differences.

Orator: What do you think of the judgments of the stars?

Citizen: I think that by the variety of the weights of the water, in several years, and certain other differences in the weights of woods, herbs, and grain, one may guess at the future plenty or scarcity of corn, better and quicker by experiments of the past, than by the motion of the stars. For if in March, there is such a proportion of weight found in water, air and woods, then fruitfulness of the earth will follow, or barrenness, or at best mediocrity. The same for wars, pestilence, and all other ordinary things. And this is the basis through which in these second causes we hunt after the judgment of the stars. Since by the increase or decrease of marrow in living creatures, fishes, and sea crabs, in trees and rushes, we seek to determine the age of the moon; and by the tides of the sea, its place in the heavens.

Orator: I have heard that the Egyptians used to predict the disposition of the year by the plentiful or scarce overflowing of the Nile.

Citizen: There is no country where one could not find some similar means of prediction; as by the fatness of fishes and creeping things, in the beginning of winter we say that there will be a long and cold winter for which nature has provided its living creatures.

Orator: What do you think of questions asked Astrologers; couldn't this device determine an equal answer for them all?

Citizen: Although not an equal one, I think (because you shall consider me a mere layman in all respects) some answer may be made in this way. But how an answer may be given of all things that are asked would require a great deal of inquiry. The way that this can be done cannot be written up in books; but by the weight of the question; for the curiosity of the inquirer seems to be caused by the foresight of the future event, though he himself may not see from where the motion comes, as someone who feels something in his eye which he does not see asks someone else if there he sees what is hurting him.

Orator: I think that you mean, as in the wheel of Pythagoras, by the various combinations of the name of the asker, his mother, the hour of the day and the light of the moon, there is a way taught of giving the answers: or as a prophet makes judgments from lots or by casual reading of Sibylline Books, or by the Psalter; or from buildings or geometric figures, or by the chattering of birds, or the bending of the flame of a fire, or the relation of a third man, or any other casual occurrence that intervenes.

Citizen: There are certain individuals who have correctly sought to give answers, by conferences which they have had with the inquirer, in making him tell some news of the disposition of this country, for the impulsive spirit has to make itself known in long discourse. For if the inquirer is inclined to talk of sad things, so shall it be; if it is a glad and merry discussion then so, also, will the event be. But I imagine conjectures might be formed according to the face, garments, motion of the eyes, form of words; and of weights looking upon the lot of those things which I ask the inquirer again and again to bring to me; yet the more valuable conjectures come from him to whom some truer thing fell without premeditation, in whom a certain spirit seemed to speak. Nevertheless, in this matter, I neither think that this art is possible,

nor that he who has it can communicate his judgment, nor that a wise man should use such a means.

Orator: What you say is very good, for St. Augustine reports that he had in his time a certain drunken companion, who would read men's minds, discover thieves, and show other secret things, in a strange manner; and yet he was at the same time a light vain fellow, and no wise man.

Citizen: I know that I myself have foretold many things as the spirit gave it to me, and at the same time was utterly ignorant of the cause. Finally I seemed to see, that it was unlawful for a serious man to speak without cause, and since then I have held my peace.

Orator: Enough said about the motions of the stars, now add something of music.

Citizen: The experiments of balance are most profitable to music. For by the differences of weights of two bells that sound a tone, it is known in what proportion of harmony the tones consist. The proportion of a Diapason, Diapente, and Diatessaron as well as all other harmonies is known by the weight of pipes, and of waters that fill the pipes, and likewise that by the weight of hammers which strike upon an anvil harmonies arise, and by the weight of drops which drop from a rock into a pond and make different sounds, and of pipes and all other musical instruments; the reason is best and most precisely reached by the balance.

Orator: Is it the same in voices and songs?

Citizen: Yes, generally all harmonic agreements are best found out by weights. Yes, the weight of a thing is properly the harmonic proportion, arising from the varying combination of various things. Also, the friendships and enmities of living creatures, and of men of the same species, and whatever else is weighed by harmonic agreement and by contrary dissonances. So the health of a man is weighed by harmony, and sickness by that which is contrary to harmony, and in the same manner, lightness and heaviness, prudence and simplicity, and many other such things, if you notice diligently.

Orator: What do you think about geometry?

Citizen: I think the nearest proportions of the circle, and the square, and all other things which belong to the difference of the capacity of figures, may be better proved by weights than in any other manner. For if you would make a vessel fashioned like a column of a known diameter and height and another cube-shaped of the same diameter and height, and then fill them both with water, by the difference of the weights you will get the proportion of the square to the circle. And in this manner you may also surmise to the squaring of the circle, and whatever else you may like to know about this. And if you would take two equal plates, shaping one into a circular column and the other into a cube and fill both with water you shall know by the differing weight of the water, the different capacity of a circle and a square of the same circumference. And having many such equal plates you may find the differences of capacities in a triangle, a five cornered, a six cornered vessel, etc. Again by using weights you may determine the capacities of vessels of any shape whatever, and to instruments of measuring and weighing,

how balances are made, how a one pound weight can lift up a thousand by its distance from the center, and the various descents either straight or angled, and how all the exact instruments of ships and other engines ought to be made. For these reasons I think that this knowledge of weights is very profitable, for anything concerning geometry. You may also, if you wish, and are curious enough, determine the number of hairs, leaves, grains, sands, or of anything else in a bushel, if you put a small quantity in the balance, and taking the weight and number of them afterwards weigh the whole. For by the proportion of the one weight to the other you may know the proportion of one number to another.

Orator: You have now explained the reasons why you wished the weights of things were taken by the balance and orderly written down. It is very likely that such a book would be very profitable; important individuals could be brought together and their knowledge of various areas could be collected into one system. This would greatly facilitate a deeper knowledge of things yet hidden from us. As for me, I will never cease in promoting this everywhere.

Citizen: If you love me, be diligent in it, and so goodby.